P9-DGL-104

THE GOOD HOUSEKEEPING COOKBOOK

THE GOOD HOUSEKEEPING COOKBOOK

EDITED BY

Zoe Coulson

Director, Foods and Cookery
Good Housekeeping Institute

Drawings by Murray Tinkelman

Photographs by James Viles

GOOD HOUSEKEEPING BOOKS · NEW YORK, NEW YORK

Manufactured in the United States of America.

ISBN 0–87851–014–1

Library of Congress Catalog Number 73–81131

Foreword

There are many ways to describe what makes a cookbook. For one, statistics—number of pages, number of color photographs, number of recipes. For another, all the elements that make the book really new and different. And so on. You can read all those things on the jacket of this book.

But there is still another element involved in this newest *Good Housekeeping Cookbook*—the same element that has been involved in every edition, beginning with the first one in 1903. That element is the *people* element.

Letters from readers tell us of their love affair with the *Cookbook*. With old editions that have been handed down from mother to daughter to daughter. For example, a recent letter speaks of a 1927 edition. "It has been in constant use all these years. The poor thing has finally given up. What can I do to hold it together for a few more years?"

Then there are the younger women, just beginning their lives as wives and homemakers. One of these wrote us to say, "I will be married soon and I need to learn to cook something more complicated than frozen pizza, which is the extent of my present skill. I need a cookbook that tells me why and how—not just a collection of recipes."

And so this newest edition of our *Good Housekeeping Cookbook* contains a great measure of inspiration from our readers. It is for them and for all those women across the country whose busy lives vary in many ways but who have one great common interest—a dedication to keeping their families well and happily fed and to making food preparation a creative and satisfying experience.

Another part of the people element is our own staff. There are not any words to describe to you the time, the work, the very loving care that went into the compilation of this book. A special staff of home economists worked on updating, developing new recipes and preparing recipes, both old and new. They are Ellen Connelly, Martha Reynolds, Wanda Veraska, Virginia Voboril. But the entire Foods and Cookery staff helped to an immeasurable degree. Supervising them, guiding them, inspiring them and doing the final editing was our Director of Foods and Cookery, Zoe Coulson.

We put our new book into your hands with the firm conviction that it is the best cookbook ever. With it comes our gratitude and best wishes to you all.

WILLIE MAE ROGERS
Director, Good Housekeeping Institute

Contents

THE GOOD HOUSEKEEPING COOKBOOK

Before you cook

Cooking success comes easy when you start with a good recipe and follow it to the letter. The recipes in this book have been kitchen-tested many times to assure success. In many of them, the use of simplified methods and time-saving products has resulted in dishes that are remarkably easy to make, yet look and taste delicious and are bursting with good nutrition.

How to Follow Our Recipes

Make it a habit to take these steps every time you try a new recipe:

Read the recipe before you begin. Be sure you understand all cooking terms used (see page 21). Check how much time it will take to prepare the recipe, and allow yourself a few extra minutes in case you are interrupted.

Check the ingredient list. Make sure you have everything you need, in the amount called for. Assemble the ingredients.

Don't substitute key ingredients, unless the recipe suggests an alternate. That goes for product forms and package sizes, too. To take one example, some packaged pudding mixes come in both regular-size and family-size packages, and in both regular and instant forms. Using either the wrong size or the wrong kind of pudding in a recipe might result in a disaster!

Seasonings and spices *can* safely be varied. But it's a good idea to follow the recipe exactly the first time, to discover the family's tastes before making changes.

Check the utensils you'll need. Assemble items for measuring, mixing, cooking and serving. Be sure pans are the right size (see How to Measure Pans, page 19).

Do as much advance preparation as possible. Chop, cut, grate, melt or otherwise prepare ingredients and have them ready before you start to mix. Grease and flour pans; turn the oven on at least 10 minutes before putting food in to bake, to allow it to preheat to the proper temperature.

Measure accurately. Our recipes are based on standard, consistent measurements. Use the proper measuring equipment and methods (see How to Measure Ingredients, page 17).

Mix carefully. Ingredients are combined in different ways (by folding, beating, stirring, etc.) to achieve different results. (See Cooking Terms, page 21.) Be sure to take note of any specific mixing times or cautions given in the recipe.

Clean up as you work. Put empty bowls, used measuring equipment in the sink; throw away paper; sponge up spills. The less cluttered the work surface, the less chance of your making a mistake.

Cook or bake as directed. For best results, use the temperature specified in the recipe. Follow the time suggested too, but to be on the safe side, start checking for doneness before the end, since ovens and heating units vary.

Be careful about doubling or halving a recipe. Though some recipes can be increased or decreased successfully, many more cannot. For best results, make the recipe as given, and repeat it until the desired amount is obtained.

Ingredients

The ingredients used in our recipes are generally available in any neighborhood supermarket. Following are helpful notes on some of them:

Artificial sweetener, or saccharin, a sugar substitute, is available in liquid, granular and tablet forms. They cannot be used interchangeably with sugar or with one another; follow label directions carefully when using, and use only in recipes developed especially for them.

They may be stored indefinitely if kept tightly closed at room temperature.

Ascorbic-acid mixture for fruit, as referred to in our recipes, is a crystalline or powdered mixture containing vitamin C and sugar. It is used to prevent darkening of fruits and vegetables after peeling. Use as recipe directs.

Baking powder is a leavening agent which makes many foods rise when they are baked in an oven, skillet or waffle iron. It is a combination of baking soda, a dry acid or acid salt and starch or flour. During mixing and baking, the acid ingredient reacts with the baking soda to produce the gas bubbles that leaven (lighten) the batter or dough, thus making it rise.

There are two types of baking powder.

- Double-acting baking powder is the most widely available type. It produces gas bubbles twice—the first time during mixing, the second during baking.
- Quick-acting baking powder (also known as tartrate baking powder) forms gas bubbles only once, during mixing. It is important that batters using this type of baking powder be baked as soon as mixed so that the leavening action is not lost.

The baking-powder label should clearly indicate which type it is. In general, the different types cannot be used interchangeably in recipes. In our recipes, we use the double-acting type.

Store, tightly covered, in a cool, dry place in the cupboard. Will keep for up to 1½ years.

Baking soda, an essential ingredient of baking powder, may be used alone as a leavening agent in mixtures containing an acid ingredient such as buttermilk, molasses, fruit juice or chocolate. It may also be used in combination with baking powder. Mixtures containing baking soda should be baked as soon as mixed, since the soda starts to react as soon as it comes in contact with the liquid.

Store and use like Baking Powder, above.

Breakfast cereals come in ready-to-eat and ready-to-cook forms; many are packaged in individual as well as family-size packages.

Ready-to-eat or cold cereals may be presweetened or regular. They offer a variety of forms—flaked, puffed, shredded, toasted, shaped. Some have fruit and spices added. Labels indicate if cereals are enriched or fortified with vitamins and minerals.

Ready-to-cook or hot cereals are available in regular, quick-cooking and instant forms.

Store all cereals in a cool, dry place. Open packages of ready-to-eat cereals carefully so they can be closed after use; they tend to lose crispness during prolonged storage. Keep ready-to-cook cereals in their original packages so cooking directions are always at hand.

Butter, made from sweet or sour cream, contains not less than 80 percent milk fat (butterfat). It comes salted or unsalted (sweet); it also comes whipped for greater volume and easier spreading. In our recipes we use solid butter only; it is not interchangeable with whipped butter. Solid butter is, however, interchangeable with margarine (page 15).

Store in refrigerator up to 2 weeks; for long periods, freezer-wrap and freeze up to 9 months.

Buttermilk: See Milk, Cultured, page 15.

Catchup is a thick tomato sauce, mildly seasoned, popular as a topping for meats and fish and as an ingredient of many foods such as barbecue sauce, meat loaf, salad dressings. It is available plain or with onion, pickle or hot spices added.

After opening, keep catchup, tightly covered, for up to one month at room temperature or in refrigerator for longer periods.

Cereals: See Breakfast Cereals, page 12.

Chili sauce is a thick tomato sauce similar to catchup, but spicier; it has bits of whole tomato, onion and other seasonings added. It is used like catchup when a more distinct flavor is desired. Store as you would catchup.

Chocolate is a product prepared from cocoa (or cacao) beans; it comes in several different forms. Each reacts differently and gives a different flavor in recipes. Be sure to use the kind the recipe calls for.

- Unsweetened (bitter) chocolate comes packaged as squares—eight 1-ounce squares to the package. It is used primarily as an ingredient; when shaved, grated or "curled," it becomes a garnish.
- Semisweet chocolate comes in bars or packages of squares, or in bags of pieces. It has cocoa butter and sugar added, and may be used as an ingredient, as a garnish and as candy.
- Sweet cooking chocolate, a combination of chocolate, sugar and cocoa butter, is sold in bars. With smooth texture and taste, it is used in recipes and for eating.
- Milk chocolate is chocolate with sugar, milk and vanilla added. Smooth, light and sweet, it is primarily an eating chocolate.
- Chocolate syrup is a sweetened liquid chocolate. Use as topping for desserts or as an ingredient in beverages.
- Chocolate sauce is chocolate syrup to which milk, cream and/or butter has been added, making it richer and thicker than the syrup.

Chocolate may be stored for about 1 year if wrapped tightly and kept in a cool, dry place. If the storage place is too warm or moist, a grayish film may develop on the surface of the chocolate. This is the fat in the chocolate, which melts and rises to the surface. The film does not harm the flavor, but it affects the color and, sometimes, the texture. Use chocolate with this film in baking, since, as it melts, the rich dark color reappears.

Chocolate may also be refrigerated for up to three months if wrapped tightly, but will become brittle and should be used in melted form.

Cocoa is powdered chocolate with part of the cocoa butter removed. Regular cocoa contains from 10 to 22 percent cocoa butter. Dutch process cocoa has been treated with alkali to give darker color and a slightly different flavor.

Instant cocoa is a mixture of cocoa, sugar, milk solids, flavors and an emulsifier which enables it to dissolve more readily; it can be prepared hot or cold with water or milk, simply by following label directions.

Cocoa products can pick up moisture and flavor from other products. Store them tightly sealed, in a cool, dry place.

Coconut comes fresh (see page 359) or packaged in flaked or shredded forms or finely grated; some is flavored. After opening a package or can, refrigerate the remainder, tightly covered.

Corn syrup is sold in pint and quart bottles and in 5- and 10-pound cans. Light corn syrup is clear, colorless and mild in flavor; dark corn syrup is dark and distinctively flavorful, and can be used as table syrup as well as an ingredient. Both are used to glaze meats and vegetables and as an ingredient in marinades, candies and desserts.

Store, tightly covered, at room temperature until opened; then refrigerate to prevent mold. If crystals form, place the bottle in a bowl of hot water to melt the crystals.

Cornmeal is finely ground white or yellow corn. It is usually enriched with thiamine, niacin, riboflavin and iron. Store at cool room temperature.

Cornstarch is a thickening agent for sauces, puddings, gravies. One tablespoon equals 2 tablespoons of flour in thickening power and makes a clearer sauce.

Store in an airtight container in a cool, dry place.

Cream is the fat portion of milk, containing at least 18 percent milk fat (butterfat) for table or coffee cream; 36 to 40 percent for heavy or whipping cream. Half-and-half is a mixture of milk and cream containing 10 to 12 percent milk fat. Sour cream usually has about 18 percent fat; sour half-and-half, 10 to 12 percent.

Store these products in the refrigerator; use as directed in recipes.

Flour: In our recipes, flour refers to wheat flour unless otherwise specified. It comes in a number of different forms, and because they cannot be used interchangeably, it is important to use the kind called for in the recipe.

• All-purpose flour, sometimes called general-purpose or family flour, is used in most general baking and as a thickening agent in gravies and sauces. It is made from hard or soft wheats, or a blend of the two, and is generally enriched with thiamine, niacin, riboflavin and iron as indicated on the label. Bag sizes range from 2 to 100 pounds.

• Instant flour is all-purpose flour which has been processed to make it fine and granular. Because it blends readily with liquids, it is particularly suitable for thickening gravies and sauces. Use only with specially developed recipes. It is packaged in convenient shakers and in 2- and 5-pound bags.

• Cake flour, blended from soft wheats, has a texture softer than most all-purpose flour. It is packaged in 32-ounce boxes.

• Self-rising flour is all-purpose flour to which leavening agents and salt have been added in proportions suitable for much general baking—not, however, for yeast breads, popovers and egg-leavened cakes such as angel food and sponge cake. To use, follow package directions.

• Whole-wheat flour is also called graham flour or entire wheat flour. It contains all the components of the entire, cleaned wheat grain in the same natural proportions. It is sold in 2-pound boxes and 5-pound bags. Do not sift before measuring.

• Other flours which are not so common are buckwheat, corn, potato, rice, rye and soy. These are used in special recipes or in special diets and can be obtained in specialty or health-food stores and occasionally in supermarkets. Follow package recipes carefully when using.

After opening, transfer flour to an airtight container and store in a cool, dry place for up to one year.

Fruit pectin is a natural substance found in many fruits which, when used in the right proportion with sugar and acid, forms a jelly. Pectin from citrus fruit is refined and bottled as liquid pectin, or packaged as a powder, to simplify the making of jelly from all kinds of fruits and fruit combinations. Use as directed in recipes; do not substitute one form for the other.

Gelatin is available in unflavored and fruit-flavor forms. Unflavored gelatin comes in boxes containing pre-measured ¼-ounce envelopes. Each envelope contains approximately 1 tablespoon gelatin, enough to jell 2 cups of liquid. Fruit-flavor gelatin has sugar and flavor added; add liquid as label or recipe directs. In our recipes do not substitute fruit-flavor for unflavored gelatin or vice versa.

Honey is the sweet, thick syrup made by honey bees. It is sold in the comb, as the extracted liquid, and in solid and granular forms. Our recipes use liquid honey. Store as for Corn Syrup, at left.

Lard is fat separated from the fatty tissue of pork. It has a characteristic nutty flavor and is usually white in color. It is often used in piecrusts, biscuits and other baked foods, and for deep-fat- and pan-frying.

Store in refrigerator; let soften at room temperature for easier measuring.

Maple sugar is made from the evaporation of maple sap or maple syrup. It is usually pressed into fancy shapes to serve as a confection; it is not generally used in baking or cooking.

Maple syrup is thick and sweet, traditionally used on pancakes and waffles and as an ice-cream topping. Pure maple syrup comes from the evaporation of the sap of maple trees. Maple-blended syrup is made from a blend of maple and cane syrups; it is milder than pure maple syrup and less expensive. Either kind may be used in our recipes.

Store as for Corn Syrup, page 14.

Margarine comes in several forms. Regular margarine, with 80 percent fat, is interchangeable with butter in our recipes. Soft margarine is readily spreadable even at refrigerator temperature and can be substituted for butter or regular margarine in cooking. Whipped margarine has air beaten in to increase volume; imitation or diet margarine has greatly reduced fat content and only half the calories of regular margarine. Do not substitute whipped or diet margarine for butter or regular margarine in recipes or frying.

Store in refrigerator or freezer; for long periods, freezer-wrap before freezing.

Meat tenderizer is a food product, obtained from papaya, which works on raw meat to make it tender regardless of kind, grade or cut. When the meat is cooked, the tenderizing action stops.

Use as directed on label or in recipes. Store, tightly covered, at room temperature.

Milk is available fresh, cultured, canned and dry. Almost all milk and cream is pasteurized. Unpasteurized milk, and products made from it, can be dangerous to health. Pasteurization consists of brief heating to kill harmful bacteria, followed by rapid chilling.

• Fresh milk: Whole milk contains not less than 3.25 percent milk fat (butterfat). Homogenized milk is pasteurized whole milk treated so the fat is uniformly distributed throughout. Skim milk has most of the fat removed; it has less than 0.5 percent milk fat. Modified skim milk has vitamins and nonfat dry milk solids added. Low-fat milk has between 0.2 and 2 percent milk fat and "2 percent" milk has, as its name implies, that amount of milk fat. Vitamin D milk, whole or skim, has added amounts of vitamin D. Most skim milk also has vitamin A added.

In our recipes we use fresh whole milk unless a specific kind is called for. Evaporated milk, diluted as directed on the label, may be substituted.

• Chocolate milk is whole milk with sugar and chocolate added; if cocoa instead of chocolate has been used, the milk is designated chocolate-flavored. Chocolate or chocolate-flavored drink contains less milk fat than the minimum for pasteurized milk.

• Cultured milk products include buttermilk, yogurt, sour cream and sour half-and-half (see Cream, page 14).

Buttermilk is thick, smooth, mildly acid; it is made by adding bacterial culture to fresh milk, usually skim milk. Butter granules, too, are sometimes added.

Yogurt is the thick, custard-like, mildly acid preparation usually made by fermenting partly skim or skim milk with a special culture. Fruit or other flavorings may be added.

Store fresh and cultured milk and milk products in the refrigerator until used; use within 3 to 5 days.

• Canned milks include evaporated milk, made from homogenized whole milk with about 60 percent of the water removed; it may be fortified with vitamin D. Sweetened condensed milk has about half of the water removed and contains about 40 percent sugar.

Evaporated milk, diluted with an equal amount of water, can be used when the recipe calls for milk. Sweetened condensed milk, however, cannot be substituted for either fresh or evaporated milk; it must be used as recipes direct.

Unopened cans of either kind of milk, stored at room temperature, will keep several months. Opened cans should be refrigerated and used within 3 to 5 days.

• Dry milk is whole milk with most of the water removed. Nonfat dry milk has also had most of the fat removed, and contains not more than 1/5 percent fat by weight. Most nonfat dry milk available is of the instant type, dissolving readily when mixed with water. Dry whole milk is also sometimes available; when properly reconstituted, it has about the same nutritive value as fluid whole milk.

Store packages or envelopes of dry milk at room temperature for up to 6 months. To use, measure like flour (see page 18). After dry milk has been reconstituted, it should be refrigerated immediately.

Molasses is a distinctively flavored syrup made from sugar-cane sap. Light molasses and unsulphured molasses have a golden color and mild flavor; they are used as a table syrup as well as an ingredient in recipes where delicate color and flavor are needed. Dark (and blackstrap) molasses is much darker and stronger flavored, and is used in recipes where pronounced flavor and color are preferred.

Store as for Corn Syrup, page 14.

Monosodium glutamate is a natural component of protein foods. When used with foods such as meat, fish, poultry and vegetables, it enhances their flavor although it adds no flavor of its own. Use as label or recipe directs.

Nuts may be purchased in the shell or shelled (cashews are an exception; they are sold only shelled). Nuts in the shell, often sold in mixed-nut combinations, are most often available during the holidays. Shelled nuts are available chopped, ground, halved, blanched, slivered, plain, toasted or salted.

Buy nuts in the shell packaged in bags; buy shelled nuts in bags, cans or jars. Containers are labeled with weight in ounces; the cup measure is sometimes given. See Equivalent Measures, page 23.

Because of their fat content, nuts become rancid if exposed to air and heat for prolonged periods. Shelled nuts, particularly those chopped or ground, are more perishable than unshelled nuts. Both kinds may be stored at room temperature in a cool, dry place for about 1 month; for prolonged storage, keep, unopened, in the refrigerator.

Store opened packages of shelled nuts, tightly covered, in the refrigerator; use within two weeks. Nuts, shelled or unshelled, may be frozen for about 3 months if tightly covered; after thawing, allow to dry out at room temperature before using.

Olives are the edible fruit of the olive tree. Both green and ripe (black) olives are processed to remove their natural bitterness. Green olives are packed in brine. They may be unpitted, pitted or pitted and stuffed with pimento, almonds or anchovies. Ripe olives are packed in light brine, sometimes with spices. They may be pitted or unpitted. Greek or Italian olives are processed by drying or salt-curing and are often sold in bulk. Most olives are sold in cans or jars.

Peanut butter is a creamy spread made from finely ground peanuts, blanched or unblanched, to which ingredients which prevent rancidity are added. Crunchy peanut butter has chopped peanuts added and can be used in any peanut butter recipe where smooth texture is not important.

Store covered at room temperature.

Pickles are made from cucumbers and come sweet, sour or dilled. Gherkins are small or immature cucumbers.

Store pickles at room temperature until opened. Then refrigerate, covered; use within a month.

Salad oils consist of one or a combination of vegetable oils. They are used for salad dressings and for dishes that require small amounts of melted fat. While they cannot be substituted for butter or other solid fats in all recipes for baked goods, they can be used in some baking recipes especially developed for liquid shortening. They are especially suitable for frying foods at high temperatures, since they have a higher smoking point than butter, margarine and some lard.

Olive oil, with its distinctive flavor, is traditionally used in Italian- and Spanish-style foods and in salad dressings.

For long storage, store olive oil in refrigerator (it may become cloudy but will still be good); store other salad oils at room temperature. After each use, wipe neck of bottle.

Shortening is produced from bleached, refined, hydrogenated vegetable oil or animal fat. It can be stored at room temperature for about 8 months without losing quality. It is good for deep-fat- and pan-frying, and as an ingredient in pastry and baked products, to which it gives a blander flavor than butter or lard.

Store at room temperature.

Sugar is derived from sugar beets or sugar cane; in our recipes, either beet sugar or cane sugar may be used.

• Granulated, white sugar is the kind used generally in cooking, for the table and in our recipes, unless otherwise specified. It may be labeled granulated, fine granulated or extra-fine granulated. Packages range from 1-pound boxes to 100-pound bags.

Superfine granulated sugar is finer than the regular type, and is often used in beverages and other foods where rapid dissolving is desirable.

White sugar is also available in tablet and cube forms for serving with beverages.

• Confectioners' sugar, sometimes called powdered sugar, is granulated sugar which has been pulverized to make a very fine, soft sugar. It usually contains a small amount of cornstarch to prevent caking.

• Brown sugars contain some molasses, which accounts for their color. Dark brown sugar contains more molasses, has a stronger flavor than light brown sugar. They usually should not be interchanged in recipes because of this flavor difference. Granulated brown sugar is dry and pourable but should not be used as a direct substitute for regular brown sugar in baking.

• Raw sugar is unrefined crystalline sugar. It consists of coarse, sticky brownish-yellow crystals. It cannot be substituted in many recipes for granulated sugar.

Keep all sugars tightly covered in a cool, dry place. Brown sugar (except the granulated type) is the most perishable; it hardens quickly if exposed to air. After opening, transfer to container with tight-fitting lid. If brown sugar becomes lumpy, roll with rolling pin and then sift before measuring. If it becomes hard, soften by placing in shallow pan in oven preheated to 250° to 300°F. just until pliable; measure immediately, since after it cools, it will become hard again.

Tapioca is a thickening agent made from tapioca flour and sold in 8-ounce packages. It thickens a mixture without making it cloudy. It is most often available as quick-cooking tapioca, but the longer-cooking pearl tapioca is also available in some areas. Be sure to use the type specified.

Vinegar is an acid liquid used for flavoring and preserving.

• Cider vinegar, made from apple juice, has a mellow fruit flavor, a fruity odor and a clear amber color. It is an all-purpose vinegar, used in general cooking, in salad dressings and in pickling.

• Distilled white vinegar is another all-purpose vinegar usually made from grain alcohol. It is clear and colorless, especially good for canning and pickling since it does not alter the color of the food.

• Special vinegars: Tarragon vinegar is made from one or more vinegars delicately flavored with tarragon. Mixed herb or salad vinegars are blended vinegars, which may be flavored with a combination of herbs, such as basil, rosemary, tarragon and thyme. Wine vinegars, made from red or white wine, have a tangy but mild flavor or may be flavored with garlic.

Store vinegar, tightly capped, at room temperature.

Wheat germ, the heart of the wheat kernel, is rich in B vitamins, vitamin E, protein and iron. It has a nutlike flavor, usually comes in vacuum-packed glass jars and should be stored in the refrigerator after opening.

Yogurt: See Milk, Cultured page 15.

How to Measure Ingredients

Accurate measurements are essential if you want the same good results every time you make a recipe. All measurements should be level, unless (as rarely happens) the recipe directs otherwise.

Pay special attention to the wording used in recipes. For example, *1 pound shelled, deveined shrimp* is a different measurement from *1 pound shrimp, shelled and deveined.* There are more shrimp to the pound when they are weighed after the shells are removed than before, and this will affect the number of servings resulting.

Use the right measuring equipment: For dry ingredients, use a set of four graduated measuring cups, consisting of ¼-, ⅓-, ½- and 1-cup measures.

For liquids, use a liquid-measuring cup—a glass or plastic 1-cup measuring cup—with a rim above the 1-cup line to prevent spilling. The cup should be marked also for measurements smaller than 1 cup. Two-cup and 4-cup liquid measuring cups are helpful for measuring larger amounts.

Measuring spoons are used for both dry and liquid ingredients. A standard set includes ¼-, ½-, 1-teaspoon and 1-tablespoon measures.

To measure liquids: Place the liquid measuring cup on a level surface. Lower your head so that the desired line of measurement is at eye level; then slowly pour liquid into the cup until it reaches the desired line. If using measuring spoons, pour the liquid just to the top of the spoon without letting it spill over.

Don't hold the cup or spoon over the mixture to which you'll be adding the liquid. You may accidentally pour out too much.

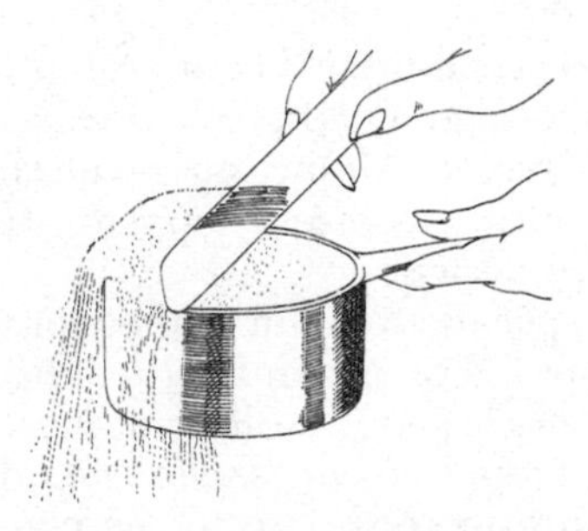

To measure dry ingredients: Lightly spoon (or lightly pack, if it's brown sugar) the ingredient into the measuring cup or spoon; then, with the edge, not the flat side, of a straight-edged knife or spatula, level off the top.

Here are tips for special ingredients:

Flour: In our recipes, we do not sift today's finely milled all-purpose and cake flours; we measure and use them right from the sack, package or canister.

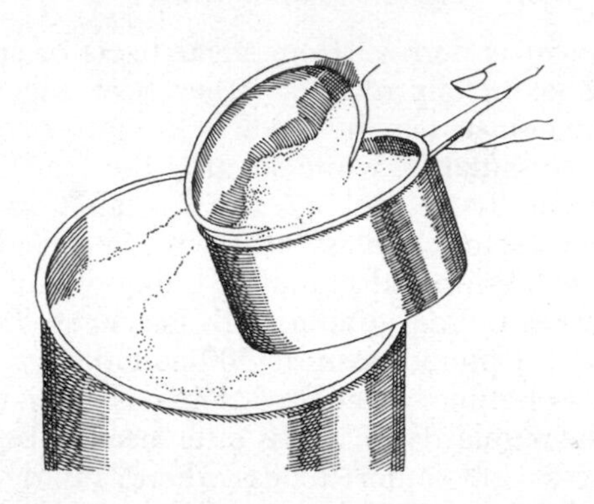

To measure: Lightly spoon the flour into the cup and level off. Never pack flour down; never shake or tap the cup.

Flour for all the recipes in this book is measured this way. However, if you are using a recipe that calls for sifted flour, you should sift the flour before measuring it, even if the label on the flour sack says "presifted." Sifting makes a difference in flour measurement; there is more flour to the cup when it's measured right from the sack. To measure sifted flour: Using a sifter or strainer, sift the flour onto waxed paper and then lightly spoon it into the cup and level off.

Granulated sugar: Spoon sugar lightly into the measuring cup and level off with the straight edge of a knife or spatula.

Brown sugar: Pack brown sugar lightly into the cup with the back of a spoon, then level off. When properly packed, it should hold its shape when inverted from the cup.

Confectioners' sugar: Because confectioners' sugar can sometimes become lumpy, many recipes call for it to be sifted. In that case, sift, then measure the same way as granulated sugar. Where the recipe does not specify, measure it without sifting. Or, if it is lumpy, or is to be used in frosting with a cake decorator, measure it and then sift out the lumps.

To measure shortenings: Liquid shortenings, such as salad oil and melted butter or margarine, should be measured in the same way as liquids, above.

Solid shortenings, such as lard, vegetable shortening, peanut butter, etc. should be spooned from the can or package and packed firmly into the graduated measuring cup or spoon right up to the top, then leveled off with the edge, not the flat side, of a knife or spatula.

Butter and margarine: Each ¼-pound stick of butter or margarine measures ½ cup; and the wrapping usually is marked off in tablespoons for measuring smaller amounts. With a sharp knife, just cut off the number of tablespoons needed, following the guidelines on the wrapping. For butter or margarine not wrapped this way, measure the same way as solid shortening.

We use regular, not whipped, butter or margarine in our recipes, since air is incorporated into the whipped product; consequently, the latter does not provide the same amount of shortening as an equal measure of the regular kind. Do not, therefore, substitute whipped for regular butter or margarine unless the recipe calls for melting the butter or margarine before measuring (the air in the whipped kind will escape during melting, and a true measurement can then be made).

How to Measure Pans

In our recipes, we tell you the kind and size of saucepan, baking dish, casserole, or other pan we have found to give best results. Where the size is not absolutely essential to the success of the recipe, we have simply said "large," "deep," etc.

However, for many recipes, particularly in baking—cakes, breads, pies, desserts—a specific measurement is essential. Here we give either the dimensions of the proper pan in inches, or its capacity in cups or quarts. Larger or smaller pans will result in spillovers in the oven or in products unevenly cooked or otherwise disappointing.

When making these recipes, be sure your pans are the same size as ours. Many pans are marked by the manufacturer with the dimensions or cup capacity. If your pans are not so marked, measure them this way: For diameter, width or length, use a ruler to measure across the top of the pan from inside edge to inside edge of ovenware, outside edge to outside edge of skillets and griddles. For capacity, using a liquid measuring cup, fill the dish to the brim with water, measuring the water as you add it.

After you've measured a baking pan or dish, use nail polish to mark the measurement on the outside bottom of the pan or dish so you won't have to measure it again.

Special Preparation Tips

Almonds: To blanch: In saucepan, cover shelled almonds with cold water. Over high heat, heat to boiling; remove at once from heat and drain. Cover almonds with cold water to cool, then press each almond between thumb and forefinger to slip off skin. Dry almonds on paper towels.

To toast: See Toasted Almonds, page 379.

To roast: Preheat oven to 375°F. In shallow baking pan, arrange a single layer of blanched, whole almonds. Bake until browned, about 15 minutes.

Avocado: To prepare: Just before using, cut avocado in half lengthwise around seed. Separate halves by twisting in opposite directions. Then pierce seed with point of paring knife; lift seed out and discard. With knife, carefully strip skin from fruit. Brush surfaces of avocado with lemon or lime juice to prevent discoloring.

Banana: To flute edges: Peel banana, then run table-fork tines lengthwise down surface. Slice banana crosswise or diagonally.

To prevent darkening, dip banana slices into an acid fruit juice such as lemon or pineapple, or into prepared ascorbic-acid mixture for fruit.

Brazil nuts: To shell: Freeze in-shell nuts overnight; then use nutcracker to shell. Or, in saucepan, cover in-shell nuts with water; over high heat, heat to boiling; boil 3 minutes. Drain; cover with cold water and let stand 1 minute to cool; drain. Use nutcracker or hammer to remove shell easily.

To slice: In saucepan, cover shelled nuts with water; over high heat, heat to simmering. Reduce heat to low and simmer 2 or 3 minutes; drain; they'll slice easily. Or, with vegetable parer, cut into slivers; slivers will curl.

Bread crumbs: *To make dried bread crumbs:* Preheat oven to 250°F. Place bread slices in one layer on cookie sheet; bake until slices are crisp and dry but not browned. (Or, let stand at room temperature several days until completely dried.) Break slices into large pieces and blend in covered blender container at high speed until reduced to fine crumbs. Or, place in strong, clean paper bag; with rolling pin, roll to make fine crumbs. Or, put through food mill or food grinder, using fine blade; tie plastic bag to blade end of grinder to collect all crumbs. Keep crumbs refrigerated.

Packaged dried bread crumbs, plain or seasoned, and crumb mixtures with different seasonings for breading foods, are available.

To make fresh bread crumbs: Crumble bread slices between your fingers to make either coarse or fine crumbs as desired.

To make Buttered Crumbs, see page 351.

California walnuts: To crack: Place each nut on end, holding by seam. With hammer, strike point sharply. Or, crack with nutcracker.

To toast: See Toasted Nuts, page 380.

Chestnuts: To roast, preheat oven to 400°F. With tip of knife, slash an X in each chestnut. Place chestnuts, cut side up, on cookie sheet. Roast about 20 minutes or until tender; to test, insert fork through cut in shell. To boil, see Chestnut Stuffing, page 204.

Chocolate: To melt: Place chocolate in double-boiler top, or in small bowl or custard cup; melt over hot, not boiling, water.

Croutons: Preheat oven to 300°F. Trim crusts from bread slices; cut slices into small squares. Place squares in one layer on cookie sheet; bake about 20 minutes or until light golden.

Orange: To section, hold peeled orange over bowl. Using paring knife, with sawing motion, cut along sides of each dividing membrane to center of fruit, then tip knife and scoop out individual sections. Or, cut halfway between membranes (membranes will now be at centers of sections); release sections by running knife down along membrane at center of fruit.

Parsley: To chop, place parsley in measuring cup. With kitchen shears, cut through parsley until desired degree of fineness is reached.

Pecans: See California Walnuts, at left.

Vanilla bean: To use in custards, hot milk beverages, etc.: Cut off the length of bean needed and split it; heat in the milk or liquid to release flavor; remove bean before using the milk; discard. Or, blot dry with paper towels and keep in sugar canister to lend aroma to sugar.

To make "vanilla sugar," used in classic baking: Split one or two beans or cut beans into pieces and stir into 3 or 4 pounds of sugar in tightly covered canister. It will take about 2 weeks for sugar to adopt vanilla aroma. Occasionally stir sugar, and add a new bean to "freshen up" aroma.

Special Cutting Tips

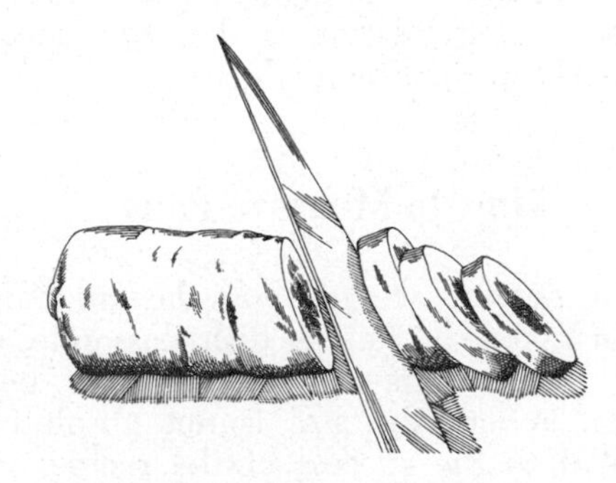

Diagonally sliced: Lay food flat on cutting board; with paring knife, cut at an angle into thin or thick slices.

To chop or mince with a French knife: Cut food into chunks, if necessary. With one hand, press down on back of blade near point. With handle of knife in other hand, cut up and down in rocking motion, pivoting knife until all food is chopped equally fine.

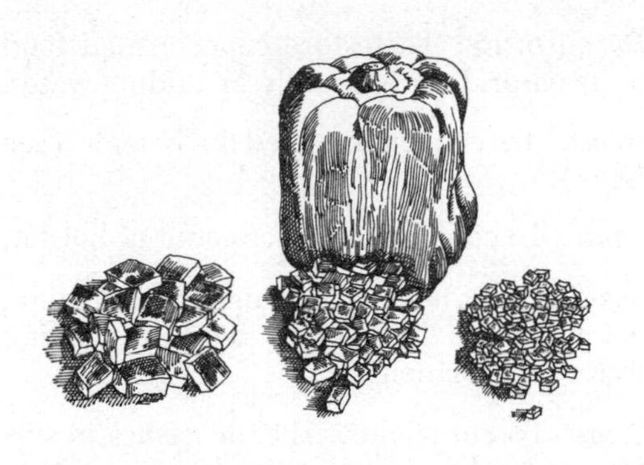

Cube, dice, mince, cut into strips: Cut with sharp knife into pieces of size or shape shown in drawing of green pepper. The whole pepper illustrates the relative sizes. Cubes, bottom left, are about ½ inch across. Diced pieces, bottom center, are about ¼ inch across. Minced pieces, bottom right, the smallest, are about ⅛ inch across. Strips can be any size.

Cooking Terms

Bake: To cook food by dry heat in an oven or oven-type appliance. When applied to meats and poultry, it is called roasting.

Barbecue: To roast or broil food on a rack or spit over coals, or under a heat unit. The food is usually brushed with a highly seasoned sauce as it cooks.

Baste: To moisten food while it cooks. Thus, the surface doesn't dry out and flavor is added. Melted fat, drippings, sauce and fruit juice are the liquids generally used.

Beat: To make a mixture smooth with rapid, regular motion using a spoon, wire whisk, hand beater or mixer. When using a spoon, the mixture should be lifted up and over with each stroke.

Blanch: To scald, either to help loosen the skin from some foods, or as a step in preparing vegetables for freezing.

Blend: 1. To thoroughly mix two or more ingredients. 2. To prepare food in blender until pureed, chopped, etc., as desired.

Boil: To cook in liquid in which bubbles rise constantly to the surface and break.

Braise: To cook food slowly in a small amount of liquid in a covered pan. (Food may or may not be browned first in a small amount of fat.)

Broil: To cook by direct heat on a rack or spit.

Brush with: To spread food lightly with salad oil, melted fat, milk, heavy cream, beaten egg, etc., with pastry brush.

Caramelize: To stir sugar in skillet over low heat until it melts and develops characteristic flavor and golden-brown color.

Chill: To refrigerate food or let it stand in ice or iced water until cold.

Chop: To cut food into small pieces with a knife or blender.

Coat: To sprinkle food with, or dip it into, flour, etc., until completely covered.

Cool: To refrigerate food, or let it stand at room temperature, until no longer warm to the touch.

Cream: 1. To make soft, smooth and creamy by beating with spoon or with mixer; usually applied to blending sugar and a fat together. 2. To cook food in, or serve it with, white or "cream" sauce.

Cube: 1. To cut food into small cubes (about ½-inch). 2. To cut the surface of meat in checkered pattern to increase tenderness by breaking tough meat fibers.

Cut in: To distribute solid fat in flour or flour mixture by using pastry blender or two knives scissor-fashion until flour-coated fat particles are of desired size.

Deep-fry: To cook in hot fat deep enough for food to float on it.

Dice: To cut food into very small pieces (about 1/4 inch).

Dot: To scatter bits, as of butter or margarine, over surface of food.

Dredge: To cover or coat food, as with flour, cornmeal, etc.

Fold in: To combine delicate ingredients (whipped cream, beaten egg whites, etc.) with other foods by using a gentle, circular motion to cut down into the mixture, slide across the bottom of the bowl and bring some of the mixture up and over the surface.

Fry: To cook in fat. See also Deep-fry, Panfry, Sauté.

Grate: To rub food on a grater (or chop in blender) to produce fine, medium or coarse particles.

Grease: To rub surface of dish or pan with fat, to keep food from sticking.

Grill: To cook by direct heat. Also, utensil or appliance used for this type of cooking.

Grind: To reduce to particles in food grinder or blender.

Knead: To work a food mixture with a press-and-fold motion.

Lukewarm: At a temperature of about 95°F. Lukewarm food will feel neither warm nor cold when sprinkled on or held to the inside of the wrist.

Marinate: To let food stand in a well-flavored mixture for a period of time to produce flavor and/or tenderness.

Mince: To cut into very small pieces, using knife, food grinder or blender.

Pan: To cook, covered, in very small amount of liquid.

Pan-broil: To cook food, uncovered, on ungreased or lightly greased hot surface, pouring off fat as it accumulates.

Pan-fry: To cook in a small amount of fat.

Parboil: To boil until partially cooked, usually before completing cooking by another method.

Peel: To remove outer covering of foods by trimming away with knife or vegetable peeler, or by pulling off.

Pit: To remove seed or pit.

Poach: To cook in simmering liquid.

Pot-roast: To cook large pieces of meat or poultry by braising.

Preheat: To heat to desired temperature before putting food in to cook.

Puree: To press food through a fine sieve or food mill, or blend in blender so it becomes a smooth, thick paste.

Reconstitute: To restore concentrated food to its natural state, usually by adding water.

Roast: To cook uncovered in hot air (see Bake).

Sauté: To cook in a small amount of hot fat.

Scald: 1. To heat to just under the boiling point. 2. To dip certain foods in boiling water (see Blanch).

Score: To cut shallow slits or gashes in surface of food to increase tenderness, or prevent fat covering from curling, or to decorate.

Sear: To brown the surface of meat quickly with high heat.

Shred: To cut food into slivers or slender pieces, using a knife or shredder.

Simmer: To cook in a liquid just below the boiling point. Bubbles form slowly and collapse just below the surface.

Steep: To allow food to stand in hot liquid to extract flavor and color.

Stew: To simmer in a liquid.

Stir: To mix food, using a circular motion.

Toast: To brown in dry heat.

Toss: To mix foods lightly with a lifting motion, using two forks or spoons.

Whip: To beat rapidly with mixer, hand beater or wire whisk, so air is incorporated and volume is increased.

Equivalent Measures

Dash	2 to 3 drops or less than ⅛ teaspoon
1 tablespoon	3 teaspoons
¼ cup	4 tablespoons
⅓ cup	5⅓ tablespoons
½ cup	8 tablespoons
1 cup	16 tablespoons
1 pint	2 cups
1 quart	4 cups
1 gallon	4 quarts
1 peck	8 quarts
1 bushel	4 pecks
1 pound	16 ounces

Equivalent Amounts

Apples	
1 pound	3 medium (3 cups sliced)
Berries	
1 pint	1¾ cups
Bread	
1 1-pound loaf	14 to 20 slices
Bread crumbs, fresh	
1 slice bread with crust	½ cup bread crumbs
Broth, chicken or beef	
1 cup	1 bouillon cube, 1 envelope powdered broth base or 1 teaspoon powdered broth or stock base dissolved in 1 cup boiling water
Butter or margarine	
¼-pound stick	½ cup
Cheese	
¼ pound	1 cup shredded
Cheese, cottage	
8 ounces	1 cup
Cheese, cream	
3 ounces	6 tablespoons
Chocolate, unsweetened	
8 ounces	8 squares
Coconut, flaked	
3½-ounce can	1⅓ cups
shredded	
4-ounce can	1⅓ cups
Cream, heavy or whipping	
1 cup	2 cups whipped cream
sour	
8 ounces	1 cup
Egg whites, large	
1 cup	8 to 10 whites
Egg yolks, large	
1 cup	12 to 14 yolks
Flour, all-purpose	
1 pound	about 3½ cups
cake flour	
1 pound	about 4 cups
Gelatin, unflavored	
1 envelope	1 tablespoon
Lemon	
1 medium	3 tablespoons juice about 1 tablespoon grated peel
Lime	
1 medium	2 tablespoons juice
Milk, evaporated	
5⅓- or 6-ounce can	⅔ cup
13- or 14½-ounce can	1⅔ cups
sweetened condensed	
14- or 15- ounce can	1¼ to 1⅓ cups
Nuts, one pound	
Almonds, in shell	1 to 1¼ cups nutmeats
shelled	3 cups
Brazil nuts, in shell	1½ cups nutmeats
shelled	3¼ cups
Filberts, in shell	2 cups nutmeats
shelled	4 cups
Peanuts, in shell	2 to 2½ cups nutmeats
shelled	4 cups
Pecans, in shell	2¼ cups nutmeats
shelled	4 cups
Walnuts, in shell	2 cups nutmeats
shelled	4 cups

Onion	
1 medium	¾ to 1 cup chopped
Orange	
1 medium	⅓ to ½ cup juice 2 tablespoons grated peel
Potatoes, white	
1 pound	3 medium
sweet	
1 pound	3 medium
Raisins	
1 pound	3 cups, loosely packed
Salad oil	
16 ounces	2 cups
Sugar, granulated	
1 pound	2¼ to 2½ cups
brown	
1 pound	2¼ cups packed
confectioners'	
1 pound	4 to 4½ cups
Syrup, corn	
16 ounces	2 cups
Syrup, maple	
12 ounces	1½ cups
Tomatoes	
1 pound	3 medium

Cooking at High Altitudes

Recipes in this book have been perfected for use at sea level; between sea level and altitudes of 2,500 to 3,000 feet, they probably need no modification. At higher altitudes, however, some adjustments may be necessary.

At sea level, water boils at 212°F. With each 500 feet of increased altitude above sea level, the boiling point drops 1 degree. Even though the boiling point is lower, it takes longer to reach at the higher altitude. Therefore, food boiled in water at high altitudes will take longer to boil and will require cooking times longer than those suggested in our recipes.

At high altitudes, cake recipes may need slight adjustments in the proportions of flour, leavening, liquid, eggs, etc. These adjustments vary from recipe to recipe and no set guidelines can be given. Many cake mixes now carry special directions on the label for high-altitude preparation.

High altitudes also affect the rising of doughs and batters, deep-frying, candy-making and other aspects of food preparation. If you are having difficulty with your recipes, call or write to the home agent at your county cooperative extension office, or to the home economics department of your local utility company or state university for information and special recipes for your area.

Microwave Cooking

Food preparation using the microwave oven is in most cases very different from that required for conventional ranges. All the recipes in this book have been developed for use with conventional ranges. If you have a microwave oven, be sure to follow the manufacturer's directions.

Special Food Terms

à la: In the manner of.

à la carte: Refers to a meal in which the diner selects individual items, paying for each, rather than taking a *table d' hôte* meal at a fixed price.

à la mode: In style. Desserts à la mode are served with ice cream; meats à la mode are braised with vegetables and served with gravy.

Amandine: Made or garnished with almonds.

Antipasto: An assortment of appetizers.

Aperitif: A drink taken before a meal to stimulate the appetite.

Aspic: Jellied meat, fish or poultry stock or vegetable liquid often used for molding meat, fish, poultry or vegetables.

au jus: Served with unthickened natural juices that develop during roasting.

au lait: With milk.

Batter: A mixture of pouring consistency, made of flour, liquid and other ingredients.

Bavarian: A molded cold dessert made with gelatin, eggs, cream and flavorings.

Bisque: A thick, rich cream soup usually made with shellfish or pureed vegetables.

Blanquette: A white, creamy stew of veal, chicken or lamb with small onions and mushrooms.

Blintz: A thin pancake rolled and filled, usually with cottage cheese.

Bombe: A dessert of frozen mixtures arranged and frozen in a mold.

Bouillabaisse: A hearty stew made with several kinds of fish and shellfish.

Bouillon: A clear, seasoned soup usually made from beef or chicken; also obtained by dissolving a bouillon cube or envelope in boiling water.

Bouquet garni: Several herbs, usually including parsley, thyme and bay leaf, tied in cheesecloth. Added to stews, soups and sauces for flavoring; bundle is easy to remove when desired.

Brochette: A skewer. Food cooked "en brochette" is cooked on a skewer.

Broth: Liquid in which meat, poultry or vegetables have simmered. Same as stock.

Canapé: Plain or toasted bread or crackers topped with a savory mixture, served as an appetizer.

Chutney: A highly seasoned relish made of fruits.

Compote: 1. A dessert of fresh or dried fruits cooked in syrup. 2. A deep bowl, often stemmed, from which such desserts and other foods are served.

Condiment: 1. Seasoning, often pungent, used to bring out the flavor of foods. 2. Sauces, relishes, etc., to add to food at the table.

Crêpe: A thin, delicate pancake.

Croissant: A rich crescent-shaped roll.

Croquette: A mixture of chopped or minced food, shaped as a cone or ball, coated with egg and crumbs and deep-fried.

Crouton: A small cube of bread toasted or fried, most often used in soups and salads.

Demitasse: A small cup ("half cup") of black coffee, usually served after dinner.

Dijon mustard: A prepared mustard (originally made in Dijon, France) which may be either mild or highly seasoned. When our recipes specify Dijon mustard, the highly seasoned type is meant.

Drippings: Fat and juices drawn from meat or poultry as it cooks.

Enchilada: A tortilla, stuffed, rolled and served with a highly seasoned sauce.

Enriched: Resupplied with vitamins and minerals lost or diminished during processing of food.

Entrée: The main dish of the meal.

Escargot: An edible snail.

Filet (or fillet): A piece of meat, fish or poultry which is boneless or has had all bones removed.

Fines herbes: A mixture of herbs used for seasoning. Traditionally includes parsley, chervil, chives and tarragon, though other herbs may be used.

Flambé: Flaming.

Foie gras: Literally translated, "fat liver"; the term usually is applied to goose liver.

Fondue: The name denotes a number of different dishes, the best known of which is a dish of melted cheese and wine or brandy. Dessert fondue may be made of chocolate or other sauces. The term also denotes a soufflé-like dish made with bread, and a dish in which cubes of beef are cooked at the table in hot fat and eaten with a variety of sauces.

Fortified: Supplied with more vitamins and minerals than were present in the natural state.

Fritter: A small quantity of a batter mixture, often containing meat, vegetables or fruit, fried until crisp.

Flute: To make decorative indentations.

Fricassee: A stew made of chicken or veal cut into pieces and cooked in a gravy.

Gazpacho: A cold Spanish soup made with tomatoes and other fresh vegetables.

Glacé: Glazed, as with a frosting; or frozen.

Glaze: 1. To coat with a glossy mixture. 2. Concentrated stock used to add flavor.

Goulash: A type of beef stew with onion and paprika.

Grenadine: Syrup flavored with pomegranates, used as flavoring and sauce.

Grenouilles: Frogs' legs.

Gumbo: A thick, Southern-style soup made with meat, poultry, fish, shellfish or vegetables.

Hibachi: Small, portable charcoal grill.

Hoisin sauce: A thick sauce made of soy beans and seasonings used in Chinese cooking.

Homogenized: With fat broken down into such small particles that it stays suspended in liquid, rather than rising to the top.

Homard: Lobster.

Hors d'oeuvres: Savory, usually small, foods used as appetizers.

Jardinière: Garnished with vegetables.

Julienne: Cut in long, thin strips.

Kabob (kebab): Cubes of meat marinated and cooked with vegetables, usually on a skewer.

Kosher: Ritually fit for use in accordance with Jewish law.

Lyonnaise: Prepared with onion.

Marinade: A seasoned liquid, often containing vinegar and oil, in which food is soaked to improve flavor.

Marinate: To soak in a marinade.

Marrons: Chestnuts.

Marrons glacés: Chestnuts preserved in syrup or candied.

Marzipan: Sweetened almond paste made into confections.

Matzoth: Thin, unleavened, cracker-like bread made of flour and water.

Meringue: Mixture of stiffly beaten egg whites and sugar.

Meunière: With sauce of butter, lemon juice and parsley.

Minestrone: Thick soup of beans, vegetables, pasta.

Mocha: Flavoring of coffee or made by combining coffee and chocolate.

Monosodium glutamate: White, crystalline salt that enhances the natural flavor of many foods.

Montmorency: With cherries.

Moules: Mussels.

Mousse: A cold dessert with whipped cream or beaten egg whites.

Nesselrode: A mixture of candied fruit, nuts and cherries used in desserts.

Oeuf: Egg.

Parfait: A dessert made of layers of fruit, syrup, ice cream and whipped cream, frozen and served in a tall slender glass.

Pasta: All macaroni products.

Pastrami: Highly spiced smoked beef, usually prepared from shoulder cuts.

Pâté: A spread of finely ground, seasoned meat or poultry.

Patty shell: A shell made from puff paste to hold creamed mixtures or fruit.

Petit four: Small, decoratively iced, rich cake.

Pilaf: Rice with seasoning, often with meat or poultry added.

Polenta: Cornmeal mush.

Potage: Soup.

Poulet: Chicken.

Profiteroles: Tiny cream puffs, filled with sweet or savory mixtures, served as dessert or hors d'oeuvres.

Prosciutto: Italian-style ham which has been aged in spices. Can be eaten without cooking and is sliced paper thin.

Puree: 1. A thick soup made from a pureed vegetable base. 2. See Puree, page 22.

Quiche: Savory egg-and-cream pie.

Ragoût: A well-seasoned stew of meat and vegetables.

Risotto: An Italian dish of rice cooked in broth and seasoned.

Roulade: Rolled meat.

Roux: Cooked paste of flour and butter or drippings, used to thicken sauces, etc.

Scaloppine: Small, thin pieces of meat sautéed or broiled until browned and tender.

Scampi: 1. Shrimp. 2. A dish of shrimp in garlic sauce.

Shish kebab: Cubes of meat cooked on a skewer, often with vegetables.

Silver dragées: Tiny, ball-shaped, silver-colored candies.

Smitane: Wine sauce with sour cream and onions added.

Stock: Broth.

Sukiyaki: Japanese dish of meat, vegetables and seasonings, usually cooked at the table.

Sub gum: A stew of Chinese vegetables.

Table d'hôte: Meal of a definite number of courses, selected by the restaurant for the price indicated.

Taco: Fried, toasted or baked tortilla with filling rolled or folded inside.

Tamale: Cornmeal spread on corn husk, filled with chili-seasoned mixture, rolled, tied and steamed.

Tempura: Japanese dish of batter-dipped, fried seafood or vegetables.

Toast points: Toast slices, cut in half diagonally.

Torte: Dessert of the cake or meringue type, usually rich in eggs and nuts.

Tortilla: Very thin, Mexican bread made of cornmeal.

Tostada: Tortilla fried until crisp.

Tournedos: Fillet of beef steak.

Truffle: 1. Species of fungus that grows below the ground; used as garnish. 2. A very rich chocolate candy.

Veau: Veal.

Wiener schnitzel: Breaded, fried veal cutlet, served plain or garnished with lemon, parsley, fried egg, etc.

Won ton: A ravioli-like Chinese dish of noodles folded around a filling of meat, fish or vegetables.

Zabaglione: Delicate dessert made of beaten eggs and wine.

HERBS AND SPICES

Herb or Spice	*Ways to Use*
ALLSPICE Available ground or whole; one spice, it resembles a blend of cloves, cinnamon and nutmeg.	In meat and poultry dishes, pickles, relishes, cakes, cookies, pastries.
ANISE SEED Seed or ground; aroma and flavor resemble licorice.	With fruits; in breads, cookies, candies.
BASIL Broken leaves or ground; sweet, faintly anise-like flavor and aroma.	In tomato sauces and dishes, soups, stuffings, salad dressings; as garnish for egg, cheese, poultry, tomato dishes.
BAY LEAVES Leaves up to 3 inches long, or ground.	In meat and poultry dishes, particularly pot roasts and stews; in fish and vegetable dishes, pickles.

CARAWAY SEED Seeds up to ¼ inch long; have characteristic aroma and slightly sharp taste.	In breads, cheese spreads and dips, sauerkraut, sweet pickles; as garnish for breads, cheese, coleslaw.
CARDAMOM SEED Whole pods with seeds; ground (seeds and pod) or decorticated (seeds only) and ground. Has pleasant aroma, slightly sharp taste.	Use whole seeds in demitasse, pickles; ground in cookies, coffeecakes, with fruits.
CELERY SEED Seeds; ground and combined with salt (celery salt); slightly bitter, fresh-celery flavor.	In meat, cheese, egg, fish dishes; barbecue sauces; pickles; soups; salad dressings.
CHERVIL Leaves resembling parsley; has pleasant aroma and flavor resembling tarragon.	In fish and egg dishes, soups, salads, meat sauces and stews.
CHILI POWDER Red to very dark red powder, with characteristic aroma and varying degrees of pungency. Refrigerate.	In meat dishes, especially Spanish- or Mexican-style; pickles; barbecue sauces; cocktail dips; salad dressings; snack foods; cheese, egg and seafood dishes.
CHIVES Fresh, thin tubular leaves; freeze-dried and chopped; flavor mild, onion-like.	In cheese, egg, fish, poultry dishes; soups; with vegetables; as garnish for salads, soups, vegetables.
CINNAMON Sticks of rolled bark in various lengths, or ground. Flavor and aroma are sweet and pungent. Short sticks (about 3 inches) are most available.	In sweet vegetable (baked beans, sweet potatoes) and fruit dishes; pickles; breads; cakes; cookies; desserts.
CLOVES Whole or ground; flavor and aroma are strong, pungent and sweet.	In meat and poultry dishes, barbecue sauces; with sweet vegetables, pickles, relishes, fruits, breads, cookies, desserts, candies; as garnish for relishes, ham, spiced fruits.
CORIANDER SEED Whole or ground; flavor and aroma are distinctively lemon-like.	In pickles, breads, cookies, cakes.
CUMIN SEED Whole or ground; flavor and aroma are strong and slightly bitter.	In Spanish-style and Mexican-style meat and rice dishes; cheese spreads; egg and fish dishes.
CURRY POWDER A blend of many ground spices; golden in color, has distinctive flavor characteristic of cooking of India.	In meat, poultry, fish, shellfish, egg and cheese dishes; sauces; salad dressings; soups.

DILL

Leaves and stems (weed) and seeds; flavor and aroma slightly sharp.

In pickles, cheese dishes, salad dressings, cocktail dips, fish and shellfish dishes; with vegetables. Fresh dill is used to garnish salads, seafood, casseroles.

FENNEL SEED

Whole or ground; flavor and aroma are sweet, anise-like.

Breads, pizza and spaghetti sauces, fish sauces, pickles; as garnish for baked goods.

GINGER

Whole, ground or cracked (in small pieces). Crystallized or candied ginger is a confection but may be added to chutneys, baked goods, used as a garnish. Flavor and aroma are pungent, sweet, taste is "hot."

In Oriental-style meat, poultry, seafood and vegetable dishes; relishes and pickles; salad dressings; breads; cookies; cakes; desserts.

MACE

Whole or ground; flavor and aroma of nutmeg but stronger, less delicate.

In soups, salad dressing, meat and poultry spreads; egg and cheese dishes; breads; cookies; cakes; fruit pies. Particularly good with chocolate.

MARJORAM

Leaves or ground; distinctive aroma similar to oregano, flavor slightly bitter.

In meat, poultry, fish, cheese, egg and vegetable dishes; vegetable sauces and Italian-style dishes.

MINT

Fresh or dried leaves, or flakes; flavor and aroma strong and sweet; provides cool after-taste.

With vegetables, fruits, desserts; in jelly, tea, relishes; a garnish for beverages, desserts.

MUSTARD SEED

Whole or powdered; yellow seeds have no odor but sharp, pungent taste when combined with water; brown seeds combined with water have sharp, irritating odor and pungent taste.

In pickles and relishes, salad dressings, egg and cheese dishes, cocktail dips, sandwich spreads.

NUTMEG

Whole seed up to 1¼ inches long, or ground; flavor and aroma are sweet, characteristic.

In beverages, vegetable dishes, breads, cookies, cakes, desserts; as garnish for beverages, sauces, desserts.

OREGANO

Leaves or ground; flavor and aroma similar to marjoram and thyme but stronger.

In Italian- and Mexican-style main-course foods and sauces, snack foods, cocktail dips; in beef, poultry, seafood, cheese and vegetable (especially tomato) dishes.

PAPRIKA

Powder, varying in color from rich bright red to brick red; flavor and aroma slightly sweet, may have slight "bite." Refrigerate.

In meat, poultry, cheese dishes; salad dressings; snack foods; cocktail dips; as garnish for cream soups, casseroles, cheese dips, salads.

Spice	Description	Uses
PARSLEY	Leaves and stems; dried flakes; flavor and aroma mild, characteristic.	In soups, salads, meat, poultry, seafood, cheese, egg, vegetable dishes; as garnish for salads, soups, main dishes.
PEPPER	Black pepper is available as whole peppercorns and cracked, coarsely ground or ground; white pepper comes whole and ground; red pepper comes as whole pods ranging from ⅜ inch to 12 inches long, and ground or crushed. All have hot biting taste and characteristic odor. White pepper is mildest; red pepper varies from mild to intense; cayenne pepper is the "hottest" spice. Refrigerate red and cayenne pepper.	In most foods: soups, main dishes, salads, salad dressings, snack and appetizer foods, pickles.
	Green peppercorns are also available.	In snack and appetizer foods; meat, fish and poultry sauces; salad dressings.
POPPY SEED	Whole; flavor and aroma are sweet, mild, nut-like.	In noodles, salad dressings, breads, rolls; fillings for breads and cakes; as garnish for cheese, snack foods.
ROSEMARY	Needle-like leaves; flavor and aroma are distinctive, tea-like, bittersweet.	In meat, poultry and fish dishes; stuffings; breads; with vegetables; in salads; as garnish for salads, breads.
SAFFRON	Strands ½ inch to ¾ inch long, or ground; aroma is strong, medicinal; flavor pleasantly bitter.	In poultry, fish and shellfish dishes; rice; breads.
SAGE	Leaves about 3 inches long, rubbed or ground; flavor and aroma slightly bitter.	In meat, poultry, cheese dishes; stuffings.
SAVORY	Leaves or ground; aroma is pine-like.	Meat, egg, rice, vegetable dishes; stuffings.
SESAME SEED	Whole; flavor and aroma slightly nut-like.	In rolls, breads, snacks, candy; as garnish for vegetables, breads, snack foods.
TARRAGON	Leaves; flavor and aroma are sweet, anise-like.	In poultry, seafood, cheese and egg dishes; with vegetables, salad dressings.
THYME	Leaves or ground; flavor is pungent, aroma distinctive.	In meat, poultry, seafood, egg, cheese and vegetable dishes; soups; stuffings; salad dressings.
TURMERIC	Ground; brilliant-yellow in color; flavor slightly bitter, aroma pepperlike.	In pickles; relishes; salad dressings; curries; cheese, egg and fish dishes.

Appetizers & snacks

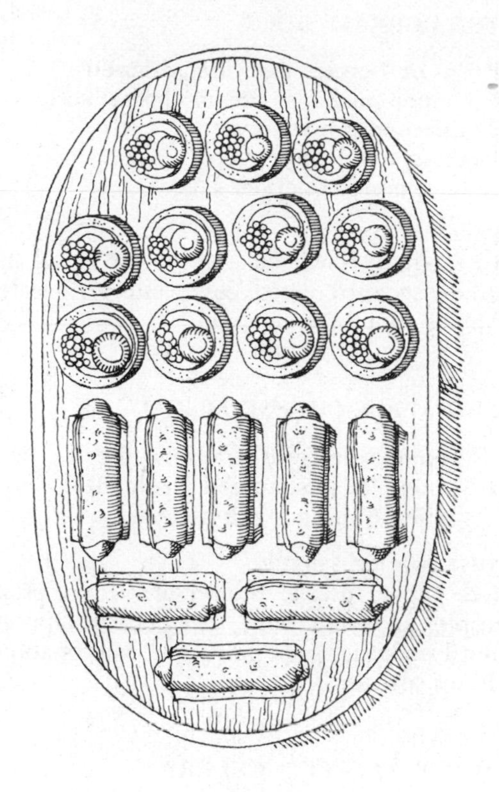

For spur-of-the-moment occasions, and for your own snacking, keep a few of these canned or packaged appetizers on hand:

Cheese wedges, chunks or slices
Potato chips
Boned chicken or turkey
Pretzels
Anchovy paste
Tuna or salmon
Onion-flavored crackers
Melba toast
Crisp rye crackers
Dill and sweet pickles
Corn chips
Shredded-wheat wafers
Popcorn
Chicken-flavored crackers
Salted nuts
Cheese spreads in variety of flavors
Ripe or green olives
Luncheon meat or chopped ham
Sardines
Deviled ham, chicken, liverwurst or corned-beef spread
Sesame crackers
Cocktail franks
Cheese crackers

Cold Appetizers

COTTAGE CHEESE DIP

1 cup creamed cottage cheese
3 tablespoons catchup
3 tablespoons minced carrot
2 tablespoons chopped chives
1 tablespoon minced pimento
½ teaspoon salt
dash hot pepper sauce

EARLY IN DAY OR DAY BEFORE:
In medium bowl, mix well all ingredients; cover and refrigerate. Makes 1½ cups dip.

BLUE CHEESE DIP

1 cup sour cream
⅓ cup milk
1 4-ounce package blue cheese
3 dashes hot pepper sauce
½ teaspoon Worcestershire

EARLY IN DAY:
In small bowl, mix well all ingredients; cover and refrigerate. Makes 1⅓ cups dip.

TUNA-CREAM DIP

1 6½- or 7-ounce can tuna, drained
2 3-ounce packages cream cheese, softened
3 tablespoons mayonnaise
1 tablespoon lemon juice
¼ teaspoon hot pepper sauce

EARLY IN DAY:
In medium bowl, flake tuna; stir in all ingredients until mixed; cover and refrigerate. Makes about 1½ cups dip.

PINEAPPLE-CHEESE SPREAD

1 8½-ounce can crushed pineapple
1 5-ounce jar pasteurized Neufchâtel cheese spread with pimento

JUST BEFORE SERVING:
On paper towels, thoroughly drain pineapple. In small bowl, beat cheese spread until smooth; stir in pineapple. Makes about 1 cup spread.

SUPER STUFFED CELERY

Cut crisp celery into 2″ to 3″ chunks; fill with peanut butter, cream cheese with chives, whipped cream cheese with onion or any of the Spur-of-the-Moment Spreads (next page).

PEPPERY DIP WITH VEGETABLES

1 cup mayonnaise
2 tablespoons grated onion
2 teaspoons tarragon vinegar
2 teaspoons chopped chives
2 teaspoons chili sauce
½ teaspoon curry powder
½ teaspoon salt
¼ teaspoon pepper
⅛ teaspoon ground thyme
raw caulifloweretts
celery and carrot sticks

SEVERAL HOURS BEFORE SERVING:
In small bowl, with spoon, stir all ingredients except vegetables; cover; refrigerate.

TO SERVE:
Spoon mixture into small bowl; set in center of plate; surround with vegetables. Makes about 1 cup dip.

AVOCADO-CRAB DIP

1 7½-ounce can Alaska King crab, drained
1 medium avocado, cut up
½ cup sour cream
¼ to ½ teaspoon salt
one-half of a .77-ounce envelope Caesar-salad seasoning mix
3 to 4 tablespoons lemon juice

UP TO 3 HOURS BEFORE SERVING:
In medium bowl, break up crab; add avocado and mash. Stir in remaining ingredients until well mixed; cover and refrigerate. Makes 1½ cups dip.

DILL DIP WITH SHRIMP AND TOMATOES

4 egg yolks
¼ cup minced fresh dill or 1 tablespoon dill weed
1 tablespoon sugar
5 teaspoons prepared mustard
1 teaspoon salt
½ teaspoon pepper
1 cup salad or olive oil
2 tablespoons cider vinegar
chilled, cooked and shelled, deveined shrimp
cherry tomatoes

AT LEAST 1 HOUR BEFORE SERVING:
In covered blender container at low speed (or in small bowl, with mixer at medium speed), blend egg yolks, dill, sugar, mustard, salt and pepper until smooth. At low speed, slowly pour in oil until blended; blend in vinegar. Cover and refrigerate.

Stir before serving. Use as dip for shrimp and cherry tomatoes. Makes 1½ cups dip.

YOGURT-CHEESE DIP

1 8-ounce package cream cheese, softened
½ cup plain yogurt
¾ teaspoon salt
⅛ teaspoon dill weed

ABOUT 15 MINUTES BEFORE SERVING:
In small bowl, with mixer at medium speed, beat cream cheese just until smooth and fluffy. Gradually beat in remaining ingredients until mixed. Makes 1¼ cups dip.

Beefy Vegetable Soup, page 53, and Corn Sticks, page 423

SPUR-OF-THE-MOMENT SPREADS

OLIVE-NUT: Into *one 3-ounce package cream cheese,* softened, stir *4 chopped, stuffed olives, 10 minced, blanched almonds, 1 tablespoon mayonnaise.*

HAM-AND-CHEESE: Mash *2 tablespoons blue cheese* with *one 3-ounce package cream cheese,* softened, *one 2¼-ounce can deviled ham, some minced green pepper.*

SHARP PINEAPPLE: Mix *one 3-ounce package cream cheese,* softened, with *¼ cup drained, canned crushed pineapple* and *1 teaspoon horseradish.*

DOTTED CHEESE: Mix *1 cup cottage cheese* with *1 tablespoon minced onion, 5 minced radishes, ½ teaspoon salt, dash pepper.*

DEVILED-HAM-CHEESE: Mix *one 2¼-ounce can deviled ham* with *one 3-ounce package cream cheese,* softened, *½ teaspoon each lemon juice and horseradish.*

CHEESE-AND-ANCHOVY: Mix *one 8-ounce package cream cheese,* softened, *6 tablespoons half-and-half, 1 teaspoon Worcestershire, 1 tablespoon anchovy paste, ½ cup chopped stuffed olives.*

NIPPY SALMON: Mix *1 cup flaked canned salmon* with *3 tablespoons mayonnaise, 1 tablespoon horseradish, 2 teaspoons bottled capers* (some juice too), and *2 teaspoons lemon juice.*

SHRIMP-TREAT: Mix *1 cup minced canned shrimp* with *¼ cup butter or margarine,* softened, *1 tablespoon lemon juice, 1 teaspoon prepared mustard, 1 teaspoon Worcestershire, ½ teaspoon salt, ¼ teaspoon paprika.*

GUACAMOLE

1 medium avocado, cut up
1 medium tomato, cut up
½ small onion, chopped
2 tablespoons lemon juice
1 teaspoon seasoned salt
¼ teaspoon hot pepper sauce

JUST BEFORE SERVING:
In covered blender container, at low speed, blend all ingredients until smooth. Makes 1¾ cups dip.

Golden Cheese-Stuffed Bread (left), page 473, and Calico Cheese-Stuffed Bread (right), page 473

CARAWAY-CHEESE BALL

1 3-ounce package cream cheese, softened
1 pound Cheddar cheese, shredded
¼ cup salad oil
2 tablespoons cooking sherry
2 tablespoons prepared mustard
caraway seed

DAY BEFORE SERVING:
In medium bowl, with mixer at medium speed, beat cream cheese until smooth. At low speed, beat in Cheddar cheese, salad oil, sherry, mustard and 1 teaspoon caraway seed until well blended. With hands, shape mixture into ball; wrap and refrigerate.

AT SERVING TIME:
Roll ball lightly in about 1½ tablespoons caraway seed. Makes 24 appetizers.

BLUE-CHEESE BALL

3 3-ounce packages cream cheese, softened
1 4-ounce package blue cheese, crumbled
2 teaspoons bourbon (optional)
¾ teaspoon dry mustard
2 tablespoons toasted sesame seed

DAY BEFORE SERVING:
In small bowl, with mixer at medium speed, beat cheeses until soft. Beat in bourbon and mustard. With hands, shape cheese mixture into ball; wrap and refrigerate overnight.

AT SERVING TIME:
With hands, reshape ball and roll in sesame seed. Makes about 32 appetizers.

HORSERADISH-CHEESE BALL

2 8-ounce packages cream cheese, softened
1 tablespoon horseradish
1 teaspoon celery salt
½ teaspoon onion salt
1 cup chopped dried beef
¾ cup chopped parsley

DAY BEFORE SERVING:
In small bowl, with mixer at medium speed, beat cream cheese until smooth. Beat in horseradish, celery salt and onion salt; mix in dried beef. With hands, shape mixture into ball; wrap and refrigerate until firm. Reshape ball; roll in parsley; cover and refrigerate. Makes about 24 appetizers.

POTTED CHEESE

1 pound very sharp Cheddar cheese, shredded (4 cups)
1 8-ounce package cream cheese, softened
1 4-ounce package blue cheese, crumbled (1 cup)
½ cup brandy
1 teaspoon dry mustard
1 teaspoon Worcestershire
¼ teaspoon hot pepper sauce

UP TO 1 MONTH BEFORE SERVING:
Into large bowl, measure all ingredients. With mixer at low speed, beat ingredients just until mixed; at high speed, beat 5 minutes, occasionally scraping bowl with rubber spatula. Pack in covered 1-quart casserole or in small containers; refrigerate at least 24 hours.

TO SERVE:
Let stand at room temperature 1 hour. Makes about 3¾ cups spread.

CRISP CHEESE TWISTS

1¼ cups all-purpose flour
½ cup yellow cornmeal
1 teaspoon salt
1 5-ounce jar Old English cheese spread
¼ cup shortening
grated Parmesan cheese

SEVERAL HOURS BEFORE SERVING:
1. In large bowl, mix flour, cornmeal and salt. With pastry blender or two knives used scissor-fashion, cut in Old English cheese and shortening until mixture resembles coarse crumbs. With fork, stir in ¼ cup water. With hands, shape dough into ball. Preheat oven to 425°F.
2. Between two 15-inch sheets of waxed paper, with rolling pin, roll half of pastry into 12" by 10" rectangle. With knife, cut dough into strips about 5" by ½".
3. With help of knife, remove each strip and, holding its ends with both hands, make twist by turning ends in opposite directions. Lay each twist on cookie sheet; press ends to sheet to prevent curling.
4. Bake twists 8 to 10 minutes until golden. When done, sprinkle with Parmesan cheese; cool twists on racks. Repeat with remaining dough. Makes about 8 dozen appetizers.

BUTTERY POPCORN

In medium saucepan over high heat, heat *2 tablespoons salad oil* until one popcorn kernel pops when added to pan. Add *⅓ cup popcorn;* cover pan; cook, shaking pan occasionally, just until corn stops popping. (Or use electric corn popper.) Sprinkle with *salt* and *melted butter or margarine.* Makes 4 cups popcorn.

CHINESE FRIED WALNUTS

4 cups California walnuts
½ cup sugar
salad oil
⅛ teaspoon salt

EARLY IN DAY:
1. In large saucepan over high heat, heat 6 cups water to boiling; add walnuts and reheat to boiling; cook 1 minute. Rinse under running hot water; drain.
2. In large bowl, in sugar, toss walnuts.
3. Meanwhile, in electric skillet, heat about 1 inch salad oil to 350°F. With slotted spoon, add about half of walnuts to oil; fry 5 minutes or until golden, stirring often.
4. With slotted spoon, place walnuts in coarse sieve over bowl to drain; sprinkle with salt; toss lightly to keep walnuts from sticking together. Transfer to waxed paper to cool. Fry remaining walnuts. Store in tightly covered container. Makes 4 cups.

SPICED NUTS

HOT-PEPPER PECANS: Preheat oven to 300°F. In 8- or 9-inch cake pan, combine *2 cups pecan halves* with *1½ tablespoons butter or margarine,* melted. Toast in oven 30 minutes, stirring occasionally. Add *1 teaspoon salt, 2 teaspoons soy sauce* and *⅛ teaspoon hot pepper sauce;* toss. Makes 2 cups.

CURRIED ALMONDS: Prepare as above but use these ingredients: *2 cups blanched whole almonds, 1½ tablespoons butter or margarine,* melted, *1 tablespoon curry powder* and *2 teaspoons salt.* Makes 2 cups.

CASHEWS WITH CHILI: Prepare as above but use these ingredients: *2 cups salted cashews, 1½ tablespoons butter or margarine,* melted, *1 tablespoon chili powder* and *2 teaspoons salt.* Makes 2 cups.

BOLOGNA WEDGES

1 3-ounce package cream cheese, softened
2 tablespoons milk
1 teaspoon instant minced onion
1 teaspoon horseradish
⅛ teaspoon hot pepper sauce
12 thin bologna slices (½ pound)

EARLY IN DAY:
In small bowl, with fork, mix all ingredients except bologna. To make a bologna stack: Spread half of mixture on 5 bologna slices; stack these and top with an unspread bologna slice; wrap and refrigerate. Repeat.

JUST BEFORE SERVING:
Cut stacks into wedges. Makes 16 appetizers.

LOBSTER COCKTAIL SUPREME

1 tablespoon salt
8 ½-pound frozen rock-lobster tails
2¼ cups catchup
½ cup horseradish
2 teaspoons Worcestershire
8 large lemons
2 bunches watercress for garnish
⅓ cup fresh lemon juice
3 tablespoons chopped parsley
2 8½-ounce cans colossal ripe olives

DAY BEFORE SERVING:
1. In large Dutch oven over high heat, heat 3 quarts water and salt to boiling; add lobster tails; reheat to boiling. Reduce heat to low; cover pan and simmer 10 minutes. Drain lobsters; cover with cold water; drain.
2. Using kitchen scissors, cut underside membrane away from each lobster tail; turn lobster over and cut tail free from shell so tail pulls away with meat in one piece. Cover and refrigerate; discard shells.
3. In medium bowl, combine catchup, horseradish and Worcestershire; cover and refrigerate.
4. With sharp knife, slice tops from lemons about one-third of way down. Scoop out lemon sections (use another day); cut a thin slice from bottom of each lemon so it stands up well. Cover and refrigerate.

ABOUT 15 MINUTES BEFORE SERVING:
On large platter or salad plates, scatter watercress. Brush lobster tails generously with lemon juice and sprinkle with parsley; arrange on one side of platter. Fill each lemon cup with catchup mixture; arrange with olives on platter. Serve with knife and fork. Makes 8 first-course servings.

MOLDED TUNA PATE

1 3-ounce can chopped mushrooms
1 envelope unflavored gelatin
2 6½- or 7-ounce cans tuna, drained
½ cup green goddess salad dressing
½ cup pitted ripe olives
¼ cup parsley leaves

UP TO 3 HOURS BEFORE SERVING:
Into blender container, drain liquid from mushrooms; sprinkle gelatin over it and soften a minute or two. Add ½ cup boiling water; cover and blend about 10 seconds on low speed, then 20 seconds on high speed. Add mushrooms, tuna, dressing, olives and parsley; cover and blend on high speed until smooth. Pour into 1-quart mold and refrigerate, covered, until firm.

TO SERVE:
Unmold. Makes 3½ cups spread.

SIX-IN-ONE COCKTAIL HASH

½ cup butter or margarine
1 tablespoon Worcestershire
¼ teaspoon celery salt
¼ teaspoon seasoned salt
¼ teaspoon onion salt
¼ teaspoon garlic salt
2 cups bite-size toasted rice cereal
2 cups bite-size shredded wheat cereal
2 cups bite-size toasted corn cereal
1 cup toasted oat cereal
1 cup thin pretzel sticks
½ cup slivered almonds

EARLY IN DAY OR SEVERAL WEEKS AHEAD:
Preheat oven to 325°F. In small saucepan over medium heat, melt butter or margarine and stir in the 5 seasonings. In large bowl, toss remaining ingredients with butter mixture; spread evenly in shallow roasting pan. Bake 20 minutes, stirring occasionally. Serve warm, or cool and store in tightly-covered container. (Flavor improves if stored several days.) Makes about 8 cups.

PICKLED SHRIMP

3 pounds uncooked medium shrimp, in shell
1 stalk celery
1 bay leaf
¼ teaspoon peppercorns
salt
1 cup salad oil
⅔ cup lemon juice
½ cup cider vinegar
3 tablespoons pickling spice, tied in cheesecloth bag
2 teaspoons sugar
2 sprigs fresh dill
Crystalline Ice Bowl (optional)

DAY BEFORE SERVING:
Shell and devein shrimp, leaving tails on. In large pan over low heat, to 6 cups boiling water, add shrimp, celery, bay leaf, peppercorns and 1 tablespoon salt. Simmer 3 minutes or until shrimp is pink; drain.

In large bowl, stir remaining ingredients except Ice Bowl; add 5 teaspoons salt. Add shrimp and toss. Cover and refrigerate, tossing occasionally.

TO SERVE:
Drain shrimp well and serve in Crystalline Ice Bowl. Makes 12 appetizer servings.

CRYSTALLINE ICE BOWL

DAY BEFORE OR SEVERAL DAYS AHEAD:
1. Cover bottom of 3-quart metal or other freezerproof bowl with *ice cubes.* Then set a 1½-quart freezerproof bowl in center on top of ice cubes. (Place a package of frozen vegetables or a can of frozen juice in small bowl to keep it from floating later.)

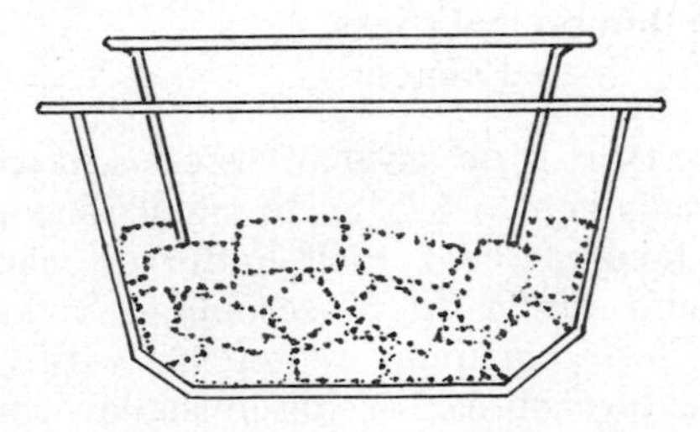

2. Fill space between bowls halfway up with ice cubes. For decoration, carefully tuck *dill sprigs, lemon or lime slices, bay leaf* and *pickling spice* between ice cubes against larger bowl. (Nontoxic fresh flowers such as sweet peas, lavender, forget-me-nots, violets, roses, carnations, may be used.)
3. Place in freezer; carefully pour cold water between bowls to about 2 inches from bottom; let freeze. (Water expands as it freezes; too much water added at one time may cause glass bowls to crack.)
4. Pour in another inch of ice water; let freeze. Repeat filling and freezing process until ice water reaches ½ inch below rim of large bowl; let freeze until needed.

AT SERVING TIME:
5. Remove weight from small bowl; fill with warm, not hot, water for about one minute; lift out small bowl. Dip large bowl in warm water for about one minute; unmold Crystalline Ice Bowl onto chilled shallow serving platter; fill center with Pickled Shrimp. (Or use to serve melon balls or carrot sticks and celery hearts.)
6. Serve immediately. Melting ice will be caught in shallow platter. Makes ice bowl to contain about 6 cups.

CHEDDAR-CHEESE THINS

1 cup all-purpose flour
¾ teaspoon salt
½ teaspoon ginger
½ teaspoon sugar
1 4-ounce package shredded Cheddar cheese (1 cup)
⅓ cup butter or margarine, softened
1 egg yolk
¼ cup toasted sesame seed

ABOUT 45 MINUTES OR SEVERAL DAYS AHEAD:
Into medium bowl, stir together dry ingredients and cheese. With pastry blender or two knives used scissor-fashion, cut in butter or margarine until mixture resembles coarse crumbs. With fork, stir in egg yolk, toasted sesame seed and 2 teaspoons cold water. Mix well and shape into ball.

Preheat oven to 350°F. With floured rolling pin on well-floured surface, roll out dough about ⅛ inch thick. Cut in 3″ by 1″ strips. Lift with pancake turner to ungreased, large cookie sheets. Reroll scraps. Bake 15 minutes or until wafers are lightly browned. Makes about 48 appetizers.

SHRIMP COCKTAIL WITH TANGY DIP

1 teaspoon salt
1 pound shelled, deveined medium shrimp
⅓ cup chili sauce
⅓ cup catchup
2 teaspoons horseradish
1½ teaspoons lemon juice
6 lettuce leaves
6 lemon wedges

EARLY IN DAY:
In large pan over high heat, heat 4 cups water and salt to boiling; add shrimp and cook over low heat until shrimp turn pink, about 3 minutes; drain. In small bowl, combine chili sauce, catchup, horseradish and lemon juice. Cover both and refrigerate.

JUST BEFORE SERVING:
On plates, on lettuce leaves, arrange shrimp; spoon on cocktail sauce; serve with lemon wedges. Makes 6 first-course servings.

EGGS A LA RUSSE

1¾ cups mayonnaise
⅓ cup chili sauce
2 teaspoons chopped chives
1 teaspoon lemon juice
dash hot pepper sauce
10 hard-cooked eggs

ABOUT 30 MINUTES BEFORE SERVING:
In small bowl, mix all ingredients except eggs. Halve eggs lengthwise; spoon mixture over them. Makes 10 appetizers.

AVOCADO APPETIZERS

3 small avocados, halved and pitted
lemon juice
1 13-ounce can consommé madrilène, chilled
6 tablespoons sour cream
6 teaspoons red caviar
cracked ice for serving
6 lemon wedges

ABOUT 20 MINUTES BEFORE SERVING:
Brush avocados with lemon juice; spoon consommé into avocados; top each with spoonful of sour cream, then caviar. Arrange avocados on ice; serve with lemon wedges. Makes 6 first-course servings.

CAVIAR-EGG ROUNDS

6 pumpernickel-bread slices
mayonnaise
2 hard-cooked eggs, sliced
3 pitted ripe olives, sliced
1 tablespoon red caviar

EARLY IN DAY:
Using 2-inch round cookie cutter, cut 2 circles from each bread slice. Spread a dab mayonnaise on center of each circle; top with egg slice. Top each with olive slice and a little caviar. Cover and refrigerate. Makes 12 appetizers.

SMOKED SALMON APPETIZER

Arrange thin slices *smoked salmon* on salad plates; sprinkle with *minced onion* and *bottled capers*. Garnish with *lemon wedges*. Serve with knife and fork.

TINY HAM-STUFFED TOMATOES

1 pint cherry tomatoes
1 4½-ounce can deviled ham
2 tablespoons sour cream
2 tablespoons horseradish

EARLY IN DAY:
Thinly slice tops from tomatoes; remove pulp and drain shells upside down on paper towels. In small bowl, combine deviled ham, sour cream and horseradish; fill tomatoes. Refrigerate. Makes 20 appetizers.

SPICED PINEAPPLE PICKUPS

1 29-ounce can pineapple chunks
1¼ cups sugar
¾ cup cider vinegar
8 whole cloves
1 short cinnamon stick
dash salt

DAY OR TWO BEFORE SERVING:
Into medium saucepan, drain syrup from pineapple; add remaining ingredients. Cook over medium heat 10 minutes; add pineapple chunks; heat to boiling. Refrigerate.

TO SERVE:
Drain pineapple and serve with cocktail picks. Makes 8 appetizer servings.

ROYAL CAMEMBERT MOUSSE

1 envelope unflavored gelatin
2 1⅓-ounce wedges Camembert cheese
¼ pound Danish blue cheese
1 teaspoon Worcestershire
1 egg, separated
½ cup heavy or whipping cream
parsley for garnish

EARLY IN DAY:
In small saucepan, into ¼ cup cold water, sprinkle gelatin; cook over low heat, stirring until gelatin dissolves.

In medium bowl, with fork, beat cheeses until smooth. Stir in Worcestershire, egg yolk and gelatin. In small bowl, with mixer at high speed, beat egg white until stiff peaks form; spoon on top of cheese mixture.

In same bowl, with mixer at medium speed, beat cream until soft peaks form. Gently fold whipped cream and beaten egg white into cheese mixture; pour into 2- or 3-cup mold. Refrigerate.

TO SERVE:
Unmold mousse on plate and garnish with parsley. Makes about 2 cups spread.

CURRIED RIPE OLIVES

To your favorite *Italian dressing*, add *curry powder* to taste. Pour over drained *ripe olives*. Refrigerate for several hours, then drain and serve as snacks.

FISH QUICKIES

SARDINES: Place *canned sardines* on *buttered rye-bread strips*. Serve with *lemon or lime wedges* to squeeze over sardines or with chili sauce to spoon over them.

CAVIAR CANAPES: Mix *¼ cup caviar, 1 teaspoon lemon juice* and *¼ teaspoon minced onion*. Spread on *toast strips*. Garnish with *sieved, hard-cooked eggs* and *tiny pearl onions*.

SARDINE-CHEESE SNACKS: Blend *1 can sardines*, drained, with *one 3-ounce package cream cheese* and *grated onion, horseradish, salt, pepper* and *paprika* to taste. Spread on *pumpernickel bread*, cut in strips. Serve with *lemon wedges*.

SWISS-CHEESE-PEPPER SQUARES

3 pumpernickel bread slices
¼ pound natural Swiss cheese, cut in short, thin strips
½ small green pepper, cut in short, thin strips
¼ cup mayonnaise
dash salt

EARLY IN DAY:
Trim crusts from bread slices; cut each into 4 squares. In small bowl, combine remaining ingredients; pile mixture onto bread. Cover and refrigerate. Makes 12 appetizers.

CRAB-SALAD APPETIZERS

2 7½-ounce cans Alaska King crab, drained
½ cup mayonnaise
⅓ cup minced celery
1 teaspoon lemon juice
¼ teaspoon pepper
1 package of 12 baked small dinner rolls
2 small heads Bibb lettuce
1 2-ounce jar red caviar

ABOUT 20 MINUTES BEFORE SERVING:
In medium bowl, flake crab; stir in mayonnaise, celery, lemon juice and pepper. Cut dinner rolls in half; on each half, place small lettuce leaf; top with crab mixture, then caviar. Makes 24 open-face appetizers.

EGG-AND-BACON APPETIZERS

½ cup mayonnaise
1 tablespoon milk
1 teaspoon salt
¼ teaspoon pepper
8 bacon slices, fried and crumbled
6 hard-cooked eggs, coarsely chopped
party rye bread
paprika for garnish

EARLY IN DAY:
In medium bowl, with fork, stir mayonnaise, milk, salt and pepper until mixed; stir in bacon and eggs. Cover and refrigerate.

TO SERVE:
Spread mixture on rye bread; sprinkle with paprika. Makes 2 cups spread, enough for about 30 appetizers.

NIPPY CARROT NIBBLERS

1 pound medium carrots
3 tablespoons salad oil
3 garlic cloves, minced
1 small onion, chopped
¼ cup cider vinegar
1 tablespoon pickling spice
1½ teaspoons salt
½ teaspoon dry mustard

DAY BEFORE OR SEVERAL DAYS AHEAD:
Cut carrots diagonally into thin slices. In large skillet over medium heat, in hot salad oil, cook garlic and onion until tender.

Add carrots and remaining ingredients to mixture. Reduce heat to low; simmer, covered, about 7 minutes or until carrots are tender-crisp, stirring occasionally. Cover and refrigerate, tossing occasionally. Makes 10 to 12 appetizer servings.

SALAMI ROLL-UPS

ABOUT 20 MINUTES BEFORE SERVING:
In small bowl, with fork, mix *two 3-ounce packages cream cheese,* softened, with *¼ cup pickle relish.* On each slice of *one 16-ounce package salami slices,* spoon some of mixture; roll up and secure each with toothpick. Makes about 20 appetizers.

MUSHROOMS WITH SHRIMP

1 pound large mushrooms, stemmed
1 cup fresh lemon juice
1 pound cooked, shelled and deveined shrimp
¼ cup Italian dressing
2 5-ounce jars cream cheese with chives
fresh dill for garnish

EARLY IN DAY:
In large bowl, toss mushroom caps and lemon juice; cover and refrigerate. In medium bowl, toss shrimp with Italian dressing; cover and refrigerate.

AT SERVING TIME:
In medium bowl, stir cream cheese with chives until smooth. Drain mushroom caps and shrimp. Fill each cap with about 1 tablespoon cheese with chives; arrange shrimp on top. Garnish with dill sprigs. Makes about 18 appetizers.

APPETIZER KABOBS

For skewers, use either toothpicks, cocktail picks or vegetable sticks (cut carrots, turnips, beets, green peppers, celery, white radishes into sticks or use thin green onions). To string food on vegetable sticks, make holes in food with metal skewer. String skewers with:

Swiss-cheese and salami chunks
Chicken chunks and pickled beets
Ham and cheese chunks
Ripe olives and carrot slices
Rolled anchovies and chicken chunks
Stuffed olives and cheese cubes
Ham and pineapple tidbits
Herring in chunks and pickled onions
Salami chunks and apple cubes
Frank chunks and mustard pickles
Shrimp and mandarin orange sections
Salami chunks and pickle slices

EGGS EN GELEE

24 hard-cooked eggs
French or Italian dressing
2 envelopes unflavored gelatin
2 10½-ounce cans condensed beef consommé
4 canned pimentos
8 pitted ripe olives

DAY BEFORE SERVING:
Halve eggs lengthwise; remove yolks. In medium bowl, combine yolks with just enough French dressing to moisten; stuff mixture into whites and level off. Press halves together, removing any excess stuffing from whites. Place each egg in muffin-size foil baking cup.

In medium saucepan, over ⅔ cup cold water, sprinkle gelatin. Stir in undiluted consommé. Over high heat, heat to boiling; cool.

Arrange baking cups in shallow pan. With star aspic cutter, cut 24 stars from pimentos and cut each ripe olive into 6 slivers; arrange on eggs in pretty design.

Carefully spoon gelatin mixture over each egg until cup is almost full. Refrigerate.

TO SERVE:
Arrange eggs in cups on platter. Makes 24 appetizers.

MARINATED-SHRIMP CANAPES

1 pound cooked, shelled and deveined medium shrimp
½ cup Italian dressing
1 medium cucumber
30 garlic toast rounds
salt and pepper
⅓ cup sour cream
parsley for garnish

SEVERAL HOURS BEFORE SERVING:
In medium refrigerator container, toss shrimp and dressing; cover and refrigerate.

JUST BEFORE SERVING:
Drain shrimp well. With fork, score sides of cucumber; cut it into ⅛-inch slices. On each toast round, place slice of cucumber; sprinkle with salt and pepper. Top each with shrimp and dot of sour cream. Garnish with parsley. Makes 30 appetizers.

MEXICAN DEVILED-HAM SNACKS

Halve *one large avocado* and remove pit; fill halves with *one 4½-ounce can deviled ham.* Guests spread ham along with avocado on *Melba toast.* Makes 20 appetizers.

CRAB LOUIS

1 cup mayonnaise
3 tablespoons catchup
2 tablespoons chopped green onion
1 tablespoon Worcestershire
1 tablespoon red wine vinegar
2 teaspoons lemon juice
½ teaspoon salt
⅛ teaspoon white pepper
1 pound cooked fresh crab or 3 6-ounce packages frozen Alaska King crab, thawed and drained
lettuce leaves
3 hard-cooked eggs, sliced
1 cucumber, sliced
1 tomato, sliced

ABOUT 1 HOUR BEFORE SERVING:
In medium bowl, combine first 8 ingredients; refrigerate 30 minutes.

In center of salad platter, heap crab; encircle it with lettuce, egg, cucumber and tomato slices; serve with dressing. Makes 6 to 8 first-course servings.

CONFETTI CHICKEN SPREAD

1 3-ounce package lemon-flavor gelatin
3 tablespoons lemon juice
2 4¾-ounce cans chicken spread
1 8-ounce package cream cheese, softened
½ cup chopped green pepper
3 tablespoons chopped pimento
3 dashes hot pepper sauce

ABOUT 3 HOURS AHEAD OR EARLY IN DAY:
In medium bowl, dissolve gelatin in 1 cup boiling water. Stir in ½ cup cold water and lemon juice; refrigerate, stirring occasionally, until mixture is consistency of unbeaten egg white. Meanwhile, in another medium bowl, with large spoon, mix remaining ingredients; refrigerate.

When gelatin is slightly thickened, fold in chicken mixture; pour into shallow 1-quart mold. Chill until firm, about 2 hours.

TO SERVE:
Unmold. Makes spread for 30 appetizers.

Hot Appetizers

CRAB APPETIZERS

butter or margarine
1½ cups minced onions
1 cup chopped green pepper
3 6-ounce packages frozen Alaska King crab, thawed and drained
2 cups chopped tomatoes
¾ cup diced potatoes
1½ teaspoons salt
¼ teaspoon pepper
¼ cup half-and-half
1 egg, slightly beaten
¼ cup dried bread crumbs
10 canned mushroom caps

ABOUT 1 HOUR AHEAD:
In large skillet over medium heat, heat 3 tablespoons butter or margarine; add onions and green pepper; cook until tender. Add crab, tomatoes, potatoes, salt and pepper; cook 20 minutes, stirring occasionally. Preheat oven to 350°F. Stir half-and-half into mixture. Brush 10 6-ounce custard cups with egg; spoon in mixture; sprinkle with crumbs; top with mushrooms; dot with butter. Place cups on cookie sheet; bake 15 minutes or until golden. Makes 10 servings.

QUICHE APPETIZERS

piecrust mix for 2-crust pie
5 tablespoons butter or margarine, softened
2 cups diced onions
1 tablespoon all-purpose flour
1½ cups shredded natural Swiss cheese (about 6 ounces)
3 eggs
1½ cups half-and-half
dash cayenne pepper
1½ teaspoons salt

ABOUT 2 HOURS AHEAD OR EARLY IN DAY:
1. Prepare piecrust mix as label directs but divide dough into two balls. On lightly floured surface, with stockinette-covered rolling pin, roll out one ball of dough into large circle about 1/16 inch thick.
2. With 5-inch circle as guide, cut about 4 pastry circles with pastry wheel or knife, reserving dough scraps. Use each circle to line an individual quiche pan; trim. Repeat with second ball of dough. Reroll leftover dough and cut to make a total of 10 circles. With fingers, rub a little butter or margarine over bottom of crusts. Chill crusts.
3. Preheat oven to 425°F. In medium skillet over medium heat, melt 2 tablespoons butter or margarine; add onions and cook 5 minutes; drain well on paper towels. On waxed paper, toss flour with cheese. In medium bowl, with fork, beat eggs well; stir in half-and-half, cayenne and salt.
4. Sprinkle about ¼ cup cheese in bottom of each crust; top each with about 1 tablespoon onion. Pour about ¼ cup egg mixture into each pan. Bake 15 minutes. Turn oven control to 325°F. and bake 30 to 35 minutes longer until knife inserted in center comes out clean.
5. Cool on wire racks 10 minutes. Carefully loosen edges of quiches with tip of knife; gently remove from pans. Serve warm (or refrigerate and serve cold). Makes 10 appetizers.

9-INCH PIE VERSION: Prepare recipe as above but instead of 2-crust mix, line one 9-inch pie plate with *1 unbaked piecrust.* Spread crust with *butter or margarine* and fill as above. Bake at 425°F. for 15 minutes, then turn oven control to 325°F. for 50 to 55 minutes. Cut into wedges to serve.

TO DO AHEAD: On day before: Line quiche pans or pie plate with crust and spread with butter or margarine. Sprinkle with cheese and onion; cover and refrigerate. Prepare filling; cover and refrigerate. On the day: Fill and bake as above.

HAM QUICHE: Sprinkle *1 cup diced cooked ham* over cheese.

LOBSTER QUICHE: Sprinkle *one 5-ounce can lobster,* drained and flaked, over cheese.

TINY QUICHE TARTS: Prepare Quiche Appetizers recipe as above but use only ⅓ cup diced onion and ⅓ cup shredded natural Swiss cheese. Cut pastry into about 35 3-inch circles, rerolling pastry scraps; use to line muffin pans with 1¾-inch cups. Into each muffin-pan cup, spoon ½ teaspoon each cheese and onion; then 1 measuring tablespoonful egg mixture. Bake tarts at 425°F. for 15 minutes; turn oven control to 325°F. and bake 20 minutes or until golden brown and puffy. Serve hot. Makes about 35 appetizers.

KING-SIZE STEAK BITES

seasoned instant meat tenderizer
1 3- to 4-pound round steak, cut about 1 inch thick
1 cup dry red wine
1 garlic clove, crushed
½ cup butter or margarine
1 tablespoon dry mustard
1 teaspoon Worcestershire
½ teaspoon salt
few drops hot pepper sauce

ABOUT 2 HOURS BEFORE SERVING:
Apply meat tenderizer to steak as label directs. In large shallow pan, mix wine and garlic. Add steak; cover and refrigerate 1½ hours, turning once.

Preheat broiler if manufacturer directs. Broil steak until medium rare, about 15 or 20 minutes, turning once.

Meanwhile, in medium saucepan over medium heat, melt butter or margarine; add remaining ingredients and 2 tablespoons marinade from steak. Cut steak into cubes and heap into chafing dish or casserole; pour on sauce and serve with cocktail picks. Makes 35 to 40 appetizers.

SPICY GLAZED WIENERS

3 5½-ounce packages little wieners
1 cup jellied cranberry sauce
3 tablespoons prepared mustard
1 tablespoon lemon juice
½ teaspoon salt

ABOUT 20 MINUTES BEFORE SERVING:
Cut 3 thin gashes on each wiener. In medium saucepan over medium heat, cook remaining ingredients, stirring, until cranberry sauce melts and becomes smooth. Add wieners and heat through. Serve hot with cocktail picks. Makes 48 appetizers.

SWEDISH MEATBALLS

1 pound ground beef
1½ cups seasoned dried bread crumbs
½ cup dry sherry
½ teaspoon mace
½ teaspoon salt
⅛ teaspoon pepper
1¼ cups heavy or whipping cream
all-purpose flour
2 tablespoons salad oil
2 tablespoons butter or margarine
1 10½-ounce can condensed beef consommé
1 bay leaf

ABOUT ONE HOUR BEFORE SERVING:
In large bowl, combine first 6 ingredients with ¾ cup cream; shape into about 40 small meatballs. On waxed paper, in about ¼ cup flour, roll meatballs to coat evenly. In large skillet over medium-high heat, in hot oil, brown meatballs well. Drain on paper towels. Wipe skillet clean.

In same skillet over medium heat, melt butter or margarine. Stir in 1 tablespoon flour until well blended and smooth. Gradually stir in undiluted consommé and ½ cup cream; heat to boiling, stirring constantly. Add meatballs and bay leaf; simmer, covered, 15 minutes or until meatballs are tender. Discard bay leaf. Serve in chafing dish to keep hot. Makes about 40 appetizers.

TO FREEZE: Cool above recipe; freeze in freezerproof container for up to 1 month. To serve, place mixture in medium saucepan; add ¾ cup water and cook over medium heat 15 minutes or until hot, stirring often.

SEAFOOD-STUFFED MUSHROOMS

2 pounds large mushrooms (about 16)
butter or margarine
2 tablespoons flour
1½ teaspoons dry mustard
1 teaspoon Worcestershire
½ teaspoon salt
⅛ teaspoon pepper
¾ cup milk
1 7½-ounce can Alaska King crab, drained
2 egg yolks, beaten
2 tablespoons chopped parsley
lemon juice
¼ cup grated Parmesan cheese

ABOUT 30 MINUTES BEFORE SERVING:
Remove stems from mushrooms; chop stems. In medium skillet over medium heat, in 3 tablespoons melted butter or margarine, cook stems until tender; stir in flour, mustard, Worcestershire, salt and pepper. Add milk and cook, stirring, until thickened; remove from heat; stir in crab, egg yolks, parsley and 1 teaspoon lemon juice.

Preheat oven to 425°F. In large skillet over medium heat, in ¼ cup melted butter or margarine, cook mushroom caps 5 minutes; fill with crab mixture; sprinkle with cheese; place in shallow baking pan. Bake 12 minutes or until hot. Sprinkle with more lemon juice, if desired. Serve with forks on small plates. Makes about 16 appetizers.

MINIATURE MEATBALLS

1½ pounds ground chuck
1 small onion, minced
1¼ teaspoons salt
1 teaspoon monosodium glutamate
¼ teaspoon pepper
3 tablespoons minced sweet gherkins
1 tablespoon chopped parsley

ABOUT 45 MINUTES BEFORE SERVING:
Preheat broiler if manufacturer directs. In medium bowl, mix chuck and next 4 ingredients. Shape into meatballs about 1 inch in diameter. Place in broiler pan; broil 8 to 10 minutes until golden, turning once.

Meanwhile, in large bowl, combinc remaining ingredients. When meatballs are done, toss in mixture to coat evenly. Makes about 36 appetizers.

RUMAKI

½ pound chicken livers
about 9 bacon slices, halved crosswise
1 8½-ounce can water chestnuts, drained
½ cup soy sauce
½ teaspoon curry powder
¼ teaspoon ginger

ABOUT 1½ HOURS AHEAD OR EARLY IN DAY:
Prepare rumaki: Cut chicken livers into chunks. Wrap each halved bacon slice around a water chestnut and chunk of liver; secure with toothpick.

In medium bowl, stir soy sauce, curry powder and ginger. Add rumaki and toss carefully. Cover and refrigerate at least 1 hour, tossing occasionally.

AT SERVING TIME:
Preheat broiler if manufacturer directs. Drain rumaki and broil on broiling pan, turning frequently, until liver is cooked, about 10 minutes. Makes about 18 appetizers.

SAUSAGE EN CROUTE

6 sweet Italian sausage links, each about 8 inches long
1 8-ounce package refrigerated crescent dinner rolls
1 egg, slightly beaten

ABOUT 2 HOURS AHEAD OR EARLY IN DAY:
In covered large skillet over medium heat, simmer sausage links and ¼ cup water for 5 minutes. Uncover skillet and cook links until browned, turning often with tongs to keep links straight; drain; cover and chill.

ABOUT 1 HOUR BEFORE SERVING:
On floured surface, unroll half of dough from dinner rolls; set aside remaining dough. Separate rectangles (not triangles) of dough; place one on top of the other. Using floured rolling pin, roll dough into 12″ by 10″ rectangle; cut crosswise into 3 pieces, each about 10″ by 4″.

Preheat oven to 375°F. Along the long edge of each piece of dough, lay a sausage link; roll up link in dough; place, seam side down, on lightly greased large cookie sheet; twist or fold dough ends to seal.

Brush egg over dough. Bake 15 minutes or until golden. Slice. Makes 24 appetizers.

APPETIZER CHEESE FONDUE

2 10¾-ounce cans condensed Cheddar-cheese soup
⅓ cup dry white wine
2 tablespoons chopped chives
1 teaspoon Worcestershire
1 large loaf French bread

ABOUT 10 MINUTES BEFORE SERVING:
In small chafing dish or fondue pot* over low heat, heat undiluted soup, wine, chives and Worcestershire until hot and bubbly, stirring occasionally.

Cut bread into 1½-inch chunks. To serve, let guests spear bread with fondue forks and dip into hot mixture. Makes about 3 cups fondue, enough for 16 appetizers.

* When cheese fondue comes into contact with aluminum, it may turn dark. But it will still be delicious.

OYSTERS ROCKEFELLER

3 tablespoons butter or margarine
½ 10-ounce package frozen chopped spinach, slightly thawed
1 tablespoon instant minced onion
1 tablespoon chopped parsley
1 bay leaf, finely crumbled
½ teaspoon salt
dash cayenne pepper, hot pepper sauce or anisette
¼ cup dried bread crumbs
rock salt (optional)
18 large or 24 small oysters on the half shell
2 bacon slices, diced
grated Parmesan cheese (optional)

ABOUT 30 MINUTES BEFORE SERVING:
Preheat oven to 425°F. In small covered saucepan over medium heat, in melted butter or margarine, cook spinach, onion, parsley, bay leaf, salt and cayenne, stirring occasionally, until spinach is heated through. Toss in bread crumbs; set aside.

If you like, place enough rock salt in bottom of large shallow baking pan to keep oysters in shell from tipping over. Place oysters in baking pan and spoon on spinach mixture. Sprinkle with bacon and cheese. Bake 10 minutes or until bacon is crisp. Serve with oyster forks. Makes 6 first-course servings.

HOT MUSHROOM TURNOVERS

all-purpose flour
3 3-ounce packages cream cheese, softened
butter or margarine, softened
½ pound mushrooms, minced
1 large onion, minced
1 teaspoon salt
¼ teaspoon thyme leaves
¼ cup sour cream
1 egg, beaten

EARLY IN DAY:
1. In medium bowl, measure 1½ cups flour, cream cheese and ½ cup butter or margarine. With mixer at medium speed, beat ingredients until well mixed, occasionally scraping bowl with rubber spatula. Wrap dough; refrigerate at least 1 hour.
2. In medium skillet over medium heat, in 3 tablespoons butter or margarine, cook mushrooms and onion until tender, about 5 minutes. Stir in salt, thyme and 2 tablespoons flour until blended; stir in cream.
3. On floured surface, thinly roll out half of dough; with cookie cutter, cut into twenty 2¾-inch circles. Roll scraps into ball; refrigerate.
4. On one-half of each circle, place a teaspoonful of mushroom mixture. Brush edges with egg; fold dough over filling; with fork, press edges together; prick tops in 3 places to let out steam; place on ungreased cookie sheets. Repeat with remaining dough, dough scraps and mushroom filling. Brush turnovers with egg. Cover and refrigerate.

ABOUT 25 MINUTES BEFORE SERVING:
Preheat oven to 450°F. Bake turnovers 12 minutes or till golden. Makes 50 appetizers.

APPETIZER SAUSAGE BALLS

1½ cups all-purpose flour
2 teaspoons curry powder
1 teaspoon paprika
¼ teaspoon salt
2 4-ounce packages shredded Cheddar cheese (2 cups)
½ cup butter or margarine
1 pound sausage meat

DAY BEFORE SERVING:
In large bowl, mix flour, curry, paprika, salt and cheese. With pastry blender or 2 knives used scissor-fashion, cut in butter or margarine until mixture resembles coarse crumbs; with hands, press into ball; cover and refrigerate.

Meanwhile, shape sausage meat into 36 small balls. In large skillet over medium heat, fry sausage until well browned; drain thoroughly. Cover and refrigerate.

ABOUT 45 MINUTES BEFORE SERVING:
Preheat oven to 400°F. Divide dough into 36 pieces; shape dough evenly around balls. Place sausage balls on cookie sheet and bake 12 to 15 minutes until golden. Serve with toothpicks. Makes 36 appetizers.

HAM-AND-CHEESE SNACKS

16 thin white-bread slices
prepared mustard
1 8-ounce package pasteurized process Swiss-cheese slices
½ pound thin boiled-ham slices
⅓ cup butter or margarine, melted

EARLY IN DAY OR DAY BEFORE SERVING:
Cut crust from bread slices; spread 8 slices with mustard. Trim cheese and ham slices to fit bread. Use cheese and ham to make 8 sandwiches; arrange on large cookie sheet; wrap and refrigerate.

ABOUT 20 MINUTES BEFORE SERVING:
Preheat oven to 450°F. Unwrap and brush sandwiches with butter or margarine; toast in oven 5 minutes or until lightly browned. Turn; brush other side and toast about 3 minutes. Cut sandwiches into thirds; serve wrapped in small paper napkins. Makes 24 appetizers.

HOT BACON BITES

Wrap half a bacon slice around one of the following; skewer with toothpick and broil until bacon is crisp, turning once or twice.

pineapple chunks
shelled and deveined shrimp
pitted prunes
canned pear chunks
chicken livers
raw scallops or oysters
luncheon meat cubes
cocktail franks

Soups

Canned condensed and ready-to-serve soups, and soups made from dry mixes, offer good eating plus good nutrition with the least possible effort. When served as is, a simple garnish or crunchy accompaniment is enough to dress them up.

Condensed soups: Among the more than 50 kinds of condensed soups are cream of asparagus, bean with bacon, beef broth, Cheddar cheese, cream of chicken, cream of mushroom, chicken broth, chicken noodle, green pea, minestrone, onion, oyster stew, tomato, tomato rice, turkey noodle, vegetable, vegetarian vegetable. Add milk or water and heat as label directs.

Ready-to-serve soups: Just open the can and heat. Ready-to-serve soups include chicken noodle and dumplings, creole, chicken gumbo, lentil and chunky chicken, turkey, beef or vegetable—and madrilène and cream vichyssoise, to be refrigerated and served cold.

Dry-soup mixes: Cream of mushroom, potato, chicken rice, onion, noodle soup with chicken broth are among the packaged mixes that need just a little simmering with water or milk before serving.

Condensed broth bases: Beef, chicken or vegetable broth comes in cubes, envelopes and jars of condensed bouillon or stock base ready for diluting with water.

CREATIVE SOUP COMBINATIONS

Soups that are good served alone take on new interest when combined with other kinds. Create your own specialties by mixing two or more kinds—or try one of these combinations, preparing them according to label directions, combining and heating:

Tomato and chicken rice
Cheddar cheese and tomato
Chicken gumbo and tomato
Cream of asparagus and cream of mushroom
Clam chowder (Manhattan style) and tomato
Cream of mushroom and cream of chicken
Turkey noodle and cream of mushroom
Chili beef and tomato

HANDSOME GARNISHES

One of these, sprinkled over soup, will add an eye-catching finishing touch:

Chopped parsley, chives, watercress
Grated orange peel
Crisp ready-to-eat cereal
Browned onion rings
Chopped green onions, green pepper
Thin lemon slices
Sour cream with nutmeg or chives
Crushed pretzels
Chopped pickles or chopped pimentos
Croutons, plain or flavored
Chopped tomatoes
Thin frankfurter slices
Bacon-flavored vegetable protein bits
Chopped toasted almonds
Thin carrot, radish or onion slices
Crumbled blue cheese
Crumbled potato or corn chips
Popcorn
Shredded or grated cheese

ACCOMPANIMENTS

Crisp accompaniments contrast pleasingly with soup. Choose one of these:

Crusty bread chunks or slices
Potato or corn chips
Plain or seasoned bread sticks
Cheese, rye, wheat or flavored crackers
Melba toast, plain or flavored
Toast with garlic or onion butter
Celery sticks, carrot sticks
Saltines or soda crackers
Oyster crackers

First-Course Soups

CURRY SOUP

2 10½-ounce cans condensed cream-of-mushroom soup
2 10¾-ounce cans condensed tomato soup
4 soup cans milk
1½ tablespoons curry powder

ABOUT 30 MINUTES BEFORE SERVING:
In medium saucepan over medium heat, heat all ingredients about 20 minutes, stirring occasionally. Makes about 10 cups or 12 first-course servings.

WATERCRESS SOUP

2 10½-ounce cans condensed cream-of-asparagus soup
½ cup cut-up watercress
2 soup cans milk
¼ teaspoon basil

ABOUT 30 MINUTES AHEAD OR EARLY IN DAY:
In covered blender container at low speed, blend undiluted soup and watercress. In medium saucepan over medium heat, heat mixture with milk, basil. Serve hot or cold. Makes 5 cups or 6 first-course servings.

SPEEDY GAZPACHO

2 11-ounce cans condensed bisque-of-tomato soup
2 beef-bouillon cubes or envelopes
¼ cup red wine vinegar
2 medium tomatoes, chopped
¼ cup chopped green pepper
2 tablespoons minced onion
1 tablespoon salad oil
1 teaspoon salt
1 teaspoon Worcestershire
6 dashes hot pepper sauce
corn chips for garnish

ABOUT 3 HOURS AHEAD OR EARLY IN DAY:
Into large bowl, pour undiluted bisque-of-tomato soup. In small saucepan over high heat, heat 2 soup cans water to boiling; remove from heat and stir in bouillon cubes until dissolved. Gradually add bouillon mixture to soup, stirring until blended.

Stir in vinegar and remaining ingredients except corn chips; cover and chill.

TO SERVE:
Sprinkle soup with corn chips. Makes about 7 cups or 8 first-course servings.

JELLIED MADRILENE SUPREME

2 13-ounce cans consommé madrilène, chilled
2 tablespoons chopped seedless green grapes
2 tablespoons chopped onion

JUST BEFORE SERVING:
In medium bowl, with fork, stir madrilène to break up. Serve topped with grapes and onion. Makes 6 first-course servings.

COLD ASPARAGUS SOUP

1 pound asparagus, cut in 1-inch pieces
salt
1 10½-ounce can condensed cream-of-potato soup
2 cups milk
1 cup sour cream
1 teaspoon lemon juice
1 tablespoon chopped chives

ABOUT 3 HOURS AHEAD OR EARLY IN DAY:
In covered, medium saucepan over medium heat, in 1 inch boiling water, cook asparagus with 1 teaspoon salt for 1 to 2 minutes until tender-crisp; drain.

In covered blender container at low speed, blend undiluted soup and one-fourth of asparagus until smooth; pour into large bowl. Blend one-fourth more asparagus and 1 cup milk; repeat step with remaining milk, then with sour cream. Stir in lemon juice and 1 teaspoon salt. Cover; refrigerate until well chilled.

TO SERVE:
Sprinkle soup with chives. Makes 5 cups or 6 first-course servings.

JELLIED ORANGE CONSOMME

3 13¾-ounce cans chicken broth
2 envelopes unflavored gelatin
2 egg whites
3 cups orange juice
½ teaspoon salt
1 unpeeled orange, thinly sliced for garnish

EARLY IN DAY:
Skim any fat from chicken broth; pour into large saucepan; sprinkle gelatin on top and let stand. Meanwhile, in small bowl, with mixer at high speed, beat egg whites until frothy; add to broth.

Over medium-high heat, heat broth with egg whites for 5 minutes, stirring constantly, until mixture starts to froth. Pour into large bowl; skim off foam; add orange juice and salt. Refrigerate at least 5 hours until thickened.

TO SERVE:
With wire whisk or hand beater, beat mixture until of good spooning consistency. Spoon into bowls; garnish with orange slices. Makes 8 cups or 10 first-course servings.

SHRIMP BISQUE

1 10½-ounce can condensed cream-of-mushroom soup, undiluted
1 10½-ounce can condensed bisque-of-tomato soup, undiluted
1 soup can milk
1 cup chopped shelled, deveined shrimp
1 tablespoon medium or dry sherry
½ teaspoon Worcestershire

ABOUT 30 MINUTES BEFORE SERVING:
In medium saucepan over low heat, heat all ingredients, stirring often, until hot and shrimp turn pink. Makes about 4¼ cups or 6 first-course servings.

CREME MONGOLE WITH SHERRY

1 10¾-ounce can condensed tomato soup
1 11¼-ounce can condensed green pea soup
1 cup half-and-half
1 teaspoon sugar
2 teaspoons Worcestershire
⅓ cup dry sherry

ABOUT 15 MINUTES BEFORE SERVING:
In medium saucepan over very low heat, heat undiluted soups and ¾ cup water. Stir in half-and-half, sugar and Worcestershire. Remove from heat; stir in sherry. Makes 4 cups or 5 first-course servings.

PEA SOUP

¼ cup butter or margarine
4 cups shredded lettuce
½ large onion, chopped
1 tablespoon all-purpose flour
1 teaspoon sugar
¼ teaspoon ground coriander
3 13¾-ounce cans chicken broth
2 10-ounce packages frozen peas
1 cup milk

ABOUT 45 MINUTES BEFORE SERVING:
In large saucepan over medium heat, in hot butter, cook lettuce and onion until tender, stirring often. Add flour, sugar, coriander. Slowly stir in broth; add peas; cook, covered, 15 minutes.

In blender, blend mixture, a cup at a time; return to pan. Add milk; heat. Makes 8 cups or 10 first-course servings.

CHILLED CUCUMBER SOUP

¼ cup butter or margarine
4 cups chopped peeled cucumbers
1 cup chopped green onions
¼ cup all-purpose flour
4 cups chicken broth
salt and pepper
½ cup half-and-half
cucumber slices for garnish

EARLY IN DAY:
In large skillet over medium-high heat, in hot butter or margarine, cook cucumbers and green onions until onions are tender; stir in flour. Gradually add chicken broth, stirring constantly; cook until mixture thickens slightly and begins to boil; add salt and pepper to taste. Reduce heat to low; simmer, covered, 10 minutes, stirring occasionally. Refrigerate until chilled.

AT SERVING TIME:
In covered blender container at medium speed, blend about 2 cups mixture until smooth; strain mixture through a sieve into a large bowl, discarding seeds. Repeat with rest of mixture. Stir in half-and-half. Garnish with cucumber slices. Makes about 5¼ cups or 6 first-course servings.

APPLE-AND-ONION SOUP

¼ cup butter or margarine
1 large onion, thinly sliced
2 large green apples, thinly sliced
3 10½-ounce cans condensed consommé
½ teaspoon curry powder
1 cup heavy or whipping cream

EARLY IN DAY OR DAY BEFORE:
In large saucepan over medium heat, in hot butter or margarine, cook onion until tender, about 5 minutes. Add apple slices and continue cooking 5 minutes. Add undiluted consommé and curry powder; cover and simmer over low heat 25 minutes.

In covered blender container at low speed, blend half of soup with half of cream; pour into large bowl. Repeat with remaining soup and cream. (Or press soup through a food mill.) Cover and refrigerate.

TO SERVE:
Stir soup well. Makes 5 cups or 6 first-course servings.

SHRIMP-AND-MUSHROOM SOUP

1 10½-ounce can condensed cream-of-mushroom soup
1 10½-ounce can condensed cream-of-asparagus soup
⅔ cup milk or half-and-half
1 cup cooked shrimp, cut in half lengthwise
½ cup dry sherry

ABOUT 15 MINUTES BEFORE SERVING:
In medium saucepan over medium heat, heat undiluted mushroom and asparagus soups, 1 soup can water and milk just to boiling, stirring occasionally. Stir in shrimp and sherry and heat through. Makes about 5 cups or 6 first-course servings.

ONION SOUP, FRENCH-MARKET STYLE

1 envelope onion-soup mix for 4 servings
French bread, thinly sliced
1 8-ounce package sliced pasteurized process Muenster cheese, shredded

ABOUT 30 MINUTES BEFORE SERVING:
Preheat oven to 475°F. In medium saucepan over medium-high heat, heat soup mix and 4 cups water, stirring occasionally; pour into 3 individual casseroles. Arrange a layer of French bread over soup; sprinkle with some cheese. Repeat layers. Bake 15 minutes or until bubbly hot. Makes 3 servings.

COLONIAL ONION SOUP

3 tablespoons butter or margarine
2 large onions, thinly sliced
2 egg yolks
6 cups milk
2 teaspoons salt
¼ teaspoon mace or nutmeg
croutons for garnish

ABOUT 30 MINUTES BEFORE SERVING:
In large skillet over medium-low heat, in melted butter or margarine, cook onions until tender-crisp, about 3 minutes. In large bowl, with fork, beat egg yolks; stir in milk, salt and mace. Add to onions and cook, stirring constantly, until soup thickens slightly. Serve sprinkled with croutons. Makes about 6 cups or 8 first-course servings.

CHICKEN PEPPER-POT SOUP

2 tablespoons butter or margarine
1 onion, thinly sliced
1 11-ounce can condensed pepper-pot soup
1⅓ cups cooked chicken, in large pieces
¼ teaspoon curry powder

ABOUT 20 MINUTES BEFORE SERVING:
In heavy, medium saucepan over medium heat, in hot butter or margarine, cook onion just until tender, about 5 minutes. Stir in soup, 1 soup can water, chicken and curry. Heat, stirring occasionally. Makes about 4 cups or 5 first-course servings.

TOMATO-CHEESE SOUP

1 10¾-ounce can condensed tomato soup
1 soup can milk
1 cup shredded sharp Cheddar cheese
¼ teaspoon salt
3 tablespoons dry sherry

ABOUT 20 MINUTES BEFORE SERVING:
In medium saucepan over medium-low heat, heat all ingredients except sherry for 10 minutes or until cheese melts. Stir in sherry. Makes 3¾ cups or 4 first-course servings.

VICHYSSOISE

2 tablespoons butter or margarine
½ cup chopped leeks (white part only)
½ teaspoon chicken stock base
1 10½-ounce can condensed cream-of-potato soup, undiluted
1 cup half-and-half
½ cup milk
chopped chives for garnish

EARLY IN DAY:
In medium skillet over medium heat, in hot butter or margarine, cook leeks 5 minutes; add chicken stock base and ⅔ cup water; heat to boiling. Reduce heat to low; cover and simmer 10 minutes. Stir in undiluted soup, half-and-half and milk. Chill.

JUST BEFORE SERVING:
In covered blender container at low speed, blend soup 30 seconds or until smooth. (Or press through fine sieve.) Garnish with chives. Makes 3½ cups or 4 servings.

AVOCADO SOUP COCKTAIL

1 13¾-ounce can chicken broth
1 medium avocado, cut in large pieces
4 teaspoons lemon juice
½ teaspoon salt
dash cayenne pepper
1 cup milk
1 teaspoon light corn syrup
1 firm, ripe tomato for garnish

ABOUT 2 HOURS AHEAD OR EARLY IN DAY:
In covered blender container at low speed, blend chicken broth and avocado until smooth. Add lemon juice, salt, cayenne, milk and corn syrup; blend until smooth. Pour into pitcher; cover; chill.

TO SERVE:
Pour soup into chilled small punch cups or old-fashioned glasses. On small cutting board, with sharp knife, chop tomato into small chunks; use to garnish soup. Makes 4½ cups or 6 first-course servings.

HOLIDAY TOMATO-ORANGE SOUP

1 6-ounce can frozen orange-juice concentrate
2 10½-ounce cans condensed tomato soup
sour cream for garnish
chopped chives for garnish

ABOUT 20 MINUTES BEFORE SERVING:
In medium saucepan, reconstitute juice as label directs. Stir in undiluted soup and heat over medium heat. Serve topped with sour cream and chives. Makes 5½ cups or 7 first-course servings.

CREAMY PIMENTO SOUP

1 4-ounce can pimentos, drained
2 cups half-and-half
2 tablespoons instant minced onion
2 10½-ounce cans condensed consommé, chilled

EARLY IN DAY:
In covered blender container at high speed, blend pimentos, half-and-half and onion for 30 seconds or until creamy. Cover and chill.

JUST BEFORE SERVING:
Stir jellied consommé into pimento mixture. Makes 6 cups or 8 first-course servings.

EGG DROP SOUP

2 chicken-bouillon cubes or envelopes
½ cup minced cooked ham
½ cup frozen peas
2 eggs
¼ teaspoon salt

ABOUT 15 MINUTES BEFORE SERVING:
In medium saucepan over high heat, heat 3 cups water to boiling. Add bouillon cubes, ham and peas; heat to boiling again; cook 3 minutes. Meanwhile, in small bowl, with fork, beat eggs and salt slightly; stir into soup and cook, stirring, until soup just begins to boil. Remove from heat immediately. Makes 4 cups or 5 first-course servings.

CONSOMME WITH PARMESAN DUMPLINGS

3 10½-ounce cans condensed consommé
4 eggs, separated
2 tablespoons seasoned dried bread crumbs
2 tablespoons grated Parmesan cheese

ABOUT 20 MINUTES BEFORE SERVING:
In Dutch oven over high heat, heat consommé and 3 soup cans water to boiling. In small bowl, with mixer at high speed, beat egg whites until stiff peaks form. In small bowl, with fork, beat yolks slightly; add crumbs and cheese; fold mixture into whites.

Drop mixture by heaping measuring tablespoonfuls into boiling consommé. Cover pan and remove from heat; let stand 10 minutes. Makes 12 first-course servings.

Hearty Soups

SWISS HAM-AND-POTATO SOUP

1 10½-ounce can condensed cream-of-potato soup, undiluted
1 cup half-and-half
¾ cup milk
1½ cups diced cooked ham
¼ cup shredded Swiss cheese
⅛ teaspoon nutmeg

ABOUT 10 MINUTES BEFORE SERVING:
In medium saucepan over low heat, heat all ingredients, stirring occasionally. Makes about 4 cups or 3 servings.

DANDY BEAN CHOWDER

2 tablespoons butter or margarine
¾ cup diced carrots
2 tablespoons minced onion
2 tablespoons minced green pepper
2 tablespoons all-purpose flour
1½ teaspoons salt
dash pepper
1½ cups milk
1 16-ounce can baked beans
3 frankfurters, minced

ABOUT 45 MINUTES BEFORE SERVING:
In large skillet over medium-high heat, in hot butter or margarine, cook carrots, onion and green pepper until tender. Stir in flour, salt and pepper until blended. Add milk and cook, stirring, until mixture thickens. Stir in baked beans and frankfurters and heat, stirring. Makes 4½ cups or 3 servings.

SEAFOOD GUMBO

butter or margarine
2 cups chopped onions
1½ tablespoons all-purpose flour
2 16-ounce cans tomatoes
1 10-ounce package frozen okra, thawed
12 oysters in shell
1 garlic clove, crushed
4 teaspoons salt
2 teaspoons Worcestershire
⅛ teaspoon hot pepper sauce
1 pound shelled and deveined shrimp
½ pound fresh or 1 6-ounce package frozen Alaska King crab, thawed and drained
hot cooked rice

ABOUT 2 HOURS BEFORE SERVING:
In Dutch oven over medium-high heat, in 2 tablespoons hot butter or margarine, cook onions until tender; stir in flour. Stir in tomatoes and okra and cook, stirring, until mixture thickens slightly.

Open oysters and drain liquid into cup; add enough water to make 1 cup liquid; refrigerate oysters. Add liquid, 6 cups water, garlic, salt, Worcestershire, hot pepper sauce. Cover; cook over low heat 1 hour.

Add oysters, shrimp and crab and simmer about 10 minutes, until shrimp are pink and edges of oysters begin to curl. Serve soup over a scoop of rice in each soup bowl. Makes about 14 cups or 8 servings.

BORSCHT

1 pound beef brisket, cut into 1-inch chunks
3 medium beets
2 medium carrots, sliced
1 medium onion, sliced
1 stalk celery, cut into chunks
1 bay leaf
salt
½ 6-ounce can tomato paste
1½ teaspoons sugar
½ small head cabbage, shredded
1 tablespoon cider vinegar
½ cup sour cream

EARLY IN DAY OR DAY BEFORE SERVING:
In covered, large kettle over medium-low heat, simmer 3 cups hot water, beef, 2 sliced beets, carrots, onion, celery, bay leaf and 1½ teaspoons salt for 2 hours.

Shred remaining beet and add to meat mixture along with tomato paste, sugar and 1 teaspoon salt. Simmer, covered, 20 minutes. Discard bay leaf. Refrigerate.

ABOUT 20 MINUTES BEFORE SERVING:
Skim fat from soup surface. Over medium heat, heat soup to boiling; add cabbage and cook until tender, about 15 minutes. Stir in vinegar. Serve garnished with sour cream. Makes 8 cups or 4 servings.

QUICK BEEF CHOWDER

2 tablespoons salad oil
1 medium onion, chopped
1 green pepper, diced
2 24-ounce cans beef stew
1 10½-ounce can condensed cream-of-celery soup
1 30-ounce can Italian tomatoes
1 12-ounce can whole-kernel corn
1 tablespoon chopped parsley
½ teaspoon salt
½ teaspoon marjoram leaves
¼ teaspoon onion salt
1 bay leaf

ABOUT 40 MINUTES BEFORE SERVING:
In Dutch oven over medium heat, in hot salad oil, cook onion and green pepper until tender, about 5 minutes. Add beef stew, undiluted celery soup and remaining ingredients and cook, covered, 15 minutes, stirring occasionally. Discard bay leaf. Makes 10 cups or 6 servings.

SKILLET CORN CHOWDER

6 bacon slices
1 medium onion, thinly sliced
1 17-ounce can cream-style white corn
1½ cups milk
1 teaspoon salt
dash pepper
2 tablespoons chopped parsley

ABOUT 30 MINUTES BEFORE SERVING:
In medium skillet over medium-high heat, fry bacon until crisp; drain on paper towels; break into large pieces. Pour off all but 2 tablespoons bacon drippings from skillet; add onion and cook over medium heat until tender, about 5 minutes. Stir in corn, milk, salt and pepper and heat through.

Serve chowder garnished with bacon and parsley. Makes 4 cups or 2 servings.

FOR 4 SERVINGS: Double recipe and use large skillet.

GERMAN LENTIL SOUP

4 bacon slices, diced
2 medium onions, sliced
2 medium carrots, sliced
1 cup sliced celery
1 ham bone*
1 16-ounce package lentils
salt
½ teaspoon pepper
½ teaspoon thyme leaves
2 bay leaves
2 tablespoons lemon juice

ABOUT 1½ HOURS BEFORE SERVING:
In Dutch oven or other large, heavy kettle over medium-high heat, fry bacon until lightly browned; push to side of pan. Add onions and carrots and celery; over medium heat, cook until onions are tender, about 5 minutes. Add ham bone, lentils, 2 teaspoons salt, pepper, thyme, bay leaves and 8 cups hot water. Cover; simmer over low heat 1 hour or until lentils are tender. Discard bay leaves.

Remove ham bone to cutting board and cut off any meat; stir meat, lemon juice and salt to taste into soup. Makes about 11 cups or 6 servings.

* Use leftover bone from cooked whole or half ham, preferably with some meat left on it.

BOUILLABAISSE, AMERICAN STYLE

2 tablespoons salad oil
1 cup chopped onions
½ cup chopped celery
2 16-ounce cans tomatoes
1 garlic clove, minced
1 tablespoon chopped parsley
1½ teaspoons seasoned salt
¼ teaspoon thyme leaves
2½ pounds striped or sea bass fillets, cut into large pieces (or 2½ pounds halibut steaks, cut in chunks)
1½ dozen clams (little necks) in shell
1 tablespoon cornstarch
1 pound shrimp, shelled and deveined

ABOUT 1 HOUR BEFORE SERVING:
In Dutch oven over medium heat, in hot salad oil, cook onions and celery until tender, about 5 minutes. Stir in tomatoes, garlic, parsley, seasoned salt, thyme. Cover; simmer 10 minutes. Add bass and cook 10 minutes or until fish is almost tender.

Meanwhile, scrub clams under running water; place them in a small kettle with ½ inch boiling water. Cover and cook until shells just open, about 5 minutes. Strain hot broth through cheesecloth; reserve 1 cup. Keep clams warm.

In small bowl, stir reserved clam juice into cornstarch; stir into tomato mixture; heat to boiling. Add shrimp and simmer 5 minutes or until shrimp are pink and tender. Add clams. Makes 8 to 10 servings.

CLASSIC OYSTER STEW

¼ cup all-purpose flour
4 teaspoons salt
4 teaspoons Worcestershire
2 8-ounce containers shucked oysters
1 quart milk
4 cups heavy or whipping cream
3 tablespoons butter or margarine

ABOUT 30 MINUTES BEFORE SERVING:
In medium saucepan, blend flour, salt, Worcestershire and ¼ cup water; add oysters and their liquid. Over low heat, simmer, stirring, 10 minutes or until oyster edges curl.

Add remaining ingredients; over medium heat, heat almost to boiling; remove from heat. Cover; let stand 10 minutes to mellow the flavor. Makes 10 cups or 6 servings.

SCALLOP STEW

¾ pound sea scallops
2 tablespoons butter or margarine
2 cups milk
1 teaspoon monosodium glutamate
1 teaspoon salt
1 teaspoon Worcestershire
dash pepper
¼ cup pasteurized process cheese spread

ABOUT 25 MINUTES BEFORE SERVING:
Slice scallops in half, across the grain. In large skillet over medium heat, in hot butter or margarine, cook scallops until fork-tender, about 5 minutes. Add milk, monosodium glutamate, salt, Worcestershire and pepper. Continue cooking just until milk is bubbly; stir in cheese spread until melted. Makes about 3 cups or 2 servings.

FOR 4 SERVINGS: Double recipe.

MEATBALL VEGETABLE SOUP

MEATBALLS:
1 pound ground beef
¼ cup dried bread crumbs
¼ cup tomato juice
2 tablespoons instant minced onion
2 teaspoons chili powder
1½ teaspoons garlic salt
¼ cup shortening

SOUP:
1 10½-ounce can condensed beef broth
1 10¾-ounce can condensed vegetable soup
1 10-ounce package frozen lima beans
1 16-ounce can tomatoes
⅓ cup packaged precooked rice
⅓ cup shredded carrots
2 tablespoons instant minced onion
¾ teaspoon salt

ABOUT 45 MINUTES BEFORE SERVING:
For meatballs: In large bowl, combine all ingredients except shortening; shape into 8 large balls. In medium skillet over medium heat, in hot shortening, brown meatballs. Cover; cook over low heat 15 minutes.

For soup: Meanwhile, in large saucepan over high heat, cook undiluted beef broth, undiluted vegetable soup and lima beans 15 minutes; add remaining ingredients and meatballs and simmer 10 minutes. Makes 8 cups or 5 servings.

BEEFY VEGETABLE SOUP

6 to 8 pounds cross-cut beef shanks
salt
3 stalks celery, diced
3 large carrots, diced
2 medium onions, diced
1 28-ounce can tomatoes
½ cup chopped parsley
½ teaspoon basil
½ teaspoon thyme leaves
½ teaspoon pepper
1 10-ounce package frozen lima beans
1 10-ounce package frozen corn
1 10-ounce package frozen peas

ABOUT 3 HOURS BEFORE SERVING:
In very large kettle over high heat, heat beef shanks, 2 tablespoons salt and 10 cups hot water to boiling. Reduce heat to low; add remaining ingredients except frozen vegetables. Cover; simmer for 2 hours.

Stir in frozen vegetables and 2 teaspoons salt; cook 30 minutes or until vegetables are tender. Makes 26 cups or 14 servings.

TO FREEZE: Cut meat from bones and add to soup; discard bones. Ladle soup into 1-quart freezer containers, leaving at least 1½ inches head space for expansion. Cover; chill; freeze up to 3 months.

CREAMED TURKEY SOUP

2 tablespoons butter or margarine
1 large onion, minced
2 13¾-ounce cans chicken broth
3 cups diced potatoes
2 cups cubed cooked turkey
1 10-ounce package frozen peas and carrots
2 teaspoons salt
½ teaspoon pepper
⅛ teaspoon rubbed sage
1 cup half-and-half
1 cup milk

ABOUT 40 MINUTES BEFORE SERVING:
In large Dutch oven over medium-high heat, in hot butter or margarine, cook onion until tender. Add chicken broth and potatoes and cook for 20 minutes. Stir in turkey, peas and carrots, salt, pepper and sage; cook 10 minutes or until vegetables are tender. Stir in half-and-half and milk; heat through. Makes 10 cups or 6 servings.

SPLIT-PEA SOUP

1 ham bone*
1 16-ounce package split peas
2 carrots, thinly sliced
1 medium onion, chopped
¼ teaspoon whole allspice
¼ teaspoon peppercorns
1 bay leaf
salt

ABOUT 1 HOUR BEFORE SERVING:
In Dutch oven or large kettle over medium heat, heat ham bone, split peas, carrots, onion and 7 cups water to boiling. Meanwhile, tie allspice, peppercorns and bay leaf in a cheesecloth bag; add to ham-bone mixture. Reduce heat to low; simmer, covered, 1 hour. Discard spice bag. Add salt to taste.

Remove bone from soup to cutting board; cut off meat and return it to soup. Discard bone. Makes about 7 cups or 6 servings.

* Use leftover bone from whole or half ham, preferably with enough meat left on it to make 1½ cups.

HAM-AND-BEAN SOUP

1 16-ounce package dried white beans
2 8-ounce packages brown-and-serve sausage links, cut in chunks
1 cup minced onions
½ cup minced celery
2 garlic cloves, minced
2 cups cubed cooked ham
1 teaspoon salt
¼ teaspoon pepper
2 10-ounce packages frozen mixed vegetables, partially thawed

ABOUT 3 HOURS BEFORE SERVING:
In large kettle over high heat, boil beans in 10 cups water for 2 minutes. Remove from heat; let stand for one hour.

In large Dutch oven over medium heat, brown sausages. Add onions, celery and garlic and cook, stirring occasionally, until celery is tender-crisp. Stir in ham and cook a few minutes; spoon off any excess fat. Add beans and their liquid, salt and pepper and cook, covered, over low heat 1 hour or until beans are tender.

Add vegetables; cook, covered, until vegetables are tender, stirring occasionally. Makes 13 cups or 8 servings.

NEW ENGLAND CLAM CHOWDER

¼ pound salt pork or bacon, diced
2 medium onions, sliced
3 dozen hard-shell clams, shucked, with liquid reserved
2 tablespoons all-purpose flour
3 large potatoes, diced (3 cups)
2 teaspoons salt
¼ teaspoon celery salt
¼ teaspoon pepper
3 cups milk
1 tablespoon butter or margarine

ABOUT 30 MINUTES BEFORE SERVING:
In large saucepan or Dutch oven over medium heat, cook salt pork until lightly browned; add onions and cook until tender, about 5 minutes. Chop clams. Add enough water to clam liquid to make 2 cups.

Stir flour into onion mixture until blended. Gradually stir in clam-liquid mixture and cook, stirring constantly, until mixture is slightly thickened. Stir in potatoes, salt, celery salt and pepper; cover and cook until potatoes are tender, about 10 minutes. Add clams, milk and butter or margarine; cover and cook until heated through, about 5 minutes, stirring often. Makes 10 cups or 4 main-dish servings.

EASY MINESTRONE

¼ cup butter or margarine
1 10-ounce package frozen peas, thawed
1 cup diced carrots
1 cup diced celery
1 cup diced onions
1 tablespoon chopped parsley
1 teaspoon basil
1 28-ounce can Italian tomatoes
3 13¾-ounce cans chicken broth
1 cup shredded cabbage
½ pound zucchini, sliced
2 16- or 17-ounce cans kidney beans
½ cup spaghetti, in small pieces
salt
grated Parmesan cheese

ABOUT 1 HOUR BEFORE SERVING:
In Dutch oven over medium heat, in hot butter or margarine, cook peas and next 5 ingredients 10 minutes. Stir in next 6 ingredients; cook 20 minutes or until spaghetti is tender. Salt to taste; serve with cheese. Makes 15 cups or 8 servings.

DINNER-IN-A-BOWL

1 3- to 3½-pound ham shank
1 pound sweet Italian sausage links, thickly sliced
4 medium potatoes, quartered
4 medium carrots, sliced
1 small head cabbage, coarsely shredded
2 large onions, thickly sliced
2 garlic cloves, crushed
¼ cup parsley sprigs
2 bay leaves
2 teaspoons salt
¼ teaspoon thyme leaves

ABOUT 1½ HOURS BEFORE SERVING:
In very large kettle over medium-low heat, simmer ham shank, sausage links and 14 cups hot water for 1 hour. Add remaining ingredients and continue simmering 30 minutes or until vegetables are tender. Remove ham to cutting board and cut meat into chunks. Discard bones and bay leaves. In large bowls, serve ham chunks with soup. Makes about 24 cups or 12 to 14 servings.

LEFTOVER SOUP: Cover and refrigerate; reheat and serve within 2 or 3 days.

MANHATTAN CLAM CHOWDER

5 bacon slices, diced
2½ cups diced onions
1½ cups diced carrots
1 cup diced celery
2 tablespoons chopped parsley
2 cups diced potatoes
3 dozen hard-shell clams, shucked, with liquid reserved
1 28-ounce can tomatoes
1 bay leaf
1½ teaspoons salt
1 teaspoon thyme leaves
¼ teaspoon pepper

ABOUT 1½ HOURS BEFORE SERVING:
In Dutch oven over medium heat, fry bacon until almost crisp; push to side of pan. Add onions and cook until tender. Add carrots, celery, parsley; cook 5 minutes.

Add 5 cups water, potatoes, clam liquid, tomatoes, bay leaf, salt, thyme, pepper; heat to boiling. Reduce heat to low; cover and simmer 20 minutes, stirring often.

Chop clams; add to mixture; simmer 5 minutes longer. Makes 14 cups or 8 servings.

JARDINIERE SOUP

¼ cup salad oil
2 pounds beef stew meat, cut in chunks
1 small onion, minced
salt
1 tablespoon basil
¼ teaspoon pepper
4 small potatoes, cubed
½ small head cabbage, shredded
1 10-ounce package frozen peas
1 9-ounce package frozen cut green beans
1 16-ounce can tomatoes

ABOUT 2 HOURS BEFORE SERVING:
In Dutch oven over medium heat, in hot salad oil, brown meat and onion. Add 8 cups hot water, 1½ tablespoons salt, basil and pepper. Reduce heat to low; cover and simmer 1 hour.

Add potatoes and cabbage; simmer, covered, 10 minutes. Add peas, beans, tomatoes and 1½ teaspoons salt; simmer 20 minutes. Makes 14 cups or 8 servings.

CHICKEN-CORN SOUP WITH RIVELS

1 4-pound stewing chicken, cut up
1 cup chopped onions
salt and pepper
2 12-ounce cans whole-kernel corn
1 cup chopped celery with leaves
1 cup all-purpose flour
1 egg
1 to 2 tablespoons milk
2 hard-cooked eggs, chopped

ABOUT 3½ HOURS BEFORE SERVING:
In covered, large kettle over medium-low heat, simmer chicken, onions, 1 tablespoon salt, ¼ teaspoon pepper and 6 cups hot water 2½ hours or until chicken is tender.

Remove chicken to cutting board; cut meat from bones into small chunks; add chunks, corn and celery to soup. Continue simmering, covered, 10 minutes. Discard bones.

Meanwhile, prepare rivels: In medium bowl, with fork, stir flour, egg, ½ teaspoon salt and enough milk to make mixture crumble coarsely. With spoon, sprinkle mixture into simmering soup. Add chopped eggs. Cook 20 minutes until rivels are tender. Add salt and pepper to taste. Makes 12 cups or 8 servings.

SHRIMP CHOWDER

¼ cup butter or margarine
4 large onions, sliced
6 medium potatoes, cubed
1 tablespoon salt
½ teaspoon seasoned pepper
6 cups milk
2 cups shredded pasteurized process sharp cheese (8 ounces)
2 pounds shrimp, shelled and deveined
3 tablespoons chopped parsley for garnish

ABOUT 1 HOUR BEFORE SERVING:
In Dutch oven over medium heat, in hot butter or margarine, cook onions until tender. Add 1 cup hot water, potatoes, salt and seasoned pepper. Reduce heat to low; cover and simmer for 15 minutes or until potatoes are tender; do not drain.

Meanwhile, in medium saucepan over low heat, heat milk with cheese until cheese has melted, stirring often; do not boil.

Add shrimp to potatoes and cook until they are pink and tender, about 3 minutes. Add hot cheese mixture. Heat but do not boil; sprinkle with parsley. Makes about 16 cups or 8 servings.

WINTER BARLEY SOUP

2½ pounds lamb stew meat, cut in chunks
2 tablespoons butter or margarine
½ cup barley
2 medium onions, sliced
2 tablespoons chopped parsley
2 teaspoons salt
¼ teaspoon pepper
1 bay leaf
1½ cups chopped celery
1½ cups sliced carrots
½ medium green pepper, diced
¼ teaspoon thyme leaves

ABOUT 2½ HOURS BEFORE SERVING:
In Dutch oven over medium-high heat, brown lamb in butter or margarine; add 6 cups hot water, barley, 1 sliced onion, parsley, salt, pepper and bay leaf. Heat to boiling; reduce heat to low; simmer, covered, about 1½ hours.

Stir in remaining sliced onion and rest of ingredients and cook 30 minutes or until meat is fork-tender. Discard bay leaf. Makes about 11 cups or 8 servings.

CREAMY CHEDDAR-CHEESE SOUP

¼ cup butter or margarine
1 medium onion, chopped
¼ cup all-purpose flour
3 cups chicken broth
3 cups milk
1 pound Cheddar cheese, shredded (about 4 cups)
3 pumpernickel-bread slices, toasted and cut in cubes

ABOUT 45 MINUTES BEFORE SERVING:
In large saucepan over medium-high heat, in hot butter or margarine, cook onion until tender, about 5 minutes. Stir in flour and cook until blended. Gradually add chicken broth; cook, stirring constantly, until mixture is slightly thickened. Add milk and heat, stirring, just to boiling.

In covered blender container at medium speed, blend about ¼ of milk mixture at a time until smooth. Return to saucepan and, over medium heat, heat just to boiling; remove from heat. With wire whisk or slotted spoon, stir in cheese until melted. If cheese does not melt completely, cook over low heat a minute, stirring constantly.

Serve soup garnished with pumpernickel cubes. Makes 8 cups or 6 servings.

SWISS SUPPER SOUP

¼ cup butter or margarine
1 cup minced onions
4 teaspoons all-purpose flour
2 teaspoons salt
5 cups milk
4 teaspoons chopped parsley
1⅓ cups shredded Swiss cheese
8 thick French-bread slices, buttered

ABOUT 30 MINUTES BEFORE SERVING:
In medium saucepan over medium heat, in hot butter or margarine, cook onions until tender, about 5 minutes. Stir in flour and salt until blended. Add 1 cup milk and stir until thickened. Add remaining milk and parsley and heat to simmering, stirring occasionally. Remove from heat; stir in cheese.

Meanwhile, preheat broiler if manufacturer directs. Arrange bread on rack and broil until golden. In each soup bowl, place 2 slices bread, then pour in cheese mixture. Serve piping hot. Makes 4 servings.

FRANKFURTER CHOWDER

¼ cup butter or margarine
2 large onions, chopped
1 stalk celery, chopped
2 cups drained sauerkraut (1 16-ounce can)
1 bay leaf
¼ teaspoon pepper
¼ teaspoon thyme leaves
2 13¾-ounce cans beef broth
2 16-ounce packages frankfurters, cut up
1½ cups sour cream
½ cup chopped fresh dill (optional)

ABOUT 45 MINUTES BEFORE SERVING:
In Dutch oven or large kettle over high heat, in hot butter or margarine, cook onions and celery until tender; stir in sauerkraut, bay leaf, pepper and thyme and cook 2 minutes. Add beef broth and simmer over medium-low heat, covered, about 15 minutes. Add frankfurters and cook 10 minutes longer. Discard bay leaf. Spoon into soup bowls; top each serving with sour cream and dill. Makes 10 cups or 6 servings.

HEARTY PRESSURE-COOKER SOUP

2 pounds chuck, cut in 1-inch chunks
⅓ cup all-purpose flour
3 tablespoons butter or margarine
3 large carrots, cut in small chunks
3 celery stalks, cut in small chunks
2 medium onions, sliced
2 large potatoes, cut in small chunks
2 12-ounce cans cocktail vegetable juice
1 tablespoon salt
½ teaspoon seasoned pepper

ABOUT 1 HOUR BEFORE SERVING:
On waxed paper, coat meat with flour. In heated 4-quart pressure cooker, without rack, in hot butter or margarine, brown meat well; add carrots, celery, onions, potatoes, cocktail vegetable juice and 2 cups hot water or enough to make cooker two-thirds full. Add salt and seasoned pepper. Bring to 15 pounds pressure as manufacturer directs; cook 15 minutes. Remove from heat and reduce pressure quickly as manufacturer directs before uncovering. Carefully remove lid. Makes about 11 cups or 8 servings.

SPRING VEGETABLE SOUP

3 tablespoons butter or margarine
3 leeks, chopped
1 small onion, chopped
½ cup regular long-grain rice
salt
3 medium potatoes, thinly sliced
1 medium carrot, thinly sliced
12 stalks fresh or frozen asparagus, cut into 1-inch pieces
1 10-ounce bag fresh spinach, chopped rather fine
dash pepper
1 cup heavy or whipping cream

ABOUT 1 HOUR BEFORE SERVING:
In large Dutch oven over medium-low heat, in hot butter or margarine, cook leeks and onion until tender. Add rice, 1½ teaspoons salt, 8 cups water. Cover; heat to boiling. Reduce heat to low; simmer 5 minutes.

Add potatoes, carrot and asparagus; cover and simmer 10 minutes. Add spinach, 4 teaspoons salt, pepper and cream. Stir gently. Makes 12½ cups or 8 servings.

FISH CHOWDER

4 large potatoes, sliced
3 medium onions, sliced
1 cup chopped celery
4 whole cloves
1 garlic clove, minced
1 tablespoon salt
1 bay leaf
¼ teaspoon dill seed
¼ teaspoon white pepper
2 16-ounce packages frozen flounder fillets, thawed
2 cups half-and-half
½ cup white wine
¼ cup butter or margarine

ABOUT 50 MINUTES BEFORE SERVING:
In covered Dutch oven or kettle over medium heat, simmer potatoes, onions, celery, cloves, garlic, salt, bay leaf, dill seed, pepper and 1 cup water about 25 minutes until vegetables are tender. Discard cloves and bay leaf.

Cut fish into large chunks. Add fish, 1 cup water and remaining ingredients to vegetables. Heat, stirring occasionally. Makes 13 cups or 8 servings.

MULLIGATAWNY SOUP

5 bacon slices, diced
1 2½-pound broiler-fryer, cut up
4 cups chicken broth
2 carrots, sliced
2 stalks celery, chopped
1 apple, chopped
1 tablespoon curry powder
6 peppercorns, coarsely crushed
2 whole cloves
1 bay leaf
3 tablespoons all-purpose flour
1 cup half-and-half or milk
1½ cups hot cooked rice
¼ cup chopped parsley

ABOUT 1½ HOURS BEFORE SERVING:
In Dutch oven over medium-high heat, fry bacon; add chicken pieces and brown well. Drain chicken pieces and bacon on paper towels; pour fat from pan. Return bacon and chicken to Dutch oven and add chicken broth, carrots, celery, apple, curry powder, peppercorns, cloves and bay leaf.

Cover; simmer over low heat 30 minutes or until chicken is tender. Remove chicken to cutting board; cut meat from bones and return to soup, discarding bones, cloves and bay leaf. Heat soup to simmering.

In cup, combine flour with ⅓ cup cold water. Gradually add to simmering soup, stirring constantly. Stir in half-and-half; heat but do not boil. To serve, spoon a mound of rice and a little parsley into each bowl of soup. Makes 8 cups or 6 servings.

Dessert Soups

BLENDER BLUEBERRY SOUP

⅓ cup sour cream
1 10-ounce package frozen blueberries, partially thawed
2 tablespoons sugar
lemon slices for garnish

ABOUT 20 MINUTES BEFORE SERVING:
In covered blender container at low speed, blend sour cream, blueberries and sugar until smooth. Add more sugar if needed. (Or, press blueberries through food mill; mix with sour cream and sugar.) Serve soup garnished with lemon slices. Makes 1¾ cups or 2 dessert servings.

STRAWBERRY-RHUBARB SOUP

1 pint strawberries, sliced
1 pound rhubarb, cut up
1¼ cups orange juice
about ½ cup sugar
¼ cup chopped orange sections

ABOUT 3 HOURS BEFORE SERVING:
Reserve 4 strawberry slices for garnish. In medium saucepan over medium heat, heat remaining strawberry slices, rhubarb and orange juice to boiling; reduce heat and simmer, uncovered, 10 minutes. Remove from heat; stir in sugar to taste; cool.

In covered blender container at low speed, blend strawberry mixture, one half at a time, until smooth. (Or put mixture through a food mill.) Fold in chopped orange sections; refrigerate, covered, until well chilled.

TO SERVE:
Garnish soup with reserved strawberry slices. Makes 4¼ cups or 4 servings.

ICED CHERRY SOUP

2 16-ounce cans pitted tart cherries
½ cup sugar
2 tablespoons lemon juice
½ teaspoon anise seed, crushed
3 tablespoons cornstarch
½ teaspoon red food color
sour cream for garnish
mint leaves for garnish

EARLY IN DAY:
Drain cherries, reserving liquid; add water to cherry liquid to make 5 cups. In covered, large saucepan over medium heat, heat cherries, liquid, sugar, lemon juice and anise seed to boiling. Reduce heat and simmer, covered, 30 minutes.

In covered blender container, blend mixture until smooth, one half at a time. (Or press mixture through a coarse sieve.) Return mixture to pan and heat to boiling. Blend cornstarch with ½ cup water; stir into hot mixture; cook, stirring, until clear and thickened. Stir in food color; refrigerate, covered, until well chilled.

TO SERVE:
Garnish soup with sour cream and mint leaves. Makes 6 cups or 6 servings.

STRAWBERRY SOUP

½ cup white wine
½ cup sugar
2 tablespoons lemon juice
1 teaspoon grated lemon peel
1 pint strawberries

EARLY IN DAY:
In covered blender container at medium speed, blend all ingredients except 3 strawberries until smooth. Cover and refrigerate.

TO SERVE:
Garnish soup with reserved strawberries, sliced. Makes 2⅔ cups or 3 dessert servings.

COLD RASPBERRY SOUP

4 10½-ounce packages frozen raspberries, thawed
2 cups port or other sweet wine
4 short cinnamon sticks
2 teaspoons cornstarch

EARLY IN DAY:
In large saucepan over medium heat, heat raspberries, wine and cinnamon sticks to boiling; reduce heat and simmer 10 minutes. In measuring cup, mix cornstarch with ½ cup water. Slowly stir into soup; cook until thickened, stirring. Cover and chill.

TO SERVE:
Remove cinnamon sticks. Makes 6 cups or 6 dessert servings.

FRUIT SOUP

1 lemon, thinly sliced
1 11-ounce package mixed dried fruits
1 8-ounce package dried apricots
⅔ cup sugar
2 tablespoons quick-cooking tapioca
½ teaspoon salt
3 short cinnamon sticks

ABOUT 3 HOURS BEFORE SERVING:
In large saucepan over medium heat, heat one-half of lemon slices, 6 cups water and remaining ingredients to boiling.

Reduce heat; cover and simmer 30 minutes or until fruits are tender. Cover; chill.

TO SERVE:
Remove cinnamon sticks. Serve with lemon slices. Makes 7 cups or 8 dessert servings.

Meats

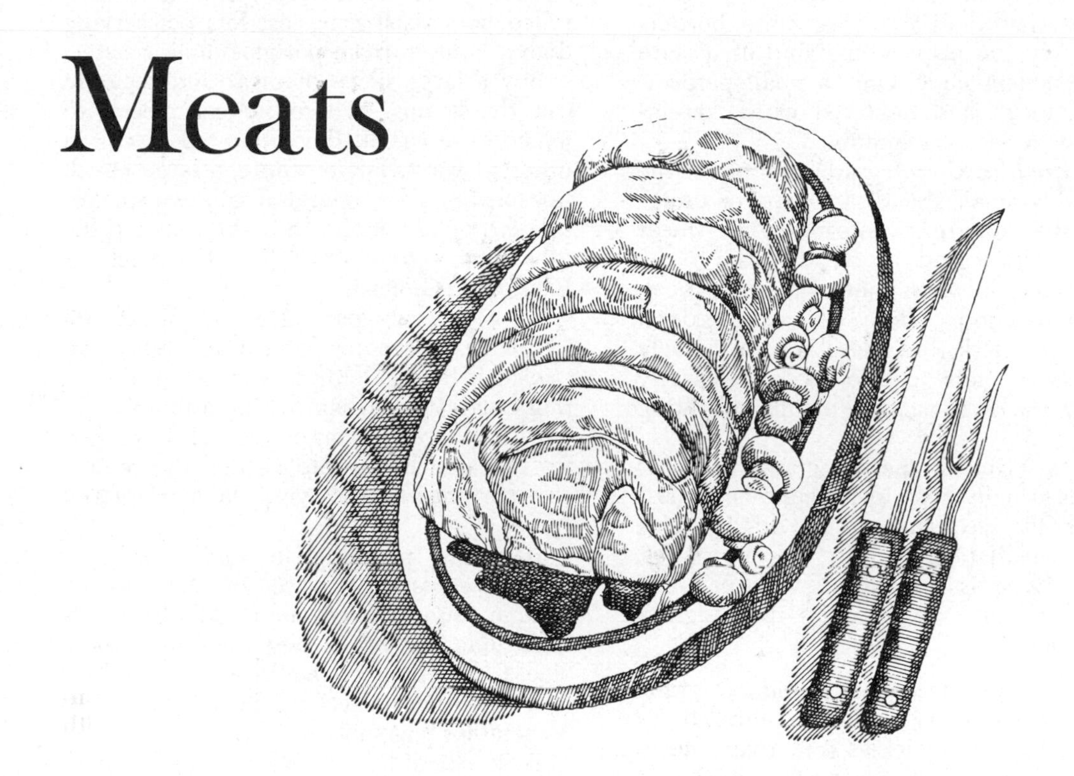

For every member of the family, meat provides good nutrition. It is a major source of the top-quality protein needed for growth and maintenance of the body and protection against disease. It supplies B vitamins (particularly thiamine, niacin and riboflavin), iron and other essential minerals. Liver is an especially good source of vitamin A (as well as iron).

Meat also supplies some of the fat needed for energy. Meat today is lean, with more lean meat in proportion to bone and fat; the small amount of fat naturally marbled through it adds to its flavor, aroma and "staying power."

How to Buy Meat

The tenderness of meat depends on the quality of the animal and the particular cut. Different cuts, and the same cuts from animals of different quality, vary in tenderness. It is important, then, to recognize the marks that indicate quality and to be able to identify the different cuts by shape and appearance.

***USDA marks:** For wholesomeness:* All meat that is sold across state lines bears the United States Department of Agriculture meat inspection stamp. On fresh meat, this is a circular mark with the abbreviated legend "U.S. inspected and passed" indicating that the meat is wholesome, was processed under sanitary conditions and is labeled honestly. This stamp is applied only to the large wholesale cuts, and so may or may not appear on the smaller cuts packaged for retail sale. The dye used does not penetrate the meat; it need not be trimmed before cooking the meat.

A similar stamp is used for processed meats such as cured and canned meats and frozen meat products. The stamp appears on the label, can or package and gives the same assurance of wholesomeness and accurate labeling.

Meat that does not cross state borders may carry the inspection stamp of a state government agency. Only a small percentage of meat is slaughtered where no inspection service is maintained.

For quality: USDA grade stamps, in the form of a small shield, are used to designate the different categories of meat quality. These grades serve as guides to the tenderness, juiciness and flavor of beef, veal and lamb. There are also Federal grades for pork, but these are not widely used, since many cuts of pork, especially cured pork, carry packers' brands indicating quality.

USDA Prime is the top grade, and this meat is usually sold to restaurants. USDA Choice, the next grade, is the quality most widely available. Of the lower grades, USDA Good is sometimes available. It is leaner and may be less juicy than higher-grade meat.

Brand names: Because the federal grade stamp is voluntary and not required by law, many meat packers and retail stores use brand names to designate the quality of their products. A packer may have several different brands, each representing a different quality of meat; some of these brands may match the federal grades.

Appearance: When buying any meat, look for freshness; the meat will be firm, finely textured and bright in color. It should also be marbled—the more flecks of fat within the lean, the greater the meat's tenderness, juiciness and flavor.

How much to buy: If the meat is boneless, plan on ¼ to ⅓ pound per serving. If it has a little bone, plan on ⅓ to ½ pound per serving. If it is very bony, allow ¾ to 1 pound per serving, and plan on two or three servings for heartier appetites. If the cut is one which requires long cooking, consider buying enough to serve for more than one meal.

Budget tips: Before you buy, figure the cost per serving. Sometimes a cut that is priced at less per pound but has considerable bone and fat may actually cost more per serving than a higher-priced cut. For example, chuck steak may be more expensive to serve than well-trimmed sirloin; rolled pork roast may cost less per serving than a bone-in fresh pork shoulder roast.

Buy a large piece of meat and separate it at the "seams"—where the lean pieces are joined. Then cook the separated pieces in different ways. For example, a large chuck pot roast may be separated into two smaller pieces, one of which can be braised and the other cut into chunks for stew such as Hungarian Goulash.

Buy several packages of meat on "special"; freeze for later use. Over-wrap packaged meat with freezer-wrap if you don't plan to use them within a month.

Buy a large amount of ground beef when it's on sale; divide into patties and recipe-size portions; freezer-wrap, label, date and freeze.

If you're planning to serve beef pot roast, compare the prices of chuck steak, bottom round, rolled rump. All three cuts make fine pot roast; buy the least expensive. Cross-cut beef shanks can be used for individual pot roasts (see Beef Shanks with Vegetables page, 92).

Pork shoulder steaks resemble pork chops in appearance, flavor and ways they can be cooked, yet as a rule they cost less.

Canned meats are fully cooked and waste-free (no bones or fat), take comparatively little time to heat. Plan menus around main dishes of luncheon meat, chopped ham, corned-beef or roast-beef hash, others.

Frozen meats: Recipe-size or serving-size amounts of frozen meats are available in supermarkets, ready to be cooked (or thawed and cooked) the same ways as fresh meat, or thawed and heated.

Cooked meats in gravy, in entrées such as veal Parmigiana, and in combination dinners make it possible to put family favorites on the table when cooking time is short.

Canned meats: Ready-to-eat or ready-to-heat-and-eat canned meats come in an impressive variety. There are single meats such as hams, chopped ham, franks, bacon, corned beef, Vienna sausages, strained or chopped meats for babies; and combination dishes such as stew, hash, sandwich spreads, chili con carne, gourmet specialties like beef Stroganoff; and many more. All are boneless, free of excess fat and fully cooked.

How to Store Meat

Fresh meat: Refrigerate fresh meat as soon as possible after purchase, in the meat compartment or in the coldest part of the refrigerator. If the meat has been prepackaged for self service, leave it in its unopened wrapping and use within two days; or store in the freezer one to two weeks. For longer freezer storage, overwrap the package with freezer-wrapping material.

If fresh meat has not been prepackaged, remove it from the market wrapping paper and wrap it loosely in waxed paper or foil; wrap variety and ground meats tightly. Refrigerate; use ground beef, stew and variety meats in one or two days; use other meats within two days.

Cured and cured-and-smoked meats: Refrigerate half or whole hams for no longer than a week; ham steaks, three or four days; sliced boiled ham and prosciutto, up to three days; bacon, five to seven days; corned beef, one week.

Sausage: Fresh pork sausage, whether bulk, links or patties, and uncooked smoked sausages should be refrigerated and used within two to three days.

Cooked sausage (page 163) should be refrigerated; if unsliced, it will keep four to six days; if sliced, use within three or four days.

Cooked smoked sausage (page 163) should be refrigerated, used within a week to 10 days.

Dry and semidry sausage (page 163) should be refrigerated, used within two or three weeks.

Cooked meat specialties (page 163) should be refrigerated, used within two or three days.

Canned hams and other perishable canned meats: If label directs, refrigerate in unopened can until ready to serve or heat. Do not freeze. Unopened canned hams keep 6 months; once opened, they should be used within a week. As a rule, canned meats weighing less than three pounds do not need refrigeration; however, be sure to check the label.

Canned meat products not marked "perishable" or "keep under refrigeration": Keep in cool dry place, not in cabinet above the range; use within a year. Once opened, cover and refrigerate; use within a few days.

Frozen meat: Store in freezer or freezer compartment as soon after purchase as possible, unless it is to be thawed for cooking. If meat is frozen and stored in a small ice-cube compartment, use within a week.

Cooked meat: Refrigerate within one or two hours, covered or wrapped to prevent drying. If meat has been cooked in liquid, cool slightly, 15 or 20 minutes, placing cooking utensil in cold or iced water, stirring occasionally. Cover and refrigerate.

Use cooked meat within two to three days.

How to Freeze Meat

For best quality in frozen meats, freeze meat that is fresh and in top condition. Cut large pieces into meal-size amounts; package together enough chops, steaks, patties and other small cuts such as short ribs for a single meal, placing foil, plastic wrap or a double thickness of waxed paper between pieces so they'll be easy to separate while thawing. Leave ground meat unseasoned (freezing intensifies seasonings and hastens rancidity); shape into patties or divide into amounts for loaves or for recipes.

Trim excess fat from cuts; wherever practical, remove bones to conserve freezer space. Wrap meat tightly in freezer-wrap; label with name of cut, weight or number of servings, and date; then freeze quickly if possible, at −10°F. or lower. Keep meat frozen at 0°F. or lower and use within the recommended storage period. For storage times see Freezer Storage, Meat (page 724).

Freezing ham for long periods is generally not recommended, since the salt used in curing can hasten flavor changes. But if you must freeze ham, wrap it in freezer wrap, seal tightly and freeze for one to two months. Canned hams should not be frozen, because expansion might cause the can to burst.

Freeze cooked meat, stuffing and gravy in separate containers.

How to Use Frozen Meat

Home-frozen meat may be thawed and cooked or cooked while still frozen.

Thaw meat in its wrappings in the refrigerator; then cook it the same way as meat that has not been frozen. Allow 5 to 7 hours per pound for thawing large roasts, 3 to 5 hours per pound for small roasts, and a total of 14 hours for 1-inch-thick steaks.

To cook meat that is still frozen, unwrap and cook as recipe directs but allow extra time. Roasts will require one-third to one-half more time than that required for unfrozen roasts. (It is not advisable to increase the cooking temperature of frozen meats. This does not change total cooking time appreciably, and it usually results in greater cooking loss, and less palatability.)

The extra time needed for steaks and chops will vary according to the thickness of the meat and the surface area, and the broiling temperature used if the meats are broiled. Frozen thick steaks, chops and ground-meat patties should be broiled farther from the heat or at a lower temperature than unfrozen ones, so that the outside of the meat doesn't brown too much before the interior is done to the desired degree.

Cuts that are to be coated with egg and crumbs, or with batter, should be thawed at least partially so the coating will adhere.

To pan-broil chops and steaks, heat the skillet until very hot before putting in the meat, so the meat will brown quickly before its surface thaws and retards browning. Then reduce the heat and turn the meat occasionally to finish cooking.

For braising pot roasts, thick frozen steaks or chops, allow approximately the same cooking time as for comparable thawed cuts.

Cook commercially frozen meat products following label directions.

Tenderizing Aids

For some less-tender meat cuts, preparation can be shortened or simplified if the tendering process is started in advance of cooking. There are several ways to do this.

Beef "tendered with papain": This is a scientific commercial process that utilizes protein derivatives from such fruits as papaya (papain) to supplement the natural tenderizing agents already present in beef. The tendering develops only as the beef cooks. This process makes it possible to cook more beef cuts by dry heat, and shortens cooking time for those cuts that must be cooked by moist heat. See Beef, page 69.

Meat tenderizers: These are derivatives of natural food-tenderizing agents found in some tropical fruits such as papaya; they tenderize by softening meat tissue, usually as the meat cooks. They are not harmful. Be sure to follow directions on the label of either unseasoned or seasoned varieties. Don't use more and don't leave it on longer than the label recommends, or meat surface might become mushy. Also, don't use it on cuts that are already tender, such as T-bone steak or on beef tendered with papain.

Mechanical methods: *Grinding* makes meat tender, as does *"cubing,"* which breaks down the connective tissue by machine. *Pounding* meat, as directed in some recipes, achieves the same results.

Aging: This improves the tenderness of some beef cuts. At the storage plant, beef is hung in rooms with controlled temperature and humidity for a specified time.

Marinating: Soaking meat, particularly in acid mixtures such as lemon juice or vinegar, tenderizes meat and adds flavor.

How to Cook Meat

Because meat cuts vary widely in tenderness, the method of cooking should be suited to the cut. Tender cuts, with a few exceptions, are best when cooked by dry heat: roasted, broiled, pan-broiled or pan-fried. Less tender cuts are best when cooked slowly in moist heat: pot-roasted, braised (in liquid or in the steam that forms when foods are cooked covered) or cooked in liquid.

Whatever the cut, meat will be at its most tender and juicy best if cooked at low to moderate temperatures; servings will be larger, too, because loss through shrinkage and evaporation will be minimized.

To estimate cooking time: The time it takes a cut of meat to cook depends on many factors: the kind of meat, its temperature at the start of the cooking period, the size and shape of the cut, the proportion of lean to fat and bone, the desired degree of doneness, whether or not the meat has been tenderized in any way. Thicker cuts will take longer than thinner cuts that weigh the same. Meat with a higher percentage of fat cooks faster than meat with little or no fat. Boned and rolled roasts require more cooking time than the same roasts with the bone in.

Cooking times in our recipes are based on meat kept refrigerated until time to cook it. Meat that is frozen or partially thawed will take longer.

There are six basic ways to cook meat: roasting, broiling, pan-broiling, pan-frying, braising and cooking in liquid.

For roasting, best results are obtained when a meat thermometer is used.

To use a meat thermometer: For meats that are roasted in an open roasting pan or baked in an oven-cooking bag or wrap, insert the point of the meat thermometer so it is centered in the thickest part of the meat; if necessary, pierce meat with skewer first to make insertion of thermometer easier. Make sure that the point does not rest on bone or in fat. If the meat is frozen, roast it at the usual roasting temperature until it has thawed enough to insert the thermometer (about halfway through the roasting period; check first with a skewer); then continue roasting until the desired temperature is reached.

For outdoor and rotisserie cooking, the dial type of thermometer is recommended. Insert the meat thermometer at a slight angle or through the end of the roast halfway between the spit and the surface of the meat; be sure the thermometer point is not resting in fat, or touching the rotisserie spit.

Do not use meat thermometer for broiling, braising, or cooking meat in liquid.

To roast: This method is recommended for large tender cuts of beef, veal, lamb, or fresh or cured and smoked pork. Some cuts suitable for roasting are pictured on pages 70, 103, 132, 144. Follow these steps:

Preheat oven to 325°F. for most meats; exceptions are 350°F. for rib eye (Delmonico) and 425°F. for beef tenderloin. Season meat with salt and pepper if desired. Place meat with fat side up on rack in open roasting pan. In some roasts, bones form a natural rack as with pork loin or standing rib roast.

Insert meat thermometer so it is centered in thickest part of meat, being careful the tip does not touch bone or rest in fat. Do not add water. Do not cover.

Roast until meat thermometer reaches desired degree of doneness. Roasts continue to cook after they are removed from the oven. If the meat is to "set" for 15 to 20 minutes before being carved, temperature could rise 5 to 10 degrees; you may wish to remove it from the oven when the reading is about 5 degrees lower than the reading for the degree of doneness desired.

To broil: Tender beef steaks, lamb or pork steaks and chops, ground beef or lamb, ham slices and bacon slices may all be broiled.

Steaks and chops should be at least ¾ inch thick; ham slices should be at least ½ inch thick. Trim excess fat from meat; slash edge of fat at 2-inch intervals so it won't curl during broiling.

Follow these steps for best results:

Preheat broiler if manufacturer directs. Rub broiling-pan rack with bit of fat trimmed from meat. Place meat on rack in broiling pan; then place pan in broiler so top of meat is two to five inches from the source of the heat. Steaks, chops and patties ¾ to 1 inch thick should be 2 to 3 inches from the heat; cuts 1 to 2 inches thick should be 3 to 5 inches from the heat.

Broil meat until the top is browned (lightly browned for cured and smoked pork). By this time the meat should be about half done.

Season top of meat with salt and pepper

if desired (omit seasoning for ham or bacon). With tongs, turn meat and broil until browned and of desired degree of doneness. Season if desired; serve at once.

To test for doneness, cut a slit near the bone or into the center of the meat and check the color.

To pan-broil: The same cuts used for broiling may be pan-broiled when cut 1 inch thick or less; this method is also convenient for cooking a small steak or a few chops.

If the meat is very lean, the pan may be brushed lightly with fat before cooking, or rubbed with a bit of fat cut from meat. However, most meats have enough fat to keep from sticking. Place meat in an unheated heavy skillet or on a griddle. Do not add fat; do not add liquid; do not cover.

Over medium to medium-low heat, cook the meat slowly, turning it occasionally so it cooks evenly. Pour off fat as it accumulates, so the meat doesn't fry. Brown meat on both sides. Gradual browning is better than quick searing, which does not hold in meat juices.

As soon as meat is done, season if desired and serve. Meat will take about half as long as if broiled in broiler.

To test for doneness of bone-in meats, cut a small slit close to bone near the end of the cooking time and check the color.

To pan-fry: This method is used to cook thin pieces of tender cuts, or meat tenderized by pounding, cubing, scoring or grinding. The pieces are cooked in a small amount of added fat or in the fat that accumulates as cooking progresses.

In skillet, over medium or medium-high heat, in a small amount of hot salad oil or other cooking fat such as bacon drippings, lard, shortening, butter or margarine, cook meat until browned on both sides. (Fat melts from some cuts, so that no salad oil need be added. Add salad oil if cuts are low in fat, such as liver, or if meat is coated with flour or bread crumbs.) Season meat with salt and pepper if desired.

Over medium or medium-low heat, cook meat, turning occasionally, until done. This way, meat cooks evenly and thoroughly without over-browning or burning. Do not cover, or crispness will be lost. Remove from pan and serve at once.

To braise: Slow cooking in a small amount of liquid, or in steam, is a preferred method for cooking many of the less-tender cuts such as beef round steaks, short ribs, pot roasts; beef, lamb and veal shanks; lamb and veal riblets. A few tender cuts, including pork steaks and cutlets, veal chops, steaks and cutlets and pork liver, can also be braised.

In a large, heavy skillet, saucepot or Dutch oven over medium-high heat, in a small amount of hot salad oil or fat melted from meat cut, cook meat until browned on all sides; pour off drippings. Slow browning helps develop flavor and long-lasting color. Some meats may not need salad oil to keep from sticking.

Season meat with salt, pepper, other seasonings if desired. Add a small amount of liquid if needed. Less tender cuts usually require liquid; tender cuts, such as pork chops, may not. The liquid may be water, vegetable juice, bouillon, soup or wine.

Cover skillet tightly, to keep in steam. Reduce heat to low; simmer (don't boil) until meat is fork-tender. This step can be done on top of the range or in an oven preheated to 325°F. to 350°F.

To test for doneness, insert a two-tined meat fork into thickest part of meat; if it goes in easily, meat is tender. If desired, make gravy or sauce from liquid in pan.

To cook in liquid: Large, less-tender cuts, such as fresh or corned-beef brisket, spareribs, smoked picnic shoulder and stews are prepared this way.

For large cuts: In large, heavy saucepot or Dutch oven over medium-high heat, cook meat until browned on all sides, if desired. This develops flavor and color. (Corned beef and other cured meats are not browned.) Add water or stock to cover meat. Liquid may be hot or cold. Season with salt, pepper, other seasonings, if desired.

Over high heat, heat mixture to boiling; reduce heat to low, cover saucepot and simmer (don't boil) until meat is fork-tender. Test for doneness as above.

If vegetables are to be added, as in "boiled" dinners, add them just long enough before the meat is done to cook them.

Continental Beef Steak, page 76

If meat is to be served cold, chill in the liquid in which it was cooked. Meat will have greater juiciness and flavor, and shrink less.

For stews: Cut meat in uniform pieces, usually 1- to 2-inch chunks. Or, cut into rectangular pieces or strips.

For a browned stew, in Dutch oven or heavy saucepot over medium-high heat, in a small amount of hot salad oil, cook pieces (coated with flour first, if desired) a few at a time, until browned on all sides, removing them as they brown; return pieces to Dutch oven when all are browned.

For a light stew, omit coating with flour and browning.

Add liquid just to cover meat. Liquid may be hot or cold; it may be water, vegetable juices, soup, stock, wine or a combination of these. Season with salt, pepper, other seasonings, if desired.

Over high heat, heat mixture to boiling; reduce heat to low; cover and simmer (don't boil) until meat is fork-tender. Test for doneness as in To Braise, above.

Add vegetables just long enough before the meat is done to cook them.

When done, remove meat and vegetables to warm dish and keep warm. If desired, thicken liquid left in pan for gravy or sauce. Serve gravy over meat and vegetables or pass it separately in a gravy boat.

To cook on a rotisserie: Tender cuts of beef and large pieces of other meats, such as boneless ham or loin, spareribs, rolled leg of lamb can be cooked on the rotisserie in the oven or outdoor grill or on a portable rotisserie.

As with other dry-heat methods, low to moderate temperatures should be used. Meat pieces should be as uniform in shape and thickness as possible. Compact boneless, or boned and rolled meats are preferred because they are easy to balance on the spit, rotate smoothly and cook evenly. Meat on the rotisserie is self-basting but may be basted occasionally to add flavor and color. If sweet sauces are used, they should be applied only during the last half hour of cooking time so they won't burn.

Insert spit through center of roast lengthwise and test for balance by rotating spit in palms of hands. Fasten meat securely so it doesn't slip as the spit turns. Insert meat thermometer (page 63). If meat thermometer doesn't fit securely, after approximate roasting time has been completed, stop rotisserie, insert thermometer and read temperature.

Following manufacturers' directions, cook meat at low to moderate temperatures to desired degree of doneness. Time will depend on the kind, size and shape of the cut, the cooking temperature and the degree of doneness desired.

GRAVY FOR MEATS

FOR ROAST MEAT: When roast is removed to a platter, pour fat from roasting pan into liquid measuring cup, leaving browned bits in pan. Pour ¼ cup of this fat (or use butter or margarine if there's not enough fat) into 2-quart saucepan; discard remaining fat. Pour 1 cup water or bouillon into roasting pan; stir and scrape to loosen browned bits.

Into fat in saucepan over medium heat, gradually stir ¼ cup all-purpose flour until smooth. Cook, stirring constantly, until mixture is slightly browned.

Slowly stir in liquid from roasting pan; add 1 cup water and heat to boiling, stirring constantly until thickened. If you like, stir in bottled sauce for gravy until gravy reaches desired brown color. Add salt and pepper to taste. Makes about 2 cups.

FOR PAN-FRIED MEAT: When meat is done, remove to warm platter. Pour drippings into 1-cup measure; if necessary add butter or margarine to make ¼ cup. Return drippings to skillet.

Over medium heat, into hot drippings, gradually stir ¼ cup all-purpose flour until smooth. Cook, stirring constantly, until mixture is lightly browned. Gradually stir in 2 cups water, milk or bouillon; heat to boiling, stirring constantly until thickened. If you like, stir in bottled sauce for gravy until gravy reaches desired brown color. Add salt and pepper to taste.

VARIATIONS FOR ROAST AND PAN-FRIED MEAT GRAVY: *For thin gravy,* use only 2 tablespoons fat and 2 tablespoons flour.

For added flavor, stir one of these into gravy: 2 tablespoons medium or dry sherry; 2 tablespoons red table wine (dry for beef,

California Beef Stew, page 87

sweet for pork) or rosé or white table wine (for lamb, veal); 2 tablespoons heavy or whipping cream; ⅛ teaspoon thyme leaves or mixed fines herbes; or sliced mushrooms or chopped parsley.

FOR BRAISED STEAKS AND CHOPS: If liquid in pan is not thick enough, thicken this way: Measure liquid; if necessary, add water, broth or milk to make about 1 cup liquid for each pound of uncooked meat; heat liquid. For each cup liquid, in cup, blend 2 tablespoons all-purpose flour with ¼ cup water until smooth; gradually stir into liquid and cook over medium heat, stirring constantly, until thickened. Season with salt and pepper if necessary.

FOR POT ROAST: Remove meat and vegetables to warm platter. Pour pan liquid into 4-cup measure or large bowl; let stand a few minutes until fat separates; spoon off and discard fat. Measure pan liquid and return to pan. For every cup of liquid, use 2 tablespoons all-purpose flour for medium-thick gravy, 1 tablespoon for thin gravy.

Over medium heat, heat pan liquid to simmering. Meanwhile, in cup, blend desired amount of flour and twice as much cold water until smooth. Gradually stir mixture into simmering liquid and cook, stirring constantly, until mixture is thickened.

FOR STEW: Pan liquid for a brown stew should be thick enough to be served as gravy. To thicken gravy for a light stew: Measure liquid and return to Dutch oven to heat. For each cup liquid, in cup, blend 1 tablespoon all-purpose flour with ¼ cup water until smooth; gradually stir into liquid and cook, stirring constantly, until thickened. Season with salt and pepper if necessary.

IN-A-HURRY GRAVY: Packaged gravy mixes are quickly made and are good with just-cooked meat or leftovers; follow label directions.

Canned gravy is ready for use after only brief heating. For variety, stir in a tablespoon or two of red or white table wine, sour cream or shredded mild or sharp cheese just until the cheese is melted.

How to Carve Meat

Correct carving helps to tenderize meat by shortening the meat fibers. Before buying a cut, consider where it will be carved. Greater skill is needed if the meat is to be carved at the table than if it's to be carved in the kitchen. And to make carving easier, more and more cuts are now available either boneless or semi-boneless.

Proper cooking also makes carving simpler. A cut roasted at too high a temperature will be crusty and hard to carve; an overcooked pot roast will fall apart during carving.

After removing a roast from the oven, let it "set" at room temperature for about 15 minutes. "Setting" firms meat so it is easier to carve.

First, remove strings, wooden picks and skewers in the kitchen. If the roast is a rolled one, and could come apart during carving, leave one or two strings in place.

When arranging meat on a platter, keep garnishes simple and leave the platter uncluttered.

Use a sharp knife and a cutting board or wooden insert in meat platter to help keep the knife sharp. Hold the meat firmly in place with a two-tined fork.

Slice across the grain or fibers of the meat. If meat is thin (as with flank steak, corned-beef brisket or some loin steaks) cut slices diagonally across the grain (with the knife held *on the slant*) to make the slices as wide as possible. Loin and rib steaks up to 1 inch in thickness are tender enough to be carved with the grain.

Carve enough for everyone, then serve.

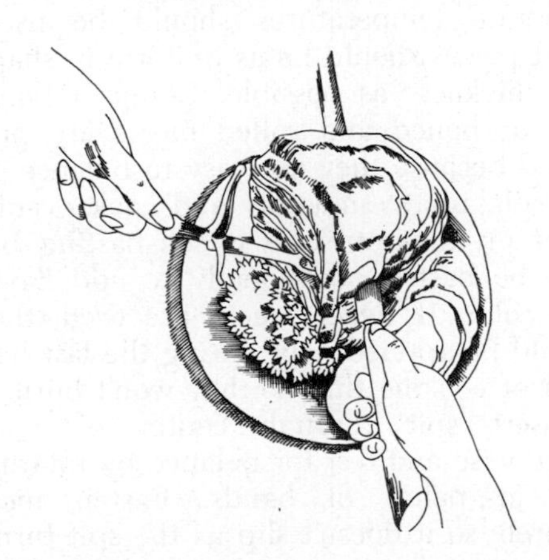

To carve standing rib roast of beef: Place cooked standing rib roast of beef on cutting board or warm platter with large end down and ribs to your left. Insert fork, tines down, between top and second ribs. Cut across meat, making a slice about ¼ inch thick. Remove knife and, with tip, cut along side of rib bone to release slice; place slice on a warm dinner plate. Continue cutting slices, removing each rib bone as it is exposed.

To carve rolled roast: Place cooked rolled roast of any meat except beef (below) on board or warm platter on its rolled side, as it was roasted. Remove all strings (or leave one or two in place if roast starts to fall apart). Using a fork to anchor meat, start cutting right side of roast into slices ¼ to ½ inch thick.

Beef rolled rib roasts are usually placed on one of their cut surfaces and sliced across top.

To carve porterhouse steak: Place cooked porterhouse steak on cutting board or warm platter, with end with most bone on your right. Cut around bone and set it aside. Using a fork to anchor meat, start at right and carve across full width of steak, through both the loin and tenderloin sections. Cut steak into slices ½ to ¾ inch thick.

To carve sirloin steak: Place cooked sirloin steak on cutting board or warm platter, with bone nearest you. Cut around bone and set it aside. Using a fork to anchor meat, and holding knife at a slight angle, cut diagonally across meat into slices about ½ to ¾ inch thick.

To carve arm and blade pot roasts: Place cooked pot roast on cutting board or warm platter. Using a fork to anchor meat, cut between the muscles and around bones, separating solid pieces of meat at natural dividing seams. Carving one solid section of meat at a time, turn section so meat fibers are parallel to length of board (this allows you to carve across grain of meat). Cut the piece into slices of desired thickness. Repeat with remaining sections of meat.

To carve loin roast: After roasting, cut back bone from ribs (meatman should have loosened back bone first). Place roast on cutting board or warm platter with rib side facing you. Using a fork to anchor meat, cut down between ribs. For pork, cut closely along each side of every rib; one slice will contain the rib, next one will be boneless.

To carve crown roast: Place crown roast, rib ends up, on cutting board or warm platter. Using a fork between ribs to anchor roast, slice down between ribs and remove each rib chop, as it is carved, to a dinner plate. Spoon any stuffing onto plate with meat.

To carve ham slice or steak: Place cooked ham slice or steak on cutting board or warm platter. Using a fork to anchor meat, cut across grain into slices about 1 to 2 inches thick; cut center slices in half for easier serving.

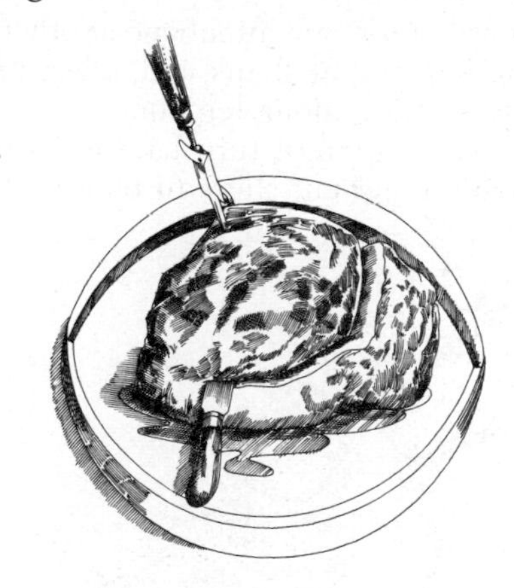

To carve picnic shoulder: Place cooked fresh or smoked picnic shoulder on cutting board or warm platter, fat side up, with shank bone to your right. Using a fork to anchor meat, cut a few slices from small meaty side; turn shoulder onto this cut surface. Starting at shank end, cut down to armbone, then follow along armbone to cut out chunky boneless meat in one piece; place it on its cut surface and cut uniform slices about ¼ inch thick from top side down to board.

Additional meat can be sliced in as large pieces as possible or cut off for chunks or for grinding for use in recipes.

To carve whole ham or leg of pork: Place cooked smoked ham or leg of pork on cutting board or warm platter, fat side up, with shank to your right. Using a fork to anchor meat, cut a few slices from thin side; turn ham onto this cut surface. Starting at shank end, slicing down to bone, cut out small wedge of meat. Continue cutting down to leg bone in slices about ¼ inch

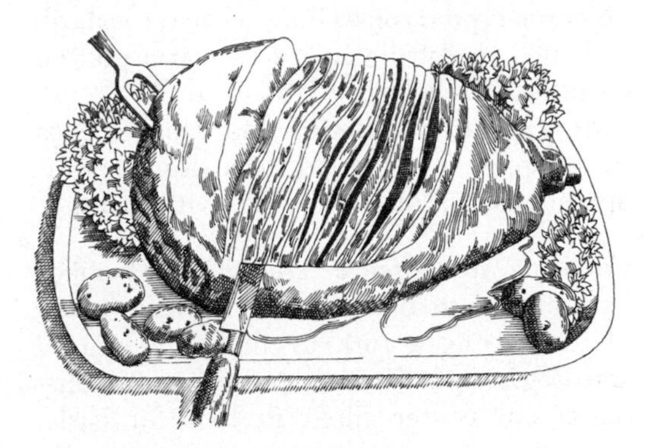

thick until you reach aitchbone at other end of ham. Starting at shank end, release meat slices by cutting along leg bone.

For more servings, turn ham to its original position and cut slices to bone.

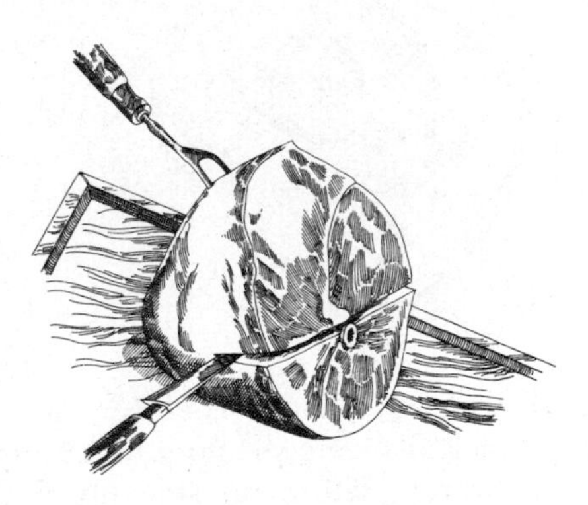

To carve shank half of ham: Place cooked shank half of ham on cutting board or warm platter with shank to your left. Using a fork to anchor meat, start at small bone on cut surface and cut off chunky boneless section in one large piece; place it on its freshly cut surface and cut uniform slices about ¼ inch thick down to board.

To carve remaining section, separate it from bone by cutting through joint; remove bone; turn meat and slice.

Additional meat can be cut off in chunks for recipes.

To carve butt half of ham: Place cooked butt half of ham on cutting board or warm platter on its cut surface. Using a fork to anchor meat, cut down along aitchbone to remove chunky boneless piece of meat. (Boneless piece may be on either the near or far side depending upon whether it is from right or left leg.) Place piece on its freshly cut surface and cut uniform slices about ¼ inch thick down to board.

Anchoring remaining butt half of ham with fork, slice across meat until knife strikes aitchbone; cut down along bone to release each slice of meat.

Additional meat can be cut off in chunks for recipes.

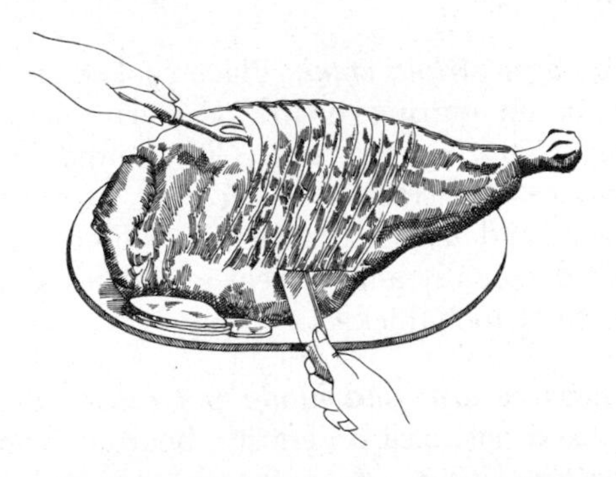

To carve leg of lamb: Place cooked leg of lamb on cutting board or warm platter with leg or shank bone to your right. Using a fork to anchor meat, cut a few slices from thin side of leg; turn leg onto this cut surface. Starting at shank end of meat, slice down to leg bone. Continue cutting down to bone in slices about ¼ inch thick until you reach aitchbone at other end of roast. Starting at shank end, release meat slices by cutting under them along leg bone.

Additional meat can be cut in as large pieces as possible or in chunks for curries, casseroles.

BEEF

Beef offers greater variety in quality, cuts and ways of cooking than any other meat. The meat comes fresh, cured, cured and smoked, frozen, canned and ready-to-serve. Cuts may be individual serving size or large enough to feed a hundred; cooking times may vary from a very few minutes to several hours.

Some beef is aged to increase its tenderness. This is usually done only with roasts and some steaks. Check with your meatman to find out if the beef you buy is aged.

Some beef is pre-tendered with papain by the meat packer so that it can be cooked more easily or in less time than regular beef. For example, when pre-tendered, some cuts normally braised, such as pot roasts, can be roasted with dry heat in the oven; they can also be cooked in the customary way, but cooking time will be shorter. Pre-tendered beef is specially labeled so it can be readily identified; cook it following label directions.

How to buy beef: Fresh beef should be uniformly bright, light to deep red, preferably with fine rather than coarse texture and firm and slightly moist. Color of the fat is no clue to quality because it varies with the age, feed and breed. Red porous bones indicate good-quality beef.

Corned beef is reddish-gray in color, owing to the mild cure that gives it its distinctive flavor. Dried beef is also cured. Available in packages and jars, it should be moist, not brittle, bright red in color with no brown spots.

How to cook beef cuts: Here are familiar beef cuts with the recommended ways to cook each (see pages 62–65):

Arm pot roast or steak—braise
Blade pot roast or steak—braise
Boston cut—braise, cook in liquid
Bottom-round pot roast—braise
Brisket, fresh or corned—cook in liquid
Chuck roll, boneless—braise
Club steak—broil, pan-broil or pan-fry
Cube steak—braise; pan-fry; broil if of high-quality beef
Delmonico (rib eye) roast or steak—roast, broil, pan-broil or pan-fry
Eye of round—braise; roast if of high-quality beef
Flank steak, fillets—braise; broil if of high-quality beef
Ground beef—roast (bake), broil, pan-broil, pan-fry, braise
Heel of round—braise, cook in liquid
Porterhouse steak—broil; pan-broil; pan-fry
Rib roasts: rib eye (Delmonico), standing —roast
Rib steak—broil, pan-broil or pan-fry
Rump, rolled—braise; roast if of high-quality beef
Round steak: top, bottom—braise, pan-fry Top round may be broiled if of high-quality beef
Shank cross cuts—braise
Short ribs—braise
Shoulder pot roast or steak, boneless—braise
Sirloin steaks: boneless; flat, pin or wedge bone—broil, pan-broil, pan-fry
Sirloin tip roast—roast if of high-quality beef; braise
Skirt-steak fillets—braise; broil, pan-broil or pan-fry if of high-quality beef
Stew meat—braise; cook in liquid
T-bone steak—broil, pan-broil, pan-fry
Tenderloin (filet mignon) roast or steak—roast, broil, pan-broil or pan-fry
Tip steak—braise; broil, pan-broil or pan-fry if of high-quality beef
Top loin steak—broil, pan-broil or pan-fry

How to test beef for doneness: Beef that is roasted or broiled may be cooked rare, medium or well done to suit individual preferences. Rare beef is brown on the outside, reddish-pink inside with lots of clear red juice. Beef cooked to a medium degree of doneness is light pink on the inside, with less juice, of a lighter color than that of rare beef. Well-done beef is brown throughout; the juice is slightly yellow. A meat thermometer will register 140°F. for rare,

SOME POPULAR BEEF CUTS

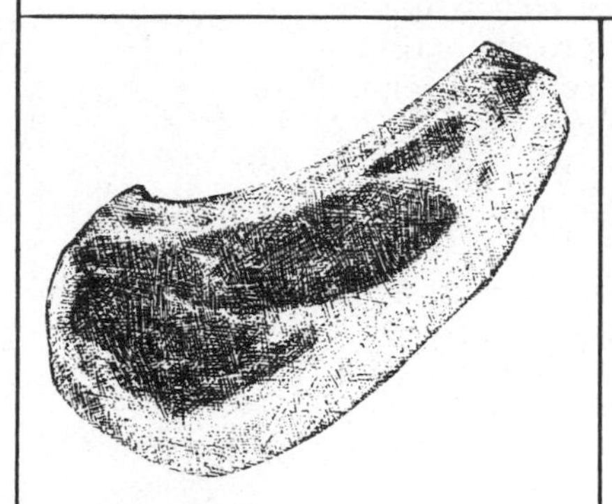

Rib Steak

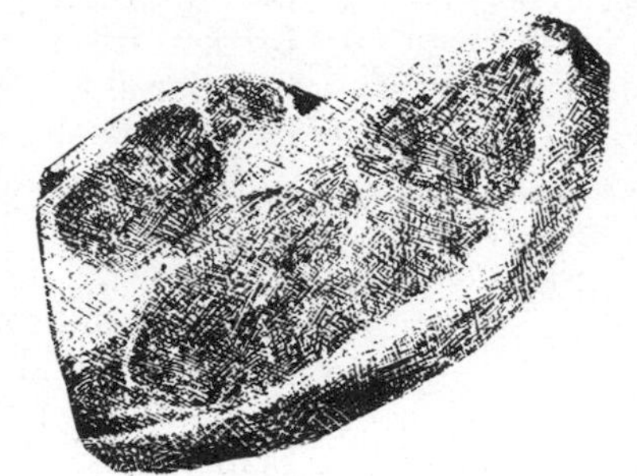

Sirloin Steak

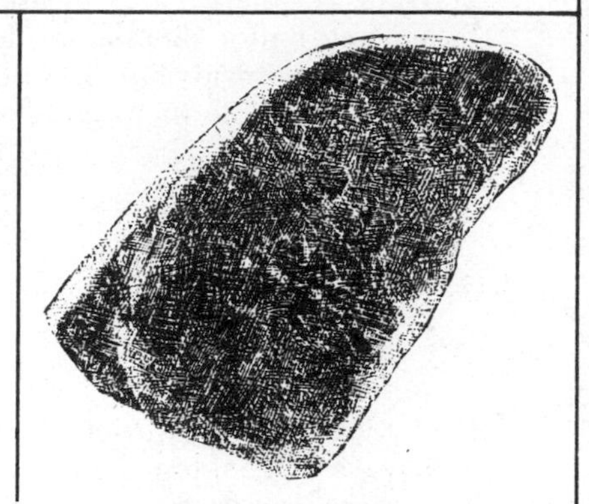

Top Round Steak

Flank Steak

Rib-Eye (Delmonico) Roast

Rolled Rump Roast

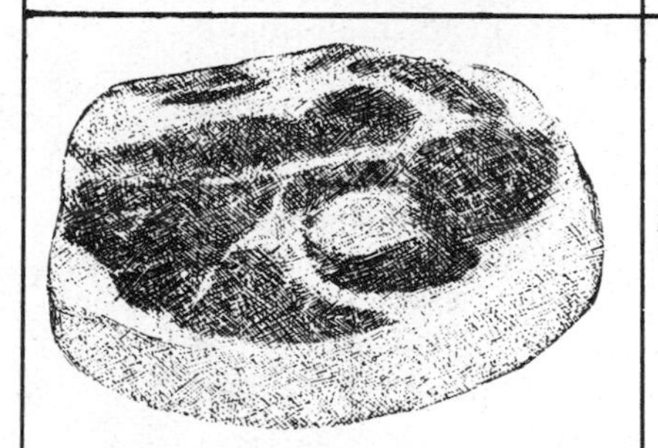

Arm Pot Roast

Blade Pot Roast

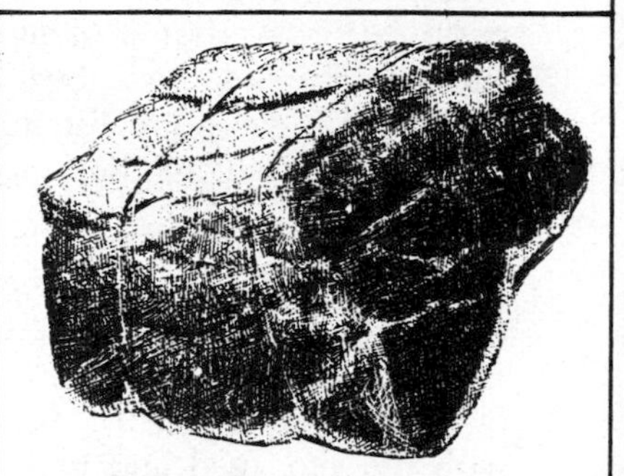

Boston-Cut Pot Roast

Brisket

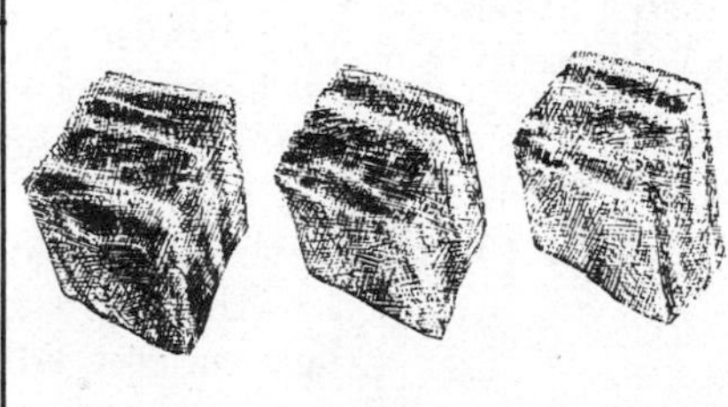

Short Ribs

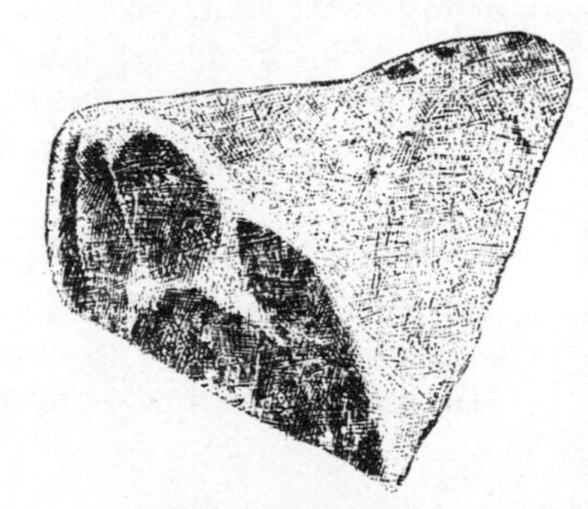

Heel of Round

160°F. for medium, 170°F. for well done.

Beef that is braised or simmered should be cooked until fork-tender.

Beef Roasts

TIMETABLE FOR ROASTING BEEF AT 325°F.

For general directions, see To Roast, page 63.

Weight of Cut (pounds)	*Approximate Hours* to Reach 140°F. (rare)*	*160°F. (medium)*	*170°F. (well done)*
Standing Rib Roast (short cut, 6 inches from tip of rib to back bone. If cut longer than 6 inches, roast will take less time.)			
4	2	2½	2¾
6	2½	3	3½
8	3	3½	4¼
10	4½	5	†
13	5	5½	†
16	4¾	5¼	†
20	4½	5	†
Rolled Rib Roast (4½ to 5 inches wide for 4-pound roast, 5½ to 6 inches wide for 6-pound roast. Thinner roasts of same weight will require less time.)			
5	2¾	3¼	4
7	3¾	4¼	5½
Rump Roast, rolled (high quality)			
5	2	2¼	2½
Sirloin Tip (high quality)			
4	2⅓	2½	2⅔
6	3	3¼	3½
Rib Eye (Delmonico) (roast at 350°F.)			
4	1⅓	1½	1⅔
6	1¾	2	2¼
Tenderloin (roast at 425°F.)			
4 to 6 (whole)	¾ to 1 hour total		
2 to 3 (half)	45 to 50 minutes total		

* Meat at refrigerator temperature, placed in oven preheated to 325°F.

† Larger roasts should be removed from oven when medium-done.

STANDING RIB ROAST WITH YORKSHIRE PUDDING

ABOUT 3½ TO 5 HOURS BEFORE SERVING: Preheat oven to 325°F. In open roasting pan, place *one 2- to 3-rib standing rib beef roast* (about 6 to 8 pounds), fat side up, on rib bones; sprinkle with *salt* and *pepper*. Insert meat thermometer into center of meat, making sure the pointed end does not touch bone or fat.

Roast until meat thermometer reaches 140°F. for rare, 160°F. for medium, and 170°F. for well done; see Timetable opposite.

Place roast on cutting board or warm platter and let stand 15 minutes for easier carving. Serve with *Yorkshire Pudding* (below) and *Creamy Horseradish Sauce* (page 167). Garnish roast with *canned crabapples* and *parsley*, if you like. Makes 14 to 18 servings.

YORKSHIRE PUDDING: About 5 minutes before roast is done, prepare pudding batter: In medium bowl, with wire whisk or fork, beat *2 eggs* until foamy; beat in *1 cup milk* and *½ teaspoon salt;* gradually beat in *1 cup all-purpose flour* until smooth.

When roast is done, turn oven control to 400°F. Spoon off *2 tablespoons clear hot beef drippings* from roasting pan and divide into twelve 3-inch muffin-pan cups; tip pans to coat cups evenly. (Use remaining drippings in pan to serve *au jus*, below.)

Heat muffin-pan cups in oven 5 minutes until drippings are very hot; remove pan from oven and quickly pour about 2½ tablespoons batter into each muffin-pan cup. Bake 30 minutes or until golden. With narrow spatula, loosen edges of each pudding and transfer it to meat platter. Serve immediately. Makes 12 servings.

ROAST BEEF AU JUS

Prepare favorite beef roast as above but, after removing roast from pan, spoon off fat from meat juices in pan; discard fat. Into pan, pour a little water (about ⅓ to ½ cup). Over medium-high heat, heat mixture to simmering, stirring and scraping until browned bits are dissolved; strain mixture. Serve over slices of meat.

STANDING RIB ROAST SUPREME

1 7-inch, 7-rib beef standing rib roast (about 16 to 18 pounds)
3 cups grated carrots
2 cups coarsely chopped celery leaves
2 teaspoons seasoned salt
½ teaspoon seasoned pepper
parsley sprigs for garnish
carrot curls for garnish

ABOUT 5 TO 6 HOURS BEFORE SERVING:

1. Preheat oven to 325°F. In large, open roasting pan, stand rib roast, fat side up, on rib bones. Insert meat thermometer into center of meat, making sure pointed end does not touch bone or fat. Roast 3 hours.
2. Meanwhile, in medium bowl, combine grated carrots, celery leaves, seasoned salt and pepper.
3. Remove roast from oven and sprinkle top with carrot mixture. Continue roasting meat until thermometer reaches 135°F. for rare, 145°F. for medium. Total roasting time should be about 4½ to 5 hours for rare, 5 hours for medium. (Because roast is large, ends of meat will be well done when inside is rare or medium done.)
4. During last of roasting time, if carrot mixture becomes dark, cover roast loosely with foil, leaving thermometer uncovered.
5. Place roast on cutting board and let stand at room temperature 15 minutes. If you like, cut roast in half crosswise, starting at backbone, between third and fourth rib bones. Arrange halves, side by side, on warm, large platter with backbones touching and cut sides facing same direction. Garnish with parsley and carrot curls. Makes about 32 to 40 servings.

FOR ABOUT 16 TO 20 SERVINGS: Roast a *6- to 8-pound standing rib roast* as above but reduce total cooking time to about 2½ to 3 hours for rare (140°F. internal temperature) to about 3 to 3½ hours for medium (160°F. internal temperature) and prepare only *half of carrot-topping mixture.*

ROAST BEEF TENDERLOIN

ABOUT 1¼ HOURS BEFORE SERVING:

1. Preheat oven to 425°F. Remove surface fat and connective tissue from *whole or half beef tenderloin.* If desired, rub meat all over with cut *garlic clove;* or, with sharp knife, make several gashes in top surface and insert piece of garlic in each slash.
2. Place meat on rack in open roasting pan; tuck narrow end under to make the roast evenly thick. Brush with *salad oil* or bacon drippings. Insert meat thermometer into center of thickest part of meat.
3. Roast whole tenderloin about 45 minutes to 1 hour total time or until meat thermometer reaches 140°F. (rare). Roast half tenderloin about 45 to 50 minutes.
4. Place tenderloin on warm platter; make gravy (page 65); or serve *au jus* (page 71) or serve with Bordelaise Sauce (page 167) or Creamy Horseradish Sauce (page 167) or Béarnaise Sauce (page 166). Accompany with Sautéed Mushrooms (page 333) and Pan-Fried Onions (page 336). Cut meat into 1-inch-thick slices. Whole tenderlion makes 8 to 12 servings; half tenderloin makes 4 to 6 servings.

BEEF WELLINGTON

Puff-Pastry dough (page 262)
Chicken Liver Pâté (below)
1 5- to 6-pound whole beef tenderloin*
1 egg
parsley sprigs for garnish

DAY BEFORE SERVING:

1. Prepare Puff-Pastry dough. Prepare Chicken Liver Pâté as directed below.

ABOUT 2 HOURS BEFORE SERVING:

2. Preheat oven to 425°F. Place tenderloin on rack in open roasting pan. Roast just 20 to 25 minutes for rare or 25 to 30 minutes for medium. Remove from oven and let stand 30 minutes. (Do not turn off oven.) Remove strings.
3. Meanwhile, in cup, with fork, beat egg with 2 teaspoons water; set aside. On lightly floured surface, with floured rolling pin, roll Puff-Pastry dough into 20″ by 13″ rectangle. With sharp knife, cut 2-inch piece of dough from 13-inch edge; reserve it for garnish.
4. Spread pâté over dough to within 1 inch

* Ask meatman to strip meat of all fat, then fold back thin end of fillet to make meat of even thickness; tie securely with strings.

of edges. Center the partially roasted tenderloin lengthwise on dough. Bring one long side of dough up over tenderloin; brush edge of dough with some of beaten egg. Bring other long side of dough up, overlapping egg-brushed dough; press lightly to seal.

5. Fold up both ends of dough; brush with beaten egg and press lightly to seal. Place dough-wrapped meat, seam side down, on large cookie sheet; brush top and sides generously with egg.

6. With canapé cutters or sharp knife, cut reserved dough into pieces to make a design; arrange on top and brush with egg. Roast 30 to 40 minutes, depending on rareness preferred. (Wellington is traditionally served rare.) Let stand 10 minutes. With 2 pancake turners, transfer roast to warm platter; garnish with parsley. Makes about 10 servings.

CHICKEN LIVER PATE: Prepare as on page 197 but omit the ½ cup softened butter or margarine after blending the chicken-liver mixture; chill.

Tender Beef Steaks

TIMETABLE FOR BROILING BEEF STEAKS

For general directions, see To Broil, page 63

Cut and Thickness (inches)	*Approximate Total Time (minutes)* *Rare*	*Medium*
Chuck, high quality		
1	24	30
1½	40	45
Rib, rib eye, club		
1	12	16
1½	18	25
2	25	30
Sirloin, Porterhouse		
1	18	25
1½	30	35
2	35	40
Filet Mignon		
1	10	15
1½	15	20

TOPPINGS FOR STEAK

Top each serving with a pat of butter or margarine. Or, offer one or more of these bottled sauces: Worcestershire, catchup, chili sauce, steak sauce. Serve sauce as is or blend with butter or margarine and spread on hot steak. Use 1 tablespoon preferred sauce with ¼ cup softened butter or margarine.

Also good on hot beef steak are these:

Butters for Broiled Beef Steaks (page 167)
Marchand de Vin Butter (page 168)
Béarnaise Sauce (page 166)
Bordelaise Sauce (page 167)
Mushroom Sauce (page 168)
Whipped Chive Butter (page 168)
Mustard Butter (page 168)
Creamy Horseradish Sauce (page 167)

PLANKED STEAK

This is a festive way to serve broiled beef steak (usually a T-bone) and vegetables. A special hardwood plank is needed; brush with salad oil.

Have at least two of the following hot cooked vegetables ready: Duchess Potatoes (page 341) or mashed potatoes; drained and buttered peas, carrots, Brussels sprouts, cauliflower, lima beans, green beans.

Broil steak; meanwhile, heat plank in oven. Place steak in center of plank and vegetables around it. If desired, spread steak with one of Toppings for Steak (above). Serve immediately.

If desired, steak may be broiled on one side until half done, then turned and broiled about 4 minutes less than recommended time on second side. Place on oiled plank, surround with vegetables and broil until steak is done and potatoes are golden.

PAN-BROILED BEEF STEAK

If cut less than 1 inch thick, beef steaks such as club, boneless rib, rib, top loin or rib eye, which would ordinarily be broiled, may be pan-broiled. Cube steaks may also be pan-broiled. To pan-broil, see page 64.

STEAK DIANE*

4 beef rib-eye steaks, each cut about ½ inch thick
salt
pepper
4 tablespoons butter or margarine
4 tablespoons brandy
2 small shallots, minced
8 teaspoons chopped chives
8 tablespoons dry sherry

ABOUT 20 MINUTES BEFORE SERVING:
On cutting board, with meat mallet, edge of plate or dull edge of French knife, pound steaks until about ¼ inch thick, turning occasionally. Sprinkle meat with salt and pepper.

In electric skillet (at the table) at high heat setting, in 1 tablespoon hot butter or margarine, cook one steak just until browned, turning once.

Pour 1 tablespoon brandy over steak and with match, set aflame. When flaming stops, stir in ¼ of shallots and 2 teaspoons chives; cook, stirring constantly, until shallot is tender, about 1 minute. Add 2 tablespoons sherry; heat. Place steak on a warm dinner plate and pour sherry mixture over steak; serve immediately. Repeat with remaining steaks. Makes 4 servings.

* Traditionally, steaks are prepared individually at the table.

BEEF STROGANOFF

1½ pounds beef tenderloin*
butter or margarine
1 large onion, minced
½ pound mushrooms, sliced
2 teaspoons dry mustard
1½ teaspoons salt
¼ teaspoon pepper
beef broth
1 tablespoon all-purpose flour
1 cup sour cream

ABOUT 45 MINUTES BEFORE SERVING:
1. On cutting board, trim fat from tenderloin; cut meat across the grain into ½-inch slices. Cut each slice into 2″ by ½″ strips. Dry strips well on paper towels.

* Meat will be easier to slice if it is partially frozen about 1½ hours ahead.

2. In 10-inch skillet over high heat, in 1 tablespoon hot butter or margarine (be careful not to let it burn), cook half of meat, stirring constantly, until lightly browned, about 1 minute (meat will be rare). Pour meat and drippings into medium bowl; set aside. In 1 tablespoon more hot butter or margarine, cook remaining meat; pour into bowl and set aside.
3. To skillet, add 2 tablespoons more butter or margarine, onion, mushrooms, mustard, salt and pepper. Cook over medium heat, stirring frequently, until vegetables are tender, about 5 minutes.
4. Into measuring cup, drain drippings from meat; add beef broth to make ½ cup. Stir flour into skillet mixture until blended. Gradually stir liquid into skillet mixture and cook, stirring constantly, until thickened.
5. Stir sour cream into mixture until smooth; add meat and heat, stirring. (Do not boil.) Makes 6 servings.

FAMILY BEEF STROGANOFF: *About 1 hour and 15 minutes before serving:* Prepare recipe only as in steps 1, 2 and 3 above but substitute *one 1½-pound top-round steak* for beef tenderloin; prepare meat with *unseasoned meat tenderizer* as label directs.

Add meat and drippings to skillet mixture and heat to boiling. Reduce heat to low; cover and simmer 35 to 45 minutes until meat is fork-tender, stirring occasionally and adding ¼ cup water or beef broth, if necessary.

In cup, blend *1 tablespoon all-purpose flour* and *2 tablespoons water* until smooth; stir into mixture in skillet and cook over medium heat, stirring constantly, until mixture is thickened. Stir in sour cream and heat. (Do not boil.) Serve over *hot rice.*

LONDON BROIL

1 1½-pound high-quality flank steak
seasoned salt
seasoned pepper
2 medium tomatoes
bottled Italian dressing
6 large mushrooms

ABOUT 30 MINUTES BEFORE SERVING:
Preheat broiler if manufacturer directs. With sharp knife, score both sides of steak;

place on rack in broiling pan. Sprinkle with 1 teaspoon seasoned salt, ⅛ teaspoon seasoned pepper.

Cut tomatoes in half; brush with Italian dressing and arrange, cut side up, around steak; broil 5 minutes. Meanwhile, slice mushrooms.

With tongs, turn steak; sprinkle with 1 teaspoon seasoned salt and ⅛ teaspoon seasoned pepper. Arrange mushroom slices in overlapping rows on rack; brush with Italian dressing. Broil about 5 more minutes for rare or 6 minutes for medium. (To check doneness, make a small cut in center of meat.) With knife in a slanting position, carve thin slices across width of steak. Serve slices with broiled vegetables. If you like, spoon drippings over slices. Makes 4 servings.

FONDUE BOURGUIGNONNE
(Beef Fondue)

1 2-pound beef tenderloin or boneless sirloin steak
3 or more Beef-Fondue Sauces (below)
1 32-ounce bottle salad oil (4 cups)
chopped parsley

EARLY IN DAY:
Trim fat from tenderloin and cut meat into 1-inch chunks; cover and refrigerate. Prepare sauces and place in serving bowls; cover and refrigerate.

ABOUT 15 MINUTES BEFORE SERVING:
In 2-quart saucepan over medium heat, heat salad oil to 375°F. on deep-fat thermometer; pour into 1½- or 2-quart metal fondue pot set over low heat (not a candle) on fondue stand. Or, heat in fondue pot as manufacturer directs. Meanwhile, on serving platter or board, arrange meat; sprinkle with parsley. Set out sauces and fondue or dinner plates.

Each diner helps himself to some of sauces; spears a meat chunk on a fondue or long-handled fork; cooks it in the hot oil until rare or of desired doneness, about 1 to 1½ minutes; places cooked meat on dinner plate and, with dinner fork, dips meat into a sauce and eats. Then each cooks more meat. Makes 6 to 8 servings.

BEEF-FONDUE SAUCES

SPICY STEAK SAUCE: In small bowl, with spoon, stir *⅓ cup mayonnaise, 3 tablespoons chili sauce, 2 teaspoons Worcestershire, 1 teaspoon bottled steak sauce* and *⅛ teaspoon hot pepper sauce;* cover and refrigerate. Makes ½ cup.

MUSTARD-SOUR-CREAM: In small bowl, with spoon, stir *½ cup sour cream, 2 tablespoons prepared mustard* and *⅛ teaspoon salt;* cover and refrigerate. Makes ½ cup.

HORSERADISH-SOUR-CREAM: In small bowl, with spoon, stir *½ cup sour cream, 2 teaspoons horseradish* and *¼ teaspoon salt;* garnish with *chopped chives;* cover and refrigerate. Makes ½ cup.

BEARNAISE SAUCE (page 166).

DILL SAUCE (page 246).

FATHER'S DAY FILETS MIGNONS

½ cup soy sauce
⅓ cup salad oil
1 garlic clove, minced
½ teaspoon ginger
6 beef tenderloin steaks, each cut about 1 inch thick
6 slices French bread, each cut diagonally about 1½ inches thick
butter or margarine
6 large Spiral Mushrooms (page 378)

EARLY IN DAY:
In shallow dish, for marinade, combine soy sauce, salad oil, garlic and ginger. Add steaks and turn over to coat with marinade; arrange steaks in one layer. Cover and refrigerate at least 4 hours, turning meat occasionally.

ABOUT 30 MINUTES BEFORE SERVING:
Preheat broiler if manufacturer directs. Place bread slices on cookie sheet; spread with butter or margarine. Broil bread 2 or 3 minutes until golden; place on warm platter; keep warm.

Place mushrooms and steaks on greased rack in broiling pan; broil about 10 minutes for rare or until meat is of desired doneness and mushrooms are tender, turning once. Serve steaks on bread, topped with mushrooms and pan drippings. Makes 6 servings.

CHATEAUBRIAND WITH BEARNAISE SAUCE

1 2-pound chateaubriand (center-cut beef tenderloin)
1 tablespoon butter or margarine, softened
1½ teaspoons salt
¼ teaspoon pepper
Béarnaise Sauce (page 166)

ABOUT 40 MINUTES BEFORE SERVING:
Preheat broiler if manufacturer directs. Spread chateaubriand on all sides with butter or margarine and sprinkle with salt and pepper. Place meat on rack in broiling pan; broil 30 minutes for rare or until of desired doneness, turning once.

Meanwhile, prepare sauce. Slice meat and serve with sauce. Makes 6 servings.

CONTINENTAL BEEF STEAK

1 4-pound high-quality, beef top-round steak, cut about 2 inches thick
unseasoned instant meat tenderizer
½ teaspoon oregano leaves
¼ teaspoon seasoned pepper
1 garlic clove, minced
3 large green peppers
3 tablespoons salad oil
1½ cups sliced celery
2 14½-ounce cans sliced baby tomatoes, drained
1 10-ounce jar colossal stuffed olives, drained and halved
2 tablespoons capers

ABOUT 1 HOUR BEFORE SERVING:
Preheat broiler if manufacturer directs. Lightly score both sides of steak. Use meat tenderizer as label directs; sprinkle both sides of steak with oregano, seasoned pepper and garlic. Place steak on greased rack in broiling pan; broil 25 minutes for rare or until of desired doneness, turning once.

Meanwhile, slice green peppers crosswise into rings; discard seeds. In large skillet over medium-high heat, in hot salad oil, cook peppers and celery 10 minutes or until tender-crisp. Add tomatoes, olives and capers; heat through.

Place steak on warm, large platter; with slotted spoon, spoon vegetables around it. Makes 10 to 12 servings.

MARINATED SIRLOIN STEAK

1 4-pound beef sirloin steak, cut about 1½ inches thick
½ cup red Burgundy, claret or other red table wine
1 tablespoon seasoned salt
¼ teaspoon seasoned pepper

EARLY IN DAY OR DAY AHEAD:
In large, shallow baking dish, place steak; for marinade, pour wine over steak. Cover and refrigerate at least 4 hours, turning meat occasionally.

ABOUT 40 MINUTES BEFORE SERVING:
Preheat broiler if manufacturer directs. With tongs, place steak on greased rack in broiling pan; reserve marinade. Sprinkle steak with seasoned salt and pepper.

Broil steak 30 minutes for rare or until of desired doneness, basting occasionally with marinade and turning once. Makes 8 to 10 servings.

BROILED HERBED CHUCK STEAK

1 0.7-ounce envelope garlic salad-dressing mix
¼ cup lemon juice
unseasoned instant meat tenderizer
1 3½- to 4-pound beef blade chuck steak, cut about 1½ inches thick
2 large tomatoes
1 medium eggplant

ABOUT 45 MINUTES BEFORE SERVING:
1. Preheat broiler if manufacturer directs. Prepare salad-dressing mix as label directs but use lemon juice instead of vinegar. Use meat tenderizer on steak as label directs.
2. Place steak on greased rack in broiling pan; brush generously with some of salad-dressing mixture. Broil steak 35 to 40 minutes until rare or of desired doneness, brushing frequently with dressing mixture and turning once.
3. Meanwhile, cut tomatoes into thick wedges; cut eggplant into thick slices and then cut each slice in half. During last 15 minutes of broiling steak, arrange eggplant and tomatoes around steak, overlapping vegetables if needed to fit on rack. Continue broiling until vegetables are tender, brushing occasionally with dressing mixture.

4. To serve, place steak on large, warm platter; arrange eggplant and tomatoes around steak. Makes about 10 servings.

STEAK AND TOMATOES ORIENTALE

1 2-pound boneless beef sirloin steak,*
cut about 1½ inches thick
2 tablespoons cornstarch
1 tablespoon soy sauce
1 tablespoon bottled sauce for gravy
1 teaspoon sugar
1 teaspoon salt
1 beef-bouillon envelope or
1 tablespoon beef-stock base
⅓ cup salad oil
1 medium onion, chopped
1 garlic clove, crushed
4 medium tomatoes, peeled and
cut into thin wedges

ABOUT 30 MINUTES BEFORE SERVING:
Trim any excess fat from steak. Slice steak lengthwise into thirds; then slice diagonally into short, very thin strips (about ⅛ inch wide). In large bowl, combine meat with next 6 ingredients; mix well; set aside.

In 12-inch skillet over high heat, in very hot salad oil, cook onion and garlic, stirring quickly and frequently (stir-frying) until almost tender, about 2 minutes.

Add meat mixture and stir-fry until meat is browned, about 5 minutes. Add tomatoes; stir-fry until tomatoes are heated through, about 2 minutes more. Makes 8 servings.

*Steak will be easier to slice if it is partially frozen about 1½ hours ahead.

CHUCK STEAK POLYNESIAN

1 0.8- or 1⅛-ounce package
meat-marinade mix
medium sherry
2 tablespoons soy sauce
2 tablespoons molasses
1 garlic clove, minced
½ teaspoon ginger
½ teaspoon dry mustard
1 2-pound beef blade chuck steak,
cut about 1 inch thick

ABOUT 1 HOUR BEFORE SERVING:
1. In shallow baking pan, prepare marinade mix as label directs but substitute ⅓ cup sherry for ⅓ cup water if using 0.8-ounce package (or 3 tablespoons sherry if using 1⅛-ounce package). Add remaining ingredients except steak; mix well. Add steak and turn over to coat both sides.
2. With two-tined fork, pierce all steak surfaces thoroughly and deeply. Let steak stand in marinade 15 minutes, turning frequently.
3. Meanwhile, preheat broiler if manufacturer directs. With tongs, place steak on greased rack of broiling pan, reserving marinade. Broil steak about 20 to 25 minutes for rare or until of desired doneness, basting occasionally with marinade and turning once.
4. With knife in slanting position, carve thin slices across the width of the steak. Makes 6 servings.

TERIYAKI BEEF KABOBS

1 2-pound high-quality, beef top-round
steak, cut about 1 inch thick
¼ cup packed light brown sugar
¼ cup soy sauce
2 tablespoons lemon juice
1 tablespoon salad oil
¼ teaspoon ginger
1 garlic clove, minced
1 small pineapple, cut
into 1-inch chunks

ABOUT 4 HOURS AHEAD OR EARLY IN DAY:
Trim any excess fat from steak and cut meat into 1-inch chunks. In medium bowl, for marinade, combine brown sugar, soy sauce, lemon juice, salad oil, ginger and garlic; stir in beef chunks. Cover and refrigerate at least 3 hours, stirring meat often.

ABOUT 30 MINUTES BEFORE SERVING:
Preheat broiler if manufacturer directs. Thread meat and pineapple chunks alternately on 12-inch metal skewers;* broil about 15 minutes until rare or of desired doneness, basting occasionally with marinade and turning once. (To check doneness, make a small slit in center of meat.) Makes 6 servings.

* Because pineapple quickly tenderizes meat, thread skewers just before broiling. If done earlier, meat becomes mushy.

CUBE STEAKS WITH SKILLET-BARBECUE SAUCE

4 beef cube steaks (about 1 pound)
2 tablespoons all-purpose flour
3 tablespoons butter, margarine or salad oil
½ teaspoon salt
⅓ cup chili sauce or catchup
1 tablespoon lemon juice
1 teaspoon dry mustard
1 teaspoon Worcestershire
⅛ teaspoon coarsely ground pepper

ABOUT 20 MINUTES BEFORE SERVING:
On waxed paper, coat cube steaks with flour. In 12-inch skillet over medium-high heat, in hot butter or margarine, cook steaks until browned on both sides; place on warm platter; sprinkle with salt and keep warm.

For barbecue sauce, to drippings left in skillet, add chili sauce and remaining ingredients; heat, stirring to loosen browned bits. Spoon barbecue sauce over steaks. Makes 4 servings.

CUBE STEAKS WITH FRESH TOMATO SAUCE

¼ cup salad oil
2 pounds beef or veal cube steaks
6 medium tomatoes, peeled
¼ cup chopped green onions
2 tablespoons sugar
2 teaspoons salt
2 teaspoons basil
2 tablespoons cornstarch

ABOUT 45 MINUTES BEFORE SERVING:
In 10- or 12-inch skillet over medium-high heat, in hot salad oil, cook steaks, a few at a time, 2 or 3 minutes on each side or until of desired doneness; place on warm platter and keep warm. Chop 3 tomatoes and slice 3.

Reduce heat to medium; to same skillet, add ¼ cup water, chopped tomatoes, green onions, sugar, salt and basil. In cup, blend cornstarch and ¼ cup cold water until smooth; gradually stir into tomato mixture and cook, stirring, until thickened.

Add sliced tomatoes; cook until heated through. Spoon tomato mixture over steaks. Makes 6 to 8 servings.

FLANK-STEAK PINWHEELS

1 1½-pound high-quality beef flank steak (or 6 flank steak fillets)
6 small wooden skewers
1 cup bottled mustard-flavored barbecue sauce

ABOUT 30 MINUTES BEFORE SERVING:
Preheat broiler if manufacturer directs. With sharp knife, score diamond pattern into both sides of steak. Starting with long side, roll steak jelly-roll fashion; fasten with skewers, placing them about 1½ inches apart. Cut between skewers. (Or, use fillets.)

Place pinwheels, cut side up, on rack in broiling pan; brush generously with some barbecue sauce; broil 20 minutes, brushing occasionally with sauce and turning once. Makes 6 servings.

Beef Pot Roasts

SAUERBRATEN

1½ cups red wine vinegar
½ cup red table or dessert wine
4 medium onions, sliced
2 tablespoons sugar
4 bay leaves
whole cloves
salt
mustard seed
peppercorns
1 4-pound beef bottom-round pot roast
3 tablespoons all-purpose flour
2 tablespoons salad oil
½ cup fine gingersnap crumbs
½ cup sour cream (optional)

2 TO 4 DAYS BEFORE SERVING:
1. For marinade, in large bowl, combine vinegar with 1 cup water, wine, 3 of the sliced onions, sugar, bay leaves, 2 teaspoons cloves, 2 teaspoons salt, 1 teaspoon mustard seed and ½ teaspoon peppercorns.
2. Add pot roast, turning to coat with marinade. Cover and refrigerate two to four days, turning meat each day.

ABOUT 5 HOURS BEFORE SERVING:
3. Remove meat; dry well with paper towels. Reserve marinade. On waxed paper, coat meat with flour.

4. In Dutch oven over medium-high heat, in hot salad oil, cook meat until well browned on all sides, about 15 to 20 minutes. Remove meat from Dutch oven and pour off all but 1 tablespoon drippings.
5. To drippings in Dutch oven, add remaining onion and cook over medium heat, stirring frequently, until tender-crisp, about 3 minutes. Add ¾ cup reserved marinade, 1½ teaspoons salt, 1 teaspoon cloves, ½ teaspoon mustard seed and 1 teaspoon peppercorns; heat to boiling. Reduce heat to low; cover and simmer 4 hours or until meat is fork-tender, turning occasionally.
6. Place meat on warm platter; slice if desired; keep warm. Into small bowl, strain liquid from Dutch oven; let stand until fat separates. Spoon off fat, then return liquid to Dutch oven (there should be about 2 cups). Strain reserved marinade; measure 1 cup. Add marinade and gingersnap crumbs to liquid in Dutch oven.
7. Over medium-high heat, heat mixture to boiling; cook, stirring constantly, until mixture is thickened. With wire whisk, stir in sour cream; heat (do not boil). If necessary, season to taste with salt and pepper. Spoon some gravy over meat; serve rest separately. Makes 10 to 12 servings.

BEEF-IN-THE-BAG

1 18″ by 12″ or 24″ by 18″ oven-cooking bag
1 tablespoon all-purpose flour
1 3½- to 4-pound beef heel-of-round
1 8-ounce can tomato sauce
1 cup sliced celery
1 teaspoon sugar
1 teaspoon salt
¼ teaspoon pepper
hot cooked noodles, spaghetti twists or macaroni (optional)

ABOUT 3½ HOURS BEFORE SERVING:
Preheat oven to 350° F. In oven-cooking bag, place flour; close bag and shake. Place bag in open roasting pan at least 2 inches deep. Trim any excess fat from heel-of-round.

Place heel-of-round in bag; add remaining ingredients except noodles. Close bag and puncture top as label directs. (Be sure that no part of bag extends over pan edges or may touch sides or top of oven when bag inflates during cooking.) Bake meat 2½ to 3 hours until meat is fork-tender. (To test for doneness, pierce meat through bag with 2-tined fork.) Remove pan from oven and let stand at room temperature for several minutes.

To serve, slit bag carefully with kitchen shears to allow steam to escape. Then place meat on warm platter; pour drippings into gravy boat; let stand until fat separates. Spoon off fat and discard; serve liquid as sauce over meat and noodles. Makes 10 to 12 servings.

BEEF-IN-WRAP: Substitute roasting wrap for oven-cooking bag. Tear off piece long enough to enclose meat with at least 3 inches extra for overlap. Sprinkle flour on wrap; place heel-of-round in center of floured wrap and top with remaining ingredients except noodles; wrap as label directs. Place in open roasting pan and puncture wrap as directed. Bake as above; remove from oven and let stand at room temperature, wrapped, for several minutes before serving.

BAKED POT ROAST WITH VEGETABLES

1 3-pound rolled beef rump roast
1 large onion, sliced
1 garlic clove, crushed
2 tablespoons Worcestershire
4 teaspoons salt
1 teaspoon sugar
¼ teaspoon pepper
4 medium parsnips, cut in chunks
1 24-ounce bag frozen lima beans, thawed

ABOUT 4 HOURS BEFORE SERVING:
Preheat oven to 350°F. In Dutch oven, place all ingredients except parsnips and lima beans; add 2 cups water. Cover and bake 2 hours. Add parsnips and lima beans and continue baking 1 to 1½ hours more until vegetables and meat are tender, turning meat occasionally.

Remove meat to warm platter. Remove strings. With large spoon, skim fat from liquid in Dutch oven. Serve liquid over meat and vegetables. Makes 8 servings.

HEARTY POT ROAST WITH ONIONS AND SQUASH

3 tablespoons salad oil
1 4-pound rolled beef rump roast
2½ teaspoons salt
1 teaspoon thyme leaves
¼ teaspoon pepper
1 pound small white onions
4 medium yellow squash, cut in chunks
3 tablespoons all-purpose flour

ABOUT 4½ HOURS BEFORE SERVING:
In Dutch oven over medium-high heat, in hot salad oil, cook rump roast until well browned on all sides. Add 2½ cups water, salt, thyme and pepper; heat to boiling. Reduce heat to low; cover and simmer 3½ hours or until meat is almost fork-tender. (Or, preheat oven to 350°F. and bake pot roast 3½ hours.)

Add onions and squash; cover and cook 30 minutes more or until meat and vegetables are tender, turning meat often.

Place meat on warm platter. With slotted spoon, arrange vegetables around meat. In cup, blend flour and ½ cup water until smooth; gradually stir into hot liquid from pot roast and cook over medium heat, stirring, until thickened. Serve gravy over meat. Makes 10 to 12 servings.

OTHER VEGETABLES: Instead of onions and squash, add 8 small carrots and 8 small potatoes. Or, instead of squash, add 1 pound green beans.

SIRLOIN-TIP POT ROAST WITH VEGETABLES

¼ cup shortening
1 5- to 6-pound beef sirloin-tip roast
1½ tablespoons salt
½ teaspoon pickling spice
⅛ teaspoon pepper
1 bay leaf
½ pound small white onions (about 15)
15 medium carrots, cut in chunks
3 9-ounce packages frozen whole green beans, partially thawed
¼ cup all-purpose flour

ABOUT 5 HOURS BEFORE SERVING:
In 8-quart Dutch oven over medium-high heat, in hot shortening, cook sirloin-tip roast until well browned on all sides. Add 3 cups water, salt, pickling spice, pepper and bay leaf; heat to boiling. Reduce heat to low; cover and simmer 4 hours or until meat is almost fork-tender, turning meat occasionally and adding more water, if necessary.

Add onions and carrot chunks and cook 30 minutes longer; add green beans and cook 10 minutes more or until meat and vegetables are fork-tender. Place meat on warm platter. With slotted spoon, arrange vegetables around meat.

Add water, if necessary, to make 2 cups pan liquid. In cup, blend flour and ½ cup water until smooth; gradually stir into hot liquid from pot roast and cook over medium heat, stirring constantly, until mixture is thickened. Remove bay leaf. Serve gravy with meat. Makes 14 to 16 servings.

FOR THREE-POUND SIRLOIN TIP: Prepare recipe as above but use a 5-quart Dutch oven and *1 tablespoon salt, 2 cups water, ½ teaspoon pickling spice, 8 onions, 8 carrots* and *two 9-ounce packages frozen whole green beans.* Simmer meat 2½ hours, then add vegetables. Makes 8 to 10 servings.

FRUITED POT ROAST

2 tablespoons shortening
1 4-pound boneless beef chuck roll
2 medium onions, sliced
1 cup apple cider
2 tablespoons brown sugar
2 teaspoons salt
1 teaspoon seasoned pepper
¼ teaspoon ground cloves
1½ cups dried apricots
1½ cups pitted prunes
2 tablespoons all-purpose flour (optional)

ABOUT 4 HOURS BEFORE SERVING:
In Dutch oven over medium-high heat, in hot shortening, cook chuck roll until well browned on all sides. Add onions, apple cider, brown sugar, salt, seasoned pepper and cloves; heat to boiling. Reduce heat to low; cover and simmer 3½ hours or until meat is almost fork-tender, turning meat occasionally and adding more cider if necessary.

Add apricots and prunes to mixture. Continue cooking 20 minutes or until meat is fork-tender. Place meat on warm platter.

Spoon fat from liquid in Dutch oven. If you like, blend flour and 1/4 cup water until smooth; gradually stir into pan liquid and cook over medium heat, stirring constantly, until mixture is thickened. Serve sauce with meat. Makes 12 to 14 servings.

BARBECUED POT ROAST

2 tablespoons salad oil
1 3½- to 4-pound beef chuck pot roast, cut about 1½ inches thick
1 18-ounce bottle onion-flavored barbecue sauce
1 tablespoon salt
¼ teaspoon pepper
2 16-ounce cans cut green beans
2 16-ounce cans whole white potatoes

ABOUT 3½ HOURS BEFORE SERVING:
Preheat oven to 350°F. In Dutch oven or 12-inch skillet with ovenproof handle, over medium-high heat, in hot salad oil, cook pot roast until well browned on both sides. Add barbecue sauce, salt and pepper; cover and bake 2 hours.

Spoon any fat from liquid; drain beans and potatoes and add. Cover and bake ½ hour longer or until meat is fork-tender and vegetables are heated through. Makes 6 to 8 servings.

POT ROAST WITH DUMPLINGS

¼ cup butter or margarine
½ cup chopped onion
1 4-pound beef arm chuck pot roast, cut about 2 inches thick
1 10½-ounce can condensed consommé
1 bay leaf, crumbled
2 tablespoons grated orange peel
1 teaspoon salt
¼ teaspoon allspice
dash pepper
2 cups buttermilk baking mix
⅔ cup milk

ABOUT 4 HOURS BEFORE SERVING:
In Dutch oven over high heat, in hot butter or margarine, cook onion until golden, about 5 minutes. Add pot roast and cook until well browned on all sides. Add undiluted consommé and next 5 ingredients; heat to boiling. Reduce heat to low; cover and simmer 3½ hours or until meat is fork-tender, turning meat occasionally.

Add 1½ cups hot water to meat and heat to boiling. Meanwhile, in medium bowl, with fork, stir baking mix with milk until blended; drop by large tablespoonfuls around meat in Dutch oven; cook, uncovered, over low heat 10 minutes; cover and cook 10 minutes longer. Makes 8 to 10 servings.

SWEDISH-STYLE POT ROAST

3 tablespoons salad oil
1 4-pound beef bottom round pot roast
2 medium onions, sliced
3 anchovy fillets
2 bay leaves
2 tablespoons cider vinegar
2 tablespoons dark corn syrup
2 teaspoons salt
1 teaspoon allspice
½ teaspoon pepper
2 tablespoons all-purpose flour
1 cup heavy or whipping cream

ABOUT 4 HOURS BEFORE SERVING:
In Dutch oven over medium-high heat, in hot salad oil, cook pot roast until well browned on all sides. Add next 8 ingredients and ½ cup water; heat to boiling. Reduce heat to low; cover and cook 3 hours or until meat is fork-tender, turning meat occasionally and adding more water, if necessary.

Place meat on warm platter; keep warm. With large spoon, skim fat from liquid in pan; remove bay leaves. Over medium heat, heat liquid to boiling. In cup, mix flour with ¼ cup cold water until smooth; gradually stir into liquid and cook, stirring constantly, until mixture is thickened; stir in cream and heat just to boiling.

Serve gravy with meat. Makes 12 to 14 servings.

LEFTOVER POT ROAST: Slice leftover pot roast and reheat in leftover gravy or in *one 10¾-ounce can beef gravy.*

BOSTON-CUT BEEF AND BREW

2 tablespoons salad oil
1 4- to 5-pound Boston-cut beef pot roast
2 large onions, diced
1 cup beer
1 tablespoon salt
2 teaspoons dry mustard
¼ teaspoon pepper
¼ cup all-purpose flour

ABOUT 4½ HOURS BEFORE SERVING:
In Dutch oven over medium-high heat, in hot salad oil, cook pot roast until well browned on all sides; remove meat from Dutch oven. Pour off all but 1 tablespoon drippings.

In drippings remaining in Dutch oven, cook onions, stirring occasionally, 5 minutes or until tender-crisp. Return meat to Dutch oven; add remaining ingredients except flour; heat to boiling. Reduce heat to low; cover and simmer 3½ to 4 hours until meat is tender, turning meat occasionally and adding more beer if necessary.

Place meat on warm platter. If necessary, spoon fat from pan liquid. In cup, blend flour and ½ cup water until smooth; gradually stir into hot liquid in Dutch oven and cook over medium heat, stirring constantly, until mixture is thickened. Serve gravy with meat. Makes 10 to 14 servings.

POT ROAST LOUISIANE

1 2½-pound boneless beef shoulder pot roast, about 1½ inches thick
2 tablespoons all-purpose flour
2 tablespoons salad oil
1 medium onion, chopped
¼ cup diced green pepper
1 stalk celery, thinly sliced
1 garlic clove, minced
1 6-ounce can tomato paste
¼ cup dry red wine
1½ teaspoons salt
2 teaspoons meat extract paste
½ teaspoon thyme leaves
¼ teaspoon hot pepper sauce
1 bay leaf
hot cooked rice for 8 servings

ABOUT 2¾ HOURS BEFORE SERVING:
1. On cutting board, trim any excess fat from pot roast. Coat meat with flour; with meat mallet, edge of plate or dull edge of French knife, pound meat well on both sides.
2. In 12-inch skillet over medium-high heat, in hot salad oil, cook meat until well browned on both sides. With tongs, remove meat. To drippings, add onion, green pepper, celery and garlic and cook until onion is lightly browned, about 2 minutes.
3. Add meat, ½ cup water, tomato paste and remaining ingredients except rice; heat to boiling. Reduce heat to low; cover and simmer about 2 hours and 15 minutes or until meat is fork-tender.
4. Place meat on warm platter. Serve pan liquid over meat and rice. Makes 8 servings.

SPANISH-STYLE POT ROAST

2 chorizos* (¼ to ½ pound)
1 4-pound rolled beef rump roast
2 tablespoons all-purpose flour
2 tablespoons olive or salad oil
1 cup chopped onions
1 garlic clove, minced
1 6-ounce can tomato paste
¼ cup red table wine
1 bay leaf
1 large green pepper, cut into chunks
1 teaspoon salt
¼ teaspoon pepper
hot cooked rice (optional)

ABOUT 4 HOURS BEFORE SERVING:
1. Cut each chorizo into 6 lengthwise strips. With long, sharp knife, into each end of rump roast, make 6 cuts, each about 5 inches deep, twisting knife to enlarge opening. Fill each opening with a sausage strip.
2. On waxed paper, coat meat with flour. In Dutch oven over medium-high heat, in hot olive oil, cook meat until browned on all sides. Remove meat from pan; pour off all but 1 tablespoon drippings.
3. In drippings in Dutch oven over medium heat, cook onions and garlic until onions are tender, about 5 minutes, stirring occasionally. Stir in remaining ingredients except rice; return meat to Dutch oven and heat to boiling. Reduce heat to low; cover

* Spanish sausage. Or, use ½ pound hard salami or cervelat, cut into 12 strips.

and simmer 3 to 3½ hours until meat is fork-tender, turning meat occasionally.
4. With large spoon, skim any fat from liquid; discard bay leaf. Slice meat and arrange on warm platter; pour a little sauce over it; serve remaining sauce in gravy boat, to be spooned over rice, if you like. Makes 10 to 12 servings.

Braised Beef Steaks

CELERY-STUFFED FLANK STEAK

1 2-pound flank steak
pepper
1 cup fresh bread crumbs
¾ cup diced celery
2 tablespoons instant minced onion
butter or margarine
½ teaspoon salt
⅛ teaspoon thyme leaves, crushed
all-purpose flour
1 tablespoon cornstarch
¼ teaspoon ginger

ABOUT 2½ HOURS BEFORE SERVING:
1. With sharp knife, score steak in diamond pattern on both sides; sprinkle with pepper.
2. In medium bowl, combine bread crumbs, celery, instant minced onion, 1 tablespoon melted butter or margarine, salt, thyme, ⅛ teaspoon pepper and 2 tablespoons water; spread evenly on one side of steak, leaving a 1-inch border. Roll steak from a long side, jelly-roll fashion; secure with toothpicks or string. On waxed paper, coat meat lightly with flour.
3. In large Dutch oven over medium-high heat, in 2 tablespoons hot butter or margarine, cook meat until well browned on all sides. Add 1 cup water; heat to boiling. Reduce heat to low; cover and simmer 2 hours or until meat is fork-tender, stirring liquid and adding water, if necessary. Place meat on warm platter; remove toothpicks; keep warm.
4. In cup, blend cornstarch and ginger with 2 tablespoons cold water until smooth; stir into hot liquid in Dutch oven and cook over medium heat, stirring constantly, until mixture is thickened. Stir in more water, if necessary. Serve gravy with steak. Makes 6 servings.

BROWNED SWISS STEAK

¼ cup bottled mild garlic-French dressing
1 2-pound beef round steak, cut about ¾ inch thick
1 10½-ounce can condensed onion soup
3 cups hot cooked noodles
2 tablespoons all-purpose flour

ABOUT 2½ HOURS BEFORE SERVING:
In Dutch oven or 10-inch skillet over medium-high heat, in hot French dressing, brown round steak well on both sides. Add undiluted onion soup and ¼ cup water. Reduce heat to low; cover and simmer 2 hours or until fork-tender, turning meat occasionally and adding more water if needed. Place steak on warm platter and surround with noodles; keep warm.

In small bowl, blend flour and ¼ cup water until smooth; gradually stir into hot liquid in Dutch oven and cook over medium heat, stirring constantly, until mixture is thickened. Serve gravy with meat and noodles. Makes 6 servings.

STUFFED CUBE STEAKS

⅓ cup butter or margarine
½ 8-ounce package herb-seasoned stuffing (2 cups)
4 beef cube steaks (about 1 pound)
2 tablespoons salad oil
1 1-ounce envelope Burgundy-wine sauce mix (or 1 1½-ounce envelope mushroom-gravy mix)

ABOUT 50 MINUTES BEFORE SERVING:
In 2-quart saucepan over high heat, heat to boiling ⅔ cup water and butter or margarine; stir in stuffing mix until well mixed. With spoon, spread about ½ cup of mixture evenly on each cube steak, leaving a ½-inch edge on all sides. Starting at a short side, roll up steaks, jelly-roll fashion; secure with toothpicks.

In 10-inch skillet over medium-high heat, in hot salad oil, cook cube steaks until browned on all sides. Stir in 1 cup water and Burgundy-wine sauce mix until sauce is blended. Reduce heat to low; cover and simmer 30 minutes or until steaks are fork-tender, stirring and turning meat occasionally. Remove toothpicks. Makes 4 servings.

CARBONNADE OF BEEF

1 2- to 2½-pound beef round steak, ½ inch thick, cut into 8 pieces
all-purpose flour
½ cup butter or margarine
8 large onions, sliced
1 12-ounce can beer (1½ cups)
2 garlic cloves, minced
1 beef-bouillon cube or envelope
2 teaspoons salt
1 teaspoon thyme leaves
¼ teaspoon pepper

ABOUT 2½ HOURS BEFORE SERVING:
On cutting board, sprinkle one side of a piece of round steak with flour; using meat mallet or edge of saucer, pound flour into meat. Repeat on other side. Pound all meat.

In 12-inch skillet over medium heat, in ¼ cup hot butter or margarine, cook onions until tender, about 5 minutes. With slotted spoon, place onions on paper towels.

In same skillet, heat remaining ¼ cup butter or margarine and cook meat, a few pieces at a time, until well browned on both sides, placing browned pieces with onions. Return onions and browned meat to skillet; add remaining ingredients; heat to boiling. Reduce heat to low; cover and simmer 1 to 1½ hours until meat is fork-tender. Makes 8 servings.

BEEF ROULADEN

1 2- to 2½-pound beef round steak,* cut about ¼ inch thick and cut into 6 pieces
6 teaspoons prepared mustard
6 bacon slices, diced
3 small dill pickles, minced
1 medium onion, minced
2 tablespoons shortening
1 8-ounce can tomato sauce
1½ teaspoons salt
1 teaspoon sugar
¼ teaspoon pepper
1 8-ounce package egg noodles
3 tablespoons all-purpose flour

ABOUT 1½ HOURS BEFORE SERVING:
1. Spread each piece of round steak with a teaspoon of mustard; in small bowl, mix raw bacon, pickles and onion and spoon along one end of each piece; roll up, jelly-roll fashion and tie securely with strings or fasten with toothpicks.
2. In 12-inch skillet over medium heat, in hot shortening, cook meat until well browned on all sides. Add tomato sauce, salt, sugar and pepper. Reduce heat to low; cover and simmer 1½ hours or until meat is fork-tender, turning once and adding water if necessary.
3. Cook noodles as label directs; drain and place in warm, deep platter.
4. Remove strings or toothpicks from meat and place on noodles. In cup, blend flour and ¼ cup water until smooth; gradually stir into pan juices and cook over medium heat, stirring constantly, until thickened; pour over meat. Makes 6 servings.

* Ask meatman to cut meat.

SUNNY CITRUS STEAK

¼ cup shortening
1 3-pound beef chuck steak, cut about 1½ inches thick
2 large onions, sliced
4 teaspoons salt
2 teaspoons light brown sugar
1 teaspoon pepper
1 cup grapefruit juice
1 large grapefruit
1 large orange
3 tablespoons all-purpose flour

ABOUT 3 HOURS BEFORE SERVING:
Preheat oven to 350°F. In 12-inch skillet over medium heat, in hot shortening, cook chuck steak until well browned on both sides. Add onions, salt, sugar, pepper and grapefruit juice; heat to boiling. Reduce heat to low; cover and simmer 2½ hours or until meat is fork-tender, turning meat once.

Meanwhile, peel and section grapefruit and orange; add sections to meat during last 5 minutes cooking time to heat through.

Place meat and fruit on warm platter. If you like, in cup, blend flour and ½ cup water until smooth; gradually stir into hot liquid and cook over medium heat, stirring constantly, until mixture is thickened; serve with meat. Makes about 8 servings.

CHILI-CHEESE STEAKS

3 tablespoons all-purpose flour
2 teaspoons salt
2 teaspoons chili powder
¼ teaspoon pepper
1 2-pound beef round steak, cut about 1 inch thick, cut into 6 pieces
¼ cup shortening
2 cups chopped onions
1 16-ounce can tomatoes
1 4-ounce package shredded sharp Cheddar cheese (1 cup)

ABOUT 2 HOURS BEFORE SERVING:
Preheat oven to 350°F. In cup, combine flour, salt, chili powder and pepper. Trim any excess fat from round steak; place meat on board and sprinkle with some flour mixture. With meat mallet or edge of saucer, pound mixture into meat. Turn and repeat on other side.

In 10-inch skillet over medium-high heat, in hot shortening, cook meat until well browned on both sides; remove meat to board. In drippings, cook onions until browned; stir in remaining flour mixture.

Into large, shallow casserole, spoon onion mixture. Arrange steaks on top, then add tomatoes and their liquid. Cover and bake 1½ hours or until meat is fork-tender. Spoon any fat from casserole. Sprinkle steaks with cheese. Heat 5 minutes or until cheese is melted. Makes 6 servings.

CHINESE PEPPER STEAK

1 2-pound beef round steak, cut about ½ inch thick*
¼ cup soy sauce
1 beef-bouillon cube or envelope
½ teaspoon ginger
½ teaspoon garlic powder
2 tablespoons shortening
3 large green peppers, cut in thin strips
3 tablespoons cornstarch
4 cups hot cooked rice

EARLY IN DAY OR DAY AHEAD:
Trim any fat from round steak and cut meat crosswise into strips about ¼ inch thick. In medium bowl, for marinade, combine soy sauce, bouillon cube, ginger, garlic powder and 1 cup boiling water; stir in meat strips. Cover and refrigerate, stirring occasionally.

ABOUT 1½ HOURS BEFORE SERVING:
Drain meat, reserving ½ cup marinade. In 10-inch skillet over high heat, in hot shortening, cook meat until it loses its red color. Add reserved marinade and 1 cup water; heat to boiling. Reduce heat to low; cover and simmer 1 hour, stirring often.

Add green pepper and cook 15 minutes or until meat is fork-tender.

In cup, blend cornstarch and ⅓ cup cold water until smooth; gradually stir into hot pan liquid and cook, stirring constantly, until mixture thickens slightly. Serve over rice. Makes 6 servings.

* Meat will be easier to slice if it is partially frozen about 1½ hours ahead.

SPICED CHUCK STEAK

⅓ cup cider vinegar
6 whole cloves
4 whole allspice
1½ teaspoons salt
1 teaspoon sugar
1 3½-pound chuck steak, cut about 2 inches thick
¼ cup shortening
1 medium onion, sliced
1 tablespoon all-purpose flour
½ cup milk

EARLY IN DAY OR DAY AHEAD:
For marinade, in small saucepan over high heat, heat ⅔ cup water and first 5 ingredients to boiling. In shallow baking dish, place chuck steak and pour mixture over meat. Cover and refrigerate at least 4 hours.

ABOUT 3½ HOURS BEFORE SERVING:
Drain marinade from meat and reserve. In Dutch oven over medium-high heat, in hot shortening, cook meat until well browned on both sides; during last of browning, add onions to brown also. Pour marinade over meat. Reduce heat to low; cover and simmer 3 hours or until fork-tender, turning meat occasionally and adding water if necessary. Place meat on warm platter.

With spoon, skim fat from pan liquid. In cup, blend flour and milk until smooth; gradually stir into hot liquid and cook over medium heat, stirring, until smooth. Serve gravy with meat. Makes 8 to 10 servings.

SAVORY CHUCK STEAK

1 3½-pound beef blade chuck steak, cut about 1½ inches thick*
3 tablespoons all-purpose flour
3 tablespoons salad oil
1 1⅜-ounce envelope onion-soup mix
½ cup chili sauce
½ teaspoon salt
⅛ teaspoon pepper

ABOUT 1½ HOURS BEFORE SERVING:
With sharp knife, cut fat and bones from chuck steak; cut meat into ¼-inch slices. On waxed paper, coat meat with flour.

In 10-inch skillet over medium-high heat, in hot salad oil, cook meat slices, a few at a time, until well browned, removing pieces as they brown. Stir in 1 cup water, onion-soup mix, chili sauce, salt and pepper; heat to boiling, stirring; add meat. Reduce heat to low; cover and simmer 45 minutes or until meat is fork-tender, stirring occasionally and adding more water, if necessary. Makes 6 servings.

* Meat will be easier to slice if it is partially frozen about 1½ hours ahead.

SWEET-SOUR BEEF WITH VEGETABLES

salad oil
sugar
cornstarch
soy sauce
2 teaspoons red table wine
1 pound beef round steak, cut into 1-inch chunks
2 large green peppers, cut in strips
2 stalks celery, sliced diagonally
⅓ cup chopped onion
3 tablespoons catchup
1½ teaspoons Worcestershire
4 medium tomatoes, cut in chunks
3 cups hot cooked rice

EARLY IN DAY:
In shallow baking dish, for marinade, combine ¼ cup salad oil, 4 teaspoons sugar, 2 teaspoons cornstarch, 4 teaspoons soy sauce and wine. Add round steak chunks and turn over to coat with marinade. Cover and refrigerate, turning meat occasionally.

ABOUT 40 MINUTES BEFORE SERVING:
In covered 8-inch skillet over medium-high heat, heat meat and marinade to boiling. Reduce heat to low; simmer 30 minutes or until meat is fork-tender, stirring occasionally. With slotted spoon, remove meat; set aside, leaving liquid in skillet. To skillet, add 1 tablespoon salad oil, green peppers, celery and onion; cover and cook over medium heat until tender-crisp.

Meanwhile, in small bowl, with fork, combine 2 tablespoons sugar, 1 tablespoon cornstarch, 1 tablespoon soy sauce, catchup and Worcestershire; gradually stir into vegetables and cook, stirring constantly, until mixture is slightly thickened.

Add tomatoes and meat and cook, stirring occasionally, until heated through. Serve with rice. Makes 4 servings.

ONIONY BRAISED ROUND STEAKS

3 bacon slices, chopped
2 1-pound beef round steaks, each cut about ½ inch thick
1 10½-ounce can condensed onion soup
¼ teaspoon pepper
1 medium green pepper, cut into 6 rings
6 lemon or orange slices
2 tablespoons all-purpose flour

ABOUT 1½ HOURS BEFORE SERVING:
1. In 10-inch skillet over medium-high heat, cook bacon until light brown; push aside.
2. Meanwhile, with sharp knife, cut each round steak into 3 serving pieces. In hot bacon drippings, cook steaks until well browned on both sides. Stir in undiluted onion soup and pepper; heat to boiling. Reduce heat to low; cover and simmer 1 hour or until steaks are fork-tender, stirring occasionally.
3. Arrange a pepper ring, then a lemon slice on each steak; cover and continue cooking until pepper rings are tender-crisp. With pancake turner, carefully place steaks with green pepper and lemon on warm platter; keep warm.
4. In cup, blend flour and ¼ cup cold water until smooth; gradually stir into hot liquid in skillet and cook, stirring constantly, until mixture is thickened. Serve gravy over steaks. Makes 6 servings.

SWISS STEAK WITH TOMATO

1 2½- to 3-pound beef arm steak, cut about 1½ inches thick
2 tablespoons all-purpose flour
3 tablespoons salad oil
2 large onions, thinly sliced
1 8-ounce can tomato sauce
1 small garlic clove, minced
1 teaspoon salt
¼ teaspoon pepper
1 bay leaf
½ cup diced green pepper
hot mashed potatoes, cooked noodles or cooked rice (optional)

ABOUT 4 HOURS BEFORE SERVING:
1. Cut bone and excess fat from arm steak. On cutting board, coat meat on one side with half of flour; with meat mallet or edge of plate, pound meat well. Turn meat and repeat on other side.
2. In 12-inch skillet over medium-high heat, in hot salad oil, cook meat until well browned on both sides. Remove meat.
3. To drippings in skillet, add onions and cook, stirring frequently, until onions are lightly browned, about 5 minutes. Add tomato sauce, garlic, salt, pepper, bay leaf and meat; heat to boiling. Reduce heat to low; cover and simmer about 3½ hours or until meat is fork-tender, turning meat once. During last 45 minutes of cooking time, add green pepper.
4. Place meat on warm platter. Discard bay leaf and spoon fat from liquid in skillet. Serve meat and liquid with mashed potatoes. Makes 6 servings.

Beef Stews

MORAVIAN GOULASH

¼ cup salad oil
2½ pounds beef stew meat, cut into 1½-inch chunks
3 cups thinly sliced onions
4 teaspoons paprika
1 8-ounce can tomatoes
2½ teaspoons salt
1 cup dill pickles, cut into chunks

ABOUT 3 HOURS BEFORE SERVING:
In 12-inch skillet or Dutch oven over medium-high heat, in hot salad oil, cook stew meat until browned on all sides, a few pieces at a time; remove and set aside. Reduce heat to medium; in drippings in skillet, cook onions until tender, about 5 minutes. Stir in paprika, meat, tomatoes with their liquid and salt; heat to boiling.

Reduce heat to low; cover and simmer 2½ hours or until meat is fork-tender, stirring occasionally and adding more water if necessary. Add pickles and cook 5 minutes longer. Makes about 8 servings.

CALIFORNIA BEEF STEW

3 bacon slices, cut into pieces
2 pounds beef stew meat
1 cup dry red wine
1 bouillon cube
2 garlic cloves, minced
1 tablespoon instant minced onion
2 teaspoons salt
¼ teaspoon thyme leaves
1 strip orange peel
18 small white onions
¾ pound small mushrooms
2 tablespoons cornstarch
1 10-ounce package frozen peas
½ cup pitted ripe olives, drained

ABOUT 3 HOURS BEFORE SERVING:
In large Dutch oven over medium-high heat, fry bacon until crisp; push bacon bits to side of pan. To drippings in pan, add stew meat and cook until well browned. Stir in 1 cup water, wine and next 6 ingredients; heat to boiling. Reduce heat to low; cover and simmer 2½ hours or until meat is fork-tender, stirring occasionally. Meanwhile, in covered, medium saucepan over high heat, in about 1 inch boiling salted water, cook onions 10 minutes; add mushrooms; cook 5 more minutes; drain.

In small bowl, mix cornstarch and 3 tablespoons water until blended; stir into stew and cook over medium heat, stirring constantly, until mixture is thickened. Add onions and mushrooms, frozen peas and olives; cover and cook 10 minutes or until peas are fork-tender. Makes 6 to 8 servings.

DELUXE: Instead of beef stew meat, use *2 pounds round steak*, cut into 1½-inch chunks. Simmer 1 hour before adding cornstarch mixture.

BROWNED BEEF STEW

2½ pounds beef stew meat, cut into 1½-inch chunks
⅓ cup all-purpose flour
⅓ cup salad oil
1 large onion, chopped
1 garlic clove, minced (optional)
4 beef-bouillon cubes or envelopes
1 teaspoon salt
½ teaspoon Worcestershire
¼ teaspoon pepper
5 medium potatoes, cut in chunks
1 16-ounce bag carrots, cut in chunks
1 10-ounce package frozen peas
hot cooked noodles or rice (optional)

ABOUT 3½ HOURS BEFORE SERVING:

1. On waxed paper, coat stew meat with flour; reserve leftover flour. In 6-quart Dutch oven over medium-high heat, in hot salad oil, cook meat, a few pieces at a time, until well-browned on all sides, removing pieces as they brown.
2. Reduce heat to medium; to drippings in Dutch oven, add chopped onion and garlic and cook until onion is almost tender, about 3 minutes, stirring occasionally. Stir in reserved flour until blended. Gradually stir in 3 cups water, bouillon, salt, Worcestershire and pepper and cook, stirring constantly, until mixture is slightly thickened. Add meat and heat to boiling, stirring occasionally. Reduce heat to low; cover and simmer about 2½ hours or until meat is almost tender, stirring occasionally.
3. Add potatoes and carrot chunks and over medium heat, heat to boiling. Reduce heat to low; cover and simmer 20 minutes. Stir in frozen peas; cover and simmer 5 to 10 minutes until all vegetables are tender.
4. Serve with or over noodles, if you like. Makes 8 to 10 servings.

WITH DUMPLINGS: Prepare as above but omit potatoes and prepare *Dumplings for Stew* (page 421); after stirring in peas, drop dough in 10 mounds on meat and vegetables and cook as directed.

HARVEST BEEF STEW: Prepare as above but substitute *½ teaspoon thyme leaves* for Worcestershire and use *1 tablespoon salt.* Omit potatoes, carrots and peas and add *3 medium zucchini,* cut into pieces; *1 medium eggplant,* cut into 1-inch chunks; *1 pound medium mushrooms* and *one 10-ounce package frozen lima beans,* slightly thawed; cover and simmer 10 minutes or until tender. Add *4 medium tomatoes,* peeled and cut into wedges, and heat through.

IRISH: Prepare as above but omit flour and do not brown meat; first, cook chopped onion and garlic in only 1 tablespoon salad oil until almost tender, about 3 minutes. Add unbrowned meat, 3 cups water, bouillon, salt, Worcestershire and pepper and proceed as directed.

BEEF PIE: Prepare as above but omit parsley and mashed potatoes in Step 4 and spoon stew into 13″ by 9″ baking dish.* Preheat oven to 425°F. Prepare Flaky Pastry (page 504) or dough for Biscuits (page 416); on lightly floured surface, with floured rolling pin, roll dough into 15″ by 11″ rectangle. Fit crust loosely over stew mixture; trim overhang to about 1 inch and make a fluted edge (page 506). With point of knife, cut wide slits in crust to allow steam to escape. Bake 20 to 25 minutes until browned. Makes 10 servings.

* Or, use 3-quart round casserole and *pastry for one-crust pie* or half biscuit recipe. Roll dough into circle 2 inches larger than top of casserole.

PRESSURE-COOKED BEEF STEW

½ cup red table wine
2 tablespoons salad oil
1 2-pound beef round steak, cut into 1½-inch chunks
¼ pound lean salt pork, cut into ½-inch cubes
1 16-ounce can tomatoes
1 large onion, minced
1 large carrot, minced
1 celery stalk, minced
½ garlic clove, minced
1 bay leaf
1½ teaspoons salt
1 teaspoon thyme leaves
3 parsley sprigs
12 stuffed olives, halved
1 3-ounce can whole mushrooms, drained
4 cups buttered, hot cooked noodles

EARLY IN DAY:

In large bowl, for marinade, combine wine

and salad oil. Add steak chunks and turn over to coat with marinade. Cover and refrigerate at least 4 hours, turning often.

ABOUT 30 MINUTES BEFORE SERVING:
Drain meat; discard marinade. In 4-quart pressure cooker over medium-high heat, fry salt pork until golden; add meat and cook until well browned. Add tomatoes and their liquid and remaining ingredients except mushrooms and noodles. Cover and bring cooker to 15 pounds pressure as manufacturer directs; cook 20 minutes.

Remove cooker from heat and reduce pressure quickly as manufacturer directs before uncovering. Add mushrooms and heat. Discard parsley and bay leaf. Serve stew over noodles. Makes 6 to 8 servings.

BEEF BOURGUIGNON

1 8-ounce package sliced bacon, cut into 1-inch pieces
20 small white onions
3 pounds beef bottom round roast, cut into 2-inch chunks
all-purpose flour
1 large carrot, chopped
1 large onion, chopped
¼ cup brandy
2 garlic cloves, crushed
2 teaspoons salt
½ teaspoon thyme leaves, crushed
¼ teaspoon pepper
1 bay leaf
3 cups red Burgundy
butter or margarine
1 pound mushrooms, sliced

ABOUT 4½ HOURS BEFORE SERVING:
1. In Dutch oven over medium-high heat, cook bacon until browned. With slotted spoon, remove bacon to paper towels to drain. Discard all but 3 tablespoons drippings. In drippings in Dutch oven, cook small white onions until lightly browned, stirring occasionally. With slotted spoon, place onions in small bowl; set aside.
2. Meanwhile, on waxed paper, coat meat chunks with 3 tablespoons flour. In drippings in Dutch oven over medium-high heat, cook meat, several pieces at a time, until well browned on all sides, removing pieces as they brown.
3. Preheat oven to 325°F. To drippings in Dutch oven, add carrot and chopped onion and cook over medium heat, stirring frequently, until tender, about 5 minutes. Return beef to Dutch oven; pour brandy over all and set aflame with match. When flaming stops, add bacon, garlic, salt, thyme, pepper, bay leaf and Burgundy. Cover and bake 3½ hours or until fork-tender.
4. About 1 hour before meat is done, in 10-inch skillet over medium heat, in 2 tablespoons hot butter or margarine, cook mushrooms until golden, about 7 minutes.
5. Meanwhile, in small bowl with spoon, mix 2 tablespoons softened butter or margarine and 2 tablespoons flour until smooth. Remove Dutch oven from oven. Into hot liquid in Dutch oven, add flour mixture, ½ teaspoon at a time, stirring after each addition, until blended. Add reserved onions and mushrooms to Dutch oven. Cover and bake until meat is fork-tender. Makes 10 servings.

HUNGARIAN-STYLE GOULASH

3 tablespoons butter or margarine
6 medium onions, thinly sliced (about 2 pounds)
2 pounds beef stew meat, cut into 1-inch chunks
¼ cup paprika (yes, this much)
2 teaspoons salt
1 bay leaf
1 cup sour cream
Poppy Seed Noodles (page 139)

ABOUT 3½ HOURS BEFORE SERVING:
In Dutch oven over medium-high heat, in hot butter or margarine, cook onions, stirring occasionally, until lightly browned, about 15 minutes. Add stew meat, paprika, salt and bay leaf. Reduce heat to low; cover and simmer 3 hours or until meat is fork-tender,* stirring occasionally. Discard bay leaf. Stir in sour cream. Serve over noodles. Makes 6 servings.

* If meat sticks to the pan, add a tablespoon or two of water.

TOMATO-BEEF GOULASH

½ cup shortening
2 teaspoons ground marjoram
1 teaspoon caraway seed
1 teaspoon grated lemon peel
6 large onions, sliced
2 pounds beef stew meat, cut into 1½-inch chunks
1 6-ounce can tomato paste
1 tablespoon paprika
2 teaspoons salt
½ *each* green and red peppers, slivered, for garnish

ABOUT 2¾ HOURS BEFORE SERVING:
In 10-inch skillet or Dutch oven over medium heat, in hot shortening, cook marjoram, caraway seed and lemon peel for 2 minutes; add onions and cook, stirring occasionally, until tender. Stir in 2 cups water, stew meat and remaining ingredients except peppers; heat mixture to boiling.

Reduce heat to low; cover and simmer 2¼ hours or until meat is fork-tender, stirring occasionally. Pour into serving dish; garnish with red- and green-pepper slivers. Makes 6 to 8 servings.

SLIVERED BEEF STEW

1 1½-pound beef round steak, cut about ¾ inch thick*
3 tablespoons all-purpose flour
¼ cup shortening
2 cups 1-inch carrot chunks
2 large onions, sliced
1 large potato, cut in 1-inch chunks
1 cup sliced celery
1 cup sliced mushrooms
1 bay leaf
salt
½ teaspoon pepper
1 cup sour cream
2 teaspoons paprika

ABOUT 45 MINUTES BEFORE SERVING:
Cut steak into strips about 3 inches long and ¼ inch thick. On waxed paper, coat meat with flour; reserve remaining flour. In large skillet over medium-high heat, in hot shortening, cook meat until well browned. Add carrots, onions, potato, celery, mushrooms, bay leaf, 2 teaspoons salt, pepper and 3 cups water; heat to boiling.

Reduce heat to low; cover and simmer 30 minutes or until meat and vegetables are fork-tender, stirring occasionally.

In cup, combine remaining flour with 1 teaspoon salt; stir into mixture and cook until thickened slightly, stirring constantly. Stir in sour cream and paprika; heat, but do not boil. Makes 6 servings.

* Meat will be easier to slice if it is partially frozen about 1½ hours ahead.

ALL-DAY BEEF STEW

3 pounds beef stew meat, cut into 1-inch chunks
½ cup all-purpose flour
4 teaspoons salt
1 10½-ounce can condensed beef broth
2 cups dry red wine
4 medium carrots, cut in 1-inch pieces
4 medium potatoes, quartered
1 20-ounce bag frozen cut green beans (about 5 cups)
1½ pounds small white onions (about 18)
1 tablespoon light brown sugar
1 bay leaf

ABOUT 6 HOURS BEFORE SERVING:
Preheat oven to 250°F. In Dutch oven, toss stew meat, flour and salt until meat is well coated. Stir in undiluted beef broth and remaining ingredients; cover and bake 5 to 6 hours until meat and vegetables are tender, stirring occasionally. Makes 8 to 10 servings.

BEEF STEW SCANDIA

1 2-pound boneless beef chuck roll or boneless shoulder roast
3 tablespoons salad oil
2 large onions, sliced
8 medium potatoes, thinly sliced (about 3 pounds)
1 12-ounce can beer (1½ cups)
1 tablespoon salt
3 tablespoons prepared mustard
¼ teaspoon pepper
1 tablespoon chopped parsley

ABOUT 2 HOURS BEFORE SERVING:
Trim any excess fat from chuck roll; cut

meat into ¼-inch-thick slices. With meat mallet, dull edge of French knife or edge of saucer, pound slices well. In Dutch oven over medium-high heat, in hot salad oil, cook meat, several pieces at a time, until lightly browned, removing pieces as they brown.

Reduce heat to medium; to drippings, add onions and cook until tender, about 5 minutes, stirring occasionally. Preheat oven to 350°F. Return meat to Dutch oven; stir in ¼ cup water and remaining ingredients except parsley; heat to boiling.

Cover Dutch oven and bake about 1¼ hours or until meat and potatoes are fork-tender, stirring once or twice. To serve, sprinkle with parsley. Makes 6 to 8 servings.

Short Ribs, Oxtails and Shanks

PEPPER SHORT RIBS

2 tablespoons salad oil
3 large sweet red and/or green peppers, cut lengthwise in ½-inch strips
3 pounds beef chuck short ribs
1 medium onion, sliced
¼ cup dry sherry or sake
soy sauce
1 tablespoon cornstarch
1 teaspoon sugar
1 cup cherry tomatoes, halved
3 cups hot cooked brown or long-grain white rice

ABOUT 4 HOURS BEFORE SERVING:

1. In Dutch oven over medium-high heat, in hot salad oil, cook red-pepper strips, stirring constantly, until tender-crisp, about 3 minutes. With slotted spoon, remove red pepper to medium bowl; cover and refrigerate.
2. In oil remaining in Dutch oven, over medium-high heat, cook chuck short ribs until browned on all sides. Add onion and cook until tender, stirring occasionally. Add sherry, 2 tablespoons soy sauce and 2 tablespoons water. Reduce heat to low; cover and simmer 3 to 3½ hours until meat is fork-tender, adding more water, if necessary, and stirring occasionally.
3. With slotted spoon, remove short ribs from Dutch oven and keep warm. For sauce, pour pan liquid into measuring cup and spoon off excess fat; add water to make 1 cup liquid; return to Dutch oven. In cup, blend cornstarch and sugar with 1 tablespoon water and 1 tablespoon soy sauce until smooth; gradually stir into hot pan liquid and cook over medium heat, stirring constantly, until mixture is thickened.
4. Return meat to Dutch oven; add peppers and tomatoes and mix gently; heat. Serve meat and vegetables over rice. Makes 5 servings.

BARBECUED SHORT RIBS

¼ cup shortening
5 pounds beef short ribs
1 medium onion, chopped
1¼ cups catchup
½ cup diced celery
¼ cup light brown sugar
¼ cup cider vinegar
1½ tablespoons Worcestershire
2 teaspoons salt
1 teaspoon prepared mustard
1 tablespoon all-purpose flour
1 8-ounce package egg noodles, cooked
chopped parsley for garnish

ABOUT 3 HOURS BEFORE SERVING:

In Dutch oven over medium-high heat, in hot shortening, cook short ribs until well browned on all sides. In medium bowl, stir ¾ cup water and remaining ingredients except flour and noodles; pour over ribs; heat to boiling. Reduce heat to low; cover and simmer 2½ hours or until ribs are fork-tender, stirring occasionally. Add more water if necessary.

With slotted spoon, place ribs on warm platter. Skim fat from pan liquid. In cup, blend flour and 2 tablespoons water until smooth; gradually stir into hot liquid and cook over medium heat, stirring constantly, until mixture is thickened. Serve gravy with meat and noodles. Garnish with parsley. Makes 5 or 6 servings.

SPICY SHORT RIBS

3 pounds beef short ribs
all-purpose flour
2 tablespoons salad oil
1 small onion, chopped
2 tablespoons catchup
2 teaspoons salt
¼ teaspoon pepper
¼ teaspoon thyme leaves, crushed

ABOUT 3 HOURS BEFORE SERVING:
Preheat oven to 350°F. On waxed paper, coat short ribs with ¼ cup flour. In 12-inch skillet with ovenproof handle, over medium-high heat, in hot salad oil, cook meat until well-browned on all sides.

Add ½ cup water, onion and remaining ingredients to meat. Cover and bake 2½ hours or until meat is fork-tender, stirring once or twice. With slotted spoon, remove meat to warm platter; keep warm.

Spoon off all but 3 tablespoons drippings from skillet, leaving browned bits in pan. Over medium heat, stir in 2 tablespoons flour until blended. Gradually stir in 1¼ cups water and cook, stirring constantly, until mixture is thickened. Serve gravy over meat. Makes 3 or 4 servings.

DILLED SHORT RIBS

2 tablespoons salad oil
6 pounds beef short ribs
1 small onion, chopped
1 cup grated carrots
2 tablespoons cider vinegar
1 tablespoon salt
¼ teaspoon pepper
1 teaspoon dill weed
1 8-ounce package egg noodles
1 tablespoon butter or margarine
2 tablespoons all-purpose flour

ABOUT 3 HOURS BEFORE SERVING:
1. In Dutch oven over medium-high heat, in hot salad oil, cook short ribs, one-half at a time, until well browned on all sides. Return all ribs to Dutch oven.
2. To Dutch oven, add 1 cup water, onion, carrots, vinegar, salt and pepper; heat to boiling. Reduce heat to low; cover and simmer 2½ hours or until meat is fork-tender, stirring occasionally. During last hour of cooking, add dill weed.
3. Prepare noodles as label directs; drain and stir in butter or margarine; arrange on warm platter. With slotted spoon, arrange short ribs on top of noodles; keep warm.
4. Skim fat from pan liquid; if necessary, add water to make 2 cups pan liquid. In cup, blend flour with ¼ cup cold water until smooth; gradually stir into hot pan liquid and cook over medium heat, stirring constantly, until mixture is thickened. Serve gravy with meat and noodles. Makes 6 or 7 servings.

BEEF SHANKS WITH VEGETABLES

2 tablespoons salad oil
8 cross-cut beef shanks, each cut about 1 inch thick (about 6 pounds)
1 large onion, sliced
½ cup white wine vinegar
1 tablespoon salt
1 teaspoon sugar
4 large potatoes, halved
8 medium carrots
8 small white onions
¼ cup all-purpose flour

ABOUT 4 HOURS BEFORE SERVING:
In 8-quart Dutch oven over medium-high heat, in hot salad oil, cook shanks, a few at a time, until well browned on both sides, removing pieces as they brown; set aside. In drippings left in Dutch oven, over medium heat, cook sliced onion until lightly browned, about 3 minutes.

Return meat to Dutch oven; add ¼ cup water, vinegar, salt and sugar; heat to boiling. Reduce heat to low; cover and simmer 2 hours, turning meat occasionally and adding more water if necessary. Add vegetables and continue cooking 1½ hours until meat and vegetables are fork-tender.

With slotted spoon, remove meat and vegetables to warm platter; keep warm. Skim fat from pan liquid. In cup, blend flour and ½ cup water until smooth; gradually stir into hot liquid in Dutch oven and cook over medium heat, stirring constantly, until mixture is thickened. Serve gravy with meat. Makes about 8 servings.

OXTAIL STEW

3 pounds oxtails, cut in 2-inch pieces
3 tablespoons all-purpose flour
2 tablespoons salad oil
2 cups pineapple juice
1 tablespoon lemon juice
2 teaspoons dry mustard
1 teaspoon salt
1 teaspoon Worcestershire
½ teaspoon chili powder
¼ teaspoon pepper
2 cups sliced celery
1 cup pitted ripe olives, halved for garnish

ABOUT 3½ HOURS BEFORE SERVING:
On waxed paper, coat oxtails with flour; reserve leftover flour.

In Dutch oven over medium-high heat, in hot salad oil, cook oxtails until well browned. Add 2 cups water, pineapple juice and next 6 ingredients; heat to boiling. Reduce heat to low; cover and simmer 3 hours or until meat is fork-tender.

During last 15 minutes cooking time, add celery. In cup, blend leftover flour and 2 tablespoons water until smooth; gradually stir into pan liquid; add olives. Cook over medium heat, stirring constantly, until mixture is slightly thickened. Makes 4 servings.

"Boiled" Beef

NEW ENGLAND "BOILED" DINNER

1 4- to 5-pound corned-beef brisket
1 large garlic clove
1 bay leaf
½ teaspoon peppercorns
3 or 4 of vegetables (below)

ABOUT 4½ HOURS BEFORE SERVING:
In 8-quart saucepot or Dutch oven over high heat, heat to boiling corned beef, garlic, bay leaf, peppercorns and enough hot water to cover. Reduce heat to low; cover and simmer 3½ to 4 hours until meat is fork-tender.

About 40 minutes before meat is done, add remaining ingredients except cabbage or Brussels sprouts. About 15 minutes before meat is done, add cabbage; simmer until all vegetables are tender.

Remove corned beef from saucepot and slice; arrange on warm, large platter. With slotted spoon, arrange vegetables around meat. Spoon fat from liquid; serve some unthickened liquid over servings or save it to make soup another day. Makes 10 to 12 servings.

VEGETABLES: 5 medium parsnips, halved; 1 medium rutabaga, cut in 8 to 10 wedges; 10 medium carrots, halved; 10 small white onions; 10 small potatoes; 1 medium head green cabbage, cut into 8 to 10 wedges; 1 pound whole green beans; 5 medium turnips, halved; one 10-ounce container Brussels sprouts.

CORNED BEEF AND CABBAGE: Prepare as above but, for vegetables, use only *1 large head cabbage,* cut into 10 to 12 wedges.

GLAZED CORNED BEEF

1 4-pound corned-beef brisket*
1 medium onion, quartered
1 stalk celery
1 carrot
1 garlic clove, quartered
1 bay leaf
½ teaspoon rosemary

GLAZE:
⅓ cup catchup
2 tablespoons red wine vinegar
2 tablespoons honey
2 tablespoons mint jelly
1 tablespoon butter or margarine
1 tablespoon prepared mustard

ABOUT 5 HOURS BEFORE SERVING:
In 5-quart saucepot over high heat, heat to boiling first 7 ingredients and enough hot water to cover. Reduce heat to low; cover and simmer 3½ to 4 hours until meat is fork-tender.

Meanwhile, preheat oven to 325°F. For glaze, in small saucepan over medium-high heat, heat remaining ingredients to boiling, stirring constantly. Place meat on rack in open roasting pan. Spoon some glaze over meat and bake 20 minutes, basting occasionally, until well glazed. Makes 10 to 12 servings.

* To use oven-roasted corned-beef brisket: Roast meat as label directs. Prepare glaze as above; spoon over meat during last 30 minutes of roasting, basting occasionally.

"BOILED" BEEF WITH HORSERADISH

2 stalks celery
1 small onion
2 garlic cloves
2 tablespoons sugar
2 tablespoons cider vinegar
1 tablespoon salt
6 whole cloves
1 bay leaf
1 4-pound beef Boston-cut pot roast or fresh boneless beef brisket
Creamy Horseradish Sauce (page 167) or Lemon Butter (page 351)
4 pounds new potatoes, boiled (optional)

ABOUT 4½ HOURS BEFORE SERVING:
In 7-quart saucepot or Dutch oven, over high heat, heat to boiling first 9 ingredients and enough hot water to cover. Reduce heat to low; cover and simmer 3½ to 4 hours until meat is fork-tender.

Serve meat with Creamy Horseradish Sauce and, if desired, potatoes. Makes 10 to 12 servings.

BEEF BRISKET WITH NOODLES

1 4-pound fresh boneless beef brisket
1 medium onion, sliced
2 tablespoons salt
1 tablespoon pickling spice
Homemade Egg Noodles (page 305) or 1 16-ounce package egg noodles
3 tablespoons butter or margarine
¼ cup all-purpose flour
1 teaspoon bottled sauce for gravy

ABOUT 5 HOURS BEFORE SERVING:
1. In 7-quart saucepot or Dutch oven over high heat, heat to boiling brisket, onion, salt, pickling spice and enough hot water to cover. Reduce heat to low; cover and simmer 3½ to 4 hours until meat is fork-tender, turning meat occasionally.
2. Meanwhile, prepare Homemade Egg Noodles but do not cook; let dry at least 2 hours.
3. When meat is done, remove to warm platter; keep warm. Strain liquid from saucepot into large bowl. Return 12 cups liquid to saucepot, adding water if necessary to make 12 cups; over high heat, heat to boiling.
4. Add noodles; when mixture returns to boiling, cook 12 to 15 minutes until tender. Drain noodles, reserving liquid. Measure 2½ cups liquid for gravy; set aside. (Refrigerate remaining liquid to make soup another day.)
5. For gravy, in 2-quart saucepan over medium heat, into hot butter or margarine, stir flour until blended. Cook, stirring constantly, until mixture is lightly browned. Gradually stir in reserved 2½ cups liquid and bottled sauce for gravy and cook, stirring constantly, until mixture is thickened. Serve meat with gravy. Makes 10 to 12 servings.

Ground Beef

Ground beef is sold by the pound or as patties. Usually taken from the less-tender cuts of beef, it is labeled as to the amount of lean meat it contains: Ground beef (70 to 75 percent); lean ground beef (75 to 80 percent) and extra-lean ground beef (80 to 85 percent). A certain amount of fat is needed to insure juiciness and tenderness, and to add flavor.

Beef from the round, chuck, flank, sirloin tip or neck may be ground to your order; have it ground coarsely once, and finer a second time.

HAMBURGERS

1 pound lean ground beef
2 tablespoons minced onion
1 teaspoon salt
¼ teaspoon pepper
Hamburger Toppings, optional (opposite)
plain or toasted hamburger buns, toasted split English muffins, rye bread slices, toasted white bread slices (optional)

ABOUT 20 MINUTES BEFORE SERVING:
In medium bowl, with spoon, mix well ground beef, onion, salt and pepper; shape mixture into 4 patties, each about 1 inch thick, or 8 patties, each about ½ inch thick. Cook in one of ways below; serve as is, with one of Hamburger Toppings and/or in buns. Makes 4 servings.

FRIED: In 10-inch skillet over medium-high heat, in 1 tablespoon hot salad oil, cook patties until of desired doneness, turning once with pancake turner. Thick patties will take about 3 to 4 minutes on each side; thin patties, 1 to 3 minutes on each side.

PAN-BROILED: Over medium-high heat, heat skillet or griddle until very hot. If desired, grease skillet lightly with salad oil, or sprinkle with salt. Cook patties as above.

BROILED: Preheat broiler if manufacturer directs. Make thick patties; arrange on rack in broiling pan. Broil patties about 2 inches from heat source, about 8 minutes or until of desired doneness, turning once. If you like, during last minutes of broiling time, top with one of these: Cheddar or American cheese slice; catchup; chili; soy or barbecue sauce; crumbled blue cheese.

HAMBURGER TOPPINGS

Spoon one of these over cooked hamburgers:
Gravy for Pan-Fried Meat (page 65)
Sour cream
Mustard Sour-Cream Sauce (page 75)
Zesty Sour-Cream Sauce (page 207)
Chive or onion dip
One of Butters for Broiled Beef (page 167)
Béarnaise Sauce (page 166)
Bordelaise Sauce (page 167)
Guacamole (page 33)

HAMBURGERS AU POIVRE

1 pound extra-lean ground beef
½ to 1 teaspoon coarsely ground pepper
1 teaspoon salt
4 slices French bread or 2 English muffins, split
3 tablespoons butter or margarine
¼ cup sauterne

ABOUT 20 MINUTES BEFORE SERVING:
Preheat broiler if manufacturer directs. Shape ground beef into 4 patties. Sprinkle patties on both sides with pepper and salt.

Toast French bread on rack in broiling pan. In 10-inch skillet over medium-high heat, in hot butter or margarine, cook patties 6 minutes or until of desired doneness, turning once. Place patties on toasted French bread; keep warm.

Spoon off all but 1 tablespoon drippings from skillet. Add wine to skillet; heat to boiling, stirring to loosen browned bits. Pour sauce over patties. Makes 4 servings.

MINUTE STEAKS AU POIVRE: Prepare as above but use *4 beef cube steaks* (about 1 pound) instead of ground beef.

SAUCY BURGERS

2 pounds ground beef
1 14½- to 16-ounce jar marinara sauce
1 cup fresh bread crumbs
1 teaspoon salt
dash pepper
1 tablespoon salad oil

ABOUT 20 MINUTES BEFORE SERVING:
In medium bowl, mix well ground beef, ½ cup marinara sauce, bread crumbs, salt and pepper; shape into 8 patties. In 12-inch skillet over medium-high heat, in hot salad oil, cook patties until well browned on both sides; drain on paper towels.

Pour drippings from skillet; return meat to skillet and pour remaining sauce over meat; heat to boiling. Reduce heat to low; cover and simmer 5 minutes. Makes 8 servings.

STUFFED BURGERS

2 pounds lean ground beef
¼ cup prepared mustard
⅓ cup minced pimento-stuffed olives
salt and pepper
6 hamburger buns

ABOUT 30 MINUTES BEFORE SERVING:
Preheat broiler if manufacturer directs. Shape ground beef into 12 thin patties. In small bowl, combine mustard and olives. Place 1 tablespoonful of mixture in center of each of 6 patties; top with remaining patties; pinch edges together to seal.

Place patties on greased rack in broiling pan; sprinkle with salt and pepper. Broil patties 8 minutes or until of desired doneness, turning once. During last minutes, toast buns. Serve burgers in buns. Makes 6 servings.

MEAT LOAF

2 pounds ground beef
2 cups fresh white or whole-wheat bread crumbs (about 4 bread slices)
½ cup milk
½ cup minced onion
2 eggs
2 teaspoons salt
¼ teaspoon pepper

ABOUT 2 HOURS BEFORE SERVING:
Preheat oven to 350°F. In large bowl, mix well all ingredients. Spoon mixture into 9″ by 5″ loaf pan;* with spoon, level top. Bake meat loaf 1½ hours.

For easier serving, let meat loaf stand at room temperature 5 minutes; pour off and discard drippings. With spatula, loosen meat loaf from pan; invert onto warm platter. (Or, with two pancake turners, lift meat loaf, top side up, to warm platter.) Makes 8 servings.

* Or, in shallow baking pan, shape mixture into 9″ by 5″ oval loaf; bake 1 hour and 15 minutes.

SUBSTITUTIONS FOR MEAT: Prepare Meat Loaf but use only 1½ pounds ground beef and add one of the following:

½ pound sweet or hot Italian sausages, diced, or pork-sausage meat
¼ pound ground veal and ¼ pound ground pork

Or, use packaged mixed ground meat for meat loaf prepared by meatman.

SUBSTITUTIONS FOR MILK: Prepare Meat Loaf but omit milk; add one of following:

1 8-ounce container creamed cottage cheese
½ 8-ounce package pasteurized process cheese spread, cut in ½-inch cubes
½ cup sour cream
½ cup tomato juice or sauce
½ cup red Burgundy
½ cup beer

SUBSTITUTIONS FOR BREAD CRUMBS: Prepare Meat Loaf but omit bread crumbs and add one of the following:

1½ cups cooked rice
1 cup uncooked rice (cover pan or loaf with foil before baking so that rice can cook)
1 cup cooked or uncooked macaroni
1 cup uncooked quick-cooking or old-fashioned oats
1 16-ounce can kidney beans, drained and mashed
2 cups fresh rye-bread crumbs
⅓ cup quick-cooking tapioca

Or, use only 1 cup fresh bread crumbs and add one of the following:

1 cup crushed saltines
½ cup nonfat dry-milk powder
½ cup wheat germ

MEAT-LOAF ADDITIONS

Prepare Meat Loaf (at left) but add one or more of the following seasonings, fruit or vegetables:

SEASONINGS:
1 garlic clove, minced
1 teaspoon hot pepper sauce
2 tablespoons horseradish
½ teaspoon basil
1 tablespoon curry powder
½ teaspoon caraway seed
½ teaspoon oregano
1 tablespoon chili powder
¼ teaspoon garlic powder
¼ cup soy sauce (use only 1 teaspoon salt)
½ cup minced green pepper
½ cup minced celery
¾ cup sweet pickle relish

VEGETABLES OR FRUIT:
1 12-ounce package frozen mashed squash, thawed, and ½ teaspoon salt (omit milk)
1 10-ounce package frozen mixed vegetables, thawed and drained, and ½ teaspoon salt
1 cup shredded carrots
1 cup shredded cored apples
1 cup sauerkraut (use only ¼ cup milk)
1 12-ounce vacuum-packed can whole kernel corn, undrained
1 12-ounce can whole kernel corn with sweet peppers, undrained
1 4-ounce can mushroom stems and pieces, drained
1 4-ounce jar diced pimentos, drained
¼ cup chopped parsley
½ cup chopped pimento-stuffed olives
½ cup chopped pitted ripe olives

FILLED MEAT LOAVES

Prepare Meat Loaf mixture but spread half of mixture in loaf pan; top with one of fillings below, then add remaining meat mixture. Bake and serve as directed.

4 or 5 whole medium mushrooms
¼ pound mushrooms, minced
1 10-ounce package frozen chopped spinach, thawed and drained
1 cup shredded mozzarella or scamorze cheese
4 hard-cooked eggs
2 frankfurters or ¼ pound knackwurst, cut lengthwise into fourths
4 or 5 pasteurized process cheese slices (overlap slightly)

DELUXE MEAT LOAVES

APPLE-RAISIN MEAT LOAF: Prepare Meat Loaf (opposite) but omit milk; add *one 4¾-ounce jar applesauce* (½ cup) and *½ cup dark seedless raisins* to mixture.

CURRIED MEAT LOAF: Prepare Meat Loaf (opposite) but add *1 cup shredded peeled apples, ½ cup minced celery* and *1 tablespoon curry powder* to mixture.

FRANKFURTER MEAT LOAF: Prepare Meat Loaf (opposite) but omit milk; add *one 8-ounce can tomatoes* and their liquid to mixture. In loaf pan, spread half of mixture. Cut *2 frankfurters* lengthwise into fourths; arrange frankfurters lengthwise on mixture; top with remaining mixture.

GERMAN-STYLE MEAT LOAF: Drain *one 8-ounce can sauerkraut,* reserving liquid. Prepare Meat Loaf (opposite) but omit milk and substitute *2 cups caraway-rye bread crumbs* for bread crumbs; add sauerkraut. To reserved liquid, add water to make ½ cup; add to mixture.

ITALIAN-STYLE MEAT LOAF: Prepare Meat Loaf (opposite) but omit milk; add *½ cup tomato juice, ¼ cup grated Parmesan cheese, ½ teaspoon basil* and *dash garlic powder* to mixture; spread *½ cup catchup* or pizza sauce on top of loaf.

MONTEREY MEAT LOAF: Prepare Meat Loaf (opposite) but add *½ teaspoon oregano* to mixture. In loaf pan, spread half of mixture; from *one 8-ounce package pasteurized process Monterey (Jack) cheese slices,* arrange 2½ cheese slices on meat. Top with remaining mixture. Bake loaf as directed but during last 10 minutes, remove loaf from oven; repeat cheese layer; top cheese with *1 medium tomato,* peeled and sliced. Finish baking loaf in oven.

PINEAPPLE MEAT LOAF: Prepare Meat Loaf (opposite) but omit milk and add juice drained from *one 8¼-ounce can sliced pineapple.* In shallow baking pan, shape mixture into 11" by 5" oval loaf; top with pineapple slices. Bake 1 hour.

SAUERBRATEN LOAF: Prepare Meat Loaf (opposite) but use only 1 cup bread crumbs; add *1 cup crushed gingersnaps, ⅓ cup red wine vinegar* and *dash ground cloves.* Serve with *sour cream.*

SPANISH-STYLE MEAT LOAF: Prepare Meat Loaf (opposite) but omit bread crumbs; add *1 cup uncooked packaged precooked rice* and *½ cup minced green pepper.* In loaf pan, spread half of mixture. With sharp knife, cut *¼ pound chorizo (Spanish sausage)* lengthwise into fourths. Arrange sausage strips lengthwise on mixture; top with remaining mixture. Spread *½ cup catchup* on top of loaf. Cover pan with foil; bake 1½ hours. Makes 10 servings.

SPINACH-CHEESE LOAF: Prepare Meat Loaf (opposite) but omit milk; add *one 8-ounce container creamed cottage cheese;* set aside. In medium bowl, combine *one 10-ounce package frozen chopped spinach,* thawed and drained, *¼ cup minced onion, ½ teaspoon salt, dash nutmeg* and *1 egg.* In 10" by 6" baking dish, spread half of meat mixture; top with spinach mixture, then with remaining meat mixture; level top. Bake 1½ hours. Makes 10 servings.

STROGANOFF MEAT LOAF: Prepare Meat Loaf (opposite) but omit milk; add *one 4-ounce can mushroom stems and pieces,* drained, *½ cup sour cream, ½ cup catchup* and *2 teaspoons dry mustard.*

WHEAT-GERM MEAT LOAF: Prepare Meat Loaf (opposite) but use only 1 cup bread crumbs and omit milk; add *1 cup shredded carrots, ½ cup wheat germ, ½ cup nonfat dry-milk powder* and *½ cup water.*

SPICY MEAT LOAF

2 pounds mixed ground meat for meat loaf (ground beef, pork and/or veal)
2 cups fresh bread crumbs (about 4 bread slices)
¼ cup minced onion
1 tablespoon horseradish
1 teaspoon salt
1 teaspoon prepared mustard
dash pepper
2 eggs
¾ cup catchup

ABOUT 1¾ HOURS BEFORE SERVING:
Preheat oven to 350°F. In medium bowl, mix well all ingredients except catchup.

In 9″ by 5″ loaf pan, spread ½ cup catchup; top with mixture. With spoon, level top. Bake meat loaf 1½ hours. Let meat loaf stand 5 minutes at room temperature; pour off and discard drippings. With spatula, loosen meat loaf from pan; invert onto warm platter; top with remaining catchup. Makes 8 servings.

LEMON BARBECUED MEAT LOAVES

1½ pounds lean ground beef
2 cups fresh bread crumbs (about 4 bread slices)
¼ cup lemon juice
¼ cup minced onion
1 egg
2 teaspoons seasoned salt
½ cup catchup
⅓ cup packed brown sugar
1 teaspoon dry mustard
¼ teaspoon allspice
¼ teaspoon ground cloves
6 thin lemon slices

ABOUT 1 HOUR BEFORE SERVING:
Preheat oven to 350°F. Grease 13″ by 9″ baking pan. In large bowl, mix well first 6 ingredients. Shape mixture into 6 individual loaves; place in baking pan. Bake 15 minutes.

In small bowl, for sauce, combine next 5 ingredients. Spoon sauce over loaves and top each with a lemon slice; bake 30 minutes longer, basting occasionally with sauce from pan. Serve sauce over loaves. Makes 6 servings.

BURGUNDY MEAT BALLS

1 pound lean ground beef
¾ cup dried bread crumbs
¾ cup milk
1 small onion, minced
1 teaspoon cornstarch
1 teaspoon salt
1 egg
¼ cup salad oil
2 tablespoons all-purpose flour
1 cup red Burgundy
1 beef-bouillon cube or envelope

ABOUT 45 MINUTES BEFORE SERVING:
In large bowl, mix well first 7 ingredients; shape into 1-inch meatballs. In 12-inch skillet over medium-high heat, in hot salad oil, cook meatballs, a few at a time, until browned, removing them as they brown.

Into drippings remaining in skillet, stir flour until blended. Gradually stir in 1 cup water, Burgundy and bouillon and cook over medium heat, stirring constantly, until bouillon is dissolved and mixture is thickened. Add meatballs and heat to boiling. Reduce heat to low; cover and simmer 15 minutes. Makes 6 servings.

POLYNESIAN MEATBALLS

2 pounds lean ground beef
2 cups fresh bread crumbs (about 4 bread slices)
½ cup milk
1 egg
⅛ teaspoon garlic salt
salt
¼ cup all-purpose flour
¼ cup salad oil
1 13¼-ounce can pineapple chunks
1 8-ounce can tomato sauce
2 small green peppers, cut into chunks
3 tablespoons white vinegar

ABOUT 1¼ HOURS BEFORE SERVING:
In large bowl, mix well first 5 ingredients and 1½ teaspoons salt; shape into 1½-inch meatballs. On waxed paper, coat meatballs with flour.

In 12-inch skillet over medium-high heat, in hot salad oil, cook meatballs, a few at a time, until well browned, removing them as they brown to drain on paper towels. Pour drippings from skillet and discard.

In skillet, heat to boiling pineapple and its liquid, tomato sauce, green peppers, vinegar and 1 teaspoon salt; return meatballs to skillet. Reduce heat to low; cover and simmer 15 minutes or until green peppers are tender-crisp, stirring frequently. Makes 8 servings.

PIZZA MEATBALLS

¼ pound Monterey (Jack) or Gruyère cheese
1 pound lean ground beef
1 cup fresh bread crumbs (about 2 bread slices)
½ cup milk
1 egg
2 tablespoons instant minced onion
½ teaspoon salt
dash pepper
2 tablespoons salad oil
1 12- to 16-ounce jar spaghetti sauce

ABOUT 45 MINUTES BEFORE SERVING:
Cut part of cheese into twenty to twenty-four ½-inch cubes. Shred remaining cheese and set aside. In large bowl, with fork, mix well all remaining ingredients except salad oil and spaghetti sauce; shape some mixture around each cheese cube to make 1½-inch meatballs.

In 12-inch skillet over medium-high heat, in hot salad oil, cook meatballs until browned on all sides. Spoon drippings from pan; add spaghetti sauce. Reduce heat to low; cover and simmer 10 minutes. Sprinkle meatballs with reserved shredded cheese. Makes 5 servings.

BAKED CHILI AND BEANS

1 pound dry pinto beans
salt
2 pounds lean ground beef
1 28-ounce can tomatoes
2 medium onions, chopped
1 garlic clove, minced
¼ cup chili powder or to taste
¼ teaspoon ground cumin
¼ teaspoon pepper

ABOUT 5½ HOURS BEFORE SERVING:
Rinse beans in cold water; discard any stones, discolored or shriveled beans. In 5-quart Dutch oven over high heat, heat beans, 5 cups hot water and 2 teaspoons salt to boiling; boil 2 minutes. Remove from heat, cover pan and let stand 1 hour.

Preheat oven to 350°F. In 12-inch skillet over medium-high heat, cook ground beef until well browned, stirring occasionally. Stir meat, 4 teaspoons salt and remaining ingredients into beans; cover and bake 3 to 3½ hours until beans are tender, stirring occasionally. Remove cover; bake 30 minutes more. Makes about 12 cups or 8 servings.

HAMBURGER STROGANOFF

¼ cup butter or margarine
½ cup minced onion
1 garlic clove, minced
1 pound lean ground beef
1 pound mushrooms, sliced
2 tablespoons all-purpose flour
1 teaspoon salt
¼ teaspoon pepper
¼ teaspoon paprika
1 10½-ounce can condensed cream-of-chicken soup
1 cup sour cream
chopped parsley, chives or dill for garnish
hot mashed potatoes, chow-mein noodles, hot cooked noodles or rice, or toast

ABOUT 40 MINUTES BEFORE SERVING:
In 12-inch skillet over medium-high heat, in hot butter or margarine, cook onion and garlic until golden, about 3 minutes. Stir in ground beef, mushrooms, flour, salt, pepper and paprika; cook, stirring often, until meat is browned, about 7 minutes.

Stir in undiluted soup; heat to boiling. Reduce heat to low and simmer 10 minutes to blend flavors. Stir in sour cream and heat (do not boil); sprinkle with parsley. To serve, spoon mixture over servings of hot mashed potatoes. Makes 5 servings.

HAMBURGER CZARINA: Prepare as above but use only ½ teaspoon salt, omit mushrooms, and substitute *one 10½-ounce can condensed cream-of-mushroom soup* for cream-of-chicken soup.

MEATBALLS IN POTATO-DILL SAUCE

1 pound lean ground beef
1 egg
1 cup fresh bread crumbs (about 2 bread slices)
¼ cup minced onion
2 tablespoons chopped parsley
¾ teaspoon salt
¼ teaspoon pepper
milk
2 tablespoons salad oil
1 10½-ounce can condensed cream-of-potato soup
1 tablespoon chopped fresh dill or ½ teaspoon dried dill weed

ABOUT 45 MINUTES BEFORE SERVING:
In medium bowl, mix well first 7 ingredients and ⅓ cup milk; shape mixture into 1½-inch meatballs.

In 12-inch skillet over medium-high heat, in hot salad oil, cook meatballs until well browned; drain on paper towels. Pour drippings from skillet and discard.

In same skillet over medium heat, heat undiluted potato soup, dill and ½ cup milk to boiling. Add meatballs and cook until heated through. Makes 4 servings.

LASAGNA

1 pound sweet or hot Italian sausages
2 pounds lean ground beef
1 garlic clove, minced
2 16-ounce cans Italian-style tomatoes
4 6-ounce cans tomato paste
¼ cup chopped parsley
2 tablespoons chopped fresh or 1 teaspoon dried basil
4½ teaspoons salt
1½ teaspoons sugar
1 teaspoon coarsely ground pepper
½ teaspoon oregano leaves
1 16-ounce package lasagna noodles
1 tablespoon olive oil
3 eggs
2 15-ounce containers ricotta cheese
4 8-ounce packages mozzarella cheese

ABOUT 3½ HOURS BEFORE SERVING:
1. In 7-quart Dutch oven over medium heat, cook sausages until well browned, about 15 minutes. Remove sausages; cool slightly; cut into ¼-inch slices.
2. Pour fat from Dutch oven; discard. In Dutch oven, cook ground beef and garlic, stirring frequently, until meat is browned. Return sausage slices to Dutch oven. Add tomatoes and their liquid and next 7 ingredients; over high heat, heat to boiling. Reduce heat to low; simmer about 25 minutes, stirring frequently until sauce is slightly thickened.
3. Meanwhile, cook lasagna noodles with olive oil as label directs; drain. In medium bowl, with fork, beat eggs; stir in ricotta cheese.
4. Preheat oven to 350°F. Grease two 13" by 9" baking pans. Thinly slice mozzarella cheese. Into each pan, spoon about 1 cup tomato sauce; arrange ⅙ of noodles in a layer over sauce; spoon on ⅙ of remaining tomato sauce, ¼ of ricotta cheese mixture and ⅙ of mozzarella slices. Repeat layers once. Top layers with remaining noodles and tomato sauce. Cut remaining mozzarella cheese into strips; arrange in attractive pattern on tops.
5. If you like, freezer-wrap, label and freeze one lasagna. Bake lasagna about 1 hour or until hot and bubbly. Let stand 15 minutes for easier serving. (Each pan makes 8 servings.) Makes 16 servings.

TO BAKE FROZEN LASAGNA: Thaw wrapped lasagna overnight in refrigerator. Preheat oven to 350°F. Cover pan with foil and bake 1½ hours or until hot and bubbly.

CHILI CON CARNE

1 tablespoon salad oil
2 pounds lean ground beef
1 cup chopped onions
¼ cup diced green pepper
2 large garlic cloves, minced
2 16-ounce cans tomatoes or 4 cups chopped, peeled fresh tomatoes
¼ to ⅓ cup chili powder
1½ teaspoons salt
2 16- or 17-ounce cans kidney beans
saltines or other accompaniments (below)

ABOUT 1½ HOURS BEFORE SERVING:
In 5-quart Dutch oven over medium-high heat, in hot salad oil, cook ground beef, onions, green pepper and garlic until onion is tender, about 10 minutes, stirring fre-

quently. Add tomatoes and their liquid, chili powder and salt; heat to boiling. Reduce heat to low; cover and simmer 1 hour, stirring occasionally. Stir in beans and their liquid; heat. Serve in soup bowls; accompany with saltines, if desired. Makes 4 servings.

ACCOMPANIMENTS: Shredded Cheddar cheese, shredded lettuce, minced onions, chopped green pepper, corn chips, French bread.

SALISBURY STEAKS

3 tablespoons butter or margarine
4 medium onions, thinly sliced
2 tablespoons cornstarch
¼ teaspoon salt
2 beef-bouillon cubes or envelopes
1 teaspoon bottled sauce for gravy
1½ pounds lean ground beef
1½ cups fresh bread crumbs
1 teaspoon seasoned salt
¼ teaspoon pepper

ABOUT 40 MINUTES BEFORE SERVING:
Preheat broiler if manufacturer directs. In 10-inch skillet over medium heat, in hot butter or margarine, cook onions until tender, about 5 minutes, stirring frequently. Stir in cornstarch, salt, bouillon, bottled sauce for gravy and 1½ cups water and cook, stirring constantly, until mixture is thickened. Reduce heat to low; cover and simmer about 10 minutes or until onions are tender; keep warm.

Meanwhile, in medium bowl, with fork, mix well ground beef, bread crumbs, salt and pepper; shape into 6 oval patties. On rack in broiling pan, broil patties 8 minutes or until of desired doneness, turning once. Place patties on warm platter; pour sauce over patties. Makes 6 servings.

PORK

Pork comes in a variety of forms: fresh, cured (pickled), cured and smoked, canned, processed alone (sausage) or in combination with other meats (cold cuts). While federal grades have been established for pork, they are not widely used, since pork, unlike beef, varies little in tenderness.

For smoked-pork information, see pages 116–130.

How to buy fresh pork: Choose meat with a high proportion of lean to fat and bone, with flesh that is firm and fine in texture. Color may range from grayish pink to light red.

How to cook fresh-pork cuts: When choosing fresh pork, consider the way you intend to cook it. Here are familiar pork cuts with the recommended way to cook each:

Arm roast—roast
Arm steak—braise, pan-fry
Back ribs—roast (bake), braise, cook in liquid
Boston roast, bone-in or rolled—roast
Chops: blade, butterfly, loin, rib, sirloin, top loin—braise, broil, pan-broil or pan-fry
Country ribs—roast (bake), braise, cook in liquid
Hocks (fresh)—braise, cook in liquid
Ground pork—roast (bake), pan-broil, pan-fry
Leg (fresh ham), bone-in or rolled—roast
Loin roasts: blade, center, sirloin, half, rolled or double rolled—roast
Neck bones—cook in liquid
Picnic (fresh)—roast
Pig's feet—braise, cook in liquid
Pork stew meat—braise, cook in liquid
Porklet (cube steak)—braise, broil, pan-broil, pan-fry
Sirloin cutlet—braise, broil, pan-broil, pan-fry
Spareribs—roast (bake), broil, cook in liquid
Tenderloin—roast, braise, pan-fry

How to test pork for doneness: For roast pork, use a meat thermometer. Fresh pork should be roasted to an internal temperature of 170°F. Pork that is broiled, pan-broiled or pan-fried should be checked for doneness by making a small slit in the center of the meat or near the bone and noting the color—it should be a uniform light gray throughout. Fresh pork is cooked well done.

Pork that is braised or cooked in liquid should feel tender when pierced with a fork.

Pork Roasts

TIMETABLE FOR ROASTING PORK

For general directions, see To Roast, page 63.

Weight (pounds)	*Approximate hours* to reach 170°F.*
Loin	
center, 3 to 5	1¾ to 2¾
half, 5 to 7	3¼ to 4
blade loin or sirloin, 3 to 4	2¼ to 2⅔
roll, 3 to 5	2¼ to 3
Crown roast, 4 to 6	2⅔ to 3½
Picnic shoulder	
bone-in, 5 to 8	3 to 4½
rolled, 3 to 5	2 to 3½
Boston shoulder	
bone-in, 4 to 6	3 to 4
rolled, 4 to 5	2½ to 3½
Leg (fresh ham)	
whole, bone-in, 12 to 16	5¼ to 6
whole, rolled, 10 to 14	4¾ to 5½
Spareribs	1½ to 2½
Tenderloin, ½ to 1	¾ to 1

* Meat at refrigerator temperature, placed in oven preheated to 325°F.

GLAZED FRESH HAM WITH GRAVY

1 14-pound whole pork leg (fresh ham)
2 teaspoons salt
1 teaspoon rubbed sage
¼ teaspoon pepper
one of Glazes (below)
3 tablespoons all-purpose flour

ABOUT 6 HOURS BEFORE SERVING:
1. Preheat oven to 325°F. Place pork leg, fat side up, on rack in open roasting pan. Roast 1½ hours.
2. Remove meat from oven; with sharp knife, cut skin and excess fat from meat, leaving a thin fat covering over meat. In cup, mix salt, sage and pepper; sprinkle over meat. Insert meat thermometer into center of thickest part of meat, being careful that it does not touch bone.
3. Return meat to oven and roast 4 hours or until meat thermometer reaches 170°F. During last 30 minutes of roasting time, baste meat occasionally with one of the glazes. Remove meat from oven.
4. Pour drippings from pan into 4-cup measure or medium bowl; spoon fat from drippings. Add water, if necessary, to make 2 cups liquid. In 2-quart saucepan over medium heat, heat liquid to boiling. In cup, blend flour and ⅓ cup water until smooth; gradually stir into hot liquid and cook, stirring constantly, until thickened. Serve gravy with meat. Makes about 28 servings.

BOURBON GLAZE: In small bowl, blend *1 cup packed brown sugar* and *¼ cup bourbon.*

ORANGE-MUSTARD GLAZE: In small bowl, mix *1 cup packed light brown sugar, ¼ cup orange juice, 2 tablespoons orange marmalade* and *2 teaspoons dry mustard.*

PORK ROAST WITH APPLE

1 3-pound pork center-loin roast*
2 teaspoons salt
1 teaspoon ground sage
½ teaspoon pepper
1 medium cooking apple, cored
½ cup apple jelly, melted

ABOUT 2¼ HOURS BEFORE SERVING:
1. Preheat oven to 325°F. With sharp knife, cut long slits between ribs into meaty side of pork roast, about ¾ way through. In cup, combine salt, sage and pepper; rub into surface and slits of roast.
2. Place roast, seasoned side up, on rack in open roasting pan. Insert meat thermometer into center of meat, being careful thermometer does not touch bone. Roast about 1¾ hours or until meat thermometer reaches 170°F.
3. About 30 minutes before end of roasting time, cut apple into same number of thin wedges as there are slits in roast. Remove roast from oven; insert one apple wedge, skin side up, into each slit, enlarging slit with knife if necessary. Brush meat and apple with jelly; return to oven for last half hour, brushing often with jelly.
4. With sharp knife, cut back bone from ribs and discard. Place roast on warm platter. Let roast stand 15 minutes for easier carving. Makes about 10 servings.

* Ask meatman to loosen back bone from ribs.

SOME POPULAR PORK AND SMOKED PORK CUTS

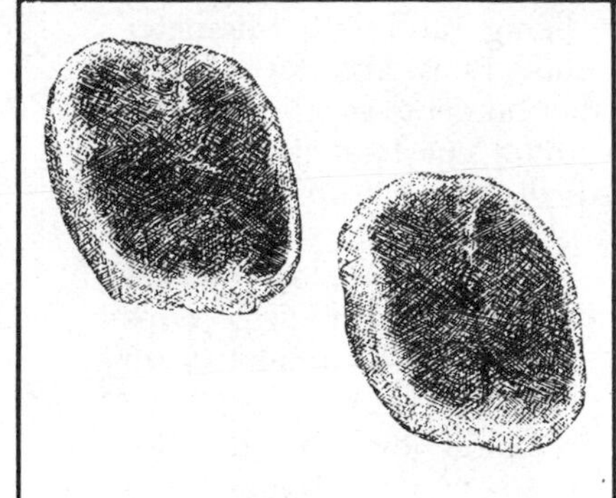

Butterfly Chops

Loin Chop

Rib Chop

Tenderloin (whole, slices, chunks)

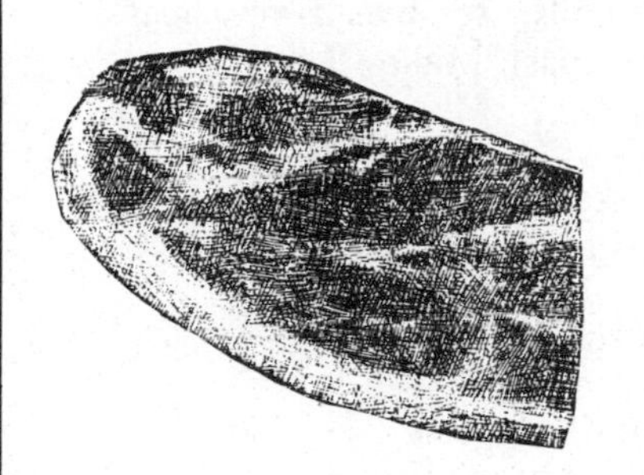

Blade Steak

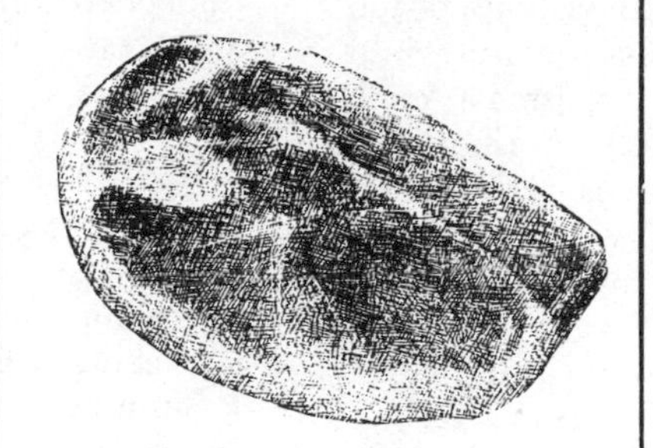

Arm Steak

Country Ribs

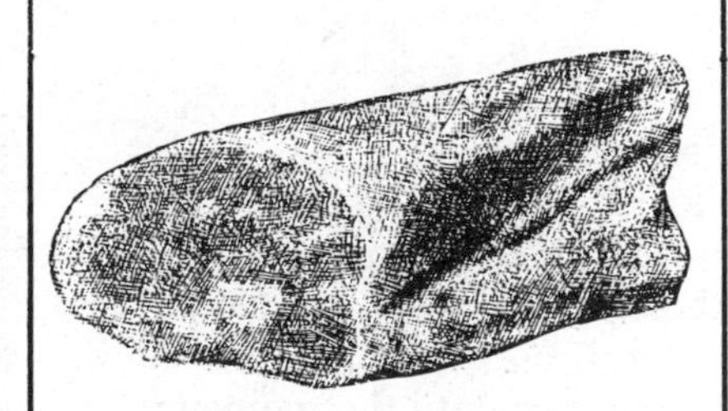

Sirloin Roast

Blade Loin Roast

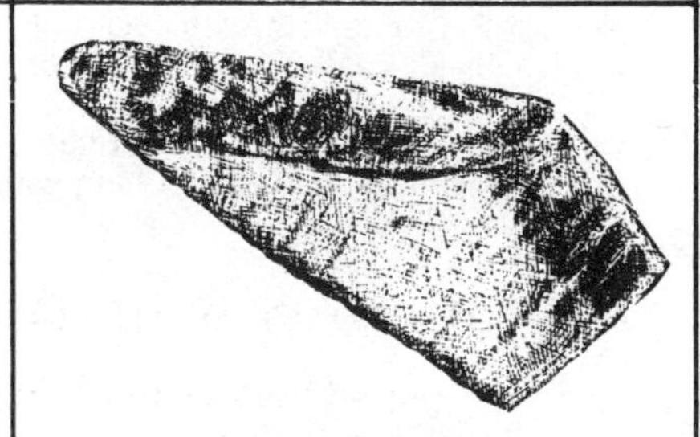

Spareribs

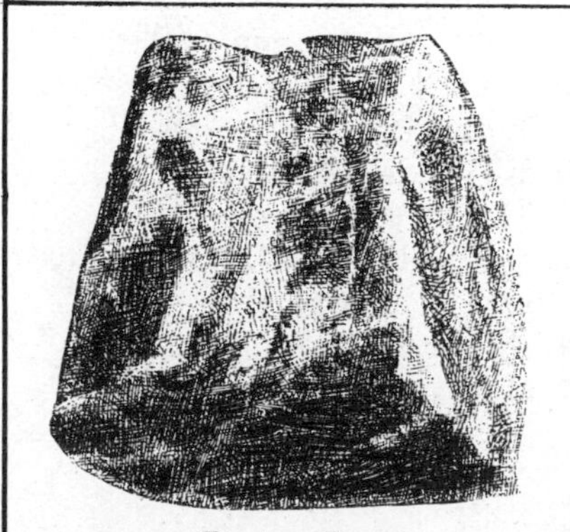

Boston Roast

Smoked Ham (Shank Half)

Smoked Ham (Butt Half)

PEACH-GLAZED PORK AND SQUASH

1 8-pound rolled pork leg (fresh ham)
1 teaspoon dry mustard
1 10-ounce jar peach preserves
½ cup butter or margarine
4 small acorn squash,* halved

ABOUT 4¾ HOURS BEFORE SERVING:

1. Preheat oven to 325°F. Place rolled pork leg on rack in 17½" by 11¼" open roasting pan. Insert thermometer into center of meat. Roast 2 hours.
2. Meanwhile, prepare glaze: In small bowl, blend dry mustard and 1 teaspoon water until smooth; add peach preserves and stir until well blended.
3. In small saucepan over low heat, melt butter or margarine. Stir in ½ cup peach glaze until blended. Spoon mixture into squash halves and place around roast; cook about 2 hours longer or until thermometer reaches 170°F. and squash is fork-tender, basting meat frequently with remaining peach glaze during last 30 minutes of cooking time.
4. To serve, place meat on warm platter and let stand 15 minutes for easier carving; remove strings. Serve squash separately. Makes 8 servings squash and 20 to 24 servings roast.

* For more squash servings, place additional halved small acorn squash on rack in a shallow baking pan and fill each half with a mixture of 1 tablespoon butter or margarine and 1 tablespoon peach preserves; bake along with other squash.

PORK ROAST WITH MADEIRA SAUCE

1 4-pound pork center-loin roast*
4 or 5 bay leaves
salt
pepper
¼ cup all-purpose flour
½ teaspoon sugar
½ cup Madeira

ABOUT 3 HOURS BEFORE SERVING:

1. Preheat oven to 325°F. With sharp knife, cut 4 or 5 slits, about 2 inches deep, between every two ribs in meaty side of pork roast. Insert bay leaves in slits. Sprinkle roast with 1 teaspoon salt and ¼ teaspoon pepper.
2. Place roast, fat side up, on rack in open roasting pan. Insert meat thermometer into center of roast, being careful thermometer does not touch bone. Roast about 2¼ hours or until meat thermometer reaches 170°F.
3. With sharp knife, cut back bone from ribs and discard; discard bay leaves. Place roast on warm platter. Remove rack from pan. For gravy, spoon off fat, leaving pan liquid and browned bits. Add 1½ cups water; over medium heat, heat mixture to boiling, stirring to loosen brown bits.
4. Meanwhile, in small bowl, blend flour, ½ teaspoon salt, sugar, dash pepper and Madeira until smooth. Gradually stir into hot mixture in pan; cook over medium heat, stirring constantly, until mixture is slightly thickened and boils; remove from heat. Serve sauce with roast. Makes 8 to 10 servings.

* Ask meatman to loosen back bone from ribs.

PORK ROAST WITH PIQUANTE SAUCE

1 4-pound pork sirloin, blade- or center-loin roast*
1 8-ounce can tomato sauce
¼ cup packed light brown sugar
¼ cup cider vinegar
¼ cup dark corn syrup
1 tablespoon cornstarch
½ teaspoon salt
⅛ teaspoon pepper

ABOUT 3 HOURS BEFORE SERVING:

Preheat oven to 325°F. Place pork roast, fat side up, on rack in open roasting pan. Insert meat thermometer into center of roast, being careful not to touch bone. Roast about 2½ hours or until thermometer reaches 170°F.

Meanwhile, prepare sauce: In 1-quart saucepan over medium-high heat, cook remaining ingredients and ¼ cup water, stirring constantly, until mixture is thickened; set aside. During last 30 minutes of roasting time, brush roast generously two or three times with tomato-sauce mixture.

Place roast on warm platter. With sharp knife, cut back bone from ribs. Let roast stand 15 minutes for easier carving. Serve sauce with roast. Makes 8 to 10 servings.

* Ask meatman to loosen back bone from ribs.

PORK ROAST WITH APRICOT STUFFING

1 8-ounce package dried apricots, coarsely chopped
¾ cup sugar
1 4-pound pork center-loin roast*
salt
½ teaspoon pepper
½ cup butter or margarine
2 cups minced celery
2 medium onions, minced
1 7-ounce package herb-seasoned stuffing croutons
1 cup finely chopped California walnuts

ABOUT 3½ HOURS BEFORE SERVING:

1. In 2-quart saucepan over medium-high heat, heat to boiling apricots and 2½ cups water. Reduce heat to low; cover and simmer 15 minutes or until apricots are tender. Stir in sugar until dissolved.
2. Meanwhile, with sharp knife, cut long slits between ribs in meaty side of pork roast, about ¾ way through, to form pockets. With fingers, force slits open slightly. In cup, combine 1 tablespoon salt and pepper; rub into surface and slits of roast.
3. Preheat oven to 325°F. In 3-quart saucepan over medium heat, in hot butter or margarine, cook celery and onions until tender, about 5 minutes. Stir in apricots and their liquid, 1 teaspoon salt, croutons and walnuts; mix well. Use some of apricot stuffing to fill slits in roast. Spoon remaining stuffing into greased 1½-quart casserole; cover and refrigerate.
4. Place roast, stuffed side up, on rack in open roasting pan. Insert meat thermometer into center of meat, being careful thermometer does not touch bone or stuffing. Roast about 2½ hours or until meat thermometer reaches 170°F. During roasting, if necessary, cover meat with a "tent" of folded foil to prevent excessive browning of stuffing. During last 45 minutes of roasting, uncover refrigerated stuffing and roast until hot.
5. With sharp knife, cut back bone from ribs and discard. Place roast on warm platter. Let roast stand 15 minutes for easier carving. Serve meat with stuffing. Makes 8 to 10 servings.

* Ask meatman to loosen back bone from ribs.

PORK CROWN ROAST WITH CRAN-APPLE STUFFING

1 14- to 16-rib pork crown roast* (about 7 pounds)
salt
pepper
2 cups cranberries, finely chopped
½ cup sugar
½ cup butter or margarine
2 small onions, diced
2 cups diced celery
8 cups white bread cubes (about 10 slices)
2 medium cooking apples, peeled and finely chopped
½ cup apple juice
1 egg
1 teaspoon poultry seasoning

ABOUT 4½ HOURS BEFORE SERVING:

1. Preheat oven to 325°F. Sprinkle pork roast with 1 tablespoon salt and ¼ teaspoon pepper. Place roast, rib ends down, on rack in open roasting pan; roast 2 hours.
2. Meanwhile, in small bowl, mix well cranberries and sugar; set aside. In Dutch oven over medium heat, in hot butter or margarine, cook onions and celery until tender, about 10 minutes. Into celery mixture, stir reserved cranberries, 2 teaspoons salt, ¼ teaspoon pepper, bread cubes and remaining ingredients and toss until well mixed.
3. Remove roast from oven; invert roast so ribs are up. Fill cavity of roast with stuffing.† Insert meat thermometer between two ribs into center of meat, being careful not to touch bone. Return meat to oven and continue roasting about 1½ hours or until meat thermometer reaches 170°F. (If stuffing becomes too brown, cover it with foil.)
4. Place roast on warm platter; let stand 15 minutes for easier carving. To carve, slice between ribs. Makes 14 to 16 servings.

* Order a crown roast from your meatman several days ahead.
† Bake any leftover stuffing in covered, greased small casserole during the last 30 minutes of roasting time.

WITH OTHER STUFFINGS: Omit stuffing ingredients and step 2; prepare Chestnut Stuffing (page 204), Mushroom Stuffing (page 205), or Mixed-Fruit Stuffing (page 206) and use to stuff crown roast.

ROTISSERIED ROLLED-PORK LOIN

1 4½- to 5-pound rolled pork loin roast
Apple-Soy Glaze (below)
1 cup applesauce

ABOUT 3½ HOURS BEFORE SERVING:
Place pork roast on rotisserie skewer as manufacturer directs. Insert meat thermometer into center of meat being careful that point does not touch skewer and thermometer does not touch heating element or oven as it turns.

Place on rotisserie and roast 2½ to 3 hours until meat thermometer reaches 170°F. During last 30 minutes of cooking time, baste meat frequently with Glaze.

Remove skewer from meat and place meat on warm platter. Let meat stand 15 minutes for easier carving; remove strings. Over medium heat, heat remaining glaze and applesauce until hot. Serve sauce with meat. Makes 14 to 16 servings.

APPLE-SOY GLAZE: In 1-quart saucepan over medium heat, in *2 tablespoons hot salad oil,* cook *½ cup minced onion* and *1 garlic clove,* minced, until tender, about 5 minutes. Stir in *½ cup applesauce, ⅓ cup dry white wine, ¼ cup soy sauce* and *½ teaspoon ginger.*

PORK SHOULDER ROAST WITH VEGETABLES

1 4- to 5-pound rolled Boston pork shoulder roast
1 16-ounce bag carrots, each halved crosswise
1 pound small white onions
2½ teaspoons salt
¼ teaspoon thyme leaves
1 bay leaf
½ pound medium mushrooms
¼ cup all-purpose flour
1 10-ounce package frozen peas
2 egg yolks

ABOUT 3½ HOURS BEFORE SERVING:
1. Preheat oven to 325°F. Place pork roast, fat side up, on rack in open roasting pan. Insert meat thermometer into center of roast. Roast 2½ to 3 hours until thermometer reaches 170°F.
2. About 30 minutes before roast is done, in 3-quart saucepan over medium heat, in 2 cups boiling water, heat carrots and next 4 ingredients to boiling; cover and cook 15 to 20 minutes until vegetables are tender-crisp. Drain vegetables, reserving liquid.
3. Place roast on warm platter; remove strings. Skim fat and measure ¼ cup liquid from pan. In same saucepan over medium heat, in ¼ cup liquid, cook mushrooms 5 minutes or until tender. Stir in flour until blended. Gradually stir in reserved vegetable liquid, then frozen peas, and cook, stirring constantly, until mixture is thickened and peas are tender. Add cooked vegetables; heat through. Reduce heat to low.
4. In small bowl, beat egg yolks slightly. Into egg yolks, stir small amount of hot sauce; slowly pour egg mixture back into the sauce, stirring rapidly to prevent lumping. Cook, stirring constantly, until mixture is thickened. (Do not boil.)
5. Serve vegetables with roast. Makes 12 to 14 servings.

FRENCH-CUT RIB PORK LOIN ROAST WITH GRAVY

2 teaspoons garlic salt
2 teaspoons paprika
pepper
1 6- to 8-rib pork loin roast, cut French style* (5 to 6 pounds)
¼ cup all-purpose flour
1 teaspoon salt
apple slices for garnish

ABOUT 3½ HOURS BEFORE SERVING:
1. Preheat oven to 325°F. On waxed paper, combine garlic salt, paprika and ¼ teaspoon pepper; rub mixture into surface of pork roast.
2. Place roast, fat side up, on rack in open roasting pan. Insert meat thermometer into center of roast, being careful not to touch bone. Roast 2½ to 3 hours until thermometer reaches 170°F.
3. With sharp knife, cut back bone from ribs; discard. Place roast on warm platter.
4. For gravy, remove rack from pan. Into 2-cup measure or large bowl, pour pan drippings (set pan aside); let stand a few seconds until fat separates from liquid.

* Ask meatman to expose about 1 inch of rib bone by cutting out meat between ribs and to loosen back bone from ribs.

Skim 3 tablespoons fat into 1-quart saucepan; skim and discard any remaining fat. Add 1/4 cup water to roasting pan; stir until brown bits are loosened; add to liquid in cup and add enough water to make 1 1/2 cups.
5. Into fat in saucepan, over medium heat, stir flour, salt and dash pepper until blended. Gradually stir in liquid mixture and cook, stirring constantly, until gravy is thickened.
6. Serve gravy with meat. Garnish meat with apple slices. Makes 10 to 12 servings.

DINNER-PARTY ROLLED PORK ROAST

1 5- to 5 1/2-pound rolled pork double-loin roast
1 teaspoon garlic salt
1 1/2 cups bottled barbecue sauce

ABOUT 4 1/4 HOURS BEFORE SERVING:
1. Preheat oven to 325°F. Sprinkle roast with garlic salt.
2. Place roast on rack in open roasting pan. Insert meat thermometer in center of roast. Roast 3 1/4 to 3 3/4 hours until meat thermometer reaches 170°F. During last 30 minutes, generously brush roast with 1 cup barbecue sauce.
3. Place meat on warm platter and let stand 15 minutes for easier carving; remove strings.
4. Meanwhile, for gravy: Skim fat from liquid in pan, leaving liquid and brown bits. Stir in 1 cup water and remaining 1/2 cup barbecue sauce; heat over medium heat, stirring to loosen brown bits; serve as gravy with roast. Makes 12 to 15 servings.

WINE-MARINATED PORK ROAST

1 3-pound rolled pork loin roast
1 garlic clove, halved
1 1/2 teaspoons salt
1 teaspoon paprika
1/2 teaspoon pepper
1 cup dry white wine
1/2 cup chicken broth
1 4-ounce jar diced pimentos, drained

DAY BEFORE SERVING:
Rub pork roast with cut edges of garlic, salt, paprika and pepper. Place in a shallow baking dish; pour wine over roast. Cover and refrigerate, turning meat occasionally.

ABOUT 2 3/4 HOURS BEFORE SERVING:
Preheat oven to 325°F. Place roast on rack in open roasting pan; reserve marinade. Insert meat thermometer into center of roast. Roast meat about 2 1/4 hours or until meat thermometer reaches 170°F. Place roast on warm platter; remove strings.

For sauce: Remove rack and pour off all but 2 tablespoons drippings from pan; strain marinade and stir into drippings with chicken broth and pimentos. Over high heat, heat mixture to boiling. Reduce heat to medium; cook 5 minutes to blend flavors, stirring occasionally. Serve sauce with roast. Makes 10 to 12 servings.

PORK SHOULDER ROAST WITH RHUBARB

1 1/2 teaspoons salt
1/2 teaspoon ginger
1/8 teaspoon pepper
1 4 1/2- to 5-pound rolled Boston pork shoulder roast
orange juice
3 1/2 pounds rhubarb, cut into large chunks
1 cup sugar

ABOUT 3 1/2 HOURS BEFORE SERVING:
1. Preheat oven to 325°F. In cup, combine salt, ginger and pepper; rub into surface of roast.
2. Place pork roast, fat side up, on rack in open roasting pan. Insert meat thermometer into center of roast. Roast about 3 hours or until meat reaches 170°F., basting occasionally with 1/2 cup orange juice.
3. Meanwhile, in 3-quart saucepan, over medium heat, heat rhubarb, sugar and 4 teaspoons orange juice to boiling. Reduce heat to low; simmer 3 to 5 minutes until rhubarb is just tender and not mushy, stirring occasionally. Remove from heat; cover and let stand 10 minutes.
4. Place roast on warm platter. Let stand 15 minutes for easier carving; remove strings. With slotted spoon, place rhubarb on platter around roast. (Serve rhubarb juice with some orange juice another day.) Makes 12 to 14 servings.

Pork Tenderloin

GLAZED PORK TENDERLOIN ROAST

1 medium lemon
1 cup apple jelly
2½ teaspoons salt
¼ teaspoon pepper
2 pork tenderloins (each about 1 pound)

ABOUT 1½ HOURS BEFORE SERVING:
Preheat oven to 325°F. Shred enough lemon peel to make 4 teaspoons; squeeze juice from lemon to make 1 teaspoon. In small saucepan over low heat, heat lemon peel and juice, apple jelly, salt and pepper until jelly melts, stirring occasionally.

Place tenderloins on rack in open roasting pan, tucking ends under to make roasts of uniform thickness. Insert meat thermometer on an angle, if necessary, into center of one tenderloin. Roast 1 hour or until thermometer reaches 170°F., brushing meat occasionally with some apple glaze. With knife slanting, carve meat into thin slices. Serve remaining glaze as sauce. Makes 6 to 8 servings.

BREADED PORK TENDERLOIN

1 pork tenderloin (about ¾ pound)
1 egg
½ teaspoon salt
¼ teaspoon rosemary, crushed
dash pepper
¾ cup dried bread crumbs
3 tablespoons salad oil

ABOUT 25 MINUTES BEFORE SERVING:
With sharp knife, cut tenderloin lengthwise almost in half, being careful not to cut all the way through. Open and flatten to "butterfly." On cutting board, with meat mallet or dull edge of French knife, pound meat to about ¼-inch thickness; cut into 3 serving pieces.

In pie plate, with fork, beat egg with 2 tablespoons water, salt, rosemary and pepper. On waxed paper, place bread crumbs. With tongs, dip meat into egg mixture, turning to coat both sides, then dip in crumbs. Repeat until each piece is coated twice.

In 12-inch skillet over medium-high heat, in hot salad oil, cook meat until well browned and fork-tender, about 10 minutes, turning once. Makes 3 servings.

PAN-FRIED BREADED PORK-TENDERLOIN PATTIES: Use about *¾ pound pork-tenderloin slices,* each cut about ½ inch thick. Pound slices to ¼-inch thickness as above; coat with egg mixture and crumbs and fry as above, turning occasionally.

BRAISED BREADED PORK-TENDERLOIN PATTIES: Use about *¾ pound pork-tenderloin slices,* each cut about ½ inch thick. Omit pounding but coat with egg mixture and crumbs as above; fry until just golden on both sides. Reduce heat to low; cover and cook until well done, about 15 minutes.

STIR-FRIED PORK AND VEGETABLES

¼ cup soy sauce
1 tablespoon dry sherry
2½ teaspoons cornstarch
1¼ teaspoons sugar
½ teaspoon minced fresh ginger or ¼ teaspoon ginger
2 pork tenderloins, thinly sliced* (each about ¾ pound)
salad oil
1 pound asparagus or ½ bunch broccoli, cut into bite-size pieces
½ pound mushrooms, sliced
¼ teaspoon salt

ABOUT 30 MINUTES BEFORE SERVING:
In medium bowl, mix well first 5 ingredients; add pork and toss lightly to coat.

In Dutch oven or 12-inch skillet over high heat, in ¼ cup hot salad oil, cook asparagus, mushrooms and salt, stirring quickly and frequently (stir-frying) until vegetables are coated; add 2 tablespoons water and stir-fry until asparagus is tender-crisp. Place vegetables and liquid on heated platter; keep warm.

In same Dutch oven over high heat, heat 6 more tablespoons salad oil until very hot; add meat mixture and stir-fry until meat loses pink color, about 2 minutes. Return vegetables to Dutch oven and stir-fry until heated through. Makes 6 servings.

* Meat will be easier to slice if it is partially frozen about 1½ hours ahead.

CREOLE PORK TENDERLOINS

2 pork tenderloins (each about 1 pound)
10 bacon slices
1 medium green pepper, coarsely chopped
1 medium onion, coarsely chopped
1 8-ounce can tomato sauce
2 tablespoons light brown sugar
4 teaspoons lemon juice
2 teaspoons seasoned salt
¼ teaspoon pepper

ABOUT 1¾ HOURS BEFORE SERVING:

1. Preheat oven to 325°F. With sharp knife, cut each tenderloin lengthwise almost in half, being careful not to cut through bottom. With meat mallet, dull edge of French knife or edge of saucer, pound meat to ½-inch thickness.
2. In 12-inch skillet over medium heat, cook bacon slices just until limp, about 4 minutes; with tongs, place bacon on paper towels; set aside.
3. In same skillet, in bacon drippings, over medium heat, cook green pepper and onion until tender, about 5 minutes; stir in remaining ingredients and cook until heated through, stirring occasionally. Spoon mixture into centers of tenderloins. Wrap bacon spiral-fashion around tenderloins, securing with toothpicks.
4. Place tenderloins on rack in open roasting pan and bake about 1 hour or until meat is fork-tender. Place meat on warm platter; remove toothpicks. Cut meat into thin slices. Makes about 8 servings.

Pork Chops and Steaks

PORK CHOPS IN VERMOUTH

8 rib, loin or top-loin pork chops, each cut about 1½ inches thick
½ cup dry vermouth or dry white wine
¾ teaspoon salt
dash pepper
1 tablespoon all-purpose flour

ABOUT 1 HOUR BEFORE SERVING:

Preheat oven to 325°F. Trim a piece of fat from edge of a pork chop. In 12-inch skillet with ovenproof handle over medium-high heat, rub piece of fat over bottom of skillet to grease it well; discard fat.

Add chops and cook until well browned, about 10 minutes. Add vermouth, salt and pepper. Cover and bake 45 minutes or until chops are fork-tender. Place chops on warm platter; keep warm.

For sauce, in small bowl, blend flour and ¼ cup water until smooth; gradually stir into hot liquid in skillet and cook over medium heat, stirring constantly, until mixture is thickened. Serve sauce over chops. Makes 8 servings.

PORK CHOPS IN ORANGE SAUCE

4 to 6 blade, rib, loin or sirloin pork chops, each cut about 1 inch thick
all-purpose flour
¾ cup orange juice
1½ to 2 teaspoons seasoned salt
1½ teaspoons sugar
1 teaspoon shredded orange peel
¾ teaspoon paprika
½ teaspoon pepper
6 whole cloves
4 to 6 thin orange slices for garnish

ABOUT 1¾ HOURS BEFORE SERVING:

1. Trim piece of fat from edge of a pork chop. On waxed paper, coat pork chops with about 2 tablespoons flour.
2. In 10- or 12-inch skillet over medium-high heat, rub piece of fat over bottom of skillet to grease it well; discard fat. Add chops and cook until well browned on both sides. In cup, stir orange juice with remaining ingredients except orange slices; pour over chops; heat to boiling. Reduce heat to low; cover and simmer about 50 minutes or until chops are fork-tender, turning occasionally. During last five minutes of cooking time, add orange slices.
3. With tongs, place chops and orange slices on warm platter. Pour liquid from skillet into 1-cup measure; spoon fat from liquid and discard cloves. Add water to make 1 cup liquid, if necessary. Return liquid to skillet.
4. In cup, blend 1 tablespoon flour and 2 tablespoons cold water until smooth; gradually stir into liquid in skillet and cook over medium heat, stirring, until thickened; serve with chops. Makes 4 to 6 servings.

SKILLET-BRAISED PORK CHOPS

4 to 6 blade, rib, loin, sirloin, butterfly or top-loin pork chops,* each cut ¾ to 1 inch thick
½ teaspoon salt
¼ teaspoon pepper

ABOUT 1 HOUR BEFORE SERVING:
Trim piece of fat from edge of a pork chop. In 10- or 12-inch skillet over medium-high heat, rub piece of fat over bottom of skillet to grease it well; discard fat.

Add chops and cook until browned on both sides. Sprinkle chops with salt and pepper; add ½ cup water. Reduce heat to low; cover and simmer 45 minutes or until meat is fork-tender. Skim any fat from pan liquid and spoon pan liquid over chops. Makes 4 to 6 servings.

* Or, use *1 to 1½ pounds pork blade or arm steaks.*

OVEN-BRAISED: Preheat oven to 350°F. Using skillet with ovenproof handle, prepare chops as above but instead of simmering on range, cover skillet and bake for 45 minutes or until meat is fork-tender.

PAN GRAVY: In cup, blend *¼ cup water* and *1 tablespoon all-purpose flour* until smooth. Remove chops from skillet; skim off fat, leaving pan liquid; gradually stir in flour mixture and cook over medium heat, stirring constantly, until mixture is thickened. Serve gravy with chops.

BRAISED PORK-CHOP VARIATIONS

Prepare Skillet-Braised Pork Chops as above but, after browning chops, use one of these variations.

APPLE: Substitute *½ cup apple juice* for water and increase salt to ¾ teaspoon. During last 5 minutes, top chops with *4 to 6 thick cooking-apple slices.*

BEEF-BOUILLON: Use only ¼ teaspoon salt; add *1 beef-bouillon cube* with water.

CRANBERRY-ORANGE RELISH: Substitute *1 cup cranberry-orange relish* for water; add a *dash of mace.*

GARDEN: Substitute *½ cup cocktail vegetable juice* for water. During last 5 minutes, top chops with *4 to 6 thin green-pepper rings* and *4 to 6 thin onion slices.*

MUSHROOM-BASIL: Omit pepper; instead of water, substitute liquid drained from *one 4-ounce can mushroom slices,* adding water to equal ½ cup; add *½ teaspoon basil* and *1 teaspoon Worcestershire* with liquid. During last 5 minutes, add mushrooms.

ORANGE-GARLIC: Substitute *½ cup orange juice* for water and increase salt to ¾ teaspoon. Add *1 small garlic clove* with juice; discard garlic before serving.

ORANGE-RAISIN: Use only ¼ cup water and add *¼ cup orange juice, ⅓ cup golden raisins* and *1 tablespoon lemon juice.* During last 5 minutes, top chops with *2 or 3 orange slices,* halved.

PEACH-CHILI SAUCE: Substitute ¼ cup syrup drained from *one 16-ounce can cling-peach halves, ¼ cup chili sauce* and *2 tablespoons lemon juice* for water. During last 5 minutes, add peach halves.

PINEAPPLE-CLOVE: Instead of water, use liquid drained from *one 8- or 8¼-ounce can pineapple slices,* adding water to equal ½ cup; add *6 whole cloves* with liquid; top chops with pineapple slices. Remove cloves before serving.

PLUM: Substitute ⅓ cup syrup drained from *one 17-ounce can purple plums* and *3 tablespoons cider vinegar* for water. During last 5 minutes, add plums.

TOMATO-THYME: Add *⅛ teaspoon thyme leaves,* crushed, with water. During last 5 minutes, top chops with *4 to 6 thick tomato slices* and sprinkle with *salt.*

THIN PORK CHOPS ORIENTALE

½ cup soy sauce
¼ cup sake or dry sherry
¼ cup salad oil
1 garlic clove, crushed
1 teaspoon ginger
1½ pounds thinly sliced pork loin chops, each cut about ½ inch thick

ABOUT 4¼ HOURS AHEAD OR EARLY IN DAY:
In shallow baking dish, for marinade, combine first 5 ingredients. Add pork chops and

turn over to coat with marinade. Cover and refrigerate at least 4 hours, turning meat occasionally.

ABOUT 15 MINUTES BEFORE SERVING:
With tongs, remove chops from marinade and drain slightly. Trim piece of fat from edge of a pork chop. In 10-inch skillet over medium-high heat, rub piece of fat over bottom of skillet to grease it well; discard fat. Add chops and cook, a few at a time, until well-browned and fork-tender, about 5 minutes, turning once. Makes 6 servings.

FRUIT-STUFFED PORK CHOPS

4 rib or top-loin pork chops, each cut about 1½ inches thick*
1 small red apple, cored and chopped
¼ cup dark seedless raisins
¼ cup minced celery
1 tablespoon minced onion
⅛ teaspoon ginger
1 teaspoon paprika
salt and pepper
¼ cup apple juice or cider
2 tablespoons all-purpose flour
½ teaspoon bottled sauce for gravy
hot cooked rice for 4 servings

ABOUT 1¾ HOURS BEFORE SERVING:
1. Preheat oven to 350°F. With sharp knife, beginning at the fat side, halve pork chops horizontally to bone to form a pocket.
2. In small bowl, for stuffing, combine apple, raisins, celery, onion and ginger. Stuff chops; place in 9″ by 9″ metal baking pan.
3. Sprinkle chops with paprika, salt and pepper; pour apple juice over chops. Cover pan with foil or lid and bake 1 hour and 15 minutes or until fork-tender.
4. Place chops on warm platter; spoon any fat from pan liquid. In cup, blend flour and ¼ cup water until smooth; gradually stir into hot liquid in baking pan and cook over medium heat, stirring constantly, until mixture is thickened. Stir in bottled sauce for gravy. Serve chops with rice and gravy. Makes 4 servings.

*Or, use 8 rib or top-loin pork chops, cut ½ inch thick. Top one chop with some stuffing. Place second chop on top and fasten chops together with toothpicks; repeat with remaining chops and stuffing.

PORK CHOPS SORRENTO

6 rib, top-loin or loin pork chops, each cut about ¾ to 1 inch thick
1 8-ounce can tomato sauce with mushrooms
1 small green pepper, cut in strips
½ teaspoon oregano leaves
1 8-ounce package mozzarella cheese, cut in 6 slices

ABOUT 1 HOUR BEFORE SERVING:
Trim piece of fat from edge of a chop. In 12-inch skillet over medium-high heat, rub piece of fat over bottom of skillet to grease it well; discard fat. Add chops and cook until browned on both sides. Add tomato sauce, green pepper and oregano.

Reduce heat to low; cover and simmer 45 minutes or until meat is fork-tender. During last 5 minutes, top each chop with a slice of cheese. Makes 6 servings.

BUTTERFLY CHOPS IN WINE SAUCE

6 butterfly pork chops, each cut about 1 inch thick
¼ pound mushrooms, thickly sliced
½ cup rosé
1½ teaspoons salt
dash pepper
3 tablespoons all-purpose flour
½ cup heavy or whipping cream
4 cups hot cooked rice or noodles

ABOUT 1 HOUR BEFORE SERVING:
Trim piece of fat from edge of a pork chop. In 12-inch skillet over medium-high heat, rub piece of fat over bottom of skillet to grease it well; discard fat.

Add chops and cook until browned on both sides, about 10 minutes. Add mushrooms, rosé, salt and pepper. Reduce heat to low; cover and simmer 40 to 45 minutes until pork chops are fork-tender.

Meanwhile, in cup, blend flour and cream until smooth. Place chops on warm platter. Over medium heat, gradually stir cream mixture into pan liquid and cook, stirring constantly, until mixture is thickened. Serve sauce over chops and rice. Makes 6 servings.

BROILED PORK CHOPS WITH CREAM-OLIVE SAUCE

6 pork chops, each cut about 1 inch thick
1 teaspoon salt
¼ teaspoon pepper
½ cup sour cream
2 tablespoons salad olives or chopped pimento-stuffed olives
1 tablespoon dry sherry
¼ teaspoon marjoram leaves
dash ginger

ABOUT 45 MINUTES BEFORE SERVING:
Preheat broiler if manufacturer directs. Place pork chops on greased rack in broiling pan; sprinkle with salt and pepper. Broil 25 to 30 minutes until well done, turning once.

Meanwhile, in heavy, small saucepan over low heat, heat sour cream and remaining ingredients until just heated through, stirring constantly. Serve sour-cream sauce over pork chops. Makes 6 servings.

BAKED STUFFED PORK CHOPS

8 rib pork chops, each cut about 1½ inches thick
2 tablespoons butter or margarine
¼ cup minced celery
2 tablespoons minced green onions
½ small garlic clove, minced
2 cups cubed rye bread with caraway seed (about 3 slices)
1 egg
salt
pepper
canned spiced peaches for garnish
Gravy for Roast Meat (page 65)

ABOUT 2 HOURS BEFORE SERVING:
Preheat oven to 325°F. With sharp knife, next to bone, cut meat of each pork chop horizontally to form a pocket.

In 2-quart saucepan over medium heat, in hot butter or margarine, cook celery, green onions and garlic until tender, about 5 minutes. Remove from heat; stir in bread, egg and ¼ teaspoon salt until well mixed. Stuff each chop with stuffing. Sprinkle meat on both sides with salt and pepper.

On rack in open roasting pan, arrange pork chops in one layer. Bake 1 hour and 15 minutes or until chops are fork-tender. Arrange pork chops on warm platter; keep warm; garnish with spiced peaches. Prepare gravy, using chicken broth for liquid. Spoon some gravy over chops and serve rest in gravy boat. Makes 8 servings.

MARINATED PORK CUBE STEAKS

½ cup soy sauce
2 tablespoons sugar
2 teaspoons ginger
1 garlic clove, halved
8 pork cube steaks (about 2½ pounds)
3 tablespoons salad oil
tomato wedges for garnish

EARLY IN DAY:
In 12″ by 8″ baking pan, combine ¼ cup water and first 4 ingredients. Add cube steaks, turning to coat well. Cover and refrigerate, turning occasionally.

ABOUT 15 MINUTES BEFORE SERVING:
In 12-inch skillet over medium-high heat, in hot salad oil, cook steaks, a few at a time, until well browned, turning once. Place steaks on warm platter; pour pan liquid over steaks. Garnish with tomato wedges. Makes 8 servings.

FRUITED FRESH PORK STEAK

1 1½-pound pork leg steak (or blade or arm pork steaks), ¾ to 1 inch thick
1 teaspoon salt
⅛ teaspoon allspice
⅛ teaspoon nutmeg
dash pepper
1 cup apple juice
1 8-ounce package mixed dried fruits
1 tablespoon all-purpose flour

ABOUT 1½ HOURS BEFORE SERVING:
Preheat oven to 350°F. Trim piece of fat from edge of leg steak. In 12-inch skillet with ovenproof handle over medium-high heat, heat piece of fat until lightly browned, rubbing fat over bottom of skillet to grease it; discard fat.

Add steak and cook until lightly browned on both sides. Add remaining ingredients except flour. Cover and bake 1 hour and 15 minutes or until steak is fork-tender.

In cup, blend flour and ¼ cup water until smooth. Place steak on warm platter. With slotted spoon, place fruit on steak. Skim fat from pan liquid. Gradually stir flour mixture into pan liquid; cook over medium heat, stirring, until thickened. Serve gravy with meat and fruit. Makes 6 servings.

BARBECUED PORK IN BUNS

2 tablespoons salad oil
6 pork sirloin cutlets, each cut about ¼ inch thick (about 1½ pounds)
1 teaspoon salt
¼ teaspoon pepper
6 hamburger buns, split and toasted
½ cup catchup
3 tablespoons molasses
1 tablespoon lemon juice

ABOUT 20 MINUTES BEFORE SERVING:
In 12-inch skillet over medium-high heat, in hot salad oil, cook pork cutlets until well browned, turning once and sprinkling with salt and pepper. With tongs, place cutlets in buns; keep warm.

Reduce heat to medium; into drippings in skillet, stir catchup, molasses and lemon juice and heat to boiling, stirring constantly. Spoon some sauce over meat in each bun. Makes 6 servings.

Spareribs and Country Ribs

MARINATED COUNTRY RIBS

1 11-ounce can mandarin orange sections
½ cup soy sauce
¼ cup salad oil
¼ cup chopped crystallized ginger
1 medium onion, quartered
4 pounds pork country ribs or back ribs

DAY BEFORE SERVING:
For marinade, in covered blender container, place mandarin orange sections with their liquid and next 4 ingredients; blend at high speed until mixture is smooth.

Cut ribs next to bones to make individual servings; place in 12″ by 8″ baking dish and pour marinade over ribs. Cover and refrigerate, turning meat occasionally.

ABOUT 2 HOURS AND 15 MINUTES AHEAD:
Preheat oven to 350°F. With tongs, arrange meat, fat side up, on rack in open roasting pan; reserve marinade. Bake 1 hour, turning meat once. Brush meat generously with reserved marinade and bake 1 hour longer or until fork-tender, turning and basting meat occasionally. Makes 4 or 5 servings.

PLUM-SAUCED SPARERIBS

8 to 10 pounds pork spareribs
1 tablespoon salt
2 tablespoons butter or margarine
1 medium onion, chopped
1 17-ounce can purple plums
1 6-ounce can frozen lemonade concentrate, thawed
¼ cup chili sauce
¼ cup soy sauce
1 teaspoon ground ginger
2 teaspoons prepared mustard
1 teaspoon Worcestershire
2 drops hot pepper sauce

ABOUT 3 HOURS BEFORE SERVING:
Cut spareribs into 2- or 3-rib portions. In large saucepot place meat, salt and enough hot water to cover meat. Over high heat, heat to boiling. Reduce heat to low; cover and simmer 1½ hours; drain. Arrange meat, fat side up, on rack in open roasting pan.

Meanwhile, in 2-quart saucepan over medium heat, in hot butter or margarine, cook onion until tender. Pour liquid from plums into blender container; remove pits from plums and add plums to container; cover and blend at low speed until smooth. (Or, force plums through food mill or coarse sieve.) Add plum mixture, undiluted lemonade concentrate and remaining ingredients to saucepan and simmer over low heat 15 minutes, stirring occasionally.

Preheat oven to 350°F. Brush some plum sauce over meat. Bake 1 hour or until fork-tender, turning and brushing meat occasionally. Serve leftover sauce with meat. Makes 10 to 12 servings.

PORK BACK RIBS WITH SAUERKRAUT

2½ pounds pork back ribs
1 tablespoon salad oil
1 12-ounce can beer
salt
4 cups well-drained sauerkraut (2 16-ounce bags)
2 tablespoons dark brown sugar
chopped parsley for garnish

ABOUT 2¼ HOURS BEFORE SERVING:
Cut back ribs into 2- or 3-rib portions. In 12-inch skillet over medium-high heat, in hot salad oil, cook ribs, a few pieces at a time, until well browned, removing pieces as they brown. Pour off drippings.

Return all ribs to skillet; add beer and ½ teaspoon salt; heat to boiling. Reduce heat to low; cover and simmer 30 minutes. Stir in sauerkraut, brown sugar and ½ teaspoon salt. Cover and simmer 1 hour longer or until ribs are tender, stirring occasionally. Garnish with parsley. Makes 6 servings.

BARBECUED SPARERIBS WITH MELON

4 pounds pork spareribs or back ribs
maple syrup
¼ cup catchup
3 tablespoons lemon juice
¼ teaspoon curry powder
¼ teaspoon garlic salt
⅛ teaspoon ground ginger
2 tablespoons chopped chutney
2 tablespoons butter or margarine
1 medium cantaloupe

ABOUT 2¼ HOURS BEFORE SERVING:
Preheat oven to 350°F. Cut meat into 2- or 3-rib portions. Arrange meat, fat side up, on rack in open roasting pan; bake 1 hour.

For sauce, in small bowl, combine ¼ cup maple syrup, next 5 ingredients and 1 tablespoon of the chutney. Brush meat with sauce and bake 1 hour longer or until fork-tender, turning and brushing meat occasionally with sauce.

Meanwhile, in 2-quart saucepan over low heat, melt butter or margarine; add 1 tablespoon maple syrup and remaining chutney; set aside. Peel and seed melon and cut into 1-inch wedges. Coat melon wedges in butter mixture. During last 15 minutes of baking time, arrange melon over meat. Makes 4 servings.

WITH PAPAYA: Instead of melon, peel and cut *2 medium papayas* into wedges; coat in butter mixture and heat as above.

OVEN-BARBECUED SPARERIBS: Bake spareribs or back ribs as above but omit sauce and melon. After one hour baking time, baste with sauce for *Oven-Barbecued Chicken* (page 180) or 1½ cups bottled barbecue sauce.

Pork Hocks and Neck Bones

HOCKS AND NAVY-BEAN STEW

4 fresh pork hocks
2 tablespoons salt
¼ teaspoon pepper
2 garlic cloves, crushed
1 bay leaf
3 cups dry navy beans (1½ 16-ounce packages)
4 whole cloves
1 pound small white onions (about 12)
1 pound carrots, cut in chunks
2 tablespoons lemon juice

ABOUT 3½ HOURS BEFORE SERVING:
1. In 8-quart saucepot, place first 5 ingredients and 5 cups hot water; over high heat, heat to boiling. Reduce heat to low; cover and simmer 1½ hours, occasionally skimming fat from liquid.
2. Meanwhile, rinse navy beans in running cold water, discarding any small stones, discolored or shriveled pieces. In 4-quart saucepan over high heat, in 9 cups boiling water, heat beans to boiling; boil 2 minutes. Remove pan from heat; cover and let soak 1 hour; drain. Add beans to hocks and continue simmering 30 minutes.
3. Stick cloves into one onion (for easy removal later). Add all onions and carrots to liquid; over high heat, heat to boiling. Reduce heat to low; cover and simmer 1 hour longer or until meat and vegetables are fork-tender. Add lemon juice last 15 minutes of cooking time.
4. Discard bay leaf and cloves. Place hocks on cutting board and, with sharp knife or kitchen shears, remove skin and bones and discard; add meat to beans. Makes about 12 cups or 6 servings.

PORK NECK BONES AND KRAUT

5 pounds pork neck bones
1 large onion, chopped
2 teaspoons salt
½ teaspoon pepper
2 27-ounce cans sauerkraut, drained

ABOUT 2½ HOURS BEFORE SERVING:
In Dutch oven over high heat, heat to boiling first 4 ingredients and 3 cups hot water. Reduce heat to low; cover and simmer 1½ hours, stirring occasionally.

Stir in sauerkraut; cover and continue cooking 30 minutes or until meat is fork-tender. Remove cover and increase heat to high; cook until water is almost cooked away, about 10 minutes, stirring often. Serve on warm platter. Makes 5 or 6 servings.

Pork Stew Meat

PORK AND VEGETABLE KABOBS

1 bunch small beets
salt
½ cup apple juice
½ cup dark corn syrup
¼ cup salad oil
1 tablespoon rosemary, crushed
1 tablespoon cider vinegar
1 pound pork stew meat, cut into 1½-inch chunks
2 medium zucchini
2 medium ears corn

ABOUT 1½ HOURS BEFORE SERVING:
In 1-quart saucepan over medium heat, in 1 inch boiling water, heat unpeeled beets and 1 teaspoon salt to boiling; cover and cook 15 minutes; drain. Peel beets and cut in halves.

Meanwhile, in medium bowl, combine apple juice, corn syrup, oil, rosemary, vinegar and 2 teaspoons salt; stir in pork. Cut zucchini and corn into 1-inch chunks.

Preheat broiler if manufacturer directs. On four 12-inch skewers, alternately arrange vegetables and pork, reserving apple-juice mixture. About 7 to 9 inches from source of heat (or at 450°F.) broil kabobs about 25 minutes until pork is well done and vegetables are tender, basting with juice mixture and turning occasionally. Makes 4 servings.

CALYPSO PORK STEW

2 pounds pork stew meat, cut into 1½-inch chunks
1 1½-pound canned ham, cut into 1½-inch chunks
¼ cup instant minced onion
1 teaspoon salt
1 bay leaf
2 cups cubed potatoes
2 yellow straightneck squash, cubed
⅓ cup chopped parsley
¼ cup lime juice
1 teaspoon coriander seed
½ teaspoon pepper
3 underripe bananas or plantains, cut into 1-inch chunks

ABOUT 2 HOURS BEFORE SERVING:
In 7-quart saucepot over high heat, heat first 5 ingredients and 2 cups water to boiling. Reduce heat to low; cover and simmer 1 hour. Add remaining ingredients except bananas; cook 30 minutes longer or until pork and squash are fork-tender. Add bananas and heat 10 minutes longer. Discard bay leaf. Makes 10 to 12 servings.

PAPRIKA PORK STEW

3 tablespoons salad oil
2 medium onions, sliced
1 garlic clove, minced
3 pounds pork stew meat, cut into 1½-inch chunks
1 cup sour cream or sour half-and-half
2 teaspoons salt
1 teaspoon paprika
2 tablespoons all-purpose flour
1 16-ounce package spinach noodles, cooked

ABOUT 2 HOURS BEFORE SERVING:
In Dutch oven over medium-high heat, in hot salad oil, cook onions and garlic until golden; push to one side of pan. Add stew meat and cook until well browned. In small bowl, combine sour cream, salt, paprika and 1 cup water; pour over meat and heat just to simmering. Reduce heat to low; cover; cook 1½ hours or until tender.

In cup, blend flour with ¼ cup water until smooth; gradually stir into hot mixture. Cook over medium heat, stirring constantly, until slightly thickened; serve over noodles. Makes 8 to 10 servings.

SMOKED PORK

Cuts of smoked pork include hams and ham slices, smoked pork loin and chops, smoked picnics and shoulder rolls, Canadian-style bacon, bacon and many forms of sausages. Pork hocks may also be smoked.

Smoked Hams and Picnics

Ham is the hind leg of pork; the picnic comes from the pork shoulder. These cuts should be labeled to identify them as *fully cooked* or *cook-before-eating;* if unlabeled, prepare as cook-before-eating ham.

Fully cooked hams: Most hams available are fully cooked and many are skinless. They may be served without further cooking, but heating to an internal temperature of 140°F. improves their flavor and texture. They are available in these styles:

Bone-in: When whole, these hams weigh from 10 to 16 pounds. Often they're cut in half and are sold as butt-half or shank-half ham. However, when a few center slices are cut from the two halves to be sold separately, the remainders are then called butt and shank portions (or ends) to indicate center slices have been removed.

Partially boned: These hams are either shankless or semi-boneless. Shankless hams have the shank bone removed and are slightly oval in shape. Semi-boneless hams have both shank bone and aitchbone removed; only the leg bone is left.

Boneless: Called "rolled," "shaped" or "formed" hams, they are sold whole, weighing 7 to 14 pounds; in halves, quarters, pieces and slices or steaks. Most fully cooked hams are boneless.

Canned hams: Always boneless and fully cooked, these weigh from one to 13 pounds. They may be unsmoked or smoked; some also are flavored and others are glazed.

Boiled ham: A fully cooked ham that comes sliced, it is usually prepackaged.

Prosciutto: An Italian-style pressed ham, it has a characteristic dark reddish color and salty flavor. It's sold thinly sliced; in some areas it comes prepackaged.

Cook-before-eating hams: Hams that need to be cooked before eating are usually available bone-in; a few come partially boned or semi-boneless. Cook-before-eating hams should be cooked to an internal temperature of 160°F.; the cured but unsmoked "Scotch" or corned ham, to 170°F.

Country hams, also known as "Smithfield," "Tennessee," "Kentucky" and "Virginia" hams, are usually heavily cured and smoked. They're sold whole with the bones in. They must be soaked and precooked (simmered) before baking, unless label directs otherwise. When labeled country-style, the ham is produced outside of the specific geographic location; for example, "Smithfield country-style" means the ham has been processed in much the same way as a Smithfield ham but not necessarily in Smithfield, Virginia. Some markets sell fully cooked, sliced "Smithfield-style" ham.

Smoked picnics: These are processed in the same way as hams; they can be baked and glazed like ham. Picnics weigh 5 to 8 pounds. Some picnics are available fully cooked (heat to 140°F.); others must be cooked to 170°F. before eating. Be sure to check label; if unlabeled, prepare smoked picnics as for cook-before-eating type.

How to buy hams and picnics: Always buy these meats from a refrigerated case, unless selecting a small canned ham labeled to indicate that refrigeration is not necessary.

Look for a label that indicates whether ham is ready-to-eat or cook-before-eating. Whole hams and picnics generally are so labeled by the meat packer; however, the supermarket may remove this label, especially when the meat is cut into halves or portions. If you're unsure whether a ham or picnic is fully cooked, prepare it as you would a cook-before-eating type.

"Water Added" on a label merely means that the meat has absorbed extra water from the curing process. This moisture produces a juicier ham or picnic.

How to cook: These cuts are most often baked; smoked picnics also can be cooked in liquid.

To roast (bake): Check timetable below to see approximately how long ham or picnic will take; plan meat to be done about

15 minutes before serving so it can "set" for easier carving. If meat is to be glazed, plan to start glazing it about half an hour before it's done.

Preheat oven to 325°F. Place meat, fat side up, on rack in open roasting pan; insert meat thermometer so it is centered in the thickest part of the meat, making sure the pointed end is not resting on bone or in fat. Do not cover; do not add water. Roast until meat thermometer reaches 160°F. for cook-before-eating hams and picnics, or 140°F. for fully cooked hams and picnics or canned hams.

During last 30 minutes of roasting time, spread meat with one of glazes at right.

When done, remove meat from oven and let stand. To carve, see pages 67–68.

If you like a decorated ham, score the surface lightly in diamond pattern and insert a whole clove in center of each diamond before baking; glaze during last 30 minutes of baking time.

TIMETABLE FOR BAKING FULLY COOKED HAMS AND PICNICS AT 325°F.

For general directions, see To Roast, page 116

Weight of Cut (pounds)	*Approximate Hours* to Reach 140°F.*
Boneless ham	
3 to 5 (half)	1½ to 1¾
7 to 10 (whole)	2½ to 3
10 to 12	3 to 3½
12 to 14	3½ to 4
Bone-in ham	
5 to 7 (half)	1½ to 1¾
10 to 13 (whole)	3 to 3½
13 to 16 (whole)	3½ to 4
Semi-boneless ham	
4 to 6 (half)	1¾ to 2½
10 to 12 (whole)	3 to 3½
Canned ham	
1½ to 3	1 to 1½
3 to 7	1½ to 2
7 to 10	2 to 2½
10 to 13	2½ to 3
Picnic	
4 to 8	1¾ to 2¾

* Meat at refrigerator temperature, placed in oven preheated to 325°F.

TIMETABLE FOR BAKING COOK-BEFORE-EATING HAMS AND PICNICS AT 325°F.

For general directions, see To Roast, page 116

Weight of Cut (pounds)	*Approximate Hours* to Reach 160°F.*
Boneless whole ham	
8 to 11	2½ to 3¼
11 to 14	3¼ to 4
Bone-in ham	
5 to 7 (half)	3 to 3¼
10 to 12 (whole)	3½ to 4
12 to 15	4 to 4½
15 to 18	4½ to 5
18 to 22	5 to 6
Picnic	
4 to 8	2½ to 4 (cook to 170°F.)

* Meat at refrigerator temperature, placed in oven preheated to 325°F.

To cook in liquid: Cook-before-eating hams, because of their mild cure, are not usually cooked in liquid. Picnics and smoked shoulder rolls (butts) are sometimes cooked in liquid. In large saucepot, place meat and enough water to cover it. Over high heat, heat to boiling; reduce heat to low; cover; simmer until meat is tender. Drain. A picnic will take about 3½ to 4 hours; a shoulder roll 1½ to 2½ hours.

To glaze after simmering, place on rack in roasting pan and bake in oven preheated to 400°F., 15 to 30 minutes, brushing on any of Glazes, below.

Ham and Pork Glazes

Prepare a glaze below and, during last 30 minutes of roasting time, brush glaze over meat 2 or 3 times.

CURRY-ORANGE GLAZE

⅔ cup light corn syrup
1 tablespoon curry powder
1 tablespoon grated orange peel

In small bowl, with fork, stir all ingredients until blended. Makes about ⅔ cup.

PINEAPPLE GLAZE

½ cup packed light brown sugar
1½ teaspoons prepared mustard
dash ground cloves
1 8¼-ounce can crushed pineapple (1 cup)

In covered blender container at low speed, blend all ingredients until smooth. Makes about 1 cup.

ORANGE-MINCEMEAT GLAZE

½ cup drained mincemeat
¼ cup orange marmalade

In covered blender container at low speed, blend mincemeat and marmalade until smooth. Makes about ¾ cup.

PEANUT GLAZE

½ cup dark corn syrup or honey
½ cup chopped salted or unsalted peanuts

In small bowl, stir corn syrup and peanuts until blended. Makes about ¾ cup.

MELBA GLAZE

⅔ cup peach preserves
½ cup red currant jelly

In small saucepan over low heat, melt preserves and jelly until blended, stirring occasionally. Makes about 1 cup.

TOMATO-ONION GLAZE

1 tablespoon butter or margarine
2 tablespoons minced onion
1 8-ounce can tomato sauce
2 tablespoons dark brown sugar
1 teaspoon Worcestershire

In small saucepan over medium heat, in hot butter or margarine, cook onion until tender, about 3 minutes, stirring occasionally. Stir in remaining ingredients and heat to boiling. Reduce heat to low; simmer 5 minutes or until slightly thickened, stirring occasionally. Makes about 1 cup.

Baked Hams and Picnics

WHOLE SMITHFIELD HAM

DAY BEFORE SERVING:

1. Prepare *one 14-pound cook-before-eating Smithfield ham* or country-style ham as label directs, or prepare as follows:
2. Place ham, skin side down, in a saucepot large enough to hold the whole ham and add enough water to cover ham completely.* Let ham stand in water at room temperature at least 12 hours or overnight.

ABOUT 6 HOURS AHEAD OR EARLY IN DAY:

3. Discard water from ham. With vegetable brush, scrub and rinse ham well. In same saucepot, again cover ham with water; over high heat, heat to boiling. Reduce heat to low; cover and simmer about 4½ hours (allow about 20 minutes per pound) or until the bone on small end of ham (shank bone) pokes out about one inch and feels loose.
4. Remove ham to rack in large open roasting pan; cool ham slightly until easy to handle.
5. Preheat oven to 325°F. With sharp knife, remove skin and trim some fat from ham, leaving about ¼ inch fat. Brush ham with *dark corn syrup*. Bake 15 minutes or until glazed. Serve ham warm or refrigerate to serve cold later.
6. To serve as appetizer, place ham on platter; garnish with *Bibb or Boston lettuce*. For carving, wrap small end of ham with a clean napkin. Set out *assorted crackers* and *sliced breads*, such as round milk crackers, sliced sprouted-wheat bread, party pumpernickel and rye. Let guests help themselves to ham, grasping napkin-covered end and cutting ham into paper-thin slices.

* Or, if you like, ask meatman to cut ham crosswise into 2, 3 or more pieces. Prepare desired amount of ham as above, soaking first, then allowing about 20 minutes per pound simmering time. Wrap uncooked portions of ham tightly with foil or plastic wrap; refrigerate to use up to 1 month later.

PRECOOKED SMITHFIELD HAMS: Follow label directions for baking and glazing precooked Smithfield hams.

LEFTOVER SMITHFIELD HAM

OPEN-FACE SANDWICH: Top rye, whole-wheat or other bread with paper-thin slice of ham; add slice or two of sweet onion.

ZESTY SANDWICH: Tuck very thin slice of ham into turkey or chicken sandwich.

HOT APPETIZER: Slice leftover ham paper thin; heat and serve in small hot biscuits.

MINCED TOPPING: Sprinkle 1 to 2 tablespoons minced ham over cooked vegetables or scrambled eggs.

VEGETABLE SEASONING: While cooking vegetables, add small chunk of ham to water.

CHICKEN SOUP: Add some diced ham to canned chicken soup as it heats.

HAM AND MELON: Arrange thinly sliced ham on melon wedges or other fruit to serve with breakfast, luncheon or as first course.

MAIN-DISH SALADS: Add chopped ham to macaroni, potato or rice salad.

HAM SPREAD OR DIP: Blend ground ham with cream cheese.

HEARTY SOUP: Use ham bone to make split-pea, bean or lentil soup.

FESTIVE ORANGE-CLAD HAM

1 12- to 14-pound whole fully cooked or cook-before-eating, bone-in ham
1 10-ounce jar orange marmalade
1 tablespoon prepared mustard
3 small oranges
whole cloves

ABOUT 4½ HOURS AHEAD OR EARLY IN DAY:

1. Preheat oven to 325°F. Place ham on rack in open roasting pan. Insert meat thermometer from top center of the thickest part, making sure pointed end is in center of ham and not resting on bone or fat.
2. Bake for 1½ hours; remove ham from oven and, with sharp knife, cut skin and any excess fat from ham, leaving a thin fat covering. Continue baking for 2 to 2½ hours or until internal temperature reaches 140°F. for fully cooked or 160°F. for cook-before-eating ham.
3. Meanwhile, prepare glaze: In small saucepan over low heat, heat orange marmalade and mustard until marmalade is melted. About 30 minutes before ham is done, with pastry brush, brush half of glaze evenly over ham.
4. Remove ham from oven; remove meat thermometer. Cut oranges into very thin slices and halve them; arrange in rows over ham, overlapping them slightly and fastening them with cloves. Carefully brush remaining warm glaze over orange slices. Return ham to oven and bake 10 minutes more or until orange slices are heated through. Serve warm or cold. Makes about 28 to 34 servings.

FESTIVE BONELESS HAM: Instead of whole ham, use *an 8- to 10-pound boneless fully cooked ham;* and prepare as above but bake about 3 hours until internal temperature reaches 140°F. on meat thermometer, glazing and garnishing as directed.

CELERY-TOPPED HAM WITH DRESSING

1 5-pound fully cooked, boneless half ham
1½ cups chopped celery leaves
2 tablespoons light brown sugar
Sweet Corn-Cake Dressing (below)

ABOUT 2½ HOURS BEFORE SERVING:

Preheat oven to 325°F. Place ham on rack in open roasting pan. In small bowl, combine celery leaves and brown sugar; pat mixture on top of ham. Insert meat thermometer into center of ham. Bake ham about 1¾ hours or until meat thermometer reaches 140°F. (Cover loosely with foil during baking if topping browns too rapidly.)

About 40 minutes before ham is done, prepare Sweet Corn-Cake Dressing; bake with ham. Makes about 18 servings.

SWEET CORN-CAKE DRESSING: In 1½-quart saucepan over medium heat, in *⅓ cup hot butter or margarine,* cook *2 medium onions,* diced, until tender, about 5 minutes. In 2-quart shallow baking dish, combine cooked onions, *two 7-ounce packages corn cakes,* cubed, *1 cup chopped California walnuts, ¾ cup chopped pitted prunes, ¾ cup milk, 1½ teaspoons poultry seasoning* and *1 teaspoon salt.* Cover with foil. Bake with ham 30 minutes. Makes 10 to 12 servings.

GLAZED SLICED HAM*

1 5- to 6-pound fully cooked boneless half ham
¼ cup sugar
2 tablespoons cornstarch
1½ cups orange juice
⅓ cup horseradish
2 tablespoons cider vinegar
1 tablespoon grated orange peel
¼ teaspoon salt

ABOUT 2¼ HOURS AHEAD OR EARLY IN DAY:
Preheat oven to 325°F. Insert a meat thermometer into center of ham slices. On rack in shallow roasting pan, bake ham for 2 hours or until meat thermometer reaches 140°F.

Meanwhile, in medium saucepan, stir sugar with cornstarch; add remaining ingredients and cook over medium heat, stirring occasionally, until mixture thickens and starts to boil. Remove from heat.

During last 30 minutes of baking time, brush ham occasionally with orange mixture. Serve warm or cover and refrigerate to serve later. Makes 18 to 22 servings.

* Ask meatman to cut ham into ¼-inch slices, then reassemble in original form by tying slices together with string.

BAKED HAM WITH CELERY AND CARROTS

1 5-pound fully cooked, semi-boneless half ham
½ teaspoon curry powder
1 teaspoon whole cloves
12 medium carrots, sliced
12 stalks celery, sliced
Curried Cream Sauce (below)

ABOUT 2½ HOURS BEFORE SERVING:
Preheat oven to 325°F. Rub ham with curry powder and stud with cloves; insert meat thermometer in center of ham, being careful thermometer does not touch bone or fat. Place ham in 15½" by 10½" roasting pan; arrange carrots and celery around ham. Bake about 2 hours until meat thermometer reaches 140°F. and vegetables are fork-tender, stirring vegetables occasionally during cooking to coat with pan drippings.

Place ham on warm large platter; with slotted spoon, arrange vegetables around meat. Prepare Curried Cream Sauce and serve with meat. Makes 15 to 18 servings.

CURRIED CREAM SAUCE: Into 4-cup measuring cup, drain pan drippings. Let stand a few minutes until fat separates. Spoon fat from drippings, reserving about ¼ cup fat. (Add butter or margarine if necessary.) To drippings left in cup, add enough *half-and-half* to make 3 cups liquid.

In 3-quart saucepan over medium heat, heat reserved fat; stir in *¼ cup all-purpose flour, 1 tablespoon chicken stock base* and *1½ teaspoons curry powder* until blended. Gradually stir in half-and-half mixture and cook, stirring constantly, until mixture is thickened. Just before serving, stir in *3 tablespoons medium sherry,* if you like.

BAKED HAM PLUS

DAY BEFORE SERVING:
Buy *one 6- to 7-pound fully cooked butt- or shank-half ham* and ask meatman to cut off center slice, about 1½ inches thick (about 2 pounds). Wrap and refrigerate both center cut and remaining ham piece. Plan to use 2 or 3 of the following ham recipes during the next 3 or 4 days.

BAKED HALF HAM: Preheat oven to 325°F. Bake *remaining half ham* (above) on rack in open roasting pan for about 2 hours until meat thermometer reaches 140°F. internal temperature. Wrap and refrigerate leftovers. Makes about 12 to 15 servings.

MANDARIN HAM STEAK: Score fat around edge of *1 fully cooked ham slice* (above). In large skillet over medium heat, brown ham until golden on each side. Add *1 cup orange juice;* drain liquid from *one 11-ounce can mandarin oranges* and add to ham along with *1 tablespoon cider vinegar, ¼ teaspoon allspice* and *½ cup golden raisins.* Stir ingredients until well mixed.

Reduce heat to low; cover and simmer 20 minutes, turning once. Add mandarin oranges and heat 5 minutes longer. In cup, stir *1 tablespoon cornstarch* with *2 tablespoons water* until blended. Gradually stir into pan liquid and cook, stirring constantly, until mixture is thickened. Serve sauce over ham. Makes 6 servings.

SKILLET HAM SANDWICHES: In large skillet over medium heat, cook *buttered split buns,* split sides down, until golden; set aside. In same skillet, cook *thin ham slices* until golden; serve in buns or serve open-faced.

HAM-AND-EGG SANDWICHES: Prepare Skillet Ham Sandwiches (above) but fry *eggs* in *butter or margarine* in skillet until yolks are set. Serve in buns with ham slices.

CHUNKY CHEF SALAD: Fill a salad bowl with *chicory* and *iceberg lettuce,* torn in bite-size pieces. In center, arrange *radish slices;* around radishes, arrange *Cheddar-cheese cubes, cubed ham* and *coarsely chopped hard-cooked eggs.* Serve with bottled *Thousand Island salad dressing.*

BARBECUED CANNED HAM AND PEACHES

1 3-pound canned ham
½ cup sugar
½ cup chili sauce
1 tablespoon lemon juice
2 teaspoons Worcestershire
½ teaspoon chili powder
5 medium peaches, peeled and halved

ABOUT 1¾ HOURS BEFORE SERVING:
Preheat oven to 325°F. Remove any gelatin from ham. Place ham in 12″ by 8″ baking dish; insert meat thermometer into center of ham. Bake 1 hour and 15 minutes.

Meanwhile, in 2-quart saucepan over medium heat, heat to boiling sugar, chili sauce, lemon juice, Worcestershire, chili powder and ½ cup water, stirring occasionally. Remove sauce from heat; add peaches and gently stir to coat peaches well.

Spoon peaches into baking dish and pour remaining sauce over ham. Bake ham and peaches about 20 minutes more, basting occasionally with sauce, until thermometer reaches 140°F. Place ham on warm platter; arrange peaches around it. Makes about 10 servings.

BARBECUED HAM

1 6- or 7-pound canned ham
1 cup dark corn syrup
¼ cup catchup
2 tablespoons prepared mustard
2 tablespoons cider vinegar
1 teaspoon liquid smoke (optional)

ABOUT 3 HOURS BEFORE SERVING:
Preheat oven to 325°F. Remove any gelatin from ham. Place ham on rack in open roasting pan. Insert meat thermometer into center of ham. Bake ham 2 hours or until thermometer reaches 140°F.

Meanwhile, in small bowl, for glaze, mix remaining ingredients. During last 30 minutes of baking time, spoon glaze over ham occasionally. Makes 20 to 24 servings.

CANNED HAM TROPICALE

1 5-pound canned ham
½ teaspoon whole cloves
1 10-ounce jar orange marmalade
2 tablespoons shredded orange peel
2 cups orange sections (about 3 large oranges)
5 medium bananas, cut in thick diagonal slices
2 tablespoons lemon juice
¼ cup packed light brown sugar
2 tablespoons cider vinegar

ABOUT 2 HOURS BEFORE SERVING:
Preheat oven to 325°F. Remove any gelatin from ham. Cut ham crosswise into slices about ½ inch thick, keeping slices in place. Tie ham with string to keep ham "shape." Place ham in 13″ by 9″ baking dish; insert cloves here and there between slices. Bake 1 hour and 15 minutes; remove string.

In 2½-quart saucepan over low heat, heat orange marmalade until of a syrup consistency. Remove from heat; gently toss in orange peel, orange sections, bananas and lemon juice; spoon mixture around ham. In small bowl, combine brown sugar and vinegar; brush over ham. Continue baking ham 30 minutes, basting ham and fruit occasionally. Makes about 16 to 18 servings.

OTHER FRUITS: Instead of oranges and bananas, use *3 large peaches,* quartered, and *2 medium pears,* cut in chunks.

CANNED HAM WITH PLUM GLAZE

1 8- to 10-pound canned ham*
1 17-ounce can plums
1½ cups packed light brown sugar
¾ cup orange juice
2 teaspoons grated orange peel
1 teaspoon dry mustard
¼ teaspoon ground cloves
curly endive for garnish

DAY BEFORE SERVING:
Remove any gelatin from ham. For marinade, into large bowl, drain liquid from plums; cover and refrigerate plums. Into liquid, mix 1 cup brown sugar, orange juice, orange peel, mustard and cloves. Add ham, turning over to coat with marinade. Cover and refrigerate, turning ham occasionally.

ABOUT 2¾ HOURS BEFORE SERVING:
Preheat oven to 325°F. Remove ham from marinade and place on rack in open roasting pan. Insert meat thermometer into center of ham. Bake ham for 2 hours, basting occasionally with marinade.

Remove ham from oven and score top in diamond-pattern; sprinkle with remaining ½ cup sugar; drizzle on remaining marinade. Continue baking ham 30 minutes or until internal temperature reaches 140°F.

Place ham on warm platter; garnish with reserved plums and curly endive. (Reserve drippings and marinade from bottom of pan; reheat to serve over any leftover ham next day.) Makes 30 to 36 servings.

* Or, use a 4- or 5-pound canned ham and bake only 1½ hours before scoring ham. Makes about 14 to 18 servings.

Ham Slices

Kinds to buy: Center-cut ham slices or steaks may be from either fully cooked or cook-before-eating ham and may be bone-in or boneless. Slices range from ½ to 2 inches in thickness.

How to cook: Ham slices 1 to 2 inches thick may be baked, broiled or braised; 1-inch-thick slices may also be pan-broiled; slices ½ to ¾ inch thick may be pan-broiled or broiled.

To bake: Follow recipe directions.

To broil: Preheat broiler if manufacturer directs. Slash fat edge, but do not cut into lean, of ham slice in several places to prevent curling; place slice on rack in broiling pan. Broil 2 to 3 inches from heat, until browned on both sides and done, turning once. One-inch-thick ham slices will take 16 to 20 minutes total time; ½-inch-thick slices will take 10 to 12 minutes total time.

To pan-broil: Trim piece of fat from one edge of ham slice and rub fat over bottom of skillet to grease it. Slash fat edge, but do not cut into lean, of ham slice in several places to prevent curling. In skillet over medium heat, cook ham slice until well browned on both sides, turning occasionally; pour off fat as it accumulates.

To braise: Trim piece of fat from edge of ham slice. In heavy skillet or Dutch oven over medium heat, rub fat over bottom of skillet to grease it. Add ham and cook until well browned on both sides. Add small amount of liquid—water, milk, tomato juice, wine; reduce heat to low; cover tightly and cook until ham is done.

HAM SLICE IN CUMBERLAND SAUCE

1 cup ruby port
½ cup dark seedless raisins
¼ cup red currant jelly
1 teaspoon dry mustard
½ teaspoon grated lemon peel
½ teaspoon grated orange peel (optional)
¼ teaspoon allspice
1 fully cooked ham slice, cut about 1½ inches thick (about 2½ pounds)
2 tablespoons cornstarch
¼ cup orange juice

ABOUT 1¾ HOURS BEFORE SERVING:
Preheat oven to 325°F. In small saucepan over medium heat, heat to boiling first 7 ingredients. Meanwhile, slash fat edges of ham slice; place in 10" by 6" baking dish.

In cup, blend cornstarch and orange juice until smooth; gradually stir into hot wine mixture and cook, stirring constantly, until mixture is thickened. Pour over ham slice in baking dish. Cover tightly with foil and bake 1¼ hours.

Place ham on warm platter; serve sauce in baking dish over ham. Makes 8 servings.

HAM SLICES WITH RICE STUFFING

2 tablespoons butter or margarine
½ cup sliced green onions
¼ cup minced celery
1 cup cooked rice
½ teaspoon poultry seasoning
2 fully cooked ham slices, each cut about ½ inch thick (about 2 pounds)
2 tablespoons dark corn syrup
2 teaspoons medium sherry

ABOUT 1½ HOURS BEFORE SERVING:
Preheat oven to 325°F. In 8-inch skillet over medium heat, in hot butter or margarine, cook onions and celery until tender, about 5 minutes. Stir in rice and poultry seasoning. Slash edges of ham to prevent curling. On rack in open roasting pan, place 1 ham slice; top with rice mixture. Place second ham slice over stuffing; secure with toothpicks.

Bake stuffed ham slices 1¼ hours or until heated through. Meanwhile, in cup, mix corn syrup and sherry. During last 15 minutes of baking time, brush mixture over top of ham to glaze. Remove toothpicks. Makes 8 servings.

ITALIAN-STYLE HAM STEAK

1 fully cooked ham slice, cut about 1 inch thick (about 1½ pounds)
1 tablespoon olive oil
1 small green pepper, diced
¼ cup diced onion
1 garlic clove, minced
1 8-ounce can tomatoes
⅛ teaspoon basil
½ 8-ounce package spaghetti twists or macaroni shells
1 tablespoon all-purpose flour
2 tablespoons dry red wine

ABOUT 45 MINUTES BEFORE SERVING:
Slash edges of ham slice to prevent curling. In 10-inch skillet over medium heat, in hot olive oil, brown ham slice well on both sides; remove ham. To drippings in skillet, add green pepper, onion and garlic; cook, stirring, about 5 minutes or until onion is tender. Add tomatoes and their liquid and basil. Return ham to skillet; heat to boiling. Reduce heat to low; cover and cook 20 minutes, turning ham once.

Meanwhile, cook spaghetti as label directs; drain and keep warm.

Place ham on warm platter. In cup, blend flour and wine until smooth; gradually stir into liquid in skillet and cook over medium heat, stirring constantly, until mixture is thickened. Spoon a little sauce over ham. Serve with spaghetti and pass sauce to spoon over each serving. Makes 4 servings.

CRANBERRY-STUFFED HAM SLICE

2 fully cooked ham slices, each cut about ½ inch thick (about 2 pounds)
1 14-ounce jar cranberry-orange relish
1 large orange, sectioned

ABOUT 40 MINUTES BEFORE SERVING:
Preheat oven to 325°F. In shallow baking dish, place one of ham slices; spread with relish. Top with second ham slice. Bake 30 minutes or until ham is heated through. Arrange orange sections in a row over ham. Continue baking 5 minutes to heat orange slices. Makes 6 servings.

HAM SLICES WITH CORN-BREAD STUFFING

2 fully cooked ham slices, each cut about ½ inch thick (about 2 pounds)
1 8¼-ounce can crushed pineapple
2 cups crumbled corn bread or corn muffins
1 egg
1 teaspoon instant minced onion
⅛ teaspoon rosemary, crushed
2 tablespoons light brown sugar

ABOUT 1¾ HOURS BEFORE SERVING:
Preheat oven to 325°F. Slash edges of ham slices to prevent curling. Drain pineapple, reserving ¼ cup liquid.

For stuffing, in medium bowl, mix reserved pineapple liquid, corn bread, egg, onion and rosemary.

On rack in open roasting pan, place 1 ham slice. Pat stuffing on ham and top with remaining ham slice. In small bowl, mix pineapple and brown sugar until blended; spread on top. Bake 1½ hours until stuffing is hot. Makes 8 servings.

MANHATTAN HAM SLICE

¼ cup bourbon
2 tablespoons sweet vermouth
dash aromatic bitters
1 medium orange
1 fully cooked ham slice, cut about 1 inch thick (about 2 pounds)
maraschino cherries for garnish

EARLY IN DAY OR DAY AHEAD:
In shallow baking dish, for marinade, combine bourbon, vermouth and bitters. Shred ½ teaspoon peel from orange and add to mixture. Slash edges of ham slice and add to marinade, turning to coat. Finish peeling orange and separate sections into small bowl. Cover orange sections and ham and refrigerate at least 4 hours, turning meat occasionally.

ABOUT 30 MINUTES BEFORE SERVING:
Preheat broiler if manufacturer directs. Drain ham slice, reserving marinade for basting.

Place ham slice on rack in broiling pan. Broil ham about 16 minutes or until meat is lightly browned, turning once and occasionally basting with marinade. Place ham on warm platter; cut orange sections in half and skewer with maraschino cherries on toothpicks for garnish. Makes 6 servings.

FRUIT-SAUCED HAM SLICE

6 boneless smoked ham slices, each cut about ½ inch thick (about 2 pounds)
1 cup pitted dried prunes
1 cup dried apricots
1¾ cups orange juice
¼ cup sugar
1 tablespoon cornstarch

ABOUT 30 MINUTES BEFORE SERVING:
Trim piece of fat from ham slice; slash edges of ham slices. In 12-inch skillet over medium-high heat, heat piece of fat until lightly browned, rubbing fat on bottom of skillet to grease it; discard piece of fat. Cook ham slices in fat, a few at a time, until lightly browned on both sides, removing them as they brown.

Into skillet, stir prunes, apricots, orange juice and sugar. Return ham to skillet, overlapping slices to fit; spoon some juice over slices; heat to boiling. Reduce heat to low; cover and simmer 20 minutes or until apricots are fork-tender. With tongs, place ham slices on warm platter; keep warm.

In cup, blend cornstarch and 2 tablespoons water until smooth; stir into hot mixture in skillet and cook over medium heat, stirring constantly, until mixture is thickened and boils. Serve fruit sauce with ham. Makes 6 servings.

COFFEE-GLAZED HAM STEAK

⅓ cup dark corn syrup
1 teaspoon instant coffee
1 fully cooked ham slice, cut about ¾ inch thick (about 1¼ pounds)

ABOUT 25 MINUTES BEFORE SERVING:
In 10-inch skillet over medium-high heat, heat corn syrup with instant coffee until coffee is dissolved, stirring constantly. Slash edges of ham slice to prevent curling. Add ham; cook 12 to 15 minutes, turning once and occasionally spooning syrup mixture over steak. Place ham on warm platter and spoon mixture over it. Makes 5 servings.

Ground Ham

Either cook-before-eating or fully cooked ham may be ground to order; or leftover ham may be ground at home. Since most dishes using ground ham are cooked thoroughly, either type of ham may be used.

PINEAPPLE HAM LOAF

1 20-ounce can sliced pineapple
2 pounds ground ham
2 eggs
2 cups fresh bread crumbs
½ cup minced celery
⅓ cup milk
1½ teaspoons dry mustard
dash pepper
1 tablespoon light brown sugar
Pineapple-Ham Sauce (opposite)

ABOUT 1¾ HOURS BEFORE SERVING:
Preheat oven to 350°F. Drain pineapple,

reserving juice to make sauce (below); pat pineapple slices dry on paper towels. In large bowl, mix remaining ingredients except sugar and pineapple slices.

In bottom of 10″ by 5″ loaf pan, sprinkle brown sugar; line bottom and sides of pan with pineapple slices. Spoon ham mixture into pan, lightly packing it around pineapple. Bake 1¼ hours. Meanwhile, prepare sauce.

For easier serving, let ham loaf stand in pan 5 minutes; invert onto platter. Serve sauce over meat. Makes 8 servings.

PINEAPPLE-HAM SAUCE: In 1-quart saucepan, blend *reserved pineapple juice* and *1 tablespoon cornstarch* until smooth; cook over medium heat, stirring constantly, until mixture is thickened; stir in *1 teaspoon butter or margarine* until blended. Makes about 1 cup.

HAM LOAF WITH CHERRY SAUCE

HAM LOAF:

1 pound ground ham
1 pound ground pork shoulder
2 eggs
2 cups fresh bread crumbs
½ cup milk
¼ cup chopped parsley
2 tablespoons chopped onion
1 teaspoon prepared mustard

SAUCE:

1 16-ounce can pitted tart red cherries
2 tablespoons sugar
4 teaspoons cornstarch
¼ teaspoon salt
¼ teaspoon grated lemon peel
⅛ teaspoon cinnamon
⅛ teaspoon nutmeg
¼ teaspoon red food color

ABOUT 2 HOURS BEFORE SERVING:
Preheat oven to 350°F. In large bowl, mix well ingredients for ham loaf. Spoon mixture into 9″ by 5″ loaf pan; with spoon, level top. Bake ham loaf 1½ hours. For easier serving, let ham loaf stand at room temperature while preparing sauce.

Meanwhile, prepare sauce: Drain liquid from cherries into measuring cup; add water to make 1 cup. In 1½-quart saucepan, mix sugar, cornstarch, salt, lemon peel, cinnamon and nutmeg; stir in liquid until blended. Cook over medium heat, stirring constantly, until thickened and clear; add cherries and food color; heat through.

Pour off liquid from ham loaf and discard. Invert loaf onto warm platter. Spoon some of sauce over loaf; serve remaining sauce in small dish to spoon over meat. Makes 8 servings.

DOUBLE HAM LOAVES

2 pounds ham
2 pounds ground pork
1 cup dried bread crumbs
1 cup milk
2 eggs
1 small onion, grated
1 teaspoon salt
¼ teaspoon pepper
1 cup packed light brown sugar
⅓ cup cider vinegar
1 teaspoon dry mustard
Raisin Sauce (below)

ABOUT 2¼ HOURS BEFORE SERVING:
Preheat oven to 350°F. Into large bowl, put ham through food grinder; mix well with ground pork and next 6 ingredients. Shape into 2 loaves and place in greased, shallow baking pan; set aside.

In small saucepan over medium heat, heat sugar, vinegar and mustard with ½ cup water to boiling; boil 1 minute. Pour brown-sugar mixture over ham loaves and bake 1½ hours, basting generously with liquid in pan 2 or 3 times. Serve with Raisin Sauce. Makes 12 to 16 servings.

RAISIN SAUCE: In 1-quart saucepan over medium heat, heat *one ¾- or ⅞-ounce envelope brown-gravy mix, 1½ cups apple juice, ½ cup dark seedless raisins* and *1 teaspoon grated orange peel* to boiling; cook, stirring occasionally, until mixture thickens. Makes about 1¾ cups sauce.

TO FREEZE AND SERVE UP TO 1 MONTH LATER:
Prepare ham loaves as directed above. Refrigerate until cool. Wrap in foil and freeze. To serve, preheat oven to 350°F. Heat one or both frozen, wrapped ham loaves on cookie sheet for 1½ hours or until heated through. Meanwhile, prepare Raisin Sauce, as above, to serve with ham loaves.

HAM BALLS IN SPICY SAUCE

HAM BALLS:

2 tablespoons butter or margarine
1 cup finely chopped celery
½ cup minced onions
¾ pound ground ham
¾ pound ground pork
¾ cup quick-cooking or old-fashioned oats, uncooked
2 eggs
½ cup milk
½ teaspoon salt
dash pepper

SPICY SAUCE:

¼ cup packed light brown sugar
2 tablespoons all-purpose flour
½ teaspoon ginger
1 12-ounce can apricot nectar
¼ cup dark corn syrup
1 tablespoon cider vinegar

ABOUT 1½ HOURS BEFORE SERVING:
Preheat oven to 325°F. In small saucepan over medium heat, in hot butter or margarine, cook celery and onions until tender, about 5 minutes. In large bowl, with fork, mix with remaining ingredients for ham balls; shape into 1½-inch balls. Place on 15½″ by 10½″ jelly-roll pan and bake 45 minutes or until lightly browned.

Meanwhile, prepare sauce: In 3-quart saucepan, mix brown sugar, flour and ginger. Stir in apricot nectar, corn syrup and vinegar and cook over medium heat, stirring constantly, until mixture is thickened.

When ham balls are done, remove from oven and transfer to saucepan containing sauce. Cook over low heat about 5 minutes to blend flavors. Makes 6 servings.

Smoked Pork Loin and Chops

Cuts to buy: Pork loin roasts and chops are available smoked.

How to cook: Smoked loin roasts should be roasted to an internal temperature of 160°F. Pan-broil or pan-fry chops if ½-inch thick or less; broil or bake if cut thicker.

To roast: Preheat oven to 325°F. Place smoked loin roast, fat side up, on rack in open roasting pan. Insert meat thermometer so it is centered in thickest part of meat, making sure pointed end does not touch bone or rest in fat. Do not add water; do not cover. Roast until meat thermometer reaches 160°F.

To pan-broil: In heavy skillet over medium heat, cook smoked pork chops until lightly browned on both sides, turning occasionally and pouring any fat from pan as it accumulates.

To pan-fry: Trim piece of fat from edge of a chop; rub fat over bottom of skillet to grease it. Then cook as in To Pan-Broil, above.

To broil: Preheat broiler if manufacturer directs. Place smoked pork chops on rack in broiling pan; broil, 2 to 3 inches from heat, until browned on both sides, turning once.

To bake smoked chops: Follow recipe directions.

BARBECUED SMOKED PORK LOIN

1 5-pound smoked pork loin*
½ cup catchup
¼ cup packed light brown sugar
¼ cup currants
1 tablespoon cider vinegar
1 teaspoon dry mustard
⅛ teaspoon ground cloves
⅛ teaspoon cinnamon
5 red cooking apples, cored and halved crosswise

ABOUT 2¼ HOURS BEFORE SERVING:
Preheat oven to 325°F. Place pork loin on rack in open roasting pan. Insert meat thermometer into center of meat, making sure pointed end is in center of roast and does not touch bone or fat. Roast about 2 hours or until meat thermometer reaches 160°F.

Meanwhile, in small bowl, combine catchup and remaining ingredients except apples.

After one hour of roasting, place apple halves, skin side up, on rack around meat. Continue roasting, occasionally brushing meat and apples with catchup mixture. With knife, cut backbone from ribs and discard. Makes 10 to 12 servings.

* Ask meatman to loosen backbone from ribs.

TANGY SMOKED PORK CHOPS AND SWEET POTATOES

1 tablespoon butter or margarine
4 smoked pork loin chops, each cut about ¾ inch thick (about 2 pounds)
⅓ cup dark corn syrup
2 tablespoons catchup
1 teaspoon prepared mustard
1 teaspoon lemon juice
1 17-ounce can vacuum-packed sweet potatoes, drained

ABOUT 45 MINUTES BEFORE SERVING:
In 12-inch skillet over medium-high heat, in hot butter or margarine, cook chops until well browned on both sides. Stir in corn syrup, catchup, mustard and lemon juice; turn chops over to coat with mixture; heat to boiling. Reduce heat to low; cover and simmer 15 minutes. Add sweet potatoes and spoon sauce over them. Cover and cook 5 to 10 minutes until sweet potatoes are hot. Serve chops and sweet potatoes with sauce spooned over. Makes 4 servings.

SMOKED PORK CHOPS WITH SWEET-SOUR CABBAGE

1 tablespoon butter or margarine
½ cup diced onion
1 medium head cabbage, coarsely shredded
2 tablespoons all-purpose flour
2 tablespoons sugar
1 teaspoon caraway seed
¼ cup cider vinegar
6 smoked pork loin chops, each cut about 1 inch thick

ABOUT 2¼ HOURS BEFORE SERVING:
Preheat oven to 325°F. In small skillet over medium heat, in hot butter or margarine, cook onion, stirring occasionally, until tender, about 5 minutes.

In 13″ by 9″ baking pan, lightly toss onion, cabbage, flour, sugar and caraway seed; pour vinegar over mixture; top with chops. Cover tightly with foil and bake 1¾ hours or until cabbage and meat are fork-tender. Makes 6 servings.

Smoked Shoulder Rolls

Kinds to buy: Smoked shoulder rolls (butts) are boneless cuts of cook-before-eating smoked pork.

How to cook: Roasting (baking) and cooking in liquid are the preferred ways to cook.

To roast: Remove any casing. Roast as in How to Cook Hams and Picnics (page 116). Smoked shoulder rolls should be roasted to an internal temperature of 170°F. A 2- to 3-pound shoulder roll will take 1½ to 2 hours to reach 170°F. on the meat thermometer. If desired, any of Glazes for Ham and Pork (pages 117–118) may be added during last half hour of roasting time.

To cook in liquid: In large saucepot or Dutch oven, place 2- to 4-pound smoked shoulder roll and enough hot water to cover meat. Over high heat, heat to boiling. Reduce heat to low; cover and simmer 1½ to 2 hours until meat is fork-tender. Drain.

If desired, shoulder roll may be glazed in oven after cooking. Place roll in baking dish and bake in oven preheated to 400°F. 15 to 30 minutes, spooning on any of Ham and Pork Glazes (pages 117–118).

SMOKED PORK WITH SWEET POTATOES

1 2½- to 3-pound smoked pork shoulder roll
1 cup packed light brown sugar
½ teaspoon nutmeg
2 17-ounce cans vacuum-packed sweet potatoes

ABOUT 2¼ HOURS BEFORE SERVING:
Preheat oven to 325°F. Remove any casing from shoulder roll. Place meat in open roasting pan. Insert meat thermometer into center of meat. Roast ½ hour.

Meanwhile, in small bowl, blend sugar, nutmeg and 3 tablespoons water.

Remove pan from oven; place sweet potatoes in one layer around meat; brush meat and potatoes with brown-sugar mixture. Roast about 1¼ hours longer or until meat thermometer reaches 170°F., brushing occasionally with pan liquid. Place meat and potatoes on warm platter; spoon pan liquid over all. Makes 8 to 10 servings.

SMOKED PORK FLORENTINE

1 2- to 2½-pound smoked pork shoulder roll
2 10-ounce packages frozen chopped spinach
1 10½-ounce can condensed cream-of-mushroom soup
¼ cup grated Parmesan cheese
1 cup milk

ABOUT 2 HOURS BEFORE SERVING:
Remove any casing from shoulder roll. In 8-quart saucepot over high heat, heat to boiling shoulder roll and enough hot water to cover. Reduce heat to low; cover and cook 2 hours or until fork-tender; drain. Near end of cooking time, in 2-quart saucepan, cook spinach as label directs but use no salt; drain; keep warm.

In 1½-quart saucepan over medium heat, heat to boiling undiluted soup, cheese and milk, stirring frequently. Slice meat and place on platter; arrange spinach on top and pour on soup. Makes 8 servings.

SMOKED PORK "BOILED" DINNER

1 2½- to 3-pound smoked pork shoulder roll
1 bay leaf
1 tablespoon peppercorns
2 or 3 of vegetables (below)

ABOUT 2½ HOURS BEFORE SERVING:
Remove any casing from shoulder roll. In 8-quart saucepot or Dutch oven over high heat, heat to boiling shoulder roll, bay leaf, peppercorns and enough hot water to cover. Reduce heat to low; cover and simmer 1 hour and 15 minutes.

Add any vegetables except Brussels sprouts, cabbage or green beans. Over high heat, heat to boiling. Reduce heat to medium-low; cover and simmer 30 minutes or until meat and vegetables are fork-tender. If using Brussels sprouts, cabbage or green beans, add them during last 15 minutes of cooking.

Slice meat and place on warm large platter. With slotted spoon, arrange vegetables around meat. Strain pan liquid and serve unthickened to ladle over servings. (Or, refrigerate and use to make soup another day.) Makes 8 to 10 servings.

VEGETABLES: 1 10-ounce container Brussels sprouts; 1 medium head cabbage, cut into 8 wedges; 1 pound whole green beans; 8 medium carrots, cut in 2-inch chunks; 8 small white onions; 4 medium parsnips, cut in 2-inch chunks; 6 medium potatoes, halved; 1 medium rutabaga, cut in 8 wedges; 4 medium turnips, halved.

CHOUCROUTE GARNI

1 2- to 2½-pound smoked pork shoulder roll
1 2- to 2½-pound rolled Boston pork roast
2 cups dry white wine
1 13¾-ounce can chicken broth
8 juniper berries or 2 tablespoons gin (optional)
6 medium onions, halved
6 medium potatoes, halved
6 fresh bratwurst (about 1½ pounds)
4 cups well-drained sauerkraut (2 16-ounce cans)
3 large cooking apples, cored and quartered

ABOUT 3 HOURS BEFORE SERVING:
In 10- to 12-quart saucepot, heat to boiling smoked pork roll (remove any casing), Boston roast, wine, chicken broth and juniper berries. Reduce heat to low; cover and simmer 2 hours. Add remaining ingredients in layers: first onions, then potatoes, bratwurst, sauerkraut and apples; cover tightly and simmer 35 to 40 minutes until meat and vegetables are fork-tender.

With slotted spoon, place apples, sauerkraut, bratwurst, potatoes and onions on warm large platter. Slice Boston roast and smoked pork roll and arrange on platter. Drain fat from pan liquid; discard juniper berries. Serve liquid over meat and vegetables. Makes 12 to 14 servings.

GLAZED SMOKED PORK AND PEARS

1 2½-pound smoked pork shoulder roll
1 tablespoon instant coffee powder
½ cup honey
4 large ripe pears, halved and cored

ABOUT 2 HOURS BEFORE SERVING:
Preheat oven to 325°F. Remove any casing from shoulder roll. Insert meat thermom-

eter into center of meat. On rack in open roasting pan, roast meat 1 hour.

Meanwhile, in cup, dissolve coffee in 1 tablespoon very hot water; stir in honey.

Arrange pear halves, cut sides up, around meat on rack. Brush meat and pears with mixture. Bake 45 minutes longer or until meat thermometer reaches 170°F., brushing frequently with mixture and pan drippings. Makes 8 servings.

Smoked Pork Hocks

Cook and use this cut the same as fresh pork hocks (page 114).

Canadian-Style Bacon

Kinds to buy: Canadian-style bacon is the large rib-eye muscle from the pork loin, cured and smoked. It is boneless and usually lean. May be sold in 2- to 4-pound pieces, or cut to order, or sliced and packed in vacuum packages.

How to cook: Roast large pieces of Canadian-style bacon; or broil, pan-broil or pan-fry slices.

To roast: Preheat oven to 325°F. Remove casing from 2- to 4-pound piece of Canadian-style bacon; place meat on rack in open roasting pan. Insert meat thermometer in center of meat. Do not add water; do not cover. Roast until thermometer reaches 140°F. for fully cooked, 1¼ to 1¾ hours; 160°F. for cook-before-eating, 1⅓ to 2⅓ hours.

To broil: Preheat broiler if manufacturer directs. Place ⅛- to ¼-inch slices of Canadian-style bacon on rack in broiling pan; broil, 2 to 3 inches from heat until browned on both sides, turning once, about 10 minutes total time.

To pan-broil: In heavy skillet over medium heat, cook meat until lightly browned on both sides, turning occasionally. Do not add fat or liquid; do not cover.

To pan-fry: In skillet over medium heat, in small amount of bacon drippings or salad oil, cook ⅛-inch slices of Canadian-style bacon until lightly browned on both sides, turning occasionally. Do not cover.

ROTISSERIED CANADIAN BACON

1 3-pound piece Canadian-style bacon
½ cup chili sauce
¼ cup dark seedless raisins
1 small onion, quartered
1 small garlic clove
2 tablespoons brown sugar
2 tablespoons red wine vinegar
2 tablespoons butter or margarine, softened
½ teaspoon dry mustard
¼ teaspoon fines herbes
dash pepper

ABOUT 1¾ HOURS BEFORE SERVING:
Preheat rotisserie as manufacturer directs. Remove any casing from Canadian bacon. Skewer Canadian bacon on rotisserie skewer as directed and cook on rotisserie 1½ hours. To check doneness, stop rotisserie and insert meat thermometer into center of thickest part of meat; it should read 160°F.

Meanwhile, for sauce, in covered blender container at high speed, blend remaining ingredients until smooth; pour into small saucepan. Over medium heat, heat sauce to boiling. Reduce heat to low; cover and simmer 10 to 15 minutes to blend flavors, stirring occasionally.

During last 30 minutes of roasting time, baste meat frequently with sauce. Makes 10 to 12 servings.

CANADIAN-BACON STACKS

1 pound Canadian-style bacon slices, each cut about ¼ inch thick (about 12 slices)
6 Cheddar or longhorn cheese slices
3 packaged corn cakes, split and toasted
6 thin onion slices or 6 thin tomato slices

ABOUT 20 MINUTES BEFORE SERVING:
Remove any casing from Canadian bacon. In 12-inch skillet over medium heat, cook bacon, a few slices at a time, until lightly browned on both sides.

On each of six bacon slices, place a cheese slice; top with remaining bacon slices. Return meat-and-cheese stacks to skillet and heat just until cheese is melted. Serve on corn cakes topped with onion slices. Makes 6 servings.

PEACH-GLAZED CANADIAN BACON

1 pound Canadian-style bacon slices, each cut about 1/4 inch thick
1 17-ounce can cling-peach slices
3 tablespoons butter or margarine
1/2 cup packed light brown sugar

ABOUT 20 MINUTES BEFORE SERVING:
Remove any casing from bacon slices. In 10-inch skillet over medium heat, cook bacon slices, a few at a time, until lightly browned on both sides, removing pieces as they brown to warm platter; keep warm.

Drain peaches and reserve 3 tablespoons liquid. Into drippings in skillet over medium heat, heat reserved liquid, butter or margarine and sugar, stirring constantly, until sugar is melted. Add peaches and heat, stirring gently; spoon over bacon. Makes 4 servings.

Bacon

Kinds to buy: Bacon is sold sliced in 8-ounce, 16-ounce and 32-ounce packages; check label to see whether bacon is thin-sliced, regular-sliced or thick-sliced.

Bacon sold in pieces is called *slab bacon;* the rind is left on. It may be sliced to order or sliced as needed at home.

Bacon varies in flavor depending upon the curing and smoking process of the packer. It also varies in thickness, width and uniformity of slices and in the proportion of lean to fat.

How to cook: Bacon, sliced, may be baked, broiled, pan-broiled or pan-fried.

To bake: Preheat oven to 400°F. Place bacon slices with fat edge of each overlapping lean edge of next slice on rack in open roasting pan and bake until browned and crisp, about 10 to 12 minutes. There's no need to turn or drain it.

To pan-fry: Remove from package in one piece the number of slices desired; place in cold heavy skillet. Over medium heat, cook bacon about 5 to 8 minutes, separating pieces with tongs so they lie flat in pan; turn pieces occasionally so they brown evenly. When browned, remove and drain on paper towels. A 10-inch skillet will hold one 8-ounce package of bacon slices at one time.

To broil: Carefully separate bacon slices so they don't tear; place on rack in broiling pan. Preheat broiler if manufacturer directs. Broil, 3 inches from heat, 3 to 4 minutes; turn and broil until browned. Watch to prevent burning.

How to store and use drippings: Strain drippings into jar; cover and refrigerate; use within 2 weeks. Use for pan-frying meats and eggs; for seasoning hot cooked vegetables; for cooking pancakes or French toast.

BACON PIECES FOR TOPPING

UP TO 2 WEEKS AHEAD:
With kitchen scissors or sharp knife, cut *one 16-ounce package bacon slices* into small pieces. In skillet over medium heat, cook bacon until browned, stirring with slotted spoon to separate pieces. When browned, remove pieces with slotted spoon; drain on paper towels. Cover; refrigerate.

To use, heat in skillet or oven just until crisp. Use as garnish for salads, casseroles, baked potatoes, hot cooked vegetables. Makes about 1 1/2 cups pieces.

Salt Pork

Kinds to buy: This favorite seasoning for baked beans, vegetables and other foods is sold sliced or by the piece to be sliced as needed. Look for a piece with streaks of lean through the fat.

How to cook: Cook slices as in Bacon, To Pan-Fry (at left) or use in recipes.

VEAL

Of all meats, veal is the most delicate in flavor; it has fine texture and little fat. Like beef, better grades of veal carry the same federal grade stamps for quality: prime, choice, good.

How to buy veal: The lean of good-quality veal is grayish-pink and fine textured; there is little external fat and no marbling. Bones should be soft and very red.

How to cook veal cuts: Veal cuts have a comparatively large amount of connective tissue for their size, and for this reason should be cooked until well done to become tender. And because veal contains so little fat, it should not be broiled. Low to moderate cooking temperatures should be used in order to obtain maximum tenderness, flavor, juiciness, uniform color and aroma.

Here are familiar veal cuts with the recommended ways to cook each:
Arm roast—roast, braise
Arm steak—braise, pan-fry
Blade roast—roast, braise
Blade steak—braise, pan-fry
Breast, whole or stuffed—roast, braise
Choplets—braise, pan-fry
City chicken—braise, pan-fry
Crown roast—roast
Cube steaks—braise, pan-fry; if rolled, braise
Cutlets: regular, rolled, thin-sliced—braise, pan-fry
Ground veal, patties—bake, braise, pan-fry
Loin chops: kidney, loin, top loin—braise, pan-fry
Mock chicken legs—braise, pan-fry
Rib chops: bone-in, boneless—braise, pan-fry
Rib roast—roast
Riblets: bone-in, boneless—braise, cook in liquid
Round roast—roast, braise
Round steak—braise, pan-fry
Rump: standing, rolled—roast, braise
Shank: whole, cross-cut—braise, cook in liquid
Sirloin roast, rolled double sirloin—roast
Sirloin steak—braise, pan-fry
Stew meat—braise, cook in liquid
Stuffed chops—braise, pan-fry

How to test veal for doneness: For roast veal, use a meat thermometer to avoid guesswork. Veal should be roasted to an internal temperature of 170°F. The exterior will be reddish-brown and the interior uniformly grayish white.

Veal that is pan-fried should be checked for doneness by making a small slit in the center of the meat or near the bone. When done, veal should be a uniform grayish-white throughout.

Veal that is braised or cooked in liquid should be tender when pierced with a fork.

Veal Roasts

TIMETABLE FOR ROASTING VEAL AT 325°F.

For general directions, see *To Roast, page 63*

Weight of Cut (pounds)	*Approximate Hours* to Reach 170°F. (well done)*
Leg (standing rump or round roast) 5 to 8	3 to 3⅓
Loin 4 to 6	2⅓ to 3
Rib (rack) 3 to 5	2 to 3
Shoulder (arm or blade roast) 6	3½
Shoulder, rolled 4 to 6	3 to 4

* Meat at refrigerator temperature, placed in oven preheated to 325°F.

LEMON-TARRAGON VEAL ROAST

2 teaspoons salt
2 teaspoons grated lemon peel
1 teaspoon tarragon leaves
1 3-pound rolled veal shoulder roast
¼ cup all-purpose flour
1 beef-bouillon cube or envelope

ABOUT 3 HOURS BEFORE SERVING:

1. Preheat oven to 325°F. In small bowl, stir salt, lemon peel and tarragon.
2. With tip of sharp knife, make about 2 dozen slits, about 2½ inches deep, over top and sides of roast; into each slit, with spoon, insert some of salt mixture. (Sprinkle remaining salt mixture over veal roast.)
3. Place meat on rack in open roasting pan; insert meat thermometer into center of thickest part of meat. Roast meat about 2 hours or until thermometer reaches 170°F. Place veal on warm platter; let stand 15 minutes for easier carving. Remove strings.
4. For gravy, spoon off any fat from drippings in roasting pan. Add 1½ cups water to drippings; stir to loosen browned bits. In cup, blend flour with ½ cup water until smooth; gradually stir into liquid in pan. Stir in bouillon cube. Cook over medium heat, stirring, until thickened; serve over meat. Makes 8 servings.

SOME POPULAR VEAL CUTS

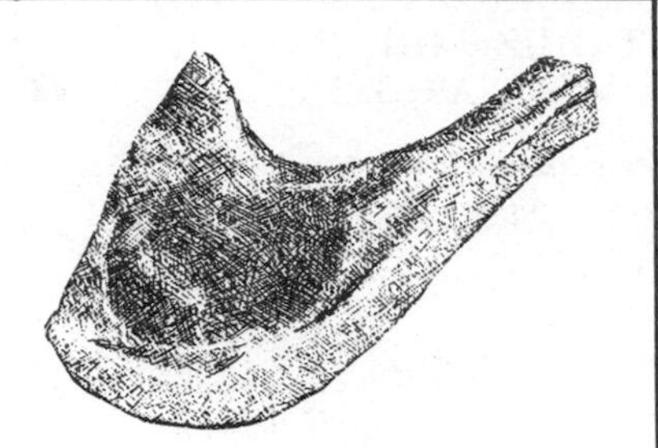

Rib Chop

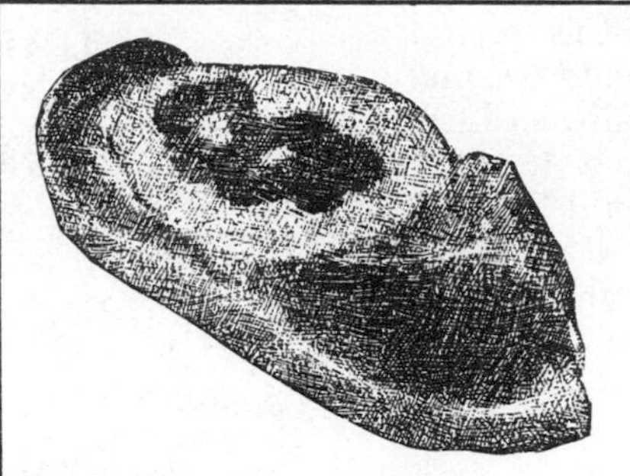

Kidney Chop

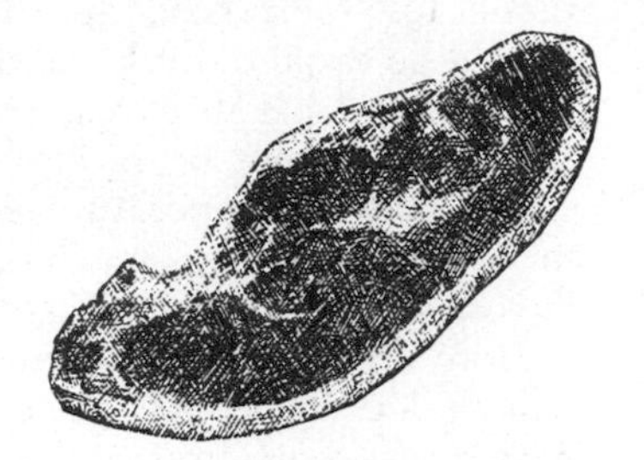

Sirloin Steak

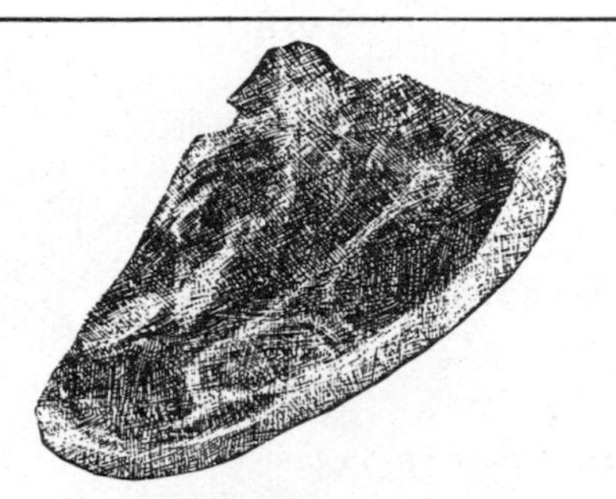

Blade Steak

Arm Steak

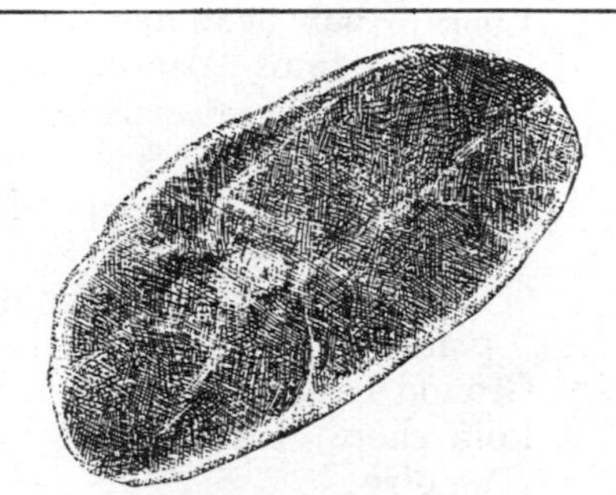

Round Steak

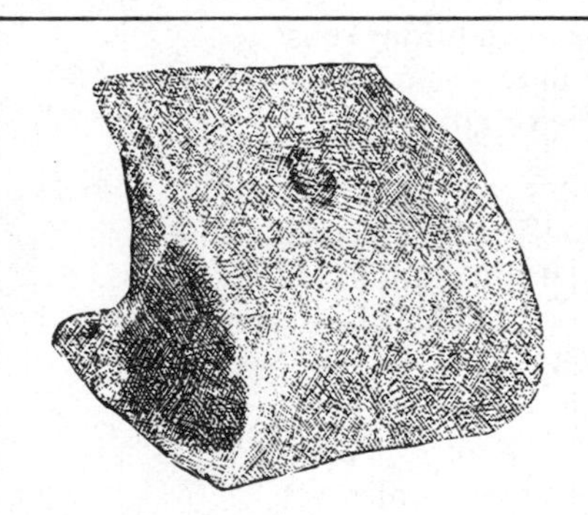

Rib Roast

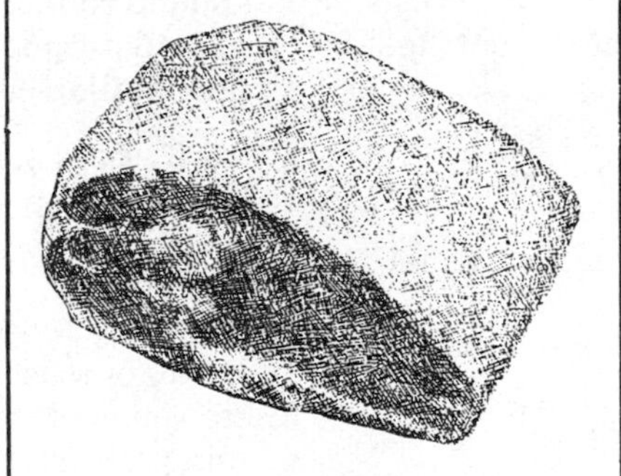

Arm Roast

Blade Roast

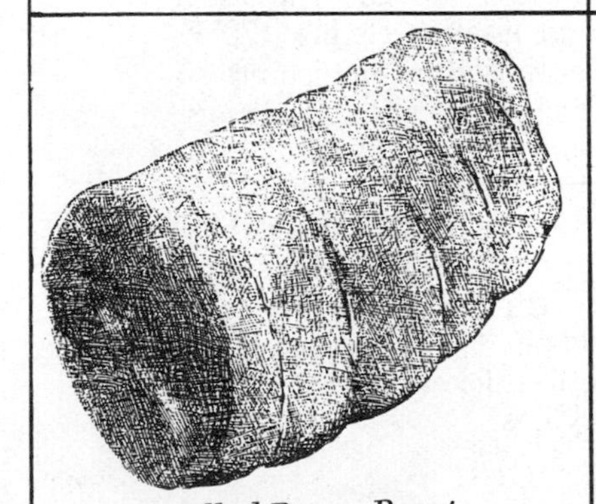

Rolled Rump Roast

Riblets

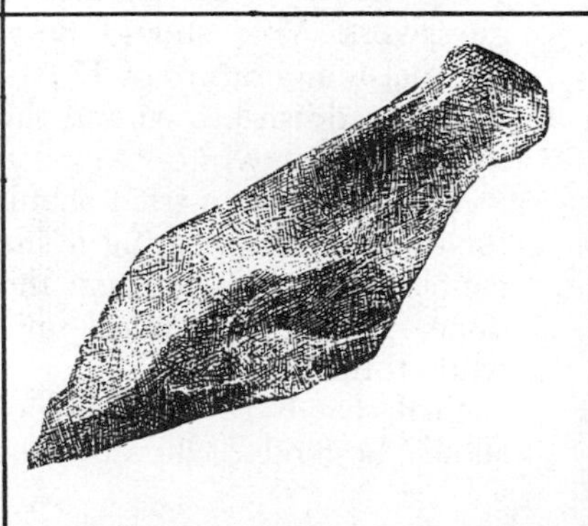

Shank

VEAL RIB ROAST MARSALA

1 6-rib veal roast,* about 4 pounds
1 teaspoon salt
¼ teaspoon pepper
¼ teaspoon thyme leaves, crushed
1 bay leaf, finely crumbled
¼ pound mushrooms, thinly sliced
1 shallot, minced
2 tablespoons all-purpose flour
¼ cup dry Marsala

ABOUT 3½ HOURS BEFORE SERVING:
Preheat oven to 325°F. On rack in shallow roasting pan, place roast. In cup, combine salt, pepper, thyme and bay leaf; rub over meat. Insert meat thermometer into center of thickest part of roast. Roast 2¼ hours or until meat thermometer reaches 170°F. Cut off backbone and discard. Place meat on warm platter. Remove rack from pan.

For gravy, into 1½-quart saucepan, spoon 2 tablespoons fat from drippings in roasting pan; spoon off any remaining fat from drippings and discard. Into roasting pan over medium heat, stir 1¼ cups water and cook, stirring to loosen browned bits.

In hot fat, in saucepan over medium heat, cook mushrooms and shallot until mushrooms are tender. Stir in flour until blended. Gradually stir in water mixture and Marsala and cook, stirring, until thickened; boil 1 minute; serve with meat. Makes 6 servings.

* Ask meatman to loosen backbone from ribs.

Veal Pot Roasts

TIMETABLE FOR BRAISING VEAL POT ROASTS

For general directions, see To Braise, page 64

Weight of Cut (pounds)	*Approximate Hours*
Arm roast, 4 to 5	2¾
Blade roast, 2½ to 3	3¼
Breast, rolled, 2 to 3	1½ to 2½
Breast, stuffed, 3 to 4	1½ to 2½
Rump, rolled, 3 to 4	2½ to 3¼
Shoulder, rolled, 3 to 5	2 to 2½
Standing rump, 5 to 6	2½ to 2¾

VEAL POT ROAST SMITANE

3 tablespoons shortening
1 4-pound boned and rolled veal rump roast
2 cups sour cream
1 package onion-soup mix for 4 servings
2 teaspoons dill seed
1 teaspoon salt
¼ teaspoon pepper

ABOUT 3 HOURS BEFORE SERVING:
In Dutch oven over medium-high heat, in hot shortening, cook rump roast until browned on all sides. In small bowl, combine remaining ingredients; spoon over meat. Reduce heat to low; cover and simmer 2½ to 3 hours until meat is fork-tender, turning meat occasionally and adding water if necessary. Serve pan liquid as gravy. Makes 12 to 14 servings.

TOMATO-PAPRIKA VEAL

2 tablespoons salad oil
1 5- to 6-pound standing veal rump roast
1 cup chopped onions
1 cup beef-and-tomato-flavored cocktail
2 tablespoons paprika
2 teaspoons salt
¼ teaspoon crushed red pepper
2 tablespoons cornstarch
½ cup sour cream or sour half-and-half
hot cooked noodles or mashed potatoes

ABOUT 3 HOURS BEFORE SERVING:
In Dutch oven over medium-high heat, in hot salad oil, cook rump roast until well browned on all sides; remove meat. In drippings, over medium heat, cook onion until tender, about 5 minutes. Stir in beef-and-tomato cocktail, paprika, salt and red pepper; return meat to Dutch oven and heat to boiling. Reduce heat to low; cover and simmer 2½ hours or until meat is fork-tender, turning meat occasionally. Place meat on warm platter; keep warm.

For sauce, in cup, blend cornstarch with ¼ cup water until smooth; gradually stir into hot mixture in Dutch oven and cook, stirring constantly, until sauce is thickened. Stir in sour cream until blended; heat (do not boil). Serve sauce over sliced veal and noodles. Makes 10 to 14 servings.

VEAL ROUND ROAST

1 18″ by 12″ or 24″ by 18″ oven-cooking bag
1 tablespoon all-purpose flour
1 5- to 5½-pound veal round roast
1 10½-ounce can condensed cream-of-mushroom soup
3 carrots, diced
1 onion, chopped
1 teaspoon salt
¼ teaspoon pepper
¼ teaspoon marjoram leaves
1 bay leaf
hot mashed potatoes or cooked noodles

ABOUT 3¼ HOURS BEFORE SERVING:
Preheat oven to 350°F. In oven-cooking bag, place flour; close bag and shake. Place bag in open roasting pan at least 2 inches deep. Place meat in bag; add undiluted soup and remaining ingredients except mashed potatoes. Close bag and puncture top as label directs. Make sure that no part of bag extends over pan edges or may touch sides or top of oven when bag inflates during cooking.

Bake meat about 3 hours until meat is fork-tender. (To test for doneness, pierce meat through bag with two-tined fork.)

To serve, carefully slit bag with kitchen shears to allow steam to escape. Place meat on warm platter; discard bay leaf. Pour drippings into gravy boat; serve as sauce over meat and potatoes. Makes 12 to 14 servings.

SPICY VEAL BLADE ROAST

2 tablespoons salad oil
1 2½- to 3-pound veal blade roast
1 tablespoon pickling spice
1 medium onion, diced
1 tablespoon curry powder
1 cup apple juice
2 teaspoons salt
dash pepper
4 small red cooking apples, halved and cored
3 tablespoons all-purpose flour

ABOUT 3½ HOURS BEFORE SERVING:
In Dutch oven over medium-high heat, in hot salad oil, cook blade roast until well browned on all sides. Meanwhile, prepare Bouquet Garni: Cut a double-thickness of cheesecloth, 5 inches square; on it, place pickling spice; pull corners up to form small bag and tie securely with colorfast or undyed cotton string.

Remove meat from Dutch oven. In drippings over medium heat, cook onion and curry powder, stirring occasionally, until onion is tender, about 5 minutes. Stir in apple juice, salt and pepper; add Bouquet Garni. Return meat to Dutch oven; heat to boiling. Reduce heat to low; cover and simmer 3¼ hours or until meat is fork-tender, turning meat occasionally.

About 30 minutes before meat is done, add apples and continue cooking until apples are tender. Place meat and apples on warm platter; keep warm.

Discard Bouquet Garni. In cup, blend flour and ⅓ cup water until smooth; gradually stir into hot liquid in Dutch oven and cook over medium heat, stirring constantly, until mixture is thickened. Serve gravy over meat. Makes 8 to 10 servings.

VITELLO TONNATO

2 tablespoons olive oil
1 3¼-pound rolled veal rump roast
2 celery stalks, diced
1 large onion, sliced
1 large garlic clove, minced
½ cup dry white wine
1 2-ounce can anchovy fillets
capers
1 chicken-bouillon cube or envelope
¼ teaspoon pepper
¼ teaspoon basil
1 6- or 7-ounce can tuna packed in olive oil
½ cup mayonnaise
lemon wedges

DAY BEFORE SERVING:
In Dutch oven over medium-high heat, in hot olive oil, cook rump roast until well browned on all sides; remove meat. In drippings over medium heat, cook celery and onion until tender, stirring occasionally, about 5 minutes. Return meat to Dutch oven; add garlic, wine, 8 anchovy fillets, 1 tablespoon capers, bouillon, pepper and basil; heat to boiling. Reduce heat to low;

cover and simmer about 2½ hours until fork-tender, turning meat occasionally.

Remove meat from Dutch oven; wrap and chill. Over medium-high heat, cook mixture remaining in Dutch oven until reduced to about 2 cups. Strain mixture, discarding vegetables. (There will be about ¾ cup broth.) In covered blender container, place broth and undrained tuna. Blend at high speed until smooth; pour into small bowl; cover and refrigerate. (Mixture will become thick.)

EARLY IN DAY OR ABOUT 4 HOURS AHEAD:
Unwrap veal roast; cut in ¼-inch slices and arrange on platter. Into tuna mixture, stir mayonnaise until blended; spoon over meat. Cover and refrigerate.

TO SERVE:
Garnish meat with 1 to 2 tablespoons capers and remaining anchovy fillets. Serve with lemon wedges to squeeze over servings. Makes 10 to 12 servings.

VEAL POT ROAST MARENGO

3 tablespoons salad oil
12 small white onions
½ pound mushrooms, quartered
1 4- to 5-pound veal arm roast
1 garlic clove, halved
1 cup Chianti
4 teaspoons salt
½ teaspoon basil
dash pepper
3 medium tomatoes, peeled, seeded and coarsely chopped
2 tablespoons all-purpose flour

ABOUT 3¼ HOURS BEFORE SERVING:
1. In 5-quart Dutch oven over medium-high heat, in hot salad oil, cook onions and mushrooms, stirring frequently, until onions are lightly browned. With slotted spoon, remove onions and mushrooms to medium bowl; set aside.
2. In drippings, over medium-high heat, cook arm roast and garlic until meat is well browned on all sides. Add Chianti, salt, basil and pepper; heat to boiling. Reduce heat to low; cover and simmer 1½ hours, turning meat occasionally.
3. Add tomatoes and reserved onions and mushrooms; cover and cook 1 hour longer or until meat is fork-tender.
4. Remove meat to warm deep platter; discard garlic. For sauce, in cup, blend flour and ¼ cup water until smooth; gradually stir into hot liquid in Dutch oven and cook over medium heat, stirring constantly, until mixture is thickened. Serve meat with sauce. Makes 8 servings.

Veal Chops and Steaks

VEAL WITH ASPARAGUS

3 tablespoons butter or margarine
4 boneless veal rib chops, each cut about 1 inch thick (about 1¼ pounds)
¼ cup minced onion
1 tablespoon all-purpose flour
½ cup chicken broth
2 tablespoons sauterne
½ teaspoon salt
¼ teaspoon marjoram leaves
¾ pound fresh asparagus
4 Swiss cheese slices

ABOUT 1 HOUR BEFORE SERVING:
1. In 10-inch skillet over medium-high heat, in hot butter or margarine, cook veal chops until browned on both sides; remove and set aside.
2. In drippings in skillet, over medium heat, cook onion, stirring occasionally, until almost tender, about 2 minutes. Stir in flour until blended. Gradually stir in chicken broth, sauterne, salt and marjoram and cook until mixture is thickened, stirring constantly to loosen browned bits.
3. Place veal chops in sauce. Reduce heat to low; cover and simmer over low heat 25 minutes. Place asparagus in small bunches on tops of chops. Continue cooking 15 minutes until meat and asparagus are fork-tender.
4. Fold cheese slices to fit tops of chops and place on asparagus. Cover skillet and continue cooking 1 or 2 minutes to melt cheese. With pancake turner, place asparagus-topped chops on warm platter. Spoon fat from sauce; serve sauce over chops. Makes 4 servings.

VEAL CHOPS WITH AVOCADO

4 veal loin chops, each cut about ¾ inch thick (about 1½ pounds)
2 tablespoons butter or margarine
¼ pound mushrooms, sliced
¼ cup minced onion
2 tablespoons medium sherry
1 teaspoon salt
dash hot pepper sauce
1 small ripe avocado
2 teaspoons cornstarch
½ cup heavy or whipping cream
1 teaspoon chopped fresh dill weed

ABOUT 1½ HOURS BEFORE SERVING:
Preheat oven to 350°F. Slash fat on edge of chops in several places. In 10-inch skillet with ovenproof handle, over medium heat, in hot butter or margarine, cook mushrooms and onion until tender, about 5 minutes. Arrange chops in skillet. Add sherry, salt and hot pepper sauce; heat to boiling. Cover and bake 1 hour or until meat is fork-tender.

Cut avocado in half; remove seed and skin. Slice avocado and arrange over chops. Bake, uncovered, 10 minutes or until avocado is heated through. With pancake turner, place chops on warm platter.

In cup, blend cornstarch and 1 tablespoon cream until smooth; stir in remaining cream. Gradually stir into hot liquid in skillet and cook over medium heat, stirring constantly, until thickened. Stir in dill. Serve chops immediately with sauce. Makes 4 servings.

VEAL CHOPS WITH MUSHROOMS

2 tablespoons butter or margarine
4 veal rib chops, each cut about ¾ inch thick (about 1½ pounds)
½ teaspoon salt
¼ teaspoon seasoned pepper
1 garlic clove, crushed
1 3-ounce can sliced mushrooms
2 teaspoons cornstarch
1 teaspoon sugar
1 tablespoon lemon juice

ABOUT 1 HOUR BEFORE SERVING:
1. In 10-inch skillet over medium-high heat, in hot butter or margarine, cook veal chops until browned on both sides. Sprinkle with salt, seasoned pepper and garlic. Add 2 tablespoons water. Reduce heat to low; cover and simmer 45 minutes or until meat is fork-tender, adding more water if necessary and turning once.
2. Drain mushrooms, reserving liquid. Place chops on warm platter.
3. Pour drippings from skillet into measuring cup; add mushroom liquid and enough water to make ¾ cup; return to skillet and heat to boiling.
4. In cup, blend cornstarch, sugar and lemon juice until smooth; gradually stir into hot liquid in skillet and cook over medium heat, stirring constantly, until mixture is thickened. Stir in mushrooms and heat. Serve sauce over meat. Makes 4 servings.

BAKED VEAL BLADE STEAKS

4 veal blade steaks, each cut about ¾ inch thick (about 2 pounds)
1 10½-ounce can condensed cream-of-potato soup
1 tablespoon instant minced onion
¼ teaspoon rosemary, crushed
¼ teaspoon salt
⅛ teaspoon pepper

ABOUT 2 HOURS BEFORE SERVING:
Preheat oven to 350°F. In 12″ by 8″ baking dish, arrange veal steaks. In medium bowl, mix undiluted soup and remaining ingredients; spoon over meat. Cover baking dish tightly with foil and bake 1¾ hours or until meat is fork-tender. Makes 4 servings.

VEAL STEAK INVERNESS

1 1½-pound veal round steak, cut about ¼ inch thick
3 tablespoons soy sauce
2 tablespoons catchup
1 tablespoon cider vinegar
¼ teaspoon pepper
1 or 2 garlic cloves, crushed (optional)
2 tablespoons salad oil
Parsley Rice (page 299)

ABOUT 4½ HOURS OR DAY AHEAD:
Cut veal steak into serving pieces. In shallow dish, for marinade, mix well next

5 ingredients and ⅓ cup water. Add meat and turn over to coat with marinade. Cover and refrigerate, turning occasionally.

ABOUT 1¼ HOURS BEFORE SERVING:
With tongs, remove veal from marinade; reserve marinade. In 10-inch skillet over medium heat, in hot salad oil, cook veal until lightly browned on both sides. Add marinade; heat to boiling. Reduce heat to low; cover skillet and cook 1 hour or until meat is fork-tender. Serve on Parsley Rice. Makes 5 or 6 servings.

LAMB CHOPS INVERNESS: Substitute *6 Frenched lamb rib chops,* each cut about 1 inch thick, for veal steak. Marinate chops as above. About 30 minutes before serving, preheat broiler if manufacturer directs. Place chops on greased rack in broiling pan and broil 15 minutes, turning once and brushing frequently with remaining marinade. Makes 3 servings.

ITALIAN-STYLE VEAL STEAKS

2 veal sirloin steaks, each cut about ¾ inch thick (about 2 pounds)
1 8-ounce package pork-sausage links
1 medium onion, diced
1 6-ounce can tomato paste
½ cup apple juice
1 teaspoon salt
½ teaspoon basil
½ teaspoon garlic salt
¼ teaspoon pepper

ABOUT 1¼ HOURS BEFORE SERVING:
Slash fat on veal steaks in several places. In 12-inch covered skillet over low heat, simmer sausages with ¼ cup water for 5 minutes; uncover and, over medium heat, cook until sausages are lightly browned, about 10 minutes. With tongs, remove sausages and cut into ½-inch pieces; set aside.

In hot drippings in skillet, over medium-high heat, cook veal steaks until browned on both sides. Remove steaks. Reduce heat to medium; add onion and cook, stirring occasionally, until tender, about 5 minutes. Stir in remaining ingredients and sausage; add steaks. Reduce heat to low; cover and simmer 40 minutes or until meat is fork-tender, turning once. Spoon off excess fat. Makes 4 servings.

VEAL STEAKS WITH SPAGHETTI

2 veal arm steaks, each cut about 1 inch thick (about 1¼ pounds)
2 tablespoons all-purpose flour
2 tablespoons olive oil
1 8-ounce can stewed tomatoes
1 6-ounce can tomato paste
1½ teaspoons seasoned salt
1 teaspoon sugar
¼ teaspoon seasoned pepper
¼ teaspoon oregano
1 8-ounce package spaghetti, cooked

ABOUT 1¼ HOURS BEFORE SERVING:
On waxed paper, coat veal steaks with flour. In 12-inch skillet over medium-high heat, in hot olive oil, cook meat until well browned on both sides.

Add remaining ingredients except spaghetti; heat to boiling. Reduce heat to low; cover and simmer 1 hour or until steaks are fork-tender, turning once. Serve with spaghetti. Makes 4 servings.

EASY VEAL PARMIGIANA

3 tablespoons butter or margarine
2 12-ounce packages frozen breaded veal steaks*
1 teaspoon sugar
1 15½-ounce can marinara sauce
1 8-ounce package mozzarella cheese, cut into 6 slices
¼ cup grated Parmesan cheese

ABOUT 30 MINUTES BEFORE SERVING:
In 12-inch skillet over medium-high heat, in hot butter or margarine, fry veal steaks, a few at a time, until browned on both sides, about 10 minutes. Arrange all steaks in skillet.

Meanwhile, in small bowl, combine sugar and marinara sauce; spoon some sauce over each steak; top each with a slice of mozzarella and sprinkle with Parmesan cheese. Reduce heat to low; cover and cook until cheese is melted, about 5 minutes. Makes 6 servings.

* Or, use *6 veal cutlets,* each cut about ¼ inch thick. On waxed paper, combine *1 cup dried bread crumbs, 1 teaspoon salt* and *dash pepper.* In pie plate, with fork, lightly beat *2 eggs.* Dip veal cutlets in egg, then bread-crumb mixture; repeat to coat each piece twice.

Veal Cutlets

VEAL PARMIGIANA

1 egg
1/3 cup all-purpose flour
3/4 cup grated Parmesan cheese
8 veal cutlets, each cut about 1/2 inch thick (about 2 pounds)
about 1/3 cup salad oil
1 teaspoon salt
1/8 teaspoon pepper
1 15-ounce jar marinara sauce*

ABOUT 45 MINUTES BEFORE SERVING:
In pie plate, with fork, beat egg with 1 tablespoon water. On waxed paper, mix flour with 1/4 cup Parmesan cheese. Dip veal cutlets, one at a time, into egg mixture, then in flour mixture, coating on both sides.

In 10-inch skillet over medium-high heat, in 2 tablespoons hot salad oil, cook cutlets, a few at a time, until browned on both sides, adding more oil as needed. Return all meat to skillet; sprinkle with salt and pepper. Pour marinara sauce over meat; sprinkle with 1/2 cup Parmesan cheese; heat to boiling. Reduce heat to medium-low; cover and cook 15 minutes. Makes 8 servings.

* Or, use *1 pint Freezer Tomato Sauce,* thawed (page 715).

SALTIMBOCCA

4 veal cutlets, each cut about 1/4 inch thick
1/4 cup butter or margarine
1/4 cup medium sherry
1/4 pound thinly sliced prosciutto or cooked ham
1/2 pound raclette or Swiss cheese, coarsely shredded

ABOUT 40 MINUTES BEFORE SERVING:
Preheat oven to 350°F. On cutting board, with meat mallet, dull edge of French knife or edge of plate, pound veal cutlets to 1/8-inch thickness, turning once. In 12-inch skillet over medium-high heat, in hot butter or margarine, cook cutlets until lightly browned on both sides. Place in 12″ by 8″ baking dish.

To drippings in skillet, add sherry and stir to loosen browned bits; pour over meat in baking dish.

Cut prosciutto into thin strips; arrange evenly over veal. Bake 5 minutes. Remove from oven and sprinkle cheese evenly over veal. Bake 4 to 5 minutes longer until cheese is melted. Makes 4 servings.

CHICKEN: Prepare as above but substitute *2 large chicken breasts,* skinned, boned and halved for veal and pound until very thin.

VEAL "BIRDS"

16 veal cutlets, each cut about 1/4 inch thick (about 2 pounds)
butter or margarine
1 medium onion, minced
1 4-ounce can mushroom stems and pieces
1 1/2 cups fresh bread crumbs
2 tablespoons chopped parsley
1/4 teaspoon salt
1/4 teaspoon pepper
1/8 teaspoon thyme leaves, crushed
1/8 teaspoon basil
3 tablespoons all-purpose flour
1 cup chicken broth
1 bay leaf

ABOUT 2 HOURS BEFORE SERVING:
1. On cutting board, with meat mallet or dull edge of French knife, pound veal cutlets lightly, turning once; set aside.
2. Prepare stuffing: In 10-inch skillet over medium heat, in 3 tablespoons hot butter or margarine, cook onion until tender, about 5 minutes. Drain mushrooms, reserving 1/4 cup liquid. Into skillet, stir mushrooms and reserved liquid, bread crumbs, parsley, salt, pepper, thyme and basil. Spread 1 rounded tablespoonful stuffing mixture on each veal cutlet; roll up, jelly-roll fashion; secure with toothpicks or small skewers. On waxed paper, coat these veal "birds" with flour.
3. Wipe skillet clean with paper towels. In skillet over medium-high heat, in 2 table-

spoons hot butter or margarine, cook veal "birds," half at a time, until well browned on all sides, adding 2 more tablespoons butter or margarine if needed, and removing pieces as they brown. Return all meat to skillet. Add broth and bay leaf; heat to boiling. Reduce heat to low; cover and simmer 40 minutes or until meat is fork-tender.

4. Arrange veal "birds" on warm platter; remove toothpicks. Discard bay leaf; spoon pan juices over meat. Makes 8 servings.

VEAL ROLLS SMITANE

6 veal cutlets, each cut about ¼ inch thick (about 1½ pounds)
butter or margarine
2 tablespoons minced onion
1½ cups fresh bread crumbs (about 3 slices)
¼ teaspoon tarragon leaves, crushed
¼ teaspoon salt
dash pepper
6 thin boiled ham slices
½ cup chicken broth
1 cup sour cream
Poppy-Seed Noodles (below)

ABOUT 1¼ HOURS BEFORE SERVING:

1. On cutting board, with meat mallet or dull edge of French knife, pound veal cutlets lightly, turning once; set aside.
2. Prepare stuffing: In 1-quart saucepan over medium heat, in 2 tablespoons hot butter or margarine, cook onion 2 or 3 minutes; remove from heat. Add bread crumbs, tarragon, salt and pepper; with fork, toss gently to mix well; set aside.
3. On each veal cutlet, place 1 ham slice; spoon some of stuffing along a narrow end; starting at same end, roll cutlet, jelly-roll fashion. Secure with toothpicks or string.
4. In 10-inch skillet over medium-high heat, in 2 tablespoons hot butter or margarine, cook veal rolls until well browned on all sides. Add chicken broth; heat to boiling. Reduce heat to low; cover and cook 30 minutes or until meat is fork-tender.
5. Place veal rolls on warm platter; remove toothpicks; keep warm. Stir drippings in skillet to loosen browned bits. Stir in sour cream; heat (do not boil). Serve sauce over meat and noodles. Makes 6 servings.

POPPY-SEED NOODLES: Prepare *three-fourths 16-ounce package wide egg noodles* as label directs; drain and add *3 tablespoons butter or margarine* and *5 teaspoons poppy seed.*

VEAL WITH HEARTS OF PALM

½ cup all-purpose flour
1 teaspoon paprika
2 pounds veal cutlets, each cut about ½ inch thick
butter or margarine
1 teaspoon salt
¼ teaspoon pepper
1 14-ounce can hearts of palm, drained and thickly sliced
2 tablespoons rum
½ cup port
⅓ cup heavy or whipping cream
1 lime, cut in wedges

ABOUT 30 MINUTES BEFORE SERVING:

On waxed paper, combine flour and paprika; use to coat veal cutlets.

In 12-inch skillet over medium-high heat, in ¼ cup hot butter or margarine, cook veal, a few pieces at a time, until lightly browned on both sides. Return all meat to skillet; sprinkle with salt and pepper and add ⅓ cup water. Reduce heat to low; cover and cook 15 minutes or until fork-tender.

Meanwhile, in 8-inch skillet over medium heat, in 2 tablespoons hot butter or margarine, cook hearts of palm just until golden brown; keep warm.

Place meat on warm platter. Over medium heat, stir rum into drippings, stirring to loosen browned bits. Stir in port; gradually stir in cream and cook about 3 minutes, stirring constantly, to blend flavors; pour over veal. Serve veal with hearts of palm and lime wedges. Makes 6 servings.

VEAL WITH MUSHROOMS: Prepare as above but omit hearts of palm. In 10-inch skillet over medium heat, in 2 tablespoons hot butter or margarine, cook *½ pound mushrooms,* sliced, stirring often, about 5 minutes or until tender. Serve with meat.

VEAL SCALOPPINE MARSALA

1 pound veal cutlets, each cut about ¼ inch thick
salt and pepper
¼ cup all-purpose flour
butter or margarine
½ cup dry Marsala
chopped parsley for garnish

ABOUT 35 MINUTES BEFORE SERVING:
On cutting board, cut veal cutlets into pieces about 3″ by 3″; sprinkle with salt and pepper. On waxed paper, coat veal lightly with flour.

In 10-inch skillet over medium-high heat, in 3 tablespoons hot butter or margarine, cook meat, a few pieces at a time, until lightly browned on both sides, adding more butter or margarine as needed and removing meat to warm platter as it browns.

Into drippings in skillet, stir Marsala and ¼ teaspoon salt; cook 1 minute, stirring to loosen browned bits; pour over veal; sprinkle with parsley. Makes 4 servings.

WIENER SCHNITZEL

6 large veal cutlets, each cut about ¼ inch thick
2 eggs
1¼ teaspoons salt
½ teaspoon coarsely ground pepper
⅓ cup all-purpose flour
1½ cups dried bread crumbs
½ cup butter or margarine
2 lemons, cut in wedges
3 tablespoons chopped parsley
6 anchovy fillets, drained (optional)
capers (optional)

ABOUT 45 MINUTES BEFORE SERVING:
On cutting board, with meat mallet or dull edge of French knife, pound veal cutlets to about ⅛-inch thickness, turning once.

In pie plate, with fork, beat eggs, salt and pepper. On one sheet of waxed paper, place flour; on another piece of waxed paper, place bread crumbs. Coat veal in flour, then dip in eggs, then coat well with crumbs.

In 12-inch skillet over medium heat, in ¼ cup hot butter or margarine, cook meat, a few pieces at a time, 3 or 4 minutes on each side until well browned, removing meat to warm platter as it browns and adding butter as needed. Garnish with lemon and parsley. Serve meat with anchovies and capers. Makes 6 servings.

A LA HOLSTEIN: Prepare cutlets as above but serve each topped with *a fried egg*.

VEAL CUTLETS A LA SUISSE

6 large veal cutlets, each cut about ½ inch thick
6 Swiss cheese slices
6 paper-thin cooked ham slices
2 tablespoons all-purpose flour
½ teaspoon paprika
3 tablespoons butter or margarine
1 cup sauterne
¼ cup half-and-half

ABOUT 1 HOUR BEFORE SERVING:
On cutting board, with meat mallet or dull edge of French knife, pound veal cutlets to about ¼-inch thickness. On each cutlet, place 1 cheese slice, then 1 ham slice. Fold each cutlet in half; fasten with toothpicks. On waxed paper, combine flour and paprika; use to coat cutlets.

In 12-inch skillet over medium-high heat, in hot butter or margarine, cook cutlets until lightly browned on both sides. Add sauterne; heat to boiling. Reduce heat to low; cover and simmer 10 to 15 minutes until meat is fork-tender.

Place cutlets on warm platter; remove toothpicks; keep warm. Simmer pan liquid, uncovered, over medium heat until reduced to ½ cup. Stir in half-and-half; heat; serve over cutlets. Makes 6 servings.

VEAL FORESTIER

1½ pounds veal cutlets, each cut about ¼ inch thick
1 garlic clove, halved (optional)
⅓ cup all-purpose flour
¼ cup butter or margarine
½ pound mushrooms, thinly sliced
½ cup dry vermouth
1 teaspoon salt
dash pepper

ABOUT 50 MINUTES BEFORE SERVING:
On cutting board, with meat mallet or dull

edge of French knife, pound veal cutlets lightly on both sides. Rub meat with cut garlic; discard garlic. On waxed paper, coat cutlets lightly with flour.

In 10-inch skillet over medium-high heat, in hot butter or margarine, cook meat, a few pieces at a time, until lightly browned on both sides, removing pieces as they brown, and adding more butter or margarine if necessary. Return all meat to skillet; add mushrooms, vermouth, salt and pepper. Reduce heat to low; cover and cook 15 minutes or until meat is fork-tender, adding 1 or 2 tablespoons of water, if necessary. Makes 6 servings.

Veal Breast and Riblets

MUSHROOM-STUFFED BREAST OF VEAL

3 tablespoons butter or margarine
½ pound mushrooms, sliced
½ cup sliced green onions
1½ cups fresh bread crumbs (about 3 slices)
1 10-ounce package frozen peas, thawed
salt and pepper
⅛ teaspoon fines herbes
1 4- to 5-pound veal breast with pocket
1½ cups Rhine wine or sauterne
¼ cup all-purpose flour
Buttered Crumbs (page 351)
chopped parsley for garnish

ABOUT 3½ HOURS BEFORE SERVING:

1. Preheat oven to 325°F. In 10-inch skillet over medium-high heat, in hot butter or margarine, cook mushrooms and green onions until tender, about 5 minutes; remove from heat. Stir in bread crumbs, peas, 2 teaspoons salt, ¼ teaspoon pepper and fines herbes.
2. Sprinkle veal inside and out with salt and pepper. Into pocket, lightly stuff mushroom mixture; secure opening with small skewers or toothpicks.
3. In large, open roasting pan, place veal; pour on wine. Cover pan tightly with foil; bake 3 hours or until meat is fork-tender.
4. Place veal on warm platter; keep warm. Pour liquid from pan into 2-quart saucepan. In cup, blend flour and ½ cup water until smooth; gradually stir into liquid in saucepan; cook over medium heat, stirring constantly, until mixture is thickened. Spoon small amount of sauce over meat; sprinkle with Buttered Crumbs and parsley. Serve remaining sauce with meat. Makes 8 servings.

BARBECUED BREAST OF VEAL

1 4-pound veal breast
1 garlic clove, cut in thin slivers
½ cup medium sherry
2 tablespoons soy sauce
¼ cup packed light brown sugar
2 teaspoons prepared mustard
thin slices French bread, toasted

ABOUT 3 HOURS AND 15 MINUTES AHEAD:
Preheat oven to 325°F. With tip of sharp knife, make 1-inch-long slits on fatty side of veal breast and insert garlic. Place meat, fat side up, in 13″ by 9″ baking pan; pour on sherry and soy sauce. Cover pan tightly with foil and bake 2½ to 3 hours until fork-tender.

Preheat broiler if manufacturer directs. In cup, blend brown sugar and mustard until smooth. Remove meat from oven. Spoon pan liquid into gravy boat; let stand until fat separates. Spoon off fat and discard. Spread brown-sugar mixture on top of meat; broil 3 to 5 minutes until mixture melts. Serve meat with French bread and sauce. Makes 6 servings.

BREAST OF VEAL IN OVEN-COOKING BAG: Place *1 tablespoon all-purpose flour* in *one 18″ by 12″ oven-cooking bag;* close bag and shake; place in baking pan. Prepare meat as above but place in bag; pour sherry and soy sauce over meat. Close bag and puncture top as label directs. Make sure that no part of bag extends over pan edges or may touch sides or top of oven when bag inflates during cooking. Bake meat as above. (To test for doneness, pierce meat through bag with two-tined fork.) Remove pan from oven and let stand at room temperature for several minutes.

To serve, slit bag carefully with kitchen shears to allow steam to escape. Place meat on warm platter; pour drippings into gravy boat. Return meat to pan; spread brown-sugar mixture on top. Broil 3 to 5 minutes until sugar mixture melts.

VEAL RIBLETS WITH VEGETABLE GRAVY

2 tablespoons salad oil
3 pounds veal riblets
2 carrots, sliced
1 medium onion, sliced
1 stalk celery, sliced
1 tablespoon all-purpose flour
1½ teaspoons salt
¼ teaspoon thyme leaves

ABOUT 2 HOURS BEFORE SERVING:
Preheat oven to 350°F. In 12-inch skillet with ovenproof handle, over medium-high heat, in hot salad oil, cook riblets, a few at a time, until well browned on all sides, removing pieces as they brown.

In drippings in skillet over medium heat, cook carrots, onion and celery, stirring occasionally, until lightly browned. Stir in flour, salt and thyme until blended. Gradually stir in ¾ cup water and cook, stirring constantly, until mixture is slightly thickened. Return meat to skillet; cover and bake 1½ hours or until meat is fork-tender, turning once or twice.

Place meat on warm platter. Spoon any excess fat from liquid in pan. In covered blender container at low speed, blend vegetables and pan liquid until smooth, adding more hot water, if necessary, to make gravy of desired consistency. (Or, press mixture through food mill.) Serve gravy with meat. Makes 4 servings.

Veal Stew Meat

VEAL PAPRIKA

3 tablespoons butter or margarine
2 pounds veal stew meat, cut into 1-inch chunks
2 cups diced onions
1 tablespoon paprika
1¾ teaspoons salt
1 8-ounce package egg noodles
1 tablespoon all-purpose flour
½ cup sour cream
chopped parsley for garnish

ABOUT 2½ HOURS BEFORE SERVING:
1. In Dutch oven over medium-high heat, in hot butter or margarine, cook veal, several pieces at a time, until well browned on all sides, removing pieces as they brown. Reduce heat to medium; add onions and paprika to drippings in Dutch oven and cook until onions are tender, about 5 minutes, stirring occasionally.
2. Return meat to Dutch oven; add ½ cup water and salt; heat to boiling. Reduce heat to low; cover Dutch oven and simmer 2 hours or until meat is fork-tender.
3. Meanwhile, cook noodles as label directs; drain.
4. In cup, blend flour and 2 tablespoons water until smooth; gradually stir into hot liquid in Dutch oven and cook over medium heat, stirring constantly, until mixture is thickened. Just before serving, stir in sour cream; heat (do not boil). Serve over noodles. Garnish with parsley. Makes 6 servings.

VEAL STEW DELUXE
(Blanquette de Veau)

1 stalk celery, diced
1 carrot, diced
2 whole cloves
1 bay leaf
2½ pounds veal stew meat, cut into 1½-inch chunks
½ cup dry vermouth or other dry white wine (optional)*
2 teaspoons salt
16 small white onions
1 pound small mushrooms
4 egg yolks
½ cup heavy or whipping cream
chopped parsley or dill for garnish
hot cooked egg noodles or rice; or mashed or boiled potatoes

ABOUT 3 HOURS BEFORE SERVING:
Prepare Bouquet Garni: Cut double-thickness of cheesecloth into 8-inch square. On it, place celery, carrot, cloves and bay leaf; pull corners up to form small bag and tie securely with undyed cotton string.

In 5-quart Dutch oven over medium-high heat, heat to boiling Bouquet Garni, veal stew meat, vermouth and salt. Reduce

* Or, omit wine and use *½ cup water;* add *1 tablespoon lemon juice* with heavy cream.

heat to low; cover and simmer 1½ hours; add onions and mushrooms. Over high heat, heat to boiling. Reduce heat to low; cover and simmer 30 minutes longer or until meat and vegetables are fork-tender. Discard Bouquet Garni.

Meanwhile, in small bowl, with wire whisk or fork, mix egg yolks and cream. Into egg-yolk mixture, stir about ½ cup hot broth; slowly pour mixture back into the stew, stirring rapidly to prevent lumping. Cook, stirring constantly, until mixture is thickened slightly. (Do not boil.) Garnish with parsley. Serve stew over noodles. Makes 8 to 10 servings.

Veal Shanks

BRAISED VEAL SHANKS
(Osso Buco)

⅓ cup olive or salad oil
6 pounds cross-cut veal shanks, each about 2 inches thick
1½ cups minced onions
½ cup minced celery
½ cup minced carrots
1 garlic clove, crushed
1 29-ounce can tomatoes
1 13¾-ounce can chicken broth
½ cup white table wine
1 tablespoon salt
½ teaspoon basil
¼ teaspoon pepper
2 bay leaves
2 tablespoons chopped parsley
1 tablespoon grated lemon peel
Baked Saffron Rice (page 301)

ABOUT 2½ HOURS BEFORE SERVING:
In Dutch oven over medium-high heat, in hot oil, cook veal shanks, half at a time until browned on all sides. In drippings in Dutch oven over medium heat, cook onions, celery, carrots and garlic until golden, stirring occasionally, about 5 minutes.

Return shanks to Dutch oven. Cut up tomatoes and add, with their liquid, to meat; add next 6 ingredients. Reduce heat to low; cover and simmer 1½ to 2 hours until veal is fork-tender. Discard bay leaves.

Place shanks on warm platter; sprinkle with parsley and lemon peel. Serve with Baked Saffron Rice. Makes 6 servings.

Ground Veal and Veal Patties

VEAL PATTIES A LA HOLSTEIN

1 pound ground veal
1 cup fresh bread crumbs
¼ cup milk
¾ teaspoon Worcestershire
salt and pepper
4 tablespoons butter or margarine
6 eggs
6 slices white bread, toasted

ABOUT 25 MINUTES BEFORE SERVING:
In medium bowl, mix well ground veal, bread crumbs, milk, Worcestershire, 1 teaspoon salt and ⅛ teaspoon pepper; shape into six thin patties. In 12-inch skillet over medium heat, in 2 tablespoons hot butter or margarine, fry patties 3 to 4 minutes on each side, until well browned. Place patties on warm platter; keep warm.

Pour drippings from skillet; add 2 tablespoons more butter or margarine to skillet. Over low heat, fry eggs; sprinkle with salt and pepper. With pancake turner, place one egg on top of each veal patty. Serve patties on toast. Makes 6 servings.

VEAL LOAF

1½ pounds ground veal
1 3-ounce can chopped mushrooms
1½ cups fresh bread crumbs
1½ cups shredded carrots
½ cup sour cream
1 small onion, minced
1 egg
1½ teaspoons salt
1 teaspoon bottled steak sauce
¼ teaspoon pepper
¼ teaspoon dill weed

ABOUT 1½ HOURS BEFORE SERVING:
Preheat oven to 350°F. In large bowl, mix well veal, mushrooms and their liquid and remaining ingredients. Spoon mixture into 9″ by 5″ loaf pan; with spoon, level top. Bake veal loaf 1¼ hours.

For easier serving, let veal loaf stand at room temperature 5 minutes. Pour off liquid and reserve. Loosen veal loaf from pan; invert onto warm platter. Serve liquid over veal loaf. Makes 6 servings.

SOME POPULAR LAMB CUTS

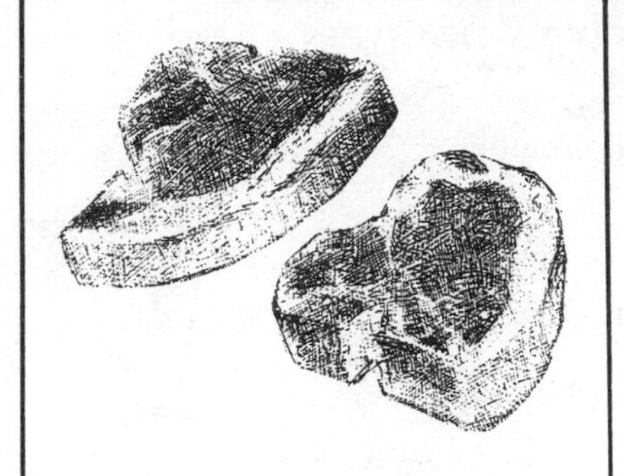

Loin Chops

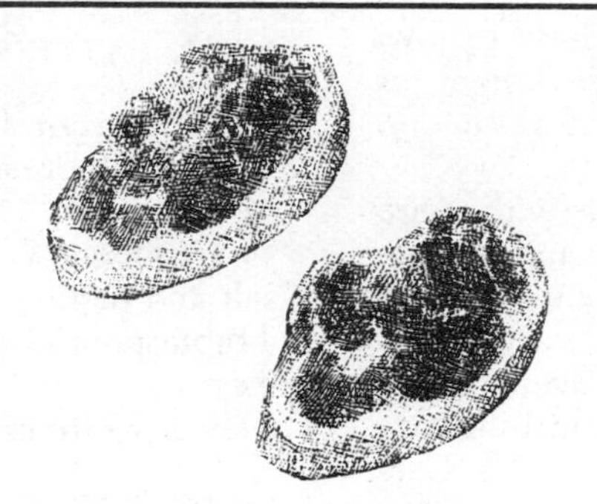

Sirloin Chops

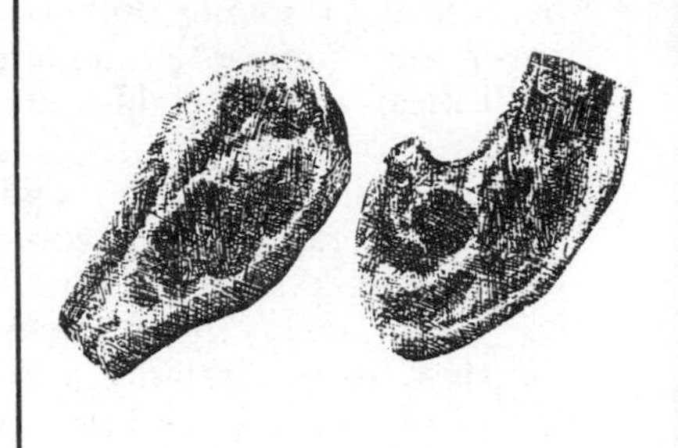

Arm Chop *Blade Chop*

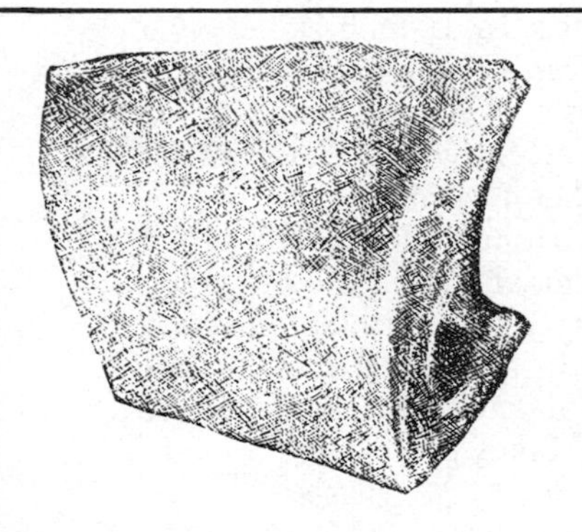

Rib Roast

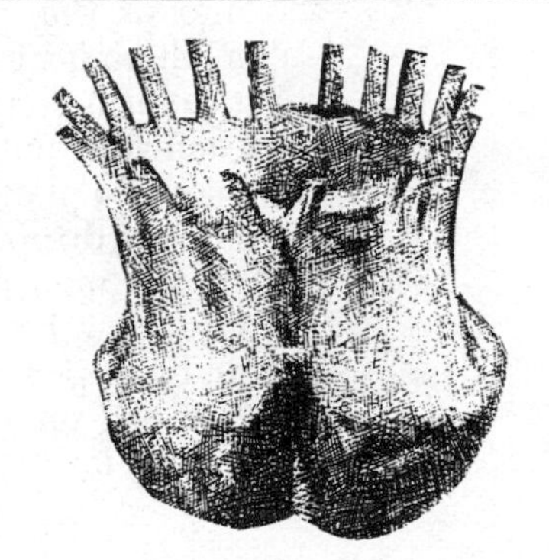

Crown Roast

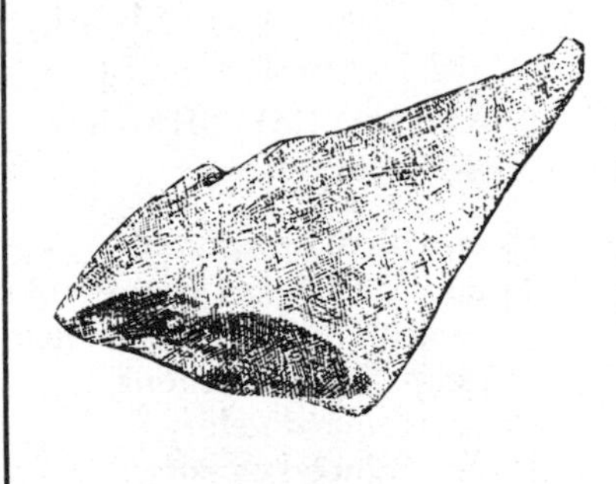

Leg of Lamb

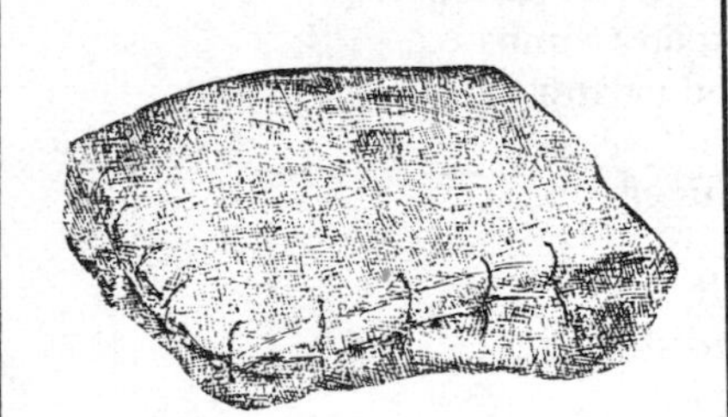

Cushion Shoulder

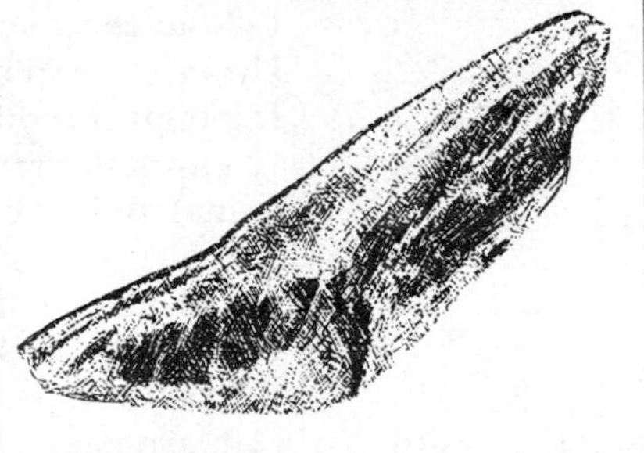

Breast

Riblets

Neck Slices

Patties

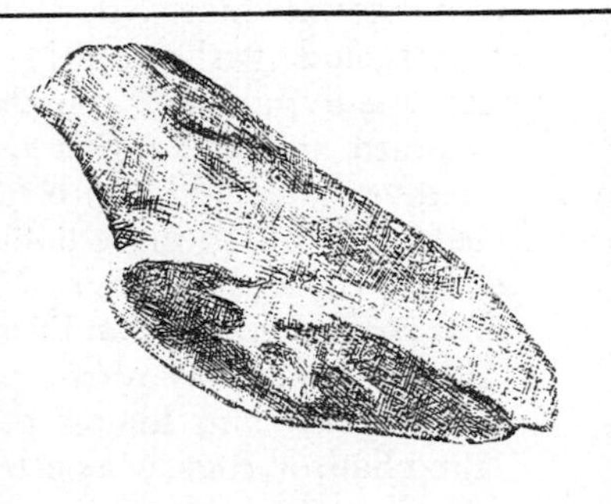

Shank

LAMB

Lamb is tender, lean meat with a delicate yet distinctive flavor. There are many cuts available and many ways of preparing them; lamb is especially favored for gourmet dishes and foreign specialties.

The thin, paperlike covering over chops, steaks and roasts is known as the "fell." Though tasteless, it should be removed from chops and steaks before cooking and should not be removed from roasts because it helps in holding their shape during cooking. If the "fell" is not removed from steaks and chops by the meatman, pull it off and discard.

How to buy lamb cuts: Meat from high-quality lamb is pink to light red, firm and fine-textured, with firm external fat. (Color of the fat is no clue to quality because it varies with age, breed and feed.) Red, porous bones also indicate high-quality lamb.

How to cook lamb cuts: Nearly all lamb cuts are tender enough to be cooked by a dry heat method, i.e., roasting, broiling, pan-broiling or pan-frying. However, these cuts are also delicious braised or cooked in liquid. Use low to moderate temperatures to retain juiciness, tenderness, flavor, uniform color and aroma.

Here are familiar lamb cuts with the recommended ways to cook each (see pages 62–65):

Arm chop—broil, pan-broil, pan-fry, braise
Blade chop—broil, pan-broil, pan-fry, braise
Breast, bone-in or rolled—roast, braise
Breast, stuffed—roast
Crown roast—roast
Cubes for kabobs—broil
Cube steak—broil, pan-broil, pan-fry
English chop—broil
Ground lamb—roast (bake), broil, pan-broil, pan-fry
Leg: American, center, combination, rolled, shank half, sirloin half, with sirloin on or off—roast
Leg chop (steak)—broil, pan-broil, pan-fry, braise
Loin chops—broil, pan-broil, pan-fry
Loin roast, rolled double loin—roast
Patties—broil, pan-broil, pan-fry
Rib chops—broil, pan-broil, pan-fry
Rib roast—roast
Saratoga chops—broil, braise
Shanks—braise, cook in liquid
Shoulder: rolled, square, cushion—roast
Sirloin chop—broil, pan-broil, pan-fry
Sirloin roast, rolled double sirloin—roast
Spareribs—braise, roast
Stew meat—braise, cook in liquid
Stuffed chops—broil, pan-broil, pan-fry

To test lamb for doneness: Lamb is generally preferred medium to well done. Medium lamb is grayish-tan with a tinge of pink; well-done lamb has no pink. A meat thermometer will register 165°F. for medium, 170° to 180°F. for well done. If you prefer lamb rare, roast to 155° to 160°F.

Lamb that is broiled, pan-broiled or pan-fried should be checked for doneness by making a small slit in the center of the meat or near the bone and checking the color.

Lamb that is braised or cooked in liquid should be cooked until fork-tender.

TIMETABLE FOR ROASTING LAMB AT 325°F.

For general directions, see To Roast, page 63

Weight of Cut (pounds)	*Approximate Hours* to Reach 165°F. (medium)*	*170° to 180°F. (well done)*
Leg, whole, bone-in		
5 to 8	2½ to 3½	3 to 4
Leg, half		
3 to 4	2¼ to 2¾	2½ to 3
Leg, boneless		
3 to 5	3¼ to 3¾	3½ to 4
Crown roast		
4 to 6	2¾ to 3¾	3 to 4
Rib (rack)		
1½ to 3	1½	2
Shoulder, bone-in		
4 to 6	2 to 2¾	2⅓ to 3
Shoulder, boneless rolled		
3 to 5	2 to 3¼	2¼ to 3½
Shoulder, cushion		
3 to 5	1¾ to 2	2¼ to 2½

* Meat at refrigerator temperature, placed in oven preheated to 325°F.

STUFFED SHOULDER OF LAMB ROMANO

¼ cup butter or margarine
1 small garlic clove, minced
2 cups fresh bread crumbs
4 teaspoons lemon juice
1 tablespoon minced anchovies
½ teaspoon seasoned pepper
1 3-pound cushion shoulder of lamb with pocket

ABOUT 2½ HOURS BEFORE SERVING:
Preheat oven to 325°F. In 2-quart saucepan over medium heat, in hot butter or margarine, cook garlic until browned, about 5 minutes; remove from heat. Stir in bread crumbs, lemon juice, anchovies and seasoned pepper; spoon into pocket in lamb shoulder; tie with string.

Place lamb, fat side up, on rack in open roasting pan. Insert meat thermometer into center of lamb, being careful not to touch stuffing. Roast about 2 hours or until meat thermometer reaches 165°F. for medium or 170° to 180°F. for well done. Let meat stand 15 minutes for easier carving. Remove string. Makes 8 servings.

ROAST LEG OF LAMB WITH CURRANT SAUCE

salt
2 teaspoons dry mustard
¼ teaspoon pepper
gin or 3 juniper berries
1 5-pound leg of lamb
8 large potatoes
½ cup currant jelly
2 tablespoons cornstarch

ABOUT 3½ HOURS BEFORE SERVING:
1. Preheat oven to 325°F. In cup, combine 2 teaspoons salt, dry mustard, pepper and 2 teaspoons gin. (Or, with handle of table knife, crush juniper berries thoroughly with salt, mustard and pepper and substitute water for gin.) Spread mixture over lamb.
2. Place lamb, fat side up, on rack in open roasting pan. Insert meat thermometer into center of thickest part of meat, being careful not to touch bone. Roast about 2½ to 3 hours until meat thermometer reaches 165°F. for medium or 170° to 180°F. for well done.
3. Meanwhile, cut potatoes into 1-inch-thick slices. About 1½ hours before meat is done, sprinkle potatoes with 1 teaspoon salt. Place on rack around meat and cook until fork-tender, brushing occasionally with pan drippings.
4. When lamb and potatoes are done, place on warm platter. For sauce, pour pan liquid into 2-cup measure or medium bowl (set pan aside); let stand until fat separates; spoon fat from liquid and discard.
5. Add 1¼ cups water to roasting pan; cook over medium heat, stirring, until browned bits are loosened; add to liquid in cup with ¼ cup gin (optional). (Add more water if needed to make 1¾ cups.) In 2-quart saucepan over medium heat, heat measured liquid and currant jelly to boiling, stirring occasionally.
6. In cup, blend cornstarch, ¼ teaspoon salt and ¼ cup water until smooth; gradually stir into hot liquid in saucepan and cook, stirring constantly, until mixture is thickened. To carve leg of lamb, see page 68. Serve sauce with lamb and potatoes. Makes 12 to 15 servings.

MARINATED LEG OF LAMB OLE

salt
½ cup orange juice
½ cup dry red wine
½ cup chili sauce
2 tablespoons salad oil
1 small onion, minced
1 garlic clove, minced
2 tablespoons sugar
2 teaspoons chili powder
1 teaspoon basil
1 6-pound leg of lamb
3 tablespoons all-purpose flour

DAY BEFORE SERVING:
1. In large shallow pan, for marinade, mix 2 teaspoons salt and remaining ingredients except leg of lamb and flour. Add lamb and turn over to coat with marinade. Cover and refrigerate, turning lamb occasionally.

ABOUT 3½ HOURS BEFORE SERVING:
2. Preheat oven to 325°F. Place lamb, fat side up, on rack in open roasting pan; reserve marinade. Insert meat thermometer into center of meat, being careful thermom-

eter does not touch bone. Roast about 3 hours or until meat thermometer reaches 165°F. for medium or 170° to 180°F. for well done, basting occasionally with marinade. Place meat on warm platter.
3. Meanwhile, for gravy: Pour pan liquid into a 4-cup measure or medium bowl (set pan aside); let stand a few minutes until fat separates from meat liquid. Skim 3 tablespoons fat from liquid into 2-quart saucepan; skim remaining fat and discard. Add 1½ cups water to roasting pan; cook over medium heat, stirring until browned bits are loosened; add mixture and reserved marinade to liquid in cup. (Add more water if needed to make 2½ cups.)
4. Over medium heat, into hot fat in saucepan, stir flour and ¼ teaspoon salt until blended; gradually stir in liquid mixture and cook, stirring, until thickened. Serve gravy with lamb. Makes 14 to 16 servings.

"STUFFED" LAMB SHOULDER ROAST

1 5-pound rolled lamb shoulder
salt and pepper
¾ cup butter or margarine
1½ cups diced celery
3 cups apple juice
1½ 8-ounce packages herb-seasoned stuffing
2 medium cooking apples, diced
2 teaspoons dill weed
½ cup apple jelly, melted
2 tablespoons all-purpose flour

ABOUT 3¾ HOURS BEFORE SERVING:
1. Preheat oven to 325°F. Rub lamb with 2 teaspoons salt and ½ teaspoon pepper. Place lamb on rack in open roasting pan; insert meat thermometer into center of meat. Roast 2¾ to 3½ hours until internal temperature is 165°F. for medium or 170° to 180°F. for well-done.
2. Meanwhile, prepare stuffing: Grease a 2-quart casserole. In Dutch oven over medium heat, in 1 tablespoon hot butter or margarine, cook celery 5 minutes or until tender. Add remaining butter or margarine and melt; remove from heat. Add 2 cups apple juice, stuffing, apples and dill and toss lightly. Place mixture in casserole and bake along with lamb for 1 hour.
3. During last 30 minutes of roasting, baste meat generously with apple jelly. Place meat on warm platter.
4. Skim fat from lamb drippings in roasting pan. Over medium heat, stir in flour until blended. Gradually stir in remaining cup apple juice and ¾ cup water and cook, stirring, until thickened. Remove strings from meat. Makes 15 to 18 servings.

ROAST RACK OF LAMB

¾ teaspoon garlic salt
¼ teaspoon salt
dash pepper
1 8-rib lamb roast* (about 2½ pounds)
¼ cup apricot preserves
2 teaspoons lemon juice

ABOUT 2 HOURS BEFORE SERVING:
Preheat oven to 325°F. In cup, combine garlic salt, salt and pepper; rub into lamb roast. Place lamb, fat side up, on rack in open roasting pan. Insert meat thermometer into center of roast, being careful not to touch bone. Roast 1½ hours or until meat thermometer reaches 165°F. for medium or 170° to 180°F. for well done.

Meanwhile, in small saucepan over medium heat, heat apricot preserves and lemon juice until preserves are melted. During last 30 minutes of roasting, brush roast with apricot mixture occasionally. Remove roast to warm platter; let stand 10 minutes for easier carving. With sharp knife, cut backbone from ribs; discard. To serve, carve between every other rib, allowing 2 ribs per serving. Makes 4 servings.

* Ask meatman to loosen backbone from ribs.

LAMB CROWN ROAST:* Using *1½ teaspoons garlic salt, ½ teaspoon salt* and *¼ teaspoon pepper* prepare *one 14- to 16-rib lamb crown roast* as above but place, rib ends down, on rack in open roasting pan and roast 30 minutes. Remove roast from oven; invert so ribs are up, then continue roasting as above about 2¼ hours more. To serve, fill cavity of roast with Wild Rice and Grape Stuffing (page 206). Decorate ribs with paper frills. Makes 7 or 8 servings.

* Order a lamb crown roast from your meatman several days ahead.

ROTISSERIED LEG OF LAMB

½ cup salad oil
½ cup white wine
½ cup red wine vinegar
1 garlic clove, crushed
2 teaspoons salt
½ teaspoon rubbed sage
½ teaspoon ginger
¼ teaspoon pepper
1 5- to 5½-pound rolled leg of lamb

DAY BEFORE SERVING:
In large shallow dish, for marinade, mix well all ingredients except leg of lamb. Add lamb and turn over to coat well with marinade. Cover and refrigerate, turning lamb occasionally.

ABOUT 3 HOURS BEFORE SERVING:
Place lamb on rotisserie skewer as manufacturer directs; reserve marinade. Insert meat thermometer into center of lamb, being careful thermometer does not touch skewer or heating element or oven as it turns. Roast on rotisserie about 2¼ to 2¾ hours until meat thermometer reaches 165°F. for medium or 170° to 180°F. for well done, brushing frequently with marinade.

Remove skewer and strings. Let meat stand 15 minutes for easier carving. Makes 14 to 16 servings.

LAMB LOIN ROAST

2 teaspoons salt
2 teaspoons thyme leaves
¼ teaspoon pepper
1 2½- to 3-pound lamb loin roast*
Avgolemono Sauce (below) or
Béarnaise Sauce (page 166)

ABOUT 2½ HOURS BEFORE SERVING:
Preheat oven to 325°F. In cup, combine salt, thyme leaves and pepper; rub into loin roast. Place roast, fat side up, on rack in open roasting pan. Insert meat thermometer into center of roast, being careful that it does not touch bone. Roast until meat thermometer reaches 165°F. for medium or 170° to 180°F. for well done, about 1½ to 2 hours. With sharp knife, cut backbone from ribs and discard.

Meanwhile, prepare Avgolemono Sauce. Serve sauce with meat. Makes about 8 servings.

AVGOLEMONO SAUCE: In 1-quart heavy saucepan, with hand beater, beat *3 egg yolks, 2 teaspoons cornstarch, 1 teaspoon salt* and *dash cayenne pepper*. In cup, combine *1 cup water, 1 envelope chicken bouillon* and *1 tablespoon lemon juice;* gradually stir into egg-yolk mixture. Cook over medium heat, stirring, until thickened. If necessary, keep warm over hot, not boiling, water, until needed; beat before serving.

* Ask meatman to loosen backbone from ribs.

MARINATED BUTTERFLIED LAMB

2 tablespoons peppercorns
½ cup Burgundy or other dry red wine
¼ cup olive oil
2 teaspoons salt
2 teaspoons oregano leaves, crushed
2 garlic cloves, slivered
1 4- to 5-pound leg of lamb, sirloin off, butterflied*

DAY BEFORE SERVING:
On cutting board, between double thickness of waxed paper, with meat mallet or clean hammer, pound peppercorns until coarsely cracked.

For marinade, in 13" by 9" baking dish, combine peppercorns and next 5 ingredients. Add meat and turn over to coat. Cover and refrigerate, turning occasionally.

ABOUT 1 HOUR BEFORE SERVING:
Preheat broiler if manufacturer directs. Drain lamb, reserving marinade for basting. Place lamb on greased rack in broiling pan. Broil lamb about 7 to 9 inches from source of heat (or at 450°F.) for 20 minutes, occasionally basting with marinade. Turn and broil 15 to 25 minutes until meat is of desired doneness. Makes 12 to 14 servings.

* Ask meatman to "butterfly" leg of lamb, or remove bones at home: Using sharp knife and keeping it next to bone, from shank end, cut meat in one piece from around leg down to joint. Place lamb, meaty side down, with leg bone exposed; cut through meat diagonally to round bone at wide end of meat, exposing rest of leg bone. With knife next to leg bone, cut meat from bone in one piece; cut out rest of bone. Discard leg bone. Cut excess fat from meat. (Butterflied lamb has uneven thickness and irregular shape.)

Glazes for Lamb Roasts

Prepare one of glazes below and, during last 30 minutes of roasting time, brush over meat 2 or 3 times.

MINT GLAZE

1 cup mint jelly
1 teaspoon rosemary, crushed
½ teaspoon salt

In small saucepan over medium heat, heat all ingredients until jelly is melted. Makes about 1 cup.

STRAWBERRY GLAZE

1 cup strawberry preserves
2 teaspoons grated orange peel
1 teaspoon lemon juice
½ teaspoon salt
¼ teaspoon cinnamon

In small saucepan over medium heat, heat all ingredients until preserves are melted. Makes about 1 cup.

MARMALADE GLAZE

1 cup orange marmalade
3 tablespoons dry sherry
½ teaspoon ginger
½ teaspoon salt

In small saucepan over medium heat, heat all ingredients until marmalade is melted. Makes about 1 cup.

APRICOT-PINEAPPLE GLAZE

½ cup apricot preserves
½ cup crushed pineapple
1 tablespoon soy sauce

In small saucepan over medium heat, heat all ingredients until preserves are melted. Makes about 1 cup.

APPLE-CURRY GLAZE

1 tablespoon butter or margarine
1 tablespoon minced green onion
1 cup apple jelly
½ teaspoon salt
½ teaspoon curry powder

In small saucepan over medium heat, in hot butter or margarine, cook green onion until tender. Stir in remaining ingredients and heat until jelly is melted. Makes about 1 cup.

Lamb Kabobs

Cubes for kabobs may be made from any thick, solid piece of boneless lamb. To cut cubes at home, buy rolled shoulder roast, unroll and cut.

INDIAN LAMB KABOBS

1 8-ounce container plain yogurt
1 medium onion, sliced
1 garlic clove, minced
2 tablespoons minced crystallized ginger
1½ teaspoons salt
1½ teaspoons ground cumin
1 teaspoon nutmeg
1 teaspoon chili powder
½ teaspoon pepper
½ teaspoon ground cloves
¼ teaspoon cinnamon
¼ teaspoon ground cardamom
2 pounds boneless lamb shoulder, cut into 1½-inch chunks

EARLY IN DAY OR DAY AHEAD:
In medium bowl, mix well all ingredients except lamb chunks; stir in lamb until well coated. Cover and refrigerate at least 4 hours, turning meat occasionally.

ABOUT 30 MINUTES BEFORE SERVING:
Preheat broiler if manufacturer directs. Drain lamb, reserving marinade. On six all-metal 10- or 12-inch skewers, skewer lamb. Place skewers on greased rack in broiling pan; broil 15 to 20 minutes until tender, basting frequently with marinade and turning kabobs once. Makes 6 servings

SHISH KEBAB

1 2½-pound rolled lamb shoulder or leg of lamb
olive oil
¼ cup red wine vinegar or lemon juice
2 garlic cloves, minced
1½ teaspoons salt
1 teaspoon oregano leaves
¼ teaspoon pepper
16 small white onions
1 large green pepper
3 firm medium tomatoes
½ pound large mushrooms

DAY BEFORE SERVING:
Cut strings and unroll lamb shoulder, trimming excess fat; cut lamb into 1½-inch chunks. In large bowl, for marinade, mix well ½ cup olive oil and next five ingredients. Add lamb and stir to coat with marinade. Cover and refrigerate overnight, turning occasionally.

ABOUT 45 MINUTES BEFORE SERVING:
Preheat broiler if manufacturer directs. In 2-quart saucepan over medium-high heat, in 2 inches boiling water, cook onions 10 minutes or until just tender-crisp. Cut green pepper into 1½-inch chunks and tomatoes into quarters. Remove stems from mushrooms.

On five 12- or 14-inch all-metal skewers, skewer lamb chunks alternately with green-pepper chunks and onions; reserve marinade. Place skewers on rack in broiling pan. Into reserved marinade, stir 3 tablespoons olive oil; brush vegetables with some of marinade mixture. Broil skewers of lamb and onions 10 to 12 minutes.

Meanwhile, on two or three more 12- or 14-inch all-metal skewers, thread mushroom caps and tomato quarters. Turn lamb; place skewers containing tomatoes and mushrooms on broiling-pan rack. Brush meat and vegetables with remaining marinade mixture and broil 10 to 12 minutes more until lamb is of desired doneness. Makes 8 to 10 servings.

MEDITERRANEAN SHISH KEBABS: Prepare as above, using lemon juice; substitute *1 teaspoon basil leaves* and *¼ teaspoon ground coriander* for oregano leaves.

Lamb Chops and Steaks

DEVILED LAMB CHOPS

all-purpose flour
1 teaspoon thyme leaves, crushed
½ teaspoon garlic salt
4 lamb arm or blade shoulder chops, each cut ½ to ¾ inch thick
3 tablespoons salad oil
4 teaspoons prepared mustard
1 medium onion, sliced
½ cup chicken broth
4 lemon slices
4 green-pepper slices

ABOUT 40 MINUTES BEFORE SERVING:
On waxed paper, combine 1 tablespoon flour, thyme and garlic salt; with meat mallet or dull edge of French knife, pound mixture into lamb chops.

In 12-inch skillet over medium-high heat, in hot salad oil, cook chops until browned on both sides; spread mustard on top of chops. Add onion and chicken broth; reduce heat to low; cover and cook 15 minutes. Add lemon and green pepper; cover and cook 5 minutes more or until chops are fork-tender.

With slotted spoon, remove chops, onion, lemon and green pepper to warm platter. For sauce, in cup, blend 1 tablespoon flour and ¼ cup water until smooth; stir into hot liquid in skillet and cook, stirring constantly, until slightly thickened. Pour sauce over chops. Makes 4 servings.

DEVILED PORK STEAKS: Substitute *4 pork shoulder steaks,* cut ½ inch thick, for lamb chops; simmer 25 minutes before adding lemon and green pepper.

LIMEY LAMB CHOPS

1 medium lime
¼ cup butter or margarine
1 teaspoon salt
¼ teaspoon marjoram leaves
4 lamb English chops, each cut about 1½ inches thick

ABOUT 45 MINUTES BEFORE SERVING:
Preheat broiler if manufacturer directs. Cut 4 thin slices from lime; set aside. From remaining lime, grate ¼ teaspoon peel.

In small saucepan over medium heat,

heat butter or margarine, salt, marjoram and grated lime peel until butter or margarine is melted. Place chops on greased rack in broiling pan; brush with half of butter mixture. Broil about 18 minutes or until of desired doneness, brushing occasionally with remaining butter mixture and turning once. Top each chop with a lime slice. Makes 4 servings.

LAMB CHOPS WITH GLAZED APPLES

4 lamb loin or sirloin chops, each cut about 1 inch thick, well trimmed
2 tablespoons butter or margarine
2 medium cooking apples, cut in wedges
½ cup packed light brown sugar
1 teaspoon salt
½ teaspoon cinnamon

ABOUT 30 MINUTES BEFORE SERVING:
Slash edges of lamb chops. In 12-inch skillet over medium heat, in hot butter or margarine, cook chops until browned on both sides and of desired doneness, about 10 to 15 minutes. Place chops on warm platter; keep warm.

In same skillet, in hot lamb drippings, cook apples until tender, turning once. Stir in remaining ingredients; heat just until brown sugar is melted, stirring constantly. Arrange apple mixture around lamb chops. Makes 4 servings.

FRENCHED LAMB CHOPS A L'ORANGE

1 10-ounce jar orange marmalade
2 tablespoons butter or margarine
1 tablespoon dry sherry
1 garlic clove, minced
1½ teaspoons salt
8 Frenched lamb rib chops, each cut about 1 inch thick

ABOUT 30 MINUTES BEFORE SERVING:
Preheat broiler if manufacturer directs. In 1-quart saucepan over low heat, combine all ingredients except lamb chops; heat until marmalade melts, stirring occasionally.

Place chops on rack in broiling pan; broil 10 to 15 minutes until of desired doneness, turning once and brushing occasionally with marmalade mixture. Makes 4 servings.

ROQUEFORT LAMB CHOPS

¼ pound Roquefort cheese
1 teaspoon salt
1 teaspoon Worcestershire
dash pepper
8 lamb 2-rib chops, each cut about 2½ inches thick
1 10½-ounce can condensed consommé

ABOUT 1½ HOURS BEFORE SERVING:
Preheat oven to 325°F. In small bowl, with fork, stir and mash Roquefort, salt, Worcestershire and pepper until well mixed. Over fat sides of lamb chops, spread mixture; set chops on bones, apart from each other, in 12″ by 8″ baking dish; add undiluted consommé. Bake 1¼ hours or until chops are well done, basting occasionally with consommé in pan. Makes 8 servings.

BROILED LAMB CHOPS DELUXE

6 lamb loin or sirloin chops, each cut about 1 inch thick
salt and pepper
butter or margarine
1 small onion, chopped
¼ pound mushrooms, chopped
2 tablespoons all-purpose flour
1 cup milk
1 slice white bread, diced
1 8-ounce package egg noodles, cooked
1 tablespoon chopped parsley

ABOUT 30 MINUTES BEFORE SERVING:
Preheat broiler if manufacturer directs. Sprinkle lamb chops with salt and pepper; broil 10 to 12 minutes, turning once.

Meanwhile, for sauce, in 8-inch skillet over low heat, in 3 tablespoons hot butter or margarine, cook onion and mushrooms 10 minutes or until onion is tender; stir in flour, 1 teaspoon salt, dash pepper and milk; cook, stirring constantly, until thickened.

In small bowl, toss bread with 1 tablespoon melted butter or margarine. Spoon 1 tablespoon mushroom sauce and some diced bread over each chop. Broil 3 to 4 minutes until bread is golden. Arrange noodles on heated platter; sprinkle with parsley; top with lamb chops. Serve remaining sauce as gravy. Makes 6 servings.

BROILED GINGERY LAMB CHOPS

2 tablespoons salad oil
1½ teaspoons ginger
½ teaspoon salt
½ teaspoon garlic powder
6 lamb loin or sirloin chops, each cut about 1 inch thick
½ pound mushrooms

ABOUT 30 MINUTES BEFORE SERVING:
Preheat broiler if manufacturer directs. In small bowl, combine oil, ginger, salt and garlic powder. Place lamb chops on greased rack in broiling pan; brush one side with some oil mixture. Broil 6 minutes; turn chops and arrange mushrooms around chops; brush both with remaining oil mixture; broil 6 minutes longer or until of desired doneness. Makes 6 servings.

BREADED LAMB SHOULDER CHOPS

2 eggs
¾ teaspoon salt
½ teaspoon dill weed
1 cup dried bread crumbs
4 lamb blade shoulder chops, each cut about 1 inch thick
1 to 2 tablespoons salad oil

ABOUT 30 MINUTES BEFORE SERVING:
In pie plate, with fork, mix well eggs, 1 tablespoon water, salt and dill weed. On waxed paper, place bread crumbs. With tongs, dip meat into egg mixture, turning to coat both sides, then dip into crumbs. Repeat until each piece is coated twice.

In 12-inch skillet over medium heat, in hot salad oil, cook chops until browned on both sides and of desired doneness, about 15 minutes. Makes 4 servings.

LAMB STEAKS AND EGGPLANT

4 lamb leg steaks or chops, each cut about ¾ inch thick
1 small eggplant, cut into 1-inch chunks
1 15-ounce can tomato-herb sauce
1 teaspoon salt

ABOUT 30 MINUTES BEFORE SERVING:
Slash edges of lamb steaks; trim piece of fat from one. In 12-inch skillet over medium-high heat, rub piece of fat to grease it well; discard fat. Add steaks and cook until browned on both sides and of desired doneness, about 15 minutes, turning often. Place steaks on warm platter; keep warm.

In drippings in same skillet over medium heat, cook remaining ingredients and ½ cup water until eggplant is tender, about 10 minutes. Arrange eggplant mixture over chops. Makes 4 servings.

MINTED LAMB CHOPS

½ cup mint jelly
1 teaspoon rosemary, crushed
6 lamb blade or arm shoulder chops, each cut about 1 inch thick
1½ teaspoons salt
¼ teaspoon pepper

ABOUT 25 MINUTES BEFORE SERVING:
Preheat broiler if manufacturer directs. In small saucepan over low heat, heat jelly and rosemary until jelly is melted; set aside.

Place lamb chops on greased rack in broiling pan and sprinkle with salt and pepper. Broil steaks about 4 minutes; brush with some of jelly mixture and broil 2 minutes longer. Turn steaks; sprinkle with salt and pepper; repeat broiling and brushing with jelly mixture until steaks are of desired doneness. Makes 6 servings.

Lamb Riblets and Breast

BONELESS LAMB RIBLETS WITH ZUCCHINI

1 tablespoon salad oil
2 pounds boneless lamb riblets
¼ cup lime juice
2 tablespoons honey
½ teaspoon marjoram leaves
½ teaspoon salt
3 medium zucchini

ABOUT 2¼ HOURS BEFORE SERVING:
In 12-inch skillet over medium-high heat, in hot salad oil, cook lamb riblets on both sides until lightly browned; spoon off fat. Add lime juice, ½ cup water, honey, marjoram and salt. Reduce heat to low; cover and simmer 2 hours or until meat is fork-tender, stirring occasionally and adding more water if necessary.

Meanwhile, diagonally slice zucchini into ½-inch pieces; add to meat during last 30 minutes of cooking. Skim fat from pan liquid; serve liquid over meat. Makes 6 servings.

LAMB RIBLETS WITH PINEAPPLE BITS

1 13½-ounce can pineapple chunks
¼ cup honey
3 tablespoons white wine vinegar
1 tablespoon salt
1 teaspoon Worcestershire
¼ teaspoon ginger
6 pounds lamb riblets

ABOUT 2½ HOURS BEFORE SERVING:
Preheat oven to 350°F. In 17¼" by 11½" roasting pan, mix liquid drained from pineapple with honey, vinegar, salt, Worcestershire and ginger. (Reserve pineapple chunks.) Add riblets; cover pan tightly with foil and bake 2 hours or until riblets are fork-tender. During last 10 minutes of cooking time, add pineapple chunks. With large slotted spoon, place riblets and pineapple on warm platter. Makes 6 servings.

OVEN-BARBECUED LAMB BREAST

1 3-pound lamb breast
3 medium oranges
½ cup chili sauce
2 tablespoons honey
1 teaspoon salt
1 teaspoon Worcestershire
¼ teaspoon pepper

ABOUT 3½ HOURS BEFORE SERVING:
Cut lamb breast into serving-size portions. Preheat oven to 325°F. Grate enough peel from 1 orange to measure 1 tablespoon; squeeze enough juice from same orange to measure ¼ cup. In small bowl, mix well orange peel, orange juice, chili sauce and remaining ingredients; set aside.

Place lamb in open roasting pan; pour chili-sauce mixture over lamb. Bake 2½ to 3 hours until fork-tender, basting with sauce occasionally.

Meanwhile, cut remaining oranges crosswise into slices. During last 15 minutes of cooking time, add orange slices to lamb to heat through. Makes 4 servings.

Lamb Shanks and Neck Slices

FRUIT-GLAZED LAMB SHANKS

4 lamb shanks
3 tablespoons all-purpose flour
2 tablespoons salad oil
2 teaspoons salt
¼ teaspoon pepper
¾ cup pitted prunes
¾ cup dried apricots
¼ cup cider vinegar
¼ cup sugar
½ teaspoon cinnamon
½ teaspoon allspice
¼ teaspoon ground cloves

ABOUT 2½ HOURS BEFORE SERVING:
Preheat oven to 350°F. On waxed paper, coat shanks with flour. In Dutch oven over medium-high heat, in hot salad oil, cook shanks until well browned on all sides. Sprinkle with salt and pepper. Cover and bake 1½ hours or until fork-tender.

Meanwhile, in medium saucepan over medium heat, heat to boiling 1 cup water, prunes and apricots. Reduce heat to low; cover and simmer 10 minutes. Add vinegar and remaining ingredients; cover and simmer 5 minutes longer.

Remove shanks from oven; spoon off pan liquid. Pour fruit sauce over shanks; bake 20 minutes more. Serve shanks and sauce on warm platter. Makes 4 servings.

BRAISED LAMB-NECK SLICES

1 tablespoon salad oil
2 pounds lamb-neck slices, each cut about ¾ inch thick
1 beef-bouillon cube or envelope
1 teaspoon caraway seed
1 teaspoon salt
dash pepper

ABOUT 1¼ HOURS BEFORE SERVING:
In 12-inch skillet over medium heat, in hot salad oil, cook neck slices until well browned, turning once. Spoon off drippings. Add 1½ cups water and remaining ingredients. Cook, stirring constantly, until bouillon is dissolved. Reduce heat to low; cover and simmer 1 hour or until meat is fork-tender, turning once. Makes 4 servings.

AEGEAN-STYLE LAMB SHANKS

6 lamb shanks
all-purpose flour
3 tablespoons salad oil
1 29-ounce can tomatoes
3½ teaspoons seasoned salt
1 teaspoon paprika
½ teaspoon garlic powder
½ teaspoon thyme leaves
3 medium onions, quartered
1 pound zucchini, cut into chunks
1 medium eggplant, cut into chunks

ABOUT 2½ HOURS BEFORE SERVING:
On waxed paper, coat lamb shanks with 3 tablespoons flour. In 8-quart Dutch oven over medium-high heat, in hot salad oil, cook shanks, a few at a time, until well browned on all sides.

Return all shanks to Dutch oven. Add tomatoes and their liquid and next 4 ingredients; heat to boiling. Reduce heat to low; cover and simmer 1 hour. Stir in onions, zucchini and eggplant; cover and simmer ½ hour longer or until shanks and vegetables are fork-tender.

With slotted spoon, place shanks and vegetables on warm platter. In cup, blend 2 tablespoons flour with ¼ cup water until smooth; gradually stir into liquid in Dutch oven and cook over medium heat, stirring constantly, until mixture is thickened. Serve sauce over shanks and vegetables. Makes 6 servings.

Lamb Stew Meat

LAMB ISRAELIENNE

1 tablespoon salad oil
2 pounds lamb stew meat, cut into 1½-inch chunks
1 cup rosé
2 garlic cloves, minced
1½ teaspoons salt
¼ teaspoon pepper
¼ teaspoon rosemary, crushed
1 pint cherry tomatoes
1 3-ounce jar almond- or pimento-stuffed olives, drained
hot buttered cooked rice

ABOUT 3 HOURS BEFORE SERVING:
In 12-inch skillet over medium-high heat, in hot salad oil, cook lamb stew meat, half at a time, until meat is well browned on all sides, removing pieces as they brown. Return all meat to skillet. Stir in rosé, garlic, salt, pepper and rosemary; heat to boiling. Reduce heat to low; cover and simmer about 2½ hours until meat is fork-tender, stirring occasionally. Add tomatoes and olives; heat 5 minutes. Serve with rice. Makes 6 servings.

MOROCCAN-STYLE LAMB STEW

1 cup dark seedless raisins
⅓ cup medium sherry
¼ cup olive oil
3 pounds lamb stew meat, cut into 1½-inch chunks
2 medium onions, chopped
1 16-ounce can tomatoes, drained and chopped
3 garlic cloves, minced
2 teaspoons salt
1 teaspoon turmeric
½ teaspoon crushed red pepper*
½ teaspoon ginger
½ cup toasted coarsely chopped filberts or almonds
hot cooked rice

EARLY IN DAY:
In small bowl, mix raisins with sherry; cover and set aside.

ABOUT 2¾ HOURS BEFORE SERVING:
In 5-quart Dutch oven over medium-high heat, in hot olive oil, cook lamb stew meat, several pieces at a time, until well browned, removing pieces as they brown. Spoon off all but 1 tablespoon drippings. Reduce heat to medium; add onions and cook until almost tender, about 3 minutes.

Return meat to Dutch oven; add ¼ cup water, raisin mixture and remaining ingredients except nuts and rice; heat to boiling. Reduce heat to low; cover and simmer about 2¼ hours or until lamb is fork-tender, adding ¼ cup more water if necessary.

Just before serving, stir in toasted nuts and heat. Serve with rice. Makes 6 servings.

* Or, use red chili peppers from pickling spice, if you prefer.

NEAR-EAST LAMB STEW

3 pounds lamb stew meat, cut into 1½-inch chunks
¼ cup all-purpose flour
¼ cup salad oil
2 medium onions, diced
2 garlic cloves, minced
2 tablespoons seasoned salt
½ teaspoon seasoned pepper
½ teaspoon thyme leaves
4 medium tomatoes, peeled and cut into wedges
2 green peppers, cut into chunks
1 medium eggplant, cut into chunks
hot cooked rice for 10 servings

ABOUT 3 HOURS BEFORE SERVING:
On waxed paper, coat lamb stew meat with flour. In Dutch oven over medium-high heat, in hot salad oil, cook lamb, several pieces at a time, until browned on all sides, removing pieces as they brown. Return meat to Dutch oven. Stir in 1 cup water, onions and next 4 ingredients; heat to boiling. Reduce heat to low; cover and simmer 2 hours. Add tomatoes, green peppers and eggplant and cook 30 minutes longer or until meat and vegetables are fork-tender, stirring occasionally. Serve over rice. Makes 10 to 12 servings.

LAMB CURRY

2 pounds lamb stew meat, cut into 1-inch chunks
¼ cup all-purpose flour
salad oil
2 medium onions, sliced
1 garlic clove, minced
1 to 3 tablespoons curry powder
2 teaspoons salt
¼ teaspoon cinnamon
¼ teaspoon ground cloves
dash pepper
1 beef-bouillon cube or envelope
½ cup tomato juice
hot cooked rice for 6 servings
Curry Accompaniments (page 240)

ABOUT 2½ HOURS BEFORE SERVING:
On waxed paper, coat lamb stew meat with flour. In 12-inch skillet over medium-high heat, in 2 tablespoons hot salad oil, cook lamb until well browned, removing pieces as they brown and adding more oil if necessary. Into drippings in skillet, stir onions, garlic and curry powder; cook over medium heat until onions are tender, about 5 minutes, stirring frequently.

Return meat to skillet; add salt, cinnamon, cloves, pepper, bouillon and 1 cup water; heat to boiling. Reduce heat to low; cover and simmer 2 hours or until meat is fork-tender, stirring occasionally. Stir in tomato juice; heat. Serve on hot rice; pass Curry Accompaniments. Makes 6 servings.

Ground Lamb

LAMB MEATBALL KABOBS

1 pound ground lamb
⅓ cup dried bread crumbs
1 egg
1 teaspoon salt
½ teaspoon grated lemon peel
dash pepper
4 bacon slices

ABOUT 30 MINUTES BEFORE SERVING:
Preheat broiler if manufacturer directs. In medium bowl, mix well first 6 ingredients; shape into 1½-inch meatballs. Onto 4 all-metal skewers, thread meatballs, weaving bacon between meatballs. Broil 10 minutes or until of desired doneness, turning once. Makes 4 servings.

TANGY LAMB PATTIES

1½ pounds ground lamb
1 tablespoon grated lemon peel
1 tablespoon chopped parsley
1 tablespoon lemon juice
1 teaspoon salt
¼ teaspoon pepper
1 small bay leaf, crushed
⅛ teaspoon rosemary, crushed
½ cup white table wine or chicken broth

ABOUT 30 MINUTES BEFORE SERVING:
In medium bowl, mix all ingredients but wine; shape into 6 patties. In large skillet over medium-high heat, in wine, cook patties, turning occasionally, about 15 minutes for medium done. Makes 6 servings.

LAMB-AND-CARROT MEATBALLS

1 pound ground lamb
1 cup fresh bread crumbs
1 cup shredded carrots
1 medium onion, minced
1 egg
2 teaspoons salt
½ teaspoon basil
¼ teaspoon pepper
¼ teaspoon thyme leaves, crushed
2 tablespoons all-purpose flour
1 8-ounce package elbow macaroni, cooked

ABOUT 45 MINUTES BEFORE SERVING:
In large bowl, mix well first 9 ingredients; shape into 1½-inch meatballs. In 10-inch skillet over medium-high heat, cook meatballs until browned on all sides.

Meanwhile, in small bowl, blend flour and 1½ cups water until smooth; add to meatballs and heat to boiling. Reduce heat to low; cover and simmer 20 minutes. Serve meatballs and sauce over hot macaroni. Makes 4 servings.

BROILED LAMBURGERS AND PEARS

6 lamb patties
1¼ teaspoons salt
¼ teaspoon pepper
6 bacon slices
¼ cup mayonnaise
¼ teaspoon curry powder
1 29-ounce can pear halves, drained

ABOUT 25 MINUTES BEFORE SERVING:
Preheat broiler if manufacturer directs. Sprinkle lamb patties evenly with salt and pepper. Wrap edge of each patty with bacon slice, securing bacon with toothpick. Place patties on greased rack in broiling pan; broil 5 minutes.

Meanwhile, in cup, stir mayonnaise and curry powder until smooth. Spread mayonnaise mixture evenly on cut sides of pear halves.

With pancake turner, turn patties; arrange pear halves around patties. Broil 5 minutes longer or until patties are of desired doneness and pears are browned. Remove toothpicks from patties. Serve lamburgers and pears on a large, warm platter. Makes 6 servings.

PEPPY LAMB LOAF

1 pound ground lamb
1 pound ground pork
2 cups fresh bread crumbs (about 4 slices)
½ cup tomato juice
¼ cup minced celery
2 eggs
2½ teaspoons salt
½ teaspoon hot pepper sauce

ABOUT 1½ HOURS BEFORE SERVING:
Preheat oven to 350°F. In large bowl, mix well all ingredients. Spoon mixture into 9" by 5" loaf pan; with spoon, level top. Bake loaf 1 hour and 15 minutes. Remove from oven and let meat loaf stand at room temperature 5 minutes for easier slicing. Makes 8 servings.

VARIETY MEATS

Liver, kidneys, sweetbreads, brains, heart, tongue and tripe are the most popular variety meats.

Liver

How to buy: Liver is a fine-textured, distinctively-flavored variety meat. Beef, veal, pork and lamb liver are all high in nutritive value. Beef liver is the least tender; beef and pork liver are the strongest in flavor. They are usually sold sliced and labeled to indicate the kind of liver. Allow 1 pound liver for 4 servings.

How to cook: Beef and pork liver are best braised, or ground for use in patties and loaves. Lamb and veal liver may be broiled, pan-broiled or pan-fried. Before cooking, trim membrane from liver. See How to Cook, pages 62–64.

To grind liver: Precook liver first, so it will be easy to grind: In skillet over medium heat, in 2 or 3 tablespoons salad oil or bacon drippings, cook slices 3 to 5 minutes, turning once. Then put through food grinder and use as recipes direct.

PAN-FRIED LIVER AND BACON

1 8-ounce package bacon slices
1 pound calves' liver, sliced about ¼ inch thick
2 tablespoons all-purpose flour
¼ teaspoon salt
4 lemon wedges (optional)
chopped parsley for garnish

ABOUT 20 MINUTES BEFORE SERVING:
In 10-inch skillet over medium heat, fry bacon until crisp but not brittle; drain on paper towels; keep warm. Meanwhile, trim any membrane from edges of liver slices. On waxed paper, coat liver with flour.

Pour off all but 2 tablespoons fat from skillet. Over medium heat, in hot fat, cook liver about 4 minutes, turning once, until crisp and browned on outside, delicate pink inside (medium done). (Don't overcook or liver will be tough.) Sprinkle with salt and squeeze a little lemon juice over slices.

Place liver and bacon on warm platter; garnish with parsley. Makes 4 servings.

LIVER AND ONIONS: Omit bacon. Use *2 tablespoons bacon drippings,* butter or margarine to cook *2 medium onions,* sliced; place on warm platter. In *2 more tablespoons drippings,* cook liver as above.

LIVER, BACON AND ONIONS: Prepare as above but, after frying bacon, pour off all drippings. In 2 tablespoons drippings, cook *2 medium onions,* sliced, until tender; add 2 more tablespoons drippings; cook liver as above.

LIVER-AND-SAUSAGE ROLLS

6 thin slices pork or beef liver, about 1 pound
¼ teaspoon salt
¼ teaspoon pepper
6 pork-sausage links
1 tablespoon salad oil
1 8-ounce can tomato sauce
⅛ teaspoon thyme leaves, crushed

ABOUT 1 HOUR BEFORE SERVING:
Trim any membrane from edges of liver slices. Sprinkle slices with salt and pepper. Place a sausage link on each slice and roll up jelly-roll fashion; fasten with small skewers or toothpicks, being sure to skewer sausage to liver.

In 10-inch skillet over medium heat in hot salad oil, cook rolls until browned on all sides. Add tomato sauce and thyme; heat to boiling. Reduce heat; cover and simmer 35 to 40 minutes until meat is well done, turning occasionally. Remove skewers. Makes 6 servings.

BROILED LIVER BEARNAISE

Béarnaise Sauce (page 166)
2 pounds calves' or lamb liver, sliced ½ to ¾ inch thick
¼ cup bacon drippings or melted butter or margarine
½ teaspoon salt

ABOUT 30 MINUTES BEFORE SERVING:
Preheat broiler if manufacturer directs. Prepare sauce; keep warm. Trim any membrane from edges of liver slices. Brush liver with drippings and sprinkle with salt. Place meat on greased rack in broiling pan; broil about 6 minutes, turning once, until lightly browned on both sides and medium or well done inside. Serve sauce over liver. Makes 8 servings.

SPANISH-SEASONED LIVER

1 pound sliced beef liver, cut into serving pieces
2 tablespoons salad oil
3 medium onions, sliced
1 1½-ounce package Spanish-rice-seasoning mix

ABOUT 45 MINUTES BEFORE SERVING:
Trim any membrane from edges of liver slices. In 10-inch skillet over medium heat, in hot salad oil, cook liver until browned. Stir in onions, Spanish-rice-seasoning mix and 1 cup water; heat to boiling. Reduce heat to low; cover and cook 20 minutes or until liver is tender, turning liver occasionally. Makes 4 servngs.

Tripe

How to buy: There are three kinds of tripe, a beef variety meat: plain, honeycomb and pocket; of these, honeycomb tripe is considered the greatest delicacy. Tripe may be fresh, pickled or canned.

Fresh tripe is generally partially cooked when bought, but requires further cooking in water to make it tender. Pickled tripe is thoroughly cooked but should be soaked before using. Use tripe within 24 hours of purchase. One pound makes 4 servings.

How to cook: Before cooking, wash tripe. Fresh tripe should be washed and precooked; then it may be broiled or pan-fried.

To precook: In heavy saucepot or Dutch oven, place tripe with enough water to cover; add 1 teaspoon salt for each 4 cups water; over high heat, heat to boiling. Reduce heat to low; cover tightly and simmer 1 to 1½ hours or until done. The cut surface will have a clear, jelly-like appearance. Drain tripe and cut into serving pieces. To broil or pan-fry, see How to Cook, pages 62–64.

To use precooked tripe: After precooking, tripe may be heated in tomato sauce, cream sauce or mushroom sauce.

TRIPE CAYENNE

1½ pounds fresh honeycomb tripe
3 tablespoons butter or margarine
1 medium green pepper, cut in slivers
1 medium onion, diced
1 garlic clove, minced
1 8-ounce can tomato sauce
½ cup minced, cooked ham
1 teaspoon Worcestershire
dash to ⅛ teaspoon cayenne

ABOUT 3 HOURS AHEAD:
Precook tripe as in To Precook (above). Cut into 1-inch pieces.

In 10-inch skillet over medium heat, in hot butter or margarine, cook pepper, onion and garlic about 5 minutes. Add tripe and remaining ingredients; heat to boiling. Reduce heat to low; cover and simmer 15 minutes, stirring occasionally. Makes 6 servings.

Sweetbreads

How to buy: These are the two lobes of the thymus gland. Considered a delicacy, sweetbreads are tender and flavorful. Most of those available come from veal and young beef. Allow 1 pound sweetbreads for 4 servings.

How to cook: Before cooking, wash sweetbreads. To use in salads or as a creamed dish, or for broiling, sweetbreads must be precooked; but they can be braised or pan-fried without precooking. However, if they are not to be used immediately after purchase, they should be precooked regardless of the way they will be prepared later.

To precook: In large saucepan or skillet, place sweetbreads with hot water to cover. For each 4 cups water, add 1 teaspoon of salt and 1 tablespoon of lemon juice, vinegar, dry or cooking sherry. If desired, add ¼ teaspoon ginger. Over high heat, heat to boiling; reduce heat to low, cover tightly and simmer 20 minutes; drain. Place in cold water; remove membrane. With sharp knife, cut out veins and thick connective tissue.

To pan-fry without precooking: Remove membrane and wash sweetbreads. If desired, coat them with flour or bread crumbs. In skillet over medium heat, in a small amount of hot butter or margarine, cook sweetbreads 20 minutes or until done, turning occasionally.

To braise without precooking: Prepare as for To Pan-Fry (above) but cover skillet during cooking, turning sweetbreads occasionally.

SWEETBREADS IN POULETTE SAUCE

1½ pounds sweetbreads
2 tablespoons butter or margarine
2 tablespoons all-purpose flour
⅔ cup chicken broth
⅔ cup half-and-half
salt
3 egg yolks
1 tablespoon lemon juice
6 Patty Shells (page 262) or toast points

ABOUT 45 MINUTES BEFORE SERVING:
Precook sweetbreads as above. Cut sweetbreads into 1-inch pieces; set aside.

In same saucepan over medium heat, into hot butter or margarine, stir flour until blended. Gradually stir in chicken broth, half-and-half and ¼ teaspoon salt; cook, stirring constantly, until thickened; reduce heat to low.

In small bowl, beat egg yolks slightly; into egg yolks, stir small amount of hot sauce; slowly pour egg mixture back into the sauce, stirring rapidly to prevent lumping. Cook, stirring constantly, until mixture is thickened. (Do not boil.) Stir in ¼ teaspoon salt and lemon juice. Add sweetbreads and heat through; serve in Patty Shells. Makes 6 servings.

SWEETBREADS MEUNIERE

1 pound veal sweetbreads (1 pair)
½ cup butter or margarine
⅓ cup dry bread crumbs
2 tablespoons lemon juice
chopped parsley for garnish

ABOUT 45 MINUTES BEFORE SERVING:
Precook sweetbreads as above. Slice sweetbreads lengthwise in half.

Meanwhile, preheat broiler if manufacturer directs. In small saucepan over low heat, melt butter or margarine. Place bread crumbs on waxed paper. Dip sweetbreads first in butter, then in bread crumbs; reserve leftover butter or margarine. Place sweetbreads on greased rack in broiling pan and broil 8 to 10 minutes until lightly browned, turning once with pancake turner. Carefully place on warm platter.

Reheat butter or margarine; stir in lemon juice and pour over sweetbreads. Garnish with parsley. Makes 3 to 4 servings.

Tongue

How to buy: Tongue may be purchased fresh, smoked, corned or pickled, also canned. Beef and veal tongues are more often available uncooked; pork and lamb tongues are usually sold ready-to-serve. One beef tongue makes 12 to 16 servings; 1 veal tongue, 3 to 6 servings; 1 pork tongue, 2 to 4 servings; 1 lamb tongue, 2 to 3 servings.

How to cook: Smoked, corned or pickled tongue may need soaking for several hours before cooking. Because tongue is a less-tender variety meat, it needs long, slow cooking in liquid to make it tender. See To Cook in Liquid, page 64.

When tongue is tender, plunge into cold water to help loosen skin. With sharp knife, slit skin on underside from thick end to tip; loosen skin all around thick end. Grasp skin at thick end and pull it off. Trim bones and gristle from thick end. If tongue is to be served cold, cover and refrigerate in cooking liquid to cool; it will be juicier. If to be served hot, cut into slices and serve.

"BOILED" FRESH TONGUE

1 3½-pound fresh beef tongue
1 medium onion, sliced
2 tablespoons salt
½ teaspoon mustard seed
½ teaspoon peppercorns
5 whole cloves
1 bay leaf
Creamy Cucumber Sauce or
Spicy Cranberry Sauce (page 160)

ABOUT 3½ HOURS BEFORE SERVING:
In 8-quart Dutch oven over high heat, heat to boiling first 7 ingredients and enough hot water to cover. Reduce heat to low; cover and simmer 3 hours or until meat is fork-tender. Plunge into cold water and remove skin, bones and gristle as in How to Cook (above). Serve with sauce. Makes 8 to 10 servings.

"BOILED" SMOKED TONGUE

1 4-pound smoked beef tongue
2 celery stalks, cut into chunks
1 carrot
2 garlic cloves, halved
1 teaspoon peppercorns
1 bay leaf
Spicy Cranberry Sauce or
Creamy Cucumber Sauce (page 160)

ABOUT 3½ HOURS BEFORE SERVING:
In 8-quart Dutch oven over high heat, heat to boiling first 6 ingredients and enough hot water to cover. Reduce heat to low; cover and simmer 3 hours or until meat is fork-tender. Plunge into cold water and remove skin, bones and gristle as in How to Cook (above). Serve with sauce. Makes 12 to 14 servings.

SPICY CRANBERRY SAUCE

1 16-ounce can whole-cranberry sauce
2 tablespoons butter or margarine
1 tablespoon light brown sugar
1 tablespoon horseradish
½ teaspoon dry mustard
¼ teaspoon allspice

ABOUT 15 MINUTES BEFORE SERVING:
In 2-quart saucepan over medium heat, heat to boiling all ingredients, stirring occasionally. Reduce heat and simmer about 5 minutes. Makes about 1⅔ cups.

CREAMY CUCUMBER SAUCE

1 medium cucumber, peeled and seeded
1 cup sour cream
1 teaspoon grated onion
½ teaspoon salt

EARLY IN DAY:
Onto waxed paper, shred cucumber; pat dry. In medium bowl, stir cucumber and remaining ingredients until blended. Makes about 1½ cups.

Brains

How to buy: Brains are soft, tender and delicate in flavor, with little difference in either tenderness or flavor whether they come from beef, veal, pork or lamb. They are very perishable and should be used within 24 hours. One pound of brains makes about 4 servings.

How to cook: Brains may be broiled, pan-fried, braised or cooked in liquid. If they are not to be used immediately after purchase, they should be precooked regardless of the way they will be prepared later. Wash them; remove the membrane before or after cooking as desired.

To precook: In large saucepan or Dutch oven, place brains with water to cover. For each 4 cups water, add 1 teaspoon salt, 1 tablespoon lemon juice, vinegar, dry or cooking sherry and any desired seasonings; over high heat, heat to boiling. Reduce heat to low; cover and simmer 20 minutes; drain. Cover with cold water to cool quickly; drain and use or cover and refrigerate.

To braise without precooking: Wash brains and remove membrane. On waxed paper, coat brains with flour or roll in dried bread crumbs. In skillet over medium-high heat, in small amount of butter or margarine, bacon drippings or salad oil, cook brains until browned on all sides. Reduce heat to low; cover and cook 20 minutes.

To pan-fry without precooking: Prepare brains as in To Braise (above) but do not cover. Turn occasionally while cooking until done, about 20 minutes.

To use precooked brains: Break brains into small pieces and heat in rich white sauce or tomato sauce; or, dip in beaten egg, coat with dried bread crumbs and pan-fry or deep-fry until golden; or, dip into melted butter and broil until golden.

BRAINS AND SCRAMBLED EGGS

1 beef brain (about 1 pound)
8 eggs
½ cup milk
1 teaspoon salt
¼ teaspoon white pepper
¼ cup butter or margarine
2 tablespoons minced onion

ABOUT 45 MINUTES BEFORE SERVING:
Precook brains as above. Meanwhile, in medium bowl, beat eggs slightly with milk, salt and pepper.

In 12-inch skillet over medium heat, in hot butter or margarine, cook onion until tender, about 2 minutes; add brains and cook about 4 minutes until lightly browned, turning once. Add egg mixture; reduce heat to low and cook until set, about 5 minutes, stirring occasionally. Makes 6 or 7 servings.

BRAINS AU BEURRE NOIR

4 lamb or pork brains (about 1 pound)
2 tablespoons all-purpose flour
6 tablespoons butter or margarine
4 French bread slices, toasted
2 tablespoons chopped parsley
1 tablespoon white vinegar
1 teaspoon capers, drained

ABOUT 1 HOUR BEFORE SERVING:
Precook brains as above. Carefully remove membrane, being careful to keep brains in

Steak-and-Kidney Pie, page 257

one piece. Pat dry with paper towels. On waxed paper, coat brains with flour.

In 10-inch skillet over medium heat, in hot butter or margarine, cook brains until lightly browned on all sides, turning with pancake turner. Carefully place each brain on a French bread slice on warm platter. Sprinkle with parsley; keep warm. Into drippings in skillet, stir vinegar and capers; pour over brains. Makes 4 servings.

BEEF BRAINS: Use 2 *beef brains,* halved (about 1½ pounds), instead of lamb.

Kidneys

How to buy: Kidneys, like sweetbreads, are considered a delicacy. Beef, veal, lamb and pork kidneys are sold alone; often, veal and lamb kidneys are left attached to chops (veal kidney chops, lamb English chops). One beef kidney makes 4 to 6 servings; 1 veal kidney, 3 to 4 servings; 1 pork kidney, 1 to 2 servings; 1 lamb kidney, ½ to 1 serving.

How to cook: Veal, lamb and pork kidneys are tender enough to be broiled. They may also be braised or cooked in liquid. Beef kidneys are less tender and should be braised or cooked in liquid.

Before cooking, remove membrane and hard white parts (tubes, fat). See step 1, Lamb Kidneys Madeira (at right). Wash kidneys. If desired, slice kidneys or cut into pieces. Lamb kidneys are usually split (butterflied) or left whole. See How to Cook Meat, pages 62–65.

SAUTEED VEAL KIDNEYS

2 veal kidneys (about 1 pound)
3 tablespoons butter, margarine or bacon drippings
¼ pound mushrooms, sliced
2 green onions, sliced
½ cup chicken broth
2 tablespoons Madeira or dry Marsala
¼ teaspoon salt
toast points
chopped parsley for garnish

ABOUT 50 MINUTES BEFORE SERVING:
Cut kidneys into 1-inch chunks, removing membrane and hard white parts. In 10-inch skillet over medium-high heat, in hot butter or margarine, cook mushrooms and onions until tender, about 5 minutes. With slotted spoon, remove from skillet; set aside.

In drippings in skillet, cook kidneys until lightly browned, about 3 minutes, stirring occasionally. Add mushroom mixture, chicken broth, Madeira and salt; heat to boiling. Reduce heat to low; cover and simmer 30 minutes or until kidneys are fork-tender. Serve over toast points. Garnish with parsley. Makes 4 servings.

LAMB KIDNEYS MADEIRA

8 lamb kidneys
2 tablespoons Madeira
1 teaspoon drained green peppercorns
⅓ cup butter or margarine, softened
¼ cup minced onion
3 tablespoons chopped parsley
1 teaspoon Worcestershire
½ teaspoon dry mustard
¼ teaspoon garlic salt
toast points

ABOUT 1 HOUR BEFORE SERVING:
1. Remove membranes from kidneys. With fingers, firmly grasp hard white piece of fat on kidney. With sharp knife next to white piece, begin splitting kidney lengthwise, carefully cutting about two-thirds of the way down into kidney, exposing thin white veins; repeat on other side. Still grasping white piece, insert knife or kitchen shears under each vein and cut vein loose from kidney. (Be careful not to cut kidney into pieces.) Discard white piece of fat and veins. Wash kidney.
2. Spread kidney open, butterfly-fashion, and place, cut side up, on greased rack of broiling pan. Repeat with remaining kidneys. Sprinkle Madeira over kidneys.
3. Preheat broiler if manufacturer directs. In small bowl, with pestle or table-knife handle, crush green peppercorns. Add softened butter or margarine and remaining ingredients except toast points; mix well. Spoon mixture over kidneys.
4. Broil kidneys about 6 minutes for rare, 8 minutes for medium and 10 minutes for well done. Serve on toast; spoon pan drippings over kidneys. Makes 4 servings.

Chicken en Cocotte, page 195

BEEF KIDNEY STEW

1 beef kidney (about 1 pound)
2½ medium onions
¼ cup shortening
all-purpose flour
3 tablespoons cider vinegar
1 tablespoon salt
¼ teaspoon pepper
2 garlic cloves, minced
6 medium carrots
4 medium potatoes
3 tablespoons minced parsley

ABOUT 2 HOURS BEFORE SERVING:
Wash kidney; cut into chunks, removing membrane and hard white parts. Chop half an onion. In Dutch oven over medium heat, in shortening, cook chopped onion until tender, about 5 minutes.

On waxed paper, in 2 tablespoons flour, coat meat; add meat to onion and cook until lightly browned. Add 4 cups water, 2 tablespoons of the vinegar, salt, pepper and garlic; heat to boiling. Reduce heat to low; cover and simmer 1 hour. Cut carrots, potatoes and 2 onions into 1-inch chunks; add to Dutch oven; cover and cook 30 minutes or until all is fork-tender.

In cup, blend 2 tablespoons flour and ¼ cup water until smooth. Gradually add to stew and cook, stirring constantly, until mixture is thickened. Stir in remaining tablespoon vinegar and parsley. Makes 4 servings.

VEAL KIDNEY STEW: Prepare as above but use *1 pound veal kidneys.*

Heart

How to buy: Beef, veal, pork and lamb hearts are flavorful, firm-textured meats with little waste. All are less-tender meats and should be braised, cooked in liquid or ground and used in recipes. One beef heart makes 10 to 12 servings; one pork or veal heart makes 2 to 3 servings; one lamb heart makes 1 serving.

How to cook: Before cooking, with sharp knife or kitchen shears, trim white tubes and fat from heart; wash heart in cold water. Braise or cook in liquid; see How to Cook Meat, pages 62–65.

BEEF HEART STEW

1 beef heart (about 3 pounds)
1 29-ounce can tomatoes
2 medium onions, chopped
1 tablespoon salt
1 teaspoon basil leaves, crushed
½ teaspoon thyme leaves, crushed
¼ teaspoon pepper
2 bay leaves
1 garlic clove, minced
3 medium carrots, cut into ½-inch pieces
3 celery stalks, cut into ½-inch pieces

ABOUT 3½ HOURS BEFORE SERVING:
Preheat oven to 350°F. With kitchen shears, split heart open; remove fat and white tubes from heart; wash heart. Cut meat into 1-inch chunks. In Dutch oven over high heat, heat meat and next 8 ingredients to boiling. Cover and bake 1½ hours. Add carrots and celery and bake 1 hour longer or until meat and vegetables are tender. Discard bay leaves. Makes about 10 servings.

STUFFED VEAL HEARTS

4 veal hearts (about 2 pounds)
butter or margarine
1 cup fresh bread crumbs (about 2 bread slices)
¼ cup minced onion
1 teaspoon salt
¼ teaspoon marjoram leaves
dash pepper
all-purpose flour

ABOUT 2½ HOURS BEFORE SERVING:
1. Preheat oven to 350°F. Trim white tubes and fat from each heart; wash heart. Inside heart, cut through wall to form a single cavity.
2. For stuffing, in 1½-quart saucepan over medium heat, melt ¼ cup butter or margarine; remove from heat. Add bread crumbs, onion, salt, marjoram and pepper; toss lightly. Stuff mixture into hearts; close openings with small skewers or toothpicks.
3. On waxed paper, coat stuffed hearts with 2 tablespoons flour. In Dutch oven over medium-high heat, in 2 tablespoons hot butter or margarine, cook hearts until

well browned on all sides. Add 1 cup water; heat to boiling. Cover and bake 1½ hours or until meat is fork-tender.

4. Place hearts on warm platter; keep warm. Pour liquid from Dutch oven into measuring cup; add water, if necessary, to make 1 cup. Return liquid to Dutch oven. Cook over medium heat, stirring to loosen browned bits.

5. In cup, blend 2 tablespoons flour and ¼ cup water until smooth; gradually stir into hot liquid in Dutch oven and cook, stirring constantly, until mixture is thickened. Serve hearts with gravy. Makes 4 servings.

SAUSAGE

Over 200 varieties of sausage are available, presenting an almost unlimited range of flavors, textures, sizes and shapes.

Kinds to buy: Varieties of sausage include the following:

Fresh sausage is made from selected cuts of fresh meat—principally pork, sometimes beef. It's the most perishable of sausages; keep refrigerated and use within two or three days after purchase. Cook thoroughly.

Uncooked, smoked sausage has characteristic smoky flavor. Should be refrigerated and used within two or three days. Cook thoroughly as for fresh sausage.

Cooked sausage is made of fresh, not cured meats. Varieties are ready-to-serve; unsliced pieces can be kept in the refrigerator for four to six days; sliced pieces, two or three days.

Cooked, smoked sausage is made of fresh meats, smoked and fully cooked and ready to eat. Some varieties have finely chopped, others coarsely chopped, ingredients. Refrigerate and serve within four or five days. When sliced, use within two or three days. If to be served hot, these sausages need only be heated through.

Dry- and semidry-sausage types are prepared by a carefully controlled drying process; they may be smoked or unsmoked. They're ready-to-eat and keep two or three weeks, refrigerated. They often cost a little more, because of the lengthy (up to six months) drying process.

Cooked meat specialties: This broad category represents prepared meat products which are ready-to-serve and keep two or three days. Most come presliced in packages; some are spreadable.

How to cook fresh-sausage links or patties or uncooked smoked sausage:

To pan-fry: Place links in cold skillet with 2 to 4 tablespoons water; cover tightly; over low heat, cook 5 to 8 minutes, depending on size or thickness. Remove cover; cook until browned, turning occasionally.

Place patties in skillet over medium heat and cook until browned, turning often.

To broil: Preheat broiler if manufacturer directs. Place links on rack in broiling pan. Broil sausage until well done, brushing occasionally with sauce, butter or margarine. With tongs, turn occasionally (a fork will pierce casings, allowing juices to escape). To test for doneness: Pierce with knife and check for uniform cooked color.

Unless label states that bratwurst or bockwurst has been precooked, place in pan of water, heat to boiling, then let stand 5 to 10 minutes; drain and broil.

To bake: Preheat oven to 400°F. Place links or patties on rack in open roasting pan; bake 20 to 30 minutes, depending on sausage size. To test for doneness: Pierce with knife and check for uniform cooked color.

How to cook frankfurters and other cooked smoked-sausage links: These sausages do not have to be cooked. They may be heated in one of these ways:

To simmer: In large saucepan, heat enough water to cover sausages to boiling. Add sausages; when water boils again, reduce heat to low; cover and simmer (don't boil) sausages until heated through, about 5 to 10 minutes depending on size.

To pan-fry: In heavy skillet or on griddle over medium heat, in 1 to 2 tablespoons hot salad oil, butter or margarine, cook sausages until browned on all sides, turning occasionally with tongs.

To broil: Preheat broiler if manufacturer directs. Brush each sausage with melted butter, margarine, bacon drippings or salad oil; place on rack in broiling pan. Broil, 3 inches from heat source, until evenly browned, turning with tongs.

KNACKWURST AND CORN SKILLET

1 pound knackwurst (about 5)
1 medium onion, diced
¼ cup chili sauce
1 teaspoon chili powder
2 12-ounce cans whole-kernel corn, drained

ABOUT 30 MINUTES BEFORE SERVING:
In 10-inch skillet over high heat, cook knackwurst and onion for 10 minutes, turning knackwurst occasionally. Spoon off fat. Add chili sauce, chili powder and corn. Reduce heat to medium; heat, stirring occasionally, about 10 minutes. Makes 4 servings.

SAUSAGE INDIENNE

1 pound pork-sausage meat
1 cup uncooked oats
½ cup finely chopped pecans
½ teaspoon curry powder
⅛ teaspoon ginger
⅛ teaspoon cloves
1 cup pineapple juice
1 tablespoon honey
1½ teaspoons cornstarch

ABOUT 40 MINUTES BEFORE SERVING:
In large bowl, mix well first 6 ingredients; shape into 4 thick patties. In 8-inch skillet over medium heat, cook patties until well browned; spoon off fat.

In small bowl, combine pineapple juice and honey; pour over patties. Cover and simmer 20 minutes, turning once. Place patties on warm platter. In cup, blend cornstarch with 1 tablespoon cold water until smooth; gradually stir into pan liquid and cook, stirring, until slightly thickened. Serve sauce over patties. Makes 4 servings.

LIVERWURST BURGERS

6 slices liverwurst
1½ pounds ground beef
prepared mustard
6 split hamburger buns

ABOUT 20 MINUTES BEFORE SERVING:
Remove casing from liverwurst. Shape ground beef into 12 thin patties, slightly larger than the liverwurst slices. Place a liverwurst slice on 6 patties. Spread liverwurst lightly with mustard and top with remaining patties. With fingers, press meat edges lightly together. In 12-inch skillet over medium-high heat, cook burgers until browned on both sides, turning occasionally, until of desired doneness. Meanwhile, toast hamburger buns. Serve patties in toasted buns. Makes 6 servings.

GLAZED BOLOGNA AND ORANGE LOAF

1 3-pound piece bologna, unsliced
2 large oranges
¼ cup orange juice
¼ cup light molasses
½ teaspoon dry mustard

ABOUT 1 HOUR BEFORE SERVING:
Preheat oven to 350°F. Remove bologna casing; slice meat crosswise about three-fourths of the way through into 12 slices. Place meat in shallow baking pan.

Grate 1 tablespoon peel from orange; set aside. Remove remaining peel from both oranges; thinly slice fruit. Place orange slices in meat cuts.

In cup, combine orange juice, molasses, mustard and reserved grated peel; brush some of mixture over bologna. Bake 45 minutes or until heated through, basting frequently with remaining orange-juice mixture. Makes 8 to 10 servings.

COLD-CUTS PLATTER

EARLY IN DAY:
Use at least three different kinds of ready-to-eat sausage: cooked, cooked and smoked, dry and semidry sausage, cooked meat specialties. Select shapes, flavors, colors and textures to furnish tempting contrasts. If you like, add sliced home-cooked or canned meat; also cheese slices, cubes or slivers, or cheese balls or spread.

Cut large slices in half; fold some slices in half, quarters or triangles; roll others or shape into cones. Slices may be rolled around asparagus spears, or sticks of cheese, pineapple, pickle or celery. Cones may be filled with drained baked beans, coleslaw, cottage cheese or fruit cocktail.

Garnish sides, ends or center of platter with foods that contrast in texture and flavor, such as gherkins, radish roses, carrot curls and cauliflowerets. Relishes such as horseradish, mustard, chili sauce and cranberry sauce may be placed in green-pepper cups and arranged on the platter.

Cover the platter with plastic wrap and refrigerate until time to serve.

SAUSAGE BALLS IN CRANBERRY GRAVY

1 pound pork-sausage meat
2 eggs
1 cup fresh bread crumbs
1 teaspoon salt
½ teaspoon poultry seasoning
1 16-ounce can jellied cranberry sauce
1 tablespoon prepared mustard

ABOUT 1 HOUR BEFORE SERVING:
In large bowl, mix well first 5 ingredients; shape into 1-inch meatballs.

In 12-inch skillet over medium-high heat, brown meatballs well; drain on paper towels. Pour all fat from skillet. In same skillet over low heat, melt cranberry sauce, stirring occasionally; stir in mustard, meatballs and ½ cup water. Cover and simmer 20 minutes or until meatballs are tender. Makes 4 servings.

POLISH SAUSAGE WITH RED CABBAGE

1 small red cabbage, coarsely shredded
1 small apple, peeled and diced
1 tablespoon lemon juice
salt
1 tablespoon butter or margarine
1 small onion, chopped
1 tablespoon wine vinegar
1 pound Polish sausage, cut into chunks

ABOUT 50 MINUTES BEFORE SERVING:
In covered 4-quart saucepan over medium heat, simmer cabbage with apple, lemon juice, 2 teaspoons salt and ½ cup water for 15 minutes, stirring occasionally.

Meanwhile, in 10-inch skillet over medium heat, in hot butter or margarine, cook onion until tender. Stir in cabbage mixture, 1 teaspoon salt, vinegar and Polish sausage chunks. Reduce heat to low; cover and simmer 30 minutes or until sausage is cooked through. Makes 4 servings.

CANNED MEATS

Check label directions to see if meat must be heated before serving. Then turn it into "something different."

If meat can be sliced: Choose from chopped ham, luncheon meat, corned beef, tongue, roast beef and similar items. Serve in one of these ways:

Slice; top cold slices with sour cream, Russian dressing, chili sauce, Guacamole (page 33), Creamy Horseradish Sauce (page 167), whole-cranberry sauce.

Cut cold meat into strips or slivers; add to fruit salad; macaroni, potato or rice salad; vegetable salad; chef's salad.

Use in Cold-Cuts Platter (page 164).

Cut into strips and arrange on top of frozen pizza; bake pizza as label directs.

Slice and pan-broil or pan-fry slices; or dip slices into beaten egg, then into dried bread crumbs and pan-fry; serve with melted currant jelly, or heated applesauce, or maple or maple-blended syrup.

Cut meat into ½-inch squares; add to White Sauce (page 352); heat and serve over waffles, baked potatoes, hot cooked rice or pasta, crumbled corn chips.

If meat product must be spooned: Use beef stew, chili con carne, ham à la king, chow mein and similar products.

Before heating, stir in a little dry red wine; if chow mein, stir in a little sherry.

Heat; stir in sour cream or sour half-and-half; add drained canned mushrooms.

Heat and top with: crumbled corn chips, canned shoestring potatoes, canned French-fried onions, chow-mein noodles, mashed potato mounds, Bacon Pieces for Topping (page 130), tiny cheese crackers. Or, top with shredded longhorn or sharp Cheddar cheese and broil until cheese melts.

Heat and serve over: corn bread, hot biscuits, toasted thick French bread slices, hot rice or pasta, waffles, toasted English-muffin halves.

GLAZED LUNCHEON MEAT

2 12-ounce cans luncheon meat
whole cloves
⅓ cup apricot preserves
2 teaspoons prepared mustard

ABOUT 35 MINUTES BEFORE SERVING:
Preheat oven to 350°F. In shallow baking dish, place luncheon meats end to end to make one long loaf; cut top of meat in diamond pattern about ¼ inch deep. Insert one clove in center of each diamond. In cup, with fork, combine preserves and mustard; spread over top of loaf. Bake about 30 minutes or until loaf is hot and glazed. Makes about 6 servings.

CHILI STEW

1 15-ounce can chili with beans
1 24-ounce can beef stew
½ loaf party rye bread slices
butter or margarine, softened
1 4-ounce package shredded Cheddar cheese (1 cup)

ABOUT 25 MINUTES BEFORE SERVING:
Preheat oven to 350°F. In 10-inch skillet with ovenproof handle, over medium-high heat, heat chili and beef stew just to boiling; remove from heat. Meanwhile, spread bread slices lightly with butter or margarine. Arrange slices, overlapping slightly, around edge of skillet; sprinkle with cheese. Bake 10 to 15 minutes or until cheese is melted. Makes 4 servings.

SWEET-SOUR LUNCHEON MEAT

1 12-ounce can luncheon meat or chopped ham
1 tablespoon butter or margarine
½ cup packed light brown sugar
1 tablespoon cornstarch
½ cup orange juice
¼ cup cider vinegar
2 teaspoons soy sauce
1 small grapefruit, sectioned and cut into chunks

ABOUT 20 MINUTES BEFORE SERVING:
Cut luncheon meat into 6 slices. In 10-inch skillet over medium-high heat, in hot butter or margarine, cook slices until browned on both sides; place on warm platter; keep warm.

Meanwhile, for sauce, in 1-quart saucepan, mix brown sugar with cornstarch until blended; stir in orange juice, vinegar and soy sauce. Over medium heat, cook mixture until thickened, stirring constantly. Add grapefruit chunks and heat through. Pour sauce over meat. Makes 3 servings.

CORNED-BEEF HASH PLUS

Cut canned corned-beef hash into slices 1 inch thick. Pan-fry slices and serve topped with pan-fried pineapple slices; Pan-Fried Onions (page 336); Sautéed Mushrooms (page 333); or warm applesauce or cranberry-orange relish; or heated pasteurized process cheese spread.

Or, break up corned-beef hash with fork; use as filling for green-pepper halves. Bake in oven preheated to 350°F. until heated through; serve topped with favorite tomato or cheese sauce.

CHILI COMBINATIONS

Use heated chili con carne as sauce for baked macaroni and cheese; or heated canned tamales; or hot frankfurters in buns; or Puffy Omelet (page 273).

MEAT SAUCES

BEARNAISE SAUCE

1½ tablespoons tarragon vinegar
3 thin onion slices
2 egg yolks
¼ teaspoon salt
dash paprika
2 tablespoons butter or margarine

ABOUT 10 MINUTES BEFORE SERVING:
In small saucepan over medium heat, heat to boiling 1½ tablespoons water, vinegar and onion. With slotted spoon, discard onion.

In double-boiler top, with wire whisk or hand beater, beat egg yolks, salt and paprika; rapidly beat in vinegar mixture.

Cook over hot, not boiling, water, beating constantly until mixture thickens slightly. Add half of butter or margarine at a time, beating until mixture is slightly thickened after each addition. Serve about 1 tablespoon hot or cold sauce over broiled beef steak or fried, poached or baked fish. Makes about 1/3 cup sauce.

CREAMY HORSERADISH SAUCE

1 4-ounce bottle horseradish (1/2 cup)
1/2 cup fresh bread crumbs
1/2 cup milk
3/4 teaspoon salt
dash cayenne pepper or hot pepper sauce
1/2 cup heavy or whipping cream

ABOUT 15 MINUTES BEFORE SERVING:
In small bowl, combine all ingredients except cream. In another small bowl, with hand beater, beat heavy cream until stiff peaks form. With rubber spatula, fold in horseradish mixture. Serve sauce with broiled or roast beef, hot tongue, baked ham, corned beef or poached, baked or fried fish. Makes about 1 3/4 cups.

BORDELAISE SAUCE

2 tablespoons butter or margarine
2 tablespoons all-purpose flour
1 tablespoon minced onion
1 tablespoon minced parsley
1 bay leaf
1/4 teaspoon thyme leaves
1/4 teaspoon salt
1/8 teaspoon coarsely ground pepper
1 10 1/2-ounce can condensed beef broth (bouillon)
1/4 cup dry red wine

ABOUT 25 MINUTES BEFORE SERVING:
In 1-quart heavy saucepan over low heat, in hot butter or margarine, cook flour until flour is lightly browned, stirring often. Stir in onion, parsley, bay leaf, thyme, salt and pepper; slowly stir in undiluted beef broth and wine.

Increase heat to medium-high; cook mixture, stirring constantly, until thickened. Discard bay leaf. Serve hot over roast or broiled beef. Makes about 1 1/3 cups.

CRANBERRY-CURRANT SAUCE

1 cup whole-cranberry sauce
1/2 cup red currant jelly
2 tablespoons medium sherry
1 teaspoon dry mustard
1/4 teaspoon cinnamon
1/4 teaspoon salt
dash ground cloves

ABOUT 10 MINUTES BEFORE SERVING:
In small saucepan over low heat, heat all ingredients, stirring constantly. Serve with ham or pork roast. Makes about 1 1/2 cups.

BUTTERS FOR BROILED BEEF STEAKS

ABOUT 15 MINUTES BEFORE SERVING:
In small bowl, stir *1/4 cup butter or margarine*, softened, with one of combinations below. Serve on broiled beef steaks or hamburgers.

ANCHOVY: *1 1/2 teaspoons anchovy paste* and *dash Worcestershire*. Makes about 1/4 cup.

CHEESE: *1/4 cup crumbled blue or grated sharp Cheddar cheese*. Makes about 1/3 cup.

CHILI: *2 tablespoons chili sauce, 1 teaspoon prepared mustard, 1/2 teaspoon chili powder*. Makes about 1/3 cup.

WINE: *2 tablespoons Burgundy* or port. Makes about 1/3 cup.

STRAWBERRY SAUCE FOR HAM

1 10-ounce package frozen strawberries, thawed
1 tablespoon cornstarch
dash ground cloves
dash cinnamon
dash salt

ABOUT 10 MINUTES BEFORE SERVING:
In 1-quart saucepan, place strawberries and their liquid. With fork, mash strawberries slightly; stir in remaining ingredients.

Cook over medium heat, stirring constantly, until strawberry mixture thickens and boils. Serve sauce with ham or roast pork. Makes about 1/2 cup.

FRUIT SAUCE

2 tablespoons cornstarch
1 tablespoon grated orange peel
½ teaspoon dry mustard
½ teaspoon nutmeg
¾ cup orange juice
¾ cup apricot nectar
1 teaspoon lemon juice

ABOUT 10 MINUTES BEFORE SERVING:
In 1-quart saucepan, blend cornstarch with orange peel, mustard and nutmeg; stir in orange juice, apricot nectar and lemon juice until smooth. Cook over medium heat, stirring constantly, until thickened. Serve hot over hot pork-sausage links or patties, roast or broiled pork or ham, roast or broiled poultry. Makes about 1⅓ cups.

MARCHAND DE VIN BUTTER

1 cup dry red wine
1 shallot, minced, or 1 teaspoon minced onion
½ teaspoon meat-extract paste
¼ teaspoon lemon juice
⅛ teaspoon pepper
¾ cup butter or margarine, softened
2 teaspoons minced parsley

ABOUT 30 MINUTES BEFORE SERVING:
In small saucepan over medium heat, heat wine and shallot to boiling; reduce heat to medium-low and simmer until mixture is reduced to ¼ cup, about 20 minutes. Stir in meat-extract paste, lemon juice and pepper; cool.

In small bowl, with mixer at medium speed, beat butter or margarine until fluffy. Gradually beat in cool (not cold) wine mixture and parsley. Serve on broiled beef steaks or hamburgers. Makes about 1 cup.

WHIPPED CHIVE BUTTER

1 cup butter or margarine, softened
2 tablespoons chopped chives

EARLY IN DAY:
In small bowl, with mixer at medium speed, beat butter or margarine until fluffy; beat in chives until blended. Cover and refrigerate. Serve cold on hot hamburgers or broiled beef steaks; or use as spread on bread for ham or cold-cuts sandwiches. Makes 1¼ cups.

DILL BUTTER: Prepare as above but substitute 2 *tablespoons chopped dill* for chives.

MUSTARD BUTTER: Prepare as above but substitute 2 *tablespoons prepared mustard* for chives.

MUSHROOM SAUCE

¼ cup butter or margarine
½ pound mushrooms, sliced
¾ cup beef broth
1 teaspoon salt
1 tablespoon cornstarch
¼ cup sauterne

ABOUT 20 MINUTES BEFORE SERVING:
In medium skillet over medium heat, in hot butter or margarine, cook mushrooms until tender, about 5 minutes, stirring occasionally. Stir in beef broth and salt and heat to boiling.

Meanwhile, in cup, blend cornstarch and sauterne until smooth; gradually stir into mushroom mixture and cook, stirring constantly, until mixture is thickened. Serve hot over broiled beef steaks or hamburgers, hot cooked green beans or peas. Makes about 2 cups.

RAISIN SAUCE

½ cup dark seedless raisins
⅓ cup currant or port-wine jelly
½ teaspoon grated orange peel
dash salt
dash allspice
1 tablespoon cornstarch
⅓ cup orange juice

ABOUT 10 MINUTES BEFORE SERVING:
In 1-quart saucepan over medium-high heat, heat to boiling ½ cup water, raisins, jelly, orange peel, salt and allspice. In cup, stir cornstarch with orange juice until blended; stir into raisin mixture and cook, stirring constantly, until thickened and clear.

Serve hot on hot broiled or baked ham, tongue, baked or broiled poultry or roast pork. Makes about 1½ cups.

Poultry

Turkey, chicken, duckling and goose are available fresh or frozen the year around. Their mild flavor goes well with other foods—whether the bird is served alone as the entrée or combined with other ingredients in a main dish.

All come ready-to-cook as whole birds; turkey and chicken also come halved, quartered or cut into pieces. In addition, there are boneless roasts and rolls of turkey that take less cooking time and make carving easy. Finally, canned and frozen prepared poultry dishes include both family favorites and gourmet specialties.

Poultry is an excellent source of high-quality protein. Chicken and turkey supply calcium, thiamine, riboflavin and niacin. Also, serving for serving, they are lower in calories than most meats.

How to Buy Poultry

USDA marks: The circular inspection mark of the United States Department of Agriculture appears on all poultry sold across state lines. This mark, usually found on label, wrapper, wing tag, package insert or giblet wrapping, indicates that the bird has been inspected for wholesomeness and has met the rigid standards set by the federal government.

Poultry may also be graded for quality. The grade mark, in the form of a shield, is usually found with or near the inspection mark. Highest-quality birds are marked USDA Grade A, indicating that they are meaty and have a good appearance.

These marks indicate wholesomeness and quality, but tenderness depends on the age or maturity of the bird.

Class names: The age (class) of the bird determines its tenderness and how it should be cooked. Young birds have tender meat and are best for roasting, frying, broiling and barbecuing. The meat of mature birds is less tender; these birds are tenderized when stewed, or simmered. Check the label for words that indicate maturity.

For young chicken, look for any of these class names: young chicken, broiler, fryer, roaster, capon, Rock Cornish hen. Young turkeys may be labeled young turkey, fryer-roaster, young hen or young tom. Duckling, broiler duckling, fryer duckling or roaster duckling are terms used to describe young duckling.

Older, less tender birds are labeled: mature chicken, old chicken, hen, stewing chicken or fowl; mature or old turkey; mature or old duck; mature or old goose.

TURKEY:

Type to buy: Turkey comes frozen or fresh-chilled; whole or, in many markets, quartered, halved, and in parts or steaks and also ground.

Whole turkeys: Most uncooked whole turkeys are frozen, unstuffed or stuffed; fresh-chilled turkeys are also available. Unstuffed turkeys, frozen or fresh, range in weight from 4 to 24 pounds; frozen stuffed turkeys come in weights from 5 to 16 pounds.

In unstuffed turkeys the giblets and neck are usually wrapped in parchment or plastic and placed inside the bird. Reserve them for separate cooking.

Most frozen turkeys are prebasted. For these, butter, fat or herb-seasoned stock has been injected into the meat of the fresh turkey and, as the turkey cooks, this inner basting keeps the meat tender and moist. There's no need for you to baste the turkey as it roasts.

Some frozen turkeys have a "built-in" meat thermometer inserted into the meat; when the turkey is done, the thermometer pops up.

Turkey parts: Whole or half breasts, thighs, legs, drumsticks, wings, halves and quarters are available, packaged by poultry processors or by the supermarket. Legs, thighs, hindquarters and wings are especially good braised; the larger pieces are suitable for roasting. Some frozen breasts are prebasted. Turkey steaks, plain or breaded, can be cooked quickly right from the frozen state. Turkey also comes ground to be used in patties, loaves, recipes.

Turkey rolls and roasts: Frozen boneless turkey rolls and boned, rolled-and-tied turkey roasts are available raw, precooked or smoked. They may be white meat, dark meat, or a combination of both. Ranging in weight from 2 to 10 pounds, they can be roasted in the oven or cooked on the rotisserie. The smaller roasts come in foil pans, some with gravy ingredients included; gravy for the others can be made from the pan drippings. These roasts are not suitable for rotisserie cooking. Prepare, following label directions.

Frozen turkey dishes: Also available are sliced turkey with gravy or giblet gravy in foil heating pans or plastic bags for heating, turkey pies, turkey dinners and other main-dish items.

Canned turkey: Canned boned turkey, packed in 5-ounce cans, is especially convenient for sandwich fillings, salads and casseroles.

Smoked turkey: Whole turkeys, breast roasts and turkey slices come cured, thoroughly smoked and cooked. The meat may be eaten as is, or heated.

Keep smoked turkey refrigerated until ready to serve.

What size to buy: When buying fresh or frozen whole, unstuffed ready-to-cook turkey, allow about 1 pound per serving if the bird weighs 12 pounds or less. If it weighs more than 12 pounds, there will be more meat on it and you should allow about ¾ pound per serving. Use this table as a guide:

AMOUNT TO BUY

Ready-to-Cook Weight (pounds)	***Number of Servings***
6 to 8	6 to 8
8 to 12	8 to 12
12 to 16	12 to 20
16 to 20	20 to 28
20 to 24	28 to 32

When buying frozen stuffed turkey, allow 1½ pounds per serving.

When buying uncooked boneless turkey, allow ⅓ to ½ pound per serving.

CHICKEN:

Type to buy: Chicken comes fresh-chilled or frozen; whole or cut into halves, quarters or serving pieces. The weight given on each chicken or package is ready-to-cook weight.

Roasting chickens weigh 3½ to 6 pounds.

Meaty, tender birds, they have enough fat to brown well at roasting temperatures. Fine for oven roasting or rotisserie cooking, they can be cooked by other methods as well. The neck and giblets are usually stuffed inside to be cooked separately.

Broiler-fryers weigh between 1½ and 4 pounds. They can be fried, broiled, roasted, braised or stewed.

Hens, stewing chickens or fowls are mature, less tender chickens, ranging in weight from 2½ to 8 pounds. They are best cooked by long, slow stewing or simmering for dishes such as chicken fricassee, stew and creamed dishes.

Capons, noted for their tenderness and generous amount of white meat, usually weigh between 6 and 8 pounds. Roasting is the favorite method of cooking them.

Rock Cornish hens are little 1- to 2-pound birds, the smallest members of the chicken family. Usually sold frozen, they can be roasted or rotisserie-cooked. Cut in half, they can be broiled, fried or roasted.

Frozen cooked chicken items come in individual or small-family packages. Frozen cooked chicken entrées such as pies, dinners and appetizers are available.

Canned chicken items include cooked whole chicken, boned meat, soups, gravies, broth and entrées sold in cans or jars. They are handy for quick serving, hot or cold.

How much to buy: Buy ¾ to 1 pound uncooked chicken per serving. When buying Rock Cornish hen, plan on 1 serving each from the 1- to 1¼-pound birds; 2 servings from the larger 1½- to 2-pound birds.

DUCKLING:

Duckling is sold fresh-chilled or frozen; whole and in parts in weights varying from 3 to 7 pounds. Allow about 1 pound of duckling per serving.

GOOSE:

Goose is sold fresh-chilled or frozen in weights varying from 4 to 14 pounds. Allow about 1 to 1½ pounds per serving.

To Store Poultry

Storing: *Uncooked,* fresh-chilled poultry and thawed, frozen unstuffed birds should be loosely wrapped and refrigerated; they will keep 2 or 3 days. Leave transparent wrap on prepackaged poultry; it is designed to control moisture loss in the refrigerator. If chicken is wrapped only in market paper, it should be unwrapped, placed on a platter or tray, loosely covered and refrigerated; wrap giblets separately and refrigerate.

Frozen unstuffed birds should be kept in the freezer until time to thaw and roast. Frozen stuffed turkeys should be kept frozen until time to roast or tempered according to label directions.

Cooked poultry should be cooled quickly, then loosely wrapped and stored in the coldest part of the refrigerator. Cooked poultry should stand at room temperature no longer than about 1½ hours after roasting. If stuffed, remove stuffing and refrigerate it separately in a covered container. Cover and refrigerate gravy promptly; before serving, heat to boiling. Use cooked poultry, stuffing and gravy within 2 or 3 days.

To Freeze Poultry

For home freezing of uncooked poultry, select only the freshest birds. Unless planing to cook it whole later, cut bird into amounts convenient for your family. Package compactly in freezer-wrapping materials, separating pieces with freezer paper, foil or plastic wrap for easier separation at thawing time. Label the package with the date, kind of poultry and weight or number of servings, and freeze. It will keep for 6 months at 0°F. or below. Use giblets within 2 months.

Do not stuff any poultry before freezing.

Commercially packaged and branded poultry parts are frozen at the height of their freshness; keep frozen in original wrapping.

If freezing cooked poultry, remove any stuffing; cool as quickly as possible; freezer-wrap and freeze meat and stuffing separately. Wrapped, cooked poultry, in pieces or slices, will retain best quality if frozen and used within about 2 months. Use frozen gravy and stuffing within 1 month.

To Thaw Poultry

Thaw unstuffed, whole ready-to-cook birds before roasting. If label does not give directions, thaw either of these ways:

In refrigerator: Leave bird in its original wrapping and place on tray. A 4- to 12-pound *turkey* takes 1 to 2 days to thaw; a 12- to 20-pound turkey, 2 to 3 days; a 20- to 24-pound turkey, 3 to 3½ days.

A 4-pound or larger *whole chicken* will take 1 to 1½ days; if smaller than 4 pounds, 12 to 24 hours. A *duckling* will take 1 to 1½ days; *goose,* 1 to 2 days.

Rock Cornish hens will take about 12 hours.

Turkey halves, quarters and *breasts* take 1 to 2 days; *cut-up pieces,* 3 to 9 hours; *rolled and tied roasts,* see label directions.

In cold water: Leave bird in its original wrapping and place in a large pan or the sink and cover with cold water. Change water frequently to speed thawing; use or refrigerate bird as soon as thawed.

A 4- to 12-pound *turkey* will thaw in 3 to 6 hours; a 12- to 20-pound turkey, 6 to 8 hours; a 20- to 24-pound turkey, 8 to 10 hours. Small *chickens* and *Rock Cornish hens* will thaw in about 1 hour; *duckling and goose,* about 3 to 6 hours.

Turkey halves and quarters will thaw in 2 to 4 hours; cut-up pieces, about 1 hour.

Refrigerate thawed birds if not cooked immediately; use within 1 or 2 days.

Tips for Stuffing Poultry

Prepare the stuffing just before roasting the bird. To save time, you can prepare ingredients ahead—chop celery, cube bread, etc.—and refrigerate them; but don't mix them and stuff the bird until you are ready to put the bird into the oven. Never stuff a bird and then refrigerate or freeze it before cooking. (Purchased prestuffed turkeys are frozen commercially under controlled sanitary conditions and at temperatures that cannot be duplicated at home.)

For homemade stuffing, use 2- or 3-day-old bread cut into ½-inch cubes. Or, use packaged prepared stuffing mix. Allow ¾- to 1-cup stuffing per pound of bird.

Pack stuffing lightly into the bird; it absorbs juices and expands during roasting.

If your family is likely to want more stuffing than the bird can hold, make an extra amount and bake it in a greased casserole along with the bird the last 30 to 45 minutes of roasting time. Or, prepare two different stuffings; use one in the bird and bake the other separately.

AMOUNT OF STUFFING NEEDED

Ready-to-Cook Weight (pounds)	*Amount of Stuffing (cups)*
1½ to 4	1 to 3
4 to 8	3 to 6
8 to 12	6 to 9
12 to 16	9 to 12
16 to 20	12 to 15
20 to 24	15 to 18

How to Cook Poultry

To roast: All kinds of poultry may be roasted. Whole birds may be roasted stuffed or unstuffed; if unstuffed, they'll take less time.

Plan to have large birds done about 30 minutes, smaller birds 15 minutes, before carving; they'll be easier to carve.

For birds stuffed at home, preheat oven as timetable (page 173) suggests. Remove giblets and neck from inside bird. (Cook as on page 175.) Rinse bird with water and drain well. If stuffing a bird over 6 pounds, spoon some of stuffing lightly into neck cavity. (Do not pack stuffing; it expands during cooking.) Fold neck skin over stuffing; with bird breast side up, lift wings up toward neck, then fold under back of bird so they stay flat and balance bird, and keep neck skin in place. If necessary, fasten neck skin to the back with 1 or 2 skewers.

Spoon stuffing lightly into body cavity. Close opening by folding skin tightly over opening; skewers may not be necessary. Depending on brand of bird, with string, tie legs and tail together; or, push drumsticks under band of skin; or use stuffing clamp. Rub skin with shortening, butter or margarine or brush with salad oil.

Insert meat thermometer into center of thigh close to body, being careful that thermometer does not touch bone. Place bird, breast side up, on rack in open roasting pan. Roast, uncovered, according to timetables below or use directions that come with bird.

When bird turns golden, cover loosely with a "tent" of folded foil. Remove foil during last ½ hour and, with pastry brush, brush bird generously with pan drippings, salad oil, melted butter or margarine or shortening (unless using duckling or a pre-basted bird) to give an attractive sheen.

Bird is done when thermometer reads 180° to 185°F. for chicken or turkey; 190°F. for goose, capon and duckling. Leg should move up and down easily and its thickest part should feel very soft when pinched with fingers protected by paper towels. Start checking for doneness of large birds during the last hour of cooking.

For unstuffed birds, skewer neck skin to back; tie drumsticks together across tail, push them under band of skin, or use stuffing clamp. Insert meat thermometer; roast and test for doneness as above. Roasting time will be slightly shorter.

TIMETABLE FOR ROASTING STUFFED WHOLE CHICKEN*

Ready-to-Cook Weight (pounds)	*Oven Temperature*	*Approximate Time (hours)**
Capon		
5 to 6½	325°F.	2½ to 3½
6½ to 8	325°F.	3½ to 4½
Roaster		
4 to 6	325°F.	2½ to 3½
Broiler-fryer		
1½ to 2	375°F.	1¼
2 to 2½	375°F.	1½
2½ to 3	375°F.	2
3 to 4	375°F.	2½
Rock Cornish Hen		
1 to 2	375°F.	1 to 1½

* For unstuffed chicken, roast about ½ hour less.

ROAST STUFFED DUCKLING

With two-tined fork, prick skin of duckling in several places. Roast stuffed duckling as above. A 4- to 5-pound stuffed bird will take 3 to 3½ hours or, if unstuffed, half an hour less. After bird reaches 185°F. to 190°F. internal temperature, and leg moves easily up and down, remove from oven; turn oven control to 400°F. Discard fat from pan and return duckling to oven to roast 15 minutes longer or until skin is crisp, basting with glaze, if desired.

ROAST STUFFED GOOSE

With two-tined fork, prick skin of goose in several places. Roast stuffed goose as above but in 350°F. oven. A 6- to 8-pound goose will take 3 to 3½ hours; an 8- to 12-pound goose will take 3½ to 4½ hours. Internal temperature should reach 190°F. and thigh should be tender when pierced with a fork. Subtract 30 minutes from cooking time if goose is unstuffed.

TIMETABLE FOR ROASTING STUFFED WHOLE TURKEY*

Ready-to-Cook Weight (pounds)	*Approximate Time at 325° F. (hours)**
4 to 8	3 to 4½
8 to 12	4½ to 4¾
12 to 16	4¾ to 5¾
16 to 20	5¾ to 6
20 to 24	6 to 7

* For unstuffed whole turkey, roast about ½ hour less.

CAUTION: Never partially roast any poultry one day and complete roasting the following day; bacteria grow readily under these conditions. Also, it does not save time.

For frozen, commercially stuffed poultry, frozen breasts and boneless turkey roasts, follow label directions. Boneless turkey roasts are done when the temperature reaches 170° to 175°F. on meat thermometer.

For turkey halves and quarters: Preheat oven to 325°F. Skewer skin to meat along cut edges so it won't shrink during roasting. With string, tie leg to tail. Lay wing flat over breast and tie in place with string. Place turkey, skin side up, on rack in open roasting pan. Brush skin with melted butter or margarine.

Insert meat thermometer in thigh next to body, being careful that thermometer does not touch any bone. Roast, uncovered, following timetable on next page or as label directs. Roast until thermometer reads 180° to 185°F.

TIMETABLE FOR ROASTING TURKEY HALVES AND QUARTERS

Ready-to-Cook Weight (pounds)	*Approximate Time at 325°F. (hours)*
5 to 8	2½ to 3½
8 to 10	3½ to 4
10 to 12	4 to 4½

To broil or grill: One-and-a-half- to 3-pound broiler-fryer chickens are most popular for broiling or outdoor grilling. Cut-up Rock Cornish hens, small fryer-roaster turkeys and ducklings may also be broiled or grilled; when whole, grill these birds in a covered outdoor grill by indirect heat (page 623).

For broiling or grilling, have birds cut in halves, quarters or serving pieces. Snap turkey or duckling wing and leg joints so they stay flat during broiling.

Preheat broiler if manufacturer directs. Or, prepare outdoor grill for barbecuing (page 623). Arrange poultry, skin side down, on rack in broiling pan or on grill; brush with salad oil or dot with butter or margarine and sprinkle with salt and pepper.

According to the type of unit, place the broiling pan at the distance from heat recommended by the manufacturer. Or, set the pan about 7 to 9 inches from the source of heat or at the lowest possible position; or, if possible, turn the broiler control to 450°F. For portable broilers, follow the manufacturer's directions.

Broil or grill *chicken* 20 to 30 minutes on one side; turn; brush with salad oil or dot with butter or margarine and sprinkle with salt and pepper. Broil 15 to 25 minutes longer, until chicken is golden-brown and skin is crisp. If you like, brush barbecue sauce or glaze over the chicken during the last 10 to 20 minutes of broiling time. (Most sauces tend to burn if brushed on the poultry the entire cooking time.)

Turkey, goose and duckling pieces are thicker than chicken and will take longer; broil 60 to 75 minutes, turning once. Do not brush duckling or goose with salad oil or melted butter or margarine.

Poultry is done when thickest parts are fork-tender. Serve with pan juices, if any.

To fry: Young chickens, capons, Rock Cornish hens, small turkeys and ducklings are suitable for frying. Birds may be halved or quartered; they'll be easiest to handle, however, if cut into serving-size pieces. They can be fried without coating if thoroughly dried before placing in hot fat; however, coating with flour, crushed cereal flakes or dried bread crumbs makes pieces crisp and helps to keep them juicy. If there's time, let coated pieces dry on wire racks about 15 minutes before frying.

In large skillet, place enough salad oil, shortening, butter or margarine to just cover bottom of pan, about ¼ to ½ cup. Over medium-high heat, heat until a drop of water added to oil sizzles. Add some of poultry pieces (don't crowd pan); cook until golden-brown on all sides, turning frequently with tongs. As pieces brown, remove and keep warm.

When all pieces are browned, return them to the skillet. For *chicken,* reduce heat to medium-low; cover skillet and cook until pieces are fork-tender; this will take 20 to 40 minutes more, depending on size of pieces. For *turkey and duckling,* add 2 to 4 tablespoons water. Cover; cook over low heat 45 to 60 minutes longer. Remove cover last few minutes to crisp skin.

Serve hot, or refrigerate and serve chilled or reheated later.

To oven-fry: Coat pieces of cut-up chicken or turkey with flour as for frying, above. Meanwhile, preheat oven to 400°F. for chicken, 350°F. for turkey. While oven heats, melt ¼ cup butter or margarine in open roasting pan in oven.

When butter or margarine is melted, with pot holders, remove pan from oven. Place poultry pieces in pan, turning once to coat both sides. Bake *chicken,* skin side up, about 40 minutes or until pieces are golden and fork-tender. Bake *turkey* 1½ hours or until fork-tender, brushing occasionally with melted butter or margarine. Serve pieces with pan juices poured over them.

To braise: Pieces from larger birds—turkey, stewing hens—are best when braised. Follow directions for frying, above, but add about ½ to 1 cup liquid (water, poultry broth, tomato juice or dry white wine) after browning. Reduce heat to low; cover and simmer until pieces are fork-tender, about

1 to 2 hours longer. Serve with pan juices.

Or, after covering pan, bake pieces in oven preheated to 350°F. about 1 to 2 hours longer or until fork-tender. Remove cover last 30 minutes to brown and crisp skin.

To simmer or stew: Leave mature bird whole, or cut into halves or pieces; place in Dutch oven or large kettle. Add water to just cover poultry; add salt, pepper and seasonings as desired (celery stalk and leaves, onion, a few whole cloves, a few peppercorns); over high heat, heat to boiling. Reduce heat to low; cover and simmer until poultry is fork-tender, 2 to 3 hours, depending on size and age of bird. See recipe, page 195.

Young poultry can be stewed the same way; it will be tender in 45 to 60 minutes.

When bird is done, remove Dutch oven from heat; keep chicken and broth covered and refrigerate. When poultry is cool, remove meat from bones in large chunks to use in recipes; strain and reserve broth.

A 4½-pound stewing chicken yields about 3 cups firmly packed, cooked chicken; a 3-pound broiler-fryer yields about 2½ cups cooked meat.

To pressure-cook: Larger birds, cut into serving-size pieces, can be pressure-cooked. Coat pieces and brown in hot fat as for frying, then add ¾ to 1 cup water as pressure-cooker manual directs. Have cooker no more than two-thirds full. Bring cooker to 15 pounds pressure as manual directs; cook 15 to 20 minutes or as directed. Remove from heat and reduce heat quickly as directed before uncovering.

To cook on rotisserie: Whole birds and large poultry pieces can be cooked on the rotisserie in the oven or outdoor grill or on the portable rotisserie.

Remove giblets. Rinse bird inside and out with water; drain well. Skewer neck skin to back, then tie wings close to body.

Mount and balance the bird, birds or pieces before starting the rotary spit. Insert spit through body lengthwise and tighten holding prongs. Tie tail and drumsticks to rod. If mounting more than one bird, mount in opposite directions to balance. Turn rod slowly to test balance.

Because rotisseries vary greatly, follow manufacturer's directions. A meat thermometer, inserted in thigh of bird next to body or in thickest part of boneless roast or turkey part (away from bone), will read 180° to 185°F. when turkey and chicken are done, 190°F. for duckling, goose and capon. Baste turkey and chicken occasionally with melted butter or margarine; baste all poultry with sauce during last 20 minutes of cooking time, if desired.

Giblets

Giblets are the heart, liver and gizzard of a bird; the neck is usually inside the bird too. If they are from a thawed frozen bird, cook within a few hours after thawing.

To cook giblets: In small saucepan over high heat, heat to boiling *giblets, neck, 1 celery stalk*, cut up, *1 medium onion, 1 teaspoon salt* and enough *water* to cover. Reduce heat to low; cover and simmer 30 minutes for small giblets, 1 hour for large ones or until fork-tender. Drain, reserving liquid for making gravy. Discard celery and onion. Coarsely chop giblets; remove meat from neck; discard bones. Use chopped giblets and neck meat in gravy or stuffing.

How to Carve Poultry

To carve turkey, chicken, capon, goose:

Place the roasted bird on a warm platter or cutting board 15 to 30 minutes ahead to allow it to "set" for easier carving. Place the bird directly in front of you with the breast of the bird at your left. Using a sharp carving knife and a fork with long tines, cut drumstick and thigh from body; disjoint it by bending it down with hand. Remove it to a separate plate and slice the dark meat from the bone.

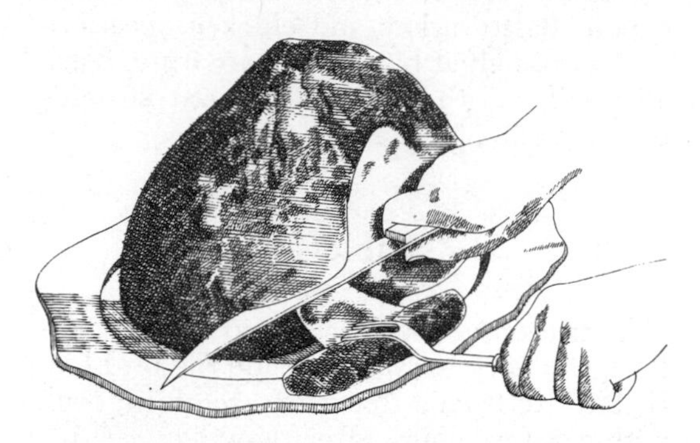

Insert the fork securely into the upper part of the wing; make a long, deep cut above the wing joint through the breast to the frame of the bird.

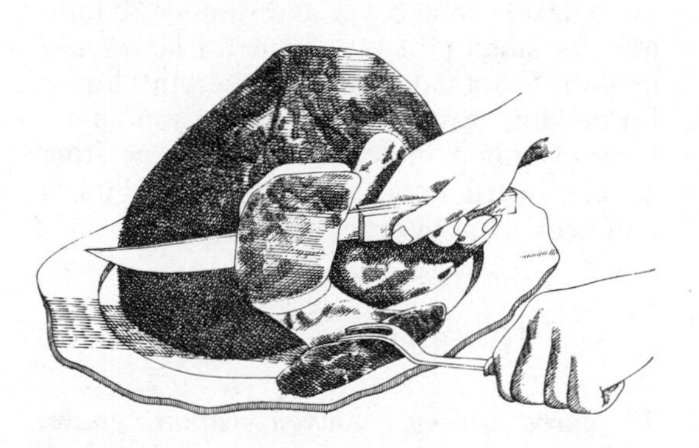

Beginning halfway up breast, carve downward with a straight motion; when the knife reaches the slice made across from the wing, the poultry slices will fall free. Continue carving in thin slices until enough has been carved for serving. Carve additional slices as needed later, repeating the same steps on the other side of the bird.

After the meal, cut all the meat from the carcass; cover and refrigerate it for use in casseroles, soups, sandwiches. Do not let the meat stand at room temperature for more than about 1½ hours after roasting.

To carve duckling, Rock Cornish hens and small game birds: Use poultry shears, kitchen shears or a sharp knife and cut the roasted bird in quarters or halves, depending upon its size.

Turkey

For general thawing, stuffing directions, roasting timetables, see pages 172–174. For Stuffings, see page 204; for Sauces and Glazes, page 207.

ROAST TURKEY WITH STUFFING

ABOUT 6 HOURS BEFORE SERVING:

1. Preheat oven to 325°F. Prepare favorite stuffing (pages 204–207). Remove neck and giblets from *one 14- to 16-pound ready-to-stuff turkey;* set aside for use in Giblet Gravy. Rinse turkey with water; drain well.
2. Stuff neck cavity of turkey lightly with stuffing. Fold neck skin over stuffing; with bird breast-side up, lift wings up, then fold under back of bird so they stay flat and balance turkey and keep neck skin in place. If necessary, fasten with 1 or 2 skewers. Stuff body cavity loosely with stuffing. Depending on brand of turkey, tie drumsticks together across tail; push them under the band of skin or use stuffing clamp. Brush skin with salad oil.
3. Insert meat thermometer in center of thigh, next to body, being careful thermometer does not touch bone. Place turkey, breast side up, on rack in open roasting pan. Roast turkey 5¼ to 5¾ hours.
4. When turkey turns golden, cover loosely with foil. During last hour of roasting, start checking for doneness and remove foil. Baste turkey with pan drippings, melted butter or margarine or salad oil (only if bird is not prebasted). Prepare *Giblet Gravy* (below).
5. Roast turkey until meat thermometer reaches 180° to 185°F. or until drumstick moves easily up and down and thickest part of drumstick feels soft when pinched with fingers protected with paper towel.
6. Remove turkey to warm platter; remove skewers, if used. Let stand 20 minutes for easier carving. Serve with Giblet Gravy. Makes 14 to 20 servings.

GIBLET GRAVY

FOR TURKEY: While bird is roasting, prepare *giblets* as on page 175, reserving broth.

When turkey is removed to platter, pour drippings from roasting pan into 4-cup measure or large bowl; let stand a few minutes until fat separates from poultry juices.

Meanwhile, add *1/4 cup water* to roasting pan; stir and scrape until all browned bits are loosened; set aside.

Spoon *6 tablespoons fat* from drippings into 2-quart saucepan; spoon off any remaining fat from drippings and discard. Add mixture from roasting pan to poultry juices; add giblet broth (and water if necessary) to make 4 cups mixture.

Over medium heat, into fat in saucepan, stir *6 tablespoons all-purpose flour* and *2 teaspoons salt* until blended; gradually stir in broth mixture and cook, stirring constantly, until mixture is smooth and thickened. Add chopped giblets and neck meat; heat. Makes about 4 cups.

FOR CHICKEN AND DUCKLING: Prepare as above but use *3 tablespoons fat, 3 tablespoons flour* and *2 cups broth mixture.*

RASPBERRY GRAVY FOR TURKEY

2 10-ounce packages frozen raspberries, thawed
1 10 1/2-ounce can condensed beef bouillon
1/2 cup red raspberry jelly
grated peel of 1 lemon
1/4 cup lemon juice
salt and pepper

ABOUT 20 MINUTES BEFORE SERVING:
Drain raspberries (use drained juice with orange juice another day). When turkey is removed to platter, pour drippings from roasting pan into medium bowl; let stand a few minutes until fat separates from meat juices.

Meanwhile, stir undiluted bouillon, 1/2 soup-can water, jelly, lemon peel and juice into roasting pan. Spoon fat from drippings; discard. Add poultry juices to pan and cook over medium heat until bubbly hot, stirring constantly to loosen browned bits. Stir in raspberries and salt and pepper to taste; heat through. Makes about 2 1/2 cups.

BARBECUED TURKEY ROLLS

ABOUT 2 HOURS BEFORE SERVING:
Roast *two 2-pound frozen, boneless turkey rolls* as label directs, but about 45 minutes before done, spoon off pan juices. (If pan is covered, remove foil.) Pour *Turkey Barbecue Sauce* (below) over turkey and continue roasting until fork-tender or internal temperature reaches 170°F. on meat thermometer. Pass remaining sauce from pan to serve with turkey. Makes 8 to 10 servings.

TURKEY BARBECUE SAUCE: In medium bowl, combine *one 18-ounce bottle all-purpose barbecue sauce* (2 cups), *1 tablespoon Worcestershire, 1/4 teaspoon hot pepper sauce* and *2/3 cup canned crushed pineapple.* Stir until thoroughly mixed.

TURKEY ROAST WITH CRANBERRY-ORANGE SAUCE

ABOUT 2 1/2 HOURS BEFORE SERVING:
Preheat oven to 325°F. or as label directs. Place *one 4-pound boned-and-tied turkey roast* on rack in open roasting pan. Insert meat thermometer into center of roast. Roast 2 to 2 1/2 hours or until internal temperature reaches 170° to 175°F. During last 50 minutes of roasting time, baste with pan drippings or melted butter or margarine.

Meanwhile, prepare Cranberry-Orange Sauce (page 208). Let roast stand 15 minutes for easier slicing; pass sauce to spoon over slices. Makes about 12 servings.

OTHER SAUCES: Watercress Sauce (page 208); Fruit-Cocktail Sauce (page 207); Lemon Sauce for Poultry (page 208).

OVEN-FRIED TURKEY THIGH

1/4 cup butter or margarine
1 cup packaged herb-seasoned stuffing
1 2-pound turkey thigh

ABOUT 2 1/4 HOURS BEFORE SERVING:
Preheat oven to 350°F. In 13" by 9" baking pan, melt butter or margarine in oven. With pot holders, remove pan from oven. On cutting board or waxed paper, with rolling pin, crush stuffing mix.

Remove bone and cut turkey into serving-size pieces. (Cover and refrigerate bone for soup another day.) With tongs, roll turkey in melted butter or margarine, then coat with crumbs on all sides; arrange, skin side up, in pan. Pat any remaining crumbs on tops of pieces. Cover pan with foil and bake 1 hour. Uncover and bake 45 to 60 minutes or until turkey is fork-tender. Makes 4 servings.

TURKEY MARYLAND

1 5- to 6-pound fryer-roaster turkey
1 egg
⅓ cup milk
all-purpose flour
1½ cups dry bread crumbs
salad oil
1½ teaspoons salt
¼ teaspoon pepper
⅔ cup half-and-half

ABOUT 2½ HOURS BEFORE SERVING:
Preheat oven to 350°F. Cut up turkey. In pie plate, with fork, beat egg with milk. Place ⅓ cup flour on sheet of waxed paper; place crumbs on another. Coat turkey and giblets with flour, then egg, then crumbs.

In 12-inch skillet over medium heat, in ¼ cup hot salad oil, cook turkey, a few pieces at a time until browned on all sides. Arrange turkey in 15½″ by 10½″ roasting pan. Sprinkle with salt and pepper; add ½ cup water. Cover pan with foil and bake 1½ hours or until fork-tender; uncover for last 30 minutes of baking time.

With tongs, place turkey on warm platter; keep warm. For sauce, into drippings in roasting pan, stir half-and-half. In cup, blend 2 tablespoons flour and ½ cup water until smooth; gradually stir into hot liquid in pan and cook over medium heat, stirring constantly, until mixture is thickened. Makes 6 to 8 servings.

TURKEY BREAST GLACE

1 5- to 6-pound frozen breast of turkey
1 envelope unflavored gelatin
1 teaspoon chicken stock base
5 teaspoons lemon juice
2 teaspoons sugar
2 teaspoons dry mustard
¼ teaspoon salt
2 cups mayonnaise (1 16-ounce jar)
1 cooked carrot and some fresh green-pepper strips for garnish

DAY BEFORE:
Roast turkey as label directs; refrigerate.

EARLY IN DAY:
In 1-quart saucepan, over 1 cup cold water, sprinkle gelatin. Over low heat, heat until gelatin is dissolved, stirring constantly. Stir in next 5 ingredients until smooth. Refrigerate to cool; stir in mayonnaise.

Remove skin from turkey; place turkey on rack over waxed paper or in shallow baking pan. Quickly spoon some mayonnaise mixture evenly over entire turkey to make a coating; refrigerate until set, about 5 minutes. If mixture becomes too thick, set in pan of hot water and stir until of saucelike consistency. Repeat coating several times, stirring mixture before spooning over turkey, until surface of turkey is well coated and smooth.

Meanwhile, for garnish, cut carrot into thin slices; cut slices into flower designs with canapé cutter. Arrange "flowers" with green-pepper strips in attractive pattern on last coating of turkey. Refrigerate. To serve, cut turkey into thin slices. Makes 10 to 15 servings.

TURKEY WITH ONION-SAGE DUMPLINGS

6 pounds turkey drumsticks and wings
¼ cup all-purpose flour
3 tablespoons salad oil
4 chicken-bouillon cubes or envelopes
2 bay leaves

DUMPLING DOUGH:
1 egg, slightly beaten
1¼ cups all-purpose flour
½ cup milk
¼ cup minced green onions
2 tablespoons salad oil
1½ teaspoons double-acting baking powder
¾ teaspoon salt
½ teaspoon rubbed sage

ABOUT 2¼ HOURS BEFORE SERVING:
1. Cut turkey wings apart at joints. On waxed paper, lightly coat all turkey with flour. In Dutch oven over medium-high heat, in hot salad oil, cook turkey until lightly browned on all sides. Add 4 cups hot water, bouillon cubes and bay leaves; heat to boiling. Reduce heat to low; cover and simmer 1½ hours or until tender.
2. About 5 minutes before turkey is fork-tender, in medium bowl, with fork, mix well all Dumpling Dough ingredients.
3. When turkey is done, discard bay leaves; place turkey on warm platter; keep warm.

Divide Dumpling Dough into 6 portions and drop by spoonfuls into simmering liquid in Dutch oven. Cook dumplings 10 minutes uncovered, then cover and cook 10 to 15 minutes more until done.

4. With slotted spoon, place dumplings on platter with turkey. Spoon excess fat from liquid in Dutch oven; discard. Pour liquid into gravy boat to serve with turkey and dumplings. Makes 6 servings.

SAUCY TURKEY WINGS

4 pounds turkey wings
2 tablespoons salad oil
1 10½-ounce can condensed cream-of-celery soup
1 teaspoon salt
½ teaspoon paprika
¼ teaspoon pepper

ABOUT 2½ HOURS BEFORE SERVING:
Preheat oven to 350°F. Separate wings at joints. (Use wing tips for broth, if you like.) In 12-inch skillet over medium-high heat, in hot salad oil, cook turkey, a few pieces at a time, until browned on all sides; arrange in 15½" by 10½" roasting pan.

In small bowl, combine undiluted soup, salt, paprika and pepper; spoon over turkey. Cover and bake 2 hours or until fork-tender. Makes 8 servings.

APRICOT-GLAZED TURKEY DRUMSTICKS

4 turkey drumsticks (about 4 pounds)
2 celery stalks, halved
1 medium onion, halved
1 tablespoon salt
½ teaspoon peppercorns, crushed
¾ cup apricot preserves
1 8¾-ounce can apricot halves, drained, for garnish

ABOUT 2½ HOURS BEFORE SERVING:
In large saucepot, place turkey, celery, onion, salt, peppercorns and add hot water to cover; over high heat, heat to boiling. Reduce heat to medium-low; cover and simmer 1½ hours or until fork-tender.

Meanwhile, preheat oven to 400°F. In small saucepan over medium heat, melt apricot preserves.

Remove turkey from broth; drain well. (Strain; cover and refrigerate broth for soup another day.) With paper towels, pull tendons from ends of drumsticks. Place turkey in open roasting pan; brush with preserves; top with apricot halves and brush them with preserves. Bake 10 minutes to glaze turkey. Makes 4 servings.

Chicken

For general thawing, cooking directions, roasting timetables and information on stuffing, see pages 172–175. For Stuffings, see page 204; for Sauces and Glazes, page 207. For leftover recipes, see Main Dishes, pages 253–268.

FRUITED SKILLET CHICKEN

3 tablespoons all-purpose flour
1 teaspoon ginger
1 3-pound broiler-fryer, cut up
¼ cup shortening
1 16-ounce jar refrigerated fruit salad
about ½ cup orange juice
2 teaspoons salt
1½ teaspoons sugar

ABOUT 1 HOUR BEFORE SERVING:
On waxed paper, combine flour and ginger; use to coat chicken. (Reserve remaining mixture.) In 12-inch skillet over medium-high heat, in hot shortening, cook chicken until browned on all sides.

Into 1-cup measuring cup, drain liquid from fruit and add enough orange juice to make 1 cup liquid; pour over chicken. (Reserve fruit.) Sprinkle mixture with salt and sugar; heat to boiling. Reduce heat to low; cover and simmer 30 to 35 minutes until chicken is fork-tender.

In cup, mix reserved flour mixture with 3 tablespoons water until smooth. Gradually stir into liquid in skillet and cook over medium heat, stirring constantly, until mixture is thickened. Add reserved fruit and heat about one minute. Makes 4 servings.

FRESH-FRUIT: Instead of using refrigerated fruit salad, simmer chicken in *1 cup orange juice* and add *1 large orange,* sectioned, and *1 large grapefruit,* sectioned.

PAN-FRIED CHICKEN

1 2½- to 3-pound broiler-fryer, cut up
¼ cup all-purpose flour
¼ cup salad oil
salt and pepper
Cream Gravy for Fried Chicken (at right), optional

ABOUT 1 HOUR BEFORE SERVING:
On waxed paper, coat chicken with flour. In 12-inch skillet, over medium-high heat, in hot salad oil, cook chicken until well-browned on all sides, turning frequently with tongs. Sprinkle chicken lightly with salt and pepper.

Reduce heat to medium-low; cover skillet and cook until pieces are fork-tender, about 25 minutes. Remove cover last few minutes to crisp skin. Serve with Cream Gravy for Fried Chicken, if you like. Makes 4 servings.

CREAM GRAVY FOR FRIED CHICKEN

ABOUT 20 MINUTES BEFORE SERVING:
After chicken is pan-fried, pour off all but *¼ cup drippings* from skillet. Stir in *¼ cup all-purpose flour* until blended (use flour left over from coating chicken, plus more flour if needed). Over medium heat, cook, stirring and scraping until browned bits are loosened from pan. Continue cooking, stirring constantly, until flour is light-golden.

Gradually stir in *2½ cups milk** and cook, stirring constantly, until mixture is smooth and thickened. Stir in *1 tablespoon chopped parsley* and *salt* and *pepper* to taste; if desired, stir in *1 tablespoon dry or medium sherry*. Makes about 2¾ cups.

* Or, use *1 cup milk* and *1½ cups half-and-half;* or 1 cup chicken broth and 1½ cups half-and-half; or 1 cup undiluted evaporated milk and 1½ cups chicken broth.

OVEN-FRIED CHICKEN

¼ cup butter or margarine
¾ cup cracker meal
1 teaspoon salt
dash pepper
1 2½- to 3-pound broiler-fryer, cut up

ABOUT 1 HOUR BEFORE SERVING:
Preheat oven to 400°F. In 13" by 9" baking dish, melt butter or margarine in oven. On waxed paper, mix cracker meal, salt and pepper. With pot holders, remove dish from oven. With tongs, roll chicken in melted butter or margarine, then coat with crumbs on all sides; return to dish. Bake 40 to 50 minutes until chicken is fork-tender. Makes 4 servings.

CORN-CRISPED: Prepare as above but omit butter or margarine; pour *⅓ cup undiluted evaporated milk* in pie plate and substitute *¾ cup cornflake crumbs* for cracker meal; use to coat chicken.

CORN-BREAD: Prepare as above but substitute *1 cup corn-bread stuffing*, crushed, for cracker meal; omit salt and pepper.

ITALIAN-SEASONED: Prepare as above but substitute *¾ cup Italian-seasoned bread crumbs* for cracker meal; omit salt and pepper.

OVEN-BARBECUED CHICKEN

2 tablespoons butter or margarine
3 garlic cloves, minced
1 cup catchup
2 tablespoons packed brown sugar
1 tablespoon Worcestershire
1 tablespoon liquid smoke (optional)
1 teaspoon salt
¼ teaspoon pepper
2 2½- to 3-pound broiler-fryers, quartered
3 medium onions, thinly sliced

ABOUT 2½ HOURS AHEAD OR DAY BEFORE:
Prepare barbecue sauce: In 1-quart saucepan over medium heat, in hot butter or margarine, cook garlic 2 or 3 minutes, until lightly browned. Add ¼ cup water, catchup and next 5 ingredients; heat to boiling. Reduce heat to medium-low; cover and simmer 10 minutes, stirring occasionally.

ABOUT 1½ HOURS BEFORE SERVING:
Preheat oven to 375°F. Arrange chicken pieces, skin side up, in large open roasting pan. Arrange onion slices over chicken; pour barbecue sauce over chicken and onions. Bake 1¼ hours or until chicken is fork-tender, basting occasionally with sauce. Serve with sauce. Makes 8 servings.

CHICKEN TARRAGON

1 2½- to 3-pound broiler-fryer, cut up
all-purpose flour
butter or margarine
¼ pound sweet Italian sausage links, diced
1 small onion, chopped
1 garlic clove, minced
1 tablespoon chopped parsley
1 12-ounce can apple juice (1½ cups)
1½ teaspoons salt
1 tablespoon tarragon

ABOUT 1 HOUR BEFORE SERVING:
On waxed paper, coat chicken with ¼ cup flour. In 12-inch skillet over medium-high heat, in 2 tablespoons hot butter or margarine, cook sausage and chicken until chicken is browned on all sides; pour off drippings.

Meanwhile, in small skillet over medium heat, in 2 tablespoons hot butter or margarine, cook onion, garlic and parsley until tender, about 5 minutes. Stir in 1½ tablespoons flour until blended. Gradually stir in apple juice and salt and cook, stirring constantly, until mixture is slightly thickened; stir in tarragon.

Pour tarragon mixture over chicken mixture. Reduce heat to low; cover and simmer 30 minutes or until chicken is fork-tender, stirring occasionally. Makes 4 servings.

CHICKEN ORIENTALE

4 green onions with tops
2 tablespoons salad oil
1 3-pound broiler-fryer, cut up
¼ cup soy sauce
2 tablespoons dry sherry
1 teaspoon sugar
¼ teaspoon ginger
3 cups hot cooked rice
2 teaspoons cornstarch

ABOUT 45 MINUTES BEFORE SERVING:
Cut green onions into 1-inch pieces. In 12-inch skillet over medium-high heat, in hot salad oil, cook green onions and chicken until chicken is browned on all sides. Stir in soy sauce, sherry, sugar and ginger. Reduce heat to low; cover and simmer 35 minutes or until chicken is tender, stirring occasionally.

Place rice on warm platter. With tongs, arrange chicken on rice; keep warm. Spoon fat from liquid in skillet. In cup, blend cornstarch and ⅓ cup water until smooth; gradually stir into hot liquid in skillet and cook over medium heat, stirring constantly, until mixture is thickened. Pour mixture over chicken. Makes 4 servings.

COUNTRY CAPTAIN

1 3½-pound broiler-fryer, cut up
¼ cup all-purpose flour
¼ cup salad oil
2 garlic cloves, halved
2 medium onions, thinly sliced
½ cup chopped celery
1 medium green pepper, chopped
1 tablespoon curry powder
2 teaspoons salt
1 29-ounce can tomatoes
1 cup regular long-grain rice
½ cup currants or dark seedless raisins
1 tablespoon butter or margarine
⅓ cup blanched whole almonds
chopped parsley for garnish

ABOUT 1 HOUR BEFORE SERVING:
1. On waxed paper, coat chicken with flour. In 12-inch skillet over medium-high heat, in hot salad oil, cook chicken until browned on all sides; remove from skillet.
2. In drippings in skillet over medium heat, cook garlic, onions, celery, green pepper, curry powder and salt until vegetables are tender, about 10 minutes, stirring occasionally. Stir in tomatoes and their liquid; add chicken pieces and heat to boiling. Reduce heat to low; cover and simmer 40 minutes or until chicken is fork-tender.
3. Meanwhile, cook rice as label directs but add currants. In small skillet over medium heat, in hot butter or margarine, brown almonds, shaking skillet occasionally.
4. To serve, arrange chicken pieces at one end of warm platter, rice at other end. Remove garlic from sauce and spoon some sauce over chicken; sprinkle chicken and rice with almonds and parsley. Pass remaining sauce in gravy boat. Makes 4 or 5 servings.

CHICKEN PROVENÇALE

1 3-pound broiler-fryer, cut up
3 tablespoons all-purpose flour
3 tablespoons salad oil
4 medium carrots, cut in 1-inch chunks
1 .6-ounce envelope old-fashioned French salad dressing mix
1 cup chicken broth
1 10-ounce package frozen peas

ABOUT 1¼ HOURS BEFORE SERVING:
On waxed paper, coat chicken with flour. In Dutch oven or 12-inch skillet over medium-high heat, in hot salad oil, cook chicken until browned on all sides. Spoon off fat.

Add carrots, salad-dressing mix and broth; heat to boiling. Reduce heat to low; cover and simmer 35 minutes. Add frozen peas and cook another 10 minutes or until chicken and peas are fork-tender. Makes 4 servings.

CHICKEN-BROCCOLI BAKE

2 tablespoons butter or margarine
1 2½- to 3-pound broiler-fryer, cut up
salt
1 bunch broccoli, cut into thin stalks
2 10½-ounce cans condensed cream-of-chicken soup
¾ cup milk
½ teaspoon ginger
3 cups hot cooked rice

ABOUT 1 HOUR BEFORE SERVING:
Preheat oven to 375°F. In 13″ by 9″ baking pan, melt butter or margarine in oven. With pot holders, remove pan from oven. With tongs, roll chicken in melted butter or margarine; sprinkle with 1 teaspoon salt. Bake 30 minutes.

Meanwhile, in 12-inch skillet over medium heat, in 1 inch boiling water, heat broccoli and 1½ teaspoons salt to boiling; cover and cook 1 minute; drain. In medium bowl, stir undiluted soup, milk and ginger until well blended.

Push chicken to one end of baking dish; arrange broccoli at other end; pour soup mixture over all. Cover with foil and bake 20 minutes more or until chicken and broccoli are tender. Serve with rice. Makes 4 servings.

CHICKEN DINNER WITH SOUR-CREAM GRAVY

3 tablespoons salad oil
1 2½- to 3-pound broiler-fryer, cut up
4 teaspoons salt
¼ teaspoon pepper
2 cups diagonally sliced celery
2 cups diagonally sliced carrots
1 cup regular long-grain rice
1 8-ounce container sour cream

ABOUT 45 MINUTES BEFORE SERVING:
In 12-inch skillet over medium-high heat, in hot salad oil, cook chicken until browned on all sides. Sprinkle with salt and pepper; add ½ cup water and heat to boiling. Reduce heat to low; cover and simmer 20 minutes. Add celery and carrot slices; cover and simmer 15 minutes more or until all is tender, stirring occasionally.

Meanwhile, cook rice as label directs; spoon onto warm platter; keep warm.

With slotted spoon, place chicken and vegetables on rice. Spoon fat from drippings. Into drippings, stir sour cream; over medium heat, heat through. (Do not boil.) Serve gravy over chicken. Makes 4 servings.

CHICKEN LOUISIANE

2 tablespoons butter or margarine
1 2½- to 3-pound broiler-fryer, cut up
1 medium onion, chopped
1 cup sliced celery
1 10-ounce package frozen whole okra, thawed and sliced
1 16-ounce can tomatoes
1 teaspoon salt
1 teaspoon chopped parsley
½ teaspoon thyme leaves
dash hot pepper sauce
hot cooked rice

ABOUT 45 MINUTES BEFORE SERVING:
In 12-inch skillet over medium-high heat, in hot butter or margarine, cook chicken until browned on all sides. Push chicken to one side of skillet; stir in onion, celery and okra; cook, stirring constantly, 2 minutes.

Arrange chicken evenly in skillet. Add tomatoes and their liquid and remaining ingredients except rice; heat to boiling. Reduce heat to low; cover and simmer 35 minutes. Serve on rice. Makes 4 servings.

CHICKEN CACCIATORE

6 tablespoons olive or salad oil
2 2½- to 3-pound broiler-fryers, cut up
1 cup coarsely chopped onions
1 medium green pepper, chopped
4 garlic cloves, minced
1 29-ounce can tomatoes
1 8-ounce can tomato sauce
½ cup Chianti
1 tablespoon salt
½ teaspoon pepper
½ teaspoon allspice
½ teaspoon thyme leaves
2 bay leaves

ABOUT 1½ HOURS BEFORE SERVING:
In 12-inch skillet or Dutch oven over medium-high heat, in hot olive oil, cook chicken, a few pieces at a time, until browned on all sides; set aside chicken.

In drippings in skillet over medium heat, cook onions, green pepper and garlic, stirring occasionally, until onions are tender, about 5 minutes. Return chicken to skillet; add tomatoes and their liquid and remaining ingredients and heat to boiling.

Reduce heat to low; cover and simmer mixture 40 minutes or until chicken is fork-tender. Discard bay leaves. Makes 8 servings.

CHICKEN CARIBBEAN

2 tablespoons butter or margarine
1 3-pound broiler-fryer, cut up
½ cup dark corn syrup
2 teaspoons grated lemon peel
3 tablespoons lemon juice
1½ teaspoons seasoned salt
¼ teaspoon oregano
dash pepper

ABOUT 1 HOUR BEFORE SERVING:
In 12-inch skillet over medium-high heat, in hot butter or margarine, cook chicken until browned on all sides. In cup, combine remaining ingredients; pour mixture over chicken and heat to boiling.

Reduce heat to low; cover skillet and simmer 35 minutes or until chicken is fork-tender, basting frequently with liquid in skillet. Makes 4 servings.

CHICKEN TETRAZZINI

2 2½- to 3-pound broiler-fryers
2 small onions
salt
¼ teaspoon pepper
1 16-ounce package spaghetti
½ cup butter or margarine
½ pound mushrooms, sliced
1 tablespoon lemon juice
½ cup all-purpose flour
¼ teaspoon nutmeg
paprika
½ cup dry sherry (optional)
1 cup half-and-half
1 3-ounce jar grated Parmesan cheese

ABOUT 2 HOURS BEFORE SERVING:
1. In large saucepot, place chickens, 1 onion, 1 tablespoon salt and pepper and water to cover; over high heat, heat to boiling. Reduce heat to low; cover and simmer 30 minutes or until fork-tender.
2. Remove chickens to large bowl; cool. Strain chicken broth, reserving 3½ cups (4 cups, if sherry is not used). (Cover and refrigerate any remaining broth for favorite soup another day.) When chickens are cool, remove chicken meat in large pieces and discard bones and skin; set chicken aside.
3. Meanwhile, cook spaghetti as label directs; drain; place in greased 13" by 9" baking dish.
4. Preheat oven to 350°F. Chop remaining onion. In 10-inch skillet over medium heat, in 2 tablespoons hot butter or margarine, cook remaining onion, mushrooms and lemon juice 5 minutes. With slotted spoon, place mixture in medium bowl.
5. In same skillet, into hot remaining butter or margarine, stir flour, 1 tablespoon salt, nutmeg and ½ teaspoon paprika until smooth. Gradually stir in sherry and reserved chicken broth and cook, stirring, until thickened. Stir in half-and-half, chicken, mushroom mixture and heat.
6. Spoon chicken mixture over spaghetti. Sprinkle with Parmesan cheese and some paprika. Bake 20 minutes or until hot and bubbly. Makes 8 servings.

QUICK TETRAZZINI: Prepare as above but omit steps 1 and 2. Instead of cooking broiler-fryers in seasonings, use *5 cups cut-up cooked chicken* or turkey and *3½ cups canned chicken broth* or bouillon.

CHICKEN ITALIANO

1 3-pound broiler-fryer, quartered
3 tablespoons all-purpose flour
2 tablespoons butter or margarine
1 14- to 16-ounce jar marinara sauce
¼ cup medium sherry
2 tablespoons chopped parsley
½ teaspoon seasoned salt
dash pepper
½ 16-ounce package fusilli
2 tablespoons salad oil
½ 8-ounce package mozzarella cheese slices

ABOUT 1½ HOURS BEFORE SERVING:
1. On waxed paper, coat chicken with flour. In 12-inch skillet over medium-high heat, in hot butter or margarine, cook chicken until browned on all sides. Stir in marinara sauce, sherry, 1 tablespoon parsley, seasoned salt and pepper and heat to boiling.
2. Reduce heat to low; cover skillet and simmer 45 minutes or until chicken is fork-tender, basting occasionally with liquid in skillet.
3. Meanwhile, preheat broiler if manufacturer directs. Cook fusilli with salad oil as label directs; drain well; place on broil-and-serve platter.
4. Arrange chicken on fusilli; spoon sauce from skillet over all. Place cheese slices over chicken. Broil 3 minutes or until cheese is melted. Sprinkle with remaining parsley. Makes 4 servings.

COQ AU VIN

4 bacon slices, cut in pieces
1 2½- to 3-pound broiler-fryer, cut up
5 tablespoons all-purpose flour
1 cup Burgundy
1 cup chicken broth or bouillon
½ pound small white onions
½ pound small mushrooms
1½ teaspoons salt
½ teaspoon pepper

ABOUT 2 HOURS BEFORE SERVING:
Preheat oven to 350°F. In 12-inch skillet over medium-high heat, fry bacon until crisp; with slotted spoon, remove bacon. In drippings in skillet, over medium-high heat, cook chicken until browned on all sides.

In 2½-quart casserole, blend flour and wine until smooth; add chicken, bacon and remaining ingredients. Cover and bake 1 hour or until chicken is fork-tender, occasionally basting chicken and vegetables with sauce. Makes 4 servings.

COQ AU VIN BLANC: Prepare as above but substitute *3 tablespoons butter or margarine* for bacon and *dry vermouth* or Chablis for Burgundy; use *2 teaspoons salt.*

EASY CHICKEN VERONIQUE

2 tablespoons salad oil
1 2½- to 3-pound broiler-fryer, cut up
1 10½-ounce can condensed cream-of-mushroom soup
1½ teaspoons paprika
½ teaspoon salt
¼ teaspoon pepper
1 cup seedless green grapes
3 cups hot cooked rice

ABOUT 1 HOUR BEFORE SERVING:
In 12-inch skillet over medium-high heat, in hot salad oil, cook chicken until browned on all sides. Add undiluted cream-of-mushroom soup, ¼ cup water, paprika, salt and pepper and heat to boiling. Reduce heat to low; cover and simmer 30 minutes or until chicken is fork-tender, stirring occasionally. Add grapes and cook until heated through. Serve with rice. Makes 4 servings.

CHICKEN MARENGO

3 tablespoons salad oil
1 garlic clove, halved
1 3- to 3½-pound broiler-fryer, cut up
paprika
½ pound mushrooms, sliced
1 16-ounce can tomatoes
12 small white onions
⅓ cup dry sherry
2 teaspoons salt
1 teaspoon sugar
3 cups hot cooked rice

ABOUT 1 HOUR BEFORE SERVING:
In 12-inch skillet over medium-high heat, in hot salad oil, cook garlic until browned; remove garlic. Add chicken and sprinkle

lightly with paprika; cook until browned on all sides.

Push chicken to one side of skillet; add mushrooms and cook until golden, about 3 or 4 minutes, stirring occasionally. Add tomatoes and their liquid and remaining ingredients except rice; heat to boiling. Reduce heat to low; cover and simmer 30 minutes or until chicken and onions are fork-tender, stirring occasionally. Serve with rice. Makes 4 servings.

LAZY CHICKEN MARENGO

3 10-ounce packages or 1 32-ounce package frozen fried chicken
1 3-ounce can sliced mushrooms
1 28-ounce can tomatoes
1 16-ounce can whole onions, drained
¼ cup cooking sherry
2 teaspoons sugar
½ teaspoon garlic salt
3 tablespoons cornstarch
salt

ABOUT 40 MINUTES BEFORE SERVING: Prepare chicken as label directs. Meanwhile, drain mushrooms, reserving liquid in cup. In 3-quart saucepan over medium heat, combine mushrooms and next 5 ingredients; heat to boiling.

Stir cornstarch into reserved mushroom liquid until smooth; gradually stir into hot mixture and cook, stirring constantly, until sauce is thickened. Add salt to taste. To serve, arrange chicken on heated platter; pour on sauce. Makes 6 servings.

CHICKEN PAPRIKA

1 2½- to 3-pound broiler-fryer, cut up
salt
paprika
3 tablespoons salad oil
1 medium onion, coarsely chopped
¾ cup sour cream
chopped parsley for garnish
hot cooked noodles

ABOUT 50 MINUTES BEFORE SERVING: Rub chicken pieces with 1 teaspoon salt and ½ teaspoon paprika. In 12-inch skillet over medium-high heat, in hot salad oil, cook chicken until browned on all sides; pour off drippings. Add onion and ½ cup water and heat to boiling. Reduce heat to low; cover and simmer 30 minutes or until chicken is fork-tender.

Remove chicken to warm platter; keep warm. In same skillet over low heat, stir sour cream with 1 teaspoon paprika and ¼ teaspoon salt; heat, stirring constantly, until mixture is hot. (Do not boil.) Pour sauce over chicken; sprinkle with parsley. Serve with noodles. Makes 4 servings.

CHICKEN CURRY WITH PAPAYA

2 3-pound broiler-fryers, cut up
¼ cup all-purpose flour
¼ cup salad oil
½ cup minced celery
½ cup minced onion
2 medium cooking apples, peeled, cored and diced
½ cup golden raisins
2 tablespoons curry powder
1 tablespoon salt
½ teaspoon dry mustard
⅛ teaspoon pepper
1 bay leaf
1 garlic clove, crushed
½ cup heavy or whipping cream
2 papayas, sliced
½ cup salted peanuts for garnish

ABOUT 1 HOUR AND 45 MINUTES AHEAD: On waxed paper, coat chicken with flour. In 12-inch skillet over medium-high heat, in hot salad oil, cook chicken, a few pieces at a time, until browned on all sides. Set chicken aside.

In same skillet over medium heat, in drippings, cook celery and onion until just tender-crisp, about 2 minutes. Stir in 2 cups water, apples and next 7 ingredients; add chicken and heat to boiling. Reduce heat to low; cover and simmer 45 minutes or until chicken is fork-tender, stirring often.

Remove bay leaf. Stir in cream. Arrange papaya slices on chicken. Cover and simmer until papaya is heated, about 5 minutes. Garnish with peanuts. Makes 8 servings.

WITH CURRY ACCOMPANIMENTS: Prepare as above but coarsely chop peanuts and omit papaya. Pass small bowls of peanuts, *coconut, chutney* and *chopped raisins.*

SINGAPORE CHICKEN

2 tablespoons salad oil
1 2½- to 3-pound broiler-fryer, cut up
2 chicken-bouillon cubes or envelopes
1 teaspoon salt
½ teaspoon ginger
1 9-ounce package frozen French-style green beans, thawed
1 6- or 8½-ounce can water chestnuts, drained and sliced
2 tablespoons cornstarch
¾ cup orange juice
2 medium oranges, sectioned

ABOUT 50 MINUTES BEFORE SERVING:
In 12-inch skillet over medium-high heat, in hot salad oil, cook chicken until lightly browned on all sides. Add 1 cup water, bouillon, salt and ginger; heat, stirring occasionally, until bouillon is dissolved.

Reduce heat to low; cover and simmer 30 minutes or until chicken is fork-tender. Add green beans and water chestnuts; increase heat to medium-high and cook until beans are tender-crisp, stirring occasionally.

Meanwhile, in cup, blend cornstarch and orange juice until smooth; gradually stir into chicken mixture and cook, stirring constantly, until mixture is thickened. Add orange sections and heat through. Makes 4 servings.

STUFFED BROILED CHICKEN

butter or margarine
2 2½-pound broiler-fryers, halved
salt
seasoned pepper
1 cup packaged herb-seasoned stuffing croutons
1 unpeeled apple, cored and chopped
1 stalk celery, chopped
1 small onion, chopped
3 brown-and-serve sausages, cut in ½-inch pieces

ABOUT 1 HOUR AND 20 MINUTES AHEAD:
1. Preheat broiler if manufacturer directs.
2. In small saucepan over medium heat, melt ¼ cup butter or margarine. Tuck chicken wings under cut side of chickens; place chickens, skin side up, on rack in broiling pan. Brush with some melted butter or margarine; sprinkle with salt and seasoned pepper. About 7 to 9 inches from source of heat (or at 450°F.), broil 20 minutes. Turn; brush with some melted butter and sprinkle with salt and seasoned pepper. Broil 15 to 20 minutes longer until fork-tender.
3. Meanwhile, in 3-quart saucepan over medium heat, melt ¼ cup butter or margarine; remove from heat; add ½ cup water, croutons, apple, celery, onion, sausage, ½ teaspoon salt and ¼ teaspoon seasoned pepper; mix well.
4. When chickens are fork-tender, spoon crouton mixture into cavities; pour any remaining melted butter in small saucepan over top.
5. Broil chickens 10 minutes more or until stuffing is hot. Makes 4 servings.

CHICKEN WITH SAVORY HERB SAUCE

2 cups packaged herb-seasoned stuffing
1 10½-ounce can condensed cream-of-chicken soup
¼ cup milk
2 teaspoons instant minced onion
1 2½- to 3-pound broiler-fryer, cut up
½ cup half-and-half
2 tablespoons chopped parsley
⅛ teaspoon thyme leaves, crushed

ABOUT 1 HOUR BEFORE SERVING:
Preheat oven to 400°F. Grease 13″ by 9″ baking pan. On waxed paper or cutting board, with rolling pin, crush stuffing. In pie plate, with fork, combine ⅓ of can of undiluted soup, milk and instant minced onion. With tongs, roll chicken in soup mixture; then coat with stuffing on all sides. Arrange chicken in pan. Bake 45 minutes or until chicken is fork-tender.

Just before chicken is done, in small saucepan over medium heat, combine remaining soup with half-and-half, parsley and thyme; heat almost to boiling; pour into gravy boat to serve over chicken. Makes 4 servings.

BROILED ROSEMARY-CHICKEN AND SQUASH

½ cup white table wine
⅓ cup packed dark brown sugar
¼ cup salad oil
¼ cup lemon juice
1 tablespoon salt
2 teaspoons rosemary, crushed
1 teaspoon Worcestershire
1 2½- to 3-pound broiler-fryer, cut up
2 small acorn squashes

EARLY IN DAY OR DAY AHEAD:
In shallow dish, for marinade, mix well first 7 ingredients. Add chicken and turn over to coat with marinade. Cover and refrigerate at least 4 hours, turning occasionally.

ABOUT 40 MINUTES BEFORE SERVING:
Preheat broiler if manufacturer directs. Cut squashes in half lengthwise; remove seeds. Drain chicken, reserving marinade for basting.

Place chicken, skin side down, and squashes, skin side up, on rack in broiling pan. About 7 to 9 inches from source of heat (or at 450°F.), broil 20 minutes, occasionally basting chicken with marinade. Turn chicken and squashes; brush generously with marinade and broil 15 minutes more or until both chicken and squashes are fork-tender. Heat any remaining marinade and serve with chicken, if you like. Makes 4 servings.

PINEAPPLE BAKED CHICKEN

2 2½- to 3-pound broiler-fryers, cut up
1 cup unsweetened pineapple juice
1 tablespoon salt
1 teaspoon rosemary, crushed
½ teaspoon ginger
½ teaspoon paprika
¼ teaspoon pepper
2 tablespoons all-purpose flour

ABOUT 1¼ HOURS BEFORE SERVING:
Preheat oven to 375°F. In open roasting pan, place chicken, skin side up. Pour in pineapple juice. In cup, combine salt, rosemary, ginger, paprika and pepper; sprinkle over chicken.

Bake chicken 50 to 60 minutes until fork-tender, basting with pan juices occasionally. Remove chicken to warm platter; keep warm. Spoon fat from pan juices.

In cup, blend flour and ¼ cup water until smooth; gradually stir into hot juices and cook over medium heat, stirring constantly, until mixture is slightly thickened. Serve sauce with chicken. Makes 8 servings.

CHICKEN SAUTERNE

¾ cup sauterne or white table wine
2 tablespoons salad oil
2 tablespoons chopped parsley
2 tablespoons chopped green onions
2 teaspoons salt
¼ teaspoon paprika
2 2-pound broiler-fryers, halved

EARLY IN DAY OR DAY AHEAD:
In 13″ by 9″ baking dish, for marinade, mix all ingredients except chicken. Add chicken; coat with marinade. Cover and refrigerate at least 4 hours, turning occasionally.

ABOUT 1 HOUR BEFORE SERVING:
Preheat oven to 375°F. Arrange chicken, skin side down, in marinade. Bake 25 minutes, basting occasionally with marinade; turn; bake 25 minutes more or until chicken is fork-tender, basting occasionally. Pour drippings into cup and spoon off fat; discard. Serve remaining liquid over chicken. Makes 4 servings.

BROILED MARINATED CHICKEN

EARLY IN DAY OR DAY AHEAD:
Into medium bowl, for marinade, pour *one 8-ounce bottle Italian dressing* or other oil-and-vinegar based dressing. Add *one 3- to 3½-pound broiler-fryer*, cut up; coat with marinade. Cover and refrigerate at least 4 hours, turning occasionally.

ABOUT 40 MINUTES BEFORE SERVING:
Preheat broiler if manufacturer directs. Drain chicken, reserving marinade. Place chicken, skin side down, on rack in broiling pan. About 9 inches from source of heat (or at 450°F.), broil chicken 20 minutes, basting occasionally with marinade. Turn chicken; brush with marinade; broil 20 minutes more or until tender, basting occasionally with marinade. Makes 4 servings.

WALNUT-ORANGE CHICKEN

2 tablespoons salad oil
3 whole large chicken breasts, halved
1 6-ounce can frozen orange-juice concentrate, thawed
1 teaspoon poultry seasoning
1½ teaspoons salt
2 tablespoons cornstarch
½ cup chopped California walnuts
¼ cup sliced green onions

ABOUT 1 HOUR BEFORE SERVING:
In 12-inch skillet over medium heat, in hot salad oil, cook chicken until browned on all sides. Stir in undiluted orange-juice concentrate, poultry seasoning, salt and ½ cup water and heat to boiling.

Reduce heat to low; cover skillet and simmer 30 to 35 minutes until chicken is tender, basting often with pan liquid. Remove chicken to warm platter; keep warm.

In cup, blend cornstarch and 2 tablespoons water until smooth; gradually stir into hot liquid in skillet and cook over medium heat, stirring constantly, until mixture is thickened. Stir in walnuts and green onions. Pour sauce over chicken. Makes 6 servings.

CRISPY CHICKEN ROLLS

3 whole large chicken breasts, skinned, boned and halved
1¼ cups cooked, shelled and deveined shrimp, chopped
¾ cup butter or margarine, softened
¼ cup chopped green onions
salt
salad oil
1 cup all-purpose flour
1¼ teaspoons double-acting baking powder

ABOUT 2½ HOURS BEFORE SERVING:
1. On cutting board, with mallet or dull edge of French knife, pound chicken pieces to about ¼-inch thickness.
2. In medium bowl, combine shrimp, butter or margarine, green onions and 1½ teaspoons salt. Spoon mixture onto centers of breasts, leaving ½ inch edge all around each. From a narrow end, roll each, jelly-roll fashion; fasten with toothpicks. Cover and refrigerate 15 minutes.
3. Meanwhile, in Dutch oven or saucepot* over medium-high heat, heat 1 inch salad oil to 370°F. on deep-fat thermometer. In medium bowl, with wire whisk or fork, mix flour, baking powder, 1 teaspoon salt and ¾ cup water until blended.
4. With tongs, roll 3 chicken rolls, one at a time, in flour mixture to coat all sides, then lower into hot salad oil. Fry rolls until golden, 10 to 15 minutes, turning occasionally. Drain chicken rolls on paper towels; keep warm. Repeat with remaining 3 rolls. Remove toothpicks. Place rolls on warm platter and serve immediately to retain crispness. Makes 6 servings.

* Or, in electric skillet, heat about 1 inch salad oil to 370°F.

CHICKEN OROBIANCO

¼ cup olive oil
2 garlic cloves, quartered
4 whole medium chicken breasts, halved
2 pounds hot Italian sausage links*
2 cups Orobianco or light muscat
½ pound mushrooms, sliced
1 teaspoon salt
toast points
2 tablespoons cornstarch

ABOUT 1¼ HOURS BEFORE SERVING:
In 12-inch skillet over medium heat, in hot olive oil, cook garlic until golden; with slotted spoon, remove garlic from oil; discard garlic. In drippings in skillet over medium-high heat, cook chicken and sausages, a few pieces at a time, until browned on all sides. Spoon off all but 2 tablespoons drippings. Return chicken and sausage to skillet. Stir in wine, mushrooms and salt; heat to boiling.

Reduce heat to low; cover skillet and simmer 30 minutes or until chicken is fork-tender, basting occasionally with liquid in skillet. On warm platter, arrange toast points; with tongs, place chicken and sausage on toast; keep warm.

In cup, blend cornstarch and ¼ cup water until smooth; gradually stir into hot liquid and cook over medium heat, stirring constantly, until mixture is thickened. Spoon some of sauce over chicken. Pass remaining sauce in gravy boat. Makes 8 servings.

* Or, use *2 pounds pork-sausage links.*

BAKED ORANGE CHICKEN

6 whole medium chicken breasts, skinned and boned
½ teaspoon paprika
¼ cup minced onion
3 tablespoons all-purpose flour
1½ teaspoons salt
¼ teaspoon rosemary, crushed
dash pepper
1½ cups orange juice
1 8-ounce package egg noodles

ABOUT 1 HOUR BEFORE SERVING:
Preheat oven to 350°F. Spread chicken breasts open; arrange in shallow baking pan, top side up, not overlapping. Sprinkle with paprika.

In small bowl, mix onion with next 4 ingredients; gradually stir orange juice into mixture; pour over chicken. Bake 35 minutes or until fork-tender, basting chicken occasionally with liquid in pan.

Meanwhile, cook noodles as label directs; drain. Arrange chicken on noodles on warm platter. Stir liquid in pan until smooth; pour over chicken and noodles. Makes 6 servings.

STIR-FRIED CHICKEN

2 whole large chicken breasts, boned and skinned, halved
2 tablespoons salad oil
1 cup thinly sliced celery
1 medium green pepper, cut in thin strips
1 small onion, sliced
1 teaspoon salt
¼ teaspoon ginger
1 16-ounce can bean sprouts, drained
1 5-ounce can water chestnuts, drained and sliced
1 envelope chicken bouillon
2 teaspoons cornstarch
2 tablespoons soy sauce
3 cups hot cooked rice or noodles (optional)

ABOUT 45 MINUTES BEFORE SERVING:
On cutting board, slice chicken crosswise into ¼-inch strips. In 12-inch skillet over high heat, in very hot salad oil, cook celery, green pepper, onion, salt and ginger, stirring quickly and frequently (stir-frying) until tender-crisp, about 3 minutes; with slotted spoon, remove vegetables to warm platter; keep warm.

To oil left in skillet, add chicken and stir-fry until chicken turns white, about 3 to 5 minutes. Return vegetables to skillet; add bean sprouts and water chestnuts, chicken bouillon and ½ cup water.

In cup, blend cornstarch and soy sauce until smooth; gradually stir into hot mixture in skillet and cook, stirring constantly, until mixture is thickened. Serve with hot rice or noodles. Makes 4 servings.

CHICKEN-AND-SHRIMP FONDUE

2 whole large chicken breasts, skinned and boned
1 pound shelled and deveined shrimp
1 bunch green onions
½ medium head cauliflower
½ pound asparagus
1 10-ounce bag spinach
Dill Fondue Sauce (below)
2 13¾-ounce cans chicken broth

ABOUT 2 HOURS AHEAD OR EARLY IN DAY:
On cutting board, slice chicken crosswise into very thin strips. Cut each shrimp in half lengthwise. Cut green onions into 2½-inch pieces. Break cauliflower into flowerets. Cut asparagus into bite-size diagonal slices.

Arrange all these ingredients with spinach on large platter or separate plates; cover and refrigerate until serving time. Prepare Dill Fondue Sauce (below).

TO COOK AND SERVE:
In electric fondue pot,* heat chicken broth to boiling at the table. Pass platter or plates of uncooked ingredients, letting each person spear a piece of vegetable or meat with a fondue fork and cook in simmering broth until vegetables and chicken are tender and shrimp turn pink. Pass sauce. Makes 6 servings.

DILL FONDUE SAUCE: In small bowl, combine *1 cup mayonnaise, 3 tablespoons milk, 2 teaspoons dill weed, 1 teaspoon horseradish* and *dash cayenne*. Pour into serving bowl. Cover and chill.

* Or, in electric skillet, heat *three 13¾-ounce cans chicken broth* to boiling at table.

CHICKEN A LA SUISSE

6 whole medium chicken breasts, skinned and boned
1 8-ounce package Swiss cheese slices
1 8-ounce package sliced cooked ham
3 tablespoons all-purpose flour
1 teaspoon paprika
6 tablespoons butter or margarine
½ cup dry white wine
1 chicken-bouillon cube or envelope
1 tablespoon cornstarch
1 cup heavy or whipping cream

ABOUT 1¼ HOURS BEFORE SERVING:
Spread chicken breasts flat; fold cheese and ham slices to fit on top; fold breasts over filling and fasten edges with toothpicks. On waxed paper, mix flour and paprika; use to coat chicken.

In 12-inch skillet over medium heat, in hot butter or margarine, cook chicken until browned on all sides. Add wine and bouillon. Reduce heat to low; cover and simmer 30 minutes or until tender; remove toothpicks.

In cup, blend cornstarch and cream until smooth; gradually stir into skillet. Cook, stirring constantly, until thickened; serve over chicken. Makes 6 servings.

CHICKEN WITH ENDIVES

4 whole medium chicken breasts, skinned and boned
butter or margarine
1 teaspoon salt
4 small Belgian endives, trimmed
2 tablespoons lemon juice
2 tablespoons bottled capers
½ cup fresh bread crumbs
1 tablespoon all-purpose flour
¼ pound natural Swiss cheese, shredded (about 1 cup)

ABOUT 45 MINUTES BEFORE SERVING:
1. Tuck under edges of chicken breasts for a more attractive shape. In 10-inch skillet over medium-low heat, heat ½ cup water and 2 tablespoons butter or margarine until melted. Arrange chicken in skillet; sprinkle with salt and place 1 endive on each breast; sprinkle endives with lemon juice.
2. Cover skillet and simmer 25 minutes or until chicken and endives are fork-tender. With slotted spoon, remove endive-topped chicken to platter. Sprinkle with capers.
3. Meanwhile, in small skillet over medium heat, heat 2 tablespoons butter or margarine and bread crumbs until crumbs are browned, stirring frequently; set aside.
4. In cup, blend flour and 2 tablespoons water until smooth; gradually stir into hot liquid in skillet (there should be about ⅔ cup liquid left in skillet) and cook over medium heat, stirring constantly, until mixture is thickened. Remove from heat; stir in cheese until melted; pour over chicken; top with crumbs. Makes 4 servings.

CHICKEN BREASTS WITH SOUR CREAM

2 tablespoons butter or margarine
2 large chicken breasts, skinned, boned and halved
¾ cup sour cream
¼ teaspoon tarragon
¼ teaspoon pepper

ABOUT 1 HOUR BEFORE SERVING:
In 10-inch skillet over medium-high heat, in hot butter or margarine, cook chicken until browned on all sides; add ¼ cup water. Reduce heat to low; cover and simmer about 25 minutes or until fork-tender.

In small bowl, combine sour cream, tarragon and pepper. Spread chicken breasts with mixture and cook 3 to 5 minutes longer to "set" sour cream. Makes 4 servings.

CHICKEN BREASTS AMANDINE

1 tablespoon butter or margarine
2 tablespoons slivered almonds
2 whole large chicken breasts, skinned, boned and halved
1 small garlic clove, minced
¼ pound mushrooms, sliced
½ teaspoon salt
¼ teaspoon pepper
1 chicken-bouillon cube or envelope
1 tablespoon cornstarch
3 cups hot cooked rice

ABOUT 40 MINUTES BEFORE SERVING:
1. In 12-inch skillet over medium-high heat, in hot butter or margarine, brown almonds, stirring constantly. With slotted

spoon, remove almonds; set aside.
2. Add chicken pieces to skillet and cook until browned on all sides. Stir in next 5 ingredients and 1 cup hot water.
3. Reduce heat to low; cover skillet and simmer 25 minutes or until chicken is fork-tender.
4. In cup, blend cornstarch and 1 tablespoon water until smooth; gradually stir into hot liquid in skillet and cook, stirring constantly, until mixture is thickened. On warm platter, arrange rice; top with chicken and spoon on sauce. Sprinkle chicken with almonds. Makes 4 servings.

CHUTNEY-GLAZED CHICKEN

¼ cup butter or margarine
3 whole large chicken breasts, halved
¾ cup chutney
1 teaspoon seasoned salt
4 cups hot cooked rice
1 tablespoon cornstarch

ABOUT 45 MINUTES BEFORE SERVING:
In 12-inch skillet over medium-high heat, in hot butter or margarine, cook chicken until browned on all sides. Stir in chutney, seasoned salt and ½ cup water; heat to boiling.

Reduce heat to low; cover skillet and simmer 25 minutes or until chicken is fork-tender, basting occasionally with liquid in skillet. Place rice on warm platter; with tongs, place chicken on rice; keep warm.

In cup, blend cornstarch and 2 tablespoons water until smooth; gradually stir into hot liquid in skillet and cook over medium heat, stirring, until thickened. Spoon sauce over chicken. Makes 6 servings.

CHICKEN PERIGORD-STYLE

½ cup butter or margarine
8 whole medium chicken breasts, halved
½ pound mushrooms, sliced
⅓ cup all-purpose flour
¼ teaspoon salt
1 13¾-ounce can chicken broth
2 tablespoons half-and-half

ABOUT 1 HOUR BEFORE SERVING:
1. In 12-inch skillet or Dutch oven over medium-high heat, in 6 tablespoons hot butter or margarine, cook chicken, a few pieces at a time, until browned on all sides. Set chicken aside.
2. In drippings over medium heat, in hot remaining 2 tablespoons butter or margarine, cook mushrooms until mushrooms are golden, about 5 minutes. With slotted spoon, remove mushrooms to small bowl.
3. Into drippings, over medium heat, stir flour and salt until blended. Gradually stir in chicken broth and half-and-half and cook, stirring constantly, until mixture is thickened.
4. Place chicken and mushrooms in sauce. Reduce heat to low; cover and simmer 25 minutes or until chicken is fork-tender. Makes 8 servings.

CHICKEN IMPERIAL

4 whole large chicken breasts, halved
all-purpose flour
½ cup butter or margarine
1 pound small mushrooms, quartered
1 tablespoon minced onion
1 cup heavy or whipping cream
¼ cup dry sherry
1½ teaspoons salt
⅛ teaspoon pepper

ABOUT 1 HOUR AND 15 MINUTES AHEAD:
With sharp knife, remove skin from chicken breasts. On waxed paper, coat chicken breasts with ¼ cup flour. In 12-inch skillet over medium heat, in hot butter or margarine, cook chicken, a few pieces at a time, until lightly browned on all sides. Set chicken aside.

In drippings in skillet over medium heat, cook mushrooms and onion 5 minutes, stirring frequently. Stir in cream, sherry, salt and pepper and stir to blend well. Return chicken to skillet.

Reduce heat to low; cover skillet and simmer 20 minutes or until chicken is fork-tender. Remove chicken to warm platter. In cup, blend 1 tablespoon flour with 2 tablespoons water. Gradually add to pan liquid, stirring constantly, and cook until mixture is thickened. Serve sauce over chicken. Makes 8 servings.

INDONESIAN CHICKEN

1 cup sour cream
2 teaspoons salt
1 garlic clove, minced
3 whole large chicken breasts, halved
⅓ cup all-purpose flour
¼ cup salad oil
¼ cup minced onion
1½ teaspoons curry powder
¼ teaspoon ginger

EARLY IN DAY:
In large bowl, mix sour cream with salt and garlic. Add chicken breasts and turn to coat with sour-cream mixture. Cover and refrigerate at least 4 hours, turning often.

ABOUT 1 HOUR BEFORE SERVING:
With rubber spatula, scrape excess sour cream from chicken breasts and reserve it. On waxed paper, coat chicken with flour. In 12-inch skillet over medium heat, in hot salad oil, cook chicken until browned on all sides. Stir in onion, curry powder, ginger and ½ cup water; heat to boiling, stirring.

Reduce heat to low; cover skillet and simmer 25 minutes or until chicken is fork-tender. With tongs, place chicken on warm platter. Stir reserved sour-cream mixture into liquid in pan; heat 2 to 3 minutes, stirring; pour over chicken. Makes 6 servings.

BROILED CHICKEN WITH PEAS AND MUSHROOMS

6 tablespoons butter or margarine
3 whole large chicken breasts, halved
salt and pepper
3 pasteurized process Swiss-cheese slices
1 10-ounce package frozen peas
½ pound mushrooms, sliced

ABOUT 45 MINUTES BEFORE SERVING:
1. Preheat broiler if manufacturer directs. In small saucepan, melt 4 tablespoons butter or margarine. Place chicken, skin side down, on rack in broiling pan; brush with some melted butter or margarine; sprinkle lightly with salt and pepper. About 7 to 9 inches from source of heat (or at 450°F.), broil chicken 20 minutes.
2. Turn chicken and brush with remaining melted butter or margarine; sprinkle lightly with more salt and pepper. Broil 15 to 20 minutes longer until fork-tender.
3. Cut cheese slices diagonally in halves; place on chicken; continue broiling until cheese is melted; place on warm platter.
4. About 10 minutes before chicken is done, cook peas as label directs; drain. In medium skillet over medium heat, in 2 tablespoons hot butter or margarine, cook mushrooms until tender, about 5 minutes. Stir in ¼ teaspoon salt and peas. Serve chicken with vegetables. Makes 6 servings.

CHICKEN WITH ARTICHOKES

2 whole large chicken breasts, halved
2 bay leaves
2 teaspoons salt
1 9-ounce package frozen artichoke hearts
2 tablespoons lemon juice
¼ cup all-purpose flour
2 egg yolks
Pilaf (page 301) or 3 cups hot cooked rice

ABOUT 50 MINUTES BEFORE SERVING:
In Dutch oven over high heat, heat chicken, 1½ cups water, bay leaves and salt to boiling. Reduce heat to low; cover and simmer 20 to 25 minutes until chicken is almost fork-tender. Add frozen artichoke hearts and cook 10 minutes more or until chicken and artichokes are fork-tender.

With slotted spoon, place chicken and artichokes in warm serving dish; keep warm. Discard bay leaves. Stir in lemon juice.

In small bowl, blend flour and ½ cup water until smooth; stir in egg yolks; stir in a small amount of the hot liquid. Slowly pour egg mixture back into hot liquid, stirring rapidly to prevent lumping. Cook over low heat, stirring constantly, until mixture is slightly thickened. Pour over chicken; serve with Pilaf. Makes 4 servings.

CRUNCHY DRUMSTICKS

1 cup orange juice
1 tablespoon salad oil
1 tablespoon salt
¼ teaspoon pepper
3 pounds chicken drumsticks
¼ cup butter or margarine
1¼ cups quick-cooking oats, uncooked

EARLY IN DAY OR DAY AHEAD:
In 13″ by 9″ baking dish, for marinade, mix

Crab Imperial, page 235, and Chicken Perigord-Style, page 191

well orange juice, oil, salt and pepper. Add chicken; coat with marinade. Cover; refrigerate at least 4 hours, turning often.

ABOUT 1 HOUR BEFORE SERVING:
Preheat oven to 400°F. Line 15½″ by 10½″ jelly-roll pan with foil; add butter or margarine and melt in oven. With pot holders, remove pan from oven and tilt pan to spread butter evenly. Meanwhile, on waxed paper, coat chicken with oats.

Arrange chicken in one layer in pan, turning pieces over to coat with melted butter. Bake 40 to 50 minutes until chicken is fork-tender, turning once. Serve hot or cold. Makes 8 servings.

SESAME MINI-DRUMSTICKS

⅓ cup butter or margarine
3½ pounds broiler-fryer chicken wings
½ cup buttermilk baking mix
¼ cup sesame seed
½ teaspoon paprika
¼ cup milk
Curry Sauce (page 352) or Currant-Mustard Sauce (below)

ABOUT 45 MINUTES BEFORE SERVING:
1. Preheat oven to 400°F. In 13″ by 9″ baking pan, melt butter or margarine in oven. With pot holders, remove pan from oven and tilt pan to spread butter evenly.
2. Meanwhile, cut chicken wings at joint between section with single bone and section with two bones. Use single-bone sections for "drumsticks." (Cover and refrigerate remaining wing parts to use for soup another day.)
3. On waxed paper, mix baking mix, sesame and paprika; place milk in small shallow dish. With tongs, roll drumsticks in milk, then coat with baking-mix mixture.
4. Place drumsticks in baking pan, turning to coat all sides with melted butter or margarine. Bake about 30 minutes or until browned and tender, turning once. Serve hot with Curry Sauce for main dish or with Currant-Mustard Sauce as first-course. Makes about 12 first-course servings or 4 main-dish servings.

CURRANT-MUSTARD SAUCE: In medium saucepan over low heat, stir *½ cup currant jelly* and *¼ cup Dijon mustard* until smooth.

POTATO-DIPPED OVEN-FRIED CHICKEN

instant potato flakes for 4 servings
2 tablespoons grated Parmesan cheese
1 tablespoon seasoned salt
¼ teaspoon pepper
1 egg
3 pounds chicken drumsticks or thighs
¼ cup butter or margarine

ABOUT 1¼ HOURS BEFORE SERVING:
Preheat oven to 400°F. In shallow dish or pie plate, mix dry potato flakes with cheese, seasoned salt and pepper. In another shallow dish, with fork, beat egg with ¼ cup water just until mixed. With tongs, roll chicken in egg mixture, then coat with potato-flake mixture; set on wire rack to dry 10 or 15 minutes.

In 15½″ by 10½″ jelly-roll pan, melt butter or margarine in oven. With pot holders, remove pan from oven and tilt pan to spread butter evenly over pan. Arrange chicken in pan, turning pieces over to coat with melted butter or margarine.

Bake chicken 40 to 50 minutes until fork-tender. Makes 8 servings.

CURRIED CHICKEN WINGS

¼ cup all-purpose flour
1 teaspoon paprika
2 pounds chicken wings
¼ cup butter or margarine
2 teaspoons curry powder
1 teaspoon salt
1 10½-ounce can condensed cream-of-chicken soup
1 16-ounce can cling-peach slices, drained

ABOUT 50 MINUTES BEFORE SERVING:
On waxed paper, combine flour and paprika; use to coat chicken.

In 12-inch skillet over medium-high heat, in hot butter or margarine, cook chicken until browned on all sides; sprinkle with curry powder and salt. In small bowl, stir undiluted soup with 1 cup water until blended; pour over chicken; heat to boiling.

Reduce heat to low; cover skillet and simmer 30 minutes or until wings are fork-tender in thickest part. Add peach slices; heat. Makes 4 servings.

Cioppino, page 268

ONION-STUFFED ROAST CHICKEN

1 5-pound roasting chicken
1 20-ounce package frozen small whole onions, cooked and drained
salad oil
milk
¼ cup all-purpose flour
salt and pepper

ABOUT 3 HOURS BEFORE SERVING:

1. Preheat oven to 325°F.
2. Remove giblets and neck from inside chicken. Rinse and drain chicken well. With breast side up, fold wings up and under back of chicken. Spoon onions into body cavity. With string, tie legs and tail together. Insert meat thermometer in center of thigh close to body.
3. Place chicken, breast side up, on rack in open roasting pan; brush with salad oil. Roast 3 to 3½ hours. When bird turns golden, cover loosely with foil. Roast until meat thermometer reaches 180° to 185°F. During last half hour remove foil and baste with pan drippings.
4. When chicken is done, place on platter.
5. Prepare gravy: Pour pan drippings into 2-cup measure (set pan aside); let stand a few minutes until fat separates from pan juice. Spoon ¼ cup fat from drippings into 1½-quart saucepan; spoon off any remaining fat and discard. Add ¼ cup water to roasting pan; stir until browned bits are loosened; add to pan juice in cup with enough milk to make 2 cups.
6. Over medium heat, into hot fat in saucepan, stir flour; gradually stir in milk mixture and cook, stirring, until thickened. Add salt, pepper to taste. Serve in gravy boat with chicken. Makes about 6 servings.

CREAMY CHICKEN STEW

1 4- to 5-pound stewing chicken, cut up
salt
1 cup dry white wine (optional)
Bouquet Garni (next page)
½ teaspoon tarragon
¼ cup all-purpose flour
1 cup heavy or whipping cream

ABOUT 3 HOURS BEFORE SERVING:

1. In 7-quart Dutch oven or large saucepot, place chicken and giblets, 4 teaspoons salt, wine and hot water to cover chicken.
2. Prepare Bouquet Garni as directed but substitute tarragon for marjoram and increase peppercorns to 1½ teaspoons; add to chicken. Over high heat, heat mixture to boiling. Reduce heat to low; cover and simmer 2½ hours or until fork-tender.
3. With slotted spoon, remove chicken pieces to warm serving dish; keep warm. Remove and discard Bouquet Garni. Spoon fat from broth.
4. Measure 2 cups broth and reserve. (Cover and refrigerate remaining broth for favorite soup another day.) Return reserved broth to Dutch oven. In small bowl, blend flour, ½ teaspoon salt and cream until smooth; gradually stir into reserved broth and cook over medium heat, stirring constantly, until mixture is thickened. Pour mixture over chicken. Makes 6 servings.

CHICKEN POT PIE

1 4- to 5-pound roasting chicken, cut up
Bouquet Garni (below)
salt
1½ pounds small white onions
2 cups carrots, cut in 1-inch chunks
2 cups celery, cut in 1-inch slices
5 tablespoons butter or margarine
⅓ cup all-purpose flour
1 cup half-and-half
¼ teaspoon pepper
1 10-ounce package frozen peas, thawed and drained
piecrust mix for 2-crust pie
1 egg yolk

ABOUT 3½ HOURS BEFORE SERVING:

1. In large saucepot or 6-quart Dutch oven, place chicken, giblets, Bouquet Garni, 4 teaspoons salt and hot water to cover chicken. Over high heat, heat mixture to boiling. Reduce heat to low; cover and simmer 1¼ hours or until chicken is fork-tender. Discard Bouquet Garni. With slotted spoon, remove chicken to large bowl; cool. Remove and discard chicken bones and skin; cut meat and giblets into bite-size pieces.
2. Meanwhile, measure 1½ cups broth; reserve. (Cover and refrigerate remaining broth for favorite soup another day.) Return reserved broth to saucepot; add

onions, carrots and celery; cover and simmer 10 minutes; drain vegetables, reserving broth.

3. In 1½-quart saucepan over medium heat, into hot butter or margarine, stir flour until blended. Gradually stir in half-and-half, reserved broth, 1¼ teaspoons salt, pepper, and cook, stirring constantly, just to boiling; pour over vegetables in saucepot. Stir in chicken and peas and pour mixture into 13″ by 9″ baking dish.*

4. Preheat oven to 400°F. Prepare piecrust mix as label directs. Roll dough into 15″ by 11″ rectangle. Fit crust loosely over chicken mixture; trim overhang to about 1 inch and make a fluted edge (page 506).

5. In small bowl, with fork, beat egg yolk with 1 teaspoon water. Brush piecrust with beaten egg yolk. With point of knife, make several slits in crust. Bake pot pie 40 minutes or until browned and bubbly. Cover loosely with foil if crust gets too brown while baking. Makes 9 servings.

*Or, use 3-quart round casserole and *pastry for one-crust pie*. Roll dough into circle 2 inches larger than top of casserole.

BOUQUET GARNI: Cut a double-thickness of 8-inch-square cheesecloth; on it, place *1 medium onion*, quartered, *1 celery stalk*, diced, 3 *parsley sprigs*, 2 *bay leaves*, ½ *teaspoon peppercorns*, ¼ *teaspoon marjoram leaves*. Pull corners up to form small bag and tie securely with colorfast or undyed cotton string.

CHICKEN EN COCOTTE

1 4- to 5-pound roasting chicken
1 teaspoon paprika
1 10½-ounce can condensed cream-of-chicken soup
9 small potatoes*
6 medium carrots, cut in 1-inch pieces
1 pound small white onions (about 12)
1½ teaspoons salt
2 tablespoons chopped parsley for garnish

ABOUT 2 HOURS BEFORE SERVING:
Preheat oven to 375°F. Remove neck and giblets from chicken. Rinse and drain chicken well. Sprinkle chicken with paprika; fold wings under bird. Place chicken and giblets in 7-quart cook-and-serve Dutch oven or covered roasting pan; pour on undiluted chicken soup. Cover and bake 45 minutes.

Place remaining ingredients except parsley in liquid around chicken in Dutch oven; cover and bake about 1 hour longer or until chicken and vegetables are fork-tender, basting vegetables occasionally with pan sauce. Remove cover and bake until chicken is light golden, about 15 minutes, basting occasionally.

Sprinkle chicken with parsley. (If you like, remove giblets; cover and refrigerate to serve next day.) Makes 5 or 6 servings.

* Or, use new potatoes and peel them just around the center.

SIMMERED CHICKEN

1 4½- to 5-pound stewing chicken, cut up
1 medium onion
3 whole cloves
3 celery tops
1 carrot, sliced
2 bay leaves
1 tablespoon salt

ABOUT 3 HOURS BEFORE SERVING:
In large saucepot or Dutch oven,* place chicken, neck and giblets, onion studded with cloves, remaining ingredients and 3 cups hot water; over high heat, heat to boiling. Reduce heat to low; cover and simmer 2 to 2½ hours until chicken is fork-tender. Discard bay leaves, celery tops and onion.

If chicken is to be used later, cool quickly by placing saucepot of chicken and broth in deep cold water in sink. Stir broth often; change water if it becomes warm. Cover and refrigerate chicken and broth after cooling in sink ½ hour. Use within 3 days.

Makes about 4 cups cut-up, cooked chicken and 4 cups broth, enough for 6 servings.

* Or, use pressure cooker and cook at 15 pounds pressure 25 to 35 minutes as manufacturer directs. Reduce pressure quickly.

CHICKEN WITH DUMPLINGS: Prepare as above but when chicken is cooked, prepare Dumplings for Stew (page 421) and drop on chicken pieces. Cook as Dumplings recipe directs. Makes 6 servings.

CHICKEN DELHI

2 3-pound broiler-fryers
1½ teaspoons ginger
⅛ teaspoon ground coriander
dash pepper
3 tablespoons butter or margarine
1 cup minced onions
1 cup plain yogurt
1 cup half-and-half
1 tablespoon turmeric
1½ teaspoons salt
about 6 cups hot cooked rice

ABOUT 2½ HOURS BEFORE SERVING:
Preheat oven to 350°F. Remove giblets and neck from chickens. (Use giblets and neck for broth, if you like.) Rinse and drain chickens well. Tie legs and tail of each chicken together. In cup, combine ginger, coriander and pepper; rub into chickens. Place chickens in open roasting pan.

In 2-quart saucepan over medium heat, melt butter or margarine; stir in onions, yogurt, half-and-half, turmeric and salt and pour over chickens. Roast 1¾ to 2 hours until fork-tender, basting frequently with sauce.

With spoon and fork, lift chickens to warm platter; cut strings. Spoon remaining pan sauce into rice and toss lightly; serve with chicken. Makes 8 servings.

CHICKEN FRICASSEE

1 5- to 6-pound stewing chicken, cut up
all-purpose flour
¼ cup salad oil
1 cup Liquid (below)
1 small onion, sliced
1 stalk celery, thinly sliced
1 tablespoon salt
½ teaspoon pepper
½ teaspoon paprika

ABOUT 3½ HOURS BEFORE SERVING:
On waxed paper, coat chicken with about ½ cup flour. In 12-inch skillet over medium-high heat, in hot salad oil, cook chicken, a few pieces at a time, until browned. Return all chicken to skillet; add remaining ingredients; heat to boiling.

Reduce heat to low; cover skillet and simmer 2½ hours or until chicken is fork-tender. Remove pieces to warm platter.

In cup, blend 1 tablespoon flour and ¼ cup cold water until smooth; gradually stir into pan juices and cook over medium heat, stirring constantly, until mixture is thickened; pour over chicken. Makes 8 servings.

LIQUIDS FOR CHICKEN FRICASSEE: Dry vermouth or other dry white wine; chicken broth; diluted canned consensed cream-of-celery, -mushroom, or -chicken soup.

ADDED EXTRAS: Sliced green onions; a few whole cloves or celery tops; 1 tablespoon lemon juice; dash nutmeg, curry powder, thyme leaves or rosemary.

WHITE CHICKEN FRICASSEE: Prepare as above but do not coat chicken in flour or brown in salad oil; after simmering, in cup, stir ⅓ cup cold water into *3 tablespoons all-purpose flour.*

ARROZ CON POLLO

¼ cup salad oil
1 4- to 5-pound roasting chicken, cut up
1 large onion, chopped
1 16-ounce can tomatoes
1 4-ounce jar pimentos, cut up
1 2-ounce jar pimento-stuffed olives
2 cups regular long-grain rice
1 tablespoon salt
¼ teaspoon pepper
2 chicken-bouillon cubes or envelopes
½ pound fresh pork-sausage links, cut in ½-inch pieces
1 10-ounce package frozen peas, thawed

ABOUT 1 HOUR AND 45 MINUTES AHEAD:
In Dutch oven over medium-high heat, in hot salad oil, cook chicken, a few pieces at a time, until browned on all sides; set aside chicken.

In drippings in Dutch oven, over medium heat, cook onion until tender, about 5 minutes. Add 1¼ cups water, tomatoes, pimentos and olives and all their liquids, and remaining ingredients except peas; top with chicken; heat to boiling.

Reduce heat to low; cover Dutch oven and simmer 35 minutes, occasionally lifting rice with fork. Add peas and cook 10 minutes more. (If mixture seems dry when peas are added, cook covered; if it seems moist, cook uncovered.) Makes 8 servings.

CHICKEN ROSA

1 5- to 6-pound roasting chicken
1 teaspoon garlic salt
¼ cup butter or margarine
1 medium onion, chopped
1 8-ounce can tomato sauce
½ cup white table wine (optional)
1 cup chicken broth
1 10-ounce package frozen peas
1 cup diced, cooked ham
1 tablespoon all-purpose flour

ABOUT 2 HOURS BEFORE SERVING:
Remove neck and giblets from chicken. (Use giblets and neck for broth, if you like.) Rinse and drain chicken well. Sprinkle chicken with garlic salt. In Dutch oven over medium heat, in hot butter or margarine, cook chicken until browned on all sides. Place chicken breast side up; add onion, tomato sauce, wine and broth; heat to boiling. Reduce heat to low; cover and simmer 1 to 1½ hours until fork-tender.

Meanwhile, cook peas as label directs but add ham before cooking; keep warm. When chicken is done, remove to warm platter. Spoon fat from pan liquid. In cup, blend flour and 2 tablespoons water until smooth. Gradually stir into hot liquid and cook over medium heat, stirring constantly, until slightly thickened. With slotted spoon, arrange peas around chicken. Pass gravy. Makes 6 servings.

CHICKEN LIVERS IN POLENTA RING

1½ cups white cornmeal
salt
2 eggs, slightly beaten
2½ cups sliced carrots
¼ cup salad oil
1½ pounds chicken livers
½ cup red table wine
4 green onions, cut in 1-inch pieces
2 tablespoons cornstarch

ABOUT 1 HOUR BEFORE SERVING:
1. Prepare Polenta Ring: In medium bowl, combine cornmeal, 1½ teaspoons salt and 2 cups water. In double-boiler top, directly over medium heat, heat 2 cups water to boiling. Stir in cornmeal mixture, and cook until thickened, stirring. Place over hot, not boiling, water; cover and cook 15 minutes or until very thick, stirring often.
2. Meanwhile, preheat oven to 350°F. Grease well 6-cup ring mold. Remove cornmeal mixture from heat. In small bowl, with wire whisk or fork, into eggs, stir small amount of hot cornmeal mixture until blended; slowly pour egg mixture back into hot cornmeal mixture, stirring rapidly to prevent lumping. Cook, stirring, until mixture is thickened. Spoon mixture into ring mold; bake 20 minutes or until set on top.
3. Meanwhile, in 1½-quart saucepan over medium heat, in 1 cup boiling water, heat carrots to boiling. Cover and cook 10 minutes or until carrots are tender-crisp.
4. While carrots are cooking, in 10-inch skillet over medium heat, in hot salad oil, cook livers until lightly browned, about 10 minutes, stirring occasionally. Spoon excess fat from skillet; stir in carrots and their liquid, wine, onions and 1½ teaspoons salt; heat to boiling, stirring occasionally. In cup, blend cornstarch with ½ cup water until smooth; gradually stir into liver mixture, and cook, stirring constantly, until mixture is thickened; keep warm.
5. Remove Polenta Ring from oven; cool on wire rack 10 minutes. With small knife, loosen Polenta Ring around edges; invert onto platter. Spoon liver mixture into center and around ring. Makes 6 servings.

CHICKEN LIVER PATE

butter or margarine
1 pound chicken livers
2 tablespoons minced onion
¼ cup dry vermouth or dry sherry
½ teaspoon salt
¼ teaspoon dry mustard
¼ teaspoon hot pepper sauce

ABOUT 4 HOURS AHEAD OR DAY BEFORE:
In 8-inch skillet over medium-high heat, in 2 tablespoons hot butter or margarine, cook chicken livers with onion, stirring often, about 5 minutes. Add vermouth; reduce heat to low; cover and simmer until livers are tender, 5 minutes longer. Cool.

In covered blender container at low speed, blend mixture until smooth. Add ½ cup softened butter or margarine and remaining ingredients; blend well. Spoon into dish; refrigerate until well chilled and firm. Makes about 2 cups.

CHICKEN LIVERS SAUTE

6 tablespoons butter or margarine
1½ pounds chicken livers
1 small onion, coarsely chopped
¼ cup all-purpose flour
¼ cup dry or medium sherry
1½ teaspoons salt
toast or toasted split English muffins

ABOUT 30 MINUTES BEFORE SERVING:
In 10-inch skillet over medium heat, in hot butter or margarine, cook chicken livers with onion about 10 minutes, stirring often; with slotted spoon, place in bowl.

Into drippings in skillet, stir flour. With spoon, gradually stir in 2 cups water and cook over medium heat, stirring, until thickened. Stir in sherry, salt and chicken-liver mixture and heat through. Serve on toast. Makes 6 servings.

MUSHROOM: Prepare as above but add *¼ pound mushrooms,* sliced, with livers.

CURRIED: Prepare as above but stir in *1 tablespoon curry powder* with flour; omit sherry.

CHICKEN LIVERS HAWAIIAN

¼ cup butter or margarine
½ cup chopped onion
1 cup chopped celery
1 medium green pepper, slivered
1½ pounds chicken livers
1 15¼-ounce can pineapple chunks, drained
2½ tablespoons brown sugar
1 tablespoon cornstarch
1½ teaspoons salt
2 tablespoons cider vinegar
hot cooked rice

ABOUT 30 MINUTES BEFORE SERVING:
In 10-inch skillet over medium heat, in hot butter or margarine, cook onion, celery and green pepper until tender-crisp, about 5 minutes. Add chicken livers; cook about 10 minutes longer, stirring; add pineapple.

In small bowl, mix brown sugar, cornstarch and salt; gradually stir in vinegar and ¾ cup water, stirring until smooth. Gradually stir mixture into chicken livers and cook, stirring constantly, until thickened. Serve with hot rice. Makes 4 servings.

Rock Cornish Hens

For basic directions, roasting information, see pages 171–175.

GLAZED ROCK CORNISH HENS

2 2-pound Rock Cornish hens, halved
½ cup chicken bouillon
1 teaspoon salt
Glaze (below)

ABOUT 1 HOUR BEFORE SERVING:
Preheat oven to 375°F. (Use giblets from hens for broth, if you like.) Arrange hens, skin side up, in 13″ by 9″ baking pan; add bouillon and sprinkle hens with salt.

Cover pan with foil and bake 30 minutes. Remove cover and brush hens with Glaze; roast 20 minutes longer or until hens are fork-tender, basting occasionally with Glaze. Makes 4 servings.

GLAZE: ½ *cup Chianti-Wine Jelly* (page 699), or ½ cup apricot preserves, melted; or ⅓ cup honey mixed with 2 tablespoons soy sauce.

ROCK CORNISH HENS WITH CURRANT SAUCE

4 1-pound Rock Cornish hens
2 cups seasoned croutons
½ cup wheat germ
½ cup finely chopped celery and leaves
½ cup chicken broth
⅓ cup butter or margarine, melted
1 teaspoon sugar
1 teaspoon salt
Currant-Raisin Sauce (below)
1 16-ounce jar spiced crabapples, drained, for garnish

ABOUT 1½ HOURS BEFORE SERVING:
1. Preheat oven to 375°F. Remove giblets and necks from hens. (Use for broth if you like.) Rinse and drain hens well. Tuck neck skin under wings to secure it.
2. In large bowl, combine croutons, wheat germ, celery, chicken broth, 2 tablespoons melted butter or margarine, sugar and salt.
3. Lightly spoon mixture into hens. With string, tie legs and tail of each hen together.
4. Brush hens generously with some of

melted butter or margarine. Place hens, breast side up, on rack in open roasting pan. Roast, brushing occasionally with melted butter or margarine, 1 hour or until a leg can be moved easily up and down.
5. Meanwhile, prepare Currant-Raisin Sauce. During last 15 minutes of roasting, brush hens generously with some of sauce; finish roasting. Serve hens garnished with crabapples. Pass remaining sauce. Makes 4 servings.

CURRANT-RAISIN SAUCE: In 1½-quart saucepan over medium-low heat, cook *one 10-ounce jar red currant jelly, ½ cup golden raisins, ¼ cup butter or margarine, 2 teaspoons lemon juice* and *¼ teaspoon allspice,* stirring occasionally, until mixture is well blended, about 10 minutes.

ROCK CORNISH HENS WITH MINCEMEAT STUFFING

2 1½- to 2-pound Rock Cornish hens
¼ cup butter or margarine, melted
4 slices whole-wheat bread, cubed
¾ cup orange juice
½ cup prepared mincemeat, drained
¼ cup diced celery
½ teaspoon salt
2 tablespoons light corn syrup
2 teaspoons medium sherry

ABOUT 1 HOUR AND 45 MINUTES AHEAD:
1. Preheat oven to 375°F. Remove giblets and necks from hens; rinse and drain hens. (Use giblets and necks for broth if you like.) Tuck neck skin under wings to secure it. Place hens, breast side up, on rack in open roasting pan. Roast hens, brushing occasionally with melted butter or margarine, about 1½ hours or until a leg can be moved easily up and down.
2. Meanwhile, for stuffing, in 1-quart casserole, combine bread cubes, orange juice, mincemeat, celery and salt; toss lightly. Bake mixture along with the hens for the last 30 minutes of roasting time.
3. In small bowl, mix corn syrup and sherry. During the last 10 minutes of roasting time, brush mixture over hens to glaze them. Serve stuffing with hens. Makes 4 servings.

PEASANT-STYLE CORNISH HENS

salt
10 large cabbage leaves
1 pound sweet Italian sausage links
¼ teaspoon pepper
¼ teaspoon ginger
2 1½-pound Rock Cornish hens
1 16-ounce bag carrots, thickly sliced

ABOUT 2 HOURS BEFORE SERVING:
1. In Dutch oven over high heat, heat 1½ cups water and 1 teaspoon salt to boiling. Add cabbage leaves; cover and cook 3 to 5 minutes until leaves become limp. Remove cabbage; set aside. Reserve liquid.
2. In same covered Dutch oven over medium heat, cook sausages and ¼ cup water for 5 minutes; uncover and brown sausages well. Meanwhile, rub 1 teaspoon salt, pepper and ginger into hens.
3. Drain sausages; discard all but 2 tablespoons fat. Remove giblets and neck from hens. Cook hens in hot fat until golden on all sides. Remove and set aside.
4. Preheat oven to 375°F. Spoon fat from Dutch oven; stir in reserved liquid. Line bottom of Dutch oven with half of cabbage leaves, overlapping slightly; place hens on top and cover with remaining leaves.
5. Cut sausages into chunks; tuck around cabbage with carrots. Cover; bake 1 hour or until hens are tender, basting often. Makes 4 servings.

ROCK CORNISH HENS NAPOLEON

¼ cup butter or margarine
3 tablespoons brandy
1 tablespoon lemon juice
1 2-pound Rock Cornish hen, halved
1 teaspoon salt

ABOUT 50 MINUTES BEFORE SERVING:
Preheat broiler if manufacturer directs. In small saucepan over low heat, melt butter or margarine; stir in brandy and lemon juice. Discard giblets and neck from hen; sprinkle hen with salt; place, skin side down, on rack in broiling pan. Brush with mixture.

About 9 inches from source of heat (or at 450°F.), broil hen 40 to 45 minutes, turning occasionally and basting with mixture, until fork-tender. Makes 2 servings.

Duckling

For basic directions, roasting information, see pages 171-175.

ROAST DUCKLING MONTMORENCY

1 4- to 5-pound duckling, quartered
1 teaspoon salt
¼ teaspoon pepper
1 17-ounce can pitted dark sweet cherries, drained
½ cup claret
2 tablespoons currant jelly
1 teaspoon cornstarch
1 tablespoon butter or margarine

ABOUT 3 HOURS BEFORE SERVING:

1. Preheat oven to 325°F. With two-tined fork, prick skin of duckling in several places; sprinkle with salt and pepper. Place duckling, skin side up, on rack in open roasting pan. Roast 2½ to 3 hours or until fork-tender.
2. Meanwhile, in medium bowl, stir cherries with claret; set aside.
3. Place duckling on warm platter; keep warm. Remove rack; pour all fat from roasting pan. Into roasting pan over medium heat, drain wine from cherries; scrape to loosen browned bits from pan. Pour mixture into 1-quart saucepan; add currant jelly.
4. In cup, blend cornstarch and ¼ cup water until smooth; gradually stir into wine mixture and cook over medium heat, stirring constantly, until mixture is smooth and slightly thickened. Add cherries and butter or margarine; heat, stirring, until cherries are hot and butter or margarine is melted and blended. Serve duckling with sauce. Makes 4 servings.

DUCKLING WITH WALNUT SAUCE

1 4- to 5-pound duckling
1 small onion, halved
½ cup apple jelly
½ cup orange juice
½ cup chopped California walnuts
2 small oranges, halved, for garnish

ABOUT 3½ HOURS BEFORE SERVING:

1. Preheat oven to 325°F. Remove neck and giblets from duckling. (Use for broth if you like.) Rinse and drain duckling. Place onion halves in duckling. With two-tined fork, pierce skin of duckling in several places. Insert meat thermometer in thickest part of duckling, between breast and thigh, being careful thermometer does not touch bone. Place duckling, breast side up, on rack in open roasting pan. Roast 2½ to 3 hours until meat thermometer reaches 185° to 190°F. and drumstick can be moved easily up and down. In small saucepan over medium heat, melt apple jelly; stir in orange juice and walnuts.

Remove pan from oven; turn oven control to 400°F. Remove duckling from rack and carefully pour off fat; discard. Return rack to pan; place duckling on rack and baste with walnut sauce. Return duckling to oven and roast 15 minutes, basting frequently with walnut sauce. Serve with remaining sauce and garnish with orange halves. Makes 4 servings.

DUCKLING, HUNTER STYLE

2 4- to 5-pound ducklings, quartered
16 small white onions
1 cup sliced celery
1 cup Chablis or other dry white wine
1 cup chicken broth
1 tablespoon seasoned salt
1 tablespoon butter or margarine
½ pound mushrooms, sliced
2 teaspoons cornstarch
chopped parsley for garnish

ABOUT 3 HOURS BEFORE SERVING:

1. In 12-inch skillet over medium heat, cook duckling, a few pieces at a time, until browned on all sides, spooning off fat as it accumulates. Place browned pieces in large Dutch oven.
2. Pour all but 1 tablespoon fat from skillet. Add onions and cook over medium heat just until lightly browned, about 5 minutes, shaking pan occasionally. Add celery and cook 5 minutes more. Stir in wine, broth and seasoned salt and heat to boiling; pour over duckling.
3. Reduce heat to low; cover Dutch oven and simmer 1 hour or until duckling is tender, turning pieces once.
4. Meanwhile, in same skillet over medium

heat in hot butter or margarine, cook mushrooms 5 minutes.
5. Remove duckling and onions to warm platter. Spoon fat from liquid in Dutch oven; discard. In small bowl, stir cornstarch and ¼ cup water until blended. Gradually stir into hot liquid in Dutch oven and cook over medium heat, stirring constantly, until sauce is thickened; add mushrooms. Serve gravy over duckling; sprinkle with parsley. Makes 8 servings.

SAUCY ORANGE DUCKLING
Pressure-Cooked

1 4- to 5-pound duckling, quartered
½ cup orange juice
2 teaspoons salt
1 teaspoon meat-extract paste
¼ teaspoon pepper
½ cup orange marmalade
2 tablespoons medium sherry
¼ cup all-purpose flour
hot cooked rice or noodles

ABOUT 1 HOUR AND 15 MINUTES AHEAD:
1. In 4-quart pressure cooker, cook duckling, a few pieces at a time, until lightly browned, spooning off fat as it accumulates. Set aside duckling and pour off all fat.
2. Place rack in cooker; add duckling, orange juice, salt, meat-extract paste and pepper. Cover and bring cooker to 15 pounds pressure as manufacturer directs; cook 20 minutes. Remove from heat and reduce pressure quickly as manufacturer directs before uncovering.
3. Preheat broiler if manufacturer directs. Meanwhile, in small saucepan over low heat, melt marmalade; stir in sherry. Place duckling, skin side up, on broil-and-serve platter; broil until skin is crisp and well-browned. Brush with marmalade mixture and broil until glazed and bubbly.
4. Meanwhile, pour pan juices into 4-cup measure; spoon off fat. Add enough water to remaining liquid to make 1½ cups; return to pressure cooker and heat to boiling.
5. In cup, stir flour and ½ cup water until smooth; gradually stir into boiling liquid and cook, stirring constantly, until mixture is thickened. Serve duckling over rice; pass sauce. Makes 4 servings.

HONEY-BARBECUED DUCKLING

1 4- to 5-pound duckling, quartered
1 teaspoon salt
¼ teaspoon pepper
½ cup honey
1 tablespoon soy sauce
½ teaspoon ginger

ABOUT 3½ HOURS AHEAD:
Preheat oven to 325°F. With two-tined fork, prick skin of duckling in several places; sprinkle with salt and pepper. Place duckling, skin side up, on rack in roasting pan. Roast 2½ to 3 hours until tender.

In small bowl, mix honey, soy sauce and ginger. Remove duckling from oven; turn oven control to 400°F. Remove duckling and rack from pan and carefully pour off fat; discard. Return duckling to pan; brush with sauce. Roast 15 minutes longer, brushing often. Makes 4 servings.

DUCKLING A L'ORANGE

2 4- to 5-pound ducklings
½ cup sauterne
½ cup orange juice
2 teaspoons sugar
½ teaspoon meat-extract paste
2 tablespoons very thin strips orange peel
1 teaspoon cornstarch
2 tablespoons brandy

ABOUT 3 HOURS BEFORE SERVING:
Preheat oven to 325°F. Remove giblets and neck from ducklings. Rinse and drain ducklings. With two-tined fork, prick skin of ducklings in several places. Insert meat thermometer into thickest part of duckling, between breast and thigh.

Place ducklings, breast side up, on rack in open roasting pan. Roast 2½ to 3 hours until meat thermometer reaches 190°F.

Place ducklings on warm platter; keep warm. Remove rack from pan and pour off fat, leaving browned bits; discard fat. Add sauterne to pan and heat over medium heat, stirring to loosen browned bits. Stir in orange juice, sugar, meat paste and orange peel; cook, stirring, until heated.

In cup, blend cornstarch and brandy; gradually stir into hot liquid and cook, stirring, until slightly thickened; pour sauce over ducklings. Makes 8 servings.

PLUM-GLAZED DUCKLINGS

2 4- to 5-pound ducklings, quartered
garlic salt
¼ cup butter or margarine
1 medium onion, coarsely chopped
1 17-ounce can purple plums
½ cup packed light brown sugar
⅓ cup chili sauce
¼ cup soy sauce
¼ cup lemon juice
1 teaspoon salt
1 teaspoon ginger
2 teaspoons prepared mustard
1 teaspoon Worcestershire

ABOUT 3 HOURS BEFORE SERVING:

1. Preheat oven to 325°F. With two-tined fork, prick skin of ducklings in several places; sprinkle with garlic salt. Place ducklings, skin side up, on racks in 2 open roasting pans. Roast 2½ hours or until tender.
2. Meanwhile, in 2-quart saucepan over medium heat, in hot butter or margarine, cook onion, stirring occasionally, 5 minutes or until tender. Into blender container, drain liquid from plums; pit plums and add to container. Add onion mixture, brown sugar and remaining ingredients. Cover and blend at high speed until smooth.
3. Pour plum mixture into saucepan. Over medium heat, simmer mixture 25 minutes, stirring occasionally.
4. When ducklings are done, remove pan from oven; turn oven control to 400°F. Remove ducklings and rack from pan; pour off fat; discard. Return rack and ducklings to pan and brush with some of sauce. Roast ducklings 15 minutes longer, brushing occasionally with sauce. Serve ducklings with sauce. Makes 8 servings.

LEMON DUCKLING WITH RICE STUFFING

1 4- to 5-pound duckling
Rice Stuffing (below)
juice of 1 lemon
½ teaspoon sugar
¼ teaspoon salt

ABOUT 4 HOURS BEFORE SERVING:

1. Remove giblets from duckling; rinse and drain duckling. Chop duckling liver and set aside; discard remaining giblets.
2. Preheat oven to 325°F. Prepare stuffing. Lightly spoon stuffing into duckling.
3. Skewer neck skin of duckling to back; fold skin of body cavity closed and tie legs together. With two-tined fork, prick skin in several places. Insert meat thermometer into thickest part of duckling, between breast and thigh, being careful that thermometer does not touch bone. Place duckling, breast side up, on rack in open roasting pan. Roast for 2½ to 3 hours until internal temperature reaches 190°F.
4. Meanwhile, into cup, squeeze juice of lemon; stir in sugar and salt. Remove duckling from oven; turn oven control to 400°F. Remove rack and duckling from pan and pour off fat. Return rack and duckling to pan; brush duckling with some of lemon mixture; roast 15 minutes more, basting frequently with mixture. Let stand 15 minutes for easier carving. Makes 4 servings.

RICE STUFFING: In large bowl, with fork, fluff *3 cups cold cooked rice.* In 10-inch skillet over medium heat, in *2 tablespoons hot butter or margarine,* cook reserved liver; *¼ pound mushrooms,* sliced; *1 cup sliced pitted ripe olives; ¼ cup minced onion; ¼ cup minced green pepper; ½ teaspoon salt* and *dash pepper* for 5 minutes. Stir in *grated peel of 1 lemon;* toss with rice mixture.

Goose

For basic directions, roasting information, see pages 171–175.

ROAST STUFFED-GOOSE DINNER

1 10- to 12-pound goose
Sage-Onion Stuffing (below)
3 pounds fresh pork-sausage links
3 10-ounce packages frozen Brussels sprouts
2 chicken-bouillon cubes or envelopes
1 13¾-ounce can chicken broth
2 tablespoons all-purpose flour

ABOUT 4½ HOURS BEFORE SERVING:

Preheat oven to 350°F. Remove neck and giblets from goose; discard fat from body cavity; rinse and drain goose. Stuff goose lightly with Sage-Onion Stuffing. Skewer neck skin to back of goose.

With string, tie legs and tail together. With two-tined fork, prick skin of goose in several places. Insert meat thermometer into thickest part of meat between breast and thigh, being careful that the thermometer does not touch bone. Place goose, breast side up, on rack in open roasting pan.

Roast goose 3½ to 4½ hours until meat thermometer reaches 190°F. and thigh is tender when pierced with fork.

ABOUT 45 MINUTES BEFORE SERVING:
In covered, 12-inch skillet over medium-high heat, cook sausages and ¼ cup water 10 minutes. Remove cover; reduce heat to low; cook until sausages are browned on all sides, turning occasionally. Meanwhile, cook Brussels sprouts as label directs but add chicken bouillon to water; drain.

When goose is done, place on warm, large platter; remove strings. Arrange sausages and Brussels sprouts around goose; keep warm.

To make gravy, spoon as much fat as possible from drippings in pan, leaving juice and browned bits; stir in chicken broth. Over medium heat, heat mixture to boiling. In cup, blend flour and ¼ cup cold water until smooth; gradually stir into hot mixture and cook, stirring constantly, until mixture is thickened. Serve gravy with goose. Makes 10 servings.

SAGE-ONION STUFFING: In small saucepan over medium heat, in *¾ cup hot butter or margarine,* cook *3 small onions,* chopped, until tender. In large bowl, mix onion with *2 teaspoons sage leaves,* crushed, *2 eggs* and *two 7-ounce packages herb-seasoned stuffing croutons.*

BOHEMIAN ROAST GOOSE

4 cups sauerkraut (about 2 16-ounce cans)
1 9- to 11-pound goose
2 cups peeled, cubed apples
1 teaspoon salt
½ teaspoon caraway seed

ABOUT 4 HOURS BEFORE SERVING:
1. In 2-quart saucepan over medium heat, heat sauerkraut and its liquid to boiling. Reduce heat to low; cover pan and cook 30 minutes; drain and rinse.
2. Meanwhile, preheat oven to 350°F. Remove giblets and neck from goose; rinse goose. (Use giblets and neck for broth if you like.) With two-tined fork, prick skin in several places.
3. Add apples, salt and caraway seed to drained sauerkraut; lightly spoon into goose. Skewer neck skin to back of goose (or, hold in place with wings). With string, tie legs and tail together. Insert meat thermometer into center of thigh next to body, being careful that the thermometer does not touch any bone. Place goose, breast side up, on rack in open roasting pan.
4. Roast goose 3¼ to 3¾ hours or until meat thermometer reaches 190°F. and thigh is tender when pierced with a fork.
5. Let goose stand at room temperature 15 minutes for easier carving. Makes 8 to 10 servings.

COUNTRY GOOSE DINNER

1 9- to 10-pound goose
paprika
1 13¾-ounce can chicken broth
1 tablespoon salt
¼ teaspoon pepper
1½ pounds small white onions (about 16)
2 medium acorn squash, quartered

ABOUT 3½ HOURS BEFORE SERVING:
Cut goose into serving pieces. In 12-inch skillet over medium-high heat, cook goose, a few pieces at a time, until browned, sprinkling lightly with paprika. Place pieces in covered roasting pan or 17½" by 11½" roasting pan. Preheat oven to 350°F.

Pour fat from skillet; discard. Add broth to skillet. Over medium heat, heat broth, stirring to loosen browned bits; add 1 broth-can water, salt and pepper and heat; pour over goose.

Cover pan with lid or foil and bake goose 2 hours, stirring once or twice. Add vegetables; cover and cook 1½ hours longer or until goose and vegetables are tender, stirring once or twice. Makes 8 servings.

Stuffings

If you prefer, instead of filling the bird with stuffing, spoon the mixture into a casserole and bake it for about 30 minutes along with the bird, or in an oven preheated to 350°F.

MOIST BREAD STUFFING

1 cup butter or margarine
2 cups diced celery
1½ cups chopped onions
¼ cup finely chopped parsley
2¼ teaspoons salt
2 teaspoons poultry seasoning
½ teaspoon pepper
16 cups lightly packed fresh bread cubes
3 eggs, slightly beaten

ABOUT 40 MINUTES BEFORE USING:
In large saucepot over medium heat, in hot butter or margarine, cook celery and onions until tender, about 10 minutes. Add parsley, salt, poultry seasoning and pepper; mix well. Stir in bread cubes and eggs; mix well. Makes enough stuffing for one 8- to 11-pound turkey, about 8 cups.

CRUMBLY BREAD STUFFING: Prepare as above but use only ½ cup butter or margarine and omit eggs.

OYSTER: Prepare as above but add *one 16-ounce can "standard" oysters,* drained, to mixture.

GIBLET: Prepare as above but add *cut-up cooked giblets* (page 175) to mixture.

CHESTNUT STUFFING

1½ pounds chestnuts
1 cup butter or margarine
1½ cups chopped celery
1 cup chopped onions
2 teaspoons salt
1 teaspoon thyme leaves
1 teaspoon marjoram
½ teaspoon seasoned pepper
8 cups fresh bread crumbs

ABOUT 1¼ HOURS BEFORE USING:
With tip of sharp knife, mark an X in each chestnut. In 3-quart saucepan, cover chestnuts with water; over high heat, heat to boiling; cook 1 minute. Remove from heat.

With slotted spoon, remove 3 or 4 chestnuts at a time; remove shells and skins. Coarsely chop nuts; set aside.

In large saucepot over medium heat, in hot butter or margarine, cook celery, onions, salt, thyme, marjoram and seasoned pepper about 10 minutes or until vegetables are tender; remove from heat. Stir in chestnuts and bread crumbs; mix well. Makes enough stuffing for one 14- to 16-pound turkey, about 11 cups.

SAUSAGE-APPLE STUFFING

1 pound pork-sausage meat
3 large apples, peeled and chopped
1 large onion, chopped
1 cup chopped celery
4 cups fresh bread crumbs
2 eggs
1½ teaspoons salt
1 teaspoon poultry seasoning

ABOUT 45 MINUTES BEFORE USING:
In large saucepot over medium heat, cook sausage until browned, breaking pieces apart with fork. With slotted spoon, remove sausage to medium bowl; set aside.

Pour all but ¼ cup drippings from saucepot. In drippings over medium heat, cook apples, onion and celery until celery is tender, about 10 minutes, stirring occasionally; remove from heat. Stir in reserved sausage and remaining ingredients; mix well. Makes enough stuffing for one 7- to 9-pound bird, about 6¼ cups.

STUFFING BALLS

8 cups firmly packed fresh bread cubes
1 cup minced celery
½ cup chopped parsley (optional)
2 tablespoons minced onion
1½ teaspoons salt
1 teaspoon poultry seasoning
¼ teaspoon pepper
½ cup butter or margarine
2 beef-bouillon cubes or envelopes
2 egg whites

ABOUT 1 HOUR BEFORE SERVING:
In large saucepot, combine bread cubes

with celery, parsley, minced onion, salt, poultry seasoning and pepper. In small saucepan over medium heat, heat butter or margarine with ½ cup water and bouillon cubes until butter or margarine is melted and bouillon is dissolved. Pour over bread mixture; toss to mix well.

In small bowl, with fork, beat egg whites just until foamy; add to bread mixture and mix well. Lightly press handful of mixture into ball; if it doesn't hold its shape, add a little more water.

With hands, shape mixture into balls, using about ½ cup mixture for each. Place on greased baking sheet. Preheat oven to 325°F. Bake stuffing balls about 30 minutes or until crisp and golden. Serve hot. Makes 10 servings.

MUSHROOM STUFFING

½ cup butter or margarine
½ pound mushrooms, sliced
¼ cup minced onion
3 tablespoons chopped parsley
1 teaspoon celery seed
¾ teaspoon salt
½ teaspoon poultry seasoning*
dash pepper
6 cups lightly packed, day-old bread cubes

ABOUT 30 MINUTES BEFORE USING:
In Dutch oven over medium heat, in hot butter or margarine, cook mushrooms and onion until mushrooms are tender, about 5 minutes, stirring occasionally. Stir in remaining ingredients except bread; add bread and toss lightly to mix well. Makes enough stuffing for one 6- to 8-pound bird, about 6 cups.

* Or, use ½ teaspoon thyme leaves, marjoram or sage.

NOODLE-SAUSAGE STUFFING

salt
½ cup uncooked tiny bowtie egg noodles
½ pound pork-sausage meat
½ cup chopped parsley
½ teaspoon thyme leaves

ABOUT 30 MINUTES BEFORE USING:
In 3-quart saucepan over high heat, heat to boiling 3 cups water and 1½ teaspoons salt. Add noodles and return to boiling; cook 10 minutes.

Meanwhile, in 8-inch skillet over medium heat, with fork, break sausage into small pieces; cook, stirring occasionally, until well browned; drain. When noodles are cooked, drain and return to saucepan; stir in sausage, parsley, thyme and ½ teaspoon salt; mix well. Makes enough stuffing for one 4- to 4½-pound bird, about 1½ cups.

CORN-BREAD STUFFING

2 12-ounce packages corn-muffin mix, or 2 10-ounce packages corn-bread mix
½ cup butter or margarine
1½ cups chopped celery
1 cup chopped onions
1½ cups orange juice
1 egg, beaten
1 teaspoon seasoned salt

ABOUT 1 HOUR BEFORE USING:
Bake corn-muffin mix as label directs for corn bread; cool in pans on wire rack.

In large saucepot over medium heat, in hot butter or margarine, cook celery and onions about 10 minutes or until tender; remove from heat. Crumble corn bread into mixture; stir in remaining ingredients; mix well. Makes enough stuffing for one 9- to 12-pound turkey, about 9 cups.

HERBED: Prepare as above but for corn-muffin mix, substitute Herbed Corn Bread (page 423) (prepare recipe twice); substitute giblet broth for orange juice.

APPLE-ORANGE STUFFING

2 tablespoons butter or margarine
1 8-ounce package herb-seasoned stuffing
1 cooking apple, cored and chopped
½ cup minced celery
1 tablespoon grated orange peel

ABOUT 15 MINUTES BEFORE USING:
In medium bowl, melt butter or margarine in 1 cup hot water; stir in remaining ingredients. Makes enough stuffing for one 6- to 8-pound bird, about 6 cups.

WHITE-AND-WILD-RICE STUFFING

1 6-ounce package white-and-wild-rice mix
¼ cup dry sherry
butter or margarine
¼ pound fresh mushrooms, sliced
½ cup diced celery
¼ cup slivered toasted almonds (optional)
2 tablespoons minced green-onion tops
⅛ teaspoon pepper

ABOUT 30 MINUTES BEFORE USING:
Prepare rice mix as label directs but substitute dry sherry for ¼ cup of the water.

Meanwhile, in 8-inch skillet over medium heat, in 3 tablespoons hot butter or margarine, cook mushrooms and celery until tender, about 5 minutes. Into rice, stir mushroom mixture, almonds, green onions and pepper. Makes enough stuffing for one 4- to 5-pound chicken or duckling, about 4 cups.

MUSHROOM-RICE STUFFING

½ cup butter or margarine
packaged precooked rice for 8 servings
1 pound mushrooms, chopped
2 cups minced celery
½ cup chopped celery leaves
½ cup chopped onion
1 tablespoon salt
½ teaspoon marjoram
⅛ teaspoon sage
⅛ teaspoon thyme leaves

ABOUT 30 MINUTES BEFORE USING:
In Dutch oven over medium heat, in hot butter or margarine, cook rice, mushrooms, celery, celery leaves and onion until celery is tender-crisp, about 8 minutes, stirring often. Add water or chicken broth as label directs for 8 servings rice. (Omit label directions for salt and butter or margarine.) Cook rice as label directs. Add salt and remaining ingredients and mix well.

Spoon mixture into serving dish and serve with roast unstuffed chicken, turkey, duckling or Rock Cornish hen. Or, use to stuff turkey and roast bird immediately. Makes enough stuffing for one 8- to 10-pound bird, about 7 cups; or 8 to 10 servings.

WILD-RICE-AND-GRAPE STUFFING

¼ cup butter or margarine
2 medium onions, diced
½ cup diced celery
1 cup seedless green grapes, halved
¼ cup medium sherry
2 cups cooked wild rice

ABOUT 1 HOUR BEFORE USING:
In medium skillet over medium heat, in hot butter or margarine, cook onions and celery until tender, about 5 minutes. Stir in remaining ingredients. Makes enough stuffing for one 4- to 5-pound bird, about 3½ cups.

SAVORY RICE STUFFING

6 tablespoons butter or margarine
2 cups diced celery
1 cup diced onions
2 cups cold cooked rice
1½ teaspoons salt
¼ teaspoon pepper
¼ teaspoon rubbed sage
¼ teaspoon thyme leaves

ABOUT 20 MINUTES BEFORE USING:
In 8-inch skillet over medium heat, in hot butter or margarine, cook celery and onions until tender, about 10 minutes, stirring frequently. Stir in remaining ingredients. Makes enough stuffing for one 4- to 5-pound bird, about 3½ cups.

MIXED-FRUIT STUFFING

1 12-ounce package mixed dried fruit, cut in pieces
1 medium onion, minced
1 16-ounce package cranberries
1 cup sugar
5 cups lightly packed, day-old bread cubes
1 teaspoon salt
½ teaspoon allspice

ABOUT 45 MINUTES BEFORE USING:
If prunes have pits, remove and discard. In 2-quart saucepan over high heat, heat 2 cups water, fruit and onion to boiling. Reduce heat to low; simmer 15 minutes or until tender; pour into large bowl.

In same pan, over medium heat, heat ¼ cup water, cranberries and sugar to boiling. Reduce heat to low; simmer 7 minutes or until berries pop, stirring occasionally. Drain liquid from berries. Pour berries into fruit mixture.

Add remaining ingredients to fruit mixture; toss lightly. Makes enough stuffing for one 8- to 10-pound bird, about 8 cups.

BEAN-AND-SAUSAGE STUFFING

1 pound fresh pork-sausage links
½ cup butter or margarine
1½ cups finely chopped celery
¼ cup finely chopped onion
1 7-ounce package herb-seasoned stuffing croutons
1 15-ounce can kidney beans, drained
2 teaspoons chili powder

ABOUT 35 MINUTES BEFORE USING:
In covered, 10-inch skillet over medium-high heat, cook sausage and ¼ cup cold water 5 minutes. Remove cover; reduce heat to low; cook sausages until browned, turning often. Drain on paper towels. Cut each into slices about ¼ inch thick.

In same skillet over medium heat, in hot butter or margarine, cook celery and onion until onion is tender, about 5 minutes. In large bowl, combine croutons with 1 cup hot water. Add all ingredients and mix well. Makes enough stuffing for one 6- to 8-pound bird, about 6 cups.

Sauces and Glazes

Sauces are always good with roast poultry, especially sliced turkey rolls. One cup sauce makes 4 or 5 servings. Glazes give a shiny finish to roast birds.

CURRANT-MINT SAUCE

1 10-ounce jar red currant jelly (1 cup)
2 tablespoons shredded orange peel
2 tablespoons chopped mint leaves*

ABOUT 10 MINUTES BEFORE SERVING:
In small bowl, with fork, stir all ingredients until well mixed. Serve cold with hot or cold roast chicken or turkey; or with roast lamb, pork or veal. Makes about 1 cup.

* Or, 2 teaspoons dried mint leaves.

FRUIT-COCKTAIL SAUCE

2 tablespoons cornstarch
1 tablespoon grated orange peel
¾ teaspoon salt
¼ teaspoon cinnamon
1½ cups orange juice
1 16-ounce can fruit cocktail, drained

ABOUT 20 MINUTES BEFORE SERVING:
In 1½-quart saucepan, combine cornstarch, orange peel, salt and cinnamon; stir in orange juice until smooth. Over high heat, cook, stirring constantly, until sauce is smooth and thickened. Stir in fruit cocktail and heat through, stirring occasionally. Serve hot. Makes about 2½ cups.

CRANBERRY-RAISIN SAUCE

1½ cups sugar
1 16-ounce package cranberries
1 cup golden raisins

ABOUT 20 MINUTES BEFORE SERVING:
In 2-quart saucepan over high heat, heat sugar and ½ cup water to boiling. Add cranberries and raisins and return to boiling. Reduce heat to low; simmer 7 minutes or until berries pop. Serve hot or cold over slices of roast chicken or turkey. Makes about 4½ cups.

ZESTY SOUR-CREAM SAUCE

2 tablespoons butter or margarine
2 tablespoons all-purpose flour
1 teaspoon horseradish
¼ teaspoon thyme leaves
¼ teaspoon salt
dash pepper
½ cup sour cream or sour half-and-half

ABOUT 15 MINUTES BEFORE SERVING:
In 1-quart saucepan over medium heat, into hot butter or margarine, with wire whisk or spoon, stir flour until smooth. Gradually stir in ½ cup water, horseradish, thyme, salt and pepper; cook, stirring constantly, until thickened. Stir in sour cream and heat through. (Do not boil.) Serve hot with fried chicken or Sesame Mini-Drumsticks, page 193; also with broiled steaks or hamburgers. Makes about 1 cup.

WATERCRESS SAUCE

1 13¾-ounce can chicken broth (about 1¾ cups)
3 tablespoons all-purpose flour
2½ cups coarsely chopped watercress
½ teaspoon salt
dash pepper

ABOUT 20 MINUTES BEFORE SERVING:
In 1½-quart saucepan over high heat, heat chicken broth to boiling. Meanwhile, in cup, with fork, blend flour and ⅓ cup cold water until smooth. Reduce heat to medium; gradually stir mixture into hot broth. Cook, stirring constantly, until sauce is smooth and thickened. Stir in remaining ingredients; simmer 2 minutes. Serve hot with hot poultry. Makes about 2 cups.

LEMON SAUCE FOR POULTRY

¼ cup sugar
¼ cup lemon juice
4 teaspoons cornstarch
1 tablespoon grated lemon peel
½ teaspoon salt
⅛ teaspoon ginger
1 drop yellow food color

ABOUT 10 MINUTES BEFORE SERVING:
In small saucepan, mix well all ingredients; stir in 1 cup water. Cook over medium heat, stirring constantly, until mixture is slightly thickened. Serve hot. Makes about 1 cup.

CRANBERRY-ORANGE SAUCE

2 tablespoons cornstarch
1 teaspoon grated lemon peel
½ teaspoon ground cloves
¼ teaspoon salt
1½ cups orange juice
1 teaspoon lemon juice
1 16-ounce can whole-cranberry sauce

ABOUT 20 MINUTES BEFORE SERVING:
In 2-quart saucepan, combine cornstarch with lemon peel, cloves and salt; stir in orange and lemon juice until smooth. Over high heat, cook, stirring constantly, until sauce is smooth and thickened. Stir in cranberry sauce and heat through, stirring occasionally. Serve hot or cold. Makes about 3 cups.

CURRIED PINEAPPLE SAUCE

1 8¼-ounce can crushed pineapple
2 tablespoons butter or margarine
1 teaspoon curry powder

ABOUT 15 MINUTES BEFORE SERVING:
In small saucepan over medium-high heat, heat to boiling pineapple and its liquid with remaining ingredients, stirring occasionally. Reduce heat to low; cover and simmer 5 minutes more to blend flavors. Serve hot with roast chicken, Rock Cornish hen or duckling; also with baked ham or roast pork. Makes about 1 cup.

GLAZES

Allow about ½ cup glaze for 4- to 10-pound birds; for larger birds, double the recipe. During the last 10 to 20 minutes of roasting time, brush the bird several times with one of these glazes.

APPLE-JELLY: In small saucepan over low heat, stir *½ cup apple jelly* with *¼ teaspoon salt* until melted. Makes about ½ cup.

APRICOT: In small saucepan over low heat, stir *½ cup apricot preserves* and *¼ cup chopped dried apricots* until blended. Makes about ½ cup.

CHUTNEY: In cup, pour ¼ cup boiling water over *2 tablespoons golden raisins* and set aside 15 to 20 minutes to "plump"; drain. In small saucepan over low heat, stir raisins, *¼ cup chutney* and *¼ cup redcurrant jelly* until blended and jelly is melted. Makes about ½ cup.

QUINCE: In small saucepan over low heat, stir *½ cup quince jelly, 1 tablespoon butter or margarine, 1 teaspoon cinnamon* and *½ teaspoon ground cloves* until blended. Makes about ½ cup.

WINE-JELLY: In small saucepan over low heat, stir *½ cup Chianti or Rosé Wine Jelly* (page 699) with *¼ teaspoon salt* until melted. Makes about ½ cup.

TANGY-CATCHUP: In small saucepan over medium heat, heat *2 tablespoons grape jelly, ⅓ cup catchup* and *¼ teaspoon bottled sauce for gravy* until blended. Makes about ½ cup.

Fish & shellfish

Fish are classified as "fat" or "lean." Fat fish, such as salmon, mackerel, whitefish, shad, bluefish, lake trout, contain up to 15 percent fat—less than most meats—and the fat is of the polyunsaturated type. Lean fish, such as ocean perch, cod, flounder, halibut, red snapper, haddock, hake, whiting, contain only 2 to 6 percent fat. All shellfish are "lean."

As a rule, seafood is generally low in calories. Fish and shellfish are a good source of complete protein; they also supply many minerals needed in the daily diet, including phosphorus, iodine, calcium. Shellfish are particularly rich in minerals. All seafoods supply vitamins of the important B complex (niacin, thiamine, riboflavin); varieties of "fat" fish are rich in vitamins A and D.

Seafood Glossary

Knowledge of some special terms is helpful when buying and using seafoods.

Court Bouillon: Seasoned liquid in which fish can be poached. See Poached Sole with Hollandaise, page 227.

Crustacean: Shellfish with segmented body covered by crusty outer skeleton: shrimp, lobster, crab, etc.

Drawn fish: Whole fish that have been eviscerated but not boned.

Dressed or pan-dressed fish: Whole fish with scales and entrails removed. Usually the head, tail and fins have been removed also. Smaller fish are generally called pan-dressed.

Fillet: See page 25.

Green shrimp: Term used in fishing industry to indicate uncooked shrimp in the shell. It does not refer to color.

Liquor: Liquid surrounding clams, oysters, mussels, scallops or other mollusks.

Mollusk: Shellfish with soft unsegmented body protected by hard shell: clam, oyster, scallop, etc.

Prawn: Term used primarily on West Coast for larger shrimp. Not the name of a variety.

Round: Fish as it comes from the water, before scaling or cleaning.

Shucked: Meat of oysters, clams, removed from shells.

Steak: Crosscut section of larger fish; usually cut at least ¾ inch thick.

How to Buy

Though the recipes that follow may specify fresh or frozen seafood, either kind may be used. Thaw frozen fish and shellfish before substituting for the fresh kind.

Fresh fish: When you buy whole fish, look for bright, clear eyes, red gills and bright, tight scales or shiny skin. Stale fish have cloudy, sunken eyes; with age, gill color fades to light pink, even gray or greenish-brown, and the color of scales or skin also fades. The flesh should be firm and springy, with bones not separated from the meat. Check, too, for fresh, mild odor; freshly caught fish has practically no fishy odor.

Fresh fillets or steaks should have flesh that appears to be freshly cut, without a dried or browned look, and firm in texture. The odor should be fresh and mild.

Frozen fish (all varieties): Wrapping should be of moisture- vapor-proof material, with little or no air space between fish and wrapping. There should be little or no odor. Look for solidly frozen flesh with clear color, free of ice crystals. Discoloration, a brownish tinge or a covering of ice crystals all indicate that the fish may have been thawed and refrozen.

If the fish is breaded, breading should be crisp, not soggy.

Fresh and frozen shellfish: Follow these guides for the various types:

Shrimp should have mild odor, firm-textured meat. Depending on variety, shell will be light gray, brownish-pink or deep red; when cooked, shell will become reddish, meat will turn an attractive pink. Fresh shrimp are sold cooked or uncooked, in the shell or shelled and deveined. Frozen shrimp also are available breaded and either cooked or uncooked.

There are about 40 small, 25 medium and 18 large shrimp to a pound before shelling. One pound of unshelled shrimp yields ½ to ¾ pound of cooked and shelled shrimp.

Oysters, clams, mussels are sold fresh in the shell, fresh-shucked or frozen. If you buy them in the shell, they should be alive, the shell tightly closed; if they are fresh, any partly opened shells will close tightly if lightly tapped. Shucked shellfish should be plump, shiny and fresh-smelling, and come with little or no liquor (liquid). Eastern oysters are sold according to size: "counts" are extra large; "extra selects" are large; "select" (preferred for frying) are medium; "standards" are small (suitable for use in soup, stew, etc.). Pacific Coast oysters include the small Olympia and the large Pacific. Hard-shelled clams come in three sizes: large (chowder), medium (cherrystone) and small (littleneck). Western clams include butter, littleneck, razor and pismo varieties. Soft-shell clams come in two sizes: the larger "soft clams in shell" and the smaller "steamer."

Crabs when sold fresh and uncooked should be alive and lively. Cooked crabs should have a bright red shell. Soft-shell crabs, which have shed their hard shells, should be a good bluish-gray color. Cooked crab meat is also available fresh or frozen. When buying, look for clear white meat with touches of pink and little or no odor.

Eastern crabs include blue crab, hard-shell and soft-shell; Pacific crabs include Dungeness, Alaska King and snow crabs; rock crabs are found on both coasts.

Lobsters, fresh and uncooked, should be alive and lively, with tails curled under, not hanging down, when picked up. Cooked lobster should have a bright red shell. Frozen rock-lobster tails should have clear white meat. Cooked lobster meat is available fresh or frozen; it should be clear white with touches of pink, little or no odor.

Two live lobsters, 1 pound each, yield about ½ pound cooked lobster meat.

Rock-lobster tails: These are the edible portion of spiny lobsters. They are available frozen or canned. The cooked meat can be used in any recipe for cooked lobster meat. One 8-ounce frozen rock-lobster tail yields about ¼ pound cooked meat.

Scallops, whether the large sea scallops or smaller bay scallops, should be practically free of liquor, creamy-pink in color and have a slightly sweet odor. Scallops are also sold frozen or frozen breaded. One pound yields about ½ pound when cooked.

Canned fish: Look for a dependable brand name and the variety that suits your needs.

Salmon: The several varieties of salmon

differ slightly in color, texture, flavor and, therefore price. In descending order of price, the canned salmons are:

• Sockeye, Red and Blueback. These are the same species, all deep salmon-pink in color, firm in texture, rich in oil. They break into medium flakes and are fine in dishes in which firmness and good color are important—salads, party casseroles.

• King and Chinook. These are rich in oil, break into large flakes, but are a bit softer in texture than the Sockeye. They are especially good in salads.

• Medium Red, Coho, Silver. These are large-flaked, good for most recipes.

• Pink. Nearly half of all salmon sold is Pink salmon. It is small-flaked, goes well in entrées, soups, sandwiches.

• Chum and Keta. Large-flaked and coarsely textured, these varieties are suitable for casseroles, cooked dishes, where their lighter color is not important.

Canned salmon is packed mainly in 16-ounce, 8-ounce and 3¾-ounce cans.

Tuna: Canned tuna comes packed in oil or water, solid-pack, chunk-style or flaked. Can sizes include 3¼ or 3½, 6½ or 7 and 12½ or 13 ounces. Select the solid or fancy pack for cold plates, party salads; chunks for salads and casseroles; and the flaked or grated for appetizers, sandwich fillings, etc. The main varieties are:

• Albacore. This is the only white-meat canned tuna; it usually comes solid-pack or chunk-style and is more expensive than other tunas.

• Yellowfin. This light-meat type accounts for most of the available canned tuna and comes in chunk, solid or flake style.

• Skipjack and Bluefin. These light-meat tunas come in chunk, solid or flake style.

Sardines: Canned sardines are soft-boned herrings packed in a variety of oils and sauces that give the characteristic flavor. Most are sold in 3¼-, 3¾- and 4-ounce cans, a few in 12-ounce cans. They are popular as appetizers or in sandwiches.

Lobster and crab meat: Both of these are sold in chunk or flaked form. Look for the kind that suits your recipe. Most popular size of Alaska King crab is the 7½-ounce can.

Shrimp: Canned shrimp, frequently deveined, range in size from small to large and are most often sold in 4½- to 5-ounce cans. While some are dry-packed, most are packed in water with a little salt. Serve cold or heat quickly in sauce or casserole.

Mackerel: Salted mackerel are available in 8-ounce cans; plain mackerel, in 15-ounce cans. The fish is usually not boned, since the bones soften during canning.

Oysters: Canned oysters are convenient for use in recipes. Different species are sold in a variety of can sizes.

Clams: Clams are canned whole or minced, stuffed, in chowder; clam juice and broth come bottled.

Amount to Buy

The amount of fish to buy depends on its type and the way it is cut; the amount of shellfish depends on whether or not it has been shelled or shucked. *For each serving,* use these amounts as a guide:

Whole or drawn fish	1 pound
Dressed fish	½ to ¾ pound
Fish steaks	½ pound
Fish fillets	¼ to ⅓ pound
Fish portions, sticks	¼ to ⅓ pound
Shrimp in shell	½ pound
Shrimp, shelled	⅓ pound
Lobster in shell	1- to 2-pound lobster
Rock-lobster tails	1 6- to 8-ounce tail or 2 or 3 smaller tails
Oysters in shell	5 or 6 oysters
Clams in shell	4 to 6 clams
Crabs in shell	Because size and variety vary so, discuss number to buy with market man.

How to Store

Fresh: Keep fresh fish and shellfish loosely wrapped, in the refrigerator, and cook within one day.

Frozen: Keep in original wrapper; use immediately after thawing. Never thaw and refreeze fish, since this will cause moisture loss, texture and flavor changes. For storing in your freezer, see page 724.

How to Thaw

The best way to thaw frozen fish or shellfish is to leave it in its wrappings and thaw it in the refrigerator or in cold water. Thawing at room temperature can cause sogginess and loss of texture. Defrost just until portions separate easily. Drain well and blot dry with paper towels before using. Many fish and shellfish need not be thawed before cooking.

How to Cook Fish

Fish cooks quickly. It is tender before it is cooked; heat simply coagulates the protein and brings out the flavor. When fish flesh becomes opaque, or a whitish, milky color, it's ready to eat. Overcooking spoils both flavor and texture.

Most fish can be cooked in essentially the same ways. So if you don't have the kind of fish called for in the recipe, or if the recipe doesn't specify any particular fish, use your favorite. Also, fresh and thawed frozen fish can be used interchangeably in recipes.

To test fish for doneness: Start checking for doneness halfway through the suggested cooking time. Insert the tines of a fork into the thickest part of the fish and lift up to see if fish "flakes" (comes up in layers).

To bake fish: Bake whole dressed fish, fillets or steaks in a preheated 350°F. oven until just tender. To prevent drying, brush fish with melted fat, oil or a sauce; there is no need to turn it while baking. A three-pound dressed fish will take 30 to 35 minutes; steaks and fillets, 12 to 15 minutes. If you bake fish without thawing it first, bake a little longer to allow for thawing. Stuffed fish requires an additional 20 to 30 minutes.

To broil or grill: Fish steaks, fillets and pan-dressed fish about one inch thick are best for broiling, since thinner ones tend to dry out too quickly and thicker ones turn brown before they are cooked through. Thaw frozen fish before broiling. Brush generously with melted fat, oil or sauce before and during broiling. Cooking time: 10 to 15 minutes. Thicker pan-dressed fish or steaks may be turned once.

To pan-fry: Bread fillets, thin steaks or pan-dressed fish (thoroughly thawed) by dipping them in a little milk or a mixture of beaten egg and milk, then in dry bread crumbs, cornflake crumbs, cornmeal or flour. Let coating dry a few minutes before cooking. Fry fish over medium-high heat in about ⅛ inch of heated fat; vegetable shortening or oil is preferred, since it has a high smoking point. Turn fish once during frying. It will begin flaking in 8 to 10 minutes, depending on thickness.

To oven-fry: Serving-size portions of breaded fish can be baked in a well-greased pan at 500°F. to simulate deep-fat frying; because of the breading, the flavorful juices don't escape in the 10 to 15 minutes it takes to cook. Bread the fish (instructions above, under To Pan-Fry). Drizzle a little salad oil or melted butter or margarine over fish before baking. No turning or basting is necessary in this method of cooking.

To deep-fry: Breaded fillets, steaks and pan-dressed fish are all suitable for frying. Bread the fish (instructions above, under To Pan-Fry). Fill a heavy, deep saucepan or deep-fat fryer half-full with vegetable shortening or oil; heat to 350°F. Place one layer of fish in the fry basket; fry until fish is golden and flakes easily, usually 3 to 5 minutes. Drain on paper towels.

To poach: Fish fillets, steaks or dressed fish simmer quickly in liquid in a covered skillet or pan. Fillets and steaks will be done in 5 to 10 minutes; thicker, dressed fish will take longer. Liquids you can use for poaching: lightly salted water, Court Bouillon (see Seafood Glossary, page 209), milk or a mixture of water and white wine.

To steam: A steam cooker or deep pan with tight cover and a rack inside is necessary for steaming fish fillets, steaks or pan-dressed fish. Thaw fish first, if frozen. Place fish on a well-greased rack, not touching water. Heat water to boiling, then cover pan and cook 5 to 10 minutes until done.

How to Cook Shellfish

Shellfish, like fish, takes very little time to cook. To test for doneness, check the appearance of the kind being prepared. Shrimp turn pink; oyster edges curl; clams and mussels open; lobsters, rock-lobster tails and crab shells turn red and the meat inside becomes opaque.

Shrimp: Shell and devein shrimp either before or after cooking, or buy it shelled and deveined, fresh or frozen.

To shell: (See illustrations, below.) Hold shrimp with outside curve up and tail away from you. Insert sharp point of kitchen shears under shell and cut along top of curve through to tail.

Peel back shell and gently begin lifting shrimp out. Then hold tip of tail firmly with fingers of one hand. With other hand, hold body of shrimp close to tail and pull gently until tail comes free of shell.

To devein: Hold shelled shrimp under running cold water. With fingers or small knife, remove black or green vein that runs along the curve. (Vein is harmless, but shrimp look more attractive without it.)

To cook shrimp for use in a recipe: In saucepot, place enough salted water to cover shrimp; heat to boiling. Add fresh or thawed shrimp. When water returns to boiling, simmer 1 to 3 minutes (depending on size of shrimp) until done; drain immediately. Shrimp are done when pink outside, opaque inside and curled up. Cut a shrimp to test inside doneness.

Oysters, Clams, Mussels: To shuck, scrub shells under running cold water with vegetable brush to remove sand. (Cut beards from mussels with kitchen shears.) Discard any that remain open when tapped with fingers. With knife or clamshucker tool, pry open shells and loosen meat. With fingers, carefully remove bits of shell from meat.

Serve oysters raw, on the half shell; or shuck and bread, then pan-fry or deep-fry or steam. Hard-shell clams may be served raw, on the half-shell, also used in recipes. Mussels are used in recipes.

To steam soft-shell clams and mussels: Place them on rack over boiling water in steam cooker or deep saucepot with tight-fitting lid; steam just until shells open, about 5 to 10 minutes.

Scallops: Pan-fry, broil, bake or deep-fry scallops as in How to Cook Fish, page 212. When cooked through, they are opaque and fork-tender.

To cook scallops for use in a recipe: In pan, place enough salted water to cover scallops; heat to boiling. Add fresh or thawed frozen scallops; when water returns to boiling, simmer 3 to 4 minutes (depending on size of scallops). Drain immediately.

Crabs: Before cooking hard- or soft-shell crabs, wash under running cold water.

SHELLING SHRIMP

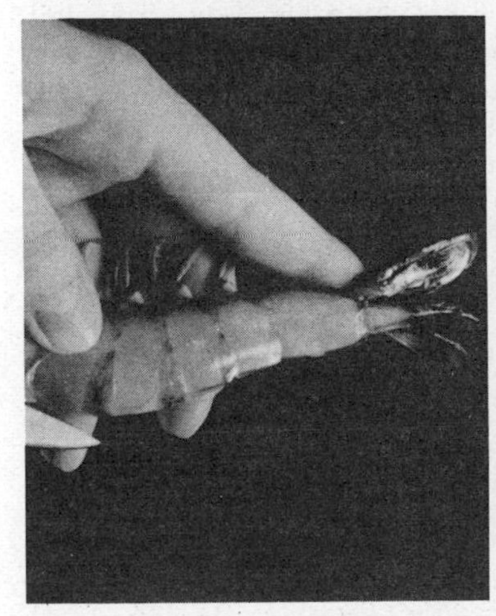
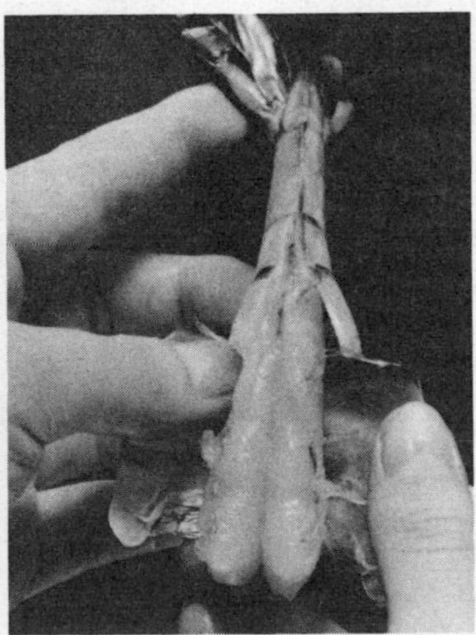
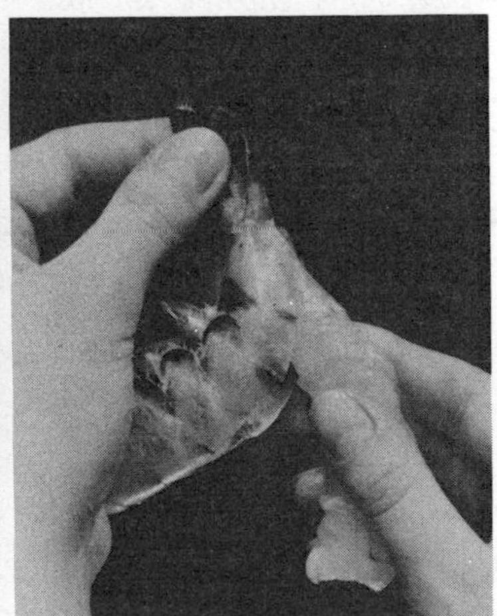

Kitchen shears make fast work of shelling shrimp. 1. Cut through shell along back to tail. 2. Open shell and start lifting shrimp out. 3. Hold tail and gently tug shrimp, with its tail intact, free of shell.

To cook hard-shell crabs: Plunge crabs, head first, into large saucepot of boiling salted water. After water returns to boiling, cook 10 minutes or until crabs are red; drain and plunge into cold water.

To remove crab meat: Twist off claws and legs; with lobster cracker, nutcracker or hammer, crack all over. With tip of knife, pick out meat; remove any cartilage. Lay each crab on its top shell. Slip knife under point of segment ("apron") that folds under body from rear; lift up, bend backward and break off. Take crab in both hands; pull upper and lower shells apart; discard top shell.

Scrape away spongy gills ("dead-man's fingers") and loose matter located in center part of body. (This is easy to do under running cold water.) Then break body in half, down center. Cut off thin shell around edges. With lobster or nut pick, remove meat between sections.

To clean soft-shell crabs for cooking: With scissors, cut across crab ½ inch behind eyes to remove head. Pull back body covering at point on each side; remove spongy gills underneath. Remove "apron" and spongy substance underneath it. Rinse crab under running cold water.

To cook cleaned soft-shell crabs: Cook as for hard-shell crabs, above; or pan-fry; or broil 8 to 10 minutes, basting with melted butter or margarine occasionally.

Lobster: Keep live lobsters refrigerated.

To cook lobster for use in a recipe: Plunge lobster, head first, into 3 inches boiling water in large saucepot; heat to boiling; cover and boil 12 to 15 minutes after water returns to boiling. For frozen lobster, follow label directions.

To remove lobster meat for salads, casseroles: Break off claws and legs. Twist off head from tail; with kitchen shears, cut away thin underside shell around tail and discard; gently pull meat from shell. With kitchen shears, cut along rounded, backside of meat, about ¼ inch deep, to expose dark vein; remove vein and discard. Reserve any red roe (coral) or greenish gray liver (tomalley) in a bowl. Cut meat into bite-size chunks; place in bowl also.

With hand, lift out bony portion from head shell. Remove any roe or liver; add to lobster meat. Discard sac and spongy grayish gills. Break bony portion into several pieces and, with lobster pick or fork, pick out any meat; crack large claws with lobster or nut cracker and remove meat.

Body and tail shells, if not broken, may be washed, dried and fitted together. Use to hold lobster salad or other dishes.

Rock-lobster tails: These are sold frozen.

To cook for use in a recipe: Cook as label directs; or drop, thawed or frozen, into boiling salted water in large saucepot; heat to boiling; reduce heat to low and cook according to timetable below. When done, drain and rinse with cold water.

Weight of Tail (ounces)	*Boiling Time (minutes)* Frozen	*Thawed*
2	2	2
3	3	3
4	5	4
5	6	4
6	8	5
7	9	6
8	11	8

To remove meat: With scissors, cut away thin underside shell. Grasp meat between thumb and fingers and pull away from shell. Use whole, slice, or cut as desired.

To Fillet a Fish

Uncooked fish: Place dressed fish (page 209) on cutting board. With sharp knife, cut through flesh along backbone from tail to just behind head. Turn knife flat and cut flesh away from backbone from head to tail. Allow knife to run over rib bones until fillet is freed at tail. Lift off entire side of fish in one piece. Then turn fish over and repeat to cut fillet from other side.

If desired, skin fillet. (Some think leaving skin on helps fish stay moist during cooking.) Lay fillet, skin side down, on cutting board. Hold tail end firmly; with knife, cut through flesh to skin, about ½ inch from end of fillet. Flatten knife against skin and cut flesh away from skin by pushing knife forward, while holding free end of skin.

Cooked fish (usually done at the table): First, remove head by slicing down behind collarbone until backbone is broken by knife; place head on another plate. Hold tail end of fish down with fork. Cut through flesh along backbone from just behind the head to the tail. Scrape flesh away from backbone and ease cooked meat away from rib bones. With fish fork and knife or two meat forks, lift top section from backbone and place on side of platter. Grasp backbone gently and lift from remaining flesh.

To Carve Whole Fish

With sharp knife, cut top side of fish into servings, just down to bone, and serve; remove and serve stuffing, if any. Lift off all bones and serve lower section in same manner.

Heat-and-Eat Seafoods

In addition to the convenience of frozen and canned fish and shellfish for use in recipes, the constantly growing number of frozen seafood dishes and complete dinners makes menu planning easier. Many, such as fish sticks and fried breaded shrimp, can be used in several ways (as appetizers, sandwich filling, etc.), as well as main dishes.

Fresh or Frozen Fish

BAKED STRIPED BASS WITH CLAMS

1 dozen hard-shell clams
1 4- to 4½-pound striped bass, dressed and boned, with tail on
1 teaspoon salt
¼ teaspoon basil
dash pepper
½ cup parsley sprigs
1 medium onion, thinly sliced
2 celery stalks with leaves, chopped
1 garlic clove, halved
2 bay leaves
½ cup dry white wine
½ cup butter or margarine, melted

ABOUT 1 HOUR BEFORE SERVING:
Preheat oven to 350°F. Grease large shallow baking pan or ovenproof serving dish. Scrub clams under running cold water; set aside. Sprinkle inside of fish with salt, basil and pepper. Arrange parsley and half of onion slices inside fish; place fish in pan.

Around fish, arrange clams, remaining onion, celery, garlic and bay leaves. Pour wine and butter or margarine over fish.

Cover pan with foil and bake 40 to 50 minutes until fish flakes easily when tested with a fork and clam shells open. Discard garlic and bay leaves. Serve fish as in To Carve Whole Fish (at left). Makes 8 servings.

STUFFED BAKED FISH

1 6-pound whole fish such as red snapper, bass, silver salmon, king mackerel, bluefish or whitefish, dressed
1 tablespoon lime juice
butter or margarine
1 medium onion, minced
½ cup minced celery
1¼ cups herb-seasoned stuffing
1 4-ounce package shredded Cheddar cheese (1 cup)
½ cup milk
¼ cup chopped parsley
1 teaspoon salt
½ teaspoon nutmeg
½ cup dry white wine

ABOUT 3 HOURS AHEAD:
1. Brush inside of fish with lime juice; refrigerate 1 hour.
2. Meanwhile, prepare stuffing: In 1-quart saucepan over medium heat, melt ¼ cup butter or margarine; add onion and celery and cook until tender, about 5 minutes. In large bowl, toss onion mixture, stuffing, cheese, milk, parsley, salt and nutmeg.
3. Preheat oven to 350°F. Line a large roasting pan with foil; grease foil. Fill inside of fish with stuffing; fasten opening with toothpicks. Place fish in pan.
4. In same small saucepan, melt ½ cup butter or margarine; add wine. Bake fish about 1 hour and 20 minutes, basting about every 15 minutes with butter mixture.
5. Lift foil with fish to warm, large platter; remove foil, then remove toothpicks. Pour pan liquid into gravy boat for sauce. Serve fish as in To Carve Whole Fish (at left). Makes 10 servings.

BAKED WHOLE FISH WITH ORANGE

1 4- to 5-pound striped bass or red snapper, dressed, with head removed
salt
½ cup butter or margarine
1 small onion, minced
4 bread slices, crumbled
2 tablespoons chopped parsley
½ teaspoon basil
⅛ teaspoon pepper
2 large oranges

ABOUT 1 HOUR AND 15 MINUTES AHEAD:
1. Preheat oven to 350°F. Line large roasting pan with foil; grease foil. Sprinkle fish inside and out with 1 teaspoon salt.
2. In 2-quart saucepan over medium heat, melt butter or margarine; pour ¼ cup into small bowl; reserve. In remaining butter or margarine, cook onion until tender, about 5 minutes. Stir in bread, parsley, ½ teaspoon salt, basil and pepper. Fill inside of fish loosely with mixture; fasten opening with toothpicks. Place fish in pan.
3. Section oranges over reserved melted butter or margarine to catch juice; reserve sections. Brush some of mixture on outside of fish. Bake fish, brushing often with butter mixture, 50 to 60 minutes until fish flakes easily when tested with a fork. During last 5 minutes of baking time, arrange orange sections on fish.
4. Lift foil with fish to warm platter; remove foil and toothpicks. Serve as in To Carve Whole Fish (page 215). Makes 8 servings.

RED SNAPPER WITH OYSTER STUFFING

1 4- to 4½-pound red snapper, dressed
salt
salad oil
¾ cup minced celery
¼ cup chopped onion
½ pint shucked "standard" oysters
3 cups fresh bread cubes
¼ cup butter or margarine, melted
1 teaspoon poultry seasoning
¼ teaspoon pepper

ABOUT 1½ HOURS BEFORE SERVING:
1. Preheat oven to 350°F. Sprinkle fish inside and outside with salt. Brush large, shallow roasting pan lightly with salad oil. Brush one side of fish with oil and place, oiled side down, in pan.
2. In 2-quart saucepan over high heat, in 1 cup boiling water, cook celery and onion until tender; drain, reserving liquid. Into cup, drain liquid from oysters; add reserved vegetable liquid to make ½ cup.
3. In large bowl, cut up oysters; stir in bread cubes, liquid, celery, onion and remaining ingredients. Fill inside of fish loosely with mixture; fasten opening with toothpicks. Brush top side of fish with salad oil. Bake 1 hour, brushing occasionally with oil.
4. With 2 large pancake turners, lift fish to warm platter; remove toothpicks. Serve fish as in To Carve Whole Fish (page 215). Makes 8 servings.

RED SNAPPER CREOLE

⅓ cup medium sherry
1 cup fresh bread crumbs
butter or margarine
2 cups minced onions
½ cup diced green or sweet red pepper
2 tablespoons chopped parsley
thyme leaves
2 tablespoons chili sauce
1 5- to 6-pound red snapper,* dressed, with head and tail removed
salt
pepper
Shrimp-Olive Sauce (page 246)

ABOUT 2 HOURS BEFORE SERVING:
1. In small bowl, pour sherry over bread crumbs. In 2-quart saucepan over medium heat, in 1 tablespoon hot butter or margarine, cook minced onions until tender, about 5 minutes. Add green pepper, parsley, ¼ teaspoon thyme leaves and chili sauce; cook a few minutes. Add crumbs; cook until mixture is almost dry, about 5 minutes more.
2. Preheat oven to 350°F. Line a large baking dish with foil; grease foil. Sprinkle inside of fish lightly with salt and pepper; fill with crumb mixture; fasten opening with toothpicks.

* Or, use bass, bluefish, cod or lake trout.

3. In small saucepan over medium heat, melt 1 tablespoon butter or margarine; stir in 1 teaspoon salt, ¼ teaspoon pepper and ¼ teaspoon thyme leaves. Brush fish with mixture; then place fish in baking dish. Bake 50 to 55 minutes until fish flakes easily when tested with a fork.
4. Remove toothpicks. Serve fish as in To Carve Whole Fish (page 215). Pass Shrimp-Olive Sauce. Makes 8 to 10 servings.

BROILED SHAD

1 3-pound shad, boned
¼ cup butter or margarine
2 tablespoons lemon juice
1½ teaspoons salt
dash pepper
1 tablespoon chopped parsley for garnish
lemon wedges (optional)

ABOUT 25 MINUTES BEFORE SERVING:
Preheat broiler if manufacturer directs. Lightly grease broiling-pan rack. Cut shad into 4 serving pieces; arrange, skin side down, on rack.

In small saucepan over medium heat, melt butter or margarine; stir in lemon juice, salt and pepper; brush over shad. Broil until fish flakes easily when tested with a fork, about 8 to 10 minutes. Garnish with parsley and serve with lemon wedges. Makes 4 servings.

BROILED SHAD WITH ROE: Prepare shad as above but place *shad roe* on rack of pan also and brush with butter mixture; broil.

SAUTEED SHAD ROE

¼ cup butter or margarine
2 shad roe (about 1 pound)
½ teaspoon salt
dash pepper
lemon wedges

ABOUT 10 MINUTES BEFORE SERVING:
In covered 10-inch skillet over medium heat, in hot butter or margarine, cook roe, turning once, 8 minutes or until roe loses its pink color and is tender when tested with a fork. Sprinkle roe with salt and pepper; serve with lemon wedges to squeeze over roe. Makes 4 servings.

SKILLET TROUT

½ cup milk
⅓ cup all-purpose flour
4 trout, dressed and boned
2 teaspoons prepared mustard
⅓ cup salad oil
½ cup butter or margarine
½ cup chopped green onions
2 tablespoons lemon juice

ABOUT 40 MINUTES BEFORE SERVING:
Into pie plate, pour milk. On waxed paper, place flour. Dip fish in milk, then in flour to coat. Spread ½ teaspoon mustard inside of each fish.

In 12-inch skillet over medium-high heat, in hot salad oil, cook fish, turning carefully with pancake turner once, for 8 minutes or until fish flakes easily when tested with a fork. Place on warm platter.

In same skillet over medium heat, in hot butter or margarine, cook onions with lemon juice until just tender, about 3 minutes; pour over fish. Makes 4 servings.

BROILED FISH STEAKS WITH CHEESE SAUCE

3 tablespoons lemon juice
salad oil
⅛ teaspoon ground ginger
1 1-ounce package cheese-sauce mix
3 small halibut steaks,* cut 1 inch thick (about 1½ pounds)
3 salmon steaks,* cut 1 inch thick (about 2 pounds)
salt
6 bay leaves for garnish

ABOUT 30 MINUTES BEFORE SERVING:
In cup, combine lemon juice, 2 tablespoons salad oil and ginger. Prepare cheese-sauce mix as label directs.

Preheat broiler if manufacturer directs. Grease broiling-pan rack. On rack, arrange halibut and salmon steaks; sprinkle with salt; brush with lemon-juice mixture. Broil 5 minutes or until lightly browned. With pancake turner, carefully turn steaks; broil 5 minutes more, brushing often with lemon mixture. Remove to large warm platter.

To serve, pour sauce around steaks; top each with bay leaf. Makes 6 servings.

* Or, use 6 steaks of one kind of fish.

HALIBUT STEAKS HAWAIIAN

2 cups cooked rice
4 teaspoons lemon juice
⅓ cup butter or margarine, melted
seasoned salt
½ teaspoon curry powder
1 8½-ounce can pineapple tidbits, drained
2 1-pound halibut steaks
1 lemon, cut in wedges, for garnish

ABOUT 1 HOUR BEFORE SERVING:
Preheat oven to 350°F. In medium bowl, combine rice with 3 teaspoons lemon juice, 2 tablespoons melted butter or margarine, ¾ teaspoon seasoned salt, curry powder and all but 10 pineapple tidbits (reserve for garnish); set aside.

Sprinkle each halibut steak with ½ teaspoon lemon juice and ½ teaspoon seasoned salt. Place one steak in a large, shallow pan; brush with half of remaining melted butter; spread with rice mixture. Top with other steak; brush with remaining butter. Secure top steak in place with metal skewers.

Bake 40 minutes or until fish flakes easily when tested with a fork. Remove skewers; garnish fish with reserved pineapple and lemon wedges. Makes 4 or 5 servings.

STUFFED HALIBUT STEAK WITH RELISH

1 large halibut steak, cut 1 inch thick (about 3 pounds)
butter or margarine
1 large onion, minced
½ pound mushrooms, sliced
¼ cup lemon juice
4 cups fresh bread crumbs
½ cup chopped parsley
3 tablespoons milk
salt and pepper
paprika
Cucumber Relish (below)

ABOUT 1 HOUR AND 10 MINUTES AHEAD:
1. Remove center bone of halibut steak and cut steak in half crosswise. In 12-inch skillet over medium heat, in 2 tablespoons hot butter or margarine, cook onion until tender, about 5 minutes. With slotted spoon, remove onion to small bowl.
2. In same skillet, covered, cook mushrooms with lemon juice until tender, about 3 minutes. Remove from heat; stir in onion, bread crumbs, parsley, milk, 1 teaspoon salt and ¼ teaspoon pepper.
3. Preheat oven to 350°F. Line 13″ by 9″ baking dish with foil; grease foil. Sprinkle both sides of steak halves with salt, pepper and paprika. In baking dish, place one steak half; spread bread-crumb mixture on top; top with other steak half. Dot with butter and sprinkle with paprika.
4. Bake 50 to 60 minutes until fish flakes easily when tested with a fork. Serve fish on warm platter with drained Cucumber Relish surrounding it. Makes 8 servings.

CUCUMBER RELISH: Into small bowl, thinly slice *1 medium cucumber;* toss with a little *Italian salad dressing.*

HALIBUT STEAK WITH EGGPLANT SAUCE

1 large green pepper
1 large onion
1 1-pound eggplant
⅓ cup salad or olive oil
2 8-ounce cans tomato sauce
½ cup dry white wine
1 garlic clove, minced
1 bay leaf
¼ cup butter or margarine
2 tablespoons lemon juice
salt and pepper
1 2-pound halibut steak

ABOUT 30 MINUTES BEFORE SERVING:
Cut green pepper into ½-inch strips; slice onion. Peel eggplant; cut in ½-inch cubes. In 12-inch skillet over medium heat, in hot oil, cook green pepper and onion until tender; add eggplant, tomato sauce, wine, garlic and bay leaf; simmer 15 minutes.

Meanwhile, preheat broiler if manufacturer directs. Grease broiling-pan rack. In small saucepan over low heat, melt butter or margarine with lemon juice, ½ teaspoon salt and ¼ teaspoon pepper.

Place halibut steak on rack and brush generously with butter mixture. Broil 5 minutes; turn and brush with butter mixture. Broil 5 minutes longer or until fish flakes easily when tested with a fork. Serve fish with sauce. Makes 6 servings.

SALMON STEAKS THERMIDOR

4 salmon steaks, cut about ¾ inch thick (about 2 pounds)
½ cup milk
¼ teaspoon salt
dash pepper
1 10½-ounce can condensed cream-of-mushroom soup
2 tablespoons medium or dry sherry
2 hard-cooked eggs, sliced
4 pasteurized process Swiss-cheese slices, halved
paprika

ABOUT 40 MINUTES BEFORE SERVING:
Preheat oven to 350°F. In greased, shallow bake-and-serve dish, place salmon steaks; pour on milk and sprinkle with salt and pepper. Bake 30 minutes or until fish flakes easily when tested with a fork. Turn oven control to broil.

Meanwhile, in 2-quart saucepan over medium heat, stir undiluted soup until smooth; stir in sherry; heat to boiling. When steaks are done, arrange sliced eggs around them; pour on sauce. Top with cheese and sprinkle with paprika. Broil until bubbling hot, about 5 minutes. Makes 4 servings.

SALMON STEAKS IN ASPIC

salt
4 salmon steaks, cut about ¾ inch thick (about 2 pounds)
1 cup cider vinegar
3 medium onions, thinly sliced
¼ cup sugar
4 whole cloves
2 bay leaves
1 envelope unflavored gelatin
12 thin cucumber slices for garnish
12 thin carrot slices for garnish

EARLY IN DAY OR DAY BEFORE:
1. Sprinkle ½ teaspoon salt on each side of each salmon steak; in 13″ by 9″ baking dish, arrange steaks side by side. Pour vinegar over all; cover and refrigerate 2 hours.
2. Prepare Court Bouillon: Into 12-inch skillet, drain vinegar from fish; add 1 cup water, onions, sugar, cloves, bay leaves and 2 teaspoons salt. Over medium-low heat, simmer mixture 15 minutes. Arrange salmon steaks in Court Bouillon; cover and simmer 20 minutes or until fish flakes easily when tested with a fork.
3. With pancake turner, carefully transfer steaks to baking dish. Strain Court Bouillon into a 2-cup measuring cup. Discard cloves and bay leaves; arrange onion slices around fish.
4. To Court Bouillon in measuring cup, add enough water to make 1½ cups. Pour into small saucepan; stir in gelatin. Over low heat, cook mixture, stirring constantly, until gelatin is completely dissolved.
5. On each steak, arrange 3 cucumber and 3 carrot slices. Pour 1 cup gelatin mixture over and around fish; refrigerate fish and remaining gelatin mixture until mixture mounds slightly when dropped from a spoon. Spoon remaining mixture over steaks as a glaze; cover and refrigerate until served. Makes 4 servings.

POACHED SALMON STEAKS

3 chicken-bouillon cubes or envelopes
2 tablespoons white vinegar
1 medium onion, sliced
1 bay leaf
dill weed
salt
pepper
4 salmon steaks, cut about 1 inch thick (about 2½ pounds)
Lemon Sauce for Fish (page 246)

ABOUT 30 MINUTES BEFORE SERVING:
Prepare Court Bouillon: In 12-inch skillet over high heat, in 4 cups boiling water, heat to boiling bouillon, vinegar, onion slices, bay leaf, 1 teaspoon dill weed, 1½ teaspoons salt and dash pepper. Reduce heat to low; cover skillet and simmer 5 minutes.

Add salmon steaks; cover and simmer 8 minutes or until fish flakes easily when tested with a fork. With pancake turner, lift steaks onto warm platter. With slotted spoon, remove and drain onion slices, placing them over steaks for garnish. Reserve 1¼ cups Court Bouillon for sauce; discard bay leaf.

Prepare Lemon Sauce. Serve sauce around steaks; sprinkle lightly with dill weed. Makes 4 servings.

FRESH TUNA STEAK PROVENÇAL

1 tuna or halibut steak, cut 1½ inches thick (about 2 pounds)
seasoned salt
pepper
¼ cup salad oil
4 medium tomatoes, peeled and chopped
2 garlic cloves, minced
2 tablespoons minced onion
½ teaspoon lemon juice
1 bay leaf
½ cup white wine
1 tablespoon butter or margarine
1 tablespoon all-purpose flour

ABOUT 50 MINUTES BEFORE SERVING:
Preheat oven to 350°F. Sprinkle tuna steak with seasoned salt and pepper. In 12-inch skillet over medium heat, in hot oil, brown steak on both sides. Place in 9″ by 9″ baking dish; add tomatoes and next 5 ingredients. Bake 30 minutes or until fish flakes easily when tested with a fork.

On warm platter, place steak, discarding bay leaf. In 1-quart saucepan over medium heat, into hot butter or margarine, stir flour until blended. Gradually stir in liquid from fish and cook, stirring constantly, until mixture is thickened; pour over fish. Makes 4 servings.

FISH FILLETS WITH SOUR CREAM

1 medium onion, thinly sliced
salt
1 16-ounce package frozen cod, ocean perch or flounder fillets, thawed
⅔ cup sour cream
½ teaspoon prepared mustard
paprika

ABOUT 40 MINUTES BEFORE SERVING:
Preheat oven to 350°F. Over bottom of 12″ by 8″ baking pan, arrange onion slices; sprinkle with salt; top with fish fillets. Cover dish with foil; bake 20 to 25 minutes until fish flakes easily when tested with a fork. Remove foil and spoon off juices. Turn oven control to broil.

In cup, stir sour cream with prepared mustard and ⅛ teaspoon salt; spread on fish; sprinkle with paprika. Broil fish about 5 minutes or until topping is golden. Makes 3 servings.

CREAMED FINNAN HADDIE

2 pounds finnan haddie or smoked cod fillets, cut in large pieces
3 tablespoons butter or margarine
4 teaspoons all-purpose flour
2 cups milk
1 cup heavy or whipping cream
4 hard-cooked eggs
parsley for garnish
Holland rusks or toast points (optional)

ABOUT 1½ HOURS BEFORE SERVING:
If using smoked cod: In large, shallow pan, place fillets and cover with cold water. Soak 1 hour, then drain.

In 12-inch skillet over medium heat, into hot butter or margarine, stir flour until blended. Gradually stir in milk and cream and cook, stirring, until mixture is slightly thickened and comes to a boil; add fish pieces. Cover; simmer 15 minutes or until fish flakes easily when tested with a fork.

Reserve 2 hard-cooked egg yolks for garnish; chop whites and other 2 egg yolks. In the sauce, with fork, coarsely flake fish; stir in chopped eggs and pour into warm dish. Through coarse sieve, press reserved egg yolks over top. Garnish with parsley. Serve on Holland rusks. Makes 8 servings.

CORNMEAL-COATED FLOUNDER FRY

2 tablespoons all-purpose flour
1 egg
⅓ cup cornmeal
⅓ cup seasoned dried bread crumbs
1 16-ounce package frozen flounder fillets, thawed
⅓ cup salad oil
Horseradish Sauce (page 245)

ABOUT 15 MINUTES BEFORE SERVING:
On one sheet of waxed paper, place flour. In pie plate, with fork, beat egg with 1 tablespoon water. On another sheet of waxed paper, combine cornmeal and bread crumbs. Dip fillets in flour, then in egg mixture, then in cornmeal mixture until coated.

In 12-inch skillet over medium heat, in hot salad oil, fry fillets, carefully turning once with pancake turner, 8 minutes or until fish flakes when tested with a fork. Serve with sauce. Makes 3 or 4 servings.

BAKED COD WITH GRAPEFRUIT

1 large grapefruit
2 16-ounce packages frozen cod fillets, thawed
¾ teaspoon salt
dash pepper
¼ cup butter or margarine
1 cup fresh bread crumbs
¼ teaspoon thyme leaves

ABOUT 40 MINUTES BEFORE SERVING:
Preheat oven to 350°F. Into small bowl, section grapefruit; let stand 5 minutes to collect juice. Brush fillets generously with juice from grapefruit; sprinkle with salt and pepper. Place in 12″ by 8″ baking pan.

In small saucepan over medium heat, melt butter or margarine; reserve 1 tablespoon; into remaining butter or margarine, stir bread crumbs and thyme; sprinkle over fish. Arrange grapefruit sections over crumbs; brush grapefruit with reserved melted butter or margarine. Bake 25 to 30 minutes until fish flakes easily when tested with a fork. Makes 6 servings.

CRUSTY FISH FOLD-UPS

½ cup bottled tartar sauce
2 tablespoons minced onion
1 16-ounce package frozen flounder fillets, thawed
⅓ cup all-purpose flour
1 egg
1 3-ounce package cheese-flavored corn snacks

ABOUT 1 HOUR BEFORE SERVING:
In measuring cup, combine tartar sauce with onion; spread on fillets. Fold each fillet in half and fasten with toothpick. Preheat oven to 350°F. Grease 10″ by 6″ baking dish.

Onto waxed paper, sprinkle flour. In medium bowl, with fork, beat egg well. On a second piece of waxed paper, coarsely crush corn snacks. Carefully dip each fillet into flour, next into egg and then into crumbs, until coated on both sides.

Arrange fillets in baking dish. Bake 40 minutes or until fish flakes easily when tested with a fork. Remove toothpicks. Serve fish at once. Makes 4 servings.

FISH FILLETS WITH CUCUMBER SAUCE

1 16-ounce package frozen cod or haddock fillets, thawed
butter or margarine
salt
dash pepper
⅓ cup grated, seeded cucumber
1 tablespoon minced parsley
1 teaspoon wine vinegar
⅛ teaspoon hot pepper sauce

ABOUT 35 MINUTES BEFORE SERVING:
Preheat broiler if manufacturer directs. Grease broiling-pan rack; arrange fillets on rack.

In small saucepan over medium heat, melt 2 tablespoons butter or margarine; brush on fillets. Sprinkle fillets with ¼ teaspoon salt and pepper. Broil 5 to 8 minutes until fish flakes easily when tested with a fork.

Meanwhile, in same saucepan over medium heat, heat ¼ cup butter or margarine, cucumber, parsley, wine vinegar, ⅛ teaspoon salt and hot pepper sauce just to boiling. Serve sauce over fillets. Makes 3 or 4 servings.

FISH FILLETS WITH GREEN MAYONNAISE

¼ cup chopped watercress
¼ cup chopped parsley
3 tablespoons chopped chives
¾ cup mayonnaise
1 10-ounce bottle lemon-lime soft drink
½ teaspoon pepper
2 16-ounce packages frozen cod, ocean perch, haddock or sole fillets, thawed

ABOUT 20 MINUTES BEFORE SERVING:
Prepare Green Mayonnaise: In cup, mix watercress, parsley and chives. In serving bowl, stir 6 tablespoons of mixture with mayonnaise; cover and refrigerate.

In 12-inch skillet over medium heat, heat lemon-lime soft drink, remaining watercress mixture and pepper to boiling. Add fillets; cover and simmer 10 minutes or until fish flakes easily when tested with a fork. Remove fillets to warm platter; serve with Green Mayonnaise. Makes 8 servings.

SWEET-SOUR FISH

1 16-ounce package frozen flounder fillets, thawed
¾ cup all-purpose flour
1 teaspoon double-acting baking powder
1 teaspoon salt
salad oil
1 16-ounce can sweet-and-sour sauce
2 tablespoons catchup
½ teaspoon chili powder

ABOUT 25 MINUTES BEFORE SERVING:
On paper towels, drain and blot fillets. In medium bowl, combine flour, baking powder, salt and ⅔ cup water.

Meanwhile, in electric skillet,* heat about 1 inch salad oil to 370°F. Dip fillets into flour mixture until coated; fry in hot oil, turning once, until golden, about 4 to 8 minutes. Drain well on paper towels; place on platter; keep warm.

In small saucepan over medium heat, heat sweet-and-sour sauce, catchup and chili powder until hot, stirring occasionally. Serve over fish. Makes 4 servings.

* Or, in 10-inch skillet over medium heat, heat oil to 370°F. on deep-fat thermometer.

FLORENTINE FILLETS

1 3-ounce can chopped mushrooms
2 tablespoons butter or margarine
½ cup chopped onion
1 cup crushed saltines
salt
¼ teaspoon pepper
⅛ teaspoon rubbed sage
4 sole or flounder fillets
1 10-ounce package frozen chopped spinach, thawed and drained
4 teaspoons lemon juice
4 medium tomatoes
bottled Italian salad dressing

ABOUT 45 MINUTES BEFORE SERVING:
Preheat oven to 350°F. Prepare stuffing: Drain mushrooms, reserving liquid. In 10-inch skillet over medium heat, in hot butter or margarine, cook onion and mushrooms until onion is tender; remove from heat. Add saltines, ¼ teaspoon salt, pepper, sage and 2 tablespoons mushroom liquid.

Sprinkle fillets with salt. Spread with spinach; sprinkle with lemon juice, then spread with stuffing. From a narrow end, roll each fillet, jelly-roll fashion; secure with toothpicks. Arrange rolls side by side in 12″ by 8″ baking dish.

Cut tops from tomatoes; place tomatoes in pan and sprinkle with salt; brush with dressing. Bake fillets and tomatoes 20 minutes or until fish flakes easily when tested with a fork. Remove toothpicks. Makes 4 servings.

TARRAGON FISH

¼ cup salad oil
1 tablespoon lemon juice
½ teaspoon tarragon
½ teaspoon salt
dash pepper
1 16-ounce package frozen flounder fillets, thawed
1 medium lemon, cut into 4 wedges
parsley sprigs for garnish

ABOUT 20 MINUTES BEFORE SERVING:
Preheat broiler if manufacturer directs. Grease broiling-pan rack. In small bowl, mix well salad oil, lemon juice, tarragon, salt and pepper. Place fillets on rack in one layer; broil 5 to 8 minutes, generously basting with oil mixture occasionally, until fish flakes easily when tested with a fork. Serve with lemon wedges and garnish with parsley sprigs. Makes 4 servings.

CLAM-STUFFED FISH FILLETS

2 16-ounce packages frozen flounder fillets, thawed
salt
2 8-ounce cans minced clams
½ cup butter or margarine
⅔ cup chopped celery
½ cup chopped onion
¼ teaspoon pepper
6 cups white-bread cubes (8 slices)
2 eggs
¼ teaspoon thyme leaves

ABOUT 1 HOUR BEFORE SERVING:
Grease eight 6-ounce custard cups. Pat fillets dry on paper towels; sprinkle with ½ teaspoon salt. Line custard cups with

fillets, cutting fillets to fit if necessary. Drain clams, reserving ¼ cup of their liquid; set aside.

Preheat oven to 350°F. In 3-quart saucepan over medium heat, in hot butter or margarine, cook celery, onion, pepper and 1 teaspoon salt until celery is tender, about 5 minutes. Stir in clams, reserved liquid and remaining ingredients until well mixed.

Spoon ½ cup clam mixture into center of each fillet-lined custard cup; place in large, shallow baking pan for easier handling. Bake fish 25 to 30 minutes until stuffing is heated through. With 2 spoons, gently lift stuffed fillets from cups to warm platter. Makes 8 servings.

SAUCY BAKED FISH FILLETS

1 16-ounce package frozen flounder or haddock fillets, thawed
1 10½-ounce can condensed cream-of-celery soup
½ cup shredded Cheddar cheese

ABOUT 25 MINUTES BEFORE SERVING:
Preheat oven to 350°F. Grease shallow bake-and-serve dish. In dish, arrange fillets in one layer. Pour undiluted soup evenly over fillets; sprinkle with cheese. Bake 15 minutes or until fish flakes easily when tested with a fork. Makes 4 servings.

BROILED FLOUNDER WITH CREAMY TOPPING

¼ cup butter or margarine
1 teaspoon salt
⅛ teaspoon pepper
2 16-ounce packages frozen flounder or ocean-perch fillets, thawed
1 8-ounce container prepared onion dip

ABOUT 20 MINUTES BEFORE SERVING:
Preheat broiler if manufacturer directs; grease bake-and-serve platter. In small saucepan over low heat, melt butter or margarine with salt and pepper. On platter, arrange fillets in a single layer; brush with butter mixture; broil 5 minutes.

Gently spread onion dip over fillets; continue broiling for 1 minute or until lightly browned and fish flakes easily when tested with a fork. Makes 6 servings.

CHEESY FLOUNDER FILLETS

1 16-ounce package frozen flounder fillets, thawed
salad oil
1 tablespoon instant minced onion
½ teaspoon seasoned salt
½ teaspoon marjoram leaves
¼ teaspoon poultry seasoning
dash pepper
2 sharp Cheddar-cheese slices, halved
1 8-ounce can tomato sauce
2 tablespoons dried bread crumbs

ABOUT 1 HOUR BEFORE SERVING:
Preheat oven to 350°F. Grease 8″ by 8″ baking dish. Brush fillets with salad oil. In cup, combine minced onion, seasoned salt, marjoram, poultry seasoning and pepper; sprinkle on fillets. Top each fillet with cheese piece and roll up from a narrow end; fasten with toothpicks; arrange in dish.

Pour tomato sauce over roll-ups; sprinkle with bread crumbs. Bake 30 minutes or until fish flakes easily when tested with a fork. Remove toothpicks. Makes 4 servings.

LIME-SAUCED FLOUNDER ROLLS

1 16-ounce package frozen flounder fillets, thawed
salt
pepper
lime juice
¼ cup minced onion
2 tablespoons butter or margarine
2 tablespoons all-purpose flour
1 cup milk
2 teaspoons chopped pimento

ABOUT 1 HOUR BEFORE SERVING:
Preheat oven to 350°F. Grease 10″ by 6″ baking dish. Sprinkle fillets with salt, pepper and lime juice; roll up from a narrow end and place in baking dish. Sprinkle onion over tops of fish.

In 1-quart saucepan over medium heat, into hot butter or margarine, stir flour until until blended. Gradually stir in milk and cook, stirring constantly, until mixture is thickened. Stir in 2 teaspoons lime juice, pimento, ½ teaspoon salt and dash pepper.

Pour sauce over fish; bake 40 to 45 minutes until fish flakes easily when tested with a fork. Makes 3 or 4 servings.

FISH AND NOODLES, HUNGARIAN STYLE

½ 16-ounce package mafalde noodles
¼ cup butter or margarine
1 medium onion, thinly sliced
1 16-ounce package frozen haddock fillets, thawed
1 teaspoon salt
paprika
1 cup sour cream
1 teaspoon dill weed

ABOUT 50 MINUTES BEFORE SERVING:
Prepare noodles as label directs; drain. Meanwhile, in 3-quart saucepan over medium heat, in hot butter or margarine, cook onion until tender, about 5 minutes. Cut fillets into 1-inch chunks. Add chunks, salt, ½ teaspoon paprika and ¾ cup water to onion; cover and cook 5 to 10 minutes until fish flakes easily when tested with a fork.

Gently stir noodles, sour cream and dill into fish mixture; continue cooking until just heated through (do not boil). Spoon mixture onto warm platter. Sprinkle lightly with more paprika. Makes 4 servings.

BROILER-BARBECUED FISH DINNER

Seafood Barbecue Sauce (below)
1 16-ounce package frozen haddock fillets, thawed
¼ pound large mushrooms
4 small zucchini
melted butter or margarine
salt and pepper
grated Parmesan cheese

ABOUT 45 MINUTES BEFORE SERVING:
Preheat broiler if manufacturer directs. Prepare sauce. Grease broiling-pan rack. Cut fillets into serving pieces and place on rack. Remove stems from mushrooms (save for use another day). Place mushroom caps beside fish. Halve zucchini lengthwise and score cut surfaces with tines of fork; arrange, cut sides up, beside mushrooms.

Brush mushrooms and zucchini generously with melted butter or margarine; sprinkle with salt and pepper. Sprinkle zucchini with cheese. Spoon sauce over fish.

Broil 10 to 12 minutes until fish flakes easily when tested with a fork and zucchini is tender; baste mushrooms occasionally with melted butter. Makes 4 servings.

SEAFOOD BARBECUE SAUCE: In small saucepan over medium heat, simmer *2 small onions*, sliced, *½ cup catchup, ⅓ cup salad oil, 2 tablespoons diced celery, 2 teaspoons dry mustard, 1 teaspoon salt, 2 teaspoons Worcestershire, 2 teaspoons lemon juice* and *¼ teaspoon pepper* for 5 minutes. Makes about 1¼ cups sauce.

FILLETS OF SOLE THERMIDOR

5 tablespoons butter or margarine
2 teaspoons salt
½ teaspoon seasoned salt
dash pepper
8 sole fillets* (about 2 pounds)
1¼ cups milk
3 tablespoons all-purpose flour
1 4-ounce package shredded Cheddar cheese (1 cup)
3 tablespoons dry sherry (optional)
paprika

ABOUT 45 MINUTES BEFORE SERVING:
Preheat oven to 350°F. In small saucepan over medium heat, melt 2 tablespoons butter or margarine with salt, seasoned salt and pepper; use to brush both sides of fillets. Roll up each fillet from a narrow end and place, seam side down, in 9" by 9" baking pan. Pour ½ cup milk over fillets and bake 25 minutes or until fish flakes easily when tested with a fork.

Meanwhile, in same saucepan over medium heat, into hot remaining butter or margarine, stir flour until blended. Gradually stir in remaining ¾ cup milk and cook, stirring constantly, until mixture is thickened. Reduce heat and stir in cheese until melted; stir in sherry.

When fish is done, remove from oven and preheat broiler if manufacturer directs. Pour off pan liquid, reserving ¼ cup; stir it into cheese sauce. (If not using sherry, use 3 tablespoons more pan liquid.) Pour sauce over fish; sprinkle with paprika. Broil about 1 minute or until sauce is slightly golden. Makes 8 servings.

* Or, use *two 16-ounce packages frozen sole fillets,* thawed. Arrange fillets in 12" by 8" baking pan (do not roll); proceed as above.

FRIED FISH ALLA MARGHERITA

¼ cup olive or salad oil
¼ cup butter or margarine
2 pounds sole or flounder fillets
1 16-ounce can tomato sauce
2 tablespoons chopped parsley
1 teaspoon oregano leaves

ABOUT 20 MINUTES BEFORE SERVING:
In 12-inch skillet over medium heat, in hot oil and butter or margarine, cook fillets 2 or 3 minutes on each side until fish flakes easily when tested with a fork.

Meanwhile, in medium bowl, stir tomato sauce, parsley and oregano; pour over fish. Reduce heat to low; cover and simmer 5 or 6 minutes, occasionally basting fish with sauce. Serve from skillet. Makes 6 servings.

BAKED SOLE WITH LEMON SAUCE

2 16-ounce packages frozen sole or flounder fillets, thawed
1 teaspoon salt
¼ teaspoon pepper
3 tablespoons butter or margarine
2 egg yolks
1 tablespoon all-purpose flour
¾ cup chicken broth
2 tablespoons lemon juice
4 stuffed olives, sliced, for garnish

ABOUT 30 MINUTES BEFORE SERVING:
Preheat oven to 350°F. Grease a large, shallow baking dish; arrange fillets in dish. Sprinkle fillets with salt and pepper; dot with 2 tablespoons butter or margarine. Bake 10 minutes or until fish flakes easily when tested with a fork.

Meanwhile, prepare sauce: In cup, mix egg yolks with 1 tablespoon water; set aside. In heavy, 1-quart saucepan over medium heat, into 1 tablespoon hot butter or margarine, stir flour until blended. Gradually stir in chicken broth and lemon juice and cook, stirring, until mixture is thickened; remove from heat.

Into egg yolks, stir small amount of hot sauce; stirring rapidly to prevent lumping, slowly pour egg mixture back into the sauce. Cook, stirring, until thickened. (Do not boil.) Spoon off any liquid from fish. Pour sauce over fish and garnish with olives. Makes 8 servings.

GOLDEN FISH FILLETS WITH ONION

butter or margarine
1 large onion, sliced
6 sole or flounder fillets (about 2 pounds)
¼ cup all-purpose flour
1 teaspoon salt
¼ teaspoon pepper
¼ teaspoon paprika
¼ cup lemon juice
½ teaspoon Worcestershire
watercress for garnish

ABOUT 45 MINUTES BEFORE SERVING:
1. In 12-inch skillet over medium heat, in 2 tablespoons hot butter or margarine, cook onion until tender, about 5 minutes; remove to plate; keep warm.
2. Meanwhile, cut fillets in half crosswise. On waxed paper, combine flour with salt, pepper, paprika; coat fillets with mixture.
3. In same skillet over medium heat, in ¼ cup hot butter or margarine, fry 6 halves, turning once, until fish is brown and flakes easily when tested with a fork; place on platter. Repeat with remaining 6 halves.
4. To mixture left in skillet, add lemon juice and Worcestershire; heat to boiling, stirring; pour over fish. Top with cooked onion; garnish with watercress. Makes 6 servings.

OCEAN PERCH FILLETS WITH DIABLO SAUCE

1 16-ounce package frozen ocean perch fillets, thawed
1 teaspoon seasoned salt
¼ teaspoon seasoned pepper
1 slice white bread
butter or margarine, softened
⅓ cup chili sauce
1½ teaspoons lemon juice
½ teaspoon Worcestershire

ABOUT 25 MINUTES BEFORE SERVING:
Preheat oven to 350°F. Grease shallow baking dish; arrange fillets in dish; sprinkle fillets with seasoned salt and pepper. Spread bread with butter or margarine and cut into cubes; sprinkle over fish. Bake 15 minutes or until fish flakes easily when tested with a fork.

Meanwhile, for sauce, in a cup, combine chili sauce, lemon juice and Worcestershire; serve over fillets. Makes 3 servings.

MIXED SEAFOOD SUPPER

2 16-ounce packages frozen ocean perch fillets
3 pounds large shrimp in shell
Curried Mayonnaise (page 246), Cucumber Sauce (page 245), Chili-Horseradish Sauce (page 246), Dill-Butter Sauce (page 246) or Soy-Onion Sauce (page 246)
2 celery stalks
1 tablespoon salt
1 bay leaf
¼ teaspoon peppercorns, crushed
parsley sprigs for garnish

EARLY IN DAY:
Thaw fillets. Shell and devein shrimp, leaving tail shells on; cover and refrigerate. Prepare two or three of sauces.

ABOUT 25 MINUTES BEFORE SERVING:
In 4-quart saucepan over high heat, heat 8 cups water to boiling with celery, salt, bay leaf and peppercorns. Add shrimp; return to boiling and cook until shrimp turn pink, about 3 minutes. Using slotted spoon, remove shrimp and arrange on one side of large warm platter; keep warm.

Then, in same cooking liquid, cook fish fillets just until fish flakes when tested with a fork, about 4 minutes. With slotted spoon, carefully remove fillets and arrange on platter with shrimp. Garnish with parsley sprigs. Serve immediately with cocktail forks and sauces. Makes about 8 servings.

SHRIMP-FILLED FILLETS HOLLANDAISE

¼ cup butter or margarine
1 garlic clove, crushed
1 small onion, minced
¼ cup minced green pepper
1 pound shelled and deveined shrimp, cooked
¼ cup dried bread crumbs
1 tablespoon chopped parsley
salt
4 sole or flounder fillets (about 1½ pounds)
Hollandaise Sauce (page 282)

ABOUT 1 HOUR BEFORE SERVING:
1. Preheat oven to 350°F. In 12-inch skillet over low heat, in 2 tablespoons hot butter or margarine, cook garlic, onion and green pepper until tender.
2. Meanwhile, reserve 4 shrimp for garnish; dice remaining shrimp; add with crumbs, parsley and ¼ teaspoon salt to mixture in skillet; mix well; remove from heat.
3. With spoon, on boned side of each fillet, spread 2 tablespoons shrimp mixture down middle. From a narrow end, roll each fillet jelly-roll fashion; tuck any extra mixture into rolls.
4. In 10″ by 6″ baking pan, put 2 tablespoons butter or margarine; place pan in oven. When butter is melted, remove pan from oven; arrange fillets in butter, seam side down; brush fillets with some melted butter. Bake 25 to 30 minutes until fish flakes easily when tested with a fork.
5. Arrange fillets on warm platter and pour some of Hollandaise Sauce over them; garnish each with a shrimp. Pass remaining sauce in gravy boat. Makes 4 servings.

SHRIMP-STUFFED ROLL-UPS

¼ cup butter or margarine
½ pound frozen shelled, deveined shrimp, partially thawed, chopped (about 1 cup)
1 cup chopped mushrooms
¼ cup dried bread crumbs
½ teaspoon dill weed
salt
6 sole fillets* (about 2 pounds)
1 cup dry white wine
2 tablespoons cornstarch
½ cup half-and-half
1 egg

ABOUT 40 MINUTES BEFORE SERVING:
1. In 10-inch skillet over medium heat, in hot butter or margarine, cook shrimp and mushrooms just until shrimp turn pink. Stir in bread crumbs, dill weed and ½ teaspoon salt until well combined; remove from heat. Spoon shrimp mixture onto center of each fillet. From a narrow end, roll each fillet jelly-roll fashion; fasten securely with toothpicks. Wipe skillet clean with paper towels.
2. In same skillet over high heat, heat to boiling wine, ½ cup water, 1½ teaspoons

* Or, use *two 16-ounce packages frozen sole fillets*, thawed.

salt and stuffed fillets. Reduce heat to low; cover and simmer 12 to 15 minutes until fish flakes easily when tested with a fork. With slotted spoon, carefully remove fillets to warm platter; remove toothpicks; keep fillets warm.

3. Meanwhile, in small bowl, with fork, stir cornstarch and half-and-half until blended; stir into simmering liquid in skillet. Cook over medium heat, stirring constantly, until sauce boils and is slightly thickened.

4. In small bowl, with fork, beat egg slightly; into egg, stir small amount of hot sauce; stirring rapidly to prevent lumping, slowly pour egg mixture back into the sauce. Cook, stirring, until thickened. (Do not boil.) Pour some sauce over fillets and pass remaining sauce in gravy boat. Makes 6 servings.

POACHED SOLE WITH HOLLANDAISE

1 carrot, sliced
1 stalk celery, sliced
1 small onion, sliced
1 medium lemon, sliced
4 peppercorns
2 bay leaves
2 parsley sprigs
1 teaspoon salt
1 16-ounce package frozen sole fillets, thawed
1 package hollandaise-sauce mix
chopped parsley for garnish
lemon wedges for garnish

ABOUT 30 MINUTES BEFORE SERVING:
Prepare Court Bouillon: In 12-inch skillet over high heat, heat to boiling 2 cups water and first 8 ingredients. Reduce heat to low; cover and simmer 10 minutes. With slotted spoon, remove vegetables, lemon and herbs; discard.

Carefully separate fillets. Cut into serving pieces and place in Court Bouillon; cover and simmer over low heat 4 minutes or until fish flakes easily when tested with a fork. With slotted pancake turner, carefully remove fillets; arrange on warm platter; discard Court Bouillon.

Meanwhile, prepare hollandaise sauce as label directs; spoon over fish. Garnish with parsley and lemon. Makes 4 servings.

SOLE WITH OYSTER SAUCE

1 pound sole fillets
¼ teaspoon pepper
¾ cup dry white wine
4 tablespoons butter or margarine
2 cups sliced mushrooms
½ cup heavy or whipping cream
1 8-ounce can or ½ pint shucked "standard" oysters, drained

ABOUT 30 MINUTES BEFORE SERVING:
Preheat oven to 350°F. In shallow baking pan, arrange fillets in a single layer; sprinkle with pepper. Pour wine over fish and bake 10 minutes or just until fish flakes easily when tested with a fork. With large pancake turner, transfer fillets to platter and keep warm; reserve pan liquid.

Meanwhile, in 10-inch skillet over medium-high heat, in 2 tablespoons hot butter or margarine, cook mushrooms until tender, stirring occasionally. Arrange mushrooms over fish. Add reserved liquid, cream and remaining butter or margarine to skillet and cook over high heat about 5 minutes until sauce cooks down to about half its original volume, stirring occasionally. Add oysters and heat through. Pour sauce over fish. Makes 4 servings.

WHITEFISH AMANDINE

2 pounds whitefish fillets
3 tablespoons lemon juice
⅓ cup all-purpose flour
2 teaspoons seasoned salt
dash seasoned pepper
¼ cup butter or margarine
½ cup blanched, slivered almonds
2 tablespoons chopped parsley

ABOUT 30 MINUTES BEFORE SERVING:
Cut fillets into serving pieces; sprinkle all sides with lemon juice. On waxed paper, combine flour, salt and pepper; dip fillets into mixture until coated.

In 12-inch skillet over medium heat, in hot butter or margarine, fry fillets, turning once, until brown and fish flakes easily when tested with a fork, about 10 minutes.

Place fillets on platter; keep warm. In same skillet over medium heat, stir almonds until golden; add parsley. Spoon over fish. Makes 6 servings.

FRIED SMELTS

1½ cups dried bread crumbs
2 teaspoons salt
½ teaspoon pepper
4 eggs
2 pounds dressed smelts
½ cup salad oil
1 lemon, cut into 6 wedges
parsley sprigs for garnish
Parsley Sauce (page 246)

ABOUT 45 MINUTES BEFORE SERVING:
On waxed paper, combine bread crumbs, salt and pepper. In pie plate, with fork, beat eggs with ¼ cup water. Dip fish, one at a time, first in egg, then in bread crumbs. Repeat, coating fish twice. Place fish on another sheet of waxed paper.

In 12-inch skillet over medium-high heat, in hot salad oil, fry fish, a few at a time, about 2 minutes on each side or until fish flakes easily when tested with a fork; drain on paper towels. Place fish on warm platter; garnish with lemon wedges and parsley sprigs.

Meanwhile, prepare Parsley Sauce. Serve sauce with fish. Makes 6 servings.

EASY SHORE DINNER

1 8- or 9-ounce package frozen fish sticks
1 8-ounce package frozen fish cakes
1 6- or 8-ounce package frozen breaded shrimp
1 8-ounce container sour cream (1 cup)
1 medium cucumber, peeled and chopped
1 teaspoon dill weed
1 teaspoon sugar
¾ teaspoon salt
dash pepper

ABOUT 30 MINUTES BEFORE SERVING:
Preheat oven to 400°F. On cookie sheet, place all frozen fish sticks, fish cakes and shrimp and bake 15 minutes or until heated through, turning once.

Meanwhile, for sauce, in small bowl, mix remaining ingredients. To serve, arrange seafood on heated platter; pass sauce to accompany seafood. Makes 6 servings.

FISH STICKS WITH ORANGE SAUCE

1 16-ounce package frozen fish sticks
½ cup orange juice
2 teaspoons lemon juice
dash nutmeg
1 tablespoon butter or margarine
1 tablespoon all-purpose flour

ABOUT 20 MINUTES BEFORE SERVING:
Bake fish sticks as label directs. Meanwhile, in cup, combine orange juice, lemon juice and nutmeg; set aside. In 1-quart saucepan over medium heat, into hot butter or margarine, with wire whisk or spoon, stir flour until blended. Add juice mixture all at once; cook, stirring, until mixture is thickened.

Place fish sticks on warm platter; serve with sauce. Makes 4 servings.

PAN-FRIED KIPPERED HERRING

ABOUT 20 MINUTES BEFORE SERVING:
For each serving, use *1 smoked kippered herring*. In shallow baking pan, cover herring with boiling water; let stand 10 minutes. Drain herring; pat dry with paper towels. In skillet over medium heat, in a little hot *salad oil*, fry herring about 5 minutes or until hot, turning once. Serve with *Lemon Butter* (page 351).

Canned Seafood

CREAMED SEAFOOD

¼ cup butter or margarine
¼ cup all-purpose flour
2 cups milk
2 eggs
2 cups canned or cooked fish* or shellfish* in flakes or chunks
2 tablespoons chopped green pepper
salt and pepper
hot cooked rice or noodles; or toast

ABOUT 20 MINUTES BEFORE SERVING:
In 3-quart saucepan over medium heat, into hot butter or margarine, stir flour until blended. Gradually stir in milk and cook, stirring, until mixture is thickened.

* Choose from fish such as tuna, salmon, cod, halibut, haddock, ocean perch; or from shellfish such as shrimp, crab, lobster, scallops.

In small bowl, with wire whisk or hand beater, beat eggs until foamy. Into eggs, stir small amount of hot sauce; stirring rapidly to prevent lumping, slowly pour egg mixture back into sauce. Cook, stirring, until thickened. (Do not boil.) Add fish, green pepper and salt and pepper to taste. Heat, stirring. Serve on rice. Makes 4 servings.

SHERRIED CRAB

6 tablespoons butter or margarine
1 cup fresh bread cubes
⅓ cup diced green pepper
½ cup chopped onion
½ pound mushrooms, thinly sliced
¼ cup all-purpose flour
2 teaspoons salt
1¾ cups milk
2 7¾-ounce cans Alaska King crab, drained and flaked
½ cup diced sweet gherkins
¼ cup medium sherry

ABOUT 40 MINUTES BEFORE SERVING:
In 10-inch skillet over medium heat, in 1 tablespoon hot butter or margarine, fry bread cubes 3 to 5 minutes until golden, tossing frequently. With slotted spoon, place bread cubes on paper towels to drain.

In same skillet over medium heat, in hot remaining butter or margarine, cook green pepper, onion and mushrooms, stirring occasionally, 8 minutes or until green pepper is tender. Stir in flour and salt. Gradually stir in milk and cook, stirring constantly, until thickened. Add crab and gherkins; cook, stirring often, until bubbling, about 15 minutes. Stir in sherry. To serve, sprinkle with bread cubes. Makes 6 servings.

SALMON PUFF

1 16-ounce can salmon
3 tablespoons butter or margarine
3 tablespoons all-purpose flour
1 teaspoon salt
½ teaspoon dry mustard
½ teaspoon Worcestershire
1 cup milk
4 eggs, separated

ABOUT 1 HOUR AND 15 MINUTES AHEAD:
Preheat oven to 375°F. Grease a 1½-quart soufflé dish or casserole. In medium bowl, flake undrained salmon. In 2-quart saucepan over medium heat, into hot butter or margarine, stir flour, salt, mustard and Worcestershire. Gradually stir in milk and cook, stirring, until thickened; cool about 10 minutes.

In cup, with fork, beat egg yolks slightly. Into yolks, stir small amount of hot sauce; stirring rapidly to prevent lumping, slowly pour egg mixture back into sauce. Cook, stirring, until mixture is thickened. Stir salmon into mixture.

In large bowl, with mixer at high speed, beat egg whites until stiff peaks form. With rubber spatula, gently fold salmon mixture into beaten whites. Pour into dish and bake 40 to 45 minutes until puffy and golden. Serve at once. Makes 4 servings.

HOT SALMON MOUSSE

2 16-ounce cans salmon
1 cup heavy or whipping cream or milk
6 eggs
2 tablespoons chopped green onion
1 tablespoon chopped parsley
½ teaspoon salt
¼ teaspoon pepper
Tomato Sauce (below)

ABOUT 1½ HOURS BEFORE SERVING:
1. Preheat oven to 400°F. Grease well a 6-cup ring mold. In large bowl, with wire whisk or spoon, combine salmon, cream, eggs, onion, parsley, salt and pepper.
2. In covered blender container at low speed, blend half of mixture at a time until smooth. (Or, with mixer at medium speed, beat until mixed.) Pour into mold.
3. Set mold in large roasting pan; place on oven rack; fill pan with boiling water to come halfway up side of mold. Bake 1 hour or until knife inserted in center of mousse comes out clean. Remove mold from pan of water; let stand on wire rack 20 minutes.
4. Meanwhile, prepare Tomato Sauce. Carefully loosen edges of mousse with narrow spatula; invert onto platter. Serve with sauce. Makes 8 servings.

TOMATO SAUCE: In small saucepan over medium heat, heat *one 10½-ounce can condensed tomato soup*, undiluted, *2 teaspoons butter or margarine, 1 teaspoon Worcestershire, ¼ teaspoon pepper* just to boiling.

SALMON-NOODLE BAKE

2 tablespoons butter or margarine
2 tablespoons all-purpose flour
1 teaspoon salt
½ teaspoon dry mustard
1 cup milk
1 16-ounce can salmon
½ pound American cheese, cut up (about 2 cups)
½ 8-ounce package medium egg noodles (2 cups), cooked and drained

ABOUT 45 MINUTES BEFORE SERVING:
Preheat oven to 350°F. In 3-quart saucepan over medium heat, into hot butter or margarine, stir flour, salt and mustard until blended. Gradually stir in milk and cook, stirring constantly, until mixture is thickened. Remove from heat. Add undrained salmon, stirring until flaked. Stir in cheese and noodles. Pour into 1½-quart casserole. Bake 30 minutes or until bubbly hot. Makes 4 servings.

SALMON LOAF SUPREME

2 eggs
1 16-ounce can salmon, drained
2 cups fresh bread crumbs (about 4 slices)
½ cup milk
½ teaspoon salt
¼ teaspoon hot pepper sauce
¼ teaspoon poultry seasoning
Creamy Pea-and-Onion Sauce (below)

ABOUT 1 HOUR BEFORE SERVING:
Preheat oven to 375°F. Grease 9″ by 5″ loaf pan. In large bowl, with fork, beat eggs slightly. Add remaining ingredients except sauce and mix well. Spoon mixture into loaf pan; with back of spoon, level the top.

Bake mixture 45 minutes or until knife inserted in center comes out clean. Meanwhile, prepare sauce. Turn out loaf onto warm platter.

To serve, cut loaf into slices and spoon some sauce over each slice; pass remaining sauce. Makes 4 servings.

CREAMY PEA-AND-ONION SAUCE: In 1½-quart saucepan over low heat, prepare *two 1½-ounce packages white-sauce mix* as label directs. Stir in *one 10-ounce package frozen peas,* thawed and *⅓ cup chopped green onions* or minced onion; heat. Makes 2 cups.

SALMON BURGERS

3 eggs
1 16-ounce can salmon, drained
2½ cups fresh bread crumbs (about 5 slices)
⅔ cup chopped celery
⅓ cup chopped green onions
3 tablespoons salad oil
2 envelopes hollandaise-sauce mix
3 English muffins, split and toasted

ABOUT 45 MINUTES BEFORE SERVING:
In large bowl, with fork, beat eggs slightly. Add salmon, crumbs, celery and green onions and mix well. With hands, shape mixture firmly into 6 patties.

In 12-inch skillet over medium heat, in hot salad oil, fry patties, turning once, 10 minutes or until lightly browned. Meanwhile, prepare hollandaise-sauce mix as label directs.

Top each muffin half with a salmon patty; spoon on sauce. Makes 6 servings.

TUNA RING WITH BLUE-CHEESE SAUCE

2 6½- or 7-ounce cans tuna, drained
½ cup minced onion
1 10-ounce package frozen mixed vegetables, thawed
½ cup shredded Cheddar cheese
¼ cup chopped parsley
1 teaspoon celery salt
½ teaspoon salt
¼ teaspoon seasoned pepper
1 egg
4 cups buttermilk baking mix
1¼ cups milk
Blue-Cheese Sauce (below)

ABOUT 1½ HOURS BEFORE SERVING:
Preheat oven to 375°F. Grease a cookie sheet. In large bowl, flake tuna and mix with onion, vegetables, cheese, parsley, celery salt, salt and pepper. In cup, with fork, beat egg and add all but about 2 tablespoons to tuna mixture.

In medium bowl, place baking mix; with fork, stir in milk until mixture forms soft dough; beat 20 strokes. Turn out onto lightly floured surface; knead dough about 6 strokes or until smooth. With lightly floured, stockinette-covered rolling pin, roll dough into rectangle 18″ by 13″. Spread with tuna mixture; from 18-inch side, roll up jelly-roll fashion.

Arrange dough in ring on cookie sheet. With kitchen shears, make 11 cuts almost, but not all the way, through ring; twist slices slightly; brush with reserved beaten egg. Bake 35 to 40 minutes until golden. Meanwhile, prepare sauce. Serve ring with sauce. Makes 6 servings.

BLUE-CHEESE SAUCE: In 1-quart saucepan, place *1 cup sour cream;* crumble in *2 to 4 ounces blue cheese.* Cook over low heat, stirring occasionally, until blended.

TUNA DIVAN

1 10-ounce package frozen broccoli spears
2 6½- or 7-ounce cans tuna, flaked
1 tablespoon lemon juice
1 10¾-ounce can condensed Cheddar-cheese soup
1 tablespoon seasoned dried bread crumbs

ABOUT 40 MINUTES BEFORE SERVING:
Preheat oven to 350°F. Cook broccoli as label directs; drain well. In medium bowl, mix well tuna, lemon juice and undiluted soup. In 8″ by 8″ baking dish or shallow casserole, evenly arrange broccoli. Spoon tuna mixture over broccoli; sprinkle with bread crumbs. Bake 25 minutes or until hot and bubbly. Makes 4 servings.

TUNA SUPPER CASSEROLE

1 10-ounce package frozen chopped spinach, thawed
2 6½- or 7-ounce cans tuna, drained
1 3- or 4-ounce can sliced mushrooms
1 tablespoon lemon juice
3 tablespoons butter or margarine
1 tablespoon all-purpose flour
1 tablespoon minced onion
½ teaspoon salt
dash pepper
1 bay leaf, crumbled
1 egg

ABOUT 45 MINUTES BEFORE SERVING:
Preheat oven to 350°F. Grease a 1½-quart casserole; place spinach in casserole. Coarsely flake tuna and arrange on spinach.

Drain mushrooms, reserving liquid in 1-cup measure. To liquid, add lemon juice and enough water to make 1 cup. In 1-quart saucepan over low heat, into 2 tablespoons hot butter or margarine, stir flour, onion, salt, pepper and bay leaf until blended; stir in mushroom liquid and cook, stirring constantly, until thickened.

In cup, with fork, beat egg. Stir small amount of hot sauce into egg; slowly pour egg mixture back into sauce, stirring rapidly to prevent lumping. Add mushrooms; spoon mixture over tuna. Dot with remaining butter or margarine. Bake 30 minutes or until heated through. Makes 4 servings.

TUNA PARTY PILAF

2 6½- or 7-ounce cans tuna, packed in oil
1 cup sliced celery
⅓ cup minced onion
1 large green pepper, cut in thin strips
3 cups cooked rice
⅓ cup diced canned pimentos
1 3- or 4-ounce can sliced mushrooms
½ cup coarsely chopped salted peanuts
1 teaspoon salt

ABOUT 20 MINUTES BEFORE SERVING:
Into 10-inch skillet, drain oil from tuna; set tuna aside. Heat oil over medium heat; add celery, onion and green pepper; cook about 3 minutes or until vegetables are tender-crisp.

Add tuna, rice, pimentos, mushrooms with their liquid, nuts and salt. Heat through, stirring often. Makes 4 servings.

QUICK CURRIED TUNA

1 10½-ounce can condensed cream-of-mushroom soup
⅓ cup milk
1 teaspoon curry powder
2 6½- or 7-ounce cans tuna, drained
4 buttered toast slices

ABOUT 20 MINUTES BEFORE SERVING:
In 1½-quart saucepan over medium heat, combine undiluted soup, milk and curry powder. Add tuna; with fork, break tuna into large flakes. Heat until mixture is bubbling, stirring often. Serve on toast. Makes 4 servings.

TUNA-CASHEW CASSEROLE

1 3-ounce can chow mein noodles
1 10½-ounce can condensed cream-of-mushroom soup
1 6½- or 7-ounce can tuna, drained and flaked
1 cup dry-roasted cashews
1 cup chopped celery
¼ cup minced onion
lemon wedges for garnish

ABOUT 40 MINUTES BEFORE SERVING:
Preheat oven to 350°F. Set aside ½ cup chow mein noodles. In 1½-quart casserole, stir rest of noodles with undiluted soup, tuna, nuts, celery, onion and ¼ cup water. Sprinkle reserved noodles over top. Bake 30 minutes or until bubbling. Serve with lemon wedges. Makes 4 servings.

SHRIMP AND TUNA GOURMET

3 tablespoons butter or margarine
1 4-ounce can mushrooms, drained
⅓ cup chopped green onions
1 10½-ounce can condensed cream-of-chicken soup
1 teaspoon Worcestershire
¼ teaspoon salt
4 drops hot pepper sauce
1 cup cooked, shelled and deveined shrimp
1 6½- or 7-ounce can chunk-style tuna
½ cup half-and-half or undiluted evaporated milk
½ cup pitted ripe olives
¼ cup diced canned pimentos
chow mein noodles

ABOUT 30 MINUTES BEFORE SERVING:
In 10-inch skillet over medium heat, in hot butter or margarine, cook mushrooms and green onions, stirring occasionally, 5 minutes.

Stir in undiluted soup, Worcestershire, salt and hot pepper sauce; cook, stirring occasionally, until mixture is hot and bubbly.

Reduce heat to low; stir in remaining ingredients except noodles. Cook mixture, stirring constantly, until mixture is hot. Serve over noodles. Makes 4 servings.

BUFFET TUNA-SHRIMP CURRY

5 tablespoons butter or margarine
½ cup sliced green onions
¼ cup minced green pepper
⅓ cup all-purpose flour
1 tablespoon curry powder
¼ teaspoon salt
¼ teaspoon ginger
1 10½-ounce can condensed chicken broth
2 cups milk
2 12½- or 13-ounce cans tuna, drained
2 cups canned or cooked, shelled and deveined shrimp, drained
6 cups hot cooked rice
Curry Accompaniments (page 240)

ABOUT 30 MINUTES BEFORE SERVING:
In electric skillet at 370°F. (or in blazer of chafing dish over direct heat), in hot butter or margarine, cook onions and green pepper until tender, about 5 minutes. Stir in flour, curry powder, salt and ginger until blended.

Gradually stir in undiluted broth and milk and cook, stirring constantly, until mixture is thickened. Add tuna in large chunks and shrimp; mix gently and heat.

Serve with rice and favorite Curry Accompaniments. Makes 8 servings.

SWEET-AND-TANGY TUNA

1 13¼-ounce can pineapple chunks
2 2-ounce envelopes sweet-and-sour sauce mix
1 medium green pepper, thinly sliced
2 6½- or 7-ounce cans tuna
2½ cups hot cooked rice or chow mein noodles

ABOUT 15 MINUTES BEFORE SERVING:
Into 2-cup measure, drain pineapple well; set aside pineapple chunks. To juice, add enough water to make 2 cups liquid.

In 2-quart saucepan over medium heat, cook sweet-and-sour sauce mix and pineapple-juice mixture until thickened, stirring occasionally. Add green pepper and cook 5 minutes. Add tuna and pineapple chunks and continue cooking until heated through. Serve over hot rice. Makes 4 servings.

CREAMED TUNA SUPREME

2 6½- or 7-ounce cans tuna
2 10½-ounce cans condensed cream-of-mushroom soup
¾ cup milk
2 tablespoons chopped canned pimento
6 eggs, separated
⅛ teaspoon salt
dash pepper

ABOUT 40 MINUTES BEFORE SERVING:
Preheat oven to 400°F. Grease 12″ by 8″ baking dish. In medium bowl, flake tuna; stir in undiluted soup, milk and pimento. Pour into baking dish; bake until mixture is bubbling, about 12 minutes.

Meanwhile, in medium bowl, with mixer at high speed, beat egg whites with salt until stiff peaks form. In small bowl, with same beaters, beat egg yolks with pepper until light and fluffy. Gently fold yolks into whites; pour over hot tuna mixture. Bake 15 minutes more or until toothpick inserted in center of egg mixture comes out clean. Serve at once. Makes 6 servings.

TUNA TETRAZZINI

1 8-ounce package spaghettini
2 2½-ounce cans sliced mushrooms
¼ cup all-purpose flour
¼ cup butter or margarine
1¼ cups milk
¼ cup medium sherry
½ pound American cheese, cubed (2 cups)
½ teaspoon seasoned salt
¼ teaspoon nutmeg
2 6½- or 7-ounce cans tuna, drained

ABOUT 1 HOUR BEFORE SERVING:
Cook spaghettini as label directs; drain and set aside. Drain mushrooms, reserving ⅓ cup liquid. Preheat oven to 350°F.

For sauce, in 2-quart saucepan over low heat, stir flour into hot butter or margarine, until blended. Gradually stir in milk, sherry and mushroom liquid and cook, stirring, until thickened. Stir in cheese, seasoned salt and nutmeg until cheese melts. Stir in spaghettini, tuna and mushrooms.

Pour mixture into 2½-quart, shallow baking dish. Bake 20 minutes or until light golden. Makes 8 servings.

BAKED TUNA CROQUETTES

2 6½- or 7-ounce cans tuna
1 cup fresh bread crumbs
wheat germ
½ cup mayonnaise
¼ cup evaporated milk
¼ cup minced onion
2 teaspoons lemon juice
½ teaspoon salt
⅛ to ¼ teaspoon pepper
Tartar Sauce (page 246)

ABOUT 30 MINUTES BEFORE SERVING:
Grease a cookie sheet. Drain liquid from tuna into medium bowl; add crumbs and ½ cup wheat germ; blend well. Stir in mayonnaise, undiluted milk, onion, lemon juice, salt, pepper and tuna and mix well.

Preheat oven to 375°F. Sprinkle some wheat germ on waxed paper. With hands, shape mixture into 8 croquettes; roll lightly in wheat germ. Place on cookie sheet and bake 20 minutes. Serve with sauce. Makes 4 servings.

Shellfish

PAN-FRIED SOFT-SHELL CRABS

8 soft-shell crabs (about 1 pound)
salt and pepper
¼ cup butter or margarine
1 tablespoon chopped parsley
1 teaspoon lemon juice
⅛ teaspoon Worcestershire
toast points (optional)
lemon wedges (optional)

ABOUT 15 MINUTES BEFORE SERVING:
Order crabs cleaned or clean as on page 214. Sprinkle crabs with salt and pepper. In 12-inch skillet over medium heat, in hot butter or margarine, fry about 3 minutes on each side or until golden. Remove from skillet and keep warm.

Into butter left in skillet, stir parsley, lemon juice and Worcestershire; pour over crabs. If you like, serve crabs on toast points with lemon wedges. Entire crab (shell and all) is eaten. Makes 4 servings.

AMANDINE: Prepare as above but just before serving, top crabs with about *¼ cup Toasted Almonds,* page 379.

STEAMED CLAMS

ABOUT 1 HOUR BEFORE SERVING:
With vegetable brush, under running cold water, scrub *6 dozen steamer clams* until free of sand.

In steamer or large saucepot over high heat, heat *1 cup water* (or enough to cover bottom) to boiling. On rack in steamer, place clams. Cover steamer with tight-fitting lid; reduce heat to low and steam clams just until they open, 5 to 10 minutes. Serve clams in soup bowls with 6 individual small dishes of butter from *1 cup melted butter or margarine.* Pour broth from clams into mugs and sprinkle with a little *chopped parsley.*

To eat: With fingers, pull clams from shells by neck; dip first in broth to remove any sand, then into butter. (All except the tough skin of the neck may be eaten.) When sand settles to bottom, the broth may be drunk. Makes 6 servings.

CLAM FRITTERS

1 cup all-purpose flour
1½ teaspoons double-acting baking powder
1 teaspoon sugar
¼ teaspoon salt
2 dozen hard-shell clams, shucked
2 eggs
1 teaspoon grated onion
salad oil
Tartar Sauce (page 246)

ABOUT 45 MINUTES BEFORE SERVING:
In medium bowl, combine flour with baking powder, sugar and salt. Drain clams, reserving ½ cup liquid; coarsely chop clams (should yield about 1¼ cups).

In second medium bowl, combine clams, eggs, onion and reserved clam liquid; with fork, beat just until mixed. Stir clam mixture into flour mixture until well mixed.

In 12-inch skillet over medium heat, in 1 tablespoon hot salad oil, drop some clam mixture by tablespoonfuls; cook several fritters at a time until golden on both sides, turning once. Place on warm platter and keep warm while cooking remaining fritters; add more oil to skillet as needed. Serve with Tartar Sauce. Makes about 2 dozen fritters or 4 servings.

PAN-FRIED CLAMS

4 dozen cherrystone clams
1 egg
2 tablespoons milk
1 teaspoon salt
dash pepper
1 cup dried bread crumbs or cracker crumbs
½ cup salad oil
chili sauce or Tartar Sauce (page 246)

ABOUT 30 MINUTES BEFORE SERVING:
Order clams shucked. Drain clams well. In cup, with fork, beat egg with milk, salt and pepper until mixed. On waxed paper, place crumbs. Dip clams in egg mixture, then in crumbs until coated.

In 12-inch skillet over medium-high heat, in hot salad oil, fry clams, turning once, 5 to 8 minutes until golden on both sides. Drain on paper towels. Serve with sauce. Makes 6 servings.

CRAB CAKES

3 cups cooked crab meat (about 1 pound)
⅓ cup fresh bread crumbs
2 tablespoons mayonnaise
2 teaspoons minced parsley
1 teaspoon Worcestershire
¾ teaspoon salt
½ teaspoon dry mustard
¼ teaspoon pepper
1 egg
about 3 tablespoons butter or margarine
Tartar Sauce (page 246) or lemon wedges

ABOUT 20 MINUTES BEFORE SERVING:
In large bowl, with fork, break crab meat into fine shreds; mix in remaining ingredients except butter or margarine and Tartar Sauce. Divide mixture into 8 portions.

In 12-inch skillet over medium heat, into hot butter or margarine, spoon portions; with pancake turner, lightly flatten portions into patties. Fry patties until golden on undersides; turn and brown other sides. Serve with Tartar Sauce. Makes 4 servings.

CRAB ROLLS: Prepare as above but serve in *hot toasted hamburger buns* or hard rolls as sandwich; garnish with *lettuce leaves* and *dill-pickle slices.* Makes 4 servings.

CRAB IMPERIAL

6 tablespoons butter or margarine
¼ cup chopped green pepper
½ cup all-purpose flour
1½ teaspoons dry mustard
1½ teaspoons salt
1½ teaspoons Worcestershire
⅛ teaspoon paprika
⅛ teaspoon pepper
3 cups milk
¼ cup lemon juice
3 egg yolks
2 pounds flaked, cooked fresh crab meat or 2 1-pound packages frozen Alaska King crab, thawed and well drained

ABOUT 1½ HOURS BEFORE SERVING:
Preheat oven to 350°F. Grease a 2½-quart casserole. In 12-inch skillet over medium heat, in hot butter or margarine, cook green pepper until tender, about 5 minutes. Stir in flour, mustard, salt, Worcestershire, paprika and pepper until blended. Gradually stir in milk and cook, stirring, until mixture is thickened and boils. Remove from heat; gradually stir in lemon juice.

In small bowl, with fork, beat egg yolks slightly. Stir in small amount of hot sauce; slowly pour egg mixture back into sauce, stirring rapidly to prevent lumping.

Cook mixture, stirring, until thickened; stir in crab meat; pour into casserole. Bake 1 hour or until golden. Makes 8 servings.

LOBSTER THERMIDOR WITH PILAF

4 1½-pound lobsters,* cooked (see page 214)
Pilaf (page 301)
6 tablespoons butter or margarine
3 tablespoons all-purpose flour
1 teaspoon salt
⅛ teaspoon nutmeg
dash paprika
1½ cups half-and-half
3 tablespoons medium sherry
½ cup shredded Cheddar cheese
parsley for garnish

EARLY IN DAY OR DAY BEFORE:
Remove meat from each lobster, leaving shell whole: Follow directions on page 214, but do not twist head from tail, and when lifting out bony portion from head shell, leave antennae on head. Put all meat, roe and liver in large bowl. Carefully wash and drain whole shells. Cover bowl and wrap shells; refrigerate both.

ABOUT 1 HOUR BEFORE SERVING:
Prepare Pilaf but substitute 2 cups chicken broth for consommé and water. Meanwhile, in 3-quart saucepan over medium heat, into hot butter or margarine, stir flour, salt, nutmeg and paprika until blended. Gradually stir in half-and-half and sherry and cook, stirring constantly, until mixture is thickened. Add lobster meat; cook just until heated through, stirring occasionally.

Arrange lobster shells on rack in broiling pan; fill with lobster mixture and sprinkle with cheese. When Pilaf is done, remove from oven. Turn oven control to broil; broil until lobster mixture is hot and cheese is melted.

To serve, spoon Pilaf on warm, large platter; arrange lobsters on Pilaf; garnish with parsley. Makes 4 servings.

* Or, use four 8-ounce rock-lobster tails.

LOBSTER IN PATTY SHELLS

1 10-ounce package frozen patty shells
⅓ cup butter or margarine
½ cup chopped celery
¼ cup chopped onion
¼ cup all-purpose flour
1 teaspoon salt
2 cups milk
2 tablespoons medium sherry (optional)
1 tablespoon lemon juice
1 4-ounce package shredded Cheddar cheese (1 cup)
3 cups cubed, cooked lobster meat (2 pounds rock-lobster tails)

ABOUT 30 MINUTES BEFORE SERVING:
Bake patty shells as label directs. Meanwhile, in 12-inch skillet over medium heat, in hot butter or margarine, cook celery and onion until tender, about 5 minutes. Reduce heat to low; stir in flour and salt until blended. Gradually stir in milk, sherry and lemon juice, and cook, stirring constantly, until mixture is thickened. Stir in cheese and lobster meat and heat over low heat, stirring occasionally, until mixture is hot and cheese is melted. To serve, spoon mixture into patty shells. Makes 6 servings.

BOILED LIVE LOBSTER

Allow *one 1- to 1½-pound lobster* per serving. Cook lobster in boiling water as in general directions, page 214.

When lobster is done, drain well; with kitchen shears, cut away thin underside shell from body. Serve whole lobster hot with lobster cracker and pick. Garnish with *lemon wedges* and *parsley* and accompany with *melted butter or margarine* in small dishes.

To eat, first break off legs and, starting from a joint, pull meat out between your teeth. Remove all lobster meat as directed on page 214.

COLD BOILED LOBSTER: When lobster is done, cool in cold water; wrap in plastic wrap and refrigerate. Serve as above or cut in half lengthwise with kitchen shears; remove dark vein. Accompany with mayonnaise, horseradish or tartar sauce.

BROILED LIVE LOBSTER

1. Allow *1 small (1 pound) or ½ large (1¾ to 2¼ pounds) lobster* per person. Order lobster split lengthwise and cleaned. Or split and clean as follows:
2. Lay lobster on its back on cutting board. Where tail and body meet, insert point of large sharp knife through to back shell (this cuts spinal cord and kills lobster). With lobster cracker, heavy mallet or hammer, crack large part of each large claw.
3. Then with sharp knife, split lobster from end of tail to head, cutting to, but not through, back shell. Spread lobster open as wide as possible. Remove dark vein down center of back of tail; leave in light-colored, greenish liver (tomalley) and dark roe (coral). Roe turns red when cooked.
4. To broil: Preheat broiler if manufacturer directs. Place lobster, cut side up, on rack in broiling pan. Brush lobster meat with *melted butter or margarine;* sprinkle with *salt, pepper, chopped parsley* and *bit of garlic powder* (optional).
5. Broil 8 to 15 minutes, depending on size of lobster, brushing occasionally with melted butter or margarine. If broiling several lobsters, arrange around sides of broiling pan, with body sections in center.
6. Serve lobster hot, cut side up, garnished with *lemon wedges* and *parsley*. Serve *melted butter or margarine* in small dishes.

BROILED ROCK-LOBSTER TAILS

Thaw *rock-lobster tails,* wrapped, in refrigerator several hours or overnight.

Preheat broiler if manufacturer directs; grease rack in broiling pan. With kitchen shears, cut away thin underside shell of each thawed rock-lobster tail. Insert skewer lengthwise through meat so tail will lie flat during broiling. Place tails, shell side up, on broiling-pan rack. Broil according to timetable below, turning once as indicated. Tails are done when meat is opaque. Serve in shell, meat side up; accompany with *melted butter or margarine* or favorite sauce in small dishes.

Weight of Tail (ounces)	*Broiling Time Shell Side*	*(minutes) Meat Side*
2	3	2
3	4	3
4	5	3
5	5	4
6	5	6
7	5	7
8	5	8

LOBSTER TAILS, ITALIAN STYLE

6 8-ounce frozen rock-lobster tails
3 tablespoons olive oil
2 tablespoons minced onion
½ garlic clove, minced
1 16-ounce can tomatoes
1 teaspoon salt
1 teaspoon lemon juice
¼ teaspoon oregano leaves
⅛ teaspoon pepper
parsley for garnish
lemon wedges for garnish

ABOUT 1 HOUR BEFORE SERVING:
Cook rock-lobster tails as label directs or as above. With kitchen shears, cut away thin underside shell of each and remove meat from shell. Cut meat into bite-size pieces; reserve empty shells.

In 10-inch skillet over medium heat, in hot oil, cook onion and garlic until onion is tender. Drain tomatoes, reserving liquid;

cut tomatoes into medium pieces. Add tomatoes, ½ cup reserved tomato liquid (use leftover tomato liquid another day), salt, lemon juice, oregano and pepper; simmer 5 minutes to blend flavors. Add cut-up rock lobster; heat just until mixture is hot and bubbling. (Shellfish toughens when overcooked.)

Fill reserved shells with mixture; garnish with parsley and lemon wedges. Makes 6 servings.

CRAB ITALIENNE: For rock-lobster tails, substitute *two 12-ounce packages frozen snow or Alaska King crab,* thawed and drained; prepare as above. Serve in individual casseroles. Makes 6 servings.

MUSSELS MARINIERE

3 pounds mussels (about 5 to 6 dozen)
butter or margarine
3 shallots, minced
1 garlic clove, minced
½ cup dry white wine
¼ teaspoon salt
dash pepper
1 tablespoon chopped parsley

ABOUT 1 HOUR AND 15 MINUTES AHEAD:

1. Scrub mussels well and rinse several times in cold water to remove all sand. Discard any that remain open when tapped with fingers. With kitchen shears, remove beards.
2. In large saucepot or Dutch oven over medium-high heat, in 2 tablespoons hot butter or margarine, cook shallots and garlic 1 minute, stirring. Add wine and mussels; sprinkle mussels with salt and pepper. Cover and simmer 6 to 8 minutes until shells open, stirring occasionally.
3. With slotted spoon, remove mussels to bowl. (Discard any that haven't opened.) Without disturbing sediment in bottom of saucepot, pour stock into 1½-quart saucepan; heat.

Meanwhile, discard halves of mussel shells to which meat is not attached. Arrange mussels in shells, open side up, in soup plates. Into hot stock, stir 1 tablespoon butter or margarine; pour over mussels; sprinkle servings with parsley. Makes 4 servings.

DEEP-FRIED OYSTERS

salad oil
1 quart shucked "select" oysters
2 eggs
1 teaspoon salt
1½ to 1¾ cups cracker crumbs
or dried bread crumbs
Tartar Sauce (page 246) or catchup

ABOUT 30 MINUTES BEFORE SERVING:

In deep-fat fryer* heat about 2 inches salad oil to 375°F.

Meanwhile, drain oysters and pat dry with paper towels. In small bowl, with fork, beat eggs with salt and 2 tablespoons water until well mixed. On waxed paper, place crumbs. Dip each oyster into egg mixture, then coat well with crumbs.

Place oysters, a few at a time, about 1 inch apart in a layer in fry basket; fry about 1 minute or until golden. Drain on paper towels; keep warm. Repeat with rest of oysters. Serve with sauce. Makes 6 servings.

* Or, in Dutch oven or deep saucepan, heat 2 inches salad oil to 375°F. on deep-fat thermometer. If fry basket is not used, remove oysters from hot fat with tongs or slotted spoon.

FRIED CLAMS: Substitute *3 dozen drained, shucked steamer clams* (about 2 cups) for oysters; use only 1 egg. Prepare and deep-fry as above; drain. Serve with Tartar Sauce. Makes 4 servings.

PAN-FRIED OYSTERS

1 pint shucked "select" oysters
3 tablespoons butter or margarine
3 tablespoons salad oil or shortening
⅔ cup finely crushed saltines
3 lemon wedges

ABOUT 20 MINUTES BEFORE SERVING:

Drain oysters; pat dry with paper towels. In 10-inch skillet over medium-high heat, heat butter or margarine and salad oil. On waxed paper, sprinkle half of crushed saltines. Place oysters on crumbs and sprinkle with remaining saltines.

In hot butter mixture, fry half of oysters at a time, turning once, about 5 minutes or until golden brown.

Serve with lemon wedges. Makes 3 main-dish servings.

SCALLOPED OYSTERS

⅓ cup butter or margarine
1½ cups finely crushed saltines
1 pint shucked "standard" oysters
¼ cup half-and-half
¾ teaspoon salt
⅛ teaspoon pepper
½ teaspoon Worcestershire
2 tablespoons chopped parsley

ABOUT 40 MINUTES BEFORE SERVING:
Preheat oven to 400°F. In 1-quart saucepan over low heat, into hot butter or margarine, stir saltines until well mixed. In 10″ by 6″ baking dish, arrange half of saltine mixture; top with undrained oysters.

In small bowl, mix half-and-half, salt, pepper and Worcestershire and pour over oysters. Sprinkle top with parsley, then with remaining saltine mixture. Bake 20 to 25 minutes until lightly browned and bubbly. Makes 4 servings.

SCALLOPED OYSTERS AND CORN: Prepare as above but sprinkle *½ cup grated American cheese food* over first layer of crumbs; top with oysters, then with *one 12-ounce can whole-kernel corn,* drained.

HANGTOWN FRY

½ pint shucked "select" oysters
6 eggs
¼ cup all-purpose flour
⅔ cup dried bread crumbs
3 bacon slices
1 tablespoon butter or margarine
½ teaspoon salt
dash pepper

ABOUT 35 MINUTES BEFORE SERVING:
Drain oysters; pat dry with paper towels. In small bowl, with fork, beat 1 egg. In another small bowl, place flour. On sheet of waxed paper, sprinkle half of bread crumbs. Roll each oyster in flour to coat well. Then dip each oyster into egg and place in single layer on bread crumbs. Sprinkle oysters with remaining bread crumbs; toss to coat well; set aside.

In 10-inch skillet over medium heat, fry bacon until crisp; remove bacon; drain on paper towels. In drippings in skillet, melt butter or margarine; add oysters in a single layer, and cook, turning once, about 5 minutes or until oysters are golden.

Meanwhile, into medium bowl, crumble bacon; add remaining 5 eggs, 2 tablespoons water, salt and pepper; beat with fork. When oysters are golden, reduce heat to low. Pour egg mixture over oysters; cook until mixture is set around edges. With metal spatula, gently lift edges as they set, tilting skillet to allow uncooked egg mixture to run underneath. Cook until mixture is set but still moist on surface. To serve, cut in wedges. Makes 4 servings.

COQUILLES ST. JACQUES

1 pound fresh or thawed frozen bay scallops
2 tablespoons dry white wine
½ teaspoon salt
dash cayenne pepper
2 tablespoons butter or margarine
½ pound mushrooms, sliced
1 small onion, minced
½ garlic clove, minced
1 tablespoon chopped parsley
¼ cup all-purpose flour
¾ cup Buttered Crumbs (page 351)
2 tablespoons grated Parmesan cheese

ABOUT 50 MINUTES BEFORE SERVING:
1. In 10-inch skillet over high heat, heat to boiling scallops, ¾ cup water, wine, salt and cayenne. Reduce heat to medium; simmer scallops 2 minutes or until tender.
2. Drain scallops, reserving liquid; set aside. Meanwhile, preheat oven to 400°F. Grease 8 baking shells or ramekins.
3. In same skillet over medium heat, in hot butter or margarine, cook mushrooms and onion 5 minutes or until tender. Stir in garlic, parsley and flour until blended. Gradually stir in reserved liquid and cook, stirring constantly, until mixture is thickened. Stir in scallops.
4. Spoon mixture into baking shells; sprinkle with Buttered Crumbs and cheese. Arrange shells on cookie sheet; bake 10 minutes or until crumbs are golden. Makes 8 first-course servings.

DEEP-FRIED SCALLOPS

1 pound fresh or thawed frozen sea scallops
1 egg
½ teaspoon salt
dash pepper
⅔ cup dried bread crumbs
salad oil
lemon wedges
Tartar Sauce (page 246), catchup or chili sauce

ABOUT 35 MINUTES BEFORE SERVING:
Cut large scallops in half. In cup, with fork, beat egg with 1 tablespoon water, salt and pepper until mixed. On waxed paper, place bread crumbs. Dip scallops in egg mixture, then in crumbs until coated.

Meanwhile, in electric skillet,* heat 1 inch salad oil to 350°F. Fry scallops, a few at a time, 1 to 2 minutes until golden. With slotted spoon, remove scallops to paper towels to drain; keep warm while frying rest of scallops. Serve with lemon wedges and Tartar Sauce. Makes 3 servings.

* Or, in 4-quart saucepan or Dutch oven over medium heat, heat oil to 350°F. on deep-fat thermometer.

OVEN-FRIED: Preheat oven to 400°F. Prepare scallops as above but, after coating, dip into about *6 tablespoons salad oil.* Place scallops in shallow baking dish; bake 20 minutes or until golden. Serve with lemon wedges and Tartar Sauce. Makes 3 servings.

SCALLOPS EN BROCHETTE

12 small mushrooms
½ large green pepper
2 tablespoons melted butter or margarine
2 tablespoons lemon juice
1 tablespoon salad oil
¼ teaspoon salt
dash pepper
1 pound fresh or thawed frozen sea scallops (about 12)
4 bacon slices
4 American-cheese slices
lemon wedges

ABOUT 1 HOUR AND 15 MINUTES AHEAD:
1. Remove stems from mushrooms. (Refrigerate stems for use another day.) Cut green pepper into eight 1-inch squares. In pie plate, combine butter or margarine, lemon juice, oil, salt and pepper. Add scallops, mushrooms and green-pepper pieces, tossing to coat with mixture; cover and refrigerate 30 minutes, tossing occasionally.
2. Preheat broiler if manufacturer directs. In 10-inch skillet over medium heat, fry bacon until light golden but still limp; drain on paper towels.
3. Run a skewer through one end of a bacon slice and then lace bacon between a fourth of the scallops, mushroom caps and green pepper pieces. Repeat with 3 more skewers. Place skewers on rack in broiling pan and broil 10 minutes, turning frequently.
4. Cut each cheese slice into 4 strips. When skewered food is done, place 4 cheese strips on top of each skewer, overlapping if necessary. Broil just until cheese melts. Serve with lemon wedges. Makes 4 servings.

PAN-FRIED SCALLOPS

1 pound fresh or thawed frozen sea scallops
⅓ cup dried bread crumbs
⅛ teaspoon salt
dash pepper
dash paprika
butter or margarine
toast points (optional)
2 tablespoons lemon or lime juice
1 tablespoon chopped parsley

ABOUT 15 MINUTES BEFORE SERVING:
Cut large scallops in half. On waxed paper, combine bread crumbs with salt, pepper and paprika; roll scallops in mixture until coated.

In 10-inch skillet over medium-high heat, in 3 tablespoons hot butter or margarine, fry scallops, turning occasionally, about 6 to 10 minutes until golden on all sides. Place toast points on warm platter. With slotted spoon, arrange scallops on toast; keep warm.

Into drippings remaining in skillet, stir 1 tablespoon butter or margarine, lemon juice and parsley; heat to melt. Pour butter mixture over scallops. Makes 3 servings.

BROILED SCALLOPS

1 pound fresh or thawed frozen sea scallops
¼ cup butter or margarine
¼ teaspoon salt
dash pepper
dash paprika
1 tablespoon chopped parsley
lemon or lime wedges

ABOUT 20 MINUTES BEFORE SERVING:
Preheat broiler if manufacturer directs. Cut large scallops in half.

In small saucepan over low heat, melt butter or margarine with salt, pepper and paprika; dip scallops into mixture until coated. Place scallops on broiling-pan rack; broil 3 minutes. Turn scallops; brush with butter mixture and broil 2 to 4 minutes longer until golden.

To serve, pour remaining butter mixture over scallops; sprinkle scallops with parsley; serve with lemon. Makes 3 servings.

FRIED SHRIMP

1 pound shelled, deveined large shrimp
1 egg
2 tablespoons all-purpose flour
½ teaspoon salt
dash pepper
½ cup salad oil
⅔ cup minced onions
¾ cup chicken broth
1 tablespoon cornstarch
1 teaspoon soy sauce
hot cooked rice

ABOUT 30 MINUTES BEFORE SERVING:
Blot shrimp well with paper towels to dry. In medium bowl, with fork, beat egg; add flour, salt and pepper; mix well. Add shrimp; stir to coat well.

In electric skillet at 370°F. (or in 10-inch skillet over medium heat), heat salad oil. With fork, lift shrimp, one by one, from batter; drop into oil and fry until golden, 2 to 3 minutes on each side. On paper towels, drain shrimp; remove to warm platter.

For sauce: In 2 tablespoons oil left in skillet, cook onions until tender, about 5 minutes. In cup, stir broth into cornstarch until smooth; add soy sauce and stir into onions; cook, stirring, until thickened. Pour over shrimp. Serve with rice. Makes 6 first-course or 3 main-dish servings.

SWEET PUNGENT: To sauce, add *2 tablespoons each vinegar and sugar, one 8½-ounce can pineapple tidbits,* drained, and *1 medium green pepper,* sliced.

BUTTERFLY SHRIMP: Shell shrimp, leaving tail segment on each. With point of knife, split each shrimp along inner curve, stopping at tail segment and cutting just deep enough to expose black vein. Spread each shrimp wide open, then rinse under running cold water to remove vein. Blot dry with paper towels.

Coat with batter and fry as above but omit sauce. Serve with bowl of soy sauce or chutney for dunking.

SHRIMP CURRY INDIENNE

5 tablespoons butter or margarine
½ cup minced onion
2½ teaspoons curry powder
⅓ cup all-purpose flour
1½ teaspoons sugar
1¼ teaspoons salt
¼ teaspoon ginger
2 cups milk
1 cup canned chicken broth
1½ pounds cooked, shelled and deveined shrimp
1 teaspoon lemon juice
3 or 4 cups hot cooked rice
Curry Accompaniments (below)

ABOUT 45 MINUTES BEFORE SERVING:
In 3-quart saucepan over medium heat, in hot butter or margarine, cook onion with curry powder until onion is tender, about 5 minutes. Stir in flour, sugar, salt and ginger until blended. Gradually stir in milk and chicken broth and cook, stirring constantly, until mixture is thickened. Add shrimp and lemon juice; heat.

Around edges of warm platter, spoon hot rice; spoon shrimp into center. Serve with Curry Accompaniments. Makes 6 servings.

CURRY ACCOMPANIMENTS: In separate small bowls, place two or more of these accompaniments, to be sprinkled over servings: chutney, raisins, tomato wedges, salted almonds or peanuts, chopped parsley, pineapple chunks, fried onion rings, crisp bacon bits, currant jelly, chopped hard-cooked eggs, sweet or sour pickles, flaked coconut, sliced avocado, shredded orange peel.

LOBSTER, CRAB OR SCALLOP CURRY: Instead of shrimp, use *4 cups flaked, cooked or canned lobster meat,* diced, cooked rock-lobster tail, Alaska King crab, snow crab or cooked scallops.

QUICK SHRIMP CREOLE

1 tablespoon salad oil
½ cup chopped green pepper
1 1½-ounce package spaghetti-sauce seasoning mix
1 16-ounce can tomatoes
1 pound shelled, deveined shrimp
hot cooked rice (optional)

ABOUT 20 MINUTES BEFORE SERVING:
In 2-quart saucepan over medium heat, in hot salad oil, cook green pepper until tender, about 5 minutes. Stir in spaghetti-sauce seasoning mix, tomatoes with their liquid and ½ cup water; cover and simmer 10 minutes. Add shrimp; cook until shrimp turn pink, about 3 minutes. If you like, serve over rice. Makes 4 servings.

SEAFOOD SUPREME

1 pound fresh or thawed frozen sea scallops
salt
1 pound shrimp, shelled and deveined
1 10½-ounce can condensed cream-of-shrimp soup
¼ cup milk
1 teaspoon paprika
1 teaspoon Worcestershire
4 drops hot pepper sauce
toast points for garnish
chopped parsley for garnish

ABOUT 30 MINUTES BEFORE SERVING:
Cut large scallops in half. In 3-quart saucepan over high heat, in 1 cup boiling water and ½ teaspoon salt, heat scallops and shrimp to boiling. Reduce heat to low; cover and simmer 3 to 5 minutes, until scallops are opaque and shrimp turn pink; drain and keep warm.

In same saucepan, stir undiluted soup, milk, paprika, Worcestershire, ¼ teaspoon salt and hot pepper sauce. Over low heat, heat, stirring frequently, until mixture is bubbly hot; add reserved seafood and heat.

Spoon mixture into warm serving dish or individual casseroles. Garnish with toast points and parsley. Makes 6 servings.

SHRIMP DE JONGHE

½ cup butter or margarine
2 tablespoons bottled garlic-spread concentrate
2 cups fresh bread crumbs
⅓ cup chopped parsley
¼ cup medium sherry
2 pounds shrimp, shelled, deveined and cooked

ABOUT 1 HOUR BEFORE SERVING:
Preheat oven to 450°F. In 2-quart saucepan over high heat, melt butter or margarine with garlic spread; stir in crumbs, parsley and sherry and mix well.

Arrange shrimp in 12″ by 8″ baking dish; top with crumb mixture. Bake 10 minutes or until hot. Makes 4 servings.

SHRIMP MARINARA

1 tablespoon olive oil
1 garlic clove, minced
1 15-ounce can tomato sauce
1 6-ounce can tomato paste
2 tablespoons chopped parsley
1 tablespoon sugar
¾ teaspoon salt
½ teaspoon oregano leaves
¼ teaspoon pepper
1 pound frozen shelled and deveined shrimp
1 16-ounce package spaghetti
¼ cup grated Parmesan cheese

ABOUT 20 MINUTES BEFORE SERVING:
In 10-inch skillet over medium-high heat, in hot olive oil, lightly brown garlic. Add next 7 ingredients; cover and simmer over low heat 10 minutes. Add frozen shrimp and cook until shrimp are tender, about 8 minutes, stirring occasionally.

Meanwhile, cook spaghetti as label directs; drain. Serve shrimp sauce over spaghetti. Sprinkle with cheese. Makes 4 servings.

SHRIMP WITH WATER CHESTNUTS

1 pound shelled and deveined shrimp
1 garlic clove, minced
1 large onion, chopped
1 8-ounce can water chestnuts, drained and thinly sliced
½ pound mushrooms, sliced
⅓ cup salad oil
2 tablespoons cornstarch
2 tablespoons medium sherry (optional)
1⅓ cups canned chicken broth
1 tablespoon soy sauce
1 teaspoon salt
½ teaspoon sugar
4 cups hot cooked rice

ABOUT 45 MINUTES BEFORE SERVING:
In medium bowl, combine shrimp, garlic, onion, water chestnuts and mushrooms. In 10-inch skillet over high heat, in hot salad oil, cook shrimp mixture, stirring constantly, until shrimp are pink, about 3 minutes.

In small bowl, combine cornstarch and sherry or 2 tablespoons water; stir until dissolved. Stir in chicken broth, soy sauce, salt and sugar. Pour mixture over shrimp and cook over medium heat, stirring constantly, until slightly thickened. Serve over rice. Makes 4 servings.

SHRIMP THERMIDOR EN CASSEROLE

1 cup regular long-grain rice
6 tablespoons butter or margarine
1 pound shelled and deveined shrimp
1 cup thinly sliced celery
¼ cup all-purpose flour
1 cup half-and-half
1 teaspoon seasoned salt
dash seasoned pepper
½ cup shredded Cheddar cheese

ABOUT 30 MINUTES BEFORE SERVING:
Preheat oven to 450°F. Prepare rice as label directs; place in 2½-quart casserole and keep warm.

Meanwhile, in 10-inch skillet over medium-high heat, in hot butter or margarine, cook shrimp and celery, stirring, 3 minutes or until shrimp are pink.

With slotted spoon, remove about 6 shrimp; set aside for garnish. Reduce heat to medium; stir flour into remaining shrimp mixture until well blended. Gradually stir in half-and-half, seasoned salt and seasoned pepper and cook, stirring constantly, until mixture is thickened.

Spoon shrimp mixture over rice in casserole; sprinkle with cheese and garnish with reserved shrimp. Bake 5 minutes or until cheese is melted and hot. Makes 4 or 5 servings.

SHRIMP CASSEROLE HARPIN

2½ pounds large shrimp, shelled, deveined and cooked
¼ cup butter or margarine
¼ cup minced green pepper
¼ cup minced onion
¾ cup slivered blanched almonds
1 10¾-ounce can condensed tomato soup
2 cups cooked regular long-grain rice
1 cup heavy or whipping cream
½ cup dry or medium sherry
1 tablespoon lemon juice
1 teaspoon salt

ABOUT 1 HOUR BEFORE SERVING:
Reserve 6 shrimp for garnish. Preheat oven to 350°F. In 10-inch skillet over medium heat, in hot butter or margarine, cook green pepper and onion about 3 minutes or until tender.

Reserve ¼ cup almonds. In 2-quart casserole, combine onion mixture with remaining shrimp and almonds, undiluted soup and remaining ingredients; mix well. Bake 30 minutes; during last 10 minutes of baking, garnish with reserved shrimp and almonds. Makes 6 servings.

BROILED SHRIMP

1 pound large or jumbo shrimp, shelled and deveined
2 tablespoons butter or margarine
1 tablespoon lemon juice
½ teaspoon seasoned salt
toast points (optional)

ABOUT 20 MINUTES BEFORE SERVING:
Preheat broiler if manufacturer directs. Arrange shrimp on broiling-pan rack. In small saucepan over low heat, melt butter or margarine with lemon juice and salt;

pour mixture over shrimp. Broil shrimp about 5 minutes or until they are pink; do not turn. Serve as is or on toast points. Makes 3 main-dish servings.

BACON-WRAPPED: Preheat broiler if manufacturer directs. Sprinkle *1 pound large shrimp,* shelled and deveined, with *salt, pepper* and *lemon juice.* Cut each of about *10 bacon slices* in half; wrap each shrimp in one half bacon slice, securing with toothpick. Place shrimp on broiling-pan rack; broil 5 minutes. Turn and broil about 3 minutes more or until shrimp are pink and bacon is done. Makes 3 main-dish servings.

DO-AHEAD SHRIMP KABOBS

1½ pounds large shrimp in shell (24 to 28)
about ¾ pound bacon slices, halved
1 14-ounce bottle catchup
1 tablespoon horseradish
1 teaspoon Worcestershire
dash pepper
2 lemons, cut in wedges

EARLY IN DAY OR DAY BEFORE:
Peel and devein shrimp. Wrap each with bacon piece; arrange 2 or 3 bacon-wrapped shrimp on each of 10 long skewers. Wrap and refrigerate. Prepare sauce: In 1-pint container with tight-fitting lid, combine catchup, horseradish, Worcestershire and pepper. Cover and refrigerate.

ABOUT 20 MINUTES BEFORE SERVING:
Preheat broiler if manufacturer directs. Broil skewered shrimp for about 10 minutes or until bacon is crisp and shrimp are pink, turning once. Serve with sauce and lemon wedges. Makes 10 first-course or 4 main-dish servings.

GARLIC-BROILED SHRIMP

1 pound large shrimp
¼ cup butter or margarine
½ teaspoon salt
1 tablespoon chopped parsley
½ to 1 teaspoon minced garlic

ABOUT 25 MINUTES BEFORE SERVING:
Shrimp may be broiled shelled or in shells. If to be broiled in shells, with fingers, pull off legs; with kitchen shears, cut shells along outside curve and remove vein that runs along the curve; close shells.

In bottom of broiling pan, melt butter or margarine; stir in remaining ingredients. Place shrimp in pan, turning in mixture to coat all sides. Broil 3 minutes; with tongs, turn shrimp and broil 3 minutes longer or until shrimp turn pink. Sprinkle with more parsley, if you like, and serve with pan juices. Makes 2 or 3 servings.

BROILED MARINATED SHRIMP

¼ cup butter or margarine, melted
1 tablespoon salad oil
2 teaspoons salt
¼ teaspoon pepper
1 large garlic clove, crushed
1½ pounds shelled and deveined medium shrimp
lemon wedges

SEVERAL HOURS BEFORE SERVING:
In large bowl, mix butter or margarine with salad oil, salt, pepper and garlic. Add shrimp; toss gently to coat shrimp. Cover and refrigerate, tossing occasionally.

ABOUT 15 MINUTES BEFORE SERVING:
Preheat broiler if manufacturer directs. Place shrimp on broiling-pan rack and broil 5 to 7 minutes or until shrimp turn pink. Serve with lemon. Makes 6 servings.

DILL-SAUCED SHRIMP ON RICE

uncooked rice for 8 servings
chicken broth
⅓ cup butter or margarine
⅓ cup all-purpose flour
2¼ teaspoons salt
1¼ teaspoons dill weed
4 cups milk
2½ pounds shelled and deveined shrimp, cooked

ABOUT 45 MINUTES BEFORE SERVING:
Prepare favorite rice for 8 servings as label directs but use chicken broth instead of water. Meanwhile, in 3- or 4-quart saucepan over medium heat, into hot butter or margarine, stir flour, salt and dill until blended. Gradually stir in milk and cook, stirring, until thickened; add shrimp. Serve on hot rice. Makes 8 servings.

SHRIMP-AND-MUSHROOM DELIGHT

1 cup regular long-grain rice
1 pound shelled and deveined shrimp, cooked
1 6-ounce can sliced mushrooms, drained
1 4½-ounce jar strained apricots
¼ cup sour cream
1½ tablespoons butter or margarine, melted
¾ teaspoon salt
dash pepper
lemon wedges for garnish
parsley for garnish

ABOUT 1 HOUR BEFORE SERVING:
Cook rice as label directs; preheat oven to 350°F. In well-greased 1½-quart casserole, combine all ingredients except garnishes; toss gently until mixed. Cover and bake 40 minutes. Garnish with lemon wedges and parsley. Makes 4 servings.

JAMBALAYA

2 6-ounce packages Spanish-rice mix
3 tablespoons butter or margarine
2 cups chopped celery
2 cups coarsely chopped green peppers
2 cups cut-up cooked ham
½ cup chopped green onions
1½ pounds shelled and deveined shrimp
2 teaspoons seasoned salt
¼ teaspoon seasoned pepper
1 16-ounce can tomatoes, drained

ABOUT 30 MINUTES BEFORE SERVING:
In Dutch oven, cook Spanish-rice mix as label directs.

Meanwhile, in 12-inch skillet over medium heat, in hot butter or margarine, cook celery and green peppers until tender, about 8 minutes. Add ham and green onions and cook a few minutes longer. Stir in shrimp, seasoned salt and seasoned pepper and cook, tossing often, until shrimp are pink, about 10 minutes. Add tomatoes and heat.

With slotted spoon, add shrimp mixture to rice; toss lightly to mix. Makes 8 servings.

SEAFOOD NEWBURG

6 tablespoons butter or margarine
3 tablespoons all-purpose flour
1 teaspoon salt
⅛ teaspoon nutmeg
3 egg yolks
2 cups half-and-half
1 cup milk
1 12-ounce package frozen cooked lobster meat, thawed (about 2 cups)
1 pound cooked, shelled and deveined shrimp
3 tablespoons medium sherry (optional)
heated patty shells or toast points

ABOUT 20 MINUTES BEFORE SERVING:
In 12-inch skillet over medium-high heat, into hot butter or margarine, stir flour, salt and nutmeg until blended. In medium bowl, with fork, beat egg yolks slightly and stir in half-and-half and milk; stir into flour mixture and cook, stirring constantly, until mixture is thickened. Add next three ingredients; cook until heated. Serve in patty shells. Makes 6 servings.

SHRIMP WITH ORIENTAL VEGETABLES

3 tablespoons salad oil
1 pound frozen, shelled and deveined shrimp
2 10-ounce packages frozen Japanese-style vegetables in sauce
1 tablespoon cornstarch
1 1¼-ounce envelope teriyaki-sauce mix
½ medium head iceberg lettuce, shredded (about 2 cups)
3 cups hot cooked rice

ABOUT 20 MINUTES BEFORE SERVING:
In covered, 12-inch skillet over medium heat, in hot salad oil, cook frozen shrimp and frozen vegetables, separating shrimp and vegetables with a fork and stirring occasionally to dissolve spice cubes. (Do not add water as label directs.)

Meanwhile, in small bowl, dissolve cornstarch and teriyaki-sauce mix in ½ cup water; stir into shrimp mixture and cook, uncovered, until mixture thickens, about 3 minutes, stirring. Add lettuce and cook 1 minute. Serve with rice. Makes 4 servings.

SHRIMP SAUTE

1 tablespoon butter or margarine
1 pound shrimp, shelled and deveined
2 green onions, sliced
¼ teaspoon salt
dash pepper
1 tablespoon medium sherry or 2 teaspoons lemon juice
1 tablespoon chopped parsley

ABOUT 15 MINUTES BEFORE SERVING:
In 10-inch skillet over high heat, in hot butter or margarine, cook shrimp with onions, salt and pepper, stirring constantly, until shrimp are pink, about 3 to 5 minutes. Stir in sherry and parsley. Makes 3 servings.

Frogs' Legs

While frogs are not members of the fish family, frogs' legs are prepared and eaten much like fish.

FRIED FROGS' LEGS

2 pounds medium frogs' legs
¼ cup milk
½ cup all-purpose flour
1 teaspoon salt
dash pepper
butter or margarine

ABOUT 20 MINUTES BEFORE SERVING:
Cut frogs' legs apart. Pour milk into pie plate or other shallow dish; combine flour, salt and pepper on sheet of waxed paper. Dip frogs' legs in milk, then in flour to coat well. In 12-inch skillet over medium heat, in ¼ cup hot butter or margarine, cook frogs' legs, several at a time, turning once, until fork-tender and lightly browned, about 5 to 8 minutes. Remove to warm platter; keep warm while cooking remaining frogs' legs; add more butter or margarine as needed. Makes 6 servings.

FROGS' LEGS SAUTÉ: Prepare as above but omit milk and flour; sprinkle frogs' legs with salt and pepper; cook as directed. Remove to platter; keep warm. Pour *2 tablespoons claret* or Chablis into drippings in skillet; heat, stirring to loosen browned bits; pour over frogs' legs.

Seafood Sauces

These sauces, quickly made, are equally delicious on cold or hot fish and shellfish. Try them as sauce or dip for cold, cooked, shelled, deveined shrimp, scallops, lobster or rock-lobster-tail meat; as dressing for seafood salad; or on hot baked, broiled, pan-fried or deep-fried fish or shellfish.

MUSTARD SAUCE FOR FISH

2 tablespoons all-purpose flour
¾ teaspoon sugar
¼ teaspoon salt
2 egg yolks
1 8-ounce bottle clam juice (1 cup)
2 tablespoons dry white wine
2 teaspoons prepared mustard

ABOUT 15 MINUTES BEFORE SERVING:
In cup, stir flour with sugar and salt until blended. In small saucepan, with wire whisk or fork, beat egg yolks slightly and stir in clam juice, wine and prepared mustard; stir in flour mixture. Over low heat, cook, stirring constantly, until sauce is smooth and thickened. Serve hot or cold with fish. Makes about 1⅓ cups.

HORSERADISH SAUCE

⅓ cup mayonnaise
¼ cup minced dill pickles
2 tablespoons horseradish
1 tablespoon milk
dash pepper

ABOUT 10 MINUTES BEFORE SERVING:
In small bowl, with spoon, stir all ingredients. Makes about ¾ cup.

CUCUMBER SAUCE

½ cup finely diced cucumber, drained
¼ cup mayonnaise or sour cream
¼ teaspoon celery salt
¼ teaspoon salt

ABOUT 10 MINUTES BEFORE SERVING:
In small bowl, with spoon, stir all ingredients. Makes about ¾ cup.

CURRIED MAYONNAISE

ABOUT 10 MINUTES BEFORE SERVING:
In small bowl, with fork, stir *1 cup mayonnaise, 1/4 cup milk* and *1 teaspoon curry powder* until blended. Makes about 1 cup.

DILL SAUCE

ABOUT 10 MINUTES BEFORE SERVING:
In small bowl, with fork, stir *1/2 cup mayonnaise* with *1 tablespoon dill weed* until well mixed. Makes about 1/2 cup.

DILL-BUTTER SAUCE

ABOUT 10 MINUTES BEFORE SERVING:
In small saucepan over low heat, melt *1 cup butter or margarine;* stir in *1 teaspoon dill weed* and *1/4 teaspoon salt.* Serve hot. Makes about 1 cup.

PARSLEY SAUCE

1 cup minced parsley
2 hard-cooked eggs, minced
1/2 cup olive oil
1/2 cup lemon juice
1/3 cup chopped bottled capers
1 garlic clove, minced

ABOUT 15 MINUTES BEFORE SERVING:
In small saucepan over medium heat, heat all ingredients until warm, stirring occasionally. Serve warm. Makes about 1 3/4 cups.

TARTAR SAUCE

1 cup mayonnaise
2 tablespoons minced parsley
1 to 2 tablespoons minced dill pickle
1 to 2 tablespoons minced onion
1 tablespoon bottled capers
1 tablespoon minced pimento-stuffed olives (optional)

ABOUT 15 MINUTES BEFORE SERVING:
In small bowl, with fork, stir all ingredients until well mixed. Makes about 1 1/4 cups.

CHILI-HORSERADISH SAUCE

1 cup chili sauce
1 tablespoon horseradish
1/4 teaspoon Worcestershire
1/8 teaspoon pepper

ABOUT 10 MINUTES BEFORE SERVING:
In small bowl, with fork, stir all ingredients until well mixed. Makes about 1 cup.

SOY-ONION SAUCE

3/4 cup soy sauce
1 tablespoon minced green onion
1 tablespoon olive oil
1/4 teaspoon sugar

ABOUT 10 MINUTES BEFORE SERVING:
In small bowl, with spoon, stir all ingredients until well mixed. Makes about 1 cup.

SHRIMP-OLIVE SAUCE

1 8-ounce can tomato sauce
1/2 pound shelled, deveined small shrimp, cooked
1/2 cup sliced pimento-stuffed olives
1/3 cup dry white wine

ABOUT 15 MINUTES BEFORE SERVING:
In 1-quart saucepan over medium heat, heat all ingredients, stirring. Serve hot. Makes about 1 2/3 cups.

LEMON SAUCE FOR FISH

3 tablespoons butter or margarine
3 tablespoons all-purpose flour
1 1/4 cups Court Bouillon (page 219)
2 tablespoons lemon juice
1/2 teaspoon salt

ABOUT 15 MINUTES BEFORE SERVING:
In 1-quart saucepan over medium heat, in hot butter or margarine, stir flour until blended. Gradually stir in Court Bouillon and cook, stirring constantly, until mixture is thickened. Remove from heat; stir in lemon juice and salt. Serve hot. Makes about 1 1/3 cups.

Game & wild birds

Most game and wild birds are supplied by hunters, but some meat markets carry them frozen or will order them. Animals and birds such as rabbits and pheasants are also raised domestically.

Cleaning, aging and otherwise readying game for cooking are done by the hunter or meatman. Weights given for meats and birds in our recipes are for dressed game, cut up if necessary, and ready to cook.

Tips for Game Cookery

Keep all game cold until cooked. Remove all visible fat, since this is where the "gamey" flavor is concentrated.

Age and diet of game animals and birds greatly affect cooking and eating qualities. For example, game that lives largely on fish may have a "fishy" flavor. Older game is usually tougher and drier. Bacon or other fat should be added when cooking it; and it should be braised or stewed. When in doubt about the age of game, it is best to braise or stew it. While cooking times are suggested in the recipes, the best rule of thumb is to cook until tender.

To Freeze Game

When freezing large game such as deer, remove all visible fat first, since game fat becomes rancid quickly even when frozen. Cut meat into pieces for cooking. Remove as many bones as possible. Trim and discard bloodshot meat. Freezer-wrap and freeze like other meats, page 61.

Refrigerate rabbit, squirrel and other small game until the meat is no longer rigid, 24 to 36 hours; then freezer-wrap and freeze, either whole or cut up.

Game birds should be refrigerated at least 24 hours before freezing. Trim any fat from wild geese; like meat fat, it too becomes rancid very quickly. Freezer-wrap birds and freeze; see Poultry, page 171.

Large and small game will keep 6 to 9 months at 0°F.; game birds, 6 months. Use stew meat and ground meat within 3 to 4 months. Thaw game meat and birds, wrapped, in the refrigerator to keep from drying out.

ROASTED GAME BIRDS

Wild goose, grouse, squab, quail, partridge and pheasant can be roasted following these directions:

Preheat oven as suggested for type of bird. Sprinkle *salt* inside bird and place *3 celery tops, 1 bay leaf* and *1 lemon slice* or lemon wedge in cavity. Tie legs closely together with string. Lightly sprinkle bird with *paprika* and *onion salt,* if you like.

Place bird on rack in open roasting pan. Cover breast and legs with *3 or 4 thick bacon slices;* roast, uncovered, until bird is tender. Bird is done when legs can be moved up and down easily, or when two-tined fork is inserted between leg and body and the juices that escape are not pink. Times vary according to size of bird. Cut string on legs; discard celery, bay leaf and lemon before serving.

WILD GOOSE: Preheat oven to 325°F. Prepare goose as above; bake 3 hours or until tender. One 6- to 8-pound wild goose makes about 6 servings.

GROUSE, QUAIL, SQUAB, PARTRIDGE OR PHEASANT: Preheat oven to 375°F. Prepare bird as above; roast grouse and quail 25 to 35 minutes, squab and partridge 45 to 55 minutes, pheasant 1 hour and 15 minutes until tender. Depending on size, two quail or one squab makes 1 serving; one grouse or partridge makes 1 or 2 servings; one pheasant makes 2 servings.

PHEASANT, HUNTER-STYLE

1 1¾- to 2-pound ready-to-cook pheasant
salt and pepper
1 small onion
1 stalk celery with leaves
5 thick bacon or salt-pork slices
Hunter Sauce (page 252)

ABOUT 1½ HOURS BEFORE SERVING:
Preheat oven to 375°F. Sprinkle cavity of pheasant with salt and pepper; place onion and celery in cavity. Tie legs together with string. Place pheasant on rack in open roasting pan. Completely cover breast and legs with bacon, securing bacon with toothpicks. Roast 1 hour and 15 minutes or until bird is tender, basting occasionally with pan juices. To test for doneness, pierce bird with two-tined fork between leg and body; juices that escape should not be pink. Remove bacon, onion and celery; discard. Serve with Hunter Sauce. Makes 2 servings.

PHEASANT IN CREAM

2 1½- to 2-pound ready-to-cook pheasants, quartered
all-purpose flour
3 tablespoons butter or margarine
2 tablespoons salad oil
½ cup diced onion
1 tablespoon salt
2 teaspoons paprika
¼ teaspoon pepper
1½ cups half-and-half

ABOUT 2 HOURS BEFORE SERVING:
Preheat oven to 350°F. On waxed paper, coat pheasant with about ½ cup flour. In 10-inch skillet over medium heat, in hot butter or margarine and salad oil, cook pheasant until browned on all sides, removing pieces to shallow 2-quart baking pan as they are browned. Pour off all but 2 tablespoons drippings from skillet; add onion and cook until tender, about 5 minutes.

Stir 3 tablespoons flour, salt, paprika and pepper into onion until blended. Gradually stir in half-and-half and cook, stirring constantly, until mixture is thickened; pour over pheasant. Cover and bake 1 hour or until fork-tender. Remove pheasant to warm platter; stir sauce until smooth and pour over pheasant. Makes 6 servings.

QUAIL WITH MUSHROOMS

⅓ cup butter or margarine
4 ready-to-cook quail
1 small onion, chopped
½ pound mushrooms, sliced
1 cup chicken broth
1¼ teaspoons salt
toast points
2 tablespoons all-purpose flour
3 tablespoons sauterne (optional)

ABOUT 45 MINUTES BEFORE SERVING:
Preheat oven to 350°F. In Dutch oven over medium heat, in hot butter or margarine, cook quail until browned on all sides; remove quail to platter. To drippings

in Dutch oven, add onion and mushrooms; cook, stirring occasionally, until onion is tender, about 5 minutes. Stir in chicken broth and salt. Add quail to mixture; cover; bake 20 minutes or until quail is tender.

Place quail on toast points on warm platter. In cup, blend flour and sauterne (or 3 tablespoons water) until smooth; gradually stir into liquid in Dutch oven and cook over medium heat, stirring constantly, until mixture is thickened. Serve sauce with quail. Makes 2 servings.

ROAST WILD DUCK

2 2-pound ready-to-cook wild ducks*
salt
pepper
1 teaspoon rosemary
2 small apples or oranges
2 small onions

ABOUT 2½ HOURS BEFORE SERVING:
Preheat oven to 325°F. Sprinkle cavities of ducks with salt, pepper and rosemary; place apple and onion in each cavity, cutting them, if necessary, to fit. Place ducks, breast side up, on rack in open roasting pan. Roast 1½ to 2 hours until ducks are tender when pierced with two-tined fork between leg and body; juices that escape should not be pink. Remove apples and onions; discard. Makes 4 servings.

* This recipe is for ducks that have been plucked but not skinned.

BRAISED WILD DUCK

2 2-pound ready-to-cook wild ducks*
all-purpose flour
¼ cup butter or margarine
½ cup chopped onion
¼ cup chopped celery
1½ teaspoons salt
¼ teaspoon coarsely ground pepper

ABOUT 2 HOURS BEFORE SERVING:
Preheat oven to 350°F. Cut ducks into serving pieces. On waxed paper, coat pieces with about ½ cup flour. In Dutch oven over medium heat, in hot butter or margarine, cook duck until browned on all sides, a few pieces at a time, removing pieces to platter as they are browned. Add onion and celery to drippings and cook until onion is tender, about 5 minutes.

Return duck to Dutch oven and sprinkle with salt and pepper; add ½ cup water. Cover and bake 1 hour or until duck is fork-tender.

Remove duck to warm platter. In small bowl, blend 1 tablespoon flour with 1 cup water until smooth. Gradually stir into drippings in Dutch oven and cook over medium heat, stirring constantly, until smooth and thickened; serve over duck. Makes 4 servings.

* Hunters sometimes skin (instead of plucking) ducks; this recipe is for skinned ducks.

STUFFED ROAST PARTRIDGE

4 1-pound ready-to-cook partridges
salt
coarsely ground pepper
2 tablespoons butter or margarine
¼ pound mushrooms, sliced
⅓ cup chopped celery
¼ cup chopped onion
1½ cups hot cooked rice
2 tablespoons chopped parsley
½ teaspoon poultry seasoning
1 8-ounce package bacon slices

ABOUT 1 HOUR AND 45 MINUTES AHEAD:
Preheat oven to 375°F. Sprinkle cavities of partridges with salt and pepper. In 10-inch skillet over medium heat, in hot butter or margarine, cook mushrooms, celery and onion until onion is tender, about 5 minutes. Stir in rice, parsley, poultry seasoning and ½ teaspoon salt; use to stuff birds lightly. Tie legs of each partridge together with string; cover each with bacon slices. Place partridges on rack in roasting pan with cover. (Or, use open roasting pan and cover with foil.) Cover and roast 1 hour; remove cover and roast 10 minutes longer or until bacon is crisp and partridges are tender when pierced with two-tined fork between leg and body; juices that escape should not be pink. Makes 4 servings.

STUFFED ROCK CORNISH HENS: Use *four 1-pound Rock Cornish hens.* Prepare as above but roast 1 hour and do not cover.

VENISON POT ROAST

1 3-pound venison shoulder roast
¼ cup all-purpose flour
2 tablespoons shortening
1 large onion, cut in chunks
salt
¼ teaspoon pepper
1 bay leaf
8 medium carrots, cut in chunks
8 medium potatoes, cut in chunks
1 20-ounce bag frozen green beans, partially thawed

ABOUT 4 HOURS BEFORE SERVING:
Trim any excess fat from meat. On waxed paper, coat meat with flour. In 8-quart Dutch oven over medium heat, in hot shortening, cook meat until browned on all sides. Add 1 cup water, onion, 1 teaspoon salt, pepper and bay leaf; heat to boiling. Reduce heat to low; cover and simmer 3 hours or until fork-tender, adding additional water if needed.

About 45 minutes before meat is done, add carrots, potatoes and beans; sprinkle them with 1 teaspoon salt; heat to boiling. Reduce heat and cook until meat and vegetables are tender, stirring vegetables occasionally. Makes 8 to 10 servings.

VENISON PAPRIKA

1 2½- to 3-pound venison rump roast
1½ cups apple cider, Chablis or other dry white wine
all-purpose flour
3 tablespoons butter or margarine
1 tablespoon paprika
½ cup sour cream
chopped parsley for garnish
1 12-ounce package egg noodles, cooked and drained

DAY BEFORE SERVING:
Trim any excess fat from meat. In large bowl, for marinade, pour cider over meat. Cover and refrigerate, turning meat occasionally.

ABOUT 3 HOURS BEFORE SERVING:
Drain meat well, reserving cider. On waxed paper, coat meat on all sides with about ¼ cup flour. In Dutch oven over medium heat, in hot butter or margarine, cook meat until browned on all sides. Add reserved cider; stir in paprika; heat to boiling. Reduce heat to low; cover and cook about 2 hours or until meat is fork-tender. Remove meat to warm platter. Measure liquid in Dutch oven; if necessary, add enough water to make 1½ cups.

In cup, blend 1 tablespoon flour and ¼ cup water until smooth; gradually stir into liquid in Dutch oven and cook over medium heat, stirring constantly, until mixture is thickened. Stir in sour cream and heat through. (Do not boil.) Spoon over meat; garnish with parsley. Serve with noodles. Makes 8 to 10 servings.

VENISON RAGOUT

2 pounds venison stew meat, cut in 2-inch chunks and trimmed of fat
1 medium onion, coarsely chopped
1½ cups dry red wine
2 teaspoons salt
¼ teaspoon rosemary
⅛ teaspoon pepper
⅓ cup all-purpose flour
¼ cup salad oil
3 celery stalks, cut up
1 12-ounce package egg noodles, cooked

DAY BEFORE SERVING:
In shallow dish, place first 6 ingredients. Cover and refrigerate, stirring mixture occasionally.

ABOUT 2½ HOURS BEFORE SERVING:
Drain meat well, reserving wine mixture. On waxed paper, coat meat with flour. In Dutch oven over medium heat, in hot salad oil, cook meat until browned on all sides, a few chunks at a time, removing chunks to platter as they are browned. When all chunks are browned, return to Dutch oven. Add reserved wine mixture; heat to boiling.

Reduce heat to low; cover Dutch oven and simmer 1½ to 2 hours until meat is fork-tender, stirring occasionally. About 30 minutes before meat is done, add celery. Cook until meat and celery are tender. Serve over noodles. Makes 8 servings.

VENISON STEAKS WITH WINE SAUCE

4 venison T-bone or loin steaks, cut about ½-inch thick (about 1½ pounds)
3 tablespoons butter or margarine
salt and pepper
½ cup dry red wine
1 tablespoon chopped parsley
1 tablespoon chopped chives
1 tablespoon quince or currant jelly
⅛ teaspoon nutmeg

ABOUT 25 MINUTES BEFORE SERVING:
Trim any excess fat from steaks. In 10-inch skillet over medium heat, in hot butter, fry steaks 3 or 4 minutes on each side until medium or well done; sprinkle lightly with salt and pepper; place on warm platter.

In drippings, heat remaining ingredients; spoon over steaks. Makes 4 servings.

VENISON BURGERS

ABOUT 25 MINUTES BEFORE SERVING:
Shape *1 pound ground venison* into 4 patties. In 10-inch skillet over medium heat, in *2 tablespoons hot butter or margarine,* cook patties until well browned on both sides; sprinkle lightly with *garlic salt* and *pepper.* Makes 4 servings.

VENISON MEAT LOAF

1 tablespoon butter or margarine
½ cup minced onion
¼ cup minced celery
2 eggs
1 cup fresh bread crumbs
½ cup milk
2 teaspoons salt
½ teaspoon thyme leaves
2 pounds ground venison
½ pound ground beef

ABOUT 2 HOURS AHEAD OR EARLY IN DAY:
Preheat oven to 350°F. In 8-inch skillet over medium heat, in hot butter or margarine, cook onion and celery until tender, about 5 minutes. Meanwhile, in large bowl, with fork, beat eggs slightly. Stir in bread crumbs and next 3 ingredients. Add venison, beef and onion mixture; mix well. Place mixture in 9″ by 5″ loaf pan and bake 1½ hours. Pour off pan juices. Serve hot or cold. Makes 8 to 10 servings.

SQUIRREL FRICASSEE

1 1-pound ready-to-cook squirrel, cut in pieces
all-purpose flour
3 tablespoons butter or margarine
1½ cups chicken broth
dash pepper

ABOUT 2 HOURS BEFORE SERVING:
On waxed paper, coat squirrel pieces with about ¼ cup flour. In 10-inch skillet over medium heat, in hot butter or margarine, cook pieces until browned on all sides. Add chicken broth and pepper; heat to boiling. Reduce heat to low; cover and simmer 45 minutes or until fork-tender. Remove pieces to warm platter.

In cup, blend 2 tablespoons flour and ½ cup water until smooth; gradually stir into pan juices in skillet and cook over medium heat, stirring constantly, until thickened; pour over squirrel. Makes 2 servings.

RABBIT FRICASSEE: Prepare as above but use *one 2-pound ready-to-cook wild rabbit.* Cook 1½ hours. Makes 4 servings.

FRIED RABBIT

⅔ cup all-purpose flour
1 teaspoon paprika
2 2-pound ready-to-cook wild rabbits or 1 5- to 6-pound domestic rabbit, cut up
¾ cup salad oil
1½ teaspoons salt
pepper

ABOUT 1½ HOURS BEFORE SERVING:
On waxed paper, combine flour and paprika; use to coat rabbit pieces.

In 12-inch skillet over medium-high heat, in hot salad oil, cook rabbit, a few pieces at a time, until browned on all sides, removing pieces to platter as they are browned. When all pieces are browned, return to skillet; sprinkle with salt and pepper. Reduce heat to low; cover and cook 45 minutes or until rabbit is fork-tender. If wild rabbit, makes 6 servings; if domestic rabbit, makes 8 servings.

FRIED SQUIRREL: Prepare as above but use *two 1-pound squirrels,* cut up, and reduce salt to 1 teaspoon. Makes 4 servings.

RABBIT SUPREME

2 2-pound ready-to-cook wild rabbits or 1 4- to 5-pound domestic rabbit, cut up
all-purpose flour
¼ cup salad oil
2 tablespoons butter or margarine
1 cup chopped onions
1 garlic clove, minced
2 teaspoons salt
¼ teaspoon pepper
1 cup milk
1 cup sour cream

ABOUT 2 HOURS BEFORE SERVING:
Preheat oven to 350°F. On waxed paper, coat rabbit pieces with about ½ cup flour. In ovenproof 10-inch skillet over medium-high heat, in hot oil and butter or margarine, cook rabbit, a few pieces at a time, until browned on all sides, removing pieces to platter as they are browned.

In drippings, over medium heat, cook onions and garlic until tender, about 5 minutes. Stir in 1 tablespoon flour, salt and pepper until blended; gradually stir in milk and cook, stirring constantly, until mixture is thickened.

Return rabbit pieces to skillet; spoon sauce over pieces. Cover and bake 1 hour and 10 minutes or until rabbit is fork-tender. Remove pieces to warm platter. Stir sour cream into gravy; heat, stirring constantly. (Do not boil.) Serve gravy over rabbit. Makes 8 servings.

HASENPFEFFER

2 2-pound ready-to-cook wild rabbits or 1 5- to 6-pound domestic rabbit, cut up
2 cups dry red wine
2 cups sliced onions
1 tablespoon pickling spice
2½ teaspoons salt
½ teaspoon coarsely ground pepper
½ teaspoon thyme leaves
2 bay leaves
6 bacon slices
about ¾ cup all-purpose flour
1 teaspoon sugar

DAY BEFORE SERVING:
In large bowl, over rabbit pieces, pour 1 cup water and wine; add next 6 ingredients. Cover and refrigerate overnight, turning pieces occasionally.

ABOUT 3 HOURS BEFORE SERVING:
1. In 12-inch skillet over medium heat, fry bacon until crisp; drain on paper towels; reserve drippings in skillet.
2. Meanwhile, remove rabbit pieces from wine mixture; reserve mixture. Pat pieces dry with paper towels. On waxed paper, coat rabbit pieces with flour. Over medium heat, in hot bacon drippings, cook rabbit, a few pieces at a time, until browned on all sides, removing pieces to platter as they are browned. Pour remaining drippings from skillet and return rabbit to skillet.
3. Crumble bacon over rabbit. Strain wine mixture, discarding seasonings; stir in sugar; pour over rabbit and heat to boiling. Reduce heat to low; cover and simmer 2 hours or until rabbit is fork-tender.
4. Remove rabbit to warm platter. Continue cooking gravy a few minutes, stirring until smooth; serve over rabbit. Makes 6 servings.

MARINADE FOR GAME

2 cups dry red wine
2 tablespoons salad oil
2 teaspoons salt
1 teaspoon coarsely ground pepper
¼ teaspoon thyme leaves
2 medium onions, thinly sliced
1 garlic clove

In saucepot or Dutch oven, mix all ingredients; add venison or other game; cover and refrigerate overnight or as recipe directs. Makes enough to marinate 5 pounds meat.

HUNTER SAUCE

½ cup red currant jelly
¼ cup catchup
¼ cup port or other sweet red wine
½ teaspoon Worcestershire

ABOUT 10 MINUTES BEFORE SERVING:
In small saucepan over low heat, cook all ingredients, stirring constantly, until smooth and jelly is melted. Serve with any game or wild birds. Makes 1 cup sauce, enough for 8 servings.

Main dishes

The main dish is generally the meal's main source of protein, supplying family members with one-fourth to one-third of their daily requirement. Meat, poultry and fish are the favorite choices; other protein-rich foods such as eggs, cheese and milk also qualify as major ingredients.

Here are recipes for favorite combination main dishes. Each supplies the protein equivalent of three ounces of lean cooked meat per serving; this meets the serving recommendations of the Basic Four Food Groups (page 727). Many of these dishes need be accompanied only by salad, bread and dessert to make a complete meal.

Recipes for combination main dishes will also be found in the chapters on Eggs (page 272), Cheese (page 285) and Salads (page 404). Others appear in Meats (page 59), Poultry (page 169), Fish (page 209), Game & Wild Birds (page 247), Cooking Outdoors (page 624), Cooking for a Crowd (page 654), Cooking for Two (page 639), Canning, Preserving & Freezing (page 715) and For Calorie Watchers (page 675). For quick reference to these, see the Index under "Main Dishes." Many Sandwiches (page 463) and Soups (page 50) can also act as main dishes if other protein foods are served at the same meal.

Skillet Main Dishes

CREAMY CHICKEN HASH

2 tablespoons butter or margarine
1 small onion, diced
1 tablespoon all-purpose flour
1 teaspoon salt
¾ cup half-and-half
2 cups cubed, cooked potatoes
2 cups cubed, cooked chicken or turkey
chopped parsley for garnish

ABOUT 25 MINUTES BEFORE SERVING:
In 10-inch skillet over medium heat, in hot butter or margarine, cook onion until tender, about 5 minutes, stirring occasionally. Stir in flour and salt; gradually stir in half-and-half and cook, stirring, until thickened.

Stir potatoes and chicken into mixture. Reduce heat to low; cover skillet and simmer about 10 minutes or until mixture is heated through, stirring occasionally. Garnish with parsley. Makes 4 servings.

FRANKFURTER BUFFET STEW

¼ cup salad oil
2 medium onions, sliced
1 garlic clove, minced
1½ 16-ounce packages frankfurters, cut into ½-inch chunks
1 29-ounce can hominy, drained
1 16-ounce can kidney beans, drained
1¾ cups tomato juice
¾ cup pitted ripe olives, chopped (1 3½-ounce can)
1 tablespoon chili powder
1½ cups shredded Cheddar cheese
8 to 10 toasted French-bread slices

ABOUT 20 MINUTES BEFORE SERVING:
In 12-inch skillet over medium-high heat, in hot salad oil, cook onions and garlic until lightly browned, about 5 minutes. Stir in frankfurters, hominy, beans, tomato juice, olives and chili powder and heat to boiling. Stir in cheese and heat until melted. Pour mixture into warm serving dish and top with bread slices. Makes 8 to 10 servings.

PAELLA

½ pound sweet Italian or large sausage links
3 tablespoons olive oil
4 chicken drumsticks
4 chicken thighs
1 large green pepper, cut into thin strips
1 garlic clove, slivered
1 29-ounce can tomatoes
1½ teaspoons salt
½ teaspoon cinnamon
¼ teaspoon pepper
¼ teaspoon saffron
1½ cups regular long-grain rice
1 2-ounce jar sliced pimentos, drained
1 pound medium shrimp, shelled and deveined
1 10-ounce package frozen peas, thawed (or 1 14-ounce can artichoke hearts, drained)
12 littleneck clams in shells or 12 mussels in shells

ABOUT 2½ HOURS BEFORE SERVING:
In covered 12-inch skillet or paella pan over low heat, heat sausages with ¼ cup water to simmering; cook 5 minutes. Uncover skillet and cook sausages over medium heat until browned, about 20 minutes, turning occasionally. Remove from skillet and cool slightly; cut into ½-inch slices; reserve drippings.

In skillet over medium-high heat, in hot drippings and olive oil, cook chicken drumsticks and thighs until lightly browned on all sides. Add green pepper and garlic and cook 2 minutes; stir in tomatoes and their liquid, salt, cinnamon and pepper; heat to boiling. Reduce heat to low; cover and simmer 30 minutes or until chicken is almost fork-tender, stirring occasionally.

In cup, mix saffron with 2 tablespoons hot water; add to chicken mixture. Add rice and pimentos. Over high heat, heat to boiling; reduce heat to medium-low; cover and cook 15 minutes, stirring occasionally. Stir sausage pieces, shrimp and peas into mixture; place clams on top; cover and simmer 5 to 10 minutes more until clams open, rice is tender and all liquid is absorbed. Serve from skillet. Makes 8 servings.

PANTRY PAELLA

1 24-ounce can clams in shells
1 6-ounce package chicken-flavored rice
3 10-ounce packages or 1 32-ounce package frozen fried chicken pieces
1 9-ounce package frozen artichoke hearts
1 5-ounce can Vienna sausage, drained
½ cup pitted large ripe olives
1 canned medium pimento, thinly sliced

ABOUT 40 MINUTES BEFORE SERVING:
Drain clams into a 4-cup measure; add enough water to make 2½ cups liquid; set aside.

In 12-inch skillet over medium-high heat, heat to boiling rice and seasoning packet with reserved clam-liquid mixture. Reduce heat to low; add chicken pieces; cover and simmer 15 minutes. Add frozen artichoke hearts; cover and simmer 10 minutes longer. Stir in clams and remaining ingredients; cover and cook 10 minutes more or until all ingredients are heated through and chicken and artichoke hearts are fork-tender. Makes 8 servings.

SKILLET MACARONI AND CHEESE

½ cup butter or margarine
2 cups elbow macaroni
¼ cup minced onion
2 tablespoons minced green pepper
1 teaspoon salt
¼ teaspoon dry mustard
2 4-ounce packages shredded Cheddar cheese (2 cups)
10 medium pimento-stuffed olives, sliced

ABOUT 45 MINUTES BEFORE SERVING:
In 10-inch skillet over medium heat, in hot butter or margarine, cook uncooked macaroni and next 4 ingredients for 5 minutes, stirring frequently. Stir in 2 cups water; heat mixture to boiling. Reduce heat to low; cover and simmer 10 to 15 minutes until macaroni is tender, stirring occasionally. Remove from heat; stir in cheese and olives until cheese is melted. Makes 4 servings.

CHOP SUEY

1 pound pork-sirloin cutlets or pork tenderloin*
2 tablespoons cornstarch
3 tablespoons soy sauce
1 tablespoon dry sherry
1½ teaspoons salt
¼ teaspoon ginger
¼ teaspoon monosodium glutamate
2 tablespoons salad oil
2 cups thinly shredded Chinese cabbage
1 cup thinly sliced celery
1 bunch green onions, cut into 1-inch pieces
1 16-ounce can bean sprouts, drained
1 6- or 8½-ounce can water chestnuts, drained and thinly sliced
1 5- or 6-ounce can bamboo shoots, drained and sliced
3 cups hot cooked rice

ABOUT 45 MINUTES BEFORE SERVING:
With sharp knife, slice pork cutlets into thin, bite-size pieces. In small bowl, combine cornstarch, next 5 ingredients and ½ cup water; set aside.

In 12-inch skillet over medium-high heat, in hot salad oil, cook pork until browned, stirring quickly and frequently, about 5 minutes. Add cornstarch mixture and all ingredients except rice; cook and stir until vegetables are tender-crisp, about 5 minutes. Serve with rice. Makes 4 servings.

SHRIMP CHOP SUEY: Use *one 16-ounce package frozen shelled and deveined shrimp,* thawed, instead of pork. Prepare as above but cook shrimp in hot salad oil only 2 minutes or until pink. Finish cooking as above.

* Meat will be easier to slice if it is partially frozen about 1½ hours ahead.

CREAMED BEEF SAUCE WITH NOODLES

1 8-ounce package fine egg noodles
1 pound ground beef
¼ cup sliced green onions
½ teaspoon dill weed
1 10½-ounce can condensed cream-of-mushroom soup
½ cup sour cream
½ teaspoon salt
dash pepper

ABOUT 20 MINUTES BEFORE SERVING:
Prepare noodles as label directs. Meanwhile, in 10-inch skillet over medium-high heat, cook ground beef, onions and dill until meat is browned. Stir in undiluted soup, sour cream, salt, pepper and ¼ cup water; cook until heated through. Serve over hot noodles. Makes 4 servings.

BACON-AND-EGGS SPAGHETTI

1 16-ounce package spaghetti
8 bacon slices, cut up
2 medium onions, coarsely chopped
4 eggs, slightly beaten
½ 8-ounce package pasteurized process cheese spread, cubed (about 1 cup)

ABOUT 30 MINUTES BEFORE SERVING:
Cook spaghetti as label directs; drain. Meanwhile, in 12-inch skillet over medium heat, cook bacon until crisp; with slotted spoon, remove to paper towels; set aside.

In drippings in skillet, cook onions until tender, about 5 minutes. Add spaghetti and bacon to onion mixture and toss until well mixed; stir in eggs and cheese and heat until cheese is melted. Makes 4 servings.

TURKEY CREOLE

2 tablespoons salad oil
½ cup chopped onion
1 large green pepper, chopped
1 small garlic clove, crushed
1 16-ounce can tomatoes
2 teaspoons chili powder
1½ teaspoons salt
1 teaspoon sugar
¾ teaspoon oregano leaves
⅛ teaspoon pepper
1 cup regular long-grain rice
3 cups cut-up cooked turkey or chicken

ABOUT 50 MINUTES BEFORE SERVING:
In 12-inch skillet over medium heat, in hot salad oil, cook onion, green pepper and garlic until onion and green pepper are tender-crisp, about 5 minutes. Add 2 cups water, tomatoes with their liquid, chili powder, salt, sugar, oregano leaves and pepper; heat to boiling; stir in rice. Reduce heat to low; cover skillet and simmer 25 minutes or until rice is tender and liquid is absorbed. Stir in turkey and heat through. Makes 4 servings.

STUFFED CABBAGE

12 large cabbage leaves
2 tablespoons butter or margarine
1 large onion, chopped
1 16-ounce can tomato sauce
2 teaspoons light brown sugar
salt
pepper
1½ pounds lean ground beef
1 cup cooked rice
1 white bread slice, crumbled
1 egg
1 teaspoon Worcestershire
½ teaspoon basil
1 small garlic clove, crushed

ABOUT 1¼ HOURS BEFORE SERVING:
1. In covered 12-inch skillet, in 1 inch boiling water, cook cabbage leaves 5 minutes; drain; set aside.
2. In same skillet over medium heat, in hot butter or margarine, cook onion 5 minutes or until tender, stirring occasionally. Add tomato sauce, brown sugar, 1 teaspoon salt and ¼ teaspoon pepper; mix well; set aside.
3. Meanwhile, in large bowl, combine remaining ingredients, 1 teaspoon salt and ¼ teaspoon pepper; divide mixture into 12 portions.
4. In center of each cabbage leaf, place portion of meat mixture. Fold 2 sides of leaf toward center; from one narrow edge of leaf, roll up jelly-roll fashion. Place filled leaves, seam sides down, in sauce in skillet. Over medium heat, heat sauce and filled leaves to simmering. Reduce heat to low; cover and simmer 45 minutes. Makes 6 servings.

SPLIT-PEA-AND-HAM SKILLET

1 cup split peas
1 teaspoon salt
½ teaspoon basil
1½ cups cubed cooked ham (about ½ pound)
1 medium green pepper, sliced into thin strips

ABOUT 50 MINUTES BEFORE SERVING:
In 10-inch skillet over medium-high heat, heat 3 cups water, peas, salt and basil to boiling. Reduce heat to low; cover and simmer 35 minutes. Add ham and green pepper; cover and cook 10 minutes longer or until peas are tender. Makes 4 servings.

FRIED STEAK WITH CREAM GRAVY

1 pound high-quality beef round steak, cut about ½ inch thick
all-purpose flour
3 tablespoons salad oil
1 cup milk
½ teaspoon salt
3 cups hot mashed potatoes

ABOUT 20 MINUTES BEFORE SERVING:
On waxed paper, coat round steak on one side with flour; with meat mallet or edge of saucer, pound steak until flour disappears; turn steak and repeat on other side. Cut steak into 4 pieces. In 10-inch skillet over high heat, in hot salad oil, fry steak pieces 3 to 5 minutes on each side until well browned. Remove to heated platter.

For gravy, into drippings in skillet over

medium heat, stir 2 tablespoons flour until well blended. Gradually stir ½ cup water into flour mixture, scraping to loosen browned bits. Stir in milk and salt and cook, stirring, until gravy is thickened. Serve steak and gravy with mashed potatoes. Makes 4 servings.

Casseroles

TURKEY-AND-DRESSING STRATA

1 10½-ounce can condensed cream-of-mushroom soup
¾ cup milk
3 cups cut-up cooked turkey or chicken
1½ cups leftover stuffing
1 tablespoon grated or shredded Parmesan cheese

ABOUT 45 MINUTES BEFORE SERVING:
Preheat oven to 350°F. Grease 1½-quart casserole. In 2-quart saucepan over medium heat, heat undiluted soup with milk; stir in turkey.

In casserole, layer stuffing and turkey mixture twice, ending with turkey mixture. Sprinkle with cheese. Bake 30 minutes or until heated through. Makes 6 servings.

STEAK-AND-KIDNEY PIE

1 beef kidney (about 1 pound)
2½ pounds beef chuck steak, trimmed and cut into 1-inch chunks
¼ cup all-purpose flour
salad oil
1 large onion, chopped
½ cup dry red wine or beer
2 beef-bouillon cubes or envelopes
2 teaspoons Worcestershire
¼ teaspoon pepper
pastry for one 9-inch unbaked piecrust (page 504)
1 egg yolk

ABOUT 3¾ HOURS BEFORE SERVING:
1. Wash kidney; remove membrane and hard white parts and cut into 1-inch chunks. On waxed paper, coat kidney and beef chunks with flour.
2. In 5-quart Dutch oven over medium-high heat, in 3 tablespoons hot salad oil, cook kidney and beef chunks, several pieces at a time, until well browned on all sides, removing pieces as they brown, and adding more oil as needed.
3. Reduce heat to medium; add onion to drippings and cook until onion is almost tender, about 3 minutes, stirring occasionally. Stir in wine, ½ cup water, bouillon, Worcestershire and pepper; add meat and heat to boiling, stirring to dissolve bouillon. Reduce heat to low; cover and simmer about 2 hours or until meat is fork-tender. Spoon mixture into 2-quart round casserole.
4. Preheat oven to 400°F. Meanwhile, prepare piecrust as recipe directs. Roll dough into circle 1 inch larger than casserole. Fit crust loosely over meat mixture; trim overhang to about 1 inch and make a fluted edge (page 506).
5. In cup, with fork, beat egg yolk with 1 teaspoon water. Brush pastry with beaten egg yolk. With point of knife, make several slits in crust. Bake pie 40 minutes or until browned and bubbly. Cover loosely with foil if crust browns too quickly. Makes about 8 servings.

TURKEY-RICE CASSEROLE

6 cups cut-up cooked turkey or chicken
2 10½-ounce cans condensed cream-of-mushroom soup
2¼ cups milk
2 cups chopped celery
¾ cup regular long-grain rice
¼ cup dry vermouth or other dry white wine
¼ cup chopped parsley
2 tablespoons butter or margarine
¼ cup dried bread crumbs

ABOUT 1 HOUR AND 45 MINUTES AHEAD:
Preheat oven to 350°F. In 2½-quart casserole, stir turkey, undiluted soup, milk, celery, rice, vermouth and parsley. Cover casserole and bake 1½ hours, stirring once or twice, until rice is cooked and mixture is hot and bubbly.

Meanwhile, in small saucepan over medium heat, melt butter or margarine; stir in bread crumbs; set aside. When turkey mixture is hot and bubbly, uncover; sprinkle with crumb mixture and bake 15 minutes more or until crumbs are golden. Makes 8 to 10 servings.

HAM STEAK AND POTATO SCALLOP

3 boneless ham slices, each cut about ½ inch thick (about 1¼ pounds)
⅓ cup butter or margarine
¼ cup minced onion
⅓ cup all-purpose flour
1 teaspoon dry mustard
¼ teaspoon salt
¼ teaspoon pepper
1½ cups milk
6 medium potatoes, each sliced about ¼ inch thick
Buttered Crumbs (page 351)

ABOUT 2 HOURS BEFORE SERVING:
Preheat oven to 350°F. Remove any casing from ham slices; cut each slice in half and arrange in 12″ by 8″ baking dish.

In 3-quart saucepan over medium heat, in hot butter or margarine, cook onion 5 minutes or until tender, stirring occasionally. Stir in flour, mustard, salt and pepper until blended. Gradually stir in milk and cook, stirring constantly, until mixture is very thick. Stir in potato slices; spoon potato mixture over ham slices. Cover tightly with foil and bake about 1½ hours or until potatoes are tender. Sprinkle with Buttered Crumbs. Makes 6 servings.

ITALIAN BEEF CASSEROLE

1 pound very lean ground beef
¼ cup diced onion
1 8-ounce can tomato sauce
1 6-ounce can tomato paste
salt
1 teaspoon basil
1 teaspoon sugar
1 small garlic clove, minced
⅛ teaspoon pepper
¼ cup fresh bread crumbs
1 3-ounce can sliced mushrooms, drained
1 10-ounce package frozen chopped spinach, thawed and drained
1 cup creamed cottage cheese
1 egg
⅛ teaspoon nutmeg
½ 8-ounce package mozzarella cheese

ABOUT 1¼ HOURS BEFORE SERVING:
In 10-inch skillet over high heat, cook ground beef and onion until meat is browned. Stir in tomato sauce, tomato paste, 1¼ teaspoons salt and next 4 ingredients. Reduce heat to low; simmer 10 minutes, stirring frequently, until mixture is thickened. Stir in bread crumbs. Reserve 6 mushroom slices; add rest of mushrooms to meat mixture.

Preheat oven to 350°F. Meanwhile, pat spinach dry with paper towels. In medium bowl, with fork, combine spinach, cottage cheese, egg, ¼ teaspoon salt and nutmeg. Cut mozzarella cheese crosswise into ¼-inch-thick slices; cut 2 slices into ½-inch-wide strips; dice remaining cheese.

In 9″ by 9″ baking pan, spread half of meat mixture; top with spinach mixture and sprinkle with diced mozzarella; spread on remaining meat mixture. Arrange cheese strips in rows on top and garnish with reserved mushroom slices. Bake 45 minutes or until hot and bubbly. Makes 6 servings.

PARTY PORK-AND-VEGETABLE PIE

3 pounds boneless lean pork,* cubed
2 medium onions, chopped
2 cups chicken broth
2 pounds small carrots, thinly sliced
1½ pounds green beans, cut into ½-inch pieces
5 teaspoons salt
1 tablespoon rubbed sage
½ teaspoon nutmeg
¼ cup cornstarch
3 packages piecrust mix for 2-crust pies
all-purpose flour
1 egg, beaten

ABOUT 3 HOURS AHEAD OR DAY BEFORE:
1. In 7-quart saucepot or Dutch oven over high heat, cook pork and onions until pork is lightly browned, about 20 minutes, stirring occasionally. Stir in chicken broth and next 5 ingredients; heat to boiling. Reduce heat to low; cover and simmer 30 minutes or until pork and vegetables are tender, stirring occasionally.
2. In cup, blend ½ cup cold water and cornstarch until smooth; gradually stir into pork mixture and cook, stirring constantly, until very thick.
3. Meanwhile, in large bowl, prepare pie-

* Meat will be easier to cut up if it is partially frozen about 1½ hours ahead.

crust mixes (together) as label directs. Shape two-thirds of pastry into large ball; shape remaining pastry into another ball. On lightly floured surface, with lightly floured rolling pin, roll large ball into an 18" by 14" rectangle, about 1/8 inch thick. Fold pastry into fourths and carefully lift into 14" by 10" open roasting or baking pan; unfold.

4. With fingers, lightly press pastry against bottom and sides of pan; brush with some beaten egg. Spoon pork mixture into pastry-lined pan; turn pastry overhang over filling; brush overhang with some beaten egg.

5. Preheat oven to 425°F. Roll remaining pastry ball into a 15" by 11" rectangle; with knife, cut design in pastry. Place pastry over filling in pan, pressing lightly around edges to seal. Brush pastry with remaining beaten egg. Bake 35 minutes or until golden. Serve warm or refrigerate to serve cold. Makes 12 servings.

TO REHEAT: Preheat oven to 425°F. Cover pie with foil and bake 50 minutes or until heated through.

BEAN-AND-BACON BAKE

3 16-ounce cans pork-and-beans in tomato sauce, lightly drained
1/2 cup catchup
1/4 cup instant minced onion
1 tablespoon horseradish
1 tablespoon prepared mustard
2 teaspoons Worcestershire
4 unpeeled orange slices, each cut about 1/4 inch thick
8 Canadian-style bacon slices, each cut about 1/4 inch thick
1/4 cup packed light brown sugar
2 tablespoons butter or margarine, melted

ABOUT 1 HOUR BEFORE SERVING:
Preheat oven to 350°F. In 2½-quart shallow casserole, stir first 6 ingredients. Arrange orange and Canadian-style bacon slices alternately on top of mixture; sprinkle with brown sugar. Bake 50 minutes or until bubbly, brushing orange slices once or twice with butter or margarine. Makes 6 servings.

HOT CHICKEN SALAD

3/4 cup mayonnaise
2 tablespoons lemon juice
1 teaspoon dry mustard
1 teaspoon salt
1 teaspoon Worcestershire
1/4 teaspoon hot pepper sauce
1 4-ounce package shredded Cheddar cheese (1 cup)
3 cups cut-up, cooked chicken
1½ cups chopped celery
1½ cups fresh bread cubes
1 cup chopped California walnuts (optional)

ABOUT 1 HOUR BEFORE SERVING:
Preheat oven to 350°F. In 1½-quart casserole, mix first 6 ingredients. Stir in half of cheese and remaining ingredients. Bake 40 to 45 minutes. Sprinkle with remaining cheese and bake 3 to 5 minutes longer until cheese is melted. Makes 6 servings.

LIVER AND CREAMED VEGETABLES

4 cups thinly sliced potatoes
2 cups thin carrot sticks
2 cups sliced onions
butter or margarine
1 pound sliced beef liver, cut into 5 serving pieces
1/2 cup all-purpose flour
1 tablespoon salt
2 cups milk

ABOUT 1¼ HOURS BEFORE SERVING:
In covered 4-quart saucepan over medium-high heat, in 1 inch boiling water, cook potatoes, carrots and onions 10 minutes; drain well. Meanwhile, in 12-inch oven-proof skillet over medium heat, in 2 tablespoons hot butter or margarine, cook liver until browned on both sides; remove from skillet.

Preheat oven to 350°F. To drippings in skillet, add 1/4 cup butter or margarine; melt. Stir in flour and salt until blended. Gradually stir in milk and cook, stirring constantly, until mixture is thickened.

Gently stir potatoes, carrots and onions into sauce. Arrange liver on top of mixture. Cover skillet and bake 30 minutes or until hot and bubbly. Makes 5 servings.

SALMON RAMEKINS

6 tablespoons butter or margarine
6 tablespoons all-purpose flour
⅛ teaspoon nutmeg
⅔ cup half-and-half
¼ cup white table wine
1 16-ounce can salmon
1 8-ounce package process Swiss cheese slices, cut in chunks
1 4-ounce can mushroom stems and pieces, drained

ABOUT 25 MINUTES BEFORE SERVING:
Preheat oven to 350°F. In 1½-quart saucepan over medium heat, into hot butter or margarine, stir flour and nutmeg until blended. Gradually stir in half-and-half and wine; cook, stirring, until mixture is thickened. Add salmon with its liquid, 1 cup Swiss cheese and mushrooms; stir briskly to break up salmon.

Spoon salmon mixture into six 10-ounce ramekins or custard cups; top each with heaping tablespoon of Swiss cheese. Bake 15 minutes or until hot and bubbly. Makes 6 servings.

Broiled Combinations

SURF AND TURF

4 4-ounce rock-lobster tails, thawed
4 bacon slices
4 beef-tenderloin steaks (filets mignons), each cut about 1 inch thick
salt
pepper
melted butter or margarine

ABOUT 30 MINUTES BEFORE SERVING:
Preheat broiler if manufacturer directs. With kitchen shears, cut away thin underside shell of each rock-lobster tail. Insert metal skewer lengthwise through lobster meat so tail will lie flat during broiling. Place tails, shell sides up, on greased rack of broiling pan.

Wrap a bacon slice around outside edge of each tenderloin steak; secure with toothpicks. Sprinkle steaks lightly with salt and pepper and arrange on rack next to lobster. About 2 or 3 inches from source of heat, broil steaks and lobster tails 5 minutes.

With tongs, turn steaks and lobster tails; brush lobster generously with melted butter or margarine. Broil 3 to 5 minutes longer until lobster meat is opaque. If meat has not reached desired doneness, remove lobster tails and keep warm. Serve steaks and lobster with individual dishes of melted butter or margarine for dipping lobster. Makes 4 servings.

SHRIMP AND SIRLOIN: Prepare as above but substitute *1 pound shelled and deveined jumbo or large shrimp* for lobster tails and *one 1½-pound sirloin steak* for tenderloin steaks. Broil steak until of desired doneness, adding shrimp last 5 minutes to cook until they turn pink.

SCALLOPS AND SIRLOIN PATTIES: Prepare as above but substitute *1 pound sea scallops* for lobster and *1 pound ground sirloin,* shaped into 4 thick patties, for tenderloin steaks.

BROILED OYSTERS AND TOMATOES

1 pint shucked "select" oysters
¾ cup dried bread crumbs
1 teaspoon salt
½ teaspoon dry mustard
¼ teaspoon paprika
3 medium tomatoes, halved crosswise
⅓ cup butter or margarine, melted
3 lemon wedges
Tartar sauce, catchup or chili sauce (optional)

ABOUT 30 MINUTES BEFORE SERVING:
1. Preheat broiler if manufacturer directs. Drain oysters well. In small bowl, combine crumbs, salt, mustard and paprika. On waxed paper, sprinkle half of crumb mixture; place oysters in single layer over it; sprinkle oysters with remaining crumb mixture.
2. Meanwhile, arrange tomatoes, cut sides up, on greased rack in broiling pan; brush with melted butter or margarine; broil 7 minutes.
3. Place crumbed oysters in one layer on rack of broiling pan. Drizzle with half of melted butter or margarine. Broil 3 to 4

minutes until golden; turn, drizzle with remaining melted butter or margarine and broil 3 to 4 minutes more until oysters are golden and tomatoes are tender.
4. Serve tomatoes and oysters with lemon wedges (to squeeze over oysters) and Tartar sauce, if you like. Makes 3 servings.

MIXED GRILL

A mixed grill is a broiled main dish made up of one or more meats, fish or poultry, or a combination of these, plus a vegetable or two and perhaps a fruit.

Choose foods from suggestions below. Preheat broiler if manufacturer directs; grease rack of broiling pan. Begin broiling food that takes longest; add other foods so that all will be done at the same time. Serve on warm platter.

MEATS: Steak, lamb chops, hamburgers, ham, lamb or veal kidneys, liver, bacon, frankfurters, sweetbreads

POULTRY: Chicken, Rock Cornish hen, duckling

SEAFOOD: Fish, lobster, rock-lobster tails, shrimp, scallops; Broiled Oysters and Tomatoes (page 260)

VEGETABLES: Mushrooms, tomatoes (see Mushroom-Capped Grilled Tomatoes, page 347)

FRUITS: Choose from Broiled Canned Fruit or Broiled Fresh Fruit (page 382)

ITALIAN-STYLE SUPPER LOAF

1 1-pound round loaf unsliced Italian bread
1 pound ground beef
1 6-ounce can tomato paste
1 4-ounce can mushroom slices
1 tablespoon instant minced onion
1 teaspoon salt
½ teaspoon oregano leaves
1 8-ounce package American cheese slices, coarsely chopped
2 medium tomatoes, chopped

ABOUT 30 MINUTES BEFORE SERVING:
With sharp knife, cut bread horizontally in half; with spoon, scoop out soft centers of bread, leaving two ½-inch-thick shells. (Use crumbs another day.)

Preheat broiler if manufacturer directs. In large bowl, combine ground beef with next 5 ingredients; spoon mixture evenly into shells. With foil, cover edges of bread shells, exposing ground beef mixture.

Place stuffed bread shells on rack in broiling pan, about 7 inches from heat source; broil 15 minutes or until ground beef is cooked through. Sprinkle cheese and tomatoes on top of ground beef; return to broiler just until cheese is melted. Cut into wedges to serve. Makes 6 servings.

Other Main Dishes

COLD SLICED BEEF A L'ORANGE

2 large garlic cloves, minced
1½ teaspoons salt
¾ teaspoon ground cumin
½ teaspoon ground cloves
½ teaspoon pepper
1 4-pound high-quality sirloin-tip beef roast
3 large oranges, peeled and sliced
2 cups orange juice

DAY BEFORE SERVING:
1. Preheat oven to 325°F. In mortar with pestle (or in small bowl, with back of spoon), crush garlic with salt; add cumin, cloves and pepper and mix to paste.
2. With tip of sharp knife, make about 2 dozen slits, about 2½ inches deep, over top and sides of beef roast; into each slit, with spoon, insert some of garlic mixture until all has been used.
3. Place roast on rack in open roasting pan; insert meat thermometer into center of meat. Roast meat about 2¼ hours or until meat thermometer reaches 140°F. for rare. Remove roast from oven; cover and refrigerate until well chilled.
4. Cut meat into thin slices. In 13" by 9" baking pan, alternately arrange roast slices and orange slices; pour orange juice over all. Cover and refrigerate.

TO SERVE:
Arrange drained meat and orange slices on chilled platter. Makes 12 to 14 servings.

CHICKEN A LA KING

6 tablespoons butter or margarine
½ pound mushrooms, sliced
¼ cup diced green pepper
6 tablespoons all-purpose flour
3 cups half-and-half or heavy or whipping cream
4 cups cubed cooked chicken or turkey
1 4-ounce jar diced pimentos, drained
2 egg yolks, beaten
2 tablespoons medium sherry
1 teaspoon salt
8 warm Patty Shells (below)

ABOUT 40 MINUTES BEFORE SERVING:
In 10-inch skillet over medium heat, in hot butter or margarine, cook mushrooms and green pepper 5 minutes or until tender. Stir in flour until blended. Gradually stir in half-and-half and cook, stirring constantly, until mixture is thickened. Add chicken and pimentos; heat to boiling, stirring often. Reduce heat to low; cover; cook 5 minutes.

In cup, into egg yolks, stir small amount of hot sauce; slowly pour egg mixture back into sauce, stirring rapidly to prevent lumping. Cook, stirring constantly, until mixture is thickened. Stir in sherry and salt. Serve mixture in Patty Shells. Makes 8 servings.

OTHER LEFTOVER MEATS: Substitute cubed cooked beef, veal, ham or lamb for chicken and add salt and pepper to taste.

PUFF PASTRY

3½ cups all-purpose flour
2 teaspoons salt
1½ cups butter or margarine

1 DAY OR UP TO 6 MONTHS AHEAD:
1. In large bowl, with fork, combine flour and salt; reserve ½ cup flour mixture. Into remaining flour mixture, pour 1 cup iced water, stirring with fork to blend well. If necessary, add 2 to 3 tablespoons more water until mixture is just moist enough to hold together. With hands, shape pastry into a ball. Wrap dough in plastic wrap; refrigerate 45 minutes or until very cold.
2. Meanwhile, soften butter or margarine just enough to be mixable. In medium bowl, with mixer at medium speed, beat butter or margarine until smooth. Gradually beat in reserved flour mixture until well blended, scraping bowl with rubber spatula. (Mixture must still be very cold but spreadable; refrigerate, if necessary.)
3. On lightly floured surface with lightly floured rolling pin, roll dough into 18″ by 8″ rectangle; with metal spatula, spread butter mixture over upper 12-inch section of dough to within ½ inch of edges; fold bottom 6-inch section of dough over butter mixture; fold top 6-inch section over bottom 6-inch section. Give dough a quarter turn.
4. Roll into 18″ by 8″ rectangle. Fold two 8-inch edges to center; fold in half so folded edges are together, one on top of other.
5. Wrap dough in plastic wrap; refrigerate at least 45 minutes to chill dough thoroughly again. (Do not shape in ball or layers will not puff evenly.)
6. Again roll dough into 18″ by 8″ rectangle; fold two 8-inch edges to center; fold in half so folded edges are together, one on top of other. Give dough a quarter turn, reroll and fold again. Wrap dough well; refrigerate at least 45 minutes.
7. Repeat step 6 once. Refrigerate at least 2 hours or until ready to use. (Or, freezer-wrap dough and freeze up to 6 months. Thaw dough overnight in refrigerator.) Makes enough dough for 12 Patty Shells or one Beef Wellington (page 72).

PATTY SHELLS: About 1½ hours before serving: 1. Roll Puff Pastry into 18″ by 8″ rectangle; cut in half; refrigerate one half. (Do not shape dough into a ball or layers will not puff evenly.) On lightly floured surface, roll pastry into ¼-inch-thick rectangle, about 12″ by 9″. With 3-inch round cookie cutter, cut pastry into rounds, pressing straight down without twisting. With 1½-inch round cookie cutter, cut center from half of rounds to make rings. Press trimmings and rounds together and reroll.
2. With water, dampen outside edge of each 3-inch round; stack a ring on each and press lightly to seal. Using small cutter, in center of each ring, press lightly into bottom round (during baking center will puff to form top). With fork, prick centers in several places. Holding knife vertically against sides of shells, lightly press at ¼-

inch intervals to make scallops. Place patty shells on 15½″ by 10½″ jelly-roll pan; cover and refrigerate. Repeat with rest of pastry. Chill shells at least 40 minutes.
3. Meanwhile, preheat oven to 425°F. In cup, with fork, beat *1 egg* with *1½ teaspoons water*. With pastry brush, lightly brush tops (not sides) of patty shells with egg mixture. Bake 20 to 25 minutes until light golden.
4. Place patty shells on wire rack; with small, sharp knife, cut out puffed top of each shell. With small spoon, gently scrape out any uncooked dough from shell and discard. Serve shells filled with creamed seafood or poultry, or pudding, or ice cream topped with sauce, or fruit mixture. After filling shells, add tops. Cover leftover shells tightly to store. Makes about 12.

TO REHEAT: Preheat oven to 425°F. Place Patty Shells on cookie sheet and bake 5 minutes to heat through.

DINNER CROQUETTES

2½ cups ground, cooked roast beef, ham, lamb, veal, chicken or turkey*
1 cup Thick White Sauce (page 352)
2 tablespoons chopped parsley
1 tablespoon minced onion
½ teaspoon lemon juice
dash rubbed sage (optional)
salt
1 egg
¼ cup all-purpose flour
½ cup dried bread crumbs
salad oil
Mushroom Sauce (page 168) or Cheese Sauce (page 352)

EARLY IN DAY OR DAY AHEAD:
1. In medium bowl, mix well first 6 ingredients. Add salt to taste. Cover and chill well, several hours or overnight.

ABOUT 30 MINUTES BEFORE SERVING:
2. Shape mixture into 8 cylinders or cones.
3. In shallow dish, with fork, beat egg and 1 tablespoon water until well blended. Place flour and bread crumbs on separate sheets of waxed paper. Roll croquettes first in flour, then in egg, then in crumbs, until well coated.
4. In electric skillet,† heat ¾ inch salad oil to 370°F. Fry croquettes until golden brown, turning frequently; drain on paper towels. Serve with sauce. Makes 4 servings.

* Or, use canned ham, chicken, turkey, luncheon meat, drained tuna or salmon.

† Or, in large skillet over medium heat, heat oil to 370°F. on deep-fat thermometer.

TACOS WITH LETTUCE, TOMATO, CHEESE

Chicken, Beef or Quick Beef Filling (below)
12 packaged taco shells*
1 small head lettuce, shredded
2 4-ounce packages shredded Cheddar cheese (2 cups)
4 medium tomatoes, chopped
hot pepper sauce

ABOUT 1 HOUR BEFORE SERVING:
Prepare desired Filling; stuff each taco shell with 2 or 3 tablespoons Filling; add lettuce, cheese, tomatoes and a few drops hot pepper sauce to taste. Eat out-of-hand. Makes 8 servings.

CHICKEN FILLING: In 10-inch skillet over medium-high heat, cook *2 medium onions*, chopped, in *¼ cup butter or margarine* until just tender; add *4 cups cooked, finely chopped chicken; 4 medium tomatoes*, chopped; *2 teaspoons salt* and *1 teaspoon pepper;* heat until piping hot.

BEEF FILLING: In 10-inch skillet over medium-high heat, cook *2 pounds ground beef* and *2 medium onions*, chopped, until browned; spoon off fat. Add *4 medium tomatoes*, chopped; *2 teaspoons oregano leaves; 2 teaspoons salt; 1 teaspoon pepper* and *2 garlic cloves*, minced; heat.

QUICK BEEF FILLING: Prepare filling with *2 pounds ground beef* as label directs for *two 1¼-ounce envelopes taco-seasoning mix* and use hot.

* Or use *two 9-ounce packages frozen tortillas*, thawed; two 11-ounce cans tortillas; or 12 refrigerated tortillas. To prepare taco shells: In small skillet over medium heat, in about ½ inch hot salad oil, fry a tortilla until it softens, just a few seconds. With tongs, fold in half, holding open about an inch to leave space for filling later; fry one side crisp; turn and fry other side. Drain on paper towels. Repeat until all tortillas are fried.

MACARONI-STUFFED GREEN PEPPERS

1 8-ounce package elbow macaroni
6 medium green peppers
salt
1 3-ounce package cream cheese, softened
1 cup sour cream
¼ cup milk
2 tablespoons minced onion
½ teaspoon dry mustard
1 8-ounce package frankfurters, sliced
¼ cup shredded Cheddar cheese

ABOUT 1 HOUR BEFORE SERVING:
Preheat oven to 350°F. Cook macaroni as label drects; drain. Cut green peppers in halves lengthwise; remove seeds. In 4-quart saucepan over high heat, in 1 inch boiling, salted water, cook peppers 5 minutes; drain on paper towels.

In large bowl, stir cream cheese with sour cream and milk until smooth; stir in onion, ½ teaspoon salt and mustard; stir in frankfurters and macaroni. Spoon mixture into pepper halves and arrange in large, shallow baking pan.

Cover pan tightly with foil and bake 25 minutes; uncover and sprinkle with cheese; bake about 5 minutes more or until cheese is melted. Makes 6 servings.

TAMALE PIE

1 cup yellow cornmeal
1 teaspoon salt
½ Tamale Meat Mixture (at right)
1 4-ounce package shredded Cheddar cheese (1 cup)
½ cup coarsely broken corn chips

ABOUT 1 HOUR BEFORE SERVING:
Preheat oven to 350°F. In medium bowl, combine cornmeal, 1 cup water and salt. In 1½-quart saucepan over medium heat, into 1 cup boiling water, stir cornmeal mixture; cook until thickened, stirring constantly; spoon into 10″ by 6″ baking dish.

Spread Tamale Meat Mixture evenly over cornmeal mixture; sprinkle with cheese and corn chips. Bake 30 minutes or until hot and bubbly. Let stand 5 minutes before serving. Makes 6 servings.

TAMALE MEAT MIXTURE

3 pounds ground beef
2 6-ounce cans tomato paste
2 1¼- or 1¾-ounce envelopes chili-seasoning mix
½ cup chopped, pitted ripe olives
1 tablespoon sugar

ABOUT 1½ HOURS OR UP TO 3 MONTHS BEFORE SERVING:
In 12-inch skillet over medium heat, cook ground beef until browned. Stir in ⅓ cup water and remaining ingredients; cook, stirring, until mixture is well blended. Spoon off any fat. Divide mixture in half to use in Tamale Pie (at left) and Tamale Pinwheels (below). Cover and refrigerate for use within 3 days or freeze. Spoon mixture into 2 freezer containers; cool in refrigerator, then cover tightly, label and freeze for up to 3 months. Thaw in refrigerator overnight before using.

TAMALE PINWHEELS

2 8-ounce packages refrigerated crescent rolls
½ Tamale Meat Mixture (above)
1 16-ounce can tomatoes

ABOUT 1 HOUR BEFORE SERVING:
Preheat oven to 375°F. Separate one package refrigerated crescent rolls into 4 rectangles. On lightly floured board, place dough rectangles with long sides slightly overlapping. With stockinette-covered rolling pin, roll dough into 14″ by 9″ rectangle.

Spread Tamale Meat Mixture evenly on dough, leaving 1-inch edge on 9″ sides. Starting at a 9″ side, roll up dough jelly-roll fashion. Cut roll into 6 pinwheels; place, cut sides up, in 15½″ by 10½″ jelly-roll pan. Repeat with remaining package of crescent rolls and meat mixture, making 12 pinwheels in all. Bake pinwheels 30 minutes or until pinwheels are golden and meat mixture is hot.

Meanwhile, in 1-quart saucepan over medium heat, heat tomatoes and their liquid until hot. Serve tomatoes as sauce over pinwheels. Makes 6 servings.

TURKEY WITH MELON AND CURRIED GELATIN

3 tablespoons butter or margarine
1 small onion, chopped
2 teaspoons curry powder
1/3 cup sugar
3 tablespoons white wine vinegar
1 1/2 teaspoons salt
1/4 teaspoon ginger
1 chicken-bouillon cube or envelope
2 envelopes unflavored gelatin
1 16-ounce container yogurt (2 cups)
2 medium cantaloupes
lettuce leaves
2 pounds sliced turkey loaf* or assorted cold cuts

EARLY IN DAY OR DAY BEFORE SERVING:
In 1-quart heavy saucepan over medium heat, in hot butter or margarine, cook onion and curry powder until onion is tender, about 5 minutes. Stir in 1 cup water, sugar and next 4 ingredients; sprinkle in gelatin; cook until gelatin is dissolved, stirring.

In covered blender container at medium speed, blend onion mixture and yogurt until smooth, about 1 minute. Pour into 4-cup mold; cover and refrigerate until set.

ABOUT 20 MINUTES BEFORE SERVING:
Cut each cantaloupe in half; discard seeds. With melon baller or metal measuring half-teaspoon, scoop melon into balls; set aside.

Unmold gelatin mixture onto large platter. Place lettuce leaves around gelatin; arrange turkey slices and melon balls on lettuce leaves. Makes 8 servings.

* Or, roast *one 2-pound frozen turkey roast* as label directs; chill and slice.

DELUXE PIZZAS

1 13 3/4-ounce package hot-roll mix
3 cups Freezer Tomato Sauce (page 715), thawed, or 2 10 1/2-ounce cans pizza sauce
1 teaspoon oregano leaves
2 of Toppings (below)
2 8-ounce packages mozzarella cheese, shredded

ABOUT 1 1/2 HOURS BEFORE SERVING:
Preheat oven to 425°F. Grease two 12- to 14-inch pizza pans or two 15 1/2″ by 10 1/2″ jelly-roll pans. Prepare hot-roll mix as label directs but use 1 cup water and omit egg; do not let rise; cut dough in half. With greased hands, pat each dough half into a pizza pan, making a 1/2-inch rim. (Or, if using jelly-roll pans, pat dough into bottom and sides.)

Over each dough half, spread half of sauce; sprinkle with half of oregano. Evenly sprinkle on toppings, using a different topping for each pizza, if you like. Sprinkle each with half of cheese. Refrigerate one pizza.

Bake second pizza on lowest rack in oven for 20 to 25 minutes until crust is browned and crisp. With kitchen shears, cut pizza into servings; serve at once. Meanwhile, bake reserved pizza. Makes 8 servings.

TOPPINGS: Quantities are enough for one pizza: 1 small green pepper, sliced in thin strips; 1 small onion, minced; 1/4 pound mushrooms, sliced; 1/2 cup chopped pitted ripe or stuffed green olives; 1/2 pound pepperoni, thinly sliced; one 2-ounce can anchovy fillets, drained; 1/4 cup chopped canned pimentos; one 8-ounce package brown-and-serve sausages, cut into 1/2-inch chunks; 1/2 pound sweet or hot Italian sausages cooked (see Paella, on page 254) and cut into small pieces; 1/2 pound pork sausage or lean ground beef, cooked in skillet until browned, then drained.

DRIED BEEF AND VEGETABLES

2 4-ounce packages dried beef
1/4 cup butter or margarine
1 medium onion, chopped
1/3 cup all-purpose flour
3 cups milk
1 10-ounce package frozen mixed vegetables, slightly thawed
6 slices toast, halved

ABOUT 30 MINUTES BEFORE SERVING:
Cut dried beef into small pieces. In 2-quart saucepan over medium heat, in hot butter or margarine, cook onion until tender. Stir in flour until smooth. Gradually stir in milk; cook, stirring, until thickened. Add dried beef and vegetables; cook over low heat 10 minutes or until vegetables are fork-tender; serve over toast. Makes 4 servings.

ROAST-BEEF HASH

2 cups diced or ground, cooked roast beef, ham, veal, pork, lamb, chicken or turkey
3 cups diced, cold cooked potatoes
½ cup minced onion
½ teaspoon salt
⅛ teaspoon pepper
⅓ to ½ cup milk or half-and-half
4 tablespoons butter or margarine
catchup, chili sauce or horseradish

ABOUT 40 MINUTES BEFORE SERVING:
In large bowl, combine first 6 ingredients. In 12-inch skillet (preferably with non-stick finish) over medium heat, in hot butter or margarine, cook mixture 20 minutes or until crusty and brown, stirring occasionally. Serve hash with catchup. Makes 4 servings.

OTHER SEASONINGS: To mixture, add 1 tablespoon minced parsley, green pepper, horseradish or sweet pickle relish.

SWEET-AND-SOUR PORK WITH PICKLED VEGETABLES

3 medium turnips, cut into 1-inch chunks
2 celery stalks, cut into 1-inch pieces
2 medium carrots, cut into ½-inch pieces
1 medium green pepper, cut into strips
1 medium cucumber, cubed
1¼ cups cider vinegar
salt
2 pounds pork stew meat, cut into 1-inch chunks
3 tablespoons cornstarch
3 tablespoons soy sauce
1½ teaspoons ground ginger
1 garlic clove, minced
3 tablespoons salad oil
¾ cup packed light brown sugar

ABOUT 1½ HOURS BEFORE SERVING:
For pickled vegetables, in medium bowl, combine first 5 ingredients with ¾ cup vinegar, ½ cup water and 1 tablespoon salt; cover and refrigerate.

In medium bowl, toss pork stew meat, cornstarch, soy sauce, ginger, garlic and 1 teaspoon salt until meat is well coated. In 12-inch skillet over medium heat, in hot oil, cook meat until well browned. Stir in brown sugar, ½ cup water and remaining ½ cup vinegar. Reduce heat to low; cover and cook 45 minutes or until meat is fork-tender and mixture is thickened, stirring occasionally.

Drain vegetables well; arrange on platter. Spoon hot pork mixture over vegetables. Makes 8 servings.

MEAT-AND-GRUYERE-STUFFED SQUASH

¾ pound lean ground beef
¾ cup minced onion
salt
pepper
1 6-ounce can tomato paste
1 tablespoon sugar
¼ pound Gruyère cheese, chopped
4 medium yellow straightneck squashes

ABOUT 1 HOUR BEFORE SERVING:
In 8-inch skillet over medium-high heat, cook ground beef, onion, 1 teaspoon salt and ¼ teaspoon pepper until meat is well browned, stirring occasionally. Stir in tomato paste, sugar and ¼ cup water. Remove from heat; stir in cheese.

Meanwhile, preheat oven to 375°F. Cut squashes into lengthwise halves; with tip of teaspoon, scoop out and discard seeds. Place squash halves, cut sides up, in 13″ by 9″ baking dish; sprinkle with ½ teaspoon salt and ⅛ teaspoon pepper. Spoon meat mixture into centers of squash halves; cover tightly with foil and bake 30 minutes or until squash is tender-crisp and meat is heated through. Makes 4 servings.

SAUSAGE-STUFFED ACORN SQUASH

1 pound pork-sausage meat
3 medium acorn squashes
¼ cup butter or margarine, melted
salt
1 10-ounce package frozen mixed vegetables, partially thawed
1 cup cubed American cheese (about ¼ pound)

ABOUT 2 HOURS BEFORE SERVING:
Preheat oven to 350°F. In 10-inch skillet over medium-high heat, cook sausage until

browned, about 10 minutes, breaking it apart with fork and spooning off fat; drain.

Meanwhile, cut squashes lengthwise into halves and remove seeds; place, cut sides up, in roasting pan. Brush inside of squash halves with some butter; sprinkle with salt.

In medium bowl, combine sausage, mixed vegetables, cheese and ½ teaspoon salt; spoon into squash halves and brush mixture with remaining butter. Cover pan tightly with foil or lid and bake 1½ hours or until squash is fork-tender. Makes 6 servings.

SAUSAGE-STUFFED EGGPLANT

2 medium eggplants
salad oil
salt
1 pound sweet Italian sausage links
1 4-ounce can mushroom stems and pieces, drained
1 cup sliced carrots, cooked
1 1¼- or 1½-ounce envelope cheese-sauce mix
½ cup milk

ABOUT 1 HOUR BEFORE SERVING:

1. Preheat oven to 375°F. Grease 12″ by 8″ baking dish. Cut each eggplant in half lengthwise. With tip of spoon or small knife, remove pulp from each eggplant half, leaving shell about ½ inch thick; reserve pulp. Brush inside of each shell with salad oil; sprinkle with salt. Place shells in baking dish; cover with foil. Bake 25 to 30 minutes until shells are tender.
2. Meanwhile, in covered, 10-inch skillet over medium heat, in ¼ cup water, cook sausage 5 minutes. Uncover and cook until well browned, about 15 minutes; drain on paper towels, reserving drippings in skillet. Cut links into 1-inch chunks.
3. Cut reserved eggplant pulp into ¾-inch chunks; add to drippings in skillet and cook until tender, adding salad oil if necessary. Return sausage to skillet with mushrooms, carrots, cheese-sauce mix and milk; cook, stirring constantly, until sauce is thickened.
4. Remove eggplant shells from oven; fill with sausage mixture; return to oven and bake, uncovered, 15 minutes to blend flavors. Makes 4 servings.

SPAGHETTI WITH CHICKEN-LIVER SAUCE

2 tablespoons salad oil
1½ pounds chicken livers
1 29-ounce jar meatless spaghetti sauce
¼ cup white table wine (optional)
1 teaspoon basil
1 teaspoon salt
1 teaspoon sugar
1 16-ounce package spaghetti, cooked
grated Parmesan cheese

ABOUT 45 MINUTES BEFORE SERVING:

In 12-inch skillet over medium heat, in hot salad oil, cook chicken livers until lightly browned, about 10 minutes, stirring occasionally. Stir in spaghetti sauce, wine, basil, salt and sugar; heat to boiling. Reduce heat to low; cover and simmer 20 minutes.

Serve chicken livers and sauce over spaghetti. Pass cheese to sprinkle on top. Makes 6 servings.

SCANDINAVIAN FISH DINNER

4 medium potatoes, quartered
1 16-ounce package frozen sole fillets, thawed
1 17-ounce can peas
¼ cup butter or margarine
½ cup all-purpose flour
2 teaspoons dill weed
2 teaspoons salt
1½ cups milk

ABOUT 1 HOUR BFEORE SERVING:

In 2-quart saucepan over medium heat, in 1 inch boiling water, heat potatoes to boiling; cover and cook 20 minutes or until just fork-tender; drain.

Meanwhile, pat fillets dry on paper towels. Drain peas, reserving ½ cup liquid. In 3-quart heavy saucepan over medium heat, into hot butter or margarine, stir flour, dill weed and salt until blended. Gradually stir in milk and reserved liquid from peas and cook, stirring constantly, until mixture is thickened. Add fish, potatoes and peas to mixture; cover and cook until fish flakes easily when tested with fork, about 10 minutes, gently stirring occasionally. Makes 4 servings.

CREAMED CHICKEN AND OYSTERS

2 8-ounce packages refrigerated buttermilk biscuits
¼ cup butter or margarine
¼ cup all-purpose flour
2 cups milk
3 cups cut-up cooked chicken or turkey
2 8-ounce cans oysters, drained
1 tablespoon cooking sherry
1 teaspoon salt
¼ teaspoon pepper
parsley sprigs for garnish

ABOUT 35 MINUTES BEFORE SERVING:
Preheat oven as biscuit-package label directs. In 10-inch skillet over medium heat, into hot butter or margarine, stir flour until blended. Gradually stir in milk and cook, stirring constantly, until mixture is thickened. Stir in chicken, oysters, sherry, salt and pepper; cook 10 minutes.

Meanwhile, bake biscuits as label directs. Serve chicken mixture over hot biscuits; garnish with parsley. Makes 6 to 8 servings.

CIOPPINO

2 tablespoons olive or salad oil
1 large onion, chopped
1 medium green pepper, chopped
1 garlic clove, minced
1 28-ounce can tomatoes
½ cup white table wine
¼ cup chopped parsley
1 tablespoon salt
¼ teaspoon basil
1½ pounds Dungeness crab (or 2 12-ounce packages frozen Alaska King crab split legs, thawed and cut into chunks)
1½ dozen hard-shelled clams (littlenecks)
1½ pounds striped-bass fillets, cut into serving pieces
1 pound shelled, deveined shrimp

ABOUT 45 MINUTES BEFORE SERVING:
In Dutch oven over medium heat, in hot oil, cook onion, green pepper and garlic until tender, about 5 minutes, stirring occasionally. Add tomatoes and their liquid, wine, parsley, salt and basil; heat to boiling. Reduce heat to low; cover and simmer 15 minutes.

Increase heat to medium-high; add crab* and clams; cook 10 minutes, stirring occasionally. Add fillet pieces and shrimp and continue cooking 5 minutes more or until fish flakes easily when tested with fork and shrimp turn pink. Serve immediately in soup bowls. Makes 6 to 8 servings.

* If using frozen Alaska King crab split legs, add during last 2 minutes of cooking time to heat through.

SPAGHETTI AND MEATBALLS

1½ pounds lean ground beef
1 cup fresh bread crumbs
1 egg
2 teaspoons salt
½ teaspoon oregano leaves
⅛ teaspoon pepper
2 tablespoons salad oil
2 pints Freezer Tomato Sauce (page 715), thawed (4 cups), or 2 16-ounce cans spaghetti sauce
1 16-ounce package spaghetti, cooked
grated Parmesan cheese

ABOUT 1 HOUR BEFORE SERVING:
In large bowl, mix first 6 ingredients; shape into 1-inch balls. In 12-inch skillet over medium-high heat, in hot salad oil, cook meatballs until browned on all sides. Spoon drippings from skillet.

Add tomato sauce; heat to boiling. Reduce heat to low; cover skillet and simmer 10 minutes. Serve meatballs and sauce over spaghetti. Pass cheese to sprinkle on top. Makes 6 servings.

FISH AND CHIPS, AMERICAN STYLE

2 8- or 9-ounce packages frozen fish sticks
1 20-ounce package frozen French-fried shoestring potatoes
malt or cider vinegar or catchup

ABOUT 30 MINUTES BEFORE SERVING:
Preheat oven to 450°F. Arrange fish sticks and potatoes in single layer on 2 cookie sheets; bake 15 to 20 minutes or until golden. To serve, sprinkle with malt vinegar or dunk in catchup. Eat out of hand. Makes 4 servings.

Eggs

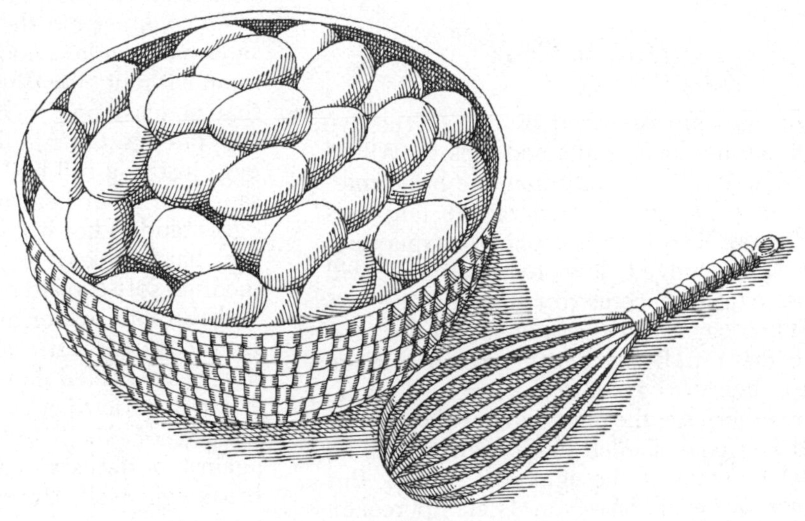

The quality of eggs depends on factors ranging from grade to storage conditions.

How to Buy

Eggs are sold by grade and by size. The grades AA and A are based on appearance; they have nothing to do with nutrition or size. Grade AA eggs, which cost slightly more, have firm, high yolks and thick whites; they spread little and are ideal for frying, poaching or cooking in the shell. Grade A eggs spread slightly more than AA and have slightly thinner whites; they are good for use in recipes.

The sizes Jumbo, Extra Large, Large, Medium or Small are in accordance with minimum weights per dozen and are set by government standard. Size does not affect nutrition or grade, but it does affect price. At Good Housekeeping, we use Large eggs for developing all our recipes.

Contrary to popular belief, the color of the shell has no effect on the quality of the egg. Color varies simply because different breeds of hens lay different color eggs.

Nor does the color of the yolk affect the quality. Yolks range in color from pale cream to yellow-orange, depending upon the diet of the hen. Blood spots, caused by the rupture of a blood vessel during the formation of the egg, have no effect on quality either; remove the spot with a spoon before cooking, if you like. The stringy white pieces in egg whites are protein fibers and anchor the yolk to the white. They are wholesome, normal parts of the egg; they tend to disappear as eggs lose freshness.

How to Store

Keep eggs in the refrigerator with large ends up. This keeps the yolks centered. Eggs sometimes absorb odors from other foods, so it is important that strong-smelling foods be kept covered. Under refrigeration, eggs keep up to one month.

If you're in doubt about an egg's freshness, break it into a saucer and sniff—a "bad" egg will have a definite off-odor or "chemical" smell. A super-fresh egg has a cloudy white and a high-standing yolk. Older eggs have less cloudy whites and flatter yolks. Leftover whites and yolks should be stored in small, tightly covered containers in the refrigerator; they keep up to one week. For freezing eggs, see page 725.

How to Cook

Most eggs are prepared by one of the five cooking methods explained below. All of these methods depend upon one basic rule: *Always cook eggs at moderate to low temperatures.* Too high a cooking temperature (or a prolonged low temperature) will cause eggs to become dry and rubbery.

When eggs are to be added to a hot mixture, first rapidly stir a little mixture into the eggs, then stir eggs into the rest of the mixture; otherwise, the eggs will curdle.

If you cook shelled eggs in an aluminum pan, the color of the eggs will darken; this is not harmful, however. Glass, porcelain enamel, stainless steel or any metal cookware with a nonstick finish are all suitable for preparing eggs and egg recipes.

Hard- or soft-cooked eggs: Eggs in the shell must be cooked at the right temperature for the right length of time. If boiled or cooked too long, the yolks will become hard and turn an unattractive greenish-gray. It is best to buy eggs for hard-cooking several days ahead, since storage allows the air space at the large end of the egg to expand and makes later peeling easier. If you like, before cooking, puncture eggs with a pin at center of large end, penetrating only the shell, to let air escape and help prevent shell from cracking during cooking.

To cook eggs in the shell: Place eggs in a saucepan wide enough to accommodate them without crowding, and deep enough so that at least one inch of water will cover tops of eggs. Over high heat, heat water and eggs just to a full boil. Immediately remove saucepan from heat and cover tightly. Let eggs stand in hot water, covered, 15 minutes for hard-cooked eggs, one minute for medium soft-cooked eggs. Pour off hot water and run cold water over eggs to stop them from cooking and also make peeling easier if eggs are peeled immediately.

To shell hard-cooked eggs, crack entire surface of shell by gently tapping egg against a flat surface, taking care not to break egg itself. Under cold running water, peel egg, starting at large end; the air space in the large end makes starting to peel easier.

Scrambled eggs: When cooked at low temperature in a lightly greased skillet, scrambled eggs won't stick. A little milk, cream or water mixed with eggs will slow the cooking and give a fluffier, more tender product.

To scramble eggs: For each serving, in bowl, beat 2 eggs slightly with 2 table-

WAYS TO CUT HARD-COOKED EGGS

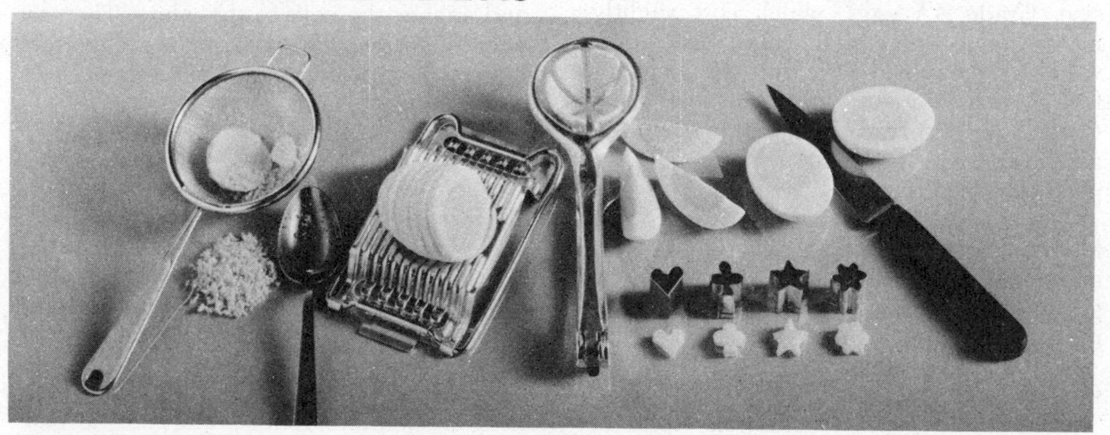

Shown here: An assortment of simple-to-use kitchen equipment that brings out the versatility of hard-cooked eggs. From left to right: Fine strainer and spoon for crumbled-egg-yolk garnish; egg slicer; egg wedger; tiny canapé cutters; small well-sharpened knife.

spoons milk or half-and-half; add salt and pepper to taste. Into medium skillet over medium heat, in 1 tablespoon butter or margarine, pour all egg mixture. As mixture begins to set, with spatula, stir cooked portion slightly so thin, uncooked part flows to bottom. Avoid constant stirring. Cook until eggs are slightly set, about 3 to 5 minutes. Serve immediately.

Fried eggs: For tender fried eggs, use moderate cooking temperature, as short a cooking time as possible to produce desired firmness, and a minimum of fat; too much fat makes fried eggs greasy.

To fry eggs: In skillet over medium heat, melt butter, margarine or bacon drippings (use 1 tablespoon of fat for a small skillet, up to 3 tablespoons for a medium skillet). One at a time, break eggs into a saucer or cup, then slip them into the skillet. Reduce heat to low. Cook eggs, basting yolks with hot butter or margarine from skillet, or turning eggs with pancake turner to cook on other side, until yolk is of desired firmness, about 10 minutes. Season and serve.

Poached eggs: Poaching means cooking shelled eggs in simmering liquid such as water, milk, consommé or soup. Eggs should be as fresh as possible and cold. Both conditions help keep egg white from spreading and produce a more compact poached egg.

To poach eggs: In lightly greased saucepan or skillet over high heat, heat 1½ inches water or other liquid to boiling. Reduce heat to low. One at a time, break eggs into saucer and slip into simmering liquid. Cook eggs 3 to 5 minutes until of desired firmness. When done, carefully remove eggs from liquid with a slotted spoon. Drain each egg (still held in spoon) over paper towels; serve.

Baked eggs: Eggs are often baked with other ingredients and may be found in a variety of recipes. Generally, the recommended oven temperature is 325°F., except when other ingredients are added or when egg whites are whipped and baked, as for meringue.

To bake eggs: Preheat oven to 325°F. For each serving, generously butter an 8-ounce ovenproof baking dish or ramekin; break 2 eggs into dish and sprinkle with salt and pepper. Bake 15 to 20 minutes until of desired doneness. Serve in baking dish.

Tips for Separating and Beating

To separate eggs, break shell at center with a quick sharp tap on the edge of a bowl. Press thumb tips into crack and pull shell apart, retaining yolk in one half and letting white pour out of other half into bowl. Pour yolk from one half to the other so that remaining white pours off. Since egg whites beat to a fuller volume when at room temperature, let egg whites stand out about 45 minutes before using.

If even a speck of yolk gets into the white, remove it with a spoon or piece of paper towel; whites do not beat to their fullest volume when any fat—yolk, butter or margarine, salad oil, etc.—is present. Fat often adheres to plastic bowls or containers.

Depending upon the recipe, egg whites are beaten to different stages: *Foamy or frothy*—air cells are large and the foam is unstable; it will separate readily into liquid. *Soft peaks*—air cells are smaller and more numerous; foam is white, shiny and moist; soft rounded peaks will form when beaters are raised. *Stiff peaks*—air cells are very small, numerous and very even in size; foam is very white, moist and glossy; pointed stiff peaks will form when the beaters are raised. When overbeaten, egg whites become dry, the air cells collapse and liquid settles out.

For tips on folding mixtures into whites, see Chiffon, Angel and Sponge Cakes, page 526.

Leftover Yolks and Whites

Use raw egg yolks in breads, cakes or other baked goods; scrambled eggs; eggnogs.

To hard-cook yolks: Place yolks in strainer and lower into small saucepan with enough simmering water to cover; simmer a few minutes until firm. Chop or mince and use within 5 days in sandwich fillings, tossed salads, salad dressings, or as garnishes.

Use raw egg whites in cakes, candies, meringues, glazes, frostings, chiffon pies.

To hard-cook whites: Bake in well-greased, shallow baking dish in 325°F. oven for 10 minutes or until firm. Chop and use in salads or as garnish for vegetables.

Main Dishes

PARTY SCRAMBLED EGGS

¼ cup butter or margarine
4 white bread slices, cubed
6 eggs
1 cup milk
1 cup sour cream
1 teaspoon salt

ABOUT 15 MINUTES BEFORE SERVING:
In medium skillet over low heat, in hot butter or margarine, fry bread cubes until golden, stirring occasionally. In medium bowl, with hand beater or spoon, beat eggs, milk, sour cream and salt until well blended; pour over bread cubes and cook over low heat, stirring occasionally, until eggs are nearly set. Serve hot. Makes 3 or 4 servings.

TOMATO-SAUSAGE SCRAMBLE

1 8-ounce package brown-and-serve sausages,* cut in ½-inch chunks
3 tablespoons butter or margarine
3 tablespoons all-purpose flour
1 cup milk
1 cup half-and-half
8 eggs
1 teaspoon salt
dash pepper
1 small tomato, cut in large chunks
¼ cup shredded Cheddar cheese

ABOUT 30 MINUTES BEFORE SERVING:
Cook sausage as label directs; drain any excess fat and keep sausage warm.

In ovenproof medium skillet over low heat, in hot butter or margarine, stir flour until smooth; gradually stir in milk and cook, stirring constantly, until mixture is thickened. In medium bowl, with fork or wire whisk, beat half-and-half, eggs, salt and pepper until blended; stir into sauce. Cook, stirring constantly, until eggs are slightly set.

Meanwhile, preheat broiler if manufacturer directs. Sprinkle sausage, tomato chunks and cheese over eggs; broil to melt cheese. Makes 8 servings.

* Or, use ½ 16-ounce package pork-sausage links. In covered skillet over medium heat, cook with 3 tablespoons water for 5 minutes. Remove cover; continue cooking until browned, turning occasionally.

SCRAMBLED-EGG VARIATIONS

When scrambled eggs are partially cooked, stir in a little of one of these:

Chopped parsley or chives
Cut-up dried beef
Minced cooked ham or chicken livers
Cooked sliced mushrooms
Minced cooked shrimp or crab
Chopped tomatoes
Shredded Cheddar or Swiss cheese

COTTAGE-CHEESE SCRAMBLED EGGS

12 eggs
1 12-ounce container dry cottage cheese*
½ teaspoon salt
⅛ teaspoon hot pepper sauce
6 tablespoons butter or margarine

UP TO 1 HOUR BEFORE SERVING:
In large bowl, with mixer at low speed, beat eggs, cheese, salt and hot pepper sauce until blended. In medium skillet over low heat, in hot butter or margarine, cook egg mixture until just set, stirring occasionally. If you like, pour into chafing dish, cover and keep warm for serving. Makes 6 servings.

* Or 1½ cups large-curd cottage cheese.

FRENCH OMELET

6 eggs
½ teaspoon salt
dash pepper
3 tablespoons butter or margarine

ABOUT 30 MINUTES BEFORE SERVING:
In small bowl, with wire whisk or hand beater, beat eggs, salt, pepper and 2 tablespoons cold water. In 10-inch skillet over medium-low heat, melt butter or margarine, tilting skillet to grease sides. Pour eggs into skillet; let set around sides.

With a metal spatula, gently lift edges as they set, tilting skillet to allow uncooked portion to run under omelet. Shake skillet occasionally to keep omelet moving freely in pan. When omelet is set but still moist on the surface, increase heat slightly to brown bottom of omelet.

Tilt skillet and, with spatula, fold omelet in half; slide onto heated platter. Makes 2 main-dish servings.

PUFFY OMELET

4 eggs, separated
¼ teaspoon cream of tartar
¼ teaspoon salt
2 tablespoons butter or margarine

ABOUT 30 MINUTES BEFORE SERVING:
Preheat oven to 350°F. In large bowl, with mixer at high speed, beat egg whites until foamy; add cream of tartar and continue beating just until stiff peaks form. In small bowl, with mixer at high speed, beat egg yolks with ¼ cup cold water and salt until very light and fluffy; carefully fold yolk mixture into beaten whites.

In ovenproof 10-inch skillet over low heat, in hot butter or margarine, cook egg mixture 3 minutes or until puffy and golden on under side when lifted with a spatula. Then bake 10 minutes or until golden and top springs back when tapped with finger.

Run a spatula around sides to loosen omelet. Make a slit part way across center of omelet; tip skillet and, with pancake turner, fold omelet in half; slide onto heated platter. Makes 2 main-dish servings.

PUFFY- OR FRENCH-OMELET FILLINGS

Immediately after sliding omelet onto platter, spoon one of these between halves:

SHRIMP FILLING: About 15 minutes before serving: In medium saucepan, prepare *one ¾- or 1½-ounce package white sauce mix* as label directs; when smooth, stir in *1 cup diced cooked shrimp, 2 teaspoons lemon juice, 1 tablespoon chopped parsley* and *⅛ teaspoon Worcestershire;* heat. Fills 2 omelets (4 servings).

CREOLE SAUCE FILLING: About 25 minutes before serving: In medium skillet over medium-high heat, heat *2 tablespoons salad oil;* add *¾ cup chopped green pepper, ¾ cup chopped celery and ¼ cup chopped onion* and cook until tender, about 5 minutes, stirring occasionally. Add *4 medium tomatoes,* chopped, *½ teaspoon oregano leaves* and *½ teaspoon salt* and simmer, covered, 10 minutes, stirring occasionally. Fills 2 omelets (4 servings).

CHEESE FILLING: Before folding omelet, sprinkle with *⅓ cup shredded Cheddar cheese.* Fills 1 omelet (2 servings).

COOKED HAM FILLING: About 15 minutes before serving: In medium skillet over medium heat, heat *2 tablespoons butter or margarine, 1½ cups cooked ham,* cut in thin strips, until hot; sprinkle with *¼ teaspoon seasoned pepper.* Fills 2 omelets (4 servings).

CHICKEN LIVER FILLING: About 15 minutes before serving: Cut *½ pound chicken livers* into pieces. In medium skillet over medium heat, heat *2 tablespoons butter or margarine;* add chicken livers and *2 tablespoons chopped green onion* and cook until tender, about 5 minutes. Stir in *2 tablespoons all-purpose flour* until blended. Add *½ cup drained canned sliced mushrooms, ⅓ cup water, ½ teaspoon salt, dash pepper* and cook until thickened, stirring occasionally. Fills 2 omelets (4 servings).

ASPARAGUS FILLING: About 15 minutes before serving: Cook *one 10-ounce package frozen cut-up asparagus* as label directs; drain. In medium saucepan over low heat, heat *1 tablespoon butter or margarine;* blend in *2 teaspoons all-purpose flour;* slowly stir in *½ cup milk, ½ teaspoon seasoned salt* and *dash pepper* and cook, stirring, until thickened. Stir in asparagus. Fills 2 omelets (4 servings).

SPECIAL ASPARAGUS OMELET

ABOUT 30 MINUTES BEFORE SERVING:
Prepare French Omelet (opposite). Spoon *2 cups cooked cut-up asparagus* into cooked omelet and spoon Hollandaise Sauce (page 282) on top. Makes 2 main-dish servings.

SHIRRED EGGS

Bake eggs as directed on page 271 and serve garnished with chopped chives or watercress.

BACONY-SHIRRED EGGS: Fry bacon slices until light brown but still limp; arrange around inside of baking dish; add eggs and bake.

CHEESE-SHIRRED EGGS: Sprinkle buttered crumbs in bottom of each baking dish; top with layer of pasteurized process cheese slices; add eggs and bake.

EGGS BENEDICT

ABOUT 20 MINUTES BEFORE SERVING:
Prepare Hollandaise Sauce (page 282) and poach *4 eggs* (page 271) until of desired doneness.

Meanwhile, preheat broiler if manufacturer directs. Split *4 English muffins;* spread each half lightly with *butter or margarine.* Place, buttered side up, on broiler pan with *4 slices Canadian bacon* or cooked ham alongside. Broil until muffin halves are toasted and Canadian bacon or ham is heated through.

For each serving, place a Canadian-bacon slice on a muffin half; top bacon with poached egg. Generously spoon Hollandaise Sauce over egg. Serve with remaining muffin half. Makes 4 servings.

POACHED EGGS IN TOMATO SAUCE

2 tablespoons butter or margarine
1 large green pepper, cut in thin strips
1 28-ounce can tomatoes
1½ teaspoons salt
dash pepper
8 eggs

ABOUT 25 MINUTES BEFORE SERVING:
In large skillet over medium-high heat, in hot butter or margarine, cook green pepper 5 minutes. Reduce heat to low and add tomatoes, salt and pepper. Cook 5 more minutes or until green pepper is tender-crisp, stirring occasionally.

One at a time, break eggs into a saucer, and slip into simmering liquid. Cover and cook gently about 5 minutes or until of desired doneness. Spoon vegetables and liquid over eggs. Makes 4 servings.

POACHED EGG VARIATIONS

Serve poached eggs over one of these:

Toasted English muffins
Buttered spinach
Toasted corn bread or muffins
Asparagus spears on toast
Breaded veal cutlets
Hot canned corned-beef hash
Buttered broccoli
Split frankfurters on toast

BAKED-EGGS-AND-SPINACH CASSEROLE

2 10-ounce packages frozen chopped spinach, thawed and drained
salt
3 tablespoons butter or margarine
3 tablespoons all-purpose flour
1 cup milk
1 4-ounce package shredded Cheddar cheese (1 cup)
6 eggs
dash pepper
toast points

ABOUT 1 HOUR BEFORE SERVING:
Preheat oven to 325°F. In 8″ by 8″ baking dish, toss spinach with ½ teaspoon salt and spread in an even layer; with spoon, make 6 indentations in spinach.

In small saucepan over low heat, in melted butter or margarine, stir in flour until smooth; gradually stir in milk and cook, stirring constantly, until sauce is thickened; stir in cheese and heat just until cheese is melted.

Break one egg into each indentation; sprinkle eggs with pepper and ¼ teaspoon salt. Pour sauce over eggs. Bake 30 to 35 minutes until eggs are of desired doneness. Serve on toast points. Makes 4 servings.

EASY CHEESE SOUFFLE

1 10¾-ounce can condensed Cheddar-cheese soup
2 tablespoons chopped parsley
½ teaspoon thyme leaves
6 eggs, separated

ABOUT 1½ HOURS BEFORE SERVING:
Preheat oven to 325°F. Grease bottom of 2-quart soufflé dish or casserole. In medium bowl, with wire whisk or fork, stir together undiluted cheese soup, parsley and thyme leaves until smooth.

In small bowl, with mixer at high speed, beat egg yolks until thick and lemon colored; fold into soup mixture. Wash beaters. In large bowl, with mixer at high speed, beat egg whites just until stiff peaks form. With rubber spatula, gently fold soup mixture into egg whites; pour into soufflé dish. Bake 1 hour and 10 minutes or until puffy and golden brown. Makes 6 servings.

CLASSIC HERBED-CHEESE SOUFFLE

¼ cup butter or margarine
¼ cup all-purpose flour
1 teaspoon salt
dash cayenne pepper
1½ cups milk
2 4-ounce packages shredded Cheddar cheese (2 cups)
6 eggs, separated
2 tablespoons chopped parsley
½ teaspoon thyme leaves

ABOUT 1¼ HOURS BEFORE SERVING:
Preheat oven to 325°F. In medium saucepan over medium heat, into hot butter or margarine, stir flour, salt and pepper until smooth. Slowly stir in milk; cook, stirring occasionally, until sauce is smooth and thickened. Add cheese; heat, stirring, just until cheese melts. Remove from heat.

In small bowl, with fork, beat egg yolks slightly. Into egg yolks, beat small amount of the hot sauce; slowly pour egg mixture into sauce, stirring rapidly to prevent lumping. Stir in parsley and thyme. Set aside.

In large bowl, with mixer at high speed, beat egg whites just until stiff peaks form. With rubber spatula, gently fold cheese mixture into egg whites; pour into 2-quart soufflé dish or casserole. With spoon, make 1-inch-deep circle in top of cheese mixture, 1 inch from side of dish. Bake soufflé for 1 hour or until puffy and golden brown. Serve immediately. Makes 6 servings.

SPINACH SOUFFLE: Cook *two 10-ounce packages frozen chopped spinach* as labels direct but add *⅓ cup chopped onion;* drain. Prepare above recipe but omit cheese, parsley, thyme; stir spinach into sauce.

CHICKEN SOUFFLE

¼ cup butter or margarine
½ cup chopped mushrooms
3 tablespoons chopped onion
2 tablespoons all-purpose flour
1 cup milk
1 chicken-bouillon cube
5 eggs, separated
2 cups finely chopped, cooked chicken
½ teaspoon salt

ABOUT 1½ HOURS BEFORE SERVING:
Preheat oven to 325°F. Grease bottom only of 2-quart soufflé dish or casserole. In medium saucepan over medium heat, in hot butter or margarine, cook mushrooms and onion until tender. Stir in flour until smooth. Reduce heat to low; add milk and bouillon cube; cook, stirring, until sauce is thickened.

In small bowl, with fork, beat egg yolks slightly; beat in small amount of the hot sauce; slowly pour egg mixture back into sauce, stirring rapidly to prevent lumping. Cook, stirring, until thickened. (Do not boil.) Remove from heat and stir in chicken.

In small bowl, with mixer at high speed, beat egg whites and salt just until stiff peaks form. Gently fold egg whites into mixture. Pour into soufflé dish. Bake 1 hour or until golden brown. Makes 6 servings.

POTATO SOUFFLE

2½ cups mashed, cooked potatoes
4 eggs, separated
½ cup grated Parmesan cheese
¼ teaspoon salt
¼ teaspoon cream of tartar
1 10½-ounce can brown gravy with onions

ABOUT 1½ HOURS BEFORE SERVING:
Preheat oven to 325°F. Grease bottom of 2-quart soufflé dish. In large bowl, with fork or wire whisk, beat mashed potatoes until smooth. Beat in egg yolks, one at a time; stir in cheese; set aside.

In small bowl, with mixer at high speed, beat egg whites, salt and cream of tartar until soft peaks form; continue beating just until stiff peaks form. Gently fold egg whites into potato mixture. Pour into soufflé dish and bake 1 hour or until puffy and golden brown.

Meanwhile, in small saucepan over medium heat, heat gravy. Serve soufflé immediately with hot gravy. Makes 6 servings.

DINNER EGGS ON TOAST

ABOUT 30 MINUTES BEFORE SERVING:
In medium saucepan, cook *one 10-ounce package frozen green beans* as label directs; drain. Add *one 10½-ounce can condensed cream-of-mushroom soup* and *1 cup milk;* cook over medium heat until hot, stirring often. Stir in *8 hard-cooked eggs,* quartered, and heat. Serve over *4 toast slices.* Makes 4 servings.

CREAMED EGGS AND MUSHROOMS

2 tablespoons salad oil
2 tablespoons chopped parsley
1 tablespoon chopped onion
1 pound mushrooms, sliced
1 tablespoon all-purpose flour
1 teaspoon salt
dash pepper
½ cup dry white wine or chicken broth
8 hard-cooked eggs, sliced

ABOUT 1 HOUR BEFORE SERVING:
In large skillet over medium heat, in hot salad oil, cook parsley and onion until onion is tender. Add mushrooms; cook, covered, over low heat for 10 minutes. Stir in flour, salt and pepper until smooth; stir in wine; simmer, covered, for 5 minutes. Add eggs and continue simmering, covered, until eggs are heated through, stirring occasionally. Makes 4 or 5 servings.

GOLDEN EGGS OLE

1 cup yellow cornmeal
1 teaspoon salt
6 hard-cooked eggs
2 tablespoons butter or margarine, melted
1 pound ground beef
1 1½-ounce envelope Sloppy Joe-seasoning mix
1 8-ounce can tomato sauce

ABOUT 1½ HOURS BEFORE SERVING:
In medium saucepan over medium heat, heat 2 cups water, cornmeal and salt to boiling; cook, stirring constantly, until very thick, about 6 minutes. Remove from heat and cool completely.

Preheat oven to 350°F. Divide cornmeal mixture into 6 equal portions. Shape each portion to cover 1 shelled cooked egg completely. Repeat with all eggs and place on cookie sheet. Brush each egg with melted butter or margarine and bake 20 minutes or until heated through.

Meanwhile, in medium cook-and-serve skillet over medium-high heat, brown ground beef; add Sloppy Joe mix, tomato sauce and 1¼ cups water. Simmer 10 minutes, covered; remove from heat. Halve eggs and arrange, cut side up, in sauce. Serve from skillet. Makes 6 servings.

CREOLE EGGS

¼ cup butter or margarine
1 large onion, chopped
1 medium green pepper, chopped
1 garlic clove, minced
1 teaspoon salt
⅛ teaspoon rosemary
⅛ teaspoon paprika
1 16- or 17-ounce can tomatoes
8 hard-cooked eggs, halved
2 cups hot cooked rice

ABOUT 45 MINUTES BEFORE SERVING:
In medium skillet over medium heat, in melted butter or margarine, cook onion and next 5 ingredients about 5 minutes. Add tomatoes and eggs; simmer, covered, 10 minutes. Serve over rice. Makes 4 servings.

EGGBURGERS

1 pound ground beef
1 teaspoon salt
dash pepper
4 hamburger buns
butter or margarine
4 eggs
Accompaniments (below)

ABOUT 30 MINUTES BEFORE SERVING:
Preheat broiler if manufacturer directs. Shape ground beef into 4 thin patties; sprinkle with salt and pepper; place patties on broiler pan. Broil 6 minutes on each side for medium or until of desired doneness. Meanwhile, split hamburger buns; spread with butter or margarine; toast with patties during last minute or two of cooking time.

While patties are broiling, fry eggs (page 271). Serve eggs on patties in buns. Serve with Accompaniments. Makes 4 servings.

ACCOMPANIMENTS: Anchovy fillets, chopped tomato, green-pepper chunks, sliced mushrooms, chopped onions, ripe-olive slices, Thousand Island dressing, blue-cheese dressing, shredded lettuce.

FRIED-EGG VARIATIONS

When fried eggs are partially cooked, sprinkle with one of these: chopped chives, chopped mushrooms, grated Parmesan cheese, cornflake crumbs.

EGGS DIVAN

6 hard-cooked eggs
$\frac{1}{4}$ cup mayonnaise
1 tablespoon instant minced onion
$\frac{1}{4}$ teaspoon salt
1 10-ounce package frozen broccoli spears
1 8-ounce jar pasteurized process cheese spread

ABOUT 1 HOUR BEFORE SERVING:
Halve eggs crosswise and remove yolks. In small bowl, combine yolks, mayonnaise, onion and salt; use to fill egg halves.

Meanwhile, preheat oven to 400°F. Cook broccoli as label directs; drain. In 10″ by 6″ baking dish, arrange broccoli spears in 3 separate piles; place stuffed eggs in between. Spoon cheese spread generously over broccoli. Bake 10 minutes or until cheese spread is bubbly. Makes 3 servings.

BEEF-EGG FOO YONG

salad oil
$\frac{1}{2}$ pound ground beef
6 eggs
$\frac{1}{2}$ teaspoon salt
$\frac{1}{4}$ teaspoon pepper
1 10-ounce package frozen mixed vegetables, slightly thawed
2 tablespoons cornstarch
2 tablespoons soy sauce

ABOUT 1 HOUR BEFORE SERVING:
In medium skillet over medium-high heat, in 2 tablespoons hot salad oil, brown meat well. With slotted spoon, remove meat and drain on paper towels.

In medium bowl, with wire whisk or fork, beat eggs, salt and pepper until well mixed; stir in meat. Brush same skillet with more salad oil; over medium-low heat, pour $\frac{1}{4}$ cup egg mixture to coat bottom of skillet. Cook until top is set and underside lightly browned; with pancake turner, turn and cook other side. Fold pancake in half; place on platter. Repeat with all mixture.

Return all egg pancakes to skillet. Sprinkle mixed vegetables on top. In small bowl, with wire whisk or spoon, stir cornstarch with soy sauce and $1\frac{1}{2}$ cups water. Pour over pancakes; cover and simmer 10 minutes. Makes 5 servings.

Desserts

MERINGUE SHELLS

EARLY IN DAY OR UP TO 5 DAYS AHEAD:
1. Preheat oven to 200°F. Have 3 *egg whites* at room temperature so they will beat to fullest volume. In small bowl, with mixer at high speed, beat whites and $\frac{1}{8}$ *teaspoon cream of tartar* until soft peaks form.
2. Gradually sprinkle in *$\frac{3}{4}$ cup sugar,* 2 tablespoons at a time, beating after each addition for about 2 minutes or until sugar is completely dissolved. To test, rub meringue between fingers; if grainy, continue beating. It takes about 15 minutes to beat in all sugar. Add *$\frac{1}{2}$ teaspoon vanilla extract* and continue beating at high speed until mixture stands in stiff, glossy peaks.
3. Onto large greased cookie sheet, spoon meringue into 6 mounds. Spread each mound into a 4-inch circle, heaping meringue at sides of circle to form a nest shape.
4. Bake $3\frac{1}{2}$ hours until meringues are crisp but not brown. Cool completely on cookie sheet. To store, wrap meringues loosely in waxed paper or place in loosely covered container; keep at room temperature. Makes 6 meringue shells.

MERINGUE PIE SHELL

EARLY IN DAY:
Preheat oven to 250°F. Prepare steps 1 and 2 of Meringue Shells (above). Into greased 9-inch pie plate, spoon meringue, smoothing it at the center and piling it high on the sides to form a pie "shell." Bake 1 hour and 15 minutes. Makes 1 pie shell.

STRAWBERRY MERINGUES

EARLY IN DAY:
Prepare Meringue Shells (above). Using ice-cream scoop or large spoon, scoop *$1\frac{1}{2}$ pints vanilla ice cream* into 6 balls onto cookie sheet; freeze. In medium bowl, thinly slice *$1\frac{1}{2}$ pints strawberries* and stir in *$\frac{1}{3}$ cup sugar;* refrigerate. (Or, thaw one 10-ounce package frozen strawberries.)

AT SERVING TIME:
Top each meringue shell with ice-cream ball and spoon on strawberries and juice. Makes 6 servings.

FRUITED CLOUD PIE

1 Meringue Pie Shell (page 277)
1 envelope unflavored gelatin
¼ cup sugar
dash salt
3 egg yolks
1¼ cups milk
¾ teaspoon vanilla extract
1 cup heavy or whipping cream
½ pint strawberries, halved
1 10-ounce package frozen sliced peaches, thawed and drained

EARLY IN DAY OR DAY BEFORE:

Make pie shell. In double boiler, stir gelatin with sugar and salt until well mixed. In small bowl, with wire whisk or fork, stir egg yolks with milk until mixed; stir into gelatin mixture. Cook over hot, not boiling, water, stirring constantly, until mixture thickens and coats a spoon, about 30 minutes; stir in vanilla. Cover and refrigerate until cool and the consistency of unbeaten egg whites.

In small bowl, with mixer at medium speed, beat cream until soft peaks form; fold into mixture; spoon into shell; chill.

TO SERVE:

Spoon fruit onto filling. Makes 10 servings.

ORANGE DESSERT SOUFFLE

1 envelope unflavored gelatin
sugar
dash salt
6 eggs, separated
1 6-ounce can frozen orange-juice concentrate, thawed
2 tablespoons lemon juice
½ teaspoon grated orange peel
Custard Sauce (page 281)

DAY BEFORE SERVING:

1. Prepare a waxed-paper collar for 1½-quart soufflé dish or casserole: Cut a 24-inch piece of 12-inch-wide waxed paper; fold in half lengthwise. Wrap around outside of dish so collar stands about 3 inches above rim. Fasten with cellophane tape.
2. In double boiler, stir gelatin with ¾ cup sugar and salt until well mixed. In small bowl, with wire whisk or fork, beat egg yolks and 1½ cups water until mixed; stir into gelatin mixture. Cook over hot, not boiling, water, stirring occasionally, until mixture is thickened and coats a spoon, about 30 minutes. Pour into large bowl; stir in undiluted orange-juice concentrate, lemon juice and orange peel.
3. Refrigerate, stirring often, until mixture mounds when dropped from a spoon.
4. In small bowl, with mixer at high speed, beat egg whites until soft peaks form; beating at high speed, gradually sprinkle in ¼ cup sugar; beat until sugar is completely dissolved. (Whites should stand in stiff peaks.) With rubber spatula, gently fold egg-white mixture into chilled orange mixture. Spoon into dish; chill until set. Remove collar. Serve with sauce. Makes 10 servings.

FROSTY LIME SOUFFLE

1 envelope unflavored gelatin
¾ cup sugar
½ teaspoon salt
4 eggs, separated
⅓ cup lime juice
grated peel of 1 lime
⅛ teaspoon green food color
1 cup heavy or whipping cream

EARLY IN DAY:

1. In double boiler, stir gelatin with ¼ cup sugar and salt until well mixed. In small bowl, with wire whisk or fork, beat egg yolks with ½ cup cold water and lime juice until mixed; stir into gelatin mixture. Cook over hot, not boiling, water, stirring constantly, until mixture thickens and coats a spoon.
2. Remove from heat and stir in 1 teaspoon of the grated lime peel and food color until well blended; pour into large bowl and cool to room temperature, stirring occasionally.
3. In small bowl, with mixer at high speed, beat egg whites until soft peaks form; beating at high speed, gradually sprinkle in ½ cup sugar; beat until sugar is completely dissolved. (Whites should stand in stiff peaks.) Wash beaters.
4. In small bowl, with mixer at medium speed, beat cream until stiff; gently fold with beaten egg whites into lime mixture. Pour into 5-cup soufflé dish; refrigerate until firm, at least 3 hours.

TO SERVE:

Garnish with remaining grated peel. Makes 8 servings.

PUMPKIN CHIFFON SOUFFLE

2 envelopes unflavored gelatin
1½ cups packed light brown sugar
salt
1 teaspoon cinnamon
¾ teaspoon nutmeg
½ teaspoon ginger
6 eggs, separated
1½ cups milk
2 16-ounce cans pumpkin
2 teaspoons lemon juice
⅔ cup sugar
whipped topping in aerosol can for garnish
pecan halves for garnish

SEVERAL HOURS BEFORE SERVING:
In medium saucepan, stir gelatin with brown sugar, 1 teaspoon salt and spices until well mixed. In small bowl, with wire whisk or fork, beat egg yolks and milk until mixed; stir into gelatin mixture. Cook over medium heat, stirring constantly, until mixture begins to boil; quickly stir in pumpkin and lemon juice; refrigerate until cooled.

In large bowl, with mixer at high speed, beat egg whites and ¼ teaspoon salt until soft peaks form; beating at high speed, gradually sprinkle in sugar; beat until sugar is completely dissolved. (Whites should stand in stiff peaks.) With rubber spatula, fold in pumpkin mixture. Spoon into individual soufflé or dessert dishes; chill.

TO SERVE:
Garnish with whipped topping and nuts. Makes 12 generous servings.

SKILLET-BAKED CUSTARD

4 large eggs
⅓ cup sugar
3 cups milk
1 teaspoon vanilla extract
⅛ teaspoon salt
nutmeg

2 HOURS AHEAD OR EARLY IN DAY:
In covered blender container at low speed (or in medium bowl with mixer at high speed), beat eggs and sugar until well blended. Beat in milk, vanilla and salt until well mixed. Pour mixture into eight 6-ounce custard cups; sprinkle with nutmeg.

Set four custard cups in each of 2 large skillets. Fill skillets with water to within ½ inch of top of custard cups. Over medium-low heat, heat water just to simmering; cover skillets. Gently simmer for 10 minutes. Immediately remove cups and refrigerate 1½ hours or until well chilled. Makes 8 servings.

BAKED CUSTARD

5 eggs
½ cup sugar
¼ teaspoon salt
3 cups milk
1½ teaspoons vanilla extract
nutmeg

ABOUT 1½ HOURS AHEAD OR EARLY IN DAY:
Preheat oven to 300°F. Grease eight 6-ounce custard cups. In large bowl, with hand beater, or mixer at low speed, beat eggs, sugar and salt until lemon-colored. Gradually beat in milk and vanilla until well blended; pour into custard cups. Sprinkle each with a dash of nutmeg.

Set cups in shallow baking pan; fill pan with hot water to within an inch of top of cups. Bake 1 hour or until knife inserted in center comes out clean. Cool on wire racks, then refrigerate. Makes 8 servings.

ONE-BOWL CUSTARD: Prepare as above but pour custard mixture into a greased 1½-quart baking dish; sprinkle with nutmeg. Bake 1½ hours or until knife inserted in center comes out clean. To serve, spoon into dessert dishes and garnish with fresh fruit, if desired. Makes 8 servings.

CREME CARAMEL

EARLY IN DAY:
Prepare Baked Custard (above) but first prepare caramel syrup: In small skillet over medium heat, melt *½ cup sugar,* stirring constantly until it is a light brown syrup; pour immediately into buttered custard cups. Pour egg mixture over syrup in cups and do not sprinkle with nutmeg. Bake as above; chill.

AT SERVING TIME:
With knife, loosen custard from cups and invert into dessert dishes, letting syrup run onto dish. Makes 8 servings.

FLOATING ISLAND

MERINGUES:
3 egg whites, at room temperature
⅛ teaspoon cream of tartar
⅓ cup sugar
½ teaspoon vanilla extract
3 cups milk

STIRRED CUSTARD:
3 egg yolks
¼ cup sugar
⅛ teaspoon salt
1 teaspoon vanilla extract

EARLY IN DAY OR DAY BEFORE SERVING:
Prepare meringues: In small bowl, with mixer at high speed, beat egg whites and cream of tartar until soft peaks form; beating at high speed, gradually sprinkle in sugar, 2 tablespoons at a time; beat until sugar is completely dissolved. (Whites should stand in stiff peaks.) To test, rub meringue between fingers; if grainy, continue beating. Add ½ teaspoon vanilla.

In medium skillet over medium heat, heat milk until tiny bubbles form around the edge (do not boil). Using half of meringue mixture at a time, drop meringue in large mounds into milk. Cook about 5 minutes, turning once. Remove and drain on paper towels. Refrigerate. Strain the remaining milk, reserving 2 cups.

Prepare custard: In double boiler over hot, not boiling, water, with wire whisk, beat egg yolks, sugar and salt until blended. Gradually stir in reserved milk; cook, stirring constantly, until mixture thickens and coats spoon, about 20 minutes. Add 1 teaspoon vanilla. Pour into shallow serving bowl; refrigerate.

TO SERVE:
Arrange meringues on top of stirred custard. Makes 6 servings.

STRAWBERRY DESSERT OMELET

ABOUT 30 MINUTES BEFORE SERVING:
Prepare Puffy Omelet (page 273) but add *2 tablespoons sugar* to egg-yolk mixture. In small bowl, toss *2 cups sliced strawberries* (or other whole berries) with *1 tablespoon sugar;* spoon into baked omelet. Sprinkle folded omelet with a *little confectioners' sugar.* Makes 4 dessert servings.

CREME BRULEE

3 cups heavy or whipping cream
6 egg yolks
⅓ cup sugar
1 teaspoon vanilla extract
⅓ cup packed brown sugar
strawberries; pineapple and bananas, cut in chunks; mandarin-orange sections

EARLY IN DAY OR DAY BEFORE SERVING:
In medium saucepan over medium heat, heat cream until tiny bubbles form around the edge (do not boil). In large, heavy saucepan with wire whisk or hand beater, beat yolks with sugar until blended; slowly stir in cream. Cook over medium-low heat, stirring constantly, until mixture just coats back of spoon, about 15 minutes. Stir in vanilla; pour into 1½-quart ovenproof, shallow serving dish or soufflé dish; refrigerate until well chilled.

ONE TO 3 HOURS BEFORE SERVING:
Preheat broiler if manufacturer directs. Carefully sift brown sugar over top of chilled mixture; broil 3 to 4 minutes until sugar melts, making a shiny top; chill.

TO SERVE:
With spoon, tap top to break crust. Place dish in center of tray; surround with fruit. Let guests help themselves to fruit, then to Crème Brûlée. Makes 10 servings.

Other Recipes

EGGNOG

ABOUT 5 MINUTES BEFORE SERVING:
In large bowl, with mixer at high speed, beat *6 eggs, 2 tablespoons sugar* and *⅛ teaspoon salt* until frothy. Turn mixer speed to low; gradually beat in *1 cup milk, 2 teaspoons vanilla extract* and *¼ teaspoon nutmeg.* Pour into pitcher or punch bowl. Sprinkle lightly with more *nutmeg.* Serve at once. Makes six ½-cup servings.

BLENDER EGGNOG: In covered blender container, at low speed, blend all ingredients in above recipe until well mixed.

SWISS CHOCOLATE-ALMOND EGGNOG: Prepare as above but substitute *2 tablespoons chocolate syrup* and *1 teaspoon almond extract* for vanilla and nutmeg.

STRAWBERRY-ORANGE EGGNOG

ABOUT 5 MINUTES BEFORE SERVING:
In large bowl, with mixer at high speed, beat *4 eggs*, *½ pint strawberry ice cream*, softened, and *4 drops red food color*; gradually beat in *½ cup milk* and *1 teaspoon orange extract*. Serve at once. Makes six ½-cup servings.

CUSTARD SAUCE

4 egg yolks
⅓ cup sugar
⅛ teaspoon salt
2 cups milk
1 teaspoon vanilla extract

ABOUT 25 MINUTES AHEAD OR EARLY IN DAY:
In double boiler over hot, not boiling, water, with wire whisk, beat egg yolks, sugar and salt until blended. Gradually stir in milk and cook, stirring constantly, until mixture thickens and coats spoon, about 25 minutes. Stir in vanilla extract. Serve warm or cold over apple pie, fruitcake or ice cream. Makes 2¼ cups.

STUFFED EGGS

ABOUT 40 MINUTES AHEAD OR EARLY IN DAY:
Slice *6 hard-cooked eggs* (page 270) in half lengthwise. Gently remove yolks and place in small bowl; with fork, finely crumble yolks. Stir in *¼ cup mayonnaise*, *¼ teaspoon salt* and *dash pepper* until smooth; with spoon, pile into egg centers. Refrigerate, covered. Makes 12 stuffed egg halves.

STUFFED-EGG VARIATIONS

Stir one of these into above egg-yolk mixture:

BACON: Add *2½ tablespoons crumbled, fried bacon*.

CARROT-RAISIN: Add *2 tablespoons grated carrot*, *1 tablespoon chopped raisins*, *¼ teaspoon ginger* and *¼ teaspoon sugar*.

PRETZEL: Add *2 tablespoons coarsely crushed pretzels* and *½ teaspoon prepared mustard*.

GREEN PEPPER: Add *3 tablespoons minced green pepper* and *¼ teaspoon vinegar*.

MEXICAN STYLE: Increase salt to ½ teaspoon; add *⅓ cup drained, chopped tomatoes* and *1 teaspoon chili powder*.

RADISH: Add *3 tablespoons minced radishes*.

SHRIMP SALAD: Add *2 tablespoons finely chopped cooked shrimp* and *2 tablespoons minced celery*.

CAPERS: Add *2 teaspoons minced capers*.

DRIED BEEF: Omit mayonnaise and salt; add *¼ cup finely chopped dried beef*, *¼ cup sour cream* and *½ teaspoon horseradish*.

CUCUMBER-DILL: Add *¼ cup minced cucumber*, *1 teaspoon dillweed*, *1 teaspoon cider vinegar*.

HAM-OLIVE: Use only 2 tablespoons mayonnaise in egg-yolk mixture and omit salt; add *one 2¼-ounce can deviled ham* and *3 tablespoons finely chopped ripe olives*.

PEANUT-BUTTER BACON: Add *2 tablespoons peanut butter*, *3 tablespoons crumbled, fried bacon*.

TUNA: Add *3 tablespoons flaked tuna* and *2 teaspoons lemon juice*.

PIZZA: Use only 2 tablespoons mayonnaise; add *1 teaspoon oregano leaves*, *⅛ teaspoon garlic powder* and *2 tablespoons catchup*.

WALNUTS: Add *⅓ cup chopped California walnuts*.

OLIVE: Add *6 pimento-stuffed olives*, minced, *2 tablespoons prepared mustard*.

ANCHOVY: Add *one-half 2-ounce can anchovies*, minced.

CURRY-CHUTNEY: Add *⅛ teaspoon curry powder* and *1 tablespoon chutney*.

SARDINE: Add *1 large sardine*, chopped.

CHEESE-BACON: Add *1 tablespoon pasteurized process cheese spread* and sprinkle each egg half with *¼ teaspoon bacon-flavor vegetable-protein bits*.

PIMENTO-WATERCRESS: *Add 3 tablespoons chopped watercress*, *1 tablespoon chopped pimento*.

HOLLANDAISE SAUCE

3 egg yolks
2 tablespoons lemon juice
½ cup butter or margarine
¼ teaspoon salt
dash cayenne pepper

ABOUT 10 MINUTES BEFORE SERVING:
In double boiler, with wire whisk, beat egg yolks and lemon juice. Add one-third butter or margarine to egg-yolk mixture and cook over hot, not boiling, water, beating constantly, until butter is melted. Repeat with another third of butter. Repeat with rest of butter, beating until mixture thickens slightly; remove from heat; stir in salt and pepper. Makes ⅔ cup sauce.

BLENDER HOLLANDAISE

¼ cup lemon juice
6 egg yolks
1 teaspoon salt
dash cayenne pepper
1 cup butter or margarine, melted

ABOUT 10 MINUTES BEFORE SERVING:
Fill blender container with hot water to warm it; discard water. In covered container at low speed, blend lemon juice, egg yolks, salt and cayenne pepper until smooth. Turn blender control to high speed; remove center of cover (or cover) and very slowly pour butter or margarine in steady stream into egg mixture. Continue blending until well mixed. Use over poached eggs, baked fish or cooked vegetables. Makes 1⅔ cups.

SOUR-CREAM HOLLANDAISE

¼ cup butter or margarine
1 cup sour cream
2 tablespoons lemon juice
4 egg yolks

ABOUT 10 MINUTES OR UP TO 2 WEEKS AHEAD:
In small saucepan over medium-low heat, melt butter or margarine. With wire whisk beat in sour cream and lemon juice. Beat in egg yolks and heat, beating constantly, 5 minutes or until slightly thickened. Use warm or refrigerate and reheat over low heat, stirring constantly. Makes 1⅔ cups.

PICKLED EGGS

4 cups white vinegar
½ cup sugar
2 tablespoons pickling spice
2 teaspoons salt
2 bay leaves
2 dozen hard-cooked eggs

DAY BEFORE SERVING:
In medium saucepan over high heat, heat vinegar, sugar, pickling spice, salt and bay leaves to boiling. Place eggs, shelled, in 2-quart jar. Add vinegar mixture. Cover and refrigerate overnight. Drain. Makes 24.

SLICED EGGS A LA RUSSE

1 cup mayonnaise
¼ cup bottled chili sauce
½ teaspoon lemon juice
dash hot pepper sauce
8 large lettuce leaves
8 hard-cooked eggs, sliced
4 medium tomatoes, sliced

ABOUT 20 MINUTES BEFORE SERVING:
In small bowl, mix mayonnaise, chili sauce, lemon juice and hot pepper sauce. Place lettuce leaves on salad plates; arrange eggs and tomatoes on top; spoon on mixture. Makes 8 salad or first-course servings.

CHUNKY EGG SALAD

¼ cup mayonnaise
3 tablespoons milk
¾ teaspoon salt
dash pepper
12 hard-cooked eggs, quartered
2 stalks celery, sliced
½ cup sliced pimento-stuffed olives
2 teaspoons chopped onion
lettuce leaves

EARLY IN DAY:
In large bowl, combine mayonnaise, milk, salt and pepper. Toss gently with remaining ingredients except lettuce. Refrigerate.

TO SERVE:
Serve on lettuce. Makes 6 servings.

EGG-SALAD SANDWICH SPREAD: Prepare egg mixture; mince eggs, celery, olives.

Cheese

Cheese offers an unlimited variety of flavors and textures. Flavors range from mild to very sharp, and textures vary from smooth and soft to hard and coarse. Of the many kinds of cheese available, there are sure to be some to please every palate.

Cheese is also nutritious, since it supplies most of the nutrients of milk: protein, calcium and riboflavin. The quality of the protein equals that in meat, fish and eggs.

Cheese eaten as is—in sandwiches, with fruit or crackers, as a snack—is at its flavorful best when served at room temperature. Take it out of the refrigerator and let it stand 30 to 60 minutes before serving. The exceptions are cottage, cream and Neufchâtel cheeses, which should always be served chilled.

Some cheeses, such as Camembert, should be almost runny when served. Let them stand at room temperature 1 to 2 hours before serving.

How to Buy

Cheese is made from milk by separating the solid portion (the curd), from the liquid (whey). For most cheeses, the curd is firmed by pressing or molding, and cured under carefully controlled conditions to develop a characteristic flavor and texture. After curing, cheese may be aged, depending on the sharpness desired. Some cheeses are made from the whey.

Natural cheese: Cheese made directly from milk is "natural" cheese. Varieties grouped by the method of making fall into these "families:"

Cheddar: includes Cheddar, Colby, Longhorn and Monterey (Jack).
Dutch: includes Edam and Gouda.
Provolone: includes Caciocavallo, Mozzarella, Provolone and Scamorze.
Swiss: includes Gruyère and Swiss.
Blue: includes Bluc, Danish Blue, Gorgonzola, Roquefort and Stilton.
Parmesan: includes Parmesan, Romano.
Fresh uncured: includes Cottage, Cream and Neufchâtel.
Surface-ripened: includes Bcl Paese, Brick, Brie, Camembert, Liederkranz, Limburger, Muenster and Port du Salut.
Whey: Gjetost, Primost, Ricotta, Sapsago.

The cheeses in each "family" may vary in texture and sharpness but in most cases are basically similar in flavor.

Natural cheese is also classified by its texture or consistency: hard-grating, such as Parmesan and Romano; hard, such as Cheddar, Swiss and Provolone; semisoft, such as Brick, Camembert, Muenster, and Roquefort; soft, such as Brie and Limburger; and soft and unripened, such as Cottage, Neufchâtel and Ricotta.

Coldpack or club cheese is a smoothly spreadable product made by blending one or more varieties of natural cheese without heating. The flavor is the same as the natural cheese used and is usually aged or sharp; some may have a smoked flavor. It is packed into jars, tubs, rolls or links.

Natural cheese may be bought in bulk, with the desired amount cut in wedges or slices from wheels, bricks, blocks or loaves. Or it may be packaged in various forms: slices, loaves, sticks, wedges, in cartons, shredded, grated.

Pasteurized process cheese: Natural cheese is the starting ingredient for all pasteurized cheese products. Different batches of one or more kinds of fresh and aged natural cheeses are ground, blended and heated or "pasteurized" with an emulsifier to halt further ripening and produce cheese that is always uniform in flavor and texture. This kind of cheese comes in a variety of types, shapes and flavors and can be counted on to give excellent results in cooking.

Process cheese made from one type of natural cheese usually carries the name of that cheese preceded by the words "pasteurized process." Popular varieties include pasteurized process Swiss, Brick, Muenster and Gruyère. One exception is American cheese, which is made from one or more members of the Cheddar cheese family. Pasteurized process cheese comes in loaves and slices in various size packages.

Pasteurized process cheese food is made by adding milk solids to pasteurized process cheese, reducing the amount of fat and increasing the moisture content, so that the cheese is softer and easy to spread. Other ingredients such as meats, fruits and vegetables may be added. These cheese foods are available in packages, slices and links.

Pasteurized process cheese spreads have ingredients added for greater softness and spreadability. They are lower in fat and higher in moisture content than pasteurized process cheese or cheese foods. A broad flavor range is available. They can be purchased as loaves and as spreads in glasses, jars, metal containers, squeeze packs and aerosol cans.

How to Store

"Keep air out and moisture in" is the basic rule of thumb in storing cheese and cheese products. Natural cheese should be tightly wrapped and stored in the refrigerator. If possible, leave in its original wrapping; cut off what is needed and rewrap the cut surface. If the outside of hard cheese becomes moldy, just scrape or cut the mold off; it won't affect flavor.

Hard or wax-coated cheeses (Cheddar, Edam, Swiss) will keep in the refrigerator 3 to 6 months unopened; 3 to 4 weeks, opened; 2 weeks, sliced.

Cottage and ricotta cheeses will keep 5 days in the refrigerator. Cream cheese and Neufchâtel will keep 2 weeks in the refrigerator.

Most pasteurized process cheese products should be refrigerated after opening. Follow instructions on the label, or seal tightly in plastic wrap or bags, foil or covered containers. Individually wrapped slices do not need to be rewrapped.

Some pasteurized process cheese products in glass jars will keep indefinitely at room temperature until opened; then they should be covered tightly and refrigerated. Products in squeeze packs and aerosol cans should never be refrigerated.

Grated Parmesan, Romano and American cheese food may be stored at room temperature unless the label directs otherwise.

How to Freeze

Freezing may make some hard cheese become crumbly and hard to cut well, though it won't affect flavor. However, if handled and stored properly, some hard and semihard cheeses can be frozen successfully for as long as 3 months. Pieces should be small—1 pound or less and not over 1 inch thick. Wrap carefully with foil or other moisture-proof freezer wrapping, pressing it tightly against the cheese to exclude air, then freeze immediately.

Among the kinds of cheese that can be frozen successfully are: Brick, Camembert, Cheddar, Edam, Gouda, Mozzarella, Muenster, Port du Salut, Provolone and Swiss. Small pieces such as Camembert can be frozen in their original package.

Freezing is not recommended for creamed cottage cheese. Uncreamed (dry) cottage cheese can be frozen for 1 to 2 weeks.

Thaw frozen cheese, wrapped, in the refrigerator and use as soon as possible after thawing. If cheese has become crumbly, use it in cooked dishes and as a topping.

How to Use

When serving cheese uncooked, let it come to room temperature for best flavor and texture. After taking it from the refrigerator let it stand 30 to 60 minutes. The exceptions are cottage and cream cheeses, which should always be chilled.

In cooking with cheese, for best results, use low to medium heat and do not overcook. Cheese needs just enough heat to melt evenly and blend with other ingredients; high heat or long cooking makes it stringy and leathery. For even, quick melting in cooked dishes, grate, shred or dice cheese before adding. When making a sauce, add cheese near the end of the cooking time and cook only until it melts. When broiling, broil just long enough to melt the cheese. When topping a casserole, add the cheese the last few minutes of baking.

To grate cheese easily, chill it thoroughly before grating.

Cheese Garnishes

CHEESE BALLS: About 2 hours before serving, with hands, shape softened cream cheese into small balls. Roll in cinnamon, paprika, chili powder, finely chopped nuts, finely chopped parsley or chives. Refrigerate until firm. Use with salads.

CHEESE CURLS: Just before serving, with vegetable parer, cut thin strip from side of chilled 8-ounce loaf pasteurized process cheese spread. Roll up strip. Use with salads, on appetizer tray, etc.

CHEESE CUTOUTS: Just before serving, with knife or fancy cutters, cut shapes from slices of cheese. Use to decorate sandwiches, two-crust fruit pies, casseroles. If you like, broil until cheese just begins to melt.

CHEESE CRUMBS: Just before serving, toss *1 cup crumbled day-old bread,* or crisp croutons, with *3 tablespoons melted butter or margarine,* then with *3 tablespoons grated Parmesan cheese* or American cheese food; sprinkle over hot vegetables, scrambled eggs, casseroles, etc.

Main Dishes

SPAGHETTI-CHEESE PIE

1 8-ounce package spaghetti
3 4-ounce packages shredded sharp Cheddar cheese (3 cups)
½ pound bacon slices, cut in 1-inch pieces
¼ pound mushrooms, sliced
½ cup chopped onion
3 eggs
1 cup milk
2 teaspoons salt
1 teaspoon Worcestershire

ABOUT 50 MINUTES BEFORE SERVING:
1. Prepare spaghetti as label directs; drain. In kettle, toss spaghetti with 2 cups cheese.
2. Meanwhile, preheat oven to 350°F. Grease 10-inch pie plate. In large skillet over medium heat, fry bacon until crisp. Push bacon to one side; spoon off all but 1 tablespoon drippings. Add mushroom slices and onion; cook, stirring occasionally, until vegetables are browned; mix with bacon.
3. Arrange spaghetti in pie plate; sprinkle with bacon mixture. In medium bowl, with hand beater, beat eggs with milk, salt and Worcestershire; stir in remaining cheese; pour over spaghetti. Bake 25 minutes or until set.
4. Remove from oven. Let stand 15 minutes before serving. Makes 6 servings.

MACARONI AND CHEESE PIE: Prepare as above but omit spaghetti and cheese; substitute *one 7½-ounce package macaroni-and-cheese dinner,* prepared as label directs. Bake 40 minutes.

QUICHE LORRAINE

1 9-inch unbaked piecrust, well chilled (page 504)
1 tablespoon butter or margarine, softened
12 bacon slices
¼ pound natural Swiss cheese, shredded (1 cup)
4 eggs
2 cups heavy or whipping cream
¾ teaspoon salt
dash nutmeg

ABOUT 2 HOURS BEFORE SERVING:
Preheat oven to 425°F. Spread piecrust with butter or margarine. In medium skillet over medium heat, fry bacon until crisp; drain on paper towels; crumble. Sprinkle bacon and cheese in piecrust.

In medium bowl, with hand beater, beat eggs with remaining ingredients; pour into crust. Bake 15 minutes. Turn oven control to 325°F. and bake 40 minutes more or until knife inserted in center comes out clean.

Remove from oven and let stand 10 minutes before serving. Makes 6 servings.

AMERICAN-CHEESE PIE

7 white-bread slices, crusts removed
2 tablespoons butter or margarine
4 slices American cheese
2 eggs, slightly beaten
1¼ cups milk
1 teaspoon Worcestershire
½ teaspoon salt
½ teaspoon dry mustard
½ teaspoon paprika

ABOUT 3 HOURS BEFORE SERVING:
Grease 9-inch pie plate. Spread bread with butter or margarine; cut each slice into fourths. Place half of bread pieces in pie plate to cover bottom.

Cut each cheese slice into 4 strips; lay over bread in bottom of pie plate. Top with remaining bread pieces. In small bowl, with fork or wire whisk, beat remaining ingredients; pour over bread. Refrigerate for about two hours.

ABOUT 1 HOUR BEFORE SERVING:
Preheat oven to 325°F. Bake pie 45 minutes. Remove from oven; let stand 10 minutes before serving. Makes 6 servings.

SWITZERLAND CHEESE-AND-ONION PIE

1 9-inch unbaked piecrust, well chilled (page 504)
butter or margarine
1 large onion, chopped (about 1 cup)
½ pound natural Swiss cheese, shredded (2 cups)
1 tablespoon all-purpose flour
3 eggs
1 cup half-and-half
1 teaspoon salt

ABOUT 1 HOUR BEFORE SERVING:
Preheat oven to 400°F. Spread piecrust with 1 tablespoon butter or margarine. In small skillet over medium heat, in 2 tablespoons melted butter or margarine, cook onion until tender, about 5 minutes, stirring occasionally; spread in piecrust. In medium bowl, toss cheese with flour; sprinkle over onion.

In same bowl, with wire whisk or hand beater, beat eggs with half-and-half and salt; pour over cheese. Bake 10 minutes. Turn oven control to 325°F. and bake 30 to 35 minutes longer until knife inserted in center comes out clean. Makes 6 servings.

ONE-APIECE QUICHES

4 white-bread slices
butter or margarine, softened
½ pound natural Swiss cheese, shredded (2 cups)
1 tablespoon minced onion
3 eggs
1 cup half-and-half
¾ cup milk
½ teaspoon dry mustard
½ teaspoon salt

ABOUT 2 HOURS AHEAD OR DAY BEFORE:
Spread bread with butter or margarine and place 1 slice in each of four 8-ounce baking dishes. Sprinkle cheese and onion over bread. In small bowl, with wire whisk or fork, mix eggs and remaining ingredients; pour into baking dishes. Cover; chill at least 30 minutes or overnight.

ABOUT 1 HOUR BEFORE SERVING:
Preheat oven to 325°F. Place dishes on cookie sheet; bake about 45 minutes or until custard is golden. Makes 4 servings.

SWISS-CHEESE-AND-TOMATO PIE

4 cups croutons
2 medium tomatoes, thinly sliced
½ pound natural Swiss cheese, shredded (2 cups)
2 eggs
1½ cups milk
¾ teaspoon salt
½ teaspoon paprika
½ teaspoon dry mustard

ABOUT 1¼ HOURS BEFORE SERVING:
Preheat oven to 350°F. Arrange croutons in 9-inch pie plate. Top with tomato slices; sprinkle with cheese.

In small bowl, with fork or wire whisk, beat remaining ingredients; pour over cheese. Bake 40 minutes or until puffy and browned. Serve at once. Makes 4 servings.

CHEDDAR-CHEESE FONDUE

2 cups half-and-half
1 tablespoon Worcestershire
2 teaspoons dry mustard
1 garlic clove, halved
1½ pounds shredded mild or sharp Cheddar cheese (about 6 cups)
3 tablespoons all-purpose flour
salt
chunks of crusty French bread or cooked, shelled and deveined shrimp or cooked ham chunks

ABOUT 30 MINUTES BEFORE SERVING:
In fondue pot or saucepan* over low heat, heat half-and-half, Worcestershire, mustard and garlic, stirring, until hot but not boiling. Discard garlic.

Meanwhile, in medium bowl, toss cheese with flour. Into hot mixture, with fork or wire whisk, gradually stir cheese. Cook over low heat, stirring constantly, until cheese is melted and mixture is smooth and bubbling. Add salt to taste. (If made in saucepan, pour into fondue pot for serving. Keep hot over low heat on fondue stand.)

Let each person spear chunks of French bread, shrimp or ham chunks on long-handled fondue fork and dip in fondue. Makes 4 cups, enough for 6 servings.

* When mixture comes in contact with aluminum, it may turn dark but will still be delicious.

CLASSIC SWISS FONDUE

1 garlic clove, halved
1½ cups dry white wine
1 tablespoon kirsch, brandy or lemon juice
1 pound shredded natural Swiss cheese (4 cups)
3 tablespoons all-purpose flour
dash pepper
dash nutmeg
chunks of crusty French bread

ABOUT 25 MINUTES BEFORE SERVING:
Rub inside of fondue pot or saucepan* with garlic; discard garlic. Pour wine into fondue pot; over low heat, heat until hot but not boiling. Stir in kirsch.

Meanwhile, in medium bowl, toss cheese with flour until mixed. Add cheese to wine by handfuls, stirring constantly with wooden spoon until cheese is melted. Stir in pepper and nutmeg. (If using saucepan, pour into fondue pot for serving; keep warm on fondue stand.)

Let each person spear chunks of bread on long-handled fondue fork and dip in fondue. Makes 3 cups, enough for 4 servings.

* When mixture comes in contact with aluminum, it may turn dark but will still be delicious.

BAKED CHEESE FONDUE

4 white-bread slices
butter or margarine, softened
1 cup shredded or slivered American cheese
4 eggs
2 cups milk
1 teaspoon salt
½ teaspoon dry mustard

ABOUT 2 HOURS BEFORE SERVING:
Preheat oven to 350°F. Spread bread lightly with butter or margarine; cut into 1-inch squares. In greased 1½-quart casserole, arrange half of squares; top with half of cheese; repeat. In medium bowl, with wire whisk or hand beater, beat eggs with rest of ingredients; pour over cheese.

Set casserole in shallow baking pan on oven rack; fill pan with hot water to come halfway up side of casserole. Bake 1 hour and 20 minutes or until puffed and golden. Serve at once. Makes 4 servings.

CHEESE STRATA

12 white-bread slices
1 8-ounce package American-cheese slices or ½ pound American cheese, thinly sliced
4 eggs
2½ cups milk
1 tablespoon minced onion
1 teaspoon salt
½ teaspoon prepared mustard
dash pepper

ABOUT 2 HOURS BEFORE SERVING:
Grease 12″ by 8″ baking dish. Cut crusts from bread. Arrange 6 bread slices to cover bottom of baking dish; cover with cheese slices, then with rest of bread.

In medium bowl, with wire whisk or hand beater, beat eggs with remaining ingredients until blended; pour over bread. Cover and refrigerate 1 hour.

ABOUT 1 HOUR BEFORE SERVING:
Preheat oven to 325°F. Bake strata about 50 minutes or until puffed and browned. Serve at once. Makes 6 servings.

RACLETTE

ABOUT 20 MINUTES BEFORE SERVING:
Preheat oven to 375°F. With sharp knife, cut rind from *1 pound Raclette cheese;* cut cheese into thin slices. Place half of slices, overlapping slightly, in shallow baking dish.* Bake until cheese is just melted and smooth, about 4 to 6 minutes; remove from oven. Place hot dish on serving plate or wooden serving board (to make serving easy while keeping cheese hot).

Sprinkle cheese with *freshly ground pepper* or paprika. Let each person help himself to serving of Raclette and eat as is or over *hot boiled potatoes;* accompany with *dill pickles* and *cocktail onions,* if you like. Repeat with rest of cheese. Makes 4 servings.

OTHER CHEESES: Among the cheeses that can be substituted for Raclette (though the flavor won't be quite the same) are Appenzeller, Fontina, Gruyère, Monterey (Jack), Muenster and Port du Salut.

* If preparing in special Raclette stove, follow manufacturer's directions.

WELSH RABBIT

¼ cup butter or margarine
½ cup all-purpose flour
½ teaspoon salt
⅛ teaspoon dry mustard
dash cayenne pepper
2 cups milk
1 teaspoon Worcestershire
2 4-ounce packages shredded sharp Cheddar cheese (2 cups)
toasted white or rye bread slices

ABOUT 20 MINUTES BEFORE SERVING:
In medium saucepan over low heat, or in double boiler over boiling water, melt butter or margarine. Stir in flour, salt, mustard and cayenne until blended; stir in milk and Worcestershire and cook, stirring constantly, until thickened. Add cheese and cook, stirring, just until cheese is melted and blended. Serve hot cheese mixture over warm toast. Makes 6 servings.

DINNER RABBIT

1 10-ounce package frozen carrots and peas
½ cup chopped celery
2 tablespoons butter or margarine
2 tablespoons all-purpose flour
1 cup milk
1 8-ounce package American-cheese slices, slivered
½ teaspoon salt
½ teaspoon Worcestershire
¼ teaspoon dry mustard
dash cayenne pepper
1 tablespoon minced green pepper
1 large tomato, cut in wedges
4 toasted, split English muffins
4 cooked ham slices

ABOUT 30 MINUTES BEFORE SERVING:
Cook carrots and peas as label directs but add celery; drain. Meanwhile, in medium saucepan over low heat, melt butter or margarine; stir in flour until smooth, then stir in next 6 ingredients.

Cook mixture, stirring constantly, until cheese is melted and sauce is thickened. Stir in cooked vegetables, green pepper and tomato wedges. For each serving, top two muffin halves with a ham slice; spoon on cheese mixture. Makes 4 servings.

WELSH RABBIT WITH BEER

1 pound American cheese, slivered or coarsely shredded (about 4 cups)
¾ cup beer
1 teaspoon dry mustard
½ teaspoon Worcestershire
¼ teaspoon salt
4 toasted white or rye bread slices

ABOUT 20 MINUTES BEFORE SERVING:
In medium saucepan over low heat, or in chafing dish over boiling water, cook cheese with next 4 ingredients, stirring constantly, until cheese is melted and mixture is smooth. Serve on toast. Makes 4 servings.

TUNA BLUSHING BUNNY

5 English muffins
1 10¾-ounce can condensed Cheddar-cheese soup
1 10¾-ounce can condensed tomato soup
1 teaspoon Worcestershire
½ teaspoon prepared mustard
2 6½- or 7-ounce cans tuna, drained

ABOUT 15 MINUTES BEFORE SERVING:
Split and toast English muffins. In medium saucepan, with spoon or wire whisk, stir undiluted soups until smooth. Stir in ½ cup water, Worcestershire, mustard and tuna. Over medium heat, cook mixture, stirring constantly, until hot and bubbly. Serve on muffin halves. Makes 5 servings.

Cheese Desserts

RICOTTA CONDITA

1 15-ounce container ricotta cheese
1 to 3 teaspoons milk
1 or 2 tablespoons sugar
1½ teaspoons cinnamon
4 small cinnamon sticks for garnish

ABOUT 1 HOUR BEFORE SERVING:
In small bowl, with mixer at high speed, beat ricotta smooth; beat in enough milk to make it creamy but still hold its shape. In cup, mix sugar and cinnamon.

In each of four 4-ounce parfait glasses, place spoonful of ricotta; sprinkle with some cinnamon-sugar; repeat, ending with ricotta; garnish; chill. Makes 4 servings.

CHEESE-AND-FRUIT TRAY

¾ pound Swiss cheese
¾ pound Cheddar cheese
¾ pound Muenster cheese
2 large apples, cut into wedges
2 large pears, cut into wedges
lemon juice
1 pound green grapes, cut into small bunches
1 pound Tokay grapes, cut into small bunches

ABOUT 4 HOURS BEFORE SERVING:
With sharp knife, cut cheeses into 1-inch chunks. Dip apple and pear wedges into lemon juice to prevent darkening.

On large serving board or platter, group fruit and cheeses attractively. Cover with plastic wrap or foil; chill. Makes 8 servings.

SHERRIED CAMEMBERT MOLD WITH FRUIT

½ pound Camembert cheese
¼ cup medium sherry
½ pound unsalted butter or margarine, softened
dried bread crumbs
apples and pears, cut in thin wedges
lemon juice
small bunches of grapes
crisp crackers

TWO DAYS BEFORE SERVING:
Scrape rind from Camembert. In small bowl, with spoon, stir cheese until creamy, then level top of cheese; pour sherry over top. Cover bowl and refrigerate overnight.

DAY BEFORE SERVING:
Drain sherry from cheese; reserve. With mixer at low speed, beat cheese with butter or margarine until blended. Slowly add reserved sherry, continuing to beat until mixture is light and fluffy. Spoon mixture into 1½-cup mold; cover and refrigerate.

ABOUT 1 HOUR BEFORE SERVING:
Onto serving tray, unmold cheese as for gelatin salad (page 390). Pat crumbs over surface; let stand at room temperature.

TO SERVE:
Dip apples and pears in lemon juice and arrange with grapes, crackers and cheese; add cocktail knife. Makes 8 servings.

NO-BAKE CHEESECAKE

2 envelopes unflavored gelatin
1 cup sugar
¼ teaspoon salt
2 eggs, separated
1 cup milk
1 teaspoon grated lemon peel
3 cups creamed cottage cheese
1 tablespoon lemon juice
1 teaspoon vanilla extract
Unbaked Graham-Cracker-Crumb Crust (page 508)
1 cup heavy or whipping cream
berries, sliced peaches, chopped nuts, preserves or canned fruit for garnish

EARLY IN DAY OR DAY BEFORE SERVING:
1. In medium saucepan, stir gelatin with sugar and salt. In small bowl, beat egg yolks with milk until mixed; stir into gelatin mixture. Cook over medium heat, stirring, until mixture thickens and coats spoon. Remove from heat; add lemon peel; cool.
2. Into large bowl, press cottage cheese through sieve. Stir in lemon juice, vanilla and gelatin mixture. Refrigerate 30 minutes, stirring often, or until mixture mounds slightly when dropped from spoon.
3. Meanwhile, prepare crust mixture; press half in bottom of 9-inch springform pan.
4. In small bowl, with mixer at high speed, beat egg whites just until stiff peaks form; spoon onto gelatin mixture. In same bowl, beat cream until soft peaks form; spoon onto gelatin mixture. With rubber spatula, fold egg whites and whipped cream into mixture; pour into pan. Sprinkle top with remaining crumb mixture and chill until firm.

TO SERVE:
Remove side of pan. With large spatula, loosen cake from pan bottom; slide onto plate. Garnish with fruit or nuts. Makes 10 to 12 servings.

SMALL NO-BAKE CHEESECAKE: Prepare as above but use *1 envelope unflavored gelatin, ½ cup sugar, ⅛ teaspoon salt, 1 egg, ½ cup milk, ½ teaspoon grated lemon peel, 1½ cups creamed cottage cheese, 1½ teaspoons lemon juice, ½ teaspoon vanilla extract, ½ cup heavy or whipping cream* and full amount of Crumb Crust in an 8- or 9-inch round cake pan or pie plate. Makes 6 servings.

CRANBERRY CHEESECAKE

3 tablespoons butter or margarine
1 cup cornflake crumbs
sugar
½ teaspoon cinnamon
2 16-ounce containers creamed cottage cheese (4 cups)
4 eggs
½ cup heavy or whipping cream
¼ cup all-purpose flour
1 tablespoon lemon juice
1 tablespoon vanilla extract
2 cups cranberries
1 envelope unflavored gelatin

DAY BEFORE SERVING:
1. In small saucepan over medium heat, melt butter or margarine; add cornflake crumbs, ¼ cup sugar and cinnamon and mix well. Spread mixture in 9-inch springform pan, packing firmly on bottom and side of pan. Preheat oven to 350°F.
2. In covered blender container, blend cottage cheese, half at a time, until smooth. (Or, into large bowl, press cottage cheese through a fine sieve.) In large bowl, with mixer at low speed, beat cheese with next 5 ingredients and 1 cup sugar until blended. At medium speed, beat 5 minutes more.
3. Pour into pan. Bake 50 minutes. Turn off oven control and leave cheesecake in oven 30 minutes longer. Cool in pan on wire rack. Refrigerate overnight. (Cracks in top are characteristic.)

EARLY ON SERVING DAY:
4. In medium saucepan over high heat, cook cranberries, 1 cup sugar and ¾ cup water 5 minutes or until skins pop, stirring occasionally. Meanwhile, in cup, sprinkle gelatin over ¼ cup water; stir into hot cranberries until dissolved. Chill until mixture begins to thicken, stirring often.
5. With spatula, loosen pan side from cheesecake and remove; loosen cake from pan bottom; slide onto plate. Spread cranberry mixture over top. Chill until topping is set, about 3 hours. Makes 12 servings.

MANDARIN CHEESECAKE: Prepare as above but omit cranberry topping. Drain *one 11-ounce can mandarin-orange sections;* arrange on cooled cake top. In small saucepan over low heat, melt *½ cup orange marmalade;* brush over oranges.

DELUXE CHEESECAKE

all-purpose flour
3/4 cup butter or margarine, softened
sugar
3 egg yolks
grated peel of 2 lemons
5 8-ounce packages cream cheese
5 eggs
1/4 cup heavy or whipping cream
1 tablespoon grated orange peel
1/4 teaspoon salt
1 cup sour cream for garnish

DAY BEFORE SERVING:

1. In small bowl, with mixer at low speed, beat 1 1/4 cups flour, butter or margarine, 1/4 cup sugar, 1 egg yolk and half of grated lemon peel until well mixed; refrigerate, covered, for 1 hour.
2. Preheat oven to 400°F. Press 1/3 of flour mixture into bottom of 10-inch springform pan; bake 8 minutes; cool. Turn oven control to 475°F.
3. Meanwhile, in large bowl, with mixer at medium speed, beat cream cheese just until smooth; slowly beat in 1 3/4 cups sugar. With mixer at low speed, beat in 3 tablespoons flour and remaining ingredients except sour cream. At high speed, beat 5 minutes, occasionally scraping bowl with rubber spatula.
4. Press rest of dough around side of pan to within 1 inch of top; do not bake. Pour cream-cheese mixture into pan; bake 12 minutes. Turn oven control to 300°F. and bake 35 minutes longer. Turn off oven; let cheesecake remain in oven 30 minutes. Remove; cool in pan on wire rack. Refrigerate.

TO SERVE:

Remove side of pan. With large spatula, loosen cake from pan bottom; slide onto plate. Spread top with sour cream. Makes 16 servings.

STRAWBERRY DELUXE CHEESECAKE: Prepare cheesecake as above but omit sour cream; cool. Meanwhile, make Strawberry Glaze: Reserve 2 cups berries from *2 pints strawberries.* In medium saucepan, stir *3/4 cup sugar, 2 tablespoons cornstarch* and *2 tablespoons lemon juice* until smooth; add remaining berries and, using potato masher or slotted spoon, crush berries; cook over low heat, stirring, until thickened; cool.

Spoon mixture on top of cooled cheesecake. Cut reserved berries in half lengthwise; arrange, cut side up, over top. In small saucepan over low heat, melt *2 tablespoons currant jelly;* brush over berries. Chill.

LONDONDERRY CHEESECAKE

1 1/2 cups all-purpose flour
sugar
grated lemon peel
1/2 cup butter or margarine
4 egg yolks
vanilla extract
4 8-ounce packages cream cheese
1 cup finely shredded very sharp Cheddar cheese
4 eggs
1/4 cup beer
1/4 cup heavy or whipping cream
1/2 teaspoon grated orange peel

EARLY IN DAY:

1. In medium bowl, combine flour, 6 tablespoons sugar and 1 teaspoon grated lemon peel. With pastry blender or 2 knives used scissor-fashion, cut in butter or margarine until mixture resembles coarse crumbs. With fork, stir in 2 egg yolks and 1/2 teaspoon vanilla to form very stiff dough; chill 30 minutes. Preheat oven to 425°F.
2. Press one-third of chilled dough evenly into bottom of 9-inch springform pan. Bake 8 to 10 minutes until golden; cool. Press rest of dough around side of pan to within 1 inch of top; do not bake.
3. In large bowl, with mixer at high speed, beat cream cheese until smooth; gradually add Cheddar cheese, beating until well blended, about 5 minutes, occasionally scraping bowl with rubber spatula.
4. At medium speed, gradually beat in 1/2 teaspoon grated lemon peel, 1/2 teaspoon vanilla, 1 3/4 cups sugar, 2 egg yolks and remaining ingredients until blended; beat 5 minutes, occasionally scraping bowl.
5. Pour mixture into crust. Bake 10 minutes. Turn oven control to 300°F. and bake 1 hour and 15 minutes longer or until top is firm when lightly pressed with finger.
6. Cool in pan on wire rack. (Cake will sink in center, leaving cracks around crust.) With spatula, loosen pan side and remove; loosen cake from pan bottom; slide onto plate; chill. Makes about 12 servings.

DELUXE CHEESE PIE

Unbaked Graham-Cracker-Crumb Crust (page 508)
1½ 8-ounce packages cream cheese, softened
2 eggs
½ cup sugar
½ teaspoon vanilla extract
1 cup sour cream

EARLY IN DAY:
Preheat oven to 350°F. Grease well 8-inch pie plate. Prepare crumb crust as recipe directs; press to bottom and side of pie plate.

In small bowl, with mixer at low speed, beat cheese with eggs, sugar and vanilla just until mixed. Beat at high speed until smooth; pour into crust. Bake 35 minutes or until set. Spread pie with sour cream and cool on wire rack. Refrigerate. Makes 8 servings.

CHERRY-CHEESE PIE: Prepare as above but omit sour cream; cool pie. Meanwhile, prepare Cherry Glaze: Drain *one 16-ounce can pitted tart red cherries,* reserving 1 cup cherries and ½ cup liquid. (Save rest of cherries and liquid for use another day.) In small saucepan, stir *1 tablespoon cornstarch* with *2 tablespoons sugar;* slowly stir in reserved cherry liquid; simmer until thickened and clear, stirring constantly. Stir in reserved cherries, *1 teaspoon lemon juice, ¼ teaspoon almond extract* and *few drops red food color;* cool. Spread on top of cooled pie.

PINEAPPLE-CHEESE PIE: Prepare as above but omit sour cream; cool pie. Meanwhile, prepare Pineapple Glaze: In small saucepan, stir *1 cup canned crushed pineapple,* undrained, with *1 teaspoon cornstarch.* Cook over low heat, stirring constantly, until thickened and clear; stir in *1 tablespoon lemon juice;* cool. Spread on top of cooled pie.

PEACH-CHEESE PIE: Prepare as above but omit sour cream; cool pie. Meanwhile, drain well *one 29-ounce can sliced cling peaches;* place peach slices on paper towels, patting dry; chill until pie is cool. Arrange peaches in overlapping rows on top of pie. In small saucepan, melt *¼ cup apricot preserves* with *1 teaspoon lemon juice;* use to brush over peach slices.

STRAWBERRY-CHEESE PIE: Prepare as above but omit sour cream; cool pie. Arrange 2 *pints whole, hulled strawberries,* stem end down, on pie top. In small saucepan over low heat, melt *½ cup red currant jelly;* use to brush over berries.

CREAM-CHEESE-RHUBARB PIE

4 cups rhubarb, cut in 1-inch pieces
sugar
3 tablespoons cornstarch
¼ teaspoon salt
1 9-inch unbaked piecrust
1 8-ounce package cream cheese
2 eggs
1 cup sour cream
almonds for garnish

EARLY IN DAY:
Preheat oven to 425°F. In medium saucepan over medium heat, cook rhubarb, 1 cup sugar, cornstarch and salt, stirring often, until mixture boils and thickens. Pour into piecrust. Bake 10 minutes; remove from oven.

Meanwhile, in small bowl, with mixer at medium speed, beat cream cheese, eggs and ½ cup sugar until smooth; pour over rhubarb mixture.

Turn oven control to 350°F. Bake pie 30 to 35 minutes until set; cool on wire rack; chill.

TO SERVE:
Spread sour cream on top of pie. Garnish with almonds. Makes 8 servings.

CREAM-CHEESE DESSERT LOAF

2 8-ounce packages cream cheese
¼ cup packed light brown sugar
1 teaspoon cinnamon
whole strawberries with hulls
crisp assorted crackers

ABOUT 20 MINUTES BEFORE SERVING:
With hands, shape cream cheese into roll. In small bowl, combine brown sugar with cinnamon; sprinkle over roll.

TO SERVE:
Arrange roll on tray; surround with berries and crackers. Let guests spread crackers with cheese, then top with berry. Makes 8 servings.

Sauces and Toppings

SOUR-CREAM CHEESE SAUCE

1 4-ounce package shredded Cheddar cheese (1 cup)
1 cup sour cream
2 tablespoons lemon juice
dash salt

ABOUT 10 MINUTES BEFORE SERVING:
In medium saucepan over low heat, stir cheese with sour cream just until cheese melts; stir in lemon juice and salt. Serve hot over fruit pie. Makes about 2 cups.

EASIEST-OF-ALL CHEESE SAUCES

Melt *pasteurized process cheese spread* over very low heat or in double boiler.

Or, heat *one 10¾-ounce can condensed Cheddar-cheese soup* with *⅓ cup milk* until blended and hot, stirring. For variety, substitute dry white wine for the milk.

Or, follow label directions for preparing *packaged cheese-sauce mix.*

SPRINKLE-ON: Sprinkle shredded cheese over hot cooked vegetables, meat patties, chops, steaks or fruit; cover pan and let the heat of cooked food melt cheese. Or, place food in heatproof serving dish; sprinkle generously with shredded cheese and broil just until the cheese melts.

BLUE-CHEESE MUSHROOM SAUCE

3 tablespoons butter or margarine
3 tablespoons all-purpose flour
½ teaspoon salt
dash pepper
2⅓ cups milk
2 ounces Danish blue cheese, crumbled (about ½ cup)
1 4-ounce can sliced mushrooms, drained

ABOUT 25 MINUTES BEFORE SERVING:
In medium saucepan over medium heat, melt butter or margarine; stir in flour, salt and pepper until smooth. Gradually stir in milk and cook, stirring, until thickened. Stir in cheese and mushrooms; heat. Serve with hot turkey, chicken, beef, veal or vegetables. Makes 2½ cups.

MORNAY SAUCE

3 tablespoons butter or margarine
2 tablespoons all-purpose flour
1 cup chicken broth
1 cup half-and-half
1 egg yolk
½ cup shredded natural Swiss cheese
¼ cup grated Parmesan cheese

ABOUT 20 MINUTES BEFORE SERVING:
In medium saucepan over medium heat, melt butter or margarine; stir in flour until smooth. Gradually stir in chicken broth and half-and-half and cook, stirring, until sauce is thickened; remove from heat.

In small bowl, with fork or wire whisk, beat egg yolk slightly; into egg yolk, beat small amount of hot sauce; slowly pour egg mixture back into the sauce, stirring rapidly to prevent lumping. Stir in shredded cheese and Parmesan cheese; cook over low heat, stirring constantly, just until sauce is thickened and cheese is melted (do not boil). Serve over poached eggs, baked chicken, poached fish or vegetables. Makes 2⅓ cups.

BLUE-CHEESE BUTTER TOPPING

ABOUT 1 HOUR BEFORE SERVING:
In small bowl, with spoon or mixer at low speed, thoroughly mix *¼ cup blue or Gorgonzola cheese* with *¼ cup butter or margarine,* softened. Use as needed; cover remainder and refrigerate for use any time up to three weeks later. Use on broiled shrimp or rock-lobster tails, hot cooked vegetables or as stuffing for celery or spread for crisp crackers. Makes about ⅓ cup.

CHEDDAR-BUTTER TOPPING: Prepare as above but use *½ cup shredded sharp Cheddar cheese, ¼ cup butter or margarine,* softened, and *a few drops hot pepper sauce.* Use on hot cooked vegetables, broiled fish or shellfish, hamburgers or hot breads. Makes about ½ cup.

PARMESAN-BUTTER TOPPING: Prepare as above but use *½ cup grated Parmesan cheese* and *¼ cup butter or margarine,* softened. Use on hot cooked vegetables or hot breads. Makes about ½ cup.

FAVORITE NATURAL CHEESE VARIETIES

Appenzeller

Look for: Wheels, cut pieces.
Characteristics: Firm, ripened. Smooth, cream-colored, with small eyes. Moister, creamier than Emmentaler (Swiss). Seasoned with wine and spices during curing.
Flavor: Robust, unique.
Uses: Appetizers, snacks, in cooking.

Bel Paese

Look for: Small wheels, wedges, segments.
Characteristics: Semisoft, ripened. Creamy-yellow interior, slightly gray or brownish surface, sometimes yellow-wax-coated.
Flavor: Mild to moderately robust.
Uses: Appetizers, snacks, sandwiches, desserts, on crackers.

Blue

Look for: Cylinders, wedges, oblongs, squares, cut portions.
Characteristics: Semisoft, ripened. White with blue-green marbling; pasty, sometimes crumbly texture.
Flavor: Piquant.
Uses: Appetizers, dips, salads, salad dressings, sandwiches, desserts, on crackers.

Brick

Look for: Loaves, bricks, cut portions, slices.
Characteristics: Semisoft, ripened. Creamy yellow, many small openings.
Flavor: Mild to moderately sharp.
Uses: Appetizers, sandwiches, snacks, desserts.

Brie

Look for: Medium and small wheels.
Characteristics: Soft, ripened. Thin whitish edible crust, creamy-yellow interior.
Flavor: Mild to pungent.
Uses: Snacks, desserts.

Caciocavallo

Look for: Spindle and tenpin shapes, bound with cord; cut pieces.
Characteristics: Firm, ripened. Clay or tan surface, light or white interior.
Flavor: Piquant, similar to Provolone but not smoky.
Uses: Snacks, sandwiches, in cooking, desserts. Suitable for grating after prolonged curing.

Camembert

Look for: Small wheels, individual wedges.
Characteristics: Soft, ripened. Edible, thin whitish crust with creamy-yellow interior.
Flavor: Distinctive, mild to pungent.
Uses: Appetizers, snacks, sandwiches, with fruit, desserts, on crackers.

Cheddar

Look for: Wheels, cylindrical loaves, wedges, oblongs, slices, cubes, shredded or grated. Longhorn cheese is a form of Cheddar.
Characteristics: Hard, ripened. Smooth, white to medium yellow-orange with some openings.
Flavor: Mild to very sharp, depending on length of ripening.
Uses: Appetizers, snacks, sandwiches, grated, in cooking, desserts.

Colby

Look for: Cylinders, wedges.
Characteristics: Hard, ripened (although softer, more open than Cheddar); light yellow to orange.
Flavor: Mild.
Uses: Snacks, sandwiches, in cooking.

Cottage

Look for: Cheese packaged in containers.
Characteristics: Soft, unripened. Small or large curd; white. Made from skim milk; creamed cottage cheese has cream added.
Flavor: Mild, acid.
Uses: Dips, salads, in cooking, desserts, cheesecake.

Cream

Look for: Foil-wrapped bars.
Characteristics: Soft, unripened. Smooth, buttery, white. Made from cream and milk.
Flavor: Mild, acid.
Uses: Dips, snacks, sandwiches, salads, desserts, cheesecake, on crackers.

Edam

Look for: Cannonball-shaped loaves, oblongs, cut pieces.
Characteristics: Hard, ripened. Grainy, red-wax-coated surface with yellow interior, small holes.

Flavor: Mild, nutlike, salty.
Uses: Appetizers, snacks, salads, sandwiches, with fruit, desserts, on crackers.

Feta

Look for: Cheese packed in brine in metal containers or jars.
Characteristics: Semisoft, ripened. Flaky, white.
Flavor: Salty, sharp.
Uses: Appetizers, snacks, salads, in cooking.

Fontina

Look for: Wheels, cut pieces.
Characteristics: Semisoft to hard, ripened. May have oiled surface. Smooth interior with few small, round eyes.
Flavor: Delicate, nutty; slightly smoky when aged.
Uses: Appetizers, snacks, in cooking, suitable for grating when fully cured, desserts.

Gjetost

Look for: Cubes and rectangles.
Characteristics: Firm, unripened. Golden-brown, buttery consistency.
Flavor: Sweetish, caramel.
Uses: Snacks, desserts, with dark breads, on crackers.

Gorgonzola

Look for: Wheels, wedges, oblongs.
Characteristics: Semisoft, ripened. Creamy-white interior with blue-green mold marbling, clay-colored surface.
Flavor: Piquant, similar to blue cheese.
Uses: Appetizers, dips, snacks, sandwiches, salads, desserts, on crackers.

Gouda

Look for: Flattened balls.
Characteristics: Hard, ripened. Grainy, small holes, yellow to medium yellow-orange interior with or without red-wax coating.
Flavor: Mellow, nutlike flavor like Edam.
Uses: Appetizers, snacks, salads, sandwiches, in cooking, desserts, with fruit.

Gruyère

Look for: Flat wheels, individual wedges.
Characteristics: Hard, ripened. Tiny gas holes or eyes, light yellow.
Flavor: Sweetish, nutlike flavor.
Uses: Snacks, in cooking, desserts.

Liederkranz (trademark name)

Look for: Small foil-wrapped loaves.
Characteristics: Soft, ripened. Russet-colored surface, creamy-yellow interior.
Flavor and aroma: Robust.
Uses: Appetizers, with fruit, with salads, desserts, on crackers.

Limburger

Look for: Cubical or rectangular pieces.
Characteristics: Soft, ripened. Reddish-yellow surface, creamy-white interior, usually with small irregular openings.
Flavor and aroma: Robust.
Uses: Appetizers, snacks, sandwiches, desserts, on crackers.

Longhorn (*see* Cheddar)

Monterey (**Jack**)

Look for: Wheels, slices.
Characteristics: Semisoft, ripened. Smooth, open texture, creamy white.
Flavor: Mild.
Uses: Sandwiches, snacks, in cooking.

Mozzarella

Look for: Small round or braided forms, slices, also packed shredded.
Characteristics: Firm, unripened. "Plastic," creamy white.
Flavor: Mild.
Uses: In cooking, sandwiches, pizza.

Muenster

Look for: Small wheels, blocks, wedges, segments, slices.
Characteristics: Semisoft, ripened. Yellow-tan surface, creamy-white interior, many small openings.
Flavor: Mild to mellow.
Uses: Appetizers, snacks, sandwiches, desserts.

Mysost (**Primost**)

Look for: Cubes, wheels, wedges.
Characteristics: Firm, unripened. Light brown, buttery consistency.
Flavor: Mild, sweetish, caramel.
Uses: Snacks, desserts, with dark bread, on crackers.

Neufchâtel

Look for: Foil-wrapped bars.
Characteristics: Soft, unripened. Creamy white.

Flavor: Mild, acid, resembles cream cheese.
Uses: Dips, spreads, snacks, sandwiches, salads, desserts, cheesecakes.

Parmesan (Reggiano)

Look for: Cylinders, wedges; also packaged grated or shredded.
Characteristics: Very hard, ripened. Granular, creamy white.
Flavor: Sharp, piquant.
Uses: Grated or shredded as seasoning.

Port du Salut

Look for: Wheels, wedges.
Characteristics: Semisoft, ripened. Creamy yellow, smooth, buttery, small openings.
Flavor: Mellow to robust.
Uses: Appetizers, snacks, with fruit, desserts.

Provolone

Look for: Pear, ball or sausage shapes; wedges, slices.
Characteristics: Hard, ripened. Compact, flaky, light brown or golden surface, pale yellow to golden interior.
Flavor: Mild to sharp, smoky, salty.
Uses: Appetizers, snacks, sandwiches, salads, in cooking, desserts. Suitable for grating when fully cured and dried.

Raclette

Look for: Wheels, cut pieces.
Characteristics: Semifirm, ripened. Thin brownish rind, pale cream interior with some tiny holes. Texture somewhat softer than Muenster.
Flavor: Cold: very mild, faintly salty; hot: much stronger, unique.
Uses: Snacks, in cooking.

Ricotta

Look for: Cheese packaged in cartons, metal cans.
Characteristics: Soft, unripened; moist or dry, white curds.
Flavor: Sweet nutlike, resembles cottage cheese.
Uses: Appetizers, snacks, salads, in cooking, desserts.

Romano

Look for: Flattened rounds, wedges; also packaged shredded or grated.
Characteristics: Very hard, ripened. Granular, greenish-black surface with yellowish-white interior.
Flavor: Sharp and piquant.
Uses: Seasoning. Suitable for grating when cured about 1 year.

Roquefort

Look for: Cylinders, wedges.
Characteristics: Semisoft, ripened. Pasty, crumbly; white with green-blue mold marbling.
Flavor: Sharp, piquant.
Uses: Appetizers, dips, snacks, sandwiches, desserts, on crackers.

Sapsago

Look for: Small cones; also packaged in shakers.
Characteristics: Very hard, ripened. Light green by addition of dried, powdered clover leaves.
Flavor: Sharp, pungent, cloverlike.
Uses: Grated as seasoning; spread for bread or crackers when mixed with butter.

Scamorze

Look for: Small pear shapes.
Characteristics: Semisoft, unripened. Smooth, light yellow.
Flavor: Mild.
Uses: In cooking, pizza.

Stilton

Look for: Wheels, wedges, oblongs.
Characteristics: Semisoft, ripened. Flaky, slightly more crumbly than Blue; creamy-white interior marbled with blue-green mold.
Flavor: Piquant, milder than Gorgonzola or Roquefort.
Uses: Appetizers, snacks, salads, desserts, on crackers.

Swiss (Emmentaler)

Look for: Segments, pieces, slices.
Characteristics: Firm, ripened; light yellow with large round eyes.
Flavor: Sweet, nutlike.
Uses: Sandwiches, snacks, salads, in cooking, desserts, on crackers.

Rice & pasta

Rice and pasta (macaroni products) provide hearty, delicious eating at relatively low cost. Both are bland-tasting and combine readily with other foods ranging in flavor from sweet and mild to savory and highly seasoned.

Rice

Rice is an economical source of carbohydrate; it also supplies B vitamins and some iron and calcium. These valuable nutrients are retained best when rice is used without being rinsed before or after cooking, and when it is cooked so that it absorbs all the cooking liquid.

Regular white rice: Packaged as long-, medium- or short-grain, this type of rice has the outer coating of bran removed by milling and may be polished or unpolished. It may be enriched with nutrients that were lost by milling; check the label.

Cooked long-grain rice has grains that are plump, tender and separate; and is best (and looks prettiest) in curries, stews, salads and main dishes. Short- and medium-grain rice is preferred for puddings, rice rings and other dishes where moist grains that tend to stick together give best results. One cup uncooked regular rice yields about 3 cups when cooked.

Precooked rice: This type of long-grain rice is cooked and then dehydrated after milling. It takes only a few minutes to prepare. Preparation and yield differ from brand to brand, so check label directions carefully. Our recipes have been developed so that, with the help of these directions, any brand can be used.

Parboiled rice: This type of long-grain rice is subjected to a combination of steam and pressure before milling so that, after milling, most of its natural vitamins and minerals are retained. It takes a little more liquid and longer cooking time than regular rice. One cup uncooked parboiled rice yields about 4 cups cooked.

Brown rice: This type is whole unpolished rice; the bran has not been removed and so the vitamins and minerals are retained. It is very light brown in color and has a nutty flavor when cooked. It requires a little more liquid and longer cooking time than white rice. One cup uncooked brown rice yields about 4 cups cooked.

Flavored rice mixes: These products, available in 6- and 7-ounce packages, contain quick-cooking or long-grain rice with seasonings. Choose from a variety of flavors including herb, curry, Spanish and others.

In-a-hurry rice dishes: Frozen seasoned rice dishes are sold in the frozen-vegetable section at the supermarket. Canned and refrigerated rice specialties are also available.

Tips on Using Rice

Store rice at room temperature in a cool, dry place away from products with strong odors. Regular, precooked and parboiled rice will keep up to one year; brown rice and wild rice, about 6 months.

Cooked rice will keep up to a week in the refrigerator. Cover it so grains won't dry out or absorb other flavors.

Reheat leftover rice in a covered saucepan this way: For each cup of rice, add 2 tablespoons of liquid. Over low heat, heat rice and liquid to simmering; simmer 4 to 5 minutes until hot.

Cooked rice can be frozen alone or combined with other foods that freeze well. Freeze in meal-size amounts. Place in freezer carton and seal; or freeze in foil-lined casserole; remove from casserole when frozen (leave foil on), freezer-wrap and store. Frozen rice keeps well 6 to 8 months. To serve, thaw at room temperature 3 to 4 hours; reheat as above.

Pasta

Pasta: This is a general term that has come to refer to all spaghetti, macaroni and noodles. It comes in over 100 shapes and sizes, some easily made at home. *Spaghetti* is a solid rod, available in various thicknesses as well as a wavy shape. Linguini and fusilli are two favorite forms. *Macaroni* is tubular, either short or long, curved or straight; and also comes in special shapes such as shells and corkscrews. Ziti and rigatoni are among the more popular styles. *Noodles* are usually flat. Unlike macaroni and spaghetti, many are made with egg solids. Along with the familiar egg noodles, lasagna and fettucini are widely used.

Look for the term "enriched" on pasta labels. It means that the products are a valuable source of B vitamins and iron. High-quality products are made with durum wheat (semolina).

Pasta pronto: Canned, packaged and frozen specialties include ravioli, macaroni-and-cheese dinner, lasagna and many others.

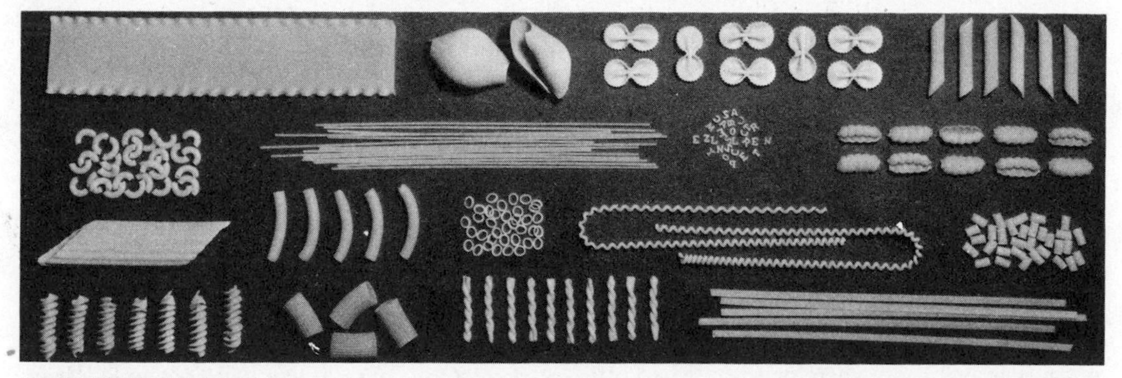

FAVORITE PASTA

Left to right: Top row: lasagna noodle, jumbo shells, bow ties, mostaccioli. Second row: elbow macaroni, spaghetti, alphabets, cavatelli. Third row: manicotti, ziti, rings, fusilli, tubettini. Bottom row: corkscrews, rigatoni, spaghetti twists, linguini.

Cooking Tips for Pasta

Most macaroni products double in size when cooked, so use a large, deep kettle, and at least four cups lightly salted water for every four ounces of pasta, to allow plenty of room to expand without sticking. Also to prevent sticking, add about a tablespoon of salad oil to cooking water.

When water is boiling briskly, gradually add pasta so that boiling does not stop. Cook, uncovered, stirring occasionally to separate. Follow label directions for cooking time—cook only until tender, yet firm. Test doneness by tasting.

Drain cooked pasta at once in colander or strainer. Do not rinse. If needed, add a bit more salad oil to prevent sticking.

Tips on Using Pasta

Store uncooked pasta at room temperature in a cool, dry place in covered containers to keep out dust and moisture. Macaroni and spaghetti will keep up to one year; noodles can be kept for about six months.

If cooked pasta is to be used in a casserole or with other ingredients in a dish that needs further cooking, shorten the boiling time slightly.

When using cooked pasta in a cold salad, add some of the salad dressing while pasta is still hot. This helps prevent sticking, helps flavors blend more thoroughly, too. Add remaining salad dressing just before serving time.

Pasta is at its best when cooked just before serving; but if it must be cooked ahead of time, or if there are leftovers, toss with a small amount of salad oil and refrigerate in a covered container. To reheat, place in pot of boiling water just long enough to heat through. Drain and use immediately.

When cooked pasta is stored in sauce, it softens and loses texture.

Different kinds of pasta are interchangeable in most recipes. For uncooked pasta, make the substitution by weight. Don't use cup measure, because a cupful of one kind of uncooked product may weigh more or less than a cupful of another kind. However, with cooked products, you *can* substitute cup for cup.

Rice Recipes

RICE PLUS

Prepare *4 servings of hot fluffy rice* as label directs; toss with one of these additions until well mixed:

ALMOND: *1/4 cup chopped or slivered toasted almonds.*

APPLE-CURRY: Cut *1 cored, unpeeled apple* into chunks. In small skillet over medium heat, in *3 tablespoons hot butter or margarine,* cook apple and *1/4 teaspoon curry powder* 5 minutes or until apple is tender.

CARROT-PARSLEY: *1 raw medium carrot,* shredded, and *2 tablespoons chopped parsley.*

CELERY: *1 small celery stalk,* chopped.

CHEESE: *1/2 cup shredded mild or sharp Cheddar cheese.*

CHUTNEY: *1/4 cup drained diced chutney* and *1/4 cup dark seedless raisins.*

CURRIED-PINEAPPLE: In small skillet over medium heat, in *2 tablespoons hot butter or margarine,* heat *one 13 1/4-ounce can pineapple tidbits,* drained, with *1/4 teaspoon curry powder,* 5 minutes or until hot.

MUSHROOM: *1/4 to 1/2 cup drained canned or cooked mushroom slices,* caps or stems and pieces.

OLIVE: *1/4 cup sliced pimento-stuffed or ripe olives.*

ONION: In small skillet over medium heat, in *2 tablespoons hot butter or margarine,* cook *1/4 cup diced onion* 5 minutes or until tender.

PARSLEY: *1/4 cup chopped parsley.*

PIMENTO: *2 tablespoons chopped pimento.*

POPPY SEED: *2 tablespoons poppy seed.*

RAISIN-CURRY: *1/2 cup golden raisins* and *1/2 teaspoon curry powder.*

TOMATO: *1/4 to 1/3 cup diced tomato.*

VEGETABLE: About *1/2 cup hot drained canned or cooked peas,* whole-kernel corn or mixed vegetables. If you like, add *2 tablespoons drained cocktail onions.*

HOT FLUFFY RICE
Saucepan Style

1 cup regular long- or medium-grain rice
1 teaspoon salt
1 tablespoon butter or margarine (optional)

ABOUT 20 MINUTES BEFORE SERVING:
In 3-quart saucepan with tight-fitting lid, over high heat, heat all ingredients and 2 cups water to boiling. Reduce heat until mixture just simmers; with fork, stir mixture once or twice. Cover pan and simmer without stirring or lifting lid, about 14 minutes or until rice is tender and all liquid is absorbed. Spoon rice into warm serving dish; fluff with fork. Makes 3 cups or 4 servings.

FOR DRIER RICE: Remove pan from heat; fluff rice lightly with fork, then cover and let stand 5 to 10 minutes.

FOR EXTRA-TENDER RICE: Increase water to 2⅓ cups; prepare as above but cook 4 to 5 minutes longer.

PARBOILED RICE: Prepare as label directs.

PRECOOKED RICE: Prepare as label directs.

BROWN RICE: Use *1 cup brown rice, 1 teaspoon salt* and *2½ cups water*. Prepare as above but simmer about 45 minutes. Or, prepare as label directs. Makes about 4 cups or 5 or 6 servings.

HOT FLUFFY RICE
Double-Boiler Style

1 cup regular long- or medium-grain rice*
1 teaspoon salt
1 tablespoon butter or margarine (optional)

ABOUT 40 MINUTES BEFORE SERVING:
In double-boiler top directly over high heat, heat all ingredients and 2 cups water to boiling. Place over gently boiling water in double-boiler bottom; cover tightly and cook without stirring or lifting lid, about 35 minutes or until rice is tender and all liquid is absorbed. Spoon rice into warm serving dish; fluff with fork. Makes 3 to 4 cups or 4 servings.

MILKY: Omit water and butter or margarine. Use *3½ cups milk;* prepare as above with regular long-grain rice but cook 40 minutes or until rice is tender and milk is absorbed.

* Or, use 1 cup parboiled rice and 2½ cups water.

COOK-IN FLAVORS FOR RICE

Prepare your favorite kind of rice but vary the liquid one of these ways:

CHERRY: Substitute *½ cup maraschino cherry liquid* for ½ cup of the water.

CHICKEN: Substitute *chicken broth* (homemade, canned or made with bouillon cubes or envelopes) for the water. Sprinkle cooked rice with *paprika* before serving.

BEEF: Substitute *canned condensed consommé,* diluted as label directs, for the water.

ORANGE OR APPLE: Substitute *½ cup orange, apple or tangerine juice* for ½ cup of the water.

VEGETABLE: Substitute *1 cup canned tomato juice* or cocktail vegetable juice for 1 cup of the water.

GOLDEN RICE

1 cup regular long-grain rice*
3 tablespoons butter or margarine
1 teaspoon salt

ABOUT 30 MINUTES BEFORE SERVING:
In medium saucepan over medium heat, cook rice, stirring constantly, until rice is golden. Stir in 2 cups water, butter or margarine and salt. Over high heat, heat to boiling; reduce heat to low, cover and simmer 15 minutes or until tender. Makes 6 servings.

* Or, use ¾ cup parboiled rice; simmer 25 minutes.

HERB RICE

ABOUT 15 TO 25 MINUTES BEFORE SERVING:
Prepare rice as label directs, but add one of these to water: about ⅛ teaspoon thyme

leaves, oregano leaves, sage leaves, rosemary, basil or savory; or about ½ teaspoon celery seed or dill weed; or about ¾ teaspoon marjoram leaves; or about 2 teaspoons poppy seed; or 1 small bay leaf. Or, substitute seasoned salt for salt.

When rice is cooked, toss with 1 or 2 tablespoons butter or margarine, if desired.

BAKED SAFFRON RICE

1 cup regular or parboiled long-grain rice
2 tablespoons butter or margarine
2 chicken-bouillon cubes or envelopes
½ teaspoon salt
½ teaspoon saffron

ABOUT 45 MINUTES BEFORE SERVING:
Preheat oven to 350°F. Grease 1½-quart casserole. Into casserole, measure rice and butter or margarine. In medium saucepan over medium heat, heat 2 cups water, bouillon cubes, salt and saffron to boiling; stir until dissolved. Pour mixture into casserole; cover and bake 30 minutes. Fluff rice with fork. Makes 6 servings.

OVEN DINNER RICE

1 cup regular long-grain rice*
2 tablespoons butter or margarine
1 teaspoon salt

ABOUT 35 MINUTES BEFORE SERVING:
Preheat oven to 350°F. Grease 1½-quart casserole. In casserole, combine all ingredients and 2 cups boiling water. Cover and bake 30 minutes or until rice is tender and all liquid is absorbed. Fluff rice with fork. Makes 4 servings.

* Or, use ¾ cup parboiled rice.

PILAF: Prepare as above but, in medium saucepan over medium heat, melt butter or margarine; cook *1 medium onion*, chopped, until tender, about 5 minutes; add *one 10½-ounce can condensed consommé* and *⅔ cup water;* heat to boiling; remove from heat; stir in rice and omit salt. Pour into casserole and bake as above. Sprinkle with *¼ cup pine nuts* or almonds if desired.

RISOTTO-STYLE: Sprinkle Pilaf with *¼ cup grated Parmesan cheese.*

CURRIED: In medium saucepan over medium heat, brown *1 cup regular long-grain rice,* stirring constantly; pour into casserole. In same pan, in *2 tablespoons hot butter or margarine,* cook *1 medium onion,* chopped, and *1½ teaspoons curry powder* until onion is tender, about 5 minutes. Add *2 cups boiling water* and heat to boiling; stir into rice. Bake as above.

ORANGE RICE

¼ cup butter or margarine
⅔ cup chopped celery (with leaves)
2 tablespoons minced onion
1 tablespoon grated orange peel
1 cup orange juice
1 teaspoon salt
⅛ teaspoon thyme leaves
1 cup regular long-grain rice*

ABOUT 45 MINUTES BEFORE SERVING:
In medium saucepan over medium heat, in hot butter or margarine, cook celery and onion until tender, about 5 minutes. Add 1½ cups water, orange peel, juice, salt and thyme. Heat to boiling; stir in rice; reduce heat to low; cover and simmer 15 to 20 minutes until rice is tender and all liquid is absorbed. Makes 6 servings.

* Or use ¾ cup parboiled rice.

RED-AND-GREEN RICE

4 cups hot cooked rice
¼ cup chopped green pepper
¼ cup sliced green onions
1 canned pimento, chopped
2 tablespoons butter or margarine
½ teaspoon seasoned salt

ABOUT 30 MINUTES* BEFORE SERVING:
In serving bowl, toss hot rice with all ingredients until butter or margarine is melted. Makes 6 servings.

* If using precooked rice, allow only 15 minutes before serving.

RED-AND-GREEN-RICE SALAD: Prepare as above but omit butter or margarine and add *½ cup Classic French Dressing* (page 411); cover and refrigerate several hours.

CURRIED RICE AND ONIONS

2 tablespoons butter or margarine
2 small onions, sliced ¼-inch thick
½ teaspoon curry powder
½ teaspoon salt
⅛ teaspoon nutmeg or mace
2 cups cooked rice
½ cup half-and-half

ABOUT 20 MINUTES BEFORE SERVING:
In medium saucepan over low heat, in hot butter or margarine, cook onions, curry, salt and nutmeg, stirring often, until onions are golden, about 7 minutes. Stir in rice and half-and-half; heat. Makes 4 servings.

SAVORY LEMON RICE

packaged precooked rice for 6 servings
3 tablespoons butter or margarine
1 13¾-ounce can chicken broth
¼ cup chopped parsley
grated peel of 1 lemon
1 tablespoon lemon juice

ABOUT 15 MINUTES BEFORE SERVING:
Prepare rice as label directs but use 3 tablespoons butter or margarine and, instead of water, use chicken broth with enough water to make amount of liquid label calls for to cook 6 servings of rice. When rice is cooked, add parsley, lemon peel and juice and toss to mix. Makes 6 servings.

RICE-AND-MUSHROOM CASSEROLE

½ cup regular long-grain rice
4 tablespoons butter or margarine
¼ pound mushrooms, sliced
½ cup chopped onion
½ cup chopped celery
1 beef-bouillon cube or envelope
½ teaspoon salt
⅛ teaspoon thyme leaves

ABOUT 1 HOUR BEFORE SERVING:
Preheat oven to 350°F. In medium skillet over medium heat, cook rice, stirring constantly, until golden, about 5 minutes; pour into 1½-quart casserole. In same skillet, in 2 tablespoons hot butter, cook mushrooms, onion and celery until tender, about 5 minutes. Add 1¼ cups water, bouillon, salt and thyme; heat to boiling; pour over rice.

Cover casserole and bake 35 minutes or until all liquid is absorbed. With fork, lightly toss in 2 tablespoons butter or margarine. Makes 4 servings.

BAKED SPANISH RICE

4 bacon slices
1 cup chopped onions
½ cup diced green pepper
1 16-ounce can tomatoes
1 8-ounce can tomato sauce
2 teaspoons sugar
1 teaspoon salt
1⅓ cups regular long-grain rice*
½ cup shredded Cheddar cheese

ABOUT 1 HOUR BEFORE SERVING:
Preheat oven to 350°F. Grease 1½-quart casserole. In large skillet over medium heat, fry bacon crisp; drain on paper towels; crumble and set aside. Pour off all but 2 tablespoons bacon drippings. In hot drippings, cook onions and green pepper until tender, stirring often, about 5 minutes.

Into measuring cup, drain tomatoes; add enough water to tomato liquid to make 1¾ cups liquid; cut up tomatoes. To onion mixture, add liquid, tomatoes, tomato sauce, sugar and salt; heat to boiling. Remove from heat and stir in rice; pour into casserole.

Cover casserole and bake 35 minutes or until rice is tender. Fluff rice with fork; sprinkle with cheese and bake 5 minutes. Garnish with bacon. Makes 6 servings.

* Or, use 1 cup parboiled rice and add enough water to tomato liquid to make 2 cups.

RICE RING

6 cups hot cooked rice
¼ cup chopped parsley
3 tablespoons butter or margarine

ABOUT 5 MINUTES BEFORE SERVING:
Grease a 5½-cup ring mold. In large bowl, toss all ingredients; lightly pack in ring mold; let stand 1 minute. Loosen edges; invert onto serving plate. Makes 6 servings.

TO KEEP RICE RING HOT: If ring is to be held awhile before serving, set mold in pan containing a little hot water; simmer on range.

FLORENTINE RICE

¼ cup butter or margarine
⅓ cup chopped onion
1 10-ounce package frozen chopped spinach, thawed and drained
1½ teaspoons salt
dash pepper
packaged precooked rice for 6 servings
½ cup shredded Cheddar cheese

ABOUT 20 MINUTES BEFORE SERVING:
In medium saucepan over medium heat, in hot butter or margarine, cook onion until tender, about 5 minutes. Add amount of water label calls for to cook 6 servings rice; add spinach, salt and pepper; heat to boiling. Stir in rice and finish cooking as label directs but add no more salt. Spoon rice into warm serving dish; fluff with fork, then sprinkle with cheese. Makes 6 servings.

PARTY RICE AND NOODLES

butter or margarine
2 medium onions, chopped
2 cups regular long-grain or parboiled rice
1 6-ounce can sliced mushrooms, drained (or ½ pound fresh mushrooms, sliced)
½ teaspoon curry powder
dash pepper
4 cups chicken broth
1½ teaspoons salt
½ 8-ounce package medium noodles (2 heaping cups)

ABOUT 1½ HOURS BEFORE SERVING:
Preheat oven to 350°F. In Dutch oven over medium heat, in ¼ cup hot butter or margarine, cook onions until tender, about 5 minutes. Add rice, mushrooms, curry and pepper and cook 5 minutes, stirring frequently. Stir in chicken broth, ¼ cup butter or margarine and salt and heat to boiling. Gently stir in uncooked noodles.

Pour mixture into 3-quart casserole; cover and bake 35 to 40 minutes until rice and noodles are tender and all liquid is absorbed. Just before serving, fluff mixture with fork. Makes 12 servings.

RICE-CHEESE PUFF

3 eggs, separated, at room temperature
1 cup cold cooked rice
½ cup milk
½ cup shredded longhorn cheese
¾ teaspoon salt
¾ teaspoon dry mustard
1 tablespoon diced pimento

ABOUT 1 HOUR BEFORE SERVING:
Preheat oven to 300°F. Grease 1-quart soufflé dish or casserole. In small bowl, with fork, beat egg yolks slightly. Stir in remaining ingredients except egg whites. In medium bowl, with mixer at high speed, beat egg whites until stiff peaks form; with rubber spatula, gently fold in rice mixture. Pour into soufflé dish. Bake 35 minutes or until knife inserted in center comes out clean. Serve immediately. Makes 6 servings.

FLUFFY WHITE AND WILD RICE

¼ cup butter or margarine
1 medium onion, chopped
½ pound mushrooms, sliced
1 10½-ounce can condensed consommé
1½ teaspoons salt
½ cup wild rice
1 cup regular long-grain rice*

ABOUT 1 HOUR BEFORE SERVING:
Preheat oven to 350°F. In ovenproof medium skillet over medium heat, in hot butter or margarine, cook onion and mushrooms until onion is tender, about 5 minutes. Stir in 1⅔ cups water, undiluted consommé and salt; heat to boiling.

Meanwhile, wash wild rice well; drain. Stir rice and wild rice into boiling mixture. Cover and bake 35 minutes or until wild rice is tender and all liquid is absorbed. Toss mixture with fork. Makes 8 servings.

* Or, use ¾ cup parboiled rice.

WILD RICE IN CONSOMME: About 1¼ hours before serving: Prepare as above but omit long-grain rice and use a total of *1 cup wild rice;* decrease water to ⅔ cup and salt to 1 teaspoon. Cover and bake 65 minutes. Makes 6 servings.

BOILED WILD RICE

1⅓ cups wild rice (8 ounces)
1½ teaspoons salt
2 tablespoons butter or margarine

ABOUT 1 HOUR BEFORE SERVING:
Wash rice well; drain. In medium saucepan over high heat, heat 2⅔ cups water to boiling. Stir in wild rice and salt. Reduce heat; cover and simmer 45 to 50 minutes until rice is tender and all liquid is absorbed. With fork, lightly toss in butter or margarine until melted. Makes 6 servings.

Macaroni, Spaghetti and Noodle Recipes

MACARONI PLUS

For each 4 to 6 servings, cook 8 ounces macaroni, spaghetti or noodles as label directs. Drain and season or garnish in one of these ways:

CRUNCHY: Sprinkle with *Buttered Crumbs* (page 351); or Polonaise Sauce (page 351); or crumbled potato or corn chips; or crumbled, canned French-fried onions; or chopped or toasted nuts.

SEEDED: Toss with *3 or 4 tablespoons butter or margarine* and *1 or 2 teaspoons poppy or celery seed.*

ONIONY: In small skillet over medium heat, in *3 or 4 tablespoons hot butter or margarine,* cook *1 small onion,* diced, and *2 tablespoons diced green pepper* 5 minutes or until tender. Toss with hot, drained cooked macaroni, spaghetti or noodles.

TOMATO: Toss with *fresh tomato chunks* or halved cherry tomatoes.

MUSHROOM: Toss with *drained canned or cooked mushrooms.*

CARROT: Toss with *shredded raw carrot.*

OLIVE: Toss with *whole or diced stuffed or ripe olives.* If you like, add 1 or 2 tablespoons olive oil.

HOLIDAY: Toss with *drained canned or cooked peas* and *diced canned pimento.*

ELENA'S MACARONI BAKE

1 8-ounce package elbow macaroni
½ pound Monterey (Jack) or American cheese, diced
1 cup sour cream
¼ cup butter or margarine
¾ teaspoon salt
¼ teaspoon pepper

ABOUT 50 MINUTES BEFORE SERVING:
Preheat oven to 350°F. Grease 2-quart casserole. Cook macaroni as label directs; drain. In casserole, stir all ingredients. Cover and bake 30 minutes. Makes 8 servings.

BAKED MACARONI AND CHEESE

1 8-ounce package elbow macaroni
4 tablespoons butter or margarine
¾ cup fresh bread crumbs
1 small onion, minced
1 tablespoon all-purpose flour
1 teaspoon salt
¼ teaspoon dry mustard
dash pepper
1½ cups milk
2 4-ounce packages shredded Cheddar cheese (2 cups)

ABOUT 45 MINUTES BEFORE SERVING:
1. Cook macaroni as label directs; drain. Preheat oven to 350°F. Grease 2-quart casserole. In small saucepan over medium heat, melt 2 tablespoons butter or margarine; add bread crumbs and toss to coat; set aside.
2. Meanwhile, in medium saucepan over medium heat, melt remaining 2 tablespoons butter; add onion and cook until tender, about 5 minutes. Stir in flour, salt, mustard and pepper until blended. Slowly stir in milk; cook until smooth and slightly thickened, stirring constantly. Remove from heat and stir in cheese until melted.
3. Place drained macaroni in casserole. Pour cheese mixture over macaroni. Sprinkle reserved crumb mixture over top.
4. Bake 20 minutes or until bubbly and bread crumbs are golden. Makes 4 servings as main dish, 6 servings as side dish.

MACARONI-STUFFED TOMATOES

6 firm medium tomatoes
seasoned salt
2 cups hot cooked elbow macaroni
1 10½-ounce can condensed cream-of-mushroom soup
2 tablespoons butter or margarine
½ cup fresh white or whole-wheat bread crumbs
1 tablespoon chopped parsley

ABOUT 45 MINUTES BEFORE SERVING:
Preheat oven to 375°F. Cut thin slice from stem end of tomatoes; scoop pulp and juice from tomatoes (save for use another day). Invert tomatoes onto paper towels 15 minutes to drain, then sprinkle inside with seasoned salt.

In medium bowl, stir macaroni with undiluted soup until well mixed; heap mixture in tomatoes. In small saucepan over medium heat, melt butter or margarine; add bread crumbs and parsley and toss to mix well; sprinkle over tomatoes. Place in 9″ by 9″ baking dish. Bake 20 minutes or until heated through. Makes 6 servings.

SPAGHETTI PATTIES

4 cups cooked spaghetti
3 eggs
4 bacon slices, fried and crumbled
¼ cup minced green onions
¼ cup grated Parmesan cheese
1 teaspoon salt
dash pepper
salad oil

ABOUT 45 MINUTES BEFORE SERVING:
In large bowl, combine all ingredients except salad oil. In large skillet over medium heat, in 3 tablespoons hot salad oil, drop three heaping ½-cup mounds of spaghetti mixture. Using a pancake turner, press each mound into a 4-inch patty.

Fry patties until golden brown, about 7 minutes, turning once; remove to platter; keep warm. Repeat with remaining spaghetti mixture, adding more oil if necessary. Serve as accompaniment to any meat, poultry or fish dish in place of potatoes or rice. Makes 6 servings.

HOMEMADE PASTA DOUGH

2¼ to 2½ cups all-purpose flour
2 eggs
1 egg yolk
1 tablespoon olive or salad oil
1 teaspoon salt

In large bowl, combine 1 cup flour, ⅓ cup water and remaining ingredients. With mixer at low speed, beat 2 minutes, occasionally scraping bowl with rubber spatula. With wooden spoon, stir in enough additional flour to make a soft dough.

Turn dough onto lightly floured surface and knead until smooth and not sticky, about 20 times. Makes 1 pound, enough dough for Cavatelli (page 308), Jumbo Ravioli (page 307) and Cannelloni (page 306).

HOMEMADE EGG NOODLES

ABOUT 3½ HOURS AHEAD OR DAY BEFORE:
Prepare Homemade Pasta Dough as above but knead until smooth and elastic, about 10 minutes. Wrap in waxed paper and let stand 30 minutes.

Cut dough in half. On floured surface, with floured rolling pin, roll half of dough into 20″ by 14″ rectangle. Fold in half crosswise, then in half again; cut into ⅛-inch strips for narrow noodles, ¼-inch strips for medium noodles, ½-inch strips for wide noodles. Open strips and place in single layer on clean cloth towels to dry. Repeat with remaining dough. Let noodles dry at least 2 hours before cooking. (Makes 1 pound.)

ABOUT 20 MINUTES BEFORE SERVING:
In large kettle over high heat, heat to boiling *3 quarts water* and *9 chicken- or beef-bouillon cubes* or envelopes (or 1 tablespoon salt) and *1 tablespoon butter or margarine.* Break noodles into smaller lengths, if desired; add to kettle and heat to boiling; cook 12 to 15 minutes until tender; drain in colander. Serve with more butter or margarine, if you like. Makes 6 servings.

NOODLES PLUS: Toss hot cooked noodles with *poppy or toasted sesame seed,* or grated American cheese food or buttered crumbs.

CANNELLONI WITH CHEESE SAUCE

Homemade Pasta Dough (page 305)
2 tablespoons butter or margarine
1 tablespoon chopped green onion
1 10-ounce package frozen chopped spinach, cooked and drained
1 cup finely chopped cooked chicken
½ cup finely chopped cooked ham
½ cup grated Parmesan cheese
1 egg, beaten
1 tablespoon dry sherry
¼ teaspoon ginger
salt
salad oil
Parmesan-Cheese Sauce or Quick Parmesan-Cheese Sauce (below)
chopped parsley for garnish

ABOUT 2½ HOURS BEFORE SERVING:
1. Prepare Homemade Pasta Dough. Cut pasta into 3 pieces. On well-floured surface, with floured rolling pin, roll 1 piece into 16″ by 8″ rectangle; cut into eight 4-inch squares. Place pasta on floured, clean cloth towel. Repeat with remaining pasta, making 24 squares in all. Cover and let pasta stand for 1 hour.
2. In medium saucepan over medium heat, in hot butter or margarine, cook green onion until tender. Stir in spinach, chicken, ham, cheese, egg, sherry, ginger and ¼ teaspoon salt; heat; set aside.
3. Preheat oven to 350°F. Grease 13″ by 9″ metal pan or broiler-proof baking dish. In large kettle over high heat, heat to boiling 5 quarts water, 2 tablespoons salt and 1 tablespoon salad oil. Cook pasta squares, a few at a time, 5 minutes. Remove pasta with slotted spoon; drain in colander and assemble while warm.
4. To assemble cannelloni: Spread rounded tablespoonful of meat mixture across center of warm pasta square; roll jelly-roll fashion. Place, seam side down, in pan. Repeat with remaining pasta squares and meat mixture.
5. Pour Parmesan-Cheese Sauce or Quick Parmesan-Cheese Sauce evenly over cannelloni; sprinkle with chopped parsley. Bake 20 minutes. Turn oven control to broil; broil 5 minutes or until golden brown. Makes 8 servings.

PARMESAN-CHEESE SAUCE: In medium saucepan over medium heat, into *¼ cup butter or margarine,* melted, stir *¼ cup all-purpose flour* until well blended. Gradually stir in *1½ cups half-and-half, 1½ cups water* and *2 chicken-bouillon cubes.* Cook, stirring constantly, until sauce is thickened; stir in *½ cup grated Parmesan cheese* and heat just until melted.

QUICK PARMESAN-CHEESE SAUCE: In medium saucepan over medium heat, heat *one 10½-ounce can condensed cream-of-chicken soup,* undiluted, *1 cup half-and-half, ½ cup water* and *½ cup grated Parmesan cheese,* shredded Fontina or Swiss cheese just until cheese is melted.

DOUBLE-DUTY STUFFED SHELLS

1 16-ounce package jumbo shell macaroni (about 40)
2 15- or 16-ounce containers ricotta or cottage cheese (4 cups)
1 8-ounce package mozzarella cheese, shredded
2 eggs
⅓ cup dried bread crumbs
¼ cup chopped parsley
1 teaspoon salt
¼ teaspoon pepper
1 29-ounce jar meatless spaghetti sauce
½ cup grated Parmesan cheese

ABOUT 1½ HOURS BEFORE SERVING:
Prepare macaroni as label directs; drain well. Meanwhile, preheat oven to 350°F. In large bowl, combine ricotta, mozzarella, eggs, bread crumbs, parsley, salt and pepper. Stuff rounded tablespoonful of cheese mixture into each cooked shell.

Spoon ¾ cup spaghetti sauce into each of two greased 13″ by 9″ baking dishes. (Or, use one 13″ by 9″ and two 9″ by 9″ baking dishes.) Arrange stuffed shells, seam side down, over sauce in one layer. Spoon remaining sauce evenly over shells; sprinkle with Parmesan cheese. Bake 30 minutes or until shells are heated through. Makes 10 servings.

TO FREEZE AND SERVE UP TO 1 MONTH LATER: Using freezerproof and ovenproof baking dishes, prepare as above but do not bake; wrap and freeze. To serve, preheat oven to 350°F. Bake frozen stuffed shells, covered, for 1 hour or until hot.

FETTUCINI ALFREDO

1 8-ounce package fettucini or medium egg noodles
¼ cup butter or margarine, melted
¼ cup grated Parmesan cheese
2 tablespoons half-and-half
salt
dash pepper

ABOUT 25 MINUTES BEFORE SERVING:
Prepare noodles as label directs; drain. Meanwhile, in warm serving dish, combine butter or margarine, cheese, half-and-half, ¼ teaspoon salt and pepper.

Carefully toss hot drained noodles with cheese mixture to coat well. Serve immediately. Pass more grated cheese, if you like, to sprinkle over servings. Makes 8 servings.

EGGPLANT LASAGNA

½ 16-ounce package lasagna noodles
1 cup dried bread crumbs
salt
dash pepper
2 eggs
1 medium eggplant, cut in ½-inch slices
salad oil
1 16-ounce package mozzarella cheese, thinly sliced
1 29-ounce jar meatless spaghetti sauce
¼ cup grated Parmesan cheese

ABOUT 1½ HOURS BEFORE SERVING:
Preheat oven to 350°F. Prepare noodles as label directs; drain. Meanwhile, on waxed paper, combine bread crumbs, ½ teaspoon salt and pepper. In small dish, with fork, beat eggs with 2 tablespoons water. Dip eggplant into egg mixture, then crumb mixture.

In large skillet over medium heat, in 2 tablespoons hot salad oil, cook eggplant slices, a few at a time, until tender, adding more oil when necessary. Drain on paper towels.

Grease 13" by 9" baking pan; in pan, layer half of noodles, eggplant slices, mozzarella and spaghetti sauce; repeat. Evenly sprinkle Parmesan cheese over sauce. Bake 30 minutes or until hot. Makes 8 servings.

JUMBO RAVIOLI WITH MARINARA SAUCE

Cheese Filling or Meat Filling (below)
Homemade Pasta Dough (page 305)
all-purpose flour
Marinara Sauce (page 309)
2 tablespoons salt
1 tablespoon salad oil
¼ cup grated Parmesan cheese for topping

ABOUT 2½ HOURS BEFORE SERVING:
Prepare Cheese or Meat Filling; set aside. Prepare Homemade Pasta Dough. Cut pasta into 4 pieces. On well-floured surface, with floured rolling pin, roll 1 piece into a 15" by 6" rectangle; with sharp knife, cut rectangle crosswise into five 6" by 3" pieces.

Spread rounded tablespoonfuls of either Cheese or Meat Filling on 3-inch side of each piece of pasta to within ¼ inch of edges. Fold dough over filling, bringing ends together; with fork dipped in flour, firmly press edges together. Place ravioli in single layer on floured, clean cloth towels. Repeat with remaining pasta and filling, making 20 ravioli in all. Let dry 30 minutes before cooking. Meanwhile, prepare Marinara Sauce; keep warm.

In large kettle over high heat, heat to boiling 4 quarts water, salt and salad oil. Cook ravioli, a few at a time, 10 minutes or until tender but firm; drain well in colander. Arrange on heated platter. Spoon Marinara Sauce evenly over ravioli; sprinkle with Parmesan cheese. Makes 4 servings.

CHEESE FILLING: In medium bowl, combine *one 15- or 16-ounce container ricotta cheese* (2 cups), *⅓ cup minced parsley, ¼ cup grated Parmesan cheese, 1 egg* and *½ teaspoon salt.*

MEAT FILLING: In medium skillet over medium-high heat, in *1 tablespoon hot olive or salad oil,* cook *¾ pound ground beef round, ½ cup minced onion* and *1 garlic clove,* minced, until meat is well browned; remove from heat and stir in *2 eggs,* slightly beaten, *¼ cup minced parsley, 2 tablespoons grated Parmesan cheese* and *1 teaspoon salt;* drain well.

NOODLES WITH HAM SAUCE

1 8-ounce package egg noodles
¼ cup butter or margarine
1 garlic clove, quartered
½ cup diced cooked ham
2 canned whole pimentos, diced
½ cup grated Parmesan cheese
1½ teaspoons salt

ABOUT 30 MINUTES BEFORE SERVING:
In large kettle, cook noodles as label directs. Meanwhile, in medium skillet over medium heat, in hot butter or margarine, cook garlic until golden. Add ham and pimentos; cook, stirring occasionally, until ham is lightly browned and heated through; discard garlic pieces.

Drain noodles well in colander; return to kettle; add ham mixture. Sprinkle grated cheese and salt over mixture and toss to mix well; spoon into warm serving bowl. Makes 6 first-course servings.

CAVATELLI WITH MEAT SAUCE

Meat Sauce (page 310)
Homemade Pasta Dough (page 305)
all-purpose flour
2 tablespoons salt
1 tablespoon salad oil
grated Parmesan cheese for topping

ABOUT 2½ HOURS BEFORE SERVING:
Prepare Meat Sauce; keep warm. Meanwhile, prepare Homemade Pasta Dough. Cut pasta into 8 pieces. With floured palms of hands, roll each piece into a 15-inch rope.

With sharp knife, cut ropes into ½-inch pieces. With finger, press each piece firmly in center, then draw your finger toward you to flatten slightly and form curled ends. Place noodles in single layer on floured, clean cloth towels. Let dry 30 minutes before cooking.

In large kettle over high heat, heat to boiling 4 quarts water, salt and salad oil; add noodles and heat to boiling; cook 10 minutes or until tender but firm, stirring occasionally; drain well in colander. Arrange on heated platter. Spoon Meat Sauce evenly over noodles; sprinkle with Parmesan cheese. Makes 4 servings.

TWO-CHEESE SPAGHETTI CASSEROLE

1 16-ounce package fusilli spaghetti
2 10¾-ounce cans condensed Cheddar-cheese soup
½ pound natural Swiss cheese, cubed

ABOUT 1 HOUR AND 15 MINUTES AHEAD:
Preheat oven to 350°F. Prepare spaghetti as label directs; drain. In greased 3-quart casserole, arrange one-third of spaghetti; spoon on one-third of undiluted cheese soup and top with one-third of Swiss cheese. Repeat layers twice. Cover and bake 45 minutes or until heated through. Makes 6 servings.

HOMEMADE SPINACH NOODLES

1 10-ounce bag spinach
salt
2 eggs
2½ to 3 cups all-purpose flour
1 tablespoon salad oil
½ cup butter or margarine

ABOUT 3 HOURS OR DAY AHEAD:
1. Wash spinach well under cold running water; trim off tough ribs and stems. In large saucepan over medium heat, heat to boiling ¼ inch water and ½ teaspoon salt. Add spinach and return to boiling; cover and cook 3 minutes. Drain spinach well and blot excess moisture with paper towels.
2. Into large bowl, press spinach through a coarse strainer with back of spoon or rubber spatula (or, puree spinach with food mill or blender). With fork, stir in eggs, 2½ cups flour and 1 teaspoon salt until mixture resembles coarse crumbs. With hands, shape mixture into a ball.
3. On well-floured surface, knead dough until smooth and not sticky, about 10 minutes, kneading in more flour if necessary. Wrap dough in waxed paper and let stand 30 minutes.
4. Cut dough in half. On floured surface, with floured rolling pin, roll half of dough into about 20″ by 14″ rectangle. With knife, cut dough into 20″ by ½″ strips. Place strips in single layer on clean cloth towels to dry. Repeat with remaining dough. Let noodles dry at least 1 hour before cooking.

ABOUT 20 MINUTES BEFORE SERVING:
Cook noodles: In large kettle over high heat, heat to boiling 4 quarts water, 2 tablespoons salt and salad oil. Add noodles and return to boiling; cook 8 minutes or until noodles are tender but firm. In colander, drain noodles and return to kettle. Add butter or margarine and toss until melted. Serve noodles on heated platter with more butter or margarine, if you like. Makes 8 servings.

NOODLE RING

ABOUT 45 MINUTES BEFORE SERVING:
Preheat oven to 375°F. Cook *one 8-ounce package egg noodles* as label directs; drain. Return noodles to kettle and toss with *¼ cup butter or margarine* and *¼ teaspoon salt;* pack into 5½-cup ring mold. Set mold in shallow roasting pan on oven rack; pour boiling water in pan to come halfway up sides of mold. Bake 20 minutes.

To unmold ring, place warm platter over ring mold; invert both and lift off ring mold. Serve immediately. Makes 6 servings.

Spaghetti Sauces

MARINARA SAUCE

2 tablespoons olive or salad oil
2 garlic cloves, minced
1 small onion, chopped
1 16-ounce can tomatoes
1 6-ounce can tomato paste
1 tablespoon sugar
2 teaspoons basil
1½ teaspoons salt

ABOUT 30 MINUTES BEFORE SERVING:
In medium saucepan over medium heat, in hot olive oil, cook garlic and onion until tender, about 5 minutes.

Stir in tomatoes and their liquid and remaining ingredients.

Reduce heat to low; cover and cook 20 minutes or until mixture is thickened, stirring occasionally. Makes about 3 cups or enough to serve over 8 ounces spaghetti, cooked, for 6 side-dish servings.

WALNUT SAUCE

¼ cup butter or margarine
1 cup coarsely chopped California walnuts
½ cup milk
2 tablespoons minced parsley
1 teaspoon salt

ABOUT 15 MINUTES BEFORE SERVING:
In small skillet over medium heat, in hot butter or margarine, lightly brown walnuts, about 5 minutes, stirring occasionally. Stir in remaining ingredients and heat through. Makes about 1⅓ cups or enough to serve over 8 ounces spaghetti, cooked, for 6 side-dish servings.

ZUCCHINI SAUCE

3 tablespoons butter or margarine
3 medium zucchini, diced
1 small onion, minced
1 16-ounce can tomato puree
2 teaspoons salt
1½ teaspoons sugar
½ teaspoon oregano leaves

ABOUT 30 MINUTES BEFORE SERVING:
In large skillet over medium heat, in hot butter or margarine, cook zucchini and onion until zucchini is tender, stirring occasionally. Stir in remaining ingredients; cook until mixture is heated through, stirring occasionally. Makes about 4 cups or enough to serve over 8 ounces spaghetti, cooked, for 6 side-dish servings.

ANCHOVY SAUCE

¼ cup olive or salad oil
1 small garlic clove, halved
1 2-ounce can anchovy fillets, chopped
2 tablespoons minced parsley
2 tablespoons grated Parmesan cheese
1 teaspoon lemon juice

ABOUT 30 MINUTES BEFORE SERVING:
In small saucepan over medium-high heat, in hot olive oil, brown garlic. Remove from heat; discard garlic. Stir in remaining ingredients until well mixed. Makes about ½ cup or enough to serve over 8 ounces spaghetti, cooked, for 6 side-dish servings.

WHITE CLAM SAUCE

3 8-ounce cans minced clams
¼ cup olive or salad oil
1 garlic clove, minced
¾ cup chopped parsley
2 tablespoons white wine (optional)
1 teaspoon basil
½ teaspoon salt

ABOUT 20 MINUTES BEFORE SERVING:
Drain juice from clams, reserving juice. In medium saucepan over medium heat, in hot olive oil, cook garlic until tender. Stir in reserved clam juice and remaining ingredients except clams; cook 10 minutes, stirring occasionally. Stir in drained clams; cook just until clams are heated through. Makes about 3 cups or enough to serve over 16 ounces spaghetti, cooked, for 4 main-dish servings.

SPINACH SAUCE

¼ cup butter or margarine
1 10-ounce package frozen chopped spinach
1 teaspoon salt
1 cup ricotta cheese
¼ cup grated Parmesan cheese
¼ cup milk
⅛ teaspoon nutmeg

ABOUT 15 MINUTES BEFORE SERVING:
In medium saucepan over medium heat, in hot butter or margarine, cook spinach and salt 10 minutes. Reduce heat to low; stir in remaining ingredients until well mixed and continue cooking until mixture is just heated through (do not boil). Makes about 2½ cups or enough to serve over 8 ounces spaghetti, cooked, for 6 side-dish servings.

MEAT SAUCE

2 tablespoons olive or salad oil
1 pound ground beef
1 medium onion, chopped
1 garlic clove, minced
1 16-ounce can tomatoes
2 6-ounce cans tomato paste
4 teaspoons sugar
2 teaspoons oregano leaves
1¾ teaspoons salt
⅛ teaspoon cayenne pepper
1 bay leaf, crumbled

ABOUT 1 HOUR AND 10 MINUTES AHEAD:
In Dutch oven or large saucepan over medium heat, in hot olive oil, cook ground beef, onion and garlic until meat is well browned; spoon off excess fat. Stir in tomatoes with their liquid and remaining ingredients. Reduce heat to low; cover and simmer 35 minutes or until sauce is very thick, stirring occasionally. Makes about 4 cups, or enough to serve over 16 ounces spaghetti, cooked, for 4 main-dish servings.

PESTO

⅓ cup olive or salad oil
¼ cup grated Parmesan cheese
¼ cup chopped parsley
1 small garlic clove, quartered
2 tablespoons basil
1 teaspoon salt
¼ teaspoon nutmeg

JUST BEFORE SERVING:
In blender container, place all ingredients; cover and blend at medium speed until well mixed. Makes about ½ cup or enough to serve over 8 ounces spaghetti, cooked, for 6 side-dish servings.

Vegetables

Variety and good nutrition are the important contributions that vegetables—fresh, frozen, canned and dry—make to menus: variety in flavor, texture and color for good eating; nutrition in the form of generous amounts of many necessary nutrients for good health. Vegetables are a source of vitamins A and C and of important minerals, particularly iron and calcium. Mature dry legumes (peas, beans and lentils) furnish protein as well as B vitamins and other nutrients. And most vegetables are low in calories.

Modern production, transportation and storage methods make available an abundance of fresh vegetables. Lettuce, tomatoes, cabbage, onions, carrots and potatoes are among those we can count on buying at any time. And canned, frozen and dry vegetables assure a supply of practically the entire range of varieties, in or out of season, the year around.

Fresh vegetables: In general, fresh vegetables are at their highest quality and lowest price when in season. Choose vegetables that look fresh and crisp, and have no skin punctures, bruises or decay. Because vegetables are perishable, buy only what you need even if the price is low; don't buy more than you can store properly or use without waste. Avoid decayed or damaged vegetables; even though you trim off visible decay, deterioration can spread quickly through the vegetable.

Vegetables should be relatively dry; excess moisture encourages decay. When selecting, handle with care to prevent bruising or damage. Many fresh vegetables are washed, trimmed and prepackaged, which helps prevent overhandling and preserves freshness.

Most fresh vegetables retain peak quality only a few days at most, so store properly. Sort before storing and separate any soft or bruised vegetables from sound ones. Nearly all green vegetables will stay crisp longer if refrigerated in plastic bags, the vegetable crisper or covered containers. Leafy vegetables that are washed before storing should be thoroughly drained.

Specific directions for buying and storing individual fresh vegetables are given in the following pages.

Canned vegetables: Wholesome and nutritious, canned vegetables are rich in minerals and vitamins because they are grown especially for canning, are harvested when at their best, and are processed quickly and in the way that best preserves their nutrients and quality. They come in many forms —among them, whole, cut, sliced and diced. As a rule, whole vegetables and fancy cuts such as julienne and French-style cost more than other styles. Short-cut, sliced and diced vegetables are the least expensive.

Some canned vegetables come in sauces, mixed with other vegetables, or with special seasonings. There are dietetic vegetables, too, for use in special diets. Check the can label for information on the contents.

Unopened cans of vegetables should be stored in a cool dry place. For best quality, use within 1 year. If kept longer, vegetables will begin to lose quality but will stay safe to eat indefinitely unless the seal is broken. (A bulging lid indicates that the seal has been broken; the can must be discarded. Avoid buying dented, rusted or damaged cans.)

Cans of vegetables to be used in salad should be chilled; refrigerate at least 8 hours before using, longer if you like. Opened cans should be covered and stored in the refrigerator; use within 2 to 3 days. A metallic taste may develop in some vegetables, particularly acid ones such as tomatoes, but it is harmless.

Frozen vegetables: Like their canned counterparts, commercially frozen vegetables are grown especially for freezing and are harvested and processed when at peak quality. They more nearly resemble fresh vegetables in appearance and flavor, and usually cost more than canned vegetables. They come in packages of various sizes, most in the familiar 10-ounce box, others in 1- to 2-pound bags, to be used as needed, with the rest returned to the freezer for storage.

Frozen vegetables come in whole, fancy-cut, short-cut, sliced, diced, chopped and other forms. Many are processed in sauces, with other vegetables, with garnishes or flavorings or in prepared dishes such as soufflés, stuffed green peppers, eggplant parmigiana and the like.

Choose firm packages; avoid those that are soft, sweating or stained by their contents; these signs indicate that the package is defrosting or has been defrosted and refrozen. In either case, quality and flavor will be less than that of the freshly frozen vegetable. Buy from a grocer who maintains the freezer cabinet at 0°F., stocks reliable brands and has rapid turnover. Buy frozen foods last when shopping, carry them home in insulated or special frozen-food bags (particularly on hot days) and get them into the freezer or freezing compartment as quickly as possible.

For home freezing of vegetables, see page 709.

Dry and dried vegetables: These vegetables include legumes in variety—peas, many kinds of beans, lentils, etc.—plus vegetables for seasoning and a wide choice of potato products. Seasoning vegetables include chopped, diced, flaked, minced and shredded onions; celery, green pepper, parsley and vegetable flakes. Dried potato products range from mashed, scalloped, au gratin and frying potatoes to potato pancakes, baked potatoes in cheese sauce or sour cream and hash browns with onions.

These vegetables take up little storage space. Store in tightly closed containers in a cool dry place; they'll keep several months.

How to Cook

To cook fresh vegetables: Fresh vegetables often need some preparation—trimming, peeling, scraping—before cooking. Remove wilted, bruised, tough or discolored portions; trim sparingly to preserve nutrients. Peel or scrape only when necessary and as thinly as possible; some of the best nutrients lie just under the skin. Rinse or scrub thoroughly under running cold water. Never soak vegetables, since some nutrients dissolve in water.

Cook vegetables only long enough to make them tender, in just enough water to prevent scorching. The less water used, the greater the food value retained. Use a pan with a tight-fitting lid to keep steam and vapor in, hasten cooking. Unpeeled vegetables cooked whole retain more vitamins and minerals; however, the cooking time will be shorter if they are pared and cut, sliced, diced or shredded.

To boil: Over high heat, heat salted water to boiling (use ½ to 1 teaspoon salt for 6 servings of vegetable). Add vegetable; heat until water boils again, cover, reduce heat and cook just until vegetable is tender-crisp. Serve immediately; flavor and food value may be lost if vegetables stand.

To pressure cook: Follow the directions that come with your pressure cooker. Pour the recommended amount of water into the cooker, add salt and vegetables; cover. Bring pressure up quickly; reduce heat to maintain constant pressure and time the cooking period exactly. When time is up, reduce pressure as quickly as possible.

To bake: Follow specific recipe directions.

To French-fry: Potatoes, sweet potatoes, batter-dipped onion rings, eggplant sticks, parsnips and breaded green-pepper rings are all good choices for French frying.

Fill French fryer, deep saucepan or heavy kettle one-third full of shortening or salad oil. With basket in place, heat to 370° to 385°F. on deep-fat thermometer. Raise basket and in it place just enough vegetable to cover bottom only. Lower basket gently into hot fat; if fat bubbles excessively, raise and lower basket several times until bubbling subsides.

Fry until vegetable is golden brown and tender; then lift basket from fat, drain a few seconds and pour vegetable out onto paper towels to drain completely. Season to taste; spread fried vegetable on a cookie sheet and keep warm in oven until all of vegetable is fried and ready to serve.

To fry: Follow specific recipe directions.

To stir-fry: Many vegetables can be cooked in this classic Chinese way that preserves flavor, color and nutrients.

In Dutch oven or skillet over high heat, heat a small amount of salad oil until very hot. Add cut-up vegetable; cook, tossing frequently, until vegetable is coated with oil. Season to taste and continue to cook until vegetable is tender-crisp. Sometimes a small amount of liquid is added after the vegetable has been coated with oil. Follow recipe directions for specific vegetables.

To pan: Cook as in To Stir-Fry, above, but cover pan after vegetables are coated; shake pan occasionally to prevent burning.

To cook frozen vegetables: Commercially frozen vegetables should be cooked according to label directions. Season and serve like cooked fresh vegetables.

To cook home-frozen vegetables, see page 709.

To cook canned vegetables: "Heat and serve" is all you need to do with commercially canned vegetables. Pour the vegetable with its liquid into a saucepan, cover and cook over medium-low heat just until hot. Serve the liquid with the vegetable, or drain and use later in sauces, soups and gravies, for it contains valuable nutrients.

To cook dry and dried vegetables: Follow package directions for cooking potato products and for using dried seasoning vegetables. For specific directions for cooking dry beans, peas and lentils, see Beans, Dry (page 315).

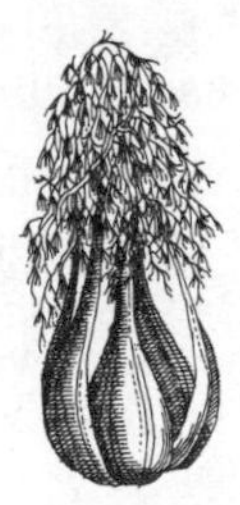

Anise, or Sweet Anise

(Fennel or Finochio)

Season: October to March.

Look for: Green, featherlike leaves and white bulbs.

To store: Refrigerate in crisper or wrapped; use within 3 to 5 days.

To prepare: Rinse in cold water. Cut ends and leaves from bulbs. Cut in sticks or pieces.

To cook: In medium saucepan over medium heat, in ½ inch boiling, salted water, heat cut-up anise to boiling; cover and cook 10 to 20 minutes or until tender.

To serve: Serve stalks fresh as snack, or use in salads like celery; use bulb and stalk cooked as vegetable with melted butter or margarine and lemon juice; use in recipes for tomato sauce or fish soups.

Artichokes, French or Globe

Season: All year. Best supplies are in March, April and May.

Look for: Compact, plump artichokes, heavy in relation to their size, with tightly closed, thick, green, blemish-free leaves. Size is not an indication of quality. Avoid over-mature artichokes with hard-tipped, spreading leaves.

To store: Refrigerate in plastic bag with a few drops water; use within a few days.

To prepare: With sharp knife, cut off stems and 1 inch straight across top. With scissors, trim thorny tips of leaves; brush cut edges with lemon juice to prevent them from turning brown. Pull loose leaves from around bottom.

To cook: In kettle over medium heat, in 1 inch boiling, salted water, place artichokes on stem ends; add a few lemon slices and heat to boiling. Then cover and cook 30 minutes or until leaf can be pulled off easily.

Seasonings to cook with: Bay leaf, garlic, oregano.

To serve: Serve as hot or cold appetizer or salad; use in recipes for stuffed main dish.

To eat: Place whole artichokes upright, with sauce on the side. With fingers, pluck off leaves one by one, starting at the bottom. Dip base of leaf (lighter-colored end) in sauce, then pull through teeth, scraping out the pulp. Discard leaves in a pile on plate. Then cut out and discard fuzzy "choke" in center of artichoke; cut solid heart into chunks and dip in sauce also.

Suggested sauces: Lemon Butter, page 351; Hollandaise Sauce, page 282.

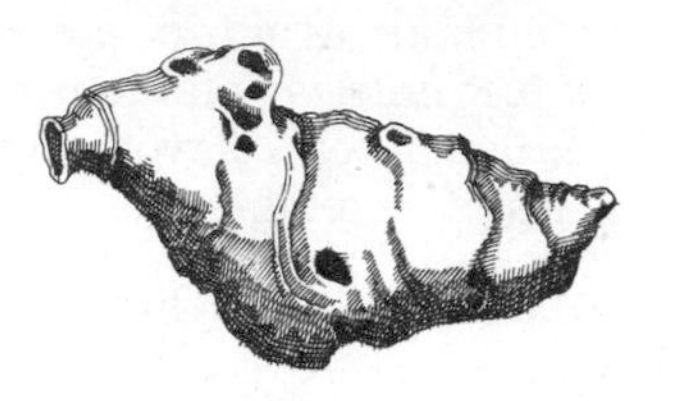

Artichokes, Jerusalem

Season: All year.

Look for: Firm, irregularly shaped artichokes, free of mold.

To store: Refrigerate in plastic bag with a few drops water; use within a week.

To prepare: Scrub with vegetable brush in cold water. Do not peel.

To cook: In medium saucepan over medium heat, in 1 inch boiling, salted water, heat Jerusalem artichokes to boiling; cover and cook 20 minutes or until fork-tender. Peel.

Seasonings to cook with: Lemon, vinegar, seasoned salt and pepper.

To serve: Serve as cooked vegetable.

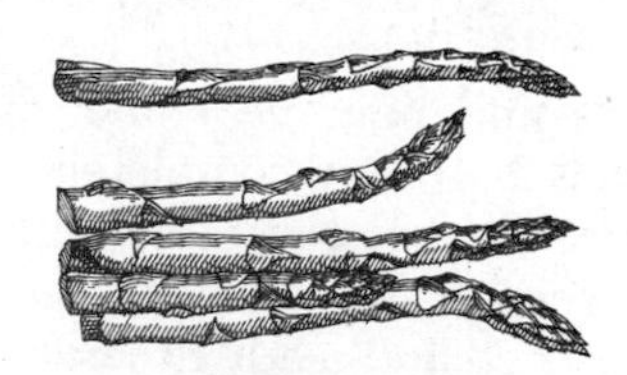

Asparagus

Season: March to July.

Look for: Straight stalks with closed, compact tips, good green color almost the entire length (the white area at the end is tough and must be discarded).

To store: Refrigerate in crisper or wrapped; use within 1 or 2 days.

To prepare: Hold base of stalk firmly and bend stalk; end will break off at spot where it becomes too tough to eat. Discard ends; trim scales if stalks are gritty.

To cook: In large skillet over medium heat, in 1 inch boiling, salted water, heat stalks to boiling; cover and cook whole asparagus about 5 minutes, cut-up asparagus about 3 to 5 minutes, until tender-crisp.

Seasonings to cook with: Allspice, mustard, coriander, lemon, seasoned salt and pepper.

To serve: Serve hot or cold, with or without sauce; use in recipes for soup, main dishes, salads, appetizers.

Suggested toppings: Toasted blanched almonds; lemon juice; Vinaigrette Sauce, page 352; nutmeg; Buttered Crumbs, page 351; Hollandaise Sauce, page 282.

PARTY ASPARAGUS

1 medium onion, chopped
1 medium green pepper, chopped
2 teaspoons salt
¼ teaspoon pepper
2 10-ounce packages frozen asparagus spears
2 teaspoons chopped pimento for garnish

ABOUT 20 MINUTES BEFORE SERVING:
In medium skillet over medium-high heat, heat ½ cup water, onion, green pepper, salt and pepper to boiling; cover and cook 5 minutes. Add asparagus and cook, covered, as label directs or until fork-tender. Serve asparagus topped with onion mixture. Garnish with pimento. Makes 6 servings.

STEAMED ASPARAGUS

ABOUT 15 MINUTES BEFORE SERVING:
In asparagus steamer or large saucepan with rack, heat ½ inch water to boiling; add *1 pound asparagus*. Cover; steam asparagus 8 to 10 minutes until tender. *Salt* to taste. Serve with Hollandaise Sauce, page 282 or Lemon Butter, page 351. Makes 4 servings.

STEAMED CUT ASPARAGUS: Cut asparagus diagonally into 2-inch pieces and steam as above, cooking 6 to 8 minutes until tender-crisp.

STIR-FRIED ASPARAGUS

1½ pounds asparagus
2 tablespoons salad oil
½ teaspoon salt

ABOUT 10 MINUTES BEFORE SERVING:
Cut asparagus diagonally into 3-inch pieces. In Dutch oven or medium skillet over high heat, in very hot salad oil, cook asparagus, stirring quickly and frequently (stir-frying) until well coated. Sprinkle with salt; continue stir-frying about 3 minutes more or until tender-crisp. Makes about 6 servings.

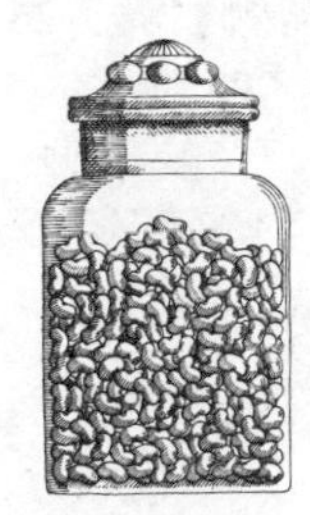

Beans, Dry

Also Dry Peas and Lentils

Season: All year.

Look for: Packaged dry beans, peas and lentils free of stones and shriveled beans.

To prepare: Rinse in running cold water and discard any small rocks or shriveled beans. Dry beans and whole peas require soaking before cooking; split peas do not. *For overnight soaking:* Cover each cup of dry beans or whole peas with 3 cups water and let stand overnight or at least 12 hours; next day, proceed with recipe, using same water. *For quicker soaking:* Add dry beans or whole peas to boiling water, allowing 3 cups water for each cup beans or peas, and, over high heat, heat to boiling; boil 2 minutes. Remove from heat, cover pan and let soak 1 hour, then cook in same water.

To cook: Cook according to recipe directions. To assure tenderer skins, add acid ingredients such as tomatoes, catchup and vinegar during last 15 minutes of cooking time. To prevent split skins, stir beans only occasionally. To prevent foaming, when cooking Great Northern, pinto or pea beans, add 2 tablespoons bacon drippings or other fat for each pound beans before cooking.

BOILED BEANS AND PEAS

Prepare and soak beans as on page 315. Add *1 teaspoon salt* for *each cup dry beans* or peas; season with *onion,* garlic or bay leaf. Cover; simmer over medium-low heat until tender, following timetable below. One cup dry vegetables yields 2 to 2½ cups cooked.

1 Cup Beans or Peas, Soaked	*Approximate Cooking Time*
Black beans	2 hours
Blackeye beans (peas or cowpeas)	25 to 30 minutes
Great Northern beans	1 to 1½ hours
Kidney beans	1½ hours
Lentils*	25 to 30 minutes
Lima beans	¾ to 1 hour
Pea beans (navy beans)	1½ hours
Peas, split*	45 minutes
Peas, whole	1 hour
Pinto beans	2 hours
Soy beans	1½ hours

* No soaking needed.

OLD-FASHIONED BAKED BEANS

2 pounds pea (navy) beans
½ cup packed brown sugar
½ cup dark molasses
4 large onions, chopped
2 tablespoons salt
4 teaspoons dry mustard
4 bacon slices, cut in 1-inch pieces

EARLY IN DAY:
Rinse beans; discard any stones or shriveled beans. In large, heavy Dutch oven over medium-high heat, heat beans and 12 cups boiling water to boiling; boil 2 minutes. Remove from heat; cover and let stand 1 hour.

Over high heat, heat covered beans to boiling; reduce heat to medium-low and simmer beans 1 hour, stirring occasionally.

Preheat oven to 350°F. Stir remaining ingredients into beans; bake, covered, 1 hour, stirring often. Remove cover; bake 1 more hour. Makes about 11½ cups or 12 servings.

Beans, Fava

Follow directions for Lima Beans, next page.

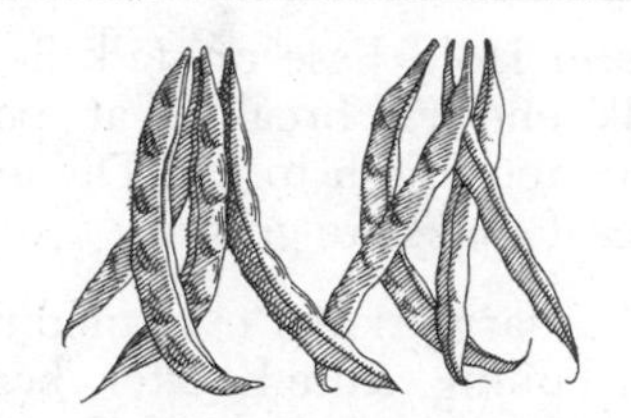

Beans, Green and Wax

Season: All year. Best supply is in June.

Look for: Crisp but tender beans without scars. Well-shaped pods with small seeds are most desirable; length is unimportant.

To store: Refrigerate in crisper or wrapped; use within 1 or 2 days.

To prepare: Rinse in cold water. Snap off ends; "string" will come off with stem end. Leave whole, or snap or cut into bite-size pieces; or pull through bean slicer for French-style beans.

To cook: In saucepan over medium heat, in 1 inch boiling, salted water, heat beans to boiling; cover and cook whole or cut-up beans 10 minutes, French-style 5 minutes, or until tender-crisp.

Seasonings to cook with: Chili powder, chives, dill, lemon, mustard, onion, sage, parsley, seasoned salt and seasoned pepper; or a few tablespoons bacon or ham drippings.

To serve: Serve hot, with or without sauce; use in recipes for stews, soups, pot roasts, main dishes and cold salads.

Suggested toppings: Hot Thousand Island Sauce, page 352; Vinaigrette Sauce, page 352; Sour Cream-Mustard Sauce, page 351; White Sauce, page 352.

GREEN BEANS IN BLUE-CHEESE SAUCE

2 pounds green beans, cut up
½ teaspoon salt
1 1½-ounce envelope white-sauce mix
⅓ cup crumbled blue cheese

ABOUT 30 MINUTES BEFORE SERVING:
In large saucepan over medium-high heat, in 1 inch boiling water, heat green beans and salt to boiling; cover and cook beans

until fork-tender, about 10 minutes; drain.

Meanwhile, prepare sauce mix as label directs for medium sauce but stir in blue cheese with liquid. Toss beans in sauce. Makes 6 to 8 servings.

TURKISH GREEN BEANS

1 9-ounce package frozen green beans
¼ cup chopped green pepper
2½ tablespoons olive oil
1 tablespoon catchup
1 teaspoon instant minced onion
½ teaspoon salt

ABOUT 1½ HOURS AHEAD OR EARLY IN DAY: Cook beans as label directs but add green pepper; drain well. Stir in remaining ingredients and heat through. Cover and refrigerate to chill. Makes 4 servings.

TURKISH GREEN-BEAN SALAD: Prepare as above and serve on lettuce.

WAX BEANS WITH ONIONS

2 tablespoons butter or margarine
2 medium onions, minced
2 15½-ounce cans whole wax beans, drained
1 teaspoon seasoned pepper

ABOUT 15 MINUTES BEFORE SERVING: In medium skillet in hot butter or margarine, cook onions until tender, about 5 minutes. Add beans and pepper; cook until hot, stirring often. Makes 6 servings.

GREEN-BEAN-AND-ONION CASSEROLE

3 9-ounce packages frozen whole green beans
12 bacon slices, fried
½ 4-ounce jar pimentos, cut up
½ cup crumbled, canned French-fried onion rings
1 teaspoon seasoned salt
½ cup sour cream

ABOUT 35 MINUTES BEFORE SERVING: Cook green beans as label directs; drain. Crumble bacon and toss with beans, pimentos, onion rings and seasoned salt. Pour into serving dish; spoon sour cream into center. Makes 10 to 12 servings.

BACON-BITS GREEN BEANS

3 bacon slices, diced
2 tablespoons minced onion
⅓ cup wine vinegar
1½ teaspoons dill seed
1½ teaspoons seasoned salt
2 9-ounce packages frozen French-style green beans, partially thawed

ABOUT 30 MINUTES BEFORE SERVING: In small skillet over medium heat, fry bacon and onion until both are limp. Stir in vinegar, dill and seasoned salt; simmer, covered, 20 minutes.

Meanwhile, in only 1 cup water, cook beans as label directs; stir in bacon mixture. Makes 12 servings.

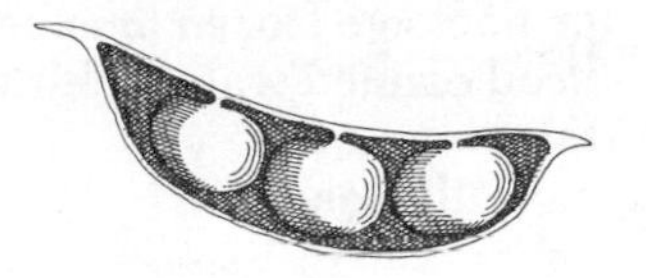

Beans, Lima

Season: All year. Best supplies are in August and September.

Look for: Well-filled, tender, green pods; avoid dried, spotty or yellowing ones. Shelled beans should be plump, with green to greenish-white skins.

To store: Refrigerate in crisper or wrapped; use within 1 or 2 days.

To prepare: Snap off one end of pod and open to remove beans. Or with knife, cut off thin strip from the inner edge of the pod and push out beans.

To cook: In saucepan over medium heat, in 1 inch boiling, salted water, heat beans to boiling; cover and cook 20 to 30 minutes until beans are tender.

Seasonings to cook with: Garlic, onion.

To serve: Serve hot, with or without sauce; use in recipes for stews, pot roasts, soups.

Suggested toppings: White or Cheese Sauce, page 352; Mushroom Sauce, page 168.

LIMA BEANS SMITANE

1 10-ounce package frozen baby lima beans
½ cup sour cream
3 tablespoons chopped chives
2 tablespoons pimento, cut into strips (optional)
¼ teaspoon garlic salt
¼ teaspoon salt
¼ teaspoon pepper

ABOUT 25 MINUTES BEFORE SERVING:
Cook lima beans as label directs; drain. Lightly toss with remaining ingredients. Makes 4 servings.

SPICY LIMA BEANS

1 10-ounce package frozen lima beans
½ cup sliced canned water chestnuts
¼ cup Italian dressing
¾ teaspoon dill weed

ABOUT 2 HOURS BEFORE SERVING:
Cook limas as label directs; drain. Add remaining ingredients and toss well. Cover and refrigerate to chill. Makes 4 servings.

Bean Sprouts

Season: All year.

Look for: Fresh-looking, crisp tops which are not dry; the shorter the sprout at the end of the bean, the more tender the bean.

To store: Place in container with water to cover and refrigerate. Use within 1 to 3 days.

To prepare: Rinse in cold water. If you like, remove roots of bean sprouts.

To cook: Use in recipes.

To serve: Use in tossed green salad. Serve as cooked vegetable.

STIR-FRIED BEAN SPROUTS

3 tablespoons salad oil
1 pound bean sprouts
1 teaspoon salt or 2 tablespoons soy sauce

ABOUT 5 MINUTES BEFORE SERVING:
In Dutch oven or medium skillet over high heat, in very hot salad oil, cook bean sprouts, stirring quickly and frequently (stir-frying) until well coated. Sprinkle with salt or soy sauce; continue stir-frying 2 minutes or more or until tender-crisp. Makes about 4 servings.

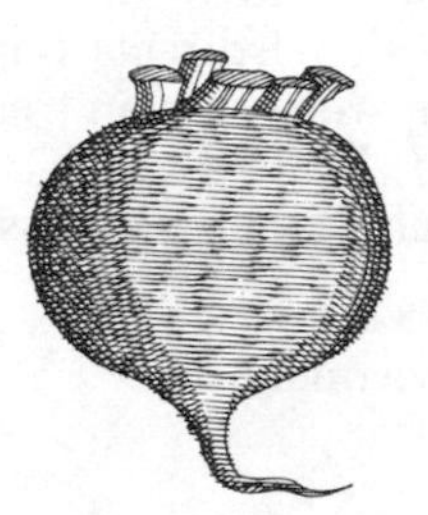

Beets

Season: All year. Best supplies are in June to October.

Look for: Smooth, rich red beets of uniform size, with no ridges or blemishes. Soft spots are telltale signs of decay. Green tops should be fresh.

To store: Remove tops; refrigerate tops and beets in crisper or wrapped. Use beets within a week or so, preferably less. Use tops as soon as possible (see Greens, page 330).

To prepare: Cut off tops and scrub beets with soft brush in cold water.

To cook: In saucepan over medium heat, in 1 inch boiling, salted water, heat beets to boiling. Cover and cook whole beets 30 to 60 minutes until tender (cooking time depends on maturity of the beets as well as their size); drain; run cold water over beets; remove skins. Or peel beets before cooking; slice or dice them; heat to boiling; cover and cook 15 to 20 minutes until tender.

Seasonings to cook with: Allspice, celery seed, cloves, dill, nutmeg, orange, lemon.

To serve: Serve hot or cold, with or without sauce; use in recipes for salads, soups.

Suggested sauces: Hollandaise Sauce, page 282; Sour Cream-Mustard Sauce, page 351; Vinaigrette Sauce, page 352.

HARVARD BEETS

¼ cup sugar
1 tablespoon cornstarch
½ teaspoon salt
⅓ cup vinegar
1 tablespoon butter or margarine
½ teaspoon instant minced onion
2 16-ounce cans sliced beets, drained (about 3 cups)

ABOUT 20 MINUTES BEFORE SERVING:
In small saucepan, combine sugar, cornstarch and salt; slowly stir in vinegar; add butter or margarine and instant minced onion; over medium heat, cook until thickened, stirring constantly. Reduce heat to low; add beets and cook just until heated through, stirring occasionally. Makes 6 servings.

BEETS IN ORANGE SAUCE: Prepare as above but use *½ cup orange juice* instead of vinegar and *1 teaspoon grated orange peel* instead of onion.

BEETS WITH LEMON-PEPPER SAUCE

1 16-ounce can sliced beets (about 2 cups)
1 1⅝-ounce package Hollandaise-sauce mix
½ teaspoon lemon-pepper marinade

ABOUT 10 MINUTES BEFORE SERVING:
In medium saucepan over medium heat, heat beets; drain and pour into serving dish. Meanwhile, in small saucepan, prepare sauce mix as label directs. Stir in marinade. Spoon over beets. Makes 4 servings.

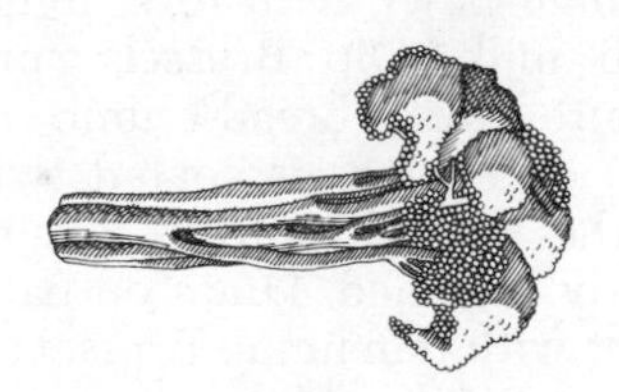

Broccoli

Season: All year. Lowest supplies are in July and August.

Look for: Tender, firm stalks and tightly closed, dark-green flowerets.

To store: Refrigerate in crisper or wrapped; use within 1 or 2 days.

To prepare: Remove large leaves and trim ends of stalk if tough or woody. Because stalks cook more slowly than the buds, split them lengthwise 2 or 3 times. Rinse well in cold water.

To cook: In skillet over medium heat, in 1 inch boiling, salted water, heat broccoli to boiling; cover and cook about 10 minutes until tender-crisp.

Seasonings to cook with: Coriander, dill, mustard, nutmeg, oregano.

To serve: Serve hot with or without sauce; use in recipes for chicken or turkey main dishes, casseroles, soups.

Suggested sauces: Hot Thousand Island Sauce, page 352; Sour Cream-Mustard Sauce, page 351; Cheese Sauce, page 352; Hollandaise Sauce, page 282.

SWISS-CHEESE BROCCOLI

1 pound broccoli, coarsely chopped
salt
3 tablespoons butter or margarine
2 tablespoons all-purpose flour
3 tablespoons chopped onion
1¼ cups milk
2 cups shredded natural Swiss cheese
2 eggs, beaten

ABOUT 1 HOUR BEFORE SERVING:
Preheat oven to 325°F. Grease a 10″ by 6″ dish. In medium saucepan over high heat, in 1 inch boiling water, heat broccoli and ½ teaspoon salt to boiling; cover and cook 10 minutes; drain; set aside.

Meanwhile, in medium saucepan over medium heat, melt butter or margarine; stir in flour and 1½ teaspoons salt until smooth. Add onion and cook 1 minute. Slowly stir in milk; cook, stirring constantly, until mixture thickens and begins to boil; remove from heat.

Stir cheese and broccoli into mixture until cheese melts slightly; stir in beaten eggs. Pour into baking dish and bake 30 minutes or until center is firm to the touch. Makes 8 servings.

BROCCOLI WITH SOUR-CREAM SAUCE

2 pounds broccoli
salt
½ cup sour cream
2 tablespoons prepared mustard

ABOUT 20 MINUTES BEFORE SERVING:
Preheat oven to 350°F. In large skillet over medium heat, in 1 inch boiling water, heat broccoli and ½ teaspoon salt to boiling; cover and cook about 10 minutes until tender-crisp; drain and arrange in shallow, medium baking dish.

In small bowl, mix sour cream, prepared mustard and ½ teaspoon salt; spoon over broccoli. Bake 8 minutes or until sauce sets. Makes 5 servings.

STIR-FRIED BROCCOLI

1 bunch broccoli
3 tablespoons salad oil
½ teaspoon salt
¼ teaspoon sugar

ABOUT 15 MINUTES BEFORE SERVING:
Cut broccoli into 2" by ½" pieces. In Dutch oven or large skillet over high heat, in very hot salad oil, cook broccoli, stirring quickly and frequently (stir-frying) until well coated. Add ¼ cup water, salt and sugar. Reduce heat to medium-high; cover and cook 2 minutes; uncover and stir-fry 5 to 6 minutes more until tender-crisp. Makes 4 to 6 servings.

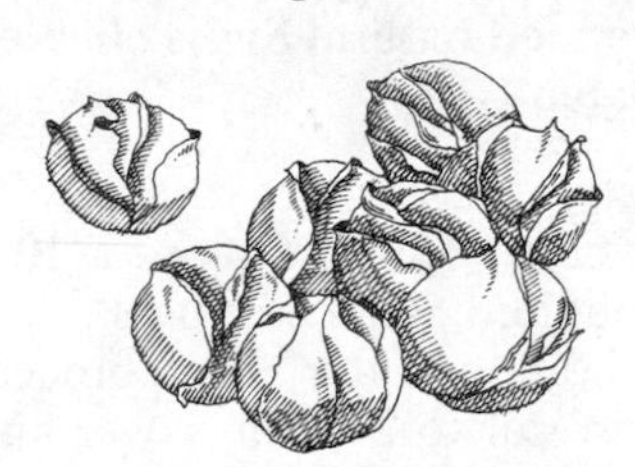

Brussels Sprouts

Season: All year. Best supplies are in September to February.

Look for: Firm, fresh, bright-green (not yellow) sprouts with tight-fitting outer leaves that are free from black spots. Puffy or soft sprouts are usually poor in quality.

To store: Refrigerate in crisper or wrapped; use within 1 or 2 days.

To prepare: Trim any yellow leaves, stem; cut an X into stem end to speed cooking. Rinse in cold water.

To cook: In saucepan over medium heat, in 1 inch boiling, salted water, heat Brussels sprouts to boiling; cover and cook about 10 minutes until tender-crisp.

Seasonings to cook with: Caraway, dill, mustard, nutmeg.

To serve: Serve hot with or without sauce; often served in combination with carrots, squash or tomatoes.

Suggested toppings: Horseradish Sauce, page 352; Sour Cream-Mustard Sauce, page 351; Vinaigrette Sauce, page 352; Buttered Crumbs, page 351.

FRENCH-FRIED BRUSSELS SPROUTS

1 13¾-ounce can chicken broth
2 10-ounce containers Brussels sprouts
salad oil
1½ cups dried bread crumbs
1½ teaspoons salt
½ teaspoon pepper
¼ teaspoon nutmeg
4 eggs
2 tablespoons milk

ABOUT 35 MINUTES BEFORE SERVING:
In medium saucepan over medium heat, heat chicken broth to boiling; add half of Brussels sprouts. Heat to boiling again; cover and cook 5 minutes or until tender-crisp; with slotted spoon, remove sprouts. Repeat with remaining sprouts. Meanwhile, in electric skillet,* heat ¾ inch salad oil to 370°F.

In small bowl or on waxed paper, mix bread crumbs, salt, pepper and nutmeg. In another small bowl, with fork, lightly beat eggs with milk. Dip Brussels sprouts in egg mixture, then bread-crumb mixture. Repeat so each piece is coated twice. Fry some of the Brussels sprouts 2 minutes or until lightly browned. Drain on paper towels. Repeat with remaining Brussels sprouts. Serve immediately. Makes 8 to 10 first-course servings or 6 vegetable servings.

* Or, in heavy saucepan over medium heat, heat salad oil to 370°F. on deep-fat thermometer.

BRUSSELS SPROUTS WITH WATER CHESTNUTS

2 10-ounce packages frozen Brussels sprouts
2 teaspoons sugar
1 teaspoon seasoned salt
¼ cup butter or margarine
½ 8-ounce can water chestnuts, sliced

ABOUT 20 MINUTES BEFORE SERVING:
Cook Brussels sprouts as label directs but omit salt and add sugar and seasoned salt; drain. Toss in butter or margarine and water chestnuts and heat over low heat. Makes 6 servings.

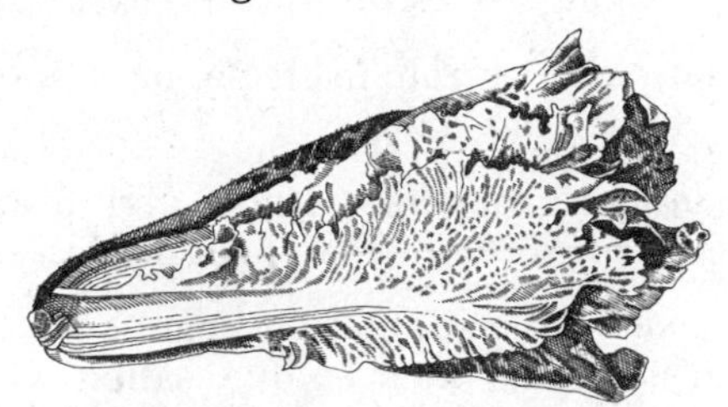

Cabbage, Chinese

Nappa, Bok Choy, Gai Choy (Chinese Mustard Greens), Gai Low (Chinese Broccoli)

Season: All year.

Look for: Crisp, fresh-appearing cabbage, free from blemishes. For Nappa, look for pale-green leaves on slender stalks. For Bok Choy, look for long, smooth, milk-white stems with large, crinkly, dark-green leaves. For Gai Choy, look for jade-green cabbage with tightly packed, curled leaves. For Gai Low, look for broccoli-like cabbage with long, irregular stalks and many leaves with white or yellow flowers.

To store: Refrigerate in crisper or wrapped; use within a week.

To prepare: Rinse; cut bottom from stalk. Slice, shred or separate into ribs.

To cook: Cook as green cabbage.

Seasonings to cook with: Soy sauce, salt and pepper.

To serve: Use Nappa sliced as salad with French dressing or tossed in green salads; use all varieties cooked as vegetable or in Chinese dishes.

STIR-FRIED CHINESE CABBAGE

1 medium head Chinese cabbage
3 tablespoons salad oil
1½ teaspoons salt or 3 tablespoons soy sauce
½ teaspoon sugar

ABOUT 15 MINUTES BEFORE SERVING:
Cut cabbage crosswise into 1½-inch pieces. In Dutch oven over high heat, in very hot salad oil, cook cabbage, stirring quickly and frequently (stir-frying) until well coated. Sprinkle with salt (use soy sauce only with Nappa) and sugar. Reduce heat; continue stir-frying 5 to 8 minutes more until tender-crisp. Makes about 4 servings.

Cabbage, Green and Red

Season: All year.

Look for: Firm heads with fresh, crisp-looking leaves. Green cabbage that has been held in storage is often trimmed of its outer leaves and lacks green color, but it is satisfactory if not wilted or discolored. Most popular green varieties include Danish, pointed and domestic. Savoy-type cabbage has finely crumpled green leaves, loosely formed heads; red varieties have distinctive reddish-purple color.

To store: Refrigerate in crisper; use within 1 or 2 weeks.

To prepare: Rinse in cold water. Cut into wedges. If core is tough, cut it away from each wedge, leaving just enough to retain shape of wedge. Or shred the cabbage, using a knife or shredder, and discard core.

To cook: In large saucepan over medium heat, in 1 inch boiling, salted water, heat cabbage to boiling; cover and cook wedges 10 to 15 minutes, shredded cabbage 3 to 10 minutes, until tender-crisp.

Seasonings to cook with: Allspice, caraway seed, cloves, curry, mustard, tarragon.

To serve: Use fresh in recipes for coleslaw, salads, pickled vegetables, sauerkraut; serve hot with or without seasonings.

Suggested toppings: Bacon bits, celery seed, grated Parmesan cheese, minced onion, chili sauce, lemon juice.

CARAWAY RED CABBAGE

2 tablespoons butter or margarine
½ cup chopped onions
2 teaspoons sugar
1 teaspoon salt
1¼ teaspoons caraway seed
2 teaspoons white vinegar
½ large red cabbage, shredded

ABOUT 20 MINUTES BEFORE SERVING:
In large saucepan over medium heat, in hot butter or margarine, cook onions until tender, about 5 minutes. Add 1 cup water and remaining ingredients; simmer, covered, for 8 minutes or until cabbage is tender-crisp. Makes 6 servings.

SKILLET CABBAGE

8 bacon slices, diced
½ cup minced onions
1 medium cabbage, shredded
2 teaspoons salt

ABOUT 30 MINUTES BEFORE SERVING:
In large skillet over medium heat, fry bacon and onions until onions are tender, about 5 minutes. Add remaining ingredients and cook, stirring occasionally, until cabbage is tender, about 10 minutes. Makes 6 to 8 servings.

STIR-FRIED CABBAGE

1 small head cabbage, coarsely shredded
3 tablespoons salad oil
1¼ teaspoons salt
¼ teaspoon sugar

ABOUT 15 MINUTES BEFORE SERVING:
In Dutch oven over high heat, in very hot salad oil, cook cabbage, stirring quickly and frequently (stir-frying) until well coated. Sprinkle with salt and sugar; continue stir-frying 4 minutes more or until tender-crisp. Makes about 4 servings.

Cardoon
(Cardoni)

Season: Fall and winter months.

Look for: Stalks with small shanks and crisp-looking leaves.

To store: Refrigerate in crisper or wrapped; use within 3 to 5 days.

To prepare: Separate stalks and discard outer, stringy stems. Rinse; cut in pieces.

To cook: In medium saucepan over medium heat, in 1 inch boiling, salted water, heat cardoon to boiling; cover and cook 20 minutes or until fork-tender.

Seasonings to cook with: Cloves, garlic.

To serve: Serve as cooked vegetable.

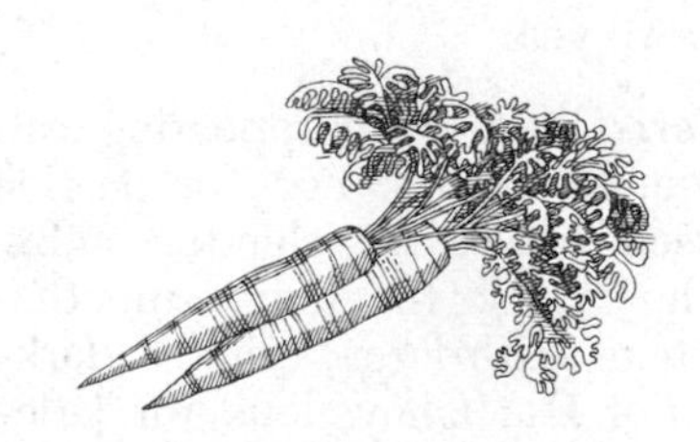

Carrots

Season: All year.

Look for: Firm, well-formed, bright-colored carrots. Avoid flabby or shriveled carrots.

To store: Refrigerate in crisper or wrapped; if carrots have tops, remove tops and refrigerate. Use within 1 or 2 weeks.

To prepare: Scrub with stiff vegetable brush in cold water or scrape. Leave carrots whole; or dice, slice or shred.

To cook: In saucepan over medium heat, in 1 inch boiling, salted water, heat carrots to boiling; cover and cook whole carrots about 20 minutes, cut-up carrots 10 to 20 minutes, until tender-crisp.

Seasonings to cook with: Cloves, curry, dill, ginger, mace, marjoram, mint, nutmeg.

To serve: Use fresh in salads, for snacks; serve hot with or without seasonings; use in recipes for stews, soups, casseroles.

Suggested toppings: Chopped parsley; White Sauce, page 352.

FRUITED CARROTS

10 medium carrots, thickly sliced
1 16-ounce can pineapple chunks
1 cup orange juice
1 tablespoon cornstarch
1 teaspoon salt
½ teaspoon cinnamon

ABOUT 20 MINUTES BEFORE SERVING:
In medium saucepan over medium heat, in 1 inch boiling water, heat carrots to boiling; cover and cook about 15 minutes or until tender-crisp; drain.

Into large saucepan, drain liquid from pineapple and add orange juice. In small bowl, mix cornstarch, salt and cinnamon; stir in a few tablespoons pineapple-orange juice and mix to a smooth paste.

Heat liquid, then stir in cornstarch mixture. Simmer, stirring constantly, until thickened. Add pineapple chunks and carrots; cook over low heat, stirring constantly, until hot and bubbly. Makes 10 servings.

SPICED CARROTS

1½ pounds carrots, sliced ¼ inch thick
½ cup dark seedless raisins
¼ cup butter or margarine
2½ tablespoons chopped onion
1 teaspoon cinnamon
¾ teaspoon salt
2 tablespoons brown sugar

ABOUT 45 MINUTES BEFORE SERVING:
In covered medium saucepan over low heat, cook all ingredients except brown sugar with ¾ cup water for 15 minutes or until carrots are fork-tender, stirring occasionally. Add brown sugar and cook until sugar is completely dissolved. Makes 6 servings.

CARROTS AND GRAPES

2 16-ounce bags carrots
½ cup orange juice
⅓ cup olive oil
½ teaspoon salt
½ teaspoon sugar
dash ginger
1 cup seedless green grapes, halved
2 tablespoons chopped parsley for garnish

ABOUT 45 MINUTES BEFORE SERVING:
Cut carrots into 1-inch-thick diagonal slices. In medium saucepan over medium heat, heat carrots, orange juice, olive oil, salt, sugar and ginger to boiling; cover and simmer 15 minutes. Add grapes and cook 5 minutes more or until carrots are fork-tender; drain. Sprinkle with parsley. Makes 8 servings.

CHEESE-AND-CARROT SCALLOP

12 medium carrots, sliced
butter or margarine
1 small onion, chopped
¼ cup all-purpose flour
2 cups milk
1 teaspoon salt
¼ teaspoon dry mustard
¼ teaspoon celery salt
dash pepper
1 cup fresh bread crumbs
1 8-ounce package American-cheese slices

ABOUT 50 MINUTES BEFORE SERVING:
1. In medium saucepan over medium heat, in 1 inch boiling, salted water, heat carrots to boiling; cover and cook 10 to 20 minutes until tender-crisp; drain.
2. Meanwhile, in another medium saucepan over low heat, melt ¼ cup butter or margarine; add onion and cook 5 minutes or until onion is tender. Stir in flour until smooth; stir in milk and next 4 ingredients. Cook mixture, stirring constantly, until thickened. Preheat oven to 350°F.
3. In small saucepan over medium heat, melt 3 tablespoons butter or margarine; add bread crumbs and toss to coat crumbs.
4. Lightly grease 2-quart casserole; in it, evenly spread half of carrots, then half of cheese; repeat. Pour sauce over all; sprinkle with bread crumbs. Bake 20 minutes or until hot and bubbly. Makes 8 servings.

GLAZED CARROTS

1 pound carrots, cut in large chunks
1 teaspoon salt
2 tablespoons butter or margarine
1 tablespoon sugar or brown sugar
¼ teaspoon nutmeg

ABOUT 25 MINUTES BEFORE SERVING:
In medium saucepan over medium heat, in 1 inch boiling water, heat carrots and ¼ teaspoon salt to boiling; cover and cook 15 minutes or until tender-crisp; drain. Add butter or margarine, sugar, ¾ teaspoon salt and nutmeg. Return mixture to heat and cook, stirring constantly, until carrots are glazed. Makes 4 servings.

SHREDDED CARROTS

2 cups shredded carrots
2 tablespoons butter or margarine
1 teaspoon sugar
½ teaspoon salt

ABOUT 15 MINUTES BEFORE SERVING:
In small saucepan over high heat, heat ¼ cup water to boiling. Add all ingredients. Reduce heat to medium; cover and cook 4 minutes. Makes 4 servings.

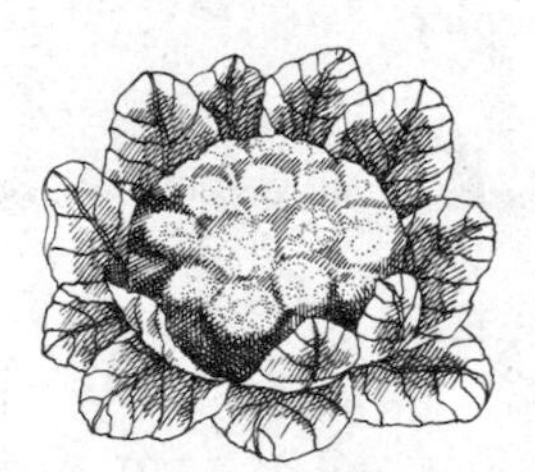

Cauliflower

Season: All year. Best supplies are in September to November.

Look for: Creamy-white, compact, tightly packed flowerets with a granular appearance. Leaves around base should be fresh and green.

To store: Refrigerate in crisper or wrapped; use as soon as possible, within 3 to 5 days.

To prepare: Rinse. Remove leaves and core. Separate into flowerets or leave whole.

To cook: In saucepan over medium heat, in 1 inch boiling, salted water, heat cauliflower to boiling; cover and cook whole cauliflower 10 to 15 minutes, flowerets about 8 minutes, until tender-crisp.

Seasonings to cook with: Chives, paprika, cloves, nutmeg, dill, rosemary, thyme.

To serve: Eat fresh in salads, for snacks; use cooked in combination with carrots, green beans.

Suggested toppings: Cheese Sauce, page 352; Bechamel Sauce, page 352; Hot Thousand Island Sauce, page 352; Vinaigrette Sauce, page 352; Hollandaise Sauce, page 282; Polonaise Sauce, page 351.

STIR-FRIED CAULIFLOWER

1 medium head cauliflower
¼ cup salad oil
¼ cup soy sauce
¼ teaspoon sugar
2 teaspoons cornstarch

ABOUT 15 MINUTES BEFORE SERVING:
Break cauliflower into small flowerets. In Dutch oven or large skillet over high heat, in very hot salad oil, cook cauliflower, stirring quickly and frequently (stir-frying) until well coated. Add ½ cup water, soy sauce and sugar. Reduce heat to medium-high; cover and cook 6 minutes more or until tender-crisp, stirring occasionally.

Meanwhile, in small bowl, stir cornstarch with 2 tablespoons cold water until smooth. Stir into cauliflower; cook, stirring, until thickened. Makes about 6 servings.

CAULIFLOWER PARMESAN

1 medium head cauliflower
½ teaspoon salt
¼ cup butter or margarine, melted
grated Parmesan cheese
seasoned pepper

ABOUT 20 MINUTES BEFORE SERVING:
In large saucepan over medium heat, in 1 inch boiling water, heat cauliflower and salt to boiling; cover and cook 10 to 15 minutes until fork-tender; drain well. Place whole cauliflower in serving dish. Pour on melted butter or margarine; sprinkle well with cheese, then with seasoned pepper. Makes 6 servings.

Celeriac
(Celery Root)

Season: October to April.

Look for: Firm, small celeriac without sprouts on top of the root. Bulb roots should be clean and tops fresh looking.

To store: Refrigerate; use within a week.

To prepare: Scrub with vegetable brush in cold water. Cut off leaves and rootlets; peel and slice for raw use.

To cook: In medium saucepan over medium heat, in 1½ inches boiling, salted water, heat celeriac to boiling; cover and cook 40 minutes or until fork-tender. Peel and slice.

Seasonings to cook with: Dill, mustard.

To serve: Serve raw as nibbler or snack or in salads. Serve as cooked vegetable.

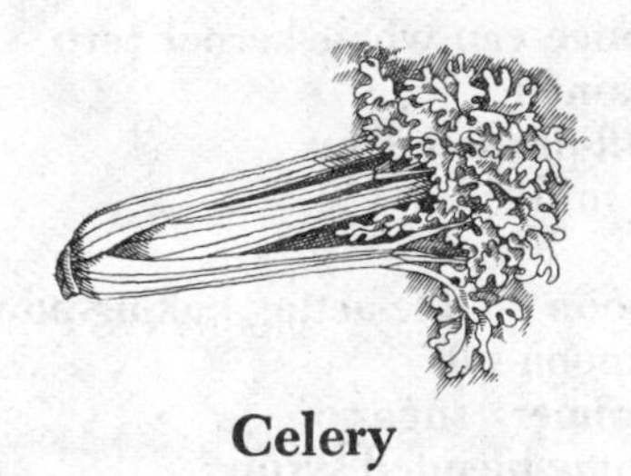

Celery

Season: All year.

Look for: Fresh, crisp, clean celery of medium length and size, pale green in color. Thin, dark-green stalks may be stringy.

To store: Refrigerate in crisper or wrapped; use within a week.

To prepare: Remove leaves (use in soups, stews); trim root end. Rinse well in cold water. Use outer stalks for cooking, cut up for salads; inner ones for serving raw.

To cook: In saucepan over medium heat, in 1 inch boiling, salted water, heat celery to boiling; cover and cook whole stalks 4 to 6 minutes, cut-up stalks 3 to 4 minutes, until tender-crisp.

Seasonings to serve with: Basil, chives, dill, mustard, tarragon.

To serve: Eat fresh for snacks, in salads; use as seasoning in casseroles, sauces; use as cooked vegetable, in soups, stews.

Suggested toppings: Buttered Crumbs, page 351; Vinaigrette Sauce, page 352; Lemon Butter, page 351.

BRAISED CELERY

2 bunches celery
1 chicken-bouillon cube
2 tablespoons butter or margarine
paprika for garnish

ABOUT 20 MINUTES BEFORE SERVING:
Pull outer stalks from celery, leaving tender center stalks intact; slice top of each bunch just below leaves. Cut bunches lengthwise into halves. (Refrigerate leftover stalks and leaves to use another day.)

In covered large skillet over medium-high heat, in 1 cup boiling water, cook celery and bouillon cube 8 to 10 minutes until celery is tender-crisp; drain. Quickly stir in butter or margarine and sprinkle with paprika; serve hot. Makes 4 servings.

CURRIED CELERY

⅓ cup butter or margarine
2 cups diagonally sliced celery
1 small onion, sliced
1 medium apple, cut in chunks
1 tablespoon all-purpose flour
1 teaspoon curry powder
½ teaspoon salt
dash pepper

ABOUT 35 MINUTES BEFORE SERVING:
In covered, medium skillet over medium-high heat, in hot butter or margarine, cook celery and onion 10 minutes or until tender-crisp, stirring occasionally. Add apple; cook, covered, 5 minutes or until tender. Add remaining ingredients and cook, stirring, until bubbling hot. Makes 6 servings.

STIR-FRIED CELERY

1 small bunch celery
2 tablespoons salad oil
1 tablespoon soy sauce
¼ teaspoon sugar

ABOUT 10 MINUTES BEFORE SERVING:
Cut celery diagonally into ½-inch pieces. In Dutch oven or medium skillet over high heat, in very hot salad oil, cook celery, stirring quickly and frequently (stir-frying) until well coated. Add soy sauce and sugar. Reduce heat to medium-high; continue stir-frying 5 minutes more or until tender-crisp. Makes about 6 servings.

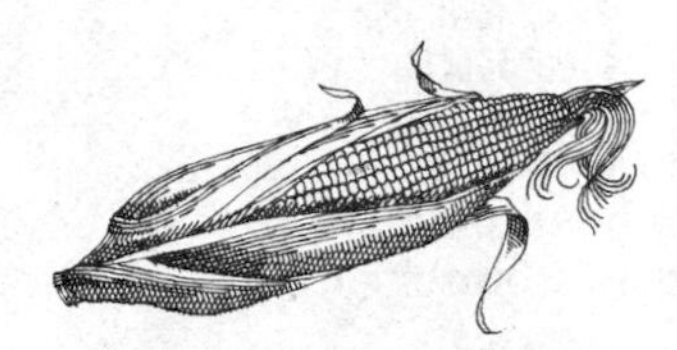

Corn

Season: All year. Best supplies are in May to September.

Look for: Medium-size ears with bright, plump, milky kernels that are just firm enough to offer slight resistance to pressure. Tiny kernels indicate immaturity; corn with very large, deep yellow kernels may be overmature and tough.

To store: Refrigerate in crisper; use as soon as possible.

To prepare: Just before cooking, remove husks and silk (small vegetable brush helps), if left on at market.

To cook: In kettle over medium heat, in 1 inch boiling, salted water, heat corn to boiling; cover and cook medium-size corn 5 to 6 minutes.

Seasonings to cook with: Basil, chili powder, chives, onions, oregano, garlic.

To serve: Spread corn-on-cob with butter or margarine, sprinkle with salt and eat in hands; cut cooked corn from cob and use in recipes for main dishes, salads, relishes, vegetable casseroles.

Suggested Toppings: Vinaigrette Sauce, page 352; Flavored Butters (next page).

SKILLET CORN

8 ears corn, husked
¼ cup butter or margarine
1 cup thinly sliced onions
½ cup green-pepper strips
1½ teaspoons salt
¼ teaspoon monosodium glutamate
¼ teaspoon oregano leaves
½ cup half-and-half
2 medium tomatoes, cut up

ABOUT 30 MINUTES BEFORE SERVING:
On cutting board, with sharp knife, cut kernels from corn (about 4 cups).

In covered large, heavy skillet over medium heat, in melted butter or margarine, cook corn, onions and next 4 ingredients until corn is tender, about 6 minutes, shaking skillet occasionally.

Remove cover; add half-and-half and tomato pieces and simmer, uncovered, 1 or 2 minutes until tomatoes are hot but still firm. Makes 6 servings.

SKILLET CORN AND OLIVES: Prepare as above but omit green pepper, tomatoes and 1 teaspoon salt; stir in *½ cup sliced stuffed olives* instead.

CORN FRITTERS

salad oil
1 16-ounce can whole-kernel corn, drained
1 cup all-purpose flour
¼ cup milk
2 eggs
1 teaspoon double-acting baking powder
½ teaspoon salt
confectioners' sugar or maple-blended syrup

ABOUT 30 MINUTES BEFORE SERVING:
In electric skillet, heat ½ inch salad oil to 400°F.* In medium bowl, with fork, stir 1 tablespoon salad oil and next 6 ingredients just until blended. Drop batter by tablespoonfuls into hot oil; fry 3 to 5 minutes, until golden brown, turning once. With slotted spoon, remove fritters to paper towels; drain. Sprinkle with sugar or serve with syrup. Makes 6 servings.

* Or, in heavy saucepan over medium-high heat, heat oil to 400°F. on deep-fat thermometer.

CUSTARD CORN PUDDING

2 cups milk
2 tablespoons butter or margarine
2 eggs
1½ teaspoons salt
1 teaspoon sugar
¼ teaspoon pepper
1 12-ounce can whole-kernel corn, drained

ABOUT 1½ HOURS BEFORE SERVING:
Preheat oven to 325°F. In medium saucepan over low heat, heat milk and butter or margarine until tiny bubbles form around edge and butter or margarine melts.

Meanwhile, in small bowl with wire whisk or fork, beat eggs, salt, sugar and pepper until well mixed; stir in corn. Slowly add milk to egg mixture, beating constantly with wire whisk or spoon.

Pour mixture into 1½-quart casserole. Set casserole in shallow baking pan on oven rack and fill pan with hot water to come halfway up side of casserole. Bake 1 hour or until knife inserted in center comes out clean. Makes 6 servings.

CREAMY CORN

1 3-ounce package cream cheese
½ cup milk
1 tablespoon butter or margarine
½ teaspoon onion salt
3 12-ounce cans whole-kernel corn

ABOUT 15 MINUTES BEFORE SERVING:
In medium skillet over low heat, stir cream cheese with milk, butter or margarine and onion salt until smooth. Add corn (do not drain corn) and heat, stirring occasionally, about 10 minutes. Makes 8 to 10 servings.

FLAVORED BUTTERS FOR CORN-ON-THE-COB

CHILI BUTTER: In small bowl, with wooden spoon, beat *½ cup butter or margarine*, softened, *2 teaspoons salt, 1 teaspoon chili powder* and *¼ teaspoon pepper* until well blended. Refrigerate until firm. Makes ½ cup.

CHIVE BUTTER: Prepare as above but substitute *2 teaspoons chopped chives* for chili powder.

DILL BUTTER: Prepare as above but substitute *1 teaspoon dill weed* for chili powder.

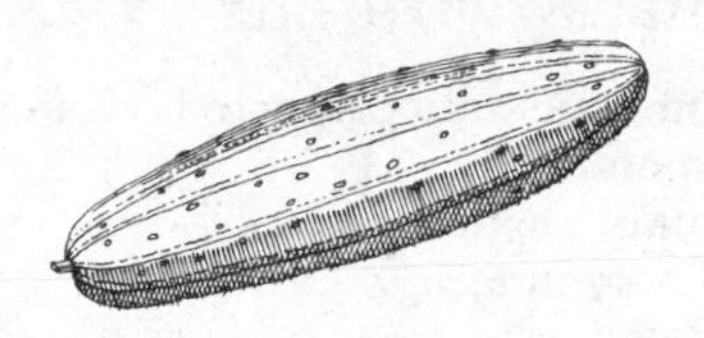

Cucumbers

Season: All year. Best supplies are in May to August.

Look for: Firm, well-shaped cucumbers with good green color. Overmature cucumbers, generally seedy, are dull or yellow and have overgrown, puffy look. Smaller varieties are preferred for pickling.

To store: Refrigerate; use within 3 to 5 days.

To prepare: Rinse in cold water. Trim ends and cut into desired shape. If skin is tender, it is not necessary to peel cucumbers. Slice, chop or cut in long wedges.

To cook: In saucepan over medium heat, in 1 inch boiling, salted water, heat lengthwise-halved cucumbers to boiling; cover and cook 5 to 10 minutes until tender-crisp.

Seasonings to sprinkle over fresh sliced cucumbers: Pepper, dill, tarragon.

To serve: Use fresh as snack, in sandwiches or salads; use in recipes for pickles, cold soup.

STIR-FRIED CUCUMBERS

3 medium cucumbers
3 tablespoons salad oil
5 teaspoons soy sauce
¼ teaspoon sugar

ABOUT 15 MINUTES BEFORE SERVING:
Peel and halve each cucumber lengthwise; remove seeds. Then cut cucumber halves into 1-inch chunks. In Dutch oven or medium skillet over high heat, in very hot salad oil, cook cucumbers, stirring quickly and frequently (stir-frying) until well coated. Add ¼ cup water, soy sauce and sugar. Reduce heat to medium-high; cover and cook about 5 minutes more or until tender-crisp, stirring occasionally. Makes about 4 servings.

CUCUMBERS WITH DILL

4 medium cucumbers, peeled
½ teaspoon salt
1 cup plain yogurt
½ cup mayonnaise
2 egg yolks
1 tablespoon chopped dill weed

ABOUT 30 MINUTES BEFORE SERVING:
Cut cucumbers into bite-size chunks. In medium saucepan over medium heat, in 1 inch boiling water, heat cucumbers and salt to boiling; cover and cook 5 minutes or until tender-crisp; drain well.

Meanwhile, in small saucepan over low heat, cook remaining ingredients except dill weed, stirring constantly, until thickened, about 10 minutes. Stir in cucumbers and dill weed. Makes 6 servings.

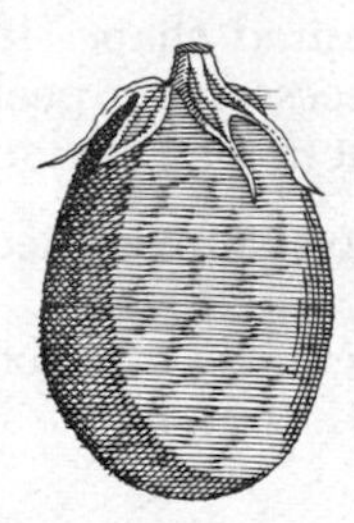

Eggplant

Season: All year.

Look for: Firm and heavy eggplant that has a uniformly dark, rich purple color and a bright green cap, and is free from scars or cuts. Wrinkled or flabby eggplant will usually be bitter-tasting.

To store: Refrigerate; use within 1 or 2 days.

To prepare: It is not necessary to peel eggplant if it is fresh and tender. Also, do not soak eggplant in salt water (you'll lose nutrients). Slice or cut into desired shape just before cooking; eggplant discolors quickly.

To cook: In large saucepan over medium heat, in 1 inch boiling, salted water, heat cut-up eggplant to boiling; then cover and cook about 5 minutes.

Seasonings to cook with: Oregano, sage, garlic.

To serve: Serve as cooked vegetable or use in recipes for casseroles, Italian dishes.

EGGPLANT WITH CARAWAY SEED

2 tablespoons salad oil
¾ cup chopped bacon slices
1 medium onion, sliced
1 teaspoon caraway seed
2 teaspoons vinegar
¾ teaspoon salt
1 small eggplant, cubed

ABOUT 25 MINUTES BEFORE SERVING:
In medium skillet over medium-high heat, in hot salad oil, cook all ingredients but eggplant 5 minutes or until bacon and onion are light brown. Reduce heat to medium; add eggplant and cook, covered, 5 to 7 minutes until tender, stirring occasionally. Makes 4 servings.

EGGPLANT PARMIGIANA

olive oil
1 garlic clove, minced
1 large onion, chopped
2 17-ounce cans tomatoes
2 teaspoons sugar
½ teaspoon oregano leaves
½ teaspoon basil
½ teaspoon salt
1 cup dried bread crumbs
2 eggs
1 large eggplant, cut into ½-inch slices
½ cup grated Parmesan cheese
1 8-ounce package mozzarella cheese, cut into ¼-inch slices

ABOUT 1½ HOURS BEFORE SERVING:
1. In medium skillet over medium heat, in 2 tablespoons hot olive oil, cook garlic and onion until tender, about 5 minutes. Add tomatoes and next 4 ingredients. Reduce heat to low and cook, covered, 30 minutes.
2. Meanwhile, grease 13″ by 9″ baking dish. On sheet of waxed paper, place bread crumbs. In small dish, with fork, beat eggs with 2 tablespoons water. Dip eggplant into egg mixture, then into crumb mixture. Repeat so each piece is coated twice.
3. In large skillet over medium heat, in 2 tablespoons hot olive oil, cook a few eggplant slices at a time until golden brown, adding a little more oil as needed.
4. Preheat oven to 350°F. Arrange half of eggplant slices in baking dish; cover with

half tomato mixture; sprinkle with half Parmesan and then top with half mozzarella; repeat. Bake 25 minutes or until lightly browned. Makes 6 main-dish servings.

STIR-FRIED EGGPLANT

1 medium eggplant
⅓ cup salad oil
2 tablespoons soy sauce
1¾ teaspoons sugar
¼ teaspoon ginger

ABOUT 15 MINUTES BEFORE SERVING:
Peel and cut eggplant into 1½-inch cubes. In Dutch oven or medium skillet over high heat, in very hot salad oil, cook eggplant, stirring quickly and frequently (stir-frying) until well coated. Add 1 cup water, soy sauce, sugar and ginger. Continue stir-frying about 8 minutes more or until tender. Makes about 4 servings.

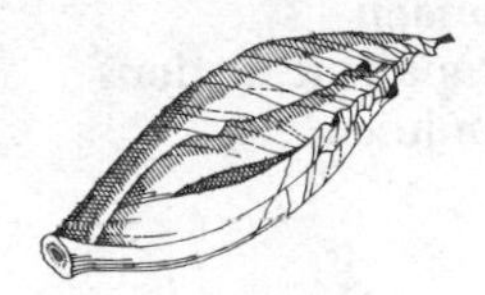

Endives, French or Belgian
(Witloof)

For curly endives, *see* Greens.

Season: September to June.

Look for: Small compact stalks with white leaves with pale green edges. Avoid wilted outer leaves.

To store: Refrigerate in crisper or wrapped; use within 1 or 2 days.

To prepare: Rinse. Trim any bruised leaves.

To cook: In saucepan over medium heat, in ½ inch boiling, salted water, heat endives to boiling; cover and cook about 15 minutes.

Seasonings to cook with: Lemon, nutmeg.

To serve: Use fresh with dressing as salad or in tossed salads; use cooked as vegetable.

Suggested toppings: Lemon Butter, page 351; Buttered Crumbs, page 351.

ENDIVES WITH SWISS CHEESE

12 small Belgian endives
salt
½ pound natural Swiss cheese, shredded
¼ cup butter or margarine
pepper
⅓ cup half-and-half

ABOUT 1 HOUR BEFORE SERVING:
Preheat oven to 350°F. In medium saucepan over medium heat, in 1 inch boiling water, heat endives and 1 teaspoon salt to boiling; cover and cook 10 minutes; drain.

Arrange 6 endives in metal 12" by 8" baking dish; sprinkle with half of cheese and dot with half of butter or margarine; sprinkle lightly with salt and pepper. Repeat. Pour half-and-half over all. Bake 10 to 15 minutes until cheese is melted. Turn heat control to broil; place dish under broiler for about 3 minutes until cheese is golden brown and bubbling. Makes 6 servings.

Escarole
See Greens

Garlic

Season: All year.

Look for: Firm, dry bulbs.

To store: Store in refrigerator or at cool room temperature in container that allows good circulaton of air. Keep dry. Will keep several months.

To prepare: Garlic is a compound bulb made up of several sections (cloves) enveloped in skin. Break off and peel cloves as needed. Leave whole, mince, chop or halve for recipes; crush in garlic press or with back of large, heavy knife to obtain garlic juice.

To cook: Use in recipes as directed.

Ginger Root

Season: All year.

Look for: Firm, irregular, knobby roots without any soft spots.

To store: Refrigerate and use within 1 or 2 weeks. (Or, put peeled, sliced ginger root in dry sherry in covered jar in refrigerator. Keeps several months.)

To prepare: Scrub with vegetable brush in cold water. Peel skin and shred or slice.

To cook: Use in recipes as directed.

To serve: Use shredded fresh ginger root as condiment on fruit salads, curries; use in recipes for main dishes, sauces, marinades.

Greens

Beet or Turnip Tops, Cilantro (Mexican or Chinese Parsley), Swiss Chard, Chicory (Curly Endive), Collards, Dandelion, Endive, Escarole, Kale, Leafy Broccoli, Mustard Greens, Parsley, Rape, Rappini, Sorrel, Spinach, Watercress

Season: Many varieties available all year.

Look for: Fresh, young, tender green leaves. Injured, dried or yellowed leaves, coarse stems or excessive sand and dirt usually indicate poor quality and may cause waste.

To store: Refrigerate in crisper or wrapped; use within 1 or 2 days.

To prepare: Wash well in cold water. Trim any rough ribs or stems. For salads, drain greens thoroughly, store in plastic bag in refrigerator to crisp.

To cook: In saucepan over medium heat, in ¼ inch boiling, salted water (using ½ teaspoon salt for 1 pound greens), heat greens to boiling; cover and cook tender, leafy greens 1 to 3 minutes, until wilted; others, 5 to 10 minutes until tender-crisp. (Parsley, cilantro should not be cooked except in recipes.)

Seasonings to cook with: Allspice, bacon drippings, lemon, onion, nutmeg, vinegar.

To serve: Serve fresh in salads with dressings; use leaves to serve molded and other salads on, in sandwiches; use as cooked vegetable or in main dishes.

SPINACH WITH GRAPEFRUIT

1 10-ounce package frozen chopped spinach
1 8-ounce can grapefruit sections
1 teaspoon lemon juice
cinnamon
pepper

ABOUT 20 MINUTES BEFORE SERVING:
Cook spinach as label directs but substitute juice drained from grapefruit for water. During last minutes of cooking time, add grapefruit sections to heat through. Drain; toss with lemon juice. Sprinkle lightly with cinnamon and pepper. Makes 6 servings.

CREAMED SPINACH

1 10-ounce bag fresh spinach or 1 10-ounce package frozen leaf spinach
½ teaspoon salt
White Sauce (page 352)
¼ teaspoon nutmeg

ABOUT 15 MINUTES BEFORE SERVING:
In medium saucepan over medium heat, in ¼ inch boiling water, heat spinach and salt to boiling; cover and cook 1 to 3 minutes until wilted; drain. Or cook frozen spinach as label directs; drain.

Meanwhile, prepare White Sauce; stir in nutmeg. Combine with spinach; mix well. Makes 4 servings.

Hominy

Hominy is corn with the hull and germ removed, available canned as whole kernels or packaged ground (hominy grits). Its chief use is as a vegetable; hominy grits are frequently served as a cereal.

HOMINY-AND-CHEESE CASSEROLE

3 tablespoons butter or margarine
3 tablespoons flour
¼ cup minced onion
1 teaspoon salt
¾ teaspoon chili powder
1½ cups milk
2 16-ounce cans white hominy
1 cup shredded longhorn cheese

ABOUT 35 MINUTES BEFORE SERVING:
Preheat oven to 350°F. In medium saucepan over medium heat, into melted butter or margarine, stir flour until smooth. Stir in onion, salt and chili powder. Slowly stir in milk; cook, stirring, until thickened.

In colander, wash and drain hominy well; stir into sauce. Pour mixture into 1½-quart casserole. Sprinkle with cheese. Bake 20 to 25 minutes. Makes 6 servings.

Horseradish Root

Season: All year.

Look for: Firm roots with no decay or soft spots; avoid shriveled roots.

To store: Refrigerate and use as needed. Keeps several months.

To prepare: Scrub with vegetable brush in cold water. Grate in blender or on grater.

To cook: Use in recipes as directed.

To serve: Use as condiment for beef, Japanese dishes; in recipes for sauces.

Kale

See Greens

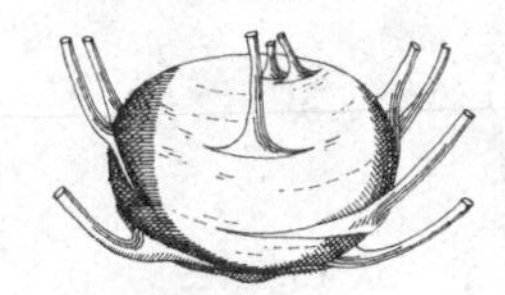

Kohlrabi

Season: May to November. Best supplies are in June and July.

Look for: Small or medium-size kohlrabi with fresh top, tender rind.

To store: Remove tops and discard; refrigerate; use within 2 or 3 days.

To prepare: Rinse in cold water. Peel thinly and slice, sliver or quarter.

To cook: In saucepan over medium heat, in 1 inch boiling, salted water, heat kohlrabi to boiling; cover and cook about 15 minutes.

Seasonings to cook with: Mustard, tarragon.

To serve: Serve peeled, fresh strips as snack or appetizer; use as cooked vegetable.

Suggested toppings: Lemon juice, parsley.

CHEESY KOHLRABI

8 medium kohlrabi, sliced ¼ inch thick
1 teaspoon salt
3 tablespoons butter or margarine
¼ cup all-purpose flour
1 10½-ounce can condensed chicken broth
¼ cup shredded American cheese
⅛ teaspoon allspice

ABOUT 45 MINUTES BEFORE SERVING:
In medium saucepan over medium heat, in 1 inch boiling water, heat kohlrabi and salt to boiling; cover and cook 30 minutes or until tender; drain.

Meanwhile, in large saucepan over low heat, into hot butter or margarine, stir flour until smooth. Gradually add undiluted chicken broth and cook, stirring constantly, until mixture is thickened. Remove from heat and stir in cheese until smooth. Add kohlrabi and cook until heated through. Sprinkle with allspice. Makes 6 servings.

Leeks

Season: All year. Best supplies are in September to November.

Look for: White bulb base with fresh green tops, usually trimmed. (Leeks are larger, milder than green onions, and give different flavor in recipes.)

To store: Refrigerate, wrapped; use within 3 to 5 days.

To prepare: Rinse in cold water. Cut off roots and stem ends. Wash. Use whole or cut into pieces.

To cook: In saucepan over medium heat, in 1 inch boiling, salted water, heat leeks to boiling; cover and cook 10 to 15 minutes until tender.

Seasonings to cook with: Ginger, rosemary, sage.

To serve: Serve fresh in salads; use as cooked vegetable or in recipes for soup or cheese pie.

Suggested toppings: Buttered Crumbs, page 351; Vinaigrette Sauce, page 352; Polonaise Sauce, page 351; White Sauce, page 352; Egg Sauce, page 352.

BUTTERED LEEKS

12 leeks
1 teaspoon salt
2 tablespoons butter or margarine
dash seasoned pepper

ABOUT 30 MINUTES BEFORE SERVING:
Cut leeks into 2-inch pieces. In medium saucepan over medium heat, in 1 inch boiling water, heat leeks and salt to boiling; cover and cook 10 to 15 minutes until fork-tender; drain. Stir in butter or margarine and seasoned pepper. Makes 6 servings.

Lentils

See Beans, Dry

Lettuce

Crisphead, Butterhead, Cos or Romaine, Looseleaf, Stem. *See also* Greens

Season: All year. Often more plentiful in summer when local supplies are available.

Look for: Clean, crisp, tender leaves, free from decay. For Crisphead varieties (Iceberg), look for solid head, heavy for its size. For Butterhead varieties (Boston, Bibb), look for soft textured leaves with lighter-color inside leaves. For Cos or Romaine, look for crisp, coarse leaves with heavy mid-rib. For Looseleaf varieties (Bunching) look for soft textured leaves in long bunches or loose. For Stem (Celtuce), look for enlarged stem (leaves are to be peeled and stem is eaten fresh or in Chinese recipes).

To store: Refrigerate in crisper or wrapped; use Crisphead lettuce within 3 to 5 days, looser, leafier kinds within 1 or 2 days.

To prepare: For Iceberg lettuce, remove core (see page 389); run cold water into core. For others, gently separate leaves; rinse thoroughly under cold running water. Trim sparingly; dark-green outer leaves are the most nutritious. Drain thoroughly; store in plastic bag in refrigerator to crisp.

To cook: Use in recipes as directed.

To serve: Fresh in sandwiches, salads; in recipes for main dishes, "wilted" salads.

STIR-FRIED ROMAINE

1 medium head romaine
3 tablespoons salad oil
½ teaspoon salt
¼ teaspoon sugar

ABOUT 10 MINUTES BEFORE SERVING:
Cut romaine crosswise into 1½-inch pieces. In Dutch oven over high heat, in very hot

salad oil, cook romaine, stirring quickly and frequently (stir-frying) until well coated. Sprinkle with salt and sugar; continue stir-frying about 2 minutes more or until wilted and tender-crisp. Makes about 4 servings.

WILTED LETTUCE

6 bacon slices
1 large head leaf lettuce
1 medium onion, thinly sliced
¼ cup vinegar
1½ teaspoons sugar
½ teaspoon dry mustard
¼ teaspoon salt
dash pepper

ABOUT 30 MINUTES BEFORE SERVING:
In large cook-and-serve skillet over medium heat, fry bacon slices until crisp; drain on paper towels. Discard all but ¼ cup bacon drippings from skillet.

Meanwhile, into medium bowl, tear leaf lettuce into bite-size pieces. Crumble bacon and add with onion slices, tossing until well mixed.

Into bacon drippings in skillet, stir remaining ingredients; over medium heat, heat to boiling, stirring constantly. Remove from heat and immediately add lettuce mixture, tossing until lettuce is slightly wilted and coated with dressing. Makes 6 servings.

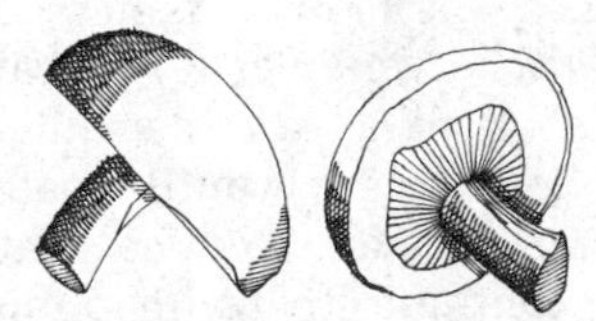

Mushrooms

Truffles are a variety of mushroom.

Season: All year.

Look for: Firm, plump, cream-colored mushrooms with short stems and caps that are closed around stem or slightly open, with pink or light-tan gills. Buy only cultivated mushrooms. (Varieties found growing wild may be poisonous.)

To store: Refrigerate, covered; use within 1 or 2 days.

To prepare: Do not peel or soak; rinse in cold water; drain well on paper towels. Cut thin slice from stem. Use mushrooms whole or slice parallel to stem; or cook as recipe directs.

Seasonings to cook with: Garlic, lemon, onion, nutmeg.

To serve: Use fresh in green salads; use as cooked vegetable or in recipes for meats, poultry, fish, casseroles, or as garnish.

SAUTEED MUSHROOMS

¼ cup butter or margarine
2 tablespoons minced onion
1 pound mushrooms, sliced
1 teaspoon lemon juice
½ teaspoon salt
dash pepper

ABOUT 20 MINUTES BEFORE SERVING:
In large skillet over medium heat, in hot butter or margarine, cook onion until tender, about 5 minutes. Add mushrooms; cook, covered, stirring occasionally, about 10 minutes. Stir in lemon juice, salt and pepper. Serve as is, or on toast; with steaks, chops, chicken or vegetables. Makes 4 servings.

MUSHROOMS IN CREAM: Prepare as above but omit lemon juice and stir in *2 tablespoons dry sherry* and *⅓ cup half-and-half.*

ONION-STUFFED MUSHROOMS

½ pound large mushrooms
¼ cup butter or margarine
½ cup minced onions
¼ teaspoon lemon juice
¼ teaspoon salt
paprika

ABOUT 30 MINUTES BEFORE SERVING:
Remove stems from mushrooms; save for use another day. In medium skillet over medium heat, in hot butter or margarine, cook onions until tender, about 5 minutes. With slotted spoon, place onions in warm bowl. To drippings in skillet, add mushroom caps, lemon juice and salt; cook, stirring occasionally, until tender, about 10 minutes. Fill each cap with onions; sprinkle with paprika. Depending on size of mushrooms, makes 3 or 4 servings.

STIR-FRIED MUSHROOMS

¼ cup salad oil
1 pound medium mushrooms, whole or sliced
1 tablespoon soy sauce
¼ teaspoon sugar
2 teaspoons cornstarch

ABOUT 10 MINUTES BEFORE SERVING:
In Dutch oven or medium skillet over high heat, in very hot salad oil, cook mushrooms, ½ cup water, soy sauce and sugar, stirring quickly and frequently (stir-frying) until coated. Reduce heat to medium-high; continue stir-frying about 5 to 6 minutes more until tender.

Meanwhile, in small bowl, stir cornstarch with 2 teaspoons cold water until smooth. Stir into mushroom mixture; cook, stirring, until thickened. Makes about 6 servings.

Mustard Greens

See Greens

Okra

Season: All year. Best supplies are in July to October.

Look for: Young, tender green pods less than 4½ inches long.

To store: Refrigerate; use within 1 to 2 days.

To prepare: Leave whole or cut into desired lengths.

To cook: In saucepan over medium heat, in 1 inch boiling, salted water, heat okra to boiling; cover and cook whole okra 5 to 10 minutes; cut-up, 3 to 5 minutes.

Seasonings to cook with: Cayenne, onion.

To serve: Serve as cooked vegetable; use in recipes for tomatoes, gumbos, soups.

Suggested toppings: Hollandaise Sauce, page 282; Hot Thousand Island Sauce, page 352; Vinaigrette Sauce, page 352.

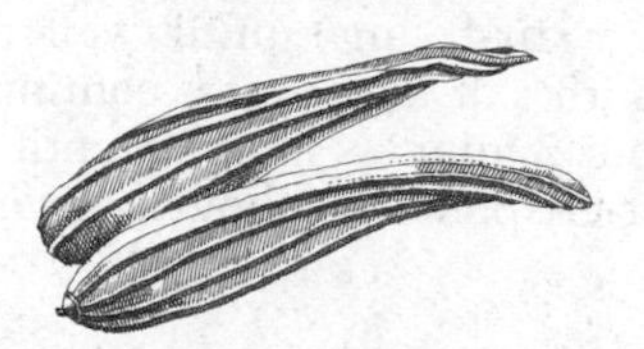

Okra, Chinese

Season: All year.

Look for: Okra up to 12 inches long, firm, with dark green color and deep ridges.

To store: Refrigerate; use within 3 to 5 days.

To prepare: Peel; or scrape ridges to remove brown edges. Cut into 1-inch pieces.

To cook: In saucepan over medium heat, in 1 inch boiling, salted water, heat Chinese okra to boiling; cover and cook 5 minutes or until tender-crisp.

To serve: Serve as cooked vegetable.

STIR-FRIED CHINESE OKRA

3 large Chinese okra, peeled
2 tablespoons salad oil
1 teaspoon salt

ABOUT 10 MINUTES BEFORE SERVING:
Cut Chinese okra into 1-inch diagonal slices. In Dutch oven over high heat, in hot salad oil, cook okra, stirring quickly and frequently (stir-frying) until coated. Add ¼ cup water and salt. Reduce heat to medium-high; continue stir-frying 5 minutes or until tender-crisp. Makes about 4 servings.

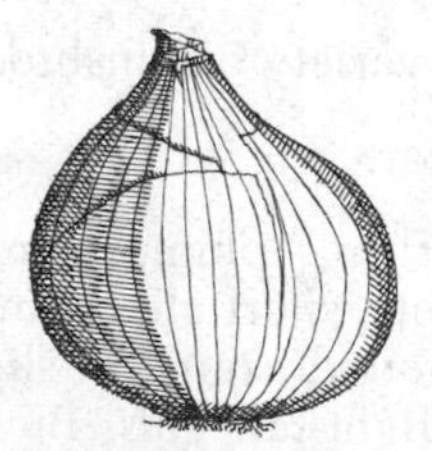

Onions, Dry

Globe, Bermuda, Spanish

Season: All year.

Look for: Clean, firm onions with dry, brittle skin. Avoid ones with sprouts.

To store: Store in refrigerator or at cool room temperature (60°F. or below) in container that allows good circulation of air. Keep dry. Will keep several months.

To prepare: Peel onion; slice it under cold running water to prevent tears. Or chill onion, then slice.

To cook: In saucepan over medium heat, in 1 inch boiling, salted water, heat whole onions to boiling; cover and cook 15 to 20 minutes until tender. Or use onions as directed in recipes.

Seasonings to cook with: Cook as vegetable with cloves, dill, nutmeg, paprika.

To serve: Serve fresh in sandwiches, salads; use as seasoning or garnish for main course, other vegetables; use in recipes.

Suggested toppings: Nutmeg; White Sauce, page 352; Mushroom Sauce, page 168; Cheese Sauce, page 352; Buttered Crumbs, page 351.

CREAMED ONIONS

2 pounds small white onions
6 tablespoons butter or margarine
3 tablespoons all-purpose flour
1½ cups milk
¼ teaspoon salt
paprika

ABOUT 30 MINUTES BEFORE SERVING:
In medium saucepan over medium heat, in 1 inch boiling, salted water, heat onions to boiling; cover and cook 10 to 15 minutes until tender.

Meanwhile, in medium saucepan over medium heat, melt butter or margarine; stir in flour until smooth; slowly stir in milk and salt and cook, stirring constantly, until thickened.

Drain onions and place in serving dish; pour on sauce and sprinkle with paprika. Makes 8 to 10 servings.

CHEDDARED ONIONS: Prepare Creamed Onions as above but stir *one 4-ounce package shredded Cheddar cheese* (1 cup) into thickened sauce; cook over very low heat, stirring constantly, until cheese is melted.

FRENCH-FRIED ONIONS

3 large onions
salad oil
½ cup milk
1 cup all-purpose flour
½ teaspoon salt

ABOUT 30 MINUTES BEFORE SERVING:
With sharp knife, slice onions ¼ inch thick; separate into rings. In electric skillet or deep fat fryer,* heat ¾ inch salad oil to 370°F.

In small dish, place milk. In small bowl, stir flour and salt until mixed. Dip onion rings in milk, then in flour mixture. Repeat so each ring is coated twice. In hot salad oil, cook onions 3 minutes or until lightly browned. Drain on paper towels. Serve immediately. Makes 6 to 8 servings.

* Or, in medium skillet over medium heat, heat oil to 370°F. on deep-fat thermometer.

GLAZED ONIONS

1½ pounds medium onions
⅓ cup sugar
2 tablespoons butter or margarine
¼ teaspoon salt

ABOUT 30 MINUTES BEFORE SERVING:
In medium saucepan over medium heat, in 1 inch boiling water, heat onions to boiling; cover and cook 15 to 20 minutes until tender-crisp; drain. In large skillet over low heat, stir sugar, butter or margarine, 2 teaspoons water and salt until mixed. Add onions; cook until golden and glazed, about 5 minutes, stirring occasionally. Makes 4 servings.

BAKED ONIONS

⅓ cup honey
¼ cup butter or margarine
½ teaspoon salt
6 large onions, sliced

ABOUT 1 HOUR BEFORE SERVING:
Preheat oven to 425°F. In small saucepan over medium heat, heat honey, butter or margarine and salt. In greased 13″ by 9″ baking dish, arrange onions; pour honey-butter mixture evenly over onions. Bake 45 minutes or until onions are fork-tender and golden brown. Makes 6 to 8 servings.

CURRIED ONIONS

¼ cup salad oil
4 cups sliced onions
1 teaspoon curry powder
1 teaspoon salt
2 teaspoons lemon juice

ABOUT 25 MINUTES BEFORE SERVING:
In medium skillet over medium heat, in hot oil, cook onions until tender, about 10 minutes, stirring occasionally. Stir in remaining ingredients. Makes 4 servings.

PAN-FRIED ONIONS

¼ cup butter or margarine
4 to 5 medium onions, thinly sliced
1 teaspoon salt

ABOUT 15 MINUTES BEFORE SERVING:
In medium skillet over medium heat, in hot butter or margarine, cook onions, covered, 5 minutes. Add salt; cook, uncovered, until onions are tender, about 8 minutes, stirring occasionally. Makes 4 servings.

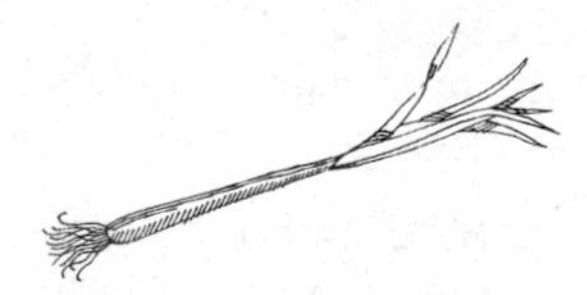

Onions, Green

Scallions, Shallots. *See also* Leeks

Season: All year. (Shallots are available October to May.)

Look for: Bunches with fresh, crisp, green tops and medium-sized necks that are well blanched at root end. Shallots have distinctive bulbs consisting of garlic-like cloves; these bulbs are sometimes cured in the same manner as onions and sold in dry form. Scallions are tiny shoots of white onions.

To store: Refrigerate; use within 1 or 2 days.

To prepare: Rinse. Cut off roots and tough ends; cut into desired lengths.

To cook: Use in recipes. Peel, then use dried shallots in same ways as fresh shallots.

To serve: Serve fresh on relish tray, in salads; use in recipes as seasoning.

Parsley

See Greens

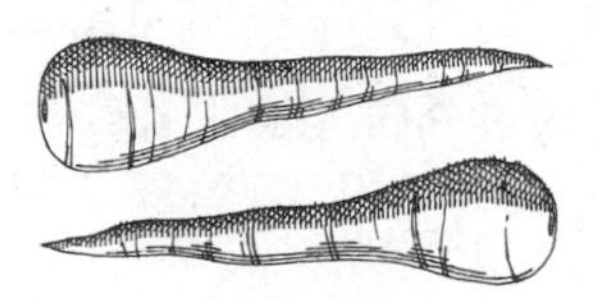

Parsnips

Season: All year. Best supplies are in October to January.

Look for: Smooth, firm, well-shaped, medium-size parsnips. Avoid large, coarse roots or ones with gray or soft spots.

To store: Refrigerate; use within 2 weeks.

To prepare: Scrub in cold water. Cut thin slice off top and bottom; peel. Leave whole; or halve, slice or cut into quarters.

To cook: In saucepan over medium heat, in 1 inch boiling, salted water, heat parsnips to boiling; cover and cook whole parsnips 20 to 30 minutes; cut-up parsnips, 8 to 15 minutes.

Seasonings to serve with: Cinnamon, ginger, orange, tarragon.

To serve: Serve as cooked vegetable; use in recipes for soups, stews, pot roasts. Or, mash and season as potatoes.

Suggested sauces: Hollandaise Sauce, page 282; White Sauce, page 352.

Peas

Season: All year. Best supplies are in March to June.

Look for: Fresh, young pods, light green in color, slightly velvety to the touch and well filled with well-developed peas. Pods with immature peas are usually flat, dark green, wilted; overmature pods are swollen, light, gray-flecked.

To store: Keep peas in pods in refrigerator; use within 1 or 2 days.

To prepare: Shell peas by pressing pods between thumb and forefinger to open.

To cook: In saucepan over medium heat, in 1 inch boiling, salted water, heat peas to boiling; cover and cook 5 to 8 minutes until tender.

Seasonings to cook with: Chives, lettuce leaves, marjoram, mint, nutmeg, oregano, onion, savory, rosemary, tarragon, thyme.

Suggested sauces: White Sauce, page 352; Mushroom Sauce, page 168.

PEAS WITH LETTUCE

3 pounds peas
½ head iceberg lettuce, shredded
½ cup sliced green onions
2 teaspoons sugar
1½ teaspoons salt

ABOUT 45 MINUTES BEFORE SERVING:
Shell peas (yield should be about 2 cups). In medium saucepan over medium heat, heat ½ cup water to boiling. Add lettuce, peas and remaining ingredients; cover and cook 6 to 8 minutes until peas are tender-crisp. Makes 6 servings.

PEAS AMANDINE

2 pounds peas
salt
⅔ cup chopped bacon slices
¼ cup minced onion
½ cup slivered almonds
½ cup heavy or whipping cream

ABOUT 20 MINUTES BEFORE SERVING:
Shell peas (yield should be about 1⅔ cups). In medium saucepan over medium heat, in 1 inch boiling water, heat peas and 2 teaspoons salt to boiling; cover and cook 5 minutes; drain. In medium skillet over medium heat, fry bacon and onion until light brown. Add peas, almonds and 1 teaspoon salt; heat through. Stir in cream. Serve in individual dishes. Makes 4 servings.

MINTED PEAS

ABOUT 20 MINUTES BEFORE SERVING:
Cook *two 10-ounce packages frozen peas* as label directs but add *1 tablespoon chopped onion* and *1 tablespoon chopped mint;* drain. Add *¼ cup butter or margarine* and toss gently until butter is melted. Serve hot. Makes 6 servings.

PEAS CONTINENTAL

2 10-ounce packages frozen peas
2 tablespoons butter or margarine
¼ cup chopped onion
1 4-ounce can sliced mushrooms, drained
2 tablespoons medium sherry (optional)
¼ teaspoon salt
¼ teaspoon nutmeg
⅛ teaspoon marjoram
dash pepper

ABOUT 15 MINUTES BEFORE SERVING:
Cook peas as label directs; drain. In medium saucepan over medium heat, in hot butter or margarine, cook onion until tender, about 5 minutes. Stir in remaining ingredients and peas and cook until thoroughly heated. Makes 6 servings.

Peas, Chinese or Snow

Season: May to September.

Look for: Fresh green, thin pea pods.

To store: Refrigerate; use within 1 or 2 days.

To prepare: Rinse in cold water. Remove stem and string along top and bottom of pod; do not shell.

To cook: In medium saucepan over medium heat, in 1 inch boiling, salted water, heat peas to boiling; cover and cook 5 to 8 minutes until peas are tender-crisp.

To serve: Serve as cooked vegetable or in Chinese dishes.

STIR-FRIED CHINESE PEAS

3 tablespoons salad oil
1 pound Chinese peas
¾ teaspoon salt

ABOUT 10 MINUTES BEFORE SERVING:
In Dutch oven or medium skillet over high heat, in very hot salad oil, cook peas, stirring quickly and frequently (stir-frying) until well coated. Sprinkle with salt; continue stir-frying 2 to 3 minutes more until tender-crisp. Makes about 6 servings.

Peas, Dry and Split

See Beans, Dry

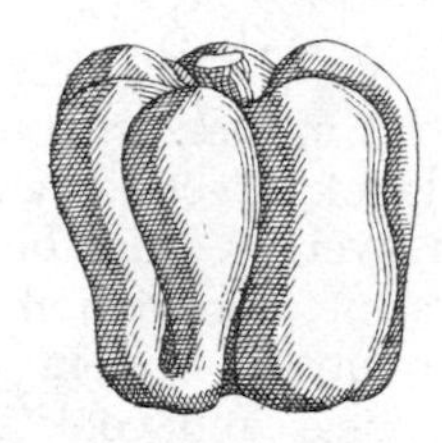

Peppers, Green

(Bell or Sweet Peppers)

Season: All year.

Look for: Peppers that are firm, shiny and thick-fleshed, medium to dark green. Wilted or flabby ones, with cuts or punctures, are of poor quality. Soft spots on the sides indicate decay. When mature, peppers turn red. Pimentos are a mild sweet pepper.

To store: Refrigerate; use within 3 to 5 days.

To prepare: Rinse in cold water. Cut slice from stem end; remove seeds and membrane. Use green peppers whole, to stuff; or cut peppers in halves, strips or rings; or dice or sliver.

To cook: Cook as recipe directs. For stuffed peppers, parboil: In large saucepan over high heat, in boiling water to cover, cook peppers 3 to 5 minutes; drain.

To serve: Serve fresh as snack, in salads; use cooked in recipes for main dishes, casseroles and as seasoning for meat, Creole, Spanish and Italian dishes.

VEGETABLE-STUFFED GREEN PEPPERS

ABOUT 15 MINUTES BEFORE SERVING:
Use 1 large green pepper for every 2 servings. Cut *peppers* in half lengthwise; remove stem, seeds and membrane. In large saucepan over medium heat, in 1 inch boiling, salted water, heat peppers to boiling; cover and simmer 5 minutes until peppers are tender-crisp; drain. Fill with *seasoned, drained hot cooked corn,* peas or any favorite combination of vegetables.

Peppers, Hot or Chili

Many hot or pungent-fleshed varieties, usually red or yellow and smaller than sweet peppers, are available for use in salads and main dishes. See Green Peppers (at left) for selection, storage, etc.

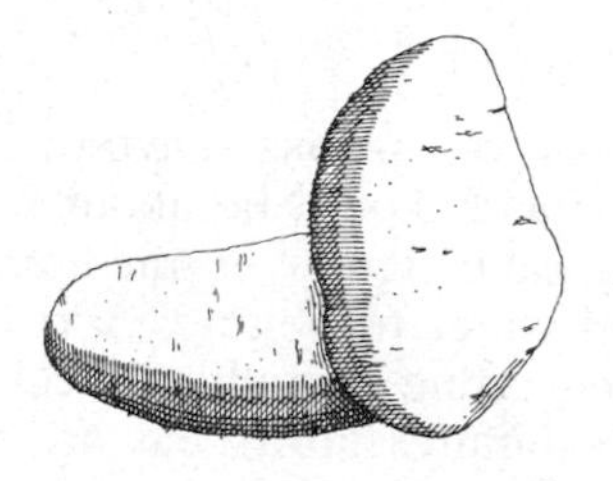

Potatoes

Season: All year.

Look for: Smooth, well-shaped, firm potatoes that are free from blemishes or sprouts. Large cuts or bruises mean waste in peeling.

To store: Store in dark, dry place at coolest room temperature. (Don't refrigerate.) Will keep a week or so.

To prepare: Scrub in cold water. When possible, cook without peeling (you'll save nutrients). After peeling, use quickly to avoid discoloration, loss of food value.

To cook: For *boiled potatoes,* in saucepan over medium heat, in 1 inch boiling, salted water, heat potatoes to boiling; cover and cook new potatoes 15 to 20 minutes, general-purpose potatoes about 30 minutes. For *baked potatoes,* see below.

Seasonings to cook with: Basil, bay leaves, caraway seed, celery seed, chives, dill, lemon, mustard, onion, thyme.

To serve: Serve as cooked vegetable, in hot or cold potato salads; use in recipes for stews, pot roasts, casseroles.

Suggested toppings: White Sauce, page 352; Sour Cream-Mustard Sauce, page 351.

BAKED POTATOES

8 medium baking potatoes, unpeeled
shortening or salad oil
toppings: sour cream, butter or margarine, shredded Cheddar or American cheese

ABOUT 30 MINUTES BEFORE SERVING:
Preheat oven to 450°F. Wash and dry potatoes. Rub potatoes with shortening and place in shallow pan. Bake 45 minutes or until fork-tender. Serve with choice of toppings. Makes 8 servings.

TWICE-BAKED POTATOES

6 medium baking potatoes, unpeeled
3 tablespoons butter or margarine
1 teaspoon salt
dash white pepper
⅓ cup milk
toppings: minced onion, chopped chives, diced American cheese or crumbled bacon

ABOUT 1½ HOURS BEFORE SERVING:
Preheat oven to 450°F. Bake potatoes 45 minutes or until fork-tender. With sharp knife, holding potato in clean pot holder, slice, lengthwise, top fourth from each potato. With spoon, carefully scoop out potatoes to form 6 shells. Scrape potato from top quarters and discard tops.

In large bowl with mixer at low speed, beat potatoes, butter or margarine, salt and pepper until fluffy. Slowly add milk, beating until smooth. Pile mashed potato mixture back into shells.

Sprinkle generously with a topping. Place potatoes on cookie sheet; bake 10 minutes or until golden. Makes 6 servings.

TO DO AHEAD: Prepare potatoes as above but after refilling, place on cookie sheet, cover and refrigerate. About 40 minutes before serving, preheat oven to 350°F. Sprinkle potatoes with a topping and bake 30 minutes or until hot and top is light brown.

FRENCH-FRIED POTATOES

salad oil
8 medium potatoes
salt

ABOUT 30 MINUTES BEFORE SERVING:
In deep-fat fryer,* heat about 2 inches salad oil to 400°F. Meanwhile, peel potatoes. Cut into ¼-inch slices; cut slices into ¼-inch lengthwise strips. Rinse in cold water; drain; dry well with paper towels.

Cover bottom of fryer basket with even layer of potatoes; gently lower potatoes into hot oil and fry 5 minutes or until golden brown; drain on paper towels. Repeat with remaining potatoes. Salt to taste. Makes 8 servings.

* Or, in large, deep heavy saucepan over medium heat, heat oil to 400°F. on deep-fat thermometer.

FRIED POTATO WEDGES

4 pounds medium potatoes
1 cup salad oil
salt
parsley sprigs for garnish

EARLY IN DAY:
Cook unpeeled potatoes in boiling water 10 to 15 minutes until partially tender. Peel potatoes; cover and refrigerate.

ABOUT 1 HOUR BEFORE SERVING:
Halve potatoes lengthwise, then cut each half lengthwise into 3 or 4 wedges. In large skillet over high heat, in hot salad oil, fry some potato wedges until golden on all sides; drain on paper towels; keep warm in foil-covered, shallow pan in 325°F. oven. Repeat with remaining potatoes, adding more oil if needed.

Sprinkle potatoes with salt and garnish with parsley. Makes 10 to 12 servings.

AMERICAN-FRIED POTATOES

3 tablespoons butter, margarine or bacon drippings
4 medium potatoes, thinly sliced (about 3 cups)
1 teaspoon salt
¼ teaspoon pepper

ABOUT 25 MINUTES BEFORE SERVING:
In large skillet (preferably with a non-stick finish), over medium heat, in hot butter or margarine, fry potatoes 15 minutes or until golden and tender, occasionally turning with pancake turner. Sprinkle with salt and pepper. Makes 4 servings.

LYONNAISE POTATOES: Prepare as above but add *½ cup chopped onions* with potatoes.

HASH BROWN POTATOES

½ cup butter or margarine
5 or 6 medium potatoes, finely diced or coarsely shredded (about 6 cups)
1 teaspoon salt
½ teaspoon paprika
¼ teaspoon pepper

ABOUT 45 MINUTES BEFORE SERVING:
In medium skillet (preferably with a non-stick finish) over medium heat, in hot butter or margarine, cook potatoes, covered, 10 minutes. Uncover and sprinkle with remaining ingredients. Continue cooking 15 minutes or until tender and brown, occasionally turning with pancake turner. Makes 6 servings.

QUICK HASH BROWN POTATOES: Dice or shred *4 cups cooked potatoes*. In medium skillet over medium-high heat, in *¼ cup hot butter or margarine*, fry potatoes 15 minutes or until browned, occasionally turning with pancake turner. Sprinkle with *1 teaspoon salt, ½ teaspoon paprika* and *¼ teaspoon pepper*. Makes 4 servings.

FRANCONIA POTATOES
(Pan-Roasted Potatoes)

ABOUT 1 HOUR AND 15 MINUTES AHEAD:
In medium saucepan over medium heat, in 1 inch boiling, salted water, heat *8 peeled medium potatoes* to boiling; cover and cook 10 minutes. Drain; arrange around beef or pork roast in roasting pan;* turn to coat with drippings in pan. Bake 40 to 60 minutes at 325°F. along with roast, turning occasionally, until tender and browned.
To serve, sprinkle potatoes with *paprika, parsley* or *thyme*. Arrange around roast on platter. Makes 8 servings.

* When not roasting with meat, preheat oven to 400°F. In shallow baking pan, melt ½ cup butter or margarine. Meanwhile, boil potatoes as above. Add boiled potatoes to melted butter or margarine, turning each to coat evenly. Bake, turning often, 40 minutes or until tender.

HOME-FRIED POTATOES

3 tablespoons bacon drippings
4 medium potatoes, cooked and thickly sliced (about 4 cups)
salt and pepper

ABOUT 25 MINUTES BEFORE SERVING:
In large skillet over medium-high heat, in hot drippings, fry potato slices 10 minutes or until browned, occasionally turning with pancake turner. Sprinkle with salt and pepper to taste. Makes 4 servings.

PAPRIKA POTATOES

2 16-ounce cans white potatoes, drained
¼ cup butter or margarine
1¼ teaspoons salt
1 teaspoon paprika

ABOUT 25 MINUTES BEFORE SERVING:
Preheat oven to 425°F. Blot potatoes with paper towels. Place butter or margarine in 12″ by 8″ baking dish and place in oven a few minutes to melt. Add potatoes; sprinkle with salt and paprika and toss until well coated. Bake 15 minutes or until golden. Makes 6 servings.

POTATOES AU GRATIN

6 cups thinly sliced potatoes
1½ teaspoons salt
2 tablespoons butter or margarine, melted
1 4-ounce package shredded Cheddar cheese (1 cup)
½ cup fresh bread crumbs

ABOUT 30 MINUTES BEFORE SERVING:
Preheat oven to 425°F. In greased 13″ by 9″

baking pan, toss potatoes and salt together and arrange in even layer. Drizzle melted butter or margarine over potatoes; sprinkle with cheese and bread crumbs. Bake 20 minutes or until tender. Makes 10 servings.

SCALLOPED POTATOES

3 tablespoons butter or margarine
⅔ cup minced onions
3 tablespoons all-purpose flour
1½ teaspoons salt
dash pepper
1½ cups milk
4 medium potatoes, thinly sliced
paprika for garnish

ABOUT 1½ HOURS BEFORE SERVING:
Preheat oven to 375°F. In medium saucepan over medium heat, in hot butter or margarine, cook onions until tender, about 5 minutes. Stir in flour, salt and pepper until blended. Gradually stir in milk and cook, stirring constantly, until mixture thickens.

In 2-quart casserole, arrange half the potatoes in a layer; pour half the sauce on top; repeat. Sprinkle with paprika. Bake, covered, 45 minutes. Uncover and bake 15 minutes or until tender. Makes 6 servings.

DELMONICO POTATOES

9 medium potatoes, unpeeled
salt
⅓ cup butter or margarine
⅓ cup all-purpose flour
2¼ cups half-and-half or milk
1 4-ounce package shredded Cheddar cheese (1 cup)
3 tablespoons dried bread crumbs

EARLY IN DAY:
In large, covered saucepan over medium heat, in 1 inch boiling water, cook unpeeled potatoes and 1 teaspoon salt for 20 to 30 minutes until potatoes are fork-tender; drain and cool.

ABOUT 1 HOUR BEFORE SERVING:
Preheat oven to 375°F. Grease 12″ by 8″ baking dish. Peel and dice potatoes. In large saucepan over medium-high heat, melt butter or margarine. With wire whisk or slotted spoon, stir in flour until well blended and smooth. Gradually stir in half-and-half and cook, stirring constantly, until mixture is thick and bubbly. Stir in 2 teaspoons salt; gently stir in potatoes.

Pour mixture evenly into baking dish; sprinkle with cheese, then bread crumbs. Bake 25 minutes or until cheese is melted and mixture is bubbly. Makes 12 servings.

MASHED POTATOES

6 medium potatoes
salt
¼ cup butter or margarine
¼ teaspoon pepper
¼ to ½ cup hot milk

ABOUT 50 MINUTES BEFORE SERVING:
In large saucepan over medium heat, in 1 inch boiling water, heat potatoes and 1 teaspoon salt to boiling; cover and cook 20 minutes or until fork-tender; drain. In large bowl, with mixer at low speed, beat potatoes, butter or margarine, 1 teaspoon salt and pepper until fluffy. Beating at medium speed, slowly add milk until mixture is moist; continue beating 2 minutes or until mixture is smooth. Makes 6 servings.

DUCHESS POTATOES

6 medium potatoes
salt
½ cup butter or margarine
2 eggs, slightly beaten

ABOUT 45 MINUTES BEFORE SERVING:
In large saucepan over medium heat, in 1 inch boiling water, heat potatoes and 1 teaspoon salt to boiling; cover and cook 20 minutes or until fork-tender; drain. Preheat broiler if manufacturer directs.

In large bowl, with mixer at low speed, beat potatoes, ¼ cup butter or margarine and 1 teaspoon salt until fluffy. Add eggs and, at medium speed, beat until mixture is smooth, about 2 minutes.

In small saucepan over medium heat, melt ¼ cup butter or margarine. On greased cookie sheet or around Planked Steak (page 73), place ten mounds of mashed potatoes. Brush with melted butter or margarine. Broil 5 to 8 minutes until golden brown. Makes 10 servings.

NEW POTATOES WITH LEMON AND CHIVES

2 pounds new potatoes, unpeeled
salt
¼ cup butter or margarine
grated peel 1 lemon
2 tablespoons chopped chives
2 tablespoons lemon juice

ABOUT 40 MINUTES BEFORE SERVING:
In large saucepan over medium heat, in 1 inch boiling water, heat potatoes and 1 teaspoon salt to boiling; cover and cook 15 to 20 minutes, until fork-tender; drain. Cool potatoes slightly, then peel; return to saucepan. Add 1 teaspoon salt and remaining ingredients and heat. Makes 6 servings.

Pumpkin

Season: Some available all year but biggest supply is in October.

Look for: Firm, bright-colored pumpkins, free from blemishes.

To store: Store in cool, dry place; use within a month.

To prepare: Halve or quarter; remove seeds and stringy portions. Cube, then peel.

To cook: In saucepan over medium heat, in 1 inch boiling, salted water, heat pumpkin to boiling; cover and cook 25 to 30 minutes.

To serve: Use in recipes for pies, breads.

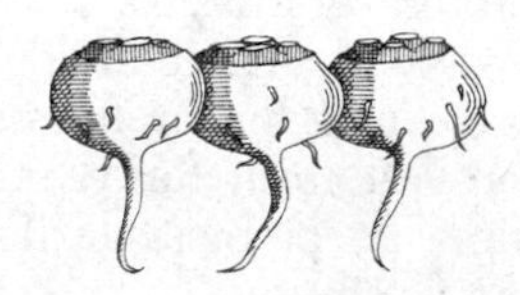

Radishes, Red and White

Season: All year.

Look for: Uniformly shaped radishes that are free of blemishes, firm and bright, deep red or white, depending upon variety.

To store: Discard tops, if any; refrigerate in crisper or wrapped; use within a week.

To prepare: Rinse. Trim roots and tops, if any. Remove leaves or leave a few for decoration. If using as garnish or relish, cut as desired and chill in ice water in refrigerator. Or, crisp in plastic bag in refrigerator.

To serve: Use fresh as snack or relish, sliced or cut up in green salads.

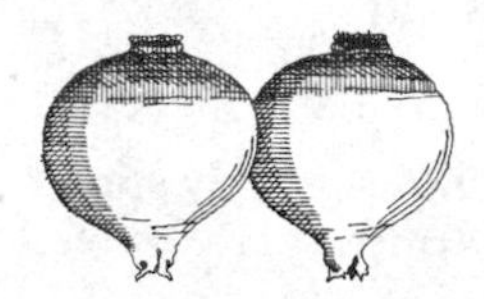

Rutabaga

Season: All year. Best supplies are in October to March.

Look for: Rutabagas that have smooth skin, are heavy for their size, free of decay.

To store: Store at cool room temperature and keep dry. Use within a week or so.

To prepare: Cut rutabaga into quarters; then peel and cut into slices or cubes.

To cook: In saucepan over medium heat, in 1 inch boiling, salted water, heat rutabaga to boiling; cover and cook about 10 minutes.

Seasonings to cook with: Bay leaf, cloves.

To serve: Use cooked as vegetable; use in recipes for soups, stews, casseroles.

Suggested sauces: White Sauce, page 352; Cheese Sauce, page 352.

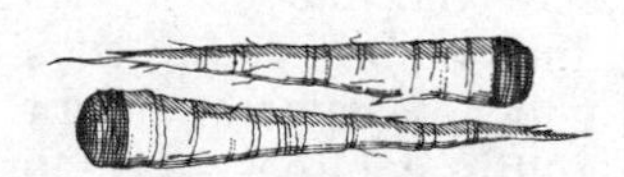

Salsify
(Oyster Plant)

Season: October and November.

Look for: Firm, well-shaped, fresh-looking roots, free from blemish.

To store: Refrigerate; use within a week or so.

To prepare: Scrub in cold water; cut off tops, peel and slice. Drop slices into pan of water with 1 or 2 teaspoons lemon juice or vinegar added to prevent discoloration.

To cook: In medium saucepan over medium heat, in 1 inch boiling, salted water, heat sliced salsify to boiling, then cover and cook 15 to 20 minutes until fork-tender.

To serve: Serve as hot cooked vegetable; use in recipes for casseroles, soups.

Suggested toppings: White Sauce, page 352; Cheese Sauce, page 352.

Sauerkraut

Sauerkraut is cabbage that has been shredded, then fermented in a brine made of its own juice and salt. Other spices may be added. It is available canned, in refrigerated plastic bags, and in bulk in delicatessens. Store cans at room temperature; refrigerate other forms and use within a few days. To serve, heat; or use in recipes.

Spinach

See Greens

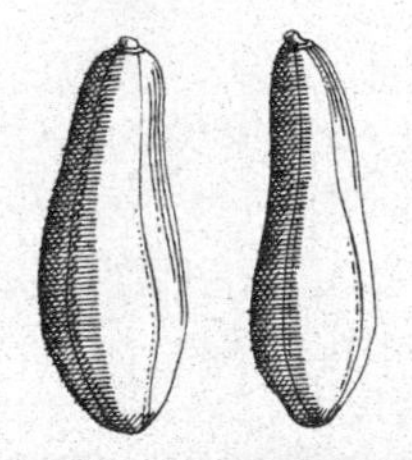

Squash, Soft-Skinned

Pattypan, Straightneck or Crookneck, Zucchini, Italian Marrow

Season: All year. Best supplies are in fall.

Look for: Small, young squash that are heavy for their size. The skin should be tender enough to yield easily to thumb pressure.

To store: Refrigerate; use within a few days.

To prepare: Scrub gently with soft vegetable brush in cold water. Cut slice from each end. Do not remove skin or seeds of squash if tender and young. Cut into desired shape.

To cook: In saucepan over medium heat, in 1 inch boiling, salted water, heat squash to boiling; cover and cook halved squash about 5 minutes; sliced squash, 3 minutes.

Seasonings to cook with: Garlic, onion, sesame seed, seasoned salt and pepper.

To serve: Serve cooked as vegetable; use in recipes for stews, casseroles, main dishes.

CHEESY SQUASH

1 chicken-bouillon cube or envelope
salt
2 pounds straightneck or crookneck squash or zucchini, cut in ½-inch slices
½ cup shredded Cheddar cheese

ABOUT 15 MINUTES BEFORE SERVING:
Preheat broiler if manufacturer directs. In large pan over medium heat, in 1 inch boiling water, stir bouillon and 1 teaspoon salt until dissolved. Add squash; cover and boil 3 to 5 minutes until just tender-crisp; drain. Arrange squash in 9-inch pie plate; sprinkle with ½ teaspoon salt and cheese. Broil 1 or 2 minutes until cheese melts and bubbles. Makes 4 servings.

STIR-FRIED ZUCCHINI

3 medium zucchini
1 tablespoon salad oil
1½ teaspoons salt
½ teaspoon sugar

ABOUT 15 MINUTES BEFORE SERVING:
Cut zucchini diagonally into ¼-inch pieces. In Dutch oven or medium skillet over high heat, in very hot salad oil, cook zucchini, stirring quickly and frequently (stir-frying) until well coated. Add ¼ cup water, salt and sugar. Reduce heat to medium-high; continue stir-frying 7 to 8 minutes until tender-crisp. Makes about 4 servings.

SQUASH WITH WALNUTS

2 tablespoons butter or margarine
4 cups zucchini, straightneck or crookneck squash, cut in ½-inch slices
¾ cup coarsely chopped California walnuts
¾ teaspoon salt

ABOUT 40 MINUTES BEFORE SERVING:
In medium skillet over medium heat, in melted butter or margarine, cook zucchini with remaining ingredients until tender-crisp, about 5 minutes, stirring occasionally. Makes 6 servings.

ZUCCHINI, ITALIAN STYLE

2 pounds medium zucchini, straightneck or crookneck squash
¼ cup bottled Italian dressing
½ teaspoon salt

ABOUT 20 MINUTES BEFORE SERVING:
Cut zucchini in half lengthwise. In large skillet over medium heat, in Italian dressing, cook zucchini, cut side down, about 5 minutes; turn and sprinkle with salt. Simmer, covered, 10 minutes or until tender. Makes 4 to 6 servings.

RICE-STUFFED ZUCCHINI

1 7- or 8-ounce package chicken-flavored rice mix
salt
4 medium zucchini (about 2¼ pounds)
1 small tomato, chopped
½ cup shredded natural Muenster cheese

ABOUT 50 MINUTES BEFORE SERVING:
Prepare rice mix as label directs. Meanwhile, in large saucepan over medium-high heat, heat 6 cups water and 1½ teaspoons salt to boiling. Cut zucchini in half lengthwise; add to water and cook over medium heat 5 to 7 minutes until just tender-crisp. Immediately drain and cool zucchini under running cold water for a few seconds.

Preheat oven to 375°F. Using tip of teaspoon, scoop out and discard seeds from zucchini halves, leaving shells about ¼ to ½ inch thick. In greased 13" by 9" baking dish, arrange zucchini halves crosswise in row; sprinkle lightly with salt.

Pile rice into zucchini halves; top each with some tomato and cheese. Bake 10 minutes or until cheese melts and rice is heated through. Makes 8 servings.

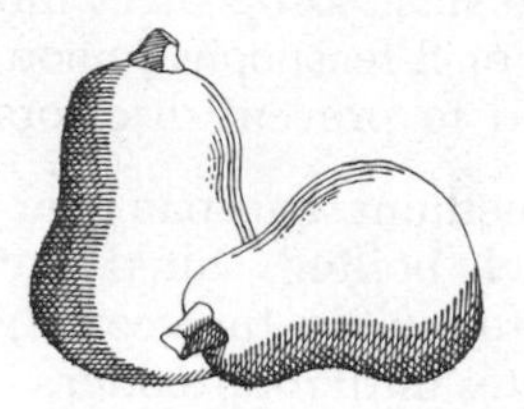

Squash, Hard-Shelled

Acorn, Banana, Butternut, Des Moines, Green and Golden Delicious, Green and Blue Hubbard

Season: All year. Best supplies are in fall.

Look for: Squash that is heavy for its size and has a hard skin; tender skin indicates immaturity, poor quality.

To store: Refrigerate or store at room temperature; use within a few weeks.

To prepare: Rinse in cold water; cut into halves or quarters; discard seeds.

To cook: For *boiled squash,* in saucepan over medium heat, in 1 inch boiling, salted water, heat squash to boiling; cover and cook halved squash about 15 minutes. For *baked squash,* preheat oven to 350°F. or 375°F. and bake squash 45 to 90 minutes until tender.

Seasonings to cook with: Basil, cloves, fennel, ginger, mustard seed, nutmeg.

To serve: Serve as cooked vegetable; use in recipes for main dishes; stuffed with meat mixtures; in stews, casseroles; or mash as potatoes with butter or margarine; in recipes for pies and puddings.

BAKED ACORN SQUASH

Preheat oven to 350°F. Cut *acorn squash* into halves lengthwise; remove seeds and place, cut side up, in shallow roasting pan. Into each half, spoon *2 tablespoons butter or margarine* and about *1 tablespoon brown sugar,* maple syrup or minced onion. Bake squash 45 minutes or until fork-tender. One acorn squash makes 2 servings.

MASHED BUTTERNUT SQUASH

2 small butternut squash (about 2 pounds)
salt
¼ cup packed brown sugar
2 tablespoons butter or margarine

ABOUT 45 MINUTES BEFORE SERVING:
Halve squash lengthwise; remove seeds. In large skillet over medium heat, in 1 inch boiling water, place squash, cut side down, and ½ teaspoon salt; heat to boiling. Cover; cook 15 minutes or until fork-tender; drain; cool slightly. With spoon, scoop out pulp into large bowl; with mixer at low speed, beat squash with ½ teaspoon salt and remaining ingredients until smooth. Makes 6 servings.

APPLE-JUICE ACORN SQUASH

3 medium acorn squash
2 cups apple juice
1¼ teaspoons salt
¼ teaspoon cinnamon

ABOUT 1 HOUR BEFORE SERVING:
Preheat oven to 350°F. Halve squash lengthwise; remove seeds and place, cut side up, in shallow roasting pan. In small bowl, combine remaining ingredients; pour into squash halves. Bake squash 45 minutes or until tender. Makes 6 servings.

Sweet Potatoes

Season: All year. Best supplies are in winter months.

Look for: Firm, uniformly shaped sweet potatoes, free of blemishes.

To store: Store in cool, dry place; use within a week or so.

To prepare: Scrub. When possible, don't peel before cooking, to save nutrients.

To cook: For *boiled sweet potatoes,* in saucepan over medium heat, in 1 inch boiling, salted water, heat sweet potatoes to boiling; cover and cook 20 minutes or until fork-tender. For *baked sweet potatoes,* preheat oven to 450°F. and bake sweet potatoes 45 minutes to 1 hour until fork-tender. When cooking meat, other foods, at lower temperatures, bake sweet potatoes longer.

Seasonings to cook with: Cinnamon, cloves, nutmeg, allspice.

To serve: Serve as vegetable; use in recipes for casseroles, pies.

CANDIED SWEET POTATOES

6 medium sweet potatoes, cooked and halved lengthwise, or 2 16-ounce cans whole sweet potatoes, drained
½ cup packed brown sugar
½ cup dark corn syrup
¼ cup butter or margarine

ABOUT 30 MINUTES BEFORE SERVING:
Preheat oven to 350°F. Arrange sweet potatoes in cook-and-serve baking dish. In small saucepan over medium heat, combine brown sugar, corn syrup and butter or margarine; heat mixture to boiling; reduce heat to low and simmer, stirring occasionally, 5 minutes. Pour mixture over sweet potatoes. Bake 20 minutes or until potatoes are well glazed, basting often. To serve, spoon syrup over potatoes. Makes 6 servings.

Swiss Chard

See Greens

Tomatoes

Season: All year.

Look for: Firm, unblemished tomatoes with some red color. (This indicates that they are mature.) Size does not indicate quality.

To store: If tomatoes are not fully ripe, leave at room temperature until they turn red. Then refrigerate; use within 1 or 2 days.

To prepare: It is not necessary to peel tomatoes before using. Rinse in cold water. If peeling is preferred, just dip tomatoes in boiling water for a minute, then cool in cold water; skin will peel off easily. Or, with fork, hold tomato over direct flame, rotating constantly until skin pops; peel.

Seasonings to sprinkle over sliced tomatoes: Basil, celery seed, chives, oregano, tarragon, thyme, coarsely ground pepper.

To serve: Serve fresh as salad, in tossed salads, as sandwich filling. Use cooked as vegetable or in recipes for soups, stews, pot roasts, sauces.

FRIED GREEN TOMATOES

⅔ cup all-purpose flour or cornmeal
2 teaspoons salt
dash pepper
3 pounds green tomatoes, cut in ½-inch slices
salad oil

ABOUT 30 MINUTES BEFORE SERVING:
In pie plate, combine flour, salt and pepper. Dip tomato slices in mixture to coat both sides.

In large skillet over medium heat, in ¼ cup hot salad oil, fry tomato slices, a few at a time, until golden on both sides and heated through. Drain on paper towels. Add more salad oil as needed. Makes 8 to 10 servings.

STEWED FRESH TOMATOES

2 pounds tomatoes, peeled
2 tablespoons butter or margarine
4 green onions, chopped
1½ teaspoons sugar
1½ teaspoons garlic salt
¼ teaspoon seasoned pepper

ABOUT 30 MINUTES BEFORE SERVING:
Cut tomatoes into wedges. In large skillet over medium heat, in hot butter or margarine, cook green onions 1 minute. Add tomatoes and remaining ingredients; cook about 10 minutes, stirring occasionally. Makes 6 servings.

SCALLOPED TOMATOES

¼ cup butter or margarine
1 small onion, chopped
2 cups fresh bread crumbs
1 teaspoon salt
½ teaspoon basil
¼ teaspoon pepper
2 14½-ounce cans sliced small tomatoes
4 teaspoons sugar

ABOUT 40 MINUTES BEFORE SERVING:
Preheat oven to 375°F. In medium saucepan over medium heat, in hot butter or margarine, cook onion until tender, about 5 minutes. Stir in bread crumbs, salt, basil and pepper.

Into 1½-quart casserole, place ¼ of tomato slices and their liquid; sprinkle with 1 teaspoon sugar and ¼ of bread-crumb mixture. Continue layering, ending with bread-crumb mixture. Bake 30 minutes or until hot and bubbly. Makes 6 servings.

SCALLOPED FRESH TOMATOES: Prepare as above but use 5 medium tomatoes, sliced, instead of canned tomatoes. Cover casserole; bake 35 minutes.

BACON-WRAPPED GRILLED TOMATOES

12 bacon slices
6 medium tomatoes
1 teaspoon marjoram leaves
1 teaspoon grated Parmesan cheese
1 teaspoon salt
½ teaspoon basil
dash pepper

ABOUT 20 MINUTES BEFORE SERVING:
Preheat broiler if manufacturer directs or prepare outdoor grill for barbecuing.

In large skillet over medium heat, fry bacon just until limp.

Cut each tomato about ¾ way through into 6 wedges, gently spreading wedges apart. In cup, combine marjoram and remaining ingredients; sprinkle on tomato wedges. Wrap 2 bacon slices around each tomato and secure with toothpicks.

For broiling, place tomatoes in broiling pan and broil 5 to 10 minutes until bacon is golden. Or for grilling, loosely wrap each tomato halfway up with foil and grill. Remove toothpicks. Makes 6 servings.

MUSHROOM-CAPPED GRILLED TOMATOES

6 to 8 small tomatoes
6 to 8 large mushrooms
2 tablespoons prepared mustard
3 tablespoons minced onion
salt
butter or margarine

ABOUT 25 MINUTES BEFORE SERVING:
Preheat broiler if manufacturer directs. Slice stem ends from tomatoes. Remove stems from mushrooms (save stems for use another day). In shallow baking pan, arrange tomatoes. Spread cut surfaces with mustard, sprinkle with minced onion and salt; dot with butter or margarine. Around tomatoes, arrange mushroom caps, rounded side down; dot with butter or margarine. Broil 12 to 15 minutes until browned.

To serve, top each tomato with a mushroom cap, rounded side down. Makes 6 to 8 servings.

BAKED PARSLIED TOMATOES

ABOUT 25 MINUTES BEFORE SERVING:
Preheat oven to 375°F. Cut stem ends from *4 medium tomatoes;* halve tomatoes crosswise. Sprinkle cut surfaces generously with *seasoned salt, chopped parsley, grated Parmesan cheese;* bake 15 minutes or until tender. Makes 4 servings.

Tomatoes, Cherry

Small, red tomatoes are sold by the box in many markets. Although too small to peel, they can be used like other tomatoes in recipes.

SKILLET CHERRY TOMATOES

¼ cup butter or margarine
¼ teaspoon garlic powder
1 pint cherry tomatoes

ABOUT 10 MINUTES BEFORE SERVING:
In large skillet over high heat, in hot butter or margarine and garlic powder, fry tomatoes just until heated and skins start to wrinkle, stirring tomatoes or shaking pan often. Makes 6 servings.

Turnip Greens

See Greens

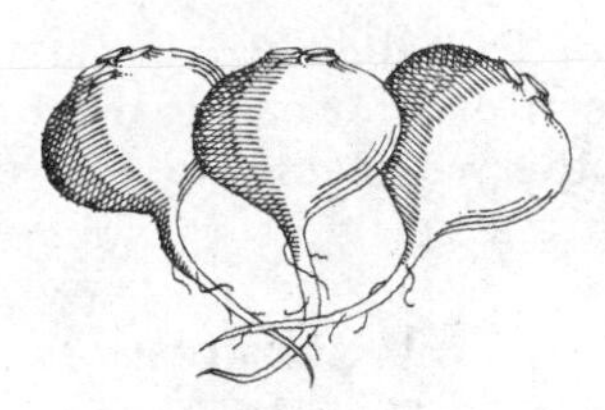

Turnips

Season: All year. Best supplies are in October and November.

Look for: Firm, unblemished turnips, heavy for their size, with fresh tops.

To store: Remove tops; refrigerate tops and turnips in crisper or wrapped. Use turnips within a week or so; use tops as soon as possible (*see* Greens, page 330).

To prepare: Rinse in cold water. Peel thinly; leave whole or cut into slices or pieces.

To cook: In saucepan over medium heat, in 1 inch boiling, salted water, heat turnips to boiling; cover and cook whole turnips 20 to 30 minutes; cut-up, 10 to 20 minutes.

Seasonings to cook with: Bay leaf, cloves.

To serve: Serve as cooked vegetable; or mash as potatoes with butter or margarine; or use in recipes for soups, stews, main dishes.

Suggested toppings: White Sauce, page 352; Cheese Sauce, page 352; paprika; parsley; nutmeg.

Water Chestnuts

Season: All year.

Look for: Firm, dark reddish-brown water chestnuts; avoid dried or shriveled ones.

To store: Refrigerate; use within 1 week.

To prepare: Rinse in cold water. Peel skin; use whole, sliced or cut into chunks.

To cook: Use in recipes as directed.

To serve: Toss sliced fresh water chestnuts with green or fruit salads; heat with peas, beans, other vegetables to add texture.

Watercress

See Greens

STIR-FRIED WATERCRESS

3 tablespoons salad oil
2 bunches watercress
¾ teaspoon salt

ABOUT 10 MINUTES BEFORE SERVING:
In Dutch oven over high heat, in very hot salad oil, cook watercress, stirring quickly and frequently (stir-frying) until well coated. Sprinkle with salt; continue stir-frying 1 or 2 minutes more until watercress is just wilted and liquid in pan starts to boil. Makes about 4 servings.

Yams

Botanically, yams are a member of another family not related to sweet potatoes. However, in the United States, many canned sweet potatoes are called yams and are used in recipes like sweet potatoes.

CINNAMON BAKED YAMS

2 tablespoons light brown sugar
½ teaspoon cinnamon
¼ teaspoon salt
2 18-ounce cans yams, drained
2 tablespoons butter or margarine, melted

ABOUT 45 MINUTES BEFORE SERVING:
Preheat oven to 350°F. In cup, combine brown sugar with cinnamon and salt. Slice yams lengthwise ¼ inch thick and place a layer in a greased shallow casserole. Sprinkle lightly with some sugar mixture and spoon on some melted butter. Repeat until yams and sugar mixture are used. Bake 25 minutes or until yams are hot and sugar is bubbly. Makes 6 to 8 servings.

Combination Vegetable Dishes

CELERY AND TOMATOES AU GRATIN

4 cups celery, cut in 1-inch chunks
salt
2 tablespoons butter or margarine
1 medium onion, chopped
1 16-ounce can tomatoes
½ teaspoon chili powder
2 teaspoons cornstarch
2 cups fresh bread crumbs
1 4-ounce package shredded Cheddar cheese (1 cup)

ABOUT 45 MINUTES BEFORE SERVING:
In large saucepan over medium-high heat, in 1 cup boiling water, heat celery and ½ teaspoon salt to boiling; cover and cook 15 minutes or until fork-tender; drain. In medium skillet over medium heat, in hot butter or margarine, cook onion until tender; add tomatoes, ½ teaspoon salt and chili powder.

Preheat oven to 350°F. In cup, stir cornstarch and ¼ cup cold water until smooth; stir into tomato mixture; cook, stirring constantly, until thickened. In greased 2-quart casserole, combine drained celery with tomato mixture. Top with bread crumbs, then with cheese; bake 25 to 30 minutes until hot. Makes 6 servings.

PEAS WITH GREEN ONIONS

2 tablespoons butter or margarine
2 bunches green onions, cut in 1-inch pieces
2 teaspoons all-purpose flour
½ teaspoon sugar
½ teaspoon salt
¼ teaspoon nutmeg
dash pepper
1 16-ounce can green peas

ABOUT 15 MINUTES BEFORE SERVING:
In medium saucepan over medium heat, in hot butter or margarine, cook onions until tender, about 5 minutes; stir in next 5 ingredients, stirring until mixed. Drain peas into 1 cup measure; add enough water to liquid to make ¾ cup; slowly stir liquid into onion mixture; cook, stirring, until thickened; add peas; heat. Makes 4 servings.

BRUSSELS SPROUTS AND BABY CARROTS

2 10-ounce packages frozen Brussels sprouts
chicken broth
2 tablespoons butter or margarine
1 16-ounce can tiny whole carrots, drained
1/8 teaspoon ginger
1/2 teaspoon seasoned salt

ABOUT 15 MINUTES BEFORE SERVING:
Cook Brussels sprouts as label directs but use chicken broth for liquid; drain.

Meanwhile, in large skillet over medium-high heat, in hot butter or margarine, cook carrots with ginger about 5 minutes; add Brussels sprouts and seasoned salt and heat. Makes about 8 servings.

SPECIAL SUCCOTASH

1 10-ounce package frozen whole-kernel corn
1 10-ounce package frozen lima beans
1/2 cup half-and-half
2 tablespoons butter or margarine
1/2 teaspoon salt
dash seasoned pepper

ABOUT 15 MINUTES BEFORE SERVING:
Prepare corn and lima beans as labels direct; drain. In medium saucepan over medium heat, cook corn, limas and remaining ingredients, stirring occasionally, about 5 minutes, until heated. Makes 6 servings.

GREEN AND GOLD VEGETABLES

1 pound small white onions
2 cups carrots, cut in 1-inch chunks
2 10-ounce packages frozen Brussels sprouts
salt
1/4 cup butter or margarine

ABOUT 35 MINUTES BEFORE SERVING:
In large saucepan over medium heat, in 1/2 inch boiling water, heat onions, carrots, Brussels sprouts and 1 teaspoon salt to boiling; cover and cook about 15 minutes or until fork-tender; drain. Add 1 1/2 teaspoons salt and butter or margarine; toss gently. Makes 8 to 10 servings.

PARSLIED CARROTS AND POTATOES

2 cups diced carrots
2 cups diced potatoes
1/4 cup chopped parsley
1/4 cup butter or margarine
1 teaspoon salt
dash pepper

ABOUT 30 MINUTES BEFORE SERVING:
In large saucepan over medium-high heat, in 3/4 cup boiling water, heat carrots and potatoes to boiling; cover; reduce heat and simmer 10 minutes or until fork-tender; drain. Stir in remaining ingredients. Makes 6 servings.

SESAME BEANS

1 1/2 pounds green beans, cut in 1-inch pieces
1 1/2 pounds wax beans, cut in 1-inch pieces
2 teaspoons salt
1 teaspoon sugar
1/4 cup butter or margarine
2 tablespoons sesame seed
1/8 teaspoon seasoned pepper

ABOUT 30 MINUTES BEFORE SERVING:
In large saucepan over medium heat, in 1 inch boiling water, heat beans, salt and sugar to boiling; cover and cook 10 to 12 minutes until vegetables are tender-crisp; drain. Stir in remaining ingredients. Makes 6 servings.

PEAS AND CELERY POTPOURRI

1 tablespoon butter or margarine
2 cups sliced celery
2 10-ounce packages frozen peas in butter sauce
1/2 teaspoon salt
1/2 teaspoon tarragon leaves
dash pepper
1/2 cup pitted ripe olives, quartered lengthwise

ABOUT 25 MINUTES BEFORE SERVING:
In medium saucepan over medium heat, in hot butter or margarine, cook celery 5 minutes. Add remaining ingredients except olives; cover and cook 12 minutes or until vegetables are tender-crisp. Stir in olives. Makes 8 servings.

RATATOUILLE

1 16-ounce can tomatoes
3 medium zucchini, sliced
1 medium eggplant, peeled and diced
1 cup diced onions
3 tablespoons all-purpose flour
3 envelopes chicken bouillon
2 teaspoons oregano leaves
½ teaspoon sugar
½ teaspoon salt
½ teaspoon garlic powder

ABOUT 1 HOUR BEFORE SERVING:
Drain tomatoes, reserving juice; set both aside. In large bowl, toss remaining ingredients except parsley until vegetables are well coated.

In 12-inch skillet or chicken fryer over high heat, heat ½ cup water and reserved tomato juice to boiling. Add coated vegetables and top with tomatoes. Reduce heat; cover and simmer about 30 minutes, stirring occasionally. Uncover and continue cooking until liquid is reduced and vegetables are tender. Makes 6 to 8 servings.

SUMMER VEGETABLE BOWL

4 bacon slices
12 small white onions
1 small green pepper, diced
1 pound green beans
6 ears corn, broken in thirds
1 tablespoon salt
2 teaspoons sugar
¼ teaspoon white pepper
6 small zucchini, cut in 1-inch chunks
2 large celery stalks, cut in 1-inch slices
1 large tomato, cut in wedges

ABOUT 1 HOUR BEFORE SERVING:
In Dutch oven over medium heat, fry bacon until crisp; drain on paper towels. To drippings in Dutch oven, add onions and green pepper; cook until golden; add 2 cups hot water and next 5 ingredients. Heat to boiling; reduce heat; cover; simmer 10 minutes.

Add zucchini and celery; cover and cook 8 to 10 minutes until all vegetables are tender. With slotted spoon, arrange vegetables on large platter; crumble bacon and sprinkle over top. (Save any leftover liquid for soup or gravy another day.) Garnish with tomato wedges. Makes 6 servings.

SKILLET VEGETABLE MEDLEY

2 tablespoons butter or margarine
2 cups sliced celery
2 cups sliced carrots
6 Belgian endives
2 tablespoons lemon juice
1 teaspoon salt
1 10½-ounce can condensed chicken broth, undiluted
chopped parsley for garnish

ABOUT 30 MINUTES BEFORE SERVING:
In large skillet over medium heat, in hot butter or margarine, cook celery and carrots 5 minutes. Add next 4 ingredients. Reduce heat to low; cover and cook 20 minutes or until endives are fork-tender. With slotted spoon, remove celery and carrots to heated platter; arrange endives on top. Sprinkle with parsley. Makes 6 servings.

ARTICHOKES AND CARROTS

4 cups sliced carrots
1 bay leaf
1 teaspoon salt
1 14-ounce can artichoke hearts

ABOUT 30 MINUTES BEFORE SERVING:
In large saucepan over medium heat, in 1 inch boiling water, heat carrots, bay leaf and salt to boiling; cover and cook 10 to 20 minutes until fork-tender. During last 5 minutes of cooking, add drained and halved artichoke hearts. Season with additional salt if you like. Makes 6 servings.

PEPPER-AND-TOMATO SAUTE

¼ cup salad oil
6 large green peppers, cut into large chunks
2 medium onions, chopped
5 large tomatoes, peeled and cut into large chunks
2½ teaspoons salt
1¼ teaspoons basil

ABOUT 30 MINUTES BEFORE SERVING:
In large skillet over medium heat, in hot salad oil, cook green peppers and onions 10 minutes. Add tomatoes, salt and basil; cover and simmer until vegetables are tender, stirring occasionally, about 15 minutes. Makes 10 servings.

GREEN BEANS AND CELERY

1 pound green beans
3 stalks celery, thinly sliced
salt
2 tablespoons butter or margarine
dash seasoned pepper
chopped parsley for garnish

ABOUT 20 MINUTES BEFORE SERVING:
Cut green beans into 1-inch pieces. In medium saucepan over medium heat, in 1 inch boiling water, heat beans, celery and 1 teaspoon salt to boiling; cover and cook 10 minutes or until tender-crisp; drain. Stir in butter or margarine, ½ teaspoon salt and seasoned pepper. Sprinkle with chopped parsley. Makes 4 servings.

VEGETABLE MEDLEY

2 10-ounce packages frozen cut asparagus
2 tablespoons butter or margarine
½ pound mushrooms, sliced
¾ teaspoon salt
dash pepper
1 12-ounce can whole-kernel corn, drained

ABOUT 20 MINUTES BEFORE SERVING:
Cook asparagus as label directs; drain. Meanwhile, in medium skillet over medium heat, in hot butter or margarine, cook mushrooms until golden. Add salt, pepper and corn and heat; stir in asparagus. Makes 6 servings.

Favorite Sauces for Vegetables

HURRY-UP SAUCES

Favorite sauces for vegetables—hollandaise, white, sour cream and others—are quickly made with the help of packaged sauce mixes.

Flavorful sauces can also be made with canned condensed soups and milk. Simply add enough milk to canned condensed cream-of-mushroom, or to Cheddar-cheese, cream-of-chicken or other soup to make it of the desired consistency. Heat and pour over drained, hot cooked vegetables.

SOUR CREAM-MUSTARD SAUCE

1 cup sour cream
1 tablespoon minced onion
1 tablespoon prepared mustard
¼ teaspoon salt
dash pepper
1 tablespoon chopped parsley

ABOUT 10 MINUTES BEFORE SERVING:
In small saucepan over very low heat, heat first 5 ingredients just until hot. Sprinkle with parsley. Makes about 1 cup.

BUTTERED CRUMBS

JUST BEFORE SERVING:
In small saucepan or skillet over medium heat, melt 2 *tablespoons butter or margarine.* Add ½ *cup fresh bread crumbs;* cook, tossing lightly, until crumbs are golden. If you like, add *1 tablespoon lemon juice,* or ½ cup shredded Cheddar or grated Parmesan cheese or American cheese food, or a pinch of thyme or basil. To serve, sprinkle over drained, hot cooked vegetables.

POLONAISE SAUCE: Prepare Buttered Crumbs with lemon juice as above. Stir in *1 hard-cooked egg,* chopped, *1 tablespoon chopped parsley* and *¼ teaspoon salt.*

LEMON BUTTER
(Maître-d'Hôtel Butter)

¼ cup butter or margarine
1 tablespoon lemon juice
1 tablespoon chopped parsley
½ teaspoon salt
dash cayenne

ABOUT 5 MINUTES BEFORE SERVING:
In small saucepan over medium heat, melt butter or margarine; stir in remaining ingredients. (Or, in small bowl, with spoon, stir butter or margarine until creamy. Slowly stir in rest of ingredients.)

Serve hot on hot cooked vegetables; broiled, fried or poached fish or shellfish. Makes about ⅓ cup.

FINES HERBES: Prepare as above but substitute *3 tablespoons dry white wine* for lemon juice; add *2 tablespoons chopped chives* and *1 teaspoon chopped fresh dill.*

WHITE SAUCE
(Cream Sauce)

2 tablespoons butter or margarine
2 tablespoons all-purpose flour
½ teaspoon salt
dash pepper
dash paprika
1 cup milk or half-and-half

ABOUT 15 MINUTES BEFORE SERVING:
In medium saucepan over low heat, or in double boiler, melt butter or margarine; stir in flour, salt, pepper and paprika until smooth. Gradually stir in milk; cook, stirring constantly, until thickened and smooth. Makes 1 cup.

THIN WHITE SAUCE: Prepare as above but use 1 tablespoon butter or margarine and 1 tablespoon flour.

THICK WHITE SAUCE: Prepare as above but use ¼ cup butter or margarine and ¼ cup flour.

BECHAMEL SAUCE: Prepare as above but substitute *½ cup chicken broth* for ½ cup of the milk.

CHEESE SAUCE: Prepare White Sauce as above but halve ingredients and, into hot sauce, stir *½ cup shredded American or Cheddar cheese* and *⅛ teaspoon dry mustard;* or *half of a 5-ounce jar sharp pasteurized process cheese spread.* Cook over very low heat, stirring, just until cheese is melted. Makes about 1¼ cups.

CURRY SAUCE: When preparing White Sauce, to butter or margarine, add *¼ cup minced onion, 2 teaspoons curry powder, ¾ teaspoon sugar, ⅛ teaspoon ginger.* Just before serving, stir in *1 teaspoon lemon juice.* Makes about 1¼ cups.

EGG SAUCE: When preparing White Sauce, use ¼ cup butter or margarine and 2 teaspoons flour; stir in *2 sliced hard-cooked eggs* and *2 teaspoons prepared mustard* or ½ teaspoon dry mustard. Makes 1¼ cups.

HOT THOUSAND ISLAND SAUCE: In cup, stir *¼ cup mayonnaise* with *¼ cup chili sauce;* stir into hot White Sauce. Makes 1½ cups.

HORSERADISH SAUCE: Into hot sauce, stir *¼ cup horseradish, ¼ teaspoon dry mustard* and *¼ teaspoon salt.* Makes 1⅓ cups.

BUTTER SAUCE FOR VEGETABLES

Into measuring cup, pour liquid from vegetables; measure and return to vegetables in pan. For each ½ cup liquid (add water to make ½ cup if necessary), in another cup, stir 1 tablespoon butter or margarine and 1 tablespoon flour to make smooth paste. Stir mixture into vegetables and liquid; over medium heat, cook, stirring gently, until sauce is thickened and smooth. Add salt and pepper to taste.

VINAIGRETTE SAUCE

¾ cup salad oil
⅓ cup cider vinegar
3 tablespoons sweet pickle relish
2 tablespoons chopped parsley
1 teaspoon salt
¾ teaspoon sugar

ABOUT 10 MINUTES BEFORE SERVING:
In covered blender container, at low speed, blend all ingredients for 1 minute. (Or, in medium bowl, combine vinegar with next 4 ingredients; slowly pour in oil, beating with fork until well mixed.) Any leftover sauce may be refrigerated, covered; beat with fork just before serving. Serve on chilled fresh or cooked vegetables. Makes 1¼ cups.

COLD CHIFFON SAUCE

1 cup White Sauce (at left)
(or 1 1-ounce package white-sauce mix)
1 egg, separated
2 tablespoons cider vinegar
1 teaspoon tarragon
¼ teaspoon salt

ABOUT 4 HOURS BEFORE SERVING:
In small saucepan, prepare White Sauce; remove from heat. In cup, beat egg yolk with fork; pour into hot sauce, stirring rapidly until blended; let stand 10 minutes. Stir in vinegar and tarragon; cool 1 hour.

In small bowl, with mixer at high speed, beat egg white and salt until stiff peaks form. With rubber spatula, fold beaten white into sauce; cover; refrigerate.

TO SERVE:
Spoon sauce over cold cooked vegetables, or cold poached fish. Makes 1⅓ cups.

Fruits

Although some fresh fruits are seasonal, the principal ones—apples, citrus fruits and bananas—are available all year round. Furthermore, there's a wonderful selection of canned, frozen and dried fruits to choose from. Great for snacks, fruits add flavor and color to desserts, sauces, meats, salads, dressings, even soups.

Fresh fruit: Several kinds of fresh fruit are always available at the market. Rapid transportation makes it possible for us to buy fruits grown elsewhere in the country (in fact, the world) any time of the year. The important factor in buying fresh fruit is being able to tell by its appearance (not by squeezing) when it will be ready to eat. Citrus fruit never needs further ripening but other fruits do, so buy them ahead of time. Fresh fruit generally is very perishable and requires refrigeration once it is ripe.

Canned fruit: Almost every kind of fruit is canned—most often in a sugar syrup, sometimes in the natural juice—for instant eating. Since many kinds are sold whole, halved, sliced, and in pieces, look for the kind and the can size that fit your needs. Sometimes fruits are mixed: e.g., fruit cocktail, orange and grapefruit sections. Canned fruits keep on the shelf for a year but should, of course, be refrigerated after opening. Some fruits—grapefruit sections, fruit salads—are sold in jars in the refrigerated section of the supermarket; these should be kept refrigerated at home. For information on home canning, see pages 691–694.

Frozen fruit: Many fruits are frozen and packaged for quick thawing and serving. Look for whole fruits such as blueberries and raspberries; cut-up fruits such as melon balls, sliced peaches; and mixed fruit combinations. Most are at their best when served with a few ice crystals remaining; when completely thawed, the texture of frozen fruits can be quite soft. If your freezer maintains 0°F., frozen fruits may be kept up to a year. For information on home freezing of fresh fruit, see pages 703–709.

Dried fruits: Raisins and prunes are staples to keep on hand, since they may be used both for snacking and in recipes. Other fruits—apricots, pears, peaches, figs—are delicious stewed or in sauces.

Apples

Season: All year. The best supplies are in October; the lowest in June, July and August.

Look for: Firm, crisp, well-colored apples, the color depending upon the variety. Avoid brown spots, shriveled or soft fruit. Select apples according to their use: Eating–Winesap, Red or Golden Delicious; cooking–Rhode Island Greening, York or Rome Beauty; cooking and eating–McIntosh, Jonathan, Yellow Newton, Stayman, Cortland or Northern Spy.

To store: Refrigerate; use within 2 weeks.

To prepare: Wash; peel and core, depending upon use. To prevent browning if apples (other than Golden Delicious or Cortland) are to stand 20 minutes or more, sprinkle with lemon juice or a little ascorbic-acid mixture for fruit, mixed as label directs.

To serve: Eat out of hand, with or without peeling; use in recipes for pies, sauces, desserts, coffeecakes.

APPLESAUCE

2 pounds cooking apples, peeled, cored and sliced
dash cinnamon
dash ground cloves
½ cup sugar

ABOUT 30 MINUTES BEFORE SERVING:
In medium saucepan over medium heat, in ½ cup boiling water, heat first 3 ingredients to boiling. Reduce heat to low; cover and simmer 8 to 10 minutes until apples are tender (for chunky applesauce), 12 to 15 minutes for smoother applesauce. During last minutes of cooking time, stir in sugar. Makes about 4 cups.

OLD-FASHIONED APPLE DUMPLINGS

pastry for 2-crust pie (pages 504–505)
sugar
1 teaspoon cinnamon
4 large cooking apples, peeled and cored
2 teaspoons butter or margarine
1 short cinnamon stick
4 drops red food color
1 egg, slightly beaten

ABOUT 1½ HOURS AHEAD OR EARLY IN DAY:
Preheat oven to 425°F. Prepare pastry and divide into four equal parts. Roll out each part into an 8-inch square. In small bowl, combine ⅓ cup sugar and cinnamon.

Center an apple on a pastry square and spoon some cinnamon mixture into cavity. Dot apple with ½ teaspoon butter or margarine. With a few drops water, moisten points of pastry square and bring up over apple, overlapping and sealing well. Repeat; place dumplings in 12″ by 8″ baking dish.

In medium saucepan over medium-high heat, heat ⅔ cup sugar, 1⅓ cups water and cinnamon stick to boiling and boil for 3 minutes. Remove cinnamon stick and stir in food color. Pour syrup around dumplings; brush top of dumplings with egg. Bake 40 minutes or until crust is golden. Makes 4 servings.

BAKED APPLES

ABOUT 1 HOUR AHEAD OR EARLY IN DAY:
Preheat oven to 350°F. Core *6 medium cooking apples* and, starting from stem end, peel them ⅓ of the way down. Arrange in shallow baking dish, peeled end up, and pour *1 cup light corn syrup* over them. Bake apples 45 minutes or until fork-tender, spooning syrup from pan over them occasionally. Serve hot or cold with cream or ice cream, if you like. Makes 6 servings.

MINCEMEAT APPLES: Fill cavities with mincemeat before baking.

ORANGE-GLAZED APPLES: Spread tops of apples with orange marmalade before baking.

APPLE PETALS: Instead of peeling apples, cut each cored apple into 6 wedges just half way down and bake as above. Serve hot topped with a spoonful of pasteurized process cheese spread.

Apples, Dried

Packaged, cut-up dried apples are available by brands. Store, tightly wrapped, at room temperature for up to 6 months. Use in recipes for sauces, compotes.

STEWED DRIED APPLES

In medium saucepan over medium heat, simmer *one 8-ounce package dried apples, 3½ cups water* and *dash salt,* 25 minutes or until apples are tender. During last few minutes, stir in *¼ cup sugar* or to taste.

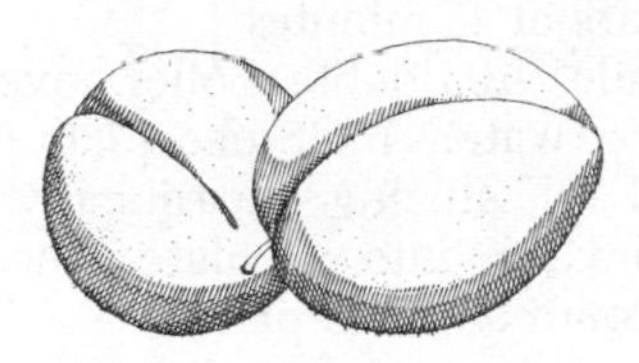

Apricots

Season: June and July.

Look for: Plump, juicy-looking orange-yellow fruit. Ripe apricots should yield to gentle pressure on the skin. Avoid dull-looking, shriveled or soft fruit.

To store: Refrigerate; use within 2 to 3 days.

To prepare: Wash and cut in half to remove seed; peel if desired. To prevent browning if apricots are not to be eaten immediately, sprinkle with lemon juice or ascorbic-acid mixture for fruits, mixed as label directs.

To serve: Eat out of hand, with or without peeling; use in recipes for salads, desserts.

CINNAMON APRICOTS IN CREAM

1 pound apricots, unpeeled
⅓ cup sugar
½ teaspoon cinnamon
¼ cup heavy or whipping cream

ABOUT 35 MINUTES BEFORE SERVING:
Preheat oven to 375°F. Halve and remove seeds from apricots. Place in 1-quart casserole. In small bowl, combine sugar, ⅓ cup water and cinnamon; pour over fruit. Bake 20 minutes or until apricots are tender. Pour on cream and bake 5 minutes longer. Makes 4 servings.

Apricots, Dried

Packaged dried medium or large apricots are available by brands. Store, tightly wrapped, at room temperature up to 6 months. Use in recipes for sauces, coffeecakes, breads, desserts.

STEWED DRIED APRICOTS

In medium saucepan over medium heat, simmer *one 8-ounce package dried apricots* and *2½ cups water,* 15 minutes or until apricots are tender. During last few minutes, stir in *¼ cup sugar* or to taste.

FOR 11- OR 12-OUNCE PACKAGE DRIED APRICOTS: Use 3 cups water and ½ cup sugar.

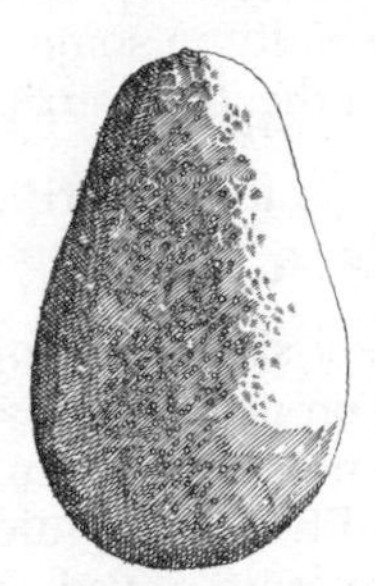

Avocados

Season: All year.

Look for: Pear-shaped, round or egg-shaped green or purplish-black avocados, depending on variety. Firm avocados should ripen at room temperature in 3 to 5 days. They are ready to eat when they yield to gentle pressure on the skin. Avoid dark spots or broken surfaces. Light-brown irregular skin markings don't affect quality, however.

To store: Refrigerate after ripening and use within 3 to 5 days.

To prepare: Cut avocado in half lengthwise to the seed; twist halves apart; remove seed. Peel and slice or cut up, depending on use. To prevent browning if avocados are not to be eaten immediately, sprinkle with lemon juice or a little ascorbic-acid mixture for fruit, mixed as label directs.

To serve: Stuff unpeeled avocado halves with salad or filling. Use slices with French dressing for salad; toss with green or fruit salads; use in recipes for dips, appetizers.

Bananas

Season: All year.

Look for: For immediate use, solid yellow bananas specked with some brown flecks. Fruit with some green will ripen at home in a few days at room temperature. (Red bananas are a specialty in some areas.) Brown skins usually indicate overripened fruit.

To store: Refrigerate after ripening and use within 2 or 3 days.

To prepare: Peel skin from top; slice or cut up, depending on use. To prevent browning if bananas are not to be eaten immediately, sprinkle with a little lemon juice or ascorbic-acid mixture for fruit, mixed as label directs.

To serve: Eat out of hand; use cut up or sliced in recipes for salads, desserts, breads.

BAKED BANANAS

3 tablespoons butter or margarine
4 slightly unripe medium bananas, peeled
salt

ABOUT 25 MINUTES BEFORE SERVING:
Preheat oven to 450°F. In oven, in pie plate or baking dish, melt butter or margarine. Remove plate from oven and roll bananas in melted butter or margarine; sprinkle lightly with salt. Bake 10 to 12 minutes until bananas are fork-tender. Serve hot as a vegetable, or ham or poultry accompaniment. Makes 4 servings.

BANANA POPS

2 teaspoons ascorbic-acid mixture for fruit
4 large bananas, peeled and sliced crosswise into thirds
1 package wooden ice-cream-bar sticks
1 6-ounce package semisweet-chocolate pieces
2 tablespoons salad oil
½ cup shredded coconut
½ cup toasted shredded coconut

2 HOURS BEFORE SERVING OR EARLY IN DAY:
In large bowl, in 3 tablespoons water, stir ascorbic-acid mixture until dissolved; gently toss bananas in mixture until coated. Insert a stick about 1 inch deep into end of each banana piece. Place on cookie sheet; freeze until firm, about 45 minutes.

Meanwhile, in double boiler, over hot, not boiling, water, melt chocolate pieces with salad oil, stirring occasionally. Pour chocolate mixture into pie plate. Place each kind of coconut on small plate.

Remove bananas from freezer and quickly roll each in chocolate; roll some bananas in shredded coconut and some in toasted shredded coconut. Return to cookie sheet and freeze for about 30 minutes. Makes 12 snacks.

Berries

Blackberries, Boysenberries, Dewberries, Loganberries, Raspberries, Youngberries. *See also* Blueberries, Cranberries, and Strawberries.

Season: Summer months, mostly June and July.

Look for: Plump, fresh-appearing, uniformly colored fruit. Berries should be free of stems or leaves. Avoid fruit that is moldy or crushed or bruised or that has leaked moisture, staining carton.

To store: Refrigerate; use within 1 or 2 days.

To prepare: Wash and remove any stems; drain well.

To serve: Serve with sugar and milk or over cereal; use in recipes for salads, pies, muffins, coffeecakes, desserts.

BLACKBERRY SAUCE

1 20-ounce bag frozen unsweetened blackberries
½ cup packed light brown sugar
2 tablespoons lemon juice
½ teaspoon cinnamon

EARLY IN DAY:
In medium saucepan over medium heat, heat frozen berries, sugar, lemon juice and cinnamon, stirring occasionally, until hot and bubbly. Cover and refrigerate. Serve over ice cream, cake, other fruits. Makes 2⅔ cups.

BLACKBERRY PARFAITS

2 3- or 3¼-ounce packages regular vanilla-pudding mix
Blackberry Sauce (above)
⅓ cup heavy or whipping cream, whipped

EARLY IN DAY:
Prepare pudding as label directs; cool. Into parfait glasses, spoon layers of pudding with layers of sauce; top with whipped cream. Chill. Makes 6 to 8 servings.

MELBA SAUCE

¼ cup red currant jelly
1½ 10-ounce packages frozen raspberries
2 tablespoons cornstarch
red food color

EARLY IN DAY:
In medium saucepan over low heat, melt jelly, stirring constantly; add frozen berries and heat. In measuring cup, mix cornstarch with 1 tablespoon cold water until smooth; stir into berries. Over medium heat, cook mixture, stirring occasionally until slightly thickened. Stir in a few drops red food color. Cover and refrigerate until serving time. Makes 2 cups.

RASPBERRY-FRUIT FONDUE

½ pint raspberries
2 tablespoons sugar
1 8-ounce package cream cheese, softened
2 pears, cut into thin wedges
lemon juice
½ pint strawberries
½ honeydew melon, scooped into balls
½ pineapple, cut into strips

ABOUT 1 HOUR BEFORE SERVING:
Prepare raspberry dip: In covered blender container, thoroughly blend raspberries and sugar. (Or, blend two 10-ounce packages frozen raspberries, thawed and drained.) Into small bowl, push raspberries through medium sieve, straining out seeds but forcing pulp through.

In medium bowl, with mixer at medium speed, beat cream cheese until smooth. Gradually beat in raspberry pulp until smooth. Refrigerate.

Meanwhile, prepare fruits for dipping: Sprinkle pears with lemon juice; arrange with other fruits on platter around bowl of dip. Let each guest dip fruit into mixture, using cocktail forks for melon. Makes 6 servings.

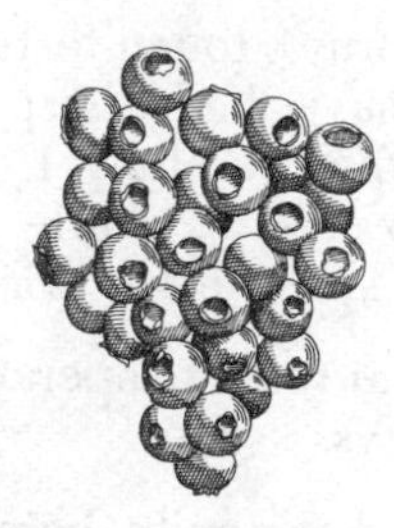

Blueberries

Season: May to September.

Look for: Plump, deep-colored berries of fairly uniform size. Silvery "bloom" on skin is natural protective waxy coating.

To store: Refrigerate; use within 2 to 3 days.

To prepare: Wash and remove any stems; drain well.

To serve: Serve with sugar and milk or over cereal; use in recipes for salads, pies, sauces, ice cream, muffins, desserts.

BLUEBERRY SAUCE

1 pint blueberries
¾ cup sugar
1 tablespoon cornstarch
dash salt
1 teaspoon lemon juice

ABOUT 20 MINUTES BEFORE SERVING:
In medium saucepan over medium heat, heat 1 cup water to boiling; add blueberries and return to boiling.

Meanwhile, in small bowl, combine sugar, cornstarch and salt; stir into blueberries and cook, stirring constantly, until thick. Add lemon juice. Makes about 2¾ cups.

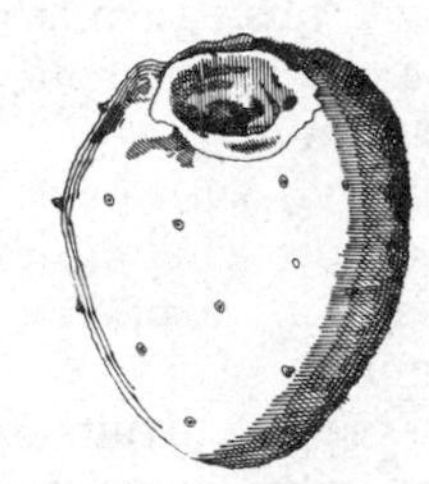

Cactus (Prickly) Pears

Season: March to May, September to November.

Look for: Thorny, tough-textured cactus pears which have had sharp spines removed. (Handle carefully!) Ripe fruit should yield to careful, gentle pressure on the skin. Avoid shriveled or dried fruit.

To store: Keep at room temperature and use within 1 to 2 days.

To prepare: Peel as apples, being careful to avoid thorns, and slice or cut up.

To serve: Eat out of hand; use in salads.

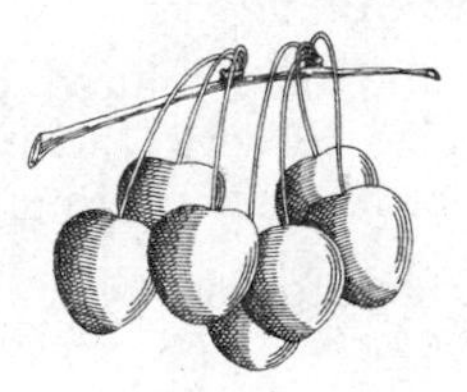

Cherries

Season: May to August.

Look for: Plump, bright-appearing cherries with color ranging from light to bright red to purplish-black, depending upon variety. Tart or sour cherries are best for cooking. Sweet cherries can be eaten fresh or used in cooking. Avoid too soft or shriveled fruit.

To store: Refrigerate; use in 2 or 3 days.

To prepare: Wash, stem and cut into center to remove seed.

To serve: Eat out of hand; use in recipes for salads, pies, desserts, jams or sauces.

CHERRY PINWHEELS

1 16-ounce can pitted, tart cherries
4 teaspoons all-purpose flour
1 8-ounce can refrigerated crescent rolls
butter or margarine, softened
⅓ cup sugar
1 tablespoon cornstarch
¼ teaspoon cinnamon

ABOUT 45 MINUTES BEFORE SERVING:
Preheat oven to 450°F. Drain and reserve liquid from cherries; drain cherries on paper towels. In medium bowl, toss cherries lightly with flour. Unroll the 2 rolls of crescent dough; spread lightly with butter or margarine; spread cherries evenly onto dough. Roll up each piece, jelly-roll fashion. Cut each roll in 3 slices and bake, cut side down, on cookie sheet for 15 to 18 minutes.

Meanwhile, in small saucepan, stir sugar, cornstarch and cinnamon with a little reserved liquid until combined; stir in remaining liquid and cook over low heat until clear and thickened, stirring. Top pinwheels with sauce. Makes 6 servings.

FRESH CHERRY PARFAIT SALAD

1 3-ounce package lemon-flavor gelatin
1 pint pineapple sherbet
2 cups sweet cherries, sliced
¼ cup chopped California walnuts

EARLY IN DAY:
In medium saucepan over medium heat, heat ¾ cup water to boiling. Add gelatin; stir until dissolved. Add sherbet, by spoonfuls, stirring until well blended. Fold in cherries and nuts. Pour into 4-cup mold; chill until set. Unmold. Makes 6 servings.

CHERRIES JUBILEE

1 10-ounce jar red currant jelly
2 17-ounce cans pitted dark sweet cherries, well drained
½ cup brandy
vanilla ice cream

AT SERVING TIME:
At table, in medium skillet or chafing dish over medium heat, melt jelly, stirring gently. Add cherries; heat until simmering. Pour in brandy; heat without stirring for a minute; light brandy with match. Spoon flaming cherries over ice cream. Makes 6 servings.

CHERRY SAUCE

1 pound sweet cherries, pitted
¼ cup sugar

ABOUT 15 MINUTES BEFORE SERVING:
In medium saucepan over medium heat, in ⅔ cup boiling water, heat cherries to boiling. Reduce heat to low; cover and simmer 5 minutes or until tender. During last minutes of cooking, add sugar. Makes 2 cups.

JIFFY CHERRIES AND CREAM

1 cup sour cream
1 tablespoon sugar
1 21-ounce can cherry-pie filling

EARLY IN DAY:
In small bowl, mix sour cream and sugar until well combined. In medium bowl, gently stir cherry-pie filling. Into six 6-ounce parfait glasses, spoon layers of cherry-pie filling and sour cream, ending with sour cream. Refrigerate. Makes 6 servings.

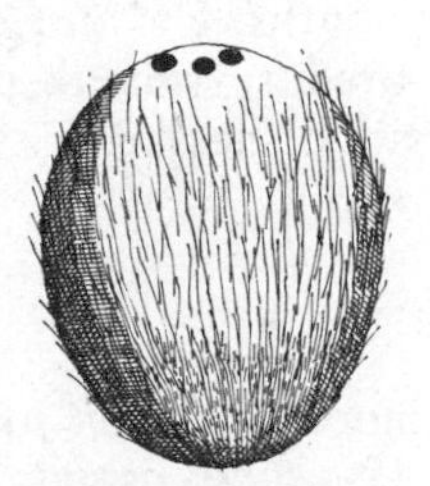

Coconuts

Season: All year with best supplies in October to December.

Look for: Coconuts heavy for their size and with juice that sloshes around inside when coconut is shaken. Avoid fruit with moldy or wet eyes.

To store: Refrigerate and use within a week. (Fresh shredded coconut will keep in refrigerator 1 or 2 days.)

To prepare: With hammer and ice pick, barbecue skewer or other sharp, pointed utensil, puncture 2 of the eyes of 1 coconut. Drain coconut juice into measuring cup and reserve, if using in a recipe.

With hammer, hit coconut very hard at widest part. If coconut shell does not crack, give it a few more extra firm hits. Hit firmly all around middle to crack open completely. With knife, pry coconut meat in pieces from shell or, with hammer, hit coconut shell pieces to crack them from meat.

To shred meat: Using small, sharp knife or vegetable peeler, peel brown outer skin from coconut meat and shred meat with coarse grater. One 1½-pound coconut yields 4 to 5 cups shredded coconut.

To serve: Use juice in beverages, salad dressings. Eat the meat out of hand or shred it to use in recipes for salads, pies, cakes, desserts.

To toast shredded coconut meat: Preheat oven to 350°F. Spread shredded coconut evenly in shallow pan. Bake until delicately browned, 20 to 30 minutes, stirring occasionally to toast evenly.

COCONUT-FRUIT DRESSING

½ cup sugar
1 tablespoon cornstarch
¾ cup coconut juice*
¼ cup lemon juice
1 egg, slightly beaten

ABOUT 1 HOUR AHEAD OR EARLY IN DAY:
In medium saucepan, mix sugar and cornstarch; stir in remaining ingredients. Cook over medium heat until thickened, stirring constantly. Chill. Serve as dressing for fresh or canned fruit salads. Makes about 1½ cups.

* If juice from one coconut does not equal ¾ cup, add water.

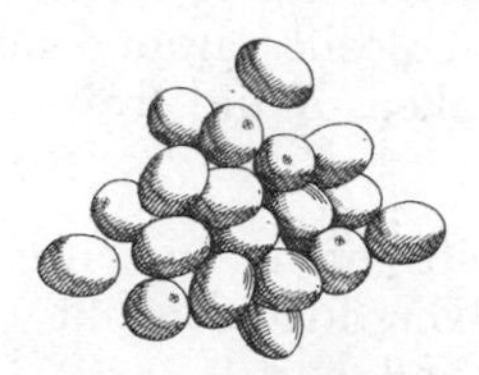

Cranberries

Season: September to January.

Look for: Plump, firm berries with high luster. Some varieties are rather large, bright red and quite tart; others are smaller, darker and sweeter. Avoid shriveled, discolored or moist cranberries. Sold prepackaged by brands.

To store: Refrigerate; use in 1 to 2 weeks.

To prepare: Wash and drain well.

To serve: Use in recipes for sauces, salads, pies, sherbets, quick breads.

CRANBERRY SAUCE

2 cups sugar
1 16-ounce package cranberries

ABOUT 10 MINUTES BEFORE SERVING:
In medium saucepan over medium heat, heat sugar and 1½ cups water to boiling. Add cranberries and return to boiling. Reduce heat to low; cover and simmer 7 minutes or until berries pop. Makes 5 cups.

Currants

Currants are not usually grown commercially. When available, use like gooseberries.

Dates

Season: All year with best supplies in November.

Look for: Lustrous golden-brown fruit. Sold prepackaged by brands, pitted and unpitted.

To store: Keep tightly wrapped; when refrigerated, will keep for several weeks.

To prepare: Cut out pits, if necessary.

To serve: Eat out of hand; use with fresh fruit as dessert; use in recipes for cakes, fruitcakes, desserts, cookies, salads.

Figs

Season: May to September.

Look for: Slightly firm fruit which yields slightly to gentle pressure on the skin. Varieties range in color from greenish-yellow to purple to black. Avoid too-soft fruit or fruit with sour odor.

To store: Refrigerate; use within 1 or 2 days.

To prepare: Wash.

To serve: Eat out of hand; use in recipes for pies or cakes.

Figs, Dried

Packaged dried figs are available by brands. Store, tightly wrapped, at room temperature up to 6 months. Eat out of hand; use in recipes for breads, fruitcakes; use cooked as breakfast fruit or dessert.

STEWED DRIED FIGS

In medium saucepan over medium heat, simmer *one 12-ounce package dried figs* with *3 cups water* for 35 minutes or until figs are tender. During last minutes of cooking, stir in *1 tablespoon lemon juice,* if desired.

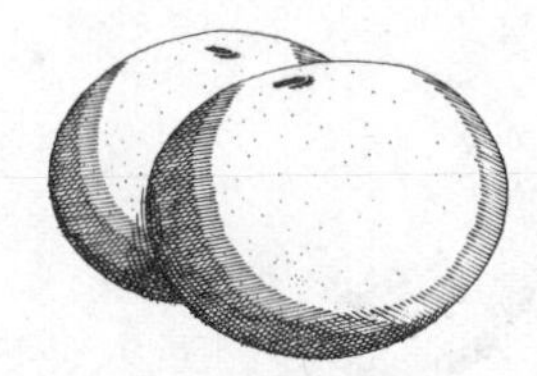

Grapefruit

Season: All year with best supplies in October to April.

Look for: Well-shaped, firm but springy-to-touch fruit that is heavy for its size. Russeting or brownish discolorations on skin usually don't affect eating quality. Varieties include seedless, with seeds, pink- or white-fleshed. Avoid fruit that is soft or discolored at stem end.

To store: Refrigerate; use in 1 to 2 weeks.

To prepare: Cut in half, parallel to stem end. With sharp, pointed knife, cut sections from membrane, leaving them in place if serving in shell. With kitchen shears, cut out core. Remove any seeds.

To serve: Eat fresh; use in recipes for salads, meat or fish.

BROILED GRAPEFRUIT

ABOUT 15 MINUTES BEFORE SERVING:
Preheat broiler if manufacturer directs. Cut *grapefruit* in halves, section and remove any seeds. Sprinkle each half with a little *brown sugar;* drizzle with melted *butter or margarine.* Broil 10 minutes or until golden and heated through.

BAKED GRAPEFRUIT: Prepare as above but bake in 450°F. oven for 20 minutes.

VARIATIONS: Sprinkle sugar with nutmeg or ground cloves. Or instead of sugar, use honey, maple-blended syrup or corn syrup.

GRAPEFRUIT AMBROSIA

JUST BEFORE SERVING:
In bowl, toss *one 16-ounce can grapefruit sections,* drained, with *1/4 cup honey* and *1/2 cup flaked coconut.* Makes 4 servings.

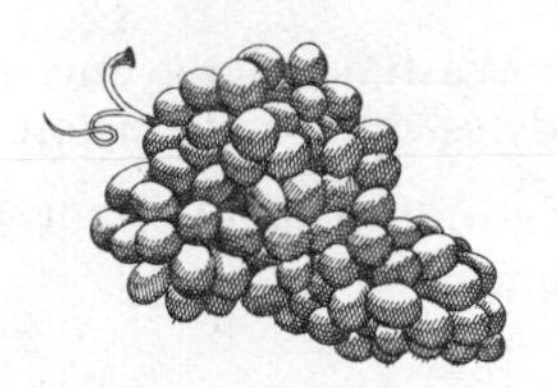

Grapes

Season: All year with best supplies from July to November.

Look for: Plump, fresh-appearing grapes with individual berries firmly attached to stems. A high color for variety usually means good flavor. Avoid dry, brittle stems or shriveled grapes or ones leaking moisture and staining carton.

To store: Refrigerate; use in 1 to 2 weeks.

To prepare: Wash and, if with seeds, cut into center to remove seeds.

To serve: Eat out of hand; use in recipes for salads, desserts, sauces, jellies and jams.

MINTED GRAPES

1 bunch seedless green grapes
1/2 cup honey
2 tablespoons lime juice
2 tablespoons finely chopped mint

EARLY IN DAY:
Stem grapes and arrange in 4 sherbet or dessert dishes. In small bowl, combine remaining ingredients; pour over grapes and refrigerate to marinate. Makes 4 servings.

Guava

Season: September to December.

Look for: Red or yellow fruit, depending on variety. Ripe guavas should yield to gentle pressure on the skin. Avoid cracked skins.

To store: Refrigerate after ripening and use within 2 or 3 days.

To prepare: Wash; cut large ones in pieces; discard seeds as with watermelon.

To serve: Eat out of hand or cut up to use in recipes for salads, sauces.

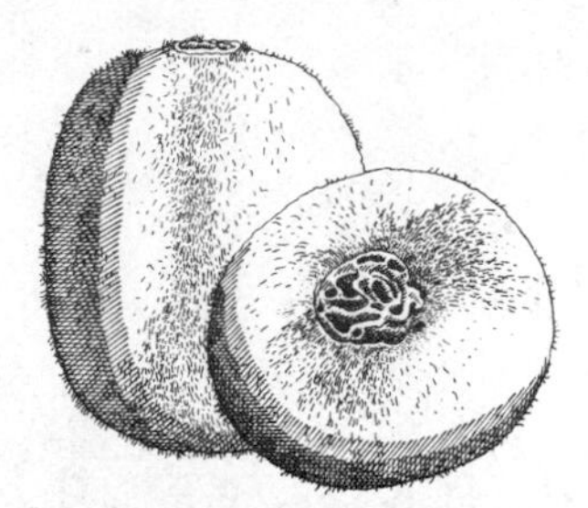

Kiwi Fruit
(Chinese Gooseberry)

Season: June to December.

Look for: Slightly firm fruit with fairly fuzzy skin. When fully ripened, kiwi fruit should yield to gentle pressure on the skin.

To store: Refrigerate after ripening and use within 1 or 2 days.

To prepare: Brush off fuzzy surface, then peel; cut in wedges or slices.

To serve: Serve cut up with sugar and milk or lemon juice as dessert or appetizer; add to fruit salads.

Kumquats

Season: November to February.

Look for: Firm, bright orange kumquats. Avoid blemished or shriveled fruit.

To store: Keep a few days at room temperature or refrigerate and use within a week.

To prepare: Wash; remove stems; cut in half to remove seeds.

To serve: Eat out of hand, peel and all; add cut-up kumquats to fruit salads.

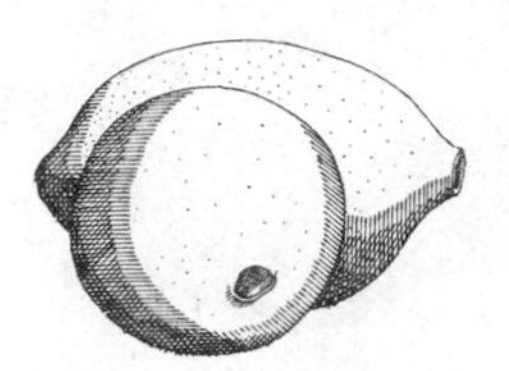

Lemons

Season: All year.

Look for: Bright, firm lemons, heavy for their size. Pale or greenish-yellow color usually means fruit of higher acidity. Avoid soft, shriveled or hard-skinned lemons.

To store: Keep a few days at room temperature; refrigerate and use within 2 weeks.

To prepare: Cut in half, parallel to stem end, for squeezing; slice in rings or cut into wedges for garnishes; remove seeds.

To serve: Use in recipes for sauces for seafood, poultry, vegetables or fruits; beverages; salad dressings; desserts. Use to garnish main dishes, desserts.

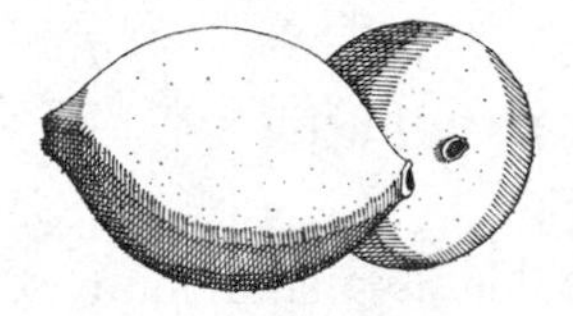

Limes

Season: All year.

Look for: Firm, glossy-skinned limes, heavy for their size. Irregular purplish-brown marks on skin don't affect flesh quality. Avoid hard, dry or soft limes.

To store: Keep at room temperature a few days or refrigerate and use within 2 weeks.

To prepare: Cut in half, parallel to stem end, for squeezing; slice in rings or cut into wedges for garnishes; remove seeds.

To serve: Use in recipes for beverages, chilled desserts, pies. Use to garnish desserts, beverages.

VIRGIN-ISLAND SALAD DRESSING

¼ cup fresh lime juice
¼ cup fresh lemon juice
¼ cup light rum
¼ cup salad oil
½ teaspoon grated lime peel
3 tablespoons light brown sugar

EARLY IN DAY:
In covered jar or bottle, shake all ingredients; refrigerate. Serve over fruits or green salads. Makes about 1 cup.

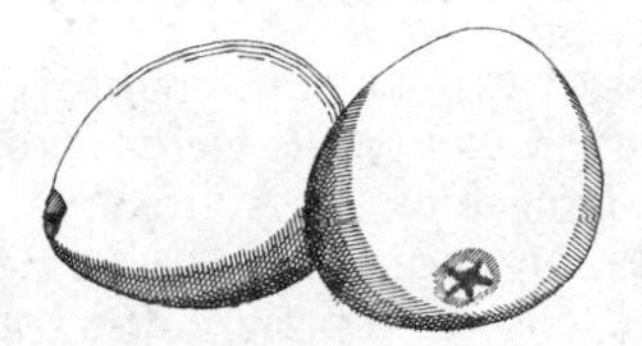

Loquats

Season: April and early May.

Look for: Deep colored, orange-yellow fruit that yields to gentle pressure on the skin.

To store: Refrigerate; use within 2 or 3 days.

To prepare: With fingers, pull off peel; cut into center to remove seeds; slice or cut up.

To serve: Eat out of hand; use in salads.

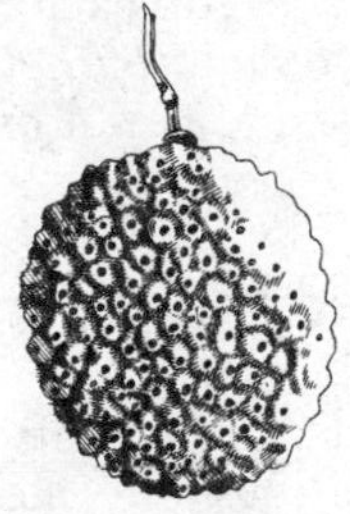

Lychees

Season: June and July.

Look for: Firm, rough and rubbery-skinned fruit with no indication of decay at stem end. Avoid blemished fruit.

To store: Refrigerate; use within 1 or 2 days.

To prepare: Beginning at stem, with thumb, peel skin as for oranges; cut around seed.

To serve: Eat out of hand; use in salads.

Lychee Nuts

Packaged dried lychees, usually called lychee nuts, are available. Store at room temperature for up to 6 months. Crack and peel skin; eat out of hand or use in recipes for sauces for meats.

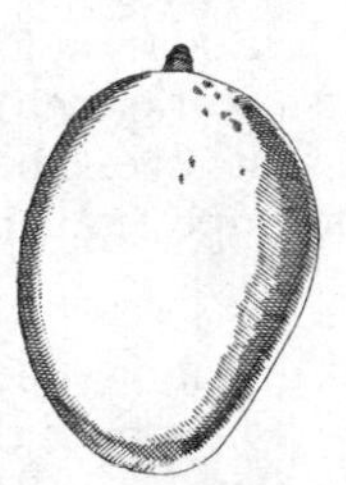

Mangoes

Season: April to August.

Look for: Oval or round, yellowish or orange fruit, perhaps with speckled skin. Ripe mangoes should yield slightly to gentle pressure on the skin. (Unripe mangoes have very poor flavor.) Avoid soft or shriveled fruit.

To store: Let ripen at room temperature; refrigerate and use in 2 or 3 days.

To prepare: Hold stem end in palm of hand and, with sharp knife, cut through skin from top to bottom in several places; peel skin down as for a banana. The mango seed is long and flat and flesh clings to it, so slice flesh from seed lengthwise.

To serve: Eat out of hand; use sliced pieces in fruit salads.

Melons

See also Watermelons

Season: May to November, depending upon variety.

Look for: Fully ripened fruit for best sweetness and flavor. (Cantaloupe are usually firm at store but ripen well at home.) Avoid bruised or cracked fruit. Use these guidelines when selecting varieties:

Cantaloupe: Scar at stem end should be smooth and without any stem remaining; the rind around the blossom end should yield slightly with gentle thumb pressure; a pleasant melon odor should be perceptible; the coarse, corky netting or veining should stand out over the background rind; the cantaloupe rind should have no green color.

Casaba: Light green or yellow color turns to gold yellow when ripe; the rind at the blossom end should yield slightly to thumb pressure; casabas have no aroma.

Crenshaw: Rind should be deep golden yellow, sometimes with small areas of lighter yellow; the rind, especially around the blossom end, should yield slightly to gentle thumb pressure; it should have a pleasant aroma.

Honey Ball: Follow tips for Honeydew except that Honey Ball is smaller and has slight, irregular netting over surface of the rind.

Honeydew: Yellowish to creamy-white; should have a soft, velvety feel; the rind should be slightly soft around the blossom end and have a faint, pleasant aroma. (Ripeness is difficult to judge.)

Persian: Follow tips for cantaloupes except that Persian melon is more nearly round and has fine netting.

To store: Let ripen at room temperature; refrigerate and use within 2 or 3 days. Keep melons with aroma well-wrapped; after cutting melons, cover cut surface.

To prepare: For wedges, cut from stem to blossom end. (For cantaloupe halves, cut parallel to stem end.) For rings, cut parallel to stem end. With spoon, scoop out seeds and connective membranes. Also cut up or scoop melons into balls.

To serve: Serve melon with lemon or lime wedges as appetizer or dessert. Use in recipes for salads, fruit cups, sherbets, gelatin desserts.

GINGERED MELON WEDGES

SEVERAL HOURS BEFORE SERVING:
Cut *1 large honeydew melon* in half lengthwise and remove seeds; slice each half into 4 wedges. Slash the pulp of wedges crisscross into bite-size pieces, then cut pulp loose from rind, leaving pulp in place.

In cup, combine *2 tablespoons confectioners' sugar* and *½ teaspoon ginger;* sprinkle over melon. Cover melon and refrigerate. Makes 8 servings.

MELON RINGS WITH STRAWBERRIES

ABOUT 30 MINUTES BEFORE SERVING:
Cut *1 large honey ball melon* crosswise into five 1-inch-thick rings; remove seeds; place slices on individual dessert plates. With knife, loosen pulp by cutting around slice ¼ inch in from rind. Slice pulp to make bite-size pieces, leaving rind intact.

From *1 pint strawberries,* spoon berries into slices; sprinkle with *confectioners' sugar.* Makes 5 servings.

CANTALOUPE RINGS A LA MODE

JUST BEFORE SERVING:
Cut *1 large cantaloupe* crosswise into four or five 1-inch-thick rings; remove seeds. Place on serving plates and cut off rind, leaving ring intact. Top each ring with sherbet from *1 pint lemon sherbet;* garnish with a few *blueberries.* Makes 4 or 5 servings.

Mixed Fruits, Dried

Packaged dried mixed fruits are available by brands. Fruits usually included in mixture are prunes, apricots, peaches and pears or apples. Store, tightly wrapped, at room temperature up to 6 months. Use cooked as breakfast fruit or dessert.

STEWED MIXED FRUITS

In medium saucepan over medium heat, simmer *one 11- or 12-ounce package dried mixed fruits* in *4 cups water* for 25 minutes or until fruit is tender. During last minutes of cooking, stir in *½ cup sugar* or to taste.

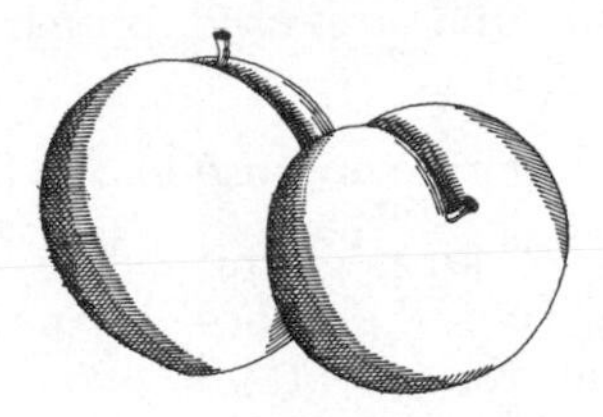

Nectarines

Season: June to September.

Look for: Plump, rich-colored fruit with slight softening along the seam side. Color will be reddish to yellowish, depending on variety. Slightly firm fruit should ripen well at room temperature. Avoid hard, soft or shriveled fruit or fruit with large proportion of green skin.

To store: Let ripen at room temperature; refrigerate and use within 3 to 5 days. To prevent browning if nectarines are not to be eaten immediately, sprinkle with a little lemon or ascorbic-acid mixture for fruit, mixed as label directs.

To prepare: Wash; peel; cut in half and remove seed.

To serve: Eat out of hand; use in recipes for salads, desserts, pies.

SPICED NECTARINE SLICES

¾ teaspoon whole cloves
¼ teaspoon cinnamon
¼ teaspoon ginger
¼ teaspoon salt
4 large nectarines, peeled and thinly sliced
½ cup sugar
3 tablespoons lemon juice

EARLY IN DAY:
In medium skillet over medium heat, heat 1½ cups water with cloves, cinnamon, ginger and salt to boiling; boil 2 minutes. Add nectarine slices and cook until fork-tender, about 10 minutes, stirring occasionally. During last minutes of cooking time, stir in sugar and lemon juice. Refrigerate until well chilled. Serve as meat accompaniment. Makes about 16 relish servings.

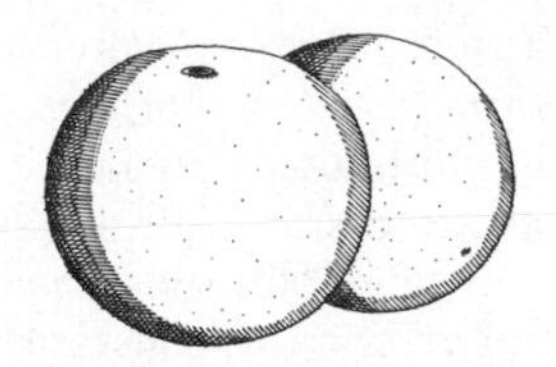

Oranges

See Tangelos

Season: All year with best supplies in winter and early spring.

Look for: Firm oranges, heavy for their size. Strict state regulations help assure tree-ripened fruits; slight greenish color or russeting of skin of certain varieties does not affect quality of the orange flesh. Navel and Temple oranges are easily peeled and sectioned; Valencia, Parson Brown, Pineapple, Hamlin varieties have abundant juice. Navel oranges are seedless, Hamlins have few, if any, seeds and Valencias usually have 6 or less seeds. Avoid dry, soft or spongy fruit.

To store: Keep at room temperature a few days or refrigerate and use within 2 weeks.

To prepare: Peel; break into sections, slice or cut up. For juice, cut in half, parallel to stem end and squeeze on reamer or electric juicer.

To serve: Eat out of hand; use in recipes for salads, desserts, beverages, sauces, cakes.

SOUTHERN AMBROSIA

1 3-ounce package egg-custard mix
6 to 8 large oranges
1½ cups shredded fresh or packaged coconut

EARLY IN DAY:
Prepare mix as label directs but do not add egg yolk; refrigerate, covered.

ABOUT 20 MINUTES BEFORE SERVING:
With hand beater, beat custard until smooth. Peel and slice oranges. Into medium serving bowl, spoon half of custard sauce; cover with half of orange slices, then half of coconut. Repeat. Makes 6 servings.

ORANGE CROWNS

ABOUT 30 MINUTES BEFORE SERVING:
Peel 8 *medium seedless oranges;* cut crosswise into slices about ½ inch thick; restack slices and arrange stacks on dessert plates. In small, deep saucepan over medium heat, melt *1 cup sugar,* stirring constantly. Reduce heat to low; stir in *¼ cup water* and *1 tablespoon vanilla extract* until well blended; pour over oranges. Garnish with *slivered almonds* and *fresh mint.* Makes 8 servings.

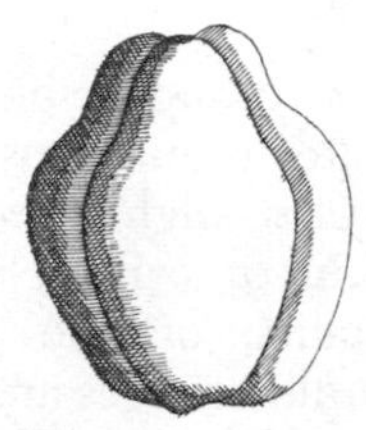

Papaya

Season: All year.

Look for: Greenish-yellow to almost-yellow fruit that should yield to gentle thumb pressure. Avoid shriveled or bruised fruit.

To store: Refrigerate; use within 3 to 4 days.

To prepare: Cut in half lengthwise and spoon out seeds; peel and slice or cut up.

To serve: Serve unpeeled halves with lemon wedges for appetizer or dessert. Use in recipes for salads, desserts.

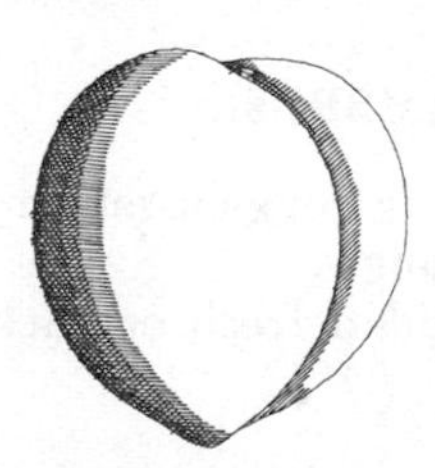

Peaches

Season: May to October.

Look for: Fairly firm to slightly softened fruit with yellow or cream color and, depending on variety, a red blush. Avoid green, shriveled or bruised fruit. Freestone varieties come readily from the seed. Clingstones do not and are used primarily by commercial canners.

To store: Refrigerate and use in 3 to 5 days.

To prepare: Wash; peel and cut in half to remove seed. To peel peaches, dip in rapidly boiling water for about 15 seconds; dip immediately in pan of cold water; with knife, peel off skins. To prevent browning if peaches are not to be eaten immediately, sprinkle with lemon juice or a little ascorbic-acid mixture for fruit, mixed as label directs.

To serve: Eat out of hand; use in recipes for salads, desserts, pies, preserves.

BUTTERY BAKED PEACHES

6 peaches
½ cup sugar
2 tablespoons lemon juice
2 tablespoons butter or margarine
mint jelly

ABOUT 1 HOUR BEFORE SERVING:
Preheat oven to 350°F. Peel, halve and seed peaches. In small saucepan over medium-high heat, heat sugar, lemon juice, butter or margarine and 1 cup water to boiling; simmer 5 minutes. Place peaches in 3-quart casserole; add syrup. Cover and bake 30 minutes or until peaches are tender. Place a little jelly in center of each half. Serve, drained, as meat garnish or warm as dessert. Makes 12 garnishes or 6 servings.

SPICED BAKED PEACHES: Prepare as above but omit lemon juice and jelly; heat *¼ teaspoon nutmeg* or 2 tablespoons dry sherry with sugar mixture.

STEWED PEACHES

¼ cup sugar
4 whole cloves
1½ pounds peaches, peeled and halved

ABOUT 20 MINUTES BEFORE SERVING:
In medium saucepan over medium heat, heat sugar, ¾ cup water and cloves to boiling. Add peaches; return to boiling. Reduce heat to low; cover and simmer 10 minutes or until tender. Makes 6 servings.

SPANISH PEACHES

1 30-ounce can cling-peach halves
3 tablespoons dark brown sugar
2 tablespoons lime juice
¼ cup dry sherry (optional)
1 tablespoon grated lime peel

EARLY IN DAY:
Drain peaches, reserving ½ cup syrup. In small saucepan over medium heat, heat reserved ½ cup syrup, sugar and lime juice for 5 minutes. Stir in sherry. Meanwhile, place peach halves, flat side down, in dish; pour syrup over them and sprinkle with lime peel. Refrigerate until serving time. Makes 8 or 9 servings.

SNOWCAPPED PEACHES

1 30-ounce can cling-peach halves, drained
strawberry jam
1 egg white
2 tablespoons sugar

ABOUT 20 MINUTES BEFORE SERVING:
Preheat broiler if manufacturer directs. Arrange peach halves, flat side up, on broiler pan; spoon a little jam into center of each half.

In small bowl, with mixer at high speed, beat egg white until soft peaks form; beating at high speed, gradually sprinkle in sugar; beat until sugar is completely dissolved. (White should stand in stiff peaks.) Heap mixture over each peach. Broil 1 or 2 minutes until golden brown. Makes 8 or 9 servings.

Peaches, Dried

Packaged dried peaches are available by brands. Store, tightly wrapped, at room temperature up to 6 months. Use in recipes for sauces, breads.

STEWED DRIED PEACHES

In medium saucepan over medium heat, simmer *one 11- or 12-ounce package dried peaches* and *4 cups water* for 25 minutes or until peaches are tender. During last minutes of cooking time, stir in *¼ cup sugar* or to taste.

Pears

Season: All year with best supplies in August to December.

Look for: Well shaped, fairly firm fruit, the color depending upon the variety. Ripen firm pears at room temperature; when ready to eat, they should yield readily to soft pressure in the palm of the hand. Avoid shriveled, discolored, cut or bruised fruit. Select Bartlett, Anjou, and Bosc pears for both eating fresh and cooking; Comice, Seckel, Nelis, Kieffer for eating fresh.

To store: Let firm pears ripen at room temperature a few days, then refrigerate and use within 3 to 5 days.

To prepare: Wash; peel; halve and remove seeds, core and stem.

To serve: Eat out of hand; slice and serve with French dressing as salad; use in recipes for salads, pies, desserts.

BUTTERSCOTCH PEARS

1 30-ounce can pear halves
⅓ cup packed light brown sugar
1 cup bite-size toasted rice cereal
2 tablespoons butter or margarine, melted
¼ teaspoon salt
¼ teaspoon nutmeg
half-and-half (optional)

ABOUT 30 MINUTES BEFORE SERVING:
Preheat oven to 425°F. Drain pears (use pear liquid with orange juice another day). In medium bowl, toss next 5 ingredients until well mixed. In buttered 9-inch pie plate, sprinkle half of cereal mixture. Arrange pear halves in plate; sprinkle with remaining mixture. Bake 10 minutes or until pears are heated through. Serve with half-and-half, if desired. Makes 4 or 5 servings.

BUTTERY BAKED PEARS WITH BRIE

6 pears
½ cup sugar
2 tablespoons lemon juice
2 tablespoons butter or margarine
1 small wheel or round Brie cheese
sesame-seed crackers

EARLY IN DAY:
Preheat oven to 350°F. Peel pears, leaving stems intact; do not core pears. In small saucepan over medium-high heat, heat sugar, lemon juice, butter and 1 cup water to boiling; simmer 5 minutes.

Place pears in 3-quart casserole; add syrup. Cover and bake 45 minutes or until tender. Refrigerate.

AT SERVING TIME:
Arrange Brie cheese and crackers on serving board with cheese spreader or knife. Place pears on dessert plates and serve to guests with dessert knives and forks. Pass cheese and crackers. Makes 6 servings.

STEWED PEARS

2 pounds pears, cut up
⅓ cup sugar

ABOUT 20 MINUTES BEFORE SERVING:
In medium saucepan over medium heat, in ⅔ cup boiling water, heat pears to boiling. Reduce heat to low; cover and simmer 10 minutes or until pears are tender. During last few minutes of cooking time, add sugar. Makes 3½ cups.

Pears, Dried

Packaged dried pears are available by brands. Store, tightly wrapped, at room temperature up to 6 months. Use in recipes for sauces, compotes.

STEWED DRIED PEARS

In medium saucepan over medium heat, simmer *one 11-ounce package dried pears* with *3 cups water* for 25 minutes or until pears are tender. During last minutes of cooking, stir in *¼ cup sugar* or to taste.

Persimmons

Season: September to January.

Look for: Slightly firm, plump fruit with smooth, unbroken skin and the stem cap attached. Avoid bruised or too-soft fruit. Oriental varieties are most common; smaller native persimmons are usually home-grown.

To store: When ripe, refrigerate and use within 1 or 2 days.

To prepare: Wash; remove caps. For pulp, peel and slice Oriental varieties and mash; press native persimmons through a food mill to remove seeds, skin.

To serve: For dessert or snack, place fruit, stem end down, on plate; cut gashes through top skin and spoon out pulp. (Pulp will cling to seed.) Use in recipes for salads, puddings.

PERSIMMON-DATE PUDDING

2 cups all-purpose flour
2 cups sugar
4 teaspoons baking soda
1 tablespoon double-acting baking powder
½ teaspoon cinnamon
¼ teaspoon ginger
¼ teaspoon ground cloves
2 cups coarsely chopped California walnuts
1 cup chopped dates
1 cup dark seedless raisins
1 teaspoon grated orange peel
2 cups persimmon pulp
1 cup milk
3 tablespoons butter or margarine, melted
2 teaspoons vanilla extract
Foamy Hard Sauce (below)

ABOUT 2½ HOURS OR UP TO 2 WEEKS AHEAD:
Preheat oven to 325°F. Into large bowl, sift

or mix well first 7 ingredients; stir in nuts, dates, raisins and orange peel; set aside.

With large spoon, stir persimmon pulp, milk, butter or margarine and vanilla extract into flour mixture until well mixed. Spoon evenly into a greased and floured 13" by 9" baking dish. Bake 50 to 60 minutes until toothpick inserted in center comes out clean. Serve warm with Foamy Hard Sauce. Makes about 12 to 14 servings.

To store, cover pudding with foil and refrigerate up to 2 weeks. To reheat, preheat oven to 325°F. Heat covered pudding about 40 minutes or until heated through.

FOAMY HARD SAUCE

In small bowl, with mixer at low speed, beat *1½ cups sifted confectioners' sugar, 1 egg* and *⅓ cup butter or margarine,* melted, until smooth. Add *½ teaspoon vanilla extract* and *½ teaspoon rum flavor;* fold in *1 cup heavy or whipping cream,* whipped. Refrigerate until ready to serve. Makes 3 cups.

Pineapple

Season: All year.

Look for: Firm fruit, heavy for its size, with distinct aroma and plump, glossy eyes. Check ease with which a leaf can be pulled from crown. Color will depend on variety, but usually dark green color indicates immaturity.

To store: Pineapples do not ripen after harvest. Refrigerate; use within 1 to 2 days.

To prepare: For rings or chunks, cut off crown and stem end; cut fruit into crosswise slices ½ to 1 inch thick. With knife, cut off rind and remove eyes. Core with biscuit cutter or knife; serve in rings or cut up. For wedges, cut fruit in halves, then quarters, through crown to stem end. Cut off core along top of wedges; run knife between rind and flesh close to rind. Leaving flesh in shell, cut it into ¼- to ½-inch slices. (Or remove flesh and use shell for serving salad.)

To serve: Use as appetizer or dessert; use in recipes for salads, pies. (Do not use fresh pineapple in gelatin; it prevents jelling.)

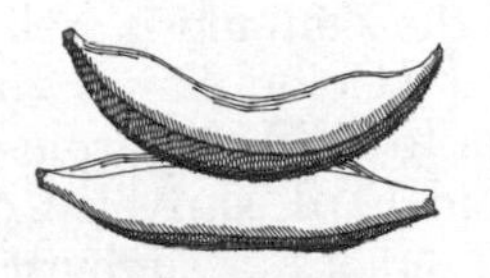

Plantains
(Cooking Bananas)

Season: All year.

Look for: Firm, large fruit with green color and some brown spots.

To prepare: Cut off ends; cut skin lengthwise in strips; with fingers, peel strips.

To serve: Use cooked in recipes as a vegetable.

FRIED PLANTAINS

ABOUT 15 MINUTES BEFORE SERVING:
In large skillet over medium-high heat, heat *¼ cup butter or margarine;* fry some of *4 very ripe plantains,* thinly sliced, until golden brown on each side; remove to warm platter. Add a little more *butter or margarine* and repeat. Makes 8 servings.

PLANTAIN CHIPS

EARLY IN DAY:
In electric skillet, heat 1 inch *salad oil* to 400°F. With potato peeler, diagonally slice, paper thin, some of *2 unripe plantains* directly into hot oil. Fry 30 seconds or until crisp; drain on paper towels. Repeat. Sprinkle with *salt.* Makes about 6 cups.

Plums
(Including Italian Prunes)

Season: June to October.

Look for: Plump fruit that yields to gentle pressure on the skin and is well colored for the variety. (Color varies from bright yellow-green to reddish purple to purplish-black.) Avoid hard, shriveled or soft fruit or fruit with cracks or sunburn marks.

To store: Refrigerate; use within 3 to 5 days.

To prepare: Wash; cut into center to remove seed. Slice or cut up for serving, with or without skin. (Varieties vary in tartness and some need more sugar when cooked.)

To serve: Eat out of hand; serve sliced with milk and sugar; use in recipes for salads, desserts, sauces, jams, coffeecakes.

STEWED PLUMS

1 pound plums, halved and seeded
⅓ cup sugar

ABOUT 20 MINUTES AHEAD OR EARLY IN DAY: In medium saucepan over medium heat, in ½ cup boiling water, heat plums to boiling. Reduce heat to low; cover and simmer 5 minutes. During last minutes of cooking time, stir in sugar. Makes 2½ cups.

QUICK PLUM DESSERTS: Spoon Stewed Plums over lemon sherbet. Or, sprinkle Stewed Plums with slivered almonds or nutmeg.

CREAMY PLUM DRESSING FOR FRUIT

4 plums, seeded
½ cup confectioners' sugar
1 8-ounce package cream cheese, softened

ABOUT 1 HOUR AND 15 MINUTES AHEAD: In covered blender container at low speed, blend plums and sugar until of sauce consistency, about 1 minute. Add cream cheese; blend for 30 seconds or just until smooth. Refrigerate at least 1 hour. Serve over fresh fruit salad. Makes about 1¾ cups.

Pomegranates

Season: September to December.

Look for: Fresh-appearing fruit, heavy for its size. Avoid shriveled fruit or broken rinds.

To store: Refrigerate; use within a week.

To prepare: With sharp knife, 1 inch from and parallel to blossom end, make shallow cut all around. With fingers, pull off top. (Kernels are very juicy.) Score fruit, through skin only, in about 6 wedges; break apart; gently remove kernels. For juice, press kernels through sieve; discard seeds.

To serve: Use juice in beverages. Eat kernels out of hand, in fruit salads or as garnish.

Prunes
(Dried Plums)

Packaged prunes are available pitted or unpitted by brands. Sizes vary from small or breakfast size to extra-large or jumbo; size has no effect on quality. Store, tightly wrapped, at room temperature up to 6 months. Use plumped or cooked as breakfast fruit or dessert or in recipes for breads, sauces.

PLUMPED PRUNES

In medium heatproof container, cover *one 16-ounce package prunes* with *4 cups boiling water* and refrigerate overnight.

COOKED PRUNES

In medium saucepan over medium heat, simmer *one 16-ounce package prunes* and *4 cups water* for about 20 minutes, depending on size of prunes. For plumper prunes, richer juice, refrigerate overnight.

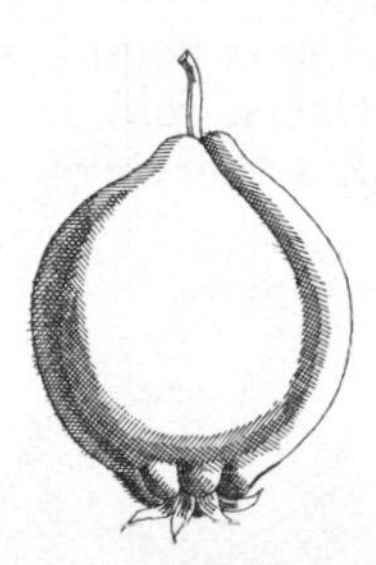

Quince

Season: October and November.

Look for: Golden-yellow, round or pear-shaped fruit with rather fuzzy skin. Avoid small, knotty fruit or ones with bruises.

To store: Refrigerate; use within 2 weeks.

To prepare: Peel, quarter and remove seeds and core.

To serve: Most often used in jelly (fresh quince has acid flavor, is never eaten raw).

Raisins
(Dried Grapes)

Packaged golden or dark seedless raisins are available by brands. Some packaged seeded muscat raisins and Zante currants also are sold by brands. Store, tightly wrapped, at room temperature up to 6 months. Eat out of hand or use in recipes for sauces, fruitcakes, cookies, breads.

RAISIN SAUCE

1 10-ounce jar red-currant jelly
½ cup dark seedless raisins
⅓ cup lemon juice
1 tablespoon cornstarch

ABOUT 15 MINUTES BEFORE SERVING:
In medium saucepan over medium heat, heat jelly, raisins and lemon juice to boiling. In cup, mix cornstarch with 2 tablespoons water; stir into jelly mixture and cook, stirring, until sauce is thickened and bubbling. Serve over ham or poultry. Makes about 1 cup.

Raspberries
See Berries

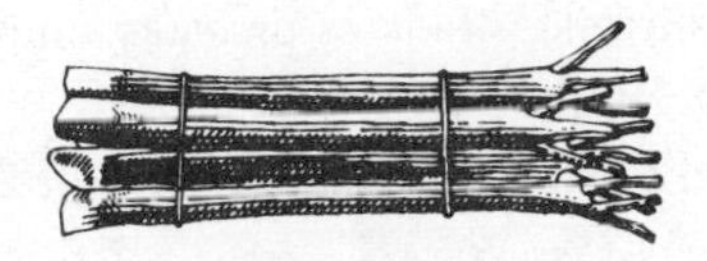

Rhubarb

Season: January to June (some areas may have rhubarb all year).

Look for: Firm, crisp, fairly thick stalks that are either red or pink in color, depending on variety. Avoid flabby stalks.

To store: Refrigerate; use within 3 to 5 days.

To prepare: Wash and trim discolored ends; cut off and discard any leaves.

To serve: Use in recipes for pies or sauce to accompany meat or poultry.

RHUBARB SAUCE

1½ pounds rhubarb, cut up
⅔ cup sugar

ABOUT 20 MINUTES BEFORE SERVING:
In medium saucepan over medium heat, in ¾ cup boiling water, heat rhubarb to boiling. Reduce heat to low; cover and simmer 5 minutes or until rhubarb is tender. During last minutes of cooking time, stir in sugar. Makes about 2⅔ cups.

STRAWBERRY-RHUBARB SAUCE: Prepare as above but stir in *1 pint strawberries,* halved, with sugar and heat to boiling. Makes about 4½ cups.

Strawberries

Season: All year with best supplies in April to July.

Look for: Full red color, uniformly shaped berries with stem cap still attached. Avoid dull or shrunken berries or leaky ones indicated by stained containers.

To store: Refrigerate; use within 1 or 2 days.

To prepare: Wash; cut out stem cap (hull).

To serve: Eat out of hand; serve whole, cut up or sliced berries with sugar and milk or over ice cream; use in recipes for desserts.

STRAWBERRY PYRAMID

2 10-ounce packages frozen raspberries, thawed
1½ tablespoons cornstarch
1 tablespoon lemon juice
3 pints strawberries
1 cup seedless green grapes

EARLY IN DAY:
In medium saucepan over medium heat, heat raspberries. In small cup, combine cornstarch with ¼ cup water and gradually stir into raspberries; heat to boiling, stirring constantly. Stir in lemon juice. Press mixture through a sieve or, in covered blender container, blend until mixed. Cover; chill.

AT SERVING TIME:
In deep 10-inch platter, heap strawberries and grapes; pour on sauce. Serve rest of sauce in small pitcher. Makes 8 servings.

STRAWBERRIES IN WINE

Slice *strawberries* into sherbet or dessert dishes; sprinkle lightly with *sugar;* chill well, about 1 hour. To serve, pour some *Chablis,* sauterne or champagne over strawberries.

STRAWBERRIES IN ALMOND YOGURT

1 8-ounce container plain yogurt
⅓ cup sugar
2 teaspoons vanilla extract
1½ to 2 teaspoons almond extract
2 pints strawberries

EARLY IN DAY:
In medium bowl, mix yogurt, sugar, vanilla and almond extracts; fold in strawberries. Refrigerate. Makes 4 servings.

Tangelos

Season: October to January.

Look for: Firm fruit, heavy for its size, with good orange color. Tangelos peel and section easily, are juicy and have few seeds.

To store: Keep at room temperature a few days or refrigerate and use within a week.

To prepare: Peel; break into sections, slice or cut up.

To serve: Eat out of hand; use in salads.

Tangerines

Season: November to March.

Look for: Deep yellow to deep orange fruit that is heavy for its size. Skin may be loose to the touch since tangerines peel easily.

To store: Refrigerate; use within 1 or 2 days.

To prepare: Pull off skin.

To serve: Eat out of hand; use in salads.

Ugli Fruit

Season: March to June.

Look for: Grapefruit-shaped fruit, yellow with greenish splotches and wrinkled, bumpy skin.

To store: Refrigerate; use within 3 to 5 days.

To prepare: Remove peel with fingers as with tangerines, or halve and section as grapefruit.

To serve: Eat out of hand or use in salads.

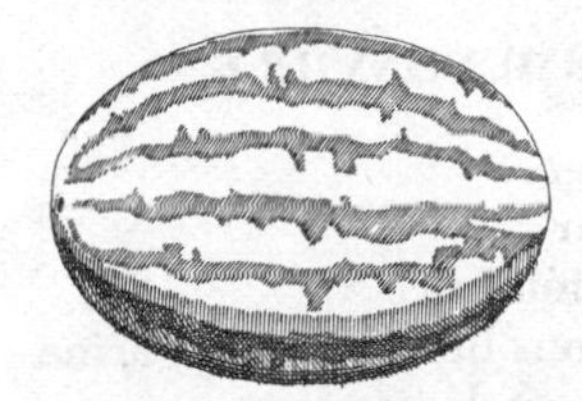

Watermelon

Season: April to October.

Look for: Firm, symmetrically shaped (round or oblong, depending on variety) watermelon with good color (some varieties have darker green stripes); the side of the melon grown next to the ground will be yellowish in appearance. Because ripeness of whole melon is most difficult to determine, look for melons sold in halves or quarters. Flesh should be firm and of good red color; seeds should be dark brown or black; avoid melons with hard white streak running through flesh.

To store: Refrigerate and use within a week. After cutting, cover cut surface with waxed paper or plastic wrap.

To prepare: For wedges, cut whole melon from stem to blossom end; for slices, cut whole melon parallel to ends. Cut off rind.

To serve: Serve in wedges, slices, cut up or scooped into balls for salads, desserts.

WATERMELON BOWL

With large, sharp knife, slice about one-fourth from the top of *1 long, medium watermelon;* remove top section.

With large spoon, scoop pulp from both sections of watermelon, being careful to leave about ½-inch of pulp inside the rind to form a shell. (Or scoop pulp into balls.) Reserve pieces; discard top section or save for making watermelon pickles.

With small, sharp knife, cut an even saw-tooth pattern about 1 inch deep around top of shell. (If watermelon is not level, cut a thin slice of rind from the bottom.) Remove seeds and cut pulp into bite-size pieces; return to shell. Cover with plastic wrap and refrigerate until serving time.

Other Fruit Recipes

SACRAMENTO FRUIT BOWL

1½ cups sugar
3 tablespoons lemon juice
2 tablespoons anise seed
½ teaspoon salt
1 small pineapple
1 small honeydew melon
1 small cantaloupe
2 oranges
2 nectarines (or 4 apricots)
2 purple plums
1 cup seedless green grapes
1 lime, sliced

EARLY IN DAY:
In medium saucepan over medium heat, cook 2 cups water with sugar, lemon juice, anise seed and salt 15 minutes or until mixture becomes a light syrup; chill.

Meanwhile, cut rind from pineapple, melon, cantaloupe and oranges and cut pulp into bite-size chunks. Slice nectarines and plums in wedges. In large bowl or other container, combine cut-up fruits with grapes and lime slices. Pour chilled syrup through strainer over fruits. Cover; chill, stirring often. Makes 10 to 12 servings.

HOT FRUITS A LA MODE

1 3½-ounce can flaked coconut (1⅓ cups)
3 pints vanilla ice cream
2 29-ounce cans plums
1 29-ounce can unpeeled whole apricots
1 20-ounce can pineapple chunks
¼ cup honey
2 tablespoons lemon juice
1 tablespoon salad oil
¾ teaspoon nutmeg

EARLY IN DAY:
Sprinkle coconut on waxed paper. Scoop ice cream into balls, roll in coconut, and place on cookie sheet. Return ice cream to freezer.

ABOUT 15 MINUTES BEFORE SERVING:
Drain plums, apricots and pineapple (use liquid with orange juice another day). In large skillet, mix honey, lemon juice, salad oil and nutmeg. Add fruits and cook over medium heat until fruit is very hot, gently spooning sauce over fruit. Serve ice-cream balls in dessert dishes with hot sauce spooned on top. Makes 10 servings.

CREME BARTLETT

6 egg yolks
3 cups skimmed milk
4 teaspoons grated orange peel
2 teaspoons sugar
1 teaspoon almond extract
¼ teaspoon salt
2 29-ounce cans pear halves
1 30-ounce can fruit cocktail, drained

EARLY IN DAY:
In medium saucepan, beat egg yolks slightly; gradually stir in skimmed milk. Over low heat, cook egg mixture, stirring constantly, until mixture coats spoon, about 30 minutes. Remove from heat; stir in orange peel, sugar, almond extract and salt. Chill custard in refrigerator until just cool but not set.

Drain pear halves well on paper towels and arrange 2 pear halves in each of 8 sherbet dishes (reserve leftover pear halves, if any, to serve next day). Spoon custard over pears. Refrigerate.

AT SERVING TIME:
Top with fruit cocktail. Makes 8 servings.

APRICOT-GLAZED PEARS AND APPLES

¾ cup sugar
¼ cup butter or margarine, softened
¼ cup lemon juice
2 large cooking apples
2 large pears
⅓ cup apricot jam
¼ cup dry sherry
⅛ teaspoon salt

EARLY IN DAY:
Preheat oven to 350°F. In 13″ by 9″ baking dish, stir together sugar, butter or margarine, lemon juice and ½ cup water. Peel, halve and core apples and pears and place in mixture, turning to coat well. Cover and bake 45 minutes or until fruit is fork-tender; refrigerate, covered.

TO SERVE:
In cup, mix apricot jam, sherry and salt. Arrange fruit in serving dish; brush generously with jam mixture. Makes 4 servings.

PEARS ARMENONVILLE

8 large pears
1 cup sugar
¼ cup lemon juice
2 tablespoons butter or margarine
2 10-ounce packages frozen raspberries, thawed
¼ cup port or other sweet wine
sour cream for garnish

DAY BEFORE SERVING:
Preheat oven to 350°F. Peel pears leaving stems intact; do not core. Place in 3-quart casserole and add sugar, lemon juice, butter or margarine and 1 cup boiling water. Bake, covered, 45 minutes or until pears are tender. Chill and drain.

In covered blender container, at low speed, blend raspberries and wine until well mixed (or force raspberries through coarse sieve). Place pears in shallow dish and pour on raspberry mixture. Refrigerate, turning pears in mixture occasionally to coat well.

TO SERVE:
Serve pears in sherbet dishes topped with sour cream. Makes 8 servings.

SPICY FRUIT BOWL

1 29-ounce can cling-peach halves
1 17-ounce can pitted dark sweet cherries, drained
6 thin lemon slices
6 whole cloves
1 short cinnamon stick
2 tangerines, sectioned
1 cup seedless green grapes

EARLY IN DAY OR DAY BEFORE SERVING:
In covered medium saucepan over medium heat, simmer peaches and peach liquid and remaining ingredients except tangerines and grapes for 10 minutes. Refrigerate.

AT SERVING TIME:
Stir tangerines and grapes into mixture. Makes 6 servings.

SUMMER TRIFLE

1 3- or 3¼-ounce package regular vanilla-pudding mix
3 cups canned pineapple juice
½ teaspoon grated lemon peel
2 teaspoons ascorbic-acid mixture for fruit
4 peaches, peeled and sliced
2 cups Ribier grapes, halved and seeded
5 figs, sliced
1 pint strawberries

EARLY IN DAY:
In medium saucepan over medium heat, cook pudding mix and juice, stirring constantly, until thickened; heat to boiling. Remove from heat and stir in lemon peel; cool.

Meanwhile, in medium bowl, mix ascorbic-acid mixture with 3 tablespoons water; toss well with peaches.

In serving bowl, layer fruits. Pour pudding over fruit; chill. Makes 8 servings.

CHUNKY FRUIT WHIP

1 cup applesauce
1 cup frozen whipped topping, thawed
1 tablespoon grated orange peel
2 large oranges

ABOUT 20 MINUTES BEFORE SERVING:
In medium bowl, combine applesauce and whipped topping; fold in orange peel. Peel oranges and cut into bite-size pieces. Reserve a few pieces for garnish, if you like, and fold remaining pieces into mixture (this will have a grainy texture). Spoon into serving dishes; garnish with reserved orange pieces. Makes 4 servings.

FRESH FRUIT WITH LEMON-SHERRY DRESSING

5 large Red Delicious apples, thinly sliced
5 large Anjou pears, thinly sliced
3 large bananas, cut in chunks
Lemon-Sherry Dressing (below)

ABOUT 30 MINUTES BEFORE SERVING:
Into large bowl, place all ingredients; gently toss to coat fruit well. Makes 12 servings.

LEMON-SHERRY DRESSING: Early in day: Into measuring cup, through strainer, squeeze *2 or 3 lemons* to make ½ cup fresh lemon juice. Add *⅓ cup sugar, ¼ cup dry sherry* and *¼ teaspoon salt,** stirring until sugar is dissolved; chill. Makes ¾ cup dressing.

* If using salted cooking sherry, omit salt.

OTHER FRUITS: Use a combination of other fresh winter fruits instead of apples and pears: oranges, grapefruit, grapes, pineapple, papaya.

SOUTH SEA SALAD

1 cup sour cream
2 tablespoons brown sugar
2 tablespoons lemon juice
1 teaspoon celery seed
2 cups sweet cherries
3 medium bananas, sliced
1 medium cantaloupe

EARLY IN DAY:
Prepare dressing: In medium bowl, stir sour cream, brown sugar, lemon juice and celery seed; chill well.

ABOUT 20 MINUTES BEFORE SERVING:
Cut seeds from cherries. In large serving bowl, combine cherries with bananas. Cut cantaloupe into six 1-inch-thick slices; cut off rind, leaving rings intact. Remove seeds. On dessert plates, place cantaloupe rings and top with cherry mixture. Serve with dressing. Makes 6 servings.

WATERMELON-BOWL SUNDAE

3 pints orange sherbet
½ oval medium watermelon, cut lengthwise
2 medium peaches, sliced
4 medium pears, sliced
1 pint strawberries

EARLY IN DAY:
Onto large cookie sheet, with ice-cream scoop, scoop orange sherbet into balls; freeze. Using melon baller, make balls from watermelon, removing seeds; chill. Prepare a watermelon bowl (page 373); chill.

ABOUT 15 MINUTES BEFORE SERVING:
Place watermelon bowl on platter; mound fruit in it and top with sherbet balls. Serve immediately. Makes 10 to 12 servings.

ORANGY FRUIT COMPOTE

2 large oranges
1 30-ounce can apricots, drained
2 29-ounce cans pear halves, drained
1½ cups orange juice
¼ cup sugar
2 or 3 short cinnamon sticks
12 whole cloves
½ teaspoon salt
¼ teaspoon ginger

ABOUT 2 HOURS AHEAD OR EARLY IN DAY:
Into large bowl, cut oranges, apricots and pears into large chunks. In medium saucepan over medium-high heat, simmer remaining ingredients 5 minutes; pour over fruit. Cover and chill. Makes 8 servings.

FRUIT AND SHERBET

1 16-ounce can pineapple chunks
1 cup orange juice
2 medium bananas, sliced
1 pint strawberries, sliced
lemon or lime sherbet

AT SERVING TIME:
Drain liquid from pineapple chunks, reserving ¼ cup liquid. In salad bowl, toss pineapple and reserved liquid with orange juice, bananas and strawberries. Serve with scoops of sherbet. Makes 6 servings.

FRUIT MERINGUE SURPRISE

1 29-ounce can cling-peach slices, drained
1 13¼-ounce can pineapple chunks
1 large red eating apple, cut into thin wedges
2 tablespoons light brown sugar
2 tablespoons lemon juice
2 egg whites
¼ teaspoon salt
2 tablespoons sugar

EARLY IN DAY:
Preheat oven to 425°F. In 12″ by 8″ shallow baking dish or cook-and-serve skillet, mix peaches and pineapple (and its syrup), apple, brown sugar and lemon juice.

In small bowl, with mixer at high speed, beat egg whites and salt until soft peaks form. Gradually sprinkle in sugar, beating at high speed. (Whites should stand in stiff glossy peaks.) Drop mixture by heaping tablespoonfuls onto fruit; bake about 4 minutes until meringue is lightly browned. Refrigerate. Makes 6 servings.

VERY-BERRY DESSERT

3 pints strawberries, halved
½ cup sugar
1 pint blueberries
½ pint raspberries
1½ pints vanilla ice cream, softened
2 tablespoons grated orange peel

ABOUT 2 HOURS BEFORE SERVING:
In large bowl, gently toss strawberries with sugar; cover and refrigerate.

JUST BEFORE SERVING:
Gently toss all berries together. In medium bowl, stir ice cream and orange peel; serve over berries. Makes 10 servings.

DECORATIVE FROSTED FRUITS

To frost grapes, oranges, apples, kumquats, dates or other whole fruits for a garnish or centerpiece: Dip fruits into egg white beaten until frothy; then dip into sugar and place on rack to dry. For extra sparkle, dip into sugar again just before drying is completed. Arrange in crystal bowl for a centerpiece or use to garnish desserts.

Relishes & garnishes

Many relishes double as garnishes and vice versa. The key is to keep them simple and edible. Just a word about garnishing: Garnishes are meant to enhance appearance and should not overwhelm the food. They should also be easy to remove when the service is buffet-style or the food is to be carved at the table.

Choose garnishes for color contrast and arrange them imaginatively. And consider both food and garnish in relation to the serving dish used; its color and shape should show off the food too.

Relishes generally fit into two groups: raw vegetable and prepared fruits or vegetables. Prepared relishes most often have vinegar or a citrus juice added during preparation. Put up jars of relishes in season when vegetables and fruits are at their plentiful best; then enjoy them whenever you like, from a few days to many months later.

Tips for Perfect Prepared Relishes

1. Before you start, read information on canning, pages 691–693.
2. Use stainless steel, aluminum, enamel, glass or stoneware utensils or pans with nonstick coating for cooking these mixtures. Copper, brass, cast iron and galvanized pans may cause undesirable color changes or chemical reactions with the food.
3. Our recipes have been made using regular table salt. Be sure salt is not iodized; iodized salt may make products dark, the liquid cloudy.
4. Fresh spices will give fullest flavor.
5. Cider vinegar is most often used because of its mellow flavor. White vinegar is often preferred for light-colored foods such as pickled watermelon rind. Vinegar should be of 4% to 6% acidity. You'll find this information on the bottle label; it may be listed as "grain strength."
6. To blender-chop vegetables, first prepare vegetables as recipe directs. Half-fill blender container with prepared vegetables. Add water to just cover; cover blender container with lid. Run blender on "chop" setting; if blender doesn't have a "chop" setting, turn control on and off until vegetables are chopped. Drain vegetables in colander and repeat until all vegetables are chopped.
7. After filling jars, remove air bubbles by running a metal spatula or knife blade between food and side of jar.

8. Because of differences in the condition of the food and the manner of packing, the liquid developed in the recipe may not be the exact amount needed every time. If not enough, add vinegar to cover the fruit or vegetable. If too much, refrigerate the excess, covered, and use later.
9. After the jars are sealed and cooled, store them in a dark, dry, cool place. Flavors will blend and mellow better if the food is allowed to stand several weeks before eating.

Garnishes

VEGETABLE GARNISHES

PICKLE FANS: Select small sweet or dill pickles. Starting at tip, cut pickles in 4 or 5 thin slices almost to stem. Spread slices to form open fan. Use on sandwich or salad plate.

RADISH TULIPS: Cut large radishes into lengthwise slices. Notch one end of each slice into 3 points. Select green-onion tops for stems and leaves. Arrange on top of baked ham.

VEGETABLE CUTOUTS: Cut peeled turnip, kohlrabi or rutabaga into thin crosswise slices. Cut with round or scalloped canapé cutters. To make flower shapes, cut evenly spaced V-shaped notches around circle; cut off corners to form rounded petals. Cut thinly sliced carrots with smaller canapé cutter or knife to make flower centers. Use with salads or sandwiches.

PEPPER CHAIN: Use thin crosswise slices of green and/or red peppers. Cut one edge of each pepper ring; slip slices together to interlock. Use on potato salad or coleslaw.

PEPPER FLOWER CUP: Cut top off small pepper that stands up straight (or use large pepper and cut in half crosswise). Remove seeds and white membranes. With sharp knife point, mark petal shapes on pepper; cut along markings. Use to hold salad dressing, tuna salad, coleslaw, olives, or gherkins. Or add a big bunch of parsley and use as a decoration.

TOMATO-PEEL ROSE: With small sharp knife, cut continuous 1-inch strip of peel from tomato. Roll tightly, skin side out; hold end in place with toothpick. (Or roll peel around finger, center with olive and run toothpick through to hold in place.) For two smaller roses, cut peel in half; use for platters of cold cuts or salads.

CUCUMBER TWISTS: Cut cucumber crosswise in thin slices. Cut each slice once from edge to center. Twist cut edges in opposite directions so slice will stand up slightly. For salads, platters of cold cuts and sandwich plates.

ONION CHRYSANTHEMUM: Peel a medium, uniformly shaped Spanish or Bermuda onion. Cut thin slice from top. Cut crosswise into quarters to within ½ inch of bottom. Slice each quarter into very thin wedges, to within ½ inch of bottom. After all wedges are cut, force toothpicks into bottom of each cut. Place onion upside down in water to cover, deeply colored with red, orange or yellow food color. Let stand at room temperature for 24 hours. Drain flower thoroughly; remove toothpicks; lightly press petals outward. Or use a purple onion but omit food color and chill in ice water to spread petals. Use for large roasts, platters of cold cuts, salads.

SPIRAL MUSHROOMS: Peel and stem large mushrooms. Hold cap, top up, in one hand. Grasp small sharp knife in other hand, blade pointing away from body; rest thumb of that hand on mushroom cap. Cut a slit from center of cap to outside edge by turning mushroom. Space several curved slits around cap. Make second set of slits parallel to first cuts to make thin wedges. Lift out wedge between each two cuts. Use fresh with salads, cold cuts; cooked, with meats, casseroles.

OTHER VEGETABLE GARNISHES: Use cherry tomatoes and watercress or tomato wedges and chicory to decorate roast chicken or beef platters.

Embellish carrot curls by putting olives, cucumber or zucchini sticks inside.

Sprinkle shredded raw carrots on potato or macaroni salad or coleslaw.

Edge salads with spinach leaves, Boston lettuce, escarole, chicory, watercress.

Garnish steaks or roasts with mushroom caps or slices; garnish beef filet, chicken breast or pâté with canned truffles.

FRUIT GARNISHES

ORANGE OR LEMON TWISTS: Slice orange or lemon crosswise in thin slices. Cut each slice once from edge to center. Twist cut edges in opposite directions so slice will stand up slightly. For pies, cakes, puddings.

LEMON, LIME OR ORANGE CARTWHEELS: Slice fruit. Cut small V-shaped notches just in peel, all around each slice. For beverages, put whole cloves or mint sprigs in center of cartwheels.

MELON FLOWERS: Peel slightly underripe cantaloupe or honeydew melon. Cut in half crosswise; remove seeds. Cut in very thin crosswise slices. Fold slices loosely in half, then in quarters, as though making a funnel. Put 2 folded slices together to form a blossom; fasten with toothpicks. For fruit or ham salads.

ORANGE-, LEMON- OR LIME-PEEL ROSES: Cut thin slice from both ends of fruit. With vegetable parer, peel continuous ½-inch strip of peel from fruit. Roll peel tightly, skin side out. Hold end in place with toothpick. (Or roll peel around finger, center with a maraschino cherry and insert pick to hold in place.) For two small roses, cut peel in half. For fruit salads, cold desserts.

STRAWBERRY FANS: Select firm berries with hulls on. Starting at tip, cut in thin slices almost to hull. Spread slices to form open fans. For fruit salads, cold desserts.

KUMQUAT FLOWERS: With knife or scissors, cut fruit into 6 or 8 sections, cutting about ¾ of way through; spread petals, remove pulp and replace with maraschino cherry. For fruit salads, cold desserts.

CHERRY BLOSSOMS: With knife or scissors, cut red maraschino cherries into 6 or 8 sections, cutting about ¾ of way through; spread petals. Add leaves cut from green maraschino cherry. For fruit salads, cakes, cold desserts.

SERRATED MELON: On honeydew or cantaloupe, mark sawtooth design evenly around center. With sharp knife, cut along marking through rind and flesh of melon. Separate halves and remove seeds. Serve as first course or dessert.

APPLE CUPS: Cut top off apple that stands up straight. Scoop out inside of apple, leaving a ¼-inch-thick shell. With pointed small knife, mark petal shapes on apple; cut along markings. Brush cut surfaces of apple with lemon juice. Use to hold fruit salad, mayonnaise, coleslaw, ambrosia.

MORE FRUIT GARNISHES: Group mandarin-orange sections in lettuce cups or stud orange slices with cloves to decorate smoked ham or tongue.

Warm peach and pear halves and fill with red or green jelly to go with lamb or ham. Or, stud canned apricots with slivered almonds.

Add one big, red strawberry, hull on, to serving of plain cake topped with custard or other light-colored sauce.

Cut long spirals of orange or lemon peel as for roses, but stud with whole cloves and float in spiced punch bowl.

Add pomegranate kernels for color and crunch to fresh-fruit or cottage-cheese salad.

Top canned pineapple slices with cream-cheese-stuffed prunes. If you like, first broil slices until golden, or brown in a little hot butter or margarine in skillet.

Cut long, very thin strips of orange peel; form into bows for gingerbread, frosted cake, sherbet.

Use scooped-out pineapple, grapefruit or orange shell for fruit salad, salad dressing, dip, cranberry sauce.

Add twists of orange, lemon or grapefruit peel to drinks, clear soups.

Perk up a fish- or chicken-salad plate with orange or grapefruit sections, melon balls, fresh cherries or raspberries; apple wedges or apple, avocado or banana slices brushed with lemon juice.

NUT AND SEED GARNISHES

TOASTED ALMONDS: *Oven method:* Preheat oven to 375°F. In jelly-roll pan, spread blanched whole, sliced, slivered or chopped almonds in single layer. Bake 5 to 10 minutes until just lightly browned, stirring occasionally.

Skillet method: In small skillet over low heat, brown almonds in a little butter or margarine, stirring constantly. Drain on paper towels.

TOASTED NUTS: Prepare as Toasted Almonds (previous page) with walnuts, pecans, filberts, Brazil nuts, or pine nuts.

TOASTED SESAME SEED: *Oven method:* Preheat oven to 350°F. In jelly-roll pan, spread sesame seed. Bake 15 minutes or until lightly browned, stirring occasionally.

Skillet method: In small skillet over low heat, brown seed in a little butter or margarine, stirring constantly.

TOASTED PUMPKIN, SUNFLOWER OR SQUASH SEEDS: Prepare hulled seeds as for Toasted Sesame Seed (above).

SWEET GARNISHES

TOASTED COCONUT: Fresh Coconut, see page 359. Canned or packaged coconut: Preheat oven to 350°F. Spread coconut evenly in jelly-roll pan. Bake 15 minutes or until delicately browned, stirring often. Use on cakes, salads, pies, cookies.

TINTED COCONUT: In medium bowl or covered jar, dilute few drops food color with 1 teaspoon water. Add 1 cup coconut; toss with fork or shake jar to tint evenly. Use on frosted cakes, cookies, puddings.

CHOCOLATE CURLS, SHAVED CHOCOLATE: With heat of hand or in very slightly warm oven, slightly soften unsweetened or semisweet-chocolate square or large milk-chocolate candy bar. With vegetable parer, shave into curls. Transfer to food with toothpick. For shaved chocolate, make shorter strokes. Use on chilled pies, puddings, frosted cakes.

GRATED CHOCOLATE: Using paring knife, shredder side of grater, or vegetable parer, grate chocolate square or bar. Use on whipped cream desserts, frosted cakes, pies.

CHOCOLATE CUTOUTS: In double boiler over hot, not boiling, water, melt 2 tablespoons semisweet-chocolate pieces and 1 teaspoon butter or margarine; stir until smooth. On waxed-paper-lined cookie sheet, spread chocolate mixture into 6″ by 4″ rectangle. Refrigerate until hard. With chilled decorative cookie cutter, cut designs from chocolate rectangle and arrange, with chilled spatula, on top of frosted cakes, chilled pies, puddings, whipped-cream desserts. Refrigerate until served.

GUMDROP POSIES: *Roses:* Use 4 large gumdrops for each flower. On surface sprinkled with sugar, roll gumdrops into ⅛-inch-thick ovals; sprinkle with more sugar. Cut ovals in half. Roll one half-oval tightly to form center. Place other halves around center, overlapping slightly; press together at base. Trim base evenly. Roll green gumdrops and cut leaves. For desserts, candy dish.

Lilies: Use 2 large gumdrops for each flower. On surface sprinkled with sugar, roll gumdrops into ⅛-inch-thick ovals; sprinkle with more sugar. Cut ovals in half; cut a triangle from each half oval. Score center of each triangle for petal marking. For flower center, roll small scrap left from cutting triangles. Overlap 4 triangles around center. Press together at base. Pull petals to elongate. Roll green gumdrops same way and cut leaves. For desserts, candy dish.

MORE SWEET ADDITIONS: Use chocolate sprinkles, red hot candies, silver dragées, nonpareils on cookies, frosted cakes, ice cream cones, glazed doughnuts.

Insert lollipops in cupcakes or ice cream cones.

Use plain or toasted nuts to garnish frosted cakes, pies, hot or cold soufflés, ice cream, gelatin and whipped-cream desserts.

Add scoops of ice cream or sherbet to fruit salad, pie, cake, beverages.

Use candied fruit—whole cherries, red, green and yellow pineapple slices, angelica—on fruitcake, steamed pudding, cookies, holiday breads.

Use marshmallows, mints, butterscotch or semisweet-chocolate pieces, chocolate-egg candies, jelly beans, gumdrops, on cookies, cupcakes, frosted cakes.

"DAIRY" GARNISHES

Add dollops of whipped cream or whipped-topping mix to cold soufflés, pies, fruit salads.

Sprinkle grated Parmesan or Romano cheese on soup, pasta, casseroles, green salads.

Use shredded Cheddar, Swiss or American cheese on fruit or vegetable salads, fish dishes, main-dish casseroles, baked vegetable dishes.

Crumble blue or feta cheese over tossed salads, on open-face sandwiches.

Add a dollop of sour cream to soups.

Put softened cream cheese through pastry bag with star tip to garnish molded salads, canapés, shrimp, lox.

Make Butter Balls or Curls (page 415) to accompany holiday breads, muffins, waffles, quick breads, hot cereals.

HERBS AND SPICES

Sprigs of fresh mint add contrast to fresh-fruit salad, interest to cold beverages.

Lemon twists and sprigs of fresh mint garnish lemon pie, lemon pudding or cake.

Fresh dill sprigs and lemon wedges or twists go with fish and shellfish.

Chopped chives or sliced green onions add interest to cottage cheese and soups.

Flat-leaf or curly parsley garnishes almost any main dish or vegetable.

Chopped fresh basil is perfect with tomatoes.

Cinnamon sticks and whole cloves garnish drinks, pickles.

Paprika adds color to egg, cheese or noodle dishes.

Poppy seed can be used on breads, cooked vegetables, noodles, dumplings, salad dressings, cottage cheese.

OTHER GARNISHES

BACON CURLS: Fry bacon slices until browned but still limp; immediately roll around two-tined fork; drain. Use on egg platters, stuffed tomato salads, macaroni-and-cheese casseroles, quiches.

EGG IDEAS: Slice, quarter or sieve hard-cooked eggs. Or, cut into wedges and dip yolk edge in finely chopped parsley, paprika or chili powder.

Garnish deviled eggs with whole capers, paprika, red or black caviar, pimento.

BREAD IDEAS: Use crumbs on casseroles and vegetables; croutons on soups and salads.

FRANKFURTERS: Slice to go on soups or hot potato salad.

PACKAGED AND CANNED: Use French-fried onion rings, crumbled potato chips, crumbled corn chips, canned shoestring potatoes to top casseroles.

Relishes

RAW VEGETABLE RELISHES

Serve a platter of these as appetizers, salads or snacks, with or without a pour-on dressing or a favorite dunk. Or, use them to garnish main dishes or salads.

RADISH ROSES: *Early in day:* Cut 4 thin slices from sides of each radish, all equidistant; next cut thin slices, not quite to stem, behind each white spot. Place on ice in bowl; cover and refrigerate until red-rimmed petals open. Drain.

RADISH ACCORDIONS: *Early in day:* From top, cut each radish lengthwise into thin slices, not quite down to stem end. Place in bowl on ice; refrigerate until served. Drain.

RADISH POMPONS: *Early in day:* From root end, cut each radish lengthwise into thin slices, not quite down to stem end. Cut again at right angle to first cuts. Place on ice in bowl; refrigerate until served. Drain.

CARROT CURLS: *Early in day:* With vegetable parer, shave lengthwise strips from long straight carrots. Curl each strip around forefinger; fasten loose end with toothpick. Refrigerate in ice water until served. Drain; remove picks.

CARROT, CUCUMBER, CELERIAC, BEET, TURNIP STICKS: Cut each chilled, peeled fresh vegetable lengthwise into ⅛-inch slices; cut each slice into thin sticks. (If carrot or cucumber is very long, first cut in half.) If you like, string pitted olives on a few of the sticks. Cover and refrigerate until served.

CELERY HEARTS: Break off heavy outer stalks, then cut tops from bunch of celery. Wash; trim root; halve bunch lengthwise through root. Cut each half lengthwise into 2 or 3 pieces, then make 3 or 4 gashes along outside stalk of each. Place on ice in bowl; cover and refrigerate until served. Drain.

CELERY CURLS: *Early in day:* With vegetable parer, remove strings from large, tender celery stalk. Shave lengthwise strips from back of stalk. Curl each strip around forefinger; fasten loose end with toothpick. Refrigerate in ice water until served. Drain and remove picks.

CELERY STICKS: Cut each large, tender stalk of celery into 3-inch pieces; cut each piece into thin sticks. Cover and refrigerate until served.

CELERY FANS: Cut each large, tender stalk of celery into 3-inch pieces; slit each piece, almost to end, into narrow, parallel strips. (Or, slit both ends almost to center.) Place on ice in bowl; refrigerate until ends curl. Drain.

CUCUMBER SLICES: Use peeled or unpeeled cucumber; run sharp-tined fork down length all around to score cucumber completely. Cut crosswise into very thin slices; cover and refrigerate until served. Serve plain or sprinkle with chopped parsley.

CUCUMBER OR ZUCCHINI WEDGES: Select 6-inch-long vegetables. Peel cucumbers; leave zucchini unpeeled. Cut each in half lengthwise, then crosswise. Cut quarters lengthwise into wedge-shaped pieces. Cover and refrigerate until served. Serve raw.

CAULIFLOWERETS: Remove outside stalks from well-chilled cauliflower. Wash and break head into small flowerets. Cover and refrigerate until served. Serve raw.

GREEN ONIONS: Cut off all but 2 inches of green tops. (Use green tops in soup.) Cover and refrigerate until served.

RUFFLED GREEN ONIONS: *Early in day:* Cut off all but 3 inches green tops; shred tops down to white with sharp knife. Refrigerate in ice water to curl. Drain.

GREEN- OR RED-PEPPER SLICES: Cut thin slice from tops of peppers; remove seeds and white membranes; cut in thin crosswise slices or cut lengthwise into thin slivers. Cover and refrigerate until served.

KOHLRABI: Cut peeled, fresh kohlrabi in thin crosswise slices. Cover and refrigerate until served.

ASPARAGUS: Clean thin, tender stalks; with vegetable parer, remove scales. Cover and refrigerate until served.

OTHER FRESH-VEGETABLE NIBBLERS: Green peas in pods—guests shell their own; cherry tomatoes; tender green beans; chunks of crisp cabbage; sliced fresh mushrooms; tender leaves of Chinese cabbage or romaine.

BUY-AND-SERVE RELISHES

Cranberry sauce—whole and jellied
Horseradish
Cranberry orange relish
Chutney
Bottled meat sauce or Worcestershire
Applesauce—plain or with cinnamon, raspberries, pineapple or apricots
Catchup
Prepared mustard—plain, hot, horseradish or with onions
Chili sauce or seafood-cocktail sauce
Mincemeat
Mixed-bean salad
Sweet-sour cabbage or sauerkraut
Watermelon pickles
Pickled onions, mushrooms, artichoke hearts, cauliflower or beets
Hot peppers or pimentos
Olives—ripe, green, stuffed
Sweet relish, India relish, piccalilli
Corn relish, onion relish
Spiced or brandied fruits—peaches, crabapples, figs, pears, pineapple
Chowchow
Pickles—mustard, dill, sweet, mixed or gherkins

BROILED CANNED FRUIT

Drain very well canned peach, pear or apricot halves or pineapple slices. Meanwhile, preheat broiler if manufacturer directs.

Arrange fruit in broiling pan and sprinkle with a little lemon juice; brush with melted butter or margarine and sprinkle with a little sugar or brown sugar, then with dash of cinnamon, nutmeg or ground cloves. Broil 8 minutes or until golden. Serve with meat, fish or poultry.

BROILED FRESH FRUIT

PEACHES OR PEARS: Peel, halve and pit or core fruit; proceed as for Broiled Canned Fruit (above). If you like, put ½ teaspoon chili sauce, catchup or cranberry sauce in fruit halves before broiling.

BANANAS: Peel firm, all-yellow or slightly green-tipped bananas. Proceed as for Broiled Canned Fruit (above) but broil bananas about 5 minutes on each side or until fork-tender.

SAUTEED FRESH PEACHES

Peel and remove pits from fresh peaches; cut peaches into quarters. Sprinkle lightly with salt and flour. In skillet over medium-high heat, in a little hot butter or margarine, fry peaches until tender, turning once with pancake turner. Serve with meat, fish or poultry or to accompany casseroles.

SAUTEED PINEAPPLE SLICES

Drain canned pineapple slices and pat dry with paper towels. In skillet over medium-high heat, in a little hot butter or margarine, fry slices until golden, turning once with pancake turner. Serve with ham, poultry or fish; main-dish salads; casseroles.

SAUTEED BANANAS

Peel firm, all-yellow or slightly green-tipped bananas; cut crosswise into halves or leave whole. In skillet, over medium heat, in a little hot butter or margarine, fry bananas until easily pierced with two-tined fork, turning to brown on all sides. Sprinkle lightly with salt. Serve with meat, fish or poultry.

CURRIED FOUR-FRUIT BAKE

1 16-ounce can pear halves
1 16-ounce can cling-peach or apricot halves
1 20-ounce can pineapple slices or chunks
6 maraschino cherries, halved
¼ cup butter or margarine
¾ cup packed brown sugar
4 teaspoons curry powder

ABOUT 2 HOURS BEFORE SERVING:
Preheat oven to 325°F. Drain fruits thoroughly. Meanwhile, in small saucepan over low heat, in melted butter or margarine, stir sugar and curry powder.

Place fruits in shallow 1½-quart casserole; spoon mixture over fruits. Bake 1 hour. Serve warm from casserole with ham, lamb or poultry. (Refrigerate leftovers to serve cold another day.) Makes 12 servings.

SPEEDY PEACH CHUTNEY

3 10-ounce packages frozen peaches, thawed and drained
1 tablespoon lime juice
1 teaspoon dried mint flakes or 2 teaspoons chopped fresh mint
1 teaspoon sugar
¼ teaspoon ginger

ABOUT 10 MINUTES BEFORE SERVING:
In medium bowl, toss all ingredients until mixed. Serve with meat or poultry. Makes about 8 servings.

FRIED APPLES

5 large cooking apples
½ cup sugar
½ teaspoon salt
¼ cup butter or margarine

ABOUT 20 MINUTES BEFORE SERVING:
Peel and core apples; cut into 1-inch wedges. In pie plate, stir sugar with salt; dip apple wedges in mixture, turning to coat all sides. In large skillet over medium-low heat, melt butter or margarine. Add apples and cook, partially covered, 15 minutes or until fork-tender, carefully turning apples occasionally with pancake turner. Serve with cooked meats. Makes 12 servings.

GLAZED APPLE QUARTERS

½ cup sugar
½ cup orange juice
2 teaspoons grated orange peel
4 firm Red Delicious or Winesap apples

ABOUT 45 MINUTES BEFORE SERVING:
In 10-inch skillet, stir sugar with orange juice and peel. Cut apples into quarters; remove cores. Place quarters, skin side up, in orange mixture. Over medium heat, heat mixture to boiling. Reduce heat to low; cover and simmer 10 to 15 minutes until apples are tender but still hold their shape. If necessary, carefully turn apples during cooking to cook evenly.

Remove apples to warm plate. Increase heat to medium and cook orange sauce until thickened; spoon over apples to glaze. Serve warm or cold with pork, ham, lamb, veal, shrimp. Makes 4 servings.

CRANBERRY-WINE SAUCE

3 cups cranberries
1½ cups sugar
1¼ cups port
1½ teaspoons cornstarch

ABOUT 15 MINUTES OR UP TO 1 WEEK AHEAD:
In medium saucepan over medium heat, heat cranberries, sugar and wine to boiling, stirring occasionally. Reduce heat to low; cover and simmer 5 minutes or until berries pop.

Meanwhile, in cup, blend cornstarch and ¼ cup cold water until smooth; gradually stir into hot cranberry mixture. Cook, stirring, until thickened. Makes 10 servings.

BLENDER CRANBERRY-RAISIN RELISH

2 cups cranberries
1 large orange with peel, cut into chunks, with seeds removed
¾ cup sugar
¾ cup dark seedless raisins
2 tablespoons finely chopped crystallized ginger
¼ cup blanched slivered almonds

EARLY IN DAY OR DAY BEFORE SERVING:
In covered blender container at low speed, blend about a fourth each of the cranberries and orange until coarsely chopped; pour into medium bowl. Repeat until all are chopped. With spoon, stir in sugar, raisins and ginger; refrigerate at least 3 or 4 hours until well chilled.

JUST BEFORE SERVING:
Stir almonds into mixture. Makes 3 cups.

CRANBERRY-ORANGE RELISH

2 medium oranges
1 pound cranberries
2 cups sugar

EARLY IN DAY OR SEVERAL DAYS AHEAD:
Cut unpeeled oranges into quarters; remove any seeds. Put oranges and cranberries through food grinder, using medium blade. Stir in sugar. Cover and refrigerate. Makes 4 cups.

CRANBERRY-TANGERINE: For oranges, substitute *3 large tangerines* and remove seeds and membrane but use peel; prepare as above. Makes 4 cups.

CRANBERRY-PINEAPPLE: For oranges, substitute *1 lemon,* unpeeled; cut into quarters and remove seeds. Grind lemon with cranberries as above. With sugar, stir in *one 8¼-ounce can crushed pineapple,* undrained. Makes 4 cups.

CRANBERRY-APPLE: Prepare as above but grind *2 unpeeled, cored cooking apples* with cranberries and grind *1 unpeeled, seeded lemon* with oranges. Increase sugar to 2½ cups. Makes 6 cups.

SPICED PRUNES

1 pound pitted dried large prunes
1 cup sugar
1 cup cider vinegar
1 teaspoon cinnamon
1 teaspoon ground cloves

DAY BEFORE OR UP TO 2 WEEKS AHEAD:
In medium saucepan over high heat, in water to cover, heat prunes to boiling; reduce heat to low; cover and simmer 10 minutes; drain. In same saucepan over high heat, heat to boiling remaining ingredients with 1 cup water; boil 1 minute. Add prunes and heat to boiling. Cover and refrigerate. Serve with poultry or meats; or as garnish for salads. Makes 10 servings.

SPEEDY PICKLED PEACHES

1 29-ounce can peach halves
½ cup sugar
½ cup cider vinegar
1 short cinnamon stick
whole cloves

DAY BEFORE OR UP TO 1 WEEK AHEAD:
Drain peach halves, reserving 1 cup syrup. In medium saucepan, combine reserved syrup, sugar, vinegar and cinnamon stick. Stud each peach half with 3 or 4 cloves; add to mixture. Over medium heat, heat to boiling; reduce heat to low and simmer 3 to 4 minutes. Cover and refrigerate. Serve with poultry, meat or fish. Makes 8 servings.

SPEEDY PICKLED PEARS: Prepare as above but use *one 29-ounce can pear halves* and syrup instead of peaches.

SPICED ORANGE SLICES

4 medium oranges
whole cloves
1 cup sugar
⅓ cup light corn syrup
¼ cup cider vinegar

TWO DAYS BEFORE SERVING:
Cut unpeeled oranges into ⅜-inch-thick slices; stud peel of each slice with 3 or 4 whole cloves. Meanwhile, in medium skillet over high heat, heat sugar with 1 cup water and remaining ingredients to boiling. Reduce heat to low; simmer 5 minutes. Add orange slices and heat to boiling; simmer 5 minutes. Cover and refrigerate.

TO SERVE:
Drain slices well. Serve with duckling, chicken or turkey. Makes 8 servings.

PICKLED BEETS

2 tablespoons sugar
¾ teaspoon salt
½ teaspoon dry mustard
⅛ teaspoon ground cloves
⅓ cup cider vinegar
1 16-ounce can sliced beets, drained
1 medium onion, sliced

EARLY IN DAY:
In medium bowl, stir first 4 ingredients until mixed. Stir in vinegar and ⅓ cup water; add beets and onion. Cover and refrigerate, stirring occasionally. Serve with meat or fish. Makes 6 servings.

CUCUMBER-MINT RELISH

3 medium cucumbers
⅔ cup white vinegar
⅓ cup chopped fresh mint
1 tablespoon sugar
1 tablespoon salt
¼ teaspoon pepper

DAY BEFORE OR UP TO 1 WEEK AHEAD:
Peel cucumbers and cut lengthwise into quarters, then crosswise into ¼-inch-thick slices. Place in bowl with ½ cup water and remaining ingredients; toss with fork to mix well. Cover and refrigerate. Serve with hot or cold meats, fish, poultry. Makes about 10 servings.

MARINATED ONIONS AND OLIVES

1 6-ounce can pitted ripe olives, drained
1 3½-ounce jar cocktail onions, drained
½ cup bottled Italian dressing

SEVERAL DAYS AHEAD:
Place all ingredients in 2-cup jar or bowl; stir with fork to mix. Cover and refrigerate several days. (Will keep, refrigerated, several weeks.) Serve with cold meats or cheeses. Makes about 8 servings.

PEAR RELISH

2 29-ounce cans pear halves
⅔ cup salad oil
½ cup lemon juice
1 large lemon, thinly sliced
1 small onion, sliced
2 tablespoons chopped parsley
½ teaspoon salt
6 drops hot pepper sauce
dash pepper

DAY BEFORE SERVING:
Drain pears, reserving 1 cup syrup. Cut pears into large chunks. In large bowl, combine pears, reserved syrup and remaining ingredients. Cover and refrigerate.

AT SERVING TIME:
Drain pears; remove lemon and onion slices; use 1 lemon slice for garnish. Makes 12 servings.

FRESH TOMATO RELISH

2 pounds tomatoes
2 medium green peppers
2 medium onions
¼ cup cider vinegar
¼ cup salad oil
2 teaspoons salt
1 teaspoon dry mustard
1 teaspoon celery seed

EARLY IN DAY:
Chop tomatoes, peppers and onions; drain slightly and place in medium bowl. Add remaining ingredients and toss to mix well. Cover and refrigerate. Serve with ham, pork, eggs, chicken, shrimp, fish. Makes 10 servings.

MIXED VEGETABLE RELISH

½ medium head cauliflower, broken into flowerets
2 carrots, cut in 2-inch strips
2 celery stalks, cut in 1-inch chunks
1 small green pepper, cut in strips
¾ cup red or white wine vinegar
½ cup olive oil
1 tablespoon sugar
1 teaspoon salt
½ teaspoon basil
¼ teaspoon tarragon
6 peppercorns
1 bay leaf
1 cup pitted ripe olives

ABOUT 1½ HOURS AHEAD OR EARLY IN DAY:
In large skillet over medium heat, in ¼ cup water, heat all ingredients except olives to boiling, stirring occasionally. Reduce heat to low; cover and simmer 3 to 5 minutes until vegetables are tender-crisp. Add olives. Cover and chill at least 1 hour.

TO SERVE:
Drain vegetables well; remove peppercorns and bay leaf. Serve with beef, pork, turkey and seafood main dishes. Makes 6 servings.

MARINATED MUSHROOMS

¾ cup olive oil
⅓ cup red-wine vinegar
1½ teaspoons salt
¾ teaspoon sugar
½ teaspoon basil
⅛ teaspoon thyme leaves
6 peppercorns
1 bay leaf
1 garlic clove, halved
1½ pounds medium mushrooms, halved

EARLY IN DAY OR DAY BEFORE SERVING:
In medium skillet over medium heat, heat to boiling all ingredients except mushrooms; cover and simmer over low heat 10 minutes. Stir in mushrooms until coated; over medium heat, cook 3 to 5 minutes until fork-tender. Cover and refrigerate.

AT SERVING TIME:
Drain mushrooms; remove peppercorns, bay leaf and garlic. Serve with beef, pasta, fish and shellfish main dishes. Makes about 8 servings.

Home-Canned Relishes

DILL PICKLES

¼ cup pickling spice
small square cheesecloth
6 cups white vinegar
¾ cup sugar
¾ cup salt
20 4-inch cucumbers (about 5 pounds)
dill seed, dill weed or heads fresh dill

Tie pickling spice in cheesecloth. In kettle or Dutch oven over high heat, heat spice bag, vinegar, sugar, salt and 6 cups water to boiling; reduce heat to medium and simmer 15 minutes.

Meanwhile, prepare jars and caps for processing (page 692). Cut cucumbers lengthwise into halves. Arrange tightly in hot jars; place 1 teaspoon dill seed or dill weed or 1 head fresh dill in each jar.

Over high heat, heat vinegar mixture to boiling; discard spice bag. Ladle hot mixture over cucumbers, leaving ½-inch head space; close jars as manufacturer directs. Process in boiling water (page 692) for 15 minutes after jars are placed in kettle. Cool. Makes 8 to 10 pints.

PICCALILLI

2½ pounds green tomatoes
6 cups cider vinegar
6 medium green peppers
6 medium red peppers
4 medium onions
3½ cups sugar
¼ cup mustard seed
¼ cup salt
2 tablespoons celery seed
2 teaspoons allspice
1 teaspoon cinnamon

1. Cut enough tomatoes into quarters to make 8 cups. (If tomatoes are large, cut in eighths.) Put 1 cup vinegar and one-fourth of tomatoes into blender container;* cover and blender-chop (page 377—but use the vinegar instead of water); do not drain vinegar after chopping. Pour chopped tomatoes with vinegar into very large kettle

* Or, put all vegetables through food grinder, using medium-fine blade; pour vegetables into large kettle; add 4 cups vinegar.

or Dutch oven. Repeat three more times until 4 cups vinegar have been used and all tomatoes have been chopped.
2. Cut peppers into eighths; remove seeds and white membranes; peel onions; cut into sixths. Blender-chop peppers and onions with water; drain. Add to tomatoes.
3. Over high heat, heat vegetable mixture to boiling; reduce heat to medium and boil, uncovered, 30 minutes, stirring often. Drain vegetables and discard liquid.
4. Meanwhile, prepare jars and caps for processing (page 692).
5. Into drained vegetables, stir remaining 2 cups vinegar and rest of ingredients. Over high heat, heat to boiling; reduce heat to medium and simmer 3 minutes. Ladle hot mixture into hot jars, leaving ½-inch head space; close jars as manufacturer directs. Process in boiling water (page 692) 5 minutes. Cool. Makes about 6 pints.

PICKLED PEACHES AND APRICOTS

4 pounds medium peaches
5 short cinnamon sticks
2 teaspoons whole cloves
small square cheesecloth
1½ pounds apricots, unpeeled
2½ cups sugar
2 cups cider vinegar

DAY BEFORE CANNING:
Peel peaches and cut in half; remove seeds. Place peaches in large kettle or Dutch oven. Cover with boiling water; cook over high heat 3 minutes (mixture does not boil). With slotted spoon, remove peaches to large bowl. Drain all but 1 cup liquid from kettle. Tie spices in cheesecloth.

In same kettle over high heat, heat apricots, spice bag, sugar, vinegar and 1 cup liquid to boiling; boil 5 minutes. Pour mixture over peaches. Let stand overnight.

NEXT DAY:
Prepare jars and caps for processing (page 692). Remove skins from apricots. In large kettle over high heat, heat fruit and liquid to boiling. Discard spice bag. Place fruit in hot jars; ladle hot syrup over fruit, leaving ½-inch head space; close jars as manufacturer directs. Process in boiling water for 15 minutes (page 692). Cool. Makes 6 pints.

SPICED CRAB APPLES

8 pounds crab apples
7 short cinnamon sticks
2 tablespoons whole cloves
2 tablespoons whole allspice
small square cheesecloth
8½ cups sugar
3 cups cider vinegar

DAY BEFORE CANNING:
Leave stems on crab apples; scrape out any hard bits in blossom ends. Run a skewer through each apple (to help prevent bursting). Tie spices in cheesecloth.

In large kettle over high heat, heat sugar, vinegar, 2 cups water and bag of spices to boiling. Reduce heat to medium; cover; cook 5 minutes. Add apples; heat to boiling; cover; simmer 10 minutes or until tender. Remove from heat; let stand overnight.

NEXT DAY:
Prepare jars and caps for processing (page 692). Drain apples, reserving syrup; discard spice bag. Heat syrup to boiling. Place apples in hot jars; ladle hot syrup over apples, leaving ¼-inch head space. Close jars as manufacturer directs. Process in boiling water 15 minutes (page 692). Cool. Makes 8 to 10 pints.

NECTARINE CHUTNEY

2½ pounds nectarines, seeded and cut into small chunks
1½ cups packed brown sugar
1 cup cider vinegar
¼ cup diced crystallized ginger
3 tablespoons instant minced onion
1 tablespoon salt
1 teaspoon dry mustard
⅛ teaspoon cinnamon
⅛ teaspoon ground cloves
½ cup slivered blanched almonds

In large, covered saucepan over low heat, cook all ingredients except almonds for 30 minutes. Over medium heat, cook, uncovered, stirring often, until thickened, about 30 minutes. Add almonds; cook 2 minutes more.

Meanwhile, prepare jars and caps for processing (page 692). Ladle hot mixture into jars, leaving ½-inch head space; close jars. Process in boiling water (page 692) 5 minutes. Cool. Makes about 4 pints.

APPLE CHUTNEY

10 cups chopped, peeled and cored green cooking apples (about 3 pounds)
8 cups chopped onions (about 3 pounds)
2 16-ounce packages brown sugar
1 15-ounce package dark seedless raisins
¼ cup molasses
1 tablespoon salt
1 tablespoon cinnamon
2 teaspoons ground cloves
2 teaspoons ginger

In large kettle, mix all ingredients. Over high heat, heat to boiling; reduce heat to medium and simmer, uncovered, stirring often, about 2 hours or until thick and dark.

Meanwhile, prepare jars and caps for processing (page 692). Ladle hot mixture into jars, leaving ½-inch head space; close jars. Process in boiling water (page 692) 5 minutes. Cool. Makes about 5 pints.

SPICY WATERMELON PICKLES

rind from 1 medium watermelon
½ cup un-iodized salt
9 short cinnamon sticks
1 tablespoon whole cloves
small square cheesecloth
4 cups sugar
2 cups white vinegar

DAY BEFORE CANNING:
Trim thin, dark green outer skin from rind. Cut rind into 1-inch pieces to make about 14 cups. In very large bowl, dissolve salt in 6 cups water; add rind. (If necessary, add water to cover.) Cover and refrigerate.

NEXT DAY:
Drain rind; rinse in running cold water; drain. In large kettle, cover rind with cold water. Over high heat, heat to boiling; reduce heat to low; simmer 30 minutes; drain. Tie spices in cheesecloth. In same kettle, combine sugar, vinegar, 2 cups water, spice bag and rind. Over high heat, heat to boiling. Reduce heat; cover; simmer 1 hour, stirring often; remove from heat. Meanwhile, prepare jars and caps (page 692).

Discard spice bag. Ladle hot mixture into jars, leaving ½-inch head space; close jars. Process in boiling water (page 692) 5 minutes. Cool. Makes 5 pints.

BREAD-AND-BUTTER PICKLES

16 cups cucumbers, sliced about ¼-inch thick (about 4 pounds)
6 cups thinly sliced onions
½ cup salt
5 cups sugar
5 cups cider vinegar
1½ teaspoons turmeric
1½ teaspoons celery seed
1½ teaspoons mustard seed

In large (7-quart) kettle, mix well cucumbers, onions and salt. Cover with cold water and 3 trays ice cubes; let stand 3 hours. Drain, rinse well and drain again; set aside.

In another large kettle, mix sugar and remaining ingredients; over high heat, heat to boiling. Reduce heat; simmer, uncovered, 30 minutes or until syrupy, stirring often.

Meanwhile, prepare jars and caps for processing (page 692). Add cucumbers and onions to syrup; over high heat, heat almost to boiling, stirring occasionally (do not boil). Ladle hot mixture into hot jars, leaving ½-inch head space; close jars. Process in boiling water (page 692) 15 minutes. Cool. Makes about 6 pints.

TANGY CORN RELISH

8 cups cooked corn cut from cobs (about 12 ears)
4 cups chopped cabbage
1 cup chopped seeded green peppers
1 cup chopped seeded red peppers
1 cup chopped onions
4 cups cider vinegar
1½ cups sugar
2 tablespoons dry mustard
2 tablespoons salt
1 tablespoon celery seed
1 tablespoon turmeric

In large kettle, combine corn with 1 cup water and remaining ingredients. Over high heat, heat to boiling; reduce heat and simmer 20 minutes, stirring often.

Meanwhile, prepare jars and caps for processing (page 692). Increase heat to high and heat corn mixture until it boils vigorously; ladle hot mixture into jars, leaving ½-inch head space; close jars. Process in boiling water (page 692) 15 minutes. Cool. Makes about 6 pints.

Salads & dressings

Starting with greens and ending with garnishes, these tips will help you make delicious salads of all types.

Choose from many kinds of greens: Different lettuces plus a tantalizing selection of other greens make variety in salads easy to achieve. For the salad of greens alone, or for the bed of greens topped with another mixture, experiment. Combine tangy greens with mild-flavored ones, crisp greens with tender ones, dark-colored greens with light ones for pleasing contrasts in flavor, texture and color. For ideas, see Lettuce (page 332) and Greens (page 330).

Greens also add good nutrition to your menus. All greens are low in calories, many are high in vitamins A and C and some are rich in minerals, including iron and calcium. Don't discard outer, darker green leaves of romaine or lettuce that are not wilted or bruised. Though sometimes not as tender as inner leaves, they are especially nutritious. Wash, dry and shred the leaves; add to the salad bowl or use in sandwiches or as a garnish for cold dishes.

Buying, storing and preparing greens: Choose fresh, crisp-looking greens; avoid those with bruised or brown-tipped leaves. Select firm, heavy heads of iceberg lettuce and cabbage. Greens may be cleaned before storing or just before using. Store in plastic bags or plastic wrap in the refrigerator.

To clean greens for salad, remove any bruised or wilted outer leaves. For tight heads (iceberg lettuce, cabbage), with sharp knife, cut out core (in cone shape), then hold head, cut side up, under running cold water to clean and to help separate leaves; drain. Or, for lettuce, place head, core up, on counter; with heel of hand, strike core to loosen; twist core out with fingers. Or whack head, core down, on counter; twist core out with fingers.

For loose heads (Boston lettuce, romaine, etc.) break off individual leaves; place in colander or in French lettuce basket and hold under running cold water; shake, then drain well. Pat dry with paper towels; place in plastic bags and refrigerate.

Parsley, watercress and mint should be

rinsed under running cold water, patted dry with paper towels and placed with stems down in covered jars, then stored in the refrigerator.

When greens are to be in bite-size pieces, tear or break them; don't cut.

To make iceberg-lettuce wedges, cut chilled head of lettuce into quarters or sixths. To shred iceberg lettuce, with sharp knife, cut chilled lettuce head in half; place one half, cut side down, then shred; repeat with other half.

Dressing the salad: For green salads, pick a dressing that will go well with your greens. Creamy dressings are best on very crisp greens such as iceberg lettuce, romaine. Light oil-and-vinegar dressings help bring out the delicate flavor and texture of tender greens such as Bibb and Boston lettuce. Dressings for other kinds of salads are suggested in the recipes.

Before making the salad, be sure chilled greens are dry; if leaves are wet, dressing may not coat them and its flavor may be diluted.

Some salads are better if mixed with dressing and allowed to stand until flavors develop. Most, however, are at their best when dressing is added and tossed or mixed just before serving. In these, dressing can cause greens to become limp; crisp vegetables, croutons, etc. to soften. Unless the recipe directs otherwise, it's best to start by adding about ⅔ of the dressing called for and toss or mix gently but well. Then add enough more dressing if needed to just coat ingredients. Leftover dressing keeps well in the refrigerator; and often small amounts can be combined with enough mayonnaise or sour cream to make a new dressing in sufficient quantity for another meal's salad.

Toss salad mixtures lightly to prevent bruising or mashing ingredients.

Storing salad dressings: Keep all homemade dressings in the refrigerator.

Ready-to-use dressings (except those you find in the dairy case) will keep, unopened, up to 3 months on the pantry shelf. After opening, keep them in the refrigerator and use within 3 months. Refrigerated ready-to-use dressings should be kept in the refrigerator before and after opening.

Store envelopes of ready-to-mix dressings on the pantry shelf until prepared; then keep the dressings refrigerated.

Salad bowl treatment: Dishwasher-safe salad bowls made of metal, glass, china, pottery, wood and plastic can be so washed; check label to be sure. A wooden salad bowl that has not been made dishwasher-proof should be washed quickly by hand in warm sudsy water. Don't allow it to soak; rinse quickly and dry thoroughly.

Unmolding gelatin salads: Individual salads may be unmolded onto salad greens. It is best to unmold large molds onto the serving platter and then surround with greens to prevent breaking. Moisten the platter first with a few drops of cold water; then it will

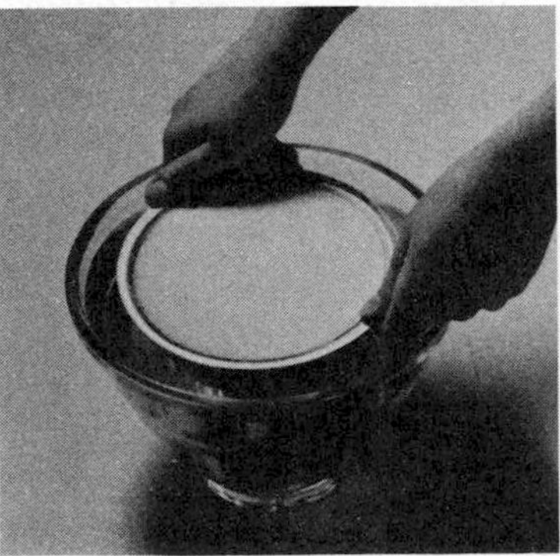
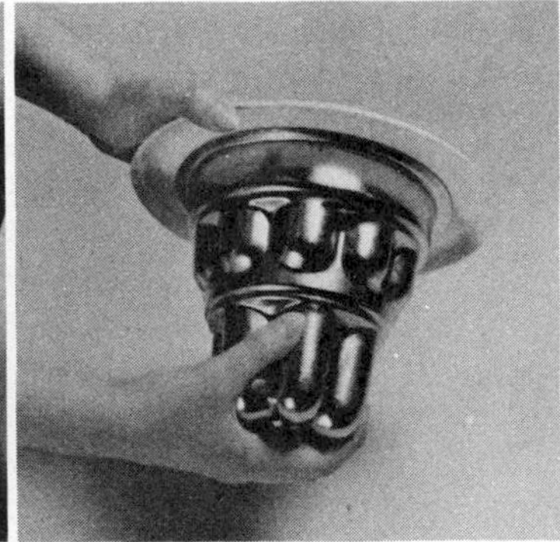

TO UNMOLD GELATIN SALADS

Carefully loosen edges of gelatin from mold with metal spatula or knife. Fill the sink or a large bowl with warm, not hot, water; dip mold into water just to rim for about 10 seconds. Be careful not to melt gelatin. Lift mold from water and gently shake to loosen gelatin. Invert platter on top of mold; quickly invert mold and platter and gently lift off mold.

be easier to slide the mold to the center if necessary.

Timesaver Salads

Canned mixed fruits, mixed vegetables, pickled beets, spiced fruits, potato salad, tomato aspic, bean salad are among the ready-to-use salad mainstays you'll find at the supermarket. Many, packed with their dressing, are ready to eat as is; others need only be topped with the dressing of your choice and served on greens. Frozen guacamole is ready to eat as soon as it's thawed. Also in the refrigerator case are ready-to-use salads: potato, macaroni, mixed fruits, gelatin mixtures, etc.

Look, too, for shredded fresh cabbage for coleslaw, and for mixed salad greens, packaged in bags in the produce section.

Quick-Fix and Quick-Mix Dressings

For hurry-up serving or for salad variety, keep a supply of ready-to-use dressings on hand. They come in jars and bottles, ready to be used as is or teamed with one another or with other ingredients. Jars of mayonnaise and salad dressing are on the supermarket shelf; jars of some specialty dressings such as blue cheese and Thousand Island and others may be found in the dairy case. Pourable dressings in bottles come thin and clear or thick and creamy; choose from a wide range, including several kinds of French- and Italian-style dressings, coleslaw dressing, Caesar and Green Goddess dressings, among others.

Packaged salad-dressing mixes, which need only to be combined with vinegar, water and salad oil, also offer a wide choice of quick dressings. Here, too, you'll find several styles of French- and Italian-style dressings, cheese dressings, and other flavors.

For the weight-conscious, "instant dressings" include lemons to be squeezed lightly over greens, creamed cottage cheese to be used right from the carton.

GARNISHES FOR SALADS

Bacon bits or curls
Cocktail onions
Shredded lemon, lime or orange peel
Pomegranate seeds
Gherkins
Carrot curls, sticks or shreds
Radish roses or sliced radishes
Sliced or minced hard-cooked egg
Anchovies
Celery curls
Whole or halved salted nuts
Stuffed dates
Cherry tomatoes
Cheese garnishes (page 285)
Croutons
Slivered or chopped nuts
Miniature marshmallows
Parsley, mint or watercress sprigs
Maraschino cherries
Ripe, green or stuffed olives
Watermelon pickles
Fresh or preserved kumquats

Green and Vegetable Salads

FRUITED GREEN SALAD

1 medium head romaine
1 medium head iceberg lettuce
1 29-ounce can fruit cocktail, chilled and drained
bottled clear French dressing

ABOUT 10 MINUTES BEFORE SERVING:
Into salad bowl, tear romaine and iceberg lettuce into bite-size pieces. Add fruit cocktail; toss gently until well mixed. Serve with French dressing. Makes 10 servings.

BOSTON-WATERCRESS SALAD

1 large head Boston lettuce
1 bunch watercress
2 medium oranges, peeled and sliced
1 medium avocado, sliced
Honey-Caraway Salad Dressing (page 412)

ABOUT 20 MINUTES BEFORE SERVING:
Into large bowl, tear lettuce and watercress into bite-size pieces. Add oranges and avocado; gently toss with dressing until well coated. Makes 8 servings.

COLONEL'S LADY'S SALAD BOWL

½ 10-ounce package frozen peas
1 small head romaine
1 small head iceberg lettuce
1 small cucumber, thinly sliced
3 green onions, chopped
1 stalk celery, sliced
½ cup Colonel's Lady's Salad Dressing (page 412)

ABOUT 10 MINUTES BEFORE SERVING:
In medium bowl, place frozen peas; cover with boiling water and let stand 5 minutes. Meanwhile, in large bowl, tear greens into bite-size pieces. Drain peas and add with remaining ingredients; toss gently to coat lettuce. Makes 12 servings.

CLASSIC TOSSED GREEN SALAD

½ head Boston lettuce
¼ head chicory
½ head romaine
¼ cup sliced radishes
½ cup Classic French Dressing (page 411)

ABOUT 20 MINUTES BEFORE SERVING:
Into large salad bowl, tear Boston lettuce, chicory and romaine into bite-size pieces. Add radishes and salad dressing; toss gently to coat lettuce well. Makes 8 servings.

OTHER DRESSINGS: Parmesan Dressing (page 412); Colonel's Lady's Salad Dressing (page 412); Blue-Cheese-and-Herb Dressing (page 410).

HEARTS OF PALM BUFFET SALAD

2 large heads iceberg lettuce
3 14-ounce cans hearts of palm, drained
2 medium avocados, sliced
Classic French Dressing (page 411)

ABOUT 20 MINUTES BEFORE SERVING:
Into large salad bowl, tear lettuce into bite-size pieces; cut hearts of palm into ¼-inch slices and add to lettuce. Add avocados and dressing; toss gently to coat lettuce well. Makes 14 to 16 servings.

ARTICHOKE BUFFET SALAD: Prepare as above but substitute *two 16-ounce cans artichoke hearts,* drained and cut into halves, for hearts of palm and omit avocado.

CAESAR SALAD

¼ cup olive or salad oil
juice of 1 lemon
1 garlic clove, halved
¼ teaspoon salt
dash coarsely ground pepper
1 medium head romaine
1 cup croutons
¼ cup grated Parmesan cheese
4 anchovy fillets, chopped
1 egg

ABOUT 1 HOUR BEFORE SERVING:
In large, glass salad bowl, combine olive oil, lemon juice, garlic, salt and pepper. Cover bowl; let stand 50 minutes. Discard garlic.

ABOUT 10 MINUTES BEFORE SERVING:
Into dressing, tear romaine into bite-size pieces. Add croutons, cheese and anchovies; toss well. Then add *raw* egg and toss again. Serve immediately. Makes 6 servings.

CALIFORNIA PARTY SALAD

1 small head chicory
1 large head Boston lettuce
1 large avocado, sliced
2 hard-cooked eggs, sliced
½ cup pecan halves
½ cup Tarragon-Vinegar Dressing (page 409)

ABOUT 20 MINUTES BEFORE SERVING:
Into large salad bowl, tear chicory and lettuce into bite-size pieces. Add remaining ingredients; toss gently to coat lettuce well. Makes 12 to 14 servings.

OLD-FASHIONED LETTUCE SALAD

1 cup half-and-half
½ cup vinegar
2 teaspoons sugar
½ teaspoon salt
2 medium heads iceberg lettuce
½ cup chopped green onions

ABOUT 15 MINUTES BEFORE SERVING:
In medium salad bowl, with fork, stir half-and-half, vinegar, sugar and salt. Tear lettuce into bite-size pieces; add with onions to dressing; gently toss to coat lettuce well. Makes 12 servings.

MIXED GREENS A LA RUSSE

½ head Boston lettuce
¼ head chicory
2 cups spinach
Russian Dressing (page 410)

ABOUT 20 MINUTES BEFORE SERVING:
Into large salad bowl, tear greens into bite-size pieces; add about ½ cup dressing and toss gently to coat greens well. Add more dressing if needed. Makes 8 servings.

HOT SPINACH-LETTUCE BOWL

½ 10-ounce bag spinach
½ medium head iceberg lettuce
2 tablespoons butter or margarine
1 tablespoon cornstarch
1 4-ounce can mushroom stems and pieces
2 tablespoons lemon juice
1 teaspoon sugar
½ teaspoon salt
¼ teaspoon onion salt
⅛ teaspoon nutmeg

ABOUT 30 MINUTES BEFORE SERVING:
Into medium salad bowl, tear spinach and lettuce into bite-size pieces.

In large skillet over medium heat, into hot butter or margarine, stir cornstarch until blended. Stir in mushrooms and their liquid, ½ cup water and remaining ingredients; cook, stirring constantly, until thickened. Immediately add spinach and lettuce, tossing until coated with dressing and slightly wilted. Return mixture to salad bowl. Serve immediately. Makes 6 servings.

ORANGE-SPINACH SALAD

1 10-ounce bag spinach
1 medium head iceberg lettuce, shredded
2 tablespoons diced onion
2 tablespoons diced green pepper
2 tablespoons diced canned pimento
2 large oranges, peeled and chopped
1 small cucumber, sliced
Honey-Caraway Dressing (page 412)

ABOUT 30 MINUTES BEFORE SERVING:
Into large salad bowl, tear spinach into bite-size pieces. Add remaining ingredients; gently toss to coat spinach well. Makes 12 to 14 servings.

SESAME-SPINACH SALAD

1 tablespoon sesame seed
2 tablespoons salad oil
1 tablespoon soy sauce
1 small garlic clove, minced
dash cayenne
1½ 10-ounce bags spinach, coarsely chopped
4 celery stalks, sliced diagonally
4 green onions, cut into pieces

ABOUT 1¼ HOURS BEFORE SERVING:
In large salad bowl, with fork, stir first 5 ingredients. Add vegetables and gently toss to coat spinach well. Refrigerate 1 hour to bring out the flavors. Makes 6 servings.

SPINACH-CUCUMBER SALAD

1 10-ounce bag spinach
1 large cucumber, sliced
1 11-ounce can mandarin-orange sections, drained or 1 cup orange sections
¾ cup Classic French Dressing (page 411) or Creamy Blue-Cheese Dressing (page 412)

JUST BEFORE SERVING:
Into large salad bowl, tear spinach into bite-size pieces. Add cucumber, oranges and Classic French Dressing; gently toss to coat spinach well. Makes 8 servings.

ROMAINE-CUCUMBER SALAD: Prepare as above but use *1 head romaine* instead of spinach.

FRESH MUSHROOM SALAD

2 pounds mushrooms, thinly sliced
½ cup chopped green onions
½ cup bottled Italian dressing or Tarragon-Vinegar Dressing (page 409)
4 Belgian endives

ABOUT 40 MINUTES BEFORE SERVING:
In large bowl, gently toss mushrooms, green onions and Italian dressing to coat mushrooms well. Refrigerate 30 minutes.

AT SERVING TIME:
Arrange leaves from endives around chilled, large salad bowl; place mushrooms in center. Makes 10 servings.

GREEK SALAD

4 large cucumbers
2 bunches radishes, sliced
1 cup Greek or pitted ripe olives
1 bunch green onions, chopped
¾ cup bottled oil-and-vinegar dressing with herbs and spices
½ pound feta cheese,* cubed
½ teaspoon oregano leaves
1 small head romaine, torn into pieces

ABOUT 1 HOUR BEFORE SERVING:
Cut cucumbers in halves lengthwise; remove seeds and cut pulp in chunks. In large bowl, gently toss cucumbers and remaining ingredients except romaine; cover and refrigerate.

TO SERVE:
Add romaine to cucumber mixture and toss gently. Makes 8 servings.

* *Or use ½ pound Muenster cheese and add 1 teaspoon salt.*

CUCUMBERS IN SOUR CREAM

1 cup sour cream
3 tablespoons minced chives or onion
2 tablespoons lemon juice
1½ teaspoons salt
dash pepper
3 large cucumbers

ABOUT 20 MINUTES AHEAD OR EARLY IN DAY:
In large bowl, combine first 5 ingredients. Peel and thinly slice cucumbers; add and mix well. Cover and refrigerate. Makes 6 servings.

HERBED TOMATO SALAD

6 medium tomatoes
2 tablespoons salad oil
1 teaspoon wine vinegar
½ teaspoon sugar
½ teaspoon oregano leaves
½ teaspoon salt
½ teaspoon pepper

ABOUT 2 HOURS BEFORE SERVING:
Slice tomatoes and arrange in serving dish in overlapping slices. In small bowl, combine remaining ingredients and sprinkle over tomatoes. Cover and refrigerate. Makes 6 servings.

CUCUMBER-AND-TOMATO SALAD

3 medium tomatoes, sliced
1 medium cucumber, sliced
Deluxe Garlic French Dressing (page 411)

JUST BEFORE SERVING:
Arrange tomato and cucumber slices on plate; pass dressing to pour over them. Makes 6 servings.

MARINATED SALAD

2 medium tomatoes, thickly sliced
1 large onion, sliced
1 medium green pepper, sliced
1 large cucumber, thinly sliced
1 cup red wine vinegar
2 tablespoons sugar
1 teaspoon salt
½ teaspoon seasoned pepper

ABOUT 3 HOURS BEFORE SERVING:
In medium bowl, arrange layers of vegetables. In another medium bowl, stir 1 cup water and remaining ingredients; pour over vegetables. Put a plate on top of vegetables and press it down with a clean, heavy can. Refrigerate.

TO SERVE:
Remove can and plate. Makes 8 servings.

ZUCCHINI SALAD

½ cup pickle relish
2 tablespoons cider vinegar
1 teaspoon sugar
½ teaspoon salt
1 pound zucchini, sliced (about 3)
romaine or other lettuce leaves
1 tomato, cut in thin wedges

ABOUT 45 MINUTES BEFORE SERVING:
In medium bowl, stir pickle relish, vinegar, sugar and salt. Add zucchini; toss gently. Cover and refrigerate about 30 minutes, tossing occasionally.

AT SERVING TIME:
Line salad bowl with romaine. Gently toss tomato with salad; spoon into romaine. Makes 6 servings.

ITALIAN-ZUCCHINI SALAD: Use ½ *cup Mixed Herb Dressing* (page 411) and omit first 4 ingredients above.

ASPARAGUS VINAIGRETTE SALAD

3 10-ounce packages frozen asparagus spears
1 cup bottled Italian dressing or Classic French Dressing (page 411)
lettuce leaves

EARLY IN DAY:
Cook asparagus as label directs; drain. Place asparagus in shallow dish and pour on salad dressing. Cover and refrigerate several hours, turning occasionally.

AT SERVING TIME:
Drain asparagus and arrange on lettuce-lined salad plates. Makes 12 servings.

CUCUMBER-GRAPEFRUIT SALAD

1 medium cucumber
bottled Italian dressing
2 large grapefruit
1 large head lettuce, shredded
⅓ cup chopped chives

ABOUT 1 HOUR BEFORE SERVING:
With fork, score unpeeled cucumber lengthwise; cut into thin slices; place in small bowl. Add enough Italian dressing to cover slices. Section grapefruit and place in another small bowl. Cover, refrigerate all.

AT SERVING TIME:
Drain grapefruit well. In salad bowl, gently toss lettuce, chives, grapefruit, cucumbers and their dressing until well coated. Makes 8 servings.

HARLEQUIN SALAD BOWL

1 20-ounce can white kidney beans, drained
1 15-ounce can red kidney beans, drained
½ cup chopped green onions
½ cup bottled oil-and-vinegar dressing
¼ cup chopped parsley
1 teaspoon salt
¼ teaspoon pepper

DAY BEFORE SERVING:
In medium bowl, mix all ingredients. Cover and refrigerate, stirring occasionally.

TO SERVE:
Lightly toss mixture and serve in chilled bowl. Makes 6 servings.

MARINATED VEGETABLE SALAD

2 pounds green beans, cut up and cooked
1 pound carrots, sliced and cooked
2 pounds lima beans, cooked
¼ cup bottled Green Goddess salad dressing
½ teaspoon salt

EARLY IN DAY:
In large serving bowl, gently toss all ingredients. Cover and refrigerate, tossing occasionally. Makes 6 servings.

FAVORITE KIDNEY-BEAN SALAD

1 16-ounce can kidney beans, drained
½ cup diced celery
½ cup sliced stuffed olives
⅓ cup diced sweet pickles
¼ to ⅓ cup mayonnaise
3 tablespoons chili sauce
2 tablespoons sliced green onion
½ teaspoon salt
lettuce leaves

ABOUT 1 HOUR AHEAD OR EARLY IN DAY:
In medium bowl, combine beans with remaining ingredients except lettuce; mix well. Cover and refrigerate.

TO SERVE: Serve on lettuce. Makes 6 servings.

THREE-BEAN SALAD

½ cup sugar
½ cup salad oil
½ cup cider vinegar
1 teaspoon salt
1 16-ounce can cut green beans, drained
1 16-ounce can cut wax beans or garbanzo beans, drained
1 16-ounce can red kidney beans, drained
½ cup chopped onion
lettuce leaves

EARLY IN DAY OR SEVERAL DAYS AHEAD:
In large bowl, stir first 4 ingredients until blended. Add remaining ingredients except lettuce leaves; toss to mix well. Cover and refrigerate.

TO SERVE:
With slotted spoon, spoon bean mixture onto lettuce leaves. Makes 8 servings.

CRISP VEGETABLE SALAD

1 medium green pepper
1 8-ounce can water chestnuts, drained and sliced
2 cups finely sliced celery
6 radishes, finely sliced
2 teaspoons minced onion
1 teaspoon lemon juice
½ teaspoon salt
dash pepper
about ⅓ cup bottled Italian dressing or Deluxe Garlic French Dressing (page 411)
lettuce leaves

EARLY IN DAY:
Into medium bowl, coarsely grate green pepper; refrigerate, covered. In medium bowl, gently toss next 5 ingredients; cover and refrigerate.

ABOUT 15 MINUTES BEFORE SERVING:
Sprinkle vegetables with salt, pepper and green pepper; add salad dressing and toss well. Serve in salad bowl lined with lettuce leaves. Makes 6 servings.

CARROT COLESLAW

1 medium head cabbage, cut in chunks
2 large carrots, cut in large chunks
about ¼ cup milk
2 teaspoons prepared mustard
1 teaspoon cider vinegar
2½ teaspoons salt
dash pepper
1 8-ounce container creamed cottage cheese

ABOUT 30 MINUTES BEFORE SERVING:
Fill blender container three-fourths full with some of cabbage and carrot chunks; cover with cold water. Blend, covered, about 5 seconds on high speed just until vegetables are grated; drain well and place in large bowl. Repeat until all have been grated.

In same blender container, place milk, mustard, vinegar, salt, pepper and cottage cheese. Cover and blend at medium speed about 3 minutes until dressing is smooth and creamy, adding 2 more tablespoons milk if needed. Add to cabbage mixture and toss until well mixed. Cover and refrigerate. Makes 10 servings.

DELUXE COLESLAW

1 medium head cabbage, shredded (8 cups)
1 small green pepper, thinly sliced
⅔ cup diced celery
⅔ cup finely shredded carrots
½ cup sliced radishes
2 tablespoons minced onion
Coleslaw Dressing (page 409)

ABOUT 1½ HOURS AHEAD OR EARLY IN DAY:
In large bowl, gently toss all ingredients. Cover and refrigerate. Makes 8 servings.

BOWL STYLE: Spread apart several outer leaves of cabbage. With sharp knife, carefully cut out center of cabbage, leaving shell about ¾ inch thick to make "bowl." Use cut-out cabbage to make coleslaw as above; heap in "bowl" to serve.

GOLDEN SLAW

1 medium head cabbage, finely shredded (8 cups)
2 cups diced, unpeeled red apple
2 cups shredded natural Swiss cheese
⅔ cup mayonnaise
¼ cup prepared mustard
2 teaspoons salt
1½ teaspoons pepper

EARLY IN DAY:
In large salad bowl, toss cabbage, apple and cheese; cover and refrigerate. In small bowl or jar, mix mayonnaise, mustard, salt and pepper; refrigerate.

JUST BEFORE SERVING:
Toss cabbage with mayonnaise mixture. Makes 12 servings.

CABBAGE-AND-PEPPER SALAD

¾ cup cider vinegar
⅓ cup sugar
1 tablespoon mustard seed
2 teaspoons salt
1 large head cabbage, cut into chunks
1 large green pepper, chopped
1 red onion, thinly sliced
2 4-ounce cans pimentos, drained and chopped

EARLY IN DAY:
In medium saucepan over medium heat,

heat to boiling vinegar, sugar, mustard seed and salt with ¾ cup water. Reduce heat and simmer, uncovered, 5 minutes; cool.

In large bowl, combine mixture with cabbage, green pepper, onion and pimentos. Cover and refrigerate; toss occasionally. Makes 8 servings.

HERBED POTATO SALAD

½ cup mayonnaise
½ cup milk
4 teaspoons salt
½ teaspoon pepper
10 cups cut-up, cooked potatoes (about 5½ pounds)
¼ cup chopped chives
¼ cup chopped fresh dill
¼ cup chopped parsley
3 medium tomatoes, cut into thick wedges
lettuce leaves

EARLY IN DAY:
In large bowl, with fork, stir mayonnaise, milk, salt and pepper until mixture is smooth. Add potatoes, chives, dill and parsley; toss gently until well coated. Cover and refrigerate.

AT SERVING TIME:
Toss tomato wedges with potato mixture. Serve on lettuce leaves. Makes 10 to 12 servings.

EASY HOT GERMAN POTATO SALAD

4 bacon slices
1 5⅝-ounce package scalloped potatoes
1 heaping tablespoon onion flakes
½ teaspoon sugar
2 tablespoons cider vinegar

ABOUT 40 MINUTES BEFORE SERVING:
In large skillet over medium-high heat, fry bacon crisp; drain on paper towels. Crumble bacon into bits and set aside. Discard bacon drippings.

Into skillet, empty potato slices and seasoned sauce mix from package of scalloped potatoes; stir in 3 cups boiling water, onion flakes and sugar; cover and cook over low heat for 30 minutes or until potatoes are tender, stirring occasionally. Stir in vinegar and bacon bits. Serve hot. Makes 4 servings.

OLD-FASHIONED POTATO SALAD

1 cup mayonnaise
1 tablespoon cider vinegar
1½ teaspoons salt
2 teaspoons prepared mustard
½ teaspoon celery seed
dash pepper
4 hard-cooked eggs, chopped
4 cups diced cooked potatoes
1½ cups sliced celery
½ cup sliced green onions
¼ cup sliced radishes
2 tablespoons chopped parsley
lettuce leaves

EARLY IN DAY:
In large bowl, stir mayonnaise with next 5 ingredients until mixed; add remaining ingredients except lettuce and mix well. Cover and refrigerate. Serve on lettuce leaves. Makes 6 servings.

MACARONI SALAD: Prepare as above but increase vinegar to 2 tablespoons and substitute *4 cups cold, drained cooked elbow macaroni* (8 ounces uncooked) for potatoes. If you like, sprinkle with *1 cup diced American or Cheddar cheese* just before serving.

RICE SALAD: Prepare as above but substitute *4 cups cold, cooked regular long-grain or packaged precooked rice* for potatoes. Sprinkle with *paprika.*

CAESAR-STYLE POTATO SALAD

½ cup salad oil
¼ cup grated Parmesan cheese
¼ cup lemon juice
1 tablespoon salt
1 tablespoon Worcestershire
¼ teaspoon pepper
5 pounds potatoes, cooked
8 bacon slices, fried and crumbled
1 medium onion, chopped
¼ cup chopped parsley
2 hard-cooked eggs, sliced

ABOUT 3 HOURS AHEAD OR EARLY IN DAY:
In large bowl, with fork, beat first 6 ingredients until well blended. Add potatoes, bacon, onion and parsley to mixture; toss gently to mix well. Arrange egg slices on top; cover and refrigerate. Makes 8 to 10 servings.

POTATOES-PLUS SALAD

5 cups sliced cooked potatoes (about 5 medium)
1 9-ounce package frozen cut green beans, cooked and drained
½ cup chopped green onions
½ cup sliced celery
½ cup sliced radishes
1½ teaspoons salt
½ teaspoon pepper
1 8¼-ounce can whole beets, well drained and halved
Horseradish Dressing (below)

EARLY IN DAY:
In large bowl, gently toss all ingredients except beets and Horseradish Dressing; cover and refrigerate.

JUST BEFORE SERVING:
Add beets and Horseradish Dressing to salad; gently toss until well mixed. Makes 8 servings.

HORSERADISH DRESSING: In small bowl, with spoon, stir *½ cup mayonnaise, ¼ cup French dressing* and *1 tablespoon horseradish* until smooth.

HERRING SALAD

1 cup heavy or whipping cream
1½ cups diced cooked potatoes (about 2 medium)
1 16-ounce can sliced pickled beets, drained
1 medium apple, diced
½ cup pickled herring in wine sauce, drained, chopped
¼ cup diced dill pickle
¼ cup minced onion
1½ teaspoons salt
¼ teaspoon pepper
2 hard-cooked eggs, cut in wedges, for garnish
parsley for garnish

EARLY IN DAY:
In medium bowl, with mixer at medium speed, beat cream until soft peaks form. Gently fold in remaining ingredients except eggs and parsley; cover and refrigerate.

TO SERVE:
Arrange salad on platter; garnish with eggs and parsley. Makes 6 servings.

TOMATO ASPIC

3½ cups cocktail vegetable juice
2 lemon slices
1 small bay leaf
2 envelopes unflavored gelatin
1 tablespoon cider vinegar
1 teaspoon salt
1 teaspoon sugar
lettuce leaves

EARLY IN DAY:
In medium saucepan over medium heat, combine 1 cup cocktail vegetable juice, lemon slices and bay leaf; sprinkle gelatin on top of mixture and cook, stirring, until gelatin is dissolved and mixture boils. With slotted spoon, remove lemon and bay leaf; discard. Stir in remaining cocktail vegetable juice and remaining ingredients except lettuce leaves. Pour mixture into eight ½-cup molds. Refrigerate until set.

TO SERVE:
Unmold gelatin onto lettuce-lined salad plates. Makes 8 servings.

TOMATO-CHEESE: Prepare as above but when mixture in each mold is partially set, drop in a small spoonful from *¼ cup creamed cottage cheese.*

TOMATO RING: Prepare as above but pour mixture into 6-cup ring mold.

TWO-TONE: Prepare as above but pour only half of mixture into molds; refrigerate until almost set. Refrigerate remaining mixture until mixture mounds slightly when dropped from a spoon; fold in *1 cup creamed cottage cheese, 1 tablespoon chopped chives, 1 tablespoon diced celery;* pour into partially filled molds. Refrigerate.

HAM OR SEAFOOD TOMATO ASPIC: Prepare as above but refrigerate mixture until mixture mounds slightly when dropped from a spoon. Fold in *¼ cup pickle relish* and *1 cup slivered, cooked ham* or 1 cup diced cooked shrimp or one 6½- or 7-ounce can tuna, drained. Pour into 6-cup mold; refrigerate.

TOMATO-OLIVE ASPIC: Prepare as above but place *pimento-stuffed olive slices* or hard-cooked egg slices in bottom of each mold; cover with small amount of mixture and refrigerate until set. Fill with remaining mixture. Refrigerate until set.

PERFECTION SALAD

½ cup sugar
2 envelopes unflavored gelatin
1 teaspoon salt
½ cup cider vinegar
2 tablespoons lemon juice
1½ cups finely shredded cabbage
⅔ cup diced celery
1 4-ounce can pimentos, drained and diced
celery leaves for garnish

EARLY IN DAY OR DAY BEFORE SERVING:
In small saucepan, stir sugar, gelatin and salt; stir in 1 cup water. Over low heat, cook until gelatin is dissolved. Remove from heat; stir in vinegar, lemon juice and 1½ cups water; chill until mixture mounds slightly when dropped from a spoon. Fold in cabbage, celery and pimentos; pour into 4-cup mold. Refrigerate until set.

TO SERVE:
Unmold salad onto plate; garnish with celery leaves. Makes 8 servings.

ARTICHOKE SALAD MOLD

1 9-ounce package frozen artichoke hearts
1 0.6-ounce package Italian salad-dressing mix
1 cup thinly sliced mushrooms
1 3-ounce package lemon-flavor gelatin
1 tablespoon diced canned pimento
1 cup mayonnaise

EARLY IN DAY:
Cook artichoke hearts as label directs; drain and cool. Cut each in half; set aside.

Prepare salad-dressing mix as label directs; in large bowl, combine with artichokes and mushrooms; cover and refrigerate 1 hour. Drain mixture, reserving salad dressing.

Meanwhile, prepare gelatin as label directs but use only 1¾ cups water and refrigerate until mixture mounds slightly when dropped from a spoon. Fold in artichoke mixture and pimento. Pour into a 4-cup mold; cover and refrigerate until set.

JUST BEFORE SERVING:
In small bowl, with fork, combine mayonnaise and reserved dressing. Unmold gelatin; serve with mixture. Makes 8 servings.

LIMELIGHT VEGETABLE MOLD

1 6-ounce package lime-flavor gelatin
2 cups sour cream
2 cups shredded carrots
2 cups diced celery
1 2-ounce jar pimentos, chopped
lettuce leaves
carrot curls and celery fans for garnish
Thick Fruit Dressing (page 412), optional

EARLY IN DAY:
In medium bowl, dissolve gelatin in only 1½ cups boiling water; refrigerate until mixture mounds slightly when dropped from a spoon. With mixer at low speed, beat gelatin for a minute until smooth; beat in sour cream until smooth. With spoon, stir next 3 ingredients into mixture; pour into 4-cup mold. Refrigerate until set.

AT SERVING TIME:
Unmold onto platter; tuck lettuce leaves around salad. Garnish with carrot curls and celery fans. Pass dressing to be spooned over servings. Makes 8 to 10 servings.

MOLDED CUCUMBER SALAD

1 3-ounce package lemon-flavor gelatin
1 teaspoon salt
3 tablespoons cider vinegar
1 teaspoon grated onion
2 cups sour cream
¼ cup mayonnaise
1 large cucumber, finely shredded and well drained
lettuce leaves
Mint Dressing (page 412)

EARLY IN DAY OR DAY BEFORE SERVING:
In medium bowl, stir gelatin and salt; add ⅔ cup boiling water and stir until gelatin is dissolved. Stir in vinegar and onion. Refrigerate until mixture mounds slightly when dropped from a spoon, about 40 minutes. With wire whisk or hand beater, beat in sour cream, mayonnaise and cucumber until well mixed. Pour into 6-cup mold. Refrigerate until set.

TO SERVE:
Unmold onto serving plate; tuck lettuce leaves around salad. Serve with Mint Dressing. Makes 8 to 10 servings.

Fruit Salads

STUFFED CANTALOUPE SALAD

2 small or medium cantaloupes
2 cups cottage cheese
1 cup strawberries, halved
½ cup blueberries or seedless green grapes
Thick Fruit Dressing (page 412)

ABOUT 20 MINUTES BEFORE SERVING:
Cut melons in half lengthwise and scoop out seeds; spoon cottage cheese into each half. Top cheese with strawberries and blueberries. Pass dressing to be spooned over servings. Makes 4 servings.

MARINATED MELON SALAD

¾ cup sugar
1½ tablespoons lemon juice
1 tablespoon anise seed
¼ teaspoon salt
2 small cantaloupes
1 large honeydew

EARLY IN DAY:
In medium saucepan over medium heat, cook sugar with 1 cup water, lemon juice, anise seed and salt for 15 minutes or until mixture reaches light syrup consistency; chill in refrigerator.

Meanwhile, into large bowl, peel melons and cut into bite-size chunks; pour chilled syrup through strainer over melons. Refrigerate, stirring often. Makes 12 servings.

WATERMELON SALAD

½ small round watermelon
1 escarole
2 large pears
lemon juice
Sour-Cream Dressing (page 409)

ABOUT 45 MINUTES BEFORE SERVING:
With melon baller or metal measuring ½ teaspoon, scoop pulp from watermelon, removing seeds. On large platter, arrange escarole leaves; thinly slice pears and dip slices in lemon juice; arrange around edge; mound watermelon balls in center. Serve with dressing. Makes 8 servings.

FRUIT-MALLOW SALAD

1 15¼-ounce can pineapple chunks
1 16-ounce can pear halves
1 11-ounce can mandarin-orange sections
1 cup seedless green grapes, halved
½ cup miniature marshmallows
¼ cup heavy or whipping cream
½ cup mayonnaise
¼ teaspoon nutmeg

EARLY IN DAY:
Drain pineapple, pears and mandarin-orange sections. (Use liquids with orange juice for breakfast another day.) Place drained fruits, grapes and marshmallows in large bowl.

In small bowl, with mixer at medium speed, beat cream until soft peaks form. With rubber spatula, gently fold in mayonnaise and nutmeg until well mixed. Thoroughly fold mayonnaise mixture into fruit; cover and refrigerate. Makes 6 salad or dessert servings.

CINNAMON-APPLE SALAD

1 cup red hot candies
sugar
6 medium cooking apples
1 cup diced celery
½ cup coarsely chopped California walnuts
½ cup seedless raisins or chopped dates
⅓ cup mayonnaise
1 tablespoon milk
lettuce leaves

ABOUT 3 HOURS AHEAD OR EARLY IN DAY:
In large saucepan over medium heat, heat candies, ½ cup sugar and 3 cups water, stirring often, until candies are dissolved.

Meanwhile, peel and core but don't slice apples; place in sugar mixture. Simmer, covered, 5 to 10 minutes until apples are just tender-crisp, turning often. Refrigerate until well chilled, spooning liquid over apples occasionally.

Prepare filling: In medium bowl, mix celery, walnuts, raisins, mayonnaise, milk and 1 teaspoon sugar; cover and refrigerate.

AT SERVING TIME:
With slotted spoon, remove apples from liquid and place on lettuce leaves. Stuff apples with filling. Makes 8 servings.

WALDORF SALAD

½ cup mayonnaise
2 tablespoons lemon juice
2 cups diced unpeeled, red apples
1 cup thinly sliced celery
½ cup chopped California walnuts
½ cup dark seedless raisins

ABOUT 20 MINUTES BEFORE SERVING:
In medium bowl, with fork, mix mayonnaise with lemon juice. Gently toss in apples, celery, walnuts and raisins. Makes 4 servings.

GINGERED: Add *½ teaspoon ginger*.

APPLE-AND-PEA SALAD

1 cup cooked peas
2 large red eating apples, unpeeled and diced
1 3½-ounce can pitted ripe olives, drained and sliced
½ cup mayonnaise
¼ cup chopped fresh mint leaves
2 tablespoons lime juice
1 teaspoon salt
lettuce leaves

EARLY IN DAY:
In medium bowl, gently toss all ingredients except lettuce leaves until apples are well coated; cover and refrigerate at least 1 hour.

TO SERVE:
Serve mixture on lettuce. Makes 6 servings.

FRUIT LUNCHEON SALAD

1 head Boston lettuce
1½ 16-ounce containers cottage cheese (3 cups)
1 small pineapple, cut into chunks
1 cantaloupe, cut into balls
1 pint strawberries
2 oranges, sectioned
Creamy Ginger-Cheese Dressing (page 412)

ABOUT 1 HOUR BEFORE SERVING:
Line large salad bowl with lettuce; spoon cottage cheese into center of lettuce; arrange pineapple, melon, strawberries and oranges around cottage cheese; chill.

TO SERVE:
Serve with dressing. Makes 6 servings.

AVOCADO-MELON SALAD

3 avocados, cut in bite-size chunks
1 cantaloupe, cut in bite-size chunks
romaine or other lettuce leaves
Creamy Ginger-Cheese Dressing or Mint Dressing (page 412)

ABOUT 30 MINUTES BEFORE SERVING:
In large bowl, gently toss avocado and cantaloupe. With slotted spoon, transfer avocado mixture to lettuce-lined platter. Serve with dressing. Makes 8 servings.

CRANBERRY-NUT GELATIN SALAD

1 6-ounce package orange-flavor gelatin
¾ cup whole-cranberry sauce
¼ cup minced celery
¼ cup chopped California walnuts
1 tablespoon lemon juice
½ teaspoon salt

DAY BEFORE SERVING:
In medium bowl or 6-cup mold, pour 3 cups boiling water into gelatin, stirring until dissolved. Refrigerate until mixture mounds slightly when dropped from a spoon, about 1 hour. Stir in remaining ingredients. Refrigerate until set. Makes 6 servings.

STUFFED PEAR SALAD

1 30-ounce can pear halves
1 8-ounce package cream cheese, softened
¾ cup finely shredded carrots
2 tablespoons raisins, chopped
¼ teaspoon cinnamon
½ medium head chicory

ABOUT 40 MINUTES BEFORE SERVING:
Drain pear halves, reserving ⅓ cup syrup. In small bowl, combine half of cream cheese, ¼ cup shredded carrot and raisins.

Onto waxed paper, drop cream-cheese mixture into as many mounds as the number of pear halves. Roll mounds in remaining shredded carrots.

For dressing, in another small bowl, with fork or wire whisk, beat remaining cream cheese, reserved syrup and cinnamon until creamy. Arrange pear halves on chicory-lined platter. Place a cheese mound in hollow of each pear half. Serve with dressing. Makes 8 to 10 servings.

CRANBERRY SALAD MOLD

2 6-ounce packages strawberry-flavor gelatin
5 medium oranges
1 16-ounce package cranberries, coarsely chopped
2 cups sugar
lettuce leaves for garnish
Orange-Cheese Dressing (below)

EARLY IN DAY OR DAY BEFORE SERVING:
In large bowl, dissolve gelatin in 3 cups boiling water; stir in 3 cups cold water. Refrigerate, stirring often, until mixture mounds slightly when dropped from a spoon.

Meanwhile, peel and chop oranges; place in another large bowl. Add cranberries and sugar and stir until sugar is completely dissolved. Stir fruit mixture into thickened gelatin. Pour into Bundt cake pan or 12-cup mold. Refrigerate until set.

TO SERVE:
Unmold gelatin onto platter; garnish with lettuce leaves. Serve with Orange-Cheese Dressing. Makes 16 servings.

ORANGE-CHEESE DRESSING: In small bowl, with mixer at low speed, beat *one 8-ounce package cream cheese* with *1/3 cup orange juice* until smooth. Stir in *2 teaspoons grated orange peel* and *dash salt.*

TWENTY-FOUR-HOUR SALAD

2 cups cooked rice, chilled
1 17-ounce can fruit cocktail, drained
1 11-ounce can mandarin-orange sections, drained
1 20-ounce can pineapple chunks, drained
1 3½-ounce can flaked coconut
1 6¼-ounce package miniature marshmallows
1 cup sour cream
lettuce leaves (optional)

DAY BEFORE SERVING:
In large bowl, gently toss all ingredients except lettuce. Cover and refrigerate, tossing occasionally.

AT SERVING TIME:
For salad, line salad bowl with lettuce leaves. Stir fruit mixture, then spoon onto lettuce. For dessert, spoon into 10 sherbet dishes. Makes 8 salad or 10 dessert servings.

APPLE-CIDER SALAD MOLD

2 envelopes unflavored gelatin
3 tablespoons sugar
½ teaspoon salt
3¾ cups apple cider
3 tablespoons lemon juice
3½ cups chopped Red Delicious apples, unpeeled
1 cup finely chopped celery

EARLY IN DAY:
In medium saucepan, stir gelatin, sugar and salt until well mixed; stir in apple cider and lemon juice. Cook mixture over low heat, stirring, until gelatin is dissolved; refrigerate until mixture mounds slightly when dropped from a spoon. Stir in apples and celery; pour into 6-cup mold; refrigerate.

TO SERVE:
Unmold onto plate. Makes 12 servings.

CREAMY LEMON-MELON MOLD

1 6-ounce package lemon-flavor gelatin
1¾ cups ginger ale
1 10-ounce package frozen melon balls, thawed and well drained
1 8-ounce package cream cheese, softened

EARLY IN DAY:
1. In medium bowl, dissolve gelatin in 2 cups boiling water; stir in ginger ale. In small bowl, reserve 2¼ cups gelatin at room temperature.
2. Pour enough remaining gelatin into 6-cup mold to form very thin layer. Arrange some melon balls in gelatin layer; refrigerate until just set but still sticky, about 15 minutes. (Reserve remaining melon balls for garnish.)
3. Carefully add enough gelatin just to cover melon balls. Refrigerate until just set, about 20 minutes. Pour in remaining gelatin; refrigerate until just firm, about 45 minutes.
4. In another small bowl, with mixer at low speed, beat cream cheese until smooth. Gradually beat in reserved 2¼ cups gelatin; carefully pour into mold. Refrigerate.

TO SERVE:
Unmold onto platter and garnish with remaining melon balls. Makes 8 servings.

CRANBERRY RELISH SALAD

2½ cups cranberry-juice cocktail
3 envelopes unflavored gelatin
1 14-ounce jar cranberry-orange relish
1 8½-ounce can crushed pineapple
1½ cups diced celery
1 cup finely chopped California walnuts
½ teaspoon salt
1 orange, thinly sliced, for garnish

EARLY IN DAY OR DAY BEFORE SERVING:
In medium saucepan, into 1 cup cranberry juice, sprinkle gelatin. Cook over low heat, stirring constantly, until gelatin is dissolved. Cool, then stir in remaining cranberry juice. Refrigerate, stirring occasionally, until mixture mounds slightly when dropped from a spoon. Fold in cranberry-orange relish, crushed pineapple, celery, walnuts and salt; spoon into a 6-cup mold. Refrigerate.

TO SERVE:
Unmold onto platter; garnish with quartered orange slices. Makes 8 to 10 servings.

PINEAPPLE-CHEESE SALAD

1 15¼-ounce can crushed pineapple
1 3-ounce package lime-flavor gelatin
⅛ teaspoon salt
⅔ cup creamed cottage cheese
¼ cup mayonnaise
¼ cup blanched almonds, finely chopped
lettuce leaves
bottled French dressing

DAY BEFORE SERVING:
Drain pineapple, reserving syrup; to syrup, add enough water to measure 1 cup. In small saucepan over high heat, heat syrup to boiling; stir in gelatin and salt and stir until gelatin is dissolved.

In medium bowl, with mixer at medium speed (or in covered blender container at medium speed), beat cottage cheese and mayonnaise until well blended; beat in pineapple, almonds and gelatin mixture. Pour into 4-cup mold or bowl; refrigerate.

TO SERVE:
Unmold; surround with lettuce and serve with French dressing. Makes 8 servings.

FROSTED FRUIT SALAD

1 6-ounce package cherry-flavor gelatin
1 10-ounce package frozen strawberries
2 large bananas
1 15¼-ounce can crushed pineapple
1 cup sour cream

DAY BEFORE SERVING:
In large bowl, combine gelatin, only 2 cups boiling water and strawberries; set aside until strawberries are thawed. In small bowl, mash bananas with pineapple until well mixed; stir into gelatin mixture.

Pour mixture into 8-inch springform pan or 13″ by 9″ baking dish. Refrigerate until set. Spread top with sour cream. Refrigerate until serving time.

TO SERVE:
Remove salad from springform pan; cut in wedges. Makes about 12 servings.

CHERRY-SURPRISE RING

1 6-ounce package cherry-flavor gelatin
2 3-ounce packages cream cheese
½ cup finely chopped California walnuts
1 17-ounce can pitted dark, sweet cherries, drained
lettuce leaves

EARLY IN DAY:
Prepare gelatin as label directs but use only 3½ cups water and refrigerate until cool. Meanwhile, in medium bowl, with fork, stir cream cheese and walnuts until well mixed. With hands, shape measuring teaspoonfuls of mixture into balls; set aside.

Spoon 3 to 4 tablespoons gelatin into a 6-cup ring mold; alternately arrange about half the cheese balls and cherries on gelatin in ring mold. Chill 20 minutes or until almost set. Spoon on ½ to ¾ cup more gelatin or enough to cover the cheese balls and cherries. Refrigerate again 20 minutes or until almost set. Spoon on remaining gelatin and alternately arrange remaining cheese balls and cherries; refrigerate.

TO SERVE:
Unmold onto lettuce-lined platter. Makes 8 to 10 servings.

Main-Dish Salads

CHICKEN SALAD

⅔ cup mayonnaise
2 tablespoons cider vinegar
1 teaspoon salt
4 to 5 cups cut-up cooked chicken or turkey
1 cup sliced celery
1 cup minced green pepper
2 teaspoons grated onion
romaine

EARLY IN DAY:
In large bowl, with fork, combine mayonnaise, vinegar and salt. Add chicken and remaining ingredients except romaine; toss well; cover and refrigerate.

TO SERVE:
On chilled platter, arrange romaine; lightly pile salad on it. Makes 6 to 8 servings.

EXOTIC CHICKEN SALAD: Prepare as above but add *⅔ cup slivered, toasted almonds* or chopped pecans and *2 cups halved, seedless green grapes* or orange sections to chicken mixture. Makes 8 to 10 servings.

NEW CHICKEN SALAD: Prepare as above but omit celery and green pepper. To chicken mixture, add *2 cups diced cucumbers* and *1 cup drained, canned pineapple chunks.* Garnish with *ripe olives.* Makes 8 servings.

HAM AND CHICKEN SALAD: Prepare as above but substitute *2 cups cooked ham chunks* for 2 cups of the chicken. Add *1 cup fresh or drained, canned pineapple chunks* to mixture. Makes 8 servings.

CHICKEN-WALDORF SALAD: Prepare as above but add *2 cups diced unpeeled red apples* and *⅔ cup chopped walnuts or pecans* to chicken mixture. Makes 8 to 10 servings.

TOASTED-WALNUT-CHICKEN SALAD: In small saucepan over medium heat, in *2 teaspoons hot butter or margarine,* cook *½ cup chopped California walnuts* and *dash salt* 3 to 4 minutes until crisp. Cool; add to chicken mixture.

HAM, VEAL OR LAMB SALAD: Halve ingredients and prepare as above but use *2 cups cooked, cut up ham, veal or lamb* for chicken. Makes 3 to 4 servings.

TUNA-MACARONI-BEAN SALAD

2 9-ounce packages frozen cut green beans
1 8-ounce package shell macaroni
2 6½- or 7-ounce cans tuna, drained and flaked
2 medium tomatoes
¼ cup chopped parsley
1 cup bottled Italian salad dressing
4 hard-cooked eggs, cut into wedges

ABOUT 3 HOURS OR DAY BEFORE SERVING:
Cook green beans as label directs; drain. Meanwhile, cook macaroni as label directs; drain. In large bowl, gently toss all ingredients except eggs until well mixed; cover and refrigerate.

AT SERVING TIME:
Garnish salad with eggs. Makes 8 servings.

INDIENNE RICE SALAD

1 6-ounce package curried rice
4 bacon slices, fried and crumbled
2 6½- or 7-ounce cans tuna, drained
½ cup diced celery
¼ cup diced green pepper
¼ cup dark seedless raisins
½ cup mayonnaise
1 teaspoon curry powder
½ cup heavy or whipping cream
lettuce leaves
salted peanuts
flaked coconut
chutney

EARLY IN DAY OR DAY BEFORE SERVING:
Cook rice as label directs; cover and refrigerate. Also refrigerate bacon and tuna.

ABOUT 4 HOURS BEFORE SERVING:
In large bowl, break tuna into chunks; add rice, bacon, celery, green pepper, raisins.

In small bowl, with fork, combine mayonnaise and curry powder. In medium bowl, with mixer at medium speed, beat cream stiff; fold in mayonnaise. Pour over rice mixture; gently toss to mix well. Cover and refrigerate.

JUST BEFORE SERVING:
Arrange lettuce leaves on platter. Toss rice mixture; pile lightly on greens. Sprinkle with peanuts and coconut. Spoon heaping tablespoonfuls of chutney onto mixture. Makes 8 servings.

CHEF'S CABBAGE SALAD

1 medium head cabbage, finely shredded
1½ pounds cooked ham, cut in thin strips
2 8-ounce packages natural Swiss cheese slices, cut in thin strips
1 large cucumber, cut in thin strips
Thousand Island Dressing (page 410)

ABOUT 1 HOUR BEFORE SERVING:
Into large salad bowl, gently toss all ingredients until well mixed; cover and refrigerate. Makes about 10 servings.

CHEDDAR-MACARONI SALAD MOLD

4 4-ounce packages shredded Cheddar cheese (4 cups)
1 cup mayonnaise
instant minced onion
¼ teaspoon prepared mustard
dash hot pepper sauce
1 16-ounce package elbow macaroni
1 2-ounce jar sliced pimentos, drained
½ cup diced celery
½ cup diced green pepper
2 tablespoons chopped pimento-stuffed olives
1½ teaspoons salt

DAY BEFORE SERVING:
Line bottom and about 1 inch up side of 10-inch springform pan with foil. In medium bowl, with mixer at medium speed, beat two packages cheese with ¼ cup of the mayonnaise, 1 teaspoon minced onion, mustard and hot pepper sauce until well mixed. Press cheese mixture evenly into bottom of pan; refrigerate.

Meanwhile, cook macaroni as label directs; drain. In large bowl, toss hot macaroni with rest of cheese until melted; toss in remaining ¾ cup mayonnaise and rest of ingredients. Refrigerate until cool. Pack mixture firmly on top of cheese. Cover and refrigerate.

TO SERVE:
Remove side of springform pan. Unmold salad onto chilled platter; peel off foil. Serve with additional mayonnaise, if you like. Cut into wedges with knife dipped in hot water. Serve with pie server. Makes 8 servings.

GREEN GODDESS SALAD

¾ cup mayonnaise
2 anchovy fillets, minced
1 tablespoon chopped parsley
1 tablespoon chopped chives
1 tablespoon chopped green onion
1 tablespoon tarragon vinegar
¾ teaspoon tarragon
1 garlic clove, halved
1 head romaine
3 cups cooked, shelled and deveined shrimp, chilled

EARLY IN DAY:
Prepare dressing: In small bowl, stir first 7 ingredients; cover and refrigerate.

TO SERVE:
Rub salad bowl with garlic clove; discard garlic. Into bowl, tear romaine into bite-size pieces. Add shrimp and dressing and toss until well coated. Makes 6 servings.

CHICKEN-STUFFED CUCUMBER SALAD

½ cup mayonnaise
2 tablespoons milk
½ teaspoon curry powder
salt
2 cups cut-up cooked chicken
¾ cup diced celery
2 large cucumbers
lettuce leaves
¼ cup salted peanuts, coarsely chopped

ABOUT 25 MINUTES BEFORE SERVING:
In medium bowl, with fork, beat mayonnaise, milk, curry powder and ¼ teaspoon salt until smooth. Add chicken and celery; toss gently until well mixed.

Peel and halve cucumbers lengthwise; using tip of teaspoon, scoop out and discard seeds; generously salt. On lettuce leaves, spoon mixture into cucumber halves; top with peanuts. Makes 4 servings.

CRAB-STUFFED CUCUMBERS: In medium bowl, combine *½ cup diced celery, ½ cup mayonnaise, ¼ cup minced and drained pimento, 2 teaspoons lemon juice, ⅛ teaspoon Worcestershire* and *dash hot pepper sauce.* Add *two 6-ounce packages frozen Alaska King crab,* thawed and well drained; toss gently. Prepare and stuff cucumbers as above. Makes 4 servings.

CHUNKY EGG SALAD

¼ cup mayonnaise
1 tablespoon cider vinegar
1¼ teaspoons salt
1 teaspoon minced onion
½ teaspoon Worcestershire
dash pepper
6 hard-cooked eggs
1 cup thinly sliced celery
2 tablespoons minced green pepper
lettuce leaves
parsley for garnish

ABOUT 1 HOUR AHEAD OR EARLY IN DAY:
In medium bowl, stir first 6 ingredients until well mixed. Cut eggs into big pieces; add eggs, celery and green pepper to mixture; mix well. Cover and refrigerate.

TO SERVE:
Spoon mixture onto lettuce leaves and garnish with parsley. Makes 4 servings.

SHRIMP SALAD

2 cups cooked, shelled and deveined shrimp, chilled
1½ cups sliced celery
½ cup chopped California walnuts (optional)
¼ cup sliced stuffed olives
¼ cup French dressing
¼ cup mayonnaise
1 teaspoon minced onion
lettuce leaves

ABOUT 1 HOUR BEFORE SERVING:
Into large bowl, cut shrimp in halves lengthwise. Add all ingredients except lettuce leaves; toss to mix well; cover and refrigerate. Serve on lettuce leaves. Makes 6 servings.

LOBSTER OR CRAB SALAD: Prepare as above but substitute *cut-up cooked lobster* or rock-lobster tails or flaked, cooked crab for shrimp.

TUNA SALAD: Prepare as above but substitute *two 6½- or 7-ounce cans tuna,* flaked, for shrimp.

SALMON SALAD: Prepare as above but substitute *one 16-ounce can salmon,* drained and coarsely flaked, for shrimp; omit walnuts; add 2 *cut-up hard-cooked eggs.*

CRAB SALAD IN PINEAPPLE SHELLS

2 6-ounce packages frozen Alaska King crab, thawed and drained
3 cups cold cooked rice
1 cup coarsely chopped ripe olives
½ cup diced celery
½ cup chopped parsley
⅓ cup mayonnaise
3 tablespoons bottled creamy French dressing
1 teaspoon curry powder
1 large pineapple*

EARLY IN DAY:
In large bowl, gently toss all ingredients except pineapple; cover and refrigerate. Cut pineapple in half lengthwise; scoop out pineapple, leaving ½-inch-thick shells (*see* page 369); cover and refrigerate. Cut scooped pineapple into chunks; toss into crab mixture; cover and refrigerate.

TO SERVE:
Gently toss mixture and spoon into pineapple shells. Makes 6 main-course servings.

* Or, use one 15¼-ounce can pineapple chunks, drained; and serve on *lettuce leaves.*

CHEESE-AND-VEGETABLE SALAD

⅓ cup mayonnaise
1 tablespoon sugar
1 tablespoon lemon juice
½ teaspoon salt
1 16-ounce can lima beans, chilled and drained
1 6-ounce package Cheddar-cheese cubes, quartered
1 cup thinly sliced radishes
½ cup diced celery
⅓ cup diced sweet pickles
4 hard-cooked eggs, sliced
lettuce leaves

EARLY IN DAY:
In medium bowl, stir mayonnaise, sugar, lemon juice and salt until blended; add remaining ingredients except lettuce and gently toss. Cover and refrigerate.

JUST BEFORE SERVING:
Line salad bowl with lettuce; toss vegetables and spoon onto lettuce. Makes 6 servings.

CALICO BEAN SALAD

1 10-ounce package frozen baby lima beans
1 16-ounce can kidney beans
2 tablespoons brown sugar
2 tablespoons sweet-pickle relish
1 tablespoon cider vinegar
1 teaspoon cornstarch
1 pound hard salami, cubed
lettuce leaves

DAY BEFORE:
Cook lima beans as label directs; drain well and set aside. Drain kidney beans, reserving liquid; set aside.

In small saucepan over medium heat, heat to boiling reserved kidney-bean liquid, brown sugar, pickle relish, vinegar and cornstarch, stirring; remove from heat.

In large mixing bowl, toss salami, lima beans, kidney beans and sauce. Refrigerate, tossing occasionally.

TO SERVE:
Gently toss salad; spoon onto lettuce leaves. Makes 6 servings.

SUMMER SALAD-SANDWICH PLATE

1 4-ounce package thin-sliced turkey breast
1 4-ounce package thin-sliced ham
1 12-ounce container vegetable cottage cheese
8 slices rye bread or cheese bread
butter or margarine, softened
3 large tomatoes
½ cup mayonnaise
1 tablespoon prepared mustard
1 tablespoon drained capers
watercress for garnish

ABOUT 15 MINUTES BEFORE SERVING:
On narrow ends of turkey and ham slices, spoon cottage cheese; roll up. Onto 6 salad plates, arrange ham and turkey roll-ups.

Spread 4 bread slices with butter or margarine; top with remaining bread slices. Cut into thirds; arrange two on each plate.

Slice each tomato into 6 slices. Arrange 3 slices in overlapping pattern on each plate. In cup, with fork, blend mayonnaise and mustard; spoon onto tomatoes; sprinkle with capers. Garnish with watercress. Makes 6 servings.

CHICKEN-MELON SALAD

3 cups cut-up, cooked chicken
2½ cups seedless green grapes, halved
2 cups diced celery
1½ cups mayonnaise
⅓ cup milk
1½ tablespoons chutney
1½ teaspoons curry powder
¼ teaspoon salt
1½ large cantaloupes
lettuce leaves

ABOUT 2 HOURS AHEAD OR EARLY IN DAY:
In medium bowl, combine chicken, grapes and celery. In covered blender container at low speed (or in medium bowl, with slotted spoon), blend mayonnaise, milk, chutney, curry powder and salt until smooth; pour over chicken mixture; toss until well mixed. Cover and refrigerate.

ABOUT 10 MINUTES BEFORE SERVING:
Cut melons into 6 wedges; remove seeds and, with sharp knife, cut rind from wedges. Place wedges on lettuce leaves on individual plates. Spoon chicken salad on top of wedges. Makes 6 servings.

CURRIED SEAFOOD SALAD

¾ cup mayonnaise
2 tablespoons lemon juice
1 teaspoon curry powder
1 6½- or 7-ounce can tuna, drained
2 cups shelled and deveined cooked shrimp
½ cup chopped celery
1 10-ounce package frozen peas, cooked
4 cups cooked rice
¼ cup bottled Italian dressing
lettuce leaves
3 hard-cooked eggs, cut in wedges for garnish

EARLY IN DAY:
In large bowl, with fork, stir mayonnaise, lemon juice and curry powder until well blended. Add tuna, separated into chunks, shrimp, celery and peas; toss well. Cover and refrigerate. In medium bowl, toss rice with Italian dressing; cover and refrigerate.

Arrange ring of rice mixture in lettuce-leaf-lined salad bowl; spoon tuna mixture into center. Garnish with egg wedges. Makes 6 servings.

CHEF'S SALAD

1 garlic clove, halved (optional)
1 large head iceberg lettuce or romaine
1 cup thin strips cooked chicken or turkey
1 8-ounce package sliced Swiss cheese, cut in thin strips
1 6-ounce package sliced cooked ham, cut in thin strips
2 medium tomatoes, cut in wedges
2 hard-cooked eggs, quartered
Classic French Dressing (page 411) or Russian Dressing (page 410)

ABOUT 30 MINUTES BEFORE SERVING:
If you like, rub large, shallow salad bowl with garlic clove; discard garlic. Into bowl, tear lettuce into bite-size pieces. On lettuce, arrange chicken, Swiss cheese, ham, tomato and egg wedges. Just before serving, toss with dressing. Makes 6 servings.

TURKEY-ROQUEFORT SALAD

1 8-ounce container sour cream (1 cup)
1 3-ounce wedge or 2 1¼-ounce wedges Roquefort cheese,* crumbled
1 teaspoon salt
3 cups cut-up, cooked turkey or chicken
lettuce leaves or chicory
1 29-ounce can cling-peach halves, drained

EARLY IN DAY:
In medium bowl, with wire whisk or fork, mix sour cream with Roquefort and salt until well blended. Gently stir in turkey until well coated; cover and refrigerate.

TO SERVE:
Arrange lettuce leaves and 6 peach halves on chilled serving plate. Gently stir turkey mixture and spoon over peach halves, dividing equally among halves. (Refrigerate remaining peach halves to use another day.) Makes 6 servings.

* Or, use one 4-ounce package blue cheese.

STUFFED TOMATOES

For each serving, use 1 medium tomato. If you like, peel tomato. Cut ¼ inch from stem end; also cut very thin slice from bottom so tomato will stay upright on lettuce leaves.

With melon baller or measuring tablespoon, scoop out pulp from tomato, leaving shell (save pulp to use in soup, sauce or gravy, another day). Sprinkle inside of tomato with salt or seasoned salt; fill with any favorite salad mixture such as Chunky Egg Salad, Shrimp or Crab Salad or Tuna Salad (page 406); Rice or Macaroni Salad (page 397); Deluxe Coleslaw (page 396); or cottage cheese. Serve on lettuce leaves.

Or, cut each tomato vertically into 5 or 6 sections almost but not quite through bottom; spread sections apart slightly; place on lettuce leaves. Spoon on (or scoop) one serving of any of salads suggested above. If you like, garnish with capers, diced green pepper or chopped green onions.

STUFFED AVOCADO SALAD

For each serving, use 1 small or ½ medium or large avocado. Halve, peel and pit avocado; cut very thin slice from underside of each half so avocado stays upright on lettuce leaves; brush halves on all sides with lemon juice. Place on lettuce leaves; top with generous spoonful or scoop of Shrimp, Lobster or Crab Salad (page 406); Chicken Salad or Ham and Chicken Salad (page 404); Chunky Egg Salad (page 406); or cottage cheese. Or, fill with halved cooked shrimp, flaked cooked crab or diced cooked lobster; top with Sauce Remoulade (page 411).

CURRIED SHRIMP SALAD

salt
2 pounds medium shrimp, shelled and deveined
⅓ cup mayonnaise
1 tablespoon lemon juice
¾ teaspoon curry powder
¼ cup chopped green onions
4 lettuce leaves

EARLY IN DAY:
In large saucepan over high heat, heat 6 cups water and 1 tablespoon salt to boiling; add shrimp and heat to boiling; cook 1 or 2 minutes until shrimp turn pink; drain. Cover and refrigerate.

JUST BEFORE SERVING:
In medium bowl, with fork, stir mayonnaise,

lemon juice, 1 teaspoon salt and curry powder. Gently toss in shrimp and green onions; serve on lettuce leaves. Makes 4 servings.

OLD-FASHIONED SHRIMP SALAD: Prepare as above but omit curry powder and add *1 cup sliced celery.*

HAM-AND-CHEESE SALAD

1 10-ounce package frozen peas
½ cup mayonnaise
¼ cup pickle relish
2 tablespoons minced onion
¾ teaspoon salt
2 cups cut-up, cooked ham
¾ cup shredded American cheese
½ cup chopped celery
lettuce leaves

EARLY IN DAY:
Prepare peas as label directs; drain and cool. In medium bowl, with fork, stir mayonnaise, relish, onion and salt until well mixed. Add peas, ham and remaining ingredients except lettuce leaves and toss until well mixed; cover and refrigerate.

AT SERVING TIME:
Spoon mixture onto lettuce leaves. Makes about 4 servings.

CURRIED TUNA SALAD

2 6½- or 7-ounce cans tuna
3 cups cold cooked rice
2 cups chopped celery
1 10-ounce package frozen mixed vegetables, cooked, drained and cooled
¾ cup bottled French dressing
½ cup chopped chutney
1 teaspoon curry powder
lettuce leaves or chicory

EARLY IN DAY:
In large bowl, gently toss all ingredients except lettuce leaves until well mixed; cover and refrigerate.

AT SERVING TIME:
Line salad bowl with lettuce. Toss tuna mixture again and spoon onto lettuce. Makes 6 servings.

Salad Dressings

TARRAGON-CREAM DRESSING

½ cup sour cream
1 tablespoon tarragon vinegar
¼ teaspoon sugar
¼ teaspoon salt
¼ teaspoon tarragon

In cup, stir all ingredients until well mixed. Makes about ½ cup.

SOUR-CREAM DRESSING

½ cup sour cream
1 tablespoon lemon juice or cider vinegar
¾ teaspoon salt

In cup, stir all ingredients until well mixed. Makes about ½ cup.

COLESLAW DRESSING

½ cup mayonnaise or cooked salad dressing
1 tablespoon milk
1 tablespoon vinegar or lemon juice
½ teaspoon sugar
¼ teaspoon salt
dash paprika
dash pepper

In cup, stir all ingredients until well blended. Cover and refrigerate. Makes about ½ cup.

TARRAGON-VINEGAR DRESSING

¾ cup salad oil
½ cup tarragon vinegar
2 tablespoons sugar
2 teaspoons garlic salt
1 teaspoon monosodium glutamate
¼ teaspoon pepper

In bowl or covered jar, combine all ingredients; stir with fork or shake until well blended. Cover and refrigerate. Stir or shake before using. Makes about 1¼ cups.

THOUSAND ISLAND DRESSING

1 cup mayonnaise
2 tablespoons chili sauce
2 tablespoons minced green pepper
1 tablespoon chopped parsley
1 teaspoon grated onion

In small bowl, stir all ingredients until well mixed. Makes about 1⅓ cups.

RUSSIAN DRESSING

1 cup mayonnaise
3 tablespoons chili sauce
1 teaspoon minced onion or chopped chives

In small bowl, stir all ingredients until well mixed. Makes about 1 cup.

ROQUEFORT MAYONNAISE

½ cup mayonnaise
½ cup French dressing
¼ cup crumbled Roquefort cheese

In small bowl, stir all ingredients until well mixed. Makes about 1⅓ cups.

TARRAGON MAYONNAISE

1 cup mayonnaise
1 tablespoon chopped parsley
1 teaspoon tarragon

In small bowl, stir all ingredients until well mixed. Makes about 1 cup.

CHUTNEY MAYONNAISE

1 cup mayonnaise
¼ cup chopped chutney

In small bowl, stir all ingredients until well mixed. Makes about 1 cup.

CURRY MAYONNAISE

1 cup mayonnaise
1 teaspoon curry powder
¼ teaspoon garlic powder (optional)

In small bowl, stir all ingredients until well mixed. Makes about 1 cup.

LOUIS DRESSING

1 cup mayonnaise
¼ cup French dressing
¼ cup chili sauce
1 teaspoon horseradish
1 teaspoon Worcestershire
dash salt
dash pepper

In small bowl, stir all ingredients until well mixed. Makes about 1⅓ cups.

CURRANT-CREAM MAYONNAISE

¼ cup heavy or whipping cream
2 tablespoons currant jelly
½ cup mayonnaise

In small bowl, with hand beater, beat cream until soft peaks form. In cup, with fork, beat jelly until smooth. Fold jelly and mayonnaise into whipped cream. Makes about 1 cup.

DILL MAYONNAISE

1 cup mayonnaise
⅓ cup chopped dill weed
¼ cup minced onion
1 teaspoon grated lemon peel

In small bowl, stir all ingredients until well mixed. Makes about 1 cup.

BLUE-CHEESE-AND-HERB DRESSING

¼ pound blue cheese
1 small garlic clove, minced
3 tablespoons lemon juice
3 tablespoons tarragon vinegar
2 tablespoons bottled steak sauce
2 tablespoons red wine (optional)
1 tablespoon Worcestershire
1 tablespoon prepared mustard
½ teaspoon salt
½ teaspoon seasoned pepper
2 cups salad oil

In large bowl, with mixer at low speed, beat all ingredients except salad oil until well blended; gradually beat in salad oil; pour into jar; cover and refrigerate.

To serve, let dressing warm to room temperature; stir with fork. Makes about 3 cups salad dressing.

COOKED SALAD DRESSING

2 tablespoons all-purpose flour
2 tablespoons sugar
1¼ teaspoons salt
½ teaspoon dry mustard
dash cayenne pepper
2 eggs
⅓ cup lemon juice or cider vinegar
few drops Worcestershire
3 tablespoons salad oil

In small saucepan, combine flour, sugar, salt, mustard and cayenne pepper. In small bowl, with wire whisk, beat eggs and 1 cup water; stir into flour mixture until smooth. Gradually stir in lemon juice and Worcestershire.

Cook over low heat, stirring constantly, until thickened. Remove from heat; stir in salad oil; pour into bowl or jar; cover; refrigerate until well chilled. Makes about 2 cups.

TANGY COLESLAW DRESSING: Prepare as above but increase mustard to 1 teaspoon.

HORSERADISH DRESSING: Prepare as above but add *1 to 2 tablespoons horseradish* after removing from heat.

BLENDER MAYONNAISE

olive or salad oil
1 egg
2 tablespoons cider vinegar
1 teaspoon sugar
1 teaspoon dry mustard
¾ teaspoon salt
dash white pepper

In covered blender container at low speed, blend ¼ cup oil and remaining ingredients for 1 or 2 seconds until thoroughly mixed. Remove center of cover (or cover) and, at low speed, very slowly pour ¾ cup oil in steady stream into mixture; continue blending until well mixed. Makes about 1¼ cups.

MIXER MAYONNAISE: In small bowl, with mixer at medium speed, combine all above ingredients except oil. At high speed, add ¼ cup oil, ½ teaspoon at a time; then, still beating, *very slowly* pour ¾ cup oil in thin steady stream into mixture; continue beating until well mixed.

SAUCE REMOULADE

1 cup mayonnaise
2 tablespoons chopped sour pickles, drained
1 tablespoon chopped capers, drained
1 tablespoon chopped parsley
1 teaspoon prepared mustard
¼ teaspoon tarragon

In small bowl, stir all ingredients until well mixed. Makes about 1¼ cups.

CLASSIC FRENCH DRESSING

¾ cup olive or salad oil
¼ cup cider or wine vinegar
¾ teaspoon salt
dash pepper

Into small bowl or covered jar, measure all ingredients; stir with fork or cover and shake until mixed. Cover; refrigerate. Stir or shake before serving. Makes 1 cup.

ANCHOVY: Prepare as above but stir in *1 tablespoon anchovy paste.* Makes 1 cup.

GARLIC: Prepare as above but add *1 garlic clove,* crushed. Makes 1 cup.

ROQUEFORT OR BLUE CHEESE: Prepare as above but add *½ cup crumbled Roquefort or blue cheese.* Makes about 1⅓ cups.

MIXED HERB: Prepare as above but add *2 teaspoons chopped parsley* and *½ teaspoon tarragon or basil.* Makes 1 cup.

DELUXE GARLIC FRENCH DRESSING

1¼ cups olive or salad oil
½ cup cider vinegar or lemon juice
3 tablespoons chili sauce
2¼ teaspoons salt
1 teaspoon sugar
1 teaspoon horseradish
1 teaspoon prepared mustard
½ teaspoon paprika
¼ teaspoon pepper
2 garlic cloves, crushed

Into small bowl or covered jar, measure all ingredients; stir with fork or cover and shake until well blended. Cover and refrigerate. Stir or shake before serving. Makes about 1¾ cups.

HONEY-CARAWAY SALAD DRESSING

¾ cup mayonnaise
2 tablespoons honey
1 tablespoon lemon juice
1 tablespoon caraway seed

In small bowl, with wire whisk or fork, stir all ingredients until blended; cover and refrigerate. Stir before using. Makes about 1 cup.

COLONEL'S LADY'S SALAD DRESSING

¾ cup salad oil
½ cup white wine vinegar
3 tablespoons sugar
3 tablespoons chopped parsley
1½ teaspoons garlic salt
1½ teaspoons salt
¾ teaspoon oregano leaves
½ teaspoon seasoned pepper

Into pint jar, measure all ingredients. Cover and shake well; refrigerate. Shake before using. Makes about 1½ cups.

CREAMY BLUE-CHEESE DRESSING

4 ounces blue cheese, crumbled (about ½ cup)
3 tablespoons half-and-half
½ cup mayonnaise or cooked salad dressing
6 tablespoons olive or salad oil
¼ cup white wine vinegar
1 teaspoon prepared mustard
⅛ teaspoon salt
⅛ teaspoon pepper

In small bowl, with fork, mash cheese with half-and-half until creamy. Add rest of ingredients; with hand beater or wire whisk, beat until well mixed. Cover and refrigerate. Makes about 1 cup.

MINT DRESSING

½ cup light corn syrup
¼ cup lime juice
2 tablespoons chopped mint leaves

In small bowl, stir all ingredients. Makes about ¾ cup.

CREAMY GINGER-CHEESE DRESSING

1 8-ounce package cream cheese, softened
¼ cup milk
2 tablespoons sugar
3 tablespoons lemon juice
¾ teaspoon ginger

In small bowl, with mixer at medium speed, beat all ingredients until smooth. Makes about 1⅓ cups.

MINT-LIME DRESSING

¼ cup lime juice
1 cup mint leaves
2 3-ounce packages cream cheese, softened
⅓ cup sugar

In covered blender container at medium speed, blend lime juice and mint until mint is finely chopped. Add cream cheese and sugar; blend at medium speed just until smooth. (Do not overblend or dressing will be thin.) Makes about 1⅓ cups.

PARMESAN DRESSING

1 garlic clove, halved
¾ cup salad oil
¼ cup lemon juice
2 tablespoons grated Parmesan cheese
¾ teaspoon salt
¼ teaspoon sugar

In covered jar, combine all ingredients; shake until well blended; refrigerate. Discard garlic and shake before serving. Makes about 1 cup.

THICK FRUIT DRESSING

½ cup sugar
1 teaspoon paprika
½ teaspoon dry mustard
½ teaspoon salt
¼ cup cider vinegar
¾ cup salad oil
2 teaspoons poppy seed

In small bowl, with mixer at low speed, beat sugar and next 4 ingredients until just mixed. At medium speed, slowly beat in oil until thickened. Beat in poppy seed. Cover and refrigerate; stir before serving, if needed. Makes about 1¼ cups.

Quick breads

Quick breads, unlike yeast breads, rise with the help of quick-acting leavening (baking powder, steam, etc.) and are generally baked or cooked as soon as the dough is mixed.

Many quick breads are at their best served hot from the oven or warm. Nut and fruit loaves, however, will have a mellower flavor and be easier to slice if they are baked the day before; if sliced while hot, they may crumble. Others, like doughnuts, are good warm *or* cold.

Tips for Perfect Quick Breads

Pans: Biscuits and muffins will brown best if shiny metal cookie sheets and pans are used for baking them. For browning loaves, use loaf pans made of dull metal, anodized aluminum or glass.

For best results, use loaf pans of the size called for. Larger pans will result in thinner loaves. If your pans are smaller, fill them no more than ⅔ full and bake the rest of the batter in greased custard cups; baking time for the cups will be shorter than that for the loaves; start testing for doneness after 20 minutes in the oven.

In our kitchens, we usually use muffin pans with 2½-inch cups. If your muffin-pan cups are a different size, fill them ⅔ full for muffins, half full for popovers.

Mixing: When assembling ingredients for these breads, unless the recipe directs otherwise, always stir dry ingredients together for even distribution.

Don't overmix. Be sure to mix ingredients only as long as the recipe specifies. Otherwise some quick breads may be coarse-textured and tough.

Biscuits: Mix the dough just until it leaves the side of the bowl; it will still be sticky. For rolled biscuits, turn dough out onto a floured surface and knead a few strokes just to blend ingredients (so biscuits are fine-textured) and make dough easy to handle.

Biscuits double in size as they bake; so roll dough to half the thickness you want in the baked biscuit. For high biscuits, roll dough ½ inch thick; for crusty, thin biscuits, roll it ¼ inch thick.

To keep biscuit tops level, when cutting, press the floured cutter straight down without twisting; or cut with firm downward strokes with floured, sharp knife. Then use a wide spatula or pancake turner to transfer biscuits to cookie sheet.

Cut biscuits close together, to keep rerolling to a minimum. To reroll, press, don't knead, trimmings lightly together; roll and cut.

For crusty biscuits, place them at least 1 inch apart on cookie sheet. For biscuits with soft sides, place them close together in a shallow baking pan.

Muffins: Perfect muffins are tender, even-textured and slightly rounded on top. Overmixing makes them tough, with tunnels and peaked tops. For best results, stir dry ingredients to mix well, then add liquid ingredients all at once and stir *just a few strokes* until flour is moistened. Batter will be lumpy, not smooth.

After spooning batter into muffin-pan cups, wipe off any that spills on the pan. Half-fill any empty cups with water.

When muffins are done, remove them at once from the cups so they don't steam and soften. If they must stand, tip each one slightly in its cup so steam can evaporate.

Nut and fruit loaves: To test for doneness, insert a toothpick into center of loaf at end of minimum baking time. If recipe says it should come out clean, there should be no crumbs clinging to it. If bread is very moist and recipe states toothpick should come out almost clean, loaf is done if only a few crumbs cling to toothpick.

Don't worry if loaf is cracked on top; a deep crack down center of quick-bread loaves is typical.

To serve, cut bread in thin slices.

Pancakes and waffles: When mixing batter, stir quickly just until flour is moistened; batter will be lumpy.

If pancake griddle or waffle baker is not automatic, test temperature by sprinkling griddle with a few drops of water; drops should sizzle. If using electric skillet, griddle or waffle baker, follow manufacturer's directions.

For a regular-size pancake, pour batter from a ¼-cup measure; for a dollar-size one, use a measuring tablespoonful of batter. After pouring batter for pancake, cook until top is bubbly. When edges begin to look dry and some bubbles burst, turn pancake and brown on underside.

When baking waffles, pour batter into center of baker; then close lid quickly and don't open until the waffle stops steaming or the light on the waffle baker goes out. Bake a little longer for crisp waffles, or leave waffle on the baker a few seconds after the cover is lifted.

If pancake or waffle batter becomes too thick on standing, thin to desired pouring consistency with a little more liquid (milk or buttermilk). Refrigerate any leftover batter and use it next day.

Keep pancakes and waffles warm by placing on rack in oven preheated to 250°F.

Doughnuts: Dough should be soft or doughnuts will be tough. After mixing dough, refrigerate at least 1 hour to make it easier to handle. Roll out on well-floured surface and cut with well-floured doughnut cutter. Cut doughnuts as close together as possible, to reduce amount of rerolling necessary (so last doughnuts are not tough). Press dough trimmings together, reroll and cut. After cutting doughnuts, lift them with pancake turner (so they don't twist or stretch); place in hot deep fat. When doughnuts rise to the surface, turn with slotted spoon, tongs or two-tined fork, being careful not to prick dough; then fry, turning occasionally, until both sides are golden. Lift from fat with slotted spoon, tongs or two-tined fork and drain on paper towels.

To Serve Breads Hot

If dish in which breads are baked is attractive, leave them in it for serving; they'll keep warm longer. Otherwise, line a basket or plate with a napkin; arrange hot bread on napkin, then bring napkin corners up to cover bread and keep heat in. Or, use range-top or electric bun warmer as manufacturer directs.

To Reheat Quick Breads

Biscuits: Wrap leftover biscuits in foil; heat in oven preheated to 375°F. about 20 minutes or until hot.

Or, put 2 tablespoons water in large skillet over low heat or electric skillet set at 200°F. Place rack in bottom; arrange biscuits on rack. Cover; heat over low heat 8 to 10 minutes until hot.

Or, preheat broiler if manufacturer directs. Split biscuits; spread split sides with softened butter or margarine. Sprinkle with shredded cheese; celery, poppy or caraway seed; or cinnamon and sugar. Or, spread with pasteurized process cheese spread, garlic spread or softened plain or flavored cream cheese. Toast in broiler until golden and hot.

Muffins: Wrap in foil; heat in oven preheated to 400°F. about 15 minutes. Or, split muffins; spread split sides with softened butter or margarine; toast in broiler.

Corn bread: Split servings; spread split sides with softened butter or margarine and toast in broiler. If you like, sprinkle with celery, poppy or sesame seed, or spread with jelly before broiling.

Boston brown bread: Place in double boiler or colander over pan of simmering water; cover and heat. Or, slice; spread slices with butter or margarine and toast in broiler.

To heat canned brown bread, *remove from can;* place in double boiler or colander over pan of simmering water; cover and heat.

Coffeecake: Wrap in foil; heat in oven preheated to 400°F. 20 to 30 minutes. Or, reheat in covered skillet as Biscuits, above.

To Store Quick Breads

Biscuits, muffins and doughnuts are at their best if served when freshly made. Leftovers may be stored at room temperature, wrapped tightly to retain moisture. Reheat and use within a day or so.

Nut and fruit loaves, at their best if made the day before using, should be cooled completely, then wrapped closely and kept at room temperature until served.

To Freeze Quick Breads

Cool nut and fruit loaves completely, then wrap in foil, heavy-duty plastic wrap or freezer-wrap and press all air from package; freeze for up to 3 months. To thaw, let stand, wrapped, at room temperature about 1½ hours. Slice and serve.

When planning to freeze waffles, bake only until lightly browned. Cool completely on wire racks; wrap as above. Or, freeze them on cookie sheets, then place in heavy-duty plastic bags and seal; freeze for 1 to 2 months. To thaw, remove from package and toast in toaster.

Doughnuts should be fried in hot, fresh salad oil or shortening, then drained well and cooled completely. Package in freezer cartons or in heavy-duty plastic bags; freeze for 4 to 6 months. To thaw, unwrap; wrap in foil and heat in oven preheated to 400°F.

Because biscuits and muffins can be made so quickly, it doesn't save time to make them ahead, freeze and then thaw them.

Double-Quick Quick Breads

At the bakery and in the bakery section of the supermarket, you'll find ready-to-eat quick breads of all types, ranging from biscuits to coffeecakes and doughnuts. When you shop, look too for other products that turn out delectable breads with very little work: mixes for biscuits, muffins, coffeecakes, corn bread, nut and fruit bread, pancakes, waffles; ready-to-bake refrigerated breads; frozen waffles, pancakes, corn cakes and sticks. Some of these products can be used to make more than one kind of bread; check the labels for directions. And of course see the recipes in this chapter that use these products.

Ways to Serve Butter or Margarine

Early in day or several days ahead, make the butter or margarine shapes below. Keep refrigerated in covered bowl of iced water until time to use; drain; arrange in chilled serving dish and serve.

BUTTER BALLS: In iced water, chill wooden

butter paddles very well. Cut firm ¼-pound bar of butter or margarine into ½-inch-thick pats. Place a pat between paddles; holding bottom paddle steady, rotate top paddle to form ball. If butter sticks, rechill paddles in iced water.

For cylinders, flatten balls and roll between paddles.

Drop balls or cylinders into iced water to cover.

BUTTER MOLDS: Dip butter molds in boiling water, then chill in iced water. Quickly pack with butter or margarine; level off with knife; press out and refrigerate molded butter. Chill molds in iced water before using again. If butter sticks, redip in boiling water; rechill.

BUTTER CURLS: Let butter curler stand in hot water 10 minutes to heat. Pulling lightly, bring curler straight across ¼-pound bar of firm butter or margarine (if bar is too cold, curls will break). Drop shell-like curls into bowl of iced water to chill; cover bowl and refrigerate. Reheat curler briefly in hot water each time.

Biscuits, Muffins, Popovers

BISCUITS

2 cups all-purpose flour
1 tablespoon double-acting baking powder
1 teaspoon salt
¼ cup shortening
¾ cup milk

ABOUT 35 MINUTES BEFORE SERVING:
Preheat oven to 450°F. In large bowl, with fork, mix flour, baking powder and salt. With pastry blender or 2 knives used scissor-fashion, cut in shortening until mixture resembles coarse crumbs; add milk. With fork, quickly mix just until mixture forms soft dough that leaves side of bowl.

Turn dough onto lightly floured surface; knead 6 to 8 strokes to mix thoroughly. With floured rolling pin, lightly roll out dough, lifting rolling pin as you near edges to keep dough evenly thick. Roll dough ½ inch thick for high, fluffy biscuits, ¼ inch thick for thin, crusty ones.

With floured 2-inch biscuit cutter, cut biscuits, using straight downward motion without twisting. With pancake turner, place biscuits on ungreased cookie sheet, 1 inch apart for crusty biscuits, nearly touching for soft-sided ones. Press dough trimmings together (don't knead); roll and cut as above until all dough is used. Bake 12 to 15 minutes until golden. Makes about 18 biscuits.

BUTTERMILK: Prepare as above but use *buttermilk* in place of milk and use only 2 teaspoons baking powder; add *¼ teaspoon baking soda* to flour mixture. Makes about 18.

SPEEDY: Prepare as above but after rolling dough, cut with knife into squares, triangles or diamonds; bake as directed.

DROP: Prepare as above but increase milk to 1 cup. With fork, stir dough until well mixed; don't knead. Onto ungreased cookie sheet, drop heaping tablespoonfuls of mixture 1 inch apart; or fill greased muffin-pan cups half full. Bake as directed. Makes about 20.

EXTRA-RICH: Prepare as above but use ⅓ cup shortening.

HEAD-START: Prepare buttermilk baking mix as label directs for rolled or drop biscuits.

SUGAR-TOP BISCUITS

Roll out and cut Biscuits or Head-Start Biscuits as above; place on cookie sheet. For each biscuit, quickly dip *small sugar cube* into *cold coffee* or orange juice; press into top of each biscuit. Bake as directed.

BISCUITS PLUS

Prepare Biscuits, Drop Biscuits or Head-Start Biscuits as recipe or label directs, but add one of suggestions below to flour mixture before adding liquid:

BACON: *½ cup crumbled cooked bacon.*

CHEESE: *¼ to ½ cup shredded sharp Cheddar cheese.*

CHIVES: *¼ cup chopped chives.*

CURRY: *¼ teaspoon curry powder.*

HAM: *⅔ cup chopped cooked ham.*

Orange-Spinach Salad, page 393

HERB: *1¼ teaspoons caraway seed, ½ teaspoon ground sage* and *¼ teaspoon dry mustard.*

LEMON: *Grated peel of 1 lemon.*

DROP BISCUITS PLUS

FRUITED DROP BISCUITS: Grease cookie sheet. Make Drop Biscuits (opposite) but add *¼ cup sugar* and *½ teaspoon cinnamon* to flour mixture. Add *one 8¾-ounce can fruit cocktail,* well drained, with milk or water.

BLUEBERRY DROP BISCUITS: Grease cookie sheet. Make Drop Biscuits (opposite) but stir *1 cup well-drained blueberries* into flour mixture. Sprinkle tops of biscuits with *sugar* before baking.

QUICK STICKY BUNS: Grease twelve 2½-inch muffin-pan cups. In small bowl, with fork, mix *½ cup packed brown sugar, ¼ cup chopped nuts, ¼ cup honey* and *2 tablespoons butter or margarine,* softened. Spoon 1 tablespoon mixture into each cup. Make Drop Biscuits (opposite); spoon dough on top of mixture in each cup. Bake. To serve, invert on serving plate; let stand a minute or two; remove pan.

THUMBPRINT BISCUITS: Grease twelve 2½-inch muffin-pan cups. Make Drop Biscuits (opposite); spoon dough into cups. With thumb, make slight indentation in top of each biscuit; fill with one of toppings, below. Bake.

Toppings: Drained, canned crushed pineapple, sprinkle of brown sugar; dot of butter or margarine, a little brown sugar, a little shredded or flaked coconut or chopped nuts; shredded orange or lemon peel, sprinkle of sugar; dot of butter or margarine, sprinkle of garlic salt or mixed herbs; 1 teaspoon favorite jelly or jam.

PARTY PINWHEELS

ABOUT 35 MINUTES BEFORE SERVING:
Preheat oven to 400°F. Grease well a cookie sheet or twelve 2½-inch muffin-pan cups, as recipe below specifies. Prepare dough for Biscuits or Head-Start Biscuits (opposite). On lightly floured surface, with floured rolling pin, roll dough into 12" by 8" rectangle. Spread dough with one of spreads below; roll up from long side, jelly-roll fashion; cut roll into 1-inch-thick slices. Place slices, flat side down, on cookie sheet or in muffin-pan cups. Bake as directed.

SAVORY: Sprinkle dough with *½ cup shredded Cheddar cheese,* deviled ham or corned-beef spread. Bake on cookie sheet about 12 minutes or until golden.

SWEET: Spread dough with *marmalade.* Bake on cookie sheet about 12 minutes or until golden.

BUTTERSCOTCH: Brush dough with *2 tablespoons melted butter or margarine.* Sprinkle with *¼ cup cinnamon-sugar mixture,* then with *½ cup golden or dark seedless raisins.* Bake in muffin-pan cups about 15 minutes or until golden.

PECAN: Prepare Butterscotch Pinwheels as above but in each muffin-pan cup, place *1 teaspoon butter or margarine, 1 teaspoon brown sugar* and *2 or 3 pecan halves;* top with pinwheels and bake.

ONION-CHEESE BISCUITS

2½ cups all-purpose flour
1 tablespoon double-acting baking powder
½ teaspoon salt
½ cup butter or margarine
2 4-ounce packages shredded Cheddar cheese (2 cups)
½ cup minced onions
1 egg
1 cup milk

ABOUT 40 MINUTES BEFORE SERVING:
Preheat oven to 425°F. Grease a large cookie sheet. In large bowl, with fork, mix flour, baking powder and salt. With pastry blender or 2 knives used scissor-fashion, cut in butter or margarine until mixture resembles coarse crumbs. Stir in cheese and onions.

In small bowl, with fork, beat egg and milk until well mixed; stir into flour mixture just until flour is moistened. Onto cookie sheet, drop heaping tablespoonfuls of dough about 1 inch apart. Bake 15 to 20 minutes until biscuits are golden. Makes about 18 biscuits.

Puffy Omelet with Fillings, page 273

GARLIC QUICK BREAD

3½ cups all-purpose flour
3 tablespoons sugar
1 tablespoon double-acting baking powder
1½ teaspoons salt
¼ cup butter or margarine
1¼ cups milk
1 egg
2 small garlic cloves, crushed

ABOUT 2 HOURS BEFORE SERVING:
Preheat oven to 375°F. Grease well a 9″ by 5″ loaf pan. In large bowl, with fork, mix flour, sugar, baking powder and salt. With pastry blender or two knives used scissor-fashion, cut in butter or margarine until mixture resembles coarse crumbs. Add remaining ingredients; stir until moistened.

Turn dough onto well-floured surface; knead until smooth and not sticky, about 5 minutes. Shape dough into a loaf; place in pan. With knife, make 6 diagonal slashes, ¼-inch deep, across top of bread. Bake 1 hour and 10 minutes or until golden. Remove from pan immediately onto wire rack; cool 30 minutes. Makes 1 loaf.

SCONES

1¾ cups all-purpose flour
2½ teaspoons double-acting baking powder
sugar
½ teaspoon salt
6 tablespoons butter or margarine
2 eggs
⅓ cup milk

ABOUT 40 MINUTES BEFORE SERVING:
Preheat oven to 425°F. Grease large cookie sheet. In medium bowl, with fork, mix flour, baking powder, 1 tablespoon sugar and salt. With pastry blender or 2 knives used scissor-fashion, cut in butter or margarine until mixture resembles coarse crumbs. In cup, with fork, beat eggs; reserve 1 tablespoon. Stir milk into remaining beaten eggs; stir egg mixture into flour mixture until well mixed.

Turn dough onto lightly floured surface; with floured rolling pin, lightly roll dough ½ inch thick. With knife, cut dough into 3-inch squares; cut each square into 2 triangles. With pancake turner, place triangles 1 inch apart on cookie sheet; brush with reserved egg and sprinkle with 2 tablespoons sugar. Bake 10 to 15 minutes until golden. Makes 10 to 12 scones.

JAM-FILLED: Prepare as above but roll dough ¼ inch thick; cut into 3-inch squares. Place 1 teaspoon of *favorite jam* in center of each square; moisten edges. Fold opposite corners together to make triangle and press with tines of fork to seal. Makes 16.

DAINTY: Cut dough into 2-inch rounds; reroll and cut trimmings. Makes about 20.

TOASTED: Bake scones day before. To serve, split and brush with *melted butter or margarine;* toast in broiler until golden.

RAISIN: Prepare as above but add *½ cup dark seedless raisins* with milk. Serve hot or cold with butter and jam.

QUICK UPSIDE-DOWN BISCUITS

ABOUT 30 MINUTES BEFORE SERVING:
Preheat oven to 400°F. In each of 8 or 10 lightly buttered muffin-pan cups, place one of Glazes below; top with biscuit from *one 8- or 9.5-ounce package refrigerated regular or flaky biscuits.* Bake 12 minutes or until golden; remove from oven and let stand ½ minute. Invert pan onto platter and let stand 5 minutes; remove pan. Makes 8 or 10 biscuits.

HONEY-NUT GLAZE: In each cup, place *3 pecan halves, 1 teaspoon honey;* sprinkle with *cinnamon.*

BUTTERSCOTCH-NUT GLAZE: In each cup, place *½ teaspoon melted butter or margarine, 1 teaspoon dark corn syrup;* stir; top with *3 pecan halves.*

PINEAPPLE GLAZE: In each cup, place *½ teaspoon melted butter or margarine* and *1 teaspoon brown sugar;* stir; top with *2 teaspoons drained, canned crushed pineapple.*

ORANGE GLAZE: In small saucepan over low heat, heat *½ cup sugar, ¼ cup orange juice, ¼ cup butter or margarine* and *2 teaspoons shredded orange peel* to boiling. Reduce heat to low; simmer 5 minutes. Spoon into muffin-pan cups.

BLUEBERRY BISCUITS

1 9.5-ounce package refrigerated flaky biscuits
½ cup blueberries
sugar
1 tablespoon grated lemon peel
melted butter or margarine

ABOUT 30 MINUTES BEFORE SERVING:
Preheat oven to 400°F. Grease ten 2½-inch muffin-pan cups. With fingers, separate each biscuit into halves horizontally.

In small bowl, combine blueberries, 2 tablespoons sugar and lemon peel. Spoon a little of the blueberry mixture in the center of one half of each biscuit; top with the other half. With fingers, pinch edges together to seal. Repeat with remaining biscuits.

Place biscuits in muffin-pan cups. Brush tops with melted butter or margarine; sprinkle with sugar. Bake 12 minutes or until rich golden brown. Makes 10 biscuits.

PAN ROLLS PRONTO

3 tablespoons butter or margarine, melted
2 8-ounce packages refrigerated flaky biscuits

ABOUT 35 MINUTES BEFORE SERVING:
Preheat oven to 400°F. In 9-inch round cake pan, melt butter or margarine. With hands, gently shape biscuits from both packages into balls; roll in butter or margarine in pan to coat balls. Bake 25 minutes or until brown. Makes 20 rolls.

QUICK BISCUIT BREAD

2 8- or 9.5-ounce packages refrigerated flaky biscuits
1 tablespoon butter or margarine, melted

ABOUT 40 MINUTES BEFORE SERVING:
Preheat oven to 400°F. Grease 9″ by 5″ loaf pan. In pan, arrange biscuits in two rows; brush with butter or margarine. Bake 25 to 30 minutes until top is golden brown. Cool bread slightly in pan. Makes 6 to 8 servings.

QUICK BOW-KNOT ROLLS

1 8- or 9.5-ounce package refrigerated biscuits
1 egg, slightly beaten
toppings: poppy or caraway seed, instant minced onion, or garlic or celery salt

ABOUT 25 MINUTES BEFORE SERVING:
Preheat oven to 425°F. Grease cookie sheet. With hands, roll each biscuit into 7-inch stick; tie each in a loose knot and place on cookie sheet. Brush with egg; sprinkle with one of toppings. Bake 10 minutes or until golden brown. Makes 8 or 10 rolls.

GARLIC STICKS

2 tablespoons butter or margarine
2 tablespoons chopped parsley
¾ teaspoon garlic salt
1 8- or 9.5-ounce package refrigerated biscuits

ABOUT 20 MINUTES BEFORE SERVING:
Preheat oven to 450°F. Grease a large cookie sheet. In small saucepan over medium heat, heat butter or margarine, parsley and garlic salt just until butter or margarine is melted.

Cut each biscuit in half; with hands, roll each half into a stick about 6 inches long. Brush each stick with butter-parsley mixture. Place on cookie sheet about 1 inch apart. Bake 5 to 8 minutes until golden. Makes 20 breadsticks.

QUICK CHEESE BREAD

2 8-ounce packages refrigerated biscuits
½ cup pasteurized process cheese spread

ABOUT 30 MINUTES BEFORE SERVING:
Preheat oven to 375°F. Grease 8″ by 8″ baking pan. Cut each biscuit into fourths; arrange in baking pan. Bake 20 minutes or until golden brown. Remove pan from oven; spread cheese spread over tops of biscuits. Return pan to oven and bake just until cheese spread melts, about 3 minutes. To serve, separate biscuits with a fork. Makes 10 servings.

QUICK FRENCH BREAD

2 8- or 9.5-ounce packages refrigerated flaky biscuits
1 egg
1 tablespoon sesame seed

ABOUT 45 MINUTES BEFORE SERVING:
Preheat oven to 350°F. Grease cookie sheet. Without separating biscuits, place rolls of dough end to end on cookie sheet, pressing biscuits together lightly and shaping into a long loaf. In cup, with fork, beat egg slightly; brush over loaf; sprinkle loaf with sesame seed. Bake 30 minutes or until golden brown. Makes 1 loaf.

BISCUITS IN THE ROUND

¼ cup butter or margarine
¼ cup chopped chives or green onions
2 8- or 9.5-ounce packages refrigerated flaky biscuits

ABOUT 45 MINUTES BEFORE SERVING:
Preheat oven to 400°F. Grease 5½-cup ring mold. In small saucepan over medium heat, melt butter or margarine. Remove from heat and stir in chives. Dip each biscuit into mixture to coat all sides. In ring mold, stand biscuits on edge, side by side, slightly touching. Pour any remaining chive mixture over biscuits.

Bake biscuits 15 to 18 minutes until golden brown. Remove from oven; cool in mold on wire rack 5 minutes. With knife, loosen ring around inside and outside edges; invert ring onto serving dish. To serve, pull ring apart, biscuit by biscuit. Makes 8 to 10 servings.

PARMESAN BISCUITS

1½ tablespoons grated Parmesan cheese
1 tablespoon chopped parsley
1 8-ounce package refrigerated biscuits
3 tablespoons butter or margarine, melted

ABOUT 20 MINUTES BEFORE SERVING:
Preheat oven to 425°F. Grease 9-inch pie plate. In cup, combine cheese and parsley. Slightly flatten each biscuit; brush generously with melted butter or margarine; sprinkle with some of cheese mixture. Fold each biscuit in half, pinching dough to seal edges.

In center of pie plate, place 5 folded biscuits with points touching to form a star; place remaining biscuits in spaces between. Brush with remaining butter or margarine. Bake 10 to 12 minutes until golden. Makes 10 biscuits.

FILLED CRESCENTS

ABOUT 30 MINUTES BEFORE SERVING:
Preheat oven to 375°F. Onto cutting board, carefully unroll dough from *one 8-ounce package refrigerated crescent rolls;* separate into triangles. On each triangle, place one of fillings below and complete as directed. Place on ungreased cookie sheet; bake until golden. Makes 8 crescents.

QUICK KOLACKY: Place *1 teaspoon of favorite jam* or preserves in center of each triangle, then fold 3 points to center, overlapping; pinch to seal. Bake 10 to 15 minutes; sprinkle with *sugar* while hot.

CINNAMON-NUT FILLING: In small bowl, with fork, mix well *¼ cup finely chopped nuts, 2 tablespoons brown sugar, 2 tablespoons sugar* and *¼ teaspoon cinnamon.* Place 1 to 2 teaspoons of mixture near wide side of each triangle. Fold wide side over filling and press edges together; continue rolling as for crescents. Place on cookie sheet; curve to form crescents. Brush with *melted butter or margarine;* sprinkle with rest of sugar mixture. Bake 10 to 12 minutes.

FRANK-CHEESE FILLING: Grease cookie sheet. Split *8 frankfurters* almost but not quite through; cut each of *2 Cheddar-cheese slices* into 4 strips. Tuck 1 strip into each frankfurter. Lay filled frank on wide end of each triangle; roll up as label directs. Place on cookie sheet with cheese side up. Bake 10 to 15 minutes.

HAM FILLING: Fold *8 cooked ham slices* in half crosswise; place one on each triangle; spread lightly with *prepared mustard.* Roll up; bake 10 to 15 minutes. Serve as is or with *cheese sauce.*

CHEESE FILLING: Generously sprinkle triangles with *grated Parmesan cheese.* Roll up and bake as label directs.

PASTRY FINGERS

ABOUT 15 MINUTES BEFORE SERVING:
Preheat oven to 375°F. Onto cutting board, carefully unroll dough from *one 8-ounce package refrigerated crescent rolls,* but do not separate into triangles. Pinch diagonal perforations together. Cut crosswise into 1-inch-wide strips. Place strips 1 inch apart on cookie sheet; bake 5 to 7 minutes until golden. Serve hot. Makes 24 to 28 fingers.

CHEESE: Prepare as above but brush dough with *melted butter or margarine* and sprinkle with *shredded Cheddar or Parmesan cheese* before cutting into strips. If using Cheddar cheese, grease cookie sheet and bake 10 to 12 minutes until browned.

SPICE: Preparc as above but brush dough with *melted butter or margarine* and sprinkle with *cinnamon-sugar mixture* before cutting into strips.

DUMPLINGS FOR STEW

1⅓ cups all-purpose flour
2 teaspoons double-acting baking powder
1 teaspoon chopped parsley or ⅛ teaspoon thyme leaves or savory
½ teaspoon salt
⅔ cup milk
2 tablespoons salad oil

ABOUT 30 MINUTES BEFORE SERVING:
In large bowl, with fork, stir flour and next 3 ingredients until mixed. In cup, combine milk with salad oil; slowly stir into flour mixture just until mixture forms soft dough (stir as little as possible). Drop dough by heaping tablespoonfuls onto pieces of chicken, meat or vegetables in simmering stew in Dutch oven or kettle.

Cook dumplings 10 minutes, uncovered; then cover and cook 10 minutes more. With slotted spoon, remove dumplings from stew. Spoon stew into serving dish; top with dumplings. Makes about 6 dumplings.

PARSLEY OR CHIVE: Prepare as above but add *¼ cup chopped parsley* or 3 tablespoons chopped chives to flour mixture.

CHEESE: Prepare as above but add *⅓ cup shredded sharp Cheddar cheese* to flour mixture.

SPEEDY: Use packaged buttermilk baking mix to make dumplings as label directs.

REFRIGERATED: Use *one 8-ounce package refrigerated biscuits.* Arrange on pieces of chicken, meat or vegetables; cover and simmer 15 to 20 minutes.

MUFFINS

2 cups all-purpose flour
2 tablespoons sugar
1 tablespoon double-acting baking powder
½ teaspoon salt
1 egg
1 cup milk
¼ cup salad oil

ABOUT 35 MINUTES BEFORE SERVING:
Preheat oven to 400°F. Grease twelve 2½-inch muffin-pan cups. In large bowl, with fork, mix flour and next 3 ingredients. In small bowl, with fork, beat egg slightly; stir in milk and oil. Add egg mixture all at once to flour mixture; with spoon, stir just until flour is moistened. (Batter will be lumpy.)

Spoon batter into muffin-pan cups. Bake 20 to 25 minutes until golden and toothpick inserted in center comes out clean. Immediately remove muffins from pan. Makes 12 muffins.

WHOLE-WHEAT: Prepare as above but use only ¾ cup flour; add *1 cup whole-wheat flour.* Increase sugar to ¼ cup and baking powder to 4 teaspoons.

SWEETER: Prepare as above but use ⅓ cup sugar.

APPLE: Prepare Sweeter Muffins as above but add *½ teaspoon cinnamon* with flour. Add *1 apple,* shredded, with egg mixture.

SURPRISE: Prepare as above but fill greased muffin-pan cups one-third full of batter; drop scant teaspoon of *favorite jelly* on center of each; cover with remaining batter.

ORANGE: Prepare as above but use ¼ cup sugar; use only ¾ cup milk. Add *¼ cup orange juice* and *1 tablespoon shredded orange peel* to egg mixture.

BLUEBERRY: Prepare as above but use ½ cup sugar and add *¾ cup fresh or frozen unsweetened blueberries* with egg mixture.

CHEESE-NUT MUFFINS

1 3-ounce package cream cheese, softened
2 tablespoons milk
1 17-ounce package nut-bread mix

ABOUT 50 MINUTES BEFORE SERVING:
Preheat oven to 350°F. Grease twelve 3-inch muffin-pan cups. In small bowl, with fork, mix cream cheese and milk until smooth. Prepare nut-bread mix as label directs but spoon 2 tablespoons batter into each muffin-pan cup; top with 1 rounded teaspoonful cream-cheese mixture; then with 1 tablespoon batter.

Bake 30 minutes or until muffins are golden and pull away from sides of cups. Cool in pan 5 minutes on wire rack; remove muffins from pan. Refrigerate any leftover muffins. Makes 12 muffins.

BRAN MUFFINS

1 cup whole bran cereal
1 cup all-purpose flour
¼ cup sugar
1 tablespoon double-acting baking powder
½ teaspoon salt
1 egg
1 cup milk
¼ cup salad oil

ABOUT 40 MINUTES BEFORE SERVING:
Preheat oven to 400°F. Grease twelve 2½-inch muffin-pan cups. In medium bowl, with fork, mix first 5 ingredients. In small bowl, with fork, beat egg slightly; stir in milk and oil. Add egg mixture all at once to flour mixture; with spoon, stir just until flour is moistened. (Batter will be lumpy.)

Spoon batter into muffin-pan cups. Bake 25 minutes or until golden and toothpick inserted in center comes out almost clean. Immediately remove from pan. Makes 12 muffins.

ORANGE-GLAZED: In cup, combine *1 tablespoon shredded orange peel* with *¼ cup sugar.* Prepare muffins as above but just before baking, sprinkle with orange-peel mixture.

RAISIN-NUT: Prepare as above but add *½ cup chopped California walnuts* and *½ cup raisins* with egg mixture.

MAPLE-BRAN MUFFINS

¾ cup maple-blended syrup
2 eggs
2½ cups bran flakes, crushed
1 cup sour cream
1 cup all-purpose flour
½ cup chopped California walnuts
1 teaspoon baking soda

ABOUT 30 MINUTES BEFORE SERVING:
Preheat oven to 400°F. Grease twelve 2½-inch muffin-pan cups. In medium bowl, with wire whisk or fork, beat syrup and eggs until blended. Beat in crushed flakes; let stand 5 minutes. Beat in sour cream until well mixed. With wooden spoon, stir in remaining ingredients just until flour is moistened. (Batter will be lumpy.)

Spoon batter into muffin-pan cups. Bake 20 minutes or until lightly browned. Immediately remove muffins from pan. Makes 12 muffins.

QUICK FILLED MUFFINS

ABOUT 40 MINUTES BEFORE SERVING:
Preheat oven as packaged muffin-mix label directs. Grease muffin-pan cups. Prepare mix as label directs but fill cups half full with batter. Top each with one of Fillings below; add more batter to fill each cup ⅔ full; bake as label directs.

FILLINGS: Several bits of mixed candied fruits; or 1 drained, cooked dried apricot or pitted prune; or 1 teaspoon drained, canned crushed pineapple mixed with a little shredded orange peel; or 1 banana slice; or a few blueberries or blackberries; or raisins.

QUICK TOPPED MUFFINS

ABOUT 35 MINUTES BEFORE SERVING:
Preheat oven as packaged muffin-mix label directs. Grease muffin-pan cups. Prepare mix as label directs and spoon into cups. Sprinkle each with one of Toppings below; bake as label directs.

TOPPINGS: Flaked or shredded coconut, as is or mixed with a little brown sugar and softened butter or margarine; or grated orange or lemon peel mixed with a little sugar; or shredded Cheddar cheese.

POPOVERS

3 eggs
1 cup milk
3 tablespoons butter or margarine, melted
1 cup all-purpose flour
½ teaspoon salt

ABOUT 1¼ HOURS BEFORE SERVING:
Preheat oven to 375°F. Grease well eight 6-ounce custard cups or twelve 2½-inch muffin-pan cups. Set custard cups on jelly-roll pan or large cookie sheet.

In medium bowl, with mixer at low speed, beat eggs until frothy; beat in milk and butter or margarine until blended. Gradually beat in flour and salt.

Pour about ⅓ cup batter into each custard cup or fill muffin-pan cups half full. Bake 50 minutes, then quickly cut small slit in top of each popover to let out steam; bake 10 minutes longer. Immediately remove popovers from cups, loosening with spatula if necessary. Serve piping hot. Makes 8 or 12 popovers.

TWEED: Prepare as above but use only ¾ cup all-purpose flour and add *¼ cup whole-wheat flour*. Bake as directed.

GIANT: Butter well eight 6-ounce deep pottery custard cups; place on jelly-roll pan or large cookie sheet. Prepare Popovers as above but use *6 eggs, 2 cups milk, 6 tablespoons melted butter or margarine, 2 cups flour* and *1 teaspoon salt* and bake 1 hour before cutting slit in top. Makes 8.

Corn Breads

GOLDEN CORN BREAD

1 cup all-purpose flour
¾ cup cornmeal
2 to 4 tablespoons sugar
1 tablespoon double-acting baking powder
1 teaspoon salt
1 egg
⅔ cup milk
⅓ cup butter or margarine, melted or salad oil

ABOUT 35 MINUTES BEFORE SERVING:
Preheat oven to 425°F. Grease 8″ by 8″ baking pan. In medium bowl, with fork, mix first 5 ingredients.

In small bowl, with fork, beat together egg, milk and butter or margarine. Pour this mixture all at once into flour mixture, stirring just until flour is moistened. Quickly pour batter into baking pan, spreading evenly. Bake 25 minutes or until golden. Cut into squares. Makes 9 servings.

BLUEBERRY CORN MUFFINS: Grease sixteen 2½-inch muffin-pan cups. Prepare as above but, to flour mixture, add *1 cup fresh or frozen blueberries*. Spoon batter into cups, filling each two-thirds full. Bake 20 minutes or until golden. Makes 16 muffins.

CORN-BREAD RING: Grease a 5½-cup ring mold. Prepare as above but spoon batter into ring mold. Bake about 25 minutes; invert from mold onto serving platter. Slice and serve as bread or fill center with creamed ham, chicken, shrimp or favorite curry mixture and serve as main dish for 8. Makes 1 corn-bread ring.

CORN MUFFINS: Grease twelve 2½-inch muffin-pan cups. Prepare as above; spoon into cups, filling each two-thirds full. Bake about 20 minutes. Makes 12 muffins.

CORN STICKS: Grease 14 corn-stick molds very well with *salad oil*. Prepare batter as above; spoon into molds, filling each three-fourths full. Bake 15 to 20 minutes. Makes about 14 sticks.

DEVILED-HAM CORN BREAD: Prepare as above but stir *one 2½-ounce can deviled ham* into egg mixture before adding to flour mixture. Cut into squares. Makes 9 servings.

CORN-BREAD SHORTCAKE: Split squares of hot corn bread. Spoon chicken à la king or creamed ham, turkey or shrimp between halves and on top of squares.

HERBED CORN BREAD

1 9½-, 12- or 14-ounce package corn-muffin mix
1 teaspoon thyme leaves
¼ teaspoon crumbled sage leaves

ABOUT 1 HOUR BEFORE SERVING:
Prepare mix as label directs for corn bread but add thyme and sage with liquid; bake as directed. Makes 9 servings.

BACONY CORN BREAD

1 8-ounce package bacon slices
2 cups all-purpose flour
1½ cups cornmeal
¼ cup sugar
2 tablespoons double-acting baking powder
2 teaspoons salt
2 eggs
1½ cups milk
¼ cup salad oil

ABOUT 2 HOURS BEFORE SERVING:
Preheat oven to 400°F. Bake bacon as on page 130; cool slightly and crumble bacon onto paper towels; set aside. Reserve ¼ cup bacon drippings.

Meanwhile, grease 13" by 9" baking pan. In large bowl, with fork, mix flour and next 4 ingredients. In medium bowl, with fork, beat together eggs, milk, salad oil and reserved bacon drippings. Pour this mixture, all at once, into flour mixture, stirring just until flour is moistened. Quickly pour batter into baking pan, spreading evenly. Sprinkle with crumbled bacon.

Bake about 25 minutes or until golden and toothpick inserted in center comes out clean. Cool corn bread in pan on wire rack 10 minutes. Cut into 15 pieces. Makes 15 servings.

CORN-FLAVOR FOLDOVERS

1 egg
¾ cup sour cream
1¼ cups all-purpose flour
½ cup cornmeal
1 tablespoon sugar
1 teaspoon double-acting baking powder
1 teaspoon salt
½ teaspoon thyme leaves
¼ teaspoon baking soda
¼ cup butter or margarine

ABOUT 45 MINUTES BEFORE SERVING:
Preheat oven to 425°F. In medium bowl, with fork, beat egg slightly; stir in sour cream. In second medium bowl, with fork, mix flour with next 6 ingredients; stir into egg mixture just until mixture forms soft dough. Turn dough onto lightly floured surface; knead 10 strokes to mix well.

With floured rolling pin, roll dough into circle about ¼ inch thick; using a floured 2¾-inch biscuit cutter, cut rounds. Press trimmings together (don't knead); roll and cut until all dough is used.

Meanwhile, in oven, melt butter or margarine in 12" by 8" baking pan. Dip rounds on both sides in melted butter or margarine; fold in half and arrange in 3 rows in pan, letting rolls touch each other. Bake 15 to 20 minutes until golden. Makes about 20 foldovers.

HERBED CORN STICKS

1 9½-, 12- or 14-ounce package corn-muffin mix
2 tablespoons instant minced onion
2 teaspoons chopped parsley
1 teaspoon basil

ABOUT 30 MINUTES AHEAD OR EARLY IN DAY:
Preheat oven to 400°F. Grease 12 to 14 corn-stick molds very well. Prepare corn-muffin mix as label directs but stir in remaining ingredients. Fill each corn-stick mold three-fourths full of batter. Bake 15 minutes or until golden. Immediately remove corn sticks from molds. Makes 12 to 14 corn sticks.

THIN CORN CRACKERS

1 cup cornmeal
½ cup all-purpose flour
½ teaspoon salt
¼ teaspoon baking soda
⅓ cup milk
3 tablespoons salad oil
melted butter or margarine
celery, sesame or poppy seed, or curry or chili powder (optional)

ONE HOUR OR UP TO 1 WEEK AHEAD:
Preheat oven to 250°F. In large bowl, with fork, combine all ingredients except melted butter or margarine and celery seed; stir until well blended. In bowl, with hands, knead just until dough holds together. (If dough seems dry, add few drops milk.)

Divide dough into 24 small pieces. On lightly floured surface, with floured rolling pin, roll each piece into paper-thin circle, 5 inches in diameter (edges will be ragged).

With pancake turner, place circles on cookie sheets. Bake 10 to 15 minutes until light golden; remove to wire racks. If serving later, cool and store in tightly covered container.

TO SERVE:
Lightly brush each Corn Cracker with melted butter or margarine. If you like, sprinkle with celery seed. Makes 24 crackers.

CORN-BREAD LOAF

ABOUT 1 HOUR BEFORE SERVING:
Preheat oven as label directs for corn bread. Grease a 9″ by 5″ loaf pan. Prepare *two 10-ounce packages corn-bread mix* as label directs but spread both batters in loaf pan; bake about 45 minutes or until toothpick inserted in center comes out clean. During last 20 minutes, loosely cover loaf with foil to prevent overbrowning.

Cool corn bread in pan on wire rack 10 minutes; remove from pan. Makes 1 loaf.

Tea Breads and Coffeecakes

CHEESE QUICK BREAD

2 cups all-purpose flour
2 teaspoons double-acting baking powder
2 teaspoons dry mustard
1 teaspoon salt
1 4-ounce package shredded Cheddar cheese (1 cup)
¼ cup butter or margarine
1 cup milk
2 eggs

DAY BEFORE SERVING:
Preheat oven to 375°F. Grease 9″ by 5″ loaf pan. In large bowl, with fork, mix flour with next 4 ingredients. In small saucepan over medium heat, melt butter or margarine; stir in milk, then eggs. With hand beater, beat mixture just until blended; add all at once to flour mixture and stir just until flour is moistened. Pour into pan.

Bake 1 hour or until toothpick inserted in center comes out clean. Cool in pan on wire rack 10 minutes; remove from pan and cool completely on rack. Makes 1 loaf.

PUMPKIN LOAVES

3 cups all-purpose flour
2 cups sugar
2 teaspoons baking soda
1 teaspoon ground cloves
1 teaspoon cinnamon
1 teaspoon nutmeg
1 teaspoon salt
½ teaspoon double-acting baking powder
1 16-ounce can pumpkin (2 cups)
⅔ cup salad oil
3 eggs, slightly beaten

DAY BEFORE SERVING:
Preheat oven to 350°F. Grease well two 9″ by 5″ loaf pans. In large bowl, with fork, mix flour with next 7 ingredients; add remaining ingredients and mix just until blended. Turn batter into pans.

Bake about 1 hour or until toothpick inserted in center comes out clean. Cool in pans on wire racks 10 minutes; remove from pans and cool completely on racks. When cool, wrap each loaf and store at room temperature. Makes 2 loaves.

EASY NUT BREAD*

3½ cups all-purpose flour
1 cup sugar
4 teaspoons double-acting baking powder
1 teaspoon salt
2 cups milk
2 eggs
1 cup coarsely chopped black or California walnuts

DAY BEFORE SERVING:
Grease two 9″ by 5″ loaf pans. In large bowl, with fork, mix flour, sugar, baking powder and salt; add remaining ingredients; stir until well mixed. Pour batter into loaf pans. Let stand for 20 minutes.

Meanwhile, preheat oven to 350°F. Bake loaves 50 minutes or until toothpick inserted in center comes out clean. Cool in pans on wire racks 10 minutes; remove from pans and cool completely on racks. Makes 2 loaves.

* This recipe has no shortening.

IRISH SODA BREAD

4 cups all-purpose flour
3 tablespoons sugar
1 tablespoon double-acting baking powder
1 teaspoon salt
¾ teaspoon baking soda
6 tablespoons butter or margarine
1½ cups dark seedless raisins
1 tablespoon caraway seed
2 eggs
1½ cups buttermilk

EARLY IN DAY:
Preheat oven to 350°F. Grease well a 2-quart round casserole. In large bowl, with fork, mix flour and next 4 ingredients. With pastry blender or 2 knives used scissor-fashion, cut in butter or margarine until mixture resembles coarse crumbs; stir in raisins and caraway seed.

In small bowl, with fork, beat eggs slightly; remove 1 tablespoon and reserve. Stir buttermilk into remaining egg; stir into flour mixture just until flour is moistened. (Dough will be sticky.) Turn dough onto well-floured surface; with floured hands, knead about 10 strokes to mix thoroughly. Shape dough into a ball; place in casserole. In center of ball, with sharp knife, cut a 4-inch cross about ¼ inch deep. Brush dough with reserved egg.

Bake about 1 hour and 20 minutes or until toothpick inserted in center comes out clean. Cool in casserole on wire rack 10 minutes; remove from casserole and cool completely on rack. Makes 1 loaf.

BANANA BREAD

1¾ cups all-purpose flour
⅔ cup sugar
1 teaspoon double-acting baking powder
½ teaspoon salt
¼ teaspoon baking soda
½ cup shortening
1 cup mashed bananas (about 2 very ripe medium bananas)
2 eggs, slightly beaten

DAY BEFORE SERVING:
Preheat oven to 350°F. Grease and flour 9″ by 5″ loaf pan. In large bowl, with fork, mix first 5 ingredients. With pastry blender or 2 knives used scissor-fashion, cut in shortening until mixture resembles coarse crumbs. With fork, stir in bananas and eggs just until blended; spread batter evenly in pan.

Bake 55 minutes to 1 hour until toothpick inserted in center comes out clean. Cool in pan on wire rack 10 minutes; remove from pan and cool completely on rack. Makes 1 loaf.

BANANA-APRICOT: Prepare as above but add *1 cup finely chopped dried apricots* with bananas.

BANANA-CRANBERRY: Prepare as above but add *1 cup cranberries,* coarsely chopped, with bananas.

BANANA-DATE: Prepare as above but add *½ cup chopped, pitted dates* with bananas.

BANANA-NUT: Prepare as above but add *½ cup coarsely chopped pecans,* almonds or walnuts with bananas.

BANANA-ORANGE: Prepare as above but add *1 teaspoon orange extract* with bananas.

BANANA-PRUNE: Prepare as above but add *1 cup finely chopped, pitted dried prunes* with bananas.

BANANA-RAISIN: Prepare as above but add *1 cup dark seedless raisins* with bananas.

PEANUT-BUTTER BREAD

¾ cup chunky or creamy peanut butter
¼ cup butter or margarine, softened
2 cups all-purpose flour
½ cup sugar
2 teaspoons double-acting baking powder
1 teaspoon salt
1 egg
1¼ cups milk
1 tablespoon grated orange peel

DAY BEFORE SERVING:
Preheat oven to 375°F. Grease 9″ by 5″ loaf pan. In small bowl, with fork, beat peanut butter and butter or margarine until light and fluffy. In medium bowl, with fork, mix flour, sugar, baking powder and salt;

add peanut-butter mixture and mix until mixture resembles coarse crumbs.

In small bowl, with fork, beat egg slightly; stir in milk and orange peel. Stir into flour mixture just until flour is moistened. Pour mixture into pan. Bake 1 hour or until toothpick inserted in center comes out clean. Cool in pan on wire rack 10 minutes; remove from pan and cool completely on rack. Makes 1 loaf.

ORANGE-NUT BREAD

3 cups all-purpose flour
1½ cups coarsely chopped California walnuts
1¼ cups sugar
5 teaspoons double-acting baking powder
1½ teaspoons salt
shredded peel of 1 orange
3 eggs
1½ cups milk
⅓ cup salad oil

DAY BEFORE SERVING:
Preheat oven to 350°F. Grease 9″ by 5″ loaf pan. In large bowl, with fork, mix flour and next 5 ingredients. In small bowl, with fork, beat eggs slightly; stir in milk and salad oil. Stir into flour mixture just until flour is moistened. Pour batter into pan.

Bake 1 hour and 20 minutes or until bread pulls away from sides of pan. Cool in pan on wire rack 10 minutes; remove from pan and cool completely on rack. Makes 1 loaf.

BLUEBERRY-ORANGE BREAD

5 cups all-purpose flour
1 cup sugar
2 tablespoons double-acting baking powder
2 teaspoons salt
1 teaspoon baking soda
4 eggs
1½ cups orange juice
¼ cup butter or margarine, melted
2 tablespoons grated orange peel
1 10-ounce package frozen blueberries

ABOUT 1½ HOURS AHEAD OR EARLY IN DAY:
Preheat oven to 375°F. Grease well two 1½-quart casseroles or one 1½-quart casserole and one 9″ by 5″ loaf pan.

In large bowl, with fork, mix flour, sugar, baking powder, salt and baking soda. In medium bowl, with fork, beat eggs; add orange juice, butter or margarine and orange peel. Stir into flour mixture just until flour is moistened. Gently stir berries into batter.

Pour batter into casseroles. Bake 50 minutes or until toothpick inserted in center comes out clean. Serve breads, cut into wedges, from casseroles to keep warm; or remove from casseroles and cool on wire racks to serve later. Best served same day made. Makes 2 loaves.

CHOCOLATE DATE-NUT LOAF

1 cup sliced pitted dates
1 6-ounce package semisweet-chocolate pieces (1 cup)
¼ cup butter or margarine
1 egg
¾ cup milk
1 teaspoon vanilla extract
2½ cups all-purpose flour
1 cup coarsely chopped California walnuts or pecans
⅓ cup sugar
1½ teaspoons salt
1 teaspoon double-acting baking powder
1 teaspoon baking soda

DAY BEFORE SERVING:
Preheat oven to 350°F. Grease 9″ by 5″ loaf pan. In small bowl, pour ¾ cup boiling water over dates; set aside. In double boiler, over hot, not boiling, water, melt chocolate with butter or margarine. In small bowl, with fork, beat egg with milk and vanilla just until mixed.

In large bowl, with spoon, mix flour and next 5 ingredients; add dates and liquid, chocolate and milk mixtures; mix just until blended. Pour mixture into loaf pan.

Bake 1 hour and 10 minutes or until toothpick inserted in center comes out clean. Cool in pan on wire rack 10 minutes; remove from pan and cool completely on rack. Wrap in plastic wrap or foil; store at room temperature. Makes 1 loaf.

DATE-NUT BREAD

1½ cups all-purpose flour
1 cup sugar
1 cup chopped pitted dates
¾ cup coarsely chopped California walnuts
2 teaspoons double-acting baking powder
½ teaspoon salt
2 eggs
¾ cup milk
3 tablespoons salad oil
1 teaspoon vanilla extract

DAY BEFORE SERVING:
Preheat oven to 350°F. Grease 9″ by 5″ loaf pan. In large bowl, with fork, mix first 6 ingredients. In small bowl, with fork, beat eggs slightly; stir in milk, salad oil and vanilla. Stir into flour mixture just until flour is moistened; pour into pan. Bake 1 hour or until toothpick inserted in center comes out clean. Cool in pan on wire rack 10 minutes; remove from pan and cool completely on rack. Makes 1 loaf.

BOSTON BROWN BREAD

1 cup whole-wheat flour
1 cup rye flour
1 cup cornmeal
1½ teaspoons baking soda
1½ teaspoons salt
2 cups buttermilk
¾ cup dark molasses

ABOUT 2½ HOURS BEFORE SERVING:
Grease and flour two tall 1-pound coffee cans and cut foil to use as lids; grease. (Or, grease and flour a 2-quart mold and its lid.) Into large bowl, measure all ingredients; with wire whisk or spoon, stir until well mixed. Pour batter into cans; cover with foil and tie foil to can with string. Place cans on rack in deep kettle; add boiling water to come halfway up sides of cans.

Cover kettle. Over low heat, simmer 2 hours or until toothpick inserted in center of bread comes out almost clean. Invert from cans onto wire rack to cool. Makes 1 large loaf or 2 small loaves.

RAISIN: Prepare as above but add *1 cup dark seedless raisins.*

HOT CINNAMON TWISTERS

⅓ cup sugar
1¼ teaspoons cinnamon
¼ cup butter or margarine
1 8- or 9.5-ounce package refrigerated biscuits

ABOUT 30 MINUTES BEFORE SERVING:
Preheat oven to 425°F. Grease cookie sheet. In small bowl, combine sugar and cinnamon. In small saucepan over low heat, melt butter or margarine. With hands, flatten each biscuit to a 4-inch circle; dip first in butter, then in cinnamon-sugar mixture. Twist 2 or 3 times; place on cookie sheet. Bake 12 to 15 minutes. Immediately remove to plate. Makes 8 or 10 twisters.

HOLIDAY CINNAMON ROLL

2½ cups buttermilk baking mix
1 egg, slightly beaten
⅓ cup milk
2 tablespoons butter or margarine, softened
¼ cup sugar
2 teaspoons cinnamon
3 tablespoons chopped citron
3 tablespoons chopped candied red cherries
¼ cup confectioners' sugar

EARLY IN DAY:
1. Preheat oven to 400°F. In medium bowl, combine baking mix, egg and milk, stirring with fork to make a soft dough. Turn onto lightly floured surface and, with floured hands, knead lightly just until smooth.
2. With lightly floured rolling pin, roll dough into 10″ by 8″ rectangle. Spread with butter or margarine; sprinkle evenly with sugar, cinnamon, 2 tablespoons each of citron and cherries. Roll dough tightly, jelly-roll fashion, beginning at 10-inch side.
3. Place, seam side down, on cookie sheet. With scissors, cut roll almost through at one-inch intervals. Bake 20 minutes or until lightly browned.
4. In small bowl, combine confectioners' sugar and 1½ teaspoons water; spread mixture evenly on warm roll and sprinkle top of roll with remaining citron and cherries. Remove roll to wire rack to cool. Makes 10 servings.

CHERRY COFFEECAKE

all-purpose flour
sugar
1 teaspoon double-acting baking powder
¼ teaspoon baking soda
¼ teaspoon salt
10 tablespoons butter or margarine, melted
½ cup milk
1 egg
1 teaspoon vanilla extract
¼ teaspoon lemon extract
1 21- or 22-ounce can cherry-pie filling

ABOUT 2 HOURS BEFORE SERVING:
Preheat oven to 350°F. Grease and flour 9″ by 9″ baking pan. In large bowl, with fork, mix 1¼ cups flour with ½ cup sugar, baking powder, soda and salt. Add ½ cup butter or margarine, milk, egg and vanilla; with spoon, beat until well mixed. Pour batter evenly in baking pan.

In small bowl, with fork, combine ½ cup flour, ¼ cup sugar and remaining 2 tablespoons butter or margarine until mixture resembles coarse crumbs; sprinkle half on top of batter. Stir lemon extract into cherry-pie filling; spread over batter, then sprinkle with rest of flour mixture. Bake 1 hour or until top is light golden. Cut into squares. Makes 9 servings.

SOUR-CREAM COFFEECAKE

½ cup finely chopped California walnuts
sugar
1 teaspoon cinnamon
½ cup butter or margarine
2 cups all-purpose flour
1 cup sour cream
2 eggs
1 teaspoon double-acting baking powder
1 teaspoon baking soda
1 teaspoon vanilla extract

ABOUT 2 HOURS AHEAD OR DAY BEFORE:
In small bowl, combine nuts, ½ cup sugar and cinnamon; set aside. Preheat oven to 350°F. Grease 9-inch tube pan.

In large bowl, with mixer at medium speed, beat 1 cup sugar with butter or margarine until light and fluffy. Add remaining ingredients and beat at low speed until blended, constantly scraping bowl with rubber spatula. At medium speed, beat 3 minutes, occasionally scraping bowl.

Spread half of batter in pan; sprinkle with half of nut mixture; spread evenly with remaining batter and sprinkle with remaining nut mixture. Bake 60 to 65 minutes until cake pulls away from side of pan. Cool in pan on wire rack 10 minutes; loosen inside edge; invert from pan onto rack to cool slightly. To serve later, cool completely and wrap. Makes 8 to 10 servings.

APPLE SOUR-CREAM: Prepare as above but spread half of batter in pan; top with ⅓ of nut mixture, then with *1 medium cooking apple,* peeled, cored and thinly sliced, and ⅓ of nut mixture. Spread with remaining batter and nut mixture. Bake 65 to 70 minutes. Cool completely in pan on wire rack.

PEACH-FILLED COFFEECAKE

1½ cups all-purpose flour
1 cup sugar
2 teaspoons double-acting baking powder
2 teaspoons grated lemon peel
⅛ teaspoon salt
1 cup butter or margarine, softened
4 eggs
1 29-ounce can sliced cling peaches, well drained
Topping (below)

ABOUT 1½ HOURS BEFORE SERVING:
Preheat oven to 350°F. Grease 13″ by 9″ baking pan. Into large bowl, measure flour and next 6 ingredients; with mixer at low speed, beat until well mixed, constantly scraping bowl with rubber spatula. Increase speed to high; beat 4 minutes, occasionally scraping bowl.

Spread batter evenly in baking pan. Arrange peaches on top of batter. Sprinkle entire top with Topping. Bake 45 to 50 minutes until light golden and toothpick inserted in center comes out clean. Cut into rectangles. Makes 12 servings.

TOPPING: In small saucepan over medium heat, melt *½ cup butter or margarine;* remove from heat. Stir in *1 cup all-purpose flour, ¼ cup sugar* and *1 tablespoon grated lemon peel* to form a soft dough.

PEAR-FILLED: Prepare as above but substitute *one 29-ounce can pear halves,* drained and sliced, for peaches.

FROSTED ALMOND TWISTS

1 8-ounce package refrigerated crescent rolls
1 egg, beaten
1 tablespoon sugar
½ cup confectioners' sugar
2½ teaspoons milk
2 teaspoons butter or margarine, softened
⅛ teaspoon almond extract

ABOUT 45 MINUTES BEFORE SERVING:
Preheat oven to 375°F. Grease cookie sheet. Unroll crescent dough onto cutting board and cut each piece in half along straight perforations; with fingers, pinch diagonal perforations together on all pieces. Cut each rectangle lengthwise into 6 strips.

Twist 2 strips together like a rope; cut each rope in half. Place ropes about one inch apart on cookie sheet; brush strips with egg and sprinkle with sugar. Bake 8 to 12 minutes until golden.

Meanwhile, in small bowl, with fork, blend confectioners' sugar, milk, butter or margarine and almond extract until smooth. Use to frost twists generously as soon as they come from oven. Makes 24 twists.

ROSETTES

salad oil
1 cup all-purpose flour
1 cup milk
2 eggs
1 tablespoon vanilla extract
2 teaspoons sugar
¼ teaspoon salt
confectioners' sugar

UP TO 1 WEEK BEFORE SERVING:
In deep-fat fryer or deep electric skillet,* heat about 1 inch salad oil to 370°F. In medium bowl, with wire whisk or hand beater, beat remaining ingredients except confectioners' sugar until smooth (or blend in covered blender container). Pour batter into pie plate or deep dish for easier dipping.

Heat rosette iron in hot oil for 2 minutes; drain excess oil on paper towel; dip hot iron into batter to cover about ¾ of rosette form; quickly return to hot oil, being careful not to touch bottom of pan.

Fry until rosette comes off iron; continue frying rosette until golden. (If rosette does not come off iron, gently ease it off with a fork.) With slotted spoon, remove rosette to paper towels to drain, leaving iron in oil to keep hot. Repeat draining iron, dipping and frying until all batter is used. Sprinkle rosettes with confectioners' sugar. Store in tightly covered container. Makes about 5 dozen rosettes.

* Or, in deep skillet or Dutch oven over medium heat, heat oil to 370°F. on deep-fat thermometer.

Pancakes, Waffles and Doughnuts

PANCAKES

1¼ cups all-purpose flour
2 tablespoons sugar
2 teaspoons double-acting baking powder
¾ teaspoon salt
salad oil
1⅓ cups milk*
1 egg, slightly beaten
butter or margarine
maple or maple-blended syrup, honey, preserves, marmalade, apple butter as desired

ABOUT 30 MINUTES BEFORE SERVING:
In large bowl, with fork, mix first 4 ingredients; add 3 tablespoons salad oil, milk and egg and stir just until flour is moistened.

Preheat electric griddle or skillet† as manufacturer directs. Unless using griddle with non-stick finish, brush lightly with salad oil. Pour batter by scant ¼ cupfuls onto hot griddle, making a few pancakes at a time; cook until bubbly and bubbles burst; edges will look dry. With pancake turner, turn and cook until underside is golden; place on heated platter; keep warm.

Repeat until all batter is used, brushing griddle with more salad oil, if necessary. Serve pancakes with butter or margarine and syrup or other topping as desired. Makes about twelve 4-inch pancakes.

* For thicker pancakes use only 1 cup milk. Makes eight 4-inch pancakes.
† Or, use griddle or skillet over medium-high heat; heat until a drop of water sizzles.

APPLE: Prepare as above but add *¼ teaspoon cinnamon* and *1 cup finely chopped, peeled and cored cooking apple* to batter.

BLUEBERRY: Prepare thicker pancakes as above but add *½ cup blueberries* to batter. Or, after pouring each pancake, sprinkle with a few blueberries.

BUCKWHEAT: Prepare as above but substitute *½ cup buckwheat flour* for ½ cup of the all-purpose flour.

PINEAPPLE TIDBIT: Prepare thicker pancakes as above but add *½ cup drained, canned pineapple tidbits* to batter.

DOLLAR PANCAKES: Prepare as above but pour batter by measuring tablespoonfuls onto hot griddle to make small pancakes. Makes about twenty-four 2-inch pancakes.

POTATO PANCAKES

2½ cups coarsely shredded raw potatoes
1 small onion, grated
⅓ cup all-purpose flour
1 egg
1 teaspoon salt
salad oil
applesauce

ABOUT 40 MINUTES BEFORE SERVING:
In medium bowl, with fork, stir all ingredients except salad oil and applesauce.

Preheat electric skillet* as manufacturer directs; spread 2 tablespoons salad oil over bottom. Pour batter by scant ¼ cupfuls into hot skillet, making a few pancakes at a time. With pancake turner, flatten mounds into 4-inch circles; cook until browned and crisp on underside, about 5 minutes. Turn and cook until other side is browned and crisp; drain on paper towels; place on warm platter; keep warm.

Repeat until all batter is used, adding more salad oil if necessary. Serve pancakes with applesauce as accompaniment to Sauerbraten (page 78), roast beef, pork or ham. Makes about 10 pancakes, enough for 5 servings.

* Or, use 12-inch skillet over medium-high heat; heat until a drop of water sizzles.

QUICK PANCAKE TREATS

Prepare pancake batter, using favorite mix (pancake or buttermilk baking mix) as label directs for pancakes. Use to make one of these variations:

APPLE: Into batter for 12 to 14 pancakes, stir *1 cup shredded, peeled and cored cooking apple, 1 tablespoon lemon juice* and *2 tablespoons sugar.* Cook pancakes until golden on both sides; serve with *sugar* and *cinnamon* or syrup.

BANANA: For each pancake, arrange *3 or 4 banana slices* on griddle; pour batter over slices. Cook until golden on both sides; serve with *butter or margarine* and *confectioners' sugar.*

BLUEBERRY: As soon as batter for pancake is poured, sprinkle with *about 1 tablespoon blueberries.* Cook until golden on both sides; serve with *honey.*

CHEESE: Into batter for 12 to 14 pancakes, stir *½ cup shredded Cheddar cheese.* Cook pancakes until golden on both sides; serve with *creamed meats, poultry or seafood;* or creamed vegetables; or syrup.

CHOCOLATE CHIP: As soon as batter for pancake is poured, sprinkle with *a few semisweet-chocolate pieces.* Cook until golden on both sides; serve with *softened ice cream* and *chocolate syrup* as dessert.

CORN: Into batter for 12 to 14 pancakes, stir *¾ cup drained, canned whole-kernel corn* and *½ teaspoon paprika.* Cook pancakes until golden on both sides; serve with *creamed dried beef or ham,* or syrup.

FRANK: As soon as batter for pancake is poured, top with *a few thin frankfurter slices.* Cook until golden on both sides; serve with *creamed vegetables,* or butter or margarine and honey.

NUT: Into batter for 12 to 14 pancakes, stir *1 cup finely chopped California walnuts* or pecans. Cook pancakes until golden on both sides; serve with *syrup* or ice cream.

PINEAPPLE: Into batter for 12 to 14 pancakes, stir *½ cup well-drained, canned crushed pineapple* and *dash of ground cloves.* Cook pancakes until golden on both sides. Serve with *syrup.*

CORNMEAL PANCAKES

2 eggs
1¼ cups buttermilk
1 cup yellow cornmeal
½ teaspoon baking soda
½ teaspoon salt
salad oil
butter or margarine
syrup

ABOUT 30 MINUTES BEFORE SERVING:
In large bowl, with fork, beat eggs slightly. Add next 4 ingredients; stir just until cornmeal is moistened.

Preheat electric griddle or skillet* as manufacturer directs. Unless using griddle with non-stick finish, brush lightly with salad oil. Pour about 2 tablespoonfuls of batter onto hot griddle, making a few pancakes at a time; cook until bubbly and bubbles burst; edges will look dry. With pancake turner, turn and cook until underside is golden; place on platter; keep warm.

Repeat until all batter is used, brushing griddle with more salad oil, if necessary. Serve pancakes with butter or margarine and syrup. Makes about eighteen 3-inch pancakes.

COUNTRY BRUNCH PANCAKES

2 cups all-purpose flour
3 tablespoons sugar
4 teaspoons double-acting baking powder
1 teaspoon salt
½ teaspoon baking soda
1½ cups milk
1 cup creamed cottage cheese
3 eggs, slightly beaten
2 tablespoons lemon juice
salad oil
Fig-Maple Syrup (below)

ABOUT 45 MINUTES BEFORE SERVING:
In large bowl, with spoon, mix well first 5 ingredients. Add remaining ingredients except salad oil and Syrup; stir just until flour is moistened.

Preheat electric griddle or skillet* as manufacturer directs. Unless using griddle with non-stick finish, brush lightly with salad oil.

* Or, use griddle or skillet over medium-high heat; heat until a drop of water sizzles.

Pour batter by scant ¼ cupfuls onto hot griddle, making a few pancakes at a time; cook until bubbly and bubbles burst; edges will look dry. With pancake turner, turn and cook until underside is golden; place on heated platter; keep warm. Prepare syrup.

Repeat until all batter is used, brushing griddle with more salad oil, if necessary. Serve pancakes with Fig-Maple Syrup. Makes about twenty 4-inch pancakes.

FIG-MAPLE SYRUP: In small saucepan over high heat, heat *1½ cups maple-blended syrup, ½ cup finely chopped dried figs, ¼ cup butter or margarine* and *1 teaspoon grated lemon peel* to boiling; reduce heat to low and simmer 3 to 4 minutes.

WAYS TO SERVE PANCAKES

As breakfast or brunch main dish, top pancakes with butter or margarine and favorite syrup, honey, molasses. Or, top pancakes with sweetened berries or sliced fruits; fruit cocktail and its syrup; canned crushed pineapple.

As luncheon or supper main dish, serve pancakes one of these ways:

HAM-FILLED: Spread each pancake with *deviled ham;* stack; top with *maple, maple-blended or buttered syrup.*

MEXICANA: Spoon heated *chili con carne* down center of each pancake; sprinkle with *1 tablespoon finely chopped sweet onion* and *1 tablespoon shredded Monterey (Jack) or Cheddar cheese.* Roll up; sprinkle with *more shredded cheese.* Serve 2 apiece.

SAUSAGE ROLL-UPS: Roll each pancake around *1 cooked sausage link;* top with *warm applesauce* or syrup. Serve 3 apiece.

BUTTERMILK WAFFLES

1¾ cups all-purpose flour
1 teaspoon double-acting baking powder
1 teaspoon baking soda
½ teaspoon salt
2 cups buttermilk
⅓ cup salad oil
2 eggs

ABOUT 30 MINUTES BEFORE SERVING:
Preheat waffle baker as manufacturer di-

rects. In large bowl, with wire whisk or slotted spoon, mix first 4 ingredients; add remaining ingredients and beat until well blended. When waffle baker is ready to use, pour batter into center of lower half until it spreads to about 1 inch from edges. Cover and bake as manufacturer directs; do not lift cover during baking. When waffle is done, lift cover; loosen waffle with fork; serve at once. Reheat baker before pouring in next waffle.* Makes 4 cups batter or about 5 waffles.

* If batter becomes too thick while standing, stir in a little more buttermilk until of good pouring consistency.

RICH: Prepare as above but use 4 eggs and substitute *½ cup melted butter or margarine* for salad oil.

PECAN: Prepare as above but add *1 tablespoon sugar* and *1 cup coarsely chopped pecans*. Stir batter each time before pouring to distribute nuts.

SWEET-MILK: Prepare as above but omit soda; use 1 tablespoon baking powder and substitute *regular milk* for buttermilk.

QUICK WAFFLE TREATS

Prepare waffle batter, using favorite mix (pancake or buttermilk baking mix) as label directs for waffles. Use to make one of these variations:

BERRY: As soon as batter for waffle is poured, sprinkle *2 tablespoons blueberries* over batter; bake.

CHEESE: Into batter, stir *½ cup shredded Cheddar cheese*. Bake; serve topped with *creamed vegetable, meat, poultry or seafood.*

CORN: Into batter, stir *1 cup drained canned whole-kernel corn*. Bake; serve topped with *creamed chicken or ham*, or syrup.

CURRY: Into batter, stir *½ teaspoon curry powder*. Bake; serve topped with *creamed chicken, turkey or shrimp.*

NUT: As soon as batter for waffle is poured, sprinkle *2 tablespoons coarsely chopped walnuts* over batter; bake.

COCONUT: Into batter, stir *1 cup chopped flaked coconut*. Bake.

WAYS TO SERVE WAFFLES

As breakfast or brunch main dish, top waffles with butter or margarine and favorite syrup (maple, maple-blended, buttered, corn or fruit-flavor); honey; molasses; apple butter; confectioners' sugar.

As luncheon or supper main dish, top with creamed dried beef, ham, tongue, poultry, seafood or eggs; creamed mushrooms; curried chicken or shrimp; Welsh rabbit, Newburg sauce.

As dessert, top with sweetened berries or sliced fruit and whipped cream; softened ice cream; favorite sundae sauce.

APPLESAUCE-RAISIN DOUGHNUTS

4 cups buttermilk baking mix
⅔ cup applesauce
½ cup golden raisins, chopped
¼ cup sugar
1 teaspoon vanilla extract
½ teaspoon nutmeg
2 eggs
salad oil
Nutmeg-Sugar (below)

ABOUT 45 MINUTES BEFORE SERVING:
In large bowl, with spoon, stir all ingredients except salad oil and Nutmeg-Sugar until well mixed. Turn dough onto well-floured surface and knead about 10 strokes or until smooth. With floured rolling pin, roll dough ¼ inch thick. With floured doughnut cutter, cut dough into rings. Press trimmings and centers ("holes") together; roll and cut until all dough is used.

Meanwhile, in deep-fat fryer,* heat 3 or 4 inches oil to 370°F. Fry 4 or 5 rings at a time in hot oil, turning as soon as they rise to the surface and turning often until golden brown. Drain on paper towels. Shake doughnuts, a few at a time, in Nutmeg-Sugar. Makes about 36 doughnuts.

* Or, in large saucepan or Dutch oven over medium heat, heat oil to 370°F. on deep-fat thermometer.

NUTMEG-SUGAR: In paper bag, combine *1½ cups sugar* and *1 teaspoon nutmeg.*

OLD-FASHIONED DOUGHNUTS

3 cups all-purpose flour
1 cup sugar
¾ cup buttermilk
2 eggs
2 tablespoons shortening
2 teaspoons double-acting baking powder
1 teaspoon baking soda
1 teaspoon salt
½ teaspoon nutmeg
salad oil
confectioners' sugar or Nutmeg-Sugar (page 433) for garnish

ABOUT 2½ HOURS BEFORE SERVING:
Into large bowl, measure 1½ cups flour and remaining ingredients except salad oil and confectioners' sugar; with mixer at low speed, beat just until smooth, constantly scraping bowl with rubber spatula. Increase speed to medium; beat 1 minute, constantly scraping bowl. Stir in remaining flour to make soft dough. Refrigerate dough at least 1 hour to make it easier to handle.

On well-floured surface with floured rolling pin, roll dough ½ inch thick. With floured doughnut cutter, cut dough into rings. Press trimmings and centers ("holes") together; roll and cut until all dough is used.

Meanwhile, in deep-fat fryer,* heat 3 or 4 inches salad oil to 370°F. Fry 4 or 5 rings at a time in hot oil, turning with slotted spoon as soon as they rise to surface and turning often until golden brown. Drain on paper towels. Serve as is or sprinkle with confectioners' sugar. Makes about 24 doughnuts.

* Or, in large saucepan or Dutch oven over medium heat, heat oil to 370°F. on deep-fat thermometer.

DOUGHNUT "HOLES": Use centers cut from doughnuts; or, using small biscuit cutter, cut all dough into small circles. Fry as above.

CHOCOLATE: In double boiler over hot, not boiling, water, melt *1½ squares unsweetened chocolate.* Prepare dough as above but use 1¼ cups sugar and omit nutmeg; add melted chocolate and *1 teaspoon vanilla extract* with milk. Roll, cut and fry as above; cool. If you like, frost doughnuts with *Chocolate Glaze* (page 487) or sprinkle with confectioners' sugar.

NUTTED: Add *½ cup chopped California walnuts* with remaining flour.

WHOLE-WHEAT: Prepare as above but substitute *1½ cups whole-wheat flour* for 1½ cups of the all-purpose flour, stirring it in after beating dough 1 minute. Roll dough about ⅜ inch thick. Fry as above. Top with Honey Glaze (below), if desired.

Honey Glaze: In small bowl, with fork, stir *½ cup honey* with *⅔ cup confectioners' sugar* until smooth. Spread over warm Whole-Wheat Doughnuts.

DOUGHNUT DROPS

salad oil
1¾ cups all-purpose flour
¼ cup sugar
1 tablespoon double-acting baking powder
1 teaspoon salt
½ teaspoon nutmeg
¾ cup milk
1 egg
Nutmeg-Sugar (page 433) or Snowy Glaze (page 559)

ABOUT 1 HOUR BEFORE SERVING:
In electric skillet or deep-fat fryer,* heat 1 inch salad oil to 370°F. In large bowl, with spoon, mix flour and next 4 ingredients; stir in ¼ cup salad oil, milk and egg until well mixed. Drop dough by rounded measuring teaspoonfuls into hot oil; fry until golden brown, turning once. With slotted spoon, remove to paper towels to drain. Serve as is or shake in bag with Nutmeg-Sugar or frost with Snowy Glaze. Makes about 4 dozen.

* Or, in large saucepan or Dutch oven over medium heat, heat oil to 370°F. on deep-fat thermometer.

Yeast breads

While the making of fragrant, delicious yeast-raised bread is an art, it is one that can be acquired readily. And the rewards in terms of good eating and good nutrition are well worth the effort. Yeast-raised breads, made with enriched flour, supply carbohydrates, protein, iron, niacin, riboflavin and thiamine, and are included in the basic groups of foods that should be eaten every day for continued good health.

Making breads with yeast is not hard. Nor does it take very much of your time. The measuring, mixing, kneading, testing, shaping often require less than half an hour. While the bread is rising and baking, you can be busy at other things about the house.

Ingredients

Yeast: Yeast is the leavening agent for the breads in this chapter. A living plant, it feeds on the sugar in the dough and produces the gas that makes the dough expand and rise. It also gives a unique aroma and flavor.

Active dry yeast dissolves and acts quickly in these recipes. It is packed in individual airtight packages and will stay fresh and give excellent results until the expiration date marked on the package.

Compressed or fresh yeast comes in 0.6-, 1- and 2-ounce cakes. It is perishable and must be kept in the refrigerator. It may be kept in the freezer for several months, but must be thawed at room temperature and then used immediately.

Active dry and compressed yeast can be used interchangeably in these recipes. One package active dry yeast equals one 0.6-ounce cake compressed yeast. Compressed yeast must be dissolved before using; see Dissolving the Yeast (page 436).

Flour: Wheat flour is best for making yeast breads since it contains gluten which stretches during beating and kneading and traps the gas formed by the yeast, producing a light, airy product. All-purpose flour is wheat flour. Whole-wheat flour has less gluten and makes heavier, smaller breads. For greater volume, whole wheat and other special flours such as rye and oatmeal usually are mixed with wheat flour.

Liquid: Milk and water are the liquids most often used for making bread. The milk may be whole, skimmed, reconstituted nonfat dry milk or evaporated milk used as is or diluted. Milk gives breads a soft crust and creamy-white crumb; water produces a crisp crust.

Be sure the liquid is at the temperature given in the recipe. If too hot, it may kill the yeast and so keep the dough from rising. If too cold, it will slow the yeast and lengthen rising times.

Sugar: Sugar is the food on which yeast grows to produce the gas that makes bread rise. White sugar is most often used; brown sugar, molasses and honey also give good results when called for in recipes.

Fat: Fats add flavor, make bread tender, help bread stay soft. Butter, margarine, shortening, salad oil or lard all may be used.

Other ingredients: Salt adds flavor, helps control yeast growth. Eggs add color, flavor and richness. Herbs, spices, fruits, nuts provide extra flavor and food value but slow the rising time.

Tips for Perfect Breads

Dissolving the yeast: In the recipes that follow, undissolved active dry yeast is mixed with some of the dry ingredients; it dissolves in the warm liquid added to the mixture. This liquid should be within a temperature range of 120° to 130°F., the temperature of very hot tap water.

In some recipes, active dry or compressed yeast is sprinkled over warm water in the mixing bowl and stirred until dissolved before adding other ingredients. In this method, the water should be at a temperature of 105° to 115°F. If the water is too hot, it will kill the yeast and the bread won't rise; if too cold, it will slow down the action of the yeast and the bread will rise slowly. Test by dropping a little of the water on the inside of your wrist; it should feel comfortably warm but not hot.

Beating: Our recipes have been developed using a mixer. If you prefer, however, a sturdy wooden spoon and vigorous beating will give equally good results.

After the first amount of flour, yeast and liquid are combined, beat the mixture vigorously (with mixer or spoon). This will hasten the formation of gluten, shorten the kneading time if the bread is to be kneaded.

If it is a batter bread requiring no kneading, the beating should continue until the batter comes away from the sides of the bowl and follows the mixer beaters or the spoon.

Adding flour to make dough: Add only enough flour to make a dough that can be handled. Additional flour will be worked in as the dough is kneaded. On days with high humidity, the dough may need more flour than the recipe indicates.

Kneading the dough: Use a counter top, board or pastry cloth that has been sprinkled lightly with flour. Rub some flour on your hands.

Turn the dough onto the surface and, with your hands, shape it into a ball. Now, pick up the edge at the point farthest from you. (See illustration, page 437.) Fold it over on top of the edge nearest you. With the heels of your hands, push the dough away in a rolling motion.

Turn the dough one quarter turn around and repeat folding, rolling and turning until it is smooth and elastic (springs back when pressed lightly), with little blisters visible under the surface, and it no longer sticks to the surface or to your hands. This will take about 8 to 10 minutes, depending on factors such as the stickiness of the dough, the strength with which you knead and the development of the gluten during beating. If the dough sticks as you work, sprinkle the surface underneath it lightly with flour and flour your hands as necessary.

If you wish, rest occasionally; a brief "break" won't affect the dough.

Rising: Unless the recipe specifies otherwise (as with freezer breads, Swedish Limpa, etc.), the dough is now ready for the "bowl rise" in a cozy, warm place with an even temperature of 80° to 85°F.

Cover the dough with a clean cloth towel while you wash, dry and lightly grease the bowl in which it was mixed. Then place the ball of dough, rounded side (top) down, in the bowl; turn it over so that the top is greased. (This helps keep top from drying.) Cover the bowl with the towel and let stand in a warm place, away from drafts, to rise until doubled.

If the kitchen is cold, you can create a warm place in one of these ways:

1. Set the covered bowl in an *unheated* oven; on a shelf underneath, place a large pan filled with hot water. Replenish the hot water once or twice as it cools.
2. Fill a large pan two-thirds full with hot water; place a wire rack across the top and set the covered bowl on the rack. Replenish the hot water as above.
3. Set the covered bowl in a deep pan of warm, *not hot*, water.
4. Set the covered bowl near, *but not on*, a radiator or warm range.

For batter breads, after stirring in the final amount of flour, leave the batter in the bowl in which it was mixed; cover the bowl and set in a warm place to rise.

Rising times suggested in the recipes are approximate, since the temperature and humidity of your kitchen may be different, and the dough may take more or less time to double.

Testing for doubling: When dough looks almost doubled, quickly and lightly press two fingertips into it to a depth of ½ inch. If dent remains, dough has doubled; if it fills in again rapidly, dough should rise longer. Test again in about 15 minutes.

For batter breads, mixture has doubled when it looks bubbly and moist, with an uneven, slightly rounded, soft top.

Punching or stirring down: When dough has doubled, punch down by pushing your fist deep into the center. Then pull the edges of the dough to the center and turn the dough over in the bowl. (If recipe directs, let dough rise again, then punch down again.) Then turn dough out onto lightly floured surface.

Batters are "stirred down" with a wooden spoon until they are nearly the original size.

Letting dough rest: Often dough is easier to shape if it is allowed to rest after it has been turned out onto the floured surface. Divide it into the number of pieces required, then cover it with the bowl or with a towel and let it stand 10 to 15 minutes. It is now ready for shaping.

Choosing baking pans: Use loaf pans of the size called for. Too large a pan will make a loaf that isn't high enough; too small a pan will result in dough sliding over the sides.

For brown bottom crust, use loaf pans made of dull metal or anodized aluminum, or use glass baking pans but reduce by 25° the temperature called for in the recipe.

KNEADING AND SHAPING BREAD

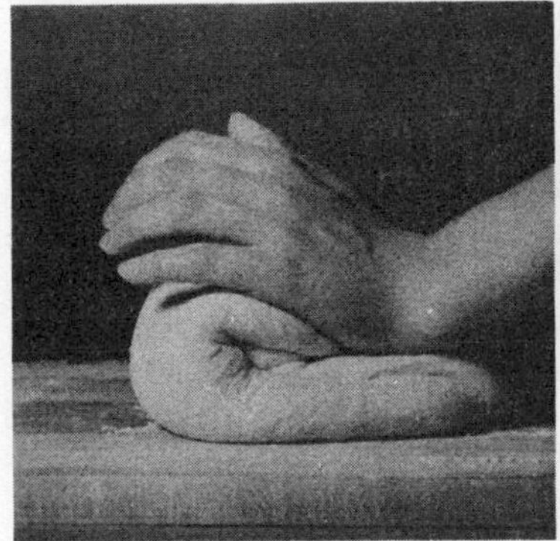
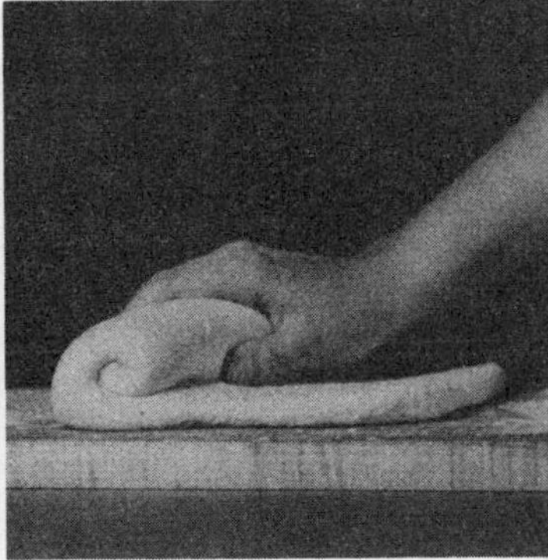
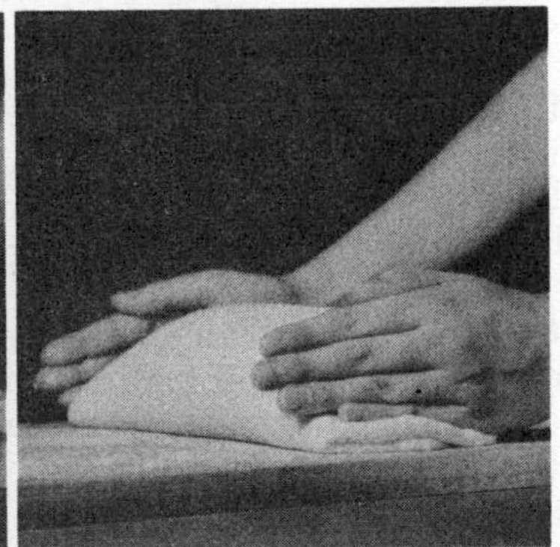

Kneading is easy and enjoyable. Fold dough toward you (photo 1); push it away with a rolling motion (photo 2); give it a quarter turn and repeat. After shaping the dough, seal the ends by pressing with the sides of your hands (photo 3); tuck the ends under and place in the loaf pan.

If shiny metal pans are used, loaves must be baked longer to brown bottom crust.

Shaping breads: Shape dough into loaves, braids, other shapes as directed in recipes.

For round loaves, hold large ball of dough in hands and pull edges under until ball is evenly rounded and smooth on top; place on cookie sheet and flatten slightly.

For small balls for rolls, hold piece of dough in one hand and with other hand tuck edges underneath as above.

Letting shaped bread rise: Cover shaped bread with a towel, set in a warm place (80° to 85°F.) and let rise until doubled. Sides of loaves baked in loaf pan should reach top of pan, center of loaf should be well rounded above pan. Bread should be puffy and light. To test, press lightly with one finger near the edge of the bread (so it won't show in finished bread). If dent remains, bread is ready for baking.

If bread is to be baked with a glaze of egg white or egg yolk, lightly brush glaze on top, brushing carefully so dough does not fall.

Baking: By the time bread has doubled, have oven preheated to proper temperature.

Carefully place loaves in oven (don't jar!) on center shelf with 2 inches between pans to allow heat to circulate. If baking 4 loaves, stagger them on 2 shelves so they bake and brown evenly. If baking breads on a cookie sheet, place the sheet on the center rack of the oven.

If top crust of bread browns too rapidly, cover with foil or brown paper.

Bake bread the minimum time given in the recipe; then test by tapping the top lightly. If loaf sounds hollow, and is browned, remove it from the oven; if not, bake a few minutes longer and test again.

Cooling: Unless the recipe says otherwise, remove bread from pan or cookie sheet to cool on wire rack away from drafts, or bottom crust may become soggy. For a soft, tender top crust, brush the top while hot with softened butter or margarine. Then let stand until slightly warm or cool.

Slicing: Fresh bread slices easily when a hot, sharp knife is used with a sawing motion. Heat the blade in hot tap water, then dry quickly and slice. Or use an unheated serrated knife.

Shaping Rolls

Directions for shaping some favorite rolls are included with recipes for Basic Roll Dough (page 442); Refrigerator Rolls (page 449); Party Rolls (page 448). These same recipes, and hot-roll mix prepared according to directions on the label, may also be used for the rolls below:

CRESCENTS: Grease large cookie sheet. On lightly floured surface, with floured rolling pin, roll dough ¼ inch thick. Using 9-inch cake pan as guide, cut dough into 9-inch circles. Cut each circle into 12 wedges. Brush with melted butter or margarine. Starting at edge opposite point, roll up each wedge. Place with center point underneath, 2 inches apart, on cookie sheet. Curve ends to form crescents. Let rise and bake as recipe or label directs.

DINNER ROLLS: Grease large cookie sheet. Shape pieces of dough into 2-inch balls. With floured hands, roll each ball 4 inches long; taper ends. Place 1 inch apart on cookie sheet. Let rise and bake as recipe or label directs. For finger or salad rolls, shape dough into 1¼-inch balls, roll 2½ inches long.

VIENNA ROLLS: Make Dinner Rolls, above. In cup, with fork, beat 1 egg white with 1 tablespoon water until frothy. Brush mixture over rolls; sprinkle rolls with caraway seed. Let rise and bake as recipe or label directs.

FAN-TANS: Grease 2½- or 3-inch muffin-pan cups. On lightly floured surface, with floured rolling pin, roll dough into rectangle ⅛ inch thick. Brush with melted butter or margarine. Cut into 1½-inch-wide strips. Stack 6 or 7 strips together; cut stacks into 1½-inch pieces; place pieces, cut sides up, in muffin-pan cups. Let rise and bake as recipe or label directs.

PAN ROLLS: Grease 8-inch cake pan. Shape pieces of dough into 2-inch balls. Dip into melted butter or margarine. Place in cake pan, letting balls just touch each other. Let rise and bake as recipe or label directs.

PARKER HOUSE ROLLS: Melt several tablespoons butter or margarine in 13″ by 9″ or 8- or 9-inch square baking pan. Roll dough about ½ inch thick and, with 2½-inch cookie cutter, cut dough into circles. Dip circles on both sides in melted butter or margarine, fold in half and arrange in rows in pan, letting rolls touch each other. Add more melted butter or margarine if necessary. Let rise and bake as recipe or label directs.

LUCKY CLOVERS: Grease 2½- or 3-inch muffin-pan cups. Shape pieces of dough into 2-inch balls; place one in each cup. With scissors, cut each ball in half, then into quarters, cutting through almost to bottom of rolls. Let rise and bake as recipe or label directs.

CURLICUES: Grease large cookie sheet. Roll dough ¼ inch thick into 12″ by 9″ rectangle. Cut crosswise into 1-inch strips. Roll each strip loosely, jelly-roll fashion; place each about 2 inches apart on cookie sheet, cut side up, and tuck end underneath; pinch to seal. Let rise and bake as recipe or label directs.

How to Store

All fresh-baked breads should be used within a few days, since bread will dry out and become moldy if kept very long. To retain moisture, wrap breads tightly in foil or plastic wrap, or place in airtight plastic bag and store in a cool, dry place in a cupboard or bread box. Crisp-crusted breads such as French bread should be wrapped loosely.

Bread may be stored in the refrigerator to retard mold growth, but it will become stale more quickly than when kept at room temperature. For longer storage, freeze.

How to Freeze

Home-baked breads and rolls should be cooled to room temperature. Don't frost or decorate before freezing. Wrap in foil, heavy-duty plastic wrap, airtight plastic bags or freezer-wrap and press all air from package. Then freeze for up to 3 months. If stored longer, they may lose flavor.

Thaw bread 2 to 3 hours at room temperature; if soft-crusted, leave wrapped; if crisp-crusted, unwrap to thaw, then use right away. Or, wrap with foil and heat in oven preheated to 375°F. for 20 minutes; unwrap the last 5 minutes to crisp the crust.

Frozen bread slices may be toasted without thawing.

Thaw sweet breads before decorating.

In-a-Hurry Breads

Choose from a vast array of bread products that make menu planning easy and shorten your time and work in the kitchen. There are packaged fully baked ready-to-eat breads and rolls, sliced (or unsliced) at bakeries and the bakery section of many supermarkets; fully baked brown-and-serve products that need only to be browned in the oven; frozen bread and roll doughs to bake; frozen baked breads that need only thawing or reheating; and yeast-roll mixes to prepare quickly and easily.

Unopened, packaged bread products will keep fresh for a few days in a cool, dry place. After opening, they should be stored as at left.

Frozen coffeecakes and rolls should be stored in the freezer until ready to thaw or to heat for serving. Or, refrigerate them to thaw and use within a week.

Brown-and-serve breads and rolls are fully baked but not browned. To serve, bake them as the label directs until hot and brown. Some are available frozen, some refrigerated, and some at room temperature. Follow label directions for storing.

Breads made from packaged mix should be stored and used within a few days, just like other fresh bread.

Frozen, unbaked yeast bread and rolls must rise before baking. Check the label for storing and preparation directions.

Breads and Rolls

WHITE BREAD

5½ to 6½ cups all-purpose flour
3 tablespoons sugar
2 teaspoons salt
1 package active dry yeast
½ cup milk
butter or margarine

ABOUT 4 HOURS BEFORE SERVING:

1. In large bowl, combine 2 cups flour, sugar, salt and yeast. In medium saucepan over low heat, heat 1½ cups water, milk and 3 tablespoons butter or margarine until very warm (120° to 130°F.). (Butter or margarine does not need to melt.) With mixer at low speed, gradually pour liquid into dry ingredients. Increase speed to medium; beat 2 minutes, occasionally scraping bowl with rubber spatula. Beat in ¾ cup flour or enough to make a thick batter; continue beating 2 minutes, occasionally scraping bowl. With spoon, stir in enough additional flour (about 3 cups) to make a soft dough.
2. Turn dough onto lightly floured surface and knead until smooth and elastic, about 10 minutes. Shape dough into ball and place in greased large bowl, turning over so that top of dough is greased. Cover with towel; let rise in warm place (80° to 85°F.), away from draft, until doubled, about 1 hour. (Dough is doubled when two fingers pressed lightly into dough leave a dent.)
3. Punch down dough by pushing center of dough with fist, then pushing edges of dough into center. Turn dough onto lightly floured surface; cut in half; cover with bowl for 15 minutes.
4. Grease two 9″ by 5″ loaf pans. With lightly floured rolling pin, roll one dough half into 12″ by 8″ rectangle. Starting with 8-inch end, tightly roll dough, jelly-roll fashion; pinch seam to seal. Press ends to seal and tuck under; place, seam side down, in loaf pan. Repeat with remaining dough. Cover with towel; let rise in warm place until doubled, about 1 hour. (Dough is doubled when one finger very lightly pressed against dough leaves a dent.)
5. Preheat oven to 400°F. If desired, brush loaves with 2 tablespoons butter or margarine, melted. Bake loaves 25 to 30 minutes until golden and loaves sound hollow when lightly tapped with fingers. Remove from pans immediately; cool on wire racks. Makes 2 loaves.

ORANGE-SWIRL LOAF: Prepare as above but in step 4, on just one rectangle of dough, evenly sprinkle *¼ cup sugar* and *grated peel of 1 large orange;* roll up as directed and place in loaf pan. (Prepare remaining dough half as above.) With scissors, cut 3 crosswise slits in top of loaf through to first layer of orange peel to allow steam to escape. Let rise, then brush with *melted butter or margarine,* and bake as directed. Serve warm with butter. Makes 1 loaf.

OLD-FASHIONED HERB RING: In small bowl, combine *2 tablespoons grated Parmesan cheese, ½ teaspoon marjoram leaves* and *½ teaspoon dill weed.* Prepare as above but in step 4, grease a large cookie sheet and, on just one rectangle of bread, brush *1 tablespoon butter or margarine,* melted; evenly sprinkle on cheese mixture. From 12-inch side, roll up as directed but place, seam side down, on cookie sheet; bring ends together to form ring and pinch to seal. With sharp knife, from outside edge of ring, make deep slash about 1½ inches toward center of ring; repeat 4 more times, evenly spacing cuts to make 5 sections of dough. Gently separate sections, keeping ring in one piece to make 5 "petals." Cover with towel; let rise in warm place until doubled, about 1 hour. (Prepare remaining dough half as above.)

Preheat oven to 400°F. Brush with *1 egg,* beaten, and sprinkle *1 tablespoon sesame seed* over top. Bake 30 minutes or until bread sounds hollow when lightly tapped with fingers. Remove from cookie sheet and cool on wire rack. Makes 1 ring.

LITTLE LOAVES: Prepare dough as above but in step 3, cut dough into five pieces. In step 4, grease five 5″ by 3″ little loaf pans. With lightly floured rolling pin, roll each piece into 10″ by 5″ rectangle. Starting at 5-inch end, tightly roll dough jelly-roll fashion; pinch seam to seal. Place, seam side down, in loaf pans. Cover with towel; let rise in warm place until doubled, about 40 minutes. Preheat oven to 400°F. Bake loaves 15 minutes or until golden and loaves sound hollow when lightly tapped with fingers. Remove from pans immediately. Serve warm or cold. Makes 5 little loaves.

MINIATURE LOAVES: Prepare dough as above but in step 3, cut dough into 10 pieces. In step 4, grease ten 4½" by 2½" miniature loaf pans. With lightly floured rolling pin, roll each piece into 10" by 4" rectangle. Starting at 4-inch end, tightly roll dough, jelly-roll fashion; pinch seam to seal. Place, seam side down, in loaf pans. Cover with towel; let rise in warm place until doubled, about 1 hour. Preheat oven to 400°F. Bake 15 minutes or until golden and loaves sound hollow when lightly tapped with fingers. Remove from pans immediately. Serve warm. Makes 10 miniature loaves.

BROWN-AND-SERVE LOAVES: Up to 1 week before serving: Prepare Miniature Loaves, above. Preheat oven only to 250°F. Bake loaves 35 minutes or until top crust is very light golden. Remove from pans immediately and cool completely on wire racks. Wrap in plastic bags and refrigerate. To serve: Preheat oven to 400°F. Bake loaves on cookie sheet 15 minutes or until browned.

ONION-BREAD SQUARES

White Bread (above)
1 4-ounce package shredded Cheddar cheese (1 cup)
2 teaspoons melted butter or margarine
½ cup onion flakes
2 tablespoons poppy seed

ABOUT 4 HOURS BEFORE SERVING:
1–3. Prepare White Bread dough as above but in step 1, add cheese with the last addition of flour and, in step 3, do not cut dough in half.
4. Grease well 15½" by 10½" jelly-roll pan. With hands, press dough into pan. Brush with melted butter or margarine; sprinkle with onion flakes and poppy seed. Cover with towel; let rise in warm place (80° to 85°F.) until doubled. (Dough is doubled when one finger very lightly pressed against dough leaves a dent.)
5. Preheat oven to 375°F. Bake bread 15 to 20 minutes until golden. Cool in pan; cut into squares. Makes 16 servings.

FREEZER WHITE BREAD

11 to 12 cups all-purpose flour
butter or margarine
⅔ cup instant nonfat dry milk powder
½ cup sugar
2 tablespoons salt
4 packages active dry yeast

UP TO 1 MONTH AHEAD:
In large bowl, combine 4 cups flour, ¼ cup butter or margarine and remaining ingredients. With mixer at medium-low speed, gradually beat in 4 cups hot tap water (120° to 130°F.) until just blended. Increase speed to medium; beat 2 minutes, occasionally scraping bowl with rubber spatula. Gradually beat in 2 cups flour or enough to make a thick batter; continue beating 2 minutes, occasionally scraping bowl. With spoon, stir in enough additional flour (5 to 6 cups) to make a soft dough.

Turn dough onto lightly floured surface and knead until smooth and elastic, about 10 minutes. Cut dough into 4 pieces; shape each piece into smooth round ball. Place balls on greased cookie sheets;* cover with plastic wrap and freeze until firm. When dough is firm, remove from cookie sheets; rewrap tightly with plastic wrap (or put in individual plastic bags). Return to freezer.

ABOUT 6 HOURS AHEAD OR EARLY IN DAY:
Remove as many breads from the freezer as needed. Unwrap; place on greased cookie sheet and let stand at room temperature, loosely covered with waxed paper, until completely thawed, about 2 to 3 hours. Then, let rise in warm place (80° to 85°F.) until slightly more than doubled, about 2 hours. (Dough is doubled when one finger very lightly pressed against dough leaves a dent.)

Preheat oven to 350°F. Bake bread 35 minutes or until loaf sounds hollow when lightly tapped with fingers. Remove from cookie sheet immediately; brush top with softened butter or margarine, if you like. Cool completely on wire rack. Makes 4 loaves.

* To bake bread same day, cover loosely with towel and let rise in warm place until slightly more than doubled, about 1 hour. Bake as directed.

BASIC ROLL DOUGH

4½ to 5½ cups all-purpose flour
⅓ cup sugar
1½ teaspoons salt
2 packages active dry yeast
½ cup milk
¼ cup butter or margarine
2 eggs

ABOUT 3½ HOURS BEFORE SERVING:

1. In large bowl, combine 1½ cups flour, sugar, salt and yeast. In medium saucepan over low heat, heat ½ cup water, milk and butter or margarine until very warm (120° to 130°F.). (Butter or margarine does not need to melt.) With mixer at low speed, gradually pour liquid into dry ingredients. Increase speed to medium; beat 2 minutes, occasionally scraping bowl with rubber spatula. Beat in eggs and ½ cup flour or enough to make a thick batter; continue beating 2 minutes, occasionally scraping bowl. With spoon, stir in enough additional flour (2 to 2½ cups) to make a soft dough.
2. Turn dough onto lightly floured surface and knead until smooth and elastic, about 10 minutes. Shape dough into ball and place in greased large bowl, turning over so that top of dough is greased. Cover with towel; let rise in warm place (80° to 85°F.), away from draft, until doubled, about 1 hour.
3. Punch down dough by pushing down the center of dough with fist, then pushing edges of dough into center. Turn dough onto lightly floured surface; cut in half; cover with towel for 15 minutes; proceed as directed for any two variations below.

PULL-APART DINNER ROLLS: Grease a cookie sheet. On lightly floured surface, roll *one-half of Basic Roll Dough* ⅛ inch thick. Using 5-inch round cookie cutter, or with edge of 5-inch plate or bowl and knife, cut 10 circles; shape each circle into an oval.

In small skillet over medium heat, in *3 tablespoons melted butter or margarine*, cook *2½ tablespoons minced green onions* until tender. Brush one oval with mixture; fold almost in half and place on cookie sheet. Brush the top folded side with melted butter or margarine mixture. Repeat with rest of ovals, making one row, with ovals slightly overlapping. Sprinkle with *sesame seed.* Cover with towel; let rise again until doubled, about 30 minutes. (Dough is doubled when one finger very lightly pressed against dough leaves a dent.)

Preheat oven to 375°F. Bake loaf 25 minutes or until golden. Remove from cookie sheet. Pull off sections to serve. Makes 1 loaf.

CLOVERLEAF ROLLS: Grease twelve 2½- or 3-inch muffin-pan cups. With sharp knife or kitchen shears, cut *one-half of Basic Roll Dough* into 36 equal pieces; shape each piece into a smooth ball. Place 3 balls into each muffin-pan cup. Brush tops with *melted butter or margarine* and sprinkle with *sesame seed,* if desired. Cover with towel; let rise in warm place until doubled, about 45 minutes. (Dough is doubled when one finger very lightly pressed against dough leaves a dent.)

Preheat oven to 400°F. Bake rolls 10 to 15 minutes until golden. Remove from pan. Makes 12 rolls.

CINNAMON-ALMOND ROLLS: Grease large cookie sheet. On lightly floured surface, with lightly floured rolling pin, roll *one-half of Basic Roll Dough* into 16" by 14" rectangle. Brush dough with *2 tablespoons butter or margarine,* melted; sprinkle with *⅓ cup slivered blanched almonds, ¼ cup sugar* and *1 tablespoon cinnamon.*

Starting with 14-inch edge, roll dough jelly-roll fashion. With sharp knife, cut roll crosswise into 18 slices. Place slices, cut side down, 2 inches apart on cookie sheet. Cover with towel; let rise in warm place until doubled, about 45 minutes. (Dough is doubled when one finger very lightly pressed against dough leaves a dent.)

Preheat oven to 350°F. Bake rolls 25 minutes or until golden. Remove from cookie sheet. Makes 18 rolls.

PINWHEEL ROLLS: Grease 2 cookie sheets. On lightly floured surface, with lightly floured rolling pin, roll *one-half of Basic Roll Dough* into 12½" by 10" rectangle. With sharp knife, cut rectangle into 2½-inch squares. With sharp knife or kitchen shears, make a 1½-inch cut from each of the 4 corners toward center of each square. (Each square will have 8 points.) Fold every other point into the center of the square. Gently press points to center to hold. Place pinwheels 2 inches apart on cookie sheets; brush with *melted butter or margarine.* Cover with towel; let rise in warm place until doubled, about 45 minutes. (Dough is doubled when one finger very lightly pressed against dough leaves a dent.)

Preheat oven to 400°F. Bake rolls 10 minutes or until golden. Remove from cookie sheets. Makes 20 rolls.

MINIATURE BRAID ROLLS: Grease cookie sheet. With sharp knife or kitchen shears, divide *one-half of Basic Roll Dough* into 30 equal pieces. On lightly floured surface, with palms of hands, roll each piece into a rope 6 inches long. Pinch 3 ropes together at one end, then braid, pinching bottom ends together to seal. Tuck ends under slightly and place on cookie sheet. Repeat with remaining strands, placing rolls several inches apart. Brush rolls with *beaten egg.* Cover with towel; let rise in warm place until doubled, about 30 minutes. (Dough is doubled when one finger very lightly pressed against dough leaves a dent.)

Preheat oven to 400°F. Bake rolls 15 to 20 minutes until golden. Remove from cookie sheet. Makes 10 rolls.

ITALIAN BREAD

4½ to 5½ cups all-purpose flour
1 tablespoon sugar
2 teaspoons salt
2 packages active dry yeast
1 tablespoon butter or margarine
cornmeal
salad oil
1 egg white

EARLY IN DAY OR DAY BEFORE SERVING:

1. In large bowl, combine 2 cups flour, sugar, salt and yeast; add butter or margarine. With mixer at low speed, gradually pour 1¾ cups hot tap water (120° to 130°F.) into dry ingredients. Increase speed to medium; beat 2 minutes, occasionally scraping bowl with rubber spatula. Beat in ½ cup flour or enough to make a thick batter; continue beating 2 minutes, occasionally scraping bowl. With spoon, stir in enough additional flour (about 1¾ cups) to make a soft dough.
2. Turn dough onto lightly floured surface and knead until smooth and elastic, about 10 minutes. Cut dough in half. Cover with towel; let stand 20 minutes. Grease large cookie sheet; sprinkle with cornmeal.
3. With lightly floured rolling pin, roll one dough half into 15″ by 10″ rectangle. Starting with 15-inch side, tightly roll dough, jelly-roll fashion; pinch seam to seal. Repeat with remaining dough. Place loaves, seam side down, on cookie sheet; taper ends. Brush loaves with salad oil; cover loosely with plastic wrap. Refrigerate 2 to 24 hours.
4. When ready to bake, preheat oven to 425°F. Meanwhile, remove loaves from refrigerator; uncover and let stand at room temperature 10 minutes. With sharp knife, cut 3 or 4 diagonal slashes on top of each loaf. Bake 20 minutes.
5. Meanwhile, in small bowl, with fork, beat egg white with 1 tablespoon cold water. Remove loaves from oven and brush with mixture; return to oven and bake 5 minutes or until golden. Makes 2 loaves.

ITALIAN ROLLS: Prepare as above but in step 2, cut dough into 6 pieces. In step 3, with lightly floured rolling pin, roll each piece into 8″ by 5″ rectangle. Beginning at 5-inch end, tightly roll each piece, jelly-roll fashion; pinch seam and ends to seal. Place, seam side down, on greased cookie sheet sprinkled with cornmeal. Brush rolls with salad oil. Cover rolls as above; refrigerate 2 to 24 hours. When ready to bake, uncover and let stand 10 minutes; preheat oven to 425°F. Bake 15 minutes; brush with egg-white mixture. Bake 5 minutes longer. Makes 6 rolls.

ITALIAN BREADSTICKS: Prepare as above but in step 2, cut dough into 16 pieces. In step 3, with hands, on lightly floured surface, roll each piece into 12-inch-long stick. Place on greased cookie sheets sprinkled with cornmeal; brush with salad oil. Cover as above; refrigerate 2 to 24 hours. When ready to bake, uncover and let stand 10 minutes; preheat oven to 425°F. Bake 10 minutes; remove from oven and brush with egg-white mixture; sprinkle with *poppy or sesame seed.* Bake 5 minutes longer or until golden brown. Makes 16 breadsticks.

COLOSSAL GOLDEN BREAD

6½ to 7½ cups all-purpose flour
⅓ cup sugar
1 tablespoon salt
1 package active dry yeast
2 cups milk
⅓ cup shortening
2 eggs
1 cup yellow cornmeal
2 tablespoons butter or margarine, softened

ABOUT 4 HOURS BEFORE SERVING:

1. In large bowl, combine 2 cups flour, sugar, salt and yeast. In medium saucepan over low heat, heat ¼ cup water, milk and shortening until very warm (120° to 130°F.). (Shortening does not need to melt.) With mixer at low speed, gradually pour liquid into dry ingredients. Increase speed to medium; beat 2 minutes, occasionally scraping bowl with rubber spatula. Beat in eggs, cornmeal and 1 cup flour or enough to make a thick batter; continue beating 2 minutes, occasionally scraping bowl. With spoon, stir in enough additional flour (about 3 cups) to make a soft dough.
2. Turn dough onto lightly floured surface and knead until smooth and elastic, about 10 minutes. Shape dough into ball and place in greased large bowl, turning over so that top of dough is greased. Cover with towel; let rise in warm place (80° to 85°F.), away from draft, until doubled, about 1 hour. (Dough is doubled when two fingers pressed lightly into dough leave a dent.)
3. Punch down dough by pushing down the center of dough with fist, then pushing edges of dough into center. Turn dough onto lightly floured surface; cut dough in half; cover with bowl for 15 minutes.
4. Grease two 9″ by 5″ loaf pans. With lightly floured rolling pin, roll one dough half into 12″ by 8″ rectangle. Starting with 8-inch end, tightly roll dough jelly-roll fashion; pinch seam to seal. Press ends to seal and tuck under; place, seam side down, in loaf pan. Repeat with remaining dough. Cover with towel; let rise in warm place until doubled, about 45 minutes. (Dough is doubled when one finger very lightly pressed against dough leaves a dent.)
5. Preheat oven to 375°F. Bake loaves 35 minutes or until golden and loaves sound hollow when lightly tapped with fingers. Brush tops with butter or margarine. Remove from pans immediately; cool on wire racks. Makes 2 loaves.

OATMEAL-RAISIN CASSEROLE LOAF

5 cups all-purpose flour
1 cup quick-cooking or old-fashioned oats, uncooked
1 tablespoon salt
2 packages active dry yeast
½ cup molasses
⅓ cup shortening
2 eggs
2 cups dark seedless raisins
¾ cup confectioners' sugar

EARLY IN DAY:

1. In large bowl, combine 3 cups flour, oats, salt and yeast. In medium saucepan over low heat, heat 2 cups water, molasses and shortening until very warm (120° to 130°F.). (Shortening does not need to melt.) With mixer at low speed, gradually pour liquid into dry ingredients. Increase speed to medium; beat 2 minutes, occasionally scraping bowl with rubber spatula. With spoon, stir in eggs, raisins and 2 cups flour. Cover with waxed paper; refrigerate 3 hours.
2. Grease 3-quart round casserole. With well-greased hands, shape dough (do not knead) into large ball. Place ball in casserole and cover with towel. Let rise in warm place (80° to 85°F.), away from draft, until doubled, about 1 hour.
3. Preheat oven to 350°F. Bake bread 1 hour and 10 minutes or until golden and loaf sounds hollow when lightly tapped with fingers. Cool in casserole 10 minutes; remove from casserole to cool completely on wire rack.
4. When loaf is cool, in small cup, stir confectioners' sugar with about 4 teaspoons water until blended; use to frost top of bread. Makes 1 loaf.

WHOLE-WHEAT BREAD

4 cups whole-wheat flour
3 to 3½ cups all-purpose flour
3 tablespoons sugar
4 teaspoons salt
2 packages active dry yeast
¾ cup milk
⅓ cup butter or margarine
⅓ cup molasses

ABOUT 4½ HOURS BEFORE SERVING:

1. In large bowl, combine 2 cups whole-wheat flour, 1 cup all-purpose flour, sugar, salt and yeast. In medium saucepan over low heat, heat 1½ cups water, milk, butter or margarine and molasses until very warm (120° to 130°F.). (Butter or margarine does not need to melt.) With mixer at low speed, gradually pour liquid into dry ingredients. Increase speed to medium; beat 2 minutes, occasionally scraping bowl with rubber spatula. Beat in ½ cup whole-wheat flour and ½ cup all-purpose flour or enough to make a thick batter; continue beating 2 minutes, occasionally scraping bowl. With spoon, stir in 1½ cups whole-wheat and enough additional all-purpose flour (about 1½ cups) to make soft dough.
2. Turn dough onto lightly floured surface and knead until smooth and elastic, about 10 minutes. Shape dough into ball and place in greased large bowl, turning over so that top of dough is greased. Cover with towel; let rise in warm place (80° to 85°F.), away from draft, until doubled, about 1 hour.
3. Punch down dough; turn dough onto lightly floured surface; cut in half; cover with bowl for 15 minutes. Grease two 9″ by 5″ loaf pans. With lightly floured rolling pin, roll one dough half into 12″ by 8″ rectangle. Starting with 8-inch end away from you, tightly roll dough jelly-roll fashion. Pinch seam to seal; press ends to seal and tuck under; place, seam side down, in loaf pan. Repeat with remaining dough. Cover with towel and let rise until doubled, about 1 hour.
4. Preheat oven to 400°F. Bake loaves 30 to 35 minutes until golden and loaves sound hollow when lightly tapped with fingers. Remove from pans immediately; cool on wire racks. Makes 2 loaves.

PUMPERNICKEL-RYE BREAD

5 cups rye flour
4 to 5 cups all-purpose flour
1 tablespoon salt
2 packages active dry yeast
3 cups beer (2 12-ounce cans)
1 cup light molasses
⅓ cup butter or margarine
1 tablespoon caraway seed

ABOUT 6½ HOURS BEFORE SERVING:

1. In large bowl, combine 3 cups rye flour and 1 cup all-purpose flour, salt and yeast. In medium saucepan over low heat, heat beer, molasses and butter or margarine until very warm (120° to 130°F.). (Butter or margarine does not need to melt.) With mixer at low speed, gradually pour liquid into dry ingredients. Increase speed to medium; beat 2 minutes, occasionally scraping bowl with rubber spatula. Beat in 2 cups rye flour or enough to make a thick batter; continue beating 2 minutes, occasionally scraping bowl. With spoon, stir in caraway seed and enough additional all-purpose flour (about 2½ cups) to make a soft dough. (Dough is traditionally sticky.)
2. Turn dough onto well-floured surface and knead until smooth and elastic, about 10 minutes. Shape dough into ball and place in greased large bowl, turning over so top of dough is greased. Cover with towel; let rise in warm place (80° to 85°F.), away from draft, until doubled, about 1 to 2 hours. (Dough is doubled when two fingers pressed lightly into dough leave a dent.)
3. Punch down dough by pushing down the center of dough with fist, then pushing edges into center. Turn dough over; let rise again until doubled, about 1½ hours.
4. Again, punch down dough; turn onto lightly floured surface; cut dough into three pieces and shape into 3 round balls. Place balls, about 5 inches apart, on greased cookie sheets. Cover; let rise in warm place until doubled, about 1 hour. (Dough is doubled when one finger very lightly pressed against dough leaves a dent.)
5. Preheat oven to 350°F. Bake loaves 50 to 60 minutes until loaves sound hollow when lightly tapped with fingers. Remove from cookie sheets immediately; cool completely on wire racks. Makes 3 loaves.

CHEESE BREAD

4 to 5 cups all-purpose flour
2 tablespoons sugar
2 teaspoons salt
2 packages active dry yeast
1 cup milk
2 4-ounce packages shredded Cheddar cheese (2 cups)
yellow and red food color

ABOUT 4½ HOURS BEFORE SERVING:
1. In large bowl, combine 1½ cups flour, sugar, salt and yeast. In medium saucepan over low heat, heat milk, ¾ cup water, cheese, 4 drops yellow and 3 drops red food color until very warm (120° to 130°F.). (Cheese does not need to melt.) With mixer at low speed, gradually pour liquid into dry ingredients. Increase speed to medium; beat 2 minutes, occasionally scraping bowl with rubber spatula. Beat in ½ cup flour or enough to make a thick batter; continue beating 2 minutes, occasionally scraping bowl. With spoon, stir in enough additional flour (about 2 cups) to make a soft dough.
2. Turn dough onto lightly floured surface and knead until smooth and elastic, about 10 minutes. Shape dough into ball and place in greased large bowl, turning over so top of dough is greased. Cover with towel; let rise in warm place (80° to 85°F.), away from draft, until doubled, about 1 hour. (Dough is doubled when two fingers pressed lightly into dough leave a dent.)
3. Punch down dough. Turn dough onto lightly floured surface; cut dough in half; cover with bowl for 15 minutes.
4. Grease two 9″ by 5″ loaf pans. With lightly floured rolling pin, roll one dough half into 12″ by 8″ rectangle. Starting with 8-inch end, tightly roll dough, jelly-roll fashion; pinch seam to seal. Press ends to seal and tuck under; place, seam side down, in loaf pan. Repeat with remaining dough. Cover with towel; let rise in warm place until doubled, about 1 hour. (Dough is doubled when one finger very lightly pressed against dough leaves a dent.)
5. Preheat oven to 375°F. Bake loaves 40 to 45 minutes until golden and loaves sound hollow when lightly tapped with fingers. Remove from pans immediately; cool on wire racks. Makes 2 loaves.

OATMEAL BREAD

5½ to 6 cups all-purpose flour
2 teaspoons salt
2 packages active dry yeast
1 tablespoon butter or margarine
½ cup light molasses
1 cup quick-cooking or old-fashioned oats, uncooked

ABOUT 4½ HOURS BEFORE SERVING:
1. In large bowl, combine 2 cups flour, salt and yeast. In medium saucepan over low heat, heat 2 cups water, butter or margarine, molasses and oats until very warm (120° to 130°F.). (Butter or margarine does not need to melt.) With mixer at low speed, gradually pour oat mixture into dry ingredients. Increase speed to medium; beat 2 minutes, occasionally scraping bowl with rubber spatula. Beat in ¾ cup flour to make a thick batter; continue beating 2 minutes, occasionally scraping bowl. With spoon, stir in enough additional flour (about 2 cups) to make a soft dough.
2. Turn dough onto lightly floured surface and knead until elastic and dough does not stick to surface, about 10 minutes. Shape dough into ball and place in greased large bowl, turning over so that top of dough is greased. Cover with towel; let rise in warm place (80° to 85°F.), away from draft, until doubled, about 1 hour. (Dough is doubled when two fingers pressed lightly into dough leave a dent.)
3. Punch down dough by pushing down the center of dough with fist, then pushing edges of dough into center. Turn dough onto lightly floured surface; cut dough in half; cover with bowl for 15 minutes.
4. Grease two 9″ by 5″ loaf pans. With lightly floured rolling pin, roll one dough half into 12″ by 8″ rectangle. Starting with 8-inch end, tightly roll dough jelly-roll fashion; pinch seam to seal. Press ends to seal and tuck under; place, seam side down, in loaf pan. Repeat with remaining dough. Cover with towel; let rise in warm place until doubled, about 40 minutes.
5. Preheat oven to 350°F. Bake loaves 50 minutes or until loaves sound hollow when lightly tapped with fingers. Remove from pans immediately; cool on wire racks. Makes 2 loaves.

SALLY LUNN

3¼ cups all-purpose flour
3 tablespoons sugar
1¼ teaspoons salt
1 package active dry yeast
1 cup milk
3 tablespoons butter or margarine
2 eggs

ABOUT 3½ HOURS BEFORE SERVING:
1. In large bowl, combine 1¼ cups flour, sugar, salt and yeast. In medium saucepan over low heat, heat milk and butter or margarine until very warm (120° to 130°F.). (Butter or margarine does not need to melt.) With mixer at low speed, gradually pour liquid into dry ingredients. Increase speed to medium; beat 2 minutes, occasionally scraping bowl with rubber spatula. Beat in eggs and ¾ cup flour or enough to make a thick batter; continue beating 2 minutes, occasionally scraping bowl. With spoon, stir in remaining 1¼ cups flour.
2. Cover bowl with towel; let dough rise in warm place (80° to 85°F.), away from draft, until doubled, about 1 hour.
3. Grease and flour well 10-inch tube pan. With spoon, stir down dough. Spoon dough into tube pan; with well-floured hands, pat dough evenly in pan. Cover with towel; let rise in warm place (80° to 85°F.), away from draft, until doubled, about 1 hour.
4. Preheat oven to 300°F. Bake bread 40 minutes or until golden and bread sounds hollow when lightly tapped with fingers. With spatula, loosen bread from sides and center of pan; remove from pan and cool on wire rack. Makes 1 loaf.

CRUSTY ONION-RYE BREAD

1 13¾-ounce package hot-roll mix
½ cup rye flour
1 envelope onion-soup mix for 4 servings
2 eggs

ABOUT 4¾ HOURS BEFORE SERVING:
1. In large bowl, combine 1 cup flour mixture from package, rye flour, yeast from package and soup mix. With mixer at medium speed, gradually pour 1 cup hot tap water (120° to 130°F.) into dry ingredients. Increase speed to medium; beat 2 minutes, occasionally scraping bowl with rubber spatula. Beat in ½ cup flour mixture and eggs; continue beating 2 minutes, occasionally scraping bowl. With spoon, stir in remaining flour mixture.
2. Turn dough onto well-floured surface and knead until smooth and elastic, about 10 minutes. Shape dough into ball and place in greased medium bowl, turning over so that top of dough is greased. Cover with towel; let rise in warm place (80° to 85°F.), away from draft, until doubled, about 2 hours.
3. Punch down dough. Turn onto lightly floured surface; cover with bowl for 15 minutes. Grease 1½-quart round casserole. Shape dough into a ball and place in casserole. Cover with towel; let rise in warm place until doubled, about 1 hour.
4. Preheat oven to 400°F. Bake bread 25 to 30 minutes until it sounds hollow when lightly tapped with fingers. Cool in casserole 10 minutes; remove from casserole and cool on wire rack. Makes 1 loaf.

ONION BUNS

1 13¾-ounce package hot-roll mix
4 teaspoons instant minced onion
2 tablespoons butter or margarine
1 cup chopped onions
1 tablespoon milk
1 egg yolk, beaten
¼ teaspoon salt

ABOUT 2¼ HOURS AHEAD:
Prepare dough for hot-roll mix as label directs but add instant minced onion with flour; let rise. In small saucepan over medium heat, in hot butter or margarine, cook chopped onions until tender. Stir in milk, egg yolk and salt; cover and refrigerate.

Turn dough onto lightly floured surface and knead slightly; shape dough into 18 balls and place in well-greased 2½-inch muffin-pan cups. Top buns with onion mixture. Cover with towel and let rise in warm place (80° to 85°F.) until doubled, about 45 minutes.

Preheat oven to 400°F. Bake buns 15 to 20 minutes until golden. Makes 18 buns.

PARTY ROLLS

3 to 4 cups all-purpose flour
¼ cup sugar
1 teaspoon salt
1 package active dry yeast
¾ cup milk
¼ cup shortening, butter or margarine
1 egg

ABOUT 3½ HOURS BEFORE SERVING:
1. In large bowl, combine 1 cup flour, sugar, salt and yeast. In small saucepan over low heat, heat milk, ¼ cup water and shortening until very warm (120° to 130°F.). (Shortening does not need to melt.) With mixer at low speed, gradually pour liquid into dry ingredients; beat in egg. Increase speed to medium; beat 2 minutes, occasionally scraping bowl with rubber spatula. Beat in ½ cup flour or enough to make a thick batter; continue beating 2 minutes, occasionally scraping bowl. With spoon, stir in enough additional flour (about 1¼ cups) to make a stiff dough.
2. Turn dough onto lightly floured surface and knead until smooth and elastic, about 10 minutes. Shape dough into ball and place in greased large bowl, turning over so that top of dough is greased. Cover with towel; let rise in warm place (80° to 85°F.), away from draft, until doubled, about 1 hour. (Dough is doubled when two fingers pressed lightly into dough leave a dent.)
3. Punch down dough by pushing down the center of dough with fist, then pushing edges of dough into center. Turn dough onto lightly floured surface; cut dough into 18 pieces. Cover with towel for 15 minutes.
4. Grease eighteen 2½-inch muffin-pan cups. Shape each piece into ball. Place one ball in each muffin-pan cup. Cover with towel; let rise in warm place until doubled, about 1 hour. (Dough is doubled when one finger very lightly pressed against dough leaves a dent.)
5. Preheat oven to 425°F. Bake rolls 12 minutes or until golden brown. Makes 18 rolls.

WHOLE-WHEAT ROLLS: Prepare as above but substitute *1½ cups whole-wheat flour* for 1½ cups of the all-purpose flour.

HONEY BUNS: Prepare as above but in step 4, into each muffin-pan cup, from *one 12-ounce jar honey,* spoon 1 tablespoon honey; and from *1 cup chopped pecans,* sprinkle some over honey; complete recipe.

CHEESE ROLLS: Prepare as above but add *1 cup shredded sharp Cheddar cheese* with egg in step 1.

VIRGINIA BUNS: Prepare as above but add *1½ teaspoons nutmeg* to ½ cup flour in step 1. If you like, dip hot buns into *melted butter or margarine,* then *cinnamon-sugar mixture.*

CHEESE BREADSTICKS

1⅔ cups all-purpose flour
¾ cup grated Parmesan cheese (3-ounce container)
1 tablespoon sugar
1 teaspoon salt
1 package active dry yeast
¼ cup salad oil
1 egg
1 tablespoon sesame seed

ABOUT 2½ HOURS BEFORE SERVING:
1. In large bowl, combine flour, cheese, sugar, salt and yeast. With mixer at low speed, gradually pour ⅔ cup hot tap water (120° to 130°F.) and salad oil into dry ingredients. Increase speed to medium; beat 2 minutes, occasionally scraping bowl with rubber spatula. (Dough will not be completely smooth because of cheese.)
2. Shape dough into ball and place in greased large bowl, turning over so top of dough is greased. Cover with towel; let rise in warm place (80° to 85°F.), away from draft, until doubled, about 1 hour. (Dough is doubled when two fingers pressed lightly into dough leave a dent.)
3. Preheat oven to 350°F. Punch down dough by pushing down the center of dough with fist, then pushing edges of dough into center; cut into 12 pieces. Roll each piece into stick about 14 inches long; place on greased cookie sheet.
4. Beat egg with 1 tablespoon water; brush on sticks; sprinkle with sesame seed. Bake 20 minutes or until golden. Cool sticks on wire rack. Makes 12 breadsticks.

Refrigerator Rolls, page 449

REFRIGERATOR ROLLS

6 to 6½ cups all-purpose flour
½ cup sugar
2 teaspoons salt
2 packages active dry yeast
½ cup butter or margarine, softened
1 egg
salad oil

EARLY IN DAY OR UP TO 1 WEEK AHEAD:
1. In large bowl, combine 2¼ cups flour, sugar, salt and yeast; add butter or margarine. With mixer at low speed, gradually pour 2 cups hot tap water (120° to 130°F.) into dry ingredients. Add egg; increase speed to medium; beat 2 minutes, occasionally scraping bowl with rubber spatula. Beat in ¾ cup flour or enough to make a thick batter; continue beating 2 minutes, occasionally scraping bowl. With spoon, stir in enough additional flour (about 2½ cups) to make a soft dough.
2. Turn dough onto lightly floured surface and knead until smooth and elastic, about 10 minutes. Shape dough into ball and place in greased large bowl, turning over so that top of dough is greased. Cover with towel; let rise in warm place (80° to 85°F.), away from draft, until doubled, about 1½ hours. (Dough is doubled when two fingers pressed lightly into dough leave a dent.)
3. Punch down dough by pushing down the center of dough with fist, then pushing edges of dough into center. Turn dough over; brush with salad oil. Cover bowl tightly with plastic wrap and refrigerate, punching down dough occasionally, until ready to use.

ABOUT 2 HOURS BEFORE SERVING:
4. Remove dough from refrigerator; grease 15½″ by 10½″ open roasting pan. Cut dough into 30 equal pieces; shape into balls and place in pan. Cover with towel; let rise in warm place until doubled, about 1½ hours. (Dough is doubled when one finger very lightly pressed against dough leaves a dent.)
5. Preheat oven to 425°F. Bake 15 to 20 minutes until golden brown. Brush rolls with melted butter or margarine. Remove from pans and serve immediately. Makes about 2½ dozen rolls.

BRIOCHE

1¾ to 2¼ cups all-purpose flour
¼ cup sugar
¼ teaspoon salt
1 package active dry yeast
⅓ cup butter or margarine
¼ cup milk
2 eggs
½ teaspoon lemon extract
salad oil

DAY BEFORE:
1. In large bowl, combine ¾ cup flour, sugar, salt and yeast. In medium saucepan over low heat, heat ¼ cup water, butter or margarine and milk until very warm (120° to 130°F.). (Butter or margarine does not need to melt.) With mixer at low speed, gradually pour liquid into dry ingredients. Increase speed to medium; beat 2 minutes, occasionally scraping bowl with rubber spatula. Beat in eggs, lemon extract and ½ cup flour or enough to make a thick batter; continue beating 2 minutes, occasionally scraping bowl. With spoon, stir in enough additional flour (about ½ cup) to make soft dough. Continue beating with spoon for 5 minutes.
2. Place dough in greased large bowl. Cover with towel; let rise in warm place (80° to 85°F.), away from draft, until doubled, about 1 hour. Stir dough down; cover bowl tightly with foil or plastic wrap and refrigerate overnight.

ABOUT 1½ HOURS BEFORE SERVING:
3. Grease 18 brioche pans or 2-inch muffin-pan cups. Turn dough onto lightly floured surface; cut off about ⅙ of dough and reserve. Shape remaining dough into an 18-inch roll. Cut roll into 18 pieces; shape each into a ball and place in a brioche pan. Cut reserved dough into 18 pieces and shape into small balls. Grease finger and make depression in center of each large ball; place small balls in depressions. Brush tops with salad oil. Cover with towel; let rise in warm place until doubled, about 45 minutes.
4. Preheat oven to 375°F. Bake brioche 10 minutes or until golden and rolls sound hollow when lightly tapped with fingers. Remove from pans immediately and serve warm. Makes 18 brioche.

Jelly Doughnuts, page 457, and Hearty Hot Cocoa, page 606

Sweet Breads, Coffeecakes and Doughnuts

BASIC SWEET DOUGH

7 to 8 cups all-purpose flour
1 cup sugar
1 teaspoon salt
2 packages active dry yeast
½ teaspoon ground cardamom or 1½ tablespoons grated lemon peel
1½ cups milk
1 cup butter or margarine
2 eggs

ABOUT 4¾ HOURS BEFORE SERVING:
1. In large bowl, combine 2 cups flour, sugar, salt, yeast and cardamom. In medium saucepan over low heat, heat milk, ½ cup water and butter or margarine until very warm (120° to 130°F.). (Butter or margarine does not need to melt.) With mixer at low speed, gradually pour liquid into dry ingredients. Increase speed to medium; beat 2 minutes, occasionally scraping bowl with rubber spatula. Beat in eggs and 1½ cups flour; continue beating 2 minutes, occasionally scraping bowl. With spoon, stir in enough additional flour (about 3½ cups) to make a soft dough.
2. Turn dough onto lightly floured surface and knead until smooth and elastic, about 10 minutes. Shape dough into ball and place in greased large bowl, turning over so that top of dough is greased. Cover with towel; let rise in warm place (80° to 85°F.), away from draft, until doubled, about 1 hour. (Dough is doubled when two fingers pressed lightly into dough leave a dent.)
3. Punch down dough. Turn dough onto lightly floured surface; cut dough into thirds or halves as directed in recipes below; cover with towel for 15 minutes. Proceed with one of the variations below.

SWEET LOAF

1. Grease 9″ by 5″ loaf pan. Use *one-third of Basic Sweet Dough.* With lightly floured rolling pin, roll dough into 12″ by 9″ rectangle. Starting from 9-inch end, tightly roll dough jelly-roll fashion; pinch seam to seal. Press ends to seal and tuck under; place, seam side down, in loaf pan. Cover with towel; let rise in warm place until doubled, about 1½ hours. (Dough is doubled when one finger very lightly pressed against dough leaves a dent.)
2. Preheat oven to 350°F. Bake loaf 35 minutes or until loaf sounds hollow when lightly tapped with fingers. Remove from pan immediately. Cool on wire rack. Makes 1 loaf.

CINNAMON-NUT BREAD: Use *one-third of Basic Sweet Dough.* In small bowl, combine *¼ cup packed light brown sugar, ¼ cup chopped pecans* and *½ teaspoon cinnamon.* After rolling dough into rectangle in step 1 of Sweet Loaf, evenly sprinkle sugar mixture on dough; roll up as directed.

LEMON LOAF: Use *one-third of Basic Sweet Dough.* In small bowl, combine *grated peel of 1 lemon, 2 tablespoons sugar* and *¼ teaspoon mace or nutmeg.* After rolling dough into rectangle in step 1 of Sweet Loaf, evenly sprinkle lemon mixture on dough; roll up as directed.

RAISIN BREAD: Use *one-third of Basic Sweet Dough.* After rolling dough into rectangle in step 1 of Sweet Loaf, evenly sprinkle *¾ cup raisins* on dough; roll up as directed.

PINE-NUT CRESCENTS

ABOUT 4½ HOURS BEFORE SERVING:
Grease cookie sheet. Cut *one-half of Basic Sweet Dough* into 2 pieces. With lightly floured rolling pin, roll one piece into a 10-inch circle; cut into 10 triangles. Using *½ cup raspberry or apricot preserves,* on base of each triangle, about 1 inch from edge, place a scant teaspoonful of preserves. For each, fold edge securely over preserves, then tightly roll up; place point down, on cookie sheet, and curve ends to form a crescent. Repeat with remaining dough. Let rise in a warm place (80° to 85°F.) until doubled. (Dough is doubled when one finger very lightly pressed against dough leaves a dent.)

Preheat oven to 350°F. Brush crescents with *1 egg,* beaten; sprinkle with *½ cup pine nuts.* Bake 15 to 20 minutes until golden. Remove from cookie sheet immediately. Makes 20 crescents.

CHERRY-GLAZED BUNS

ABOUT 4½ HOURS BEFORE SERVING:
Grease large cookie sheet. Cut *one-half of Basic Sweet Dough* (opposite) into 16 pieces. With hands, roll one of pieces into a 12-inch rope; twist rope by turning its two ends in opposite directions. Snugly wind twisted rope round and round, making a flat, coiled bun; tuck end under, then place on cookie sheet. Repeat with rest of dough pieces. Let rise in warm place (80° to 85°F.) until doubled. (Dough is doubled when one finger very lightly pressed against dough leaves a dent.)

Preheat oven to 350°F. Bake buns 20 minutes or until golden. Remove from cookie sheet immediately.

Meanwhile, in small bowl, blend *½ cup confectioners' sugar* with *4 to 5 teaspoons hot water* until smooth. Spread on buns. Cut *8 candied cherries* in half; use to garnish buns. Makes 16 buns.

FRUITED BRAID

½ of Basic Sweet Dough (opposite)
1 cup golden raisins
¾ cup finely chopped fresh or candied orange peel
¼ cup finely chopped candied citron
1 tablespoon all-purpose flour
1 egg yolk, slightly beaten
½ cup confectioners' sugar

ABOUT 4¾ HOURS BEFORE SERVING:
Grease large cookie sheet. Cut Basic Sweet Dough into 3 pieces. With lightly floured rolling pin, roll each piece of dough into a 12" by 4" strip.

In medium bowl, toss raisins, orange peel and citron with flour. Spread ⅓ of mixture on lengthwise center of each strip; brush edges with egg yolk. Fold edges of each strip over fruit and each other, forming a roll; pinch seam to seal. Braid the 3 rolls together, tucking ends under; place on cookie sheet. Cover with towel; let rise in warm place (80° to 85°F.), away from draft, until doubled, about 1 hour. (Dough is doubled when one finger very lightly pressed against dough leaves a dent.) Brush braid with egg yolk.

Preheat oven to 350°F. Bake 35 minutes or until golden and loaf sounds hollow when lightly tapped with fingers. Remove from cookie sheet immediately and cool completely on wire rack. In small bowl, mix sugar and 1 tablespoon water; brush over braid. Makes 1 loaf.

RAISIN BRAID

Basic Sweet Dough (opposite)
¾ cup dark seedless raisins
½ cup sliced blanched almonds
1 egg, beaten

ABOUT 4½ HOURS BEFORE SERVING:
1–3. Prepare Basic Sweet Dough as directed but in step 1, before stirring in last 3½ cups flour, stir in raisins and ¼ cup almonds and, in step 3, cut dough into 3 pieces; cover with towel for 15 minutes.
4. Grease 9-inch springform pan. With hands, roll each piece of dough into a roll 22 inches long. Place rolls side by side and braid; pinch ends to seal. Coil braid into pan; brush with beaten egg and sprinkle with ¼ cup almonds. Cover with towel; let rise in warm place until doubled, about ½ hour. (Dough is doubled when one finger very lightly pressed against dough leaves a dent.)
5. Preheat oven to 350°F. Bake 1 hour and 15 minutes or until bread sounds hollow when lightly tapped with fingers. Cool in pan about 10 minutes. Remove from pan and cool on wire rack. Makes 1 loaf.

BRAIDED ROLLS

ABOUT 4½ HOURS BEFORE SERVING:
Grease large cookie sheet. Cut *one-half of Basic Sweet Dough* (opposite) into 12 pieces. Cut one piece into thirds; with hands, roll each third into a 10-inch rope. Braid these three ropes, tucking ends under; place on cookie sheet. Repeat with remaining pieces of dough. Let rise in warm place (80° to 85°F.) until doubled. (Dough is doubled when one finger very lightly pressed against dough leaves a dent.)

Preheat oven to 350°F. Brush rolls with *1 egg*, beaten, then bake 15 to 20 minutes until golden. Remove from cookie sheet immediately and cool on wire racks. Makes 12 rolls.

CINNAMON-ORANGE BUNS

½ of Basic Sweet Dough (page 450)
sugar
½ cup orange juice
¼ cup butter or margarine
1 tablespoon grated orange peel
3 egg yolks
1 tablespoon cinnamon

ABOUT 5 HOURS BEFORE SERVING:
1. Grease twelve 3″ by 1½″ muffin-pan cups. In medium saucepan over medium heat, cook ½ cup sugar, orange juice, butter or margarine and orange peel 5 minutes, stirring occasionally. Pour 1 tablespoon of mixture into each muffin-pan cup.
2. With lightly floured rolling pin, roll dough into 16″ by 13″ rectangle. In small bowl, with fork, beat 1 tablespoon water and egg yolks; lightly brush some of mixture over dough. In cup, mix ¼ cup sugar and cinnamon; sprinkle evenly over dough.
3. From 16-inch side, roll dough jelly-roll fashion; pinch seam to seal. With seam side down, cut roll into twenty-four ¾-inch crosswise slices. Brush all sides with yolk mixture. Into each muffin-pan cup, press 2 slices, side by side with a cut side down. Cover and let rise in warm place until doubled. (Dough is doubled when one finger very lightly pressed against dough leaves a dent.)
4. Preheat oven to 350°F. Brush tops with yolk mixture; bake 25 minutes or until golden. Remove from pan immediately and cool on wire rack. Makes 12 buns.

KNOTTED ROLLS

ABOUT 4½ HOURS BEFORE SERVING:
Grease large cookie sheet. Cut *one-half of Basic Sweet Dough* (page 450) in half. With lightly floured rolling pin, roll one piece into 12″ by 8″ rectangle; cut rectangle into eight 8″ by 1½″ strips. Loosely tie each strip into knot; with scissors, make 3 or 4 cuts in each end; place on cookie sheet. Repeat with remaining piece of dough. Let rolls rise in warm place (80° to 85°F.) until doubled.

Preheat oven to 350°F. Lightly brush rolls with *1 egg*, beaten; bake 15 to 20 minutes until golden. Remove from cookie sheet immediately. Makes 16 rolls.

CINNAMON BUNS

½ of Basic Sweet Dough (page 450)
½ cup packed light brown sugar
½ cup chopped pecans
½ cup dark seedless raisins
1 teaspoon cinnamon
¼ cup butter or margarine, melted
Sugar Glaze (below)

ABOUT 4 HOURS BEFORE SERVING:
Grease well 13″ by 9″ baking dish. In small bowl, combine brown sugar, pecans, raisins and cinnamon; set aside. With lightly floured rolling pin, roll dough into 18″ by 12″ rectangle. Brush generously with melted butter or margarine; sprinkle sugar mixture over dough.

Starting with 18-inch side, roll dough jelly-roll fashion; pinch seam to seal. With seam side down, cut dough crosswise into 18 slices; place in baking dish, cut sides down; brush with remaining melted butter or margarine. Cover with towel; let rise in warm place until doubled, about 40 minutes. (Dough is doubled when one finger very lightly pressed against dough leaves a dent.)

Preheat oven to 400°F. Bake buns 20 minutes or until golden brown. Cool slightly in pan on wire rack. Spread with Sugar Glaze. Serve warm. Makes 18 buns.

SUGAR GLAZE: In small bowl, stir *2 cups confectioners' sugar, ½ teaspoon vanilla extract* and about *3 tablespoons water* until smooth.

POTICA

3½ to 3¾ cups all-purpose flour
sugar
salt
1 package active dry yeast
1 cup milk
butter or margarine
2 eggs, separated
2 cups ground California walnuts
⅓ cup half-and-half
½ teaspoon vanilla extract
2 tablespoons fresh bread crumbs

ABOUT 4 HOURS BEFORE SERVING:
1. In large bowl, combine 1¼ cups flour, ¼ cup sugar, 1 teaspoon salt and yeast. In medium saucepan over low heat, heat milk,

¼ cup water and ¼ cup butter or margarine until very warm (120° to 130°F.). (Butter or margarine does not need to melt.) With mixer at low speed, gradually pour liquid into dry ingredients. Increase speed to medium; beat 2 minutes, occasionally scraping bowl with rubber spatula. Beat in 2 egg yolks and 1½ cups flour or enough to make a thick batter; continue beating 2 minutes, occasionally scraping bowl. With spoon, stir in enough additional flour (about ¾ cup) to make a soft dough.
2. Turn dough onto lightly floured surface and knead until smooth and elastic, about 10 minutes. Shape dough into ball and place in greased large bowl, turning over so that top of dough is greased. Cover with towel; let rise in warm place (80° to 85°F.), away from draft, until doubled, about 1 hour. (Dough is doubled when two fingers pressed lightly into dough leave a dent.)
3. Meanwhile, prepare filling: In medium bowl, stir walnuts, ⅔ cup sugar, half-and-half, ½ teaspoon salt and vanilla. In small saucepan over medium heat, melt 2 tablespoons butter or margarine; add bread crumbs and cook until golden; add to walnut mixture. In small bowl, with mixer at high speed, beat 2 egg whites until stiff; with rubber spatula, gently fold nut mixture into beaten whites.
4. Punch down dough by pushing down the center of dough with fist, then pushing edges of dough into center. Turn dough onto lightly floured surface; cut in half; cover with bowl for 15 minutes.
5. Grease two 9″ by 5″ loaf pans. With lightly floured rolling pin, roll one dough half into a 16″ by 9″ rectangle. Spread with half of filling; starting with 9-inch end, tightly roll dough jelly-roll fashion; pinch seam to seal. Press ends to seal and tuck under; place, seam side down, in loaf pan. Repeat with remaining dough and filling. Cover with towel; let rise in warm place until doubled, about 30 to 40 minutes. (Dough is doubled when one finger very lightly pressed against dough leaves a dent.)
6. Preheat oven to 375°F. Bake 35 to 40 minutes until golden and loaves sound hollow when lightly tapped with fingers. Remove from pans immediately; cool on wire racks. Makes 2 loaves.

SWEDISH LIMPA

3½ to 4 cups all-purpose flour
2 cups rye flour
¼ cup sugar
1 tablespoon salt
2 packages active dry yeast
1 cup milk
2 tablespoons molasses
2 tablespoons butter or margarine
2 teaspoons anise seed
salad oil

DAY BEFORE OR EARLY IN DAY:
1. On waxed paper, combine 3½ cups all-purpose flour and rye flour. In large bowl, combine 2 cups flour mixture, sugar, salt and yeast. In medium saucepan over low heat, heat 1 cup water, milk, molasses, butter or margarine and anise seed until very warm (120° to 130°F.). (Butter or margarine does not need to melt.) With mixer at low speed, gradually pour liquid into dry ingredients. Increase speed to medium; beat 2 minutes, occasionally scraping bowl with rubber spatula. Beat in ¾ cup flour mixture or enough to make a thick batter; beat 2 minutes, occasionally scraping bowl. With spoon, stir in remaining flour mixture and enough additional all-purpose flour to make a soft dough.
2. Turn dough onto lightly floured surface and knead until smooth and elastic, about 10 minutes. Cut dough in half; cover with towel; let stand 20 minutes. Grease large cookie sheet.
3. Shape dough into 2 balls; with hands, flatten dough into ovals, each about 12″ by 4″. Place ovals at least 3 inches apart on cookie sheet; brush with salad oil. Cover loosely with plastic wrap and refrigerate 2 to 24 hours.

ABOUT 2 HOURS BEFORE SERVING:
Preheat oven to 375°F. Uncover loaves and let stand at room temperature 10 minutes. Bake 35 minutes or until loaves sound hollow when lightly tapped with fingers. Remove from cookie sheet immediately and cool on wire racks. Makes 2 loaves.

HOLIDAY LIMPA: Prepare as above but stir *¾ cup dark seedless raisins* and *½ cup finely chopped candied orange peel* into batter before adding remaining flour mixture at end of step 1.

HOT CROSS BUNS

5½ to 6 cups all-purpose flour
⅔ cup sugar
1 teaspoon salt
1 teaspoon nutmeg
2 packages active dry yeast
1 cup milk
½ cup shortening, butter or margarine
1 egg
1 4-ounce container candied citron (½ cup), minced
¾ cup dried currants
1 egg white, slightly beaten
1 cup confectioners' sugar
½ teaspoon vanilla extract

ABOUT 4 HOURS BEFORE SERVING:
1. In large bowl, combine 1½ cups flour, sugar, salt, nutmeg and yeast. In small saucepan over low heat, heat ½ cup water, milk and shortening until very warm (120° to 130°F.). (Shortening does not need to melt.) With mixer at low speed, gradually pour liquid into dry ingredients; beat in egg. Increase speed to medium; beat 2 minutes, occasionally scraping bowl with rubber spatula. Beat in ¾ cup flour or enough to make a thick batter; continue beating 2 minutes, occasionally scraping bowl. With spoon, stir in citron, currants and enough additional flour (about 2¾ cups) to make a soft dough.
2. Turn dough onto lightly floured surface and knead until smooth and elastic, about 10 minutes. Shape dough into ball and place in greased large bowl, turning over so that top of dough is greased. Cover with towel; let rise in warm place (80° to 85°F.), away from draft, until doubled, about 1½ hours. (Dough is doubled when two fingers pressed lightly into dough leave a dent.)
3. Punch down dough by pushing down center of dough with fist, then pushing edges of dough into center. Turn out onto lightly floured surface. Cut dough into 18 pieces; cover with towel for 15 minutes.
4. Grease 13″ by 9″ baking pan. Shape dough into balls. Place in pan. With kitchen scissors, cut deep cross in top of each bun. Cover with towel; let rise in warm place until doubled, about 1½ hours. (Dough is doubled when one finger very lightly pressed against dough leaves a dent.)
5. Preheat oven to 375°F. Brush tops of buns with egg white. Bake 20 to 25 minutes until golden brown. Meanwhile, prepare icing: In small bowl, with spoon, stir confectioners' sugar, vanilla and 1 to 2 teaspoons hot water until smooth. Cool buns slightly in pan; fill cross in each bun with icing. Serve warm or cold. Makes 18 buns.

NORWEGIAN CHRISTMAS CAKE

5 to 6 cups all-purpose flour
½ cup sugar
2 teaspoons ground cardamom
1 teaspoon salt
2 packages active dry yeast
1 cup milk
⅔ cup butter or margarine
2 eggs
1 15-ounce package dark seedless raisins
1 4-ounce container candied citron
1 egg white, slightly beaten

ABOUT 4 HOURS BEFORE SERVING:
1. In large bowl, combine 2 cups flour, sugar, cardamom, salt and yeast. In medium saucepan over low heat, heat milk, butter or margarine and ½ cup water until very warm (120° to 130°F.). (Butter or margarine does not need to melt.) With mixer at low speed, gradually pour liquid into dry ingredients. Increase speed to medium; beat 2 minutes, occasionally scraping bowl with rubber spatula. Beat in eggs and ¾ cup flour or enough to make a thick batter; continue beating 2 minutes, occasionally scraping bowl. With spoon, stir in enough additional flour (about 1½ to 2 cups) to make a soft dough.
2. Turn dough onto lightly floured surface and knead until smooth and elastic, about 10 minutes. Shape dough into ball and place in greased large bowl, turning over so that top of dough is greased. Cover with towel; let rise in warm place (80° to 85°F.), away from draft, until doubled, about 1½ hours. (Dough is doubled when two fingers pressed lightly into dough leave a dent.)
3. Punch down dough by pushing down center with fist, then pushing edges of dough into center. Turn dough onto lightly floured surface; knead in raisins and

citron. Cut dough in half; cover with bowl 15 minutes. Grease two 9″ by 5″ loaf pans.
4. With lightly floured rolling pin, roll one dough half into 12″ by 8″ rectangle. Starting with 8-inch end, tightly roll dough jelly-roll fashion; pinch seam to seal. Press ends to seal and tuck under; place, seam side down, in loaf pan. Repeat with remaining dough. Cover with towel; let rise in warm place until doubled, about 1 hour. (Dough is doubled when one finger very lightly pressed against dough leaves a dent.)
5. Preheat oven to 350°F. Brush tops of loaves with egg white. Bake 45 to 50 minutes until loaves sound hollow when lightly tapped with fingers. Remove from pans immediately; cool on racks. Makes 2 loaves.

FREEZER PANETTONE BUNS

5½ to 6½ cups all-purpose flour
¾ cup sugar
½ cup butter or margarine, softened
1 teaspoon salt
¾ teaspoon anise seed
3 packages active dry yeast
3 eggs
¼ cup dark seedless raisins
¼ cup chopped candied cherries
¼ cup slivered blanched almonds
Sugar Glaze (page 452)

UP TO 1 MONTH AHEAD:
In large bowl, combine 1¼ cups flour with next 5 ingredients. With mixer at low speed, gradually add 1 cup hot tap water (120° to 130°F.). Increase speed to medium; beat 2 minutes, occasionally scraping bowl with rubber spatula. Beat in eggs and ¾ cup flour or enough to make a thick batter; continue beating 2 minutes, occasionally scraping bowl. With spoon, stir in enough flour (about 3 cups) to make a soft dough.

Turn dough onto lightly floured surface and knead until smooth and elastic, about 10 minutes. Knead in raisins, cherries and almonds until evenly distributed. Cut dough into 3 equal pieces. Shape one piece into 8 balls; arrange in greased 8-inch round cake pan;* wrap with plastic wrap; freeze. Repeat with remaining dough.

* To bake bread same day, cover loosely with towel and let rise in warm place until slightly more than doubled, about 2 hours. Bake as directed.

ABOUT 6 HOURS BEFORE SERVING:
Remove as many breads from freezer as needed. Unwrap; let stand at room temperature, loosely covered with waxed paper, until completely thawed, about 3 hours. Then let rise in warm place (80° to 85°F.), away from draft, until slightly more than doubled, about 1½ hours.

Preheat oven to 350°F. Bake bread 20 to 25 minutes until golden. Meanwhile, make Sugar Glaze. Remove bread from pan and place on serving plate; spread top with glaze. Serve warm or cold. Each bread makes 8 servings. Makes 3 breads.

COMING-OF-THE-KINGS BREAD

1 13¾-ounce package hot-roll mix
2 eggs
¼ cup butter or margarine, melted
¼ cup sugar
1 teaspoon vanilla extract
½ cup chopped California walnuts
½ cup golden raisins
¾ cup diced mixed candied fruits
1 cup confectioners' sugar

ABOUT 4 HOURS BEFORE SERVING:
1. In large bowl, dissolve yeast from hot-roll mix in ½ cup warm water; stir in mix, eggs, butter or margarine, sugar and vanilla until mixed. Cover with towel; let rise in warm place (80° to 85°F.), away from draft, until doubled, about 1 hour. (Dough is doubled when two fingers pressed lightly into dough leave a dent.)
2. Grease cookie sheet. Stir walnuts, raisins and ½ cup candied fruits into dough. Turn dough onto well-floured surface; knead until elastic and not sticky, about 5 minutes. Shape dough into 20-inch-long roll; join ends to form a ring; place on cookie sheet. Cover with towel; let rise in warm place until doubled, about 30 minutes. (Dough is doubled when one finger very lightly pressed against dough leaves a dent.)
3. Preheat oven to 375°F. Bake loaf 30 minutes or until golden and loaf sounds hollow when lightly tapped with fingers. Remove from cookie sheet to cool on rack.
4. When bread is cool, in small bowl, stir confectioners' sugar and 2 tablespoons water until blended; stir in remaining candied fruits; use to glaze top. Makes 1 loaf.

STOLLEN

5½ to 6½ cups all-purpose flour
½ cup sugar
1½ teaspoons salt
2 packages active dry yeast
¾ cup milk
⅔ cup butter or margarine
3 eggs
1 cup toasted slivered almonds
1 cup cut-up candied cherries
⅓ cup golden raisins
confectioners' sugar

EARLY IN DAY:

1. In large bowl, combine 2 cups flour, sugar, salt and yeast. In small saucepan over low heat, heat milk, ½ cup water and butter or margarine until very warm (120° to 130°F.). (Butter or margarine does not need to melt.) With mixer at low speed, gradually pour liquid into dry ingredients. Increase speed to medium; beat 2 minutes, occasionally scraping bowl with rubber spatula. Beat in eggs and ½ cup flour or enough to make a thick batter; continue beating 2 minutes, occasionally scraping bowl. With spoon, stir in enough flour (about 2¾ cups) to make a soft dough.
2. Turn dough onto lightly floured surface and knead until smooth and elastic, about 10 minutes. Shape dough into ball and place in greased large bowl, turning over so that top of dough is greased. Cover with towel; let rise in warm place (80° to 85°F.), away from draft, until doubled, about 1 hour. (Dough is doubled when two fingers pressed lightly into dough leave a dent.) In small bowl, mix almonds, cherries and raisins.
3. Punch down dough. Turn dough onto lightly floured surface; knead nut mixture into dough. Cut dough into 3 pieces. Cover 2 pieces; refrigerate.
4. With lightly floured rolling pin, roll one piece of dough into 12" by 7" oval; fold in half lengthwise. Place on large cookie sheet. Cover with towel. Repeat with second piece of dough. Let both rise in warm place until doubled, about 1 hour. (Dough is doubled when one finger very lightly pressed against dough leaves a dent.) After 30 minutes of rising time, repeat with third piece of dough.
5. Preheat oven to 350°F. Bake 25 to 30 minutes until stollens sound hollow when lightly tapped with fingers. Remove from cookie sheets and cool completely on wire racks. Bake third stollen and cool. Sprinkle tops with confectioners' sugar. Each stollen makes 8 servings. Makes 3 stollens.

LEMON BUBBLE RING

5 to 6 cups all-purpose flour
sugar
1 teaspoon salt
2 packages active dry yeast
1 cup milk
butter or margarine
2 eggs
grated peel of 2 lemons
¼ teaspoon mace

ABOUT 4 HOURS BEFORE SERVING:

1. In large bowl, combine 2 cups flour, ½ cup sugar, salt and yeast. In medium saucepan over low heat, heat milk, ½ cup water, ¼ cup butter or margarine until very warm (120° to 130°F.). (Butter or margarine does not need to melt.) With mixer at low speed, gradually pour liquid into dry ingredients. Increase speed to medium; add eggs and beat 2 minutes, occasionally scraping bowl with rubber spatula. Beat in ½ cup flour or enough to make a thick batter; continue beating 2 minutes, occasionally scraping bowl. With spoon, stir in enough additional flour (about 2 cups) to make a soft dough.
2. Turn dough onto lightly floured surface and knead until smooth and elastic, about 10 minutes. Shape dough into ball and place in greased large bowl, turning over so that top of dough is greased. Cover with towel; let rise in warm place (80° to 85°F.), away from draft, until doubled, about 1 hour. (Dough is doubled when two fingers pressed lightly into dough leave a dent.)
3. Punch down dough by pushing down center with fist, then pushing edges of dough into center. Turn dough onto lightly floured surface; cut dough in half; cover with bowl and let stand 15 minutes. Meanwhile, in small bowl, combine ½ cup sugar, lemon peel and mace; set aside. In small saucepan, melt 2 tablespoons butter or margarine. Grease 10-inch tube pan.
4. Cut each dough half into 16 pieces. Shape each piece into ball by tucking ends under. Place half of balls in tube pan, brush with half of melted butter or margarine,

sprinkle with half of lemon mixture. Repeat with remaining balls, melted butter and lemon mixture. Cover with towel; let rise in warm place until doubled, about 45 minutes. (Dough is doubled when one finger very lightly pressed against dough leaves a dent.)
5. Preheat oven to 350°F. Bake 35 minutes or until golden and loaf sounds hollow when lightly tapped with fingers. Cool in pan 5 minutes; remove from pan and cool on wire rack. Makes 1 loaf.

JELLY DOUGHNUTS

5 to 6 cups all-purpose flour
⅓ cup sugar
2 teaspoons nutmeg
1 teaspoon salt
½ teaspoon cinnamon
2 packages active dry yeast
1¼ cups milk
⅓ cup butter or margarine
2 eggs
about 4 cups salad oil
2 10-ounce jars apple, blackberry, grape or other jelly (2 cups)
confectioners' sugar

ABOUT 4 HOURS BEFORE SERVING:
1. In large bowl, combine 1½ cups flour, sugar, nutmeg, salt, cinnamon and yeast. In medium saucepan over low heat, heat milk and butter or margarine until very warm (120° to 130°F.). (Butter or margarine does not need to melt.) With mixer at low speed, gradually pour liquid into dry ingredients. Increase speed to medium; add eggs and beat 2 minutes, occasionally scraping bowl with rubber spatula. Beat in ¾ cup flour or enough to make a thick batter; continue beating 2 minutes, occasionally scraping bowl. With spoon, stir in enough additional flour (about 1¾ cups) to make a soft dough.
2. Turn dough onto lightly floured surface and knead until smooth and elastic, about 10 minutes. Shape dough into ball and place in greased large bowl, turning over so that top of dough is greased. Cover with towel; let rise in warm place (80° to 85°F.), away from draft, until doubled, about 1 hour. (Dough is doubled when two fingers pressed lightly into dough leave a dent.)
3. Punch down dough by pushing center of dough with fist, then pushing edges of dough into center. Turn dough onto lightly floured surface; cut dough in half; cover with bowl for 15 minutes. Grease 2 cookie sheets.
4. With lightly floured rolling pin, roll one-half of dough ¼ inch thick. Using 2¾-inch round biscuit cutter, cut circles. Repeat with remaining dough and trimmings (or roll each half into 18″ by 9″ rectangle; cut into eighteen 3-inch squares). Place doughnuts on cookie sheets; cover with towels and let rise in a warm place (80° to 85°F.), away from draft, until doubled, about 1 hour. (Dough is doubled when one finger very lightly pressed against dough leaves a dent.)
4. In deep fat fryer,* heat 1 inch salad oil to 370°F. Fry 4 or 5 doughnuts in hot oil until golden brown, 45 seconds to 1 minute on each side, turning with slotted spoon. Remove to paper towels to drain; repeat with remaining dough.
5. With sharp thin knife, pierce doughnut from one side almost to opposite side. Place jelly in cake decorator or cookie press. Using tip with about ¼-inch hole in end, gently squeeze small amount jelly into each doughnut through slit. Sprinkle with confectioners' sugar. Makes about 3 dozen doughnuts.

* Or, in Dutch oven over medium heat, heat oil to 370°F. on deep-fat thermometer.

SUGARED DOUGHNUTS: Prepare as above but use doughnut cutter to cut rolled dough. Reroll trimmings, "holes" (or fry "holes" separately). Let rise; then fry as above. Sprinkle warm doughnuts with *sugar* or shake doughnuts with sugar in a paper bag to coat well; omit jelly.

CREAM: Prepare as above but omit jelly. For filling, use *canned vanilla or chocolate pudding* or pudding prepared with regular vanilla, chocolate, butterscotch or lemon pudding mix as label directs. Refrigerate.

PARTY: Prepare Cream Doughnuts as above. Frost with Sugar Glaze (page 452); sprinkle with *chopped nuts,* or flaked or shredded coconut, or chocolate shot or nonpareils.

Special Breads

Start with plain or sweet bread or rolls you make or buy. Dress them up in one of the ways below for breakfast, lunch, dinner or snack-time.

FRENCH TOAST

2 eggs
¼ cup milk
1 tablespoon sugar
½ teaspoon salt
butter, margarine or bacon drippings
6 white- or whole-wheat-bread slices
maple syrup, honey, marmalade, confectioners' sugar or applesauce for topping (optional)

ABOUT 20 MINUTES BEFORE SERVING:
In pie plate, with fork, beat eggs slightly; beat in milk, sugar and salt. Meanwhile, in large skillet over medium heat, heat 1 tablespoon butter or margarine.

Quickly dip bread slices into egg mixture, turning to coat both sides. Place in hot skillet; fry until browned on both sides, turning once and adding more butter or margarine if needed. Serve immediately with topping. Makes 6 servings.

DELUXE: Prepare as above but substitute *half-and-half* or heavy cream for milk and add *2 teaspoons sherry* to egg mixture.

BAKED CINNAMON: Preheat oven to 500°F. Grease cookie sheet. Prepare egg mixture as above but add *1 teaspoon cinnamon.* Dip bread slices into mixture; place on cookie sheet. Bake 5 minutes on each side or until golden. Serve with syrup.

FRENCH TOAST CUPS: Preheat oven to 350°F. Grease six 6-ounce custard cups. Prepare as above but press each dipped bread slice into a custard cup. Bake 20 minutes or until golden. Use to hold scrambled eggs or creamed meat, seafood or poultry.

PETITE MAPLE TOAST: Prepare as above but for bread, use *hard rolls* or French bread cut into ½-inch or ¾-inch slices. Or, omit egg mixture and dip slices into maple or maple-blended syrup; then fry in hot butter or margarine until golden on both sides.

TOAST TREATS

The electric toaster makes short and easy work of toasting bread just the way you like it. Here are other ways, however, to turn bread into toast with a difference:

BAKED: Preheat oven to 425°F. Spread bread slices with butter or margarine; then top with chopped parsley or chives. Bake 8 minutes or until crisp and golden.

Or, spread with butter or margarine; top with cream cheese, then with marmalade, or thinly sliced jellied cranberry sauce or crumbled blue cheese. Bake 8 minutes or until topping is hot and bubbly.

BROILED: Preheat broiler if manufacturer directs. Toast bread slices on one side in broiler; turn slices and spread with softened butter or margarine, then with one of these toppings: garlic spread (in jar); or honey and sprinkling of cinnamon; or honey mixed with grated orange peel; or brown sugar and chopped nuts or coconut; or prepared mustard and thin onion slices. Broil until golden.

WAFFLED: Set waffle baker at medium heat. Bake unbuttered bread slices until golden.

PANNED: In skillet over medium heat, in a little hot butter or margarine, sprinkle paprika, celery, garlic, onion or seasoned salt. Place bread slices in mixture and fry, turning once, until golden.

CINNAMON TOAST

In cup, stir *3 tablespoons sugar* with *1 teaspoon cinnamon* (or, use 3 tablespoons prepared cinnamon-sugar); sprinkle over *hot buttered toast;* cut toast into strips or triangles.

Or, broil bread slices on one side until golden; turn, spread with butter or margarine; sprinkle with cinnamon-sugar mixture; broil until hot and mixture is bubbly.

MELBA TOAST

Preheat oven to 325°F. Cut unsliced loaf of bread into ⅛-inch-thick slices. If you like, remove crusts, then cut slices diagonally into triangles. Place on cookie sheet; bake 15 minutes or until golden, crisp and curled, turning once.

SAVORY BREAD SLICES

ABOUT 25 MINUTES BEFORE SERVING:
Preheat oven to 450°F. Cut slices of sandwich loaf in half crosswise; stand with cut edges up in loaf pan or in shallow "box" made of folded foil. Between slices and over top of "loaf," spread one of mixtures below. Bake 15 minutes or until hot and golden.

CHEESE: Mix shredded Cheddar cheese with enough mayonnaise to make of spreading consistency. Or, combine softened chive cream cheese with milk to make spreadable.

SAVORY: Spread with softened butter or margarine combined with a little garlic or onion salt, prepared mustard, horseradish, thyme leaves, curry powder or chopped parsley.

SWEET: Spread bread with softened butter or margarine, then sprinkle with sugar and cinnamon, or brown sugar and coconut. Or, spread with marmalade; top with honey and shredded orange or lemon peel or cinnamon, or softened cream cheese and marmalade.

PIZZA SLICES

ABOUT 20 MINUTES BEFORE SERVING:
Preheat broiler if manufacturer directs. Broil bread slices on 1 side until golden. Turn slices; spread with softened butter or margarine, then spread with pasteurized process cheese spread. Top each slice with a little chili sauce, a sprinkle of oregano leaves and 2 anchovy fillets. Broil until hot and bubbly. Cut in half to serve.

RYE TOASTIES

ABOUT 20 MINUTES BEFORE SERVING:
Preheat oven to 400°F. In cup, combine *2 tablespoons butter or margarine,* softened, with *2 tablespoons grated Parmesan cheese.* Spread on *24 slices party rye bread;* place on cookie sheet. Bake 10 minutes or until hot and bubbly. Makes 24.

GARLIC: Prepare as above but add *¼ teaspoon garlic salt* to mixture. If you like, omit cheese.

EASY BREADSTICKS

1. Preheat oven to 425°F. or preheat broiler if manufacturer directs. Cut hard or frankfurter rolls lengthwise into quarters. Spread all sides with softened butter or margarine. Roll quarters in chopped parsley or chives; or finely chopped nuts; or poppy, caraway, celery or sesame seed; or grated Parmesan cheese. Or, roll in cinnamon and sugar. Place, cut sides up, on cookie sheet; bake 5 to 10 minutes, or broil, until golden.

2. Preheat oven to 350°F. or preheat broiler if manufacturer directs. Trim crusts from loaf of unsliced white, rye or wholewheat bread. Cut loaf lengthwise into ¾-inch slices; then cut each slice crosswise into 4-inch strips. Brush strips on all sides with melted butter or margarine or spread thinly with mayonnaise. Sprinkle with grated cheese and crumbled cooked bacon; or finely chopped nuts; or poppy, sesame, dill or caraway seed; or thyme leaves, oregano or dill weed. Place on cookie sheet; bake 20 minutes, or broil, until golden.

3. Trim crusts from white-bread slices; cut slices into 1-inch-wide strips. Prepare as in step 2, above.

BUTTERY RYE FINGERS

ABOUT 25 MINUTES BEFORE SERVING:
Preheat oven to 350°F. Make sandwiches with rye bread and softened butter or margarine; cut each sandwich into 1-inch-wide strips. Wrap every 8 or 10 strips in foil. Bake packages 15 minutes or until bread is heated through.

HOT ONION-RYE LOAF

ABOUT 30 MINUTES BEFORE SERVING:
Preheat oven to 425°F. Through top of unsliced oval loaf of rye bread, make 11 crosswise cuts *almost* to bottom crust. Spread each cut surface with softened butter or margarine. Insert a thin onion slice in every other cut. Wrap loaf in foil; place on cookie sheet. Bake 15 minutes or until bread is hot. To serve, cut through slits that have no onion. Makes 6 "sandwiches."

SAVORY LONG LOAVES

Preheat oven to 375°F. Cut *1 loaf French, Italian or Vienna bread* into slices (thick, thin or diagonal) almost through to bottom crust. Spread all cut surfaces with one or more of spreads below; if you wish, sprinkle loaf with *grated Parmesan cheese.* Bake 15 to 20 minutes until hot. For softer crust, loaf may be wrapped in foil before baking; leave top open part way.

GARLIC: In small bowl, with spoon, combine *½ cup butter or margarine,* softened, with *1 garlic clove,* minced or ½ teaspoon garlic salt and *1 tablespoon chopped parsley.* (Or, use garlic spread in jar as label directs.) If you like, sprinkle cut surfaces with *oregano* and *grated Parmesan cheese.*

CHEESE: In small bowl, with spoon, combine *½ cup butter or margarine,* softened, with *2 cups shredded American cheese* or ½ cup crumbled blue cheese and, if you like, *2 tablespoons chopped chives.*

SEEDED: In small bowl, with spoon, combine *½ cup butter or margarine,* softened, with *1 teaspoon poppy, celery or caraway seed.*

HERBED: In small bowl, with spoon, combine *½ cup butter or margarine,* softened, with *generous pinch herbs* such as marjoram, thyme leaves, rosemary, savory.

CURRY: In small bowl, with spoon, combine *½ cup butter or margarine,* softened, with *¼ teaspoon curry powder.*

PAPRIKA-CREAM: Into *½ cup sour cream,* stir *1 teaspoon paprika* until blended.

CHIVE-CHEESE CREAM: Into *one 3-ounce package chive cream cheese,* softened, stir *½ cup sour cream* until blended.

ONION-CHEESE: Spread cut surfaces with Garlic, Seeded or Herbed Spreads (above); insert *1 thin onion slice* and *1 cheese slice,* cut to fit, between bread slices.

JUNIOR LOAVES

Preheat oven to 425°F. Use hard or soft white, wheat, French or frankfurter rolls. Cut each almost through to bottom crust into 2 or 3 thick slices. Spread with one of spreads above. Bake 10 minutes.

FAN-TAN LOAF

Preheat oven to 425°F. In 10″ by 5″ loaf pan, place sliced loaf white bread, top side up. Fill, then top as below. (If baking only part of loaf, use inverted custard cup to prop slices up in loaf pan.) Bake 15 minutes or until hot and toasted.

CHEESY: Between bread slices, spread softened butter or margarine mixed with a little prepared mustard; spread with some grated cheese or cheese spread (or insert halved cheese slices). Spread top of loaf with a little mayonnaise or softened butter or margarine. Sprinkle with grated cheese, then with a little grated onion, chopped chives or a few sliced green onions, tossed with melted butter or margarine. If necessary, cut slices apart with scissors.

RELISH: Between slices and over top of loaf, spread softened butter or margarine mixed with a little garlic salt and one of these: prepared mustard, horseradish, chopped parsley or crumbled blue cheese.

SAVORY: Between slices and over top of loaf, spread softened butter or margarine mixed with one of these: celery, garlic, seasoned or onion salt; thyme leaves; curry or chili powder plus garlic salt. Sprinkle with celery or poppy seed or paprika.

TOASTED ROLLS-IN-LOAF

ABOUT 30 MINUTES BEFORE SERVING:
Preheat oven to 400°F. Grease shallow baking pan. Trim crusts from top and sides of *1 unsliced loaf of white or whole-wheat bread.* (For rounded top, peel, don't cut off, top crust.)

Cut almost through to bottom crust in very thin slices or 1-inch-thick slices; or cut lengthwise down middle, then crosswise into 1½-inch slices to make squares; or cut diagonally into 2-inch slices one way, then cut diagonally in opposite direction to make diamonds. Place in baking pan.

Spread cut surfaces, top and sides of loaf with one of mixtures below. Bake 18 minutes or until golden. To serve, cut "rolls" apart.

ZESTY CHEESE: In small bowl, combine *½ cup butter or margarine,* softened, with ¼ *cup minced onion, 1 tablespoon poppy seed* and *1 tablespoon prepared mustard.* Spread on all loaf surfaces. Place *Swiss-cheese slices,* cut to fit, between cuts. Top loaf with *bacon slices.*

BUTTER PLUS: In small bowl, combine *½ cup butter or margarine,* softened, with one of these: *2 cups shredded sharp Cheddar cheese* (two 4-ounce packages); or ¼ cup chopped parsley or chives or minced onion; or ½ teaspoon savory, ½ teaspoon thyme leaves, 1 tablespoon chopped parsley and dash of garlic salt; or ¼ cup crumbled blue cheese and 1 tablespoon grated onion; or ⅓ cup packed brown sugar and 1 teaspoon cinnamon.

FLUFFY CHEESE: In small bowl, combine *1 cup shredded sharp Cheddar cheese* (one 4-ounce package) with *¼ cup butter or margarine,* softened, and *2 egg yolks.* In another small bowl, with mixer at high speed, beat *2 egg whites* until stiff peaks form; fold in cheese mixture.

DOUBLE CHEESE: In small bowl, combine *one 3-ounce package cream cheese,* softened, with *1 cup shredded sharp Cheddar cheese* (one 4-ounce package), *2 tablespoons milk, 1 tablespoon chopped parsley, 1 tablespoon diced pimento, 1 tablespoon horseradish, 1 teaspoon grated onion, 1 teaspoon lemon juice* and *¼ teaspoon salt.* After spreading on mixture, wrap loaf in foil, leaving top open.

FILLED BUTTER-FLAKE ROLLS

Preheat oven to 425°F. Gently separate leaves of *baked fan-tan or packaged butter-flake rolls* almost to bottom. Spread all leaves with *softened butter or margarine;* spread a few leaves with one of fillings below.

For toasted rolls, set filled rolls in greased muffin-pan cups; for soft rolls, place side by side on foil and wrap. Bake 5 to 10 minutes or until hot.

ZESTY CHILI: In small bowl, combine *½ cup chili sauce* or catchup with *1 teaspoon horseradish.* Makes enough for 12 rolls.

SWEET NUT: In small bowl, combine *½ cup marmalade* or other preserves with *¼ cup coarsely chopped nuts.* Or, sprinkle with brown sugar and chopped nuts. Makes enough for 12 rolls.

HAM AND CHEESE: Spread some leaves with *deviled ham,* some with *shredded Cheddar* or natural Swiss cheese.

SEED: Sprinkle leaves with *sesame or poppy seed.*

HERB: Sprinkle leaves with *garlic, onion or curry powder.* Or, omit butter and spread leaves with garlic spread in jar.

HONEY PEANUT: In small bowl, combine *½ cup peanut butter* with *2 tablespoons honey* and *½ teaspoon grated orange peel.* Makes enough for 12 rolls.

CHEESE: Sprinkle leaves with *crumbled blue cheese* or grated or shredded Parmesan cheese. Or, spread leaves with softened, pasteurized process smoky- or pimento-cheese spread, or chive cream cheese. (If necessary, thin with milk to make of good spreading consistency.)

MUSHROOM: Preheat oven to 375°F. Drain, then coarsely chop *one 2½-ounce can sliced mushrooms.* In small bowl, combine mushrooms with *½ cup butter or margarine,* softened. Spread on leaves and over tops of *12 butter-flake or fan-tan rolls;* place rolls side by side on foil; wrap. Bake 15 minutes or until hot and crisp.

GLAZED BROWN-AND-SERVE ROLLS

ABOUT 25 MINUTES BEFORE SERVING:
Preheat oven to 400°F. Grease 1 muffin-pan cup for each roll. In each cup, place one of mixtures below; top mixture with *1 brown-and-serve soft roll,* upside down. Bake 15 minutes; let stand 1 minute; invert pan onto serving platter and remove.

COCONUT: For each muffin-pan cup, mix *2 teaspoons brown sugar, 1 teaspoon chopped flaked coconut, 1 teaspoon butter or margarine,* softened, and *½ teaspoon water.*

BUTTERSCOTCH: In small saucepan over medium heat, heat to boiling *¼ cup butter or margarine* with *½ cup packed brown sugar* and *1 tablespoon water.* Reduce heat to low; simmer 8 minutes; place 1 tablespoon in each muffin-pan cup. Makes enough for about 8 rolls.

BROWN-AND-SERVE STICKIES

ABOUT 35 MINUTES BEFORE SERVING:
Preheat oven to 400°F. In bottom of 9″ by 5″ loaf pan, spread one of mixtures below. Place *8 brown-and-serve soft rolls* upside down on mixture. Bake 25 minutes; let stand 1 minute; invert pan onto serving platter and remove. Serve rolls hot.

NUT: In small saucepan over medium heat, melt *3 tablespoons butter or margarine;* stir in *⅓ cup packed brown sugar* and *3 tablespoons chopped nuts.*

CARAMEL-ORANGE: In small bowl, mix *¼ cup sugar, 1½ tablespoons orange juice, 1 tablespoon butter or margarine,* softened, *1 teaspoon grated orange peel* and *¼ teaspoon nutmeg* or mace.

QUICK COFFEECAKE

ABOUT 35 MINUTES BEFORE SERVING:
Preheat oven to 375°F. Trim crusts from *1 unsliced loaf of white bread.* Cut loaf lengthwise in half. Cut each half into 1½-inch slices, almost through to bottom, to form squares.

Spread cut surfaces, top and sides with *softened butter or margarine.* Then cover each half with one of mixtures below. Bake 15 to 20 minutes until hot and golden. To serve, break "rolls" apart.

NUT: In small bowl, combine *¼ cup packed brown sugar* with *2 tablespoons chopped California walnuts or pecans.*

COCONUT: Spread with *sweetened condensed milk,* then sprinkle with *shredded or flaked coconut.*

HONEY: In cup, stir *2 tablespoons honey* and *2 tablespoons brown sugar* until smooth. After spreading on bread, sprinkle with *2 tablespoons chopped walnuts.*

SUGAR AND SPICE: Sprinkle with *sugar,* then with *cinnamon.*

RUM-RAISIN: In cup, stir *¼ cup light corn syrup* with *1 tablespoon rum.* After spreading on bread, top with *2 tablespoons dark seedless raisins* and *2 tablespoons chopped California walnuts,* then with *1 tablespoon sugar* and *¼ teaspoon cinnamon* or nutmeg.

TOASTED ENGLISH MUFFINS

Before toasting, pull English muffins apart (don't cut) this way: With tines of dinner fork, puncture from edge to center of muffin all the way around, halfway between muffin top and bottom; gently separate the halves. This makes little hills and valleys which, after toasting and buttering, hold the melting butter or margarine in little pools, making the muffin extra delicious. Toast muffin halves, split side up, in broiler; or toast in toaster.

TOPPINGS: Spread split muffins with butter or margarine; top with one of these and then toast under broiler:

Soft cream cheese and jelly or marmalade
Caraway, poppy or sesame seed
Shredded Cheddar or crumbled blue cheese
Cinnamon, sugar, chopped nuts
Grated Parmesan cheese, garlic salt

FRENCH TOASTED: Dip English muffin halves into French-toast mixture (page 458). In skillet over medium heat, in a little hot butter or margarine, cook muffin halves, first on split side, then on other side, until golden. Serve with jelly or jam, maple-blended syrup or honey; or, top with creamed seafood or poultry mixture.

MOCK PATTY SHELLS

TOAST CUPS: Preheat oven to 375°F. Trim crusts from thin bread slices. Brush slices with melted butter or margarine; press each into 3-inch muffin-pan cup. Bake 12 minutes or until golden. Remove from cups; use as patty shells to hold creamed food.

CROUSTADES (TOAST CASES): Preheat oven to 375°F. Trim crusts from loaf of unsliced bread; cut loaf into 2-inch-thick slices. Cut slices into squares or oblongs; or with cookie cutter, cut into rounds or hearts. With fingers, pull out center of each, leaving ⅜-inch-thick shell (save crumbs for use another day). Brush with melted butter or margarine; place on cookie sheet; bake 12 to 15 minutes until golden.

CHEESE CROUSTADES: Prepare Croustades as above but about 5 minutes before end of baking, brush again with melted butter or margarine and sprinkle with grated Cheddar cheese.

Sandwiches

Sandwich making goes faster when you use production-line techniques. First make up the filling. Then line up the bread slices in rows, two by two, and with a flexible spatula, spread softened butter or margarine to the edges of all the slices. Spread filling on one row of slices; top with remaining slices; cut and wrap sandwiches. When making more than one variety of sandwich, cut and wrap it before proceeding to another variety.

Crisp lettuce, sliced tomatoes and similar ingredients should be wrapped separately, to be added to the sandwich at the last minute. If added ahead, they make the bread soggy, moisten the filling.

Freezing Sandwiches

Many sandwiches can be prepared and frozen up to 2 weeks before serving. It is important to use fresh bread and the freshest ingredients for the filling. To prevent fillings from soaking into the bread, spread a protective coating of butter, margarine or peanut butter to the edges of the bread slices; avoid moist spreads like mayonnaise, salad dressing or jelly. Frozen mayonnaise or salad dressing may separate, so use sour cream, applesauce, or milk in fillings.

Crisp lettuce, onion rings, tomato slices should never be frozen; just add them fresh at serving time.

Wrap sandwiches of different flavors separately to prevent flavors mingling. (See Freezing, pages 703–705, for information on wrapping and storage.) Sandwiches thaw in about an hour at room temperature but will stay fresh for 3 or 4 hours after thawing, if kept wrapped.

Some filling ingredients freeze well: Hard-cooked egg yolk, Roquefort or blue cheese, cream cheese, cheese spread, sliced cheese, sour cream, butter or margarine, canned or cooked chicken, turkey, meats or fish, dried beef, deviled ham, bologna, mild-flavored salami, boiled ham, canned pineapple, applesauce, raisins, peanut butter, prepared mustard, catchup, chili sauce, pickles.

Other filling ingredients do not freeze well: Hard-cooked egg white, cottage cheese, cooked bacon, fresh vegetables and lettuce, apples, preserves, jellies, jams, mayonnaise or salad dressing as spread.

Everyday Sandwiches

EASY SANDWICH FILLINGS

These fillings freeze well:

BOLOGNA-AND-EGG FILLING: Mince *½ pound bologna* with *2 hard-cooked egg yolks.* Combine with *¼ cup sour cream.* Makes about 2 cups.

CHEESE-AND-RAISIN FILLING: Combine *1½ 4-ounce packages shredded Cheddar cheese* (1½ cups) with *3 tablespoons raisins.* (Use *applesauce or peanut butter* as spread on bread.) Makes about 2 cups.

DEVILED-HAM-AND-RELISH FILLING: Combine *three 4½-ounce cans deviled ham* with *⅓ cup sweet relish.* Makes about 2 cups.

CHICKEN-CRANBERRY FILLING: Combine *2 cups diced cooked or canned chicken* with *3 tablespoons cranberry-orange relish, 1 tablespoon orange juice* and *¼ teaspoon salt.* Makes about 2 cups.

SALMON-AND-PARSLEY FILLING: Combine *one 15-ounce can salmon,* drained, with *3 tablespoons chopped parsley, 2 tablespoons pineapple juice* and *¼ teaspoon salt.* (Use *butter or margarine* as spread on bread.) Makes about 2 cups.

These fillings do not freeze well:

CHEESE SALAD: Combine *2 cups diced natural or pasteurized process Swiss cheese, ¾ cup mayonnaise, ½ cup diced green pepper, 1 tablespoon chili sauce* and *dash pepper.* Makes about 2½ cups.

ORIENTAL CHICKEN SALAD: Mix *2½ cups diced cooked chicken* with *⅓ cup diced water chestnuts* and *⅓ cup diced celery;* stir *2 tablespoons soy sauce* into *⅔ cup mayonnaise,* then combine with chicken mixture. Makes about 3 cups.

SHRIMP SALAD: Mix *1½ cups chopped, cooked shrimp, 2 chopped hard-cooked eggs, ½ cup bottled relish sandwich spread, ¼ cup diced celery, 2 tablespoons milk, ¼ teaspoon salt.* Makes about 2 cups.

EGG SALAD: Mix *6 chopped hard-cooked eggs, ¼ cup minced onion, ½ cup mayonnaise, 3 tablespoons prepared mustard* and *1 teaspoon salt.* Makes about 2 cups.

ZESTY TUNA BUNS

⅔ cup evaporated milk (1 5½-ounce can)
2 cups fresh white-bread cubes
2 6½- or 7-ounce cans tuna
2 tablespoons prepared mustard
2 tablespoons pickle relish
2 teaspoons lemon juice
½ teaspoon salt
6 hamburger buns, split and buttered
6 lettuce leaves
1 large tomato, cut into 6 slices

ABOUT 25 MINUTES BEFORE SERVING:
Preheat broiler if manufacturer directs. In medium bowl, with fork, stir milk and bread cubes until almost smooth.

Stir in drained tuna, mustard, pickle relish, lemon juice and salt. Spread tuna mixture over bottom bun halves and broil until golden, about 8 minutes. During last minutes of broiling time, toast bun tops. Top tuna mixture with lettuce, tomato slices and bun tops. Makes 6 sandwiches.

CANADIAN-BACON BUNS

1 16-ounce package Canadian-bacon slices
6 hamburger buns or English muffins
butter or margarine, softened

ABOUT 15 MINUTES BEFORE SERVING:
Preheat broiler if manufacturer directs. In medium skillet over medium-high heat, fry bacon just until heated. Meanwhile, split hamburger buns and spread with butter or margarine; broil until golden. Serve 2 or 3 slices bacon in each bun; cut in half. Serve hot. Makes 6 sandwiches.

FRANKFURTER-EGG-SALAD BUNS

4 frankfurters, finely chopped
3 hard-cooked eggs, coarsely chopped
3 tablespoons chili sauce
1 teaspoon prepared mustard
½ teaspoon minced onion
salt
4 frankfurter buns, split and toasted

ABOUT 15 MINUTES BEFORE SERVING:
In medium bowl, stir first 5 ingredients; add salt to taste. Spoon mixture onto bun halves. Makes 8 open-face sandwiches.

HOT MEAT-LOAF SANDWICH

1 pound ground beef
1 10¾-ounce can condensed vegetable soup
1 slice white bread, crumbled
4 hamburger buns, split
butter or margarine

ABOUT 25 MINUTES BEFORE SERVING:
Preheat oven to 450°F. In medium bowl, combine ground beef, undiluted soup, and bread; shape mixture into 4 patties about ½ inch thick. Bake in jelly-roll pan or shallow baking pan for 15 minutes.

Meanwhile, spread bun halves with butter or margarine.

During last minutes of baking time, add buns and bake until hot. Serve patties (they will be moist) in buns. Makes 4 sandwiches.

SLOPPY-JOE BUNWICHES

1 pound ground chuck
1 small onion, chopped
⅔ cup bottled barbecue sauce
¼ cup chopped parsley
1 tablespoon soy sauce
2 teaspoons sugar
1 teaspoon salt
½ teaspoon ginger
dash seasoned pepper
2 8-ounce packages refrigerated buttermilk biscuits
1 egg, beaten

ABOUT 45 MINUTES BEFORE SERVING:
In large skillet over medium-high heat, cook meat and onion until meat is browned, stirring constantly. Stir in barbecue sauce, parsley, soy sauce, sugar, salt, ginger and seasoned pepper.

Preheat oven to 450°F. On lightly floured surface, with floured rolling pin, roll 2 biscuits together into 5-inch circle. Place biscuit circle in palm of hand; spoon about 2 rounded measuring tablespoonfuls meat mixture in center. With other hand, gather circle along circumference to form closed pouch; pinch firmly to seal. Place, sealed side up, on foil-lined cookie sheet, 2 inches apart. Repeat, making 9 more.

Brush with beaten egg; bake 15 minutes or until lightly browned. Remove immediately from cookie sheet; serve warm. Makes 10 sandwiches.

MINI-SUBMARINE SANDWICHES

6 hard rolls, about 4 inches long
1 cup shredded lettuce
¼ cup minced onion
1 large tomato, chopped
3 tablespoons Italian dressing
1 8-ounce package bologna slices
1 6-ounce package provolone-cheese slices

ABOUT 15 MINUTES BEFORE SERVING:
Slice rolls almost in half horizontally, leaving one side attached. In small bowl, toss lettuce, onion, tomato with Italian dressing. In each roll, arrange 1 or 2 slices each of bologna and cheese and top with some lettuce mixture. Makes 6 sandwiches.

GRILLED CHEESE SANDWICHES

For each sandwich, spread 1 bread slice with butter or margarine; top with slices of favorite cheese or cheese spread. If you like, spread with mustard or barbecue sauce. Top with another bread slice.

In medium skillet over medium heat (or in electric frypan or griddle), in small amount of butter or margarine, cook sandwiches on both sides until golden.

HOT MOZZARELLA-SALAMI SANDWICHES

1 loaf Italian bread, about 8 inches long
1 8-ounce package hard salami slices
1 8-ounce package mozzarella-cheese slices
oregano leaves
2 eggs
¼ cup milk
dash salt
dash pepper
½ cup butter, margarine or salad oil

ABOUT 20 MINUTES BEFORE SERVING:
Cut Italian bread diagonally into slices about ½ inch thick, to make at least 12 slices. On half the bread slices place salami, then mozzarella, then sprinkle with oregano; top with remaining bread.

In pie plate, with fork, beat eggs with milk, salt and pepper; *quickly* dip each sandwich into mixture, turning to coat both sides. In medium skillet, in hot butter, brown sandwiches on both sides, pressing them firmly but gently with pancake turner. Serve hot. Makes at least 6 sandwiches.

ITALIAN HERO SANDWICHES

12 sweet Italian sausages
2 medium onions
5 green or red peppers
2 tablespoons olive or salad oil
4 hard rolls, split

ABOUT 45 MINUTES BEFORE SERVING:
In large covered skillet over low heat, simmer sausages and 1/4 cup water for 5 minutes. Remove cover and continue cooking 15 minutes or until sausages are browned, turning occasionally. Keep sausages warm.

Meanwhile, slice onions into thin rings; cut peppers into 1/2-inch strips. In same skillet over medium heat, in hot oil, cook onions and peppers until tender, about 10 minutes, stirring occasionally.

Fill each roll with 3 sausages and some onion mixture. Makes 4 sandwiches.

SUBMARINES

Submarines, heroes, hoagies, poorboys—all are the same king-size sandwich: Fill a long loaf of crisp-crusted bread with one or more kinds of meat and cheese slices, pickle slices, green-pepper rings, lettuce leaves, tomato and onion slices; spread with mayonnaise. Cut into hefty pieces to serve.

SALMON BURGERS

1 16-ounce can salmon, drained
3 eggs
2 1/2 cups fresh bread crumbs
2/3 cup chopped celery
1/3 cup chopped green onions
3 tablespoons salad oil
2 1 1/4- or 1 1/2-ounce envelopes hollandaise-sauce mix
3 English muffins, split, toasted and buttered

ABOUT 45 MINUTES BEFORE SERVING:
In large bowl, combine first 5 ingredients. With hands, shape mixture into 6 patties.

In large skillet over medium heat, in hot salad oil, fry patties 5 minutes or until lightly browned; with pancake turner, carefully turn and fry a few minutes longer. Meanwhile, prepare mix as label directs.

Top each muffin half with patty; spoon on sauce. Makes 6 open-face sandwiches.

ST. LOUIS CHEESEBURGERS

2 tablespoons butter or margarine
1/2 small onion, minced
2 tablespoons all-purpose flour
1/2 cup milk
1/2 4-ounce package blue cheese
1 1/2 pounds ground round
1/2 teaspoon salt
6 hamburger buns, split and buttered

ABOUT 30 MINUTES BEFORE SERVING:
Preheat broiler if manufacturer directs. In medium saucepan over medium heat, in hot butter or margarine, cook onion until tender; stir in flour. Gradually add milk and cook, stirring constantly, until thickened. Stir in cheese (mixture will be lumpy); set aside.

Shape meat in 6 patties; sprinkle with salt and broil 10 minutes or until of desired doneness, turning once. During last minutes of broiling, toast buns and spoon some cheese mixture onto each patty. Makes 6 sandwiches.

SAVORY HAMBURGERS

1 egg
1/3 cup fresh whole-wheat bread crumbs
1/4 cup milk
1 pound ground beef
1 tablespoon minced onion
seasoned salt and seasoned pepper
6 hamburger buns, split
3 tablespoons butter or margarine
1/2 cup watercress leaves
2 medium tomatoes, thickly sliced

ABOUT 25 MINUTES BEFORE SERVING:
1. Preheat broiler if manufacturer directs. In large bowl, combine egg, crumbs and milk. With fork, stir in beef, onion, 1 1/2 teaspoons seasoned salt, 1/4 teaspoon seasoned pepper; shape into 6 patties.
2. On rack in broiler pan, broil patties 4 minutes; turn and broil 4 minutes more or until of desired doneness. Toast buns.
3. Meanwhile, in medium skillet over medium heat, in hot butter or margarine, cook watercress and tomato slices until tender, 3 to 5 minutes; sprinkle lightly with seasoned salt and seasoned pepper.
4. Serve patties topped with vegetables in buns. Makes 6 sandwiches.

PEANUT-BUTTER-PLUS SANDWICHES

Peanut-butter sandwiches can be as varied and interesting as you want them to be. Use white, pumpernickel, whole wheat, raisin or rye bread. Spread the bread with either creamy or chunky peanut butter. And, instead of adding the usual jelly, try one of these combinations:

PEANUT BUTTER AND EGG SALAD: In medium bowl, stir *2 hard-cooked eggs,* finely chopped, with *2 tablespoons minced celery, 2 tablespoons mayonnaise, ½ teaspoon salt, ¼ teaspoon prepared mustard* and *dash pepper* until well mixed. Use as filling for 4 peanut-butter sandwiches.

PEANUT BUTTER AND CHEESE-OLIVE: For each sandwich, spread 1 bread slice with softened *cream cheese;* add a layer of *thinly sliced, large pimento-stuffed olives* or pitted ripe olives. Spread other slice of bread with peanut butter.

PEANUT BUTTER AND MARSHMALLOW CREAM: For each sandwich, spread 1 bread slice with *1 tablespoon marshmallow cream;* sprinkle with coarsely chopped *Spanish peanuts.* Spread other bread slice with creamy peanut butter.

PEANUT BUTTER AND CRANBERRY SAUCE: For each sandwich, spread 1 bread slice with *jellied cranberry sauce;* top with *lettuce leaf.* Spread other slice with peanut butter.

PEANUT BUTTER AND COLESLAW: In small bowl, toss *2 cups finely shredded cabbage, 2 tablespoons diced pimento, 2 tablespoons mayonnaise, 1 teaspoon wine vinegar, ½ teaspoon salt* and *¼ teaspoon sugar.* Refrigerate about an hour, tossing occasionally. Use as filling for 4 peanut-butter sandwiches.

PEANUT BUTTER AND TUNA: In medium bowl, thoroughly mix *one 6½- or 7-ounce can tuna,* well drained; *¼ cup minced green pepper; 2 tablespoons mayonnaise; ½ teaspoon salt; ½ teaspoon lemon juice* and *¼ teaspoon instant minced onion.* Use as filling for 4 peanut-butter sandwiches.

PEANUT BUTTER AND DATE-NUT: In small bowl, combine *½ cup diced pitted dates* and *¼ cup chopped pecans.* Use as filling for 4 peanut-butter sandwiches.

PEANUT BUTTER AND CANADIAN BACON: For each sandwich, cook *2 Canadian-bacon slices;* arrange on 1 bread slice; sprinkle with *chopped parsley.* Spread other bread slice with peanut butter.

PEANUT BUTTER AND BANANA: For each sandwich, spread peanut butter on both bread slices; use *thinly sliced bananas* as filling.

PEANUT BUTTER SUNSHINE: For each sandwich, spread 1 bread slice with peanut butter and top with *3 or 4 tablespoons grated carrots* and *1 tablespoon seedless raisins.* Top with another bread slice.

PEANUT BUTTER AND CUCUMBER CRISPS: For each sandwich, spread 1 bread slice with peanut butter and sprinkle with about *1 tablespoon minced green pepper* and about *5 thin cucumber slices.* Top with another bread slice.

HOT FILLED FRANKFURTERS

Split frankfurters almost all the way through lengthwise and broil until lightly browned. Into split frank, sprinkle shredded or diced cheese, chopped onion, drained sauerkraut or coleslaw, baked beans, chili con carne or catchup. Serve in split frankfurter buns, toasted along with franks.

CLUB SANDWICHES

For each sandwich, spread 3 slices of plain or toasted bread with butter, margarine, mayonnaise, whipped cream cheese or other soft spread; fill with 2 or more Hearty Fillings (below) and tuck in lettuce or watercress, sliced tomatoes, onions or pickles. For a junior club sandwich, use only 2 slices of bread. Cut sandwiches into thirds or fourths and skewer pieces with decorated toothpicks. Serve sandwiches, cut sides up, garnished with lettuce, tomato wedges, cherry tomatoes, pickles or olives.

HEARTY FILLINGS: Sliced chicken, turkey, beef, pork, lamb, veal, ham, corned beef, pastrami, luncheon meat, Canadian bacon, meat loaf, crisp bacon, sliced cheese, cream cheese, cheese spread, meat spread, split frankfurters, canned pâté, chopped cooked liver, sardines, egg, meat or seafood salad.

FRENCH TOASTED SANDWICHES

Using favorite bread and one of fillings below, make up sandwiches. For every *6 sandwiches,* prepare Dip: In pie plate, with fork, beat *3 eggs* with *½ cup milk, 1 teaspoon sugar* and *¼ teaspoon salt.* Dip each sandwich *quickly* into mixture, turning to coat both sides. In medium skillet over high heat, in *¼ cup hot butter or margarine,* brown sandwiches on both sides.

Cut each sandwich in half and accompany with cranberry sauce, pickle relish or pickled peaches. Makes 6 sandwiches.

FILLINGS: Ham and cheese slices; turkey or chicken slices; corned beef and Swiss cheese slices; peanut butter and ham slices.

BOLOGNA BURGERS

1 8-ounce package bologna slices
¼ cup catchup
¼ cup mayonnaise
8 hamburger buns, split
1 8-ounce package American cheese slices

ABOUT 45 MINUTES BEFORE SERVING:
Preheat oven to 375°F. Into medium bowl, put bologna through food grinder;* mix in catchup and mayonnaise. Spoon mixture onto bottom halves of buns; top each with a cheese slice, then top of bun. Wrap in foil.

Place wrapped burgers on large cookie sheet; bake 20 to 25 minutes until piping hot. Makes 8 sandwiches.

* Or, with sharp knife, finely chop bologna.

END-OF-THE-ROAST SANDWICH FILLING

2 cups cut-up leftover roast beef, veal, pork, turkey or chicken
½ small onion
¼ cup mayonnaise
1 teaspoon dry mustard
½ teaspoon celery salt

ABOUT 20 MINUTES BEFORE SERVING:
Into medium bowl, put meat through food grinder;* mix in remaining ingredients. Makes 1⅓ cups, enough for 4 sandwiches.

* Or, with sharp knife, finely chop meat.

Hot Supper Specials

CUBE-STEAK SANDWICHES

6 French-bread slices, cut on diagonal, ¾ inch thick
2 teaspoons prepared mustard
1½ pounds cube steaks
unseasoned instant meat tenderizer
seasoned pepper
⅓ cup butter or margarine
6 lettuce leaves
6 tomato slices
salt

ABOUT 15 MINUTES BEFORE SERVING:
Preheat broiler if manufacturer directs. Broil bread slices until golden on one side; then spread other side with mustard and broil until golden; keep warm.

Sprinkle steaks with tenderizer as label directs, then with seasoned pepper. In large skillet over medium-high heat, in hot butter or margarine, fry steaks 2 minutes on each side or until of desired doneness.

On mustard-spread bread slices, arrange lettuce, steaks and tomato slices. Sprinkle with salt and seasoned pepper. Makes 6 servings.

DEVILED STEAK SANDWICHES

2 tablespoons salad oil
1 pound cube steaks
1 medium onion, sliced
⅓ cup bottled steak sauce
3 tablespoons light brown sugar
2 tablespoons prepared mustard
1 teaspoon salt
4 or 5 bread slices, toasted and buttered
2 hard-cooked eggs, sliced

ABOUT 30 MINUTES BEFORE SERVING:
In large skillet over medium-high heat, in hot salad oil, fry steaks 2 minutes on each side or until of desired doneness; remove from skillet.

Reduce heat to medium; in same skillet, cook ½ cup water, onion, steak sauce, brown sugar, mustard and salt until onion is tender, stirring occasionally. Return steaks to skillet; heat in onion mixture, turning to coat both sides.

Spoon steaks and sauce over toast. Top with egg slices. Makes 4 or 5 servings.

BAKED SLOPPY-JOE SANDWICHES

1 can (about 15 ounces) barbecue sauce and beef or pork for sloppy joes
½ cup shredded pasteurized process Swiss cheese
¼ cup grated Parmesan cheese
1 egg, beaten
1 10-ounce package corn-bread mix

ABOUT 30 MINUTES BEFORE SERVING:
Preheat oven to 400°F. In medium bowl, stir barbecue sauce and beef or pork with cheeses and egg.

Prepare corn-bread mix as label directs. Spread half of corn-bread mixture in bottom of greased 8″ by 8″ baking dish; top with sloppy-joe mixture. Spread with rest of corn-bread mixture (don't worry about spreading it evenly or exactly to the edges). Bake 20 minutes or until golden brown. Makes 4 or 5 servings.

HOT HAM-AND-ASPARAGUS TOAST

1 10-ounce package frozen asparagus spears
¾ cup mayonnaise
milk
¼ teaspoon dry mustard
¼ cup butter or margarine
6 white-bread slices
12 boiled-ham slices

ABOUT 30 MINUTES BEFORE SERVING:
Prepare asparagus as label directs but cook only until asparagus is tender-crisp; drain and keep warm.

Meanwhile, in small bowl, combine mayonnaise with 2 tablespoons milk and mustard.

Pour ½ cup milk into pie plate. In medium skillet over medium heat, melt butter or margarine. *Quickly* dip bread slices, one at a time, into milk, turning to coat both sides. Immediately fry until golden on each side. Place slices in broiler pan; top each with 2 ham slices, then 3 or 4 asparagus spears. Spoon mayonnaise over them; broil 3 to 5 minutes until mayonnaise bubbles and turns golden. Makes 6 servings.

OTHER VEGETABLES: Use *one 9-ounce package frozen whole green beans* or *one 10-ounce package frozen broccoli spears* instead of asparagus, cooking just until fork-tender.

TOASTED SALMON SANDWICHES

⅓ cup butter or margarine, melted
12 white-bread slices
1 16-ounce can salmon
1 10-ounce package frozen peas, cooked and drained
¼ cup instant minced onion
1 10½-ounce can condensed cream-of-mushroom soup
4 eggs
2 cups milk

ABOUT 1½ HOURS BEFORE SERVING:
Preheat oven to 325°F. Brush melted butter or margarine on one side of each bread slice; arrange 6 slices, buttered side up, in one layer in well-buttered 13″ by 9″ baking dish.

In medium bowl, with fork, flake salmon; stir in peas and onion; spread evenly over bread slices in baking pan; cover with remaining bread slices, buttered side up. In another bowl, with hand beater, bcat undiluted soup, eggs and milk until well blended; slowly pour over and around bread. Bake 1 hour or until knife inserted in custard portion comes out clean. Serve at once. Makes 6 servings.

DIVAN SANDWICHES

1 tablespoon butter or margarine
2 tablespoons all-purpose flour
1 cup milk
1 4-ounce package shredded Cheddar cheese (1 cup)
4 buttered toast slices
4 large cooked turkey or chicken slices
1 10-ounce package frozen asparagus spears, cooked and drained
1 3- or 4-ounce can sliced mushrooms

ABOUT 20 MINUTES BEFORE SERVING:
Preheat broiler if manufacturer directs. In small saucepan over low heat, melt butter or margarine; stir in flour until blended; add milk and cook, stirring constantly, until thickened. Stir in cheese until melted.

Place toast on cookie sheet. Arrange turkey slices, asparagus spears and drained mushrooms on top; spoon on cheese sauce. Broil 3 to 5 minutes until golden. Makes 4 servings.

OPEN-FACE PEPPER-STEAK SANDWICHES

1½ pounds round steak, cut about ½ inch thick
unseasoned instant meat tenderizer
butter or margarine
2 medium green peppers, cut into thin strips
1 ⅞- or 1-ounce package brown gravy-seasoning mix
1 loaf Italian bread, about 12 inches long
½ teaspoon garlic salt
½ teaspoon basil (optional)

ABOUT 40 MINUTES BEFORE SERVING:
Preheat broiler if manufacturer directs. Sprinkle steak with tenderizer as label directs; cut into ½-inch-wide strips. In large skillet over high heat, in 2 tablespoons hot butter or margarine, fry meat 3 minutes, stirring occasionally. Stir in green peppers, gravy-seasoning mix and 1 cup water; continue cooking 5 minutes or until meat is fork-tender, stirring occasionally.

Meanwhile, cut bread in half horizontally; spread with butter or margarine; sprinkle with garlic salt and basil. Broil bread halves until toasted.

Spoon meat mixture over bread halves; cut each half crosswise into 3 sections. Makes 6 servings.

BAKED HAM-AND-CHEESE SANDWICHES

8 white-bread slices
butter or margarine, softened
8 American-cheese slices
4 boiled-ham or bologna slices
2 eggs
2 cups milk
1 teaspoon seasoned salt
¼ teaspoon dry mustard

ABOUT 1 HOUR AND 15 MINUTES AHEAD:
Preheat oven to 350°F. Spread bread lightly with butter or margarine. Make 4 sandwiches, using half the cheese and all ham slices; arrange in well-greased 9″ by 9″ baking pan; top each with a cheese slice.

In medium bowl, with fork, beat eggs slightly; stir in remaining ingredients and pour over sandwiches. Bake 1 hour or until golden. Makes 4 servings.

WAFFLEWICHES

1 15½-ounce can corned-beef hash
½ cup chopped California walnuts
¼ cup minced sweet gherkins
1 teaspoon prepared mustard
½ teaspoon salt
dash pepper
10 rye-bread slices (without seeds)
3 eggs
⅓ cup milk
4 teaspoons sugar
melted butter or margarine
1 15-ounce jar applesauce (2 cups)
ground nutmeg

ABOUT 30 MINUTES BEFORE SERVING:
1. In medium bowl, combine hash, walnuts, gherkins, mustard, salt and pepper.
2. On each of 5 bread slices, ¼ inch in from edges, evenly spread hash mixture; top with remaining bread slices.
3. In pie plate, with fork, beat eggs, milk and sugar until sugar is dissolved. Preheat waffle baker to medium-low heat, brushing generously with melted butter or margarine. Quickly dip one or two sandwiches into egg mixture, turning to coat on both sides. Grill until golden, about 4 minutes. Repeat with rest of sandwiches.
4. Meanwhile, in small saucepan over low heat, heat applesauce until hot; sprinkle with nutmeg; serve over sandwiches. Makes 5 servings.

FOR CORNED-BEEF LOVERS: Substitute *one 12-ounce can corned beef* mixed with *¼ cup minced sweet gherkins* and *½ cup chopped California walnuts* for mixture in step 1.

FOR AN INFORMAL FAMILY LUNCH OR SUPPER: Place sandwiches, prepared for grilling, on buffet and let each person dip his own into egg mixture and grill on greased waffle baker.

BUNS STROGANOFF

6 hard rolls
Hamburger Stroganoff (page 99)
chopped parsley or fresh dill for garnish

ABOUT 35 MINUTES BEFORE SERVING:
Cut thin slice from tops of rolls; hollow out rolls. Fill with Hamburger Stroganoff; sprinkle with parsley. Makes 6 servings.

HAM-AND-CHEESE BISCUIT BAKE

2 cups buttermilk-biscuit mix
½ cup milk
3 tablespoons salad oil
⅔ cup mayonnaise
1 teaspoon prepared mustard
1 12-ounce can chopped ham
3 American-cheese slices

ABOUT 45 MINUTES BEFORE SERVING:
Preheat oven to 450°F. In medium bowl, with fork, combine biscuit mix, milk and salad oil to make soft dough; beat vigorously until stiff. With fingers, press dough into well-greased 13″ by 9″ baking dish.

In small bowl, combine mayonnaise with prepared mustard; spread evenly over dough. Cut ham into 6 crosswise slices, then cut each slice into 2 triangles; arrange on mayonnaise mixture in 2 rows. Bake 15 minutes. Turn oven control to 350°F.

Meanwhile, cut each cheese slice into 3 strips. Arrange over ham and bake until cheese is bubbly. Makes 4 servings.

BAKED TUNA SANDWICHES

8 white-bread slices
butter or margarine
1 6½- or 7-ounce can tuna, drained
¼ cup diced celery
2 tablespoons chopped onion
½ teaspoon salt
¼ teaspoon caraway seed
4 Cheddar-cheese slices
2 eggs
1 cup milk
paprika for garnish

ABOUT 1 HOUR BEFORE SERVING:
Preheat oven to 350°F. Spread 4 bread slices with butter or margarine and place, buttered side down, in bottom of 9″ by 9″ baking dish. Bake 10 minutes; remove from oven.

In medium bowl, with fork, flake tuna; mix in celery, onion, salt and caraway seed; spoon onto bread in dish, spreading to edges; top with layer of Cheddar cheese, then with remaining bread.

In small bowl, with fork, beat eggs well; gradually stir in milk; pour over sandwiches; sprinkle with paprika. Bake 40 to 45 minutes until set. Makes 4 servings.

WESTERN-OMELET SANDWICH

6 eggs
¾ cup milk
½ teaspoon salt
dash pepper
¾ cup minced cooked ham
⅓ cup minced onions
⅓ cup minced green pepper
3 tablespoons fat (butter, margarine, bacon drippings or shortening)
6 frankfurter rolls, split, buttered and toasted

ABOUT 25 MINUTES BEFORE SERVING:
1. In medium bowl, with wire whisk or hand beater, beat eggs with milk, salt and pepper. Add ham, onions and green pepper.
2. In large skillet over medium-low heat, melt fat, tilting skillet to grease sides. Pour egg mixture into skillet; cook until set around edges.
3. With metal spatula, gently lift edges as they set, tilting skillet to allow uncooked portion to run under omelet.
4. Shake skillet occasionally to keep omelet moving freely in pan. When omelet is set but still moist on the surface, increase heat slightly to brown bottom. Cut omelet into wedges; roll each wedge from point and use as filling for one of buns. Makes 6 servings.

Party Sandwiches

PACIFIC RIBBON SANDWICHES

1 cup sour cream
1 envelope onion-soup mix for 4 servings
18 white-bread slices
12 boiled-ham slices
12 Muenster-cheese slices

EARLY IN DAY:
Combine sour cream and soup mix. Trim crusts from bread; trim ham and cheese slices to fit bread. Spread all bread with soup mixture; top each of 6 slices with ham, bread slice, cheese, bread slice with spread side down, to make 3-decker sandwiches. Refrigerate, covered.

TO SERVE:
Cut each sandwich into fourths and insert decorated toothpicks into each fourth to hold layers together. Makes 6 servings.

TEA SANDWICHES

Trim crusts from sliced white, whole wheat or other bread. Spread bread to the edges with Cream-Cheese Filling (below) or spread with softened butter or margarine, then with any easily spread filling that firms up when chilled. Wrap sandwiches in waxed paper, foil or plastic wrap and refrigerate several hours, or overnight.

To serve, cut sandwiches into halves, thirds, 2 or 3 triangles, or into fancy shapes with sharp cookie cutters. (If cutting ahead of time, arrange on plate and cover with plastic wrap; refrigerate.)

RIBBON SANDWICHES: Use 5 bread slices for each stack; fill and press gently but firmly together. (If you like, alternate light and dark slices.) With sharp knife, using sawing motion, cut crusts from bread. Wrap and refrigerate until filling is firm.

To serve, cut each stack into slices about ½ inch thick, then cut each slice into thirds, halves or 2 or 3 triangles.

CHECKERBOARDS: Use 4 bread slices of 2 contrasting colors for each stack. Alternating light and dark slices, fill and press gently but firmly together. With sharp knife, using sawing motion, cut crusts from bread. Wrap and refrigerate until filling is firm.

Slice stacks into thirds; spread slices with filling and put stack back together, reversing center slice so that contrasting breads alternate in checkerboard fashion. Press together; wrap and refrigerate.

To serve, cut each stack into slices about ½ inch thick.

PINWHEELS: With long sharp knife, cut off all crusts except bottom from unsliced loaf white bread. Turn loaf on its side; cut lengthwise into slices about ½ inch thick. (Retaining bottom crust makes cutting easier.) From narrow end, lightly roll each slice with rolling pin to help prevent cracking.

Spread bread to edges with filling. If you like, place 2 or 3 stuffed olives or 2 Vienna sausages or 2 small gherkins across one narrow end. Starting at that end, roll tightly, jelly-roll fashion. Wrap rolls separately and refrigerate.

To serve, cut rolls into ½-inch slices. If you like, broil slices to serve hot.

MOSAICS: Trim crusts from breads of 2 contrasting colors. With sharp canapé or cookie cutter, cut a shape from the center of 1 light and 1 dark slice and insert the dark center into the light slice and vice versa; use as the top slices of sandwiches. If you like, with large, sharp cookie cutters, cut sandwiches into shapes.

CREAM-CHEESE FILLING

With rubber spatula, thoroughly stir softened cream cheese to make it easy to spread on bread. Mix or top cream cheese with one of these:

Bacon bits and minced, drained chutney
Minced watermelon pickle
Chopped chives and crushed pineapple
Ground salami
Minced nuts and pimento-stuffed olives
Flaked sardines and lemon juice
Minced clams and dill pickles
Chopped salted peanuts

REUBEN SANDWICH LOAF

1 1½-pound oval loaf rye bread
butter or margarine, softened
bottled Thousand Island or Russian dressing
3 3-ounce packages wafer-thin, ready-to-eat corned beef slices
2 8-ounce packages natural Swiss-cheese slices
1½ cups well-drained sauerkraut

ABOUT 1 HOUR BEFORE SERVING:
Preheat oven to 425°F. Without slicing through bottom crust, cut rye bread into 16 slices. To make "sandwiches," spread every other slice with butter or margarine; spread facing slices with dressing; then tuck in meat and cheese; spoon in sauerkraut.

Wrap loaf in foil; bake 40 minutes or until hot. To serve, cut through bottom crust into sandwiches. Makes 8 sandwiches.

HAM SANDWICH LOAF: Prepare sandwich loaf as above but spread *prepared mustard* lightly on buttered slices and use *three 4-ounce packages boiled-ham slices, two 8-ounce packages Cheddar- or Muenster-cheese slices* and *1½ cups well-drained coleslaw.* If you like, do not bake.

GOLDEN CHEESE-STUFFED BREAD

2½ cups shredded Cheddar cheese
½ cup mayonnaise
½ teaspoon curry powder
⅔ cup finely diced celery
½ cup chopped parsley
2 canned whole pimentos, drained
1 loaf French bread, about 12 inches long

DAY BEFORE SERVING:
In medium bowl, with mixer at medium speed, combine cheese, mayonnaise and curry powder. With spoon, stir in celery and parsley. Pat pimentos very dry with paper towels; chop coarsely and stir into cheese mixture.

With sharp knife, cut bread in half crosswise; hollow out halves, leaving a shell about ½ inch thick. (Use scooped-out bread later for making crumbs, if you like.) With rubber spatula, press cheese mixture into bread shells. (Use any leftover filling as sandwich spread.) Put cut ends together; wrap with plastic wrap or foil and refrigerate at least 24 hours.

AT SERVING TIME:
With sharp knife, cut chilled loaf into ½-inch slices. Makes about 20 sandwiches.

CALICO CHEESE-STUFFED BREAD

1 8-ounce package cream cheese
1 3-ounce package cream cheese
1 4-ounce package blue cheese
½ cup bottled piccalilli
1 4-ounce jar pimentos, drained
1 cup chopped parsley
1 teaspoon onion salt
1 teaspoon Worcestershire
several dashes hot pepper sauce
1 loaf rye or whole-wheat Italian bread, about 12 inches long

DAY BEFORE SERVING:
Soften cheeses at room temperature. In medium bowl, with mixer at medium speed, combine cream and blue cheeses. Thoroughly drain piccalilli; pat pimentos very dry with paper towels, then chop coarsely. With spoon, stir piccalilli, pimentos, parsley, onion salt, Worcestershire and hot pepper sauce into cheeses.

With sharp knife, cut bread in halves crosswise; hollow out each half, leaving a shell ½ inch thick. (Use scooped-out bread for making crumbs later, if you like.) With rubber spatula, press cheese mixture into the two bread shells. Put cut ends together; wrap with plastic wrap or foil and refrigerate at least 24 hours.

AT SERVING TIME:
With sharp knife, cut chilled loaf into ½-inch slices. Makes about 20 sandwiches.

CHICKEN-SALAD-STUFFED ROLLS

1 6-ounce can chicken, diced
1 cup diced celery
½ cup chopped green pepper
½ cup mayonnaise
¼ cup sour cream
1 teaspoon salt
½ teaspoon curry powder (optional)
4 small rectangular hard rolls
salad greens
paprika for garnish

UP TO 30 MINUTES BEFORE SERVING:
In medium bowl, stir first 7 ingredients until well mixed.

Cut ½-inch slice from top of each roll, then scoop out soft center. (Use for bread crumbs later, if you like.) Fill hollow in each roll with chicken mixture.

Serve rolls on platter with greens; sprinkle with paprika. Makes 4 sandwiches.

CRUSTY HOT SANDWICH LOAF

1 cup cut-up bologna
1 6-ounce package cubed Cheddar cheese
¼ cup mayonnaise
1 teaspoon curry powder
1 loaf French bread, about 14 inches long
1 medium onion, thinly sliced

EARLY IN DAY OR DAY BEFORE:
In small bowl, stir bologna, cheese, mayonnaise and curry powder. Split French bread lengthwise into halves. Spoon bologna-cheese mixture onto bottom half. Arrange sliced onion on top; set top half of bread in place; cut into 6 crosswise slices. Wrap tightly in foil and refrigerate.

40 MINUTES BEFORE SERVING:
Preheat oven to 400°F. Bake wrapped loaf 30 minutes. Makes 6 sandwiches.

PIZZA-BY-THE-YARD

1 pound ground beef
1 6-ounce can tomato paste
⅓ cup grated Parmesan cheese
¼ cup chopped ripe olives
1 tablespoon instant minced onion
1 teaspoon salt
1 teaspoon oregano leaves
dash pepper
1 loaf Italian or Vienna bread, about 14 inches long
4 slices Cheddar cheese
2 medium tomatoes, sliced

ABOUT 30 MINUTES BEFORE SERVING:
Preheat broiler if manufacturer directs. In medium bowl, combine first 8 ingredients.

Split bread lengthwise in halves. Spread meat mixture on bread halves. Broil 12 minutes or until meat is well browned. Cut Cheddar-cheese slices in half diagonally. Top pizzas with tomato and cheese slices, alternating them along length of bread. Broil just until cheese is melted; cut each pizza into 5 or 6 slices. Makes 10 or 12 open-face sandwiches.

SALAMI-AND-SWISS LOAF

1 cup mayonnaise
½ cup prepared mustard
1 12-inch loaf rye bread, thinly sliced
chicory
2 medium red onions, thinly sliced
2 8-ounce packages natural Swiss-cheese slices, cut in thirds
1 8-ounce package hard salami slices
3 medium tomatoes, thinly sliced
radish roses for garnish

UP TO 3 HOURS BEFORE SERVING:
In small bowl, combine mayonnaise and mustard. Place sliced loaf on large sheet of foil or plastic wrap. Spread mayonnaise mixture on every other bread slice, keeping loaf in shape.

Insert some chicory and a couple of slices each of onion, Swiss cheese, salami and tomatoes to make sandwiches. Wrap sandwich loaf; refrigerate.

TO SERVE:
Unwrap loaf; serve from large platter or on wooden board. Garnish with radish roses. Makes about 16 sandwiches.

CHICKEN AND HAM ON TOAST

2 1½-ounce envelopes white-sauce mix
2 cups cooked or canned chicken, cut in chunks
3 tablespoons dry sherry
butter or margarine
4 large baked ham slices
4 English muffins, split and toasted

ABOUT 20 MINUTES BEFORE SERVING:
Prepare white-sauce mix as label directs; add chicken and sherry and heat, stirring occasionally. In medium skillet over high heat, in a little butter or margarine, fry ham slices. Serve ham on split muffins; spoon mixture over ham. Makes 4 servings.

HAM-AND-EGG SANDWICH LOAF

1 loaf unsliced white bread, about 12 inches long
Ham-Horseradish Filling (below)
Curry-Egg Filling (below)
14 stuffed medium olives for garnish

EARLY IN DAY OR DAY BEFORE SERVING:
With long, sharp knife, cut all crusts from bread; cut bread horizontally into 4 slices, each about ¾ inch thick, using ruler as guide. For sandwich loaf, use 3 slices; use remaining slice for toast another day.

Place bottom bread slice on large sheet of foil or plastic wrap; spread with Ham-Horseradish Filling in even layer. Top filling with second bread slice; spread with Curry-Egg Filling. Top with third bread slice. Carefully wrap loaf and chill.

JUST BEFORE SERVING:
Remove foil; garnish top of loaf with row of olives, secured with toothpicks. Slice between olives. Makes 14 sandwiches.

HAM-HORSERADISH FILLING: In medium bowl, mix *1¼ cups ground cooked or canned ham* with *⅓ cup chili sauce, ¼ cup minced onion, ¼ cup mayonnaise, 2 tablespoons minced green pepper* and *1 tablespoon horseradish.* Refrigerate, covered.

CURRY-EGG FILLING: In medium bowl, mix *6 hard-cooked eggs,* chopped, with *⅓ cup mayonnaise, 2 tablespoons minced parsley, 1½ teaspoons seasoned salt, ¾ teaspoon curry powder.* Refrigerate, covered.

JUMBO STACKS

1 3½-pound frozen turkey roll
1 2½-pound smoked boneless pork butt
1 or 2 round loaves rye or white bread
1 pound Swiss-cheese slices
½ pound olive-loaf slices
1 4-ounce can pimentos, drained
1 small head lettuce, shredded
bottled oil-and-vinegar dressing
Condiments (below)

EARLY IN DAY:
Roast turkey roll and pork butt as labels direct; refrigerate.

ABOUT 20 MINUTES BEFORE SERVING:
On large sandwich tray or wooden board, slice turkey, pork and bread; arrange with Swiss cheese and olive loaf.

Slice pimentos. In medium bowl, toss lettuce and pimentos with enough oil-and-vinegar dressing to moisten. Place Condiments and bowl of lettuce on tray. Everyone makes his favorite sandwich combination. Makes at least 16 sandwiches.

CONDIMENTS: Prepared mustard, mayonnaise, catchup, chowchow, sliced pickles.

STRAWBERRY-BLINTZ SANDWICHES

1½ cups creamed cottage cheese
4 eggs
2 tablespoons sugar
12 white-bread slices
2 10-ounce packages frozen strawberries in quick-thaw pouch
⅓ cup milk
butter or margarine

ABOUT 30 MINUTES BEFORE SERVING:
In medium bowl, with fork, beat cottage cheese, 1 egg and sugar until well mixed; spread about ¼ cup mixture on each of 6 bread slices; top with remaining slices. Thaw strawberries as label directs.

In pie plate, with fork, beat 3 eggs and milk together well. In large skillet over medium-high heat, melt a little butter or margarine. Quickly dip sandwiches, one at a time, into egg mixture, turning to coat both sides; brown on both sides in skillet; place on warm platter while frying remaining sandwiches. Serve with berries spooned over them. Makes 6 sandwiches.

HOT TUNA BISCUITS

2 8-ounce cans refrigerated biscuits
2 6½- or 7-ounce cans tuna, drained
½ cup diced sharp Cheddar cheese
⅓ cup mayonnaise

ABOUT 30 MINUTES BEFORE SERVING:
Preheat oven to 425°F. Pat each biscuit into a thin 4-inch oval. Arrange half of biscuits on greased cookie sheet. In small bowl, mix tuna, cheese, mayonnaise. Spread on biscuits on cookie sheet. Top with remaining biscuits; with fingers, press edges together.

Bake sandwiches 10 to 15 minutes until browned. Makes 10 sandwiches.

HOT CHEESE-CHIVE LOAF

½ cup butter or margarine, softened
½ cup shredded Cheddar cheese
¼ cup chopped chives
2 tablespoons prepared mustard
1 1-pound round loaf white bread

EARLY IN DAY:
In medium bowl, with spoon, mix all ingredients except bread. Cut bread into 12 slices, not quite through bottom crust. Spread mixture on every other slice; wrap loaf in foil; refrigerate.

ABOUT 30 MINUTES BEFORE SERVING:
Preheat oven to 425°F. Heat loaf 20 minutes. Unwrap and cut through bottom crust between sandwiches. Makes 6 sandwiches.

HOT CRAB SANDWICHES

1 7½-ounce can crab, drained and flaked
mayonnaise
2 tablespoons pickle relish
¼ teaspoon salt
8 bread slices, toasted
2 medium tomatoes, thinly sliced
8 natural Swiss-cheese slices

ABOUT 20 MINUTES BEFORE SERVING:
Preheat oven to 400°F. In medium bowl, combine crab, ¼ cup mayonnaise, pickle relish and salt; spread on 4 toast slices. Top with tomato slices. Spread remaining toast with mayonnaise; place on tomatoes. Cover each with 2 slices cheese. Bake 10 minutes until hot. Makes 4 sandwiches.

KEEP-TRIM SANDWICHES

Lower-calorie sandwiches can be as tasty and appealing as heartier ones when made with "keep-trim" fillings and thinly sliced breads. Spread the bread with a thin layer of filling, omitting butter or margarine, mayonnaise or salad dressing; use lettuce to make a fuller sandwich without adding calories. (If the sandwich is to be carried, pack lettuce separately and tuck it into the sandwich at mealtime.)

Season keep-trim sandwiches generously—a thin but tasty sandwich is more satisfying than a thick, tasteless one. If the sandwich is part of lunch, plan fresh fruit, vegetable nibblers and a beverage to round out the meal.

DOUBLE-CHEESE SANDWICH: Combine *Roquefort and Neufchâtel* cheeses* with a bit of *minced onion* or dash of onion juice and some *well-drained, chopped canned mushrooms.* Spread on *dark bread.*

BACON-AND-COTTAGE-CHEESE SANDWICH: Combine *crumbled cooked bacon* or bacon-flavored vegetable-protein bits with *chopped sweet gherkins* and moisten with *blended cottage cheese.*** Spread on *toast.*

CHICKEN-AND-OLIVE SANDWICH: Mix *chopped cooked chicken* with *chopped ripe olives* and *just enough low-calorie mayonnaise**** to moisten. Spread on *raisin bread.*

CRUNCHY TUNA SANDWICH: Spark *tuna* with *minced celery, chopped nuts, salt* and *a bit of blended cottage cheese.*** Spread on *thin, thin slices of date-nut bread.*

CURRIED SHRIMP SANDWICH: Mix *canned shrimp* and *chopped apple* with *low-calorie mayonnaise**** and *curry powder.* Spread on *dark bread.*

CHEESE-AND-ORANGE SANDWICH: Spread *Neufchâtel cheese** and *orange marmalade* on *raisin bread* or toast.

* Neufchâtel cheese has 32 percent fewer calories than cream cheese.

** Cottage cheese, blended smooth in blender with a bit of water or milk, makes a tasty, lower-calorie alternate for sour cream.

*** Salad dressing has about two-thirds the calories of regular mayonnaise. Low-calorie mayonnaise has about one-fifth the calories of regular mayonnaise.

APPLE-AND-HAM SANDWICH: Spread *rye or pumpernickel bread* with *apple butter;* add a *couple of boiled ham slices.*

HAWAIIAN SANDWICH: Mix *cottage cheese* with *drained canned crushed pineapple* and *a bit of onion salt.* Spread on *raisin bread.*

CHICKEN LIVER SPECIAL SANDWICH: Chop *cooked chicken livers* with *stuffed olives.* Spread on *pumpernickel bread.*

DELI-SANDWICH: Place *a baked-ham or roast-beef* slice between 2 *rye- or pumpernickel-bread slices* plus *coleslaw* made with *low-calorie mayonnaise.**** (If sandwich is to be carried, pack coleslaw separately.)

PEPPERY SANDWICH: Make a sandwich of *thinly sliced green pepper* and *ham or beef slices* on *dark or white bread.*

CHILI-MEAT SANDWICH: Chop *canned luncheon meat* and moisten it with *chili sauce.* Spread on *rye bread.*

SANDWICH GARNISHES

Orange or grapefruit sections
Cucumber sticks
Raw zucchini slices
Orange cups filled with cranberry sauce
Pimento strips
Olives—green, ripe or stuffed
Raisins
Lemon or lime wedges dipped in chopped parsley or paprika
Caulifowerets
Pickled onions
Cream-cheese balls, rolled in chopped nuts
Spiced crab apples
Grape jelly in small pear halves
Potato chips, corn curls or chips
Cherry tomatoes filled with seasoned cottage cheese
Green onions, radishes, carrots, celery
Pickled peppers
Watercress, curly endive, mint, parsley
Apple or pear wedges, dipped in lemon juice
Grape clusters
Stuffed eggs
Jellied cranberry-sauce cutouts
Chutney or piccalilli
Tomato wedges
Sweet or dill pickles

Desserts

Keep the rest of the meal in mind when you plan dessert. When the meal is hearty, serve a light sweet such as fruit or gelatin. A hearty dessert such as bread pudding makes a good ending for a light meal.

Dessert can also balance the meal nutritionally. If the main dish is predominantly vegetable, follow it with a dessert of eggs, cheese, milk or yogurt. No fruit in the meal? Put it in the dessert. If potatoes, rice, macaroni or spaghetti are not on the bill of fare, serve a dessert featuring bread, rice or cake as the follow-up.

Select a dessert that can be made at the time most convenient for you—one to make ahead, or one that you can put together along with the rest of the meal.

If you're planning a new treat for guests, try it out on the family first. This preview will turn an ordinary menu into something special and give you practice for the big event. But remember too that simple desserts can top off a company meal just as deliciously as elaborate creations.

When serving spoonable desserts, use pretty stemmed wine, sherbet or saucer champagne glasses or even dainty teacups instead of the usual shallow dessert dishes. Serve very rich desserts in demitasse cups or the *petits pots* used for *pot de crème.*

Tips for Special Desserts

Puddings made with milk: To keep cooked puddings creamy and free of "skin," press waxed paper directly against the surface of the hot pudding, then cool pudding; remove paper. For smoother texture, beat pudding with hand beater or wire whisk before serving.

Creamy puddings double nicely as sauces or toppings for gelatin desserts, ice cream, fruit or cake squares.

Steamed puddings: To save work on busy days, make these puddings ahead and refrigerate or freeze. Reheat thawed puddings at serving time as recipe or package directs. (Of course you can make and steam just before serving.)

Use pudding molds with lids; or use heatproof bowls and cover with greased foil. Cut foil 1 inch larger all around than top of bowl and grease. Crimp edges to bowl to seal before steaming pudding.

To flame pudding: For large pudding, heat ½ cup brandy to lukewarm in small saucepan. For individual puddings, heat 1 tablespoon brandy per pudding. Place pudding on heated serving platter. Pour lukewarm brandy over and around hot pudding. Touch lighted match to brandy; when alcohol burns off, flame will die, and pudding is ready to be served.

If you like, instead of brandy, use cubes of sugar that have been soaked in lemon extract; place cubes around pudding and light each with match.

Gelatin desserts: Both unflavored gelatin and fruit-flavored gelatin must be dissolved completely for molds to set properly. Make sure there are no granules visible in the hot liquid. Stir gelatin constantly, but not vigorously, when dissolving; gelatin splashed on sides of bowl or pan is difficult to dissolve.

When using unflavored gelatin, sprinkle it evenly over the surface of the liquid in a medium saucepan. Cook over direct low heat, stirring constantly, until granules are no longer visible. (When using milk or milk-base liquids, sprinkle gelatin on liquid and let it soften a few minutes before dissolving; when dissolving gelatin in water or water-base liquids, gelatin does not need pre-softening.)

While mixture chills, stir occasionally so it cools and thickens evenly. If mixture thickens too much before other ingredients are added or it is poured into a mold, melt it over low heat and chill again.

When recipe says mixture should be refrigerated until it mounds or reaches the consistency of unbeaten egg white, test it this way: Drop some mixture from spoon back into mixture. If it forms a small mound that does not quickly blend back into mixture, it is the right consistency.

When adding whipped cream or beaten egg whites to a thickened gelatin mixture, gently fold in with wire whisk or rubber spatula. Vigorous beating reduces volume.

To hasten setting of gelatin mixture, place bowl of mixture in bowl of ice water; refrigerate. Stir often until mixture reaches desired consistency. Or, put bowl of gelatin mixture in freezing compartment of refrigerator; stir occasionally until of desired thickness. Don't try to chill until set; ice crystals may form, make gelatin watery.

To unmold gelatin mixtures, see Unmolding Gelatin Salads (page 390).

Use canned or cooked pineapple with gelatin; fresh pineapple prevents setting.

Whipped cream and whipped toppings: For topping desserts, these are interchangeable —heavy cream, whipped; whipped cream or whipped topping in aerosol can; whipped topping prepared from packaged mix; frozen whipped topping. One cup heavy or whipping cream makes about 2 cups, whipped, and equals one 2-ounce package or envelope whipped-topping mix prepared by label directions or 2 cups thawed, frozen whipped topping.

Heavy cream should be fresh and cold to beat to fullest volume; use mixer at medium speed to avoid overbeating.

Desserts That Freeze Well

The desserts below can be made days or weeks ahead and stored in the freezer. Prepare as recipe directs; cool, freezer-wrap and freeze or follow these directions:

Cream puffs and éclairs: Fill with ice cream or whipped cream before freezing. Serve ice-cream-filled puffs without thawing; thaw other puffs about 30 minutes at room temperature. Top with hot sauce.

Crêpes: To freeze, don't fill; stack with waxed paper between; wrap stack and freeze. Thaw at room temperature about 1 hour; complete as recipe directs.

Steamed puddings: To thaw, unwrap; place in steamer or double boiler; heat (time will depend on size of pudding).

Baba au Rhum: Don't add sauce before freezing. Thaw large or small babas at room temperature about 2 hours. Pour warm sauce over them and let soak; complete as recipe directs.

Apple Betty: Leave in casserole; cover. Thaw, covered, in oven at 350°F.

Whipped cream: Drop spoonfuls onto cookie sheet; freeze, then place dollops in freezer bag and store in freezer.

Sauces: Chocolate, butterscotch, caramel, fruit and hard sauces may be stored in freezer. Thaw in refrigerator several hours.

Garnishes for Desserts

See Fruit Garnishes (page 379); Sweet Garnishes (page 380); "Dairy" Garnishes (page 380).

Easiest-of-All Desserts

Ready-to-eat and ready-to-make desserts come in a wide range of types and flavors.

Gelatin desserts come ready to eat, in cans on the supermarket shelf or in plastic containers in the refrigerator case. Packaged gelatin mixes offer a delightful array of fruit flavors. To vary gelatin, mold, whip or combine it with fruits or whipped cream. Packages come in two sizes.

Ready-to-eat puddings also make menu variety easy. Rice, tapioca and creamy cooked puddings come canned or refrigerated; the creamy type is also available frozen. Ready-to-make packaged pudding mixes include the regular kind that needs short cooking (just heat to boiling with milk) and the instant type that needs no cooking at all (just a brief beating with cold milk). For variety, there are tapioca and custard-pudding mixes.

PUDDING DRESS-UPS

To dress up puddings, use one of the following to ripple in, spoon on or layer with pudding.

FOR VANILLA: A little sundae sauce and sweetened whipped cream
Spoonful of melted semisweet chocolate
Cut-up oranges and shredded coconut
Just-thawed frozen orange, grape or pineapple-orange-juice concentrate
Melted currant jelly tossed with coconut
Sweetened fresh, canned or thawed frozen berries or other fruit
Almond extract, cream sherry or brandy to taste; also fold in drained canned crushed pineapple or sweet cherries, if desired

FOR VANILLA OR LEMON: Drained fresh, frozen or canned peach slices, mixed fruit, pineapple tidbits or banana chunks
Raspberry, strawberry or peach preserves
Canned crushed pineapple, flavored with mint extract and tinted with green food color
Fresh blueberries, sliced peaches, halved strawberries
Blueberry- or cherry-pie filling and toasted slivered almonds
Just-thawed frozen raspberries, strawberries, blackberries
Flaked coconut tossed with grated lemon peel
Chopped, pitted dates or dried figs and chopped nuts (moistened first with thawed frozen orange-juice concentrate, if desired)
Drained canned sweet cherries
Rhubarb sauce

FOR VANILLA OR CHOCOLATE: Crushed peanut brittle or peppermint candy
Chocolate or butterscotch sauce, then sweetened whipped cream and/or chopped nuts
Vanilla, chocolate or strawberry ice cream
Melted semisweet-chocolate or butterscotch pieces and chopped nuts
Instant coffee powder (add 2 teaspoons per 4 servings; cook with pudding); also, fold in ½ cup heavy or whipping cream, whipped

FOR CHOCOLATE: One square semisweet chocolate, grated
Sherry, rum or brandy to taste; top with shredded coconut or mixed candied fruit
One pint coffee ice cream stirred into cooked pudding while still warm
Flaked coconut tossed with grated orange peel
Whipped cream with raspberry jam
Drained canned pear halves and chocolate sauce
Sliced banana and apricot preserves

ALL FLAVORS: Scoops of ice cream
Miniature marshmallows, folded in while pudding is still warm
One of Whipped-Cream Toppings (page 499) for topping or layering
Flaked coconut, plain or toasted
Cookie or cake crumbs for topping or making parfaits

GELATIN DRESS-UPS

Read Gelatin Desserts (page 478). Vary fruit-flavor gelatins with these ideas:

CUBES: Prepare gelatin as label directs but reduce liquid by 1/4 cup for every cup of cold liquid used and pour into shallow pan to depth of about 1/2 inch; chill until set or overnight. Cut into cubes with knife dipped in warm water. Remove cubes by dipping pan in warm water, then inverting onto waxed paper. Arrange cubes with fruit in dessert dishes. Or, mix two flavors of cubes. Or, serve topped with softened ice cream, sweetened whipped cream or Custard Sauce (page 281). Or, use cubes to garnish tops of other desserts.

WHIP: When gelatin is slightly thickened, set in bowl of ice water and beat with mixer at high speed until frothy; spoon into dessert dishes; chill until set. Or, chill gelatin until very thick. With mixer at high speed, beat until fluffy (about double in volume); chill until set. Serve with fruit, Custard Sauce (page 281) or whipped topping.

FLAKES: Prepare as for Cubes (above) but run fork through gelatin or force through a ricer instead of cutting into cubes. Serve with Custard Sauce (page 281); fold into chilled vanilla pudding or fold sweetened whipped cream or well-drained fruit into gelatin.

CUT-OUTS: Prepare as for Cubes (above) but cut into animal or other shapes with cookie cutters dipped in warm water. Use as a garnish for pudding, children's birthday cake or a whipped dessert such as Snow Pudding (page 497).

FRUITED MOLD: When there's no time to wait for gelatin to thicken before adding fruit, remember that some fruits float in gelatin and others sink. Use a combination of these in liquid gelatin for a self-layered dessert. Fruits that sink include frozen sweetened raspberries, fruit cocktail, apricots, canned grapefruit sections, cherries, canned pineapple, peaches, pears, plums, fresh grapes. Fruits that float include banana slices, fresh grapefruit and orange sections, canned orange sections, apple cubes, fresh and canned strawberries, mandarin oranges. Marshmallows and nut meats also float.

SOFT-SET: Prepare gelatin as label directs but increase cold water by 1/2 cup per cup cold water called for on label. When set, serve with pour cream. Or, use in parfaits with fruit or softened ice cream. Or, use as sauce on plain cake or fruit.

PERKY FLAVOR: Prepare gelatin as label directs but substitute ginger ale or lemon-lime flavor carbonated beverage for cold water.

QUICK SPANISH CREAM: Prepare gelatin as label directs but substitute half-and-half for cold water. (Or, use 1/2 cup heavy or whipping cream in place of 1/2 cup cold water.) Mixture may have a curdled appearance at this point. Chill until almost set. Then with mixer at high speed, beat until fluffy. Chill until set.

QUICK CAKE DESSERTS

COTTAGE PUDDING: Top unfrosted squares of yellow or white cake, or slices of poundcake, with any sauce (pages 499–500).

CHARLOTTE RUSSE: Line sherbet dishes with ladyfingers. Center mound of Sweetened Whipped Cream (page 499) in each dish; top with maraschino cherry. Serve at once or refrigerate.

COCONUT FINGERS: Spread poundcake slices with butter or margarine and cut into fingers; sprinkle with flaked coconut. Broil until toasted.

FRENCH-TOASTED SLICES: Dip poundcake slices into French-Toast mixture (page 458). Fry in butter or margarine until golden. Serve with jelly or maple-blended syrup.

MAKE-YOUR-OWN SHORTCAKES: On a tray, arrange bakers' dessert shells and poundcake slices; vanilla ice cream, whipped cream or whipped topping in aerosol can; sliced peaches, bananas, blueberries or strawberries. Everyone makes his own shortcake.

SPUR-OF-THE-MOMENT SHORTCAKES: Fill bakers' dessert shells or sponge or angel-food-cake slices with a filling (below) and add a topping:

Berries and/or sliced peaches with sour cream

Whipped cream or marshmallow cream with chocolate sauce and salted nuts
Orange chunks and banana slices with sprinklings of sherry, flaked coconut
Orange sherbet with whipped cream
Sprinkling of rum, then ice cream with strawberries or butterscotch sauce
Spiced applesauce or crushed pineapple
Sweetened, sliced strawberries with pineapple chunks or sliced bananas
Thawed peach slices or dark sweet cherries with almond-flavored whipped cream

DOUGHNUT DECKERS: Put split doughnut halves together with melted semisweet chocolate as filling; top with scoop of vanilla or coffee ice cream.

FRUITCAKE DESSERTS

In covered double-boiler top over hot water, heat fruitcake slices through. Serve with Hard Sauce or Eggnog Sauce (page 500) or Sweetened Whipped Cream (page 499).

YOGURT DESSERTS

In sherbet dishes, parfaits or tall glasses, alternate layers of sweetened fresh, canned or just-thawed frozen fruits with plain, vanilla or fruit-flavor yogurt.

Serve plain or vanilla-flavor yogurt with fresh strawberries, raspberries or blueberries and brown sugar or honey.

Serve coffee-flavor yogurt with chocolate syrup or layer with chopped nuts, toasted flaked coconut, cake or cookie crumbs.

YOGURT FRUIT PUDDING

1 3⅝- or 3¾-ounce package vanilla instant-pudding mix
1 cup milk
1 8-ounce container strawberry-flavor yogurt
strawberries for garnish (optional)

ABOUT 15 MINUTES BEFORE SERVING:
In small bowl, with mixer at low speed, beat pudding mix and milk just until thickened. Fold in yogurt. Pour into 4 dessert dishes. Refrigerate at least 5 minutes before serving. Garnish with strawberries. Makes 4 servings.

APRICOT CREAM

1 3⅝- or 3¾-ounce package vanilla instant-pudding mix
1 cup apricot nectar, chilled
1 cup sour cream
1 teaspoon lemon juice

ABOUT 15 MINUTES BEFORE SERVING:
In small bowl, with mixer at low speed, beat all ingredients just until blended. Spoon into 4 dessert dishes; refrigerate at least 5 minutes before serving. Makes 4 servings.

LAYERED APPLESAUCE

½ cup butter or margarine
2 cups quick-cooking oats, uncooked
2 tablespoons sugar
1 16-ounce can applesauce, chilled
whipped cream for garnish

ABOUT 20 MINUTES BEFORE SERVING:
In medium skillet over medium heat, melt butter or margarine. Add oats and cook, stirring constantly, until oats are golden; stir in sugar.

Spoon applesauce into 6 dessert dishes; top with oat mixture and whipped cream. Serve at once. Makes 6 servings.

STRAWBERRY TAPIOCA

2 10-ounce packages frozen sliced strawberries, thawed
¼ cup quick-cooking tapioca
¼ teaspoon salt
2 tablespoons lemon juice
⅓ cup heavy or whipping cream

ABOUT 3 HOURS BEFORE SERVING:
Drain berries, reserving liquid. To liquid, add enough water to make 2 cups. In medium saucepan over medium heat, heat liquid with tapioca and salt, stirring constantly, until mixture boils. Remove from heat; cool, stirring occasionally. When cold, stir in berries and lemon juice. Cover and refrigerate.

TO SERVE:
In small bowl, with mixer at medium speed, beat cream until stiff peaks form; with rubber spatula, gently fold into strawberry mixture. Spoon into dessert dishes. Makes 6 to 8 servings.

GINGERED FRUIT

3 cups pitted sweet cherries
1 cup raspberries
1 cup pineapple chunks
1 10-ounce jar orange marmalade (1 cup)
2 tablespoons syrup drained from canned, preserved ginger
1 tablespoon preserved ginger, chopped
mint leaves for garnish

SEVERAL HOURS AHEAD OR DAY BEFORE:
Layer fruits in glass bowl. In small bowl, stir marmalade with ¼ cup hot water, ginger syrup and ginger; drizzle over fruits. Cover and refrigerate.

AT SERVING TIME:
Garnish with mint. Makes 6 servings.

PRUNE WHIP

1½ cups pitted cooked prunes
¼ cup confectioners' sugar
½ teaspoon grated orange peel
1 cup heavy or whipping cream

EARLY IN DAY:
In covered blender container at high speed, blend prunes, sugar and orange peel until smooth. In small bowl, with mixer at medium speed, beat cream until stiff peaks form; with rubber spatula, gently fold in prune mixture. Spoon into dessert dishes. Refrigerate at least 4 hours. Makes 6 servings.

PEARS A LA CREME

1 29-ounce can pear halves
2 tablespoons butter or margarine
⅓ cup packed light brown sugar
½ teaspoon cinnamon
¼ teaspoon nutmeg
¼ teaspoon ginger
1½ pints vanilla ice cream

ABOUT 20 MINUTES BEFORE SERVING:
Drain pear halves (use liquid with breakfast orange juice another day). In medium skillet over low heat, melt butter or margarine; stir in next 4 ingredients. Add pear halves and simmer 10 minutes, turning pears once.

Spoon ice cream into dessert dishes; top each with hot pear and some sauce. Makes 8 to 10 servings.

STRAWBERRIES MANHATTAN

Wash large strawberries but leave hulls and stems on; heap into serving bowl. On each dessert plate, set small cup or tiny bowl of sour cream and generous spoonful of brown sugar. Each guest helps himself to strawberries and dips berries in sour cream, then in brown sugar.

STRAWBERRY SHORTCAKE

2 pints strawberries
sugar
1¾ cups all-purpose flour
½ cup shortening
⅓ cup milk
1 egg
1 tablespoon double-acting baking powder
1 teaspoon grated lemon peel
¾ teaspoon salt
butter or margarine, softened
1 cup heavy or whipping cream, whipped

ABOUT 45 MINUTES BEFORE SERVING:
Reserve a few strawberries for garnish. Wash and hull remaining berries and sprinkle with ⅓ cup sugar; mash slightly; set aside.

Preheat oven to 450°F. Grease 9-inch round cake pan. Into medium bowl, measure ¼ cup sugar and next 7 ingredients. With mixer at medium speed, beat mixture until well combined and a soft dough forms. Pat dough evenly into pan. Bake 15 minutes or until golden.

Invert shortcake onto platter; with long, sharp knife, split hot shortcake horizontally. Spread cut surfaces with butter or margarine. Onto bottom half, spoon half of berries; top with other cake half; spoon remaining berries over top. Spread whipped cream over berries and garnish with whole strawberries. Makes 8 servings.

INDIVIDUAL SHORTCAKES: Prepare as above but onto greased cookie sheet, drop dough in 8 equal mounds about 2 inches apart. Bake 10 minutes or until golden. Split and serve as above.

PEACH SHORTCAKE: Prepare as above but substitute *4 cups sliced peaches* for strawberries.

PEACH NOODLE KUGEL

1 8-ounce package wide egg noodles
3 tablespoons butter or margarine
3 eggs
½ cup sugar
1½ tablespoons grated lemon peel
¼ teaspoon salt
2 cups milk
½ cup dark seedless raisins
1 16-ounce can sliced cling peaches, drained
Streusel Topping (below)

ABOUT 2 HOURS BEFORE SERVING:
Preheat oven to 350°F. Grease 12″ by 8″ baking dish. Prepare noodles as label directs; drain. In large bowl, toss hot noodles with butter or margarine. In medium bowl, with wire whisk or fork, beat eggs, sugar, lemon peel and salt until well mixed; stir in milk and raisins. Stir mixture into noodles; pour into dish. Bake 30 minutes.

Remove dish from oven; arrange peach slices on top and sprinkle evenly with Streusel Topping. Return to oven and bake 15 minutes more. Let stand about 30 minutes for easier cutting. Serve warm. Makes 10 servings.

STREUSEL TOPPING: In small saucepan over low heat, melt *2 tablespoons butter or margarine;* stir in *¼ cup dried bread crumbs* and *½ teaspoon cinnamon.*

QUICK FRUIT COBBLER

2 10-ounce packages frozen mixed fruit, thawed
2 tablespoons sugar
2 tablespoons cornstarch
1 tablespoon lemon juice
½ teaspoon salt
1 9.5-ounce package refrigerated cinnamon rolls

ABOUT 30 MINUTES BEFORE SERVING:
Preheat oven to 375°F. In medium saucepan over medium heat, heat fruit, sugar, cornstarch, lemon juice and salt, stirring constantly, just until thickened. Pour mixture into 8″ by 8″ baking dish. Arrange cinnamon rolls in one layer over fruits; reserve icing from package. Bake 20 minutes or until golden brown. Spread icing evenly on top of rolls. Serve hot. Makes 8 servings.

PEAR-BUTTERSCOTCH CRISP

1 29-ounce can pear halves, drained
½ cup packed light brown sugar
½ cup all-purpose flour
¼ teaspoon salt
¼ teaspoon cinnamon
¼ cup butter or margarine
half-and-half, softened vanilla ice cream or Custard Sauce (page 281)

ABOUT 40 MINUTES BEFORE SERVING:
Preheat oven to 425°F. In greased 9-inch pie plate, arrange pear halves, cut side down. Into small bowl, measure next 4 ingredients; with fork or pastry blender or 2 knives used scissor-fashion, cut in butter or margarine until mixture resembles coarse crumbs; sprinkle over pears. Bake 15 to 20 minutes until crumbs are golden. Serve warm with half-and-half. Makes 4 servings.

QUICK PEAR COBBLER

5 pears, halved and cored
2 tablespoons lemon juice
⅓ cup packed light brown sugar
5 tablespoons butter or margarine, melted
sugar
cinnamon
1 8-ounce package refrigerated buttermilk biscuits
1 cup sour cream

ABOUT 45 MINUTES BEFORE SERVING:
Preheat oven to 400°F. Place pear halves, cut side up, in 13″ by 9″ baking pan; sprinkle with lemon juice, then with brown sugar. Pour 3 tablespoons melted butter or margarine evenly over pear halves. Cover and bake 20 minutes or until just tender.

Meanwhile, on waxed paper, mix together ½ cup sugar and ½ teaspoon cinnamon. Separate refrigerated biscuits; dip each in remaining melted butter or margarine, then coat with sugar-cinnamon mixture. At the end of 20 minutes baking time, uncover pears and place a sugared biscuit on top of each pear half. Bake 10 minutes longer or until biscuits are done.

While biscuits are baking, in small bowl, combine sour cream, 3 tablespoons sugar and ¼ teaspoon cinnamon. Serve pear halves warm with sour-cream mixture spooned on top. Makes 10 servings.

PLUM KUCHEN

5 plums or 16 prune plums
sugar
1 cup all-purpose flour
¼ cup shortening
¼ cup milk
1 egg
1½ teaspoons double-acting baking powder
½ teaspoon salt
3 tablespoons butter or margarine
1 teaspoon cinnamon
¼ teaspoon nutmeg
⅓ cup apricot jam or currant jelly

ABOUT 1¼ HOURS BEFORE SERVING:
Pit plums; cut into eighths (cut prune plums in half). Preheat oven to 400°F. Grease 12″ by 8″ baking dish. Into large bowl, measure ¼ cup sugar and next 6 ingredients. With mixer at low speed, beat until mixture leaves sides of bowl and clings to beaters, constantly scraping bowl.

Spread dough in baking dish. Arrange plums, skin side up, in slightly overlapping rows. In small saucepan, over medium heat, melt butter or margarine; stir in ¼ cup sugar, cinnamon and nutmeg; spoon over plums. Bake 30 to 35 minutes until plums are tender.

In small bowl, with fork, stir jelly with 1 tablespoon hot water until smooth; brush over hot fruit. Makes 6 servings.

PEACH OR APPLE: Prepare as above but, for plums, substitute 5 *peaches,* peeled and sliced, or *4 cups peeled and cored, thinly sliced cooking apples.*

GLAZED GRAPE KUCHEN

1 8-ounce package refrigerated crescent dinner rolls
½ cup vanilla-wafer crumbs
1 tablespoon sugar
1 teaspoon cinnamon
¼ teaspoon nutmeg
2 cups seedless green grapes
3 tablespoons butter or margarine, melted
⅓ cup currant jelly

ABOUT 45 MINUTES BEFORE SERVING:
Preheat oven to 400°F. Unroll package of crescent dinner rolls. In 12″ by 8″ baking dish, lay the 2 strips of dough side by side, rolling up ends of strips so they fit the dish.

In small bowl, combine crumbs, sugar, cinnamon and nutmeg; sprinkle over top of dough. Spread grapes evenly over crumb mixture; brush grapes with butter or margarine. Bake 30 minutes or until golden.

Meanwhile, in cup, combine jelly with 1 tablespoon hot water; brush over grapes. Serve warm. Makes 6 to 8 servings.

BANANA-COCONUT BETTY

2 cups lightly packed fresh bread cubes
⅓ cup butter or margarine, melted
⅓ cup sugar
1 tablespoon grated lemon peel
½ teaspoon nutmeg
½ teaspoon cinnamon
4 bananas, thinly sliced
2 tablespoons lemon juice
½ cup shredded coconut
half-and-half for topping

ABOUT 1 HOUR BEFORE SERVING:
Preheat oven to 375°F. Grease 1½-quart casserole. In small bowl, toss bread cubes with butter or margarine. In small bowl, stir sugar, lemon peel, nutmeg, cinnamon.

Place one-third of bread cubes in even layer in casserole; cover with half of bananas; sprinkle with half of sugar mixture. Repeat layering once. (Bread cubes will be left over.)

In cup, mix ¼ cup water with lemon juice; pour over mixture. Toss remaining bread cubes with coconut; sprinkle over mixture. Cover and bake 30 minutes; uncover and bake 5 minutes longer or until coconut is golden. Serve warm with half-and-half. Makes 6 servings.

APPLE BETTY: About 2 hours before serving: Prepare as above but use 2-quart casserole and substitute *6 cups peeled and cored, sliced cooking apples* for bananas and use ½ to ⅔ cup sugar, depending on tartness of apples; reduce lemon juice to 1 tablespoon and omit lemon peel and coconut. Cover and bake 30 minutes; uncover and bake 30 minutes longer or until apples are tender. Makes 6 servings.

CARAMEL BREAD PUDDING

3 or 4 white- or raisin-bread slices
butter or margarine, softened
½ cup packed dark brown sugar
3 eggs
1 cup milk
dash salt
½ teaspoon vanilla extract
vanilla ice cream or whipped cream for garnish

ABOUT 2 HOURS BEFORE SERVING:
Spread bread slices lightly with butter or margarine; cut into ½-inch squares; measure 2 cups. Generously spread butter or margarine in double boiler. Spread brown sugar in an even layer in double boiler; top with bread cubes. Do not mix.

In small bowl, with wire whisk or hand beater, beat eggs with milk, salt and vanilla extract until well mixed; pour over bread. Do not stir. Cover and, over medium-low heat, cook over simmering water 1 hour or until puffed and knife inserted in center comes out clean. Serve warm topped with ice cream. Makes 4 servings.

CHERRY BREAD PUDDING

12 white-bread slices
butter or margarine, softened
cinnamon
1 10-ounce jar cherry preserves (1 cup)
4 eggs
2⅔ cups milk
2 tablespoons sugar

EARLY IN DAY:
Preheat oven to 325°F. Cut crusts from bread (save for use another day); spread butter or margarine on one side of each slice. Grease 8" by 8" baking dish. Arrange 4 bread slices in bottom of dish; sprinkle lightly with cinnamon. Spread spoonful of cherry preserves on each slice. Repeat, making 2 more layers.

In medium bowl, with wire whisk or fork, beat eggs, milk and sugar until well mixed. Pour over bread and bake 1 hour or until knife inserted in center comes out clean. Refrigerate. (If preferred, serve warm.) Makes 6 servings.

BREAD PUDDING

3 cups milk
2 eggs
⅓ cup sugar
1 teaspoon vanilla extract
½ teaspoon salt
¼ teaspoon nutmeg
3 cups lightly packed white-bread cubes
half-and-half

ABOUT 2 HOURS BEFORE SERVING:
Preheat oven to 325°F. In medium saucepan over medium heat, heat milk until tiny bubbles form around the edge. Meanwhile, in 1½-quart casserole, with wire whisk or fork, beat eggs, sugar, vanilla, salt and nutmeg until well mixed. Gradually beat hot milk into egg mixture; stir in bread cubes.

Set casserole in baking pan; place on oven rack; fill pan halfway up side of casserole with boiling water. Bake 1 hour or until knife inserted in center comes out clean. Serve pudding warm with half-and-half. Makes 8 servings.

FRUITED BREAD PUDDING: Prepare as above but stir in *1 cup chopped pitted dried prunes* or 1 cup golden raisins with bread cubes.

QUEEN OF PUDDINGS: Prepare as above but use *1 egg and 2 egg yolks* (reserve egg whites) and beat egg-milk mixture in medium bowl. Pour mixture into eight 6-ounce custard cups. Set cups in shallow baking pan; place on oven rack and fill pan halfway up side of cups with boiling water. Bake 40 to 50 minutes until knife inserted in center comes out clean. Remove from oven. Turn oven control to 350°F.

In small bowl, with mixer at high speed, beat 2 *reserved egg whites* until soft peaks form; beating at high speed, gradually sprinkle in *¼ cup sugar;* beat until sugar is completely dissolved. (Whites should stand in stiff peaks.) Do not scrape sides of bowl during beating.

Heap meringue on top of puddings, leaving depression in center of each. Return to oven and bake 10 to 15 minutes until golden. Serve warm or cold, with dab of *currant jelly* in center of each. Makes 8 servings.

RICE CUSTARD

3 eggs
3⅓ cups milk
1½ cups cooked rice
½ cup dark seedless raisins
½ cup sugar
1½ teaspoons grated lemon peel
1 teaspoon vanilla extract
1 teaspoon nutmeg
half-and-half, Whipped Cream (page 499), maple-blended syrup, Chocolate Sauce or Hot Butterscotch Sauce (page 500)

ABOUT 1 HOUR AND 40 MINUTES AHEAD:
Preheat oven to 300°F. In 2-quart casserole, with wire whisk or fork, beat eggs slightly; stir in next 6 ingredients; sprinkle with nutmeg.

Set casserole in baking pan; place on oven rack; fill pan halfway up side of casserole with boiling water. Bake 1 hour and 25 minutes, stirring once after first 30 minutes. (To avoid breaking top, lower spoon down side of pudding; stir gently back and forth along bottom of casserole.) When custard is done, knife inserted in center will come out clean. Serve warm or cool with half-and-half. Makes 8 servings.

RICE CREAM

6 cups milk
1 cup regular long-grain rice
3 tablespoons sugar
½ teaspoon salt
1 cup heavy or whipping cream
1 14¾-ounce jar lingonberries

EARLY IN DAY OR DAY BEFORE SERVING:
In large, heavy saucepan over medium heat, heat milk, rice, sugar and salt until tiny bubbles form around the edge. Reduce heat to low; cover and simmer 45 to 50 minutes until rice is tender, stirring occasionally. Refrigerate until well chilled.

In small bowl, with mixer at medium speed, beat heavy or whipping cream until soft peaks form; with rubber spatula, gently fold into rice mixture. Place in serving dish. Refrigerate to chill well.

TO SERVE:
Spoon lingonberries over Rice Cream. Makes 8 servings.

LADY NAPOLEON

½ cup heavy or whipping cream
1 3½- or 3¾-ounce package instant lemon-pudding mix
1 3-ounce package ladyfingers (12)
¼ cup confectioners' sugar
2 tablespoons semisweet-chocolate pieces
1 teaspoon light corn syrup

EARLY IN DAY:
In small bowl, with mixer at medium speed, beat cream until soft peaks form. Prepare pudding as label directs but use only 1 cup milk; with rubber spatula, gently fold in whipped cream. Place layer of 6 ladyfinger halves, unseparated, on plate; spread with ⅔ cup pudding mixture. Repeat layering, ending with ladyfingers.

In cup, into confectioners' sugar, gradually blend in 1½ teaspoons water until smooth; spread over ladyfingers, letting some drip over sides.

In double boiler over hot, not boiling, water, melt chocolate pieces with corn syrup and 1 teaspoon water. Drizzle mixture from tip of teaspoon across center of each ladyfinger. With toothpick, make 3 lengthwise marks through chocolate lines, 1 inch apart, to form zigzag design. Refrigerate.

TO SERVE:
Cut between ladyfingers into slices. Makes 6 servings.

CREAM PUFFS

½ cup butter or margarine
¼ teaspoon salt
1 cup all-purpose flour
4 eggs
Cream-Puff Filling (opposite), ice cream, or sweetened whipped cream
Chocolate Coating or Glaze (opposite), Hot Butterscotch Sauce (page 500) or confectioners' sugar

EARLY IN DAY:
Preheat oven to 375°F. Grease large cookie sheet. In medium saucepan over high heat, heat 1 cup water, butter or margarine and salt until butter melts and mixture boils. Reduce heat to low; with wooden spoon, vigorously stir in flour until mixture forms ball and leaves sides of pan; remove from heat.

Beat eggs into mixture until thoroughly blended. Drop batter on cookie sheet in 8 large mounds, 3 inches apart, swirling top of each. Bake 50 minutes or until golden; cut slit in side of each puff; bake 10 minutes longer. Place puffs on wire rack to cool.

TO SERVE:
Slice off top of each puff; fill as suggested above; replace tops; top with Coating or sauce. Makes 8 servings.

ECLAIRS: Prepare batter as directed above but drop in 12 mounds, 2 inches apart, and in rows 6 inches apart. With small spatula or knife, spread each mound of batter into 5″ by ½″ rectangle, rounding sides and piling dough on top. Bake 40 minutes or until golden. Cut slit in side of each éclair; bake 10 minutes longer. Cool on wire rack.

To serve, slice top from each éclair; fill with Eclair Filling (below); replace tops and top with Chocolate Glaze (at right). Makes 12 servings.

CREAM-PUFF FILLING

½ cup sugar
¼ cup cornstarch
¼ teaspoon salt
2 cups milk
2 eggs
2 teaspoons vanilla extract
3 drops yellow food color

EARLY IN DAY:
In medium saucepan, combine sugar, cornstarch and salt; stir in milk. Cook over medium heat, stirring constantly, until mixture thickens, about 10 minutes. In small bowl, with fork, beat eggs slightly; beat small amount of hot mixture into eggs; slowly pour egg mixture into milk mixture, stirring rapidly to prevent lumping. Cook, stirring constantly, until thickened (do not boil). Stir in vanilla and food color. Refrigerate until cold. Makes enough to fill 8 cream puffs.

ECLAIR FILLING: Prepare Cream-Puff Filling as above but substitute *½ teaspoon almond extract* for vanilla, and with rubber spatula, gently fold *½ cup heavy or whipping cream,* whipped, into cold filling.

CHOCOLATE COATING

2 squares semisweet chocolate
2 tablespoons butter or margarine
1 cup confectioners' sugar
1 tablespoon milk

ABOUT 10 MINUTES BEFORE USING:
In small saucepan over low heat, melt chocolate and butter or margarine, stirring constantly. Stir in confectioners' sugar and milk until smooth. Spread on cream puffs or éclairs. (If icing gets too thick, return to low heat, stirring constantly, until of spreading consistency.) Makes enough to coat 8 cream puffs.

CHOCOLATE GLAZE: Prepare as above but use *3 to 4 tablespoons milk* to make thin glaze; drizzle over cream-puff tops.

FUDGE PUDDING

¾ cup all-purpose flour
sugar
salt
½ cup milk
¼ cup butter or magarine, softened
1 square unsweetened chocolate, melted
1½ teaspoons double-acting baking powder
1 teaspoon vanilla extract
½ cup packed brown sugar
3 tablespoons cocoa
half-and-half for topping

ABOUT 1½ HOURS BEFORE SERVING:
Preheat oven to 350°F. Into large bowl, measure flour, ⅔ cup sugar, ½ teaspoon salt and next 5 ingredients. With mixer at low speed, beat ingredients until just mixed; increase speed to medium and beat 4 minutes, occasionally scraping bowl with rubber spatula. (Batter will have curdled appearance.) Pour into 8″ by 8″ baking dish.

Into medium bowl, measure ½ cup sugar, ¼ teaspoon salt, brown sugar and cocoa; sprinkle over chocolate mixture. Pour 1½ cups boiling water over all. Do not stir. Bake 60 minutes. (Batter will separate into cake and sauce layers.) Cool slightly. Serve warm with half-and-half. Makes 9 servings.

FUDGE NUT: Add *½ cup coarsely chopped California walnuts* to cocoa mixture.

BAKED LEMON-CAKE PUDDING

2 eggs, separated
¼ teaspoon salt
sugar
1 cup milk
⅓ cup lemon juice
3 tablespoons all-purpose flour
2 tablespoons butter or margarine, melted
1 tablespoon grated lemon peel
whipped cream for garnish

ABOUT 1¾ HOURS AHEAD OR EARLY IN DAY: Preheat oven to 350°F. Grease 1-quart casserole. In small bowl, with mixer at high speed, beat egg whites with salt until soft peaks form; beating at high speed, gradually sprinkle in ½ cup sugar, 2 tablespoons at a time, beating until sugar is completely dissolved. (Whites should stand in stiff peaks.) Do not scrape sides of bowl during beating.

In another small bowl, with same beaters and mixer at medium speed, beat egg yolks with ¼ cup sugar; add remaining ingredients except whipped cream and beat until well mixed. With wire whisk or rubber spatula, gently fold egg-yolk mixture into egg whites just until mixed. Pour batter into casserole.

Set casserole in shallow pan; place on oven rack. Fill pan halfway up side of casserole with boiling water. Bake 55 to 65 minutes until top is golden and firm. (Pudding separates into cake layer on top, sauce layer underneath.) Cool in casserole on wire rack. Serve slightly warm or cold, as is, or topped with whipped cream. Makes 6 servings.

BOSTON CREAM PIE

1 package yellow-cake mix for 2-layer cake
Creamy Custard Filling (page 552)
Chocolate Glaze (page 551)

EARLY IN DAY: Prepare cake mix as label directs, using two 8-inch round cake pans; cool. Meanwhile, prepare Creamy Custard Filling; cool.

Cut 1 cake layer horizontally in half. (Save second layer to serve another day.) On plate, place one half of layer, cut side up; spread evenly with cold custard. Top with second half layer, cut side down. Frost top of cake with Chocolate Glaze, allowing it to drip down sides. Refrigerate until serving time. Makes 8 servings.

TORTE SUPREME

1¾ cups all-purpose flour
1½ cups sugar
5 eggs, separated, at room temperature
1 cup butter or margarine
3 tablespoons milk
1 teaspoon grated lemon peel
1 teaspoon vanilla extract
½ teaspoon double-acting baking powder
about 1 10-ounce jar raspberry preserves (1 cup)
1 3½-ounce can flaked coconut (1⅓ cups)
1½ cups heavy or whipping cream

EARLY IN DAY: Preheat oven to 350°F. Grease well three 9-inch round cake pans. Into large bowl, measure flour, ½ cup sugar, egg yolks and next 5 ingredients. With mixer at low speed, beat ingredients until just mixed; increase speed to high; beat 4 minutes, occasionally scraping bowl with rubber spatula. Spread dough evenly into pans; spread each layer with ¼ cup raspberry preserves. Wash beaters.

In medium bowl, with mixer at high speed, beat egg whites until soft peaks form; beating at high speed, gradually sprinkle in 1 cup sugar, 2 tablespoons at a time; beat until sugar is completely dissolved. (Whites should stand in stiff peaks.) With rubber spatula, gently fold in coconut.

Spread ⅓ of mixture over each layer. Bake 30 to 35 minutes until light golden. Cool in pans on wire racks 15 minutes; remove and finish cooling.

TO SERVE: In large bowl, with mixer at medium speed, beat cream until stiff peaks form. Place 1 layer on plate; spread with ⅓ of the whipped cream; repeat with remaining layers and whipped cream. If you like, garnish with small spoonfuls of preserves around edge of torte. Makes 10 servings.

HOLIDAY PETITS FOURS

4 eggs, at room temperature
¾ cup sugar
¾ cup all-purpose flour
1 teaspoon double-acting baking powder
½ teaspoon salt
½ teaspoon almond extract
1 10-ounce jar apple jelly (1 cup)
Almond Paste (below)
Sugar Icing (below)
decorations: red candied cherries, cake or cookie decorator in aerosol can, dragées and nonpareils

EARLY IN DAY:
1. Preheat oven to 350°F. Grease 15½″ by 10½″ jelly-roll pan; line with waxed paper and grease paper. In large bowl, with mixer at high speed, beat eggs until foamy. Beating at high speed, gradually sprinkle in sugar, a few tablespoons at a time; beat until mixture is fluffy and very pale yellow, about 7 minutes. Reduce speed to low; beat in flour, baking powder, salt and almond extract until well mixed. Spread batter evenly in pan; bake 20 minutes or until cake springs back when lightly touched with finger. Cool cake on wire rack 10 minutes; invert from pan onto rack; peel off waxed paper and cool completely.
2. In small saucepan over low heat, melt jelly. With pastry brush, glaze cake with some of jelly. Cut cake crosswise in half, forming two rectangles about 10½″ by 7¾″.
3. Between 2 sheets of waxed paper, roll Almond Paste (below) to about 10½″ by 7¾″ rectangle. Peel off top sheet; invert the bottom sheet with Almond Paste onto 1 cake rectangle and peel off paper. Top with second cake rectangle, glazed side down, pressing layers firmly.
4. With serrated knife, cut assembled cake lengthwise into 6 strips, each about 1¼ inches wide. Then cut each strip crosswise into 5 pieces. Brush cut surfaces of cake pieces with remaining jelly. Place them 1 inch apart on wire racks over waxed paper.
5. With small spoon, drizzle Sugar Icing over cake pieces, letting excess icing drip onto waxed paper. (Return dripped icing to bowl and beat until smooth to use again, adding ½ teaspoon water if necessary.) When icing is dry, decorate with candied cherries, cake decorator, dragées and nonpareils. Makes 30.

ALMOND PASTE: In small bowl, mix well *1 cup ground almonds, 1 cup confectioners' sugar, 1 egg yolk, 2 teaspoons lemon juice* and *½ teaspoon almond extract*. Sprinkle work surface generously with confectioners' sugar; with sugared hands, knead mixture until smooth and not sticky.

SUGAR ICING: In large bowl, mix well *one 16-ounce package confectioners' sugar, 5 tablespoons water, 1 teaspoon almond extract* and *2 drops red food color.*

DESSERT CONES

¾ cup all-purpose flour
¾ cup sugar
2 eggs
2 teaspoons grated lemon peel
2 teaspoons lemon juice
1 4-ounce package whipped-topping mix (2 envelopes)
about 16 candied cherries for garnish

DAY BEFORE SERVING:
Preheat oven to 375°F. Grease well and flour large cookie sheet. Into small bowl, measure first 5 ingredients. With mixer at low speed, beat ingredients until smooth. Drop by rounded tablespoonfuls, 5 inches apart, onto cookie sheet; with metal spatula, spread each mound of batter to form circle 5 inches in diameter. (Do not place more than 3 or 4 circles on sheet, since they must be shaped quickly after baking.)

Bake 6 to 8 minutes until edges are golden. Using pancake turner, loosen a circle from cookie sheet (leave remaining circles on cookie sheet in oven with oven door ajar). Holding the circle, top side out, gently in both hands, quickly fold two sides toward center, to form a cone. Place cone, seam side down, on wire rack to cool. Quickly shape remaining circles.

Repeat baking and shaping cones, using a freshly greased and floured cookie sheet each time. Store cones in containers with loose-fitting covers. Makes about 16 cones.

ABOUT 10 MINUTES BEFORE SERVING:
Prepare topping mix as label directs. Spoon into cones; arrange in serving bowl. Top each with cherry. Makes about 16 servings.

CREPES SUZETTE

CREPES:

⅔ cup all-purpose flour
½ teaspoon salt
3 eggs
1½ cups milk
about ¼ cup melted butter or margarine

SAUCE:

⅓ cup orange juice
¼ cup butter or margarine
2 tablespoons sugar
½ teaspoon grated orange peel
¼ cup orange-flavor liqueur

EARLY IN DAY OR UP TO 2 MONTHS AHEAD: Prepare crêpes: In medium bowl, with wire whisk or hand beater, beat flour, salt and eggs until smooth; gradually beat in milk and 1½ tablespoons melted butter or margarine until well blended. Cover and refrigerate at least 2 hours.

Brush bottom and side of 7-inch skillet generously with melted butter or margarine. Over low heat, heat skillet; pour in scant ¼ cup batter; tip pan to coat bottom with batter. Over low heat, cook batter until top is set and underside lightly browned, about 3 minutes. With metal spatula, turn crêpe and cook other side until golden, about 1 minute. Slip crêpe onto waxed paper.

Repeat making crêpes until all batter is used, stacking with waxed paper between crêpes. Wrap in foil and refrigerate or freeze.* Makes 12 crêpes.

ABOUT 20 MINUTES BEFORE SERVING: Prepare sauce: In large chafing dish, suzette pan or large cook-and-serve skillet over low heat, heat orange juice, butter or margarine, sugar and orange peel until butter or margarine melts. Fold crêpes in quarters; arrange in sauce. Simmer over medium-low heat 10 minutes; pour liqueur in center (do not stir). Heat liqueur a minute or two; light with a long match and let mixture flame. Serve immediately. Makes 6 servings.

* To freeze up to 2 months ahead: Wrap crêpes and freeze. Thaw, wrapped, at room temperature for about 1 hour.

ORANGE-MINCE CREPES: Prepare crêpes as above but omit sauce; fold crêpes in fourths, then prepare this sauce: In small bowl, combine *1 cup mincemeat, ¼ cup orange juice, ¼ cup dry or medium sherry* and *2 tablespoons slivered almonds.* In large chafing dish or skillet over medium heat, melt *2 tablespoons butter or margarine;* arrange folded crêpes in skillet. Spoon mincemeat sauce around crêpes; heat.

STRAWBERRY BLINTZES: Prepare crêpes as above but omit sauce. In small bowl, with mixer at medium speed, beat *one 8-ounce container creamed cottage cheese* (1 cup), *one 3-ounce package cream cheese,* softened, *¼ cup sugar* and *½ teaspoon vanilla extract* until smooth. Spread a spoonful of mixture along center of each crêpe; fold two sides toward middle, then roll up in opposite direction. In large skillet over medium heat, in 2 tablespoons hot butter or margarine, cook until golden. Serve topped with some of *one 10-ounce package frozen strawberries,* thawed.

CHEESE-FILLED CREPES: Prepare crêpes as above but omit sauce and fill as for Strawberry Blintzes. Then prepare Cherry Sauce (page 359). Place filled crêpes in cook-and-serve skillet; pour sweet Cherry Sauce over crêpes. Over low heat, simmer crêpes 10 minutes.

CHOCOLATE-MINT FONDUE

ABOUT 30 MINUTES BEFORE SERVING: Arrange bite-size chunks of *assorted fruits:* pineapple, strawberries, cherries, melon, grapes and pears, apples, bananas (dipped in lemon juice to prevent browning); *poundcake* or angel-food cake, *pretzels, dates* and *large marshmallows* on large platter.

In medium saucepan over low heat, melt *three 4-ounce bars sweet cooking chocolate* (or use one 12-ounce package semisweet-chocolate pieces) with *½ cup half-and-half* or milk and *½ teaspoon peppermint extract.* Pour mixture into fondue pot or chafing dish; place over low heat.

Guests dip fruits, cake, pretzels, dates and marshmallows into hot chocolate fondue. (Provide fondue forks for dipping all but pretzels.) Fondue should stand up well over low heat for 45 minutes to 1 hour, but if chocolate becomes too thick, stir in 1 or 2 tablespoons half-and-half or milk. Makes about 1½ cups fondue, enough for 8 to 10 dessert servings.

TWO-DIP DESSERT FONDUE

2 medium pears, cut in small chunks
2 medium apples, cut in small chunks
ascorbic-acid mixture for fruit
4 plain doughnuts, cut in pieces
1 7½-ounce package thick ring pretzels
1 6-ounce can pecans, finely chopped

HOT CARAMEL SAUCE:
½ cup butter or margarine
2 cups half-and-half
1½ cups packed light brown sugar
½ cup sugar
⅛ teaspoon salt
⅛ teaspoon nutmeg
⅛ teaspoon cinnamon

ABOUT 45 MINUTES BEFORE SERVING:
Toss fruits in ascorbic-acid mixture as label directs to prevent them from turning brown. Arrange fruits, doughnuts and pretzels on large platter. Place chopped pecans in small serving bowl.

Prepare sauce: In fondue pot,* on range over medium heat, heat butter or margarine, half-and-half, sugars, salt and spices to boiling. Boil about 15 minutes until mixture sheets when dropped from side of a spoon. Do not stir mixture.

Place fondue pot on stand over low heat. Guests dip fruits, doughnuts and pretzels into hot sauce, then into pecans. (Provide fondue forks for dipping fruits and doughnuts.) Makes 8 to 10 dessert servings.

* If using an electric fondue set, prepare sauce directly on fondue base, using high-heat setting; reduce heat to low setting to serve.

BABA AU RHUM

about 3½ cups all-purpose flour
¼ cup sugar
¼ teaspoon salt
2 packages active dry yeast
½ cup butter or margarine, softened
6 eggs
1 4-ounce jar candied citron or
1 cup dried currants
Rum Sauce (below)
⅓ cup apricot jam
1 tablespoon lemon juice

EARLY IN DAY OR DAY BEFORE:
1. In large bowl, combine ¾ cup flour, sugar, salt and yeast. In medium saucepan over low heat, heat ½ cup water and butter or margarine until very warm (120° to 130°F.). (Butter or margarine does not need to melt.) With mixer at low speed, gradually add liquid to dry ingredients. At medium speed, beat 2 minutes, occasionally scraping bowl with rubber spatula.
2. Add eggs and 1 cup flour or enough to make a thick batter. With mixer at low speed, beat until mixed. Increase speed to high; beat 2 minutes, occasionally scraping bowl. With spoon, stir in citron and enough flour (about 1¾ cups) to make soft dough.
3. Spread dough evenly in greased 10-inch tube pan. Cover; let rise until tripled in volume and nearly to top of pan.
4. Preheat oven to 375°F. Place pan carefully on oven rack (jarring may make baba fall). Bake 35 to 45 minutes until rich brown. Cool in pan on wire rack to lukewarm. Prick top of baba in many places with metal skewer or two-tined fork; spoon on Rum Sauce. Let stand at least 2 hours.

TO SERVE:
Invert baba from pan onto plate. Into small bowl, press apricot jam through sieve; stir in lemon juice until smooth; spread over top of baba. Makes about 16 servings.

RUM SAUCE: In small saucepan over medium heat, heat *2¼ cups sugar, 3 cups water, 6 thin orange slices* and *6 thin lemon slices* to boiling. Reduce heat; cover and simmer 5 minutes. Cool to lukewarm. With slotted spoon, remove fruit slices; discard. Stir in *1¼ cups light rum.*

INDIVIDUAL BABAS: Prepare steps 1 and 2 above. Grease 24 baba molds 2 inches deep and 2 inches in diameter or 3-inch muffin-pan cups. Fill molds half full with dough. Let rise in warm place until tripled in volume (about 1 hour and 15 minutes). (Dough will rise slightly above tops of cups.) Preheat oven to 375°F.

Bake babas 15 to 20 minutes until rich brown. Cool in molds on wire racks until lukewarm. Remove from molds; place babas, top side up, in large, shallow roasting pan. Prick tops 3 or 4 times with two-tined fork. Spoon on Rum Sauce (above). After 30 minutes, roll babas in sauce. Serve, top sides up, spooning on any excess sauce. Makes 24 servings.

CHOCOLATE MOUSSE

1 6-ounce package semisweet-chocolate pieces (1 cup)
6 eggs, separated
2 teaspoons vanilla extract
Coffee Whipped Cream (page 499)
1 1-ounce square semisweet chocolate for garnish

EARLY IN DAY:
In double boiler, over hot, not boiling, water, melt chocolate pieces; remove from heat. With rubber spatula, rapidly stir in egg yolks all at once; stir in vanilla.

In small bowl, with mixer at high speed, beat egg whites until stiff peaks form; with rubber spatula, gently fold beaten whites into chocolate mixture. Spoon mixture into dessert dishes. Refrigerate at least 4 hours.

TO SERVE:
Top mousse with Coffee Whipped Cream and Chocolate Curls (page 380) made from semisweet-chocolate square. Makes 8 servings.

RASPBERRY MOUSSE

2 10-ounce packages frozen raspberries, thawed
2 envelopes unflavored gelatin
sugar
1 teaspoon lemon juice
dash salt
4 egg whites, at room temperature
2 cups heavy or whipping cream

EARLY IN DAY:
In covered blender container at low speed, blend raspberries until smooth; strain into medium saucepan; discard seeds. Sprinkle gelatin evenly over liquid; cook over low heat, stirring until dissolved. Remove from heat; stir in ¼ cup sugar, lemon juice and salt. Chill, stirring occasionally, until mixture mounds when dropped from a spoon, about 20 minutes.

In large bowl, with mixer at high speed, beat egg whites until soft peaks form. Beating at high speed, gradually sprinkle in ¼ cup sugar; beat until sugar is completely dissolved. (Whites should stand in stiff peaks.) With rubber spatula, gently fold raspberry mixture into beaten whites. Wash beaters.

In small bowl, with mixer at medium speed, beat 1½ cups cream until soft peaks form. With rubber spatula, gently fold into raspberry mixture; pour into 2-quart serving bowl or 10 dessert dishes. Refrigerate until set, at least 4 hours.

TO SERVE:
In small bowl, with mixer at medium speed, beat remaining ½ cup cream with 1 tablespoon sugar until soft peaks form; use to garnish mousse. Makes 10 servings.

CHOCOLATE SOUFFLE

butter or margarine
sugar
⅓ cup all-purpose flour
1½ cups milk
3 squares unsweetened chocolate, coarsely chopped
6 eggs, separated
¼ teaspoon salt
2 teaspoons vanilla extract
Sweetened Whipped Cream (page 499), optional
Chocolate Sauce (page 500), optional

ABOUT 1½ HOURS BEFORE SERVING:
1. Preheat oven to 375°F. Grease 2-quart soufflé dish or casserole with butter or margarine and sprinkle with sugar. Into medium saucepan, measure flour and ¼ cup sugar; with wire whisk or spoon, slowly stir in milk until smooth. Cook over medium heat, stirring constantly, until mixture is thickened and smooth; remove from heat.
2. Stir chocolate into mixture until melted. Rapidly beat in egg yolks, all at once until well mixed; cool to lukewarm.
3. In large bowl, with mixer at high speed, beat egg whites and salt until soft peaks form; beating at high speed, gradually sprinkle in ½ cup sugar; beat until sugar is completely dissolved. (Whites should stand in stiff peaks.) With rubber spatula, gently fold chocolate mixture and vanilla into beaten whites until blended.
4. Pour mixture into soufflé dish; with back of spoon, about 1 inch from edge of dish, make 1-inch indentation all around. Bake 35 to 40 minutes until knife inserted under "top hat" comes out clean. Serve at once with Sweetened Whipped Cream and Chocolate Sauce. Makes 8 servings.

ORANGE MERINGUE SOUFFLES

¾ cup orange marmalade
1 tablespoon lemon juice
3 egg whites, at room temperature
⅛ teaspoon salt
3 tablespoons sugar
¼ cup slivered blanched almonds or coarsely chopped California walnuts

ABOUT 30 MINUTES BEFORE SERVING:
Preheat oven to 350°F. In small saucepan over low heat, melt orange marmalade; add lemon juice; set aside.

In medium bowl, with mixer at high speed, beat egg whites and salt until soft peaks form; beating at high speed, gradually sprinkle in sugar; beat until sugar is completely dissolved. (Whites should stand in stiff peaks.) With rubber spatula, gently fold in marmalade mixture.

Spoon mixture into six 5-ounce soufflé dishes or 6-ounce custard cups. Top each with some slivered almonds. Bake 15 minutes or until golden; serve immediately (soufflés will fall if they stand). Makes 6 servings.

LEMON REFRIGERATOR CAKE

1 3-ounce package ladyfingers (about 12)
1½ cups sugar
2 envelopes unflavored gelatin
¾ teaspoon salt
6 eggs, separated, at room temperature
½ cup lemon juice
1 tablespoon grated lemon peel
1 cup heavy or whipping cream or 1 2-ounce package whipped-topping mix
½ cup shredded or flaked coconut for garnish

DAY BEFORE SERVING:
Split ladyfingers and line side of 9-inch springform pan with them. In medium saucepan, stir ¾ cup sugar, gelatin and salt until well mixed. In small bowl, with wire whisk or fork, beat egg yolks with ½ cup cold water until well mixed; stir in lemon juice.

Stir yolk mixture into gelatin mixture until well mixed. Cook over medium-low heat, stirring constantly, until mixture coats spoon, about 10 minutes. Remove from heat; stir in lemon peel.

In large bowl, with mixer at high speed, beat egg whites until soft peaks form; beating at high speed, gradually sprinkle in ¾ cup sugar; beat until sugar is completely dissolved. (Whites should stand in stiff peaks.) With rubber spatula, gently fold lemon mixture into whites. Spoon mixture into lined pan; refrigerate overnight.

TO SERVE:
Carefully remove side of springform pan. In small bowl, with mixer at medium speed, beat cream until soft peaks form. Spread whipped cream over top of cake; sprinkle with coconut. Makes 12 servings.

ALMOND TORTE

1⅓ cups all-purpose flour
sugar
1 teaspoon double-acting baking powder
1 cup butter or margarine, softened
3 eggs
1 cup ground almonds*
½ teaspoon almond extract
3 tablespoons raspberry preserves
½ cup confectioners' sugar
1 tablespoon lemon juice

EARLY IN DAY:
In medium bowl, mix flour, ⅓ cup sugar and baking powder. With fork, mix in ½ cup butter or margarine and 1 egg until flour is moistened; press mixture evenly onto bottom and 1 inch up side of a 9-inch springform pan. Cover and refrigerate.

Preheat oven to 350°F. Into large bowl, measure ½ cup butter or margarine, ½ cup sugar, almonds, almond extract and 2 eggs. With mixer at low speed, beat mixture until well mixed, constantly scraping bowl with rubber spatula. Beat at medium speed 3 minutes, occasionally scraping bowl.

Pour batter into chilled crust and bake 45 to 50 minutes until toothpick inserted in center comes out clean and top is lightly browned. Cool on wire rack 1 hour. Carefully remove side of springform pan; spread cake with a thin layer of preserves. In cup, mix confectioners' sugar with lemon juice; drizzle over preserves. Makes 10 servings.

* If you like, grind *one 4½-ounce can blanched almonds* in blender.

BAVARIAN CREAM

1 envelope unflavored gelatin
sugar
¼ teaspoon salt
2 eggs, separated
1¼ cups milk
1 cup heavy or whipping cream
1½ teaspoons vanilla extract
Melba Sauce (page 357), optional

DAY BEFORE SERVING:
In medium saucepan, stir gelatin, 2 tablespoons sugar and salt until well mixed. In small bowl, with wire whisk or fork, beat egg yolks with milk until well mixed; stir into gelatin mixture. Cook over low heat, stirring constantly, until mixture coats spoon. Refrigerate until mixture mounds slightly when dropped from a spoon.

In small bowl, with mixer at high speed, beat egg whites until soft peaks form; beating at high speed, gradually sprinkle in ¼ cup sugar; beat until sugar is completely dissolved. Spoon whites over gelatin.

Using same bowl and beaters, beat cream with vanilla until soft peaks form; add to gelatin. With rubber spatula, gently fold whites and cream into gelatin. Pour into 6-cup mold; refrigerate.

TO SERVE:
Unmold mold onto serving plate. Serve with Melba Sauce. Makes 6 to 8 servings.

CHEESE BAVARIAN MOLD

1 cup sugar
2 envelopes unflavored gelatin
¾ teaspoon salt
2 eggs, separated
1 cup milk
1 lemon
3 cups creamed cottage cheese
1 cup heavy or whipping cream
orange sections for garnish

EARLY IN DAY:
In small saucepan, stir sugar, gelatin and salt. In small bowl, with wire whisk or hand beater, beat egg yolks with milk until mixed; stir into gelatin mixture. Cook over low heat, stirring constantly, until mixture thickens slightly and coats a spoon, about 8 minutes. Remove from heat; cool slightly.

Grate lemon peel and squeeze juice from lemon. Add lemon peel and juice and cottage cheese to milk mixture. With mixer at medium speed, beat until well blended; refrigerate until mixture mounds when dropped from a spoon. Wash beaters.

In small bowl, with mixer at high speed, beat egg whites just until stiff peaks form. In large bowl, with same beaters, beat cream until stiff. With rubber spatula, gently fold beaten whites into whipped cream; gently fold in chilled milk mixture just until blended. Pour into 8-cup mold or 8 dessert dishes. Refrigerate until set.

TO SERVE:
Unmold mold onto large dessert plate. Garnish with oranges. Makes 8 servings.

PINEAPPLE BAVARIAN

2 envelopes unflavored gelatin
1 cup sugar
⅛ teaspoon salt
3½ cups canned pineapple juice
2 teaspoons grated lemon peel
¼ cup lemon juice
1½ cups heavy or whipping cream
1 3½-ounce can flaked coconut
2 cups halved strawberries
1 8½-ounce can pineapple slices, drained and quartered

EARLY IN DAY:
In small saucepan, stir gelatin, sugar and salt until well mixed. Stir in 1 cup pineapple juice. Cook over low heat, stirring constantly, until gelatin is dissolved. In large bowl, combine remaining 2½ cups pineapple juice, lemon peel, lemon juice and gelatin mixture. Refrigerate until mixture mounds when dropped from a spoon.

In small bowl, with mixer at medium speed, beat cream until soft peaks form; set aside. In large bowl, with same beaters and mixer at high speed, beat gelatin mixture until fluffy. With rubber spatula, gently fold whipped cream and ¾ cup coconut into mixture. Pour into 6-cup mold; refrigerate until set.

TO SERVE:
Unmold Bavarian onto large platter; arrange strawberries and pineapple around mold. Sprinkle with remaining coconut. Makes 12 servings.

NECTARINE-CHEESE DESSERT

¾ cup all-purpose flour
⅓ cup butter or margarine, softened
sugar
2 egg yolks
1 tablespoon grated lemon peel
1 envelope unflavored gelatin
⅛ teaspoon salt
½ cup milk
1 8-ounce package cream cheese, softened
2 tablespoons grated orange peel
1 egg white, at room temperature
1 3-ounce package lemon-flavor gelatin
3 or 4 nectarines, cut in thick slices

EARLY IN DAY:

1. Preheat oven to 400°F. Into medium bowl, measure flour, butter or margarine, 2 tablespoons sugar, 1 egg yolk and lemon peel. With pastry blender or 2 knives used scissor-fashion, cut mixture into pieces the size of peas. With hands, shape mixture into ball; spread in bottom (not on side) of 10-inch springform pan. Bake 8 minutes or until light golden; cool.
2. In small saucepan, stir unflavored gelatin with ⅓ cup sugar and salt. In cup, with fork, beat remaining egg yolk with milk until well blended; stir into gelatin mixture. Cook mixture over low heat, stirring constantly, until mixture is thickened and coats spoon. Remove from heat.
3. In small bowl, with mixer at medium speed, beat cream cheese with orange peel until smooth. Reduce speed to low; gradually beat in gelatin mixture until well blended. Wash beaters.
4. In another small bowl, with mixer at high speed, beat egg white just until soft peaks form. With rubber spatula, gently fold into cheese mixture. Refrigerate 10 minutes or until mixture mounds slightly when dropped from a spoon. Pour over crust; refrigerate 30 minutes.
5. In small bowl, dissolve lemon gelatin in ¾ cup boiling water; stir in ¾ cup cold water; cool until lukewarm. Meanwhile, arrange nectarine slices on cheese mixture. Place dessert in refrigerator; carefully pour gelatin over nectarines. Refrigerate until set, at least 3 hours.

TO SERVE:

Dip spatula in hot water to loosen edge of dessert from pan; carefully remove side of springform pan. Makes 8 to 10 servings.

PEACH-CHEESE DESSERT: Prepare as above but use *3 or 4 peaches,* peeled and cut into thick slices, instead of nectarines.

CHOCOLATE-CUP CREAMS

16 fluted, paper baking cups (to fit 3-inch muffin-pan cups)
1 12-ounce package semisweet-chocolate pieces (2 cups)
2 tablespoons shortening
1 3- or 3¼-ounce package regular vanilla-pudding mix
1 envelope unflavored gelatin
1 teaspoon instant coffee powder
2 cups half-and-half
1 cup heavy or whipping cream, whipped
chocolate sprinkles for garnish
16 maraschino cherries with stems, well drained, for garnish

SEVERAL DAYS BEFORE SERVING:

Place each paper cup in 3-inch cup of a muffin pan; set aside. In double boiler over hot, not boiling, water, melt chocolate pieces with shortening; keep warm. Starting from top rim of each paper cup, drizzle chocolate, 1 heaping measuring teaspoonful at a time, down inside of cup. About 3 of these teaspoonfuls will cover entire inside of each cup. Refrigerate. (If you do not have 16 muffin-pan cups, remove and refrigerate firm cups and reuse pans.)

EARLY ON SERVING DAY:

Remove a few cups at a time from refrigerator; gently but quickly peel paper away from each, leaving a chocolate cup. Set cups on serving plate and refrigerate. Repeat until all cups are peeled.

In medium saucepan, combine pudding mix, gelatin and coffee powder; stir in half-and-half; cook as label directs. Cover surface with waxed paper and refrigerate just until cool. With rubber spatula, gently fold whipped cream into mixture. Fill chocolate cups with mixture and refrigerate.

TO SERVE:

Sprinkle each cup with chocolate sprinkles and top with a cherry. Makes 16 servings.

SPANISH CREAM

1 envelope unflavored gelatin
sugar
¼ teaspoon salt
3 eggs, separated, at room temperature
2 cups milk
1 teaspoon vanilla extract
Hot Butterscotch Sauce or Chocolate Sauce (page 500), whipped cream or sweetened crushed berries for topping

EARLY IN DAY:
In medium saucepan, stir gelatin with ¼ cup sugar and salt. In small bowl, with wire whisk or fork, beat egg yolks with milk until well mixed; stir into gelatin mixture. Cook over low heat, stirring constantly, until mixture is thickened and coats spoon, about 10 minutes. Stir in vanilla. Refrigerate, stirring occasionally, until mixture mounds when dropped from a spoon.

In medium bowl, with mixer at high speed, beat egg whites until soft peaks form; beating at high speed, gradually beat in ¼ cup sugar; beat until sugar is completely dissolved. (Whites should stand in stiff peaks.) Do not scrape sides of bowl during beating. With rubber spatula, gently fold gelatin mixture into beaten whites; pour into 6-cup bowl. Refrigerate until set.

TO SERVE:
Spoon mixture into dessert dishes. Serve plain or with a sauce. Makes 8 servings.

EGGNOG CHARLOTTE RUSSE

2 envelopes unflavored gelatin
sugar
½ teaspoon salt
½ teaspoon nutmeg
4 eggs, separated
2 cups milk
¼ cup brandy or bourbon (or 2 tablespoons brandy-flavor extract)
1 3-ounce package ladyfingers, split
1½ cups heavy or whipping cream
1 square semisweet chocolate, grated, for garnish

EARLY IN DAY OR DAY BEFORE:
1. In double boiler, stir gelatin with ½ cup sugar, salt and nutmeg. In small bowl, with wire whisk or fork, beat egg yolks with 1 cup milk until well mixed; stir into gelatin mixture. Cook over hot, not boiling, water, stirring constantly with spoon or rubber spatula, until mixture thickens and coats spoon, about 30 minutes. Stir in remaining 1 cup milk and brandy. Cover surface closely with waxed paper and refrigerate until mixture mounds slightly when dropped from a spoon, about 1 hour. Remove waxed paper.
2. Meanwhile, line side of 8-inch springform pan with ladyfingers.
3. In large bowl, with mixer at high speed, beat egg whites until soft peaks form; beating at high speed, gradually sprinkle in ¼ cup sugar; beat until sugar is completely dissolved. (Whites should stand in stiff peaks.) Do not scrape sides of bowl during beating. Fold in chilled mixture.
4. In small bowl, with mixer at medium speed, beat 1 cup heavy cream until soft peaks form; with rubber spatula, gently fold into dessert mixture. Spoon mixture into lined pan; refrigerate until set.

TO SERVE:
Carefully remove side of springform pan. In small bowl, with mixer at medium speed, beat remaining ½ cup heavy cream until soft peaks form; use to garnish top. Sprinkle with grated chocolate. Makes 12 servings.

CHERRY-SHERRY JUBILEE

2 17-ounce cans pitted dark sweet cherries
1 3-ounce package cherry-flavor gelatin
½ cup medium or cream sherry
⅓ cup toasted slivered almonds
1 pint vanilla ice cream, softened

EARLY IN DAY:
Drain cherries, reserving liquid. To liquid, add enough water to make 1¾ cups. In medium saucepan over high heat, heat liquid to boiling. Place gelatin in medium bowl; stir in liquid until gelatin is dissolved. Add cherries, sherry and almonds. Refrigerate until set.

TO SERVE:
With fork, gently break up gelatin. Spoon into dessert dishes; top with ice cream. Makes 8 servings.

ORANGE ANGEL MOLD

1 7-inch bakery angel-food cake
1 envelope unflavored gelatin
⅔ cup sugar
⅛ teaspoon salt
1 6-ounce can frozen orange-juice concentrate, partially thawed
2 cups heavy or whipping cream
3 drops red food color
2 drops yellow food color
¼ pound seedless green grapes, halved, for garnish
1 11-ounce can mandarin orange sections, drained, for garnish

DAY BEFORE SERVING:
With sharp knife, cut brown crust from cake, then break cake into 2-inch pieces. (Save crumbs for use in another day's dessert.) In medium saucepan, combine gelatin, sugar and salt until well mixed; stir in ½ cup cold water. Cook over low heat, stirring constantly, until gelatin is dissolved; stir in undiluted orange-juice concentrate. Refrigerate until mixture mounds when dropped from a spoon.

In medium bowl, with mixer at medium speed, beat cream until soft peaks form. With rubber spatula, gently fold in orange-juice mixture. Stir in food colors to tint orange.

Lightly oil 2½-quart mixing bowl. Spoon in ¼ of orange mixture, top with about ⅓ of cake pieces; repeat layering, ending with orange mixture. Cover and refrigerate.

ABOUT 1 HOUR BEFORE SERVING:
Unmold dessert onto platter. Garnish with grapes and orange sections; refrigerate until served. Makes 10 servings.

SNOW PUDDING

1 envelope unflavored gelatin
¾ cup sugar
¼ cup lemon or lime juice
1 egg white
1 teaspoon grated lemon or lime peel
Custard Sauce (page 281)
sliced bananas or peaches, whole or sliced berries

DAY BEFORE OR EARLY IN DAY:
In medium saucepan, combine gelatin and sugar; stir in ¾ cup water. Cook over low heat, stirring constantly, until gelatin is dissolved. Stir in ½ cup water and lemon juice. Pour into large bowl; refrigerate, stirring occasionally, until mixture mounds when dropped from a spoon.

Add egg white to mixture; with mixer at high speed, beat 10 minutes or until mixture mounds slightly when dropped from a spoon. With rubber spatula, gently fold in lemon peel. Spoon into 6-cup mold; refrigerate until set.

TO SERVE:
Unmold mold onto platter; serve with Custard Sauce and garnish with fresh fruit. Makes 8 servings.

NO-BAKE PLUM PUDDING

1 6-ounce package lemon-flavor gelatin
⅛ teaspoon salt
1 teaspoon cinnamon
½ teaspoon ground cloves
1½ cups finely chopped dark seedless raisins
1½ cups finely chopped cooked prunes
1½ cups finely chopped California walnuts
1½ cups Grape-nuts cereal
½ cup finely chopped candied citron
10 to 12 California walnut halves
Custard Sauce (page 281) or Eggnog Sauce (page 500)

DAY BEFORE OR EARLY IN DAY:
In large bowl, dissolve gelatin and salt in 2 cups boiling water. Add 2 cups cold water, cinnamon and cloves. Refrigerate until mixture mounds when dropped from a spoon.

Fold raisins, prunes, chopped walnuts, cereal and citron into mixture; spoon 2 to 3 tablespoons gelatin mixture into 8-cup mold. Arrange walnut halves in a circle on top of mixture. Chill 20 minutes or until almost set.

Over walnut halves, spoon ½ cup gelatin mixture or enough to cover. Refrigerate again 20 minutes or until almost set. Spoon in remaining mixture; chill until set.

TO SERVE:
Unmold pudding onto plate. Serve with sauce. Makes 10 to 12 servings.

HOLIDAY BAKED PUDDING

2¼ cups all-purpose flour
1 cup sugar
1 cup fresh bread crumbs
1 cup chopped dates
1 cup chopped apple
1 cup ground suet
1 cup buttermilk
2 eggs
½ cup chopped California walnuts
½ cup molasses
1 teaspoon double-acting baking powder
1 teaspoon salt
½ teaspoon cinnamon
½ teaspoon ground cloves
2 pints vanilla ice cream, softened

ABOUT 4 HOURS BEFORE SERVING:
Preheat oven to 325°F. Grease 8-cup pudding mold and its lid (or, cut foil to cover 2-quart casserole with 1-inch overhang; grease both). In large bowl, measure all ingredients except ice cream; with spoon, stir until well mixed. Pour mixture into mold; cover with lid or foil and seal tightly around edges. Bake 2½ hours or until toothpick inserted in center comes out clean. Cool on wire rack 5 minutes; loosen pudding and invert onto platter. Serve warm with ice cream. Makes 12 servings.

TO DO AHEAD: Several days ahead: Bake pudding; cover and refrigerate. To serve: Reheat, covered, at 325°F. for 1 hour.

SPICY OATMEAL STEAMED PUDDING

1 cup quick-cooking or
old-fashioned oats, uncooked
¾ cup dark seedless raisins
¾ cup all-purpose flour
¾ cup sugar
¾ teaspoon salt
1¼ teaspoons baking soda
1 teaspoon cinnamon
1¼ cups buttermilk
3 tablespoons salad oil
1½ teaspoons vanilla extract
vanilla ice cream, softened

ABOUT 2 HOURS BEFORE SERVING:
Grease 8-cup pudding mold and its lid. (Or, cut foil to cover 8-cup ring mold with 1-inch overhang; grease both.) Into large bowl, measure all ingredients except ice cream; with spoon, stir until well blended. Pour into mold; cover. Place mold on trivet in deep kettle. Add boiling water to come halfway up side of mold but not touching cover. Cover and simmer 1½ hours or until toothpick inserted in center comes out clean. Cool mold on wire rack 5 minutes; loosen pudding and invert onto platter. Serve with ice cream. Makes 10 servings.

TO DO AHEAD: See Holiday Baked Pudding (above).

CRANBERRY STEAMED PUDDING

3 cups cranberries, coarsely chopped
3 cups finely crumbled vanilla wafers
1½ cups sugar
¾ cup milk
¾ cup butter or margarine, melted
3 eggs, beaten
½ cup all-purpose flour
½ cup slivered blanched almonds,
coarsely chopped
1 tablespoon double-acting baking powder
1 teaspoon cinnamon
¾ teaspoon salt
½ teaspoon ginger
Hard Sauce or Eggnog Sauce (page 500),
or whipped cream for garnish

ABOUT 4 HOURS BEFORE SERVING:
Grease 12-cup ring mold. Cut foil to cover mold with 1-inch overhang; grease foil. Into large bowl, measure all ingredients except Hard Sauce; with spoon, stir until well blended. Pour into mold; cover with greased foil and seal tightly around edges.

Place mold on trivet in deep kettle. Add boiling water to come half way up side of mold, not touching foil. Cover and simmer 3 hours and 15 minutes. Remove mold from kettle and cool on wire rack 20 minutes; loosen pudding and invert onto platter. Serve with Hard Sauce. Makes 12 servings.

TO DO AHEAD: See Holiday Baked Pudding (at left).

ZABAGLIONE

ABOUT 20 MINUTES BEFORE SERVING:
In doubler-boiler top, not over water, with portable mixer at high speed, beat *6 egg yolks* and *¼ cup sugar* until thick and light

colored, about 5 minutes. Reduce speed to medium; beat in *½ cup dry or sweet Marsala.*

Place mixture over simmering water; cook, beating constantly at medium speed, until mixture is fluffy, warm and mounds slightly when beater is lifted, about 10 minutes. Remove from over water at once and serve immediately in dessert dishes. Makes 6 servings.

FRUITED: Ladle Zabaglione over *fresh berries* or other fruit. Makes 8 to 10 servings.

OTHER DESSERTS

For other desserts, see Eggs (page 277), Cheese (page 289), Fruits (page 353), Soups (page 57).

Dessert Sauces

WHIPPED CREAM

With hand beater or mixer at medium speed, beat well-chilled heavy or whipping cream just until soft or stiff peaks form, depending on use. (Overbeating causes cream to curdle and turn to butter.) On hot days, chill bowl and beaters. Cream doubles in volume when beaten.

SWEETENED: For *each cup heavy or whipping cream,* add *1 to 2 tablespoons sugar* and *1 teaspoon vanilla extract* or ¼ teaspoon almond extract or dry sherry to taste. Beat as above.

BERRY: Beat cream as above until soft peaks form; fold in *drained and crushed, slightly sweetened strawberries,* raspberries, blackberries or blueberries.

CHOCOLATE: Place *2 tablespoons instant-cocoa mix* (or 2 tablespoons sugar and 2 tablespoons cocoa) in small bowl; add *1 cup heavy or whipping cream.* With hand beater or mixer at low speed, beat just until soft peaks form.

ROSETTES: Beat heavy or whipping cream (or Sweetened, Chocolate or Coffee versions) just until stiff peaks form; spoon into pastry bag with decorative tip. Force cream through tip onto cake or dessert.

COFFEE: Place *2 teaspoons instant coffee powder* and *2 tablespoons sugar* in small bowl; add *1 cup heavy or whipping cream.* With mixer at medium speed, beat just until soft peaks form.

SUNSHINE FOAMY SAUCE

1 egg, separated
dash salt
light brown sugar
½ teaspoon vanilla extract
¼ cup heavy or whipping cream, whipped

ABOUT 15 MINUTES BEFORE SERVING:
In small bowl, with mixer at high speed, beat egg white and salt until soft peaks form; beating at high speed, gradually sprinkle in 2 tablespoons brown sugar; beat until sugar is completely dissolved. (Whites should stand in stiff peaks.) Do not scrape sides of bowl during beating.

In another small bowl, with same beaters, beat egg yolk, 2 tablespoons brown sugar and vanilla until light and fluffy. With rubber spatula, gently fold yolk mixture and whipped cream into beaten white. Makes 1⅓ cups.

ORANGE-FLUFF SAUCE

½ cup sugar
½ cup frozen orange-juice concentrate,* thawed
⅛ teaspoon salt
2 egg yolks
1 cup heavy or whipping cream, whipped

EARLY IN DAY:
In medium saucepan over low heat, cook sugar, undiluted juice concentrate and salt, stirring constantly, until sugar dissolves; set aside. In small bowl, with mixer at high speed, beat egg yolks until light and fluffy; reduce speed to medium and gradually beat in orange-juice mixture.

Return mixture to saucepan; over low heat, cook, stirring constantly, until slightly thickened. Cool, then fold in whipped cream. Refrigerate until well chilled. Makes 2½ to 2⅔ cups.

* After measuring ½ cup frozen orange-juice concentrate, reconstitute remainder of 6-ounce can by adding 1 cup cold water; to remainder of 12-ounce can add 3 cups cold water.

EGGNOG SAUCE

½ cup heavy or whipping cream
2 egg yolks
¾ cup confectioners' sugar
3 tablespoons brandy

ABOUT 15 MINUTES BEFORE SERVING:
In small bowl, with mixer at medium speed, beat cream until stiff peaks form; set aside. In another small bowl, with mixer at high speed, beat egg yolks until lemon-colored; beat in sugar and brandy. With rubber spatula, gently fold in whipped cream. Makes about 1¾ cups.

HARD SAUCE

⅓ cup butter or margarine, softened
1 cup confectioners' sugar
½ teaspoon vanilla extract

EARLY IN DAY:
In small bowl, with mixer at medium speed, beat butter or margarine with sugar until creamy; beat in vanilla. Spoon mixture into serving dish; refrigerate until serving time. Makes ⅔ cup.

DELUXE: Prepare as above but fold in *¼ cup heavy or whipping cream,* whipped.

PEACH SAUCE

ABOUT 10 MINUTES BEFORE SERVING:
In covered blender container at low speed, blend *one 10-ounce package frozen peaches,* thawed, *¼ teaspoon almond extract* and *dash nutmeg* until smooth. Makes 1 cup.

BRANDIED STRAWBERRY SAUCE

3 10-ounce packages frozen sliced strawberries, thawed
½ cup currant jelly
1 tablespoon cornstarch
few drops red food color
¼ cup brandy

UP TO 2 WEEKS BEFORE SERVING:
Drain berries, reserving ½ cup juice. In medium saucepan over low heat, melt jelly, stirring constantly. In small bowl, mix reserved juice and cornstarch until smooth. Gradually stir cornstarch mixture into melted jelly, stirring constantly; increase heat to medium and cook until thickened, stirring. Add food color; stir in berries and brandy. Cover; refrigerate. Makes 2½ cups.

CHOCOLATE SAUCE

1 6-ounce package semisweet-chocolate pieces (1 cup)
½ cup light corn syrup
¼ cup half-and-half
1 tablespoon butter or margarine
1 teaspoon vanilla extract

ABOUT 15 MINUTES BEFORE SERVING:
In medium saucepan over low heat, melt chocolate with corn syrup, stirring constantly. Remove from heat; stir in remaining ingredients until mixed. Serve warm. Makes 1⅓ cups.

DATE-NUT SAUCE

1 7¼- or 8-ounce package pitted dates, chopped
⅛ teaspoon salt
½ cup light or dark corn syrup
½ cup chopped California walnuts

ABOUT 10 MINUTES BEFORE SERVING:
In medium saucepan over medium heat, heat dates, salt and ¾ cup water to boiling; remove from heat. Stir in remaining ingredients. Serve warm. Makes 2 cups.

HOT BUTTERSCOTCH SAUCE

1 cup packed light brown sugar
¼ cup half-and-half
2 tablespoons butter or margarine
2 tablespoons light corn syrup

ABOUT 10 MINUTES BEFORE SERVING:
In small saucepan over medium heat, heat all ingredients to boiling, stirring occasionally. Serve warm. Makes 1 cup.

HOT CARAMEL SAUCE

ABOUT 15 MINUTES BEFORE SERVING:
In small saucepan over low heat, heat *½ 14-ounce package vanilla caramels* (about 25 caramels) and *½ cup milk,* stirring constantly, until mixture is smooth and thickened. Serve warm. Makes about 1 cup.

Pies

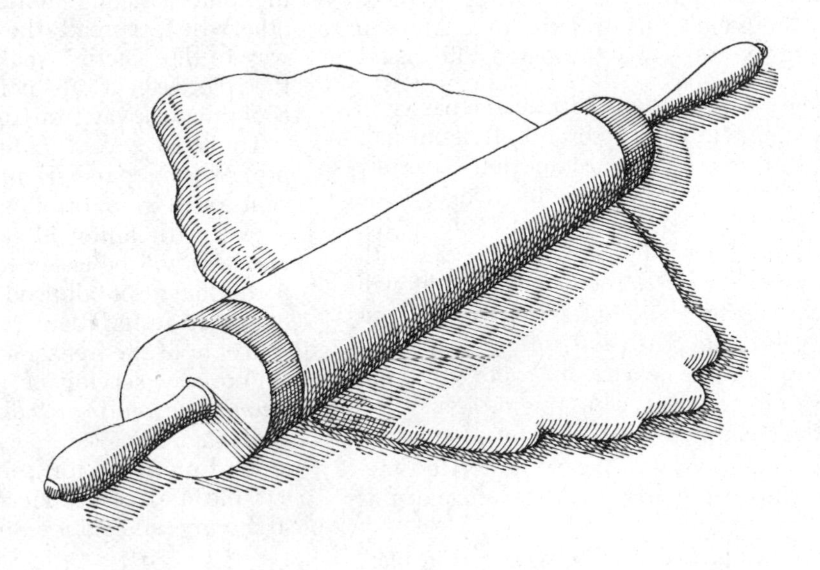

Nothing shows off your baking skills to better advantage than a luscious, melt-in-the-mouth pie. Making one isn't difficult, but it does require care and close attention to detail.

Tips for Perfect Pies

Choosing the pie plate: Pie plates come in a wide choice of materials. Choose from anodized aluminum (dull), tin-coated or enamel-coated steel, porcelain-coated aluminum with nonstick finish or glass; all these materials help piecrusts to brown. Shiny metal pans reflect heat and do not allow the crust to brown as well; place these on a cookie sheet for baking to improve browning.

Sometimes pie plates, though marked the same size, vary in capacity. Should your pie look skimpy, just add a little more filling. If you have too much filling, bake the extra in a custard cup along with the pie (cover the cup with foil if the pie has a top crust) and save it for a one-serving dessert later on. Before starting to bake, check your pans (see Measuring Pans, page 19). Our recipes are sized to fit the larger-capacity pie plates.

Don't grease pie plates unless the recipe says so.

When making a one-crust pie, make enough piecrust for two or more pies with one mixing. Complete one pie; store or freeze the extra piecrust, baked or unbaked, for use later on. (See page 502.)

Rolling the pastry: Pastry should be rolled out with a stockinette-covered rolling pin, on a surface that's been lightly and evenly floured. (Sprinkle surface with flour and then rub flour over or into it.) Roll the stockinette-covered rolling pin over the floured surface so the cover absorbs some of the flour.

Place the ball of pastry on the floured surface. Flatten it slightly with your hand, then roll it from center to edges, lifting the rolling pin as it nears the edges, so they won't be too thin. Keep the pastry circular in shape, pushing the edges in with your hands occasionally. Pinch together any cracks or breaks as they appear. Occasionally lift the entire piece of pastry carefully to be sure it is not sticking. If it does stick, use a spatula to loosen it and sprinkle more flour on the surface underneath. If the pastry tears, patch it by cutting a piece from the edge to fit over the tear. Moisten torn edges and press the patch into place.

Lining the pie plate: To transfer pastry to pie plate, gently and loosely roll about half the pastry circle onto rolling pin. Carefully lift pastry to pie plate; center it over plate and unroll. Ease pastry into pie plate, lightly pressing it to bottom and sides with fingertips; do not stretch pastry or it will shrink during baking. After rolling out pastry for top crust, cut design in center, then roll pastry circle onto rolling pin and transfer to filled pie, centering design.

After making a fluted or rope edge (page 506), hook points of pastry under the pie-plate rim so the edge will stay in place as it bakes.

Leftover pastry may be wrapped in plastic wrap or foil, stored in the refrigerator a day or so. Be sure to allow it to warm up to room temperature before using, or it will be too stiff to roll out.

Baking the pie: If the top crust of the pie seems to be browning too much, cover it loosely with foil during the last 15 minutes of baking time.

To prevent edges from overbrowning: Before putting pie in oven, fold a 2- or 3-inch-wide strip of foil over edges. Bake pie as directed; remove foil during last 15 minutes of baking time.

When baking a single piecrust, even though it's been very well pricked (see Baked Piecrust, page 505), look at it after it's been in the oven 5 minutes. If it has puffed, prick the puffed area again with a fork to let the air underneath escape; then finish baking.

Special pies: To prevent spilling of *custard and pumpkin-pie mixtures,* place the pastry-lined pie plate in the center of the oven rack; pull the rack out part way and pour the filling into the crust, then carefully push the rack back in place and bake.

Chiffon-pie filling will be a little higher and lighter if, after it is mixed, it is chilled about 5 minutes, then heaped in the piecrust.

Meringue-topped pies require special care to prevent the meringue from shrinking. Before baking (unless the recipe directs otherwise), spread the meringue all the way to the piecrust, making sure it touches the piecrust at all points. After baking, cool the pie away from drafts.

To cool *cooked filling* for cream pies, press waxed paper right to surface to prevent a skin from forming; chill.

Pies with filling of *ice cream or frozen mixtures* will be easier to cut and will have better flavor if allowed to stand at room temperature for about 15 minutes after they come out of the freezer.

For easy serving of pies with *unbaked crumb, coconut or chocolate crusts,* dip cloth in warm water; wring out and wrap around pie plate for a minute or two, then cut pie and serve. Heat will loosen crust so servings come out easily.

How to Store Pies

Keep pies with cream, custard, whipped cream or chiffon fillings in the refrigerator after they are cooled; use within a day or so.

Fruit pies may be stored at room temperature; use within 2 or 3 days.

How to Freeze Pastry and Pies

Pastry, piecrusts, double-crust and deep-dish fruit pies and chiffon pies all freeze well. Homemade cream and custard pies do not freeze well; the filling may separate or "weep." Meringue topping also does not freeze well; meringue may shrink or become tough.

If you like to keep several pies at a time in the freezer, make them in the reusable aluminum-foil pie plates that come in packages.

Pastry: Shape pastry into balls, freezer-wrap and freeze. To use, thaw, wrapped, at room temperature 2 to 4 hours, depending on size, then complete pies as desired.

Or, roll pastry into circles 3 inches larger than pie plates, stack with 2 sheets of waxed paper between each, wrap and freeze. To use, remove as needed, place on pie plate and allow to thaw 10 to 15 minutes before shaping. Shape, prick, and bake in oven preheated to 425°F. 10 to 12 minutes, or complete pie as recipe directs.

Use frozen pastry within 2 months.

Piecrust: Shape piecrust in pie plate; bake and cool, or leave unbaked. Do not remove from pie plate. If preparing more than one crust, wrap, then stack with crumpled waxed paper between each.

To use, unwrap and thaw baked piecrust at room temperature 15 minutes or in oven, preheated to 350°F., 10 minutes. Unwrap unbaked crust; prick and bake without thawing in oven preheated to 425°F., 15 to 20 minutes. Or fill and bake as recipe directs.

Use baked piecrusts within 4 to 6 months, unbaked piecrusts within 2 to 3 months.

Fruit pies: Freeze fruit pies baked or unbaked. Many think frozen unbaked pies have a fresher flavor than those baked before freezing.

To freeze unbaked fruit pies, if fruit is very juicy, add 1 to 2 tablespoons more thickening per pie. Make pie as usual but do not cut slits in top crust. Freeze before or after wrapping; if pie seems too tender to handle, freeze until firm; then cover top with a paper plate for protection; freezer-wrap and store. To use, unwrap; cut slits in top crust and bake, still frozen, in preheated oven as recipe directs, allowing 15 to 25 minutes additional baking time or until fruit is bubbling. If top crust seems to be browning too much, cover with foil last 15 minutes of baking time; to prevent edges from overbrowning, wrap a 3-inch-wide strip of foil around them.

Do not put pies frozen in oven-glass pie plates into oven until it has been fully preheated to proper baking or thawing temperature.

Let frozen baked pie thaw at room temperature 30 minutes, then heat in oven preheated to 350°F. about 30 minutes or until warm.

Use baked or unbaked fruit pies within 3 to 4 months.

Pumpkin pies: For best results bake, then freeze pumpkin pies or crust may become soggy. Use within 4 to 6 months. Thaw as for fruit pies, above. Or freeze filling and crust separately; thaw both and complete pie as recipe directs.

Chiffon pies: Freeze chiffon pies until firm; wrap and store. Use within 1 month. To thaw, unwrap and let stand at room temperature 2 to 4 hours or in refrigerator overnight if you like.

GARNISHES FOR PIES

Two-crust pies
Whipped cream
Hard Sauce (page 500)
Cheese balls
Snowy Glaze (page 559)
Sliced or shredded Cheddar cheese
Sour cream
Maple-blended syrup
Cream-cheese wedges

One-crust pies
Candied fruits
Small bunches of grapes
Chocolate curls
Nuts
Whipped cream
Shredded or flaked coconut
Baked pastry cutouts
Shredded lime, lemon or orange peel
Crushed hard candies
Sliced Cheddar-cheese cutouts

HEAD-START PIECRUSTS

Excellent pastry with little effort is easy to achieve with packaged piecrust mix. Frozen piecrusts can be used baked or unbaked in pie recipes. Complete crumb piecrusts that need only to be filled with ready-to-eat filling are also available.

Pastry and Piecrusts

Flaky Pastry (page 504), Flaky Oil Pastry (page 505) and piecrust mix may all be used interchangeably. For one-crust pies that do not have to be baked, you may use any baked pastry, crumb or coconut piecrust, or unbaked crumb or coconut pie-crust, or Meringue Pie Shell (page 277).

FLAKY PASTRY
(for one 2-crust pie or two 8- or 9-inch piecrusts)

2 cups all-purpose flour
1 teaspoon salt
¾ cup shortening

1. In medium bowl, with fork, stir flour and salt. With pastry blender or two knives used scissor-fashion, cut shortening into flour until mixture resembles coarse crumbs.
2. Sprinkle 5 to 6 tablespoons cold water, a tablespoon at a time, into flour mixture, mixing lightly with a fork after each addition until pastry is just moist enough to hold together. With hands, shape pastry into a ball. (If it is a hot day, wrap in waxed paper and refrigerate ½ hour.)
3. *For two-crust pie:* Divide pastry into 2 pieces, one slightly larger. Shape each piece into a ball. For bottom crust, on lightly floured surface, with lightly floured stockinette-covered rolling pin, roll larger ball into a circle ⅛ inch thick and about 2 inches larger all around than pie plate. Roll pastry circle gently onto rolling pin; transfer to pie plate and unroll, easing into bottom and side of plate.

For two pie crusts: Divide pastry evenly in half; roll out and line pie plates as directed above.

4. For top crust, roll smaller ball as for bottom crust but, with sharp knife, cut a few short slashes or a design in center of circle; center over filling in bottom crust. With scissors or sharp knife, trim pastry edges, leaving a 1-inch overhang. Fold overhang under, then bring up over pie-plate rim; pinch to form a high edge, then make a decorative edge (page 506). Bake pie as directed in recipe.

MIXER-STYLE: Into large bowl, measure flour, salt and shortening; with mixer at low speed, beat 1 minute or just until mixture resembles coarse crumbs, scraping bowl constantly with rubber spatula (do not overbeat). Sprinkle in 5 tablespoons cold water, continuing to beat just until mixture is moistened and cleans sides of bowl. Gather dough into ball; complete as in steps 3 and 4 of Flaky Pastry, above.

UNBAKED PIECRUST (8- or 9-inch): Prepare as above in steps 1 and 2 but use *1 cup all-purpose flour, ½ teaspoon salt, ¼ cup plus 2 tablespoons shortening, 2 to 3 tablespoons water.* Shape all of pastry into one ball.

On lightly floured surface, with lightly floured stockinette-covered rolling pin, roll pastry into circle ⅛ inch thick and about 2 inches larger all around than pie plate. Roll pastry circle gently onto rolling pin; transfer to pie plate and unroll, easing into bottom and side of plate. With kitchen scissors or sharp knife, trim pastry edges, leaving a 1-inch overhang. Fold overhang under;

SECRETS OF FLAKY PASTRY

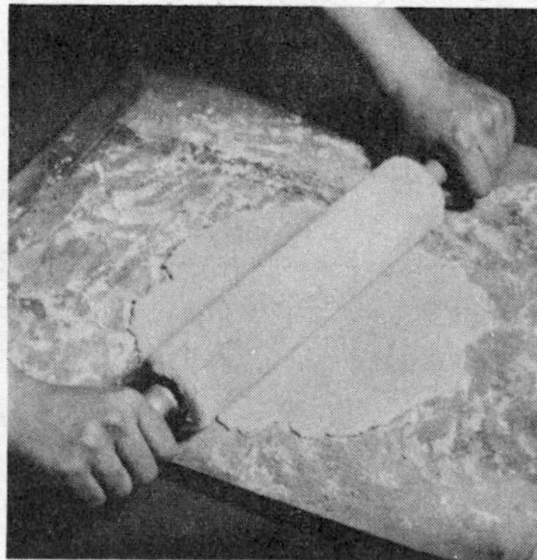
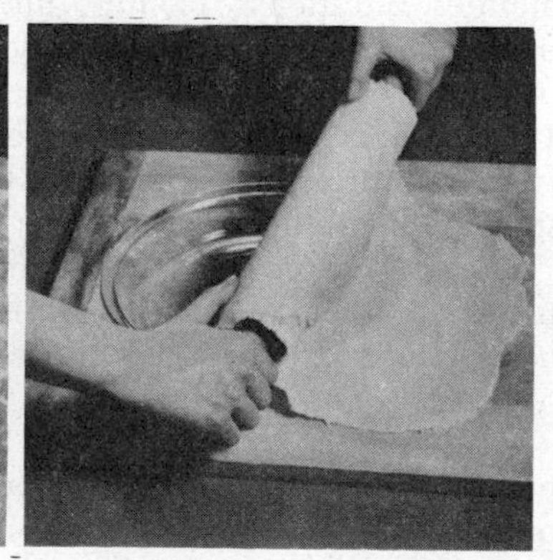

1. Cut in shortening until flour mixture resembles coarse crumbs. 2. Roll dough from center to edges, in all directions, keeping circle even. 3. Roll dough onto rolling pin, then center it over pie plate and unroll it carefully into plate.

pinch to form a high edge, then make a decorative edge. Fill and bake as directed in recipes.

BAKED PIECRUST (8- or 9-inch): Preheat oven to 425°F. Prepare as above for unbaked piecrust. With four-tined fork, prick bottom and side of crust in many places to prevent puffing during baking. Bake 15 minutes or until golden. Cool.

FLAKY OIL PASTRY

(for one 2-crust pie or two 8- or 9-inch piecrusts)

2⅓ cups all-purpose flour
1 teaspoon salt
½ cup plus 1 tablespoon salad oil

1. In medium bowl, with fork, stir flour and salt. Stir in oil until mixture resembles coarse crumbs.
2. Sprinkle 3 to 4 tablespoons cold water, a tablespoon at a time, into flour mixture, mixing lightly with fork after each addition, until pastry is moist and cleans sides of bowl. With hands, shape pastry into a ball.
3. *For two-crust pie:* Divide pastry into 2 pieces, one slightly larger; shape each piece into ball. To roll, wipe counter top with damp cloth; center 12-inch square of waxed paper on dampened surface. For bottom crust, place larger ball on waxed paper. Cover with second square of waxed paper. With rolling pin, roll pastry into a circle ⅛ inch thick and about 2 inches larger all around than pie plate. Gently peel off top sheet of paper. Transfer pastry on bottom sheet of waxed paper to pie plate, pastry side down; gently peel off waxed paper and ease into bottom and sides of plate.

   For two piecrusts: Divide pastry evenly in half. Roll out and line pie plates as directed above.
4. For top crust, roll smaller ball as for bottom crust, but with sharp knife, cut a few short slashes or a design in center of circle. Center over filling in bottom crust; peel off waxed paper. With scissors or sharp knife, trim pastry edges, leaving a 1-inch overhang. Fold overhang under, then bring up over pie-plate rim to form a high edge; make a decorative edge (page 506). Bake pie as directed in recipe.

UNBAKED OIL PIECRUST (8- or 9-inch): Prepare as above in steps 1 and 2 but use *1⅓ cups all-purpose flour, ½ teaspoon salt, ⅓ cup salad oil* and *2 tablespoons cold water.* Shape all of pastry into 1 ball.

To roll, wipe counter top with damp cloth; place 12-inch square of waxed paper on dampened surface. Center pastry on waxed paper; cover with second square of waxed paper. With rolling pin, roll pastry into circle ⅛ inch thick and about 2 inches larger all around than pie plate. Gently peel off top sheet of paper.

Transfer pastry on bottom sheet to pie plate, pastry side down; gently peel off paper and ease into bottom and side of plate. With kitchen scissors or sharp knife, trim pastry edges, leaving a 1-inch overhang. Fold overhang under; pinch to form a high edge, then make decorative edge. Fill and bake as directed in recipes.

BAKED OIL PIECRUST (8- or 9-inch): Preheat oven to 425°F. Prepare as above for unbaked piecrust. With four-tined fork, prick bottom and side of crust in many places to prevent puffing during baking. Bake 15 minutes or until golden. Cool.

COBBLER OR TOP CRUST

Prepare Flaky Pastry (page 504) or Flaky Oil Pastry for one unbaked piecrust (above).Roll 2 inches larger all around than 9½" by 1½" deep pie plate; place over filling; trim edges leaving a 1-inch overhang; pinch to form a high edge and make decorative edge. Cut a 4-inch "X" in center of crust; fold back points from center of "X" to make square opening. Bake as directed in recipe.

PIE TOPS

GOLDEN BROWN: Before baking two-crust pie, brush top (not edge) with milk, half-and-half, undiluted evaporated milk, or slightly beaten egg white. If you like, sprinkle top with sugar.

LATTICE: Prepare bottom crust; fill; trim pastry to 1-inch overhang. Roll top crust into 12-inch circle; cut into ½-inch strips.

Moisten edge of bottom crust with water.

Place pastry strips about 1¼ inches apart across pie; press each at both ends to seal. Repeat with an equal number of strips placed at right angles to first ones to make lattice design.

Turn bottom crust overhang up over ends of pastry strips; pinch to seal well and make high stand-up edge that will hold pie juices in; flute.

TWISTED LATTICE: Make Lattice Top as above, twisting pastry strips before attaching to rim.

WOVEN LATTICE: Make Lattice Top as above but place first layer of strips on pie; do not seal ends. Fold every other strip back halfway from center. Place center cross-strip on pie and replace folded part of strips. Now fold back alternate strips; place second cross strip in place. Repeat to "weave" cross-strips into lattice. Seal ends; make high fluted edge.

DIAMOND LATTICE: Make any Lattice Top as above but attach cross-strips on diagonal to make diamond design.

TRELLIS: Cut pastry into 7 strips; place on filling with all going in same direction; omit cross-strips.

DECORATIVE EDGES

OLD-FASHIONED FORKED: Trim pastry even with rim of pie plate. With back of floured four-tined fork, press pastry to plate rim all around edge.

FLUTED: Trim pastry, leaving 1-inch overhang; fold overhang under to make stand-up edge. Firmly place left index finger on inside of pastry edge; with right thumb and index finger, pinch pastry at that point. Repeat every ¼ inch around edge. Leave points rounded or pinch again to sharpen. (This makes a high edge, especially suitable for custard, pumpkin and juicy fruit pies.)

MODIFIED FLUTE: Make Fluted Edge but leave ½ inch between flutes; don't sharpen points. With floured four-tined fork, flatten each flute.

ROPE: Trim pastry, leaving 1-inch overhang; fold overhang under to make stand-up edge. Press right thumb into pastry at angle, then pinch pastry between this thumb and knuckle of index finger. Place thumb in groove left by index finger and repeat all around edge.

SCALLOPED: Trim pastry, leaving 1-inch overhang. Fold overhang under, making a stand-up edge.

Position left thumb and forefinger about 1¼ inches apart on outside of stand-up edge. Using a floured round-bowl measuring tablespoon, press inside edge gently outward and between fingers to form scallop. Gently press pastry against spoon to round evenly. Repeat around edge. Pinch points between scallops to sharpen.

TURRET: Trim pastry, leaving 1-inch overhang; fold overhang under, making stand-up edge. With sharp knife, cut down through edge to rim of pie plate, making cuts ½ inch apart. Leave one pastry piece between cuts standing; flatten piece next to it; repeat around edge.

COIN: Trim pastry even with rim of pie plate. Using bottle cap dipped in flour, cut rounds from pastry trimmings. Moisten edge of pie; place rounds on edge, overlapping slightly; press lightly with fingertips.

NO-ROLL PASTRY

(one unbaked 8- or 9-inch piecrust with topping)

2 cups all-purpose flour
1 teaspoon salt
¾ cup shortening

In medium bowl, with fork, stir flour and salt. With pastry blender or 2 knives used scissor-fashion, cut shortening into flour mixture until mixture resembles coarse crumbs. Reserve 1 cup of mixture.

Sprinkle 2 to 3 tablespoons cold water into flour mixture, a tablespoon at a time, mixing lightly with fork after each addition, until pastry is just moist enough to hold together. Press to bottom and side of 8- or 9-inch pie plate; flute edges. Fill crust with fruit, mincemeat or pumpkin-filling mixture; sprinkle reserved flour mixture over top and bake as recipe directs.

CORNMEAL PASTRY
(one unbaked 9-inch piecrust)

1 cup all-purpose flour
½ cup cornmeal
½ teaspoon salt
½ cup shortening
⅓ cup shredded Cheddar cheese

In bowl, stir flour with cornmeal and salt. With pastry blender or 2 knives used scissor-fashion, cut in shortening and cheese until mixture resembles fine crumbs.

Sprinkle ¼ cup water, a tablespoon at a time, into flour mixture, mixing lightly with fork after each addition, until pastry is just moist enough to hold together. With hands, shape into flattened ball. Roll out and line 9-inch pie plate as in Unbaked Piecrust (page 504). Fill and bake as recipe directs.

TART SHELLS
(12 tart shells)

1½ cups all-purpose flour
1 tablespoon sugar
¼ teaspoon salt
⅓ cup shortening

Preheat oven to 425°F. In medium bowl, with fork, mix together flour, sugar and salt. With pastry blender or 2 knives used scissor-fashion, cut shortening into flour mixture. Sprinkle 3 to 4 tablespoons cold water, a tablespoon at a time, into flour mixture, mixing lightly with fork after each addition, until pastry is just moist enough to hold together. With hands, shape dough into a ball; divide into 12 equal parts; shape each piece into a ball.

On lightly floured surface, with lightly floured stockinette-covered rolling pin, roll 1 ball into circle ⅛ inch thick and 5 inches in diameter; press circle into 3¼″ by 1¼″ fluted tart pan; trim even with top; prick bottom with fork. Repeat with remaining balls. Bake 10 to 12 minutes until light golden. Turn shells out of pans onto wire rack; cool completely; fill with chilled chiffon, cream or whipped-cream pie filling, or ice cream.

UNBAKED: Prepare dough and line tart pans as above; do not prick. Fill and bake as directed in recipes.

BAKED CRUMB CRUST
(one 8- or 9-inch piecrust)

Preheat oven to 375°F. Prepare crumbs in blender, following blender manufacturer's directions; or place cookies or cereal in strong paper bag and roll fine with rolling pin; or grind cookies in food grinder.

Measure crumbs into medium bowl; toss with remaining ingredients until well mixed. If you like, set aside about 3 tablespoons mixture. With back of spoon, press rest of mixture to bottom and side of 8- or 9-inch pie plate, making small rim.

Bake 8 minutes; remove to wire rack to cool completely. Fill as recipe directs or with favorite chilled pie filling; top with reserved crumb mixture or garnish as recipe directs.

GRAHAM-CRACKER: For 8-inch pie, use *1¼ cups graham-cracker crumbs, 3 tablespoons sugar, ¼ cup melted butter or margarine.*

For 9-inch pie, use *1½ cups crumbs, ¼ cup sugar, ⅓ cup melted butter or margarine.*

VANILLA- OR CHOCOLATE-WAFER: For 8-inch pie, use *1¼ cups wafer crumbs, ¼ cup melted butter or margarine.*

For 9-inch pie, use *1½ cups crumbs, ⅓ cup melted butter or margarine.*

DOUBLE-CRUMB: Use half vanilla- and half chocolate-wafer crumbs in Vanilla Wafer Crust above.

GINGERSNAP: For 8-inch pie, use *1¼ cups gingersnap crumbs, ¼ cup melted butter or margarine.*

For 9-inch pie, use *1½ cups crumbs, ⅓ cup melted butter or margarine.*

NUT-CRUMB: Substitute *½ cup finely chopped nuts* for ½ cup crumbs in any of recipes above.

SPEEDY: *Packaged graham-cracker crumbs* can be used for either baked or unbaked crumb crusts. Just measure and mix.

CORN- OR WHEAT-FLAKES: For 8-inch pie, use *1¼ cups corn- or wheat-flake crumbs, 2 tablespoons sugar, ¼ cup melted butter or margarine.*

For 9-inch pie, use *1½ cups crumbs, 3 tablespoons sugar, ⅓ cup melted butter or margarine.*

UNBAKED CRUMB CRUST
(one 8- or 9-inch piecrust)

Prepare as Baked Crumb Crust (page 507) except do not make rim and do not bake. Chill piecrust well; fill as recipe directs or with chilled pie filling; top with reserved crumb mixture or garnish. Refrigerate.

GRAHAM-CRACKER: For 8-inch pie, use *1⅓ cups graham-cracker crumbs, ¼ cup packed brown sugar, ¼ teaspoon cinnamon, ¼ cup melted butter or margarine.*

For 9-inch pie, use *1½ cups crumbs, ⅓ cup packed brown sugar, ½ teaspoon cinnamon, ⅓ cup melted butter or margarine.*

PRETZEL: For 8-inch pie, use *¾ cup coarse pretzel crumbs, 3 tablespoons sugar, ¼ cup melted butter or margarine.*

For 9-inch pie, use *1 cup crumbs, ¼ cup sugar, ⅓ cup melted butter or margarine.*

NO-ROLL NUT PASTRY
(one 9-inch piecrust)

1 cup all-purpose flour
½ cup butter or margarine, softened
¼ cup confectioners' sugar
¼ cup finely chopped California walnuts

Preheat oven to 400°F. In 9-inch pie plate, with hands, mix all ingredients until soft and pliable. Press evenly against bottom and side of pie plate. With fork, prick bottom of crust well. Bake 12 minutes or until golden; cool on wire rack. Fill with favorite chilled pie filling.

NUT CRUST
(one 8- or 9-inch piecrust)

Preheat oven to 400°F. In small bowl, with spoon, thoroughly mix finely ground Brazil nuts, pecans, California walnuts, blanched almonds or peanuts with sugar and softened butter or margarine. With back of spoon, press to bottom and side of pie plate; do not spread on rim. Bake about 8 minutes, just until golden. Remove to wire rack to cool completely. Fill as recipe directs.

For 8-inch pie, use *1 cup nuts, 2 tablespoons sugar, 1½ tablespoons butter or margarine.*

For 9-inch pie, use *1½ cups nuts, 3 tablespoons sugar, 2 tablespoons butter or margarine.*

CHOCOLATE-ALMOND CANDY CRUST
(one 9-inch piecrust)

1 6-ounce package semisweet-chocolate pieces (1 cup)
2 tablespoons butter or margarine
1 cup finely chopped almonds

Line 9-inch pie plate with foil. In double boiler over hot, not boiling, water, melt chocolate with butter or margarine. Stir in almonds. With spatula, spread mixture evenly on bottom and side of foil-lined pie plate. Refrigerate until firm, about 2 hours.

Lift piecrust from pan and peel off foil; replace in pan. Fill with chilled chiffon or Bavarian-type filling; refrigerate.

Let stand at room temperature 5 minutes before serving. (Or, fill with ice cream; cover and freeze.)

COCONUT CRUST
(one 9-inch piecrust or one 8-inch piecrust with topping)

TOASTED: Preheat oven to 300°F. On bottom and side of 9-inch pie plate,* evenly spread *2 tablespoons butter or margarine,* softened. Pat *one 3½-ounce can flaked or one 4-ounce can shredded coconut* evenly into butter or margarine. Bake 15 to 20 minutes until golden. Remove to wire rack to cool completely. Fill with chilled filling.

CHOCOLATE: Grease 9-inch pie plate.* In small saucepan over low heat, melt *2 squares unsweetened chocolate* with *2 tablespoons butter or margarine, 2 tablespoons water* and *⅔ cup confectioners' sugar;* stir to blend well. Stir in *one 3½-ounce can flaked or one 4-ounce can shredded coconut* (1⅓ cups). Press to bottom and side of pie plate. Refrigerate about 1 hour or until firm. Fill with chilled filling.

SNOWY: In 9-inch pie plate,* lightly toss *1½ cups flaked or shredded coconut* with *½ cup confectioners' sugar* until mixed. Add *3 tablespoons melted butter or margarine;* mix well, then press to bottom and side of pie plate. Refrigerate about 1 hour or until firm. Fill with chilled filling.

* For 8-inch piecrust, prepare as above; reserve some of coconut mixture to garnish finished pie and press rest to side and bottom of 8-inch pie plate. Bake or refrigerate as directed.

Fill-and-Bake Pies

PEACH PIE

pastry for one 2-crust, 9-inch pie (pages 504–505)
6 cups peeled, sliced peaches
¾ to 1 cup sugar
⅓ cup all-purpose flour
1 tablespoon lemon juice
½ teaspoon grated lemon peel
½ teaspoon cinnamon

ABOUT 2 HOURS AHEAD OR EARLY IN DAY:
Preheat oven to 425°F. Roll out half of pastry and line 9-inch pie plate as directed in steps 1 through 3 of pastry recipe.

In large bowl, lightly toss peaches with remaining ingredients; spoon into crust.

Prepare top crust as directed in step 4 of pastry recipe; make a decorative edge. Bake 45 to 50 minutes until golden. Serve warm or cold. Makes 6 servings.

APPLE PIE

pastry for one 2-crust, 9-inch pie (pages 504–505)
⅔ to ¾ cup sugar (half brown sugar, if you like)
2 tablespoons all-purpose flour
½ teaspoon cinnamon
¼ teaspoon nutmeg
½ teaspoon grated lemon peel
1 to 2 teaspoons lemon juice
6 to 7 cups thinly sliced, peeled and cored cooking apples (2 pounds)
1 tablespoon butter or margarine.

ABOUT 2 HOURS AHEAD OR EARLY IN DAY:
1. Roll out half of pastry and line 9-inch pie plate as directed in steps 1 through 3 of pastry recipe. Preheat oven to 425°F.
2. In small bowl, combine sugar with next five ingredients (amount of sugar depends on tartness of apples).
3. Place half of apples in piecrust; sprinkle with half of sugar mixture. Top with rest of apples, then with rest of sugar mixture. Dot with butter or margarine.
4. Prepare top crust as directed in step 4 of pastry recipe; make a decorative edge.
5. Bake 40 to 50 minutes until golden. Serve warm or cold. Makes 6 servings.

APPLE-CUSTARD PIE

1 9-inch unbaked piecrust (pages 504–505)
6 cups thinly sliced, peeled and cored cooking apples
sugar
3 tablespoons all-purpose flour
½ teaspoon salt
¼ teaspoon cinnamon
2 eggs
¾ cup half-and-half or milk
dash nutmeg

EARLY IN DAY:
Prepare piecrust with Fluted Edge (page 506). Preheat oven to 375°F. In large bowl, toss apple slices with ¾ cup sugar, flour, salt and cinnamon until well coated. Arrange apple slices in overlapping circles in piecrust.

In small bowl, with wire whisk or fork, beat eggs with ¼ cup sugar, half-and-half and nutmeg; pour over apple slices; cover loosely with foil. Bake 45 minutes; remove foil and bake 30 minutes more or until knife inserted in custard comes out clean. Cool, then refrigerate. Makes 6 to 8 servings.

OPEN-FACE APPLE PIE

1 9-inch unbaked piecrust (pages 504–505)
6 cups thinly sliced, peeled and cored cooking apples
⅔ cup sugar
2 tablespoons all-purpose flour
1 teaspoon grated lemon peel
2 teaspoons lemon juice
½ teaspoon cinnamon
¼ teaspoon nutmeg
⅛ teaspoon salt
1 tablespoon butter or margarine
light corn syrup

ABOUT 2 HOURS AHEAD OR EARLY IN DAY:
Prepare piecrust with Fluted Edge (page 506). Preheat oven to 425°F. In large bowl, toss apples with next 7 ingredients; arrange in piecrust. Dot with butter or margarine.

Cover top of pie with sheet of foil; place another sheet of foil on oven shelf below pie to catch any drips. Bake 45 minutes; remove foil from top of pie. Bake 10 to 15 minutes more until apples are tender. Drizzle corn syrup over top of hot pie. Serve warm or cold. Makes 6 servings.

CHERRY PIE

1 cup sugar
¼ cup cornstarch
½ teaspoon salt
5 cups pitted fresh tart cherries
pastry for one 2-crust, 9-inch pie (pages 504–505)
1 tablespoon butter or margarine

ABOUT 2 HOURS AHEAD OR EARLY IN DAY: Preheat oven to 425°F. In large bowl, combine sugar, cornstarch, salt and cherries; toss well; let stand while preparing pastry.

Roll out pastry and line 9-inch pie plate as directed in steps 1 through 3 in pastry recipe. Spoon cherry filling evenly into crust; dot with butter or margarine. Prepare top crust as directed in step 4. Bake 50 to 60 minutes until crust is golden. Serve warm or cold. Makes 6 servings.

PEAR PIE

pastry for one 2-crust, 9-inch pie (pages 504–505)
6 pears
¾ cup sugar
3 tablespoons quick-cooking tapioca
2 tablespoons lemon juice
2 tablespoons butter or margarine
1 teaspoon grated lemon peel
½ teaspoon nutmeg
½ teaspoon cinnamon
¼ teaspoon salt
milk

ABOUT 2 HOURS AHEAD OR EARLY IN DAY: Roll out half of pastry and line 9-inch pie plate as directed in steps 1 through 3 of pastry recipe. Preheat oven to 425°F.

Peel, core and slice pears into large bowl; add remaining ingredients except milk and toss to mix well; spoon into piecrust.

Roll remaining pastry into 10″ by 4½″ rectangle. Cut lengthwise into 6 strips. Place strips parallel across pie; twist, then fasten ends to crust. Trim; make a decorative edge. Brush strips with milk. Bake 50 to 60 minutes until pears are tender. Serve warm or cold. Makes 6 servings.

CANNED PEAR PIE: Prepare as above but use *two 29-ounce cans pears,* drained and sliced, instead of fresh pears. Bake 40 minutes or until crust is golden.

CANNED CHERRY PIE

2 16-ounce cans pitted tart cherries
1 cup sugar
3 tablespoons quick-cooking tapioca*
¼ teaspoon salt
¼ teaspoon cinnamon
½ teaspoon vanilla extract
⅛ teaspoon red food color
pastry for one 2-crust, 9-inch pie (pages 504–505)

ABOUT 3 HOURS BEFORE SERVING:
1. Drain cherries well, reserving ½ cup juice. In medium bowl, combine sugar, tapioca, salt and cinnamon; stir in reserved cherry juice, cherries, vanilla and food color; let stand while preparing pastry.
2. Preheat oven to 425°F. Roll out half of pastry and line 9-inch pie plate as directed in steps 1 through 3 of pastry recipe.
3. Pour cherry mixture into piecrust. Prepare top crust as for Lattice Top (page 505).
4. Bake 20 minutes; cover top of pie with sheet of foil and bake 30 minutes more. Cool on wire rack at least 1 hour before serving. Makes 6 to 8 servings.

* Or use cornstarch and omit tapioca; prepare recipe as above but in medium saucepan over medium heat, cook sugar, 3 tablespoons cornstarch, salt, cinnamon, reserved cherry juice and food color, stirring, until thickened. Stir in cherries and vanilla. Pour into piecrust; place lattice strips over filling. Bake 30 minutes or until crust is golden. (Foil is not needed for this version.)

RHUBARB PIE

1½ cups sugar
¼ cup all-purpose flour*
1 tablespoon grated orange peel (optional)
¼ teaspoon salt
4 cups rhubarb, cut into 1-inch pieces (about 3 pounds)
pastry for one 2-crust, 9-inch pie (pages 504–505)
2 tablespoons butter or margarine

ABOUT 1¼ HOURS AHEAD OR EARLY IN DAY: Preheat oven to 425°F. In large bowl, combine sugar, flour, orange peel and salt. Add rhubarb and toss well; let stand while preparing pastry.

* For thicker filling, use ⅓ cup all-purpose flour.

Roll out half of pastry and line 9-inch pie plate as directed in steps 1 through 3 of pastry recipe. Spoon filling evenly into crust; dot with butter or margarine.

Prepare top crust as directed in step 4 of pastry recipe. Bake 40 to 50 minutes until crust is golden. Serve warm or cold. Makes 6 servings.

CALIFORNIA LEMON PIE

1 9-inch unbaked piecrust (pages 504–505)
3 eggs, separated
1 cup sugar
¼ cup butter or margarine, softened
1 cup milk
¼ cup lemon juice
1 tablespoon all-purpose flour
1 tablespoon grated lemon peel

EARLY IN DAY:

1. Preheat oven to 425°F. Prick piecrust with fork; bake only 8 minutes; set aside.
2. Turn oven control to 350°F. In small bowl, with mixer at high speed, beat egg whites until soft peaks form; beating at high speed, gradually sprinkle in ½ cup sugar; beat until sugar is completely dissolved.
3. In large bowl, with same beaters and with mixer at medium speed, beat ½ cup sugar with butter or margarine and egg yolks until well mixed; at low speed, beat in milk, lemon juice, flour and lemon peel.
4. With wire whisk, gently fold whites into yolk mixture; pour into piecrust.
5. Bake pie 35 to 40 minutes until knife inserted about 1 inch in from side comes out clean. Refrigerate. Makes 8 servings.

CRANBERRY-NUT PIE

¾ cup sugar
1 tablespoon cornstarch
¾ cup light corn syrup
1 teaspoon grated lemon peel
3 cups cranberries
½ cup dark seedless raisins
½ cup chopped California walnuts
2 tablespoons butter or margarine
pastry for one 2-crust, 9-inch pie (pages 504–505)

ABOUT 2 HOURS AHEAD OR EARLY IN DAY:

In medium saucepan, stir sugar with cornstarch; stir in ¼ cup water, corn syrup and lemon peel; over medium heat, heat to boiling. Stir in cranberries, raisins, and walnuts; cover and cook until cranberry skins pop, about 4 minutes. Remove from heat and stir in butter or margarine. Cool 30 minutes but do not stir while cooling. Meanwhile, prepare pastry.

Preheat oven to 425°F. Roll out half of pastry and line 9-inch pie plate as directed in steps 1 through 3 of pastry recipe.

Pour cooled cranberry mixture into piecrust. Prepare top crust as for Lattice Top (page 505). Bake 40 minutes or until crust is golden. Serve warm or cold. Makes 8 to 10 servings.

GOOSEBERRY PIE

4 cups gooseberries (about 2 pints)
1½ to 2 cups sugar
¼ cup cornstarch*
½ teaspoon cinnamon
¼ teaspoon salt
pastry for one 2-crust, 9-inch pie (pages 504–505)
1 tablespoon butter or margarine

ABOUT 2 HOURS AHEAD OR EARLY IN DAY:

Preheat oven to 450°F. If gooseberries are large, slice in half. In medium bowl, combine sugar, cornstarch, cinnamon and salt; add gooseberries and toss well; with slotted spoon, mash berries so that all sugar mixture is moistened; let stand while preparing pastry.

Roll out half of pastry and line 9-inch pie plate as directed in steps 1 through 3 of pastry recipe. Spoon gooseberry filling evenly into crust; dot with butter or margarine. Prepare top crust as directed for Lattice Top (page 505).

Bake 10 minutes; turn oven control to 350°F. and bake 1 hour more or until pastry is golden. (During last 15 minutes or so of baking, place sheet of foil just below shelf with pie to catch any drips.) Serve warm or cold. Makes 6 servings.

CURRANT PIE: Prepare as above but use *2 pints currants* instead of gooseberries.

* For thicker filling, use 6 tablespoons cornstarch.

CONCORD-GRAPE PIE

4 cups Concord grapes
¾ cup sugar
3 tablespoons quick-cooking tapioca
1 tablespoon lemon juice
pastry for one 2-crust, 9-inch pie (pages 504–505)
2 tablespoons butter or margarine

ABOUT 2 HOURS AHEAD OR EARLY IN DAY: Slip skins from grapes; reserve skins. In medium saucepan over high heat, heat grape pulp to boiling, stirring occasionally; reduce heat to low and simmer 5 minutes, stirring. Press pulp through sieve into medium bowl to remove seeds. Add grape skins, sugar, tapioca and lemon juice; mix well; let stand while preparing pastry.

Preheat oven to 425°F. Roll out half of pastry and line 9-inch pie plate as directed in steps 1 through 3 of pastry recipe. Fill with grape mixture; dot with butter or margarine. Prepare top crust as directed in step 4 of pastry recipe; make a decorative edge. Bake 25 minutes or until golden. Serve warm or cold. Makes 8 servings.

BLACKBERRY PIE

⅔ to ¾ cup sugar
¼ cup all-purpose flour
½ teaspoon cinnamon
½ teaspoon grated lemon peel
¼ teaspoon nutmeg
5 cups blackberries
pastry for one 2-crust, 9-inch pie (pages 504–505)
1 tablespoon butter or margarine

ABOUT 2 HOURS AHEAD OR EARLY IN DAY: Preheat oven to 425°F. In large bowl, combine first 6 ingredients; let stand.

Roll out half of pastry and line 9-inch pie plate as directed in steps 1 through 3 of pastry recipe. Spoon filling evenly into crust; dot with butter or margarine. Prepare top crust as directed in step 4 of pastry recipe; make a decorative edge. Bake 50 minutes or until golden. Makes 6 servings.

BLUEBERRY COBBLER: Prepare filling as above but use *6 cups blueberries* instead of blackberries; add *2 teaspoons lemon juice*. Top with Cobbler Crust (page 505). Bake as above. Makes 6 to 8 servings.

SOUR-CREAM PUMPKIN PIE

1 9-inch unbaked piecrust (pages 504–505)
3 eggs, separated
1 16-ounce can pumpkin (2 cups)
1 cup sugar
1 cup sour cream
1 teaspoon cinnamon
½ teaspoon ginger
¼ teaspoon nutmeg
¼ teaspoon ground cloves
¼ teaspoon salt

EARLY IN DAY OR DAY BEFORE SERVING: Prepare piecrust with Fluted Edge (page 506); refrigerate. Preheat oven to 450°F.

In small bowl, with mixer at high speed, beat egg whites just until soft peaks form. In large bowl, with same beaters and with mixer at low speed, beat pumpkin with egg yolks and remaining ingredients until well blended. With wire whisk or rubber spatula, gently fold whites into mixture.

Place pie plate on oven rack; pour pumpkin mixture into piecrust. Bake 10 minutes; turn oven control to 350°F. and bake pie 1 hour and 5 minutes more or until filling is set. Refrigerate. Makes 6 to 8 servings.

PILGRIM PUMPKIN PIE

1 9-inch unbaked piecrust (pages 504–505)
1 16-ounce can pumpkin (2 cups)
1 13-ounce can evaporated milk
2 eggs
½ cup packed brown sugar
½ cup sugar
1½ teaspoons cinnamon*
½ teaspoon ginger
½ teaspoon nutmeg
½ teaspoon allspice
½ teaspoon ground cloves
½ teaspoon salt
whipped cream for garnish

ABOUT 3 HOURS AHEAD OR EARLY IN DAY: Prepare piecrust with Fluted Edge (page 506); refrigerate. Preheat oven to 425°F.

In large bowl, with mixer at medium speed, beat pumpkin with next 10 ingredients until well mixed. Place pie plate on oven rack; pour pumpkin mixture into pie-

* Or, instead of cinnamon and next 4 spices, use 2 teaspoons pumpkin-pie-spice mix.

crust; bake 15 minutes; turn oven control to 350°F. and bake 35 minutes more or until filling is set. Cool. Serve topped with whipped cream. Makes 8 servings.

HONEY-NUT PUMPKIN PIE: Prepare as above. Just before serving, spread *1/3 cup honey* over top; sprinkle with *1/3 cup sliced Brazil nuts,* almonds, filberts, peanuts, pecans or California walnuts.

SQUASH PIE: Prepare as above but substitute *2 cups mashed, cooked or thawed frozen butternut squash* (about 1 1/3 12-ounce packages) for pumpkin.

SLIPPED CUSTARD PIE

1 9-inch unbaked piecrust (pages 504–505)
4 eggs
1/2 cup sugar
1/2 teaspoon salt
1 teaspoon vanilla extract
2 cups hot milk
softened butter or margarine
1/4 teaspoon nutmeg
whipped cream, berries, toasted coconut or maple-blended syrup for garnish

EARLY IN DAY:
Prepare piecrust. Turn oven control to 350°F. In medium bowl, with hand beater or wire whisk, beat eggs, sugar, salt and vanilla. Slowly pour milk into egg mixture, stirring rapidly to prevent lumping.

Butter a second 9-inch pie plate; set in shallow baking pan on oven rack. Pour egg mixture into pie plate; sprinkle with nutmeg. Pour enough hot water into baking pan to come half way up side of pie plate. Bake 35 minutes or until knife inserted about 1 inch from edge comes out clean. Cool.

When custard is cool, loosen from side of pie plate with spatula; shake gently to loosen bottom. Hold far edge of plate over far edge of piecrust; tilt custard gently; as it slips into crust, pull plate back quickly until custard rests in crust. Let filling settle a few minutes. Serve topped with one of garnishes above. Makes 6 servings.

SLIPPED COCONUT-CUSTARD PIE: Prepare as above but add *1/2 cup shredded coconut* to egg mixture.

CUSTARD PIE

1 9-inch unbaked piecrust (pages 504–505)
1 tablespoon butter or margarine, softened
2 1/2 cups milk
1/2 cup sugar
3 eggs
1 teaspoon vanilla extract
1/2 teaspoon salt
1/4 teaspoon nutmeg
whipped cream, toasted coconut or chopped nuts for garnish

EARLY IN DAY:
Rub unbaked piecrust with butter or margarine; refrigerate. Preheat oven to 425°F.

In medium bowl, with hand beater or wire whisk, beat well remaining ingredients except garnish. Place pie plate on oven rack; pour milk mixture into piecrust. Bake 20 to 25 minutes until knife inserted about 1 inch from edge comes out clean. Cool. Serve topped with one of garnishes above. Makes 6 servings.

COCONUT-CUSTARD PIE: Prepare pie as above but sprinkle *1/2 cup shredded or flaked coconut* over bottom of prepared crust.

MERINGUE-TOPPED BUTTERMILK PIE

Cornmeal Pastry (page 507)
3 eggs, separated
sugar
1 tablespoon butter or margarine, softened
2 cups buttermilk
1/4 cup all-purpose flour
1/4 teaspoon grated lemon peel
2 tablespoons lemon juice

EARLY IN DAY:
Preheat oven to 425°F. Prepare pastry as recipe directs; make a decorative edge.

In large bowl, with mixer at low speed, beat egg yolks, 1 cup sugar and butter or margarine until mixed. Beat in remaining ingredients except egg whites until smooth. Pour mixture into crust. Bake 10 minutes; turn oven control to 350°F. and bake 40 to 45 minutes more until almost set. Cool.

When pie is cool, preheat oven to 400°F. Use egg whites to make 3-Egg-White Meringue (page 524). Spread over filling, sealing to edges; bake 10 minutes or until meringue is golden. Cool. Refrigerate until served. Makes 8 servings.

DOUBLE PEANUT PIE

1 9-inch unbaked piecrust (pages 504–505)
3 eggs
1 cup dark corn syrup
½ cup sugar
½ cup creamy peanut butter
½ teaspoon vanilla extract
1 cup salted peanuts
whipped cream for garnish

EARLY IN DAY:
Preheat oven to 350°F. Prepare piecrust. In large bowl, with mixer at medium speed, beat eggs with corn syrup, sugar, peanut butter and vanilla until smooth; stir in peanuts. Place pie plate on oven rack; pour mixture into piecrust. Bake 55 to 60 minutes until knife inserted about 1 inch in from edge comes out clean. Cool. Garnish servings with whipped cream. Makes 12 servings.

FUDGE-NUT PIE

1 9-inch unbaked piecrust (pages 504–505)
2 squares unsweetened chocolate
¼ cup butter or margarine
¾ cup sugar
½ cup packed light brown sugar
½ cup milk
¼ cup corn syrup or maple-blended syrup
1 teaspoon vanilla extract
¼ teaspoon salt
3 eggs
1 cup finely chopped California walnuts
coffee, vanilla or chocolate ice cream for garnish

EARLY IN DAY:
Preheat oven to 350°F. Prepare piecrust. In medium saucepan over low heat, heat chocolate with butter or margarine just until melted; remove from heat. Add sugar and next 6 ingredients; with hand beater or wire whisk, beat until well mixed. Stir in walnuts.

Pour mixture into piecrust. Bake 45 to 55 minutes until filling is puffed. Cool.* Serve topped with ice cream. Makes 8 servings.

RICH WALNUT PIE: Prepare as above but omit chocolate; increase butter or margarine to ½ cup.

* Filling will shrink to original size while cooling.

PECAN PIE

1 9-inch unbaked piecrust (pages 504–505)
3 eggs
1 cup dark corn syrup
½ cup sugar
¼ cup butter or margarine, melted
1 teaspoon vanilla extract
1 cup pecan halves

EARLY IN DAY:
Preheat oven to 350°F. Prepare piecrust. In medium bowl, with hand beater or wire whisk, beat eggs well. Beat in next 4 ingredients until well blended. Arrange pecans in bottom of piecrust; carefully pour egg mixture over them. Bake 1 hour or until knife inserted 1 inch in from edge comes out clean. Cool. Makes 8 servings.

PECAN TARTS: Prepare Unbaked Tart Shells (page 507). Prepare filling as above but coarsely chop pecans; distribute pecans evenly among tart shells; pour filling over pecans. Bake 25 to 30 minutes. Cool 10 minutes; remove from pans and cool on wire rack. Serve topped with *whipped cream.* Makes 12 tarts.

MINCE PIE

1 18-ounce jar prepared mincemeat (2 cups)
1½ cups coarsely broken California walnuts
2 large apples, cored and diced
½ cup packed brown sugar
¼ cup brandy or rum (optional)
1 tablespoon lemon juice
pastry for one 2-crust, 9-inch pie (pages 504–505)
Hard Sauce (page 500) or Frozen Cheese Cream (page 575) for garnish

DAY BEFORE:
In medium bowl, stir first 6 ingredients until well mixed; cover and refrigerate overnight to allow flavors to blend.

ABOUT 3 HOURS BEFORE SERVING:
Roll out half of pastry and line 9-inch pie plate as directed in steps 1 through 3 of pastry recipe. Preheat oven to 425°F. Fill with undrained mincemeat mixture.

Prepare top crust as for Lattice Top (page 505). Bake 30 to 40 minutes until golden. Serve warm, topped with one of garnishes above. Makes 8 servings.

CUSTARD MINCEMEAT PIE

1 9-inch unbaked piecrust (pages 504–505)
1 18-ounce jar prepared mincemeat, drained
2 eggs
1½ cups milk
¼ cup sugar
1 teaspoon vanilla extract
½ teaspoon nutmeg

ABOUT 2 HOURS AHEAD OR EARLY IN DAY: Preheat oven to 350°F. Prepare piecrust.

Spoon mincemeat unevenly into piecrust. In small bowl, with hand beater or wire whisk, beat eggs with remaining ingredients until well mixed. Pour egg mixture over mincemeat. Bake 45 minutes or until custard is set. Serve warm or refrigerate and serve chilled. Makes 8 to 10 servings.

DEEP-DISH PLUM PIE

pastry for one 9-inch unbaked piecrust (pages 504–505)
2 pounds plums, halved
2 tablespoons butter or margarine
1¼ cups sugar
3 tablespoons all-purpose flour
¼ teaspoon almond extract

ABOUT 2 HOURS AHEAD OR EARLY IN DAY: Preheat oven to 425°F. Roll pastry ⅛ inch thick to fit top of 10″ by 6″ baking dish with ½-inch overhang; fold pastry in half; cut several slits at center fold.

Arrange plums in baking dish; dot with butter or margarine. In small bowl, combine sugar, flour and extract; sprinkle over plums. Unfold pastry over filling; turn overhang under. Moisten edge of baking dish with water; press pastry firmly to edge of dish and flute. Bake 45 to 50 minutes until plum filling is bubbly and crust is golden brown. Serve warm. Makes 6 servings.

DEEP-DISH APPLE PIE: Preheat oven and prepare crust as directed above but use *6 peeled, cored medium cooking apples,* sliced; dot with *2 tablespoons butter or margarine.* In small bowl, combine *¾ cup sugar, ¼ cup flour, 1 teaspoon cinnamon, 1 teaspoon lemon juice, ½ teaspoon nutmeg* and *¼ teaspoon salt;* sprinkle over apples. Top with pastry as directed above; bake as above. Makes 6 servings.

DEEP-DISH PEACH PIE

pastry for 2-crust, 9-inch pie (pages 504–505)
10 cups sliced, peeled peaches (about 5 pounds)
3 tablespoons butter or margarine
1 cup sugar
¼ cup cornstarch
½ teaspoon cinnamon
⅛ teaspoon salt

ABOUT 2 HOURS AHEAD OR EARLY IN DAY: Preheat oven to 425°F. On large floured surface with floured rolling pin, roll out ¾ of the pastry into 18″ by 12″ rectangle; use to line 12″ by 8″ baking dish. Spoon peaches into dish; dot with butter or margarine. In small bowl, stir sugar with cornstarch, cinnamon and salt; sprinkle over peaches.

Roll remaining pastry into 10″ by 6″ rectangle. With pastry cutter, cut dough lengthwise into six 1-inch-wide strips; place crosswise over peaches, twisting strips. Fold edges of bottom crust up over strip ends, pinching to seal; form a fluted edge.

Bake 50 minutes or until filling is bubbly and crust is golden. Let stand 15 minutes, then serve warm. Or cool completely. Makes 10 servings.

CHERRY-BERRY DEEP-DISH PIE

1 16-ounce can pitted tart cherries
1 10-ounce package frozen blueberries, thawed
¾ cup sugar
¼ cup quick-cooking tapioca
3 tablespoons lemon juice
¼ teaspoon salt
pastry for one 9-inch unbaked piecrust (pages 504–505)

ABOUT 2 HOURS BEFORE SERVING: Drain cherries and blueberries. In 1-quart baking dish, combine fruits and next 4 ingredients; let stand while preparing pastry.

Preheat oven to 425°F. Roll pastry to fit top of baking dish with ½-inch overhang; fold pastry in half; cut several slits in center fold. Unfold pastry over filling; turn overhang under. Moisten edge of baking dish with water; press pastry to edge of dish and flute or mark with floured tines of fork.

Bake pie 50 minutes or until crust is golden; serve warm. Makes 8 servings.

APPLE TURNOVERS

piecrust mix for 2-crust pie
1 22-ounce can apple-pie filling
1 egg
1 tablespoon sugar
¼ teaspoon cinnamon

ABOUT 1 HOUR AHEAD OR EARLY IN DAY:
Preheat oven to 425°F. Prepare pastry as label directs; divide in half. On lightly floured surface with lightly floured rolling pin, roll half of dough ⅛ inch thick. With sharp knife, cut dough into 10-inch square; cut into four 5-inch squares.

Spread scant ¼ cup apple-pie filling on half of each square, leaving ½-inch margin along edges; lightly moisten edges with water. Fold over other half of square and seal edges with fork dipped in flour. Repeat with remaining dough, re-rolling scraps to make 10 turnovers. Place turnovers on cookie sheet.

In small bowl, with fork, beat egg with sugar and cinnamon; brush over pastries. Bake 15 minutes or until golden. Remove from cookie sheet to cool. Serve warm or cold. Makes 10 turnovers.

FRIED APPLE PIES: In deep fat fryer, heat about *3 inches salad oil* to 400°F.* Prepare turnovers as above but omit egg, sugar and cinnamon. Place 2 or 3 pies in fry basket; gently lower into hot oil. Fry 3 to 5 minutes until golden; drain on paper towels. Fry remaining pies. Sprinkle, while warm, with *confectioners' sugar* or cinnamon-sugar. Serve warm or cold. Makes 10 fried pies.

* Or, in large, deep saucepan over medium-high heat, heat salad oil to 400°F. on deep-fat thermometer. (Remove pies with slotted spoon.)

QUICK FRENCH FRUIT TART

ABOUT 1 HOUR BEFORE SERVING:
Preheat oven to 425°F. Onto cookie sheet, unroll 1 roll of dough from *one 14-ounce package refrigerated apple, cherry or blueberry turnover pastries;* overlap serrated cuts ¼ inch; press together. Repeat with second roll. Bake 8 to 10 minutes until golden. Cool on cookie sheet on wire rack.

To serve, spread both pastry strips with fruit filling from package; drizzle frosting from package over filling. Cut each into four pieces. Makes 8 servings.

Fill-and-Chill Pies

LEMON MERINGUE PIE

1 9-inch baked piecrust* (page 505)
sugar
⅓ cup cornstarch
salt
grated peel of 1 lemon
½ cup lemon juice
4 eggs, separated
1 tablespoon butter or margarine

EARLY IN DAY:
Prepare piecrust. Turn oven control to 400°F. In medium saucepan, stir 1 cup sugar with cornstarch and ⅛ teaspoon salt. Stir in 1½ cups warm water, lemon peel and juice; cook over medium heat, stirring constantly, until mixture is thickened and boils; remove from heat.

In small bowl, with wire whisk or spoon, beat egg yolks; into yolks, stir small amount of hot sauce. Slowly pour egg mixture back into sauce, stirring rapidly to prevent lumping. Return to heat; cook, stirring, until thickened (do not boil). Stir in butter or margarine; pour into piecrust.

Use egg whites to make 4-Egg-White Meringue (page 524). Spread meringue over filling, sealing to edges; bake 10 minutes or until meringue is golden. Cool, then refrigerate. Makes 6 servings.

* For 8-inch pie, use *¾ cup sugar, ¼ cup cornstarch, ⅛ teaspoon salt, 1¼ cups water, grated peel of 1 lemon, ⅓ cup lemon juice, 3 eggs,* separated, *1 tablespoon butter or margarine* for filling; turn into *baked 8-inch piecrust.* Make 3-Egg-White Meringue (page 524).

LEMON SNOW: Prepare as above but fold meringue into hot filling; pour into piecrust. Refrigerate until set.

ORANGE MERINGUE: Prepare as above but reduce sugar to ⅓ cup, water to ½ cup, lemon juice to 2 tablespoons; substitute *grated peel of 1 orange* for lemon peel; add *1 cup orange juice* with water.

PINEAPPLE MERINGUE: Drain *one 8-ounce can crushed pineapple,* reserving liquid. To liquid, add water to make 1½ cups; use as liquid in filling. Prepare as above but reduce sugar to ½ cup, lemon juice to 1 tablespoon; add pineapple to hot filling.

QUICK LEMON MERINGUE: For filling, use *one 3-ounce package regular lemon-flavor pudding-and-pie-filling mix;* prepare as label directs; add *1 tablespoon butter or margarine* and *1 tablespoon grated lemon peel;* pour into piecrust.

HURRY-UP LEMON MERINGUE PIE

1 8-inch Baked Crumb Crust (page 507)
1 14- or 15-ounce can sweetened condensed milk
1 teaspoon grated lemon peel
½ cup lemon juice
2 eggs, separated

EARLY IN DAY:
Prepare crumb crust. Turn oven control to 400°F. In medium bowl, with wire whisk or spoon, stir sweetened condensed milk with lemon peel, lemon juice and egg yolks until thickened; pour into piecrust.

Use egg whites to make 2-Egg-White Meringue (page 524); spread over filling, sealing to edges. Bake 10 minutes or until golden. Cool; chill. Makes 6 servings.

KEY LIME: Prepare as above but substitute *grated lime peel* and *lime juice* for lemon peel and juice.

FREEZER LEMON PIE

piecrust mix for 1-crust, 9-inch pie
lemon juice
1 13-ounce can evaporated milk
1 6-ounce can frozen lemonade concentrate, thawed
¼ cup sugar

EARLY IN DAY OR DAY BEFORE:
Prepare piecrust mix as label directs but use lemon juice instead of water. Bake; cool.

Meanwhile, in 8″ by 8″ baking pan, freeze undiluted evaporated milk until ice crystals appear at edges of the milk, about 30 minutes. In large bowl, with mixer at high speed, beat chilled milk until stiff peaks form. Slowly beat in lemonade concentrate and sugar. Pour into cool piecrust. Freeze.

TO SERVE:
Let pie stand at room temperature 5 minutes for easier cutting. Makes 12 servings.

FROZEN LEMON-CREAM PIE

1 9-inch Baked Vanilla-Wafer Crumb Crust (page 507)
2 eggs, separated
sugar
1 teaspoon grated lemon peel
⅓ cup lemon juice
1 cup heavy or whipping cream
1 teaspoon nutmeg for garnish

SEVERAL DAYS AHEAD:
Prepare crumb crust; cool. In medium saucepan, stir egg yolks with ½ cup sugar, lemon peel and lemon juice until well mixed; cook over low heat, stirring constantly, until slightly thickened; cool. In small bowl, with mixer at high speed, beat egg whites until soft peaks form; beating at high speed, gradually sprinkle in ¼ cup sugar; beat until sugar is completely dissolved. Set aside.

In small bowl, with mixer at medium speed, beat cream until soft peaks form. With rubber spatula, fold whipped cream and whites into lemon mixture; pile into crust; freeze, then wrap and store in freezer.

ABOUT 20 MINUTES BEFORE SERVING:
Remove pie from freezer; let stand, unwrapped. Sprinkle with nutmeg. Makes 8 servings.

FREEZER PINEAPPLE-ORANGE PIE

1 9-inch Unbaked Graham-Cracker Crumb Crust (page 508)
1½ pints orange sherbet, softened
2 8½-ounce cans crushed pineapple
2 tablespoons cornstarch
¼ cup orange marmalade

UP TO 1 WEEK AHEAD:
Place crumb crust in freezer 15 minutes. Fill with sherbet; freeze. Meanwhile, drain pineapple, reserving 2 tablespoons liquid. In medium saucepan, combine pineapple, reserved liquid and cornstarch; cook over medium heat, stirring constantly, until thickened. Cool. Spread on pie; freeze, then freezer-wrap and store in freezer.

20 MINUTES BEFORE SERVING:
Unwrap pie; spread with marmalade. Let stand 15 minutes, then cut into wedges. Makes 10 servings.

SATIN-SMOOTH CREAM PIE

1 8-inch baked piecrust (page 505) or 8-inch Baked Crumb Crust (page 507)
1 3- or 3¼-ounce package regular vanilla-flavor pudding mix
2 tablespoons butter or margarine
¼ teaspoon vanilla or almond extract
½ cup heavy or whipping cream
Chocolate Curls (page 380), chopped nuts or toasted coconut for garnish

EARLY IN DAY:
Prepare piecrust; cool. Meanwhile, prepare pudding mix as label directs; stir in butter or margarine and extract. Cover pudding surface with waxed paper; refrigerate 30 minutes or until cool. With wire whisk or hand beater, beat mixture until smooth. Pour into piecrust; refrigerate until firm.

TO SERVE:
In small bowl, with mixer at medium speed, beat cream until soft peaks form; spread over filling. Top with one of above garnishes. Makes 6 servings.

SUPREME: Prepare as above but reduce milk to 1½ cups; fold whipped cream into cooled filling.

MERINGUE-TOPPED: Preheat oven to 400°F. Prepare as above but add *3 egg yolks* to milk; omit whipping cream. Use *3 egg whites* to make 3-Egg-White Meringue (page 524); spread over filling, sealing to edges. Bake 10 minutes or until golden. Cool, then refrigerate.

BANANA: Slice *2 medium bananas* ½ inch thick; arrange in baked shell. Pour cooled filling into pie shell; refrigerate until firm. Top with whipped cream and garnish with more banana slices, dipped in *lemon juice*.

COCONUT: Fold *½ cup flaked coconut* into hot filling. Sprinkle whipped cream (or meringue topping before baking) with *¼ cup shredded or flaked coconut*.

PINEAPPLE-TOPPED: In small saucepan, combine *1½ teaspoons cornstarch* with *1 tablespoon sugar;* add *one 8¼-ounce can crushed pineapple, 1 teaspoon grated lemon peel* and *1½ teaspoons lemon juice*. Cook over medium heat, stirring, until mixture thickens and boils; cool. Spoon over pie filling. Omit whipping cream. Refrigerate.

BLUEBERRY-TOPPED: Spoon Blueberry Sauce (page 358) over cooled filling. Omit whipping cream. Refrigerate.

RASPBERRY: Prepare Supreme variation, above; refrigerate. Meanwhile, from *3 cups raspberries*, sort out 1 cup small or broken berries; reserve perfect berries. In medium saucepan over medium heat, cook sorted berries with *2 tablespoons sugar, 1 tablespoon cornstarch, 1 teaspoon grated lemon peel, 1 tablespoon lemon juice* and *½ cup water*, stirring constantly, until thickened. Refrigerate until cold, then press through strainer or food mill into medium bowl. Fold in reserved berries. Carefully spoon over pie filling; refrigerate about 5 hours or until set. Makes 6 servings.

BUTTERSCOTCH CREAM PIE

1 9-inch baked piecrust (page 505) or 9-inch Baked Crumb Crust (page 507)
¾ cup packed light brown sugar
⅓ cup all-purpose flour
¼ teaspoon salt
2 cups milk
3 eggs, separated
3 tablespoons butter or margarine
1 teaspoon vanilla extract

EARLY IN DAY:
Prepare piecrust; cool. Turn oven control to 400°F. Meanwhile, in medium saucepan, stir brown sugar with flour and salt; stir in milk until smooth. Cook mixture over medium heat, stirring constantly, until mixture is thickened and boils; remove from heat.

In cup, with fork, beat egg yolks; into egg yolks, stir small amount of hot sauce. Slowly pour egg mixture back into sauce, stirring rapidly to prevent lumping. Return to heat; cook, stirring, until thickened (do not boil). Stir in butter or margarine and vanilla extract; pour into piecrust.

Use egg whites to make 3-Egg-White Meringue (page 524). Spread meringue over filling, sealing to edge; bake 10 minutes or until meringue is golden. Cool, then refrigerate. Makes 6 servings.

SHADOW-TOP: Prepare as above but omit meringue. Cool pie; top with sweetened whipped cream and garnish with shaved semisweet chocolate.

CHOCOLATE CREAM: Prepare as above but substitute ½ cup sugar for light brown sugar; add *2 squares unsweetened chocolate,* coarsely chopped, to milk mixture and cook mixture over low heat, stirring constantly, until chocolate is melted. Beat with wire whisk or spoon until blended; increase heat to medium and continue as directed.

BLACK-BOTTOM PIE

1 9-inch Baked Gingersnap-Crumb Crust (page 507)
2 squares unsweetened chocolate
1 envelope unflavored gelatin
sugar
2¼ teaspoons cornstarch
3 eggs, separated
1¼ cups milk
1 teaspoon vanilla extract
1 tablespoon light rum
½ cup heavy or whipping cream, whipped

EARLY IN DAY OR DAY BEFORE SERVING:
1. Prepare crust; cool. In small saucepan over very low heat, melt 1½ squares chocolate; set aside.
2. In second small saucepan, stir gelatin with ¼ cup sugar and cornstarch, until well mixed. In small bowl, with fork, beat egg yolks with milk; stir into gelatin mixture. Cook over medium-low heat, stirring, until mixture is thickened and coats spoon. Remove from heat; divide in half.
3. Into one half of mixture, stir melted chocolate and vanilla; with spoon, beat smooth. Refrigerate until mixture mounds when dropped from spoon. Pour into crust; refrigerate. Refrigerate remaining custard until it mounds when dropped from spoon.
4. Meanwhile, in small bowl, with mixer at high speed, beat egg whites until soft peaks form; gradually sprinkle in ¼ cup sugar; beat until sugar is completely dissolved. With rubber spatula, gently fold whites and rum into chilled custard; pour as much custard mixture as crust will hold over chocolate mixture in crust. Refrigerate pie a few minutes, then pour rest of custard mixture on top. Refrigerate until set.

TO SERVE:
Garnish pie with whipped cream. Sprinkle with remaining chocolate, shaved. Makes 8 servings.

NESSELRODE PIE

1 9-inch Unbaked Graham-Cracker-Crumb Crust (page 508)
1 envelope unflavored gelatin
sugar
¼ teaspoon salt
4 eggs, separated
1¼ cups milk
1 tablespoon rum
1 teaspoon grated lemon peel
1 4-ounce jar diced mixed candied fruit (about ½ cup)
1 2-ounce package whipped-topping mix
red and green candied pineapple, cut in slivers, for garnish

EARLY IN DAY OR DAY BEFORE SERVING:
Prepare piecrust. In medium saucepan, stir gelatin with 3 tablespoons sugar and salt until well mixed. In small bowl, with wire whisk or spoon, beat egg yolks with milk until mixed; stir into gelatin mixture. Cook mixture over medium-low heat, stirring constantly, until mixture is thickened and coats spoon. Remove from heat and stir in rum and lemon peel. Refrigerate until cold but not firm, about 40 minutes.

In large bowl, with mixer at high speed, beat egg whites until soft peaks form; gradually sprinkle in ¼ cup sugar; beat until sugar is completely dissolved. (Whites should stand in stiff peaks.) With wire whisk or rubber spatula, gently fold gelatin mixture into whites with mixed candied fruit. Spoon filling into piecrust; refrigerate about 1 hour or until set (or overnight).

TO SERVE:
Prepare whipped-topping mix as label directs; spread on pie. Garnish with candied pineapple. Refrigerate until served. Makes 8 servings.

KING-SIZE NESSELRODE: For 10-inch pie, use *1½ cups graham-cracker crumbs* in crust; prepare crust as directed on page 508. For filling, use: *1 envelope plus 1 teaspoon unflavored gelatin, 1½ cups milk, ½ teaspoon salt, 8 eggs, 2 tablespoons rum, 2 teaspoons grated lemon peel, one 4-ounce jar mixed candied fruit, two 2-ounce packages whipped-topping mix.* Prepare and garnish as above.

RICH BAVARIAN PIE

1 9-inch baked piecrust (page 505) or 9-inch Baked Crumb Crust (page 507) or Nut Crust (page 508)
1 envelope unflavored gelatin
sugar
1/8 teaspoon salt
3 eggs, separated
1 1/4 cups milk
1 teaspoon vanilla extract
1/2 to 1 cup heavy or whipping cream
1/4 teaspoon nutmeg
shaved unsweetened chocolate for garnish

EARLY IN DAY OR DAY BEFORE SERVING:
1. Prepare piecrust; cool. In small saucepan, stir gelatin with 1/4 cup sugar and salt until well mixed. In small bowl, with wire whisk, beat egg yolks with milk until mixed; stir into gelatin mixture. Cook over medium-low heat, stirring constantly, until mixture is thickened and coats spoon. Remove from heat and stir in vanilla.
2. Refrigerate until mixture mounds when dropped from spoon, about 40 minutes. With hand beater, beat mixture smooth.
3. In large bowl, with mixer at high speed, beat egg whites until soft peaks form; beating at high speed, gradually sprinkle in 1/4 cup sugar; beat until sugar is completely dissolved.
4. In small bowl, with same beaters and with mixer at medium speed, beat heavy cream until stiff peaks form. With wire whisk or rubber spatula, gently fold whipped cream and gelatin mixture into whites.* Spoon mixture into piecrust; sprinkle filling with nutmeg. Refrigerate.

TO SERVE:
Sprinkle with chocolate. Makes 8 servings.

* Or, if you like, don't fold whipped cream into filling; use as topping for pie.

COFFEE: Prepare as above but add *2 tablespoons instant coffee powder* to egg whites before beating. Omit whipped cream and shaved chocolate. For topping, melt *3/4 cup semisweet-chocolate pieces* over hot, not boiling water; stir in *1/4 cup water* until smooth; drizzle over top of pie.

Or, into beaten whites, fold *1/2 cup sliced pitted dates* and *1/4 cup chopped pecans.* Omit chocolate topping; sprinkle with *cocoa.*

STRAWBERRY: Prepare as above but fold *1 cup sliced strawberries* into filling. Omit chocolate; garnish pie with *berries.*

EGGNOG: Prepare as above but omit vanilla; add *1/2 teaspoon rum extract;* use *1 teaspoon nutmeg.* Especially good in *Unbaked Pretzel Crumb Crust* (page 508).

COCONUT: Prepare as above but omit nutmeg; add *1/2 cup flaked or grated fresh coconut* with gelatin mixture. If fresh coconut, add *1/4 teaspoon almond extract* with vanilla.

CRANBERRY-TOPPED: Prepare as above but substitute *almond extract* for vanilla; use only 1/2 cup heavy cream; omit nutmeg and chocolate. For topping, in medium saucepan over medium heat, cook *one 16-ounce can whole-cranberry sauce* with *1 tablespoon cornstarch* until clear and thickened; cool; spread on pie when filling is set.

BANANA: Prepare as above but line cooled piecrust with *sliced bananas* before spooning in filling.

CHOCOLATE-COCONUT: Prepare *Chocolate-Coconut Crust* (page 508) and *Coconut* filling (above). For garnish, in small bowl, toss *1/2 cup flaked coconut* with *2 tablespoons shaved unsweetened chocolate.*

PUMPKIN CHIFFON PIE

1 3 1/2-ounce can flaked coconut
1/4 cup finely crushed graham-cracker crumbs
1/3 cup melted butter or margarine
sugar
1 envelope unflavored gelatin
3/4 teaspoon cinnamon
1/2 teaspoon ginger
1/2 teaspoon nutmeg
1/2 teaspoon salt
3 eggs, separated
1/2 cup milk
1 1/4 cups canned pumpkin
1 2-ounce package whipped dessert-topping mix for garnish

EARLY IN DAY OR DAY BEFORE SERVING:
1. Preheat oven to 375°F. Spread coconut evenly on cookie sheet; bake 8 to 10 minutes until lightly browned; reserve 2 tablespoons for garnish. In 9-inch pie plate,

mix well remaining coconut, crumbs, butter or margarine and 2 tablespoons sugar; press firmly to bottom and side of pie plate. Bake 6 to 8 minutes until golden; cool.

2. In double-boiler top, stir gelatin with ½ cup sugar, cinnamon, ginger, nutmeg and salt until well mixed. In small bowl, with wire whisk, beat egg yolks with milk until well mixed; stir into gelatin mixture; stir in pumpkin. Cook over boiling water 20 minutes or until thickened, stirring frequently. Refrigerate until cool but not set.

3. In large bowl, with mixer at high speed, beat egg whites until soft peaks form; gradually sprinkle ¼ cup sugar into whites, beating at high speed. With rubber spatula, gently fold chilled pumpkin mixture into whites. Pour into crust; refrigerate until set.

TO SERVE:

Prepare mix as label directs; use to garnish pie; sprinkle with coconut. Makes 10 servings.

LEMON CHIFFON PIE

1 9-inch baked piecrust (page 505)
1 envelope unflavored gelatin
sugar
¼ teaspoon salt
4 eggs, separated
1 tablespoon grated lemon peel
¼ cup lemon juice
½ cup heavy or whipping cream
shredded lemon peel for garnish

EARLY IN DAY OR DAY BEFORE SERVING:

Prepare piecrust; cool. In small saucepan, stir gelatin with ⅓ cup sugar and salt until well mixed. In small bowl, with wire whisk, beat egg yolks with ⅓ cup water, grated lemon peel and lemon juice until mixed; stir into gelatin mixture. Cook over medium-low heat, stirring, until mixture is thickened and coats spoon; remove from heat.

In large bowl, with mixer at high speed, beat egg whites until soft peaks form; beating at high speed, gradually sprinkle in ½ cup sugar; beat until sugar is completely dissolved. With rubber spatula, gently fold lemon mixture into whites; spoon mixture into piecrust; refrigerate until set.

TO SERVE:

In small bowl, with mixer at medium speed, beat cream until stiff peaks form; spoon in mounds around pie edge. Sprinkle with shredded peel. Makes 8 servings.

LIME-SWIRL PIE: Omit the ⅓ cup sugar; substitute *1 teaspoon grated lime peel* for lemon peel, *lime juice* for lemon juice. Prepare as directed but swirl whipped cream through filling in shell; top pie with *shredded lime peel.*

ORANGE CHIFFON PIE

1 9-inch baked piecrust (page 505)
or Unbaked Crumb Crust (page 508)
1 envelope unflavored gelatin
sugar
¼ teaspoon salt
3 eggs, separated
1 teaspoon grated orange peel
1 cup orange juice
2 tablespoons lemon juice
few drops yellow food color
1½ cups heavy or whipping cream
orange sections, drained, for garnish

EARLY IN DAY OR DAY BEFORE SERVING:

Prepare piecrust; cool if baked. In small saucepan, stir gelatin with ½ cup sugar and salt until well mixed. In small bowl, with wire whisk or hand beater, beat egg yolks with orange peel, orange juice and lemon juice until mixed; stir into gelatin mixture. Cook over medium-low heat, stirring constantly, until mixture is thickened and coats spoon; remove from heat. Stir in food color and refrigerate, stirring occasionally, until mixture mounds when dropped from a spoon, about 45 minutes.

In large bowl, with mixer at high speed, beat egg whites until soft peaks form; beating at high speed, gradually sprinkle in ¼ cup sugar; beat until sugar is completely dissolved. With wire whisk or rubber spatula, gently fold gelatin mixture into whites.

In small bowl, with same beaters and with mixer at medium speed, beat ½ cup heavy cream until soft peaks form; fold into gelatin mixture. Spoon mixture into crust; refrigerate until set, about 30 minutes.

TO SERVE:

In small bowl, with mixer at medium speed, beat remaining heavy cream with 2 tablespoons sugar until stiff peaks form. Spoon on pie; garnish with orange sections. Makes 8 servings.

CHOCOLATE MOUSSE PIE

1 9-inch Graham-Cracker-Crumb Crust (page 507)
1 6-ounce package semisweet-chocolate pieces (1 cup)
1 egg
2 eggs, separated
1 teaspoon rum extract
1 9-ounce container frozen whipped topping, thawed
Chocolate Curls for garnish (page 380)

EARLY IN DAY:
Prepare crumb crust; cool. In double boiler, over hot, not boiling, water, melt chocolate pieces; remove from heat and cool slightly. With hand beater, beat in egg and 2 egg yolks, one at a time; add extract.

In small bowl, with mixer at high speed, beat 2 egg whites until soft peaks form; fold into chocolate mixture. With wire whisk, gently fold ½ container whipped topping (2 cups) into chocolate mixture; pour into cooled crust. Refrigerate until set.

TO SERVE:
With spatula, swirl remaining whipped topping on pie. Garnish with Chocolate Curls. Makes 8 to 10 servings.

CHRISTMAS PIE

1 9-inch Nut Crust (page 508)
sugar
1 envelope unflavored gelatin
3 eggs, separated
1¾ cups milk
¼ cup chopped candied cherries
3 tablespoons light rum or 2 teaspoons vanilla extract
whipped topping in aerosol can

EARLY IN DAY OR DAY BEFORE SERVING:
Prepare piecrust, using Brazil nuts; cool. Meanwhile, in medium saucepan, stir ¼ cup sugar with gelatin until mixed. In small bowl, with wire whisk or hand beater, beat egg yolks with milk until mixed; stir into gelatin mixture. Cook over medium-low heat, stirring, until mixture is thickened and coats spoon; remove from heat. Refrigerate until mixture mounds when dropped from spoon, about 40 minutes.

With hand beater, beat mixture until smooth; stir in cherries and rum.

In small bowl, with mixer at high speed, beat egg whites until soft peaks form. Beating at high speed, gradually sprinkle in ¼ cup sugar; beat until sugar is completely dissolved. With wire whisk or rubber spatula, gently fold whites into gelatin mixture. Spoon filling into crust; refrigerate until set, about 4 hours.

TO SERVE:
Garnish pie with whipped topping. Makes 8 servings.

PEPPERMINT PIE

1 9-inch Chocolate-Wafer Crumb Crust (page 507)
1 envelope unflavored gelatin
¼ cup sugar
½ cup finely crushed hard peppermint candies
6 eggs, separated
¾ cup milk
whipped cream in aerosol can for garnish

EARLY IN DAY OR DAY BEFORE SERVING:
Prepare crust but do not bake; refrigerate. In medium saucepan, stir gelatin with sugar and crushed candy until well mixed. In small bowl, with wire whisk, beat egg yolks with milk just until mixed; stir into gelatin mixture. Cook over medium-low heat, stirring constantly, until mixture is thickened and coats spoon. Refrigerate until consistency of unbeaten egg white.

In large bowl, with mixer at high speed, beat egg whites until stiff peaks form. With wire whisk or rubber spatula, gently fold gelatin mixture into whites; pour into crust. Refrigerate mixture until set.

TO SERVE:
Garnish pie with whipped cream. Makes 8 servings.

CHERRY ANGEL PIE

Meringue Pie Shell (page 277)
1 3½- or 3¾-ounce package instant vanilla-pudding mix
¾ teaspoon almond extract
Cherry Topping (opposite)

EARLY IN DAY:
Prepare Meringue Pie Shell; cool. Prepare

instant pudding as label directs but use only 1¼ cups milk; stir in almond extract. Pour mixture into pie shell; spoon Cherry Topping over pudding; chill. Makes 8 servings.

CHERRY TOPPING: Drain *one 16-ounce can pitted tart cherries;* reserve liquid. Add enough water to reserved liquid to make 1 cup. In medium saucepan, combine *¼ cup sugar, 5 teaspoons cornstarch, ¼ teaspoon red food color, dash salt* and reserved liquid. Cook over medium heat, stirring constantly, until mixture is clear and thickened; remove from heat. With rubber spatula, gently fold cherries into sauce. Makes about 2 cups.

RASPBERRY RIBBON PIE

1 9-inch baked piecrust (page 505)
1 3-ounce package raspberry-flavor gelatin
¼ cup sugar
1 10-ounce package frozen raspberries
1 tablespoon lemon juice
1 3-ounce package cream cheese or Neufchâtel cheese, softened
⅓ cup confectioners' sugar
1 teaspoon vanilla extract
dash salt
1 cup heavy or whipping cream
fresh raspberries or whipped cream for garnish

EARLY IN DAY OR DAY BEFORE SERVING:
Prepare piecrust; cool. In medium bowl, stir gelatin and sugar with 1¼ cups boiling water until dissolved. Add frozen raspberries and lemon juice; stir until berries thaw. Cover and refrigerate, stirring often, until mixture mounds when dropped from spoon.

In small bowl, with wire whisk, mix cream cheese with confectioners' sugar, vanilla and salt until smooth.

In second small bowl, with mixer at medium speed, beat heavy cream until soft peaks form. With wire whisk or rubber spatula, gradually fold cream-cheese mixture into whipped cream. Spread half of whipped-cream mixture in piecrust; top with half of raspberry mixture; repeat. Refrigerate until set.

TO SERVE:
Garnish with fresh raspberries or spoonfuls of whipped cream. Makes 8 servings.

GRASSHOPPER PIE

1 9-inch baked Chocolate-Wafer Crumb Crust (page 507)
1 envelope unflavored gelatin
sugar
⅛ teaspoon salt
3 eggs, separated
¼ cup crème de menthe
¼ cup cold coffee
1 cup heavy or whipping cream
angelica for garnish

DAY BEFORE SERVING:
1. Prepare crumb crust; cool. In medium saucepan, stir gelatin with ¼ cup sugar and salt. In small bowl, with wire whisk, beat egg yolks with ½ cup water; stir into gelatin mixture. Cook over low heat, stirring, until gelatin is dissolved and mixture is thickened, about 10 minutes. Remove from heat; stir in crème de menthe and coffee.
2. Refrigerate mixture, stirring often, until mixture is consistency of unbeaten egg white, about 20 minutes.
3. In large bowl, with mixer at high speed, beat egg whites until soft peaks form; beating at high speed, gradually sprinkle in ¼ cup sugar; beat until sugar is completely dissolved. With wire whisk or rubber spatula, gently fold in gelatin mixture.
4. In small bowl, with same beaters and with mixer at medium speed, beat cream until stiff peaks form; fold into gelatin mixture. Spoon mixture into crust; garnish with angelica. Refrigerate pie until set. Makes 10 servings.

BANANA-SPLIT PIE

1 9-inch baked piecrust (page 505)
1 pint vanilla ice cream, softened
1 large banana
1 21-ounce can cherry-pie filling

UP TO 1 WEEK AHEAD:
Prepare piecrust; cool. In crust, evenly spread ice cream; freeze, then freezer-wrap and store in freezer.

ABOUT 20 MINUTES BEFORE SERVING:
Peel, then cut banana into diagonal slices. Reserve 5 slices for garnish; arrange rest of slices on top of ice cream. Spoon pie filling over banana. Garnish with reserved banana slices. Makes 6 servings.

RASPBERRY LEMON PIE

1 8-inch Unbaked Graham-Cracker-Crumb Crust (page 508)
1 3½- or 3¾-ounce package instant lemon-pudding mix
1 4½-ounce container frozen whipped topping, thawed
1 10-ounce package frozen raspberries, thawed and drained

EARLY IN DAY OR DAY BEFORE SERVING:
Prepare crumb crust; refrigerate. Meanwhile, in medium bowl, with mixer at medium speed, beat instant pudding mix with only 1½ cups milk until well mixed, no more than 2 minutes; let stand 5 minutes. With wire whisk or rubber spatula, gently fold in whipped topping; swirl in berries; pour into crust; freeze. Makes 8 servings.

FRUIT CREAM TARTS

12 baked Tart Shells (page 507)
¼ cup sugar
2 tablespoons cornstarch
¼ teaspoon salt
1 cup milk
1 egg
1 teaspoon vanilla extract
½ cup heavy or whipping cream, whipped
fruit for garnish
1 cup currant jelly (optional)

EARLY IN DAY OR DAY BEFORE SERVING:
1. Prepare Tart Shells; cool. Meanwhile, in medium saucepan, stir sugar with cornstarch and salt until well mixed. Stir in milk until smooth. Over medium heat, cook, stirring, until mixture boils; boil 1 minute.
2. In cup, with fork, beat egg; stir in small amount of hot sauce. Slowly pour egg mixture back into sauce, stirring rapidly to prevent lumping. Cook, stirring, until thickened (do not boil). Cover and refrigerate until cold, about 40 minutes; stir in vanilla.
3. With wire whisk or rubber spatula, gently fold whipped cream into custard.
4. Spoon custard into Tart Shells. Top with whole or sliced strawberries; blueberries; raspberries; peach slices; apricot halves; mandarin-orange sections, drained.
5. If you like, in small saucepan, melt jelly with 1 tablespoon water; cool slightly. Spoon jelly over fruit; refrigerate until jelly sets. Makes 12 servings.

STRAWBERRY-RHUBARB SUPREME PIE

1 pound rhubarb, cut up
¾ cup sugar
1 tablespoon lemon juice
dash salt
1 9-inch Nut Crust (page 508)
1 3-ounce package strawberry-flavor gelatin
1 5⅓-ounce can evaporated milk, chilled (⅔ cup)
½ pint strawberries, sliced

DAY BEFORE SERVING:
In medium saucepan over medium heat, heat ¼ cup water to boiling; add rhubarb, sugar, lemon juice and salt; simmer 5 minutes, stirring occasionally. Refrigerate mixture about 2 hours or until well chilled. Meanwhile, prepare crust; cool.

In small bowl, dissolve gelatin in ½ cup boiling water; refrigerate 20 minutes or until consistency of unbeaten egg white.

In medium bowl, with mixer at high speed, beat undiluted evaporated milk and gelatin until soft peaks form. With rubber spatula, fold strawberries and rhubarb into mixture; refrigerate about 20 minutes longer; pour into piecrust. Refrigerate overnight. Makes 6 servings.

MERINGUE PIE TOPPINGS

Preheat oven to 400°F. In small bowl, with mixer at high speed, beat egg whites (at room temperature) with salt until soft peaks form. Beating at high speed, gradually sprinkle in sugar, 2 tablespoons at a time, beating until sugar is completely dissolved after each addition. (Whites should stand in stiff peaks.) Rub a bit of the meringue between thumb and forefinger; if it doesn't feel grainy, sugar is dissolved.

Spread meringue over filling; *seal to piecrust all around edge*. Swirl or pull up points with back of spoon to make attractive top. Bake 10 minutes or until golden. Cool away from drafts.

3-EGG-WHITE MERINGUE: Use *3 egg whites, ¼ teaspoon salt, 6 tablespoons sugar.*

4-EGG-WHITE MERINGUE: Use *4 egg whites, ¼ teaspoon salt, ½ cup sugar.*

2-EGG-WHITE MERINGUE: Use *2 egg whites, ⅛ teaspoon salt, ¼ cup sugar.*

Cakes & frostings

Unlike many others, recipes for cakes are carefully balanced, with ingredients in definite proportion to one another. We think you'll have the most successful cakes if you follow our directions carefully.

Tips for Perfect Cakes

Ingredients: The ingredients used in the following recipes are described in Ingredients, pages 12–17. Our recipes have been made without sifting the flour, so don't you sift when making them. To measure flour, see page 18.

Don't substitute! If the recipe calls for shortening, use shortening, not butter or margarine; if it calls for cake flour, don't substitute the all-purpose kind. Different ingredients give different results in recipes.

Pans: Before starting to mix the batter, prepare the pans. Be sure to use pans of the size called for in the recipe.

For even browning and tender crust, use bright, shiny metal pans, or pans with non-stick finish. Avoid dull, dark or enamel pans; these can cause uneven and excessive browning. Glass and porcelain-coated aluminum pans with non-stick finish may be used if oven temperature is reduced 25°F.

If pan should be greased and floured, grease bottom and sides generously with shortening; sprinkle with a little flour and shake pan until coated; invert pan and tap to remove excess flour. Pans with non-stick finish should be greased and floured if recipe specifies. Or grease pan, then sprinkle with sugar. Cake slides out and frosting goes on readily.

For angel, chiffon and sponge cakes, do not grease pans. In our kitchens, when a recipe calls for a Bundt pan, we use the heavy, cast-aluminum kind. If yours is the lightweight variety, you may find the baking time needed different from that given in the recipe.

Oven: Set oven rack so the center of the cake or layers is close to the center of the oven. If 2 oven racks are needed, place them so they divide oven into thirds. If more than one pan is used, place them so they don't touch the sides of the oven or each other. If pans are on different racks, stagger them so one is not directly underneath another. For cakes baked in tube pans, set oven rack in lowest position.

Preheat oven at least 10 minutes.

Shortening cakes: When making our one-bowl layer cakes, loaves and cupcakes, beat ingredients at the recommended mixer speed for the recommended amount of time. Scrape the mixing bowl frequently with a rubber spatula so that all ingredients are mixed thoroughly.

The electric mixer helps you make shortening cakes easily and quickly. If you use a wooden spoon instead, you'll need to give ingredients *150 vigorous strokes for every minute of beating time* to blend ingredients.

Pour batter into prepared pans and smooth the top with the rubber spatula. With a knife, cut through the batter several times to break large air bubbles.

Bake as directed. Do not open oven door until the minimum baking time has passed; you can cause the cake to "fall."

When minimum time is up, test for doneness by inserting toothpick in center of cake. If it comes out clean and dry, cake is done and should be removed immediately to cool. If crumbs stick to toothpick, bake cake 2 to 5 minutes longer and test again.

Cool cake in pan on wire rack 10 minutes. With small spatula, loosen cake edges from pan and invert a second wire rack over top of pan. Invert pan and both racks; cake should drop from pan. Remove upper rack and pan so cake bottom is up. Now place inverted wire rack lightly over cake and again invert cake and both racks; remove upper rack, leaving cake top up. Cool cake thoroughly before frosting or storing.

Fruitcakes: Measure the flour, then toss about ½ cup of the amount with chopped fruits and nuts to coat them and help distribute them evenly in the batter.

Grease pans generously; line with foil and grease the foil.

When cake is done, remove to wire rack and cool completely in pan. Remove from pan, wrap and store. (See opposite page.)

Make fruitcake at least 2 weeks ahead so flavors mellow during storage.

Chiffon, angel and sponge cakes: Don't grease the pan. Batter clings to side and tube as it rises and cake stays high and light.

Eggs vary in size. In our recipes we use Large eggs. If your eggs are a different size, follow our cup measurements when given. Be sure that the bowl into which the whites are to be placed is free from grease. Separate eggs when cold, being careful that no bits of yolk remain in white. Cover and let warm to room temperature. Egg whites cannot be beaten stiff if any grease or egg yolk is present.

Fold ingredients into beaten egg whites with wire whisk or rubber spatula by cutting down through center of egg whites, across bottom and up side of bowl. Give bowl a quarter turn; repeat until egg whites are broken to size of small peas.

With rubber spatula, push batter into pan, then smooth and level it very lightly. Cut through with knife to break any large air bubbles.

When cake has baked minimum time, check for doneness. Cake is done if top springs back when lightly pressed with finger. If it does not, bake cake 2 to 5 minutes more and test again. Cracks in top, which are typical of cakes baked in tube pans, should feel dry.

To cool cake, invert pan on bottle or funnel so cake top does not touch counter. Let cake cool completely in pan.

To remove cake from pan, gently cut around side and tube of pan with knife, using an up-and-down motion and pressing knife firmly against pan. Invert pan and gently shake cake onto plate.

How to Frost Cakes

Be sure the cake is cool. Brush off crumbs and, with kitchen scissors, trim off any crisp edges, if necessary. To keep the cake plate clean, arrange strips of waxed paper to form a square covering the plate edges; center the cake or layer on the strips and frost; then gently pull out strips.

Make fluffy frostings just before using. Most uncooked creamy frostings may be made in advance, but cover tightly to prevent a crust forming. If they are refrigerated and become firm, let them warm to room temperature or stir well after removing from the refrigerator so they'll soften to proper spreading consistency.

Turning a cake as you work makes frosting it easier. Place cake on a plate on turntable, lazy Susan or top of a bowl.

Layer cake: Place first layer, top side down, on cake plate; spread with filling or frosting almost to edge. If filling is quite soft, spread only to within 1 inch of edge; weight of upper layer will push it to edge.

Place second layer, top side up, on frosted layer so that flat bottoms of the 2 layers face each other; this way the top layer does not tend to slide off. Frost sides of cake thinly to set crumbs (so they won't show in finished frosting). Then again frost the sides, generously this time, swirling frosting up to make a ½-inch ridge above cake top. Now frost cake top, swirling frosting or leaving it smooth if you like. Decorate if you wish.

When making a torte cake, split layers evenly before frosting. With a ruler and toothpicks, mark midpoint all around layer; cut with long sharp knife, using toothpicks as a guide. Remove toothpicks.

Oblong cake: Place cake, top side up, on plate with waxed paper strips. Frost top and sides. For easy storage or to pack for a picnic, leave cooled cake in its baking pan; frost top only.

Tube cake: Place cake, top side down, on plate with waxed paper strips. Brush crumbs from top and sides. To set crumbs on sides, spread sides thinly with frosting, then frost generously, making ridge at top; frost top and inside center of cake.

To glaze, brush crumbs from top of cake only. Drizzle glaze over top of cake from spoon, letting it run down sides.

To split tube cake into layers, with ruler, measure depth of cake and divide into desired number of layers; place toothpicks around cake to mark cutting line. With long sharp knife, cut across cake, using toothpicks as guide; remove toothpicks.

Ring cake (baked in Bundt pan, ring mold): Place cake, top side down, on plate with waxed paper strips. Glaze as above.

Cupcakes: To frost quickly, dip tops in frosting, turning slightly to coat; remove. If cupcakes were baked in paper liners, leave liners on.

Easy Decorative Touches

1. Use back of spoon to swirl circles, S's, wavy lines in frosting; pull up for peaks.
2. For spiral: Place cake on turntable, lazy Susan or rotating base of mixer (remove mixer head). Press spatula into frosting at center and turn cake in one direction, slowly moving spatula toward cake edge.
3. On creamy-frosted cake, draw tines of fork across top in parallel rows; repeat at right angles to first rows, reversing direction of every other row if you like.
4. On unfrosted cake, place paper doily with open design. Sprinkle with confectioners' sugar; lift doily straight up to remove. Design will remain on cake.

Garnishes for Cakes

You can make these attractive garnishes for cakes: Gumdrop Posies, page 380; Chocolate Curls, page 380; Tinted Coconut, page 380; Frosted Grapes, page 376.

Hurry-up Frostings

All the old favorites and many new taste-tempters are to be found among the frostings that can be made with packaged mixes. Choose from fluffy, fudgy and creamy types.

Also available are canned, ready-to-spread frostings that need no mixing at all. Use them as is or, if you like, stir in chopped nuts, shredded orange or lemon peel, or a few drops of flavoring extract.

Tubes and aerosol cans of ready-to-use frostings in many colors make decorating cakes and cookies easy. There is a selection of different decorating tops to use with each. Tubes of glossy decorating gel for writing are also available.

To Store Cakes

Unfrosted cakes should be cooled completely before storing. To store cakes, frosted or unfrosted, left in the pan, cover the top of the pan tightly with its lid, plastic wrap or foil. Layer cakes and frosted tube cakes should be kept in a cake keeper or under an inverted large bowl or pan.

Plan to serve cake with fluffy frosting the day it's made; the frosting gradually dissolves during storage. Store leftovers in cake keeper or under an inverted bowl, but insert a spoon or knife handle under the top so air can circulate and help to keep the frosting fluffy.

Cakes with whipped-cream frosting or cream fillings should be kept refrigerated.

To store fruitcakes, wrap closely in plastic wrap or foil; keep in a cool place. If desired, pour brandy or wine over cake before wrapping; or dampen a cloth with brandy or wine and wrap cake in it, then in foil. Re-dampen cloth weekly. Glaze and decorate fruit cake after storing.

To Cut Cakes

Cut layer and loaf cakes with long, thin, sharp knife, using a sawing motion. Cut angel, chiffon and sponge cakes with a long serrated knife, using a sawing motion; or use a cake breaker. Fruitcakes can be cut into thin slices easily if thoroughly chilled.

To Freeze Cakes

Baked cakes freeze well; cake batter does not. Unfrosted cakes should be closely wrapped with freezer wrap, plastic wrap or foil and sealed with tape. Freeze and keep for as long as 4 to 6 months. Fruitcake will keep up to 12 months.

Frosted cake should be placed on foil-covered cardboard and frozen until frosting hardens; then wrap, seal and return to freezer. Creamy and fudge frostings freeze best. Frosted cakes may be kept 2 to 3 months in the freezer.

Do not freeze cakes with custard or fruit fillings; they may be soggy when thawed.

Thaw cakes with whipped-cream toppings or fillings, unwrapped, in the refrigerator for 3 to 4 hours. Thaw cakes with fluffy frostings, unwrapped, at room temperature. Other cakes, frosted or unfrosted, should be thawed, wrapped, at room temperature. Unfrosted layers take 1 hour to thaw; frosted tube cakes and layer cakes, 2 to 3 hours; cupcakes, 30 minutes.

Layers, Loaves and Cupcakes

FAVORITE YELLOW CAKE

2¼ cups cake flour
1½ cups sugar
¾ cup shortening
¾ cup milk
3 eggs
2½ teaspoons double-acting baking powder
1 teaspoon salt
1 teaspoon vanilla extract
½ teaspoon almond extract

EARLY IN DAY:
Preheat oven to 375°F. Grease and flour two 9-inch round cake pans. Into large bowl, measure all ingredients; with mixer at low speed, beat until well mixed, constantly scraping bowl with rubber spatula. Beat at medium speed 5 minutes, occasionally scraping bowl. Pour batter into pans and bake 25 minutes or until toothpick inserted in center comes out clean. Cool layers in pans on wire racks 10 minutes; remove from pans and cool completely on wire racks. Makes 2 layers.

Fill and frost with: Any Butter-Cream Frosting, page 549; Fluffy Boiled Frosting, page 549; Quick Fudge Frosting, page 549. Or fill with any Quick Cream Filling, page 552 and frost with "Four-Minute" Frosting, page 550.

PINEAPPLE-UPSIDE-DOWN CAKE: Before making above cake, prepare topping: In 13″ by 9″ baking pan, place *½ cup butter or margarine;* place pan in preheated 375°F. oven until butter melts. Sprinkle *2 cups packed brown sugar* over butter. Meanwhile, drain *one 15¼-ounce can pineapple chunks;* use pineapple to form "flowers" in sugar mixture. Use a drained *maraschino cherry* for center of each flower.

Prepare cake batter as above and carefully spoon over design. Bake 35 to 40 minutes until toothpick inserted in center comes out clean. Cool in pan on wire rack 10 minutes. Then loosen cake from sides of pan; place platter on top of pan and invert both; lift off pan. (If fruit sticks to pan, lift off with spatula and replace in design on cake.) Serve cake warm or topped with cream, whipped cream or vanilla ice cream.

NUT-SWIRL CAKE: Prepare and cool 2-layer cake as above. Prepare *1 package fluffy white-frosting mix* as label directs; use to fill and frost cake. With tip of spoon, swirl petal design on top of cake. Fill spaces between swirls with *1 cup chopped nuts.*

FRESH ORANGE CAKE: Prepare as above but substitute *2 teaspoons grated orange peel* for vanilla extract.

TWO-EGG YELLOW CAKE

3 cups cake flour
1¾ cups sugar
1¼ cups milk
½ cup shortening
2 eggs
2½ teaspoons double-acting baking powder
1 teaspoon salt
1½ teaspoons vanilla extract

EARLY IN DAY:
Preheat oven to 350°F. Grease and flour two 9-inch round cake pans or one 13″ by 9″ baking pan. Into large bowl, measure all ingredients; with mixer at low speed, beat until well mixed, constantly scraping bowl with rubber spatula. Beat at medium speed 4 minutes, occasionally scraping bowl. Pour batter into pans and bake round layers 30 to 35 minutes, or 13″ by 9″ cake for 40 to 45 minutes, until toothpick inserted in center comes out clean. Cool cake in pans on wire racks 10 minutes; remove from pans and cool completely on wire racks. Makes 2 layers or 1 cake.

Fill and frost cake with: Any Butter-Cream Frosting, page 549; any Cream-Cheese Frosting, page 550; Quick Fudge Frosting, page 549; Easy Penuche Frosting, page 549; Rich Chocolate Frosting, page 550.

CHOCOLATE-CHIP CAKE: Prepare cake batter as above but, after beating, stir in *½ cup semisweet-chocolate pieces,* chopped. Pour into 13″ by 9″ baking pan. Prepare topping: In small bowl, stir *½ cup packed brown sugar, ½ cup chopped nuts* and *½ cup semisweet-chocolate pieces;* spread over batter. Bake 40 to 45 minutes until toothpick inserted in center comes out clean. Cool in pan on wire rack.

MARSHMALLOW-NUT TOPPED CAKE: Prepare and bake cake as above in 13″ by 9″ baking dish. Meanwhile, prepare topping: In small saucepan over medium heat, melt *¼ cup butter or margarine;* stir in *½ cup packed brown sugar;* remove from heat. Stir in *1 cup coarsely chopped California walnuts* and *1 cup miniature marshmallows.* Sprinkle over cake when it comes from oven. Turn oven control to broil and broil cake 3 to 5 minutes until marshmallows are melted and golden. Cool in pan on rack.

YELLOW CUPCAKES: Preheat oven to 350°F. Place paper liners in 2 dozen 3-inch muffin-pan cups, or grease and flour cups. Prepare batter as above but pour it into cups, filling each half full. Bake 20 minutes or until toothpick inserted in center of one comes out clean. Cool in pans on wire racks 10 minutes; remove from pans and cool completely on wire racks. Frost as above, if you like. Makes 2 dozen.

BITTERSWEET CHOCOLATE CAKE

1½ cups cake flour
1½ cups sugar
1 cup buttermilk
⅓ cup shortening
3 egg whites
3 squares unsweetened chocolate, melted
1 teaspoon baking soda
1 teaspoon salt

EARLY IN DAY:
Preheat oven to 350°F. Grease and flour two 8-inch round cake pans. Into large bowl, measure all ingredients; with mixer at low speed, beat until well mixed, constantly scraping bowl with rubber spatula. Beat at high speed 5 minutes, occasionally scraping bowl. Pour batter into pans and bake 30 to 35 minutes until toothpick inserted in center comes out clean. Cool layers in pans on wire racks 10 minutes; remove from pans and cool completely on wire racks. Makes 2 layers.

Fill and frost cake with: Quick Fudge Frosting, page 549; Mocha Butter Cream, page 549; Harvest Moon Frosting, page 550; Marshmallow "Seven-Minute" Frosting, page 550.

WALNUT-FUDGE CAKE

2 cups California walnuts
8 eggs, separated
1½ cups confectioners' sugar
1 cup unsalted butter, softened
6 1-ounce squares semisweet chocolate, melted
3 tablespoons all-purpose flour
1½ teaspoons vanilla extract
Chocolate-Walnut Filling (below)
Thin Chocolate Glaze (at right)
California walnut halves for garnish

EARLY IN DAY OR DAY BEFORE SERVING:
1. Preheat oven to 325°F. In blender or with knife, chop 2 cups walnuts. Grease and flour three 9-inch round cake pans.
2. In large bowl, with mixer at high speed, beat egg whites until soft peaks form; beating at high speed, gradually sprinkle in ½ cup of the sugar, 2 tablespoons at a time; beat until sugar is completely dissolved. (Whites should stand in stiff, glossy peaks.)
3. In another large bowl, at low speed, beat yolks and butter with remaining sugar, chopped walnuts, chocolate, flour and vanilla until well mixed, constantly scraping bowl with rubber spatula. Beat 4 minutes at medium speed, occasionally scraping bowl. With rubber spatula, gently fold in egg whites just until blended.
4. Pour batter into pans and bake 35 minutes or until toothpick inserted in center comes out clean. Cool layers in pans on wire racks 10 minutes; remove from pans and cool completely on wire racks.
5. Fill between layers with Chocolate-Walnut Filling. Spread Thin Chocolate Glaze over top and down sides of cake. Garnish with walnut halves; refrigerate.

TO SERVE:
Cut into thin wedges. Makes 16 servings.

CHOCOLATE-WALNUT FILLING: In blender, finely chop *2 cups California walnuts.* In double boiler, over hot, not boiling, water, melt *two 1-ounce squares semisweet chocolate.* Stir in *⅓ cup sugar,* chopped walnuts and *½ cup milk.* Cook over boiling water 5 minutes until sugar is completely dissolved. Remove from heat; with spoon, beat in *¼ cup butter or margarine,* softened, and *1 teaspoon vanilla extract* just until blended. Refrigerate just until cool.

THIN CHOCOLATE GLAZE: In double boiler over hot, not boiling, water, melt *one 6-ounce package semisweet-chocolate pieces* with *2 tablespoons shortening;* remove from heat. Beat in *2 tablespoons light corn syrup* and *3 tablespoons milk* until smooth; spread while still warm.

SPICE CAKE

2 cups cake flour
¾ cup sugar
¾ cup milk
½ cup packed brown sugar
½ cup shortening
2 eggs
2½ teaspoons double-acting baking powder
1 teaspoon salt
1 teaspoon cinnamon
1 teaspoon allspice
½ teaspoon ground cloves
½ teaspoon nutmeg
1 teaspoon vanilla extract

EARLY IN DAY:
Preheat oven to 350°F. Grease and flour two 8-inch round cake pans. Into large bowl, measure all ingredients. With mixer at low speed, beat just until blended, constantly scraping bowl with rubber spatula. Beat 3 minutes with mixer at high speed, occasionally scraping bowl. Pour batter into pans. Bake 25 to 30 minutes until toothpick inserted in center comes out clean. Cool layers in pans on wire racks 10 minutes; remove from pans and cool completely on wire racks. Makes 2 layers.

Fill and frost cake with: Fluffy Beige Frosting, page 550; Browned Butter-Cream Frosting, page 549. Or fill with Quick Butterscotch Filling, page 552; frost with Whipped-Cream Frosting, page 551.

SPICE CUPCAKES: Preheat oven to 350°F. Place paper liners in 2 dozen 3-inch muffin-pan cups, or grease and flour cups. Prepare batter as above but pour it into cups, filling each half full. Bake 20 minutes or until toothpick inserted in center of one comes out clean. Cool in pans on wire racks 10 minutes; remove from pans and cool completely on wire racks. Frost as above, if you like. Makes 2 dozen.

ORANGE-JUICE CAKE

2 cups sugar
¾ cup butter or margarine, softened
2½ cups all-purpose flour
1 cup buttermilk
3 eggs
1 teaspoon salt
1 teaspoon baking soda
1 teaspoon vanilla extract
1 cup chopped dark seedless raisins
1 cup coarsely chopped pecans
3 tablespoons grated orange peel
½ cup orange juice

DAY BEFORE SERVING:
Preheat oven to 350°F. Grease a 9- or 10-inch tube pan. In large bowl, with mixer at medium speed, beat 1½ cups sugar and butter or margarine until fluffy; at low speed, beat in flour, buttermilk, eggs, salt, soda and vanilla until well mixed, constantly scraping bowl with rubber spatula. Beat at medium speed 3 minutes, occasionally scraping bowl.

Stir in raisins, pecans and orange peel. Pour batter into pan and bake 55 minutes or until toothpick inserted in center comes out clean. Cool cake in pan on wire rack 10 minutes; remove from pan and place on wire rack over a sheet of waxed paper.

While cake is still very warm, in small bowl, stir orange juice with ½ cup sugar and pour over cake, spooning any drips from waxed paper back over cake. Cool completely. Makes 12 to 16 servings.

CHOCOLATE CAKE

2 cups cake flour
1¾ cups sugar
¾ cup cocoa
1¼ cups milk
¾ cup shortening
3 eggs
1¼ teaspoons baking soda
1 teaspoon salt
1 teaspoon vanilla extract
½ teaspoon double-acting baking powder

EARLY IN DAY:
Preheat oven to 350°F. Grease and flour two 9-inch round cake pans. Into large bowl, measure all ingredients; with mixer at low speed, beat until well mixed, constantly scraping bowl with rubber spatula. Beat at high speed 5 minutes, occasionally scraping bowl. Pour batter into pans and bake 30 to 35 minutes until toothpick inserted in center comes out clean. Cool layers in pans on wire racks 10 minutes; remove from pans and cool completely on wire racks. Makes 2 layers.

Fill and frost cake with: Coffee-Cream-Cheese Frosting, page 550; Coconut "Seven-Minute" Frosting, page 550.

CHOCOLATE CUPCAKES: Preheat oven to 350°F. Place paper liners in 2 dozen 3-inch muffin-pan cups, or grease and flour cups. Prepare cake batter as above but pour into cups, filling each half full. Bake 20 minutes or until toothpick inserted in center of one comes out clean. Cool in pans on wire racks 10 minutes; remove from pans and cool completely on wire racks. Frost as above, if you like. Makes 2 dozen.

APPLESAUCE CAKE

2¼ cups all-purpose flour
1 15-ounce jar applesauce (1½ cups)
1¼ cups sugar
⅔ cup shortening
⅓ cup milk
2 eggs
2 teaspoons baking soda
1 teaspoon cinnamon
½ teaspoon salt
½ teaspoon nutmeg
½ teaspoon ground cloves
1 cup dark seedless raisins
½ cup California walnuts, chopped
confectioners' sugar (optional)

EARLY IN DAY:
Preheat oven to 350°F. Grease and flour a 13″ by 9″ baking pan. Into large bowl, measure all ingredients except raisins, nuts and confectioners' sugar; with mixer at low speed, beat until well mixed, constantly scraping bowl with rubber spatula. Beat at high speed 3 minutes, occasionally scraping bowl. Stir in raisins and nuts.

Pour batter into pan and bake 40 to 45 minutes until toothpick inserted in center comes out clean. Cool cake in pan on wire rack. If you like, sprinkle with confectioners' sugar. Makes 12 servings.

THREE-LAYER PARTY CAKE

BATTER:
3 cups all-purpose flour
2 cups sugar
¾ cup butter or margarine, softened
4 eggs
3½ teaspoons double-acting baking powder
1 teaspoon salt
1 teaspoon vanilla extract

FILLING AND FROSTING:
1 9-ounce package coconut-pecan caramel-frosting mix
1 package fluffy white-frosting mix
1 tablespoon instant coffee
2 tablespoons toasted coconut for garnish

EARLY IN DAY:
Preheat oven to 350°F. Grease and flour three 9-inch round cake pans. Into large bowl, measure all batter ingredients and 1¼ cups water; with mixer at low speed, beat until well mixed, constantly scraping bowl with rubber spatula. Beat at high speed 4 minutes, occasionally scraping bowl. Pour batter into pans and bake 25 to 30 minutes until toothpick inserted in center comes out clean. Cool layers in pans on wire racks 10 minutes; remove from pans and cool completely on wire racks.

For filling, prepare coconut-pecan caramel-frosting mix as label directs; use to fill between cake layers. For frosting, prepare fluffy white-frosting mix as label directs, but stir instant coffee into mix before adding water; use to frost cake. Garnish cake with coconut. Makes 14 servings.

GERMAN GOLD POUNDCAKE

2 cups sugar
1 cup butter or margarine, softened
3½ cups cake flour
1 cup milk
6 egg yolks
1½ teaspoons double-acting baking powder
2 teaspoons vanilla extract
⅛ teaspoon salt

EARLY IN DAY:
Preheat oven to 350°F. Grease and flour 10-inch Bundt pan* or two 9″ by 5″ loaf pans. Into large bowl, measure sugar and butter or margarine; with mixer at high speed, beat until light and fluffy. Add flour and rest of ingredients; at low speed, beat until well mixed, constantly scraping bowl with rubber spatula. Beat at high speed 4 minutes, occasionally scraping bowl.

Pour batter into pan and bake in Bundt pan 1 hour or in loaf pans 45 to 50 minutes until toothpick inserted in center comes out clean. Cool cake in pan on wire rack 10 minutes; remove from pan; cool completely on rack. Makes 1 ring or 2 loaves.

* Bundt pan will give best, most attractive results.

SELF-FROSTING GERMAN CHOCOLATE CAKE

butter or margarine
½ cup packed light brown sugar
⅔ cup pecan halves
⅔ cup shredded coconut
¼ cup evaporated milk
1½ cups cake flour
1 cup sugar
½ teaspoon baking soda
½ teaspoon double-acting baking powder
½ teaspoon salt
¾ cup buttermilk
1 teaspoon vanilla extract
1 4-ounce bar sweet cooking chocolate, melted
2 eggs

ABOUT 1½ HOURS BEFORE SERVING:
1. Preheat oven to 350°F. In small saucepan over low heat, melt ¼ cup butter or margarine with brown sugar; spread in 9-inch square cake pan; sprinkle with pecans and coconut, then with evaporated milk.
2. In medium bowl, stir together flour, sugar, soda, baking powder and salt.
3. In large bowl, with mixer at medium speed, beat ⅓ cup butter or margarine until smooth. Add flour mixture, half of buttermilk and vanilla; beat at low speed until well mixed, constantly scraping bowl.
4. Add chocolate, eggs and remaining buttermilk; beat at medium speed 3 minutes, occasionally scraping bowl. Pour batter into pan and bake 45 to 50 minutes until cake springs back when lightly pressed with finger. Cool cake in pan on wire rack for 5 minutes; invert onto cake plate. Serve warm. Makes 1 small cake.

DELUXE MARBLE CAKE

2 squares unsweetened chocolate
1¼ cups sugar
1 teaspoon vanilla extract
½ cup butter or margarine, softened
2 cups all-purpose flour
¾ cup evaporated milk
3 eggs
2 teaspoons double-acting baking powder
1 teaspoon orange extract
½ teaspoon salt
½ teaspoon baking soda
confectioners' sugar

EARLY IN DAY:
1. Preheat oven to 350°F. Grease well one 9-inch springform pan. In small saucepan over very low heat, melt chocolate, ¼ cup sugar and ¼ cup water, stirring constantly. Stir in vanilla; cool.
2. Into large bowl, measure 1 cup sugar and all ingredients except chocolate mixture and confectioners' sugar; with mixer at low speed, beat until well mixed, constantly scraping bowl with rubber spatula. Beat at high speed 5 minutes, occasionally scraping bowl. Remove 2½ cups batter; beat chocolate mixture into remainder.
3. Alternately spoon batters into pan; with knife cut through batter a few times. Bake 55 to 60 minutes. (Top will be cracked.) Cool cake in pan on wire rack 10 minutes; remove sides of pan; cool cake on rack.
4. Sprinkle cake lightly with confectioners' sugar. Makes 10 to 12 servings.

ENGLISH LEMON CAKE

2 cups sugar
⅔ cup butter or margarine, softened
3 cups all-purpose flour
1 cup milk
4 eggs
2 teaspoons double-acting baking powder
2 teaspoons salt
1 4-ounce can blanched almonds, ground
¼ cup grated lemon peel
½ 6-ounce can frozen lemonade
  concentrate, thawed
confectioners' sugar

DAY BEFORE SERVING:
Preheat oven to 350°F. In large bowl, with mixer at medium speed, beat sugar with butter or margarine until light and fluffy; at low speed, beat in flour, milk, eggs, baking powder and salt until well mixed, constantly scraping bowl with rubber spatula. Beat at high speed 5 minutes, occasionally scraping bowl. Stir in almonds and lemon peel. (Batter will appear slightly curdled.)

Pour batter into ungreased 9-inch tube pan. Bake 65 minutes or until toothpick inserted in center comes out clean. Cool cake in pan on wire rack 1 hour; remove from pan to cake plate. Brush surface of cake with undiluted lemonade concentrate. Cover with foil; let stand overnight.

JUST BEFORE SERVING:
Sprinkle cake lightly with confectioners' sugar. Makes 12 to 16 servings.

MERRYFIELD APPLE CAKE

3 cups all-purpose flour
2 cups sugar
1 cup salad oil
3 eggs
1 teaspoon baking soda
1 teaspoon salt
2 teaspoons vanilla extract
3 cups diced, peeled cooking apples (about
  3 medium apples)
1 cup chopped California walnuts
½ cup chopped dark seedless raisins
confectioners' sugar

UP TO 1 WEEK AHEAD:
Preheat oven to 325°F. Grease well and flour two 8-inch square cake pans or one 13" by 9" pan. Into large bowl, measure flour and next 6 ingredients; with mixer at low speed, beat until well mixed, constantly scraping bowl with rubber spatula. Beat 3 minutes more, occasionally scraping bowl.

With spoon or rubber spatula, stir in apples, nuts and raisins; spread batter evenly into pans. Bake 1 hour or until cake is golden brown. Cool cakes in pans on wire racks 10 minutes; remove from pans and cool completely on wire racks. Wrap and refrigerate.

TO SERVE:
Place a paper doily over cake surface and sprinkle with confectioners' sugar; remove doily. Makes 18 servings.

SILVER-WHITE CAKE

4 egg whites
1½ cups sugar
2¼ cups cake flour
1 cup milk
½ cup shortening
1 tablespoon double-acting baking powder
1 teaspoon salt
1 teaspoon vanilla extract
¼ teaspoon almond extract

EARLY IN DAY:
Preheat oven to 375°F. Grease and flour two 8-inch round cake pans; line with waxed paper. In small bowl, with mixer at high speed, beat egg whites until soft peaks form; beating at high speed, gradually sprinkle in ½ cup sugar, 2 tablespoons at a time; beat until sugar is completely dissolved. (Whites should stand in stiff peaks.) Do not scrape bowl at any time. Set aside.

Into large bowl, measure 1 cup sugar and remaining ingredients; with mixer at low speed, beat until well mixed, constantly scraping bowl with rubber spatula. Beat at medium speed 3 minutes, occasionally scraping bowl. With mixer at low speed, beat in egg whites.

Pour batter into pans and bake 25 minutes or until toothpick inserted in center comes out clean. Cool layers in pans on wire racks 10 minutes; remove from pans and cool on racks. Makes 2 layers.

Fill and frost cake with: Mocha Butter-Cream Frosting, page 549; Peppermint "Seven-Minute" Frosting, page 550. Or fill with Creamy Custard Filling, page 552; or Fresh Lemon Filling, page 552; frost with Snow Peak Frosting, page 550.

LUSCIOUS COCONUT LAYER CAKE: Prepare cake as above and fill and frost with Coconut "Seven-Minute" Frosting, page 550.

LADY BALTIMORE CAKE: Prepare and cool 2-layer cake as above. With sharp knife, split layers. In small bowl, combine *½ cup candied cherries,* chopped; *⅓ cup dried figs,* chopped; *⅓ cup raisins,* chopped; and *¼ cup chopped pecans;* set aside. Prepare 2 *packages fluffy white-frosting mix* as label directs; stir fruit mixture into 3 cups of the frosting; use as filling. Spread remaining frosting on top and sides of cake.

DEVIL'S FOOD CAKE

2 cups cake flour
1½ cups sugar
1¼ cups buttermilk
½ cup shortening
3 eggs
3 squares unsweetened chocolate, melted
1½ teaspoons baking soda
1 teaspoon salt
1 teaspoon vanilla extract
½ teaspoon double-acting baking powder

EARLY IN DAY:
Preheat oven to 350°F. Grease and flour two 9-inch round cake pans. Into large bowl, measure all ingredients; with mixer at low speed, beat until well mixed, constantly scraping bowl with rubber spatula. Beat at high speed 5 minutes, occasionally scraping bowl. Pour batter into pans and bake 25 to 30 minutes until toothpick inserted in center comes out clean. Cool on wire racks 10 minutes; remove from pans; cool completely on racks. Makes 2 layers.

Fill and frost cake with: Quick Fudge Frosting, page 549; Snow Peak Frosting, page 550; Mocha Butter Cream, page 549; Orange Cream-Cheese Frosting, page 550.

CHOCOLATE RUM CAKE

Devil's Food Cake (above)
¼ cup sugar
½ cup dark rum
1 cup heavy or whipping cream, whipped
Dark Chocolate Coating (page 551)

EARLY IN DAY:
Preheat oven to 350°F. Grease well 15½" by 10½" jelly-roll pan; line with waxed paper; grease paper. Prepare Devil's Food Cake as directed but pour into jelly-roll pan and bake 30 minutes or until toothpick inserted in center comes out clean. Cool on rack 10 minutes; invert from pan. Remove paper and cool cake, top side up, on rack.

With fork, prick holes in cake. In small saucepan over medium heat, heat sugar and ⅓ cup water to boiling; boil 3 minutes. Stir in rum. Pour evenly over cake. Let stand 30 minutes.

Cut cake lengthwise into 3 strips. Place a cake strip on platter and spread with half of whipped cream. Stack with second strip; spread with remaining whipped cream, then top with third strip and frost top of cake with Dark Chocolate Coating. Refrigerate. Makes 12 to 16 servings.

BANANA CAKE

2¼ cups cake flour
1¼ cups sugar
1½ cups well-mashed ripe bananas (3 to 4)
½ cup shortening
2 eggs
2½ teaspoons double-acting baking powder
1 teaspoon vanilla extract
½ teaspoon baking soda
½ teaspoon salt

EARLY IN DAY:
Preheat oven to 375°F. Grease and flour two 8-inch round cake pans. Into large bowl, measure all ingredients; with mixer at low speed, beat until well mixed, constantly scraping bowl with rubber spatula. Beat at high speed 5 minutes, occasionally scraping bowl. Pour batter into pans and bake 25 minutes or until toothpick inserted in center comes out clean. Cool layers in pans on wire racks 10 minutes; remove from pans and cool on racks. Makes 2 layers.

Fill and frost cake with: Whipped-Cream Frosting, page 551. Garnish with thin slices of banana that have been dipped into lemon juice. Or fill and frost with Browned Butter-Cream Frosting, page 549.

SPICY GINGERBREAD

2½ cups all-purpose flour
1 cup molasses
½ cup sugar
½ cup shortening
1 egg
1½ teaspoons baking soda
1 teaspoon cinnamon
1 teaspoon ginger
¾ teaspoon salt
½ teaspoon ground cloves
1 cup boiling water

EARLY IN DAY:
Preheat oven to 350°F. Grease and flour one 9-inch square cake pan. Into large bowl, measure all ingredients; with mixer at low speed, beat until well mixed, constantly scraping bowl with rubber spatula. Beat at medium speed 3 minutes, occasionally scraping bowl. Pour batter into pan and bake 55 to 60 minutes until toothpick inserted in center comes out clean. Cool cake in pan on wire rack. Makes 1 small cake.

Frost with: Chocolate Cream-Cheese Frosting, page 550; "Four-Minute" Frosting, page 550. Or top with whipped cream.

Chiffon, Angel and Sponge Cakes

CHOCOLATE-CHIP CHIFFON CAKE

1 cup egg whites, at room temperature (7 or 8 egg whites)
½ teaspoon cream of tartar
1¾ cups sugar
2¼ cups cake flour
½ cup salad oil
5 egg yolks
1 tablespoon double-acting baking powder
1 teaspoon salt
2 teaspoons vanilla extract
3 squares semisweet chocolate, grated
Peppermint "Seven-Minute" Frosting (page 550)

EARLY IN DAY OR DAY BEFORE SERVING:
1. Preheat oven to 350°F. In large bowl, with mixer at high speed, beat egg whites and cream of tartar until soft peaks form; beating at high speed, gradually sprinkle in ½ cup sugar, 2 tablespoons at a time; beat until sugar is completely dissolved. (Whites should stand in stiff peaks.) Do not scrape sides of bowl during beating.
2. In another large bowl, with mixer at low speed, beat flour, 1¼ cups sugar, ¾ cup cold water, salad oil and next 4 ingredients until blended. Beat at medium speed until smooth, scraping bowl often. Fold in chocolate; gently fold mixture into egg whites.
3. Pour batter into ungreased 10-inch tube pan and bake 60 to 65 minutes until top springs back when touched lightly with finger. Invert cake in pan on bottle to cool completely. With spatula, loosen cake from pan and invert onto plate.
4. Frost with Peppermint "Seven-Minute" Frosting. Makes 12 servings.

BIG ORANGE CHIFFON

1 cup egg whites, at room temperature (7 or 8 egg whites)
½ teaspoon cream of tartar
1½ cups sugar
2¼ cups cake flour
¾ cup orange juice
½ cup salad oil
5 egg yolks
1 tablespoon double-acting baking powder
3 tablespoons grated orange peel
1 teaspoon salt

EARLY IN DAY:
Preheat oven to 325°F. In large bowl, with mixer at high speed, beat egg whites and cream of tartar until soft peaks form; beating at high speed, gradually sprinkle in ½ cup sugar, 2 tablespoons at a time; beat until sugar is completely dissolved. (Whites should stand in stiff peaks.) Do not scrape sides of bowl during beating. Set aside.

In another large bowl, with mixer at medium speed, beat 1 cup sugar with remaining ingredients until blended. With rubber spatula, gently fold in flour mixture.

Pour batter into ungreased 10-inch tube pan and bake 1 hour and 15 minutes or until top springs back when lightly touched with finger. Invert cake in pan on bottle; cool completely. Makes 1 cake.

JELLY ROLL

¾ cup all-purpose flour
1 teaspoon double-acting baking powder
½ teaspoon salt
4 eggs, separated, at room temperature
sugar
½ teaspoon vanilla extract
confectioners' sugar
1 10-ounce jar favorite jam or jelly

EARLY IN DAY:
1. Preheat oven to 375°F. Grease 15½" by 10½" jelly-roll pan; line with waxed paper. In small bowl, with fork, stir flour, baking powder and salt; set aside. In small bowl, with mixer at high speed, beat egg whites until soft peaks form; beating at high speed, gradually sprinkle in ⅓ cup sugar; beat until sugar is completely dissolved. (Whites should stand in stiff peaks.)
2. In large bowl, with mixer at high speed, beat egg yolks until thick and lemon-colored; beating at high speed, gradually sprinkle in ½ cup sugar. Beat in vanilla.
3. Sprinkle flour mixture over egg yolks; add beaten whites. With rubber spatula, gently fold mixture until thoroughly blended. Spread batter evenly in pan and bake 15 minutes or until top springs back when lightly touched with finger.
4. Meanwhile, sprinkle clean cloth towel with about ⅓ cup confectioners' sugar. Immediately invert cake onto towel; gently remove waxed paper; cut off crisp edges, if you like. Roll cake and towel from narrow end; cool completely on rack. Unroll and spread with jelly; reroll without towel.
5. Sprinkle roll with confectioners' sugar. Makes 10 servings.

COFFEE CLOUD CAKE

¾ cup egg whites, at room temperature (6 egg whites)
½ teaspoon cream of tartar
2 cups sugar
6 egg yolks
2 cups all-purpose flour
1 cup cold coffee
1 tablespoon double-acting baking powder
1 teaspoon vanilla extract
½ teaspoon salt
1 cup California walnuts, finely chopped

EARLY IN DAY:
Preheat oven to 350°F. In large bowl, with mixer at high speed, beat egg whites and cream of tartar until soft peaks form; beating at high speed, gradually sprinkle in ½ cup sugar, 2 tablespoons at a time; beat until sugar is completely dissolved. (Whites should stand in stiff peaks.) Do not scrape sides of bowl during beating. Set aside.

In another large bowl, with mixer at medium speed, beat 1½ cups sugar and egg yolks with flour, coffee, baking powder, vanilla extract and salt until light and fluffy. Sprinkle egg whites with nuts; with rubber spatula, gently fold flour mixture into whites, just until blended.

Pour mixture into ungreased 10-inch tube pan and bake 60 to 70 minutes until top springs back when lightly touched with finger. Invert cake in pan on bottle; cool completely. Makes 1 cake.

ANGEL-FOOD CAKE

1¼ cups confectioners' sugar
1 cup cake flour
1⅔ cups egg whites, at room temperature (12 to 14 egg whites)
1½ teaspoons cream of tartar
½ teaspoon salt
1¼ cups sugar
2 teaspoons vanilla extract
½ teaspoon almond extract

EARLY IN DAY:
Preheat oven to 375°F. In small bowl, stir confectioners' sugar and flour; set aside. In large bowl, with mixer at high speed, beat egg whites and cream of tartar, until soft peaks form; beat in salt. Beating at high speed, gradually sprinkle in sugar, 2 tablespoons at a time; beat until sugar is dissolved. (Whites should stand in stiff peaks.) Do not scrape sides of bowl during beating. With rubber spatula, fold in flour mixture and extracts just until they disappear.

Pour mixture into ungreased 10-inch tube pan. Bake 30 to 35 minutes until cake springs back when lightly touched with finger. Invert cake in pan on bottle; cool completely. With spatula, loosen cake from sides and remove to plate. Makes 1 cake.

SUGAR BUSH WALNUT CAKE

1 cup egg whites, at room temperature (7 or 8 egg whites)
½ teaspoon cream of tartar
1½ cups sugar
2¼ cups all-purpose flour
7 egg yolks
⅔ cup California walnuts, finely chopped
½ cup salad oil
1 tablespoon double-acting baking powder
1 teaspoon vanilla extract
1 teaspoon maple extract

EARLY IN DAY:
Preheat oven to 325°F. In large bowl, with mixer at high speed, beat egg whites and cream of tartar until soft peaks form; beating at high speed, sprinkle in ½ cup sugar, 2 tablespoons at a time; beat until sugar is dissolved. (Whites should stand in stiff peaks.) Do not scrape bowl during beating.

In another large bowl, with mixer at medium speed, beat flour with 1 cup sugar, ¾ cup cold water and remaining ingredients until blended. Gradually pour flour mixture over whites and, with rubber spatula, gently fold until just blended.

Pour batter into ungreased 10-inch tube pan and bake 1 hour and 15 minutes or until top springs back when lightly touched with finger. Invert cake in pan on bottle; cool completely. Makes 1 cake.

Start-with-a-Mix Cakes

FROSTED POUNDCAKE TORTE

1 16-ounce package poundcake mix
1 8-ounce package cream cheese, softened
¼ cup nonfat dry-milk powder
3 tablespoons heavy or whipping cream
1 teaspoon orange extract
1½ cups confectioners' sugar
½ cup California walnuts
1½ squares semisweet chocolate
1 teaspoon diced candied citron
Easy Mocha Frosting (below)

DAY BEFORE SERVING:
1. Bake poundcake mix in 9″ by 5″ loaf pan as label directs; cool. Cut thin slices from ends and top of cake to make even edges. Cut cake horizontally into 4 slices.
2. To make filling: In small bowl, with mixer at medium speed, beat cream cheese until smooth, about 1 minute. Beat in milk powder, cream and orange extract until well blended. Gradually add confectioners' sugar, beating at low speed until smooth.
3. On cutting board, chop and mix nuts, ½ square chocolate and citron; with rubber spatula, fold nut mixture into cheese mixture.
4. Place a cake slice on platter and spread generously with filling. Repeat with two more slices and filling; top with last slice. Frost. Grate 1 square chocolate and garnish top. Chill. Makes 10 servings.

EASY MOCHA FROSTING: In double boiler over hot, not boiling, water, melt *4 squares semisweet chocolate, 6 tablespoons butter or margarine* and *¼ cup strong coffee,* stirring constantly until smooth. Remove from heat. With mixer at medium speed, gradually beat in *1 cup confectioners' sugar* until smooth. Chill about 5 minutes. If too thick, add more coffee.

COCONUT-CREAM ROLL

1 package angel-food-cake mix
1½ cups heavy or whipping cream
2 cups shredded coconut
green grapes for garnish

EARLY IN DAY:
Line 15½" by 10½" jelly-roll pan with waxed paper. Preheat oven to 350°F. Prepare cake mix as label directs but spread in paper-lined pan. Bake 35 to 40 minutes until cake springs back when lightly touched with finger.

Cool cake in pan on wire rack 15 minutes, then invert cake onto cloth towel and peel off paper. Cut crisp edges from cake. From narrow end, roll cake and towel together; place, seam side down, on wire rack to cool.

ABOUT 15 MINUTES BEFORE SERVING:
Unroll cake and towel. In small bowl, with mixer at medium speed, whip cream until soft peaks form. With 1 cup whipped cream, spread cake to within ½ inch of edges; sprinkle cream with 1 cup coconut.

Reroll cake from narrow end. Place, seam side down, on platter. Completely frost roll with rest of whipped cream and sprinkle with rest of coconut. Garnish with grapes. To serve, cut into slices. Makes 8 servings.

APRICOT-BRANDY CAKE

1 18.5-ounce package sour-cream cake mix
1 2-ounce envelope whipped-topping mix
4 eggs
½ cup sugar
½ cup apricot brandy
Apricot Glaze (below)
canned apricots for garnish

EARLY IN DAY OR DAY BEFORE:
1. Preheat oven to 350°F. Grease and flour *well* 10-inch heavy cast-aluminum Bundt pan. In large bowl, with mixer at low speed, beat cake mix and whipped-topping mix with eggs and 1 cup water until moistened. Increase speed to medium and beat for 4 minutes.
2. Pour batter into pan and bake 45 minutes or until toothpick inserted in center comes out clean. Cool in pan on wire rack.
3. Meanwhile, in small saucepan over medium heat, heat sugar and ½ cup water to boiling; lower heat and simmer 1 minute. Remove from heat and stir in brandy.
4. While cake is still warm, using a long skewer or hibachi stick, make many holes through cake to bottom of the pan; with spatula, loosen cake from edges of pan. Slowly pour brandy mixture over cake, allowing mixture to soak in. Let stand at least 3 hours or overnight.
5. Onto wire rack over waxed paper, remove cake from pan, catching any excess brandy mixture on paper; spoon mixture over cake.
6. Transfer cake to platter; brush with Apricot Glaze and garnish with apricots. Makes 12 to 14 servings.

TO PREPARE UP TO ONE WEEK AHEAD: Prepare cake and soak with brandy mixture as in steps 1 through 5. Store in tightly covered container. At serving time, complete with Apricot Glaze.

APRICOT GLAZE: In medium saucepan over medium heat, heat *½ cup apricot preserves* and *2 tablespoons sugar* to boiling. Remove from heat and stir in *2 tablespoons apricot brandy;* use immediately to glaze cake.

COCONUT POUNDCAKE

2 16-ounce packages poundcake mix
1 cup shredded coconut
½ cup sugar
1 tablespoon lemon juice
grated orange peel for garnish

EARLY IN DAY:
Grease and flour 10-inch tube pan. In large bowl, prepare mixes as label directs but fold in shredded coconut. Pour batter into pan and bake 1 hour and 15 minutes or until toothpick inserted in center comes out clean. Cool cake in pan on wire rack 10 minutes; remove from pan and set on wire rack.

Meanwhile, in small saucepan over medium heat, cook sugar, lemon juice and ¼ cup cold water for 10 minutes or until mixture becomes syrupy.

With pastry brush, brush syrup mixture over warm cake. Garnish with orange peel. Cool cake completely before serving. Makes 10 to 12 servings.

STRAWBERRY-CHEESE ROLL

1 package angel-food-cake mix
confectioners' sugar
2 pints strawberries
1 8-ounce package cream cheese, softened
3 tablespoons milk
½ teaspoon nutmeg

ABOUT 1½ HOURS AHEAD OR EARLY IN DAY: Preheat oven to 350°F. Line a 15½" by 10½" jelly-roll pan with waxed paper. Prepare cake mix as label directs but spread evenly in paper-lined pan. Bake 35 to 40 minutes until top springs back when lightly touched with finger.

Sprinkle a cloth towel well with confectioners' sugar. Invert cake onto towel; peel off waxed paper. Cut crisp edges from cake. Then, from narrow end, roll cake and towel together; place, seam side down, on wire rack to cool.

When cake is cool, thinly slice 1 pint strawberries. In small bowl, with mixer at medium speed, beat cream cheese, milk and nutmeg smooth. Gently unroll cake; spread with cheese mixture. Cover cheese with sliced berries; reroll cake and sprinkle generously with confectioners' sugar. Place, seam side down, on platter; refrigerate.

TO SERVE:
Slice cake and serve with rest of strawberries. Makes 8 to 10 servings.

SIX-LAYER PARTY CAKE

2 packages yellow-cake mix for 2-layer cakes
1½ cups butter or margarine, softened
5 squares unsweetened chocolate, melted
5 cups confectioners' sugar
1½ teaspoons vanilla extract
¼ teaspoon salt
sweet cooking chocolate or semisweet squares for garnish

EARLY IN DAY:
1. Bake 1 package cake mix as label directs for two 9-inch round cake pans; repeat with second package; cool layers. Wrap and freeze one layer to use another day. With sharp knife, cut each of remaining three layers in half horizontally.
2. Prepare frosting: In large bowl, with mixer at high speed, beat butter or margarine until creamy. At low speed, beat in unsweetened chocolate, confectioners' sugar, vanilla and salt until well blended, occasionally scraping bowl with rubber spatula. If necessary, add 1 or 2 teaspoons hot water to make of spreading consistency.
3. Place first layer on cake plate, cut side up; spread with ½ cup frosting. Repeat until 4 more frosted layers are stacked on top. Top with last layer, top side up. Frost sides and top of cake.
4. From sweet cooking or semisweet chocolate, make chocolate curls (page 380); carefully arrange over top of cake.

TO SERVE:
With long, sharp knife, cut cake in half, then cut each half into 6 wedges. With help of knife and pie server, place each wedge on a dessert plate. Makes 12 servings.

ICE-CREAM-FILLED SPICE RING

2 pints coffee ice cream
1 package spice-cake mix for 2-layer cake
1 cup coarsely chopped California walnuts
Butterscotch Glaze (below)

DAY BEFORE SERVING:
With medium (number 16) ice-cream scoop, scoop ice cream into balls and arrange on chilled jelly-roll pan or cookie sheet. Freezer-wrap and freeze.

Grease and flour 12-cup ring mold. Prepare cake mix as label directs but fold walnuts into batter and bake in ring mold 40 minutes or until toothpick inserted in center comes out clean. Cool in mold on wire rack 10 minutes; remove from mold and cool completely on wire rack.

Spread Butterscotch Glaze on top of cake and garnish; cover.

TO SERVE:
Arrange ice-cream balls in center of cake. Serve immediately. Makes 8 to 10 servings.

BUTTERSCOTCH GLAZE: Set aside 2 tablespoons butterscotch pieces from *one 6-ounce package butterscotch pieces.* In double boiler over hot, not boiling, water, melt remaining candy with *2 tablespoons butter or margarine, 1 tablespoon milk* and *1 tablespoon light corn syrup* until smooth, stirring occasionally. Spread on cake; garnish cake with reserved butterscotch pieces.

PEANUT-BRITTLE CAKE

1 package orange chiffon-cake mix
2 2-ounce envelopes whipped-topping mix
1 teaspoon almond extract
½ pound peanut brittle

EARLY IN DAY:
Prepare cake mix as label directs; cool. Prepare topping mixes as label directs, substituting almond extract for vanilla; use to frost cake. With rolling pin, crush peanut brittle; sprinkle over cake. Refrigerate. Makes 10 to 12 servings.

CREAM-LEMON GINGER SQUARES

1 package gingerbread mix
½ cup orange juice
1 teaspoon instant coffee
1 teaspoon grated orange peel
1 teaspoon mace
1 2-ounce package whipped-topping mix
1 8-ounce package cream cheese, softened
¼ cup sugar
3 tablespoons milk
1 3¼- or 3⅝-ounce package regular lemon-pudding mix
1 tablespoon butter or margarine

EARLY IN DAY:
Add enough water to orange juice to make liquid required in gingerbread mix. Prepare mix as label directs but add instant coffee, orange peel and mace; use orange-juice mixture for liquid.

Prepare fluffy cream sauce: Make up topping mix as label directs. In small bowl, with mixer at low speed, whip cream cheese, sugar and milk until fluffy; fold topping into mixture. Refrigerate.

Prepare lemon sauce: In medium saucepan over low heat, heat pudding mix and 3 cups water to boiling, stirring constantly until slightly thickened; stir in butter until melted. Cover; refrigerate.

AT SERVING TIME:
Cut cake into 9 squares; top each with a spoonful of fluffy cream sauce and some lemon sauce. Use leftover sauces to make dessert (below). Makes 9 servings.

REFRIGERATED LEMON CREAM DESSERT: Stir leftover sauces together until smooth; chill until firm. Serve in dessert dishes next day.

MINI NESSEL-ROLLS

1 package orange chiffon-cake mix
confectioners' sugar
Nessel-Roll Filling (below)

EARLY IN DAY:
1. Preheat oven to 350°F. Line 15½" by 10½" jelly-roll pan with waxed paper; grease and flour. Line bottom and sides of 9" by 5" loaf pan with waxed paper. Prepare cake mix as label directs but pour half of batter (about 5 cups) into jelly-roll pan; pour remaining batter into loaf pan. Place pans in oven. Bake batter in jelly-roll pan 12 to 15 minutes or until cake comes away from sides of pan. Do not overbake. Continue baking loaf 40 more minutes; cool loaf completely in pan. (See below.)
2. While jelly roll is baking, sprinkle thin layer confectioners' sugar onto an 18-inch length of waxed paper. Cut another 18-inch length waxed paper into quarters and set aside. When jelly-roll cake is done, immediately invert onto sugared paper. Working quickly, peel off paper. Sprinkle another thin layer of confectioners' sugar over cake.
3. With sharp knife, cut cake in half lengthwise, then crosswise to make quarters. (With kitchen shears, cut waxed paper beneath cake, too.) Place reserved papers over cake pieces. Starting with long edge, tightly roll each cake piece with waxed paper; place rolls close together, seam side down, on rack; cool.
4. Unroll and peel waxed paper from one cake roll. Spread ¼ cup Nessel-Roll Filling in center of cake almost to edge. Roll cake just so edges touch, holding edges together for a few seconds to help seal. Place, seam down, on cutting board; cut into thirds. Repeat with remaining rolls; refrigerate.

JUST BEFORE SERVING:
Sprinkle thin layer confectioners' sugar over tops of rolls. Makes 12 servings.

ORANGE CHIFFON LOAF: Wrap and freeze loaf to serve later with ice cream or fruit sauce. Makes 8 to 10 servings.

NESSEL-ROLL FILLING: In small bowl, fold *1 cup frozen whipped topping* with *2 tablespoons chopped mixed candied fruit, 1 tablespoon grated orange peel* and *¼ teaspoon rum extract.*

APPLE-UPSIDE-DOWN GINGERBREAD

1 package gingerbread mix
2 tablespoons butter or margarine
¼ cup packed light brown sugar
1 large unpeeled cooking apple, cored
whipped cream for topping

ABOUT 45 MINUTES BEFORE SERVING:
Preheat oven as gingerbread-mix label directs. In 9-inch square cake pan, in oven, melt butter or margarine; stir in brown sugar until well mixed; spread evenly in bottom of pan. Cut apple into ½-inch-thick slices; arrange over sugar mixture.

Prepare gingerbread mix as label directs and pour evenly over apple slices. Bake as label directs or until toothpick inserted in center comes out clean. Cool in pan on wire rack 10 minutes; then invert plate over cake in pan; invert both and lift off pan. To serve, cut into squares; top with whipped cream. Makes 9 servings.

BANANA-GINGER PARTY CAKE

2 packages gingerbread mix
6 medium bananas, sliced
lemon juice
Whipped-Cream Frosting (page 551)

EARLY IN DAY:
Preheat oven to 350°F. Grease and flour 10-inch springform pan. Prepare gingerbread mixes as label directs but bake in springform pan 40 to 45 minutes or until toothpick inserted in center comes out clean. Cool in pan on wire rack 10 minutes; remove from pan; cool completely on rack. Dip banana slices in lemon juice.

Cut gingerbread in half horizontally, making 2 layers. Place one layer, cut side up, on serving plate; spread thinly with some Whipped-Cream Frosting. Cover with banana slices; spread half of remaining frosting over bananas. Top with second layer, top side up. Spread with rest of frosting; garnish with remaining banana slices. Refrigerate. Makes 16 servings.

FAMILY-SIZE BANANA-GINGER CAKE: Prepare as above but use 1 package gingerbread mix and bake in one 8-inch round cake pan as label directs. Use 4 bananas and half of frosting. Makes 8 servings.

RUBY PEACH ANGEL CAKE

1 package angel-food-cake mix
2 10-ounce packages frozen raspberries, thawed
1½ teaspoons lemon juice
1½ teaspoons cornstarch
1 peach, sliced

EARLY IN DAY:
Prepare cake mix and bake in 10-inch tube pan as label directs; cool.

In medium saucepan, place raspberries and their juice, reserving a few berries for garnish. Add lemon juice. Over medium heat, heat mixture to boiling, stirring constantly to mash raspberries.

In cup, stir cornstarch with 1½ teaspoons cold water until smooth. Over medium heat, slowly stir mixture into raspberry mixture; cook, stirring constantly, until slightly thickened. Press mixture through medium sieve into medium bowl; discard seeds. Refrigerate.

JUST BEFORE SERVING:
Place cake on platter; arrange peach slices on top, pinwheel fashion. Garnish with reserved berries. Spoon syrup over peaches, letting it drizzle down sides; pass remaining syrup. Makes 12 servings.

HATBOX DATE-FILLED CAKE

1 package white-cake mix for 2-layer cake
3 cups finely chopped pitted dates
dash salt
3 tablespoons brandy (optional)
1 can vanilla creamy frosting

EARLY IN DAY:
Prepare cake mix as label directs for two 8-inch round cake pans; cool.

Meanwhile, in medium saucepan over medium heat, cook dates, 1 cup water and salt, stirring occasionally, until water is absorbed; cool. Stir in brandy.

With sharp knife, cut layers into halves horizontally. Spoon ⅓ of date mixture evenly over 3 layers and stack; top with final layer, top side up. Frost top layer with vanilla frosting. (Use any leftover frosting on cupcakes next day.) Nice for picnics; pack carefully in hatbox to carry. Makes 12 to 14 servings.

AMBROSIA CAKE

1 package white- or yellow-cake mix for 2-layer cake
Quick Orange-Cream Filling (page 552)
Orange Glaze (below)
¾ cup flaked coconut

EARLY IN DAY:
Prepare cake mix as label directs for 2-layer cake. When cooled, fill with Quick Orange-Cream Filling; cover; refrigerate.

JUST BEFORE SERVING:
Prepare Orange Glaze and use to brush top and sides of cake. Sprinkle top with coconut. Makes 1 cake.

ORANGE GLAZE: In small saucepan over medium heat, heat *⅓ cup light corn syrup, 2 tablespoons orange juice* and *1 teaspoon grated orange peel* to boiling, stirring often.

ORANGE ANGEL SUPREME

1 package angel-food-cake mix
1 envelope unflavored gelatin
1 cup sugar
6 eggs, separated
½ cup lemon juice
½ teaspoon grated lemon peel
3 cups thinly sliced oranges, well drained
1½ cups heavy or whipping cream, whipped

EARLY IN DAY OR DAY BEFORE:
1. Prepare cake mix as label directs; cool. Remove cake from pan and wash pan.
2. In double boiler, stir gelatin with ½ cup sugar until well mixed. In small bowl, with fork, beat egg yolks with lemon juice and peel until mixed; stir into gelatin mixture. Cook over boiling water, stirring constantly, until mixture coats spoon. Add gelatin and stir until dissolved. Remove from heat; cool, stirring occasionally.
3. In small bowl, with mixer at high speed, beat egg whites until soft peaks form; beating at high speed, gradually sprinkle in ½ cup sugar, 2 tablespoons at a time; beat until sugar is completely dissolved. (Whites should stand in stiff peaks.) Do not scrape sides of bowl during beating. With rubber spatula, gently fold in slightly cooled custard.
4. With sharp knife, slice cake horizontally into fourths; return bottom layer to tube pan. Spoon ⅓ of filling evenly over cake layer and arrange 1 cup orange slices over filling. Repeat layers twice.
5. Add top layer; refrigerate, covered.

JUST BEFORE SERVING:
Loosen cake from pan and carefully invert onto cake platter. Frost with whipped cream. Makes 12 to 14 servings.

STRAWBERRY-FILLED ANGEL CAKE

1 package angel-food-cake mix
2 10-ounce packages frozen sliced strawberries, thawed
1 3-ounce package strawberry-flavor gelatin
confectioners' sugar

EARLY IN DAY:
Prepare cake mix as label directs; cool. Meanwhile, into small bowl, drain thawed berries, reserving syrup. In another small bowl, dissolve gelatin in 1 cup hot water; stir in reserved syrup. Refrigerate, stirring occasionally, until mixture is consistency of unbeaten egg white. Add strawberries; chill until almost set, stirring often, about 2 hours.

With sharp knife, cut cake crosswise into thirds. Spread bottom third with half of gelatin mixture almost to edge; top with second layer and spread with rest of gelatin mixture. Top with third layer, top side up; refrigerate.

TO SERVE:
Sprinkle cake with confectioners' sugar; cut into wedges. Makes 10 to 12 servings.

FLUFF-TOPPED SPICY CHOCOLATE CAKE

1 package chocolate-cake mix for 2-layer cake
2 teaspoons cinnamon
1 teaspoon nutmeg
1 2-ounce package whipped-topping mix
grated semisweet chocolate for garnish

EARLY IN DAY:
Prepare cake mix as label directs for two 8-inch round cake pans but add cinnamon and nutmeg to dry ingredients; cool. Prepare whipped-topping mix as label directs; use to fill and frost cake layers. Garnish with grated chocolate. Makes 10 servings.

PEPPERMINT-CHOCOLATE CAKE

1 package devil's food-cake mix for 2-layer cake
1½ teaspoons peppermint extract
Picnic Chocolate Frosting (below)
¼ cup coarsely crushed peppermint candy

DAY BEFORE:
Prepare cake mix as label directs for 13″ by 9″ cake but add peppermint extract to batter. Cool cake completely in pan; spread top of cake with Picnic Chocolate Frosting and sprinkle with candy; cover and refrigerate. Makes 12 servings.

PICNIC CHOCOLATE FROSTING: In small saucepan over very low heat, stir *5 squares unsweetened chocolate* and *¼ cup butter or margarine* until melted; remove from heat. In small bowl, combine *1½ cups confectioners' sugar, ⅛ teaspoon salt* and *⅓ cup milk;* stir into chocolate mixture until smooth. Chill in refrigerator for about 10 minutes until frosting is slightly thickened, stirring occasionally.

APRICOT ANGEL CAKE

1 package angel-food-cake mix
1 17-ounce can apricot halves
2 teaspoons lemon juice
2 drops red food color
2 drops yellow food color
5 teaspoons butter or margarine
2 tablespoons cornstarch

EARLY IN DAY:
Prepare angel-food cake as label directs; cool. Meanwhile, make apricot topping: Drain apricots, reserving syrup in measuring cup; to syrup, add lemon juice, red and yellow food colors; set aside.

In small skillet over medium heat, melt butter or margarine; add cornstarch, stirring constantly until mixture is well blended. Add syrup mixture and stir rapidly until sauce is thickened. Remove from heat.

In covered blender container at low speed, blend apricots 2 or 3 minutes until pureed. (Or, press fruit through food mill or coarse sieve.) Add pureed fruit to sauce and mix thoroughly; refrigerate. When chilled, spread mixture on top of cake and drizzle down sides. Makes 12 servings.

LEMON-GLAZED POUNDCAKE

1 16-ounce package poundcake mix
Lemon Glaze (below)
mint or lemon leaves for garnish

EARLY IN DAY:
Prepare poundcake mix as label directs but bake in greased 9-inch tube pan or 9-cup ring mold. Invert cake onto wire rack; remove pan and cool completely on wire rack.

With small spatula, spread glaze over top of cooled cake, allowing it to drip down sides. Garnish with lemon slices and mint or lemon leaves. Makes 10 servings.

LEMON GLAZE: Cut a few thin slices from one end of *1 large lemon;* set aside for garnish. Grate *1 tablespoon lemon peel* from remaining lemon into small bowl with *½ cup confectioners' sugar.* Gradually add *2 to 3 teaspoons lemon juice,* stirring with fork until well blended and of spreading consistency.

ORANGE-RAISIN CAKE

1 package yellow-cake mix for 2-layer cake
1 teaspoon orange extract
grated peel of 1 orange
1 cup dark seedless raisins
¾ cup brown sugar
1 cup orange juice
¼ cup lemon juice

ABOUT 1 HOUR BEFORE SERVING:
Preheat oven to 350°F. Prepare cake mix as label directs but, after beating, stir in orange extract, orange peel and raisins and bake in 13″ by 9″ baking pan. Bake 30 to 35 minutes until toothpick inserted in center comes out clean. Cool in pan on wire rack 10 minutes.

Meanwhile, prepare sauce: In small bowl, stir brown sugar with orange and lemon juices until sugar dissolves.

Invert deep platter over cake in pan; invert both and lift off pan. Prick top of cake with fork, then pour sauce over it; spoon any sauce that drips to bottom of platter back over cake. Serve warm. Makes 12 or 15 servings.

RAISIN-WHITE CAKE: Prepare recipe as above but use *1 package white-cake mix for 2-layer cake* and *golden raisins.*

DOUBLE-CHOCOLATE TORTE

1 package chocolate-cake mix for 2-layer cake
½ cup butter or margarine, softened
⅛ teaspoon salt
2 squares unsweetened chocolate, melted
1 teaspoon vanilla extract
2 eggs
2½ cups confectioners' sugar
2 tablespoons pistachio nuts, chopped, for garnish

EARLY IN DAY:
Prepare cake mix as label directs for two 8-inch round cake pans; cool.

To prepare frosting: In medium bowl, with mixer at low speed, beat butter or margarine with next 5 ingredients until well blended.

With sharp knife, cut cake layers in half horizontally. Spread each layer with ¼ of frosting; stack layers. Garnish top edge with chopped nuts. Makes 10 to 12 servings.

ANGEL-BERRY SHORTCAKE

1 package angel-food-cake mix
confectioners' sugar
2 2-ounce envelopes whipped-topping mix
3 pints large strawberries, halved
¼ cup blueberries for garnish

EARLY IN DAY:
Preheat oven to 350°F. With waxed paper, line bottom of 15½" by 10½" jelly-roll pan.

Prepare cake mix as label directs but spread batter evenly in paper-lined pan; bake 35 to 40 minutes until cake springs back when lightly touched with finger.

Meanwhile, cover large wire rack with sheet of waxed paper, then lightly sprinkle paper with confectioners' sugar. When cake is done, with spatula, loosen it from sides of pan; invert onto waxed paper. Lift off pan and peel off paper. Let cake stand at room temperature until cool, then return it to pan; wrap.

ABOUT 30 MINUTES BEFORE SERVING:
Prepare whipped-topping mix as label directs. With spatula, spread topping evenly over cake. Top with strawberries in rows; garnish with blueberries. To serve, cut into rectangles. Makes 9 to 12 servings.

CREAM-AND-CANDY CAKE

1 package angel-food-cake mix
4 1.1-ounce chocolate-wafer candy bars
1½ cups heavy or whipping cream

EARLY IN DAY:
Prepare cake mix as label directs; cool. Remove from pan.

Coarsely chop candy bars; set aside. In small bowl, with mixer at medium speed, beat cream until stiff peaks form; use to frost cake. Sprinkle candy on top and sides of cake. Refrigerate. Makes 12 servings.

BURNT SUGAR CAKE

⅓ cup packed dark brown sugar
¼ cup boiling water
1 package yellow-cake mix for 2-layer cake
Easy Penuche Frosting (page 549)

EARLY IN DAY:
In heavy skillet over medium heat, stir brown sugar constantly until melted. Then cook, stirring, until it smokes. Slowly stir in boiling water until sugar is dissolved; pour into measuring cup; set aside.

Preheat oven as cake-mix label directs. Prepare mix for two 9-inch round cake pans as directed but substitute burnt-sugar syrup for an equal amount of liquid called for in cake. Bake and cool as label directs.

Fill and frost with Easy Penuche Frosting. Makes 12 to 16 servings.

COCONUT-ORANGE-TOPPED GINGERBREAD

1 package gingerbread mix
1 orange
1 3½-ounce can flaked coconut (1⅓ cups)
½ cup packed light brown sugar

ABOUT 1 HOUR BEFORE SERVING:
Prepare gingerbread mix as label directs; cool in pan on wire rack 10 minutes.

Meanwhile, into medium bowl, measure 1 tablespoon peel grated from orange and 2 tablespoons juice from orange. Cut orange pulp into chunks. Stir orange chunks, coconut and sugar with orange peel and juice.

Preheat broiler if manufacturer directs. Spread orange mixture over cake; broil 1 minute until browned. Makes 9 servings.

Bittersweet Chocolate Cake, page 529, with Marshmallow "Seven-Minute" Frosting, page 550, and Chocolate Curls, page 380

MAPLE-NUT SQUARES

1 package yellow-cake mix for 2-layer cake
2 teaspoons imitation maple flavoring
1½ cups finely chopped pecans
½ cup packed light brown sugar
⅓ cup all-purpose flour
¼ cup milk
¼ cup butter or margarine, softened
2 teaspoons cinnamon

ABOUT 1½ HOURS BEFORE SERVING:
Prepare cake mix as label directs for 13″ by 9″ baking pan but add flavoring and ½ cup pecans; bake; cool in pan on wire rack 20 minutes.

Meanwhile, preheat broiler if manufacturer directs. For topping: In small bowl, thoroughly mix brown sugar with next 4 ingredients; stir in remaining pecans. Spread topping over cake; broil 2 minutes or until bubbly. Cut cake into squares; serve warm or cold. Makes 12 servings.

STRAWBERRY FESTIVAL CAKE

1 package yellow-cake mix for 2-layer cake
½ cup light rum (optional)
1 4-ounce package whipped-topping mix
1 10-ounce jar strawberry jam
6 strawberries, halved, for garnish

EARLY IN DAY OR DAY BEFORE:
Prepare cake mix as label directs for two 9-inch round cake pans; cool. With sharp knife, cut cakes in half horizontally to make 4 layers. If you like, spoon rum over layers.

Prepare 1 envelope whipped-topping mix as label directs; set aside. Spread ⅓ cup jam over each of three layers; then spread whipped topping over jam. Stack cake, putting plain layer on top.

Prepare second envelope whipped-topping mix and spread on sides and top of cake; garnish with berries. Makes 10 to 12 servings.

ANGEL DELIGHT

2 tablespoons butter or margarine, softened
2 tablespoons light brown sugar
4 angel-food-cake wedges

ABOUT 20 MINUTES BEFORE SERVING:
Preheat broiler if manufacturer directs. In cup, with spoon, mix butter or margarine with brown sugar. Lightly spread each cake wedge with ¼ of sugar mixture. Place wedges on cookie sheet; broil 2 minutes or until topping is golden. Makes 4 servings.

QUICK PARTY CAKE

1 pint lemon sherbet
1 10-ounce package frozen red raspberries, thawed
1 tablespoon cornstarch
1 tablespoon butter or margarine
1 9-inch round yellow- or white-cake layer

EARLY IN DAY OR DAY BEFORE:
With medium (number 16) ice-cream scoop, scoop sherbet into 8 balls; place on jelly-roll pan; cover, then freeze.

Drain raspberries, reserving syrup. In small saucepan, combine raspberry syrup with enough water to make 1 cup; stir in cornstarch and butter or margarine; cook over low heat until thickened and clear; add raspberries. Refrigerate.

AT SERVING TIME:
Reheat raspberry sauce, if desired. Cut cake into wedges and arrange each on dessert plate; top with sherbet ball; spoon sauce over all. Makes 8 servings.

BROILED FRUIT CAKE

1 9-inch yellow-cake layer
⅓ cup strawberry jelly
1 30-ounce can apricot halves, well drained
1 8-ounce can sliced cling peaches, well drained
2 tablespoons light brown sugar
⅛ teaspoon cinnamon
2 tablespoons butter or margarine

ABOUT 1 HOUR BEFORE SERVING:
Set cake layer on heatproof plate or tray. Over it, spread jelly, then top with well drained fruits. (Refrigerate any leftover fruits for another day.) In small bowl, stir brown sugar with cinnamon and butter or margarine until blended; dot over fruit. Refrigerate cake.

AT SERVING TIME:
Preheat broiler if manufacturer directs. Broil cake just until fruit starts to brown, about 5 minutes. Makes 8 servings.

Deluxe Cheesecake, page 291

QUICK RUM CAKE DE MAISON

1 package yellow-cake mix for 2-layer cake
1 teaspoon grated orange peel
½ cup light rum
Whipped-Cream Frosting (page 551)
Rich Chocolate Frosting (page 550)
1½ cups chopped California walnuts

DAY BEFORE SERVING:
Prepare cake mix as label directs for two 9-inch round cake pans but fold grated orange peel into batter; bake and cool.

With long sharp knife, cut layers in half horizontally to make 4 layers. Sprinkle each layer with 2 tablespoons rum. Place first layer on cake plate, cut side up; spread with one-third of Whipped-Cream Frosting. Repeat with 2 more layers. Top with last layer, top side up.

With Rich Chocolate Frosting, frost sides and top. Sprinkle nuts around sides of cake. Refrigerate overnight. Makes 12 servings.

FROZEN PINK ANGEL CAKE

1 package angel-food-cake mix
2 10-ounce packages frozen mixed fruits, thawed and drained
2 cups heavy or whipping cream
1 pint raspberry sherbet, softened

DAY BEFORE OR UP TO 1 MONTH AHEAD:
1. Prepare cake mix and cool cake in pan as label directs. Then remove from pan and place cake, top up, on platter. Wash pan.
2. With sharp knife, carefully cut a 1-inch slice from top of cake; set aside. Carefully hollow out cake, leaving shell about ¾ inch thick. (Reserve cake scraps to serve another day.) Return cake to pan.
3. Cut peaches from mixed fruits into bite-size pieces. In large bowl, with mixer at medium speed, beat heavy cream until soft peaks form. Reduce mixer speed to low and beat in softened sherbet until well blended; stir in cut-up peaches and rest of mixed fruits.
4. Spoon all but 1 cup mixture into hollowed cake. Replace top of cake and frost top with remaining sherbet mixture. Freeze until firm, then wrap tightly with plastic wrap and return to freezer.

TO SERVE:
Carefully remove cake from pan to serving plate. Let cake stand at room temperature about 15 minutes for easier cutting. Makes 14 to 16 servings.

ALMOND-PINEAPPLE ANGEL CAKE

1 package angel-food-cake mix
⅓ cup toasted chopped almonds
⅓ cup minced candied pineapple
almond extract
Whipped-Cream Frosting (page 551)
toasted blanched almonds for garnish

EARLY IN DAY:
Prepare cake mix as label directs but fold in almonds, pineapple and ¼ teaspoon almond extract just before pouring batter into pan. Bake and cool in pan.

ABOUT 1 HOUR BEFORE SERVING:
Prepare Whipped-Cream Frosting but add ½ teaspoon almond extract. Remove cake from pan; place on platter; frost. Garnish with almonds. Chill. Makes 12 servings.

CRANBERRY-ORANGE MERINGUE CAKE

1 package yellow-cake mix for 2-layer cake
1 14-ounce jar cranberry-orange relish
Meringue Frosting (below)

EARLY IN DAY:
Prepare cake mix as label directs for two 9-inch round cake pans; bake and cool.

About 1 hour later, preheat oven to 375°F. Place a cooled layer on cookie sheet; frost with ½ of cranberry-orange relish; top with remaining layer. Frost sides only with Meringue Frosting, making ¾-inch rim above cake top. Bake cake 10 to 15 minutes until meringue is golden.

With 2 pancake turners, lift cake to serving plate. Spread remaining cranberry-orange relish over top of cake. Makes 10 servings.

MERINGUE FROSTING: In small bowl, with mixer at medium speed, beat *3 egg whites* and *dash salt* until soft peaks form; at high speed, gradually sprinkle in *⅓ cup sugar*, 2 tablespoons at a time; beat until sugar is completely dissolved. (Whites should stand in stiff peaks.) Do not scrape sides of bowl during beating.

Fruitcakes

BRAZIL-NUT SENSATION FRUITCAKE

3 cups Brazil nuts
2 cups whole pitted dates
1 cup maraschino cherries, well drained
¾ cup all-purpose flour
¾ cup sugar
½ teaspoon double-acting baking powder
½ teaspoon salt
3 eggs
1 teaspoon vanilla extract

SEVERAL WEEKS AHEAD:
Preheat oven to 300°F. Grease 9″ by 5″ loaf pan; line with foil. In large bowl, stir Brazil nuts, dates and cherries. Measure flour, sugar, baking powder and salt into mixture; mix until nuts and fruits are well coated; set aside.

In small bowl, with mixer at medium speed, beat eggs and vanilla until foamy; stir into nut mixture until well mixed.

Pour mixture into loaf pan, leveling top. Bake 2½ hours or until toothpick inserted in center comes out clean. Cool loaf in pan on wire rack 15 minutes. Turn loaf out of pan; peel off foil; cool completely on wire rack. Wrap and refrigerate. Makes one 3-pound fruitcake.

MARASCHINO FRUITCAKE

1 28-ounce jar maraschino cherries, drained
1 15-ounce package dark seedless raisins
1 cup coarsely broken California walnuts
2½ cups all-purpose flour
1 cup sugar
½ cup butter or margarine
4 eggs
1 teaspoon vanilla extract
½ teaspoon salt

SEVERAL WEEKS AHEAD:
Preheat oven to 300°F. Grease very well a 10-inch Bundt pan.* Halve cherries; drain on paper towels. In medium bowl, toss cherries, raisins and nuts with ½ cup flour until fruit is well coated; set aside.

In large bowl, with mixer at medium speed, beat sugar and butter or margarine until light and fluffy. At low speed, beat in remaining flour, eggs, vanilla and salt until well mixed, constantly scraping bowl with rubber spatula. Beat at high speed 5 minutes, occasionally scraping bowl. Fold fruit into batter.

Pour batter into pan, level top and bake 1½ hours or until toothpick inserted in center comes out clean. Cool cake in pan on wire rack 15 minutes; remove from pan and cool completely on rack. Wrap; refrigerate. Makes one 3¾-pound fruitcake.

* If you prefer, use well-greased 10-inch tube pan and bake for 2 hours and 15 minutes or until done.

GRAHAM-CRACKER FRUITCAKE

2 cups dark seedless raisins
2 cups golden raisins
1 cup pitted dates, chopped
½ cup halved candied cherries
⅔ cup slivered candied pineapple
⅓ cup diced candied orange peel
¼ cup diced candied citron
1 cup chopped California walnuts
2 cups port wine
1 tablespoon vanilla extract
1 cup butter or margarine, softened
1 cup sugar
6 eggs
5 cups graham-cracker crumbs (1½ 13¼-ounce packages)
Fruitcake Glaze (page 551)

TWO TO 4 WEEKS BEFORE SERVING:
1. In large bowl, mix fruits and nuts, 1 cup port wine and vanilla. Cover tightly; let stand overnight or preferably 2 or 3 days.
2. Preheat oven to 250°F. In large bowl, with mixer at medium speed, beat butter or margarine and sugar until creamy. Beat in eggs, two at a time, until blended. Alternately beat in graham-cracker crumbs, a fourth at a time, with fruit mixture (including any excess wine) until thoroughly mixed.
3. Grease one 10-inch tube pan or two 9″ by 5″ loaf pans; line with foil; grease. Pour batter in pan; bake 3½ hours or until toothpick inserted in center comes out clean.
4. Cool cake in pan on wire rack; remove from pan and carefully peel off foil. Store at least 2 weeks, sprinkling with remaining wine. Glaze with Fruitcake Glaze before serving. (To store, see page 527.) Makes one 5- to 5½-pound fruitcake.

GOLDEN FRUITCAKE

2 cups golden raisins
1½ cups chopped dried figs (1 12-ounce package)
1 cup diced candied citron (2 4-ounce containers)
1 cup diced candied lemon peel
1 cup diced candied orange peel
1 cup chopped pitted dates
1 cup slivered blanched almonds or pecans
½ cup diced candied pineapple (1 4-ounce container)
½ cup candied cherries, halved (1 4-ounce container)
½ cup dried currants
all-purpose flour
1 cup butter or margarine, softened
2 cups sugar
2 teaspoons double-acting baking powder
½ teaspoon salt
6 eggs
1 teaspoon lemon or orange extract
1 cup dry sherry or orange juice
Fruitcake Glaze (page 551)

SEVERAL WEEKS AHEAD:
Preheat oven to 300°F. Line 10-inch tube pan with foil. In large bowl, combine first 10 ingredients and toss lightly with ¾ cup flour until fruits and nuts are well coated.

In another large bowl, with mixer at medium speed, beat butter or margarine with sugar until light and fluffy. Add 3 cups flour, baking powder, salt, eggs, extract and sherry or orange juice. Beat at low speed until well mixed, constantly scraping bowl with rubber spatula. Beat 4 minutes at medium speed, occasionally scraping bowl. Stir in fruit mixture until well mixed.

Pour batter into pan; bake 3 hours or until toothpick inserted in center of cake comes out clean. Cool cake in pan on wire rack; remove from pan and peel off foil. (To store, see page 527.) Before serving, top with Fruitcake Glaze. Makes one 7-pound fruitcake.

GOLDEN FRUIT CAKELETS: Place about 125 2-inch miniature foil baking cups in jelly-roll pans or on cookie sheets. Fill each ⅔ full with batter and bake at 325°F. for 30 to 35 minutes until toothpick inserted in center comes out clean. Makes 125 miniature fruitcakes.

DARK CHRISTMAS FRUITCAKE

3 cups dark seedless raisins
1½ cups diced candied citron (3 4-ounce containers)
1 cup candied cherries, halved (2 4-ounce containers)
1 cup diced candied pineapple (2 4-ounce containers)
1 cup pecan halves
1 cup slivered blanched almonds
1 cup dried currants
½ cup diced candied orange peel
½ cup diced candied lemon peel
all-purpose flour
6 eggs, separated, at room temperature
sugar
1½ teaspoons cinnamon
1½ teaspoons ground cloves
1 teaspoon nutmeg
½ teaspoon baking soda
1 cup shortening
½ square unsweetened chocolate, melted
¼ cup lemon juice
¼ cup orange juice
Fruitcake Glaze (page 551)

SEVERAL WEEKS AHEAD:
1. Preheat oven to 300°F. Line 10-inch tube pan with foil. In large bowl, combine first 9 ingredients and toss lightly with 1 cup flour until fruits and nuts are well coated.
2. In another large bowl, with mixer at high speed, beat egg whites until soft peaks form; beating at high speed, gradually sprinkle in ½ cup sugar, 1 tablespoon at a time; beat until sugar is completely dissolved. (Whites should stand in stiff peaks.) Do not scrape sides of bowl during beating. Set aside.
3. Into medium bowl, measure 1 cup flour, ½ cup sugar, egg yolks and rest of ingredients except Glaze; with mixer at low speed, beat until well mixed, constantly scraping bowl with rubber spatula. Beat at high speed 5 minutes, occasionally scraping bowl. With spoon, stir batter into fruit mixture. Gently fold egg whites into batter.
4. Pour batter into pan and bake 2 hours and 10 minutes or until toothpick inserted in center comes out clean. Cool cake completely in pan on wire rack; remove from pan and peel off foil. (To store, see page 526.) Before serving, top with Fruitcake Glaze. Makes one 5-pound fruitcake.

Fillings and Frostings

BUTTER-CREAM FROSTING

1 16-ounce package confectioners' sugar
6 tablespoons butter or margarine, softened
3 to 4 tablespoons milk or half-and-half
1½ teaspoons vanilla extract
⅛ teaspoon salt

In large bowl, with mixer at medium speed (or with spoon), beat all ingredients until very smooth, adding more milk if necessary to make of good spreading consistency. Fills and frosts 2-layer cake; frosts 13″ by 9″ cake, tube cake, or 2 dozen cupcakes.

LEMON: Prepare as above but substitute *lemon juice* for milk and omit vanilla.

MOCHA: Prepare as above but add *½ cup cocoa;* substitute *⅓ cup hot coffee* for milk and reduce vanilla to ½ teaspoon.

ORANGE: Prepare as above but add *2 egg yolks, 1 teaspoon grated orange peel* and use only about 2 tablespoons milk.

BROWNED: In small skillet over medium heat, heat butter or margarine until lightly browned; cool. Prepare as above.

CHOCOLATE: Increase butter to ½ cup. Melt, then cool, *3 squares unsweetened chocolate;* add with *2 egg yolks* to rest of above ingredients.

EASY PENUCHE FROSTING

½ cup butter or margarine
1 cup packed dark brown sugar
6 tablespoons milk
1 14- or 15.4-ounce package creamy vanilla-frosting mix

In medium saucepan over medium heat, in melted butter or margarine, heat brown sugar to boiling, stirring constantly; reduce heat to low and boil 2 minutes, stirring. Add milk; cook, stirring, until mixture boils again. Remove from heat; cool.

Pour cooled mixture into small bowl. With mixer at medium speed, gradually beat in frosting mix until smooth. Fills and frosts 2-layer cake; frosts 13″ by 9″ cake, tube cake, or 2 dozen cupcakes.

FLUFFY BOILED FROSTING

1¼ cups sugar
⅛ teaspoon cream of tartar
pinch salt
3 egg whites, at room temperature
1 teaspoon vanilla extract

In small saucepan over medium heat, heat sugar, cream of tartar, salt and 6 tablespoons water to boiling; boil without stirring to 260°F. on candy thermometer or until a little mixture dropped in cold water forms hard ball. Remove from heat.

In small bowl, with mixer at high speed, beat egg whites until soft peaks form. Pour syrup in thin stream into egg whites, beating constantly; add vanilla and continue beating until mixture forms stiff peaks. Fills and frosts 2-layer cake; frosts tube cake, 13″ by 9″ cake, or 2 dozen cupcakes.

QUICK FUDGE FROSTING

2 6-ounce packages semisweet-chocolate pieces (2 cups)
¼ cup shortening
3 cups confectioners' sugar
½ cup milk

In double boiler, over hot, not boiling, water, melt chocolate pieces with shortening. Stir in sugar and milk; remove from heat. With spoon, beat until smooth. Fills and frosts 2-layer cake; frosts 13″ by 9″ cake, tube cake, or 2 dozen cupcakes.

ORNAMENTAL FROSTING

1 16-ounce package confectioners' sugar
½ teaspoon cream of tartar
3 egg whites, at room temperature
½ teaspoon vanilla or almond extract

Into large bowl, sift sugar and cream of tartar (or press through very fine sieve). With mixer at low speed, beat in egg whites and vanilla; at high speed, beat until knife drawn through mixture leaves clean-cut path. (On humid days you may need to beat in more sugar.) Cover bowl with damp cloth. Use to make cake and cookie decorations with cake decorator or pastry tube. To tint, in small bowl, place some of frosting and stir in food color a drop at a time.

CREAM-CHEESE FROSTING

2 3-ounce packages cream cheese, softened
2 tablespoons evaporated milk
1 teaspoon vanilla extract
dash salt
1 16-ounce package confectioners' sugar

In small bowl, with mixer at medium speed, beat cream cheese with milk just until smooth. Gradually beat in vanilla, salt and sugar until blended. Fills and frosts 2-layer cake; frosts 13″ by 9″ cake, tube cake, or 2 dozen cupcakes.

CHOCOLATE: Prepare as above but increase milk to 3 tablespoons and add *2 squares unsweetened chocolate,* melted, to cheese.

ORANGE: Prepare as above but substitute *orange juice* for milk and *1 teaspoon shredded orange peel* for vanilla.

COFFEE: Prepare as above but, with sugar, add *4 teaspoons instant coffee.*

"SEVEN-MINUTE" FROSTING

1½ cups sugar
2 egg whites
1 tablespoon light corn syrup
1 teaspoon vanilla extract
½ teaspoon salt

In top of double boiler, with mixer at high speed, beat all ingredients with ½ cup water* until blended, about 1 minute. Place over rapidly boiling water; beat at high speed until soft peaks form (this may take more than 7 minutes). Pour into large bowl; beat until thick enough to spread. Fills and frosts 2-layer cake; frosts tube cake, 13″ by 9″ cake, or 2 dozen cupcakes.

* For crusty surface, use only ⅓ cup water.

CHOCOLATE: Melt *2 squares unsweetened chocolate;* cool. Prepare above frosting; fold in (don't beat) chocolate.

COCONUT: Prepare as above but use 1½ teaspoons vanilla extract and add *½ teaspoon orange extract* and *1 teaspoon almond extract.* Sprinkle filled and frosted cake with *shredded or flaked coconut.*

HARVEST MOON: Prepare as above but use *1½ cups packed brown sugar* for sugar.

MARSHMALLOW: Beat frosting over boiling water as above. Add *1 cup miniature marshmallows* (marshmallows will not dissolve). Pour into large bowl and finish beating.

PEPPERMINT: Prepare as above but substitute *¼ teaspoon peppermint extract* for vanilla; tint pink with *red food color.*

"FOUR-MINUTE" FROSTING (for small cakes): Halve each ingredient, using 1½ teaspoons light corn syrup. (If making variations, halve their ingredients also.) Cook as directed; beating over boiling water will take about 4 minutes; finish beating as directed. Fills and frosts 8-inch 2-layer cake; or frosts square cake or 1 dozen cupcakes.

RICH CHOCOLATE FROSTING

6 squares unsweetened chocolate, melted
1½ cups confectioners' sugar
3 eggs
½ cup butter or margarine, softened

In medium bowl, with mixer at low speed, (or with spoon), beat chocolate with sugar and 3 tablespoons hot water until blended. Add eggs, one at a time, beating well after each addition. Add butter or margarine; beat until smooth. Fills and frosts 2-layer cake; frosts tube cake, 13″ by 9″ cake, 2 dozen cupcakes.

SNOW-PEAK FROSTING

1¼ cups light corn syrup
2 egg whites, at room temperature
dash salt
1 teaspoon vanilla extract

In small saucepan over medium heat, heat corn syrup until boiling; remove from heat.

In large bowl, with mixer at high speed, beat egg whites until foamy; add salt and continue beating just until soft peaks form. Slowly pour in hot syrup, continuing to beat for 6 to 8 minutes until frosting is fluffy and forms peaks when beater is raised. Beat in vanilla. Fills and frosts 2-layer cake; frosts 13″ by 9″ cake, tube cake, or 2 dozen cupcakes.

FLUFFY BEIGE FROSTING: Prepare as above but use *1⅓ cups dark corn syrup.*

WHIPPED-CREAM FROSTING

2 cups heavy or whipping cream
¼ cup confectioners' sugar
dash salt
1 teaspoon vanilla extract

In small bowl, with mixer at medium speed, beat cream with sugar and salt until stiff peaks form; fold in vanilla. Keep frosted cake refrigerated until serving time. Fills and frosts 2-layer cake; frosts tube cake.

CHOCOLATE: Over hot, not boiling, water, melt *one 6-ounce package semisweet-chocolate pieces* (1 cup); cool. Prepare frosting as above but fold in cooled chocolate.

COFFEE: Prepare as above but add *1 teaspoon instant coffee* with sugar.

ORANGE: Prepare as above but add *1 teaspoon shredded orange peel* with vanilla.

PEPPERMINT: Beat cream and salt (no sugar) as above and fold in *¼ cup crushed peppermint candy;* omit vanilla.

CHOCOLATE GLAZE

In small saucepan over low heat, melt *2 squares semisweet chocolate* and *1 tablespoon butter.* With wire whisk or fork, beat in *½ cup confectioners' sugar* and *2 to 3 tablespoons milk* until smooth.

DARK CHOCOLATE COATING

2 squares unsweetened chocolate
2 tablespoons butter or margarine
1 cup confectioners' sugar

In small saucepan over very low heat, melt chocolate with butter and 3 tablespoons water, stirring constantly. Remove from heat; stir in sugar and beat with spoon just until smooth. Use immediately; coating stiffens as it cools. Frosts top of 2-layer cake; Boston Cream Pie, page 488; Eclairs, page 487.

FRUITCAKE GLAZE

In small saucepan over low heat, melt *¼ cup apple jelly;* brush over fruitcake. For garnish, make flower designs with *candied cherries* in centers and *blanched whole almonds* around cherries, pressing garnishes into cake. Let glaze set before serving.

COOK-ON PRALINE TOPPING

½ cup butter, margarine or shortening
1½ cups chopped, flaked coconut
¾ cup chopped nuts
¾ cup packed brown sugar
¾ teaspoon vanilla extract

ABOUT 10 MINUTES BEFORE CAKE IS BAKED: In medium saucepan over low heat, into melted butter, margarine or shortening, stir remaining ingredients until well mixed.

When cake is done, turn on broiler control. Spread mixture over hot cake. Broil 13" by 9" cake 2 minutes until golden.

FOR 8- OR 9-INCH CAKE LAYER: Prepare as above but use *⅓ cup butter, margarine or shortening, 1 cup chopped coconut, ½ cup chopped nuts, ½ cup packed brown sugar,* and *½ teaspoon vanilla extract.*

COOK-ON HONEY-COCONUT TOPPING

¼ cup butter or margarine
1½ cups shredded or flaked coconut
½ cup honey

ABOUT 10 MINUTES BEFORE CAKE IS BAKED: Prepare as Cook-on Praline Topping above.

FOR ONE 8- OR 9-INCH LAYER CAKE: Use *2 tablespoons butter or margarine, 1 cup coconut* and *⅓ cup honey.*

PINEAPPLE FILLING

¼ cup sugar
3 tablespoons cornstarch
⅛ teaspoon salt
¾ cup canned pineapple juice
2 tablespoons butter or margarine
1 tablespoon lemon juice
1 teaspoon grated lemon peel

In medium saucepan, mix sugar, cornstarch and salt; slowly stir in pineapple juice, then add remaining ingredients. Over low heat, heat mixture to boiling, stirring constantly; boil 1 minute until smooth and thickened; cool. Fills 2-layer cake.

FRESH LEMON FILLING

¼ cup sugar
2 tablespoons cornstarch
¼ teaspoon salt
1 tablespoon grated lemon peel
2 tablespoons lemon juice
1 tablespoon butter or margarine

In medium saucepan, stir sugar, cornstarch and salt with ⅓ cup water. Over medium heat, cook until mixture is very thick and boils briskly, stirring constantly. Reduce heat; simmer 1 minute, stirring occasionally. Remove from heat; stir in lemon peel, lemon juice and butter or margarine. Cool at room temperature. Fills 2-layer cake.

ORANGE: Prepare as above but substitute *grated orange peel* for lemon peel and *¼ cup orange juice* for lemon juice. Add *½ teaspoon lemon juice.*

QUICK VANILLA-CREAM FILLING

1 3- or 3¼-ounce package regular vanilla-pudding mix
½ cup heavy or whipping cream, whipped
vanilla or almond extract

Prepare pudding mix as label directs but reduce milk to 1½ cups; place piece of waxed paper on surface of pudding; refrigerate. When pudding is well chilled, remove paper; fold in whipped cream with a few drops of extract. Fills and tops 3-layer cake; fills 4-layer cake or 2 split layers.

QUICK ORANGE: Prepare as above but substitute *1½ cups orange juice* for milk. With whipped cream, add *1 tablespoon grated orange peel.*

QUICK PINEAPPLE: Prepare as above but substitute *½ cup drained canned crushed pineapple* for whipped cream.

QUICK CHOCOLATE: Prepare as above but substitute *one 3¾- or 4-ounce package regular chocolate-pudding mix* for vanilla pudding; reduce milk to 1½ cups. Into hot pudding, stir *2 tablespoons brown sugar.* Omit cream if you prefer a less rich filling.

QUICK BUTTERSCOTCH: Prepare as above but substitute *one 3¾- or 4-ounce package regular butterscotch-pudding mix* for vanilla pudding; reduce milk to 1½ cups. Into hot pudding, stir *2 tablespoons brown sugar* and *3 tablespoons butter or margarine* until blended. Omit cream, if you like.

QUICK LEMON: Substitute *one 3¼- or 3⅝-ounce package regular lemon-pie-filling mix* for vanilla pudding. Prepare as label directs. Omit cream, if you like.

CREAMY MOCHA FILLING

2 eggs, separated, at room temperature
confectioners' sugar
1 cup butter or margarine, softened
2 squares unsweetened chocolate, melted
2 teaspoons instant coffee
1 teaspoon vanilla extract

In small bowl, with mixer at high speed, beat egg whites until soft peaks form; beating at high speed, gradually sprinkle in ¼ cup sugar; beat until sugar completely dissolves. (Whites should stand in stiff peaks.) Do not scrape sides of bowl during beating.

In large bowl, with same beaters, and with mixer at medium speed, beat 1¼ cups confectioners' sugar with egg yolks, ⅓ cup water and rest of ingredients until well mixed. With rubber spatula, fold in egg whites. Fills and tops 1 large angel-food cake, split into 3 layers.

CREAMY CUSTARD FILLING

¼ cup sugar
2 tablespoons cornstarch
dash salt
1 cup milk
2 eggs
1 teaspoon vanilla extract

In medium saucepan, stir sugar, cornstarch and salt with milk until smooth. Over medium heat, cook until mixture is thick and boils, about 5 minutes, stirring constantly. In small bowl, with fork, beat eggs slightly; into eggs, beat small amount of hot milk mixture. Reduce heat to low; slowly pour egg mixture back into milk mixture, stirring rapidly to prevent lumping. Cook, stirring, until thickened (do not boil). Stir in vanilla; cover surface with waxed paper; cool completely. Fills 2-layer cake.

Cookies

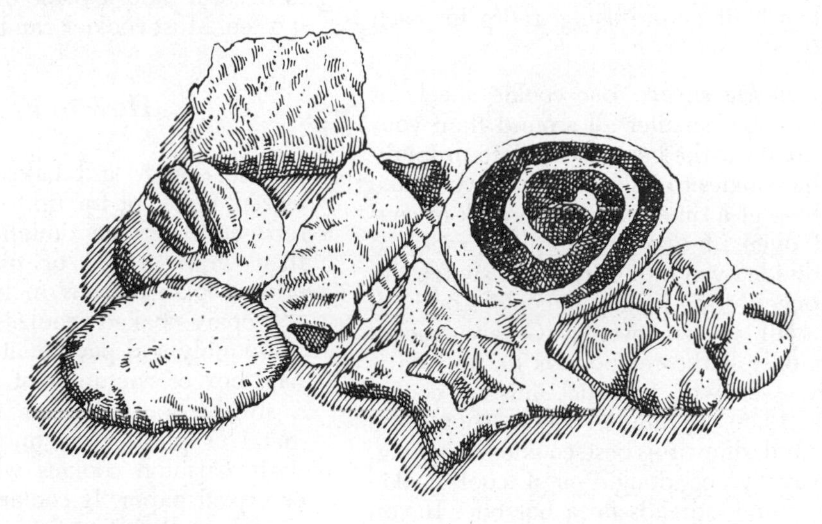

Basically the ingredients for all cookies are the same—flour, shortening, eggs, leavening, liquid, flavorings. But proportions vary, producing the soft or stiff doughs that make possible the many delightful kinds of cookies.

Baked cookies fall into six basic types:

Drop: Easiest and speediest of all. Soft dough is simply dropped from a spoon onto cookie sheets.
Bar: Easily mixed soft dough is turned into a shallow pan and baked, then cut into bars or squares. Individual cookies are baked in special molds or muffin cups.
Molded: Stiff dough is shaped between the hands into logs, crescents, balls, canes, wreaths and similar designs.
Pressed: Dough is forced through a cookie press or pastry tube into various shapes.
Refrigerator: Very stiff, rich dough is shaped into long rolls, chilled well so rolls can be sliced and baked hours or days later.
Rolled: Stiff dough is rolled out, cut into fancy shapes with knife and a pattern, or a cookie cutter or pastry wheel.

Into these classes also fall the cookies made from packaged mixes and refrigerated doughs, and those made with cereals and cookie crumbs that take no baking at all.

Tips for the Cookie Baker

Mixing ingredients: Ingredients used in these recipes are described in Ingredients, pages 12–17. Our recipes have been developed using flour that needs no sifting. To measure flour, see page 18.

The mixer will help you whip up a batch of cookies in no time. However, if you're using a spoon, use a wooden one with a comfortable, long handle so you can mix, stir and beat effectively.

Chilling dough: Chill the dough for molded cookies so it will be easy to handle. Flatten balls of dough in the palm of your hand, or with the bottom of a glass that has been greased or dipped in flour or sugar, or with the floured tines of a fork. Redip glass or fork for each cookie.

Chill rich dough for pressed cookies well, to help cookies hold their shape while baking.

Chill rolled cookie dough if it is too soft

to handle easily. To keep cookies for second rollings as tender as possible, save trimmings and reroll all at one time. When dough is chilled before using, use just a portion at one time, and keep the rest refrigerated until ready to use.

Roll dough for cookies on lightly floured surface, using floured stockinette-covered rolling pin. Dip cookie cutters or pastry wheel in flour before using; redip for each cookie.

Using cookie sheets: Use cookie sheets at least 2 inches smaller all around than your oven, to allow the heat to circulate properly and the cookies to bake evenly. If you bake one sheet at a time, place oven rack in center of oven; if two sheets, place racks so they divide oven into thirds, and switch the pans once during baking so cookies on both pans will brown evenly. Grease cookie sheets only if the recipe says to, and do it lightly, even with non-stick-finished cookie sheets. Plain aluminum sheets should be clean and shiny for best cookie browning.

Always place dough on a cool cookie sheet; dough spreads on a hot one. If you need extra cookie sheets, inverted baking pans may be used. Or cut a piece of heavy-duty foil to fit the cookie sheet. While the sheet of cookies is baking, place more dough on the foil; as soon as the cookie sheet comes out of the oven and is emptied, place foil with dough on it and return to oven immediately.

Drop dough for drop cookies 2 inches apart unless the recipe directs otherwise. With a teaspoon, scoop up the dough and with rubber spatula or tip of another teaspoon, push it off onto cookie sheet.

Cooling cookies: To prevent overbaking, with pancake turner, remove cookies from cookie sheets to racks as soon as they come from the oven, unless the recipe directs otherwise. Never overlap cookies, or place them on top of one another, until they are cold.

Cool bar cookies in the pan slightly before cutting them. If cut too warm, they will be crumbly.

Cookies that are to be dipped in confectioners' sugar after baking will look snowier if dipped twice—once while they are warm and again after they are cool.

How to Store

Keep cookies in a container with a tight-fitting cover. If crisp cookies soften, heat in 300°F. oven for 3 to 5 minutes before serving. Bar-type cookies may be stored right in the baking pan, tightly covered with foil or plastic wrap. If cookies tend to dry out, add a piece of apple, replacing it often. Most cookies can be frozen.

How to Freeze

Cookie dough and baked cookies can be frozen and kept for up to 6 months. Shape refrigerator-cookie dough in rolls or bars, then wrap in foil or plastic wrap. Pack other cookie doughs in freezer containers.

Prepare baked cookies as usual; cool thoroughly and pack gently in any freezing bag, box or container of suitable size. Use a sturdy container for fragile cookies—a metal or plastic box or coffee can if you wish. Cushion cookies with crumpled foil or waxed paper. If cookie has soft frosting or is decorated, first freeze cookies on clean cookie sheet until frozen; then pack.

Thaw refrigerator-cookie dough in refrigerator for about 1 hour or until it slices easily. Thaw other cookie doughs until they can be handled easily; shape and bake as usual. Unwrap frozen baked cookies and thaw them about 10 minutes.

How to Pack for Mailing

1. Choose travel-wise cookies that can stand a few knocks, such as long-lived soft drop cookies and packable bars and squares. Some good cookie travelers from this chapter include all bar cookies, Walnut Clusters, Soft Molasses Cookies, Chocolate Crackle-tops, Chocolate-Chip Cookies, Oatmeal Cookies, Peanut-Butter Cookies, Hermits.
2. Use a sturdy cardboard packing box, tightly covered plastic food containers or covered metal containers such as coffee or shortening cans. Metal containers are particularly recommended for mailing overseas. Line boxes with waxed paper, foil or plastic wrap; place cushion of crumpled waxed paper, paper towels or excelsior on bottom.

3. Put cookies in pairs, back to back, with waxed paper between; wrap in plastic wrap or bags, foil or waxed paper. Or wrap cookies individually, taping to seal well.
4. Place heaviest cookies at bottom and arrange layers with the cushion material between. Top with a layer of cushioning; seal top securely with freezer, adhesive or plastic tape.
5. Wrap box or container in heavy brown paper. Tie securely. Using permanent ink that won't smear if wet, label front with mailing address and return address; cover with clear tape or colorless nail polish. Mark the package "Perishable–Food."
6. Add correct amount of postage. For long distance and overseas shipment, cookies should be sent by air parcel post.

Short-Cut Cookies

Not much time to measure and mix? Then take a short cut; start with products designed to cut your time and work to a minimum.

Refrigerated slice-and-bake cookies offer a variety of flavor favorites–oatmeal-raisin, sugar, fudge brownie, peanut butter, chewy almond and others. They can be shaped and baked as the label directs or in delightfully surprising ways as in our recipes.

Packaged cookie mixes make possible a galaxy of brownies ranging from fudge to German sweet chocolate to butterscotch; date bars; chocolate-chip drops; oatmeal cookies; and others. There are treats to be made from buttermilk-biscuit mix and piecrust mix as well.

Packaged ready-to-eat cookies are the easiest of all. Serve them as is, or dress them up in one of these easy ways:

1. Spread plain or unfrosted filled cookies with canned frosting; sprinkle with chopped nuts, nonpareils, coconut or colored sugar.
2. For cookie sandwiches, spread filling of canned frosting between bottoms of two butter, oatmeal or chocolate cookies.
3. Spread chocolate or butter cookies with peanut butter; top with miniature marshmallows; broil just until bubbly.
4. Spread plain cookies with melted semisweet chocolate or butterscotch pieces.

Drop Cookies

SOFT MOLASSES COOKIES

2 cups all-purpose flour
½ cup sugar
½ cup shortening
½ cup light molasses
1 egg
2 teaspoons baking soda
1 teaspoon ginger
1 teaspoon cinnamon
¼ teaspoon salt
raisins for garnish

EARLY IN DAY:
Preheat oven to 400°F. Grease cookie sheets. Into large bowl, measure all ingredients except raisins. Add ⅓ cup cold water. With mixer at medium speed, beat until well mixed, occasionally scraping bowl.

Drop mixture by rounded tablespoonfuls, at least 2 inches apart, onto cookie sheets; place 4 or 5 raisins on top of each cookie. Bake 8 minutes or until top springs back when lightly pressed with finger. With pancake turner, remove cookies to wire racks; cool. Makes about 2½ dozen cookies.

WALNUT CLUSTERS

1½ squares unsweetened chocolate, melted
½ cup all-purpose flour
½ cup sugar
¼ cup butter or margarine, softened
1 egg
½ teaspoon salt
1½ teaspoons vanilla extract
¼ teaspoon double-acting baking powder
2 cups California walnuts, chopped
confectioners' sugar for garnish

EARLY IN DAY:
Preheat oven to 350°F. Grease cookie sheets. Into large bowl, measure all ingredients except walnuts and confectioners' sugar. With mixer at medium speed, beat ingredients until well mixed, occasionally scraping bowl with rubber spatula. With spatula, stir in walnuts.

Drop mixture by rounded teaspoonfuls, ½ inch apart, onto cookie sheets. Bake 10 minutes. With pancake turner, remove cookies to wire racks; cool. Sprinkle with confectioners' sugar. Makes 3 dozen cookies.

FRUITCAKE DROPS

1½ cups golden raisins
½ cup bourbon
¾ cup all-purpose flour
¼ cup packed light brown sugar
2 tablespoons butter or margarine, softened
1 egg
¾ teaspoon baking soda
¾ teaspoon cinnamon
¼ teaspoon nutmeg
¼ teaspoon ground cloves
2 cups pecans, chopped
3 4-ounce jars candied cherries, chopped (1½ cups)
1 4-ounce jar candied lemon peel, diced (½ cup)
1 egg yolk

EARLY IN DAY:
In medium bowl, stir raisins and bourbon until mixed; set aside for about 1 hour.

Preheat oven to 325°F. Grease cookie sheets. Into large bowl, measure flour and next 7 ingredients. With mixer at medium speed, beat ingredients until well mixed, stirring occasionally with rubber spatula. With spatula, stir in raisin mixture, nuts, candied cherries and lemon peel. Drop mixture by level tablespoonfuls, about 1 inch apart, onto cookie sheets.

In cup, beat egg yolk with 1 teaspoon water; brush on each cookie. Bake about 15 minutes or until firm. With pancake turner, immediately remove to wire racks; cool. Makes about 4 dozen cookies.

BRANDIED FRUITCAKE DROPS: Substitute ½ cup brandy for bourbon.

HERMITS

3¾ cups all-purpose flour
2 cups packed light brown sugar
1 cup butter or margarine, softened
4 eggs
¼ cup milk
1 teaspoon baking soda
1 teaspoon nutmeg
½ teaspoon cinnamon
½ teaspoon salt
2 cups dark seedless raisins
1 cup California walnuts, chopped

EARLY IN DAY:
Into large bowl, measure all ingredients except raisins and walnuts. With mixer at medium speed, beat ingredients until well mixed, occasionally scraping bowl with rubber spatula. With spatula, stir in raisins and nuts. Refrigerate, covered, until well chilled, about 3 hours.

TO BAKE:
Preheat oven to 375°F. Grease cookie sheets. Drop mixture by heaping tablespoonfuls, 2 inches apart, onto cookie sheets. Bake 15 minutes or until golden brown. With pancake turner, immediately remove cookies to wire racks; cool. Makes about 3 dozen cookies.

CHOCOLATE-COOKIE CAKES

3 squares unsweetened chocolate, melted
1¾ cups all-purpose flour
¾ cup packed light brown sugar
⅔ cup milk
½ cup butter or margarine
1 egg
1 teaspoon vanilla extract
½ teaspoon double-acting baking powder
¼ teaspoon baking soda
¼ teaspoon salt
Chocolate Frosting (below)
½ cup chopped pistachio nuts

EARLY IN DAY:
Preheat oven to 350°F. Grease cookie sheets. Into large bowl, measure all ingredients except Chocolate Frosting and nuts. With mixer at medium speed, beat until well mixed, occasionally scraping bowl with rubber spatula.

Drop mixture by heaping tablespoonfuls, 2 inches apart, onto cookie sheets. Bake 10 minutes or until firm when lightly pressed with finger. With pancake turner, immediately remove cookies to wire racks; cool.

Meanwhile, prepare Chocolate Frosting. Generously frost each cookie; sprinkle with nuts. Makes about 2½ dozen cookies.

CHOCOLATE FROSTING: In double boiler over hot, not boiling, water, melt *1½ cups semisweet-chocolate pieces* with *⅓ cup milk* and *3 tablespoons butter or margarine;* remove from heat and, with spoon, beat in *3 cups confectioners' sugar* and *1½ teaspoons vanilla extract;* use immediately to frost cooled cookies.

ALMOND LACE ROLLS

⅔ cup blanched almonds, ground
½ cup sugar
½ cup butter or margarine
1 tablespoon all-purpose flour
2 tablespoons milk
confectioners' sugar

EARLY IN DAY:*
Preheat oven to 350°F. Grease and flour large cookie sheet. Into large skillet, measure all ingredients except confectioners' sugar. Cook over low heat, stirring, until butter or margarine is melted and mixture is blended. Keeping mixture warm over very low heat, drop 4 heaping teaspoonfuls, 2 inches apart, onto cookie sheet. Bake 5 minutes or until golden.

Remove cookie sheet from oven and, with pancake turner, quickly remove cookies, one by one, and roll around handle of wooden spoon. (If cookies get too hard to roll, reheat in oven a minute to soften.) Cool. Repeat until all batter is used, greasing and flouring cookie sheet each time.

TO SERVE:
Lightly dust cookies with confectioners' sugar. Makes about 2½ dozen cookies.

* Mixture will be hard to handle on humid days.

PECAN COOKIES

2 egg whites, at room temperature
2 cups confectioners' sugar
1 teaspoon cider vinegar
1 teaspoon vanilla extract
2 cups pecan halves

EARLY IN DAY:
Preheat oven to 300°F. Grease cookie sheets. In small bowl, with mixer at high speed, beat egg whites until soft peaks form. Beating at high speed, gradually sprinkle in sugar, a few tablespoons at a time; beat until sugar is completely dissolved. (Whites should stand in stiff peaks.) Do not scrape sides of bowl during beating. Beat in vinegar and vanilla. Fold in pecan halves.

Drop mixture by heaping teaspoonfuls, 2 inches apart, onto cookie sheets. Bake 12 to 15 minutes. (Cookies remain light.) With pancake turner, remove cookies to wire racks; cool. Makes 3½ dozen cookies.

DATE-NUT COOKIES

2¾ cups all-purpose flour
1½ cups sugar
1 cup shortening
3 eggs
1 teaspoon baking soda
1 teaspoon cinnamon
¼ teaspoon salt
1 8-ounce package pitted dates, chopped
1 cup California walnuts, chopped

EARLY IN DAY:
Preheat oven to 375°F. Into large bowl, measure all ingredients except dates and walnuts. With mixer at medium speed, beat until well mixed, occasionally scraping bowl. Stir in dates, walnuts, 1 tablespoon water.

Drop mixture by heaping teaspoonfuls, 1 inch apart, onto cookie sheets. Bake 12 to 15 minutes until golden. With pancake turner, immediately remove cookies to wire racks; cool. Makes about 6 dozen cookies.

CHOCO-PEANUT DROPS

all-purpose flour
2 squares unsweetened chocolate, melted
½ cup sugar
½ cup shortening
1 egg
1 teaspoon salt
1 teaspoon vanilla extract
½ cup packed light brown sugar
¼ cup peanut butter
2 tablespoons butter or margarine, softened

EARLY IN DAY:
Preheat oven to 325° F. Into large bowl, measure 1 cup flour and next 6 ingredients. With mixer at medium speed, beat ingredients until well mixed, occasionally scraping bowl; set aside. Wash beaters.

In small bowl, with mixer at medium speed, beat 3 tablespoons flour, brown sugar, peanut butter and butter or margarine until well mixed, occasionally scraping bowl. (Mixture will be crumbly.)

Drop chocolate dough by teaspoonfuls, 1 inch apart, onto cookie sheet; top each with ½ teaspoon peanut-butter dough. Dip a fork into flour and press gently across top of each cookie. Bake 12 minutes or until firm. With pancake turner, remove cookies to racks; cool. Makes 4 dozen cookies.

CHERRY BITES

1 cup all-purpose flour
½ cup sugar
⅓ cup shortening
1 egg
2 tablespoons milk
1 teaspoon grated lemon peel
1 teaspoon vanilla extract
½ teaspoon double-acting baking powder
¼ teaspoon baking soda
¼ teaspoon salt
½ cup golden raisins
½ cup chopped California walnuts
1½ cups wheat flakes, crushed
1 4-ounce jar candied cherries (½ cup)

EARLY IN DAY:
Preheat oven to 400°F. Grease cookie sheets. Into large bowl, measure first 10 ingredients. With mixer at medium speed, beat ingredients until well mixed, occasionally scraping bowl; stir in raisins, walnuts.

Onto waxed paper, scatter wheat flakes. Drop dough by rounded teaspoonfuls, a few at a time, onto wheat flakes; toss lightly to coat. Place 2 inches apart on cookie sheets.

Halve cherries. Place a half on each cookie. Bake 12 minutes or until edges are golden. With pancake turner, remove cookies to racks; cool. Makes 3 dozen cookies.

OATMEAL COOKIES

1 cup uncooked quick-cooking oats
¾ cup all-purpose flour
½ cup packed brown sugar
½ cup California walnuts, chopped
½ cup shortening
¼ cup sugar
1 egg
½ teaspoon salt
½ teaspoon baking soda
½ teaspoon vanilla extract

EARLY IN DAY:
Preheat oven to 375°F. Into large bowl, measure all ingredients. With mixer at medium speed, beat ingredients until well mixed, occasionally scraping bowl.

Drop by teaspoonfuls, 1 inch apart, onto cookie sheet. Bake 12 minutes or until lightly browned. With pancake turner, immediately remove cookies to wire racks; cool. Makes about 4 dozen cookies.

CHOCOLATE-CHIP COOKIES

1¼ cups all-purpose flour
½ cup packed light brown sugar
½ cup butter or margarine, softened
¼ cup sugar
1 egg
1 teaspoon vanilla extract
½ teaspoon baking soda
½ teaspoon salt
1 6-ounce package semisweet-chocolate pieces
½ cup chopped California walnuts

EARLY IN DAY:
Preheat oven to 375°F. Grease cookie sheets. Into large bowl, measure all ingredients except chocolate pieces and nuts. With mixer at medium speed, beat until well mixed, occasionally scraping bowl with rubber spatula. Stir in chocolate and nuts.

Drop mixture by rounded teaspoonfuls, 2 inches apart, onto cookie sheets. Bake 10 to 12 minutes until lightly browned. With pancake turner, remove cookies to wire racks; cool. Makes about 4 dozen cookies.

PEANUT-BUTTER-AND-JELLY COOKIES

1 12-ounce jar peanut butter with marshmallow*
¾ cup milk
2 cups buttermilk-biscuit mix
½ cup shredded, chopped coconut
½ cup grape jelly

EARLY IN DAY:
Preheat oven to 400°F. In large bowl, with mixer at low speed, beat peanut butter with marshmallow and milk. Gradually beat in biscuit mix. Stir in coconut. Drop dough by teaspoonfuls, about 2 inches apart, onto cookie sheets.

With greased and sugar-coated bottom of glass, flatten each spoonful of dough into a 2½-inch circle. Bake 8 to 10 minutes until cookies are slightly browned around edges. With pancake turner, immediately remove cookies to wire racks; cool.

On bottoms of half of cookies evenly spread 1 teaspoon jelly; top with remaining cookies, tops up, to form sandwiches. Makes about 2 dozen sandwich cookies.

* Or, use ¾ cup creamy peanut butter and ¾ cup marshmallow cream.

Bar Cookies

MINCEMEAT SQUARES

1½ cups uncooked quick-cooking or old-fashioned oats
1 cup all-purpose flour
½ cup butter or margarine, softened
¼ cup packed light brown sugar
¼ cup milk
1 teaspoon grated lemon peel
½ teaspoon cinnamon
½ teaspoon nutmeg
¼ teaspoon salt
¼ teaspoon baking soda
1 cup mincemeat

EARLY IN DAY:
Preheat oven to 350°F. Grease well an 8″ by 8″ baking pan. Into large bowl, measure all ingredients except mincemeat. With mixer at medium speed, beat ingredients until well mixed, occasionally scraping bowl with rubber spatula.

Pat half of mixture into bottom of pan; spoon mincemeat evenly over layer. Drop spoonfuls of remaining oat mixture evenly over mincemeat; gently pat into even layer to cover mincemeat. Bake 25 to 30 minutes. Cool in pan on rack; cut into squares. Makes 16 cookies.

APRICOT-CARAMEL BARS

1 14-ounce package vanilla caramels
¼ cup butter or margarine
1 cup marshmallow cream
½ teaspoon vanilla extract
5 cups puffed-wheat cereal
¾ cup chopped dried apricots

EARLY IN DAY:
In double boiler over boiling water, melt caramels with butter or margarine until blended, about 30 minutes, stirring occasionally. With fork, beat in marshmallow cream and vanilla.

Meanwhile, grease 9″ by 9″ pan. In large bowl, mix cereal and apricots. Pour hot caramel mixture over cereal mixture and mix well; press mixture firmly into pan and set aside to become firm, about 1 hour. Cut into bars. Makes 12 cookies.

ROCKY-ROAD BROWNIES

1 16½- or 17¼-ounce package walnut-brownie mix
2 squares unsweetened chocolate
2 tablespoons butter or margarine
1 cup confectioners' sugar
2 cups miniature marshmallows

EARLY IN DAY:
Prepare brownies as label directs. Meanwhile, in medium saucepan over low heat, melt chocolate and butter or margarine with 3 tablespoons water; stir well. Remove pan from heat and stir in sugar until smooth.

Immediately on taking brownies from oven, cover with marshmallows; drizzle with icing. Cool in pan. Cut into 12 cookies.

LEBKUCHEN

2 cups all-purpose flour
1 cup coarsely broken California walnuts
1 8-ounce jar mixed candied fruits (1 cup)
1 teaspoon double-acting baking powder
1 teaspoon cinnamon
½ teaspoon ground cloves
½ teaspoon salt
3 eggs
1 egg yolk
1½ cups packed dark brown sugar
½ cup strong coffee or sherry
Snowy Glaze (below)

UP TO 2 WEEKS BEFORE SERVING:
Preheat oven to 375°F. Grease 15½″ by 10½″ jelly-roll pan. Onto waxed paper, measure first 7 ingredients; set aside.

In large bowl, with mixer at high speed, beat eggs and egg yolk until thick and lemon-colored, about 10 minutes; continue beating and sprinkle in sugar, a few tablespoons at a time. With rubber spatula, thoroughly blend in coffee and flour mixture; pour into pan.

Bake 25 minutes or until toothpick inserted at several points comes out clean. Cool in pan on wire rack. Frost with Snowy Glaze. Before frosting dries, with wet knife, mark into 2″ by 2½″ bars; when dry, cut. Makes about 2½ dozen cookies.

SNOWY GLAZE: In medium bowl, mix *1 cup confectioners' sugar* with *2 to 3 tablespoons milk* and *¼ teaspoon vanilla extract.*

CHEWY CARAMEL BROWNIES

2 cups packed light brown sugar
1 cup all-purpose flour
1 cup chopped nuts
½ cup shortening
2 eggs
2 teaspoons double-acting baking powder
2 teaspoons vanilla extract
¾ teaspoon salt

ABOUT 1 HOUR AHEAD OR EARLY IN DAY:
Preheat oven to 350°F. Grease and flour 15½" by 10½" jelly-roll pan. Into large bowl, measure all ingredients. With mixer at medium speed, beat ingredients until well mixed, occasionally scraping bowl with rubber spatula; evenly spread in pan.

Bake 25 minutes or until golden brown. Cool brownies in pan 5 minutes. Cut, and with pancake turner, remove to wire rack. Serve warm or cooled. Makes 2½ dozen cookies.

HOLIDAY FRUITCAKE BARS

1 cup diced mixed candied fruits (about ½ pound)
1 cup candied cherries, halved (about ½ pound)
1 cup diced candied pineapple (about ½ pound)
2 cups raisins
¾ cup sweet white wine (cream sherry, Marsala, muscatel, Madeira)
1⅓ cups all-purpose flour
1 cup packed light brown sugar
6 tablespoons butter or margarine, softened
2 eggs
1 teaspoon cinnamon
1 teaspoon ground cloves
¼ teaspoon baking soda
¼ teaspoon salt

UP TO 3 WEEKS AHEAD:
In medium bowl, mix fruits and wine. Cover and let stand overnight.

NEXT DAY:
Preheat oven to 350°F. Grease and flour 15½" by 10½" jelly-roll pan.

Into large bowl, measure flour and remaining ingredients. With mixer at low speed, beat ingredients until well mixed, occasionally scraping sides of bowl with rubber spatula. With same spatula, stir in fruit mixture.

Spread batter evenly in pan. Bake about 30 minutes or until toothpick inserted in center comes out clean. Cool in pan; cut into bars. Makes about 4 dozen cookies.

FUDGY BROWNIES

1 cup butter or margarine
4 squares unsweetened chocolate
2 cups sugar
4 eggs
1 cup all-purpose flour
1 teaspoon vanilla extract
½ teaspoon salt
2 cups coarsely chopped nuts

EARLY IN DAY:
Preheat oven to 350°F. Grease 13" by 9" baking pan. In large saucepan over very low heat, melt butter or margarine and chocolate, stirring constantly. Remove from heat and stir in sugar. Cool slightly.

Add eggs, one at a time, beating until well blended after each addition. Stir in flour, vanilla and salt; stir in nuts. Pour into pan. Bake 30 to 35 minutes until toothpick inserted in center comes out clean. Cool in pan on wire rack; cut into pieces. Makes about 2 dozen brownies.

NO-BAKE BROWNIES

1 12-ounce package semisweet-chocolate pieces
¼ cup butter or margarine
2½ cups graham-cracker crumbs
1½ cups chopped California walnuts
1 14-ounce can sweetened condensed milk
1 teaspoon vanilla extract

EARLY IN DAY:
In double boiler over hot, not boiling, water, melt chocolate and butter or margarine until smooth, stirring occasionally. Meanwhile, grease well 12" by 8" baking dish.

In large bowl, combine graham-cracker crumbs and walnuts; stir in condensed milk and vanilla extract until crumbs are moistened; then stir in chocolate mixture until mixed. Pat evenly into baking dish. Let stand at room temperature about 2 hours before cutting. Makes 24 brownies.

SHORTBREAD

2 cups all-purpose flour
1 cup butter or margarine, softened
½ cup confectioners' sugar
¼ teaspoon salt
¼ teaspoon double-acting baking powder
2 tablespoons sugar
1 teaspoon cinnamon

EARLY IN DAY:
Preheat oven to 350°F. Into large bowl, measure all ingredients except sugar and cinnamon. With mixer at medium speed, beat ingredients until well mixed, occasionally scraping bowl with rubber spatula; pat dough in 9″ by 9″ baking pan. In cup, mix sugar and cinnamon and sprinkle over dough. Bake 30 to 35 minutes. Cut into bars while warm. Makes about 20 cookies.

LUSCIOUS APRICOT SQUARES

⅔ cup dried apricots
all-purpose flour
½ cup butter or margarine, softened
¼ cup sugar
1 cup packed light brown sugar
2 eggs
½ cup chopped California walnuts
½ teaspoon double-acting baking powder
½ teaspoon vanilla extract
¼ teaspoon salt
confectioners' sugar

EARLY IN DAY:
1. In covered small saucepan over low heat, in enough water to cover apricots, cook apricots 15 minutes; drain and finely chop.
2. Preheat oven to 350°F. Grease 8″ by 8″ baking pan. Into large bowl, measure 1 cup flour, butter or margarine and sugar. With mixer at medium speed, beat ingredients until well mixed and crumbly; pat evenly into pan. Bake 25 minutes or until golden.
3. Meanwhile, into same bowl, measure ⅓ cup flour, apricots, brown sugar and remaining ingredients except confectioners' sugar. With mixer at medium speed, beat ingredients until well mixed, occasionally scraping bowl with rubber spatula; pour over baked layer and return to oven; bake 25 minutes longer or until golden.
4. Cool in pan; cut into squares. Sprinkle with confectioners' sugar. Makes 16 cookies.

COFFEE BROWNIES

⅓ cup butter or margarine
2 squares unsweetened chocolate
1 cup sugar
¾ cup all-purpose flour
2 eggs
2 tablespoons instant coffee powder
1 teaspoon vanilla extract
½ teaspoon double-acting baking powder
¼ teaspoon salt
½ cup chopped nuts

EARLY IN DAY:
Preheat oven to 375°F. Grease 8″ by 8″ baking pan. In small saucepan over very low heat, melt butter or margarine with chocolate. Pour into large bowl; add remaining ingredients except nuts. With mixer at medium speed, beat ingredients until well blended, occasionally scraping bowl with rubber spatula. With spatula, stir in nuts. Pour into pan.

Bake 25 minutes or until toothpick inserted in center comes out clean. Cool in pan; cut into squares. Makes 16 cookies.

MADELEINES

2 eggs
dash salt
⅓ cup sugar
1 teaspoon grated lemon peel
½ cup all-purpose flour
¼ cup butter or margarine, melted and cooled

EARLY IN DAY:
Grease and flour well each 3⅜″ by 2″ shell of one frame of 12 Madeleine shells. Preheat oven to 400°F.

In small bowl, with mixer at high speed, beat eggs and salt until soft peaks form; beating at high speed, gradually sprinkle in sugar, 2 tablespoons at a time; beat until mixture is thick and lemon-colored, 15 to 20 minutes.

With rubber spatula, fold in lemon peel. Sprinkle flour, about 2 tablespoons at a time, over egg mixture and gently fold into mixture. Fold in butter or margarine, about 1 tablespoon at a time. Fill shells about three-fourths full. Bake 8 minutes or until golden. Immediately remove from shells to wire rack; cool. Makes 12 cookies.

TOFFEE BARS

1¾ cups all-purpose flour
1 cup sugar
1 cup butter or margarine, softened
1 teaspoon vanilla extract
1 egg, separated
½ cup finely chopped California walnuts

3 TO 5 DAYS BEFORE SERVING:
Preheat oven to 275°F. Grease 15½" by 10½" jelly-roll pan. Into large bowl, measure all ingredients except egg white and walnuts. With mixer at medium speed, beat ingredients until well mixed, occasionally scraping bowl with rubber spatula; pat evenly in pan.

In cup, with fork, beat egg white slightly; brush over top of dough and sprinkle with nuts.

Bake 1 hour and 10 minutes or until golden. Immediately cut into 50 bars and remove from pan to cool on wire rack. Store in tightly covered container for at least 3 days before serving. Makes about 4 dozen cookies.

ALMOND-TOFFEE BARS: Prepare recipe as above but substitute ½ cup finely chopped, blanched almonds for walnuts.

BUTTERSCOTCH-CHEESE SQUARES

1 15-ounce roll refrigerated butterscotch-nut slice-and-bake cookies
1 8-ounce package cream cheese, softened
½ cup sugar
1 egg
½ teaspoon vanilla extract
California walnuts for garnish

EARLY IN DAY:
Preheat oven to 375°F. Grease well 8- or 9-inch square pan. Cut cookie dough into ¼-inch slices and arrange in 2 layers in bottom of pan. Bake 15 minutes or until puffy. Remove from oven and cool slightly.

In small bowl, with mixer at medium speed, beat cream cheese, sugar, egg and vanilla until smooth; pour over baked cookie layer and bake 25 minutes more or until toothpick inserted in center comes out clean. Cool in pan on wire rack; refrigerate. Cut into squares; garnish with walnuts. Keep refrigerated. Makes 16 cookies.

Molded Cookies

PEANUT-BUTTER COOKIES

2¼ cups all-purpose flour
1 cup creamy peanut butter
⅔ cup honey
½ cup sugar
½ cup butter or margarine, softened
2 eggs
½ teaspoon double-acting baking powder

UP TO 2 WEEKS BEFORE SERVING:
Preheat oven to 350°F. Into large bowl, measure all ingredients. With mixer at medium speed, beat ingredients until well mixed, occasionally scraping bowl.

With hands, shape dough into 1½-inch balls; place 3 inches apart on cookie sheets. Dip a fork into flour and press deeply across top of each cookie; repeat in opposite direction. Bake 15 minutes or until lightly browned. With pancake turner, immediately remove cookies to wire racks; cool. Makes about 3 dozen cookies.

FROSTY CRINKLES

2 cups all-purpose flour
1⅔ cups sugar
1 cup dark seedless raisins, chopped
½ cup California walnuts, chopped
½ cup butter or margarine, softened
⅓ cup milk
2 squares unsweetened chocolate, melted
2 teaspoons double-acting baking powder
1 teaspoon salt
confectioners' sugar

EARLY IN DAY:
Into large bowl, measure all ingredients except confectioners' sugar. With mixer at medium speed, beat ingredients until well mixed, occasionally scraping bowl. Cover and refrigerate 4 hours or until firm.

TO BAKE:
Preheat oven to 350°F. Grease cookie sheets. Sprinkle confectioners' sugar onto waxed paper. With hands, shape dough into 1½-inch balls. Roll balls in sugar until heavily coated; place about 2 inches apart on cookie sheets. Bake 12 to 15 minutes. With pancake turner, remove cookies to racks; cool. Makes about 3 dozen cookies.

CHOCOLATE CRACKLETOPS

2 cups finely ground pecans
3 squares unsweetened chocolate, finely grated
1 cup sugar
2 eggs
¼ cup dried bread crumbs
2 tablespoons all-purpose flour
½ teaspoon cinnamon
½ teaspoon ground cloves
confectioners' sugar

EARLY IN DAY:
Preheat oven to 325°F. Grease cookie sheets. Into large bowl, measure all ingredients except confectioners' sugar. With mixer at medium speed, beat ingredients until well mixed, occasionally scraping bowl with rubber spatula.

Sprinkle confectioners' sugar onto waxed paper. With hands, shape dough into 1-inch balls; roll in sugar; place 1 inch apart on cookie sheet. Bake 12 to 15 minutes (they'll be soft with crackled tops). With pancake turner, immediately remove cookies to wire racks; cool. Makes about 4 dozen cookies.

NO-BAKE COOKIE BALLS

1 6-ounce package semisweet-chocolate pieces
3 tablespoons light corn syrup
2 teaspoons instant coffee
confectioners' sugar
1¾ cups finely crushed vanilla wafers (about 3 dozen)
1 cup chopped California walnuts

DAY BEFORE SERVING:
In double boiler, over hot, not boiling, water, melt chocolate; remove from heat. Stir in corn syrup. In cup, dissolve coffee in ⅓ cup hot water and stir into mixture.

Thoroughly mix in 3 cups confectioners' sugar, crushed wafers and walnuts. Sprinkle some confectioners' sugar onto waxed paper. With hands, shape mixture into 1-inch balls; roll in sugar. Store at least a day in a covered container, to mellow flavors. Makes about 5 dozen cookies.

CHOCO-ORANGE BALLS: Substitute *⅓ cup orange juice* for instant coffee and hot water.

DATE BALLS

2 cups corn, wheat or bran flakes
¾ cup pitted dates, chilled
½ cup pecans
2 tablespoons honey
1 tablespoon butter or margarine, softened
2 teaspoons lemon juice
confectioners' sugar

EARLY IN DAY:
Put cereal, dates and pecans through food chopper (or, in covered blender container at low speed, blend ingredients just until well chopped). In large bowl, mix cereal mixture with honey, butter or margarine and lemon juice; knead until well mixed.

Sprinkle some confectioners' sugar onto waxed paper. With hands, shape dough into small balls and roll in sugar. Makes 2½ dozen cookies.

DANISH ALMOND CAKES

1⅔ cups all-purpose flour
½ cup sugar
½ cup diced toasted almonds
½ cup butter or margarine, softened
½ cup shortening
1 egg
1 tablespoon cinnamon
½ teaspoon double-acting baking powder
½ teaspoon ground cardamom
1 egg yolk, slightly beaten
blanched almonds, halved

EARLY IN DAY:
Into large bowl, measure all ingredients except 1 egg yolk and almonds. With mixer at medium speed, beat ingredients until well mixed, occasionally scraping bowl with rubber spatula. Cover; refrigerate 2 hours.

TO BAKE:
Preheat oven to 375°F. With hands, shape dough into 1-inch balls; place 2 inches apart on cookie sheets and flatten slightly with flat-bottomed glass that has been covered with a damp cloth.

In cup, blend egg yolk with 1 tablespoon water; brush on tops of cookies; top each cookie with an almond half. Bake 10 minutes or until golden. With pancake turner, immediately remove cookies to wire racks; cool. Makes about 3½ dozen cookies.

PEPPERMINT SNOWBALLS

confectioners' sugar
2¼ cups all-purpose flour
1 cup butter or margarine, softened
1 teaspoon vanilla extract
½ cup crushed hard peppermint candy
2 tablespoons cream cheese, softened
1 teaspoon milk
1 drop red food color

EARLY IN DAY:
Into large bowl, measure ½ cup confectioners' sugar, flour, butter or margarine and vanilla. With mixer at medium speed, beat ingredients until well mixed, occasionally scraping bowl with rubber spatula.

In small bowl, toss together peppermint candy and ¼ cup confectioners' sugar.

In another small bowl, prepare filling: With spoon, blend cream cheese with milk until smooth. Gradually stir in ½ cup confectioners' sugar, food color and 3 tablespoons of reserved candy mixture.

TO BAKE:
Preheat oven to 350°F. With hands, shape dough into ¾-inch balls. With handle of wooden spoon, make a deep hole in center of each ball. Fill each hole with about ¼ teaspoon of filling; cover with a bit of dough to seal.

Bake cookies 12 minutes or until set but not brown. Remove; while cookies are hot, roll in remaining candy mixture; sprinkle any leftover mixture over cookies. Refrigerate until served. Makes about 3 dozen cookies.

BOURBON BALLS

confectioners' sugar
2½ cups finely crushed vanilla wafers (about 60 wafers)
1 cup finely chopped California walnuts
2 tablespoons cocoa
¼ cup bourbon
3 tablespoons corn syrup

UP TO 4 WEEKS BEFORE SERVING:
In large bowl, thoroughly mix 1 cup confectioners' sugar and remaining ingredients.

Sprinkle some confectioners' sugar onto waxed paper. With hands, shape mixture into 1-inch balls; roll each in sugar. For best storing, wrap each ball in plastic wrap or foil. Makes about 3½ dozen cookies.

KING-SIZE GINGERSNAPS

sugar
1¾ cups all-purpose flour
¾ cup shortening
1 egg
¼ cup light molasses
1 tablespoon baking soda
1 teaspoon ground cloves
1 teaspoon ginger
1 teaspoon cinnamon
½ teaspoon salt

EARLY IN DAY:
Preheat oven to 350°F. Into large bowl, measure 1 cup sugar and remaining ingredients. With mixer at medium speed, beat ingredients until well mixed, occasionally scraping bowl with rubber spatula. Sprinkle some sugar onto waxed paper. With hands, shape dough into 1½-inch balls; roll each in sugar; place 3 inches apart on cookie sheets. Flatten balls with fingers and sprinkle with more sugar. Bake 12 to 15 minutes. With pancake turner, immediately remove cookies to wire racks; cool. Makes 18 cookies.

SUGAR-AND-SPICE COOKIES

1 18-ounce roll refrigerated sugar slice-and-bake cookies
1 egg white
½ cup sugar
1½ teaspoons cinnamon
1 teaspoon nutmeg

EARLY IN DAY:
Preheat oven to 375°F. Grease cookie sheets well. Cut cookie roll into 1-inch-thick slices; cut each slice into quarters. With hands, shape each into small ball.

In small bowl, with fork, beat egg white with 1 tablespoon water. In another small bowl, combine sugar, cinnamon and nutmeg. Brush each ball with egg-white mixture, then roll in sugar mixture.

Place about 2 inches apart on cookie sheets. Bake 10 minutes or until golden. Remove cookies to wire racks; cool. Makes about 3½ dozen cookies.

COOKIE CANES

3 eggs
4 cups all-purpose flour
2 cups packed brown sugar
1 cup finely chopped pecans
1 cup butter or margarine, softened
¾ cup natural-flavor malted milk powder
⅓ cup sour cream
2 teaspoons double-acting baking powder
2 teaspoons vanilla extract
½ teaspoon baking soda
½ teaspoon salt
red-colored sugar or nonpareils for garnish

EARLY IN DAY:
Into large bowl, measure 2 eggs and remaining ingredients except colored sugar or nonpareils. With mixer at low speed, beat ingredients until well mixed, occasionally scraping bowl with rubber spatula. Cover; refrigerate 4 hours or until dough is firm.

TO BAKE:
Preheat oven to 350°F. Grease cookie sheets. With hands, shape dough into 1-inch balls; on lightly floured surface, with hands, roll each ball into pencil-size stick, about 6 inches long. Place sticks 2 inches apart on cookie sheets, bending one end of each slightly to make candy-cane shape.

In cup, beat 1 egg slightly; brush on canes and sprinkle with colored sugar or nonpareils. Bake 10 minutes or until lightly browned. With pancake turner, immediately remove cookies to wire racks; cool. Makes about 5 dozen cookies.

QUICK CRUNCHIES

½ cup butter or margarine
2 eggs
1 cup chopped dates
¾ cup sugar
dash salt
2 cups crisp rice cereal
1 cup chopped pecans
1 teaspoon vanilla extract
1 4-ounce can shredded coconut

ABOUT 1 HOUR BEFORE SERVING:
In large skillet over medium heat, melt butter or margarine. In small bowl, with fork, beat eggs well and stir in dates, sugar and salt; pour into skillet. Cook over medium heat for 10 to 15 minutes until thickened, stirring often. Remove from heat.

Stir in cereal, pecans and vanilla. With hands, shape mixture by teaspoonfuls into balls. On waxed paper, sprinkle coconut; roll balls in coconut until well coated. Let stand on waxed paper to harden. Makes 3 to 4 dozen cookies.

QUICK PEANUT-BUTTER COOKIES

piecrust mix for 2-crust pie
1 cup packed light brown sugar
½ cup peanut butter
sugar

EARLY IN DAY:
Preheat oven to 375°F. Into medium bowl, measure piecrust mix, brown sugar, peanut butter and 3 tablespoons water; stir until mixture forms ball.

Divide dough into about 48 pieces; with hands, shape each into ball and place 2 inches apart on cookie sheets. Flatten with fork dipped in sugar. Bake 8 minutes or until light golden and slightly puffy. With pancake turner, immediately remove cookies to racks; cool. Makes 4 dozen cookies.

HAZELNUT DROPS

1 cup all-purpose flour
½ cup shortening
¼ cup sugar
1 teaspoon grated orange peel
½ teaspoon grated lemon or lime peel
¼ teaspoon salt
1 egg, separated
⅔ cup finely ground hazelnuts

EARLY IN DAY:
Into large bowl, measure 1 tablespoon water and remaining ingredients except egg white and hazelnuts. With mixer at medium speed, beat ingredients until well mixed, occasionally scraping bowl with rubber spatula. Refrigerate dough until easy to handle.

Preheat oven to 350°F. Put egg white in saucer; put nuts on waxed paper. With hands, shape dough into 1-inch balls; roll in egg white, then in ground nuts. Place 1 inch apart on cookie sheets. Bake 18 to 20 minutes until firm. Immediately remove to wire racks; cool. Makes 2 dozen cookies.

Pressed Cookies

SPRITZ

3¾ cups all-purpose flour
1⅓ cups butter or margarine, softened
¾ cup sugar
¼ cup orange juice
1 egg yolk

EARLY IN DAY:
Into large bowl, measure all ingredients. With mixer at medium speed, beat ingredients until well mixed, occasionally scraping bowl. Cover; refrigerate about 1 hour.

TO BAKE:
Preheat oven to 375°F. Use part of dough at a time; keep rest refrigerated. Using bar-plate tip, press dough through cookie press in long strips, about 1 inch apart, down length of cookie sheets; cut each strip into 2½-inch pieces, leaving pieces in place.

Bake 8 minutes or until light golden, being careful not to overbake. Immediately cut again between cookies to separate them. With pancake turner, immediately remove cookies to wire racks; cool. Makes about 9 dozen cookies.

SPRITZ VARIATIONS

RINGLETS (Molded Cookies): Preheat oven to 375°F. Divide chilled Spritz dough into quarters; refrigerate ¾ of dough. Divide remainder into 16 pieces. On lightly floured surface, with hands, roll each piece into thin, pencil-like rope about 7 inches long; twist 2 ropes together tightly and shape into ring. Place 1 inch apart on cookie sheet. Brush with *1 egg*, slightly beaten.

Bake 12 minutes or until golden. With pancake turner, immediately remove to racks; cool. Repeat. Makes 2½ dozen cookies.

RASPBERRY THUMBPRINTS (Molded Cookies): Use ½ of chilled Spritz dough. Preheat oven to 375°F. With hands, shape rounded teaspoonfuls of dough into balls. Place 1 inch apart on cookie sheets. Press thumb into centers of cookies, making deep indentations.

Bake 10 minutes; remove from oven and, with *⅓ cup red raspberry preserves* (or other fruit preserves), fill indentations. Return cookies to oven and bake 5 minutes more. With pancake turner, immediately remove cookies to wire racks; cool. Makes about 6 dozen cookies.

CINNAMON HALF-MOONS (Rolled Cookies): Use ½ chilled Spritz dough. Preheat oven to 375°F. On lightly floured surface, with floured rolling pin, roll dough ⅛ inch thick; with 2½-inch round cutter, cut out rounds. Cut each round in half.

On cookie sheets, place about 1 inch apart; brush with *1 egg*, beaten. Sprinkle tops with mixture of *3 tablespoons sugar* and *½ teaspoon cinnamon*. Bake 10 minutes or until edges are lightly browned. With pancake turner, immediately remove cookies to wire racks; cool. Makes about 6 dozen cookies.

Refrigerator Cookies

CRAZY COOKIES

1 18-ounce roll refrigerated sugar slice-and-bake cookies
1 16-ounce roll refrigerated Swiss-style chocolate-chunks slice-and-bake cookies
confectioners' sugar

EARLY IN DAY:
Let both refrigerated cookie rolls stand at room temperature 2 to 3 hours until soft enough to roll out. Spread thin layer of confectioners' sugar onto sheet of waxed paper. On sugared paper, with lightly sugared rolling pin, roll sugar-cookie dough into 16″ by 10″ rectangle.

On another sugared paper, repeat with chocolate-chunks-cookie dough; invert dark dough on top of light dough; peel waxed paper from top.

Trim doughs to same size. Starting with short end, roll doughs jelly-roll fashion, peeling back waxed paper while rolling. Discard waxed paper. Wrap roll in waxed paper and refrigerate several hours until firm enough to slice.

TO BAKE:
Preheat oven to 350°F. Grease cookie sheets. Slice roll into ¾-inch-thick slices; cut each into quarters. Place quarters upright on rounded edge, 2 inches apart on

cookie sheets. Bake 12 minutes or until golden brown. With pancake turner, immediately remove cookies to wire racks; cool. Makes about 4 dozen cookies.

SLICE-AND-BAKE COOKIES

2¾ cups all-purpose flour
1½ cups packed light brown sugar
1 cup shortening
2 eggs
2½ teaspoons double-acting baking powder
1 teaspoon cinnamon
1 teaspoon vanilla extract
½ teaspoon nutmeg
½ teaspoon salt

DAY BEFORE OR UP TO 1 WEEK AHEAD:
Into large bowl, measure all ingredients. With mixer at medium speed, beat ingredients until well mixed, occasionally scraping bowl with rubber spatula. Shape dough into rolls about 1½ inches in diameter. Wrap rolls in waxed paper; refrigerate overnight or up to 1 week.

TO BAKE:
Preheat oven to 375°F. Making only as many cookies as desired, cut cookie rolls into ¼-inch-thick slices; rewrap and return rest of roll to refrigerator. Place slices 1 inch apart on cookie sheet. Bake 8 minutes or until lightly browned. With pancake turner, immediately remove cookies to wire racks; cool. Makes about 8 dozen cookies.

CANDY-TOPPED SUGAR COOKIES

1 18-ounce roll refrigerated sugar slice-and-bake cookies
2 1⅜-ounce packages nonmelting chocolate-covered peanut candies

EARLY IN DAY:
Preheat oven to 375°F. Cut refrigerated cookie roll into ¼-inch-thick slices; place about 2 inches apart on cookie sheets.

In covered blender container at low speed, grind peanut candies (or chop with knife). Sprinkle about ¼ teaspoon ground candy onto each cookie. Bake 8 to 10 minutes until golden. With pancake turner, immediately remove cookies to wire racks; cool. Makes about 3½ dozen cookies.

Rolled Cookies

SUGAR COOKIES

3¼ cups all-purpose flour
1½ cups sugar
⅔ cup shortening
2 eggs
2½ teaspoons double-acting baking powder
2 tablespoons milk
1 teaspoon vanilla extract
½ teaspoon salt
Decorative Toppings, below (optional)

EARLY IN DAY:
Into large bowl, measure all ingredients except toppings. With mixer at medium speed, beat ingredients until well mixed, occasionally scraping bowl with rubber spatula. With hands, shape dough into ball; wrap; refrigerate dough 2 to 3 hours until easy to handle.

Preheat oven to 400°F. Lightly grease cookie sheets. Roll half or third of dough at a time, keeping rest refrigerated. For crisp cookies, roll dough paper thin. For softer cookies, roll ⅛″ to ¼″ thick. With floured cookie cutter, cut into shapes. Reroll trimmings and cut.

Place cookies ½ inch apart on cookie sheets; sprinkle with decorative toppings. Bake 8 minutes or until very light brown. With pancake turner, remove cookies to racks; cool. Makes about 6 dozen cookies.

DECORATIVE TOPPINGS: Brush cookies with *heavy or whipping cream,* or with mixture *of 1 egg white* slightly beaten with *1 tablespoon water;* sprinkle with *sugar, nonpareils, chopped nuts, shredded coconut, cut-up gumdrops, butterscotch pieces.*

BUTTERSCOTCH-PECAN: Substitute *2 cups packed brown sugar* for sugar. Add *1 cup finely chopped pecans* to ingredients.

CHOCOLATE: Increase milk to 3 tablespoons. Add *3 squares unsweetened chocolate,* melted, and *1 cup finely chopped California walnuts* to ingredients.

COCONUT: Add *1 cup shredded coconut,* chopped, to ingredients.

LEMON: Substitute *4 teaspoons lemon juice* and *grated peel of 1 lemon* for vanilla.

JELLY TART COOKIES

2¼ cups all-purpose flour
1 cup shortening
½ cup confectioners' sugar
2 tablespoons milk
2 teaspoons vanilla extract
½ teaspoon salt
¼ teaspoon double-acting baking powder
red currant jelly or green mint jelly

EARLY IN DAY:
Into large bowl, measure all ingredients except jelly. With mixer at medium speed, beat ingredients until well mixed. Cover; chill until easy to handle, about 4 hours.

TO BAKE:
Preheat oven to 350°F. On lightly floured surface, with floured rolling pin, roll dough ¼ inch thick; cut into 2½-inch rounds. To make rings: From half the rounds, cut a ¾-inch circle from center; brush rings with milk. Place all rounds and rings 1 inch apart on cookie sheets. Bake 10 minutes or until light golden. With pancake turner, immediately remove cookies to wire racks; cool. Shape dough scraps and circles into ball; roll out and use for more rounds and rings.

Place 1 teaspoon currant jelly on bottom of each cookie round; top with rings, right side up. Makes about 1½ dozen cookies.

STRAWBERRY PILLOWS

1½ cups all-purpose flour
3 3-ounce packages cream cheese, softened
½ cup butter or margarine, softened
½ 10-ounce jar strawberry preserves
½ cup ground California walnuts
1 egg, beaten

EARLY IN DAY:
Into medium bowl, measure flour, cream cheese and butter or margarine. With mixer at low speed, beat ingredients until well mixed, occasionally scraping bowl with rubber spatula. Cover; chill at least 1 hour.

Meanwhile, prepare filling: In small bowl, stir preserves and nuts; set aside.

TO BAKE:
Preheat oven to 450°F. Divide dough in half; refrigerate one half. On well-floured surface, with floured rolling pin, thinly roll out dough into large rectangle. Cut into small rectangles 3″ by 2″. Place ½ teaspoon of filling close to 2-inch end of each rectangle. Fold dough over filling, bringing ends together; with fork dipped in flour, press edges together.

Brush with egg and place on cookie sheet. Repeat with remaining dough. Bake 12 minutes or until golden. Remove cookies to wire racks; cool. Reroll trimmings for more cookies. Makes about 3½ dozen cookies.

JAM TIES: Prepare as above but cut dough into 5″ by 1″ strips. Place strips on lightly greased cookie sheets. Spoon ¼ teaspoon of filling into center of each strip. Cross ends of each strip around but not over filling; brush dough with egg. Bake 10 minutes or until golden. Makes 4 dozen cookies.

CINNAMON STARS

3 egg whites, at room temperature
confectioners' sugar
2 cups blanched almonds, ground
1 teaspoon cinnamon
½ teaspoon grated lemon peel

SEVERAL DAYS BEFORE SERVING:
1. Preheat oven to 350°F. Grease cookie sheet. In medium bowl, with mixer at high speed, beat egg whites until soft peaks form. Beating at high speed, beat in 2 cups confectioners' sugar, 2 tablespoons at a time. Do not scrape sides of bowl. Spoon out ¾ cup for frosting; cover and set aside.
2. Into remaining mixture, beat almonds, cinnamon, lemon peel and ½ cup confectioners' sugar. Cover; refrigerate about 2 hours or until workable.
3. On waxed paper, well dusted with confectioners' sugar, pat out one-third of dough and generously sprinkle with confectioners' sugar. Cover with waxed paper and roll out ⅛ inch thick. Peel off paper; with well-floured, 2¾-inch star cutter, cut cookies.
4. With pancake turner, place stars on cookie sheet. Bake 8 minutes or until lightly browned. With pancake turner, remove cookies to wire racks; cool. Repeat with remaining dough and trimmings.
5. Frost cookies with reserved frosting; return to cookie sheets. Turn oven control to 325°F. Bake 5 minutes or until frosting is set but not browned; cool. Store tightly covered. Makes about 4 dozen cookies.

GUMDROP COOKIES

3¼ cups all-purpose flour
1 cup sugar
1 cup butter or margarine
1 egg
2 teaspoons double-acting baking powder
1 teaspoon vanilla extract
small gumdrops, halved crosswise

DAY BEFORE:
Into large bowl, measure all ingredients except gumdrops. With mixer at medium speed, beat ingredients until well mixed, occasionally scraping bowl with rubber spatula. Cover and refrigerate overnight.

TO BAKE:
Preheat oven to 375°F. On lightly floured surface, with floured rolling pin, roll about half of dough to ¼-inch thickness. (Keep remaining dough refrigerated.) With fluted 2¾-inch cookie cutter, cut cookies; place on cookie sheets. Place 3 or 4 gumdrop halves on each cookie. Repeat with remaining dough and trimmings.

Bake 10 minutes or until golden. With pancake turner, remove cookies to wire racks; cool. Makes about 3 dozen cookies.

GINGERBREAD-MEN COOKIES

2¼ cups all-purpose flour
½ cup sugar
½ cup shortening
½ cup light molasses
1 egg
1½ teaspoons cinnamon
1 teaspoon double-acting baking powder
1 teaspoon ginger
1 teaspoon ground cloves
½ teaspoon nutmeg
½ teaspoon baking soda
½ teaspoon salt
Ornamental Cookie Frosting (opposite)

EARLY IN DAY:
Preheat oven to 350°F. Into large bowl, measure all ingredients except Ornamental Cookie Frosting. With mixer at medium speed, beat ingredients until well mixed. Cover and refrigerate 1 hour.

On lightly floured surface, with floured rolling pin, roll dough ⅛ inch thick. With cutters, cut out gingerbread men (or other desired shapes). Place cutouts ½ inch apart on cookie sheets. Reroll trimmings and cut. Bake 8 minutes or until browned. With pancake turner, remove cookies to racks.

With frosting in paper cone or cake decorator, decorate cookies. Makes 2 dozen 5-inch cookies.

ORNAMENTAL COOKIE FROSTING

1¼ cups confectioners' sugar
⅛ teaspoon cream of tartar
1 egg white

JUST BEFORE USING:
Into small bowl, sift sugar and cream of tartar through very fine sieve; add egg white. With mixer at high speed, beat mixture so stiff that knife drawn through leaves clean path. (On humid days you may need to beat in more sugar.)

ALMOND BUTTER COOKIES

sugar
1¾ cups all-purpose flour
¾ cup butter or margarine, softened
1 teaspoon almond extract
dash salt
1 egg white, slightly beaten
⅛ teaspoon cinnamon
⅓ cup toasted diced and buttered almonds

EARLY IN DAY OR DAY BEFORE:
Into large bowl, measure ¼ cup sugar, flour, butter or margarine, almond extract and salt. With mixer at medium speed, beat ingredients until well mixed, occasionally scraping bowl with rubber spatula. (Mixture will be crumbly.) With hands, shape mixture into ball. (If dough is too soft to roll out, cover and refrigerate until firm.)

TO BAKE:
Preheat oven to 325°F. On lightly floured surface, with floured rolling pin, roll dough into 12″ by 8″ rectangle. With pastry wheel or knife, cut into 3″ by 1″ strips; place on cookie sheets; brush with egg white.

In small bowl, mix a scant ¼ cup sugar with cinnamon and almonds; sprinkle on cookies. Bake 15 minutes or until golden. With pancake turner, remove cookies to racks; cool. Makes about 3 dozen cookies.

MINCEMEAT POCKETS

3 cups all-purpose flour
1 cup sugar
½ cup packed light brown sugar
½ cup shortening
¼ cup butter or margarine, softened
2 eggs
1 teaspoon baking soda
2 teaspoons milk
1 teaspoon vanilla extract
¼ teaspoon salt
5 tablespoons mincemeat

EARLY IN DAY OR DAY AHEAD:
Into large bowl, measure all ingredients except mincemeat. With mixer at low speed, beat ingredients until well mixed, occasionally scraping bowl with rubber spatula. Cover; chill till firm or overnight.

TO BAKE:
Preheat oven to 350°F. Grease cookie sheets. On lightly floured surface, with floured rolling pin, roll dough about ⅛ inch thick; using 2¾-inch round cookie cutter, cut dough into about 54 rounds, rerolling scraps.

On each round, place ¼ teaspoon mincemeat; fold over to make a half round; press curved edges together with 4-tined fork to seal. Place on cookie sheets and bake 10 minutes or until golden. With pancake turner, immediately remove cookies to wire racks; cool. Makes about 4½ dozen cookies.

SPICE COOKIES

sugar
3⅔ cups all-purpose flour
1 cup butter or margarine, softened
2 eggs
1 tablespoon milk
1½ teaspoons baking soda
1½ teaspoons cinnamon
½ teaspoon nutmeg
¼ teaspoon ground cloves
1 cup dried currants

DAY BEFORE:
Into large bowl, measure 1½ cups sugar and remaining ingredients except currants. With mixer at medium speed, beat ingredients until well mixed, occasionally scraping bowl with rubber spatula. With spatula, stir in currants. Cover; refrigerate overnight.

TO BAKE:
Preheat oven to 375°F. On lightly floured board, with floured rolling pin, roll dough as thin as possible; lightly sprinkle with sugar. With pastry wheel or knife, cut dough into diamonds about 2 inches in length. Bake 8 minutes or until very lightly browned. With pancake turner, immediately remove cookies to wire racks; cool. Makes about 10 dozen cookies.

RAISIN-SPICE COOKIES: Use *1 cup chopped golden or dark seedless raisins* instead of currants in above recipe.

ORANGE-ALMOND COOKIES

2½ cups all-purpose flour
1 cup sugar
1 cup butter or margarine, softened
2 tablespoons orange juice
grated orange peel
½ cup toasted slivered almonds
¼ cup packed light brown sugar
1 egg yolk

EARLY IN DAY:
Into large bowl, measure flour, sugar, butter or margarine, orange juice and 1 tablespoon orange peel. With mixer at medium speed, beat ingredients until well mixed, occasionally scraping bowl with rubber spatula. With hands, shape dough into ball; wrap and refrigerate for at least 3 hours or place in freezer 30 minutes.

TO BAKE:
Preheat oven to 325°F. Prepare Topping: In small bowl, stir almonds, brown sugar and ½ teaspoon orange peel.

Between 2 sheets waxed paper, with rolling pin, roll dough ¼ inch thick. With 2½-inch scalloped or round cookie cutter, cut out as many cookies as possible. With pancake turner, place on cookie sheets. (Refrigerate cookie trimmings.)

In cup, mix egg yolk with 1 tablespoon water; use to brush on dough. Sprinkle tops with Topping. Bake 20 minutes or until golden. With pancake turner, immediately remove cookies to wire racks; cool. Repeat with remaining trimmings. Makes about 2½ dozen cookies.

Ice creams & sherbets

Ice cream, ice milk and sherbet are favorite frozen desserts. Their commercial versions are all milk products; the difference lies in their milk-fat (butterfat) and milk-solids content. In commercial products, there is from 10 to 16 percent milk fat and about 20 percent total milk solids in ice cream; from 2 to 7 percent milk fat and at least 11 percent total milk solids in ice milk. (Most of the soft frozen dairy desserts sold at roadside stands are ice milks.) Sherbets have 1 to 2 percent milk-fat content and total milk-solids content of 2 to 5 percent.

Ice cream with a large percentage of milk fat is usually higher both in calories and in cost. Ice cream with 16 percent milk fat contains approximately 165 calories in a half-cup serving. Ice cream with 10 percent milk fat has about 125 calories in a half cup. There are about 100 calories in a half cup of ice milk, and 130 calories in the same amount of sherbet. (Sherbet, though low in milk fat, has a higher sugar content than ice cream, to balance the tartness of the fruit juices used for flavoring.)

Fruit ices, also known as water ices or Italian ices, have no milk fat or milk solids. As with sherbet, the sugar content is high, to balance the flavoring.

Dietetic ice creams are sweetened with mannitol, sorbitol or saccharin instead of sugar. In most such products, the fat content has not been decreased, and many contain about the same number of calories as regular ice cream. Some have the calorie content listed on the label.

Tips for Frozen Desserts

When freezing ice cream in a churn-type ice-cream freezer, be sure to fill the freezer can only as full as the manufacturer directs, to allow for expansion of the mixture as it freezes. If there is too much mixture, freeze the excess in a special ice-cube tray. About 1 hour before serving, remove from tray to small bowl and beat with mixer at medium speed until smooth; return to tray and keep frozen until serving time.

Since ice cubes tend to stick in trays previously used for freezing dessert mixtures—the finish can be removed by washing—it's best to keep special ice-cube trays just for frozen desserts and other foods. Baking pans, paper cups and mixing bowls may also be used.

Mixtures will freeze faster in shallow pans or trays than in deep ones. Freeze them uncovered, but before storing, cover to prevent drying out.

How to tell when a mixture is partially frozen? It should be frozen firm to 1 inch in from the edge; the center, however, will still be mushy and soft.

Chill bowl for beating partially frozen mixture to keep it from melting too much.

After freezing mixture in ice-cream freezer, transfer to chilled container and place in home freezer a few hours to harden, or pack in ice-cream freezer as directed in recipe.

In those Special Ice-Cream Desserts (pages 578–582) which use ice cream, ice milk may be substituted with equally good results.

How to Store

Store commercially made ice cream, ice milk and sherbet in their cartons, tightly closed, in the freezer at 0°F. or lower. For long storage, freezer-wrap the cartons. These products will be at their best, however, if used within 1 month; prolonged storage can cause them to become grainy. Cut surfaces should be covered closely with plastic wrap or foil to prevent drying.

If you store ice cream, ice milk and sherbet in the refrigerator freezing compartment, use them within 2 or 3 days.

Homemade custard-base ice cream and fruit ice, made in a churn-type freezer, should be transferred to a freezer container for storage. Cover the surface with plastic wrap or foil and adjust the lid. Store 1 to 2 months.

Before serving, remove these products from freezer and let stand 20 minutes to soften slightly for easier scooping.

Mix-and-Freeze Desserts

HOMEMADE VANILLA ICE CREAM

2 cups sugar
6 tablespoons all-purpose flour
1 teaspoon salt
5 cups milk
6 eggs
4 cups half-and-half
3 tablespoons vanilla extract
about 20 pounds cracked ice
2 to 3 pounds rock salt (about 3 cups)

EARLY IN DAY OR UP TO 1 MONTH AHEAD:
1. In large, heavy saucepan, with spoon, combine sugar, flour and salt. In medium bowl, with hand beater or wire whisk, beat milk and eggs until well blended; stir into sugar mixture until smooth. Cook over low heat, stirring constantly, until mixture thickens and coats spoon, about 30 to 45 minutes. Cover surface with waxed paper and refrigerate to cool, about 2 hours.
2. Pour half-and-half, vanilla and cooled mixture into 4- to 6-quart ice-cream freezer can. Place dasher in can; cover and place can in freezer bucket; attach motor or hand crank. (If using 5- or 6-quart can, add 2 cups water to bucket.) Fill bucket half full with ice; sprinkle with about ¼ cup rock salt. Add about an inch of ice and about ¼ cup rock salt; repeat thin layers of ice and salt until about an inch below can lid.
3. Freeze according to manufacturer's directions, adding more ice and salt as needed. It will take about 35 to 45 minutes to freeze.
4. After freezing, ice cream will be soft. Remove motor; wipe lid carefully before removing. Remove dasher; with spoon, pack down ice cream. Cover opening of can with waxed paper, plastic wrap or foil. Replace lid and put cork in hole in center; add more ice and salt to cover lid. Let stand to harden ice cream about 2 to 3 hours, adding more ice and salt as needed. (Or, place ice cream in a home freezer to harden, about 2 to 3 hours.) Makes about 3 quarts or 12 servings.

CHOCOLATE: Prepare egg mixture (step 1) as above but omit 1 cup milk. While mixture is cooling, in small saucepan over low heat, melt *8 squares unsweetened chocolate;* stir in *3/4 cup sugar* and *1 cup hot water* until blended; chill. In 4- to 6-quart freezer can, combine egg mixture, chocolate mixture, half-and-half and vanilla; freeze. Makes about 3 quarts or 12 servings.

BLUEBERRY SWIRL: Prepare as above but, while mixture is freezing (step 3), in covered blender container at low speed, blend *1 pint blueberries, 2 tablespoons sugar, 1 teaspoon lemon juice* and *1/4 teaspoon allspice* until smooth. Remove dasher and spoon out 6 cups ice cream into large bowl. Add berry mixture and, with spoon, swirl it through ice cream; pour mixture into three 1-pint containers and place in home freezer to harden. Let remaining 3 pints of ice cream harden. Makes 3 pints or 6 servings. of Blueberry Swirl and 3 pints of Vanilla.

CHOCOLATE CHIP: Prepare as above but, while mixture is freezing (step 3), finely chop *one and one-half 4-ounce packages sweet cooking chocolate.* Remove dasher. With long-handled spoon, stir in chocolate until well mixed. Cover can and harden. Makes about 3 quarts or 12 servings.

FRENCH VANILLA: Prepare as above but use *8 egg yolks* instead of whole eggs.

PEACH: Prepare egg mixture (step 1) as above; while mixture is cooling, in covered blender container at low speed, blend *10 to 12 ripe medium peaches,* peeled and cut up, and *1/2 cup sugar* until smooth. Makes about 3 cups puree. (Or, use three 10-ounce packages frozen sliced peaches and 3 tablespoons of their liquid.) In 4- to 6-quart freezer can, stir peaches, egg mixture, only *2 cups half-and-half* and *3/4 teaspoon almond extract* instead of vanilla; freeze. Makes about 7 pints or 14 servings.

PISTACHIO: Prepare egg mixture (step 1) as above but use *1 cup sugar, 3 tablespoons flour, 1/2 teaspoon salt, 2 1/2 cups milk* and *3 eggs* and cook about 15 minutes. In step 2, use only *2 cups half-and-half* and, for vanilla, substitute *1/8 teaspoon green food color* and *1/4 teaspoon almond extract;* freeze about 20 minutes. While mixture is freezing, coarsely chop *1 1/2 cups salted green pistachio nuts.* Remove dasher. With long-handled spoon, stir in nuts. Cover can and harden. Makes 3 pints or 6 servings.

RASPBERRY RIPPLE: Prepare as above but, while mixture is freezing (step 3), thaw *one 10-ounce package frozen raspberries* in large bowl. With potato masher, crush berries. Remove dasher and spoon 6 cups ice cream over berries. With 2 or 3 motions with spoon, swirl berries through ice cream (over-stirring ruins "ripple" effect); pour mixture into three 1-pint containers and place in home freezer to harden. Let remaining 3 pints of ice cream harden. Makes 3 pints or 6 servings of Raspberry Ripple and 3 pints of Vanilla.

SPICED BANANA: Prepare egg mixture (step 1) as above but use *1 cup sugar, 3 tablespoons flour, 1/2 teaspoon salt, 2 1/2 cups milk* and *3 eggs;* cook about 15 minutes. While mixture is cooling, in blender container, dissolve *1 tablespoon ascorbic-acid mixture for fruit* in *1/4 cup water;* add *6 ripe, firm medium bananas,* cut up, to mixture. (Completely ripened bananas will give strong flavor and dark color to ice cream.) Add *1/3 cup sugar* and *1 1/2 teaspoons cinnamon;* cover and blend until smooth. In 4- to 6-quart freezer can, stir egg mixture, banana mixture, only *2 cups half-and-half;* omit vanilla. Freeze about 20 minutes. Makes 5 pints or 10 servings.

STRAWBERRY: Prepare as above but, while egg mixture is cooling, in medium bowl, with potato masher, crush *1 1/2 pints strawberries,* hulled, *1 cup sugar* and *2 tablespoons lemon juice;* let stand about an hour. In 6-quart freezer can, stir well egg mixture, half-and-half, strawberries and *1/4 teaspoon red food color;* freeze. Makes about 4 quarts or 16 servings.

TOASTED WALNUT: Prepare as above but, while mixture is freezing (step 3), preheat oven to 375°F. In jelly-roll pan, spread *3 cups chopped California walnuts* in single layer; bake 10 minutes or until just lightly browned; cool. Remove dasher. Stir in nuts until well mixed. Cover can and harden. Makes about 3 quarts or 12 servings.

HOME-FREEZER METHOD: Prepare egg mixture (step 1) but use *1 cup sugar, 3 tablespoons flour, 1/2 teaspoon salt, 2 1/2 cups milk, 3 eggs;* cook about 15 minutes; cool. Stir in *2 cups heavy or whipping cream, 5 teaspoons vanilla.* Pour into 9" by 9" pan;

cover; freeze until frozen but still soft, 3 to 4 hours; spoon into large bowl. With mixer at medium speed, beat until smooth but still frozen; return to pan; cover; freeze until firm. Makes 6 cups or 6 servings.

PEPPERMINT ICE CREAM

½ pound peppermint-stick candy
2 cups milk
2 cups half-and-half
about 20 pounds cracked ice
2 to 3 pounds rock salt

EARLY IN DAY OR UP TO 1 MONTH AHEAD:
Between sheets of waxed paper, with rolling pin, crush candy to a fine powder. Add candy, milk and half-and-half to 4- to 6-quart ice-cream freezer can and freeze as directed in Homemade Vanilla Ice Cream (page 572), about 30 minutes.

After freezing, ice cream will be soft. Remove motor; wipe lid carefully before removing. Remove dasher; with spoon, pack down ice cream. Cover opening of can with waxed paper, plastic wrap or foil. Replace lid and put cork in hole in center; add more ice and salt to cover lid. Harden ice cream 2 to 3 hours, adding ice and salt as needed. (Or, harden in a home freezer, 2 or 3 hours.) Makes about 3 pints or 6 servings.

EASY BANANA ICE CREAM

½ cup orange juice
3 ripe, firm medium bananas, cut in large chunks
12 regular marshmallows
1 tablespoon sugar
dash salt
2 or 3 drops yellow food color
1 cup heavy or whipping cream

DAY BEFORE OR UP TO 2 WEEKS AHEAD:
In covered blender container at high speed, blend all ingredients except cream until smooth, about 1 minute. (Completely ripened bananas will give a strong flavor.)

In medium bowl, with mixer at medium speed, beat cream until stiff peaks form. With rubber spatula, gently fold in banana mixture; pour into an 8″ by 8″ baking pan; cover with foil and freeze until firm. Makes about 4 cups or 4 servings.

FROZEN COEUR A LA CREME

1½ cups heavy or whipping cream
6 egg yolks
½ cup sugar
1 teaspoon vanilla extract
Peach Sauce (page 500)

EARLY IN DAY OR 2 WEEKS AHEAD:
In medium bowl, with mixer at medium speed, beat cream until soft peaks form; set aside.

In large bowl, with mixer at high speed, beat egg yolks and sugar until thick and lemon-colored. Beat in vanilla. With rubber spatula, gently fold whipped cream into mixture; pour into 8″ by 8″ baking pan. Cover with foil or plastic wrap and freeze until firm.

TO SERVE:
Let Crème stand at room temperature 10 minutes for easier scooping. Serve with Peach Sauce. Makes 10 to 12 servings.

FROZEN APPLE CREAM

¼ small lemon
1 8-ounce package cream cheese
1 cup half-and-half
1 15- or 16-ounce can applesauce (about 2 cups)
¾ cup sugar
1 teaspoon vanilla extract

DAY BEFORE OR UP TO 2 WEEKS AHEAD:
Cut lemon (with peel) into 3 or 4 pieces. Cut cream cheese into large chunks. In covered blender container, place half-and-half, lemon and cream-cheese pieces and remaining ingredients; blend at low speed until smooth, about 2 minutes, occasionally stopping and scraping container with rubber spatula. Pour mixture into an 8″ by 8″ baking pan; cover with foil or plastic wrap and freeze until partially frozen, about 2 hours.

Spoon mixture into blender container and blend at high speed, just until smooth; return mixture to pan; cover and freeze until firm.

TO SERVE:
Let cream stand at room temperature about 10 minutes for easier serving. Makes about 5 cups or 10 servings.

FROZEN LEMON CREME

1 envelope unflavored gelatin
1½ cups milk
1 cup sugar
3 tablespoons lemon juice
2 teaspoons grated lemon peel
2 teaspoons vanilla extract
¼ teaspoon salt
1 cup heavy or whipping cream

EARLY IN DAY OR UP TO 1 MONTH AHEAD:
In small saucepan, sprinkle gelatin over 1 cup milk. Cook over low heat, stirring constantly, until gelatin is dissolved; set aside. In large bowl, combine ½ cup milk with remaining ingredients except cream; gradually stir in gelatin mixture (mixture may have curdled appearance). Cover bowl with foil or plastic wrap and freeze until partially set, about 1 hour.

In small bowl, with mixer at medium speed, beat cream until soft peaks form. With mixer at medium speed, beat mixture in large bowl until smooth but still frozen; with rubber spatula, carefully fold in whipped cream. Cover and freeze until firm.

TO SERVE:
Let Crème stand at room temperature 10 minutes. Makes 6 cups or 12 servings.

FROZEN CHEESE CREAM

1½ cups creamed cottage cheese
½ cup sugar
1 teaspoon vanilla extract
1 egg
2 pints vanilla ice cream, slightly softened

ABOUT 4 HOURS OR UP TO 2 WEEKS AHEAD:
In covered blender container at low speed, blend cottage cheese with sugar, vanilla and egg until smooth.

In large bowl, with mixer at low speed, beat ice cream with cheese mixture until blended. Pour into 10″ by 5″ loaf pan; cover with foil or plastic wrap; freeze until firm.

TO SERVE:
Let stand in refrigerator about 30 minutes for easier scooping. Serve as dessert or over apple or mincemeat pie. Makes about 4 cups or 8 servings.

DOUBLE RASPBERRY FREEZE

1 3-ounce package raspberry-flavor gelatin
½ cup sugar
dash salt
2 cups milk
1 pint raspberries or 1 10-ounce package frozen raspberries, thawed

EARLY IN DAY OR SEVERAL DAYS AHEAD:
In medium saucepan, into 1 cup boiling water, stir gelatin, sugar and salt until gelatin is dissolved. Refrigerate until cool, about 20 minutes. Stir in milk; refrigerate until mixture mounds slightly when dropped from a spoon, about 1 hour.

Meanwhile, if using frozen raspberries, drain well on paper towels. Fold raspberries into gelatin mixture; pour into 12 paper-lined 2-inch muffin-pan cups. Wrap with foil or plastic wrap and freeze until firm.

TO SERVE:
Remove desserts from muffin-pan cups; peel off paper. Place upside down on paper-doily-lined dessert plates. Let stand at room temperature about 10 minutes to soften slightly. Makes 12 servings.

STRAWBERRY-ORANGE FROST

1½ cups orange juice
½ cup lemon juice
¼ cup orange-flavor liqueur
3 pints strawberries
2 cups sugar

DAY BEFORE OR UP TO 1 MONTH AHEAD:
In covered blender container,* at high speed, blend all ingredients until smooth, blending about half at a time; pour mixture into a 9″ by 9″ baking pan and mix well. Cover with foil or plastic wrap and freeze until partially frozen, about 4 hours.

Spoon mixture into large bowl and, with mixer at medium speed, beat until smooth but still frozen; return mixture to pan. Cover and freeze until firm.

TO SERVE:
Let mixture stand at room temperature 10 minutes for easier scooping. Makes about 10 cups or 12 servings.

* Or, press berries through food mill.

MELBA CREAM DESSERT

2 envelopes unflavored gelatin
4 medium peaches, peeled and cut up
½ cup sugar
2 teaspoons lemon juice
½ teaspoon salt
3 cups heavy or whipping cream
1 10-ounce package frozen raspberries, thawed

EARLY IN DAY OR UP TO 1 MONTH AHEAD:
1. In small saucepan, sprinkle gelatin over ½ cup water. Over low heat, heat mixture, stirring constantly, until gelatin is dissolved. Pour ¼ cup of mixture into blender container; add peaches, ¼ cup sugar, 1 teaspoon lemon juice and ¼ teaspoon salt. Cover and blend until smooth; pour mixture into medium bowl; set aside.
2. In large bowl, with mixer at high speed, beat 1½ cups cream until stiff peaks form. With rubber spatula, gently fold peach mixture into whipped cream. Spoon into 10-cup mold and refrigerate until partially set, about 30 to 40 minutes.
3. Meanwhile, in same blender container, blend remaining gelatin mixture, raspberries and their liquid, ¼ cup sugar, 1 teaspoon lemon juice and ¼ teaspoon salt until smooth; cover and set aside.
4. When peach mixture is partially set, in large bowl, beat remaining 1½ cups cream; fold in raspberry mixture; pour over peach mixture. Cover; freeze until firm.

TO SERVE:
Unmold dessert; let stand 10 minutes at room temperature. Makes 12 servings.

ORANGE MILK SHERBET

1 envelope unflavored gelatin
3 cups milk
2 cups half-and-half
1½ cups sugar
1 cup orange juice
¼ cup grated orange peel
¼ cup lemon juice
¾ teaspoon salt
¼ teaspoon yellow food color
⅛ teaspoon red food color

EARLY IN DAY OR UP TO 1 MONTH AHEAD:
In small saucepan, sprinkle gelatin over 1 cup milk. Cook over low heat, stirring constantly, until gelatin is dissolved; set aside. In large bowl, combine 2 cups milk with remaining ingredients; gradually stir in gelatin mixture (mixture may have curdled appearance). Pour mixture into two 8″ by 8″ or 9″ by 9″ baking pans. Cover with foil or plastic wrap and freeze until partially frozen, about 3 hours.

Spoon mixtures from both pans into chilled large bowl; with mixer at medium speed, beat until smooth but still frozen; return mixture to pans. Cover and freeze until firm.

TO SERVE:
Let sherbet stand at room temperature 10 minutes for easier scooping. Makes 4 pints or 10 servings.

TO MAKE IN ICE-CREAM FREEZER: Prepare as above but, instead of mixing in large bowl, add everything to 4-quart ice-cream freezer can and freeze as directed in Homemade Vanilla Ice Cream (page 572). Makes about 5 pints.

LIME: Prepare as above but use *2 cups sugar* and substitute *¾ cup lime juice* and *2 tablespoons grated lime peel* for orange juice and peel; omit lemon juice; substitute *4 drops green food color* for yellow and red food colors.

APRICOT ICE

2 30-ounce cans apricot halves
1 cup sugar
2¼ cups orange juice
⅓ cup lemon juice
about 20 pounds cracked ice
2 to 3 pounds rock salt

EARLY IN DAY OR UP TO 1 MONTH AHEAD:
Drain apricots (use juice another day) and place apricots in blender container; cover and blend at low speed until apricots are pureed.

In large bowl, mix well pureed apricots, sugar, orange juice and lemon juice; pour into 4- to 6-quart ice-cream freezer can and freeze as directed in Homemade Vanilla Ice Cream (page 572). Mixture will take about 30 minutes to freeze.

After freezing, ice will be soft. Remove motor; wipe lid carefully before removing.

Homemade Strawberry Ice Cream, page 573

Remove dasher; with spoon, pack down Apricot Ice. Cover opening of can with waxed paper, plastic wrap or foil. Replace lid and put cork in hole in center; add more ice and salt to cover lid. Harden ice about 2 to 3 hours, adding more ice and salt as needed. (Or, place ice in a home freezer to harden, about 2 to 3 hours.) Makes about 1½ quarts or 8 servings.

CANTALOUPE ICE

2 medium cantaloupes, peeled and seeded
½ cup sugar
3 tablespoons lemon juice
½ teaspoon salt

DAY BEFORE OR UP TO 1 MONTH AHEAD:
Cut cantaloupes into chunks to make about 6 cups. In covered blender container at medium speed, blend chunks and remaining ingredients, half at a time, until smooth, stopping and occasionally scraping container with rubber spatula. Into 8″ by 8″ or 9″ by 9″ baking pan, pour cantaloupe mixture. Cover with foil or plastic wrap; freeze until firm.

ABOUT 30 MINUTES BEFORE SERVING:
Let ice stand at room temperature about 20 minutes, occasionally breaking up mixture with spoon. In large bowl, with mixer at low speed, beat mixture until mushy, about 3 to 5 minutes. Spoon into chilled dessert dishes; serve immediately. Makes 5 cups or 10 servings.

CRANBERRY-ICE RELISH

1 cup sugar
1 pound cranberries
1 3-ounce package lemon-flavor gelatin

DAY BEFORE OR UP TO 1 MONTH AHEAD:
1. In medium saucepan over high heat, heat sugar and 2½ cups water to boiling; add cranberries. Reduce heat to medium; cover and cook about 7 minutes or until skins of berries "pop"; remove from heat. Add gelatin and stir until dissolved.
2. In covered blender container at low speed, blend mixture, half at a time, until pureed* (about 20 seconds) and pour into 9″ by 9″ baking pan. Cover with foil or plastic wrap and freeze until frozen about 3 inches from edge, about 5 hours.
3. Spoon mixture into chilled, large bowl and, with mixer at medium speed, beat until smooth but still frozen, about 2 minutes; return mixture to pan. Cover and freeze until firm.

TO SERVE:
4. Let cranberry ice stand at room temperature 10 minutes for easier scooping. Makes 6 cups or 12 to 14 servings.

PINEAPPLE ICE: In large bowl, combine 2 *20-ounce cans crushed pineapple in pineapple juice* with *¾ cup sugar* and *2 tablespoons lemon juice*. In small saucepan, over *1 cup cold water*, sprinkle *1 envelope unflavored gelatin*. Cook over low heat, stirring constantly, until gelatin is dissolved. Stir into pineapple mixture. Complete recipe as in steps 2, 3 and 4, above. Makes 6 cups or 12 servings.

* Or, press cranberry mixture through food mill.

TOMATO-ICE APPETIZER

3 cups tomato juice
2 tablespoons minced onion
1 tablespoon lemon juice
2 teaspoons sugar
¾ teaspoon salt
½ teaspoon basil
1 stalk celery, chopped
2 drops hot pepper sauce
2 tablespoons minced parsley

EARLY IN DAY OR UP TO 1 WEEK AHEAD:
In medium saucepan over medium-high heat, heat to boiling all ingredients except parsley. Reduce heat to low; cover and simmer 5 minutes, stirring occasionally. Into 8″ by 8″ baking pan, strain tomato mixture through fine sieve; stir in parsley. Cover with foil or plastic wrap and freeze until firm.

ABOUT 30 MINUTES BEFORE SERVING:
Let tomato ice stand at room temperature about 20 minutes, occasionally breaking up mixture with spoon. In large bowl, with mixer at low speed, beat mixture until mushy, about 3 to 5 minutes. Spoon into 6 chilled appetizer dishes. Serve immediately. Makes 6 first-course servings.

Clockwise: Sugar Cookies, page 567; Almond Lace Rolls, page 557; Walnut Clusters, page 555; Spritz, page 566; Toffee Bars, page 562

Special Ice-Cream Desserts

PARFAITS

JUST BEFORE SERVING:
In parfait, sherbet or small iced-tea glasses, spoon ice cream in layers with any of toppings for Sundaes (below); top, if desired with whipped cream and maraschino cherries. Or, arrange one of these combinations:

TWO-TONE: Alternate layers of 2 different ice creams, or 1 ice cream and 1 sherbet, plus chocolate, butterscotch or fruit sauce.

RAINBOW: Alternate layers of vanilla ice cream and 2 or more kinds of jelly or preserves. Top with whipped cream and nuts.

MIXED FRUIT: Alternate layers of sherbet with thawed frozen mixed fruits or canned fruit cocktail; top with shredded lime or orange peel.

CHERRY CORDIAL: Alternate layers of chocolate ice cream with finely diced maraschino cherries; top with chocolate sauce.

ORANGE: Alternate layers of orange sherbet or vanilla ice cream with orange marmalade.

MOCHA: Alternate layers of coffee ice cream with chocolate sauce; top with candy coffee beans.

SUNDAES

JUST BEFORE SERVING:
Top your favorite ice cream or sherbet with one or more of these:

Any of sauces on page 582
Eggnog Sauce, Peach Sauce, Brandied Strawberry Sauce, Chocolate Sauce, Date-Nut Sauce, Hot Butterscotch Sauce (page 500); Melba Sauce (page 357); Cherry Sauce (page 359)
Crushed pineapple
Mandarin orange sections
Canned apricots; or slightly thawed or thawed frozen peaches, strawberries, raspberries, blueberries, blended in covered blender container until smooth
Banana slices
Maple, maple-blended or fruit-flavor syrup
Honey
Crème de menthe, crème de cacao or coffee-flavored liqueur
Grenadine syrup
Fruit preserves or marmalade
Jelly, melted or beaten with fork
Whole-cranberry sauce
Frozen grape-juice concentrate, slightly thawed
Warm prepared mincemeat
Peanut butter, stirred with honey or pancake syrup until of pouring consistency
Marshmallow cream, stirred with milk, chocolate syrup, fruit juice or cold coffee until of pouring consistency
Whipped cream
Crushed candy: peanut brittle, toffee, peppermint, fruit-flavor hard candy
Crumbled milk chocolate or peppermint patties
Shaved sweet or semisweet chocolate
Coconut, plain or toasted
Chopped plain or salted nuts
Crumbled cookies or macaroons
Crumbled pretzels
Shredded orange or lime peel

QUICK RIPPLED ICE CREAM

SEVERAL HOURS AHEAD:
Spoon *1 pint ice cream*, slightly softened, into 8″ by 8″ baking pan. Swirl or fold one of flavors below through ice cream; freeze until firm. Makes 4 servings.

BERRY: With fork, swirl *1 cup crushed fresh or thawed frozen strawberries or raspberries* through vanilla ice cream.

QUICK BISCUIT TORTONI: Fold *⅓ cup macaroon crumbs, 2 tablespoons diced candied cherries* and *¼ cup chopped salted almonds* into vanilla ice cream.

GINGER: Fold *1 cup coarsely broken gingersnaps* into vanilla ice cream.

FRUITED: Fold *1 cup crumbled fruitcake* into vanilla ice cream.

MAPLE: Swirl *maple or maple-blended syrup* through butter-pecan ice cream.

MINCEMEAT: Swirl *½ cup prepared mincemeat* through vanilla ice cream.

ICE-CREAM SANDWICHES

JUST BEFORE SERVING:
For each serving, make "sandwich" using *2 thin slices angel, chiffon or sponge cake,* plain or toasted, with *slightly softened ice cream* as filling. Top with favorite *sundae sauce* or any of fruit toppings listed in Sundaes (opposite).

PARTY: Split *one 8-inch or 9-inch cake layer,* unfrosted, in half horizontally. Place one half, cut side up, on plate; spread with *1 pint favorite ice cream,* slightly softened; top with second cake half, cut side down; freeze. To serve, cut into wedges; top wedges with *favorite sundae sauce.* Makes 6 servings.

PORTABLE: For each serving, spread each of *2 graham-crackers* thinly with *strawberry preserves.* From a pint ice-cream "brick," cut 1-inch-thick slice of *ice cream;* trim to fit crackers; place on spread side of one cracker; top with other cracker, spread side down. Serve immediately in paper napkin.

ICE-CREAM SNOWBALLS

SEVERAL HOURS OR UP TO 1 MONTH AHEAD:
With large spoon or ice-cream scoop, spoon or scoop balls of ice cream. Roll each ball in one of coatings below. Arrange on tray if serving same day; freeze. If storing for later use, freezer-wrap and freeze. To serve, unwrap if necessary; place one or two balls on dessert plates and top, if you like, with sauces or fruits suggested for Sundaes (opposite).

COATINGS: Fine cake crumbs; grated fresh coconut; plain or tinted shredded or flaked coconut; chopped plain or salted nuts; crumbled sugar-coated cereal flakes; grated chocolate; crushed peppermint candy or peanut brittle.

PEACH MELBA

JUST BEFORE SERVING:
For each serving, spoon *vanilla ice cream* into dessert dish; top with *fresh or canned peach half;* spoon Melba Sauce (page 357) over peach.

BAKED ALASKA

1 package poundcake mix
1 pint strawberry ice cream, slightly softened
1 pint chocolate-chip ice cream, slightly softened
3 egg whites, at room temperature
1/8 teaspoon cream of tartar
6 tablespoons sugar

EARLY IN DAY OR UP TO 2 WEEKS AHEAD:
Prepare cake mix as label directs in 9" by 5" loaf pan; cool. Wash loaf pan.

Line loaf pan with waxed paper. Spread ice creams in two even layers in pan; freeze until firm.

Slice cake horizontally in half; place one half of cake, cut side up, in center of a sheet of foil. Unmold frozen ice cream on top of cake; peel off waxed paper. Wrap ice-cream cake and freeze until needed. (Use remaining cake half another day.)

ABOUT 25 MINUTES BEFORE SERVING:
Preheat oven to 500°F. For meringue: In small bowl, with mixer at high speed, beat egg whites and cream of tartar until soft peaks form; beating at high speed, gradually sprinkle in sugar, 2 tablespoons at a time; beat until sugar is completely dissolved. (Whites should stand in stiff peaks.) To test, rub a small bit of the meringue between thumb and forefinger; if it doesn't feel grainy, sugar is dissolved.

Unwrap ice-cream cake and place on chilled cookie sheet, ice-cream side on top. Quickly spread meringue over entire surface of ice-cream cake, right down to cookie sheet. Bake 3 minutes or until meringue is lightly browned. Slip 2 pancake turners under Baked Alaska and carefully transfer to chilled platter. Slice and serve immediately. Makes 8 to 10 servings.

INDIVIDUAL: Preheat oven to 500°F. Prepare meringue as above but use *4 egg whites, 1/8 teaspoon cream of tartar* and *1/2 cup sugar.* Place *6 bakers' or packaged dessert shells* on chilled cookie sheet; top each with large scoopful from *2 pints favorite ice cream.* Quickly spread each with meringue right down to cookie sheet; bake 3 minutes or until meringue is lightly browned. Transfer to chilled dessert plates; serve immediately. Makes 6 servings.

HOLIDAY ICE-CREAM MOLD

1 cup heavy or whipping cream
1 cup chopped candied red cherries
½ cup ground almonds
½ teaspoon ground cardamom
2 pints vanilla ice cream, softened

EARLY IN DAY OR UP TO 1 WEEK AHEAD:
In large bowl, with mixer at medium speed, beat heavy or whipping cream until soft peaks form. Reduce mixer speed to low; beat in remaining ingredients just until blended. Pour into 6-cup mold. Cover with foil or plastic wrap and freeze until firm.

ABOUT 1 HOUR BEFORE SERVING:
With metal spatula, loosen edges of frozen mixture from mold. In large bowl or sink of very hot water, dip frozen mixture almost to top to loosen; dry mold with towel. Invert mixture onto platter. Return to freezer.

TO SERVE:
Let mold stand at room temperature about 10 minutes for easier slicing. Makes 10 to 12 servings.

BOMBE GLACE WITH FRUIT

3 pints strawberry-ripple ice cream,*
slightly softened
⅓ 3-ounce package ladyfingers
¼ cup orange-flavor liqueur
1 pint strawberries, sliced
1 banana, sliced
1 peach, sliced
small bunches seedless grapes

DAY BEFORE SERVING:
Spoon 2 pints ice cream into 6-cup mold; with back of spoon, press ice cream to sides and bottom of mold to make a smooth shell. Split ladyfingers and arrange against ice cream, overlapping slightly; drizzle with orange-flavor liqueur. Spoon remaining ice cream into center, pressing to pack firmly. Cover with foil or plastic wrap and freeze.

ABOUT 1 OR 2 HOURS BEFORE SERVING:
With metal spatula, loosen edges of frozen mixture from mold. In large bowl or sink of hot water, quickly dip frozen mixture almost to top to loosen; dry mold. Invert mixture onto platter. Return to freezer.

TO SERVE:
Let mold stand at room temperature 10 minutes for easier slicing. Arrange fruits around ice cream. Makes 8 to 10 servings.

* Or, use any favorite-flavor ice cream.

ICE-CREAM BOMBE

DAY BEFORE OR UP TO 1 MONTH AHEAD:
Spoon 2 *pints favorite-flavor ice cream,* slightly softened, into a 6-cup mold; with back of spoon, press ice cream to sides and bottom of mold to make a smooth shell. Into hollow center, spoon *1 pint sherbet,* slightly softened, pressing to pack firmly. Freezer-wrap mold; freeze.

AT SERVING TIME:
With metal spatula, loosen edges of frozen mixture from mold. In large bowl or sink of hot water, quickly dip frozen mixture almost to top to loosen; dry mold with towel. Invert mixture onto platter. Cut into wedges. Makes 6 servings.

RAINBOW ICE-CREAM ROLLS

2 pints raspberry sherbet, slightly softened
2 pints orange sherbet, slightly softened

EARLY IN DAY OR UP TO 2 WEEKS AHEAD:
Line a 15½" by 10½" jelly-roll pan with waxed paper, extending waxed paper about 2 inches beyond short ends of pan. Refrigerate until well chilled. Spread raspberry sherbet evenly in pan; freeze until firm, about 3 hours. Then spread orange sherbet evenly over raspberry; freeze until firm but not solid, about 3 hours. (When frozen solid, sherbet does not roll well.)

To roll, with spatula, loosen sherbet from waxed paper along long sides of pan. Working quickly, roll jelly-roll fashion: Lift a narrow end of waxed paper and turn over end of sherbet, pressing with fingers to start roll. Peel paper back, then continue lifting paper and rolling sherbet until completely rolled. Discard paper. (If necessary, use spatula to help separate paper from sherbet as you roll.)

Quickly place roll, seam side down, on chilled freezerproof platter. Return to freezer until serving time. Makes 8 servings.

OTHER COMBINATIONS: Use chocolate and pistachio or strawberry and vanilla ice creams or lime and lemon sherbets instead of raspberry and orange sherbets.

BANANA SPLIT

JUST BEFORE SERVING:
For each serving, peel and split *1 ripe large banana* lengthwise; place halves, cut side up, on dessert plate. Top with *3 scoops of ice cream,* using different flavors if you like. Then top each ice-cream mound with 2 or 3 tablespoons sauce, using *3 different ice-cream sauces.* Sprinkle ice cream with *chopped nuts;* top center mound with *whipped cream* and *maraschino cherry.*

ICE-CREAM PIES

EARLY IN DAY:
Prepare any of piecrusts (pages 504–508); cool if baked. Refrigerate to chill well.

AT SERVING TIME:
Fill chilled *piecrust* with 1, 2 or 3 flavors of *ice cream* or sherbet, using 1 to 2 pints for 8-inch pie, 2 to 3 pints for 9-inch pie. Top with any of toppings for Sundaes (page 578); cut into wedges. Makes 6 to 8 servings.

TO DO AHEAD: Fill piecrust with ice cream or sherbet; freezer-wrap and freeze up to 1 month. To serve, unwrap; let stand at room temperature 20 minutes for easier cutting. Add topping, if desired.

TARTS: Prepare as above, using Tart Shells (page 507), *1½ pints ice cream* or sherbet.

PUMPKIN ICE-CREAM PIE

1 18-ounce can pumpkin-pie filling
1 pint butter-pecan ice cream, softened
1 8-inch graham-cracker piecrust
½ cup packed brown sugar
2 tablespoons butter or margarine
½ cup chopped pecans

EARLY IN DAY OR UP TO 1 MONTH AHEAD:
In large bowl, with mixer at medium speed, beat pie filling and ice cream until well mixed. Spoon into crust and freeze 1 hour.

In small saucepan over medium heat, heat brown sugar, butter or margarine and 1 tablespoon water to boiling. Remove from heat; stir in pecans. With spoon, drizzle mixture over pie. Freeze until firm.

TO SERVE:
Let pie stand at room temperature 15 minutes. Makes 8 servings.

MINTED SHERBET RING WITH BERRIES

3 pints lemon sherbet, slightly softened
⅓ cup green crème de menthe
2 pints strawberries
shredded coconut for garnish

EARLY IN DAY OR DAY AHEAD:
In large bowl, with mixer at medium speed, beat lemon sherbet with crème de menthe until smooth; spoon into a 5½-cup ring mold; freezer-wrap and freeze.

AT SERVING TIME:
With metal spatula, loosen edges of frozen mixture from mold. In large bowl or sink of hot water, quickly dip frozen mixture almost to top to loosen; dry mold with towel. Invert mold onto platter; remove mold. Fill center of ring with strawberries; sprinkle with coconut. Serve immediately. Makes 8 to 10 servings.

FROZEN SNACK POPS

Fill each plastic pop mold to within ¼ inch of top with one of fillings below. (Each mold holds about ¼ cup filling.) Cover; freeze 12 hours or overnight.

VANILLA-RAISIN: Spoon *¼ cup prepared regular or instant vanilla pudding* into mold; swirl *1 tablespoon dark seedless raisins, dash cinnamon* and *dash nutmeg* through pudding. Makes 1 pop.

OTHER FLAVORS: Pour ¼ cup any of these into mold: orange juice, grape juice, chocolate milk drink, ready-to-use eggnog, tropical fruit punch. Makes 1 pop.

VANILLA-CHOCOLATE: Spoon *¼ cup vanilla yogurt* into mold; swirl *1 teaspoon chocolate syrup* through yogurt. Makes 1 pop.

YOGURT FLAVORS: Spoon *¼ cup vanilla, strawberry, blueberry, or other favorite-flavor yogurt* into mold. Makes 1 pop.

ICE SNOWBALLS OR "SLUSH"

JUST BEFORE SERVING:
Crush *ice* fine in electric ice crusher or slush-maker. For each serving, fill paper cup with crushed ice, heaping slightly; top with a few tablespoonfuls of *thawed undiluted frozen orange-juice, red tropical fruit punch or grape-juice concentrate.* Serve with spoon and straw.

ORANGE-SHERBET CUPS

DAY OR SO BEFORE SERVING:
Slice tops from *6 small oranges* about one-fourth of the way down. Slice a thin strip from bottom so each will stand evenly. With sharp knife, cut out all fruit sections. (Serve sections next day.)

From *2 pints orange sherbet,* fill each shell. Place in shallow pan and freeze.

TO SERVE:
Let orange cups stand at room temperature about 10 minutes until slightly softened. Sprinkle each with *flaked coconut.* Makes 6 servings.

Sauces for Frozen Desserts

HOT CHOCOLATE-MINT SAUCE

20 chocolate-covered peppermint candies (about 9 ounces)
2 tablespoons butter or margarine
3 tablespoons half-and-half

ABOUT 5 MINUTES BEFORE SERVING:
In small saucepan over low heat, melt peppermints with butter or margarine and half-and-half. Serve hot. Makes 1 cup.

CHOCOLATE-MARSHMALLOW SAUCE

2 cups miniature marshmallows
⅓ cup heavy or whipping cream
⅓ cup honey
1½ squares unsweetened chocolate
⅛ teaspoon salt

ABOUT 15 MINUTES BEFORE SERVING:
In medium saucepan over low heat, cook all ingredients, stirring constantly, until marshmallows and chocolate are melted. Serve hot. Makes 1½ cups.

HOT FUDGE SAUCE

1½ cups sugar
½ cup milk
⅓ cup light corn syrup
2 squares unsweetened chocolate
1 tablespoon butter or margarine
1 teaspoon vanilla extract
dash salt

ABOUT 20 MINUTES BEFORE SERVING:
In 2-quart saucepan over medium heat, heat first 4 ingredients to boiling, stirring constantly. Set candy thermometer in place and continue cooking, stirring occasionally, until temperature reaches 228°F. or until a small amount of mixture dropped from tip of spoon back into mixture spins a ¼-inch thread. Remove from heat; immediately stir in butter or margarine, vanilla and salt. Serve hot. Makes 1⅔ cups.

BUTTER-CARAMEL SAUCE

1 cup half-and-half
¾ cup sugar
½ cup light corn syrup
¼ cup butter or margarine
⅛ teaspoon salt
½ teaspoon vanilla extract

ABOUT 45 MINUTES BEFORE SERVING:
In 1½-quart saucepan over medium heat, combine ½ cup half-and-half and next 4 ingredients. Cook, stirring frequently, until candy thermometer reads 250°F. or a little mixture dropped in cold water forms a hard ball. Remove from heat; gradually stir in remaining half-and-half. Cook, stirring constantly, just until blended; remove from heat; stir in vanilla. Serve hot. Makes about 1⅓ cups.

In addition to those above, the following sauces are also especially good on frozen desserts:

Brandied Strawberry Sauce (page 500)
Cherry Sauce (page 359)
Chocolate Sauce (page 500)
Date-Nut Sauce (page 500)
Eggnog Sauce (page 500)
Hot Butterscotch Sauce (page 500)
Melba Sauce (page 357)
Peach Sauce (page 500)

Candy

For those family members with a sweet tooth, serve candy as dessert for luncheon or dinner. That way it doesn't spoil the appetite for meals, yet satisfies a natural desire for sweets.

Tips for Perfect Candies

Getting ready: Don't double candy recipes; increased amounts of ingredients will lengthen the cooking time. If you want more than the recipe makes at one time, make it again until you have the amount needed.

The pan used for cooking the mixture is important. It should be large enough to allow the mixture to boil freely without running over and heavy enough to lessen the chance that the mixture will stick to the bottom.

Cooking the candy mixture: Use a wooden spoon for stirring and beating. A metal spoon might get too hot to handle.

Undissolved sugar crystals can cause candy to be grainy. Either butter the sides of the saucepan before cooking so crystals can't cling to the sides, or wash crystals down from the sides with a pastry brush dipped in hot water and drained. When starting to cook the mixture, stir until all the sugar is dissolved; then stir only if the recipe says to.

Testing the candy with a thermometer: A candy thermometer takes the guesswork out of testing the boiling mixture.

To check your candy thermometer, let it stand in boiling water for a few minutes. If it registers 212°F., it is accurate. (If you live at high altitude, see page 24.) If it registers above (or below) 212°F., determine the number of degrees difference and add this to (or subtract it from) the temperature given in the recipe. Use this adjusted temperature in making the candy. Repeat for each new recipe.

For an accurate reading, place the candy thermometer so that it stands upright and the bulb is well covered with the boiling (not foaming) mixture. *Be sure the bulb is not resting on the bottom of the pan.* When reading, be sure your eye is level with the mercury. After the temperature reaches 220°F. on the candy thermometer, watch it carefully, since it rises rapidly from that point.

Temperatures for cooking candy vary: For example, some mixtures reach the soft ball stage at 236°F. and others at 240°F. When using a candy thermometer, cooking to any temperature within a given range will give acceptable results, but cooking to the precise temperature specified in the recipe will produce the very best candy.

When finished with the candy thermometer, remove it from the candy mixture and place it where it can cool before washing; if put at once into dish water it may break.

Using the cold-water test: If you do not have a candy thermometer, use the cold-water test. Have ready a measuring cup filled with water that is very cold but not iced. *Remove the pan of candy mixture from the heat* and, with a clean spoon, drop about ½ teaspoon of the mixture into the water. Let it stand a minute; then, with fingers, note the firmness of the mixture. Use this chart as a guide:

230° to 234°F.—Thread:
Syrup spins a 2-inch thread in the air as it falls from spoon.
234° to 240°F.—Soft ball:
Syrup (in cold water) forms a soft ball which flattens on removal from water.
244° to 248°F.—Firm ball:
Syrup (in cold water) forms a firm ball which does not flatten on removal from water.
250° to 266°F.—Hard ball:
Syrup (in cold water) forms a ball which is hard enough to hold its shape, yet pliable.
270° to 290°F.—Soft crack:
Syrup (in cold water) separates into threads which are hard but not brittle.
300° to 310°F.—Hard crack:
Syrup (in cold water) separates into threads which are hard and brittle.

Cooling candy mixture: When the recipe for creamy candies such as fudge says to cool until lukewarm, remove the saucepan from the heat and let the mixture stand without stirring to 110°F. on the candy thermometer, or until the bottom of the saucepan feels lukewarm to your hand. Don't move or jar the saucepan; don't beat the mixture while it is hot, or large sugar crystals will form and make the candy grainy.

Finishing the candy: When the mixture is ready for pouring, hold the saucepan close to the pan and pour quickly. With a rubber spatula, push the mixture into the pan; don't scrape the saucepan, since the mixture on the sides may be sugary.

Cut or break the candy when cool; store when cold.

How to Store

Most candies keep best when stored in a tightly covered container and kept in a cool place. Creamy candies such as fudge and penuche will keep fresh longer, and chewy candies such as caramels and taffy will be prevented from sticking together, if individual pieces are wrapped in plastic wrap, waxed paper or foil. If recipe says to keep candy refrigerated, cover or wrap and refrigerate until served.

How to Pack for Mailing

Choose candies that travel well, such as fudge, taffy, candied nuts and fruit peels. Some of the candies from this chapter that "go places" well include cooked fudge (Chocolate, Merry Christmas, etc.); Pecan Penuche; Maple Kisses; Molasses Taffy; Divinity Drops; Peanut Brittle; Crispy Candy Squares; Apricot Snowballs; Sherried Walnuts; Christmas Popcorn Balls. Follow directions for packing and mailing cookies, steps 2 through 6, page 554. In step 3, wrap each piece of candy individually in waxed paper, plastic wrap or foil.

NO-COOK CHEESE-NUT FUDGE

1 3-ounce package cream cheese, softened
2½ cups confectioners' sugar
¼ teaspoon almond extract
½ cup chopped blanched almonds, walnuts, pecans, Brazil nuts or flaked coconut

ABOUT 30 MINUTES BEFORE SERVING:
Butter 9″ by 5″ loaf pan. In small bowl, with mixer at medium speed (or with spoon), beat cream cheese with sugar and almond extract until smooth. Stir in nuts. Press into pan. Refrigerate until firm; cut

into squares. Keep refrigerated until served. Makes 30 squares or about 1 pound.

CHOCOLATE-NUT: Prepare as above but reduce confectioners' sugar to 2 cups; add 2 *squares unsweetened chocolate,* melted, to cream cheese and substitute *vanilla extract* for almond.

PEANUT BUTTER: Prepare as above but substitute 2 *tablespoons creamy peanut butter* for almond extract and, for nuts, use ¼ *cup chopped salted peanuts.*

CHERRY NUT: Prepare as above but add *one 4-ounce container red or green candied cherries,* chopped, and use only ¼ cup chopped blanched almonds.

PECAN PENUCHE

2 cups packed light brown sugar
2 cups sugar
1 cup milk
3 tablespoons butter or margarine
1½ teaspoons vanilla extract
1 cup coarsely chopped pecans

EARLY IN DAY:
In large saucepan over medium heat, heat sugars and milk to boiling, stirring constantly. Set candy thermometer in place and continue cooking, without stirring, until temperature reaches 238°F., or until a small amount of mixture dropped into very cold water forms a soft ball. Remove mixture from heat; add butter or margarine and vanilla.

Cool mixture, without stirring, to 110°F. or until outside of saucepan feels lukewarm to hand. Meanwhile, butter 8″ by 8″ pan.

With spoon, beat until mixture becomes thick and begins to lose its gloss; quickly stir in pecans. Pour into pan. (Don't scrape saucepan; mixture on side may be sugary.) Cool in pan on wire rack; when cold, cut into squares. Makes 25 pieces or 2 pounds.

CHOCOLATE-DRIZZLED: Prepare as above. In double boiler over hot, not boiling, water, melt ½ *cup semisweet-chocolate pieces* and, with teaspoon, drizzle over top of candy. From about 1 *cup pecan halves,* place a pecan half on top of each piece.

COCONUT: Prepare as above but substitute 1 *cup chopped shredded coconut* for pecans.

MARSHMALLOW NUT FUDGE

1⅔ cups sugar
⅔ cup evaporated milk (1 6-ounce can)
2 tablespoons butter or margarine
½ teaspoon salt
1½ 6-ounce packages semisweet-chocolate pieces (1½ cups)
2 cups miniature marshmallows
½ cup chopped California walnuts
1 teaspoon vanilla extract

ABOUT 1½ HOURS BEFORE SERVING:
Butter 8″ by 8″ baking pan. In a small saucepan over medium heat, heat sugar, undiluted milk, butter or margarine and salt to boiling; boil 5 minutes, stirring constantly. Remove from heat and add remaining ingredients. Beat vigorously until marshmallows melt. Pour into pan; sprinkle with more chopped nuts, if desired. Cool in pan on wire rack; cut into small squares. Makes 64 pieces or about 2 pounds.

MAPLE KISSES

1 cup packed light brown sugar
½ cup sugar
½ cup evaporated milk
¼ cup light corn syrup
1 tablespoon butter or margarine
1 teaspoon maple flavor
1½ cups chopped California walnuts

ABOUT 1½ HOURS BEFORE SERVING:
In medium saucepan over very low heat, heat sugars, undiluted milk and corn syrup to boiling, stirring constantly. Set candy thermometer in place and continue cooking, stirring constantly, until temperature reaches 235°F. or until a small amount of mixture dropped into very cold water forms a soft ball. (This takes about 30 minutes.) Remove mixture from heat.

With spoon, beat butter or margarine, maple flavor and nuts into mixture. Quickly drop mixture by teaspoonfuls onto waxed paper; cool on wire racks. When cold, store in tightly covered container up to 1 week. Makes about 24 pieces or ¾ pound.

PEANUT: Prepare as above but substitute *chopped salted peanuts* for walnuts.

MERRY-CHRISTMAS FUDGE

3 cups sugar
1½ cups milk
¾ teaspoon salt
3 tablespoons butter or margarine
1½ teaspoons vanilla extract
½ cup marshmallow cream
¾ cup sliced candied cherries or candied orange peel

ABOUT 4 HOURS BEFORE SERVING:
In large saucepan over medium heat, heat sugar, milk and salt to boiling, stirring until sugar is dissolved. Set candy thermometer in place and continue cooking, without stirring, until temperature reaches 234°F. or until a small amount of mixture dropped into very cold water forms soft ball. Remove mixture from heat; add butter or margarine and vanilla.

Cool mixture, without stirring, to 110°F. or until outside of saucepan feels lukewarm to hand. Meanwhile, butter 8″ by 8″ baking pan.

With spoon, beat until mixture begins to hold its shape. Add marshmallow cream; beat until mixture becomes thick and begins to lose its gloss. Quickly stir in cherries; pour into pan. (Don't scrape saucepan; mixture on side may be sugary.) Cool in pan on wire rack; when cold, cut into squares. Makes 36 pieces or about 1¾ pounds.

OPERA FUDGE: Prepare as above but omit marshmallow cream and candied cherries. If you like, stir in *¾ cup chopped nuts* before pouring into pan.

CHOCOLATE FUDGE

3 cups sugar
1 cup milk
2 tablespoons corn syrup
2 squares unsweetened chocolate
3 tablespoons butter or margarine
1 teaspoon vanilla extract
1 cup chopped California walnuts or pecans

ABOUT 2½ HOURS BEFORE SERVING:
In large saucepan over medium heat, heat sugar and next 3 ingredients to boiling, stirring constantly. Set candy thermometer in place and continue cooking, stirring occasionally, until temperature reaches 238°F. or until a small amount of mixture dropped into very cold water forms a soft ball. Remove from heat; immediately add butter or margarine and vanilla.

Cool mixture, without stirring, to 110°F., or until outside of saucepan feels lukewarm to hand. Meanwhile, butter 8″ by 8″ pan.

With spoon, beat until mixture becomes thick and begins to lose its gloss. Quickly stir in nuts; pour into pan. (Don't scrape saucepan; mixture on side may be sugary.) Cool in pan; when cold, cut into 32 squares. Makes 32 pieces or about 1¼ pounds.

PEANUT BUTTER: Prepare as above but use *¼ cup creamy peanut butter* for butter or margarine and substitute *1 cup chopped salted peanuts* for walnuts.

CHOCOLATE MARSHMALLOW: Prepare as above but stir in *1 cup miniature marshmallows* just before pouring mixture into pan.

ORANGE-ALMOND CARAMELS

3 cups sugar
1 cup evaporated milk
dash salt
2 teaspoons grated orange peel
1⅓ cups toasted slivered almonds

ABOUT 1½ HOURS BEFORE SERVING:
In heavy medium saucepan over medium heat, heat 1 cup sugar, stirring constantly, until entirely melted and a deep golden color. Stirring constantly, slowly add ¼ cup boiling water; cook until mixture is a smooth syrup. Stir in remaining 2 cups sugar, undiluted evaporated milk and salt.

Set candy thermometer in place and continue cooking over medium heat, stirring constantly, until temperature reaches 238°F., or until a small amount of mixture dropped into very cold water forms a soft ball. Remove from heat; add orange peel and stir until mixture cools slightly; add 1 cup nuts and continue stirring until a little of mixture retains its shape and looks slightly dull when dropped on waxed paper.

Drop by heaping teaspoonfuls onto waxed paper; press a few more nuts on top of each piece. Wrap; store up to one week. Makes about 50 pieces or 1½ pounds.

EASY BRAZIL-NUT CARAMELS

1 14-ounce package vanilla and chocolate caramels
2 tablespoons shortening
¾ cup chopped Brazil nuts

ABOUT 1½ HOURS AHEAD OR EARLY IN DAY: In double-boiler top, over boiling water, melt caramels with shortening, stirring occasionally; stir in Brazil nuts. Remove from heat; keep mixture over hot water and drop by teaspoonfuls onto foil.

Cool until firm. Wrap each caramel in plastic wrap; store in refrigerator or cool place. Makes about 36 pieces or 1 pound.

MOLASSES TAFFY

butter or margarine
1⅓ cups sweetened condensed milk (1 14- or 15-ounce can)
½ cup light molasses
⅛ teaspoon salt

ABOUT 2 HOURS BEFORE SERVING: Butter large platter or 8″ by 8″ pan. In medium saucepan over medium heat, heat sweetened condensed milk, molasses and salt to boiling, stirring occasionally. Set candy thermometer in place and continue cooking, stirring constantly, until temperature reaches 244°F. or until a small amount of mixture dropped into very cold water forms a firm ball, about 20 minutes. Remove from heat; pour onto platter.

Let mixture stand until cool enough to handle. With buttered fingers, pull mixture until shiny and light colored. Twist into rope about ¾ inch thick; with kitchen scissors, cut into 1-inch pieces. Wrap each piece in plastic wrap. Makes about 50 pieces or ¾ pound.

DIVINITY DROPS*

3 cups sugar
½ cup light corn syrup
2 egg whites, at room temperature
1 teaspoon vanilla extract

UP TO 1 WEEK AHEAD: In medium saucepan over medium-high heat, heat sugar, corn syrup and ½ cup water to boiling, stirring until sugar is dissolved. Set candy thermometer in place and continue cooking, without stirring, until temperature reaches 248°F.

Meanwhile, in medium bowl, with mixer at high speed, beat egg whites until stiff peaks form. Beating at medium speed, slowly pour half of syrup into whites. Continue beating while heating other half of syrup to 272°F.

While turning bowl and continuing beating, slowly pour hot remaining syrup into mixture (mixture will be stiff). (Don't scrape saucepan; mixture on side may be sugary.) Add vanilla; beat until mixture holds stiff, glossy peaks. Working quickly, drop by heaping teaspoonfuls onto waxed paper. Cool; store tightly covered. Makes about 60 candies or 1½ pounds.

NUT DIVINITY: Prepare as above but add *1 cup chopped hazelnuts* with vanilla.

* Avoid making on humid day; candy will not harden. This recipe requires a candy thermometer.

MARSHMALLOW SQUARES

1 3-ounce package strawberry-, cherry-, or lime-flavor gelatin
sugar
¼ cup light corn syrup
red or green food color

DAY BEFORE SERVING: Line 8″ by 8″ baking pan with waxed paper. In small saucepan over low heat, dissolve gelatin in ⅔ cup hot water. Stir in 1 cup sugar until dissolved (do not boil). Stir in corn syrup; pour into medium bowl and refrigerate until slightly thickened, about 45 minutes.

With mixer at medium speed, beat mixture 5 minutes or until it starts to mound, adding enough food color to achieve desired color. Spoon into pan. Refrigerate to set thoroughly.

TO SERVE: Invert mixture onto a surface heavily sprinkled with sugar. Rub waxed paper lightly with dampened cloth; let stand a few minutes; carefully peel off paper. Sprinkle additional sugar on top of candy. Cut candy into 1-inch squares and roll sides in sugar. Keep refrigerated. Makes about 48 pieces or 1 pound.

NEAPOLITAN DIVINITY*

7½ cups sugar
1½ cups light corn syrup
¾ teaspoon salt
6 egg whites, at room temperature
2 squares unsweetened chocolate, melted
1 teaspoon vanilla extract
½ cup chopped California walnuts
½ teaspoon mint extract
¼ teaspoon green food color
½ cup chopped red candied cherries
½ teaspoon almond extract
¼ teaspoon red food color

UP TO 1 WEEK BEFORE SERVING:
1. Grease well 13″ by 9″ baking pan and line with foil; set aside. In large saucepan over medium heat, heat 5 cups sugar, 1 cup corn syrup, ½ teaspoon salt and 1 cup water to boiling, stirring constantly. Set candy thermometer in place and continue cooking, without stirring, until temperature reaches 248°F.
2. Meanwhile, in large bowl, with mixer at high speed, beat 4 egg whites until stiff peaks form. Beating at medium speed, slowly pour half of syrup into whites. Continue beating while heating other half of syrup to 272°F. Continuing to beat, slowly pour hot remaining syrup into mixture; beat until mixed. Into medium bowl, pour half of mixture.
3. Into remaining mixture in large bowl, with mixer at medium speed, beat melted chocolate and vanilla until mixture thickens and begins to lose its gloss. Into mixture in medium bowl, with spoon, stir chopped nuts, mint extract and green food color until well mixed and mixture thickens and begins to lose its gloss. Quickly spread green mixture evenly in pan; evenly spread with chocolate mixture.
4. In medium saucepan over medium heat, heat 2½ cups sugar, ½ cup corn syrup and ¼ teaspoon salt with ½ cup water to boiling, stirring constantly. Repeat procedure for cooking syrup as in step 1. Meanwhile, in small bowl, with mixer at high speed, beat 2 egg whites until stiff peaks form. Beating at medium speed, slowly pour half of syrup into whites. Continue beating while heating other half of syrup to 272°F. Continuing beating, slowly pour syrup into mixture; beat until mixed. Stir in remaining ingredients until mixture thickens and begins to lose its gloss; quickly spread evenly over chocolate layer in pan.
5. Let candy cool in pan on wire rack; remove from pan and remove foil. On cutting board, with knife, cut candy into 24 crosswise strips; then cut each strip into 4 pieces, wiping knife as needed with damp cloth for easier cutting. Wrap each piece in plastic wrap; store tightly covered. Makes 96 pieces or about 4 pounds.

* This recipe requires a candy thermometer.

NUTTY MALLOW POPS

For each candy, use *1 regular marshmallow.* Insert two-tined fork in marshmallow and hold marshmallow over pan of boiling water, turning in steam until sticky on all sides. Quickly roll marshmallow in *finely chopped California walnuts* until well coated. Let stand on waxed paper until no longer sticky. Insert *lollipop stick* or short colored straw into marshmallow.

CRISPY CANDY SQUARES

butter or margarine
1 10-ounce bag regular marshmallows
2 squares unsweetened chocolate
5 cups packaged crisp rice cereal
½ teaspoon vanilla extract

EARLY IN DAY:
Butter 9″ by 9″ baking pan and 3-quart bowl. In double-boiler top over boiling water, melt marshmallows with 6 tablespoons butter or margarine and chocolate, stirring often, until smooth and blended. Meanwhile, place rice cereal in bowl.

Into mixture, stir vanilla; remove from heat. Pour mixture over cereal and quickly stir until all cereal is moistened. Press mixture into pan; refrigerate.

TO SERVE:
Cut mixture into squares. To store, leave in pan and cover with foil; keeps several days. Makes about 16 pieces or 1 pound.

CHOCOLATE-TOPPED: Prepare as above but omit chocolate from mixture and melt it separately; spread over candy just before cutting.

FRENCH CHOCOLATES

1 12-ounce package semisweet-chocolate pieces
1 cup chopped California walnuts
¾ cup sweetened condensed milk
1 teaspoon vanilla extract
dash salt
1⅓ cups chopped, flaked coconut, finely chopped California walnuts or chocolate sprinkles for garnish

EARLY IN DAY:
In double-boiler top over hot, not boiling, water, melt chocolate pieces; stir in next 4 ingredients until well mixed. Cool mixture about 5 minutes or until easy to shape. With buttered hands, shape small amount of mixture into 1-inch ball; roll immediately in chopped coconut. Repeat with remaining mixture. Makes about 56 pieces or 1¾ pounds.

TRUFFLES: Line 9″ by 5″ loaf pan with waxed paper. Prepare as above but after mixing, press mixture into pan. Cool in pan on wire rack several hours or until firm. When firm, invert from pan onto cutting board; peel off waxed paper and cut into 4 lengthwise strips; cut each strip into 9 pieces. Omit coconut. Makes 36 pieces or about 1½ pounds.

CHOCOLATE RUM STICKS

3 6-ounce packages semisweet-chocolate pieces (3 cups)
1 14-ounce can sweetened condensed milk
dash salt
2 cups chopped California walnuts
2 teaspoons rum extract

DAY BEFORE SERVING:
Line 9″ by 9″ pan with waxed paper. In medium saucepan over low heat, melt chocolate pieces, stirring frequently. Stir in milk and salt; remove from heat. Pour into medium bowl and, with mixer at medium speed, beat until smooth. Stir in nuts and extract; pour into pan; refrigerate.

TO SERVE:
Invert candy onto cutting board; peel off waxed paper. With sharp knife, cut into ½-inch slices; cut each slice into thirds. Makes 48 pieces or about 2¼ pounds.

CRUNCHY BRIDGE BITES

ABOUT 1 HOUR BEFORE SERVING:
In double-boiler top over hot, not boiling, water, melt *one 6-ounce package semisweet-chocolate pieces;* stir in *1½ cups crumbled corn chips* from one 6-ounce package until completely coated; remove from heat. Onto waxed-paper-lined cookie sheet, drop mixture by rounded teaspoonfuls. Refrigerate until firm, about 40 minutes. Makes 36 pieces or ¾ pound.

COBBLESTONE CANDY

2 12-ounce packages butterscotch pieces
2 tablespoons shortening
3 cups miniature marshmallows
2 cups chopped nuts

EARLY IN DAY:
In double-boiler top over hot, not boiling, water, melt butterscotch pieces with shortening, stirring occasionally. Meanwhile, line 13″ by 9″ baking pan with foil. Into mixture, stir marshmallows and nuts. (Marshmallows need not melt.) Spread mixture in pan; refrigerate 3 hours or until firm.

TO SERVE:
Let candy stand at room temperature 5 minutes; peel off foil; cut candy into 1-inch squares. Makes about 120 pieces or 2⅓ pounds.

HAYSTACKS

1 6-ounce package butterscotch or semisweet-chocolate pieces
2 teaspoons salad oil
1 3-ounce can chow mein noodles (2 cups)
2 cups miniature marshmallows

ABOUT 2 HOURS BEFORE SERVING:
Line large cookie sheet with waxed paper. In double-boiler top over hot, not boiling, water, melt butterscotch pieces with salad oil, stirring occasionally. In large bowl, mix chow mein noodles and marshmallows; pour on butterscotch; with fork, mix well.

Onto cookie sheet, drop mixture by heaping teaspoonfuls. (If mixture thickens, place over hot water a few minutes.) Refrigerate until set. Makes about 30 pieces or ¾ pound.

PEPPERMINT PATTIES

1 14- or 15-ounce can sweetened condensed milk
2 teaspoons peppermint extract
12 drops red food color
1½ to 2 16-ounce packages confectioners' sugar
1½ cups pecan halves

ABOUT 3 HOURS OR UP TO 2 WEEKS AHEAD: In large bowl, mix sweetened condensed milk, peppermint extract and food color. With spoon, stir in 1½ packages sugar. On cutting board generously sprinkled with confectioners' sugar, gradually knead in enough additional sugar so that mixture forms a smooth, firm ball that doesn't stick to hands or board.

Pat mixture into 8″ by 8″ square. With knife, cut into 1-inch squares. Shape each piece into a ball and, with fingers, flatten into 2-inch patty; top with pecan half. Repeat with remaining pieces. (Keep pieces covered with plastic wrap while preparing patties.) Let patties dry at least 1 hour. Store in covered container; keeps 2 weeks. Makes 64 patties or about 2½ pounds.

DATE-STUFFED CANDIES: From *3 cups pitted dates,* cut each date in half crosswise. Prepare recipe as above but use *2 teaspoons vanilla extract* instead of peppermint and pat mixture into 11″ by 11″ square; cut into 1-inch squares. Wrap each piece around a date half. Makes about 120 candies or 3¼ pounds.

CARAMEL-POPCORN BALLS

16 cups popped corn (about 1 cup popcorn)
salt
1 cup salted peanuts
1 14-ounce bag vanilla and chocolate caramels

ABOUT 1 HOUR BEFORE SERVING: In a large greased kettle, sprinkle popped corn lightly with salt; add peanuts; toss to mix. Meanwhile, in large saucepan over low heat, melt caramels with ¼ cup water, stirring until smooth; pour over popped-corn mixture, tossing until popped corn is well coated. Wet hands with ice-water; shape mixture into 2½-inch balls. Makes 18 to 20 balls.

POPCORN CRUNCH

8 cups popped corn (about ½ cup popcorn)
2 cups bite-size shredded wheat
1 4-ounce can blanched whole almonds, toasted (page 379)
1½ cups sugar
1 cup dark corn syrup
½ cup butter or margarine
1 teaspoon vanilla extract
¼ teaspoon cinnamon

UP TO 1 WEEK BEFORE SERVING: Preheat oven to 250°F. In large kettle, combine popped corn, shredded wheat and almonds. Heat in oven 20 minutes; keep warm. Grease 2 large cookie sheets; set aside.

Meanwhile, in medium saucepan over medium heat, heat sugar, corn syrup and butter or margarine to boiling, stirring until sugar is dissolved. Set candy thermometer in place and continue cooking, without stirring, until temperature reaches 290°F. or until a small amount of mixture dropped into very cold water separates into thin threads which are hard but not brittle. Remove from heat; immediately stir in vanilla and cinnamon.

Pour sugar mixture over popped-corn mixture, a little at a time, stirring constantly, until popped-corn mixture is well coated; immediately spread mixture onto cookie sheets. When cool, break mixture into pieces. Store in tightly covered container. Makes about 10 cups or 2 pounds.

CHRISTMAS POPCORN BALLS

12 cups popped corn (about ¾ cup popcorn)
½ pound candied cherries, halved
1 16-ounce bottle light corn syrup (2 cups)
1 tablespoon white vinegar
1 teaspoon salt
2 teaspoons vanilla extract

DAY BEFORE SERVING: In greased large kettle, toss popped corn with cherries until well mixed.

In medium saucepan over medium-high heat, heat to boiling corn syrup, vinegar and salt, stirring occasionally. Set candy thermometer in place and continue cooking, without stirring, until temperature reaches 250°F. or until a small amount dropped into very cold water forms a hard ball. Remove syrup from heat; stir in vanilla.

Slowly pour syrup over popped-corn mixture, tossing until kernels are well coated. With greased hands, shape popped-corn mixture into 3-inch balls, using as little pressure as possible, so balls will not be too compact. (If mixture hardens, place kettle over very low heat until mixture is pliable.) Makes 12 balls.

CANDIED CITRUS PEEL

2 medium oranges
2 medium lemons
1 medium grapefruit
sugar
½ cup light corn syrup
1 3-ounce package lemon-flavor gelatin

UP TO 2 WEEKS BEFORE SERVING:
With sharp knife, score peel of fruits into quarters; pull away from pulp. (Use fruit in salad another day.) With sharp knife, cut peel into long, thin strips. In large kettle over high heat, heat peels and 8 cups hot water to boiling; boil 15 minutes. Drain peels in colander and rinse. With 8 more cups of hot water, boil peels 15 minutes again; drain.

In same kettle over high heat, heat 1¾ cups sugar, corn syrup and 1½ cups water until boiling and sugar is dissolved, stirring frequently. Gently stir in peels. Reduce heat to medium-low and cook until most of the syrup has been absorbed, about 40 minutes, stirring occasionally.

Remove from heat; gently stir in gelatin until dissolved; cool 10 minutes. (Mixture will be thick and sticky.) Onto waxed paper, place 1 cup sugar. Lightly roll peels, a few at a time, in sugar, adding more sugar if necessary. Place sugar-coated peels in single layer on wire racks; let dry overnight or about 12 hours. Store in tightly covered container. Makes about 8 cups or 2 pounds.

GRAPEFRUIT, ORANGE OR LEMON: Prepare as above but use enough peel from just one kind of citrus fruit to make 4 cups strips, lightly packed, and any fruit-flavor gelatin.

FRUITCAKE MINIATURES

½ pound dark fruitcake
¾ cup confectioners' sugar
½ teaspoon cocoa
½ teaspoon vanilla extract
cashews for garnish

EARLY IN DAY OR SEVERAL DAYS AHEAD:
Place wire rack over waxed paper. With sharp knife, cut fruitcake into 1-inch cubes and place on wire rack. In small bowl, with spoon, mix confectioners' sugar, cocoa, vanilla and 3 to 4 teaspoons water until smooth and thick. Drizzle mixture over each cake cube, covering top and sides as it falls. (Return mixture that drips onto waxed paper to bowl and use again.)

Top each cube with a cashew. Let stand 1 hour to set. Store in tightly covered container. Makes 12 pieces or about ½ pound.

CANDY APPLES

8 small Red Delicious apples
8 wooden ice-cream-bar sticks
3 cups sugar
½ cup light corn syrup
¼ cup red-hot candies
½ teaspoon red food color

EARLY IN DAY:
Wash and thoroughly dry apples; insert a wooden stick part way through stem end of each apple. Grease large cookie sheet; set aside.

In medium saucepan over medium heat, heat remaining ingredients and 1 cup water to boiling, stirring until sugar and candies are dissolved. Set candy thermometer in place and continue cooking, without stirring, until temperature reaches 290°F. or until a small amount of mixture dropped into very cold water separates into thin, hard threads, about 20 minutes.

Immediately remove syrup from heat and dip apples: Tip saucepan and swirl each apple in mixture to coat evenly; lift out apple and swirl over saucepan a few more seconds to catch drips. Place apples on greased cookie sheet to cool. Work quickly before syrup hardens; if it does harden, place over very low heat to soften. Cool apples for at least 1 hour before serving. Makes 8 candy apples.

MARZIPAN FRUITS

UP TO 2 WEEKS BEFORE SERVING:
Prepare Marzipan Dough: In large bowl, knead *2 cups canned almond paste* with *4 egg whites;* slowly knead in *12 cups confectioners' sugar* or enough to make a stiff dough. Cover dough to keep moist for easy handling. Shape (below), then glaze fruits with *Glossy Sugar Glaze* (below). Store in tightly covered container. Makes about 4¼ pounds.

GLOSSY SUGAR GLAZE: In medium saucepan over medium heat, cook *4½ cups sugar* with *1 cup water* just until sugar dissolves and candy thermometer registers 223°F. Remove from heat very gently; do not stir. Let stand undisturbed until cool. Place Marzipan Fruits, letting none touch another, on a rack in shallow, open pan. With spoon, carefully remove any crystallized sugar on top of mixture. To coat Marzipan Fruits, evenly pour on sugar mixture with as little agitation as possible to prevent glaze from crystallizing. Dry overnight.

APPLES: On waxed paper, knead about *2 drops green food color* into *1½ cups Marzipan Dough.* Divide dough into 14 pieces and shape into apples; stick *stems from whole cloves* part way into tops of apples. Using fine brush, tint apples with *red food color* diluted with water. Dry on tray. Makes 14 apples.

BANANAS: On waxed paper, knead about *6 drops yellow food color* into *½ cup Marzipan Dough.* Divide dough into 7 pieces and shape into bananas. Prepare brown color as label of food color directs; using brush, paint characteristic lines. Dry on tray. Makes 7 bananas.

PEARS: On waxed paper, knead about *4 drops green* and *4 drops yellow food color* into *1 cup Marzipan Dough.* Divide dough into 12 pieces and shape into pears. In top of each pear, insert a leaf of *dried rosemary* part way. Dry on tray. Makes 12 pears.

APRICOTS: On waxed paper, knead about *6 drops yellow* and *4 drops red food color* into *1 cup Marzipan Dough.* Divide dough into 16 pieces and shape into apricots. Insert *stems from whole cloves* part way into tops of apricots. Dry on tray. Makes 16 apricots.

CHERRIES: On waxed paper, knead about *½ teaspoon red* and *4 drops blue food color* into *½ cup Marzipan Dough.* Divide dough into 16 pieces and shape into cherries. Insert *stems removed from maraschino cherries.* Dry on tray. Makes 16 cherries.

STRAWBERRIES: Divide *¾ cup Marzipan Dough* into 20 pieces and shape into strawberries. Using fine brush, tint berries with *red food color* diluted with water. On waxed paper, knead about *5 drops green food color* into *¼ cup Marzipan Dough.* Using lightly cornstarch-dusted cutting board and rolling pin, roll dough ⅛-inch thick. With 1¼-inch star-shaped canapé cutter, cut 20 stars; press a star on large end of each berry. Dry on tray. Makes 20 strawberries.

APRICOT SNOWBALLS

1 8-ounce package dried apricots
1½ cups flaked coconut
2 tablespoons confectioners' sugar
2 teaspoons orange juice
sugar (optional)

UP TO SEVERAL WEEKS AHEAD:
Into small bowl, using medium blade of food grinder, grind apricots. With hands, mix with coconut, confectioners' sugar and orange juice. Shape mixture into ½-inch balls; roll in sugar, if you like. Store in tightly covered container. Makes about 30 balls or ¾ pound.

PEANUT-DATE CHIPPEROOS

1½ cups peanut butter
1 8-ounce package pitted dates, chopped
¾ cup confectioners' sugar
½ cup flaked coconut
1 teaspoon lemon juice
½ teaspoon grated lemon peel
¾ cup finely crushed potato chips

EARLY IN DAY:
In large bowl, stir all ingredients except potato chips until well mixed. With hands, shape mixture into 1-inch balls. Roll balls in crushed potato chips. Keep refrigerated. Makes about 36 pieces or 1½ pounds.

FIG CANDY SLICES

1 8-ounce package dried figs
½ cup golden raisins
1 cup creamy peanut butter
½ cup confectioners' sugar
grated peel of 1 lemon

DAY BEFORE SERVING:
Into medium bowl, using coarse blade of food grinder, grind figs and raisins. With spoon, stir in remaining ingredients until well mixed. Divide mixture in half and roll each half into a 10-inch roll. Wrap each roll in plastic wrap or waxed paper and refrigerate overnight to blend flavors.

TO SERVE:
On cutting board, with sharp knife, cut rolls into ¼-inch-thick slices. Keep refrigerated. Makes about 60 pieces or 1¼ pounds.

SHERRIED WALNUTS

1½ cups sugar
½ cup medium or sweet sherry
½ teaspoon cinnamon
3 cups California walnuts

ABOUT 30 MINUTES BEFORE SERVING:
In medium saucepan over medium heat, heat sugar and sherry to boiling, stirring until sugar is dissolved. Set candy thermometer in place and continue cooking, without stirring, until temperature reaches 240°F. or until a small amount of mixture dropped into very cold water forms a soft ball. Meanwhile, butter a large cookie sheet.

Remove mixture from heat; add cinnamon and walnuts and stir until mixture loses its gloss and becomes cloudy. Turn onto cookie sheet and separate nuts; cool. Makes about 1½ pounds candy.

CHOCOLATE-STUFFED FIGS

ABOUT 45 MINUTES AHEAD OR EARLY IN DAY:
Cut a small slice from stem end of each of *20 whole dried figs* (about one 12-ounce package). With finger, gently press through cut end into center of each fig to make it hollow, being careful not to tear sides. Unwrap *20 candy kisses* from a 10-ounce package and gently push each into center of a fig. Pinch fig opening closed and place, cut side down, in jelly-roll pan. (If early in day, cover figs with plastic wrap and keep at room temperature.)

ABOUT 20 MINUTES BEFORE SERVING:
Preheat oven to 350°F. Bake figs 5 minutes; turn cut sides up and bake 5 minutes more. Remove from oven and immediately press an almond from *about one half 4-ounce can whole blanched almonds* into center of each fig. Let cool 10 minutes, then serve warm. Makes 20 pieces or about 1 pound.

DATE-NUT BITES

1 cup finely chopped pitted dates
½ cup slivered blanched almonds
½ cup sugar
½ teaspoon vanilla extract
1 egg white
about 12 candied cherries, halved

EARLY IN DAY:
In medium bowl, combine dates, almonds, sugar, vanilla and egg white; refrigerate 1 hour. Preheat oven to 325°F. Grease large cookie sheet. Shape date mixture into balls; top each with a cherry half and place on cookie sheet.

Bake 15 to 20 minutes. Cool on cookie sheet 5 minutes, then remove balls to wire racks to cool. Makes about 24 pieces or 1 pound.

COCONUT CONFETTI

1 6-ounce package semisweet-chocolate pieces (1 cup)
2 tablespoons light corn syrup
1 3½-ounce can flaked coconut (1⅓ cups)
nonpareils for garnish

TWO HOURS AHEAD OR EARLY IN DAY:
Line large cookie sheet with waxed paper. In double boiler over hot, not boiling, water, melt chocolate pieces with corn syrup and 1 tablespoon water; stir in coconut.

Drop mixture by heaping teaspoonfuls onto cookie sheet; sprinkle each with nonpareils. Keep refrigerated. Makes about 24 pieces or ½ pound.

WALNUT CRUNCH

1¼ cups sugar
¾ cup butter or margarine
1½ teaspoons salt
½ teaspoon baking soda
1½ cups coarsely chopped California walnuts
⅓ cup semisweet-chocolate pieces, melted
½ cup finely chopped California walnuts

ABOUT 3½ HOURS BEFORE SERVING:
Butter 15″ by 10″ jelly-roll pan. In medium saucepan over medium heat, heat sugar, butter or margarine, salt and ¼ cup water to boiling, stirring often. Set candy thermometer in place and continue cooking, stirring often, until temperature reaches 290°F. or until a small amount of mixture dropped into very cold water separates into threads which are hard but not brittle.

Remove mixture from heat; stir in soda and coarsely chopped walnuts; pour at once into pan. Spread mixture with chocolate and sprinkle with finely chopped walnuts; cool. With hands, snap candy into small pieces. Store in tightly covered container. Makes about 1½ pounds.

PEANUT BRITTLE

1 cup sugar
½ cup light corn syrup
¼ teaspoon salt
1 cup shelled raw peanuts*
2 tablespoons butter or margarine, softened
1 teaspoon baking soda

UP TO 2 WEEKS BEFORE SERVING:
Grease large cookie sheet. In heavy, medium saucepan over medium heat, heat to boiling, sugar, corn syrup, salt and ¼ cup water, stirring until sugar is dissolved. Stir in peanuts. Set candy thermometer in place and continue cooking, stirring frequently, until temperature reaches 300°F. or until a small amount of mixture dropped into very cold water separates into hard and brittle threads.

Remove from heat; immediately stir in butter or margarine and baking soda; pour at once onto cookie sheet. With 2 forks, lift and pull peanut mixture into rectangle about 14″ by 12″; cool. With hands, snap candy into small pieces. Store in tightly covered container. Makes 1 pound.

* Or, use *1 cup salted peanuts* and omit the salt.

Beverages

Call on a variety of china and glassware to add interest to beverages. Hot drinks keep hot attractively in mugs, steins and demitasse cups as well as in regular cups. To make cold drinks look special, serve them in water goblets, pilsners, mugs, brandy snifters, tankards, wine or champagne glasses as well as in tumblers.

Ladle punch and party beverages from punch bowls, glass salad bowls or mixing bowls, or pour from attractive pitchers.

Ice for Beverages

Keep extra ice cubes on hand in a plastic bag or freezer container in the freezer. To make ice cubes, use water, coffee, leftover punch or fruit juice diluted with water. Don't use creamy mixtures unless you freeze them in an ice-cube tray reserved just for them, since washing to remove the fat film could destroy the finish and ice cubes frozen later would stick.

Garnished ice cubes: Place one or more of the following in each section of the tray; then fill tray with water and freeze: halved or sliced maraschino cherry; tiny mint sprig; grape; canned mandarin-orange section; tiny chunk of orange, lemon or lime; pineapple chunk; gumdrop; whole berry; dark sweet cherry; small melon ball.

Tinted ice cubes: With food color, tint water to desired delicate shade; pour into tray; freeze.

Crystalline Ice Bowl (page 36): Prepare as recipe directs, using flowers listed in step 2 of recipe as decoration.

Ice Float: Day before serving: Freeze plain or tinted water, fruit juice, ginger ale, lemonade or punch in 8″ by 8″ baking pan, heart-shaped cake pan or ring mold. To unmold, dip pan just to rim in hot water, then invert into punch. If you like, top square or heart-shaped float with fruits or non-toxic flowers (see step 2, Crystalline Ice Bowl, page 36).

Or, arrange about 1 cup mint leaves and maraschino cherries, or mixed cut-up fruits, in ring mold or metal loaf pan; pour in about ¼-inch liquid; freeze. When firm, fill mold with liquid and freeze. Unmold as above.

Holiday Ice Ring: Under running cold water, wash excess color from equal number of red and green maraschino cherries. Arrange cherries, alternating colors, in ring mold. Cover cherries with water; freeze. When firm, fill mold to top with cold water; freeze. Unmold as in Ice Float (page 595).

Frozen fruits: Fruits and berries, frozen whole, can be used to chill beverages as ice does. They add color, don't dilute the mixture and can be eaten later. Choose from peaches, pears, nectarines, plums, apricots, grapes, cherries and strawberries. Grapes and cherries stay close to the bottom of the bowl; the other fruits float.

Day before serving, freeze this way: Wash and dry fruit; arrange on cookie sheet; freeze. Arrange in punch bowl at serving time; carefully pour in punch.

Using Fruit Juices

If a recipe calls for both juice and grated peel, grate the peel first and then squeeze the juice; it's easier!

For best flavor, squeeze lemons, limes, oranges, grapefruit just before using, since loss of flavor is rapid. If juice must stand, cover and refrigerate to preserve both flavor and vitamin C content. Bottled lemon and lime juices may be used instead of fresh; follow label directions.

Unless recipe directs otherwise, don't strain pulp from juice; it contains valuable vitamins and minerals.

Garnishes for Drinks

Add extra color and eye-appeal to cold beverages with one or more of these:

Mint sprigs or leaves
Orange, lemon or lime slices,
  wedges or twists (page 379)
Thick banana slices
Strawberries
Maraschino cherries with stems
Pineapple chunks
Small scoops of sherbet or ice cream
Melon balls
Thin candy sticks or canes
Frosted Grapes (page 376)

These will add flavor as well as color to hot beverages:

Cinnamon sticks
Whipped cream
Marshmallows or marshmallow cream
Thin candy sticks or canes
Clove-studded lemon or lime
  slices or orange wedges

Quickest-of-All Drinks

Refrigerated beverages such as milk, buttermilk, chocolate milk and orange and grapefruit juices are of course ready to serve. There are also soft drinks in at least 30 different flavors, some in low-calorie form, which need only be chilled or served over ice. Remember too, the many canned juices, nectars, juice blends and drinks, punches and ades available in single- or multiple-fruit flavors. Chill and serve.

Along with instant coffee, tea and hot-chocolate mixes, there are soft-drink mixes and frozen concentrated fruit juices and beverages that are easy to mix or reconstitute for speedy serving.

Some of the favorite cocktails come bottled or canned, ready to chill and pour. Mixes, to which liquor must be added, are also available.

Cocktails and Mixed Drinks

Glasses: The right glass makes a drink look and taste better. The glasses most often used for drinks are: jigger, 1½ ounces; cocktail, 4 ounces; old-fashioned, 6 to 12 ounces; table wine, 8 to 10 ounces; cordial, 1 ounce; champagne, 5 to 6 ounces; whiskey sour, 6 ounces; highball, 8 to 12 ounces.

Bar equipment: These tools make mixing drinks easier: bottle opener, corkscrew, ice bucket and tongs, mixing glass and long-handled stirring spoon, shaker (or use blender), muddler, bar strainer or small kitchen strainer, knife and cutting board, lemon squeezer, jigger or drink measure.

Mixing drinks: The basic drink measure used in our recipes is the jigger, which holds 1½ ounces or 3 tablespoons. One-half jigger is equal to 1½ tablespoons.

Use glasses large enough to hold a full serving. (Never fill glasses right to the top; fill about ⅔ full.)

Drinks are smoother when served icy cold. If you have refrigerator space, chill liquors, mixers and glasses. Chill glasses at least 30 minutes; or, fill with ice while you mix the drinks, then discard ice before pouring. Or, place glasses in freezer 5 minutes to chill, 10 minutes if you want them frosted.

Use fresh ice for every drink, even "seconds." Always put it in the glass before adding other ingredients; that way the ingredients are chilled as they are poured over it, and splashing is reduced.

Except for drinks with carbonated beverages, add liquor last to other ingredients in recipes. Sugar does not dissolve readily in spirits. Dissolve it first in a teaspoonful of water (or fruit juice if the recipe calls for it). Strain cocktails as directed.

If recipe says to "shake," shake vigorously to insure thorough blending. If directions say to "stir," stir just enough to chill the drink and combine delicate flavors. Most drinks containing clear liquors only, like the Martini, are stirred; drinks containing eggs, cream or other ingredients difficult to mix are shaken. Never shake drinks containing carbonated beverages (mixers); add the mixer last and stir very gently.

Don't leave drinks too long in the shaker. Melting ice dilutes them and makes them flat, and even if the ice is removed, the taste of the drink in a metal shaker may be affected. If the shaker is glass and the drink must stand, remove the ice.

ALEXANDER

1 cup crushed ice
1 jigger brandy or gin
½ jigger crème de cacao
½ jigger heavy or whipping cream

JUST BEFORE SERVING:
Over crushed ice in cocktail shaker, pour remaining ingredients; shake well. Strain mixture into cocktail glass. Makes 1 serving.

BLACK RUSSIAN

2 or 3 ice cubes
1 jigger vodka
½ jigger coffee-flavor liqueur

JUST BEFORE SERVING:
Over ice cubes in old-fashioned glass, pour vodka and liqueur; stir. Makes 1 serving.

BLOODY MARY

ice cubes
⅔ cup tomato juice
1 jigger vodka
dash Worcestershire
dash each salt and pepper
dash hot pepper sauce
1 large lime wedge

JUST BEFORE SERVING:
Over ice cubes in 10-ounce highball glass, measure all ingredients except lime wedge; squeeze lime wedge into mixture and stir well. Makes 1 serving.

COMPANY BLOODY MARY

2 18-ounce cans tomato juice (4½ cups)
1 cup vodka
2 teaspoons Worcestershire
½ teaspoon salt
¼ teaspoon coarsely ground pepper
few dashes hot pepper sauce
ice cubes
2 limes, quartered lengthwise

JUST BEFORE SERVING OR EARLY IN DAY:
In large pitcher, combine first 6 ingredients. Cover and refrigerate if made ahead. To serve, stir mixture; pour over ice cubes in eight 10-ounce highball glasses. Squeeze a lime wedge into each glass; stir. Makes about 5½ cups or 8 servings.

BULLSHOT

2 or 3 ice cubes
1 jigger vodka
½ cup canned condensed beef broth

JUST BEFORE SERVING:
Over ice cubes in old-fashioned glass, pour vodka and undiluted beef broth; stir and serve. Makes 1 serving.

CHAMPAGNE COCKTAIL

1 sugar cube
dash aromatic bitters
1 lemon twist
champagne, chilled

JUST BEFORE SERVING:
In champagne glass, place sugar; add bitters and lemon twist. Slowly pour in champagne to fill glass. Makes 1 serving.

DAIQUIRI

1 jigger lime juice
3 to 4 teaspoons sugar
1½ cups cracked ice
2 jiggers light rum

JUST BEFORE SERVING:
Into cocktail shaker, measure lime juice and sugar; stir or cover and shake until sugar is dissolved. Add ice and rum; shake well. Strain mixture into two cocktail glasses. Makes 2 servings.

BACARDI: Prepare as above but reduce sugar to 2 teaspoons and add *1 tablespoon grenadine syrup.*

COMPANY FROZEN DAIQUIRIS

1 6-ounce can frozen limeade concentrate
2½ cans light rum (use limeade can to measure)

DAY BEFORE OR SEVERAL DAYS AHEAD:
In 1½-quart freezer-proof bowl or container, combine limeade concentrate, rum and 3 cans water; cover and freeze. (Mixture does not freeze solid.)

JUST BEFORE SERVING:
Place a portion of frozen mixture in blender container; cover and blend until smooth and slushy. Pour into cocktail glasses. Serve with 2 short straws. Makes about 5 cups or thirteen 3-ounce servings.

FROZEN WHISKEY SOURS: Prepare as above but substitute *one 6-ounce can frozen lemonade concentrate* for limeade and *blended whiskey* for rum. Use only 2 cans water and add *1 can orange juice* (use lemonade can to measure). Just before serving, garnish each drink with *maraschino cherry* and *half an orange slice.*

DUBONNET COCKTAIL

cracked ice
1 jigger Dubonnet
½ jigger gin

JUST BEFORE SERVING:
Over cracked ice in cocktail shaker or large glass, pour Dubonnet and gin; stir well; strain into cocktail glass. Makes 1 serving.

FRAPPE

shaved ice
1 jigger liquor (brandy, cordials, crème de menthe, crème de cacao, fruit liqueurs, sloe gin)

JUST BEFORE SERVING:
Fill cocktail glass with shaved ice; pour liquor over ice. Serve with 2 short straws. Makes 1 serving.

GIMLET

1½ cups cracked ice
2 jiggers gin or vodka
½ jigger bottled sweetened lime juice

JUST BEFORE SERVING:
Over cracked ice in small pitcher or cocktail shaker, pour gin and lime juice; stir well. Strain mixture into two cocktail glasses. Makes 2 servings.

GIMLET WITH FRESH LIME JUICE: In small pitcher or cocktail shaker, stir or cover and shake *½ jigger fresh lime juice* and *3 to 4 teaspoons sugar* until sugar is dissolved. Add *1½ cups cracked ice;* pour in *2 jiggers gin or vodka* and stir well. Strain mixture into two cocktail glasses. Makes 2 servings.

GIN AND TONIC

ice cubes
1 jigger gin
quinine water (tonic water)
lime or lemon slice or wedge

JUST BEFORE SERVING:
Over ice cubes in highball glass, pour gin; add quinine water to fill glass; add lime slice. Makes 1 serving.

VODKA AND TONIC: Use *vodka* instead of gin.

GRASSHOPPER

1½ cups cracked ice
1 jigger green crème de menthe
1 jigger crème de cacao
1 jigger heavy or whipping cream

JUST BEFORE SERVING:
Over cracked ice in cocktail shaker, pour remaining ingredients; shake well; strain into cocktail glasses. Makes 2 servings.

HIGHBALL

ice cubes
1 jigger liquor (applejack, blended whiskey, bourbon, brandy, Canadian whisky, crème de menthe, gin, Irish whisky, rum, rye, Scotch, vodka)
club soda, ginger ale or water

JUST BEFORE SERVING:
Over ice cubes in highball glass, pour liquor; add club soda to fill glass; stir and serve. Makes 1 serving.

HOT BUTTERED RUM

1 jigger dark rum
1 to 2 teaspoons maple-blended syrup
1 teaspoon butter
nutmeg

JUST BEFORE SERVING:
Into 10-ounce mug, measure rum, syrup and butter. Stir in ¾ cup boiling water. Sprinkle with nutmeg. Makes 1 serving.

HOT TODDY

½ teaspoon sugar
2 whole cloves
1 small cinnamon stick
1 lemon slice
1 jigger liquor (blended whiskey, bourbon, brandy, Canadian whisky, gin, Irish whisky, rum, Scotch, vodka)

JUST BEFORE SERVING:
Into old-fashioned glass, measure all ingredients. Place teaspoon in glass; add boiling water to fill glass. (Teaspoon helps prevent glass from breaking when boiling water is added.) Stir mixture. Makes 1 serving.

COLD TODDY: In old-fashioned glass, dissolve *½ teaspoon sugar* in *1 tablespoon cold water;* add *2 or 3 ice cubes* and *1 jigger liquor* (above); fill with cold water. Garnish with *lemon slice.* Makes 1 serving.

IRISH COFFEE

1½ teaspoons sugar
1 jigger Irish whisky
hot strong black coffee
whipped cream

JUST BEFORE SERVING:
Into 6- or 8-ounce stemmed glass or coffee cup, measure sugar and Irish whisky; add hot coffee to fill glass to within ½-inch of top; stir to dissolve sugar. Top with whipped cream; do not stir. Sip coffee through cream. Makes 1 serving.

JACK ROSE

1 cup cracked ice
1 jigger applejack
½ jigger lemon or lime juice
2 teaspoons grenadine syrup

JUST BEFORE SERVING:
Over cracked ice in cocktail shaker, pour remaining ingredients; shake well. Strain mixture into cocktail glass. Makes 1 serving.

MANHATTAN

1½ cups cracked ice
2 jiggers bourbon, blended or Canadian whisky
1 jigger sweet vermouth
2 dashes aromatic bitters
2 maraschino cherries for garnish

JUST BEFORE SERVING:
Over ice in cocktail shaker or large glass, pour next three ingredients; stir. Strain mixture into two cocktail glasses. Garnish each with cherry. Makes 2 servings.

DRY MANHATTAN: Prepare as above but substitute *dry vermouth* for sweet vermouth.

PERFECT MANHATTAN: Prepare as above but use *½ jigger each sweet and dry vermouth* for sweet vermouth.

MARGARITA

lime or lemon peel
salt
1 cup crushed ice
1 jigger tequila
½ jigger triple sec
½ jigger lime or lemon juice

JUST BEFORE SERVING:
Rub rim of cocktail glass with lime peel; dip rim in salt; set aside. Over ice in cocktail shaker or large glass, pour remaining ingredients; stir; carefully pour into prepared glass. Makes 1 serving.

MARTINI

1½ cups cracked ice
2 jiggers gin
¼ jigger dry vermouth (2 teaspoons)
2 small stuffed green olives or lemon twists for garnish

JUST BEFORE SERVING:
Over cracked ice in cocktail shaker or small pitcher, pour gin and vermouth; stir. Strain mixture into two chilled cocktail glasses. Garnish each with olive or lemon twist. Makes 2 servings.

EXTRA-DRY MARTINI: Prepare as above but use only 1 teaspoon dry vermouth.

VODKA MARTINI: Prepare as above but substitute *vodka* for gin. Garnish with lemon twists.

GIBSON: Prepare as above but garnish with *cocktail onions.*

MINT JULEP

4 sprigs mint
1 teaspoon sugar
finely crushed or shaved ice
1½ jiggers bourbon

UP TO 30 MINUTES BEFORE SERVING:
In 12-ounce highball glass or tankard (preferably silver or aluminum), place 3 sprigs mint and sugar. Crush mint with muddler or handle of wooden spoon until sugar is dissolved, about 5 minutes. Fill glass to brim with ice; pour in bourbon; don't stir. Add more ice to fill glass. Set in freezer until serving time. Just before serving, garnish with mint sprig. Serve with long straw. Makes 1 serving.

MIST

shaved ice
1 jigger liquor (applejack, blended whiskey, bourbon, brandy, Canadian whisky, gin, Irish whisky, rum, rye, Scotch, vodka)
lemon twist for garnish

JUST BEFORE SERVING:
Pack ice into an old-fashioned glass; pour liquor over ice. Garnish with lemon twist. Serve with short straw. Makes 1 serving.

OLD-FASHIONED

1 sugar cube
dash aromatic bitters
cracked ice
1½ jiggers liquor (applejack, blended whiskey, bourbon, brandy, Canadian whisky, gin, Irish whisky, rum, rye, Scotch or vodka)
maraschino cherry and slice of orange or lemon twist for garnish

JUST BEFORE SERVING:
In old-fashioned glass, with muddler, stir sugar with bitters and 1 tablespoon water until dissolved. Add cracked ice to fill glass; pour in liquor. Garnish with fruit and serve with muddler. Makes 1 serving.

ON-THE-ROCKS

2 or 3 ice cubes
1 jigger liquor (blended whiskey, bourbon, brandy, Canadian whisky, cordials, Irish whisky, rum, rye, Scotch, sloe gin) or 1 serving favorite cocktail
lemon twist for garnish

JUST BEFORE SERVING:
Over ice cubes in old-fashioned glass, pour liquor; add lemon twist. (With liquor, some people may request a dash of water.) Makes 1 serving.

ORANGE BLOSSOM

1 teaspoon sugar
2 tablespoons orange juice
1 cup cracked ice
1 jigger gin

JUST BEFORE SERVING:
In covered cocktail shaker, shake sugar and orange juice until sugar is dissolved. Add ice and gin; shake well; strain mixture into cocktail glass. Makes 1 serving.

PINK LADY

1 cup cracked ice
1 jigger gin
½ jigger lemon juice
1 tablespoon grenadine syrup
1 egg white

JUST BEFORE SERVING:
Over cracked ice in cocktail shaker, pour all ingredients; shake well. Strain mixture into cocktail glass. Makes 1 serving.

ROB ROY

1 cup cracked ice
1 jigger Scotch
½ jigger sweet vermouth
dash aromatic bitters
maraschino cherry or lemon twist for garnish

JUST BEFORE SERVING:
Over cracked ice in cocktail shaker or large glass, measure Scotch, vermouth and bitters; stir well. Strain mixture into cocktail glass; garnish with cherry. Makes 1 serving.

DRY ROB ROY: Prepare as above but substitute *dry vermouth* for sweet vermouth. Use lemon twist for garnish.

SCREWDRIVER

2 or 3 ice cubes
1 jigger vodka
orange juice

JUST BEFORE SERVING:
Over ice cubes in 6-ounce glass, pour vodka; add enough orange juice to fill glass; stir and serve. Makes 1 serving.

SOUR

1 jigger lemon juice
3 to 4 teaspoons sugar
1½ cups cracked ice
2 jiggers liquor (applejack, blended whiskey, bourbon, brandy, Irish whisky, Scotch, rum, rye or vodka)
maraschino cherries and orange slices for garnish

JUST BEFORE SERVING:
In cocktail shaker, stir or cover and shake lemon juice and sugar until sugar is dissolved. Add ice and liquor; shake well. Strain mixture into two whiskey-sour or cocktail glasses. Garnish each with a maraschino cherry and half an orange slice. Makes 2 servings.

STINGER

1 cup cracked ice
1 jigger brandy
½ jigger white crème de menthe

JUST BEFORE SERVING:
Over cracked ice in cocktail shaker, pour brandy and crème de menthe; shake well. Strain mixture into cocktail glass. Makes 1 serving.

TOM COLLINS

2 tablespoons lemon juice
2 teaspoons sugar
1 cup cracked ice
1 jigger gin*
ice cubes
club soda
maraschino cherry and orange slice or lime twist for garnish

JUST BEFORE SERVING:
In covered cocktail shaker, shake lemon juice and sugar until sugar is dissolved. Add cracked ice and gin; shake well. Strain mixture over ice cubes in highball glass. Add club soda to fill glass; stir. Garnish with fruit and serve. Makes 1 serving.

* Or, use bourbon, brandy, Canadian whisky or applejack.

JOHN COLLINS: Prepare as above but in place of gin, use any *whiskey*, rum, Scotch or vodka.

Coffee

Coffee can be mild or robust, full-bodied or mellow or highly aromatic, depending on the beans used and the length of the roasting time. Most of the coffee sold in this country is American roast, which is the lightest and mildest in flavor. French-roast coffee, a little darker and stronger, is popular for use in *café au lait* and breakfast coffee. Both American and French roast are used to make demitasse. Italian-roast coffee is darkest and strongest and is used for making espresso.

The blend of coffee you like depends on your own taste. If you are not satisfied with your coffee, try different blends until you find one you prefer; then stay with it.

Coffee for brewing may be bought already ground and canned or packaged, or as roasted beans to be ground to order in the store or in a home coffee grinder.

There's no special secret for brewing good coffee. Observance of the few simple rules below will assure delicious coffee every time.

1. Choose the grind that's right for your type of coffee maker. A percolator uses regular (coarse) grind; a drip pot, drip (medium) grind; a vacuum pot, fine grind.
2. Use fresh coffee. Although unopened cans will keep at least a year at room temperature, it's best to buy only as much as you will use in a week. After opening a can of coffee, cover it tightly and store it in the refrigerator. It will retain optimum freshness for about a week. Keep coffee beans in an airtight container in the refrigerator; use within 3 weeks.
3. Start with a thoroughly clean coffee maker. Wash it and all of its washable parts in hot sudsy water; rinse thoroughly in clear water. Occasionally scrub hard-to-reach places with a small brush. Whenever you notice darkening by coffee oils, use a packaged coffee-stain remover according to directions. Store the coffee maker uncovered or loosely covered.
4. Use cold, fresh water. Mineral deposits in some hot tap water can give an off-flavor to brewed coffee.
5. Your coffee maker brews the best coffee when filled at least three-quarters full.
6. Use the correct measurements. For *each serving, use 2 level measuring tablespoons of coffee* (1 Approved Coffee Measure) and *¾ cup cold, fresh water.*
7. Time the brewing properly. In the time given for each method below, all the good-tasting elements of coffee are extracted. Longer brewing extracts less desirable elements, may make coffee bitter.
8. Never boil coffee; boiling causes undesirable flavor changes.
9. Always remove basket with used grounds before serving coffee.
10. Serve coffee as soon as possible after brewing; flavor and aroma are at their best. Coffee tastes better if it is kept warm rather than reheated; if necessary, hold it at serving temperature but no longer than an hour. For non-automatic coffee makers, place over low heat on an asbestos pad or pour into a server and place over a candle warmer or on an electric trivet.

Drip method: Just before serving, measure ¾ cup cold water per serving into kettle; over high heat, heat to boiling. Meanwhile, preheat coffee pot by rinsing it with very hot water.

Into cone lined with filter paper or filter section of coffee pot, measure 2 tablespoons drip-grind coffee per serving.

Pour measured boiling water into cone or upper container of drip pot. With a cone, half of the water should be poured in a slow circular manner, the infusion stirred and the remainder poured after the first half drips through. Cover, depending on pot used. When dripping is completed in 4 to 6 minutes, remove grounds or upper section. Stir brew and serve.

Vacuum method: Just before serving, into lower bowl of coffee pot, measure ¾ cup fresh cold water per serving. Place on high heat; heat to boiling. Meanwhile, place filter in upper bowl. Into upper bowl, measure 2 tablespoons fine-grind coffee per serving.

Remove boiling water from heat. Insert upper bowl, twisting slightly to insure seal. Reduce heat to very low (if using electric range, turn off unit); place coffee-maker on reduced heat. Most of water will rise into upper bowl. Let stand 1 minute, stirring in zig-zag fashion first 20 seconds.

Remove coffee pot from heat. Brewed

coffee will return to lower bowl within 2 minutes. Remove upper bowl and serve coffee.

Percolator method*: Just before serving, remove basket and stem from percolator. Measure ¾ cup fresh cold water per serving into percolator. Over high heat, heat water to boiling; remove from heat.

Meanwhile, into basket, measure 2 tablespoons regular-grind coffee per serving. Insert basket and stem into percolator when water is boiling; cover; place over low heat and percolate slowly 6 to 8 minutes. (When using a party-size percolator, estimate perking time at 1 minute per cup.) Water level should always be below bottom of basket. Remove basket and stem and serve coffee.

* For automatic coffee makers, follow manufacturers' directions.

Instant coffee: Steaming hot, or frosty iced coffee is ready in an "instant" when instant coffee is dissolved in water. Packed in sealed jars, instant coffee should be stored in a cool dry place before and after opening. It keeps up to 6 months unopened; opened, it should be kept tightly covered and used within 2 weeks for best flavor. Choose from 2 kinds and prepare each by label directions:
Instant coffee powder is strong brewed coffee that is dried by a hot air process, leaving a fine powder.
Freeze-dried coffee is strong brewed coffee that is dried by rapidly freezing, then removing ice in a special process that leaves coarse, dark-brown crystals.

Decaffeinated coffee: This is coffee which is almost or completely free of the stimulant caffein. The caffein is extracted from the beans before roasting to protect the full coffee flavor. Decaffeinated coffee is available in ground, instant coffee powder or freeze-dried form.

COFFEE ACCOMPANIMENTS

Serve hot coffee with sugar and cream, half-and-half or milk; or offer one of these for extra flavor:

Semisweet-chocolate pieces
Brown sugar
Chocolate-covered mints
Shredded lemon or orange peel
Chopped candied ginger
Maple or maple-blended syrup
Thin lemon or orange slices
Chocolate- or butterscotch-sundae sauce
Red hot candies
Crushed peppermint candy
Slivered candied orange peel
Sweetened whipped cream

DEMITASSE

Prepare coffee by one of the methods above but use only ½ cup water with 2 tablespoons coffee per serving. Serve in demitasse cups.

CAFE AU LAIT

To make this breakfast drink in the French manner, hold a pot of *hot coffee* in one hand, a pot of *hot milk* in the other; pour both at the same time to fill large cups. Serve *sugar* separately.

CAFE ROYALE

For each serving, place a *sugar cube* in a demitasse spoon or regular teaspoon; hold over *hot coffee* in cup and pour *brandy* over cube. Carefully ignite with match. When sugar is melted, stir into coffee.

CAFE COCOA

½ cup heavy or whipping cream
1 teaspoon confectioners' sugar
4 heaping tablespoons quick chocolate-flavor-milk mix
about 4 cups hot coffee
shredded orange peel for garnish

JUST BEFORE SERVING:
In small bowl, with mixer at medium speed, beat cream and confectioners' sugar until soft peaks form. Place 1 heaping tablespoon quick chocolate-flavor-milk mix in each of 4 coffee mugs or large cups. Add coffee to fill cups almost full; top with whipped cream and sprinkle with shredded orange peel. Makes 4 cups or four 1-cup servings.

CAFFE ESPRESSO

Use a drip pot or a *macchinetta*, following directions that come with it. For 4 demitasse servings, use *8 tablespoons Italian-roast coffee* to *1½ cups water*. Serve in demitasse cups or 4-ounce glasses, with *sugar* and *lemon twist*, never with cream.

CAFFE CAPPUCCINO: Prepare hot Caffè Espresso as above; combine with an equal quantity of *hot milk*. Pour into tall cups; sprinkle each with cinnamon. Makes 4 servings.

SPICED COFFEE

4 short cinnamon sticks
8 whole allspice
8 whole cloves
¾ cup favorite-grind coffee
cream and sugar

EARLY IN DAY:
In medium saucepan over high heat, heat 6 cups water and spices to boiling; reduce heat to low; simmer 5 minutes; chill.

ABOUT 20 MINUTES BEFORE SERVING:
Strain spices from liquid. Use liquid with ground coffee for preparing coffee by favorite method. Guests add cream and sugar as desired. Makes 9 servings.

CARDAMOM COFFEE: Prepare as above but substitute *12 whole cardamom*, crushed, for spices and serve with sugar.

CAFE BRULOT

1 cup brandy
peel of 1 medium orange
6 whole cloves
4 whole allspice
2 small cinnamon sticks
3 tablespoons sugar
3 cups hot double-strength coffee

JUST BEFORE SERVING:
On serving table, in blazer of chafing dish* over direct heat, heat all ingredients except coffee, until brandy is hot. Carefully ignite brandy with match; let flame for 1 to 2 minutes. Slowly pour coffee into flaming brandy. Ladle into demitasse cups. Makes 8 servings.

* Or, in small saucepan over medium heat, heat all ingredients except coffee until brandy is hot; pour into warmed heatproof serving bowl; ignite and continue as above.

ICED COFFEE

REGULAR COFFEE: Brew hot coffee but use twice the amount of ground coffee as usual. Fill tall glasses with ice cubes and slowly pour in hot coffee. Serve with cream and sugar, if desired.

REGULAR COFFEE WITH COFFEE ICE CUBES: Brew coffee as usual; cool, then pour into ice cube trays. Freeze. At serving time, fill glasses with coffee cubes. Pour fresh-brewed, regular-strength coffee over cubes. Serve with cream and sugar, if desired.

INSTANT COFFEE: In bottom of a tall glass, dissolve instant coffee with a little warm water. (Use about twice as much instant coffee as you use for a cup.) Fill glass with ice cubes, then cold water; stir. Serve with cream and sugar, if desired.

AFTER-DINNER ICED COFFEE

SEVERAL HOURS AHEAD:
Make *4 cups Regular Iced Coffee* (above) but, when brewing, add *¼ teaspoon anise seed* to water; chill.

JUST BEFORE SERVING:
Into glasses containing *regular or coffee ice cubes*, strain coffee (to remove anise seed). Top with generous spoonful of *whipped cream* or thawed frozen whipped topping; garnish with *curls of semisweet chocolate*. Serve as beverage or light summer dessert. Makes four 1-cup servings.

ICY LEMON COFFEE

2 cups cold strong coffee
1 pint lemon sherbet
2 tablespoons grenadine syrup

JUST BEFORE SERVING:
In covered blender container at medium speed, blend all ingredients until well blended, about 30 seconds. Serve in four 10-ounce glasses. Makes 4 cups or four 1-cup servings.

PLANTATION FROST

1½ cups cold strong coffee
3 tablespoons sugar
1 banana, cut in chunks
½ pint vanilla ice cream

JUST BEFORE SERVING:
In covered blender container at high speed, blend coffee, sugar and banana until mixture is smooth, about 20 seconds. Add ice cream; reduce speed to medium and blend until smooth, about 10 seconds. To serve, pour into chilled 8-ounce glasses. Makes about 3 cups or four ¾-cup servings.

Tea

Varieties: Tea comes in a wide assortment of flavors, ranging from hearty and smoky to delicate and flowery. Though there are thousands of varieties, teas are generally grouped according to how the leaves are processed, and fall into three classifications.
Black tea: A special process of oxidation (fermentation) turns the leaves black and produces a brew with hearty, rich flavor. Most of the tea drunk in this country is black tea. Darjeeling, Earl Grey, English Breakfast, Keemun, Lapsang Souchong are among the black teas available.
Oolong tea: Tea leaves are only partly oxidized and turn a greenish brown. The brew is light in color, and has a subtle flavor and bouquet. Formosa Oolong and Canton Oolong are popular varieties.
Green tea: The tea leaves are not oxidized and retain their green color. The brew is light in color, and has a mild and distinctive flavor. Favorite green teas include Gunpowder, Hyson and Basket Fired.

Terms such as pekoe and orange pekoe indicate the size of the tea leaf, not a special variety or flavor.

Loose tea and tea bags should be stored at room temperature. After opening, transfer tea to an airtight container and use within 6 months.

For full-bodied, fragrant, delicious tea, follow these easy steps every time you brew:
1. Use a teapot for brewing, and preheat it by rinsing it out with hot water. This keeps the tea hot while brewing.
2. Heat fresh, cold tap water to a rapid boil. Water that has been standing or reheated gives tea a flat taste. Also, only boiling water can extract the full flavor from the leaves.
3. Allow ¾ measuring cup water per serving.
4. Use 1 teaspoon of loose tea or 1 tea bag per serving and pour the boiling water over the tea.
5. Brew by the clock—3 to 5 minutes. Don't judge the strength of the tea by its color; some teas brew light, some dark.
6. If you like tea less strong, add a little hot water after the full brewing period.
7. After brewing, stir tea to make sure the flavor is uniform, and serve.
8. Serve tea with milk (not half-and-half or cream); milk lets the full tea flavor come through. Or serve with lemon, lime or orange slices or wedges; mint sprigs; cinnamon sticks for stirring; cherry preserves.

Instant tea: Hot tea by the cup or potful, or iced tea by the glass or pitcherful, is ready in minutes when instant tea is prepared according to label directions. Instant tea is the dried extract of freshly brewed tea. Packaged in jars, it is available plain or lemon-flavored. Instant iced-tea mixes in jars or envelopes are instant tea with fruit flavoring and sweetening added. Liquid iced tea, plain or sweetened, is available in cans.

ICED TEA

For perfect iced tea, prepare as for hot tea (at left) but use 50 percent more tea to allow for dilution by melting ice. For example, use 4 teaspoons tea or 4 tea bags to make 4 servings of hot tea. For 4 glasses of iced tea, use 6 teaspoons tea or 6 tea bags.

COLD-WATER WAY: About 6 hours ahead or day before: Into pitcher, measure *4 cups cold tap water*. Add *8 to 10 tea bags* (remove tags); cover and let stand at room temperature or in refrigerator 6 hours or overnight; remove tea bags and stir. Serve as above. Makes 4 cups or about five ¾-cup servings. For 10 to 12 servings, double recipe.

FAMILY STYLE: About 15 minutes or several hours ahead: In large saucepan over high heat, heat *4 cups fresh cold water* to boiling. Remove from heat; immediately stir in *⅓ cup loose tea* or 15 tea bags. Stir; cover and let stand (steep) 5 minutes. Stir again; strain mixture (or remove tea bags and pour mixture) into pitcher holding an additional *4 cups fresh cold water.* Cover and let stand until serving time.*

To serve, pour tea over *ice cubes* in 12-ounce glasses; serve with *sugar* and *lemon;* garnish if desired (see Garnishes for Drinks, page 596). Makes 8 cups tea or ten ¾-cup servings.

* Don't refrigerate tea; it may become cloudy. If it should cloud, add a little boiling water until it clears.

FROST-RIMMED ICED TEA

ABOUT 15 MINUTES BEFORE SERVING:
Brew and cool tea, or prepare your favorite plain or flavored instant iced-tea mix as label directs. For *each glass of iced tea,* run the cut side of a *lemon or lime wedge* around rim of glass to moisten; then invert moistened rim in saucer of *sugar* to coat well. Fill each glass with ice and tea, being careful not to disturb sugared rim. Garnish with additional *lemon or lime wedge* or sprig of mint.

When drinking, rotate the glass with each sip for a slightly sweetened flavor. Makes 1 serving.

SPARKLING ICED TEA

1 envelope from one 3.6-ounce package lemon-flavor iced-tea mix
1 envelope from one 3.2-ounce package mint-flavor iced-tea mix
2 trays ice cubes
2 12-ounce bottles ginger ale, chilled

JUST BEFORE SERVING:
In large pitcher, stir iced-tea mixes with 2 cups water until dissolved. Add ice cubes. Slowly pour ginger ale down side of pitcher (to prevent foaming); stir gently to mix. To serve, pour into chilled 8-ounce glasses. Makes 5 cups tea or six to seven ¾-cup servings.

SPICE BAGS FOR TEAS

For each spice bag, cut a 5-inch square, double-thickness of *cheesecloth.* Spoon one combination of spices (below) in the center; pull corners up to form a small bag and tie securely with a *colorfast or undyed cotton string.* For gifts, on gift tag, print the brewing directions (below) and attach. Store in covered container.

ORANGE-ANISE: Use *½ teaspoon dried orange peel, ¼ teaspoon anise seed* and *2 whole allspice.*

To brew: Steep spice bag in one 5- or 6-ounce cup hot *apple juice* for 1 to 2 minutes. Discard bag. Makes 1 serving.

CARDAMOM-CINNAMON: Use *2 whole cardamom,* cracked, and *1 large cinnamon stick,* broken.

To brew: Steep spice bag in one 5- or 6-ounce cup hot *cranberry juice* for 1 or 2 minutes. Discard bag. Makes 1 serving.

CRYSTALLIZED GINGER TEA: Use *1 tablespoon minced crystallized ginger* and *1 teaspoon black tea.*

To brew: Steep spice bag in one 5- or 6-ounce cup *boiling water* for 3 to 5 minutes. Discard bag. Makes 1 serving.

Milk and Ice-Cream Drinks

HEARTY HOT COCOA

½ cup plus 1 tablespoon cocoa
½ cup sugar
dash salt
6 cups milk (or 3 cups evaporated milk plus 3 cups water)
½ teaspoon vanilla extract
6 regular marshmallows or whipped cream, optional

ABOUT 15 MINUTES BEFORE SERVING:
In large saucepan, stir cocoa with sugar and salt until mixed. Stir in a small amount of milk to make a smooth paste; stir in remaining milk. Over medium-low heat, heat mixture, stirring occasionally, until tiny bubbles form around edge (do not boil). Remove from heat; add vanilla; beat with hand beater until smooth and foamy. Pour into mugs or cups. Top each serving with

a marshmallow or whipped cream, if you like. Makes 6 cups or six 1-cup servings.

SPEEDY HOT COCOA: Use quick chocolate-flavored-milk mix or cocoa mix as label directs. Serve in mugs.

HOT PEPPERMINT CHOCOLATE: Prepare *Hearty Hot Cocoa* or 6 cups Speedy Hot Cocoa as above but add *1 cup crushed peppermint candy* to milk before heating. Heat until candy is melted. Garnish each serving with *small peppermint stick* or candy cane. Makes six 1-cup servings.

CINNAMON-STICK CHOCOLATE: Prepare *Hearty Hot Cocoa* or 6 cups Speedy Hot Cocoa as above but add *2 short cinnamon sticks* to milk before heating. To serve, remove cinnamon sticks and top each serving with *heaping tablespoon of marshmallow cream.* Garnish each serving with *cinnamon stick,* if you like. Makes six 1-cup servings.

ICED COCOA: Prepare *Hearty Hot Cocoa* as above; cool; pour over *ice cubes* in 7 or 8 glasses. Stir well. Top with *whipped cream;* sprinkle with *nutmeg* or cinnamon, if you like.

ICE CREAM SODAS

Making ice cream sodas at home is easy. For each soda, place *2 to 3 tablespoons syrup* (from list below) in a tall glass. Stir in about *¼ cup milk.* Add a *scoop of ice cream* and pour in chilled *club soda* until glass is almost filled; stir. If you like, top with *whipped cream and maraschino cherry.* Serve with iced-tea spoon and long straws.
Syrups: Chocolate, maple or maple-blended syrup; fruit-flavored pancake syrup; light molasses; thawed frozen lemonade concentrate (omit milk); cherry sundae topping.

FLOATS

In each tall glass, place a scoop of favorite ice cream. Pour in chilled soft drink until glass is almost filled; stir.

PARTY BLENDER SHAKES

Borrow two or three blenders; place with yours and surround with several kinds of *ice cream* and *sherbet* (kept cold in an insulated chest), *fruits, milk, dessert sauces, fruit juices, nuts* and *jams.* Let guests make their own milk shakes. Set out plenty of tall glasses or mugs, straws and iced-tea spoons. Blender strategy: first put in liquids; add fruit, then ice cream. Blend until thick and smooth. Serve immediately.

FOR DIETERS: Mix only fruit juice and fruit; then, with blender still running, add one *ice cube* at a time until drink becomes thick and frosty. (Omit milk, sauces, nuts and jams.)

MOCHA FLOAT

¾ teaspoon quick chocolate-flavor-milk mix
¾ teaspoon instant coffee powder
½ teaspoon sugar
club soda, chilled
2 small scoops chocolate-ripple ice cream

JUST BEFORE SERVING:
Into an 8-ounce glass, measure first 3 ingredients. Gradually add enough club soda to fill glass ¾ full; stir until sugar is dissolved. Add ice cream; stir well. Serve with spoon and straw. Makes 1 serving.

CHOCOLATE-ORANGE SODAS

1 6-ounce can frozen orange-juice concentrate, thawed
1½ cups quick chocolate-flavor-milk mix
2 pints vanilla ice cream
1 28-ounce bottle club soda, chilled

JUST BEFORE SERVING:
In medium bowl, stir unreconstituted orange-juice concentrate with chocolate-milk mix until smooth; stir in only 1 juice-can water. Pour ¼ cup chocolate-orange mixture into each of eight 12-ounce glasses. Add 1 large scoop ice cream to each glass. Add club soda to fill glasses almost to top. Serve with straws and iced-tea spoons. Makes eight 1½-cup servings.

STRAWBERRY SODAS

1½ cups milk
1 10-ounce package frozen sliced strawberries, partially thawed
1 pint strawberry ice cream
1 16-ounce bottle strawberry soft drink, chilled

JUST BEFORE SERVING:
In covered blender container, with blender at high speed, blend milk and strawberries 15 seconds; pour into five 12-ounce glasses. Add scoop of ice cream to each glass; slowly add soft drink to fill glasses almost to top. Makes five 1½-cup servings.

HOT MOCHA FLOAT

4 cups milk
½ cup sugar
⅓ cup cocoa
3 tablespoons instant coffee
½ pint vanilla ice cream

ABOUT 20 MINUTES BEFORE SERVING:
In 3-quart saucepan, with wire whisk or hand beater, beat milk, sugar, cocoa, instant coffee and 2 cups water until well blended. Over medium heat, heat until mixture is hot but not boiling, stirring occasionally. Remove mixture from heat; ladle into six 8-ounce mugs. Top each mug with a spoonful of ice cream. Makes about 5 cups or six ¾-cup servings.

ONE-AT-A-TIME FLOATS: In mug, stir *1 cup hot milk* into *2 tablespoons chocolate syrup;* spoon in some *vanilla ice cream.*

Coolers and Aperitifs

BEEF AND BITTERS

ice cubes
2 10½-ounce cans condensed beef broth
6 lemon wedges
aromatic bitters

JUST BEFORE SERVING:
Partially fill 6 old-fashioned glasses with ice cubes; pour undiluted beef broth over ice. Into each glass, squeeze a lemon wedge and stir a dash or two of bitters. Makes 6 first-course or snack servings.

EASY-WAY LEMONADE

2 lemons, thinly sliced
½ cup sugar
ice cubes

EARLY IN DAY:
Into large heatproof bowl or pitcher, measure lemons and sugar. Pour in 4 cups boiling water; stir until sugar is dissolved. Refrigerate until chilled.

TO SERVE:
Pour mixture over ice cubes in chilled 8-ounce glasses. Makes 4 cups lemonade or five ¾-cup servings.

LEMONADE

1½ cups sugar
1 tablespoon finely grated lemon peel
1½ cups lemon juice (8 to 10 lemons)
ice cubes
club soda (optional)

ABOUT 2 HOURS OR UP TO 1 WEEK AHEAD:
Prepare syrup: In 1-quart jar with tight-fitting lid, shake sugar and lemon peel with 1½ cups very hot water until sugar is dissolved. Add lemon juice. Refrigerate.

TO MAKE LEMONADE:
Over ice cubes in 12-ounce glass, pour ¼ cup syrup. Stir in ¾ cup cold water or club soda. Makes sixteen 1-cup servings.

FOR 8 SERVINGS: In 2½-quart pitcher or container, combine half of the syrup with 6 cups water. Pour over ice cubes.

LIMEADE: Prepare as above but substitute grated *lime peel* for lemon peel and *lime juice* for lemon juice (about 10 limes). Reconstitute with water only.

RUBY TREAT

1 18-ounce can tomato juice, chilled (2¼ cups)
1 cup unsweetened pineapple juice, chilled
1 tablespoon fresh lemon juice

JUST BEFORE SERVING:
In quart pitcher, mix juices. Pour into juice glasses. Makes about 3 cups or 6 first-course or snack servings.

SPARKLING FRUITADE

2 cups cranberry-apple drink, chilled
1 cup cool double-strength iced tea
1 10-ounce bottle lemon-lime soft drink, chilled
ice cubes

JUST BEFORE SERVING:
In pitcher, combine cranberry-apple drink, iced tea and lemon-lime soft drink. Pour over ice cubes in six 8-ounce glasses. Makes about 4¼ cups or six ¾-cup servings.

GRAPEFRUIT-AND-APPLE MIST

1 18-ounce can grapefruit juice
1½ cups apple juice (1 12-ounce can)
¼ cup lime juice
2 tablespoons sugar (or sugar to taste)
1 12-ounce bottle ginger ale
ice cubes

JUST BEFORE SERVING:
In large pitcher, stir juices and sugar until sugar dissolves. Gently stir in ginger ale. To serve, pour over ice cubes in chilled 12-ounce glasses. Makes about 5 cups or five 1-cup servings.

SPICED GRAPE-JUICE COCKTAIL

2 2-inch cinnamon sticks
4 whole cloves
2 whole allspice
2 tablespoons sugar
1 6-ounce can frozen grape-juice concentrate
crushed ice
8 thin lemon slices for garnish

EARLY IN DAY:
In 1-quart saucepan over medium heat, heat 2½ cups water and first 4 ingredients to boiling; cover and simmer 5 minutes. Strain; discard spices. Cool. Add undiluted concentrate; refrigerate.

JUST BEFORE SERVING:
Fill eight 6-ounce glasses halfway with crushed ice; pour spiced grape-juice mixture over ice to fill glasses. Garnish each serving with a lemon slice. Makes eight 3-ounce first-course servings.

CRANBERRY-ORANGE COCKTAIL

1 32-ounce bottle cranberry-juice cocktail
1 cup orange juice
1 teaspoon mace
orange-peel twists (page 379)

EARLY IN DAY:
In pitcher, combine cranberry-juice cocktail, orange juice and mace. Place an orange-peel twist in each section of an ice-cube tray. Half fill tray with juice mixture; freeze. Refrigerate remaining mixture.

ABOUT 20 MINUTES BEFORE SERVING:
Remove tray from freezer. Thaw cubes slightly. Place 2 or 3 cubes in each of 6 old-fashioned glasses. Pour refrigerated mixture over them. Serve with teaspoons. Makes about 5 cups cocktail and cubes or 6 first-course servings.

CLAM-JUICE STINGER

1 7½-ounce bottle clam juice, chilled
1 12-ounce can vegetable-juice cocktail, chilled
1 tablespoon lemon juice
2 dashes hot pepper sauce
ice cubes (optional)
lemon slices or wedges for garnish

JUST BEFORE SERVING:
In medium pitcher, stir juices and hot pepper sauce. To serve, pour into chilled 6-ounce glasses. If you like, add ice cubes. Garnish with lemon slices or wedges. Makes about 2½ cups or four 5-ounce first-course servings.

Party Drinks and Punches

APPLE-LEMON PUNCH

4 cups apple juice, chilled
2 cups lemonade, chilled
2 16-ounce bottles lemon-lime soft drink, chilled
ice cubes

JUST BEFORE SERVING:
In large pitcher, combine juice, lemonade and soft drink. Serve over ice cubes. Makes 10 cups or twenty ½-cup servings.

DANISH BRANDIED COFFEE

6 eggs
very finely grated peel of 1 lemon
½ cup sugar
3 cups cold strong coffee
⅔ cup brandy

JUST BEFORE SERVING:
In large bowl, with mixer at high speed, beat eggs with lemon peel until frothy, about 1 minute. Beating at high speed, gradually sprinkle in sugar; beat until mixture is thick, about 3 minutes. Reduce speed to low; slowly beat in coffee, then brandy. Serve in 6-ounce glasses. Makes about 6 cups or twelve ½-cup servings.

WASSAIL BOWL WITH BAKED APPLES

3 large cooking apples, cored
1 gallon apple cider (16 cups)
6 whole cloves
6 whole allspice
2 teaspoons nutmeg
1 6-ounce can frozen lemonade concentrate
1 6-ounce can frozen orange-juice concentrate
1 cup packed brown sugar
sugar
short cinnamon sticks for garnish

ABOUT 45 MINUTES BEFORE SERVING:
Preheat oven to 350°F. Cut apples in half crosswise and place, cut sides down, in 13″ by 9″ baking dish. Bake 25 minutes or until apples are fork-tender.

Meanwhile, in covered, large kettle over low heat, simmer 2 cups apple cider, cloves, allspice and nutmeg 10 minutes. Add remaining apple cider, undiluted lemonade and orange-juice concentrates and brown sugar; heat until hot but not boiling, stirring occasionally. Pour hot mixture into heated large punch bowl. Float apples, skin sides up, in punch; sprinkle tops with a little sugar. To serve, pour hot punch into punch cups; add a cinnamon stick to each serving. Makes 18 cups or thirty-six ½-cup servings.

LEFTOVER APPLES: Drain and refrigerate apples after serving punch; serve as dessert next day.

GLOGG

2 teaspoons dried orange peel
1 teaspoon whole cloves
4 whole cardamom, cracked
3 short cinnamon sticks
cheesecloth
2 ⅘-quart bottles Burgundy
1 cup dark seedless raisins
1 8-ounce package dried apricots
1 ⅘-quart bottle vodka, gin or aquavit
¾ cup sugar
1 cup whole blanched almonds

DAY BEFORE SERVING:
Place orange peel and spices on a piece of cheesecloth; tie securely with string to form a bag. In covered, 4-quart saucepan over medium-low heat, simmer 1 bottle Burgundy, raisins, apricots and spice bag 30 minutes. Remove from heat and discard spice bag; stir in remaining Burgundy, vodka and sugar; cover mixture and let stand at room temperature overnight.

TO SERVE:
Over high heat, heat wine mixture until piping hot, but not boiling, stirring occasionally. Carefully ignite wine mixture with a long match; let burn a few seconds; then cover pan to extinguish flame. Add almonds; pour into heated punch bowl. Serve hot. Makes about 10 cups or twenty ½-cup servings.

LIME PUNCH BOWL

2 6-ounce cans frozen daiquiri mix, thawed
1 28-ounce bottle lemon-lime soft drink
½ cup light rum (optional)
3 or 4 drops green food color
ice cubes
1 small banana
1 lime, thinly sliced

JUST BEFORE SERVING:
Pour daiquiri mix into chilled punch bowl. Using daiquiri-mix can as a measure, stir in 2 cans water. Add soft drink, rum and green food color; add ice. Slice peeled banana into punch, then float lime slices on top. Makes about 8 cups or sixteen ½-cup servings.

SPARKLING GARNET PUNCH

1 1-pound bunch seedless green grapes
6 cups cranberry-juice cocktail
2 tablespoons sugar
4 whole allspice
1 short cinnamon stick
3 16-ounce bottles club soda, chilled
2 drops almond extract

DAY BEFORE:
Freeze grapes in 1 bunch on cookie sheet. In large saucepan over high heat, heat cranberry juice, sugar, allspice and cinnamon to boiling; simmer 10 minutes. Strain mixture, discarding spices. Refrigerate.

JUST BEFORE SERVING:
Place frozen grapes in bottom of large pitcher or punch bowl. Add cranberry mixture, club soda and almond extract. Serve immediately. Makes 12 cups punch or eighteen ¾-cup servings.

EGGNOG

12 eggs, separated
1 cup sugar
1½ cups bourbon
½ cup brandy
6 cups milk
1¼ teaspoons nutmeg

DAY BEFORE SERVING OR EARLY IN DAY:
In large bowl, with mixer at high speed, beat egg yolks until thick. Beating at high speed, gradually sprinkle in sugar; beat until mixture is thick and light-colored, about 15 minutes, frequently scraping bowl with rubber spatula. Beat in bourbon and brandy, drop by drop, to prevent curdling yolks. Cover and chill.

ABOUT 20 MINUTES BEFORE SERVING:
In large bowl, with mixer at high speed, beat egg whites until soft peaks form. In chilled large punch bowl, stir yolk mixture with milk and nutmeg until blended. With rubber spatula or wire whisk, fold beaten whites into mixture. To serve, ladle into 6-ounce punch cups or glasses. Makes about 19 cups or thirty-eight ½-cup servings.

CREAMY EGGNOG: At the last, fold in *1 cup heavy or whipping cream,* whipped.

EGGNOG ROYALE

2 pints coffee ice cream
2 quarts ready-to-use eggnog
3 cups cold coffee
2 cups bourbon or rum (optional)
2 cups heavy or whipping cream
nutmeg

DAY BEFORE SERVING:
Scoop up about 10 large ice-cream balls; place on jelly-roll pan; freeze. Refrigerate eggnog.

JUST BEFORE SERVING:
Into chilled large punch bowl, stir eggnog, coffee and bourbon. In medium bowl, with mixer at medium speed, beat cream just until soft peaks form; fold into eggnog mixture. Place ice cream balls on top and sprinkle lightly with nutmeg. Serve at once. Makes about 15 cups or thirty ½-cup servings.

PARTY FRENCH CHOCOLATE

½ cup semisweet-chocolate pieces
½ cup light corn syrup
1 teaspoon vanilla extract
2 cups heavy or whipping cream
8 cups milk

1 HOUR BEFORE SERVING OR EARLY IN DAY:
In medium saucepan over low heat, heat chocolate pieces and ¼ cup water, stirring constantly, until chocolate is melted. Stir in corn syrup and vanilla; refrigerate until cold.

In medium bowl, with mixer at medium speed, gradually pour chocolate mixture into cream; continue beating just until mixture holds soft peaks; spoon into serving bowl; refrigerate until serving time.

JUST BEFORE SERVING:
In 3-quart saucepan over medium heat, heat milk until tiny bubbles form around the edge (don't boil); pour into warmed coffeepot (rinsed with hot water). Place coffeepot on tray with bowl of chocolate whipped cream, cups and saucers.

Spoon some chocolate whipped cream into each guest's cup, then fill the cup with hot milk. The guest stirs the two together before sipping. Makes sixteen ¾-cup servings.

FROSTED MOCHA PUNCH

½ gallon vanilla ice cream
⅔ cup instant freeze-dried coffee
¼ cup sugar
1 cup chocolate syrup
4 cups milk
1 cup heavy or whipping cream, whipped
1 28-ounce bottle club soda, chilled

ABOUT 20 MINUTES BEFORE SERVING:
Remove ice cream from freezer and spoon half into punch bowl to soften; return rest of ice cream to freezer. Into medium bowl, measure coffee and sugar; stir in 2 cups cold water until dissolved.

Stir chocolate syrup and milk into mixture. Pour over ice cream in punch bowl; stir until blended. Fold in whipped cream; gently pour in club soda. Spoon remaining ice cream onto punch. To serve, ladle into 6-ounce punch cups or glasses. Makes about 24 cups or forty-eight ½-cup servings.

SYLLABUB

5 cups half-and-half
2 cups Chablis
1 cup sugar
½ cup brandy
⅓ cup lemon juice
shredded peel of 1 lemon for garnish

ABOUT 10 MINUTES BEFORE SERVING:
In large bowl, with mixer at low speed, beat half-and-half until frothy; gradually beat in remaining ingredients except lemon peel until well mixed; pour into chilled punch bowl. Sprinkle with lemon peel. Makes about 8 cups or sixteen ½-cup servings.

HOT SPICED-TEA PUNCH

4 tea bags or 4 teaspoons loose tea
1 3-inch stick cinnamon
1 teaspoon whole cloves
¾ cup sugar
2 cups orange juice
½ cup lemon juice

ABOUT 20 MINUTES BEFORE SERVING:
In 3-quart saucepan over medium heat, heat 4 cups water to boiling. Remove from heat; immediately add tea and spices. Cover and let steep 5 minutes; remove tea and strain spices. Add sugar, fruit juices and 3 cups water; heat until hot but not boiling. Makes about 9½ cups or twelve ¾-cup servings.

COLD SPICED-TEA PUNCH: Prepare as above but do not heat last time and stir until sugar is dissolved. Chill.

GRAPE WINE SPRITZER

1 1-quart bottle Concord grape wine
½ cup lemon or lime juice
1 28-ounce bottle club soda, chilled
ice cubes
lemon and orange slices for garnish

ABOUT 2 HOURS AHEAD OR EARLY IN DAY:
In large pitcher, combine wine with lemon juice; refrigerate until well chilled.

TO SERVE:
Pour ½ cup wine mixture into each of nine 10-ounce glasses. Slowly add club soda to fill each glass three-fourths full; add ice cubes and fruit slices. Makes 9 servings.

SANGRIA

½ cup lemon juice
½ cup orange juice
½ cup sugar
1 ⅘-quart bottle dry red wine
¼ cup brandy
1 7-ounce bottle club soda, chilled
1 cup fruit (sliced orange, lemon, apple, peach, banana)
1 tray ice cubes

JUST BEFORE SERVING:
Into large pitcher, pour juices and sugar; stir to dissolve. Stir in remaining ingredients. Makes about 6 cups punch or eight 6-ounce servings.

TO DO AHEAD: Prepare as above but omit club soda, fruit and ice; stir these in at serving time; serve immediately.

MOCK SANGRIA: In large pitcher, combine *4 cups grape juice* and *one 16-ounce bottle club soda,* chilled. Add *ice cubes;* garnish with *orange slices*. Makes about 6 cups punch or eight ¾-cup servings.

Wines

Wines can be divided into five basic classes and, within these classes, into a few well-known generic types. All other wines are similar to these types:

Appetizer Wines	Sherry, Vermouth, Flavored wines
White Table Wines	Sauterne, Rhine wine, Chablis
Red Table Wines	Claret, Burgundy, Rosé
Sweet Dessert Wines	Port, Muscatel, Tokay
Sparkling Wines	Champagne, Sparkling Burgundy

Wines can be enjoyed before meals or with them—accompanying appetizer, main course and dessert. Some wines complement certain foods more than others.

Traditionally, white meat such as poultry, fish and seafood, and egg-and-cheese main dishes are accompanied by white wines. Red meat and other rich, fuller-flavored foods are served with red wine. Rosé and the sparkling wines go well with any food. However, let personal preference be your guide. Here are serving suggestions.

Appetizer wines: Serve appetizer wines well chilled, either straight (undiluted) or over ice. Of the *Sherries,* dry and medium sherries are best choices for an appetizer, while cream (or sweet) sherries are fine to serve with dessert or after dinner. Sherry is also a favorite wine for cooking. *Vermouth* is flavored with aromatic herbs. Serve dry (French-style) or sweet (Italian-style) alone as an appetizer or in cocktails. *Flavored wines* are light, sweet and fruity, with such flavors as apple and cola added.

White table wines: All white wines should be served chilled. *Sauterne* comes dry, semisweet and very sweet; serve dry and semisweet types with main courses; serve semisweet and very sweet with desserts or between meals. *Aurora, Sauvignon Blanc, Sémillon, Catawba* and *Haut* or *Chateau* are similar to sauterne. *Rhine wine* varies from dry to slightly sweet and goes well with main dishes; *Riesling, Sylvaner* and *Traminer* are Rhine-wine types. *Chablis* is similar to Rhine wine but fuller bodied; try *Delaware, Folle Blanc, Pinot Blanc, Chardonnay* for variations.

Red table wines: Depending on the type, red wines are served either cool or chilled. *Claret* is a dry wine of medium body and rich, full flavor. Serve it at cool room temperature with hearty meats and cheeses. Leading varieties include *Cabernet Sauvignon, Zinfandel, Chelois. Burgundy,* probably the best-known red table wine, is usually preferred cool and is especially good with red meats, game and turkey. *Barbera, Gamay, Pinot Noir* and *Baco Noir* are good choices of Burgundy-type wines. *Red Chianti* and *"Vino"-type* wines, served cool, are also nice red table wines. *Rosé* wines, the lightest of the red table wines, served chilled, come dry to sweet with a fruity flavor; serve them with any food.

Sweet dessert wines: Most dessert wines may be served cool or chilled, and are delicious with or after dessert and with between-meal refreshments. *Port* is a medium-sweet to sweet wine, usually deep red in color and especially good with cheese and nuts. *White Port* is light straw to pale gold in color and likely to be sweeter than red port. *Muscatel* is semisweet to sweet and ranges from golden to dark amber in color. *Tokay* has a sweetness between port and sherry and a nutty flavor. Other dessert wines: *Angelica,* the sweetest; *Madeira,* semisweet, served at room temperature or chilled as an aperitif; *Marsala,* similar to but sweeter than sherry. *Sweet Sauternes* and *Cream Sherry* also make nice dessert wines.

Sparkling wines: This festive class of wine is always served well chilled and goes well with any food and any occasion. *Champagne* comes very dry (*naturel*), dry (*brut*), semidry (*sec*) and sweet (*doux*). The color of pink champagne is the result of leaving the skins of the grapes with the juice during part of the fermentation process. In flavor, quality and degree of dryness, pink champagne resembles its pale-gold relative. *Red Sparkling Burgundy* and *Golden Sparkling Muscat* are semisweet to sweet. *Cold Duck* is a combination of champagne and sparkling Burgundy.

The best way to learn which you like is to experiment. Try a few of the wines in each of the five classes, writing down the names and label information of ones you particularly like. Buy small bottles when you're tasting a wine for the first time; they contain half the volume of the usual fifth (four-fifths of a quart), enough for two or three servings.

If you feel that you need additional guidance in buying wines, select a knowledgeable wine dealer and put yourself in his hands. He will suggest suitable wines in the price range you decide upon.

How to Read a Wine Label

All wine labels, on both U.S.-produced and imported wines, have some things in common. The *brand name of* the wine (usually the name of the winery) appears near the top of the label and is often accompanied by an emblem of that particular winery.

The *name of the wine* appears beneath the brand name. It may be a generic name such as Burgundy, Chablis or port, in which case the wine is a blend of several different varieties of grapes. Or it may be the name of the grape used, such as Riesling or Sauvignon Blanc, in which case the majority of the grapes used in making the wine were of that variety. Some wineries invent and trademark names for their wines, such as Emerald Dry or Prince Noir. Such a wine may be similar to other wines, but the name is exclusive to the winery it comes from.

Some statement of *geographic origin* is always present on a wine label. Often, in the case of imported wines, the smaller the region listed, the higher the quality of the wine. Therefore, if a French wine label indicates that the wine was produced on a chateau (the grower's own property), it will probably be of higher quality than a wine labeled with a whole region of France or simply "France." In the case of U.S.-produced wines, the label must list the name of the state or region in which the wine was produced. Unlike the case with imported wines, this is not necessarily an indication of quality.

The alcohol content of a wine is usually stated on the label. Federal law requires a minimum content of 7 percent for table wines; they may, however, contain 10 to 14 percent alcohol. Dessert and appetizer wines may contain as much as 21 percent.

The label may also tell you the *vintage*, the year the wine was made. Growing conditions in the wine-producing areas of the U.S. are consistently good, resulting in wines of consistent quality, and the date on U.S.-produced wines indicates that the grapes were grown and fermented in that year. For imported wines, however, the vintage is an indication of the level of quality. The variations in climates of some other parts of the world can result in vast differences in wine quality from year to year. For these wines, "vintage charts" are used as guides to wines of the better years.

Other information on the label of a U.S.-produced wine includes such phrases as "produced and bottled by," which indicates that 75 percent of the wine was crushed, aged and finished by the bottler; and "estate bottled," which indicates that the vintner grew all his own grapes and fermented all the wine. Sometimes a back label also appears on U.S.-produced wines. It describes the wine's flavor, and sometimes the grapes from which it was made and foods it goes specially well with.

Imported wines have the names of the producer and/or shipper, and sometimes the importer, on the label. Experience is the best guide to the names to look for here.

How Much to Buy

Many imported wines come in 24-ounce bottles. In this country, the fifth (four-fifths of a quart) is the most common size for wine. It contains 25.6 ounces or enough for six servings of table and sparkling wines or eight servings of dessert and appetizer wines. Other popular sizes are the tenth (also called a small bottle), which is 12.8 ounces; quart, 32 ounces; half-gallon, 64 ounces; and gallon, 128 ounces.

The shape of the bottle frequently indicates the kind of wine, an old bottling tradition of European winemakers. For example, claret and claret-type wine bottles usually have straight sides, curving shoulders and short, slender necks; they are made of dark green glass. Sauterne-type wine bottles are very similar, but the glass is lightly tinted or clear. Burgundy bottles are stocky with sloping shoulders and long necks. These, too, are made of dark-green glass. Chablis-type wines have similar bottles. Rhine-wine bottles are tall, slender and gently curving, of green or brown glass. Some winemakers, however, have developed their own bottle shapes.

If you want to start a wine cellar, you should probably include some of each of the five classes of wines. Beyond that, choose other wines that you like. A good representative start: Three red table wines—a mellow red or vino type, a Burgundy and a Zinfandel. Three white table wines—a Riesling, a sauterne and a Chablis. A bottle of rosé and a bottle of dry or medium-dry sherry; a bottle of port, two of vermouth, one sweet and one dry, and a bottle of champagne. U.S.A. wines offer good value within a range of $1 to $4, so the cost of such a cellar may be surprisingly modest.

How to Store

If stored for long periods of time, wines should be kept in dimly lighted places that have a constant, relatively cool (below 60°F.) temperature. Lay cork-bottled wines on their sides to keep corks moist and airtight. Bottles with plastic corks and metal screwcaps may remain upright. Wines may be refrigerated for a few weeks with no bad effects. Once opened, table wines should either be used entirely or reclosed tightly and refrigerated so they will remain fresh for several days. Appetizer and dessert wines, because of their higher alcoholic content, will keep well this way for a month or more after being opened.

How to Serve Wine

Sometimes two or more wines are served at a meal. Generally, only one wine is served with each course. An exception might be a buffet dinner at which several main dishes are served. Then, at least two wines—a red and a white—might be offered. Or, guests might be offered a choice of wines with a single main dish—as in the case of baked ham. Some prefer white wine with ham, some red, some rosé.

When serving a different wine with each course, plan to serve a white wine before a red wine; dry before sweet, light before full, and young before old. Otherwise a red wine served first, for example, might overpower a more delicate white wine served later. The exception is the sweet white dessert wines, which are always served at the end of a meal. When serving more than one wine, be sure to provide a wine glass for each type of wine at each place setting.

Glassware for wines: A good all-purpose wine glass is tulip-shaped, clear and stemmed, with a capacity of 9 ounces. The large size and tulip shape permit generous servings with ample room for the distinctive fragrance (bouquet) to collect above the wine. The stem prevents your hand from warming the wine. Fill the glasses about one-third full for appetizer and dessert wines; one-half full for table and sparkling wines.

If you prefer the more formal, classic service or if you frequently serve more than one wine at a meal, you may wish to select a variety of glassware. Appetizer and dessert wines may be served in conical, 5- to 6-ounce sherry glasses. To distinguish white wine glasses from red wine glasses at a formal place setting, use an 8-ounce glass for the white; a 10-ounce glass for the red. Champagne and other sparkling wines are best served in narrow flute or tulip-shaped glasses, with hollow stems if you like, since these will hold and display the characteristic bubbles better than the saucer-shaped glasses often associated with sparkling wines.

To serve any wine, bring the bottle to the proper temperature; then uncork and wipe the mouth of the bottle clean. The host pours a little for himself first, to make sure no bits of cork remain in the bottle and to taste for satisfactory flavor. Then he pours for the rest of the diners, twisting the bottle as he fills the glasses to prevent dripping; or he passes the bottle so diners may pour for themselves. If the bottle is chilled, wrap a towel around it but allow the label to show.

Red wine may be opened an hour or so ahead; at serving time, the host usually tastes the wine immediately before filling the glasses of other diners.

How to Cook with Wine

Wine adds decided zest to cooking. As cooking progresses, the alcohol evaporates, but the delicious flavor remains and mellows. (Alcohol vaporizes sooner than water boils; it is cooked out in simmering.)

Recipes usually specify a type of wine—dry sherry, sauterne, port—to be used, but others of similar nature in the same basic class usually can be substituted satisfactorily. Experts recommend cooking with wine of a quality you would like to drink. Use some in the recipe and serve more to enjoy as a beverage with the food.

Here are a few suggestions for cooking with wine.

For soups, add about a tablespoon of wine for each cup of soup. To consommé, add dry sherry or white table wine. To brown soups such as lentil and black bean, add dry or medium sherry. To meat and vegetable soups, add dry red or white wine.

For meat dishes, add a few tablespoons as the meat cooks to improve both the flavor of the meat and the gravy. If you like, substitute wine for the water or bouillon called for in the recipe; a rule of thumb is about ¼ cup wine for each pound of meat. To beef pot roasts, stews, other braised beef dishes, add red table wine. To veal shoulder roasts, shoulder chops, add any white table wine. To lamb stews, shoulder roasts, add either white or a light red table wine.

For chicken dishes, add a few tablespoons of white table wine to the cooking liquid or use the wine as part of the liquid called for in the sauce.

For fish dishes, add white table wine as the recipe directs.

For game, use any hearty red table wine as part of the cooking liquid. Some recipes call for marinating the meat overnight in wine to help mellow the flavor and slightly tenderize the meat.

For French dressing, substitute dry red table wine for part of the vinegar.

For fruits, pour a few tablespoons of wine over cut-up fresh, canned or frozen varieties, or over fruit combinations. To sliced strawberries, peaches and pears, add port. To bananas, add red wine. To melon, grapes, pears, add sauterne.

BRIEF U.S.A. WINE DIRECTORY

Wine Characteristic	When to Serve
Appetizer Wines	
SHERRY Dry, medium dry and sweet. Color ranges from pale to dark amber.	Dry: Before meal as appetizer. Sweet: With dessert; with between-meal refreshments.
VERMOUTH Sweet or dry, flavored with aromatic herbs. Sweet (Italian type) is dark amber. Dry (French type) is pale amber.	Before meal as appetizer.
OTHER SPECIAL NATURAL WINES (Flavored Wines) Semisweet to sweet, with added natural flavors varying from orange and lemon to vanilla.	As aperitif or for afternoon or evening refreshments with or without food. Use in fruit punches.
White Table Wines	
CATAWBA Both dry and semisweet. Made in Eastern and Midwestern states from native hybrid grapes that give it characteristic flavor and aroma.	Same as sauterne.
CHABLIS Dry and slightly fuller-bodied than Rhine wine. Fruity flavor. Straw-colored to pale gold wine.	With main course; especially good with fish, poultry, veal, lamb.
CHARDONNAY Dry, full-flavored wine with pronounced flavor characteristic of Pinot Chardonnay grape. Pale to light golden color.	Same as Chablis.
CHENIN BLANC Dry to semisweet. Light-bodied, fragrant white wine. Made from Chenin Blanc (White Pinot and Pinot de la Loire) grape.	Same as Chablis.
DELAWARE Dry to semisweet. Made from Delaware grape grown in Eastern states.	Same as Rhine wine.
FOLLE BLANCHE Dry. Made from Folle Blanche grape.	Same as Chablis.
LIGHT MUSCAT Dry or semisweet. (Also called dry muscat.) Light wine of muscat grapes with characteristic flavor and aroma.	Dry: With poultry or fish. Semisweet: With or after dessert; with between-meal refreshments.

PINOT BLANC Chablis type. Dry, tart; made from Pinot Blanc grape.	Same as Chablis.
RHINE WINE (HOCK OR MOSELLE) Dry to semisweet with delicate pale-gold, slightly greenish color. Often flowery, fruity.	With main course; especially good with poultry, veal or fish.
RIESLING Rhine-wine type made from one or a blend of the Riesling grapes. White (or Johannisberg) Riesling is the classic Rhine-wine grape of Germany; it produces a fruity, dry wine with a flowery fragrance. Emerald Riesling, developed by the University of California, is fruity, slightly "spicy."	Same as Rhine wine.
SAUTERNE Sometimes dry but often semisweet with golden hue. Very sweet sauternes are labeled Haut Sauterne or frequently Chateau Sauterne. Eastern Sauterne is often less sweet, with characteristic aroma and Labrusca-grape taste.	Dry: With poultry and fish. Sweet: With dessert, between meals or with poultry and fish. Very sweet: After dessert.
SEMILLON Either dry or semisweet. Sauterne-type wine made from Sémillon grape.	Same as sauterne.
SYLVANER Rhine-wine type. Dry, sometimes tart, but fruitier and more fragrant. Made from Sylvaner (Franken Riesling) grape.	Same as Rhine wine.
TRAMINER Dry or slightly sweet, with medium body. Light, crisp wine. Made from Traminer grape. Gewurztraminer is a "spicy" Traminer from the grape of the same name.	Same as Rhine wine.

Red Table Wines

BARBERA Heavy-bodied, typical Italian. Strong in flavor.	With main course; delicious with highly seasoned food, rice and spaghetti dishes.
BURGUNDY Medium to heavy-bodied, dark ruby in color. (Usually a blend of several grape varieties.) Eastern Burgundy has characteristic "grapy" perfume and flavor of Eastern grapes.	With main course, especially red meats, turkey, duck, game.

CABERNET SAUVIGNON Dry and aromatic. Appealing ruby-red color. Ages well. Made from Cabernet Sauvignon grape, famous Bordeaux grape of France and one of the best red-wine grapes of California. Has distinctive flavor.	Same as claret.
CHIANTI Medium-bodied, ruby-red wine, strongly flavored; dry, fruity, slightly tart.	Same as claret.
CLARET Medium-bodied, moderately dry. Usually a blend of several grapes.	With beef, spaghetti, game.
GAMAY Light in body. Made from Gamay grape. Often a rosé wine.	Same as Burgundy.
PINOT NOIR Body and flavor vary greatly with amount of Pinot Noir grape present in wine (by law, at least 51 percent). Finest are velvety to taste, with a beautiful red color. Ages well.	Same as Burgundy.
ROSÉ Dry to semisweet. Fruity wine. Lightest of red table wines, pink in color and light in body.	Ideal for luncheons, picnics, light main courses.
RUBY CABERNET Fruity, medium-bodied red wine. Made from a new variety of California grapes.	Same as claret.
ZINFANDEL Light to medium-bodied, fruity claret type. Has distinct taste and aroma of Zinfandel grape, produced only in California.	Same as claret.

Sweet Dessert Wines

ANGELICA Sweet; straw- or amber-colored; mild and fruity in flavor.	With or after dessert; with between-meal refreshments.
MADEIRA Semisweet, deep amber. Resembles sherry but is sweeter and darker.	As aperitif; with or after dessert; with plain cake or cookies as refreshments.
MARSALA Medium-bodied. Deep amber. Resembles sherry but is sweeter and darker. Usually is sweeter than Madeira but drier than Tokay.	With or after dessert; with cheese and nuts.

MUSCATEL Medium-bodied. Ranges in color from golden to amber. Has distinctive flavor, aroma and sweetness of muscat grapes.	With or after dessert; with between-meal refreshments; with cheese and nuts.
PORT Sweet, heavy-bodied, rich-tasting wine, ranging from deep-red to tawny color. (Some white port is produced, usually straw-colored.)	With or after dessert; especially good with cheese, nuts and fruits.
TOKAY Sweet, amber-colored. Usually made by blending angelica, port, and sherry. (It in no way resembles Hungarian Tokay in flavor.)	With or after dessert; with fruitcake, nuts, raisins or between-meal refreshments.

Sparkling Wines

CHAMPAGNE Very dry, usually labeled *naturel;* dry, usually labeled *brut;* semidry, labeled *sec;* sweet, labeled *doux*. Pale-gold color. Made sparkling by secondary fermentation of finished wine, creating natural effervescence. There also are pink champagnes.	Dry: As appetizer; with main course—especially poultry, game, sweetbreads, fish. Sweet: With dessert; with between-meal refreshments.
COLD DUCK Medium dry to fairly sweet. Light-red color. Blend of Sparkling Burgundy and champagne.	Most popular as refreshment beverage between meals.
SPARKLING BURGUNDY Smooth, slightly sweet, light-bodied. Red wine made naturally sparkling by same method as champagne.	With main course—especially poultry, game, sweetbreads; with between-meal refreshments.

Cooking outdoors

Directions, and even recipes, for cooking outdoors must be more general than for food preparation in the kitchen. Much depends on the amount of heat from the grill, camp stove or open fire as well as the current air temperature and even the amount of wind. However, by selecting simple, easy-to-cook foods, you can prepare many great meals in the open.

In high country (more than 3000 feet above sea level), even simple camp-style cooking can be a problem. For information on high-altitude cooking, see page 24.

How to Select Meat, Fish and Poultry for the Grill

Many kinds of beef, poultry, pork, lamb, veal, sausages, fish and shellfish are suitable for outdoor grilling. Select from the list below or see how-to-cook instructions for Meats (page 59), Poultry (page 169), Fish and Shellfish (page 209). Chops cut about an inch thick and steaks cut 1 to 2 inches thick are best for grilling. These thicker cuts take longer to cook than thin cuts, but the extra thickness assures that there will be enough time for the outside to brown well while the inside cooks to rare, medium or well-done as you prefer.

Beef

Hamburgers

Tender steaks: rib, sirloin, T-bone, porterhouse, club, rib-eye

Less-tender steaks: round steak or blade-bone chuck treated with a meat tenderizer or marinade; steaks commercially pre-tendered with papain; flank (served carved diagonally across the grain)

Oven roasts: rib-eye; high-quality, choice-grade rump, sirloin-tip; oven roasts pre-tendered with papain

Corned beef brisket (precooked)

Poultry

Whole or cut-up chicken, turkey, duckling, goose, Rock-Cornish hens

Lamb

Chops

Steaks

Ground patties

Boned and tied or netted leg or shoulder roasts (or roasts cut in chunks)

Pork*

Chops

Steaks treated with meat tenderizer

Spareribs; country ribs or back ribs (precooked)

Ham: canned; boneless rolled ham; slices or steaks

Rolled Boston shoulder

Rolled pork loin

Shoulder, cut in chunks

Boned and rolled fresh leg of pork

Canned chopped ham

Canadian-style bacon, whole or cut in thick slices

Canned luncheon meat

* Pork must be cooked until well done; use a meat thermometer for larger cuts and cook to 170°F. internal temperature for fresh pork, 160°F. for smoked pork and 130°F. for fully cooked ham.

Veal

Chops or cutlets

Steaks

Shoulder, cut in chunks

Rolled shoulder roast

Sausage

Frankfurters

Vienna sausage

Brown-and-serve sausage

Fresh sausage links (be sure to cook thoroughly); smoked sausage links

Precooked bratwurst

Knackwurst

Bologna

Fish

Whole, fillets or steaks

Shellfish

Lobsters

Rock-lobster tails

Shrimp, scallops, oysters on skewers

Tips on the Fire

• Read the manufacturer's instructions for using the grill before you start to cook.

• Always do your grilling in the open air. Fires produce carbon monoxide; if this accumulates in closed porches or garages, it can be extremely hazardous.

• Take care when starting a fire. Start it with wood shavings scattered around the charcoal; or with an electric starter, efficient and easy to use. Or use liquid starters, or solid and semisolid starters according to label directions. *Never* use gasoline or alcohol.

• For open grilling, the fire bed should be larger than the items being cooked and deep enough to maintain an even temperature. For covered grilling, follow the grill manufacturer's directions.

• Allow plenty of time for the coals to reach the cooking temperature you want. With charcoal, always start the fire 15 to 30 minutes ahead; for even, maximum heat, charcoal should be covered with white ash. For quick-cooking foods, use a single layer of briquets, covering an area a little larger than food to be cooked. For longer cooking, use two or more layers. Never add charcoal starter after the fire is ignited.

• To gauge the temperature of the fire, use a grill thermometer. Or, hold your hand, palm down, above the coals and count in long seconds, so: "one-second-one, two-seconds-two," etc. If you can keep your hand over the coals for no more than 2 seconds, the coals are hot (about 400°F.). If you can keep your hand there 3 to 4 seconds, the coals are medium-hot (about 350°F.); 4 or 5 seconds, the coals are at low heat (about 300°F.).

If need be, and the grill is adjustable, move the rack away from or closer to the heat to get the temperature you want. During cooking of large cuts of meat or poultry, check temperature occasionally, and add more fuel if necessary.

• Fire flares up and chars foods when fat, sauces and food particles drop into it. To help prevent this: If using an open grill, slightly tip the rack (or the entire grill) so that drippings run down the rack beyond the coals. Keep a water-filled clothes sprinkler handy to douse flare-ups. (Check instructions before using on gas or electric grills.) For a covered grill, prepare a drip pan as the manufacturer directs.

• Most grills let you adjust the distance between grid and heat. Experiment until you find a position which gives maximum heat with minimum charring or flame. A grill with cover and damper (used closed for roasting and smoking) can be used for open grilling, too. Control a too-hot fire by closing the damper and/or covering when necessary.

How to Grill Meats, Fish and Poultry

Prepare the outdoor grill for barbecuing, following the manufacturer's directions and the particular recipe. Depending upon their design, grills cook by different methods of heat:

Open grill for direct heat: Arrange a layer of coals in the grill so that food can be cooked directly over it. This method is used for cooking steaks, chops, ribs, patties, frankfurters, chicken pieces, fish, shellfish and all rotisserie cooking.

Covered grill for direct heat: Arrange the coals in a layer directly under the meat cuts, as above. (Gas and electric grills as well as charcoal grills with covers use this method.)

Covered grill for indirect heat: Arrange a drip pan made of heavy-duty, broiling or double-thickness foil the size of the meat in the center of the grill; arrange coals around the drip pan. Roasts, whole turkeys, chickens are cooked by this method. Because it's similar to oven roasting, no turning of the meat is necessary.

Low, even heat is best for grilling meats and poultry; the meat shrinks less, cooks more uniformly and will not be charred.

Control the intensity of the heat by using a specific number of briquets. Allow 10 to 15 briquets per pound of meat and add 10 to 15 each hour to maintain even heat.

Score edges of steaks, chops and ham slices so they don't curl during grilling; trim fat from edges of meat so it doesn't drip onto the coals during cooking and cause smoky flare-ups. Brush a little salad oil over the grids of the grill before adding the food.

For easier handling of fish, hamburger patties, sausage links and other small foods, place them in a large folding wire grill; brush sauce onto the food right over the wire grill.

Marinades and barbecue sauces add flavor to meats, fish and poultry cooked outdoors. Select milder-flavored preparations to accent fish, veal and poultry, heartier ones to bring out the flavor of beef, lamb or pork. Choose from the wide collection of bottled and packaged products at the supermarket or see our recipes, pages 637–638. For long-cooking foods such as spareribs or chicken, it is best to use low heat and to brush tomato-based or sweet sauces on during the last 20 minutes of cooking time; this helps prevent too dark a color and a "charred" flavor.

The time needed to cook meats, fish and poultry is dependent not only on the thickness of the meat but also on the amount of heat from the grill. For 2-inch-thick beef steaks, done medium-rare, allow approximately 12 to 15 minutes on each side; a 1-inch-thick, fully cooked ham slice will grill in about 8 to 10 minutes on each side; chicken pieces will take 45 to 60 minutes with frequent turning; a 1-pound, pan-dressed fish will take 4 or 5 minutes on each side.

Shellfish take about 2 or 3 minutes on each side, depending on the type and the thickness. Small rock-lobster tails and lobsters (about 1 pound) take about 8 to 10 minutes.

For a rich smoky flavor, add apple, hickory, oak or cherry wood chips to the briquets while the food is cooking. Soak the chips in water at least an hour before using so they will give maximum smoke and not burn too rapidly.

When the meat or poultry is ready to turn, use barbecue tongs or a long-handled pancake turner; a fork would pierce the meat, causing flavorful juices to run out. Season the meat just before serving, or let your guests season their own pieces.

Hints for Traveler-Cooks

Foods to take on the road: When planning a trip by car or boat, keep menus simple and select foods that are easy to carry. Along the way, replenish the fresh foods—milk, bread, fruits and vegetables—at roadside stands, vending machines or markets, and keep them organized in plastic bags inside insulated bags or coolers, perhaps one for beverages and milk and another for sandwich makings, fruits, and so on. For long-keeping ice, freeze water in washed milk cartons and put one or two cartons in the cooler.

Use plastic containers with tight-fitting

lids to carry moist foods such as freshly washed lettuce, potato salad. Clean jars with tight-fitting lids are also good for sugar, flour and other dry ingredients.

Stash cans of baked beans, sandwich spreads, beef stew and chunky chicken or other favorite soups in the corner of the trunk or trailer for an emergency meal.

Good organization is important, so keep foods and utensils separated in small boxes and plastic bags. It's handy to carry along extra plastic bags for garbage disposal as well as for keeping food. Pack cooking utensils, portable stoves and food chests last, ready to unload first. That way, the meal can be started while the tent is being pitched or the luggage unpacked.

Consider tucking in some of the following for cooking or eating while traveling:

Individual breakfast cereals (dry or instant)
Canned puddings, fruits, vegetables
Canned meat and fish
Catchup, mustard, pickles
Salad oil, butter or margarine
Dehydrated or canned soups
Evaporated or instant nonfat dry milk
Flour in shaker containers
Hard or canned cheeses
Instant coffee, tea, cocoa
Instant potato mixes
Packaged precooked rice
Instant fruit drinks
Packaged spaghetti or macaroni dinners
Packaged sauce mixes
Pancake or biscuit mix
Seasonings (salt, pepper, minced onion)

Cooking equipment to carry: Check your kitchen for appropriate cooking equipment —electric skillet, pressure cooker, Dutch oven, saucepan, etc.—that can be "toted." Before you buy any special cooking, heating or carrying equipment, see what's available by browsing through camping and picnic sections of department, sporting goods and drug stores, even supermarkets.

In pans, look for nested camping sets; they pack easily. Consider a simple-to-use portable gasoline, charcoal or propane stove. Or, try a tiny one-burner unit that uses canned fuel—fine for roadside heating of canned soup or hash, beverages. Or, select a portable bucket grill, hibachi or folding grill. Learn how to start and control your portable stove before you start.

Pack heavy-duty foil—doubled, it makes extra pans to use over the grill. Other great aids for on-the-go living are portable coolers, insulated bags, picnic jugs and bottles, wide-mouth vacuum bottles, portable tables and picnic kits.

Carry-in-Car Treats

For car journeys, adults as well as children enjoy snacking as they go along. Select several treats from the list below. Also keep dampened sponges in plastic bags for quick cleanup—one color for sticky fingers, another for car surfaces.

Assorted cheese-spread snacks, packed five flavors to a plastic bag
Presweetened cereals in individual boxes
Candy bars, wrapped hard candies
Shelled peanuts, mixed nuts
Apples, pears, bananas, oranges, grapes
Peanut-butter sandwiches, quartered and wrapped individually
Individual cans of puddings, fruit
Packets of crackers, cookies

Main Dishes

EASY GRILLED MAIN DISHES

SKEWERED SAUSAGES: Cut brown-and-serve sausages in halves and skewer with cherry tomatoes and pineapple chunks. Cook over grill, brushing often with bottled sweet-and-sour sauce.

TERIYAKI LAMB: Let chunks of lamb shoulder stand in teriyaki barbecue marinade overnight. Place lamb on skewers; grill until of desired doneness, brushing occasionally with leftover marinade.

HAM AND APPLES: Thread chunks of fully cooked ham onto skewers with large pieces of unpeeled apple. Grill until apples are tender and ham is browned, brushing near the end of grilling time with honey or light corn syrup.

GLAZED ROCK CORNISH HENS: Brush Rock Cornish hens (or small broiler-fryers) with salad oil and cook in a covered grill until tender. During last minutes of cooking time, brush with orange marmalade.

STUFFED FRANKS: Split frankfurters almost halfway through; stuff some with potato salad from individual cans, others with pork and beans. Top mixture with shredded cheese; wrap each frank with a bacon slice and grill until bacon is done.

PIZZA BURGERS: Grill split English muffins along with hamburger patties. Use to make sandwiches, adding a spoonful of tomato sauce and some oregano leaves to each.

APRICOT-GLAZED BEEF BRISKET

1 4½-pound fresh boneless beef brisket
1 medium onion, quartered
2 bay leaves
salt
1 17-ounce can unpeeled apricot halves, drained
2 tablespoons sugar
2 tablespoons cider vinegar
2 tablespoons salad oil
¼ teaspoon ground cloves

EARLY IN DAY OR DAY BEFORE SERVING:
In covered saucepot over high heat, heat to boiling brisket, onion, bay leaves, 1 tablespoon salt and enough water to cover. Reduce heat to low; simmer 2½ hours or until brisket is fork-tender. Drain; discard onion and bay leaves. Place brisket on plate; cover and refrigerate.

ABOUT 1 HOUR AND 10 MINUTES AHEAD:
Prepare outdoor grill for barbecuing. In blender container, place 1 teaspoon salt, apricot halves and remaining ingredients; cover and blend at low speed until well mixed; pour into small bowl. Place cooked brisket on grill over medium coals; grill 30 to 40 minutes until heated through, turning occasionally. During last 10 minutes of grilling, baste brisket frequently with apricot mixture. Makes 10 to 12 servings.

TO BROIL: Precook brisket and prepare apricot mixture as above. Preheat broiler if manufacturer directs. Broil brisket 30 to 40 minutes until hot, turning occasionally. During last 10 minutes of broiling, baste brisket frequently with mixture.

SPICED RIB STEAKS

½ cup soy sauce
2 tablespoons brown sugar
2 tablespoons Worcestershire
2 tablespoons cooking sherry
1 teaspoon salt
4 rib steaks, each cut about 1 inch thick

ABOUT 3 HOURS AHEAD OR EARLY IN DAY:
In large, shallow baking dish, for marinade, mix well all ingredients except steaks. Add steaks to mixture; cover and refrigerate at least 2 hours, turning steaks occasionally.

ABOUT 30 MINUTES BEFORE SERVING:
Prepare outdoor grill for barbecuing. With tongs, place steaks on grill; reserve marinade for basting. Grill steaks about 5 minutes on each side for rare or until of desired doneness, basting occasionally with marinade. Makes 4 servings.

TO BROIL: Preheat broiler if manufacturer directs. Broil steaks 3 or 4 minutes on each side or until of desired doneness, turning and basting once with marinade.

GRILLED INDIVIDUAL SUPPERS

1 pound round steak, cut in 1-inch chunks
¾ cup bottled barbecue sauce
4 medium carrots, sliced
4 medium potatoes, cubed
1⅓ cups sliced celery
2 teaspoons salt

ABOUT 3 HOURS AHEAD OR EARLY IN DAY:
In small, shallow baking dish, arrange meat; pour on barbecue sauce. Cover and refrigerate about 2 hours, turning meat occasionally.

ABOUT 1 HOUR BEFORE SERVING:
Prepare outdoor grill for barbecuing. Cut heavy-duty foil into four 18″ by 12″ pieces. Divide meat and vegetables among pieces of foil and sprinkle each with ½ teaspoon salt. Fold foil over and seal ends tightly. Place directly on hot coals and cook 35 to 45 minutes until meat and vegetables are fork-tender. Serve from foil packages. Makes 4 servings.

TO BAKE IN OVEN: Preheat oven to 425°F. Place wrapped suppers on cookie sheet and bake 30 minutes.

MARINATED CHUCK STEAK

1 3½- to 4-pound beef blade chuck steak,* cut about 1½ inches thick
unseasoned meat tenderizer
1 cup catchup
¼ cup cider vinegar
1 tablespoon brown sugar
1 tablespoon Worcestershire
1 tablespoon prepared mustard
1½ teaspoons oregano leaves
1 teaspoon salt

DAY BEFORE SERVING:
Trim excess fat from steak. Prepare steak with meat tenderizer as label directs. In 13″ by 9″ baking pan, for marinade, mix well remaining ingredients. Add meat, turning to coat with marinade. Cover and refrigerate overnight.

ABOUT 1 HOUR AND 15 MINUTES AHEAD:
Prepare outdoor grill for barbecuing. With tongs, place steak on grill over medium coals; grill 30 to 45 minutes until of desired doneness, basting frequently with remaining marinade and turning occasionally. Makes 6 to 8 servings.

TO BROIL: Marinate steak as above. Preheat broiler if manufacturer directs. Broil steak 35 to 40 minutes until of desired doneness, basting occasionally with marinade and turning once.

* Select high-quality, choice-grade chuck steak.

SEAFARER'S STEW

3 tablespoons salad oil
2 pounds beef stew meat, cut in 2-inch chunks
1 medium onion, sliced
1 tablespoon salt
¼ teaspoon pepper
6 large carrots, cut into chunks
6 stalks celery, cut into chunks
1 teaspoon dill weed
1 bay leaf
French bread (optional)

ABOUT 30 MINUTES BEFORE SERVING:
In 4-quart pressure cooker, in hot oil, brown stew meat and onion. Add remaining ingredients (except bread) and ¾ cup water. (Use 1 cup water if recommended in pressure-cooker manual.) Bring to 15 pounds pressure as manufacturer directs; cook 15 minutes.

Remove from heat and reduce pressure quickly as manufacturer directs before uncovering. Serve with French bread. Makes 6 servings.

TO COOK ON TOP OF RANGE: In Dutch oven over medium heat, brown stew meat and onion as above. Add remaining ingredients (except bread) and *1½ cups water;* cover and simmer over low heat until fork-tender, about 2 hours, stirring occasionally.

CHILI-ON-THE-GO

2 tablespoons shortening
1 pound ground beef
¼ pound hot Italian sausage links, skinned
1 cup chopped onions
1 28-ounce can tomatoes
1 16-ounce can kidney beans
½ cup catchup
1 tablespoon chili powder
2 teaspoons brown sugar
1½ teaspoons salt
1 teaspoon prepared mustard

EARLY IN DAY:
In 3-quart heavy saucepan over medium heat, in hot shortening, cook beef, sausage and onions until browned, stirring. Stir in tomatoes with their liquid, liquid from kidney beans (reserve beans) and remaining ingredients. Simmer 45 minutes. Stir in kidney beans and heat 15 minutes longer. Carefully spoon chili into wide-mouth vacuum bottles. Makes 8 servings.

BARBECUED SPARERIBS

4 pounds spareribs
1 10-ounce jar red currant jelly
½ cup lemon juice
3 tablespoons cornstarch
1 tablespoon salt
1 tablespoon grated lemon peel
1 garlic clove, minced

EARLY IN DAY OR DAY BEFORE SERVING:
Cut spareribs into 2- or 3-rib portions. In large saucepot over high heat, heat to boiling spareribs and enough water to cover.

Reduce heat; cover; simmer 1 hour; drain. Place ribs on plate; cover and refrigerate.

ABOUT 50 MINUTES BEFORE SERVING:
Prepare outdoor grill for barbecuing. In small saucepan over medium heat, heat remaining ingredients until mixture is thickened and jelly is melted, stirring constantly. Place spareribs on grill over medium coals; grill 20 minutes or until fork-tender, basting often with mixture and turning ribs occasionally. Makes 4 servings.

TO BROIL: Precook spareribs and prepare jelly mixture as above. Preheat broiler if manufacturer directs. Broil ribs 20 to 30 minutes until fork-tender, basting often with mixture and turning occasionally.

HOT AND SPICY COUNTRY RIBS

4 pounds pork country ribs or back ribs, cut into serving pieces
1 15-ounce can tomato sauce
¾ cup packed light brown sugar
½ cup red wine vinegar
1 tablespoon salt
1 tablespoon celery seed
1 tablespoon chili powder
2 teaspoons garlic salt
2 teaspoons oregano leaves
1 teaspoon pepper
½ teaspoon ground cloves

EARLY IN DAY OR DAY BEFORE SERVING:
In large saucepot over high heat, heat to boiling ribs and enough water to cover. Reduce heat to low, cover and simmer 1 hour; drain. Place ribs on plate; cover and refrigerate.

ABOUT 1 HOUR BEFORE SERVING:
Prepare outdoor grill for barbecuing. In 1-quart saucepan or bowl, combine tomato sauce and remaining ingredients. Place ribs on grill over medium coals; grill 30 minutes or until fork-tender, brushing generously with tomato-sauce mixture last 20 minutes, turning often. Makes 4 servings.

TO BROIL: Precook ribs as above. Preheat broiler if manufacturer directs. Prepare tomato-sauce mixture as above. Broil ribs 30 minutes, brushing last 20 minutes with tomato-sauce mixture and turning often.

TUMBLE-ROASTED RIBS AND CHICKEN

2 pounds spareribs
2 tablespoons salt
1 tablespoon paprika
1½ teaspoons celery seed
¼ teaspoon pepper
1 2½- to 3-pound broiler-fryer, cut up

EARLY IN DAY:
With sharp knife, cut spareribs between bones into individual ribs. In large saucepot, over high heat, heat to boiling spareribs and enough water to cover. Reduce heat to low; cover and simmer 45 minutes; drain. Place ribs on plate; cover and refrigerate.

ABOUT 2 HOURS BEFORE SERVING:
Prepare outdoor grill with rotisserie and wire rotisserie basket as manufacturer directs for barbecuing.

In cup, combine seasonings. On waxed paper, sprinkle chicken and spareribs with seasonings. Place chicken and ribs in rotisserie basket; tumble-roast over medium coals 1½ hours or until ribs and chicken are fork-tender. Makes 6 servings.

TO BAKE IN OVEN: Preheat oven to 350°F. Do not precook ribs. Season spareribs and chicken as above; place ribs on rack in shallow, open roasting pan and bake 45 minutes. Add chicken; continue baking 45 minutes, turning and basting occasionally with pan drippings, until all is tender.

SPICY HAM SLICE

½ cup catchup
⅓ cup sweet pickle relish
1 tablespoon cider vinegar
⅛ to ¼ teaspoon cayenne pepper
1 2-pound fully cooked ham slice

ABOUT 1 HOUR BEFORE SERVING:
Prepare outdoor grill for barbecuing. In small saucepan, combine first 4 ingredients. Place ham slice on grill over medium coals; grill 20 minutes or until heated through, basting frequently with mixture and turning occasionally. Makes 6 servings.

TO BROIL: Preheat broiler if manufacturer directs. Prepare catchup mixture as above. Broil ham 20 minutes or until heated through, basting with mixture and turning once.

ROTISSERIE HAM WITH APPLE GLAZE

ABOUT 2 HOURS BEFORE SERVING:
Prepare outdoor grill with rotisserie for barbecuing. Place *one 4- to 5-pound fully cooked, rolled ham* on rotisserie skewer, with drip pan in place, as manufacturer directs. Insert meat thermometer at slant into center of ham with dial close to one end of ham.

Grill ham on rotisserie, about 1½ hours or until meat thermometer reaches 130°F., basting during last 15 minutes with *Apple Glaze* (below). Remove ham from skewer; let stand 15 minutes before serving for easier carving. Pass remaining glaze to serve with ham. Makes 16 to 20 servings.

APPLE GLAZE: In small saucepan over low heat, heat *two 10-ounce jars apple jelly, 1 tablespoon lemon juice* and *1 teaspoon cinnamon,* stirring, until jelly is melted.

TO BAKE IN OVEN: Preheat oven to 325°F. Place ham on rack in shallow, open roasting pan. Insert meat thermometer into center of ham. Bake ham 1 hour and 45 minutes or until meat thermometer reaches 130°F., basting during last 15 minutes with glaze. Serve as above.

GRILLED CHOPPED HAM AND PEACHES

2 cups orange juice
⅓ cup sugar
2 tablespoons cornstarch
1 teaspoon thyme leaves
3 12-ounce cans chopped ham
4 peaches, peeled and halved

ABOUT 4 HOURS AHEAD OR EARLY IN DAY:
In 9″ by 9″ baking pan, for marinade, mix well first 4 ingredients. Lightly score large surfaces of canned chopped hams in diamond pattern; place in marinade. Cover; refrigerate at least 3 hours, turning often.

ABOUT 1 HOUR BEFORE SERVING:
Prepare outdoor grill for barbecuing. Thread chopped ham on two parallel 16-inch skewers; thread 4 peach halves on each of two 16-inch skewers. Pour marinade into small saucepan; heat on grill 10 minutes or until slightly thickened, stirring occasionally; keep warm.

Grill ham over low coals 15 to 20 minutes until heated through, brushing frequently with marinade and turning occasionally. During last 5 minutes of grilling time, add peaches and heat, brushing with mixture and turning once. Serve remaining marinade over ham and peaches. Makes 8 servings.

TO BROIL: Prepare and marinate ham as above. Preheat broiler if manufacturer directs. Broil ham 10 minutes, turning and basting occasionally with marinade. Add peaches and broil until heated through, turning and basting occasionally.

To serve, place ham and peaches on heated platter; keep warm. Pour remaining marinade into small saucepan; heat over medium heat 5 minutes or until thickened, stirring; serve over ham and peaches.

GRILLED PORK STEAKS WITH PINEAPPLE

6 pork blade steaks, each cut ½ inch thick
1 29½-ounce can pineapple slices
½ cup soy sauce
⅓ cup salad oil
¼ cup minced onion
½ garlic clove, crushed
1 tablespoon brown sugar

AT LEAST 4 HOURS OR DAY AHEAD:
Slash fat edges of pork steaks. Drain 6 pineapple slices and reserve with ¼ cup syrup. (Use remaining pineapple and syrup another day.) Cover and refrigerate pineapple.

In 13″ by 9″ metal baking pan, for marinade, mix well reserved pineapple syrup and remaining ingredients except steaks and pineapple. Add steaks and turn over to coat with marinade. Cover and refrigerate at least 3 hours, turning occasionally.

ABOUT 1 HOUR BEFORE SERVING:
Prepare outdoor grill for barbecuing. Grill steaks over medium coals until fork-tender, about 30 minutes, brushing occasionally with remaining marinade.

Immediately after removing steaks from marinade, add pineapple slices, turning to coat both sides; let heat in pan on grill over edge of coals. Serve a hot pineapple slice over each steak. Makes 6 servings.

TO BROIL: Marinate steaks as above. Preheat broiler if manufacturer directs. Broil steaks 20 to 30 minutes, until fork-tender, basting occasionally with marinade and turning once. During last 5 minutes of broiling, dip pineapple slices in marinade and place on top of steaks to heat through.

BOLOGNA KABOBS

1 pound bologna (in one piece)
1 16-ounce can small whole onions, drained
2 peaches, peeled and halved
¾ cup bottled barbecue sauce

ABOUT 50 MINUTES BEFORE SERVING:
Prepare outdoor grill for barbecuing. Cut bologna into 16 chunks. On four 14-inch skewers, alternately thread bologna chunks with onions; add 1 peach half to end of each skewer. Place kabobs on grill over low coals; grill 15 minutes or until bologna is heated through, occasionally turning kabobs and basting frequently with barbecue sauce. Makes 4 servings.

TO BROIL: Preheat broiler if manufacturer directs. Using all-metal skewers, prepare kabobs as above; broil kabobs 10 minutes or until heated through, occasionally turning and basting with barbecue sauce.

CAMP-STOVE STEW

3 tablespoons butter or margarine
1 medium onion, coarsely chopped
1 16-ounce package frankfurters, quartered lengthwise
1 tablespoon all-purpose flour
1½ teaspoons chili powder
1 teaspoon salt
2 15-ounce cans red kidney beans
1 16-ounce can tomatoes
1 12-ounce can whole-kernel corn, drained

ABOUT 30 MINUTES BEFORE SERVING:
In large saucepot or Dutch oven over medium heat, in hot butter or margarine, cook onion with frankfurters until lightly browned; with spoon, stir in flour, chili powder and salt. Add beans and tomatoes with their liquid and corn. Cover and simmer 15 minutes. Makes 6 servings.

SKILLET FRANKS AND VEGETABLES

1 16-ounce package frankfurters
1½ pounds lima beans, shelled
1 15-ounce can tomato sauce
1 6- or 8½-ounce can water chestnuts, drained
¼ cup packed light brown sugar
2 tablespoons bottled steak sauce
1½ teaspoons salt

ABOUT 1 HOUR BEFORE SERVING:
Prepare outdoor grill for barbecuing. Cut each frankfurter in half crosswise. In metal-handled, 10-inch skillet (if nonmetal-handled skillet is used, keep handle away from direct heat when cooking), mix remaining ingredients. Arrange franks over bean mixture. Cover and cook on grill over medium coals 35 to 45 minutes until lima beans are tender, stirring occasionally. Makes 4 or 5 servings.

TO COOK ON CAMP STOVE OR TOP OF RANGE: In 10-inch skillet, prepare franks and lima beans as above; cook over medium-high heat about 25 minutes.

SKILLET BRATWURST DINNER

2 pounds precooked bratwurst
1 2-pound package frozen hash-brown potatoes
4 medium green onions, chopped
3 celery stalks, thinly sliced
1½ teaspoons salt

ABOUT 1 HOUR AND 15 MINUTES AHEAD:
Prepare outdoor grill for barbecuing. In metal-handled 12-inch skillet (if nonmetal-handled skillet is used, keep handle away from direct heat) on grill over medium coals, brown bratwurst well on all sides; drain on paper towels; keep warm.

Spoon off all but about ⅓ cup of fat from skillet; add frozen potatoes and remaining ingredients. Cook 20 minutes or until potatoes are browned and celery is tender-crisp, occasionally turning mixture with pancake turner. Add bratwurst and serve from skillet. Makes 8 servings.

TO COOK ON CAMP STOVE OR TOP OF RANGE: In large skillet, prepare as above over medium heat.

CHICKEN WITH CHILI-SAUCE MARINADE

1 12-ounce bottle chili sauce
½ cup white wine vinegar
1 tablespoon horseradish
1 garlic clove, quartered
1 teaspoon salt
1 3-pound broiler-fryer, cut up

EARLY IN DAY:
In 13″ by 9″ baking pan, for marinade, mix all ingredients except chicken. Add chicken; coat with marinade. Cover; refrigerate at least 4 hours, turning occasionally.

ABOUT 1 HOUR AND 15 MINUTES AHEAD:
Prepare outdoor grill for barbecuing. With tongs, place chicken on grill over medium coals; grill 45 minutes or until fork-tender, basting with marinade and turning occasionally. Makes 4 servings.

TO BROIL: Prepare chicken as above. Preheat broiler if manufacturer directs. Broil chicken 45 minutes or until fork-tender, basting with marinade and turning often.

BARBECUED CHICKEN WITH PLUM SAUCE

1 2½- or 3-pound broiler-fryer, quartered
salad oil, melted butter or margarine
2 teaspoons salt
¼ teaspoon pepper
¼ cup light corn syrup
3 plums, pitted

ABOUT 1 HOUR AND 15 MINUTES AHEAD:
Prepare outdoor grill for barbecuing. Brush chicken lightly with salad oil; sprinkle with salt and pepper.

In covered blender container, place corn syrup and plums; blend at low speed until plums are pureed.

Place chicken on grill over medium coals; grill 45 minutes or until fork-tender, turning occasionally. During last 5 minutes of grilling, baste frequently with plum mixture. Makes 4 servings.

BARBECUED CHICKEN WITH SPICY PEANUT GLAZE: Prepare as above but instead of plum-corn-syrup mixture, brush chicken during last 10 minutes with Spicy Peanut Glaze: In small bowl, mix well *⅓ cup chunky peanut butter, 2 tablespoons soy sauce, 1 tablespoon cider vinegar, 1 tablespoon honey, 1 small garlic clove,* crushed, *¼ teaspoon ground cardamom* and *¼ teaspoon cinnamon.*

TO BROIL: Preheat broiler if manufacturer directs. Prepare chicken and plum mixture or peanut glaze as above. Broil chicken 45 minutes or until fork-tender, turning occasionally. During last 5 minutes of broiling, baste frequently with mixture.

CAMPGROUND CHICKEN DINNER

2 2½-pound broiler-fryers, cut up
salt and pepper
6 medium potatoes
6 medium onions
6 medium carrots
⅓ cup white wine vinegar
¼ cup sugar
1 tablespoon Worcestershire
3 bay leaves, crushed
6 ears corn, husked
butter or margarine

ABOUT 1¾ HOURS BEFORE SERVING:
Sprinkle chicken pieces with salt and pepper. In 16-quart saucepot, place chicken pieces in center. Surround with potatoes, onions and carrots.

In bowl or jar, combine 3 cups boiling water with vinegar, sugar, 2 tablespoons salt, Worcestershire, bay leaves and ¼ teaspoon pepper; pour over chicken and vegetables. Over high heat, heat to boiling.

Reduce heat to low; cover and simmer about 1½ hours until chicken and vegetables are fork-tender, occasionally ladling liquid in saucepot over all. About 15 minutes before end of cooking, add corn. Serve with salt and butter or margarine for corn. Makes 6 servings.

TURKEY WITH ORANGE-WALNUT GLAZE

ABOUT 4 HOURS BEFORE SERVING:
1. Prepare outdoor covered grill, using indirect-heat method with drip pan as manufacturer directs for barbecuing. Remove giblets and neck from inside *one 12-pound frozen, ready-to-stuff, prebasted turkey,* thawed. (Use giblets and neck in favorite

soup recipe.) Rinse and drain turkey well.
2. Lift wing tips up, then fold under back of bird so they stay flat and balance turkey. Depending on brand of turkey, tie drumsticks together across tail with string, or push under band of skin or use stuffing clamps. Brush turkey with *salad oil.* Insert meat thermometer into center of thigh next to body, being careful thermometer does not touch bone.
3. Place turkey on grill over drip pan. Cover; roast 2½ to 3 hours, adding more briquets to each side of grill at the end of each hour as manufacturer directs. During last 15 minutes of roasting time, baste turkey generously with *Orange-Walnut Glaze* (below). Turkey is done when thermometer reads 180° to 185°F., or when thickest part of drumstick feels soft when pinched with fingers protected with paper towels.
4. Remove turkey to platter; let stand 15 minutes for easier carving. Makes about 16 servings.

ORANGE-WALNUT GLAZE: In small saucepan over medium heat, heat *1 cup orange marmalade, ½ cup finely chopped California walnuts, 3 tablespoons lemon juice, 1 tablespoon instant minced onion* and *2½ teaspoons salt* until marmalade is melted.

TO COOK ON ROTISSERIE OVER OUTDOOR GRILL: Prepare outdoor grill with rotisserie for barbecuing. Prepare turkey as in step 1 and Orange-Walnut Glaze as directed above. Skewer turkey on rotisserie skewer as manufacturer directs. Insert meat thermometer into center of thigh as in step 2. Roast turkey 5 to 5½ hours until meat thermometer reads 180° to 185°F. Baste with glaze during last 15 minutes.

TO BAKE IN OVEN: Preheat oven to 325°F. Prepare turkey as in steps 1 and 2 and Orange-Walnut Glaze as directed above. Place turkey, breast side up, on rack in shallow, open roasting pan. Roast turkey 3 to 3½ hours or until meat thermometer reads 180° to 185°F. (When skin turns golden, cover with a "tent" of folded foil to prevent excess browning.) Baste with glaze during last 15 minutes of roasting.

SAUCY GRILLED FISH

Buttery Lemon Sauce (page 637)
8 serving-size bluefish or other locally available fish, pan-dressed

ABOUT 45 MINUTES BEFORE SERVING:
Prepare outdoor grill for barbecuing. Prepare sauce. Place fish in large folding wire grill or directly on grill; cook over medium coals, basting frequently with sauce, about 5 minutes on each side or until fish flakes easily when tested with a fork. Makes 8 servings.

TO BROIL: Preheat broiler if manufacturer directs. Broil fish 5 minutes on each side, brushing often with sauce.

GRILLED SESAME TROUT

6 serving-size rainbow trout or other locally available fish, pan-dressed
½ cup lemon juice
4 teaspoons salt
¼ teaspoon pepper
¼ cup sesame seed
¾ cup butter or margarine

EARLY IN DAY:
With sharp knife, make three light slashes on each side of fish. In 13″ by 9″ baking pan, for marinade, mix well lemon juice, salt and pepper. Add fish and turn over to coat with marinade. Cover and refrigerate at least 3 hours, turning occasionally.

ABOUT 45 MINUTES BEFORE SERVING:
Prepare outdoor grill for barbecuing. In small saucepan over medium heat, toast sesame seed until golden, stirring and shaking pan occasionally; add butter or margarine and heat until melted. Drain marinade from baking pan into sesame-seed mixture.

Place fish in large folding wire grill or directly on grill; cook over medium coals, basting frequently with sesame-seed mixture, about 5 minutes on each side or until fish flakes easily when tested with a fork. Makes 6 servings.

TO BROIL: Prepare fish and sesame-seed mixture as above. Preheat broiler if manufacturer directs. Broil fish about 5 minutes on each side, basting frequently with sesame-seed mixture.

CLAMBAKE

ABOUT 4 OR 5 HOURS BEFORE SERVING:
1. At the beach, dig a pit in the sand about 1 foot deep and 3½ feet across; line it with *dry, smooth flat rocks,* each about 6 inches thick. (Do not use rocks that are wet or that have baked before.) With *wood,* build a fire on the rocks and keep it going 1½ to 2½ hours to heat the rocks white-hot. Meanwhile, gather and wash about *3 bushels wet rock seaweed.* Wet a *tarpaulin* at least 5 feet by 5 feet and have *more large rocks* ready to secure it over the pit later. Have a pail of salt water handy.
2. Prepare the food for steaming: Pull outer husks from *2 to 2½ dozen ears corn;* reserve husks. Pull inner husks back and remove silks, then re-cover kernels with inner husks. Cut up *four 2½-pound broiler-fryers* and wrap individual servings in cheesecloth. Scrub about *6 dozen hard-shell clams.* Scrub *12 medium sweet potatoes.* If you like, kill *twelve 1½-pound lobsters* (see Broiled Live Lobster, page 236).
3. When stones are hot, quickly rake and shovel embers from the pit. Line the pit with about 6 inches of seaweed. Place a sheet of *chicken wire* about 3½ feet square to cover the seaweed. Working quickly, layer chicken, potatoes, corn, lobsters and clams; separate each food by more seaweed. Top layers with reserved corn husks. Sprinkle salt water over all.
4. Quickly cover the food completely with the wet tarpaulin, anchoring it in place with the large rocks. Let the food steam about one hour. If steam billows the tarpaulin, unfasten a corner occasionally to let steam escape. To test for doneness, check to see that chicken is tender, clams are opened and lobster is pink.
5. Serve the clams first, then lobsters, then corn, potatoes and chicken with lots of *butter or margarine* and *salt* and *pepper.* Beer is the traditional beverage, and watermelon is often the dessert. Provide lots of napkins. Makes 12 generous servings.

OTHER COMBINATIONS: Use soft-shell clams instead of hard-shell clams; use dressed blue-fish, cod, haddock or striped bass wrapped in cheesecloth instead of chicken or lobsters; use white potatoes, peeled and in cheesecloth, instead of sweet potatoes.

INDOOR CLAMBAKE

1 3-pound bluefish, boned
cheesecloth
2 to 3 dozen hard-shell clams
2 to 3 dozen soft-shell clams
1 pound seaweed (optional)
6 1½-pound lobsters
12 ears corn, husked
1 pound butter or margarine, melted
salt

ABOUT 1½ HOURS BEFORE SERVING:
1. Cut bluefish into 3 pieces; wrap each piece in a square of cheesecloth. Scrub clams. Rinse seaweed.
2. In clam steamer or large kettle (about 20 quarts) over high heat, heat about 2 inches hot water to boiling. Place lobsters, head first, in steamer. Arrange in layers corn, bluefish, hard-shell clams, soft-shell clams and seaweed; cover steamer. Over high heat, heat to boiling. Reduce heat to low; let steam 20 to 30 minutes until fish flakes easily and clams open.
3. To serve: Remove and discard seaweed. Serve clams first, then bluefish, then corn and lobsters. Each person dips clams and lobster meat into melted butter and spreads some butter over the corn. Serve with salt and provide plenty of napkins.
4. If you like, strain sand from broth through double layer of cheesecloth and serve the broth in mugs. Makes 6 servings.

CAMPER'S PAN-FRIED FISH

4 small trout, catfish or other locally available fish, pan-dressed
salt and pepper
¼ cup evaporated milk
½ cup all-purpose flour
¼ cup cornmeal
2 tablespoons shortening

ABOUT 20 MINUTES BEFORE SERVING:
Sprinkle each fish well with salt and pepper. Pour undiluted milk in shallow pan. In another shallow pan, combine flour and cornmeal. Dip fish in milk, then into flour mixture until well coated.

In 12-inch skillet over medium heat, in hot shortening, fry fish 4 minutes on each side or until fish flakes easily when tested with a fork. Makes 4 servings.

OUTDOOR BREAKFAST IDEAS

PANCAKES: Packaged pancake mix with fresh berries, semisweet-chocolate pieces or chopped nuts added.

EGGS ON TOAST: English muffins, toasted and buttered, topped with scrambled eggs, bacon bits, canned French-fried onions.

FISH AND FLAPJACKS: Fried fresh-caught fish with cornmeal flapjacks or pancakes.

WESTERN EGGS: Scrambled eggs, bacon pieces, chopped onion and green pepper between buckwheat cakes.

HOMINY SCRAMBLE: A mixture of eggs scrambled with crumbled bacon and drained, canned hominy.

STEAK AND POTATOES: Cube steaks or pieces of boneless sirloin, fried with cooked potato chunks or served on onion rolls.

CANADIAN GRILL: Canadian-bacon slices plus brown-and-serve sausages, basted with maple-flavored syrup while they cook.

HEARTY OATMEAL: Hot oatmeal with brown sugar, huckleberries or blueberries and milk.

Vegetables

Grill these vegetables along with the main dish. Some vegetables take longer than meat, so check to see when to start the fire.

MARJORAM POTATOES AND ONIONS

4 medium potatoes, thickly sliced
2 medium onions, thickly sliced
2 teaspoons marjoram leaves
1½ teaspoons salt
¼ cup butter or margarine

ABOUT 1 HOUR AND 15 MINUTES AHEAD:
Prepare outdoor grill for barbecuing. On a large sheet of heavy-duty foil, mix first 4 ingredients in a single layer; dot with butter or margarine. Fold foil over vegetables and seal ends. Place packet directly on top of medium coals; cook 30 to 40 minutes until potatoes and onions are tender, turning once. Makes 4 servings.

TO BAKE IN OVEN: Preheat oven to 400°F. In 9″ by 9″ baking pan, combine ingredients. Cover pan; bake 40 minutes or until vegetables are tender.

VEGETABLE PACKETS

½ pound carrots (about 4), cut into julienne strips
½ pound green beans, cut up
¼ pound mushrooms, sliced
1 teaspoon salt
½ teaspoon thyme leaves
3 tablespoons butter or margarine

ABOUT 1½ HOURS AHEAD:
Prepare outdoor grill for barbecuing. On sheet of heavy-duty foil, mix first 5 ingredients; spread in layer; dot with butter or margarine. Fold foil over vegetables and seal ends. Cook packet on grill over medium coals 1 hour or until vegetables are tender-crisp. Makes 4 servings.

TO COOK ON CAMP STOVE OR TOP OF RANGE:
In 2-quart saucepan over medium heat, place all ingredients. Cover and cook, stirring occasionally, 15 minutes or until vegetables are tender-crisp.

SKILLET EGGPLANT PARMESAN

1 small eggplant, cut into ½-inch slices
1 15- to 16-ounce jar meatless spaghetti sauce
½ teaspoon salt
¼ teaspoon seasoned pepper
½ 8-ounce package mozzarella cheese, thinly sliced
2 tablespoons grated Parmesan cheese

ABOUT 1 HOUR BEFORE SERVING:
Prepare outdoor grill for barbecuing. In metal-handled 10-inch skillet (if nonmetal-handled skillet is used, keep handle away from direct heat when cooking), mix well first 4 ingredients. Cover and cook on grill over medium coals 20 minutes or until eggplant is tender, stirring occasionally. Arrange mozzarella slices on top and sprinkle with Parmesan cheese; cover and cook until cheese is melted. Makes 6 servings.

TO COOK ON CAMP STOVE OR TOP OF RANGE:
In 10-inch skillet, prepare eggplant and cook over medium heat as above.

GRILLED ROSEMARY ZUCCHINI

6 medium zucchini, cut in ½-inch slices
½ cup chopped onion
1 teaspoon rosemary
1 teaspoon salt
½ cup butter or margarine

ABOUT 1 HOUR BEFORE SERVING:
Prepare outdoor grill for barbecuing. In 13″ by 9″ disposable aluminum cake pan or on a large sheet of heavy-duty foil, mix zucchini with onion, rosemary and salt. Dot mixture with butter or margarine; cover pan with foil or fold sheet of foil over and seal ends. Cook in pan on grill over medium coals 25 minutes or until zucchini is tender-crisp. Makes 8 servings.

TO COOK ON CAMP STOVE OR TOP OF RANGE: In 10-inch skillet over medium heat, melt butter; add remaining ingredients; cover and cook 15 minutes or until zucchini is tender-crisp, stirring occasionally.

VEGETABLE KABOBS

2 medium ears corn, husked
12 cherry tomatoes
1 green pepper, cut into chunks
½ small eggplant, cut into chunks
1 8-ounce bottle Italian dressing

ABOUT 2 HOURS AHEAD OR EARLY IN DAY:
Break each ear of corn in half. In large bowl, toss corn, tomatoes, green pepper and eggplant with Italian dressing; cover and refrigerate at least 1 hour, stirring occasionally.

ABOUT 1 HOUR BEFORE SERVING:
Prepare outdoor grill for barbecuing. Drain vegetables, reserving dressing. On four 14-inch skewers, alternately thread vegetables. Grill vegetables over medium coals about 20 minutes or until vegetables are tender, occasionally turning skewers and brushing frequently with reserved dressing. Makes 4 servings.

TO BROIL: Refrigerate vegetables in dressing as above. Preheat broiler if manufacturer directs. Using all-metal skewers, prepare kabobs; broil in bottom of broiling pan 15 minutes or until tender, occasionally turning kabobs and basting frequently with dressing.

BARBECUED CORN-ON-THE-COB

ABOUT 1 HOUR BEFORE SERVING:
Prepare outdoor grill for barbecuing. Remove husks and silk from *6 medium ears corn.* Place each ear on sheet of heavy-duty foil; brush corn with *⅓ cup bottled barbecue sauce;* fold foil over each ear tightly to seal. Grill corn over medium coals 30 minutes, turning often. Makes 6 servings.

PAPRIKA BUTTERED: In small bowl, mix well *6 tablespoons butter or margarine,* softened, *2 tablespoons salt, 2 teaspoons paprika* and *dash pepper.* Prepare corn as above but spread with butter mixture instead of barbecue sauce.

TO BAKE IN OVEN: Preheat oven to 450°F. Prepare and wrap corn in foil as above; bake 10 minutes or until piping hot.

VEGETABLES THAT COOK ALONG WITH THE MEAT

GRILLED FROZEN VEGETABLES: Season frozen green beans, corn, peas, asparagus, broccoli, lima beans or cauliflower with salt, pepper; place in layer about ½ to 1 inch thick on heavy-duty foil; wrap tightly. Grill 20 to 30 minutes, turning occasionally.

ONIONS IN FOIL: For each serving, peel 3 or 4 small white onions and cut an X in one end of each. Dot with butter or margarine; wrap tightly in heavy-duty foil and cook directly on coals for about 30 minutes.

GRILLED EGGPLANT: Place chunks of eggplant on skewers; brush with salad oil; sprinkle with garlic salt. Grill, turning often, until tender, about 10 minutes.

POTATOES PLUS: Scrub 2 or 3 large potatoes (do not peel) and cut into thick slices. Overlap slices slightly on sheet of heavy-duty foil and dot with butter or margarine; sprinkle with minced chives. Wrap tightly; cook directly on coals about 45 minutes or until tender, turning once.

BARBECUED ZUCCHINI: Score zucchini in medium diamonds all around, about ⅛-inch deep; cut in about 2-inch chunks and thread on skewers. Grill until tender-crisp, about 20 minutes, turning often and brushing with Italian salad dressing.

Breads and Snacks

BREADS AND SNACKS FROM THE GRILL

FILLED RAISIN TOAST: Spread softened cream cheese between raisin-bread slices. Toast on both sides over grill. Cut in half diagonally.

PEPPERY BREADSTICKS: Mix a dash or two of hot pepper sauce with some melted butter or margarine. Roll Italian breadsticks in this mixture, then wrap in foil and heat on grill about 10 minutes.

GRILLED PEANUT-BUTTER SANDWICHES: Make sandwiches with Vienna bread, peanut butter and a favorite jelly. Grill, turning once, on both sides until heated through; cut into strips.

CHICKEN APPETIZER ROUNDS: Spread party-rye slices with canned chicken-salad-sandwich spread and sprinkle with shredded Cheddar cheese; top with another bread slice; toast on both sides.

CHEESY POPCORN: Cook ready-to-pop popcorn in its disposable container right on the grill; toss with grated Parmesan cheese.

HAM SNACKS: Fill split hot-dog buns with canned ham-salad-sandwich spread. Grill on both sides; slice into thirds.

CHEESE-ON-RYE NIBBLERS: Make sandwiches with cream-cheese-with-chives spread and rye bread. Toast on both sides; cut into triangles.

FILLED BROWN-AND-SERVE ROLLS

ABOUT 1 HOUR BEFORE SERVING:
Prepare outdoor grill for barbecuing. With sharp knife, horizontally split rolls from *one 8- or 10-ounce package brown-and-serve rolls;* fill with one of the *Spreads* below. Press roll halves together; brown on grill over medium coals about 5 to 7 minutes on each side. Makes 6 servings.

ANCHOVY-BUTTER SPREAD: In small bowl, with spoon, mix well *½ cup butter or margarine,* softened, *2 tablespoons minced anchovies, 2 teaspoons minced parsley* and *1 teaspoon lemon juice.* Makes about ½ cup.

CHEESE-PICKLE SPREAD: In small bowl, with spoon, mix well *½ cup pasteurized process cheese spread* and *¼ cup drained pickle relish.* Makes about ½ cup.

SPICED ORANGE-BUTTER SPREAD: In small bowl, with spoon, mix well *¼ cup butter or margarine,* softened, *¼ cup orange marmalade, ½ teaspoon grated orange peel* and *⅛ teaspoon ginger.* Makes ½ cup.

PARMESAN-TARRAGON-BUTTER SPREAD: In small bowl, with spoon, mix well *½ cup butter or margarine,* softened, *2 tablespoons grated Parmesan cheese* and *1½ teaspoons tarragon.* Makes about ½ cup.

TO BROWN ROLLS IN OVEN: Preheat oven to 425°F. Split and fill rolls as above; place on cookie sheet and bake 12 to 15 minutes until rolls are golden.

CHILI BREAD

½ cup butter or margarine, softened
2 teaspoons chili powder
1 long loaf Italian bread

ABOUT 1 HOUR BEFORE SERVING:
Prepare outdoor grill for barbecuing. In small bowl, with fork, mix well butter or margarine and chili powder. Cut Italian bread crosswise into 1-inch slices, being careful not to cut through bottom crust. Spread chili butter between bread slices; wrap in foil. Grill bread over hot coals 20 minutes or until hot. Makes 6 servings.

GARLIC: Prepare as above but use *¼ teaspoon garlic powder* instead of chili powder.

ONION: Prepare as above but use *2 tablespoons minced green onions* instead of chili powder.

PIZZA: In small bowl, mix *6 tablespoons butter or margarine,* softened, with *2 tablespoons grated Parmesan cheese* and *2 teaspoons Italian herb seasoning;* slice *1 round loaf Italian bread* horizontally in half and spread cut sides with mixture; press halves together. Wrap and grill as above. Slice into wedges to serve.

TO HEAT BREAD IN OVEN: Preheat oven to 400°F. Heat wrapped bread 15 minutes.

CAMPFIRE SNACKS

COATED MARSHMALLOWS: Skewer, then toast marshmallows just until golden; swirl in shredded coconut or chopped nuts.

BACONY TIDBITS: Wrap cooked prunes or drained, canned water chestnuts with bacon; skewer and grill until bacon is crisp.

BARBECUED VIENNAS: Roast skewered Vienna sausages, bologna cubes or pineapple chunks over a fire. Then dunk in bottled barbecue sauce heated in a small pan.

SUGARY POPCORN: Pop corn in a covered skillet or wire corn popper; sprinkle with sugar and cinnamon.

CAMPER'S COFFEECAKE

1½ cups packaged buttermilk baking mix
⅓ cup sugar
1 egg, well beaten
¼ cup milk
½ cup finely chopped California walnuts

ABOUT 50 MINUTES BEFORE SERVING:
Prepare outdoor grill for barbecuing. Thoroughly grease bottom of heavy 10-inch skillet or Dutch oven with tight-fitting cover. Line bottom of skillet with two thicknesses of heavy-duty foil; grease again.

In medium bowl, with spoon, stir baking mix with sugar. Add egg and milk and stir just until batter is thoroughly mixed; pour into skillet and sprinkle with walnuts. Cover and grill over low coals without removing cover 20 to 25 minutes until cake springs back when pressed lightly with fingers. Makes 6 servings.

TO COOK ON CAMP STOVE OR TOP OF RANGE: Prepare as above but "bake" over low heat.

CHEESE-CHIVE PUMPERNICKEL

½ cup butter or margarine, softened
½ cup shredded Cheddar cheese
¼ cup chopped chives
2 tablespoons prepared mustard
1 1-pound round loaf pumpernickel bread

ABOUT 1 HOUR BEFORE SERVING:
Prepare outdoor grill for barbecuing. In small bowl, with fork, mix well butter or margarine, cheese, chives and mustard. Cut bread into 12 vertical slices, about ¾ inch thick, not quite through bottom crust.

Spread cheese mixture onto every other slice; wrap in foil. Grill bread over hot coals 25 minutes or until heated through. Unwrap and pull sandwiches apart to serve. Makes 6 to 8 servings.

TO HEAT BREAD IN OVEN: Preheat oven to 400°F. Heat wrapped bread 25 minutes.

Desserts

JIFFY GRILLED DESSERTS

CHOCOLATE FONDUE: Melt canned ready-to-spread chocolate frosting in saucepan on grill, stirring constantly; keep warm. For dippers, use marshmallows, apple chunks, pretzels, cookies.

WAFFLES A LA MODE: Toast frozen waffles on the grill; top with scoops of ice cream; drizzle with pecan topping from a jar.

SAUCY SHERBET: Heat canned raspberry applesauce in a saucepan on the grill; serve over scoops of lemon sherbet.

HOT DOUGHNUTS: Thread frozen sugar-and-spice doughnuts on skewers and grill until heated through.

CHEESE-TOPPED APPLE PIE: Arrange slices of American or Cheddar cheese on top of a purchased, baked apple pie. Cover loosely with foil and heat on grill until cheese starts to melt.

GLAZED FRUIT: Drain canned cling-peach or pear halves. In a skillet, melt a little butter or margarine with a few tablespoons brown sugar; add peaches or pears and heat on grill, spooning mixture over them.

CAKE KABOBS: Alternate chunks of poundcake with marshmallows on skewers. Grill until marshmallows begin to melt.

HOT APPLE SLICES: Cook thick wedges of unpeeled apples in melted butter or margarine in disposable aluminum cake pan on grill. When apples are heated through, sprinkle with sugar on all sides.

HOT FRUIT SUNDAE

3 large nectarines, cut into wedges
3 large plums, cut into wedges
½ cup orange juice
½ cup sugar
2 tablespoons brandy (optional)
3 pints vanilla ice cream

ABOUT 45 MINUTES BEFORE SERVING:
Prepare outdoor grill for barbecuing. In metal-handled 1½-quart saucepan (if non-metal-handled saucepan is used keep handle away from direct heat), place fruit wedges and orange juice. On grill over low coals, cook 10 to 15 minutes until fruits are tender, stirring occasionally. Remove from heat; stir in sugar and brandy. Serve over ice cream. Makes 8 servings.

TO COOK ON CAMP STOVE OR TOP OF RANGE:
In 1½-quart saucepan over low heat, simmer fruit and orange juice 10 minutes or until tender. Stir in sugar and brandy and serve as above over vanilla ice cream.

Barbecue Sauces and Marinades

CHILI-PINEAPPLE SAUCE

1 14-ounce bottle catchup
1 cup pineapple juice
¾ cup chopped green onions
½ teaspoon chili powder

ABOUT 5 MINUTES BEFORE USING:
In medium bowl, combine all ingredients. Use to baste shrimp, meat, fish or poultry during grilling. Serve additional sauce with meat. Makes about 1½ cups.

PIQUANT BARBECUE SAUCE

1½ cups catchup
3 tablespoons cider vinegar
2 tablespoons dark corn syrup
2 teaspoons salt
1 teaspoon paprika
¾ teaspoon chili powder

ABOUT 5 MINUTES BEFORE USING:
In medium bowl, combine all ingredients. Use to baste spareribs, beef or lamb during grilling. Makes about 1¾ cups.

BUTTERY LEMON SAUCE

1 cup butter or margarine
⅓ cup lemon juice
¼ cup chopped parsley
1 tablespoon salt
1 tablespoon grated lemon peel
1 teaspoon sugar
¼ teaspoon pepper

ABOUT 10 MINUTES BEFORE USING:
In small saucepan over medium heat, in hot butter or margarine, heat remaining ingredients, stirring until smooth. Use to baste fish or shellfish during grilling. Makes about 1½ cups.

SWEET-SOUR MUSTARD SAUCE

2 tablespoons salad oil
1 small onion, minced
2 tablespoons all-purpose flour
1 cup chicken broth
1 tablespoon sugar
3 tablespoons Dijon mustard
1 teaspoon salt

ABOUT 15 MINUTES BEFORE SERVING:
In small saucepan over medium heat, in hot salad oil, cook onion until tender, about 5 minutes. Stir flour into onion mixture until blended. Gradually stir in chicken broth, then remaining ingredients and cook, stirring constantly, until mixture is thickened. Serve hot. Serve over grilled steak or beef patties. Makes about 1 cup, enough for 4 servings.

HONOLULU SAUCE

¼ cup butter or margarine
½ cup catchup
½ cup orange juice
½ cup honey
¼ cup lemon juice
2 tablespoons soy sauce
½ teaspoon ginger

ABOUT 10 MINUTES BEFORE USING:
In small saucepan over medium heat, in hot butter or margarine, heat remaining ingredients, stirring until smooth. Use to baste poultry, pork or ham during grilling. Makes about 2 cups.

PEPPERY BLUE-CHEESE SAUCE

1 tablespoon butter or margarine
1 tablespoon all-purpose flour
¾ cup milk
½ cup crumbled blue cheese
½ teaspoon salt
¼ teaspoon coarsely ground pepper

ABOUT 15 MINUTES BEFORE SERVING:
In small saucepan over medium heat, into hot butter or margarine, stir flour until blended. Gradually stir in milk and cook, stirring constantly, until mixture is thickened. Remove mixture from heat; stir in cheese and remaining ingredients. Serve hot. Serve over grilled steak, lamb or beef patties or lamb chops. Makes about 1 cup.

BACON-BARBECUE SAUCE

6 slices bacon
½ cup minced onion
½ cup minced green pepper
1 10½-ounce can condensed tomato soup
¼ cup bottled steak sauce
2 teaspoons sugar
1 teaspoon cider vinegar
½ teaspoon salt

ABOUT 30 MINUTES BEFORE SERVING:
In 8-inch skillet over medium heat, fry bacon until crisp; drain on paper towels. Pour all but 3 tablespoons fat from skillet. Add onion and green pepper and cook over medium heat until tender, about 5 minutes. Stir in undiluted soup, ½ cup water and remaining ingredients. Cover and simmer 15 minutes, stirring occasionally.

Crumble, then add bacon pieces to sauce. Serve hot as sauce for hamburgers, steaks, spareribs, chicken or frankfurters. Makes about 2 cups.

SOY-SESAME MARINADE

½ cup minced onion
½ cup soy sauce
2 tablespoons light brown sugar
2 tablespoons sesame seed
2 tablespoons salad oil
2 teaspoons salt
2 teaspoons lemon juice
½ teaspoon pepper
½ teaspoon ginger

ABOUT 5 MINUTES BEFORE USING:
In medium bowl, combine all ingredients. Use to marinate shrimp, scallops, beef or lamb before grilling. Makes about 1 cup.

MEXICALI MARINADE

⅓ cup olive oil
2 garlic cloves, crushed
⅓ cup cider vinegar
⅓ cup apple juice
1 teaspoon chili powder
1 teaspoon sugar
1 teaspoon salt
¼ teaspoon pepper

ABOUT 30 MINUTES BEFORE USING:
In small saucepan over medium heat, in hot olive oil, cook garlic 2 or 3 minutes. Stir in remaining ingredients and heat through, stirring until smooth; cool. Use to marinate beef, pork, lamb or veal before grilling; also use to baste during cooking. Makes about 1 cup.

GINGER MARINADE

ABOUT 5 MINUTES BEFORE USING:
In medium bowl, combine *one 7-ounce bottle lemon-lime soft drink* (about 1 cup), *¼ cup soy sauce, 2 tablespoons sugar, 1 tablespoon garlic salt* and *1 tablespoon ground ginger*. Use to marinate shrimp, beef, veal, lamb, pork or poultry. Makes about 1¼ cups.

Cooking for two

Cooking for two can be easy and enjoyable. Here are some of the secrets.

- Keep menus simple. Serve just a few items at each meal, but in more generous portions.
- Cook once for two or more meals. For example, cook small roasts over the weekend. Serve hot for the first meal, then use leftovers for hot or cold sandwiches and in casseroles.
- Let the freezer help. Prepare casserole dishes that make 6 to 8 servings; after baking, divide casserole into two-portion amounts and freeze. For best results, thaw before heating. Heat at the temperature given in the recipe; most dishes will be hot in about 30 minutes.
- Use basic cooking directions for meats (page 62), poultry (page 172), fish (page 212) and vegetables (page 312); they apply to the smaller amounts for two as well as to family-size quantities.
- When you want to halve a recipe, use Equivalent Measures (page 3) to help in reducing amounts of ingredients. Be sure to write down reduced amounts beside each ingredient so you won't forget to halve any.

Shopping for Two

Buy carefully to avoid waste, save storage space and make small-scale cooking and serving easy.

Miscellaneous items: Buy butter by the quarter pound, eggs by the half dozen.

- Use fresh fruit often. It's easy to serve a banana, apple, orange, tangerine, half a cantaloupe, etc.
- For variety, buy the one-serving-size cans of fruit and vegetable juices occasionally. Then you can serve different ones without taking up much refrigerator space.
- Buy hot or cold cereals packaged in individual portions.
- Pick the 6-, 7- or 8-ounce-can sizes of fruits, vegetables, fish and meat products. Low-calorie fruits come in small-size cans, too.
- Look for frozen dinners and individual portions of main dishes. Other packaged frozen entrees, combination dishes and desserts are ideal for 2 or 3 servings.
- Choose crackers and cookies that come in resealable inside wrappings. Or, transfer regularly packed ones to airtight containers.

• Keep instant nonfat dry milk on hand; reliquify just what you need for drinking and cooking.
• Buy instant coffee in small jars so it's used quickly; flavor deteriorates if opened jars are kept too long.
• Dry coffee lighteners keep indefinitely at room temperature; the frozen lighteners keep several weeks in the refrigerator.

Meat, poultry and fish: Here's a quick buying guide: Count on one pound of poultry or meat with lots of bone (short ribs, chicken) for 2 servings; plan on one pound of fish fillets or meat with little bone (pot roast, round steak) for 3 servings; one pound of boneless meat (ground meat, rolled roast) will make 4 servings. Buy hamburger in one-pound lots; divide and shape into patties; freezer-wrap patties individually and freeze. Day before using, let thaw, wrapped, overnight in refrigerator.
• Buy chicken parts in the amount needed for one serving apiece; or buy extras, freezer-wrap and freeze. Whole chicken, cut up, is often on "special." Use half, freeze half.
• Frozen fish steaks come two or three in 10- or 16-ounce packages. Because they're easy to separate without thawing, they're a better choice than fillets.

Vegetables: Buy fresh cabbage, cauliflower, broccoli and Brussels sprouts in regular amounts. Cut off or separate enough for one meal; cover and refrigerate the remainder and cook it fresh within a day or two.
• Get the large-size bags of frozen vegetables. You can pour out enough for a meal, then twist-tie the bag and return it to the freezer.
• Avoid "two-for" sales of fresh vegetables unless the vegetable is a real favorite. The half cent or so saved may be wasted if the unused portion of the vegetable perishes before you get a chance to use it.
• Packaged precooked rice and instant mashed potatoes are easy to cook in one- or two-serving portions.

Breads: Look for the refrigerated biscuits that come just five to the package.
• Buy a regular-size loaf of bread; freezer-wrap and freeze what you won't use in a few days. Keep several different kinds of bread on hand this way for variety from meal to meal.

Desserts: Choose packaged one-layer cake mixes, or packaged cake-and-frosting combination mixes; they're a good size for two.
• Favorite desserts come canned in individual servings; top them with whipped topping from an aerosol can.
• Buy slice-and-bake refrigerated cookies; cut off and bake just the amount needed each time.

Tricks with Leftovers

Many recipes can be made in the full amount and leftovers reheated or refrigerated for use later.

• Soups and chowders: Refrigerate leftovers, reheat next day in double boiler or over very low heat.
• Molded salads and desserts: Refrigerate and serve as is a day or so later. If salads, serve with fresh salad greens.
• Many salad dressings keep well for a long time in the refrigerator; for those with perishable ingredients—sour cream, cream cheese, cottage cheese—make half the recipe.
• Quick breads can be served fresh and hot when made, reheated (page 415) in a day or so. For yeast breads, see Special Breads, pages 458–462, for ways to serve.
• Give desserts a new sauce or topping the second time around. Frozen desserts keep beautifully in freezer or freezing compartment of refrigerator.

Fruit juice: Add liquid from canned fruits to regular fruit juices—for example, add a little peach or pear liquid to the orange juice for breakfast.

Main dishes: Freeze leftover meats or casseroles in individual ovenproof containers, or wrap them securely in foil, ready for convenient cooking in their container later.
• Stir a few tablespoonfuls of sour cream into heated leftover gravy for meat or poultry, to give it new zest.
• Stir curry powder to taste into heated leftover gravy to serve over leftover roast beef, lamb, turkey, chicken.

Vegetables: Mix bread crumbs with a little melted butter or margarine. Sprinkle over reheated green beans, broccoli or Brussels sprouts.

• Reheat green beans or lima beans; add a few spoonfuls of leftover sour-cream dip and toss gently to mix well.

• Dice a slice or two of Cheddar or American cheese. Stir it into drained hot carrots until the cheese melts into an easy and delicious glaze.

• Empty a can of beef stew into a casserole. Spoon on leftover mashed potatoes in a ring; bake in oven preheated to 375°F. until potatoes are browned, stew is hot.

• Add leftover corn kernels to pancake batter to make corn cakes or fritters.

• Add leftover rice to tomato or vegetable soup or to consommé or bouillon to make it heartier.

Desserts: Stir extra apricots, prunes or raisins into dessert sauces, use to top ice cream or cake; or, stir into custard or vanilla pudding.

• Place cake slices, frosted or unfrosted, on foil; broil just to heat and toast. Then top each hot slice with a scoop of ice cream.

• Sprinkle leftover canned pears, peaches or pineapple with lemon juice; brush with melted butter or margarine; sprinkle with brown sugar and cinnamon or ground cloves. Broil until bubbly. Use as garnish for meat or as topping for vanilla ice cream.

• Line a loaf pan or pie plate with strips of leftover cake; spread with softened ice cream. Freeze. To serve, cut into slices or wedges; top servings with favorite dessert sauce.

Breakfast for Two

Breakfast need never be humdrum! These menus for a week combine good nutrition with flavorful variety and easy preparation. With each one, serve the favorite morning beverage: coffee, tea or milk.

Grapefruit and Orange Sections
Poached Eggs
Toasted English Muffins with Butter or Margarine
Strawberry Jam

Cranberry Juice
Hot Instant Oatmeal with Sliced Bananas
Fruit-Filled Toaster Pastries

Orange Juice
French Toast with Maple Syrup

Raspberry Applesauce
Soft-Cooked Eggs
Hot Corn Muffins
Marmalade

Stewed Prunes
Shredded Wheat
Warm Coffeecake with Butter or Margarine

Tomato Juice
Canadian Bacon
Fried Eggs
Whole-Wheat Toast with Butter or Margarine and Honey

Broiled Grapefruit Halves
Brown-and-Serve Sausages
Scrambled Eggs
Hot Cinnamon Buns

Lunch or Supper for Two

Mystery Mushroom Soup (below)
Rye Crackers
Chutney
Chicken-and-Grape Salad (page 642)

MYSTERY MUSHROOM SOUP

ABOUT 15 MINUTES BEFORE SERVING:
In 1½-quart saucepan over medium-low heat, prepare *one 10½-ounce can condensed cream-of-mushroom soup* with *milk* as label directs; stir in *1 cup shredded lettuce* and *dash pepper;* simmer 3 to 4 minutes until lettuce is tender-crisp. Makes about 2½ cups or 2 servings.

CHICKEN-AND-GRAPE SALAD

1/4 cup mayonnaise
1 tablespoon milk
1/2 teaspoon salt
1/4 teaspoon dry mustard
1/8 teaspoon pepper
1 1/2 teaspoons lemon juice
1 1/2 cups cut-up cooked chicken
1 1/2 cups halved and seeded grapes
1/2 cup thinly sliced celery

ABOUT 15 MINUTES BEFORE SERVING:
In medium bowl, stir first 6 ingredients. Add chicken, grapes and celery; stir well. Makes 2 servings.

Zesty Vegetable Soup (below)
Tuna Cheeseburgers (below)
Pickles
Chocolate Milk

ZESTY VEGETABLE SOUP

1 10 3/4-ounce can condensed vegetable soup
1 tablespoon lemon juice
1/4 teaspoon basil

ABOUT 10 MINUTES BEFORE SERVING:
Prepare soup as label directs but add lemon juice and basil. Makes about 2 1/2 cups or 2 servings.

TUNA CHEESEBURGERS

1 6 1/2- or 7-ounce can tuna
1/4 cup diced celery
1/4 cup mayonnaise
1 tablespoon lemon juice
1 tablespoon milk
1/4 teaspoon salt
3 hamburger buns, split
3 process American cheese slices

ABOUT 15 MINUTES BEFORE SERVING:
Preheat broiler if manufacturer directs. In medium bowl, flake tuna; stir in celery, mayonnaise, lemon juice, milk and salt. Spoon mixture on top of 3 bun halves; place cheese slices on remaining halves. Place all bun halves on rack in broiling pan; broil just until cheese melts, about 3 minutes. Makes 3 sandwiches.

Cocktail Vegetable Juice
Cheese-and-Bacon Soufflé (below)
Buttered Asparagus Hard Rolls
Sweetened Strawberries

CHEESE-AND-BACON SOUFFLE

3 tablespoons butter or margarine
2 tablespoons all-purpose flour
1/2 teaspoon salt
1 cup evaporated milk
1 4-ounce package shredded Cheddar cheese (1 cup)
3 eggs, separated
1/4 cup crumbled, fried bacon pieces

ABOUT 1 HOUR AND 20 MINUTES AHEAD:
Preheat oven to 350°F. Grease 1 1/2-quart soufflé dish or casserole. In 1-quart saucepan over medium heat, into hot butter or margarine, stir flour and salt until smooth. Gradually stir in undiluted milk and cook, stirring constantly, until mixture is thickened. Stir in cheese; heat until melted.

In small bowl, with wire whisk or fork, beat egg yolks slightly. Stir in a small amount of hot cheese sauce; slowly pour egg mixture back into cheese sauce, stirring rapidly to prevent lumping. Cook over low heat, stirring, until mixture is thickened, about 1 minute. (Do not boil.) Set aside.

In medium bowl, with mixer at high speed, beat egg whites until stiff peaks form. With wire whisk or rubber spatula, fold bacon and cheese mixture into egg whites. Pour into soufflé dish; bake 40 to 50 minutes until puffed and golden brown. Serve at once. Makes 2 servings.

Island Chicken Sandwiches (below)
Nippy Tomato Soup (page 643)
Chocolate Fudge Cake

ISLAND CHICKEN SANDWICHES

JUST BEFORE SERVING:
Top 2 *buttered rye-bread slices* with 4 *cooked chicken slices*. Thinly slice 1/2 *medium cucumber* and arrange on top. Spoon on *Thousand Island salad dressing*. Makes 2 open-face sandwiches.

NIPPY TOMATO SOUP

JUST BEFORE SERVING:
Prepare *one 10¾-ounce can condensed tomato soup* with water as label directs but add *1 tablespoon Worcestershire.* Makes about 2½ cups or 2 servings.

Curried Onion-and-Pea Soup (below)
Saltines
Boston Fish Salad (below)
Peach Tarts

CURRIED ONION-AND-PEA SOUP

1 11¼-ounce can condensed green-pea soup
1 beef-bouillon envelope
½ teaspoon instant minced onion
½ teaspoon curry powder

ABOUT 15 MINUTES BEFORE SERVING:
In 1½-quart saucepan, with wire whisk or spoon, stir undiluted soup and remaining ingredients until smooth. Gradually add 1 soup-can water, stirring to blend well. Over medium heat, heat to boiling, stirring often. Makes about 2½ cups or 2 servings.

BOSTON FISH SALAD

1 16-ounce package frozen cod, perch or flounder, thawed and drained
1 cup mayonnaise
1 cup finely chopped celery
½ cup shredded carrot
1 tablespoon capers, drained
2 teaspoons lemon juice
½ teaspoon salt
¼ teaspoon onion salt
1 small head Boston lettuce
2 hard-cooked eggs, sliced
1 cup sliced, cooked or canned beets

ABOUT 1 HOUR BEFORE SERVING:
Bake fish as label directs. In large bowl, flake fish and combine with next 7 ingredients. Cover and refrigerate.

JUST BEFORE SERVING:
Line small platter with lettuce leaves; top with fish mixture. Arrange egg slices on fish and beets on lettuce. Keep leftovers refrigerated. Makes 3 or 4 servings.

Cheese-and-Fruit Salad (below)
Tangy Ham Sandwiches (below)
Hot Cocoa

CHEESE-AND-FRUIT SALAD

¼ cup mayonnaise
¼ teaspoon prepared mustard
¼ teaspoon lemon juice
½ large apple, cut up
½ large pear, cut up
¾ cup cubed Swiss cheese

JUST BEFORE SERVING:
In medium bowl, combine mayonnaise with mustard and lemon juice; stir in apple, pear and cheese. Makes 2 salad servings.

TANGY HAM SANDWICHES

JUST BEFORE SERVING:
Spread *pumpernickel bread slices* with *butter or margarine,* then with *horseradish;* fill with *thin slices cooked ham.* Cut into finger sandwiches.

Shrimp Scramble (below)
Molded Vegetable Salad
Canned Peaches
Chocolate Cookies

SHRIMP SCRAMBLE

4 eggs
2 tablespoons milk
1 4½-ounce can shrimp, drained
½ teaspoon salt
⅛ teaspoon pepper
¼ teaspoon prepared mustard
2 English muffins, split
butter or margarine

ABOUT 15 MINUTES BEFORE SERVING:
In medium bowl, with fork, beat eggs and milk slightly; stir in shrimp, salt, pepper and mustard. Meanwhile, toast English muffins; spread with butter; keep warm.

In 8-inch skillet over medium heat, melt 1 tablespoon butter or margarine. Add egg mixture and cook, stirring once or twice with fork, until eggs are set; spoon over muffin halves. Makes 2 servings.

Quick Senegalese (below)
Deviled-Ham Sandwiches (below)
Celery Sticks
Coconut Cupcakes

QUICK SENEGALESE

1 cup half-and-half or milk
1 10½-ounce can condensed cream-of-chicken soup, chilled
2 teaspoons curry powder

ABOUT 10 MINUTES BEFORE SERVING:
In covered blender container, at low speed, blend half-and-half, undiluted soup and curry powder 10 seconds or until smooth. Makes about 2¼ cups or 2 servings.

DEVILED-HAM SANDWICHES

JUST BEFORE SERVING:
Spread *one 2¼-ounce can deviled ham* on 2 of *4 rye-bread slices;* spread *mayonnaise* on other slices. Make sandwiches; cut each in halves. Makes 2 servings.

Eggs Celestine (below)
Escarole Salad with French Dressing
Papaya with Lemon Wedges

EGGS CELESTINE

2 tablespoons butter or margarine
2 tablespoons all-purpose flour
¼ teaspoon curry powder
½ cup chicken broth
½ cup milk
½ teaspoon salt
¼ teaspoon pepper
1 8¼-ounce can asparagus tips, drained and cut into pieces
4 hard-cooked eggs, sliced
toast points

ABOUT 20 MINUTES BEFORE SERVING:
In 8-inch skillet over medium heat, into hot butter, stir flour and curry powder until blended. Gradually stir in chicken broth and milk; cook, stirring, until thickened. Stir in salt, pepper, asparagus and eggs; heat. Serve over toast. Makes 2 servings.

Blended Fruit Juice
Salmon Custard Casseroles (below)
Cucumber Salad
Hot Buttered Biscuits
Lemon Sherbet

SALMON CUSTARD CASSEROLES

2 eggs
½ cup evaporated milk
1 7¾-ounce can salmon, drained
1 tablespoon chopped chives
½ teaspoon dry mustard
¼ teaspoon salt
dash pepper
paprika

ABOUT 45 MINUTES BEFORE SERVING:
Preheat oven to 350°F. Grease 2 individual 10-ounce casseroles very well. In medium bowl, with fork, beat eggs slightly; stir in undiluted evaporated milk, salmon and next 4 ingredients; mix well to flake salmon. Pour into casseroles; sprinkle with paprika.

Set casseroles in shallow baking pan; fill pan with hot water to come half-way up sides of casseroles. Bake 25 to 30 minutes until knife inserted in center comes out clean. Makes 2 servings.

Hearty Coleslaw for Two (below)
Corn Muffins
Cheesecake

HEARTY COLESLAW FOR TWO

¼ pound bologna slices
¼ cup mayonnaise
¼ teaspoon salt
1¾ cups finely shredded cabbage
1 8¾-ounce can pineapple tidbits, drained
lettuce
4 hard-cooked eggs, quartered

ABOUT 20 MINUTES BEFORE SERVING:
Cut bologna in thin strips. In medium bowl, stir mayonnaise and salt. Add cabbage, pineapple and bologna and toss lightly; serve on lettuce topped with eggs. Makes 2 generous servings.

Dinners for Two

Artichokes with Lemon Butter
Mustard-Glazed Ham Steak (below)
Sweet Potatoes
Whole Green Beans
Rolls
Belgian-Endive Salad
Fruit Tarts

MUSTARD-GLAZED HAM STEAK

2 tablespoons butter or margarine
¼ cup packed light brown sugar
2 teaspoons prepared mustard
1 ¾- to 1-pound boneless ham steak

ABOUT 20 MINUTES BEFORE SERVING:
Preheat broiler if manufacturer directs. In small saucepan over medium heat, melt butter or margarine; stir in brown sugar and mustard. Place ham on rack in broiling pan; brush with half of sugar mixture; broil 5 to 7 minutes; turn and brush with remaining sugar mixture. Broil 5 minutes longer or until mixture is bubbly and ham is glazed. Makes 2 generous servings.

Saucy Swiss Steak (below)
Mashed Potatoes
Buttered Spinach
Lettuce with Green Goddess Dressing
Maple-Nut Sundae

SAUCY SWISS STEAK

1 ¾- to 1-pound boneless beef round steak, cut about ½ inch thick
1½ tablespoons all-purpose flour
1 tablespoon salad oil
1 16-ounce can tomatoes
½ small green pepper, sliced
1 medium onion, sliced
1½ teaspoons basil
1 teaspoon salt
⅛ teaspoon pepper

ABOUT 1 HOUR AND 15 MINUTES AHEAD:
On cutting board, with sharp knife, trim any excess fat from meat and cut meat into 2 serving pieces. Coat meat on one side with half of flour; with meat mallet, edge of plate or dull edge of French knife, pound meat well. Turn meat and repeat on other side.

In 8-inch skillet over medium heat, in hot oil, cook meat until browned on both sides. Add tomatoes with their liquid and remaining ingredients; heat to boiling. Reduce heat to low; cover and simmer about 1 hour or until meat is fork-tender. Makes 2 generous servings.

Pork Chops Jardinière (below)
Whole Artichokes
Buttered New Potatoes
Bread Sticks
Apple and Pear Wedges with Provolone Cheese

PORK CHOPS JARDINIERE

1 tablespoon salad oil
4 pork chops, each cut about ¾ inch thick
1 13¾-ounce can chicken broth
¼ teaspoon salt
⅛ teaspoon pepper
⅛ teaspoon sugar
2 medium celery stalks
1 medium carrot
1 tablespoon all-purpose flour

ABOUT 1 HOUR AND 20 MINUTES AHEAD:
In 10-inch skillet over medium heat, in hot oil, cook pork chops until lightly browned on both sides. Pour off any excess fat. Add chicken broth, salt, pepper and sugar. Cover; reduce heat to low and simmer 1 hour or until pork chops are almost fork-tender.

Meanwhile, cut celery and carrot into 3-inch-long pieces; cut pieces into thin strips. Push pork chops to one side of skillet; add celery and carrot strips. Reduce heat to low; cover and simmer 5 minutes or until vegetables are tender. Place chops on warm platter. With slotted spoon, place vegetables on chops.

In cup, with fork, blend flour with 2 tablespoons water until smooth; gradually stir into hot liquid in skillet and cook over medium heat, stirring often, until liquid is thickened. Pour sauce over chops and vegetables. Makes 2 servings.

Tomato-Topped Fish Fillets (below)
Parslied Potatoes Minted Peas
Sliced Hard-Cooked Egg-and-Beet Salad
Rolls
Cherry Tarts

TOMATO-TOPPED FISH FILLETS

1½ tablespoons butter or margarine
2 tablespoons lemon juice
1 16-ounce package frozen cod, ocean perch or flounder fillets, thawed
onion salt
½ teaspoon salt
¼ teaspoon pepper
1 medium tomato, sliced

ABOUT 30 MINUTES BEFORE SERVING:
Preheat oven to 350°F. In large, shallow baking dish in oven, melt butter or margarine. With pot holders, remove dish from oven; stir in lemon juice. Dip fillets in mixture, turning to coat both sides.

Arrange fillets in dish; sprinkle with ½ teaspoon onion salt, salt and pepper. Arrange tomato slices over fillets; sprinkle with ¼ teaspoon onion salt. Bake 20 to 25 minutes until fish flakes easily when tested with a fork. Makes 3 or 4 servings.

LEFTOVER FISH: Add to potato soup later.

Apricot Nectar
Lemony Liver (below)
Hash-Browned Potatoes
Green Beans with Pimento
Sliced Tomatoes
Strawberry Shortcake

LEMONY LIVER

1½ tablespoons all-purpose flour
½ teaspoon salt
¼ teaspoon pepper
¾ pound calves' liver, thinly sliced
2 tablespoons butter or margarine
1 tablespoon lemon juice
1 tablespoon chopped parsley

ABOUT 10 MINUTES BEFORE SERVING:
On waxed paper, combine flour, salt and pepper; use to coat liver. In 10-inch skillet over medium heat, in hot butter or margarine, cook liver until tender, about 2 minutes on each side; sprinkle with lemon juice and parsley. Makes 2 servings.

Chicken à l'Orange (below)
Buttered Zucchini Slices
Cucumber-and-Radish Salad
Pumpernickel Bread
Coconut-Covered Ice-Cream Balls

CHICKEN A L'ORANGE

¼ cup all-purpose flour
1 teaspoon chili powder
1 1½- to 2-pound broiler-fryer, cut up
3 tablespoons butter or margarine
1 tablespoon shredded orange peel
1 cup orange juice
1 teaspoon sugar
½ teaspoon salt
1 orange, sectioned

ABOUT 1 HOUR BEFORE SERVING:
In pie plate, combine flour with chili powder; use to coat chicken. In 10-inch skillet over medium-high heat, in hot butter or margarine, cook chicken until browned on all sides. Stir in remaining flour mixture, orange peel, orange juice, sugar and salt. Reduce heat to low; cover and simmer 30 to 40 minutes until chicken is tender. Add orange sections and heat. Makes 2 servings.

Broiled Rib-Eye Steaks
Broccoli with Toasted Almonds
Avocado-Orange Salad (below)
Rye Bread with Butter Balls (page 415)
Toasted Poundcake

AVOCADO-ORANGE SALAD

1 tablespoon white vinegar
1½ teaspoons salad oil
¼ teaspoon salt
1 medium avocado
2 small oranges, sectioned

ABOUT 15 MINUTES BEFORE SERVING:
In medium bowl, with fork, mix vinegar

with salad oil and salt. Cut avocado in half lengthwise; remove seed (do not peel). With sharp knife, scoop out some of meat from avocado halves, leaving a shallow rim all around to make shells.

Cut avocado meat into cubes; add with orange sections to vinegar mixture and toss gently. Arrange orange sections around edges of avocado shells and spoon remaining mixture into centers. Makes 2 servings.

Potato Soup Laced with Lime (below)
Country Scallops (below)
Peas and Celery (below)
Lettuce and Red-Pepper Salad
Club Rolls
Apple Turnovers à la Mode

POTATO SOUP LACED WITH LIME

1 10½-ounce can condensed cream-of-potato soup
milk
1 lime

ABOUT 15 MINUTES BEFORE SERVING:
Prepare soup as label directs, using all milk. Cut lime in half horizontally; squeeze juice from one half into soup. Slice remaining lime half for garnish. Makes 2 or 3 servings.

COUNTRY SCALLOPS

4 bacon slices, cut in small pieces
2 tablespoons minced onion
⅓ cup catchup
2 teaspoons Worcestershire
¼ teaspoon salt
⅛ teaspoon pepper
1 16-ounce package frozen scallops, thawed and drained

ABOUT 20 MINUTES BEFORE SERVING:
In 10-inch skillet over medium heat, fry bacon 3 minutes. Add onion and continue cooking 5 minutes longer or until bacon is lightly browned. Stir in catchup, Worcestershire, salt and pepper. Add scallops and cook until tender, about 5 to 8 minutes, stirring occasionally. Makes 4 servings.

LEFTOVER SCALLOPS: Use in salad or hearty sandwich filling for hamburger buns next day.

PEAS AND CELERY

⅓ cup coarsely chopped celery
1 10-ounce package frozen peas
½ teaspoon thyme leaves
¼ teaspoon salt
2 tablespoons butter or margarine

ABOUT 20 MINUTES BEFORE SERVING:
In covered 1-quart saucepan over medium heat, cook celery with ½ cup water 5 minutes or until tender-crisp. Add peas; heat to boiling. Reduce heat to low; cover and cook as label directs; drain. Add remaining ingredients; toss. Makes 3 servings.

Two-in-One Main Dishes

ENCORE MEATBALLS

1 pound ground chuck
2 eggs
½ medium onion, minced
½ cup dried bread crumbs
1 teaspoon salt
dash pepper
dash allspice
3 tablespoons salad oil
one of Sauces (below)

ABOUT 45 MINUTES BEFORE SERVING:
In large bowl, with spoon, mix thoroughly ½ cup water and all ingredients except salad oil and Sauces; shape into 1-inch balls. In 10-inch skillet over medium-high heat, in hot salad oil, cook meatballs until well browned. Remove half of meatballs; cover and refrigerate. Add remaining meatballs to one of the Sauces. Reduce heat to low; simmer 5 to 10 minutes, stirring occasionally. Makes 2 servings.

WITHIN 2 DAYS: Prepare other Sauce; add meatballs; heat as above. Makes 2 servings.

SAUERBRATEN SAUCE: In 1-quart saucepan, combine *one 10¾-ounce can beef gravy, 2 tablespoons red wine vinegar, 2 teaspoons brown sugar* and *dash ginger.* Over medium heat, heat to simmering.

CHEESE-MUSTARD SAUCE: In small pan, prepare *one 1¼-ounce package cheese-sauce mix* as label directs but use *1¼ cups milk;* stir in *1 tablespoon Dijon mustard.*

LAMB-SHANK-AND-VEGETABLE ENTREES

1 beef-bouillon cube or envelope
½ cup salad oil
¼ cup packed brown sugar
¼ cup soy sauce
8 peppercorns
2 teaspoons oregano leaves
garlic cloves
4 lamb shanks
2 tablespoons shortening

NIGHT BEFORE FIRST MEAL:
In shallow dish, dissolve bouillon in 1 cup boiling water; add salad oil, brown sugar, soy sauce, peppercorns and oregano; crush 2 garlic cloves and add; mix well. Add lamb shanks, turning to coat on all sides (mixture does not entirely cover the meat). Cover dish with lid or foil and refrigerate overnight to marinate shanks, turning shanks once or twice.

ABOUT 2 HOURS BEFORE SERVING:
Drain shanks, reserving soy-sauce mixture. Cut 2 more garlic cloves into slivers. Slit lamb shanks in several places and insert garlic slivers. In Dutch oven over medium heat, in hot shortening, cook lamb until browned on all sides. Add soy-sauce mixture. Reduce heat to low; cover and simmer 1½ to 2 hours until meat is fork-tender.

Remove shanks and discard liquid. Cover and refrigerate 2 shanks for use within two days (or cool, freezer-wrap and freeze). Keep remaining shanks warm for one of recipes below.

LAMB AND LIMAS: Cook *one 9-ounce package frozen lima beans* or one 10-ounce package frozen succotash as label directs; spoon on one end of heated platter; add heated lamb shanks to other end. Makes 2 servings.

LAMB AND CABBAGE: Thaw shanks if necessary. About 25 minutes before serving: Place shanks and 1 cup water in Dutch oven. Over high heat, heat to boiling; cover. Reduce heat to low and simmer 15 minutes. Add about *3 cups coarsely shredded cabbage* or Chinese cabbage, *1 teaspoon onion salt;* cover and cook 10 minutes or until cabbage is tender-crisp. Place lamb shanks on warm platter; surround with cooked cabbage. Makes 2 servings.

POT ROAST REPEATED

1 2- to 2½-pound beef round steak, cut about 1¼ inches thick
3 tablespoons shortening
3 celery stalks, chopped
1 medium onion, chopped
1 beef-bouillon cube or envelope or 1 teaspoon beef-stock base
4 peppercorns
1 bay leaf
2 teaspoons salt
½ teaspoon pepper
2 medium carrots, cut into small chunks
1 10-ounce package frozen Brussels sprouts
1 tablespoon all-purpose flour

ABOUT 2 HOURS AND 45 MINUTES AHEAD:
Cut meat into 2 pieces. In 10-inch skillet over medium heat, in hot shortening, cook celery and onion about 3 minutes or until tender-crisp; push to side of skillet. Add meat and cook until browned on all sides. Add bouillon cube, peppercorns, bay leaf, salt, pepper and 1 cup water; heat to boiling. Reduce heat to low; cover and simmer 2 to 2½ hours until meat is fork-tender. Add carrots and Brussels sprouts during last 20 minutes.

When meat and vegetables are tender, remove with slotted spoon to warm platter. Discard peppercorns and bay leaf. In cup, stir 3 tablespoons cold water into flour until smooth; stir into liquid in skillet and cook, stirring, until thickened.

Cover and refrigerate one piece of meat for use within two days (or freezer-wrap and freeze meat and half of gravy). Slice remaining meat; serve hot with vegetables and remaining gravy. Makes 2 generous servings.

ZESTY HOT BEEF SANDWICHES: Thaw meat, if necessary. About 15 minutes before serving: In small saucepan, combine *1 cup leftover gravy* (or if no gravy is left over, use canned beef gravy) with *¾ teaspoon prepared mustard* and *3 tablespoons minced sweet pickles.* Thinly slice remaining pot roast; add to mixture, spooning some of mixture over slices. Cook over low heat until meat is heated through. Serve on 2 *toasted bread slices.* Makes 2 servings.

TWO-WAY BEEF STEW

3 tablespoons shortening
1 medium onion, sliced
1½ pounds boneless beef shoulder pot roast, cut into 1-inch chunks
1¼ teaspoons salt
¼ teaspoon pepper
¼ teaspoon ginger

ABOUT 1 HOUR BEFORE FIRST MEAL: In 10-inch skillet over medium heat, in hot shortening, cook onion 5 minutes or until tender; with slotted spoon, remove onion. To drippings in skillet, add meat and cook, stirring often, until browned on all sides. Return onion to skillet; add salt, pepper, ginger and 1 cup water; heat to boiling. Reduce heat to low; cover and simmer 45 minutes or until meat is tender. (Add more water, if necessary, while simmering.) Divide meat mixture in half; cover and refrigerate one-half and use within two days (or wrap and freeze). Use remaining meat for Austrian Goulash to serve same day.

AUSTRIAN GOULASH: Cook *half of 8-ounce package medium egg noodles* as label directs; drain. Into remaining meat mixture in skillet, stir *¼ cup sour cream, 1 teaspoon caraway seed* and *¼ teaspoon paprika.* Place noodles on warm platter and top with meat mixture. Makes 2 generous servings.

SWEET-AND-SOUR BEEF: Thaw meat, if necessary. About 20 minutes before serving: In 8-inch skillet over medium heat, in *2 tablespoons hot shortening,* cook *1 medium green pepper,* cut into strips, and *1 small onion,* thinly sliced, about 5 minutes or until tender. Stir in *1 tablespoon cornstarch;* add *one 8½-ounce can crushed pineapple* and its liquid. Cook, stirring constantly, until thickened. Add *2 tablespoons lemon juice* and *1 tablespoon soy sauce.* Add meat to skillet and heat through, about 5 minutes. Makes 2 generous servings.

DOUBLE-ENTREE FLANK STEAK

FIFTEEN MINUTES BEFORE FIRST MEAL: Cut *one 2-pound flank steak* in half crosswise. Prepare one half as for London Broil (page 74); wrap and refrigerate one-half for use within two days (or freezer-wrap and freeze). Makes 2 servings.

BEEF STRIPS WITH ONIONS: Thaw meat, if necessary. About 40 minutes before serving: Slice remaining *half flank steak* diagonally across grain into very thin strips. In 10-inch skillet over medium heat, in *2 tablespoons hot shortening,* lightly brown strips. Add *1 beef-bouillon cube* or envelope, *1 cup water, 2 medium onions,* sliced and *1 teaspoon bottled sauce for gravy.* Heat to simmering; cover. Reduce heat to low and simmer 25 minutes or until meat is fork-tender. Makes 2 servings.

DOUBLE-DUTY SPAGHETTI SAUCE

3 bacon slices, cut in small pieces
1 medium onion, chopped
1 celery stalk, thinly sliced
1 garlic clove, minced
1 15- or 16-ounce can tomato puree
1 8-ounce can tomato sauce
1 teaspoon salt
¾ teaspoon oregano
½ teaspoon basil
¼ teaspoon pepper

ABOUT 30 MINUTES BEFORE FIRST MEAL: In 2-quart saucepan over medium heat, fry bacon until crisp. Add onion, celery and garlic; cook 5 minutes or until onion and celery are tender. Add ⅓ cup water and remaining ingredients; heat to boiling. Reduce heat to low and simmer, stirring occasionally, about 15 minutes. Use half of sauce in a recipe below; refrigerate other half to use in the other recipe within 2 or 3 days. Makes 1½ cups sauce.

SPAGHETTI WITH CLAM-TOMATO SAUCE: Cook *half of 8-ounce package spaghetti* as label directs; drain. Into half of above sauce, stir *one 7½-ounce can minced clams,* drained; simmer 5 minutes. Serve mixture over spaghetti; sprinkle with *grated Parmesan cheese.* Makes 2 servings.

SAUCY BURGERS: Shape *¾ pound ground chuck* into 4 patties. In 8-inch skillet over medium heat, in *1 tablespoon hot shortening,* brown patties on both sides; drain on paper towels. Pour fat from skillet; return patties to skillet and pour on half of above sauce; cover. Reduce heat to low and simmer 5 minutes. Makes 2 or 3 servings.

ROAST CHICKEN ALFREDO

1 5-pound roasting chicken
2 cups chicken broth
½ 8-ounce package egg noodles
¼ cup butter or margarine
½ pound mushrooms, chopped
¼ cup grated Parmesan cheese
¼ cup heavy or whipping cream
salad oil
1 small onion, quartered
1 celery stalk, cut up
1 bay leaf
salt
3 tablespoons all-purpose flour
¼ teaspoon pepper

ABOUT 4 HOURS BEFORE FIRST MEAL:

1. Preheat oven to 325°F. Remove neck and giblets from chicken; rinse and drain chicken. (Cover and refrigerate neck and giblets.) In 3-quart saucepan over high heat, heat chicken broth to boiling; add noodles and cook 5 minutes; drain noodles, reserving broth.
2. Meanwhile, in 10-inch skillet over medium heat, in hot butter or margarine, cook mushrooms 5 minutes or until tender. Stir in noodles, cheese and cream.
3. Stuff noodle mixture into chicken. Skewer neck skin to back; skewer opening closed. Tie legs and tail closely together. Fold wings up and under back of chicken. Insert meat thermometer in center of thigh close to body, being careful the thermometer doesn't touch bone. Place chicken, breast side up, on rack in open roasting pan. Brush chicken with salad oil.
4. Roast chicken 3 to 3½ hours until meat thermometer reaches 180° to 185°F. or until drumstick moves easily up and down, basting occasionally with pan drippings.
5. Meanwhile, in 2-quart saucepan, pour reserved broth over chicken neck and giblets; if necessary, add boiling water to cover giblets; add onion, celery, bay leaf and 1 teaspoon salt. Over high heat, heat to boiling. Reduce heat to low; cover and simmer until tender, about 30 minutes. Strain giblets, reserving liquid; remove meat from neck; dice meat and giblets for gravy.
6. When chicken is tender, remove to warm platter. Remove skewers and string. Pour all but 3 tablespoons drippings from roasting pan. Into drippings in pan, over medium heat, stir flour until blended. Gradually stir in reserved giblet liquid (about 2 cups) and cook, stirring constantly, until mixture is thickened. Season with 1 teaspoon salt and pepper. Serve roast chicken with gravy. Refrigerate leftover chicken and gravy for use in Chicken Alfredo Casserole recipe within two days. Makes 6 servings.

CHICKEN ALFREDO CASSEROLE

2 cups cut-up cooked chicken
1 cup chicken gravy
½ cup chopped almonds
3 tablespoons heavy or whipping cream
1 tablespoon chopped parsley
1 tablespoon lemon juice
½ teaspoon salt
¼ teaspoon curry powder
⅛ teaspoon onion salt
2 tablespoons butter or margarine
⅓ cup dried bread crumbs

ABOUT 45 MINUTES BEFORE SERVING:

Preheat oven to 350°F. Grease two 12-ounce (1½ cups) individual casseroles. In medium bowl, mix all ingredients except butter or margarine and bread crumbs; spoon into casseroles. In small saucepan, melt butter or margarine; stir in bread crumbs; sprinkle over chicken mixture. Bake 30 minutes or until hot. Makes 2 servings.

Quick Breads

For each of the breads suggested below, use *one 4.5-ounce package refrigerated biscuits* and complete as recipe directs, halving rest of ingredients:

Blueberry Biscuits (page 419), Quick Upside-Down Biscuits (page 418), Garlic Sticks (page 419)
Parmesan Biscuits (page 420): Bake on cookie sheet.
Quick Bow-Knot Rolls (page 419): Use egg white instead of whole egg.

Cooking for a crowd

Serving 24 or more at one time is quite different from preparing a meal for just a few guests.

If you're planning a wedding reception at home, or a large shower or anniversary party, you'll find special recipes on pages 663–666. Other recipes in this chapter and many of the suggestions on planning the menu and cooking in quantity will also be helpful.

If you are asked to "chair" a church or club money-raising or social function, these are some of the things you'll need to know:

Serving as Chairman

The details of meals to raise money are many and diverse. They include publicity, planning, buying, cooking and serving the food; operating the dining room efficiently; cleaning up afterwards. As chairman, it's your job to assign duties to committees, appoint committee heads (your co-chairmen), and help with the selection of their workers. With your co-chairmen, you decide on the purpose of the function (is it to make a profit or just cover costs?) and plan the menu. You should be available to help direct all stages of the meal, and have the final word on matters involving a conflict of opinion.

Planning the Menu

What you serve will depend on a variety of factors, including the kitchen equipment and utensils available, the dining-room facilities, the way the food is to be served, and the size of the crowd expected.

Choose foods that are popular with your particular group, look appetizing and are easy to serve in controlled portions. Look for items that can be prepared ahead, completely or in part, or served without much last-minute preparation. Select foods which will hold up well if they have to stand. Take advantage of foods in season and special sales, and encourage food donations.

Then, after the menu is chosen, it's a good idea to have a run-through on a small scale at home first, to make sure the complete menu tastes and looks as good in reality as it sounds in planning.

Figuring Costs

Estimating expenses: Whether you plan to make a profit or just break even, you'll first have to estimate what the meal will cost before you can decide how much to charge. Start by choosing a tentative menu and add up the costs of all the groceries needed to serve the expected number of diners. Include the cost of donated foods.

Then figure in the cost of decorations, tablecloths and napkins, rented items such as chairs, the printing of tickets and posters, clean-up supplies, wages of workers. Don't forget to include such expenses as delivery charges, meals for workers, postage, waxed paper and other items that may seem minor but can mount up.

Finally, to the total figure, add 10 percent more, to cover any costs that may have been overlooked or may arise unexpectedly later. This is the entire cost of the function.

Pricing the meal: Divide the entire cost by the number of people expected; the result is the actual cost of one meal. This is the price to charge per person if you plan only to make expenses.

If you want to make a profit, double the one-meal price. If this new figure is higher than you think the diners will want to pay, you'll have to revise the menu or cut costs in other ways to achieve your profit goal.

Buying the Food

Estimate the number of people you expect to feed, and add the number of workers. Then make out the shopping list, based on the menu and the recipes you will use; include the clean-up supplies, paper towels and other items that will be needed. Place the meat order at least one week ahead and plan to have nonperishables on hand as early as possible.

For amounts needed to serve 24 people, see chart on page 666.

Cooking in Quantity

Most of the recipes in this chapter are given in amounts to make 24 servings. Helpers who aren't professional chefs will find this amount can be prepared in the kind of equipment usually available in church and school kitchens, or in equipment borrowed from home. If larger quantities are needed, it is better to repeat the recipe as many times as necessary than to double or triple it at one time.

General hints: Foods partially prepared ahead and refrigerated may take longer to cook or bake than indicated in the recipe. The baking time may also be longer if two large pans are placed in the same oven.

Position oven racks and make sure pans fit before preheating the oven.

Don't use salt lavishly when preparing foods; it's better to let diners add salt at the table than to have to correct for too much seasoning.

Large-size disposable aluminum pans can be used for making baked beans, corn pudding and the like. However, they are too fragile for roasting heavy foods; for these, use sturdy metal pans.

After foods are prepared, taste each one to make sure it is seasoned properly.

Meats: Raw meat that is to be cut into strips or cubes will be easier to slice if it is first frozen just until firm, about 1½ hours. Remove from freezer and let stand a few minutes, then cut with a sharp knife on a cutting board.

If oven space is limited, have helpers prepare roasts, hams, turkeys at home and bring them (hot) just before serving time.

If cooking more than one roast in an oven, be sure to leave space between roasts so heat can circulate evenly.

Shape hamburger patties, meat loaves and meat balls early in day; cover with waxed paper or plastic wrap and refrigerate until time to cook. Fry hamburger patties just before serving.

Baked meat loaves will be easier to slice if you let them stand about 10 minutes after they come out of the oven.

Handle frankfurters with tongs during and after cooking, to avoid pricking the skins.

Vegetables: If possible, cook vegetables just before serving so they'll be at their best. Cook only the amount needed at one time; plan to cook more just in time to serve the next group.

Cut vegetable stalks by the bunch: Firmly hold celery stalks, green onions or asparagus together and cut through the bunch with a sharp, heavy knife, to make uniform pieces.

Scrub baking potatoes the day before and arrange on baking sheets, ready to bake next day.

If tomatoes are to be peeled, early in the day, dip them in boiling water a few seconds, then into cold water and place on trays (don't stack trays!). Refrigerate; peel just before using.

Ready-to-cook frozen vegetables can be bought in large packages. However, don't cook more than 5 pounds at a time; it may take too long to reheat the water to boiling after the vegetables have been added. Once the water boils again, start counting cooking time; drain vegetables as soon as they're done, and keep warm.

Sauces: Such sauces as cheese, curry, mushroom, "cream" or white and others can be made the day before and refrigerated, then reheated over boiling water. Stir often to keep smooth.

Desserts: Whip cream one hour ahead; refrigerate.

Cut pies and cakes up to one hour before serving.

For easy, uniform servings, bake cake mix in 13" by 9" cake pans as directed on label; cool in pan; frost and cut into servings when cold. See also Tea Cakelets (page 662). For large two-layer cake, bake cake mix as in Bridal-Shower Cake (page 664); fill and frost as directed but omit frosting decorations.

Punches: When punch is garnished with Frozen Fruits (page 596), Ice Float (page 595), Holiday Ice Ring (page 596) and bowl is to be refilled several times, it's a good idea to have one or more extra fruit or ice garnishes on hand to add when needed.

Serving the Meal

Be sure workers know how much food is to be served in each portion. Over-generous servings eat up profits; skimpy servings mean leftover food. Our recipes are prepared in pans which make it easy to divide the food into 24 uniform portions. It's a good idea to lightly score the top of a panful of food to indicate portions before starting to serve.

If the service is buffet- or cafeteria-style, arrange the foods with the proper serving silver in this order: meat, potatoes, gravy, vegetable, rolls, butter or margarine (if not placed on tables in advance), salads, then desserts and beverages, if these last two items are not to be served at the table by the waitresses.

If the plates are filled in the kitchen for a sit-down meal, set up an assembly line; have each helper place one item on the plate and pass the plate on to the next helper for another item. Filled plates are placed on a tray which a waitress carries into the dining room.

Tables should be cleared as quickly, and as unobtrusively, as possible.

You'll find serving ideas in greater detail in Entertaining, pages 735–754.

Safety First

Be sure all work surfaces, utensils and tableware are spotless before and after the function. Wash thoroughly in hot, soapy water and rinse in scalding water.

Those who cook and serve should scrub their hands thoroughly before starting, wash again if they must interrupt their work. Don't let anyone with a cold or a skin problem handle food or tableware.

To avoid food poisoning, refrigerate all food mixtures, particularly those with mayonnaise, such as sandwich fillings and salads of meat, chicken, fish and eggs; also cakes and pies with cream and custard fillings, cream puffs and similar foods. Cool hot mixtures quickly by placing them in their container in cold water or crushed ice; then cover and refrigerate until time to use. Cover foods left at room temperature as well as those in refrigerator.

Main-Course Foods

AMERICAN-STYLE CHEESE LASAGNA

3 tablespoons salad oil
2 medium onions, minced
2 29-ounce cans tomato sauce
2 8-ounce cans mushroom stems and pieces, drained
3 6-ounce cans tomato paste
1 tablespoon salt
2 teaspoons oregano leaves
1 teaspoon basil
3 16-ounce containers cottage cheese
3 eggs, slightly beaten
2 16-ounce packages lasagna noodles
2 pounds American-cheese slices

ABOUT 3 HOURS AHEAD OR DAY BEFORE:
1. For sauce, in Dutch oven over medium heat, in hot salad oil, cook onions 5 minutes or until tender.
2. Stir in 3 cups water, tomato sauce and next 5 ingredients; heat to boiling. Reduce heat to low; simmer 15 minutes, stirring occasionally. Remove and reserve 6 cups sauce. Into remaining sauce, stir cottage cheese until well mixed; stir in eggs.
3. Meanwhile, preheat oven to 375°F. Grease two 15½" by 10½" roasting pans. Cook lasagna noodles as label directs; drain. Reserve 4 cheese slices for garnish; cut remaining cheese slices into halves. Into each pan, spoon 1 cup reserved sauce; arrange ⅙ of noodles in a layer over sauce; spoon on ¼ of cottage-cheese mixture and top with ¼ of cheese pieces. Repeat layers of noodles, cottage-cheese mixture and cheese slices; top layers with remaining noodles. Spoon remaining sauce over each pan. Cut reserved cheese slices into ½-inch strips; use to garnish tops.
4. Bake about 1 hour or until lasagna is hot and bubbly. Let stand 15 minutes before serving. Makes 24 servings.

ITALIAN-STYLE LASAGNA: Prepare as above but in step 2, substitute *three 29-ounce jars* and *one 16-ounce jar spaghetti sauce with mushrooms* for water, tomato sauce, mushrooms, tomato paste, salt, oregano and basil; substitute *three 15-ounce containers ricotta cheese* for cottage cheese. Omit simmering; reserve 6 cups spaghetti sauce and stir ricotta cheese and eggs into remaining sauce. In step 3, substitute *four 8-ounce packages mozzarella cheese slices* or 32 ounces mozzarella cheese, sliced, for American cheese.

TO DO AHEAD: Day before serving: Prepare steps 1 through 3; cover pans with foil and refrigerate. On serving day: Preheat oven to 375°F. Bake, covered, 1 hour; uncover and bake 30 minutes more or until hot.

TANGY MEAT PATTIES AND FRANKS

2½ cups fresh bread crumbs
1½ cups milk
4 eggs
5 pounds ground beef chuck
5 teaspoons salt
1 tablespoon instant minced onion
½ teaspoon pepper
2 tablespoons shortening
2 12-ounce bottles chili sauce
1½ cups grape jelly (1½ 10-ounce jars)
3 tablespoons lemon juice
1¼ teaspoons dry mustard
1½ pounds frankfurters, cut diagonally into chunks
hot cooked rice for 24 servings (about 16 cups)

ABOUT 1½ HOURS BEFORE SERVING:
Preheat oven to 350°F. In large bowl, mix bread crumbs and milk. Stir in eggs, then chuck, salt, onion and pepper; shape into 48 patties, using a scant ¼ cup mixture for each patty. In 12-inch skillet in hot shortening, cook patties, a few at a time, until browned on both sides, removing as they brown to two 13" by 9" baking pans.

Pour excess drippings from skillet; in skillet, place chili sauce, jelly, lemon juice and mustard; cook over low heat, stirring occasionally, until jelly is melted. Meanwhile, evenly sprinkle frankfurter chunks over meat patties. Pour chili-sauce mixture over all. Bake 25 minutes or until hot and bubbly. Serve over rice. Makes 24 servings.

TURKEY CURRY FOR 24

1 cup butter or margarine
6 cups sliced celery
3 cups coarsely chopped onions
1¼ cups all-purpose flour
3 tablespoons salt
6 chicken-bouillon cubes or envelopes
¼ cup curry powder
12 cups milk
12 cups cut-up cooked turkey or chicken
8 5-ounce cans chow mein noodles

ABOUT 1 HOUR BEFORE SERVING:
In 8-quart Dutch oven over medium-high heat, in hot butter or margarine, cook celery and onions until tender, about 15 minutes. Stir in flour, salt, bouillon cubes and curry powder. Gradually stir in milk and cook, stirring, until thickened. Add turkey and heat, stirring often. Makes twenty-four 1-cup servings. Spoon each serving over 1 cup noodles.

BEEF-VEGETABLE SOUP

⅓ cup salad oil
6 pounds beef stew meat, cut in 1-inch chunks
1 large onion, chopped
3 tablespoons salt
2 tablespoons basil
6 large potatoes, peeled and cut up
1 medium head cabbage, shredded
1 32-ounce bag frozen peas
1 32-ounce bag frozen cut green beans
2 28-ounce cans tomatoes, chopped

ABOUT 3 HOURS BEFORE SERVING:
In 12-quart saucepot over medium-high heat, in hot salad oil, cook meat, a few pieces at a time, until browned on all sides, removing pieces with slotted spoon to a bowl as they brown. Add onion to drippings and cook until tender, about 5 minutes. Return meat to saucepot; add 18 cups hot water, salt and basil; heat to boiling. Reduce heat to low; cover and simmer 1½ hours or until meat is fork-tender.

Increase heat to high; add potatoes; cover and heat to boiling; cook 10 minutes. Add cabbage, peas and beans and cook 20 minutes or until tender. Add tomatoes and their liquid and heat. Makes about 42 cups or twenty-eight 1½-cup servings.

CHILI FOR A CROWD

5 pounds ground beef
2 pounds onions, coarsely chopped (about 5 large)
2 30-ounce cans chili beans
1 53-ounce can red kidney beans (or 3 20-ounce cans red kidney beans)
1 46-ounce can tomato juice
1 8-ounce package elbow macaroni
3 tablespoons chili powder (or to taste)
2 tablespoons salt
1 teaspoon pepper

ABOUT 1½ HOURS BEFORE SERVING:
In heavy 10-quart saucepot or 2 large Dutch ovens over medium-high heat, cook ground beef and onions until meat loses its pink color, stirring often. Add remaining ingredients; heat to boiling. Reduce heat to medium and cook 15 minutes, stirring frequently. Makes about 32 cups or twenty-four 1⅓-cup servings.

APPLE-GLAZED HAM AND DRESSING

1 9-pound fully cooked, boneless ham
Corn-Bread-Ham Dressing (below)
1 10-ounce jar apple jelly

ABOUT 2½ HOURS BEFORE SERVING:
Preheat oven to 325°F. From rounded end of ham, slice enough to dice to make 2 cups; reserve for dressing. Place remaining ham on rack in shallow, open roasting pan. Insert meat thermometer into center of ham. Roast ham about 2 hours or until temperature reaches 140°F.

About 45 minutes after putting ham in oven, prepare Dressing; bake with ham. During last 20 minutes of baking, for glaze, brush ham with apple jelly. Makes about 24 servings.

CORN-BREAD-HAM DRESSING: Grease 17¼" by 11½" baking pan. In 10-inch skillet over medium heat, in *1 cup hot butter or margarine*, cook *3 cups diced celery*, *1½ cups chopped onion* and *1½ cups chopped green pepper* until tender-crisp, about 10 to 12 minutes. In baking pan, mix well *three 8-ounce packages corn-bread stuffing* and *2 cups water*, vegetable mixture and *2 cups reserved diced cooked ham;* cover and bake along with ham for 40 minutes. Makes twenty-four ⅔-cup servings.

TUNA LOAVES WITH CUCUMBER SAUCE

TUNA LOAVES:
4 eggs
3 cups milk
2 cups finely crushed saltines
5 12½- or 13-ounce cans tuna, drained and flaked
3 cups finely chopped celery
⅓ cup grated onion
2¼ teaspoons salt

CUCUMBER SAUCE:
6 medium cucumbers, peeled, seeded and coarsely chopped
½ cup butter or margarine
½ cup all-purpose flour
1 tablespoon salt
shredded peel of 1 lemon
1 tablespoon lemon juice
6 egg yolks
chopped dill or parsley for garnish

ABOUT 2 HOURS BEFORE SERVING:
1. Preheat oven to 350°F. Grease well three 9" by 5" loaf pans. Prepare Tuna Loaves: In large bowl, with wire whisk or fork, beat eggs slightly; stir in milk and saltines; let stand 5 minutes, stirring occasionally. Stir in tuna, celery, onion, salt; spoon mixture into pans. Bake 1 hour or until knife inserted in center comes out almost clean.
2. Meanwhile, prepare Cucumber Sauce: In 3-quart saucepan over high heat, cook cucumbers in 3 cups water about 5 minutes or until tender-crisp. Drain, reserving liquid. To liquid, add enough water to make 5¼ cups.
3. In Dutch oven over medium heat, into hot butter or margarine, stir flour until blended. Gradually stir in liquid and cook, stirring constantly, until mixture is thickened. Add salt, lemon peel, juice and cucumber; cook, stirring, just until boiling.
4. In small bowl, with fork, beat egg yolks slightly. Stir in small amount of hot cucumber mixture. Slowly pour egg mixture back into sauce, stirring rapidly to prevent lumping. Cook, stirring, until thickened. (Do not boil.)
5. Set loaf pans on racks; let stand 15 minutes. With spatula, loosen edges of loaves; invert onto warm platters. Cut each loaf into 8 slices. Spoon ⅓ cup sauce over each serving; top with dill. Makes 24 servings.

SPAGHETTI BEEF CASSEROLE

2 16-ounce packages spaghetti twists or 2 16-ounce packages spaghetti, broken
2 tablespoons shortening
4 pounds ground beef chuck
1 cup minced onions
2 16-ounce cans tomato sauce
1 to 2 tablespoons chili powder
4 teaspoons salt
¼ teaspoon pepper
1 16-ounce loaf pasteurized process cheese spread, cut in cubes
1 1½-ounce container grated Parmesan cheese

ABOUT 1½ HOURS BEFORE SERVING:
Cook spaghetti as labels direct; drain. Meanwhile, preheat oven to 350°F. Grease a 17¼" by 11½" baking pan or two 4-quart casseroles. In two 12-inch skillets over medium-high heat, in hot shortening, cook meat until browned.

Reduce heat to medium and add onions; cook until onions are tender, about 5 minutes. Spoon off any excess fat. Stir in tomato sauce, chili powder, salt and pepper; cook 5 minutes, stirring occasionally. In baking pan, combine cooked spaghetti with cheese cubes and meat mixture.

Cover with foil and bake 30 to 45 minutes until hot. Just before serving, sprinkle with Parmesan cheese. Makes 24 servings.

TO DO AHEAD: Day before serving: Prepare as above but do not bake; cover with foil and refrigerate. About 1¾ hours before serving, preheat oven to 350°F. Bake mixture, covered, about 1 hour and 30 minutes or until hot. Just before serving, sprinkle with Parmesan cheese.

ROAST BEEF FOR 24

Order meat about one week ahead to be sure to get this special roast. Plan roast to be done about 30 minutes before serving.

3¾ TO 4½ HOURS BEFORE SERVING:
Preheat oven to 325°F. Place *one 8-pound boneless inside round roast** on rack in shallow, open roasting pan; sprinkle with *salt* and *pepper*. Insert meat thermometer

* Or, use rolled and tied rump or sirloin-tip roast.

in center of thickest part of roast. Roast until meat thermometer reads 140°F. for rare, 150° to 160°F. for medium or 170°F. for well done, about 3¼ to 4 hours. Remove from oven. Let roast stand about 20 minutes; then slice. Meanwhile, make Brown Gravy (below). Serve slices with gravy. Makes 24 servings.

BROWN GRAVY: Pour fat and pan juices from roasting pan into bowl; let stand a few minutes to separate. With large spoon, skim off fat, reserving *¾ cup fat;* set aside. Pour small amount of hot water into roasting pan and stir to loosen browned bits; add mixture to pan juices in bowl. Measure pan juices; add water, broth or milk if necessary to make *6 cups liquid.*

In 3-quart saucepan over medium-high heat, stir *¾ cup flour* with reserved fat until smooth and bubbling. Rapidly stir in liquid; cook, stirring constantly, until mixture is thickened and boils. Reduce heat to medium; boil 3 minutes, stirring often. Add *salt* and *pepper* to taste. Serve about ¼ cup gravy over sliced meat or over mashed potatoes, hot cooked rice or noodles. Makes about 6 cups or 24 servings.

LEMON-BARBECUED CHICKEN

1½ cups lemon juice (about 7 lemons)
½ cup salad oil
1 large onion, minced
2 tablespoons salt
1 tablespoon pepper
1 tablespoon thyme leaves
1 large garlic clove, crushed
6 2½- to 3-pound broiler-fryers, quartered
16 cups hot cooked rice (optional)

ABOUT 2¼ HOURS BEFORE SERVING:
Preheat oven to 375°F. In medium bowl, combine first 7 ingredients; mix well. In two 17¼″ by 11½″ roasting pans, arrange chicken quarters, skin side up. Pour lemon mixture over pieces. Bake 1½ hours or until chicken is fork-tender, spooning the pan juices over chicken 3 times during baking.

To serve, spoon some of pan juices over chicken and rice. Makes 24 servings.

HEARTY SEAFOOD CASSEROLE

1 32-ounce package frozen flounder or cod fillets, thawed (or 2 16-ounce packages)
2 pounds shelled and deveined shrimp
4 8-ounce cans minced clams
3 16-ounce packages small shell macaroni
3 cups butter or margarine
10 cups coarsely sliced celery (about 2 medium bunches)
3 cups all-purpose flour
8 cups milk
2 bunches green onions, cut in 1-inch pieces
6 chicken-bouillon cubes or envelopes
salt
pepper

ABOUT 2½ HOURS BEFORE SERVING:
1. With knife, cut fillets into serving pieces; drain fillets and shrimp on paper towels. In strainer, over 4-cup measure or large bowl, drain 2 cans clams; add enough water to clam liquid to measure 4 cups. Repeat with another 4-cup measure and remaining 2 cans clams. Using 1 or 2 large saucepots, prepare macaroni as label directs; drain well. Set these ingredients aside.
2. Preheat oven to 350°F. In 8-quart Dutch oven over medium-high heat, in 1½ cups hot butter or margarine, cook half of celery until tender, about 10 minutes, stirring occasionally. With large spoon, stir 1½ cups flour into celery mixture until well blended.
3. Gradually stir in 4 cups reserved clam liquid, 4 cups milk, half of chopped green onions, 3 bouillon cubes, 5 teaspoons salt and ¼ teaspoon pepper; cook, stirring constantly, until mixture is thickened, about 15 minutes.
4. Gently stir in half of each of the cooked macaroni, fillets, shrimp and clams; cover and set aside. In another 8-quart Dutch oven, repeat with remaining ingredients.* Bake 35 minutes or until shrimp are tender when tested with a fork. Serve hot. Makes 24 servings.

*Or, prepare recipe as above but spoon mixture into 4 greased 3-quart casseroles; cover and bake 25 minutes or until shrimp are tender when tested with a fork.

STEAK-AND-VEGETABLE BAKE

6 pounds beef round steaks, each cut about ½ inch thick
¾ cup all-purpose flour
½ cup salad oil
8 pounds potatoes, sliced
salt
pepper
3 pounds carrots, cut in 1-inch chunks
2 1⅜-ounce envelopes onion-soup mix
chopped parsley for garnish

ABOUT 4 HOURS BEFORE SERVING:
1. Trim fat and remove any bones from steaks. Coat steaks on one side with flour; with meat mallet, pound steaks well; turn steaks and repeat on other side. Cut steaks into 24 serving pieces.
2. In 12-inch heavy skillet over medium-high heat, in ¼ cup hot salad oil, cook meat, a few pieces at a time, until well browned on both sides, adding more oil as needed and removing pieces as they are browned.
3. In one of two 15½" by 11½" roasting pans, arrange half of potatoes; sprinkle with 1½ teaspoons salt; top with half of meat. Sprinkle meat with 1½ teaspoons salt and ¾ teaspoon pepper. Top meat with half of carrots; sprinkle with 1 envelope onion-soup mix and pour in 2 cups water. Repeat, using second pan. Meanwhile, preheat oven to 350°F.
4. Cover pans with foil; bake 2 hours or until meat is fork-tender. Garnish with chopped parsley. Keep one pan hot while serving the other. Makes 24 servings.

SESAME-SEED CORN BREAD

¾ cup sesame seed
3 10-ounce packages corn-bread mix

ABOUT 40 MINUTES BEFORE SERVING:
In small saucepan over medium heat, toast sesame seed until golden, stirring and shaking pan frequently; set aside.

In large bowl, prepare mixes, all at one time, as label directs, using 3 times the eggs and milk used for one package; stir in sesame seed. Pour mixture into pans. Bake as label directs. Makes 24 servings.

BAKED BEANS MEXICALI

2 tablespoons salad oil
3 medium onions, chopped
2 medium green peppers, chopped
¼ cup packed brown sugar
4 28-ounce cans baked beans in New England-style sauce
4 teaspoons chili powder
2 teaspoons salt
1 teaspoon oregano leaves
2 cups coarsely crumbled corn chips

ABOUT 1 HOUR BEFORE SERVING:
Preheat oven to 350°F. Grease a 13" by 9" baking dish. In 10-inch skillet over medium heat, in hot salad oil, cook onions and green peppers with brown sugar until tender, about 10 minutes.

In baking dish, combine onion mixture with beans, chili powder, salt and oregano; mix well. Sprinkle with corn chips. Bake 45 minutes or until hot. Makes twenty-four ½-cup servings.

CORN PUDDING FOR 24

¼ cup bacon drippings, butter or margarine
1 medium onion, minced
6 cups milk
6 cups fresh bread crumbs
2 17-ounce cans cream-style corn
2 17-ounce cans whole-kernel corn, drained
6 eggs, beaten
3 tablespoons sugar
1 tablespoon salt*
½ teaspoon pepper

ABOUT 2 HOURS BEFORE SERVING:
Preheat oven to 350°F. Grease two 13" by 9" baking pans or twenty-eight 6-ounce custard cups. In 6-quart saucepot over medium heat, in hot bacon drippings, cook onion until tender, about 5 minutes. Stir in milk and heat through; remove from heat. Stir in remaining ingredients until well mixed; ladle into pans. Set pans in larger pans; place on oven racks. Pour boiling water into each larger pan to come halfway up sides of corn-pudding pans. Bake 55 minutes or until knife inserted 1 inch from edge of pudding comes out clean. Makes 24 to 28 servings.

* If using butter or margarine, use 4 teaspoons salt.

CANDIED SWEET POTATOES FOR 24

12 large sweet potatoes
1 16-ounce bottle dark corn syrup (2 cups)
¼ cup butter or margarine
1 teaspoon salt

ABOUT 2 HOURS BEFORE SERVING:
In 2 large saucepots over high heat, in boiling, salted water to cover, heat sweet potatoes to boiling; cover and cook about 20 minutes or until fork-tender.

Preheat oven to 400°F. Drain sweet potatoes; peel, cut into halves and arrange, cut side up, in two 13" by 9" baking pans. In 1-quart saucepan over medium heat, heat remaining ingredients to boiling; boil 5 minutes. Pour mixture over sweet potatoes.

Bake 30 minutes or until sweet potatoes are heated through, basting once with syrup. Serve potatoes topped with syrup. Makes 24 servings.

SCALLOPED POTATOES FOR 24

2 32-ounce bags frozen cottage-fried potatoes
½ cup butter or margarine
½ cup all-purpose flour
1 tablespoon salt
½ teaspoon pepper
6 cups milk
⅓ cup instant minced onion
paprika

ABOUT 1½ HOURS BEFORE SERVING:
Preheat oven to 350°F. Grease 17¼" by 11½" roasting pan; arrange frozen potatoes in pan. In 3-quart saucepan over medium heat, into hot butter or margarine, stir flour, salt and pepper until blended. Gradually stir in milk and cook, stirring constantly, until mixture is thickened and smooth; stir in onion. Pour mixture over potatoes in pan; sprinkle with paprika. Bake 40 to 45 minutes until hot. Makes 24 servings.

POTATOES AU GRATIN FOR 24: Prepare as above but use only 5 cups milk; stir *one 16-ounce loaf pasteurized process cheese spread,* diced, into hot milk mixture and cook over low heat, stirring, until cheese spread is melted; sprinkle potatoes with *one 8-ounce loaf pasteurized process cheese spread,* coarsely shredded, during last half of baking time.

GARDEN ASPIC

8 envelopes unflavored gelatin
2 46-ounce cans cocktail vegetable juice
4 cups sliced celery
1½ cups chopped ripe olives
1 cup diced green peppers
1 teaspoon garlic salt
1 teaspoon seasoned salt
lettuce leaves (about 3 large heads lettuce)
1 16-ounce bottle French dressing

DAY BEFORE SERVING:
In Dutch oven, sprinkle gelatin over 2 cups water; cook over medium heat, stirring constantly, until gelatin is completely dissolved. Stir in cocktail vegetable juice and next 5 ingredients. Pour mixture into 17¼" by 11½" roasting pan; refrigerate until set.

TO SERVE:
Cut mixture into 24 portions; arrange each portion on a lettuce leaf on a salad plate. Serve each with about 1½ tablespoons French dressing. Makes 24 servings.

GLORIFIED WALDORF SALAD

1⅓ cups mayonnaise
¼ cup milk
2 tablespoons lemon juice
1½ teaspoons nutmeg
4 large apples, diced
4 large pears, diced
4 cups grapes, halved
2 cups diced celery
2 cups coarsely chopped pecans or black walnuts
3 large heads lettuce

ABOUT 1 HOUR BEFORE SERVING:
Prepare dressing: In small bowl, with wire whisk or fork, stir mayonnaise, milk, lemon juice and nutmeg until smooth. In large bowl, combine remaining ingredients except lettuce; add dressing and toss gently until well mixed.

AT SERVING TIME:
For each serving, heap about ¾ cup of mixture onto a lettuce leaf on a salad plate. Makes about twenty-four ¾-cup servings.

POTATO SALAD FOR A CROWD

7 pounds potatoes
salt
1 32-ounce jar mayonnaise
½ cup cider vinegar
2 tablespoons sugar
2 tablespoons salt
1 teaspoon pepper
4 cups sliced celery
1½ cups chopped parsley
½ cup finely chopped onion
3 large heads lettuce (optional)

ABOUT 8 HOURS AHEAD OR DAY BEFORE:
In 2 Dutch ovens over medium heat, in boiling salted water to cover, cook unpeeled potatoes about 30 minutes or until tender.

Meanwhile, in 8-quart saucepot, with wire whisk or slotted spoon, combine mayonnaise with next 4 ingredients.

When potatoes are tender, drain and peel; slice into saucepot. Add celery, parsley and onion; mix gently but well. Spread mixture into 15½" by 11½" roasting pan; cover and refrigerate to chill well.

TO SERVE:
Serve salad on lettuce leaves, if you like. Makes about twenty-four ¾-cup servings.

CRANBERRY-MALLOW SALAD

3 3-ounce packages strawberry-flavor gelatin
3 14-ounce jars cranberry-orange relish
3 3-ounce packages lime-flavor gelatin
⅛ teaspoon green food color
1½ cups heavy or whipping cream
1 8-ounce package cream cheese, softened
1½ cups mayonnaise
1 10½-ounce bag miniature marshmallows
24 lettuce leaves

EARLY IN DAY OR DAY BEFORE:
In large bowl, stir 3 cups boiling water into strawberry-flavor gelatin until gelatin is dissolved. Stir in cranberry-orange relish. (Do not add more water.) Pour into two 13" by 9" pans. Chill until set. Rinse bowl.

In same bowl, prepare lime-flavor gelatin as label directs. Stir in food color; refrigerate until mixture mounds slightly when dropped from a spoon.

In another large bowl, with mixer at medium speed, beat cream until soft peaks form. In medium bowl, with mixer at medium speed, beat cream cheese until fluffy; beat in mayonnaise until smooth. Beat cream-cheese mixture into lime gelatin; with rubber spatula, fold mixture into whipped cream. Evenly spread marshmallows over strawberry layers. Pour lime mixture over layers. Refrigerate until set.

AT SERVING TIME:
Cut each salad into 12 servings; serve on lettuce. Makes 24 servings.

EXOTIC CHICKEN SALAD

18 pounds chicken*
salt
2⅔ cups mayonnaise
1 cup half-and-half
½ cup cider vinegar
3 tablespoons grated onion
½ teaspoon pepper
7 cups seeded, halved green grapes
4 cups thinly sliced celery
2 cups slivered almonds
3 large heads lettuce
parsley for garnish

DAY BEFORE SERVING:
In large saucepot or 2 or 3 Dutch ovens place chickens, 4 tablespoons salt and hot water to cover chicken; over high heat, heat to boiling. Reduce heat to low; cover and simmer whole chickens until fork-tender. (Broiler-fryers will take about 45 minutes; stewing chickens, 3 to 4 hours.)

Place saucepot of chicken and broth in deep cold water in sink. Stir broth often; change water when it becomes warm. Cover and refrigerate saucepot after ½ hour in sink to cool completely.

Remove fat from broth; place chicken on cutting board. (Refrigerate broth to use in soup another day.) Remove meat from bones in large pieces; discard skin and bones. Into large bowl or saucepot, cut meat into chunks; cover and refrigerate.

ABOUT 3 HOURS BEFORE SERVING:
Prepare dressing: In medium bowl, with wire whisk or fork, stir mayonnaise with

* Select either broiler-fryers (about 3½ pounds each) or stewing chickens.

half-and-half, vinegar, onion, pepper and 5 teaspoons salt until smooth. Combine chicken with grapes, celery and almonds. Add dressing and toss gently until well mixed. Cover and refrigerate.

AT SERVING TIME:
Heap about 1 cup of mixture onto lettuce leaves on individual plates. Garnish with parsley. Makes about twenty-four 1-cup main-dish servings.

TOSSED SALAD FOR A CROWD

3 large heads iceberg lettuce (8 quarts)
1 medium head romaine
½ small head chicory
4 medium tomatoes, cut up
1 to 1½ cups favorite pourable salad dressing
1 medium onion, thinly sliced and separated into rings

ABOUT 1 HOUR BEFORE SERVING:
In chilled, large salad bowl or 10-quart saucepot, tear iceberg lettuce, romaine and chicory into bite-size pieces. Add tomatoes and dressing; toss gently until lettuce is well-coated with dressing. To serve, spoon into individual salad bowls; top servings with onion rings. Makes about 8 quarts or twenty-four 1⅓-cup servings.

Desserts

DEEP-DISH APPLE PIE FOR 24

20 cups peeled, cored and sliced cooking apples (about 7 pounds)
3 cups sugar
⅓ cup quick-cooking tapioca
1¼ teaspoons cinnamon
¾ teaspoon nutmeg
½ teaspoon salt
¼ cup butter or margarine
pastry for one 2-crust 9-inch pie
whipped cream or softened ice cream for topping

ABOUT 3 HOURS AHEAD OR EARLY IN DAY:
Preheat oven to 425°F. In 17¼" by 11½" roasting pan, place apples. In small bowl, stir sugar with tapioca, cinnamon, nutmeg and salt; toss with apples. Pour ½ cup water over apples; dot with butter or margarine.

On lightly floured surface, with lightly floured rolling pin, roll pastry ⅛ inch thick and 1 inch larger than top of pan. Fold pastry in quarters; place over apples and unfold. Press pastry to pan edges and trim off excess pastry. Cut slits or design in pastry. Bake 50 minutes or until crust is golden. Cut into 24 portions; serve hot or cold topped with whipped cream. Makes 24 servings.

APPLE BROWN BETTY FOR A CROWD

1 22-ounce loaf white bread
1 cup butter or margarine
1½ cups packed brown sugar
1 cup sugar
1 tablespoon grated lemon peel
2 teaspoons nutmeg
1 teaspoon cinnamon
2 tablespoons lemon juice
20 cups peeled, cored and sliced cooking apples (about 7 pounds)
half-and-half or softened ice cream for topping

ABOUT 2 HOURS BEFORE SERVING:
Leave crusts on bread; cut bread into small cubes. (Makes about 17 cups loosely packed cubes.) Preheat oven to 425°F. In large saucepot, over medium heat, melt butter or margarine; remove from heat. Lightly toss bread cubes with melted butter or margarine until well mixed. In medium bowl, combine 1 cup brown sugar, sugar, lemon peel, nutmeg and cinnamon. In small pitcher, combine lemon juice with 2 cups water.

In one of two 13" by 9" baking pans, arrange ¼ of bread-cube mixture; top with half of apples; sprinkle with half of brown sugar mixture; pour half of lemon mixture over apples. Repeat with other pan. Sprinkle remaining bread cubes and brown sugar over mixtures in both pans.

Cover pans with foil and bake 30 minutes. Uncover; bake 25 minutes or until apples are tender. Serve warm with half-and-half. Makes 24 servings.

PARTY MELBA SAUCE

1 10-ounce jar peach preserves (1 cup)
½ cup raspberry preserves
½ cup currant jelly
½ cup lemon juice
½ teaspoon salt

ABOUT 1 HOUR AHEAD OR DAY BEFORE:
In small saucepan over medium heat, heat ingredients until blended, stirring; cool.

TO SERVE:
Spoon scant 2 tablespoons per serving over vanilla ice cream, tapioca or rice pudding. Makes about 2½ cups or 24 servings.

FLUFFY HARD SAUCE

1 cup butter or margarine, softened
3 cups confectioners' sugar
1 teaspoon lemon or vanilla extract

ABOUT 15 MINUTES AHEAD OR EARLY IN DAY:
In small bowl, with mixer at low speed, beat all ingredients until blended. At high speed, beat until mixture is fluffy, about 5 minutes. Makes about 1½ cups or twenty-four 1-tablespoon servings.

TEA CAKELETS

Grease and flour a 15½" by 10½" jelly-roll pan. Prepare *1 package favorite-flavor cake mix for 2-layer cake* as label directs; pour into pan. Bake about 25 minutes or until toothpick inserted in center comes out clean. Cool cake in pan on wire rack. Spread cake with *1 can favorite-flavor ready-to-spread frosting;* cut into squares. Makes 24 squares.

Beverages

HOT COFFEE FOR A CROWD

Use *½ pound ground coffee* (about 2½ cups) and *20 cups fresh-from-the-faucet cold water;* prepare coffee in coffee maker, following manufacturer's directions. Or, prepare in one of these ways:

SAUCEPOT STYLE: Place *½ pound regular-grind coffee* in *piece of cheesecloth* or muslin large enough to hold about double amount of coffee; tie loosely to make bag.

Meanwhile, in 6-quart saucepot over high heat, heat *16 cups cold water* to boiling. Add bag of coffee. Cover; reduce heat to low and simmer 10 to 12 minutes. With tongs, move bag back and forth in liquid several times, then remove. Cover saucepot; keep coffee hot but do not boil. Makes about 24 servings.

INSTANT: In 5-quart saucepot, stir *one 2-ounce jar instant coffee* with part of *16 cups cold water* until dissolved. Add remaining cold water. Over high heat, heat to boiling; remove from heat. (Or, stir boiling water into instant coffee until coffee is dissolved; cover and let stand 5 minutes.) Makes about 24 servings.

INSTANT ICED COFFEE FOR A CROWD

In 6-quart saucepot, stir part of *17 cups cold water* into *1⅔ cups instant coffee* until coffee is dissolved. Stir in remaining water. Pour over ice in tall glasses. Makes about 24 servings.

HOT TEA FOR A CROWD

UP TO 4 HOURS BEFORE SERVING:
For tea concentrate: Into large bowl, measure *⅔ cup tea leaves.* In 2-quart saucepan over high heat, heat *4 cups water* to boiling; pour over tea leaves. Cover and let stand 5 minutes. Stir; strain concentrate into pitcher or tea pot. Keep at room temperature until time to use.

TO SERVE:
Pour 2 tablespoons concentrate into each tea cup; add *hot water* to fill cup. Makes about 24 servings.

INSTANT: In 5-quart saucepot over high heat, heat *16 cups water* to boiling. Pour over *½ cup instant tea;* stir until tea is dissolved. Makes about 24 servings.

ICED TEA FOR A CROWD

UP TO 4 HOURS BEFORE SERVING:
Prepare concentrate as in Hot Tea for a

Crowd (above) but use *1 cup tea leaves* and 6 *cups boiling water*. To serve, in 7-quart saucepot, pour concentrate into *18 cups cold water;* pour over *ice cubes* in tall glasses. Makes about 30 servings.

INSTANT: Dissolve *¾ cup instant tea* in *6 cups cold water;* add *18 cups cold water*. Serve as above. Makes about 30 servings.

TEA PUNCH

4 cups hot tea
2 cups sugar
2 cups orange juice, chilled
1 cup lemon juice, chilled
2 16-ounce bottles ginger ale, chilled
1 pint orange or lemon sherbet, softened

EARLY IN DAY:
In large bowl or pitcher, stir tea with sugar until sugar is dissolved; refrigerate.

AT SERVING TIME:
Into chilled large punch bowl, stir tea, orange juice, lemon juice and ginger ale. Spoon sherbet onto mixture. Makes about 12 cups or twenty-four ½-cup servings.

Wedding and Shower Refreshments

MINT PATTIES OR ROSES

BASIC DOUGH:
3 egg whites, at room temperature
2 to 2½ 16-ounce packages confectioners' sugar
2 tablespoons light corn syrup
1 teaspoon mint extract
¼ teaspoon yellow food color

UP TO 1 WEEK BEFORE SERVING:
In large bowl, place egg whites, 1 package sugar, corn syrup, mint extract and food color. With mixer at low speed, beat ingredients until just mixed; increase speed to high and beat until soft peaks form, occasionally scraping bowl with rubber spatula. With spoon, stir in another package sugar to make a stiff mixture.

Turn mixture onto surface sprinkled with confectioners' sugar and gradually knead in enough sugar to form a smooth, firm dough. Cut dough into 3 pieces; work with 1 piece of dough at a time, covering remaining dough with plastic wrap to keep soft.

Between two 12-inch sheets of waxed paper, with rolling pin, roll piece of dough ⅛ inch thick. Prepare Mint Patties or Mint Roses (below).

MINT PATTIES: Remove top sheet of waxed paper from rolled Basic Dough (above). With 1-inch round cookie or canapé cutter, cut out circles. With small spatula, lift circles or patties onto sheet of waxed paper; let dry several hours before storing. Knead scraps until smooth and pliable again, adding drops of water if necessary. Reroll and cut to make more patties, wiping spatula, cutter and fingers occasionally with a damp cloth to remove any sugar crystals which may form. Repeat rolling and cutting with 2 more reserved dough pieces. Patties store well in tightly covered container up to 1 week. Makes about 20 dozen or 1¼ pounds.

MINT ROSES: Lift top sheet of waxed paper from a part of the rolled Basic Dough (above). With 1-inch round cookie or canapé cutter, cut out only 5 circles. With small spatula, lift out circles; set aside. With fingers, roll some scraps into a ½″ by ⅛″ rod-shaped piece for center of rose.

With rod-shaped piece as center of rose, mold a dough circle around it to resemble a petal. Overlap the next 4 circles around first petal, pressing at base and moving slightly above the previous petal with each circle. Cut thick slice from rose at base so rose will stand. Place rose on sheet of waxed paper; let dry before storing. Continue making more roses from rolled dough, keeping uncut portion covered.

Knead scraps until smooth and pliable again, adding drops of water if necessary. Reroll to make more roses, wiping spatula, cutter and fingers occasionally with damp cloth to remove any sugar crystals which may form. Repeat with 2 more reserved dough pieces. Place dried roses in single layer on large tray or jelly-roll pan; cover with foil or plastic wrap. Roses store well in tightly covered container up to 1 week. Makes about 4 dozen.

BRIDAL-SHOWER CAKE

2 packages white-cake mix for 2-layer cakes
2 3-ounce packages egg-custard mix
3 cups milk
2 cups sliced blanched almonds (2 3½-ounce cans), ground
½ teaspoon almond extract
Butter-Cream Icing (below)
Decorator Frosting (below)
blue and yellow food colors
Mint Roses (page 663)

DAY BEFORE SERVING:

1. Prepare one package cake mix as label directs but bake in a well-greased and floured 15½" by 10½" jelly-roll pan about 20 to 25 minutes until toothpick inserted in center comes out clean. Invert cake from pan onto large wire rack to cool completely. Repeat with second package cake mix.
2. Meanwhile, in 3-quart saucepan over medium heat, combine both packages of egg-custard mix and milk; cook, stirring constantly, until boiling. Remove from heat; stir in ground almonds and almond extract. Cover custard surface with waxed paper and refrigerate until set.
3. Place one cake, top side down, on large platter and spread top of cake with chilled custard, leaving ½-inch edge all around. Top with second cake, top side up. Frost top and sides of cake with Butter-Cream Icing. Refrigerate until ready to decorate.
4. Decorate cake: Spoon about ⅔ cup Decorator Frosting into decorating bag (or waxed-paper cone). With tip number 30 (or small rosette tip), make borders around top and bottom edges of cake. In small bowl, with spoon, combine ½ cup Decorator Frosting with 4 drops blue food color and 3 drops yellow food color to make a pretty green color; spoon into another decorating bag (or waxed-paper cone). With tip number 4 (or medium writing tip), make decorative stems and with tip number 67, make leaves on top of cake. (Wrap any remaining Decorator Frosting in plastic wrap to decorate cake or cookies another day.)
5. Gently press 12 to 16 Mint Roses around green stems and leaves on cake. Cover cake loosely with foil or plastic wrap; keep refrigerated. Makes 24 servings.

BUTTER-CREAM ICING: In large bowl, with mixer at low speed, beat *one and one-half 16-ounce packages confectioners' sugar* (about 6 cups), *½ cup butter or margarine*, softened, *½ cup milk* and *2 teaspoons vanilla extract* until smooth, adding more milk or sugar if necessary for good spreading consistency.

DECORATOR FROSTING: In small bowl, with mixer at low speed, beat *2¾ cups confectioners' sugar, 2 egg whites*, at room temperature, *¼ teaspoon cream of tartar, ¼ teaspoon vanilla extract* and *9 drops yellow food color* until just mixed. Increase speed to high and beat until mixture is so stiff that knife drawn through mixture leaves clean-cut path. (On humid days, you may need to beat in more sugar to stiffen frosting.)

WEDDING CAKE
(Round 14", 10" and 6" tiers)

5 packages white-cake mix for 2-layer cakes
almond extract
6 recipes for Butter-Cream Frosting (page 549)
Decorations (below)

DAY BEFORE SERVING:

Each tier is made of two layers, filled and frosted.

1. To make layers: Set out enough wire racks to cool cake layers, including two large enough for 14-inch layer (or use oven or refrigerator racks); also large cookie sheet for handling large layers. Generously grease and flour 14-inch, 10-inch and 6-inch round cake pans. Preheat oven to 350°F.
2. Prepare 1 package cake mix as label directs, but add ¼ teaspoon almond extract; pour into 10-inch and 6-inch pans, filling each ¾ to 1 inch deep. Bake 6-inch layer 20 to 25 minutes, and 10-inch layer 30 to 35 minutes until toothpick inserted in center comes out clean. (Layers baked in deep pans will not be very brown on top.) Remove from oven; tap side of pans and shake pans to loosen layers; cool layers in pans 10 minutes on wire racks. Remove layers from pans and cool completely on wire racks.
3. Meanwhile, prepare 1 package of cake mix as label directs but add ¼ teaspoon

almond extract. Pour into 14-inch pan; set aside. Prepare another package of cake mix same way and add half to batter in pan, shaking pan to spread evenly. (Batter in pan will be about ¾ inch deep.) Cover and refrigerate remaining batter. Bake layer 40 to 55 minutes until toothpick inserted in center comes out clean. Remove from oven; tap sides of pan and shake pan to loosen layer; cool in pan 10 minutes on wire rack. Shake pan again to loosen layer and invert onto large cookie sheet. Place wire rack over layer and invert cookie sheet and rack so layer is top side up on rack; remove cookie sheet. Wash, dry, grease and flour pan. Cool layer completely on rack.

4. While first 14-inch layer is cooling for 10 minutes, prepare another package cake mix, adding almond extract. Combine this batter with refrigerated batter. When 14-inch pan is ready, pour batter into pan; bake. Remove from pan and cool as in step 3.

5. Use last package cake mix to make second set of 10-inch and 6-inch layers as in step 2.

6. Frost cake: In large bowl, prepare 2 times Butter-Cream Frosting; as you work, make additional double batches as needed.

7. If tops of layers are rounded, with long, sharp knife, slice off enough to make them flat across most of surface. (Use sliced-off portion for another day's dessert—as crumbs to roll ice cream balls in, to fold into creamy pudding, to sprinkle over fruit sauce, etc.)

8. For bottom tier, place one 14-inch layer, top side down, on large platter or foil-covered cardboard. Spread Butter-Cream Frosting almost to edge. Place second 14-inch layer, top side up, on frosted layer. Thinly frost sides and top of both layers to set crumbs.

9. For next tier, center one 10-inch layer on top of bottom tier, top side down; spread with frosting; top with second 10-inch layer, top side up; thinly frost sides and top of both layers.

10. If top tier is to be reserved for first-anniversary party, place 6½-inch round of foil-covered cardboard in center of 10-inch tier; then fill and frost 6-inch cake layers on cardboard. Omit cardboard if entire cake is to be served at one time.

11. Now, frost entire cake generously, smoothing or swirling frosting as desired. Add decorations; if using fresh flowers, place on cake just before guests arrive. Fourteen-inch tier makes 70 servings; 10-inch tier makes 35 servings, 6-inch tier makes 10 servings; makes total of 115 servings.

DECORATIONS: Make flowers using Ornamental Frosting (page 549), frosting in aerosol cans, ready-to-use frosting ornaments or fresh flowers (see list of non-toxic flowers, Crystalline Ice Bowl, page 36).

CHAMPAGNE-PUNCH FRUIT BOWL

4 cups fresh strawberries
½ cup sugar
1 ⅘-quart bottle sauterne
1 cup cognac
Frozen Fruits (page 596)
4 ⅘-quart bottles champagne, chilled

AT LEAST 2 HOURS BEFORE SERVING:
In large bowl, sprinkle strawberries with sugar. Add sauterne and cognac; chill.

AT SERVING TIME:
Arrange Frozen Fruits in chilled, large punch bowl. Pour in strawberry mixture; slowly add champagne. Makes 18 cups or thirty-six ½-cup servings.

GOLDEN ANNIVERSARY PUNCH

2 20-ounce cans crushed pineapple in pineapple juice
2 6-ounce cans frozen lemonade concentrate
¼ cup sugar
1 28-ounce bottle club soda, chilled
1 tray ice cubes

ABOUT 10 MINUTES BEFORE SERVING:
In covered blender container at high speed, blend crushed pineapple with its liquid, one can at a time, 15 to 20 seconds until thick; pour into chilled punch bowl.

To pineapple, add undiluted lemonade concentrate and sugar; stir. Stir in soda. Add ice and serve at once. Makes about 10 cups or twenty ½-cup servings.

GOLDEN CHAMPAGNE PUNCH: Prepare as above but add *one ⅘-quart bottle champagne,* chilled, with club soda. Makes about twenty-six ½-cup servings.

SPARKLING CINNAMON PUNCH

¾ cup sugar
4 short cinnamon sticks
2¾ cups orange juice, chilled
⅓ cup lemon juice
3 16-ounce bottles lemon-lime soft drink, chilled
ice cubes

EARLY IN DAY:
In 1½-quart saucepan over medium heat, heat to boiling 3 cups water, sugar and cinnamon sticks. Reduce heat and simmer 5 minutes; cover and refrigerate to let flavors develop.

JUST BEFORE SERVING:
Discard cinnamon sticks from mixture. In chilled, large punch bowl, combine cinnamon mixture, juices and soft drink. Add ice cubes. Makes 12 cups or twenty-four ½-cup servings.

AMOUNTS TO BUY FOR 24

Items are given in units most available at supermarkets. However, larger sizes of many products can often be found. Buy the largest available to reduce cost per serving.

Food for 24	*Serving Size*
Apples	
8 pounds medium	1 apple
diced	
4 to 8 pounds	½ to 1 cup
Applesauce, canned	
7 16-ounce cans	½ cup
Apricots	
6 pounds	4 or 5 halves
Asparagus	
6 pounds	4 or 5 stalks
Avocados	
12 pounds	1 half
Bacon	
2 pounds	2 slices
Bananas	
8 pounds medium	1 banana
sliced	
9 pounds	about ¾ cup
Beans	
dry	
2½ pounds	½ cup
green, cut up	
6 to 8 pounds	½ cup
limas, shelled	
4 pounds	⅓ cup
Beets	
6 pounds	½ cup
Blueberries	
8 pints	½ cup
Bread	
4 16-ounce loaves	2 slices
2 24-ounce loaves	2 slices
1½ Pullman loaves	2 slices
Brown bread, canned	
3 16-ounce cans	1 slice, ½ inch thick
Broccoli	
8 pounds	½ cup
Butter	
½ pound	1 pat (12 pats per quarter pound)
Cabbage	
6 pounds	½ cup, cooked
Carrots	
8 pounds	½ cup
Catchup	
1 20-ounce bottle	1 tablespoon
Cauliflower	
8 pounds	½ cup
Celery	
3 medium bunches	½ cup
Cheese	
American slices	
1½ pounds	1 slice
cottage	
4 to 6 pounds	⅓ to ½ cup
cream cheese	
1½ 8-ounce packages	1 tablespoon
grated Parmesan	
1½ 3-ounce containers	1 tablespoon
Cherries	
6 pounds	½ cup
Chicken	
broiler-fryer	
12 2- to 2½-pound chickens	½ chicken
6 3- to 3½-pound chickens	¼ chicken
roaster	
18 pounds	3 to 4 ounces, sliced
stewing	
18 pounds	¾ cup, diced

Food for 24	*Serving Size*
Chili sauce	
1½ 12-ounce bottles	1 tablespoon
Coffee	
ground	
½ pound	¾ cup, brewed
instant	
1 2-ounce jar	¾ cup, brewed
Corn-on-the-cob	
2 dozen ears	1 ear
Crackers	
1 8-ounce package	2 crackers
Cranberries for sauce	
1½ pounds	¼ cup sauce
canned jellied sauce	
3 16-ounce cans	1 slice, ½ inch thick
Cucumbers	
6 medium	¼ cup
Eggplant	
5 pounds	½ cup
Eggs	
4 dozen	2 eggs
Fish fillets and steaks	
8 pounds, fresh	4 ounces, cooked
8 16-ounce packages, frozen	4 ounces, cooked
Frankfurters	
5 to 6 16-ounce packages	2 frankfurters
Fruit juice,canned	
2 46-ounce cans	½ cup
Fruit-juice concentrates	
4 6-ounce cans	½ cup
Fruits, canned cocktail	
4 30-ounce cans	½ cup
Fruits, frozen mixed	
9 12-ounce packages	½ cup
Grapefruit	
12 medium	½ grapefruit
canned sections	
6 16-ounce cans	½ cup
Grapes	
seeded	
6 pounds	½ cup
seedless	
5 pounds	½ cup
Half-and-half (for coffee)	
¾ pint	1 tablespoon
Heavy or whipping cream	
1 pint	2 tablespoons, whipped

Food for 24	*Serving Size*
Ice cream	
1½ half-gallon containers	½ cup
Jelly	
1½ 10-ounce jars	1 tablespoon
Lemonade concentrate	
3 12-ounce cans	1 cup
Lemons	
1 dozen makes:	
2 cups juice	
¾ cup grated peel	
for tea or garnish	
3 medium	1 thin slice
Lettuce	
4 medium heads	⅙ head
Mayonnaise	
1 pint	1 tablespoon
Meat, canned	
ham	
6 pounds	4 ounces, sliced
luncheon meat or chopped ham	
6 12-ounce cans	2 slices
Meat, fresh	
boned, boneless or ground	
8 pounds	4 ounces, cooked
cuts with medium bone (steaks, roasts, chops)	
12 pounds	depends on bone
cuts with large bone (spare ribs, short ribs)	
24 pounds	depends on bone
Melon balls, frozen	
8 12-ounce packages	½ cup
Milk	
3 half-gallon containers	1 cup
Mushrooms	
4 pounds	¼ cup
Onions (for creaming)	
8 pounds medium	1 onion
Oranges	
diced or sectioned	
2 dozen	½ cup
juice	
3 dozen	½ cup
Pasta	
macaroni	
3 16-ounce packages	1 cup

Food for 24	*Serving Size*
noodles	
3 16-ounce packages	1 cup
spaghetti	
3 16-ounce packages	1 cup
Peaches	
6 pounds medium	1 peach
canned, halves	
4 29-ounce cans	1 large half
canned, sliced	
4 29-ounce cans	½ cup
sliced	
6 pounds	½ cup
Pears	
6 pounds	1 pear
canned, halves	
4 29-ounce cans	1 large half
sliced	
5½ pounds	½ cup
Peas	
black-eyed	
6 pounds	½ cup
in pod	
12 pounds	½ cup
Pineapple	
4 medium	½ cup
canned chunks, tidbits	
4 29-ounce cans	½ cup
canned, sliced	
3 30-ounce cans	1 large slice
Plums, canned whole	
4 30-ounce cans	2 or 3 plums
Potatoes	
sweet	
8 pounds medium	½ to 1 potato
white	
8 pounds medium	1 potato
Prunes	
canned	
8 16-ounce jars	4 or 5 prunes
dried	
4 pounds	4 or 5 prunes
Rhubarb	
6 pounds	½ cup
Rice	
packaged precooked (see label)	⅔ cup
parboiled (see label)	⅔ cup
regular long-grain	
1 24-ounce package	⅔ cup
Rolls	
2 dozen	1 roll
Salad dressing	
1 16-ounce bottle	1½ to 2 tablespoons
Sherbet	
1½ half-gallon containers	½ cup
Soup, canned condensed	
10 10½-ounce cans	1 cup
Spinach	
8 10-ounce bags	½ cup
Squash, hard-shelled	
acorn	
12 squash	½ squash
Hubbard, butternut	
12 pounds	½ cup, mashed
Squash, soft skinned	
8 pounds	½ cup
Strawberries	
8 pints	½ cup
frozen, sliced	
12 10-ounce packages	½ cup
Sugar	
cubes	
½ pound	2 cubes
granulated	
¼ pound	1 teaspoon
Tea	
bags	
1½ 16-bag packages	¾ cup, brewed
instant	
1 1-ounce jar	¾ cup, brewed
leaves	
½ 4-ounce package	¾ cup, brewed
Tomatoes	
canned	
4 29-ounce cans	½ cup
juice, canned	
2 46-ounce cans	½ cup
sliced	
5 pounds medium	⅔ tomato
Turkey	
18 pounds	4 ounces, sliced
Vegetables, canned	
6 16- or 17-ounce cans	½ cup

For calorie watchers

The best way to lose weight successfully, and to keep it off, is to develop the right eating habits. Dieters, like everyone else, need balanced meals and should choose them from the Basic Four Food Groups (page 727). The minimum servings listed will furnish about 1200 calories a day, the amount recommended for women dieters, and will produce an average weight loss of 1 to 2 pounds a week. Men dieters, to lose the same amount safely, need about 1800 calories each day.

Since it is not practical to fit a woman's full iron requirement (18 milligrams a day) within the 1200-calorie limit, ask your physician to recommend an iron supplement. Men won't need this supplement; and a good diet such as the one which follows meets all other nutrient needs. If you want to lose more than 5 pounds, get your doctor's approval before you start.

Here is a plan that features hearty, traditional meals, yet limits calories to 1200 for women, 1800 for men. It can easily be adjusted for other family members: for boys and girls aged 7 to 12, use the basic 1200-calorie plan and add 1 glass of skimmed milk daily. For teenage girls, use the basic 1200-calorie plan and add 2 glasses of skimmed milk. For teenage boys, use the "for men" portions and add 2 glasses of skimmed milk daily.

Choose one menu from breakfast, lunch and dinner choices each day. Men should follow "for men" servings and add the Snacks for Men Only on page 671.

Breakfast
300 calories for women, 400 for men

Juice, eggs, toast, milk
4-ounce glass orange or grapefruit juice
1 soft- or hard-cooked, poached or scrambled egg (no added fat)
1 toast slice* lightly spread with butter or margarine and jelly
8-ounce glass skimmed milk
Coffee or tea**
For men: Add extra toast slice

* Use whole-grain or enriched breads and crackers wherever possible.
** Have coffee or tea with any meal. Use no more than 1 teaspoon sugar; save part of milk to use as "cream."

Juice, cereal and fruit, milk
4-ounce glass orange or grapefruit juice
1 cup ready-to-eat or ¾ cup cooked cereal with 1 teaspoon sugar and ½ sliced banana or ½ cup fresh or unsweetened frozen strawberries
8-ounce glass skimmed milk
For men: Have 8-ounce glass juice and extra half serving of cereal

Fruit, pancakes, milk
½ cup fresh or unsweetened canned orange or grapefruit sections or fruit cocktail
2 4-inch pancakes (made from mix using skimmed milk) with 1 tablespoon maple-flavored syrup
8-ounce glass skimmed milk
For men: Have 3 pancakes

Lunch
450 calories for women, 500 for men

Soup, sandwich, salad, milk
1 cup soup: beef, chicken or turkey noodle; tomato; onion; vegetable beef or vegetarian vegetable
Sandwich on bread, toast or large roll with low-calorie mayonnaise and lettuce, filled with 2 slices lean beef, chicken, turkey or ham or ¼ cup flaked tuna or salmon
Large tossed salad with low-calorie dressing; or celery, carrot and pickle sticks
8-ounce glass skimmed milk
For men: Add extra slice of meat to sandwich

Soup, main-dish salad, bread, milk
1 cup soup: beef or chicken bouillon or consommé
½ cup egg, tuna, salmon, shrimp or crab salad prepared with low-calorie mayonnaise and lettuce; celery and tomatoes as garnish
1 bread or toast slice lightly spread with butter or margarine
For men: Have ¾ cup salad

Cottage cheese or yogurt, bread, fruit
8-ounce container creamed cottage cheese or vanilla-flavor yogurt
1 cup fresh-fruit cocktail or dietetic-packed canned fruit
8 saltine squares or Melba rounds (each lightly spread with butter or margarine)
For men: Add large tossed salad with low-calorie dressing

Omelet, toast, milk
2-egg plain, onion or mushroom omelet (skimp on butter or margarine to make omelet)
2 toast slices or 1 toasted English muffin or 1 large roll (do not butter)
8-ounce glass skimmed milk
For men: Butter bread or roll

Hamburger on roll or toast, salad, milk
1 4-ounce hamburger served on hamburger or hard roll, or on toast with catchup, mustard, lettuce and tomato or onion, as desired
Small serving coleslaw or tossed salad with low-calorie dressing
8-ounce glass skimmed milk
For men: Add small apple, peach or tangerine

Frankfurter on roll, sauerkraut, fruit, milk
1 grilled or boiled frankfurter with mustard, catchup, or relish as desired, on toasted frankfurter roll
¾ cup sauerkraut
1 serving fruit from list (page 671)
8-ounce glass skimmed milk
For men: Add ¾ cup tomato, noodle or vegetable-beef soup

Dinner

450 calories for women, 600 for men
Meat, vegetable, salad, potatoes or bread, fruit
¼ pound (weigh uncooked) lean beef, veal, lamb, pork or liver, panbroiled or simmered until tender in tomato juice or water
2 servings vegetables from list (page 671) —one cooked and one as salad with low-calorie dressing
½ cup mashed or baked potato or 1 bread slice, 1 small roll, muffin or biscuit (all lightly buttered)
1 serving fruit from list (opposite)
For men: Have ⅓ pound meat

Fish, potatoes or pasta, vegetable, salad, fruit

⅓ pound (weigh uncooked) cod, flounder, haddock, halibut, sole or any seafood, brushed with a little salad oil and broiled, or poached in chicken bouillon or dry white wine

¾ cup rice, noodles or diced potatoes or 1 small baked potato (all lightly buttered)

2 servings vegetables from list (at right)—one cooked and one as salad with low-calorie dressing

1 serving fruit from list (at right)

For men: Have ½ pound fish or seafood; add 1 lightly buttered bread slice or extra serving potatoes

Chicken, potatoes or pasta, salad, dessert, fruit as snack

1 half chicken breast (about ⅓ pound), broiled, baked or simmered until tender in pineapple juice, chicken bouillon or dry white wine

1 serving vegetables from list (at right)—cooked or as salad with low-calorie dressing

½ cup rice, noodles or diced potatoes or 1 small baked potato (all lightly buttered)

1 serving any dessert with up to 150 calories such as those on pages 682–683

1 serving fruit from list (at right) as snack

For men: Have 1 whole chicken breast (about ¾ pound)

Casserole, vegetable, potatoes or pasta, salad, fruit

1 serving any 200- to 250-calorie main dish such as those on pages 675–679

2 servings vegetables from list (at right)—one cooked and one as salad with low-calorie dressing

½ cup mashed or boiled potatoes (no butter), rice or pasta

1 serving fruit from list (at right)

For men: Have 1½ servings main dish

Snacks for Men Only:

Have any two of the following:

1 toasted buttered English muffin

15 potato chips

25 to 30 peanuts

½ cup pudding (made with skimmed milk)

12-ounce bottle soft drink

12-ounce bottle beer

1 small cocktail

1 10″ by 3″ wedge watermelon

5 saltines spread with 1 tablespoon peanut butter

1 plain doughnut

1½ buttered toast slices

2 medium apples, peaches or oranges

1 medium slice angel-food cake

½ cup ice milk or sherbet

2 homemade small chocolate chip or other cookies

3 chocolate wafers and 1 cup skimmed milk

8 small pretzels

Fruit and Vegetable Choices

Vegetables: Asparagus, broccoli, Brussels sprouts, cabbage, carrots, cauliflower, celery, green beans, greens, okra, sauerkraut, spinach or tomatoes

Fruits: 1 small fresh peach or apple; ½ fresh pear or banana; 2 fresh apricots or plums; 1 cup fresh grapes, cherries, berries or melon cubes; ½ cup dietetic-packed canned or frozen fruit

Everyday Calorie Cutters

Never underestimate the value of saving a few calories here and there! Eating an extra 50 calories a day can cause a weight gain of 5 pounds a year; conversely, by eliminating 50 calories a day, you can lose 5 pounds a year. What's more, you can cut calories without resorting to expensive specialty items, or changing your family's style of eating. Here are 50 suggestions to help you save calories painlessly:

Main Dishes

1. Pan-broil hamburger and other meats.

Place the meat in a cool skillet and quickly heat to cooking temperature. Enough fat comes from the meat to prevent sticking, and no extra fat is needed.

2. Halve the amount of fat used to pan-fry poultry and fish. Use a pan with nonstick finish for cooking; 2 tablespoons of salad oil will then be enough to fry a pound of fish or 2 chicken breasts.

3. Serving for serving, Canadian bacon has less than half the calories of regular cooked bacon.

4. Save nearly half the calories in oil-packed tuna by draining the oil. Or use water- or broth-packed tuna and save one-third the calories compared with drained oil-packed tuna.

5. Frozen prepared dinners have natural portion-control—no seconds are available. The fish (without breading), meat loaf and sliced turkey dinners have the fewest calories. After heating, just pour off most of the gravy and you'll have an easy 250- to 350-calorie meal.

6. Roast or broil chicken with the skin on to keep meat moist—but don't eat the skin.

7. Oven-bake chicken instead of deep-frying it. Remove the skin before breading.

8. Try canned spaghetti sauces or packaged mixes. Both have fewer calories than homemade sauces.

9. Liver is rich in iron and very low in calories. Serve it with mushrooms or onions that have been simmered in a little broth, instead of the traditional bacon or fried onions.

10. All cottage cheese is made with skimmed milk. Although creamed cottage cheese has slightly more calories (130 per half cup) than uncreamed (85 calories per half cup), both are good choices for a protein-rich diet main course.

Fruits and Vegetables

11. Try canned pineapple that's packed in its own juice. It's delightfully tart and has 35 calories less per serving than pineapple packed in heavy syrup.

12. Freeze unsweetened cherries, strawberries and blueberries. Let them thaw slightly and they'll form their own syrup without the extra calories from sugar.

13. Herbs and spices—which have no calories—give any meal extra flair for mere pennies. Use them instead of butter or margarine to season vegetables; season fruit with spices and just a sprinkle of sugar.

14. Drain syrup from canned fruit and substitute unsweetened orange or pineapple juice for a flavor change and calorie saver.

15. Always keep "rabbit food" available for snacks. The best choices are celery, cabbage, carrots, lettuce, green peppers and tomatoes.

16. For variety without calories, there's a wide range of low-calorie greens to use in salads and as garnishes: raw spinach, chicory, romaine, escarole, Chinese cabbage.

17. Use low-calorie dressings on salads. They contain about 50 fewer calories per tablespoon.

18. Buy frozen vegetables in large plastic bags. Cook just what you need and eliminate leftovers. That way you won't be tempted by calorie-adding second helpings.

19. Start the meal with low-calorie appetizers that quickly curb your hunger. Vegetable soup, broth, spiced fruit or vegetable juice are ideal.

20. Serve two leafy green (lettuce, spinach) or yellow vegetables (squash, carrots) at every meal. Go easy on rice, potatoes, noodles, corn and beans.

Breads and Cereals

21. Restrict yourself to ½-cup servings for potatoes, rice, spaghetti, macaroni; 1-cup servings for flaked or puffed cereals, ⅔-cup servings for cooked cereals. All contain about 100 calories.

22. Cook rice in broth or bouillon for rich flavor and just a few added calories. You won't have to add butter or margarine for seasoning.

23. Hot breads like muffins, rolls, biscuits and cornbread have almost twice the calories of plain bread. The exception is refrigerated buttermilk biscuits, which have only 50 calories each. Buy the ones that come in the 8-ounce package—not the 9.5-ounce package—they're smaller.

24. For variety, try French bread, hard rolls, pumpernickel, oatmeal, onion or rye bread.

25. If you must use white bread, select the thin-sliced sandwich kind.

26. Or make herb toast: Lightly spread a slice of bread with butter or margarine and sprinkle with celery seed, sesame seed or poppy seed; place in the broiler to brown edges. Herb toast has 100 calories per slice.
27. Melba rounds and slices, at about 20 calories apiece, are available in numerous flavors.
28. When using instant rice and potatoes, prepare just enough for one serving per person, to avoid the temptation of leftovers and seconds.
29. Packaged frozen French fries, heated in the oven, yield only 125 calories for a small serving; deep-fried or the homemade kind yield 155 calories.
30. Serve sandwiches open-faced, eliminating an extra slice of bread. They're attractive, too.

Milk and Milk Products

31. Select milk in terms of its calories. For instance, reliquified non-fat dry milk, regular skimmed milk and buttermilk contain only 90 calories per cup. Modified skim milk, or 2 percent milks with some fat and added non-fat dry-milk solids to give a flavor like whole milk, contain 130 to 145 calories per cup.
32. Yogurt, made with partially skimmed milk, has a cool, refreshing taste, few calories. Plain yogurt offers the fewest calories (125 calories per 8-ounce container); next come coffee and vanilla flavors with about 200. But beware of the fruit flavors—they have up to 225 to 275 calories, depending on brand and flavor.
33. Ice milk has fewer calories than ice cream and contains more milk solids and proteins.
34. Look for "imitation cheese" and "imitation cheese spreads." They have fewer calories and less fat than regular cheese.
35. Make instant-breakfast mix with skimmed milk and save 70 calories per serving.
36. When making cream sauces, use half the fat you normally would. Mix in the flour and cook slightly, then slowly stir in milk until smooth; heat until thickened.
37. In sauces calling for light cream, substitute half-and-half and save almost 200 calories per cup! Substitute sour half-and-half for sour cream.
38. When you make dips, try plain yogurt as a substitute for sour cream or cream cheese. Delicious in the onion-soup dip.
39. Prepare chocolate milk or cocoa with skimmed milk and chocolate syrup. It will have about the same calories as a glass of plain whole milk.

Sauces, Desserts and Snacks

40. Whipped cream or topping in aerosol cans is much "lighter" than homemade whipped cream. Tablespoon for tablespoon, it has ⅕ the calories.
41. Inexpensive ice creams contain less milk fat and therefore fewer calories than the more expensive brands. Ice milk is also a slimming substitute for ice cream. Lowest of all in calories: Italian ices.
42. Whipped butter or margarine has 66 calories per tablespoon compared with 100 for regular butter or margarine. Serve it soft and it will spread further on bread and toast.
43. Snack on pumpkin and sunflower seeds. Buy the in-shell variety; they're less expensive and because you must shell them, you'll eat more slowly.
44. Snack on unbuttered popcorn—only 25 calories per cup. Flavor it with onion salt or garlic salt.
45. Cut desserts into smaller servings. Get 10 servings from a 9-inch pie. Or, use cake mixes to make cupcakes—one package of cake mix for a 2-layer cake makes 36 cupcakes.
46. Neufchâtel cheese has ¾ the calories of cream cheese, and can be used in all the same ways.
47. Prepare sauce mixes and gravy mixes but use skimmed milk when package calls for milk.
48. Small sour balls and hard candies can be savored for a long time, average only 20 calories each.
49. Prepare packaged pudding mixes with skimmed milk and eliminate 40 calories per half cup serving.
50. For a low-calorie dessert, whip partially set fruit-flavor gelatin until frothy to "stretch" a 4-serving package of gelatin to 6 servings. If you like, add cut-up, drained canned fruit to whipped gelatin and let set a couple of hours.

A Word about Breakfast

Don't skip breakfast if you're cutting down on calories. You may be hungrier than usual by noon and tend to overeat at lunch. Here are some quick breakfast menus, complete with their total calorie counts. Note: We haven't added calories for coffee or tea. If you take half-and-half, add 20 calories per tablespoon; if you take sugar, 20 calories per teaspoon. Keep both to a minimum.

Half grapefruit, poached egg, lightly buttered rye-bread slice, glass whole milk, coffee or tea. 360.
Sliced orange, 1 cup of cornflakes with ½ cup milk and 1 tablespoon sugar, 2 bacon slices, coffee. 395.
Half cup tomato juice, 1 toaster waffle topped with 2 tablespoons applesauce, cup of hot cocoa made with whole milk, coffee or tea. 360.
Half cup orange and grapefruit sections, soft-cooked egg, lightly buttered English muffin, glass skimmed milk, coffee or tea. 405.
Sliced banana in ½ cup orange juice, ¾ cup hot oatmeal with ½ cup whole milk and 1 tablespoon brown sugar, coffee or tea. 370.
Half cup vegetable cocktail juice, packaged frozen pancake-and-sausage-patties breakfast entrée, coffee or tea. 365.
Packaged instant breakfast made with whole milk, slice of buttered toast. 380.

LOW-CALORIE SNACKS

Keep a supply of low-calorie snacks in the refrigerator or cupboard and you won't be tempted by rich foods. Here's a calorie-keyed list of possibilities to post in a prominent spot.

Apple, medium-sized 75
Banana, small 75
Bouillon, 1 cup 10
Candy, hard, 1 large 35
Carrot, raw 20
Cauliflowerets, about ½ cup 15
Celery, 3 small stalks 10
Cheese, Cheddar, Swiss or
  cream, 1 ounce 105
Crackers:
  4 small grahams 55
  1 two-inch-square saltine 15
  1 round, average size 15
Cookies:
  1 fig bar 55
  1 small gingersnap 30
  1 small sugar wafer 25
Gelatin, flavored, ½ cup 75
Grapefruit juice, ½ cup 45
Gumdrop, 1 small 10
Melba toast, 1 regular 20
Milk, skimmed, 1 cup 85
Orange, 1 medium 75
Pear, 1 small 75
Pickle, dill or sour, 1 large 15
Popcorn, unbuttered, 1 cup 25
Pretzels, 5 small sticks 20
Radishes, 4 small 5
Raisins, 3 tablespoons 90
Tangerine, 1 small 40
Tomato juice, 1 cup 50
Zwieback, 1 regular 35

BLUSHING BUTTERMILK

70 calories per serving

JUST BEFORE SERVING:
In glass, stir *½ cup chilled tomato juice* and *½ cup buttermilk;* stir in *½ teaspoon lemon juice,* if you like. Makes 1 serving.

LOW-CALORIE CHEESE-DIP APPETIZER

270 calories per cup of dip

1 8-ounce container creamed cottage cheese
2 tablespoons milk
2 green onions, minced
1 canned pimento, well drained and chopped
½ teaspoon seasoned salt
dippers: carrot sticks, celery sticks, apple wedges, cucumber sticks

EARLY IN DAY:
In small bowl, with fork, stir cottage cheese with milk until smooth. Stir in green onions, pimento and salt. Cover and refrigerate. Prepare dippers and refrigerate.

TO SERVE:
With fork, stir mixture and pour into small serving bowl. Arrange bowl on tray surrounded by dippers. Makes 1 cup dip.

FRUIT-GLAZED BAKED CHICKEN

230 calories per serving

1 6-ounce can frozen pineapple-grapefruit juice concentrate, thawed
1 teaspoon salt
1 teaspoon mint flakes (optional)
¼ teaspoon ginger
dash pepper
1 2-pound broiler-fryer

ABOUT 1½ HOURS BEFORE SERVING:
Preheat oven to 375°F. In small saucepan over medium heat, heat ½ can undiluted juice concentrate, salt, mint, ginger and pepper just to boiling. (Dilute remaining ½ can concentrate with 1½ cups water for use another day.) Place chicken on rack in shallow, open baking pan. Roast 1 hour, or until chicken is fork-tender and golden brown, basting with mixture twice during last 15 minutes of roasting time. Makes 4 servings.

CHICKEN TROPICALE

285 calories per serving

¼ cup all-purpose flour
salt
¼ teaspoon pepper
4 small whole chicken breasts, skinned and halved (about 3 pounds)
5 teaspoons salad oil
8 medium new potatoes, halved
1 cup orange juice
2 tablespoons brown sugar
1 teaspoon basil
¼ teaspoon nutmeg
1 17-ounce can cling-peach slices, drained
2 tablespoons cider vinegar
chopped parsley for garnish

ABOUT 1½ HOURS BEFORE SERVING:
On waxed paper, combine flour, 1 teaspoon salt and pepper; coat chicken in mixture; shake off excess flour. In large skillet over medium-high heat, in hot oil, brown chicken breasts on both sides. Add potatoes, orange juice, brown sugar, basil, nutmeg and 1 teaspoon salt. Reduce heat to low; cover and simmer 30 minutes or until potatoes are tender.

Stir in peaches and vinegar; cook until heated through. Sprinkle with parsley. Makes 8 servings.

HAMBURGER-VEGETABLE SOUP

130 calories per serving

6 beef-bouillon cubes or envelopes
1 16-ounce can tomatoes
1 large onion, diced
¾ cup diced celery
1 medium carrot, diced
1 garlic clove, crushed
1 bay leaf
½ teaspoon salt
dash pepper
½ pound ground beef round steak
1 10-ounce package frozen peas
3 tablespoons chopped parsley for garnish

ABOUT 1 HOUR BEFORE SERVING:
In large saucepan over high heat, heat 5 cups water to boiling; add bouillon cubes and stir until dissolved. Add tomatoes and their liquid and next 7 ingredients; cover and simmer over low heat 20 minutes.

Meanwhile, in small skillet over medium-high heat, cook meat, stirring constantly, until lightly browned. Add meat and peas to soup and cook 10 minutes or until peas are fork-tender; discard bay leaf. Stir in parsley just before serving. Makes about 9 cups or 6 servings.

DO-AHEAD SOUP: Up to 2 months before serving: Prepare a double quantity of above recipe but do not stir in parsley. Divide soup into portions and freeze. On serving day, thaw portion; heat over medium heat until bubbly and stir in a little chopped parsley for garnish.

SURPRISE HAM STEAK

230 calories per serving

1-pound fully cooked boneless ham slice
¾ cup large-curd creamed cottage cheese
1 tablespoon horseradish
1 tablespoon white vinegar

ABOUT 30 MINUTES BEFORE SERVING:
Preheat oven to 325°F. Trim any excess fat from ham. Place ham on bake-and-serve platter. Bake 15 minutes, turning once.

Meanwhile, in small bowl, mix cottage cheese, horseradish and vinegar. Spread over ham. Continue baking 5 minutes more to heat through. Makes 4 servings.

APRICOT-TOPPED HAM SLICES
210 calories per serving

¾-pound fully cooked boneless ham slices (4 slices, each about ⅓-inch thick)
3 tablespoons apricot preserves
1 tablespoon salad oil

ABOUT 10 MINUTES BEFORE SERVING:
Trim any fat from ham. In large skillet over medium heat, heat preserves and oil until bubbly. Add ham slices; cook, turning once, until heated through. To serve, roll up slices and serve with sauce from pan. Makes 4 servings.

LOW-CALORIE CHILI
280 calories per serving

1 tablespoon salad oil
2 cups sliced celery
1 cup chopped onions
½ cup chopped green pepper
1 garlic clove, minced
1 pound ground beef round steak
1 16-ounce can kidney beans, thoroughly drained
1 28-ounce can tomatoes
½ teaspoon salt
chili powder

ABOUT 1¼ HOURS BEFORE SERVING:
In large kettle over medium heat, in hot oil, cook celery, onions, green pepper and garlic until onions are tender, about 5 minutes. Add meat and cook until meat is browned, stirring occasionally. Stir in kidney beans, tomatoes and their liquid, salt and 1½ teaspoons chili powder; heat to boiling. Reduce heat to low and simmer 40 to 45 minutes, stirring occasionally. Just before serving, stir in enough chili powder to give desired "hotness." Makes 6 servings.

CHILIBURGERS
270 calories per serving

ABOUT 20 MINUTES BEFORE SERVING:
In medium bowl, mix *1 pound ground beef round steak* with *½ cup chili sauce*. With hands, shape into 4 patties. In medium skillet over medium heat, pan-broil patties on each side until of desired doneness. Makes 4 servings.

TANGY LAMB PATTIES
315 calories per serving

1½ pounds ground lamb
1 tablespoon grated lemon peel
1 tablespoon chopped parsley
1 tablespoon lemon juice
1 teaspoon salt
¼ teaspoon pepper
⅛ teaspoon crushed bay leaf
⅛ teaspoon crushed rosemary
½ cup white wine or chicken broth

ABOUT 30 MINUTES BEFORE SERVING:
In medium bowl, mix all ingredients but wine; with hands, shape mixture into small patties. In large skillet over medium-high heat, in wine, cook patties, turning occasionally, about 15 minutes for medium doneness or 20 minutes for well-done. Makes 6 servings.

PEPPERCORN STEAK
305 calories per serving

1 2½-pound boneless beef round steak
instant meat tenderizer
⅓ cup dry red wine or beef broth
¼ cup minced onion
1 tablespoon salad oil
2 teaspoons peppercorns

ABOUT 50 MINUTES BEFORE SERVING:
1. Trim any excess fat from meat. Prepare steak with meat tenderizer as label directs. Place steak in large baking dish.
2. In cup, combine wine, onion and salad oil as marinade; pour over steak. Cover; refrigerate 30 minutes, turning occasionally.
3. Preheat broiler if manufacturer directs. Coarsely crush peppercorns in pepper mill (or wrap peppercorns in cloth, then crush coarsely with rolling pin). Remove steak from marinade; press pepper well into both sides of steak.
4. Place steak on broiling pan; pour remaining marinade over steak. Broil 15 minutes or until of desired doneness, turning once. Serve steak cut in very thin slices. Makes 8 servings.

FLANK STEAK: Prepare recipe as above, using flank steak, but before tenderizing, score it by cutting diagonal slashes on both sides.

LOW-CALORIE VEAL MARSALA
230 calories per serving

1-pound veal round steak, cut about ¼-inch thick
¼ cup all-purpose flour
1 teaspoon salt
generous dash pepper
2½ tablespoons butter or margarine
¼ cup dry Marsala

ABOUT 45 MINUTES BEFORE SERVING:
If necessary, cut meat into pieces about 3 inches square; trim any connective tissue or fat. With mallet, edge of saucer or back edge of French knife, pound meat into very thin slices (about ⅛-inch thick).

On waxed paper, stir flour with salt and pepper; coat meat with mixture. In large skillet over medium heat, in hot butter or margarine, cook meat, a few pieces at a time, until lightly browned, about 1 minute on each side.

Return all meat to skillet; add Marsala and ¼ cup water; cook until gravy thickens slightly, gently scraping bottom of skillet to loosen browned bits. Makes 4 servings.

LIVER-AND-BACON BAKE
245 calories per serving

1 pound beef liver
all-purpose flour
1 teaspoon salt
¼ teaspoon pepper
1 4-ounce package Canadian bacon slices (10 to 12 slices)
1 large onion, sliced

ABOUT 1½ HOURS BEFORE SERVING:
Preheat oven to 350°F. Cut liver into 4 serving pieces. On waxed paper, stir 2 tablespoons flour with salt and pepper; coat liver with mixture. Trim any fat from bacon.

In 2-quart shallow casserole, place liver, bacon, onion slices and 1 cup water. Cover and bake 1 hour and 10 minutes or until liver is fork-tender.

For thicker gravy, in cup, blend 2 tablespoons flour with 2 tablespoons water until smooth; stir into liquid in casserole last 10 minutes of baking time. Makes 4 servings.

PEPPERS AND STEAK
200 calories per serving

1 2-pound boneless beef top round steak, cut ½-inch thick
1 cup beef bouillon
¼ cup soy sauce
½ teaspoon ginger
½ teaspoon garlic powder
2 tablespoons salad oil
3 large green peppers, cut into thin strips
3 tablespoons cornstarch

DAY BEFORE OR EARLY IN DAY:
Trim any fat from meat; cut meat into strips about ¼-inch wide. In medium bowl, stir bouillon, soy sauce, ginger and garlic powder. Add meat strips; cover and refrigerate.

ABOUT 1¼ HOURS BEFORE SERVING:
Drain meat, reserving ½ cup marinade. In large skillet over high heat, in hot oil, cook meat until lightly browned. Add reserved marinade and 1 cup water. Reduce heat to low; cover and simmer 45 minutes. Add green peppers; cook 15 minutes or until meat is tender.

In cup, blend cornstarch and ¼ cup water until smooth; gradually stir into skillet; cook, stirring, until mixture thickens slightly. Makes 8 servings.

GRAVY JARDINIERE FOR MEAT
20 calories per ¼-cup serving

1 medium onion, thinly sliced
2 stalks celery, diced
1 10½-ounce can condensed beef consommé
2 tablespoons cornstarch
¼ teaspoon bottled sauce for gravy

ABOUT 20 MINUTES BEFORE SERVING:
In covered medium saucepan over high heat, heat to boiling onion, celery, consommé and 1 soup-can water. Reduce heat to low and simmer until onion is tender, about 5 minutes.

In cup, stir cornstarch with 2 tablespoons water and bottled sauce for gravy until smooth; slowly stir into consommé and heat to boiling, stirring. Serve over beef or other meat. Makes 2 cups.

SHRIMP AMANDINE
245 calories per serving

butter or margarine
½ cup slivered almonds
2½ pounds medium shrimp, shelled and deveined
1 teaspoon salt
dash pepper
2 tablespoons chopped chives

ABOUT 15 MINUTES BEFORE SERVING:
In medium skillet over medium heat, in 1 tablespoon hot butter or margarine, cook almonds until golden. With slotted spoon, remove almonds to paper towels to drain. In same skillet, in 1 tablespoon additional butter or margarine, cook half of shrimp, stirring constantly, 3 or 4 minutes until they turn pink; sprinkle with salt and pepper. Remove shrimp from skillet to warm platter. Repeat with remaining shrimp. Sprinkle shrimp with almonds and chives. Makes 6 servings.

TOMATO-CURRY LOBSTER TAILS
265 calories per serving

12 frozen rock-lobster tails (about 5 ounces each)
2 tablespoons butter or margarine
½ cup minced onion
½ cup chopped green pepper
1 garlic clove
1 16-ounce can tomatoes
2 teaspoons curry powder
1 teaspoon salt
1 bay leaf

ABOUT 1 HOUR BEFORE SERVING:
Boil lobster tails as on page 214. Cut away underside membrane and remove meat from shells; cut meat into bite-size pieces and reserve empty shells.

In large saucepan over medium heat, in hot butter or margarine, cook onion, green pepper and garlic until green pepper is tender, about 5 minutes. Add tomatoes and their liquid, curry, salt and bay leaf; heat to boiling. Reduce heat to low; cover and simmer 10 minutes, stirring occasionally.

Add lobster meat and heat through, about 5 minutes. Remove garlic and bay leaf. Fill reserved shells with lobster mixture. Serve hot. Makes 6 servings.

FLOUNDER TURBANS
220 calories per serving

1 tablespoon salad oil
¼ cup chopped onion
¼ cup chopped celery
2 cups packaged herb-seasoned stuffing
1 16-ounce package frozen flounder fillets, thawed
salt and pepper
chopped parsley for garnish
lemon wedges for garnish

ABOUT 40 MINUTES BEFORE SERVING:
In medium skillet over medium heat, in hot oil, cook onion and celery until onion is tender, about 5 minutes. Stir in ⅔ cup water, then stuffing mix until mix is evenly moistened. Preheat oven to 350°F.

Lightly oil four 2-cup casseroles. To make turbans, lightly sprinkle fillets with salt and pepper; arrange around side and over part of bottom of each casserole. Top fish in each with ¼ of stuffing mixture. Cover with foil and bake 20 minutes or until fish flakes easily when tested with a fork.

Turn turbans out of casseroles onto warm platter; garnish with parsley and lemon wedges. Makes 4 servings.

SOLE WITH CHEESE SAUCE
260 calories per serving

½ cup dry white wine
2 tablespoons minced onion
salt and pepper
4 small sole fillets (about 1½ pounds)
1 tablespoon butter or margarine
2 tablespoons all-purpose flour
½ cup half-and-half
⅛ teaspoon nutmeg
½ cup shredded natural Swiss cheese

ABOUT 30 MINUTES BEFORE SERVING:
Preheat broiler if manufacturer directs. In large skillet over medium heat, heat wine, onion, 1 teaspoon salt and dash pepper to boiling. Add fish fillets; reduce heat to low; cover and simmer 10 minutes or until fish flakes easily when tested with a fork. With slotted pancake turner, remove fish to

cook-and-serve platter, thoroughly draining liquid from fish.

Drain liquid from skillet, reserving ½ cup. In same skillet over medium heat, melt butter or margarine; with wire whisk or fork, stir in flour; slowly stir in reserved liquid, half-and-half, ½ teaspoon salt, nutmeg and dash pepper. Cook, stirring constantly, until thickened and smooth; stir in ⅓ cup cheese. (Spoon off any liquid that has drained from fish.) Pour sauce over fish; top with remaining cheese. Broil just until golden. Makes 4 servings.

ZESTY SAUCED HADDOCK
200 calories per serving

1 pound haddock fillets (or 1 16-ounce package frozen haddock fillets, thawed and drained)
salt
½ cup sour cream
⅛ teaspoon dry mustard
⅛ teaspoon ginger
generous dash thyme leaves
paprika for garnish
chopped parsley for garnish

ABOUT 30 MINUTES BEFORE SERVING:
Preheat oven to 350°F. Lightly grease 10" by 6" baking dish. Cut haddock into 3 serving pieces; sprinkle each on both sides with salt; place in single layer in baking dish.

In small bowl, stir sour cream, mustard, ginger and thyme until smooth; spread mixture on top of fillets. Bake 20 to 25 minutes until fish flakes easily when tested with a fork. Serve sprinkled with paprika and parsley. Makes 3 servings.

GREEN BEANS WITH MARJORAM
30 calories per serving

1 9-ounce package frozen green beans
2 chicken-bouillon cubes or envelopes
½ teaspoon marjoram leaves

ABOUT 15 MINUTES BEFORE SERVING:
Cook green beans as label directs but omit salt and add bouillon cubes and marjoram leaves; drain. Makes 3 servings.

SEASONED ASPARAGUS SPEARS
25 calories per serving

ABOUT 20 MINUTES BEFORE SERVING:
In large skillet over medium heat, in 1 inch boiling, salted water, heat *2 pounds asparagus spears* to boiling; cover and cook 5 minutes or until tender-crisp; drain. Sprinkle lightly with *nutmeg*. Makes 6 servings.

LEMON-MINT BEANS
20 calories per serving

1 9-ounce package frozen cut green beans
1 9-ounce package frozen wax beans
salt
2 tablespoons lemon juice
1 teaspoon mint flakes, crushed
½ teaspoon grated lemon peel

ABOUT 15 MINUTES BEFORE SERVING:
In medium saucepan, cook together green beans and wax beans as labels direct but use 1 cup boiling, salted water; drain. Add lemon juice, mint flakes, lemon peel and ½ teaspoon salt; toss well. Makes 8 servings.

CURRIED CARROTS AND PINEAPPLE
90 calories per serving

1 13½-ounce can pineapple chunks
8 medium carrots, cut into strips
½ teaspoon curry powder
½ teaspoon salt
dash pepper

ABOUT 20 MINUTES BEFORE SERVING:
Drain pineapple syrup into measuring cup, reserving pineapple chunks. Add enough water to syrup to make 1 cup liquid; pour into medium skillet. Add carrot strips, curry, salt and pepper; cover and cook over medium heat about 10 minutes or until fork-tender. Stir in pineapple chunks and cook, covered, a few minutes to heat through. Makes 5 servings.

TO USE CANNED CARROTS: Prepare recipe as above but instead of fresh carrots, use *two 16-ounce cans cut whole-style carrots*, drained; cook only about 5 minutes to heat through.

CARROTS CAROLINA
90 calories per serving

⅓ cup packed brown sugar
2 tablespoons orange juice
dash salt
2 16-ounce cans cut whole-style carrots, well-drained

ABOUT 30 MINUTES BEFORE SERVING:
Preheat oven to 375°F. In ovenproof saucepan over medium heat, cook brown sugar, orange juice and salt, stirring constantly, until sugar is dissolved. Add carrots; stir to coat with sugar mixture. Bake, stirring once or twice, 20 minutes. Makes 6 servings.

CELERY WITH CARAWAY SEED
25 calories per serving

3 cups diagonally-sliced celery
1 teaspoon salt
1 tablespoon butter or margarine
½ teaspoon caraway seed
dash pepper

ABOUT 30 MINUTES BEFORE SERVING:
In medium saucepan over medium heat, in 1 inch boiling water, heat celery and salt to boiling; cover and cook 3 to 4 minutes until tender-crisp; drain. Add remaining ingredients and toss until well mixed. Makes 6 servings.

CREAMED POTATOES
125 calories per serving

2½ pounds potatoes (8 medium), cut up
1 medium onion, thinly sliced
1 cup thinly sliced celery
2 teaspoons salt
dash pepper
2½ cups skimmed milk
1 tablespoon cornstarch

ABOUT 40 MINUTES BEFORE SERVING:
In large saucepan over high heat, heat all ingredients but cornstarch to boiling. Reduce heat to low; cover and cook 10 minutes or until potatoes are tender. In cup, stir cornstarch with 2 tablespoons water until smooth; stir into potato mixture and cook, stirring constantly, until thickened and smooth. Makes 8 servings.

HOT GERMAN COLESLAW
70 calories per serving

4 bacon slices
¼ cup cider vinegar
¾ teaspoon salt
¼ teaspoon pepper
1 small cinnamon stick or ⅛ teaspoon cinnamon
1 small head cabbage, shredded

ABOUT 30 MINUTES BEFORE SERVING:
In large saucepan over high heat, heat to boiling 6 cups hot water, bacon, vinegar, salt, pepper and cinnamon. Add cabbage and cook over medium-high heat until cabbage is tender-crisp; drain. Remove bacon and cinnamon stick. Makes 4 servings.

MUSHROOM SALAD
25 calories per serving

⅔ cup tarragon vinegar
1 tablespoon salad oil
1 small garlic clove, crushed
1 bay leaf
¼ teaspoon thyme leaves
3 6-ounce cans whole mushrooms, drained

AT LEAST 1¼ HOURS BEFORE SERVING:
In large bowl, mix all ingredients and ⅓ cup water. Cover and refrigerate at least 1 hour.

TO SERVE:
Drain mixture (reserve liquid for salad dressing another day); discard bay leaf. Serve mushrooms as salad. Makes 5 servings.

ORANGES OREGANO
95 calories per serving

1 tablespoon olive oil
1 teaspoon oregano leaves
½ teaspoon salt
4 pitted ripe olives, sliced
2 large oranges, sliced
lettuce leaves

ABOUT 10 MINUTES BEFORE SERVING:
In small bowl, stir olive oil with 1 tablespoon hot water, oregano and salt. Add olives and orange slices and toss until well coated. Serve on lettuce. Makes 4 servings.

SARDINE-CARROT SANDWICHES
235 calories per serving

12 medium carrots
⅓ cup pickle relish
1 teaspoon salt
12 whole-wheat bread slices, toasted
2 3¾-ounce cans sardines
12 lemon wedges

ABOUT 30 MINUTES BEFORE SERVING:
Into small bowl, finely shred carrots. Stir in relish and salt. Spread mixture over toast slices. Drain sardines. With handle of wooden spoon, press 2 or 3 parallel lines into carrot spread. Lay a sardine in each impression. (Cover and refrigerate any leftover sardines to use later.) Serve with lemon wedges and knives and forks. Makes 6 servings.

GLAZED PINEAPPLE-CHEESE PIE
180 calories per serving

Special Graham-Cracker Crust (at right)
1 8-ounce container creamed cottage cheese (1 cup)
1 envelope unflavored gelatin
sugar
1 cup pineapple juice
1 teaspoon grated lemon peel
3 tablespoons lemon juice
3 egg whites, at room temperature
¼ teaspoon salt
1 16-ounce can pitted tart cherries
1 tablespoon cornstarch
¼ teaspoon almond extract
few drops red food color

EARLY IN DAY OR DAY AHEAD:
Prepare crust. Into large bowl, press cottage cheese through fine sieve. In small saucepan, stir gelatin and ¼ cup sugar until well mixed. Stir in pineapple juice. Cook over low heat, stirring constantly, until gelatin is dissolved. Into cottage cheese, stir gelatin mixture, lemon peel and 2 tablespoons lemon juice. Refrigerate until mixture mounds when dropped from a spoon.

In medium bowl, with mixer at high speed, beat egg whites and salt until soft peaks form; beating at high speed, gradually beat in ¼ cup sugar; beat until sugar is completely dissolved. (Whites should stand in stiff peaks.) Do not scrape sides of bowl during beating. With rubber spatula, gently fold beaten whites into gelatin mixture; pour into crust. Refrigerate until set.

Meanwhile, prepare glaze: Drain cherries well, reserving ½ cup liquid. In small saucepan, mix cornstarch with 2 tablespoons sugar; slowly stir in reserved liquid. Over medium heat, cook mixture until clear and thickened, stirring constantly. Stir in cherries, 1 tablespoon lemon juice, almond extract and food color; cool to room temperature. When pie is set, spoon on glaze, spreading to edges of pie. Chill until well set. Makes 10 servings.

SPECIAL GRAHAM-CRACKER CRUST
(one 8- or 9-inch piecrust)
575 calories per piecrust

¾ cup graham-cracker crumbs
1 tablespoon sugar
2 tablespoons butter or margarine, melted
dash salt

Preheat oven to 350°F. In 8- or 9-inch pie plate, mix all ingredients and 1 tablespoon water. With back of spoon, press mixture to bottom and side of plate. Bake 6 to 8 minutes. Cool.

SPRINGTIME STRAWBERRY PIE
160 calories per serving

Special Graham-Cracker Crust (above)
2 10-ounce packages frozen sweetened strawberries, thawed
1 envelope unflavored gelatin
⅓ cup fresh lemon juice
2 egg whites

EARLY IN DAY:
Prepare crust. Into small saucepan, drain liquid from strawberries; sprinkle with gelatin and cook over medium heat, stirring constantly, just until gelatin dissolves; stir in lemon juice. Refrigerate, stirring occasionally, until mixture mounds when dropped from spoon.

In medium bowl, with mixer at high speed, beat gelatin mixture and egg whites until light and fluffy. With rubber spatula, gently fold in drained berries; heap into piecrust. Refrigerate at least 3 hours. Makes 8 servings.

DANISH FRUIT PUDDING

120 calories per serving

2 10-ounce packages frozen raspberries, thawed
2 tablespoons cornstarch
juice of ½ lemon (about 2 tablespoons)
½ teaspoon vanilla extract
dash cinnamon
dash salt
2 tablespoons slivered almonds

EARLY IN DAY:
Into medium saucepan, drain liquid from raspberries; reserve raspberries. In cup, with wire whisk or spoon, combine cornstarch with lemon juice, vanilla, cinnamon and salt until smooth; stir into raspberry liquid. Over medium-high heat, heat mixture to boiling, stirring constantly; boil one minute. Remove from heat; stir in reserved raspberries. Cover surface of pudding with waxed paper and refrigerate until well chilled.

TO SERVE:
Spoon raspberry mixture into serving dishes. Top each serving with some slivered almonds. Makes 6 servings.

MERINGUE MELBA

125 calories per serving

1 30-ounce can cling-peach halves
1 10-ounce package frozen raspberries, thawed
¾ teaspoon almond extract
4 egg whites, at room temperature
⅛ teaspoon cream of tartar
¼ cup sugar

ABOUT 1½ HOURS AHEAD OR EARLY IN DAY:
1. Drain 6 peach halves; set aside (reserve any leftover peaches for use another day).
2. Drain raspberries well, reserving juice. In covered blender container at low speed, blend raspberries and almond extract until smooth; if necessary, stir in enough reserved juice to make ¾ cup. (Or, in small bowl, with fork, vigorously stir and mash berries until well blended.)
3. Into each of six 6-ounce custard cups, place 1 tablespoon raspberry mixture; top with a peach half, cut side up and spoon on 1 tablespoon raspberry mixture.
4. Preheat oven to 425°F. In medium bowl, with mixer at high speed, beat egg whites and cream of tartar until soft peaks form; beating at high speed, gradually sprinkle in sugar; beat until sugar is completely dissolved. (Whites should stand in stiff peaks.) Spoon meringue over peaches, spreading it to edges of cups and mounding it high in the centers.
5. Place custard cups on cookie sheet; bake 2 to 3 minutes until meringue is lightly browned. Refrigerate until well chilled. Makes 6 servings.

PEAR MERINGUE: Prepare as above but use *one 29-ounce can pear halves* instead of peaches and *one 10-ounce package frozen strawberries* instead of raspberries.

ORANGE CREAM

115 calories per serving

1 envelope unflavored gelatin
sugar
2 eggs, separated
1 cup skimmed milk
⅔ cup whole milk
2 teaspoons grated orange peel
2 teaspoons orange extract
1 teaspoon lemon juice
3 drops yellow food color
2 drops red food color
dash salt
1 orange for garnish

EARLY IN DAY:
In double-boiler top, stir gelatin and 2 tablespoons sugar. In small bowl, with wire whisk or hand beater, beat egg yolks with both milks until mixed; stir into gelatin mixture. Cook over hot, not boiling, water, stirring constantly, until mixture thickens slightly and coats spoon, about 20 minutes.

Remove from heat; cool slightly. Stir in orange peel, orange extract, lemon juice, food colors and salt. Refrigerate until mixture mounds when dropped from spoon.

In small bowl, with mixer at high speed, beat egg whites until soft peaks form; beating at high speed, gradually sprinkle in 2 tablespoons sugar; beat until sugar is completely dissolved. (Whites should stand in stiff peaks.) With rubber spatula, gently fold beaten whites into gelatin mixture; spoon into serving dishes. Chill for at least 2 hours. Garnish with orange sections cut into small pieces. Makes 6 servings.

MOCHA MOUSSE

55 calories per serving

1 envelope unflavored gelatin
sugar
¾ cup strong coffee
4 chocolate cookie wafers
3 egg whites, at room temperature
¼ teaspoon cream of tartar
½ teaspoon vanilla extract
¼ teaspoon imitation maple flavor

EARLY IN DAY:
In medium saucepan, stir gelatin and 2 tablespoons sugar. Stir in coffee and cook over low heat, stirring, until gelatin is dissolved. Chill, stirring occasionally, just until mixture mounds slightly when dropped from spoon.

Meanwhile, in covered blender container, grind cookies into crumbs (or crush with rolling pin). Stir crumbs into thickened gelatin mixture.

In large bowl, with mixer at high speed, beat egg whites and cream of tartar until stiff peaks form. Beating at high speed, gradually beat in 1 tablespoon sugar and beat until sugar is completely dissolved. (Whites should stand in stiff peaks.) Beat in vanilla and maple flavors. With rubber spatula, gently fold beaten whites into coffee mixture and spoon into dessert dishes. Refrigerate until set, at least 3 hours. Makes 6 servings.

PINEAPPLE AND ORANGE COMPOTE

90 calories per serving

2 13¼-ounce cans pineapple chunks, drained
1 cup orange juice
1 cup miniature marshmallows

ABOUT 1 HOUR BEFORE SERVING:
In large bowl, gently toss all ingredients to mix well; cover and refrigerate 45 minutes to blend flavors and soften marshmallows. Makes 6 servings.

RASPBERRY RUBY ICE

130 calories per serving

2 10-ounce packages frozen raspberries, thawed
2 egg whites, at room temperature
¼ cup sugar

AT LEAST 5 HOURS BEFORE SERVING:
Press raspberries through sieve and discard seeds. In medium bowl, with mixer at high speed, beat egg whites until soft peaks form. Beating at high speed, gradually sprinkle in sugar; beat until sugar is completely dissolved. (Whites should stand in stiff peaks.) With rubber spatula, gently fold in raspberries. Freeze, stirring occasionally, until consistency of soft sherbet. Makes 6 servings.

WINTER SHERBET

120 calories per serving

1 15¼-ounce can crushed pineapple
1 16-ounce can cling-peach slices
2 tablespoons lemon juice
¼ teaspoon vanilla extract
dash salt

EARLY IN DAY:
In covered blender container at low speed, blend pineapple and its syrup until smooth; pour into shallow baking pan. Blend peaches and their liquid until smooth; add to pineapple. Stir in remaining ingredients. Freeze mixture until mushy, about 2 hours, stirring occasionally. Again blend mixture, a third at a time, until smooth. Freeze until consistency of sherbet. If softer texture is preferred, let stand at room temperature a few minutes before serving. Makes 6 servings.

PINEAPPLE FRAPPE

70 calories per serving

JUST BEFORE SERVING:
Drain *one 30-ounce can pineapple chunks* (serve juice another day). In covered blender container at high speed, blend pineapple, *1½ cups cracked ice* and *⅛ teaspoon mint extract* just until large chunks of ice disappear. Serve immediately in chilled dessert dishes. Makes 6 servings.

FIGURING CALORIES

Every member of the family has his own calorie requirement depending on age, size and activities. If you're cooking for a family with different requirements, it's important to provide enough calories—and not too many—for everyone. The following table, drawn up by the National Research Council, lists recommended daily dietary allowances designed for the maintenance of good nutrition.

Age	Calories
Children	
1–3 years	1100–1250
3–6	1400–1600
6–10	2000–2200
Males	
10–14	2500–2700
14–18	3000
18–22	2800
25	2800
45	2600
65	2400
Females	
10–14	2250–2300
14–18	2400–2300
18–22	2000
25	2000
45	1850
65	1700

CALORIE VALUES OF FOOD

This table has been abstracted from *Composition of Foods—Raw, Processed, Prepared* and the *Home and Gardens Bulletin Number 72*, both available from the Superintendent of Documents, U.S. Government Printing Office, Washington, D.C. 20402.

Food	Amount	Calories
Alcoholic beverages:		
ale	1 bottle (12 oz.)	160
beer	1 bottle (12 oz.)	160
bourbon (86-proof)	1 jigger (1½ oz.)	125
brandy	1 jigger (1½ oz.)	75
champagne	1 glass (4 oz.)	85
daiquiri	1 average	120
gin (90-proof)	1 jigger (1½ oz.)	110
Manhattan	1 average	130
old-fashioned	1 average	130
rum (80-proof)	1 jigger (1½ oz.)	100
rye (90-proof)	1 jigger (1½ oz.)	110
Scotch (86-proof)	1 jigger (1½ oz.)	105
vodka (86-proof)	1 jigger (1½ oz.)	105
wine, dry	1 glass (3½ oz.)	85
sweet	1 glass (3½ oz.)	140
Almonds	12 to 14	85
Apple	1 medium (2½" diam.)	70
Apple, baked	1 medium	130
Apple brown betty	½ cup	175
Apple butter	1 tablespoon	35
Apple juice (Cider)	½ cup	60
Applesauce:		
sweetened	½ cup	115
unsweetened	½ cup	50
Apricots:		
canned in syrup	4 medium halves, 2 tablespoons syrup	110
dried	5 halves	50
fresh	3 medium	55
stewed, sweetened	½ cup	200
Asparagus	4 medium stalks	10
Avocado	½ 10-oz. avocado	185
Bacon:		
crisp, fried	2 slices	90
Canadian, uncooked	3 oz.	185
Banana	1 medium (6" long)	100
Bagel	1 large (1¾ oz.)	165
Bass, striped, raw	3 oz.	90
Beans:		
baked, with pork and tomato sauce, canned	1 cup	320
green, fresh	1 cup (1" pieces)	30
kidney, canned	1 cup	230
limas, fresh	½ cup	95
wax, canned	1 cup	45
Beef, uncooked:		
chuck, lean meat only	4 oz.*	180

* 4 oz. raw meat will make 3 oz. cooked.

Food	Amount	Calories
Beef, uncooked:		
as purchased, with bone	1 lb.	985
flank, lean meat only	4 oz.*	165
as purchased	1 lb.	655
porterhouse, lean meat only	4 oz.*	185
as purchased	1 lb.	1,605
rib roast, lean meat only	4 oz.*	220
as purchased, no bone	1 lb.	1,820
round, lean meat only	4 oz.*	150
as purchased, no bone	1 lb.	895
rump, lean meat only	4 oz.*	180
as purchased, no bone	1 lb.	1,375
sirloin, lean meat only	4 oz.*	160
as purchased, no bone	1 lb.	1,510
Beef, dried	2 oz.	115
Beef stew, canned	1 serving (1 cup)	210
Beets	2 (½ cup, diced)	25
Baking mix	1 cup	530
Biscuits:		
baking powder	1 (2″ diam.)	90
refrigerated	1 biscuit	60 to 80**
Blackberries	½ cup	40
Blueberries	½ cup	40
Bluefish:		
cooked, baked	4 oz.	180
uncooked fillets	1 lb.	530
Bologna (all meat)	1 oz.	80
Bouillon cubes	1 cube	5
Brazil nuts	2 medium	55
Breads, fresh or toasted:		
Boston brown	1 slice	100
cornbread	1 slice	190
cracked wheat	1 slice	65
French or Italian	1 slice	65
Melba toast	1 slice	15
rye, light	1 slice	60
white	1 slice	70
white, raisin	1 slice	65
whole wheat	1 slice	65
Bread crumbs:		
fresh, unbuttered	2 slices (1 cup)	140
packaged dry	¼ cup	100
Broccoli, cooked	½ cup	20
Brownies, with nuts	1 square from mix	85
Brussels sprouts	1 cup	55
Butter or margarine	1 tablespoon	100
	1 cup	1,630
Buttermilk	1 cup (8 oz.)	90
Cabbage:		
cooked	½ cup	15
raw	½ cup shredded	10
	1 lb.	100
Cakes:		
angel-food	1/12 of 10″ cake	135
cheesecake (cream-cheese base)	1 slice (⅛ of cake)	450
chiffon	1/16 of 10″ cake	215
chocolate cake, fudge frosting	1/16 of 9″ 2-layer cake	235
cupcake, unfrosted	1 medium	90
fruitcake	1/30 of 8″ loaf	55
poundcake	½″ slice	140
spongecake	1/12 of 10″ cake	195
yellow cake, chocolate frosting	1/16 of 9″ 2-layer cake	275
Candy:		
caramel, plain	1 small piece	40
chocolate cream	1 medium piece	50
chocolate, milk	1 oz.	145
fondant	1 oz.	105
fudge	1 oz.	115
gumdrops	1 small	10
hard candy	1 large sour ball	35
Life Savers	1	10
peanut brittle	1 oz.	120
Cantaloupe	½ (5″ diam.)	60
Carrots:		
cooked	½ cup, diced	20
raw, sliced	1 cup (½ cup grated)	20
	1 lb. (tops trimmed)	155
Catchup, chili sauce	1 tablespoon	15
Catfish, raw	4 oz.	115
Cauliflower:		
cooked	1 cup	25
raw	1 lb. (trimmed)	50
Caviar, pressed	1 oz.	90
Celery, raw	1 cup, diced	15
	1 lb.	60
Cereals, cooked:		
cornmeal, grits	1 cup	120
farina	1 cup	105
oatmeal	1 cup	130
Cereals, ready-to-eat:		
bran flakes	1 cup	105
corn flakes	1 cup (about 1 oz.)	100
oat cereal	1 cup (⅔ oz.)	100
puffed rice, wheat	1 cup (about ½ oz.)	55

* 4 oz. raw meat will make 3 oz. cooked.
** Varies according to brand.

Food	Amount	Calories
Cereals, ready-to-eat:		
crisp rice	1 cup (1 oz.)	105
shredded wheat	1 medium biscuit	90
Cheese:		
American	1 slice (1 oz.)	105
Camembert	1 oz.	85
Cheddar	1 slice (1 oz.)	115
cheese spread	1 oz.	80
cottage, creamed	⅓ cup	85
plain	⅓ cup	60
cream	2 tablespoons (1 oz.)	105
Mozzarella, whole milk	1 oz.	90
Neufchâtel	1 oz.	70
Parmesan/Romano, grated	2 tablespoons (⅓ oz.)	50
Ricotta, partially		
skimmed milk	⅓ cup	85
whole milk	⅓ cup	120
Roquefort or blue	1 oz.	105
Swiss, processed or natural	1 slice (1 oz.)	105
Cheese soufflé	1 serving (1½ cups)	320
Cherries		
canned in syrup	½ cup, 3 tablespoons syrup	115
canned, tart	1 cup	105
sweet, fresh	1 cup	80
Chewing gum	1 stick	10
Chicken, fryers, raw:		
breast, whole	1 small (¾ lb.)	295
breast, skinned	1 small (¾ lb.)	265
leg and thigh	1 small (½ lb.)	190
roasted, no bone	average serving (4 oz.)	205
	5 oz. (1 cup diced)	225
Chicken à la king	1 cup, no biscuit	410
Chicken pot pie	1 4" pie	535
Chili con carne, canned	1 cup	335
Chocolate:		
milk	1 oz.	145
semisweet	1 oz.	145
unsweetened (baking)	1 oz.	145
Chocolate milk drink (skim milk)	1 glass (8 oz.)	190
Chocolate syrup	1 tablespoon	50
Chop suey, canned	1-cup serving	145
Clams, uncooked	6 (4 oz., meat only)	85
canned	3 oz.	45
Cocoa	1 tablespoon	20

Food	Amount	Calories
Cocoa, prepared with milk	1 cup	245
Coconut, shredded	½ cup	225
Cod, uncooked	4 oz.	90
Coffee, without sugar and cream	1 cup	0
Coffee lighteners	1 tablespoon	20 to 30*
Cola drinks	6 oz. bottle	70
Cookies:		
chocolate chip	1 (1" diam.)	50
fig bar	1 square	50
gingersnap	1 small (2" diam.)	30
macaroon	1 (2½" diam.)	85
oatmeal	1 large (3" diam.)	65
sandwich-type	1 cookie	50
sugar	1 medium (3" diam.)	80
sugar wafer	1 2½" x ¾" rectangle	25
Corn		
fresh	1 ear (5" long)	70
whole kernel or creamed, canned	½ cup	85
	1 lb.	300
Corned-beef hash, canned	3 oz.	155
Cornmeal, uncooked	1 cup	500
Cornstarch	1 tablespoon	30
Cornstarch pudding	½ cup	140
Crab, cooked	4 oz.	105
Crackers:		
graham	4 (2½" square)	110
oyster	10 crackers	45
saltine	4 squares	50
soda	2 (2½" square)	50
whole rye	1 double cracker	20
Cranberries, fresh	1 cup	45
Cranberry juice	½ cup	80
Cranberry sauce	1 tablespoon	20
	½ lb.	330
Cream:		
half-and-half	1 tablespoon	20
heavy	1 tablespoon	55
	1 cup	840
sour	1 tablespoon	25
Cucumbers, fresh	6 slices (⅛" thick)	5
	1 lb.	65
Custard, baked	½ cup	150
Danish pastry, plain	4½" piece	275
Dates, dried and pitted	¼ cup	125
Dessert topping	1 tablespoon	10 to 25*
Doughnuts (cake type)	1 medium	125
Duck, uncooked	1 average serving (4 oz.)	185
Eggs:		
baked or poached	1 large	80

* Varies according to brand.

Food	Amount	Calories
Eggs:		
fried	1 egg, 1 teaspoon butter	110
omelet	2 eggs, 2 teaspoons butter, milk	215
fresh:	1 large	80
white	1 large	15
yolk	1 large	60
scrambled	1 egg, milk and butter	110
Eggplant, raw	1 slice (5″ diam.)	20
	1 lb.	90
Escarole, raw	4 leaves	5
Figs, dried	1 large	60
Finnan haddie	4 oz.	120
Fish sticks	1 breaded stick	40
Flounder, uncooked fillets	4 oz.	90
Flour:		
all-purpose	1 cup	455
cake	1 cup, sifted	415
whole wheat	1 cup, stirred	400
Frankfurters	1 medium (8 per lb.)	170
French toast	1 slice (no syrup)	140
Frozen custard	½ cup	200*
Fruit cocktail, canned	½ cup fruit and syrup	95
Gelatin, flavored	½ cup prepared	70
Gelatin, unflavored	1 envelope (1 scant tablespoon)	25
Ginger ale	1 glass (8 oz.)	85
Gingerbread	2″ square (unfrosted)	175
Goose, cooked	4 oz.	260
Grapefruit	½ medium	45
Grapefruit juice:		
sweetened, canned	½ cup	65
unsweetened	½ cup	50
Grapefruit sections	½ cup, 1 tablespoon syrup	90
Grape juice	½ cup	85
Grapes	1 cup	65
Gravy:		
canned beef	2 tablespoons	15
homemade (from drippings)	2 tablespoons	30
Haddock:		
pan fried	1 fillet (3 oz.)	140
uncooked fillets	1 lb.	360
Halibut:		
broiled	1 steak (4½ oz.)	240
uncooked fillets	1 lb.	455
Herring:		
pickled	3 oz.	185
smoked kippered	3 oz.	180

* Varies according to brand.

Food	Amount	Calories
Honey	1 tablespoon	65
Honeydew melon	2″ wedge from 7″ x 6½″ melon	50
Ice cream, vanilla	1 cup (10 percent butterfat)	255
	1 cup (16 percent butterfat)	330
Ice-cream soda	1 regular (vanilla)	270
Ice milk	1 cup	200
Jam	1 tablespoon	55
Jelly	1 tablespoon	50
Kale, cooked	½ cup	15
Kidneys, beef, raw	3 oz.	110
Kohlrabi, cooked	½ cup	25
Lamb:		
chop, lean only	4 oz., cooked	140
leg, lean meat only	1 lb., uncooked	610
roast, lean only	3 oz., cooked	155
Lard	1 tablespoon	115
Lemon or lime juice	4 tablespoons	15
Lemonade, concen- trated, frozen	1 cup prepared as directed	110
Lentils, uncooked	2½ tablespoons	85
Lettuce	2 large leaves	10
	1 lb.	55
Liver:		
beef, uncooked	4 oz.	155
calf, uncooked	4 oz.	155
chicken, uncooked	4 oz.	145
Liverwurst	2 oz.	175
Lobster, cooked meat	½ cup (3 oz.)	80
Loganberries	½ cup	45
Macaroni and cheese	1 serving (1 cup)	430
Macaroni:		
cooked	½ cup	95
uncooked	1 lb.	1,675
Mackerel, fillets	4 oz.	215
Mangoes	1 medium	85
Margarine	1 tablespoon	100
	1 cup	1,630
Marmalade, jam	1 tablespoon	55
Marshmallows, plain	1 average regular	25
	½ cup miniature	140
Matzoth:		
egg	1 regular	135
plain	1 regular	120
Meat loaf	1 serving (1″ slice)	370
Milk:		
buttermilk	1 glass (8 oz.)	90
condensed, sweet-ened	½ cup	490

Food	Amount	Calories
Milk:		
evaporated	½ cup, undiluted	175
half-and-half	½ cup	165
liquid, skimmed	1 glass (8 oz.)	90
liquid, 98% fat-free	1 glass (8 oz.)	145
liquid, whole	1 glass (8 oz.)	160
malted, dry powder	3 tablespoons (1 oz.)	115
milk shake	1 glass (8 oz.)	400
nonfat dry milk, instant	⅓ cup (dry powder)	85
yogurt (made with partially skimmed milk):		
plain	1 cup (8 oz.)	120 to 150*
coffee, vanilla	1 cup (8 oz.)	200 to 250*
fruit flavored	1 cup (8 oz.)	230 to 290**
Molasses, light	1 tablespoon	50
Muffins:		
blueberry	1 (2½″ diam.)	140
bran	1 (2½″ diam.)	100
corn	1 (2⅜″ diam.)	125
English	1 (3½″ diam.)	145
plain	1 (3″ diam.)	120
Mushrooms:		
canned	1 cup	40
fresh	1 lb.	125
fresh	4 large	10
Noodles:		
cooked	½ cup	100
chow-mein	1 cup	240
uncooked	½ lb.	880
Oatmeal, cooked	1 cup	130
uncooked	1 cup	310
Oils:		
corn, cottonseed, olive, peanut, soybean	1 tablespoon	125
	½ cup	975
Okra, cooked	8 pods	25
Olives:		
green, pimento-stuffed	4 medium	15
ripe	3 small	15
Onion, raw	1 medium	40
	1 lb.	155
Orange	1 medium (2⅝″ diam.)	65
Orange juice, fresh, frozen or canned	½ cup	55
Orange sections	½ cup	45

* Varies according to brand.
** Varies according to brand *and* flavor.

Food	Amount	Calories
Oysters, eastern, uncooked	6 to 8 medium (4 oz., meat only)	75
Pancakes, from mix	2 (4″ diam.)	120
Parsley	⅓ cup chopped	5
Parsnips, cooked	½ cup	50
Peach nectar	½ cup	60
Peaches:		
canned, syrup pack	½ cup with syrup	100
	16 oz., undrained	355
fresh	1 medium	35
	1 lb.	150
frozen, sweetened	½ cup	100
Peanuts, roasted	8 to 10	55
	½ lb., shelled	1,320
Peanut butter	1 tablespoon	95
Pear nectar	½ cup	65
Pears:		
canned, syrup pack	½ cup with syrup	100
	16 oz., undrained	345
fresh	1 medium	100
	1 lb.	250
Peas:		
fresh, cooked	½ cup	60
fresh, shelled	1 lb., uncooked	380
green, canned	½ cup	80
	16 oz.	300
split, uncooked	½ cup	345
Pecans	9 medium nuts	70
	1 cup, halves	740
Peppers, green, raw	1 medium	15
Perch (ocean), raw	4 oz.	105
Pickles:		
dill	1 medium	10
sour	1 large	15
sweet	1 small	20
Piecrust:		
homemade, double crust	1 9″ crust	1,800
homemade, single crust	1 9″ crust	900
packaged mix, double crust	1 (8″ or 9″ crust)	1,480
Pies:		
apple, double crust	⅐ of 9″ pie	350
butterscotch	⅐ of 9″ pie	350
cherry, double crust	⅐ of 9″ pie	350
custard	⅐ of 9″ pie	285
lemon meringue	⅐ of 9″ pie	305
mince	⅐ of 9″ pie	365
pecan	⅐ of 9″ pie	490
pumpkin	⅐ of 9″ pie	275

Food	Amount	Calories
Pineapple:		
crushed, canned	½ cup	100
	16 oz.	335
juice	½ cup	65
sliced, canned	1 large or 2 small slices	90
sliced, fresh	1 cup, chopped	75
	1 lb., untrimmed	125
Pizza, cheese	⅛ of 14″ pie	185
Plums:		
canned, syrup pack	½ cup with syrup	100
	16 oz. (undrained)	360
fresh	1 (2″ diam.)	25
Popcorn, popped, with oil	1 cup	40
Popover	1 medium	120
Pork:		
ham, boiled	1 slice (1 oz.)	70
ham, cured, uncooked	3 oz. (lean meat)	140
ham, fresh, uncooked	3 oz. (lean meat)	130
loin chop, uncooked	4 oz. (lean meat)	210
Potatoes:		
baked or boiled	1 medium (1 cup, diced)	90
French-fried	10 pieces (2″ long)	155
mashed	½ cup, milk and butter added	95
scalloped	½ cup	120
sweet, baked/boiled	1 medium (5″ x 2″)	155
sweet, candied	1 small (3½″ x 2¼″)	295
Potato chips	10 medium (2″ diam.)	115
Poultry stuffing	1 cup	195
Pretzels	5 3⅛″-long sticks	10
Prune juice, canned	½ cup	100
Prunes, uncooked	4 medium	70
Pudding:		
chocolate	½ cup	175
cornstarch	½ cup	140
vanilla	½ cup	140
Pumpkin, canned	½ cup	40
Pumpkin seeds:		
shelled	1 tablespoon	60
unshelled	¼ cup	60
Rabbit, uncooked, no bones	4 oz.	180
Radishes, raw	4 small	5
Raisins, seedless	¼ cup	120
Raspberries	½ cup	35
Rhubarb:		
stewed/sweetened	½ cup	190
uncooked	1 lb.	55
Rice:		
brown, uncooked	½ cup	300
cooked	1½ cups	300
precooked	1 cup cooked	180

Food	Amount	Calories
Rice:		
regular long grain, uncooked	½ cup	325
	1 lb.	1,645
cooked	½ cup	90
wild, uncooked	½ cup	295
Rice pudding	1 serving (¾ cup)	225
Rolls, plain	1 small (16 per lb.)	85
	1 medium (12 per lb.)	115
	1 large (8 per lb.)	175
Rye wafers	2 wafers	45
Salad dressings:		
blue or Roquefort	1 tablespoon	75
French	1 tablespoon	65
Italian	1 tablespoon	80
mayonnaise	1 tablespoon	100
salad, cooked type	1 tablespoon	65
Thousand Island	1 tablespoon	80
Salmon:		
baked	1 steak (4 oz.)	210
sockeye or red, canned	½ cup, flaked (3 oz.)	120
Sardines, canned in oil	4 medium (1½ oz.)	85
Sauces:		
barbecue	¼ cup	80
chocolate syrup	2 tablespoons	100
hard	2 tablespoons	140
hollandaise	2 tablespoons	175
spaghetti, canned meat sauce	½ cup	100
tomato puree	½ cup	45
white, medium	½ cup	210
Sauerkraut	½ cup	20
Sausage, cooked	2 links (16 per lb.)	125
brown-and-serve	4 oz., uncooked	445
Scallops, uncooked	8 medium (4 oz.)	90
Sherbet	½ cup	130
Shortening, solid	1 tablespoon	110
	1 cup	1,770
Shrimp:		
canned	3 oz.	100
shelled, uncooked	12 to 14 medium (3½ oz.)	90
unshelled	1 lb.	285
Shrimp creole	1 serving (½ cup rice, ¾ cup sauce)	300
Soups (canned soups are prepared according to label directions):		
bean, black	scant cup (⅓ can)	80
beef broth	scant cup	20
beef-noodle	scant cup	60
chicken broth	scant cup	20
chicken, cream of (with milk)	scant cup	135

Food	Amount	Calories
Soups (canned soups are prepared according to label directions):		
chicken-gumbo	scant cup	50
chicken-noodle	scant cup	55
chicken with rice	scant cup	45
clam chowder:		
Manhattan	scant cup	65
New England	scant cup	145
consommé	scant cup	30
minestrone	scant cup	85
mushroom, cream of	scant cup	185
onion	scant cup	30
pea, green	scant cup	115
potato, cream of	scant cup	160
tomato, clear	scant cup	70
cream of	scant cup	140
turkey-noodle	scant cup	65
vegetable	scant cup	60
Spaghetti, cooked	1 cup	155
Spaghetti sauce:		
canned mushroom	1 cup	155
canned with cheese	1 cup	190
Spinach or other greens, cooked	½ cup	20
Squash:		
soft-skin, cooked	½ cup	15
hard-shell, cooked	½ cup	65
Starch (arrowroot, cornstarch, etc.)	1 tablespoon	30
Strawberries	½ cup	25
Sugar:		
brown	1 tablespoon	50
	1 cup	820
confectioners'	1 tablespoon	30
	1 cup	460
granulated	1 tablespoon	40
	1 cup	770
Sundaes:		
chocolate ice cream with chocolate sauce and chopped pecans	½ cup ice cream, 2 tablespoons sauce and 2 tablespoons pecans	355 to 405*
vanilla ice cream with butterscotch sauce	½ cup ice cream, 2 tablespoons sauce	250 to 300*
Sunflower seeds, shelled	1 tablespoon	45
Sweetbreads, calves, cooked	¾ cup (3½ oz.)	170

* Varies according to brand.

Food	Amount	Calories
Sweet potatoes	See Potatoes	
Swordfish, cooked	1 steak (4 oz.)	195
Syrup:		
corn	1 tablespoon	60
maple	1 tablespoon	50
Tangerine	1 (2½″ diam.)	40
Tapioca, quick-cooking	4 tablespoons	140
Tea without sugar or cream	1 cup	0
Tomato juice	½ cup (4 oz.)	25
Tomatoes:		
canned	½ cup	25
	16 oz.	95
fresh	1 medium	40
Tongue, uncooked	4 oz.	180
Tripe, cooked	4 oz.	115
Trout, uncooked	4 oz. (fillets)	220
Tuna:		
canned in oil	⅔ cup, drained (3 oz.)	170
	7 oz. (undrained)	576
canned, water pack	⅔ cup (3 oz.)	110
Turkey, roasted (white and dark meat)	3 oz.	160
	1 lb.	855
Turnips, white, cooked	½ cup	15
Veal, cooked:		
cutlet, no bone	3 oz.	185
roast, no bone	1 slice (3 oz.)	180
Vegetable juice, canned	½ cup (4 oz.)	20
Vienna sausage, canned	1 sausage	40
Vinegar	1 cup	30
Waffle	1 7″ waffle	205
Walnuts, chopped	1 tablespoon	50
	1 cup halves, chopped	790
Watercress	1 bunch, 3″ long	20
Watermelon	1 wedge, 8″ x 4″	115
Wheat germ	1 tablespoon	15
Whipped toppings:		
aerosol	1 tablespoon	10*
frozen or mix	1 tablespoon	10 to 25*
Whitefish, uncooked fillets	4 oz.	175
Yams	See Potatoes, sweet	
Yeast:		
dried	1 package active dry	25
cake	1 cake, compressed	20
Yogurt	See Milk	
Zwieback	1 cracker	30

Canning, preserving & freezing

Canning food preserves it by destroying spoilage microorganisms with heat and sealing the container so that more microorganisms cannot enter. Freezing food preserves it by delaying the action of these substances. In jellies and jams, sugar is the preserving agent.

Some varieties of fruits and vegetables are better than others for freezing and canning because they retain truer color, flavor and texture. Check with your county or state cooperative extension service or college of agriculture for these varieties in your area.

CANNING

Foods are canned by heating them hot enough and long enough (processing) to destroy harmful organisms and stop enzyme action. The method of processing is determined by the acid content of the food.

Acid foods include all fruits and these vegetables: tomatoes, pimentos and sauerkraut; also pickles and relishes. They can be canned safely at the temperature of boiling water; the processing is done in a water-bath canner.

Low-acid foods include all other vegetables, meats, poultry, fish and soups. These must be processed at above-boiling temperatures; the processing is done in a steam-pressure canner.

In these pages we give directions for canning fruits and vegetables only. For information on canning meats, poultry, fish and other foods, or for canning all foods if you live at high altitudes, contact the home agent for your county cooperative extension office or the home service department of your local public utility company.

Special Equipment

Before starting to prepare the food, make sure you are using the right kind of canner and that it is in good working order.

Water-bath canner for acid foods: Use a boiling-water-bath canner (also called "cold-pack canner") or any deep saucepot or kettle with a rack to keep jars at least ½ inch above pot bottom and a tight-fitting cover. The canner should be deep enough so the rim is at least 4 inches above the jars and large enough so jars do not touch the sides or one another.

Pressure canner for low-acid foods: Use a pressure canner with an accurate gauge for maintaining pressure at 10 pounds, a petcock (vent) and safety valve, and a rack in the bottom. Have the pressure gauge checked at least once a year; the home agent for your county cooperative extension office, or a canner dealer or manufacturer, can tell you where.

Jars and caps: Use only tempered glass jars made for home canning. Mason jars are the most widely used. Don't reuse jars originally filled with bought foods such as mayonnaise; they may break at canning temperatures, and caps and lids for true canning jars are not likely to fit them.

Caps are of two styles: the two-piece type consisting of lid and screw band, or the one-piece glass or porcelain-lined zinc cap, which is used with a rubber ring. Be sure the caps are the correct type and size for your jars. Screw bands and zinc or glass caps can be reused (unless rusty or damaged by prying off); metal lids with sealing compound and rubber rings must be replaced after each use. Each package of caps contains instructions for adjusting them for processing.

Steps in Canning

Preparing jars and caps for processing: Check jars to be sure there are no nicks, cracks or sharp edges that will prevent an airtight seal or cause breakage. Wash jars and zinc or glass caps and rubber rings, or lids and screw bands, in hot soapy water; rinse. Leave jars and caps in hot water until ready to use; if using rubber rings, keep them wet until placed on jars.

Packing jars: Packing foods into jars is done by one of these two methods:

Raw or cold pack: Raw, unheated food is packed firmly into jar and is then covered with boiling liquid to ½ inch from top of jar. It will take about ½ to 1½ cups liquid per quart. Corn, peas and lima beans should be packed only to 1 inch from top, since they expand during processing.

Hot pack: Hot foods, precooked or heated in liquid, are packed loosely into jars and covered with boiling liquid to ½ inch (1 inch for corn, peas and lima beans) from top.

After filling each jar, run a narrow rubber spatula between food and side of jar to remove air bubbles. Then wipe jar rim and threads clean and cover with cap, following manufacturer's directions.

Don't pack more jars than canner can hold at one time.

Processing in boiling-water bath: Place a rack in bottom of canner or deep, large kettle; fill canner half full with hot water. Over high heat, heat almost to boiling for raw-pack foods, to full boiling for hot-pack. Carefully place filled jars in kettle far enough apart so that water can circulate freely; add additional boiling water if needed to come to 1 to 2 inches over jars. (Do not pour water directly on jars.) Heat to boiling. Start timing when water boils. Cover canner and boil gently for time indicated in recipe. If necessary, add boiling water during processing to keep jars covered. With jar lifter or tongs, remove jars from canner; seal caps as manufacturer directs.

Processing in pressure canner: Follow manufacturer's directions for model you are using. Start counting processing time when pressure gauge reaches 10 pounds.

Cooling jars: As each processed jar is lifted from canner, complete sealing if necessary. If some of liquid has boiled out of jar, do not open jar to add more. To cool, place jars, top side up, on wire rack or folded cloth, away from drafts; set 2 or 3 inches apart so air can circulate.

To test for airtight seal: When jars are cool, at least 12 hours after processing, check seal. If using two-piece caps, carefully remove screw band; if center of lid has a slight dip or stays down when pressed, jar is sealed; store without screw bands if you like. Jars with zinc caps and rubber rings are sealed if caps are low in center; do not tighten caps further. Jars with glass caps and rubber rings: turn jar partly over; if there is no leakage, jar is ready to be stored. If jar is not airtight, refrigerate food and use within a day; do not re-process.

To detect spoilage: Don't taste and don't use *any* canned food if it shows any one of these signs: Before opening—bulging jar caps or can ends, or leakage; after opening —spurting liquid, gas bubbles, an off-odor, contents that are soft, mushy, slimy or moldy, sediment in bottom of jar or can. Discard contents immediately.

Some spoilage is not so readily detected; for that reason, home-canned low-acid foods such as meats, poultry, fish, soups and vegetables (except tomatoes) should be heated to boiling and then boiled for 10 minutes before tasting. (Boil spinach and corn 20 minutes.) If foaming or an off-odor develops during boiling, or if, after boiling, the food does not look or smell right, discard it without tasting.

Clouding of liquid in jar may be due to hard water, starch in overripe vegetables or spoilage. Boil food as above, without tasting; if foaming or an off-odor develops, discard food.

To Can Fruit

Select fruits in perfect condition and as fresh as possible. Fruit may be canned in water, in syrup or in fruit juice.

Rinse fruit well, either in running cold water or several changes of water, lifting it out of water each time so that dirt rinsed off doesn't get back on. Prepare, following Fruit Preparation Directions for specific fruit, below.

To treat fruit to prevent darkening: Before packing, prepare ascorbic-acid mixture for fruit as label directs and drop peeled or cut apples, apricots, peaches or pears into mixture as pieces are prepared; drain before packing into jars. Or, in large bowl, combine 4 quarts water, 2 tablespoons salt and 2 tablespoons cider or white vinegar; drop fruit pieces into mixture; remove within a few minutes and rinse well.

FRUIT JUICE FOR CANNING

JUST BEFORE PREPARING FRUIT:
In large saucepan, with potato masher, crush soft, sound, ripe, juicy fruit well. Over low heat, heat to simmering. Strain through clean cotton cloth; discard pulp. Use juice as liquid to pour over fruit packed in jars or to make Sugar Syrup.

SUGAR SYRUP FOR CANNING

JUST BEFORE PREPARING FRUIT:
Into 2-quart saucepan, measure *4 cups water* or fruit juice and *sugar* for desired syrup below. Over high heat, heat mixture, stirring, until sugar is dissolved. Reduce heat to low; keep syrup hot but don't boil. Pour hot over fruit in jars, or use to cook fruit for hot pack. Usually 1 to 1½ cups syrup are required for each 1-quart jar.

LIGHT: Use 1⅓ cups sugar. Makes 4½ cups.

MEDIUM: Use 2 cups sugar. Makes 5 cups.

HEAVY: Use 4 cups sugar. Makes 6 cups.

FRUIT PREPARATION DIRECTIONS

APPLES: Peel, core, cut up or slice. Treat to prevent darkening. Heat to boiling in water or in light sugar syrup; boil 5 minutes. Pack mixture hot into jars. Adjust caps. Process in boiling-water bath 15 minutes for pints, 20 minutes for quarts.

APPLESAUCE: Cut apples into quarters; place in large saucepot with water to cover bottom ½ inch deep. Heat to boiling; cover and cook until fruit is tender. Press mixture through food mill or sieve to remove seeds and skins. Add sugar to taste. Heat to simmering; pack into jars leaving ¼ inch head space. Adjust caps. Process in boiling-water bath 10 minutes for pints and quarts.

APRICOTS: Peel if desired. (To peel, dip fruit quickly into boiling water, then into cold water to help loosen skins.) Cut in half and remove seeds, or leave whole. If peeled, treat to prevent darkening. Pack fruit cold into jars; cover with boiling light or medium sugar syrup or water. Adjust caps. Process in boiling-water bath 25 minutes for pints, 30 minutes for quarts.

BERRIES (blackberries, blueberries, boysenberries, gooseberries, loganberries, raspberries): Pack fruit cold into jars; cover with boiling light sugar syrup or water. Adjust caps. Process in boiling-water bath 10 minutes for pints, 15 minutes for quarts.

CHERRIES: Remove stems and seeds. Pack fruit cold into jars; cover with boiling light or medium sugar syrup or water. Adjust caps. Process in boiling-water bath 20 minutes for pints, 25 minutes for quarts.

Or, pack hot this way: Measure cherries into large saucepot; for each quart, add ½ cup sugar; cover saucepot. Heat to boiling; remove from heat. Pack mixture hot into jars; if necessary, add boiling light sugar syrup to cover fruit. Adjust caps. Process in boiling-water bath 10 minutes for pints, 15 minutes for quarts.

PEACHES: Peel peaches (see Apricots, page 693); cut in half and remove seeds. Scrape cavities to remove red fibers; these may turn brown later. Slice if desired. Treat to prevent darkening. Pack fruit cold into jars, cavity side down; cover with boiling light or medium sugar syrup or water. Adjust caps. Process in boiling-water bath 25 minutes for pints, 30 minutes for quarts.

Or, pack fruit hot this way: Heat peaches, a few at a time, in liquid just until hot. Pack hot fruit and liquid as above. Adjust caps. Process in boiling-water bath 20 minutes for pints, 25 minutes for quarts.

PEARS: Peel; cut in half and remove cores. Treat to prevent darkening. Pack and process as for Peaches, above.

PLUMS: Cut in half and remove seeds; or, leave whole and prick skins with needle so plums don't burst when heated (they still may crack). Pack fruit cold into jars; cover with boiling light or medium sugar syrup or water. Adjust caps. Process in boiling-water bath 20 minutes for pints, 25 minutes for quarts.

Or, pack hot this way: Heat plums in liquid to boiling; remove from heat. Fill jars with hot mixture; process as above.

To Can Vegetables

Select vegetables in perfect condition and as fresh as possible. Rinse vegetables well, scrubbing if necessary, in running cold water or several changes of water, lifting out of water each time. Drain well before cutting; prepare as recipe directs.

Most vegetables can be packed either hot or cold. If packed hot, they should be covered with the liquid in which they were heated. However, if this cooking liquid is dark, strong-flavored or gritty, discard it and cover vegetables with boiling water.

Salt may be added for seasoning, or omitted if desired. Add ½ teaspoon salt to each pint jar, 1 teaspoon salt to each quart.

Pack lima beans, corn and peas loosely into jars, without shaking down, to at least 1 inch from tops; these vegetables expand during cooking. All other vegetables should be packed tightly to ½ inch from tops.

For greater safety, all the vegetables which follow, except tomatoes, should be processed in a pressure canner (page 692).

Use processing time specified in Vegetable Preparation Directions, below. Some vegetables which cook quickly for table use need much longer processing time to destroy all spoilage microorganisms.

VEGETABLE PREPARATION DIRECTIONS

ASPARAGUS: Remove scales and tough ends; cut into 1- to 2-inch pieces. Pack cold into jars; add salt if desired. Cover with boiling water. Adjust caps. Process in pressure canner at 10 pounds pressure 25 minutes for pints, 30 minutes for quarts.

Or, pack hot this way: In large saucepot, cover asparagus with boiling water; when mixture returns to boiling, boil 3 minutes. With slotted spoon, loosely pack hot asparagus into jars; cover with boiling liquid or, if liquid is gritty, with boiling water. Add salt if desired; process as above.

BEANS, GREEN AND WAX: Snap off ends ("string" will come off with stem end). Cut beans into 1- to 2-inch pieces. Pack beans cold into jars; add salt if desired. Cover with boiling water. Adjust caps. Process in pressure canner at 10 pounds pressure 20 minutes for pints, 25 minutes for quarts.

Or, pack hot this way: In large saucepot, cover beans with boiling water; when mixture returns to boiling, boil 5 minutes. With slotted spoon, loosely pack beans into jars; add salt if desired. Cover beans with boiling liquid. Process as above.

BEANS, LIMA: Shell beans; pack cold into jars to 1 inch from tops; don't press or shake down. Add salt if desired. Cover beans with boiling water, leaving ½ inch head space. Adjust caps. Process in pressure canner at 10 pounds pressure 40 minutes for pints, 50 minutes for quarts.

Or, pack hot this way: In large saucepot, heat beans with boiling water to cover to boiling; reduce heat to keep mixture simmering. With slotted spoon, pack hot beans loosely into jars to 1 inch from tops. Add salt if desired. Cover beans with boiling water, leaving 1 inch head space. Adjust caps. Process as above.

BEETS: Cut off tops and roots; cover beets with boiling water and boil 15 to 25 minutes until skins slip easily. Cool quickly in cold water; remove skins. Leave baby beets whole; slice medium or large beets, or cut into ½-inch cubes; cut very large slices into halves or quarters. Pack beets into jars; add salt if desired. Cover with boiling water. Adjust caps. Process in pressure canner at 10 pounds pressure 30 minutes for pints, 35 minutes for quarts.

CARROTS: Scrape or peel carrots; slice or dice. Pack cold into jars; add salt if desired. Cover with boiling water. Adjust caps. Process in pressure canner at 10 pounds pressure 25 minutes for pints, 30 minutes for quarts.

Or, pack hot this way: In large saucepot, heat carrots with boiling water to cover to boiling; reduce heat to keep mixture simmering. With slotted spoon, pack carrots into jars; add salt if desired; cover with boiling liquid. Adjust caps. Process as above.

CORN, CREAM-STYLE: Remove corn husks and silk. Cut tip ends from kernels; scrape pulp from cobs. Use pint jars only; pack corn kernels and pulp loosely to 1½ inches from jar tops; don't press or shake down. Add ½ teaspoon salt to each pint if desired. Cover corn with boiling water, leaving ½ inch head space. Adjust caps. Process in pressure canner at 10 pounds pressure 1 hour and 35 minutes.

Or, pack hot this way: Measure corn kernels and pulp; to each 4 cups, add 2 cups boiling water. Heat mixture to boiling; reduce heat to keep mixture simmering. In pint jars only, pack mixture to 1 inch from tops; add salt if desired. Adjust caps. Process in pressure canner at 10 pounds pressure 1 hour and 25 minutes.

CORN, WHOLE-KERNEL: Remove husks and silk. Cut kernels from cob; don't scrape cob. Pack corn cold into jars to 1 inch from tops; add salt if desired. Cover corn with boiling water leaving ½ inch head space. Adjust caps. Process in pressure canner at 10 pounds pressure 55 minutes for pints, 1 hour and 25 minutes for quarts.

Or, pack hot this way: Measure corn; to each 4 cups, add 2 cups boiling water. Heat mixture to boiling; reduce heat to keep mixture simmering. With slotted spoon, pack corn loosely into jars to 1 inch from tops; cover with boiling liquid, leaving 1 inch head space. Add salt if desired. Adjust caps. Process as above.

GREENS: Can beet or turnip tops, kale, mustard greens, Swiss chard, following directions for Spinach (page 696).

OKRA: Use only young, tender okra pods; remove stem ends without cutting into pods. Leave pods whole or cut into 1-inch pieces. Cover okra with boiling water; when mixture boils again, boil 1 minute. With slotted spoon, pack okra into jars; add salt if desired. Cover with boiling water. Adjust caps. Process in pressure canner at 10 pounds pressure 25 minutes for pints, 40 minutes for quarts.

PEAS: Shell peas; pack cold into jars to 1 inch from tops; don't press or shake down. Add salt if desired. Cover with boiling water, leaving 1 inch head space. Adjust caps. Process in pressure canner at 10 pounds pressure 40 minutes for pints or quarts.

Or, pack hot this way: In large saucepot, heat peas with boiling water to cover to boiling; reduce heat to keep mixture simmering. With slotted spoon, pack peas loosely into jars to 1 inch from tops. Add salt if desired; cover peas with boiling liquid, leaving 1 inch head space. Adjust caps. Process as above.

POTATOES: Peel whole potatoes 1 to 2½ inches in diameter. Cover potatoes with boiling water; when water returns to boiling, boil 10 minutes. With slotted spoon, pack potatoes into jars. Add salt if desired. Cover potatoes with boiling water. Adjust caps. Process in pressure canner at 10 pounds pressure 30 minutes for pints, 40 minutes for quarts.

PUMPKIN, MASHED: Cut pumpkin into large pieces; remove seeds and stringy portions. In large saucepot, in 1 inch boiling water, cook pumpkin, covered, about 25 minutes or until tender. Scoop pulp from rind and mash with potato masher or back of spoon. Return mashed pumpkin to saucepot; heat until simmering, stirring to prevent sticking. Spoon hot pumpkin into jars; do not add liquid; do not add salt. Adjust caps. Process in pressure canner at 10 pounds pressure 1 hour and 5 minutes for pints, 1 hour and 20 minutes for quarts.

SPINACH AND OTHER GREENS: Wash spinach well; remove tough ribs or stems. Place spinach in large saucepot with water remaining on leaves. Cover and heat just until spinach is wilted. Pack spinach loosely into jars; add ¼ teaspoon salt for each pint, ½ teaspoon salt for each quart if desired. Cover with boiling water. Adjust caps. Process in pressure canner at 10 pounds pressure 1 hour and 10 minutes for pints, 1 hour and 30 minutes for quarts.

SQUASH, HARD-SHELLED: Follow directions for Pumpkin, above.

SQUASH, SOFT-SKINNED: Cut unpeeled squash into ½-inch slices, then cut slices into halves or quarters. Pack squash cold tightly into jars to 1 inch from tops. Add salt if desired. Cover with boiling water, leaving ½ inch head space. Adjust caps. Process in pressure canner at 10 pounds pressure 25 minutes for pints, 30 minutes for quarts.

Or, pack hot this way: In large saucepot, heat squash with boiling water to cover to boiling; reduce heat to keep mixture simmering. With slotted spoon, loosely pack squash into jars to ½ inch from tops; cover with boiling liquid, leaving ½ inch head space. Add salt if desired. Process in pressure canner at 10 pounds pressure 30 minutes for pints, 40 minutes for quarts.

SWEET POTATOES: In covered large saucepot, in water to cover, boil sweet potatoes 20 minutes or until skins slip off easily. Remove skins; leave potatoes whole or cut into pieces. Pack potatoes "dry" into jars to 1 inch from tops, pressing gently to fill spaces. Don't add salt or liquid. Adjust caps. Process in pressure canner at 10 pounds pressure 1 hour and 5 minutes for pints, 1 hour and 35 minutes for quarts.

Or, pack "wet" this way: Pack potatoes into jars to 1 inch from tops. Add salt if desired. Cover with boiling light or medium sugar syrup, leaving 1 inch head space. Adjust caps. Process in pressure canner at 10 pounds pressure 55 minutes for pints, 1 hour and 30 minutes for quarts.

TOMATOES: Place tomatoes in colander or wire basket and dip into boiling water for ½ minute, then plunge into cold water. Cut out stem ends and pull off skins. Leave tomatoes whole, or cut into halves or quarters.

Pack tomatoes into jars, pressing gently to fill spaces with juice; don't add water. Add salt if desired; if tomatoes are sweet, add 1 teaspoon fresh lemon juice to each pint jar, 2 teaspoons to each quart jar if desired. Adjust caps. Process in boiling-water bath 35 minutes for pints, 45 minutes for quarts.

Or, pack hot this way: Cut peeled tomatoes into quarters. In large saucepot, heat to boiling; reduce heat to keep tomatoes simmering. Pack into jars. Add salt and lemon juice if desired. Adjust caps. Process in boiling-water bath 10 minutes for pints and quarts.

To Store Canned Foods

Home-canned foods will be at their best if used within a year. Store in a cool dry place, preferably at a temperature below 70°F. An unheated closet in kitchen or basement is fine.

JAMS, JELLIES AND OTHER FRUIT SPREADS

Jelly, jam, preserves, conserve, marmalade and fruit butter provide excellent ways to use fruit that may not be ideal for freezing or canning owing to variations in size, shape and degree of ripeness.

INGREDIENTS: Fruit supplies flavor and color; acid enhances flavor and aids jelling; sugar helps preserve the mixture and contributes to flavor; and pectin is the substance which makes these mixtures jell.

Pectin is a natural component of fruit; it varies with the kind and degree of ripeness of each fruit. Some fruit has more pectin than others; all fruit when underripe has more pectin, but less flavor, than when ripe.

Commercial fruit pectins can be used with all fruit if specially developed recipes are followed. Because these pectins permit the use of fully ripe fruit, shorten cooking time and eliminate guessing as to how long to cook the fruit mixtures, we use them in all our jelly recipes and most of our recipes for other sweet fruit spreads.

Two types are available: liquid and powdered. Be sure to use the kind the recipe calls for, and follow directions for combining it in the mixture. The two kinds cannot be used interchangeably.

Lemon juice can be added to fruit that is low in acid.

Granulated, white cane or beet sugar may be used; do not use brown sugar or confectioners' sugar.

Special Equipment

For cooked mixtures: Use a 7- to 10-quart saucepot or kettle with a broad, flat bottom. Pan should be about three times larger than amount of ingredients.

Jelly glasses with tight-fitting covers, and canning jars with lids and screw bands or porcelain-lined zinc caps and rubber rings, may be used. For preserves and soft jams, use canning jars with lids that can be tightly sealed. In warm, humid climates, seal all jellies, jams and conserves in canning jars with caps.

For freezer jams: Use a large bowl for mixing. Use jelly glasses; or 1-pint or smaller jars or other glass or plastic containers that can stand scalding-water or dishwasher temperatures, have tight-fitting lids and are designed to hold food. This way you know they can withstand changes in temperature from scalding to freezing at 0°F.

Steps in Making Fruit Spreads

Don't try to double recipes for fruit spreads. It's easier and safer to make the recipe as many times as needed than to try to cook larger amounts of ingredients.

Before you start to cook, assemble all equipment and prepare jars or containers; prepare and measure all ingredients.

Preparing jelly glasses, jars or freezer-proof containers: Check glasses or jars to be sure there are no nicks, cracks or sharp edges. Wash glasses, jars or containers and lids in hot soapy water; rinse. Pour boiling water over all, inside and out; invert on dish rack or clean towel, away from draft, to drain dry. Or, wash in an automatic dishwasher with a very hot (150°F. or higher) rinse cycle and let remain in dishwasher until ready to fill.

Melting paraffin: Use a small, clean metal can with a plastic cover, such as a 1-pound coffee can. Then paraffin can be left in can, covered and stored for later use.

To melt paraffin, put it in can and place can in a medium saucepan filled with about 1 inch of water. Over medium heat, heat, uncovered, until paraffin is melted. Never melt paraffin over direct heat. Keep hot.

Preparing fruit: Rinse fruit gently, either in running cold water or in several changes of water, lifting it out of water each time so that dirt rinsed off doesn't get back on. Don't soak fruit, or flavor and food value might be lost. Drain well.

To chop fruit, chop on cutting board with sharp knife, or use meat grinder or blender. Fruits turn dark faster when chopped in blender.

Making cooked mixtures: The "rapid boil" called for in our recipes means that mixture is bubbling all across its surface and cannot be stirred down.

To measure ½ bottle liquid fruit pectin, invert bottle straight down over boiling mixture and let it drain until pectin reaches ½-bottle mark, then quickly turn bottle upright.

After cooking, remove mixture from heat and skim off any foam, using a metal spoon. The foam is harmless but detracts from appearance of the product in glass or jar.

If jam, preserves or marmalade is to be covered with paraffin, stir and skim off foam (discard) for several minutes as recipe specifies, to cool jam slightly and prevent fruit from floating to top. However, if jam is to be sealed in jars with caps, skim it as soon as cooked and pour into jars; seal. Occasionally shake jars as they cool to prevent fruit from floating.

Sealing glasses with paraffin: Fill glasses with hot mixture, leaving ½-inch space at top. Dip a tablespoon into melted paraffin, then rest spoon on edge of glass and tilt to let paraffin flow onto surface of hot mixture. With tip of spoon, spread paraffin so it covers surface and touches glass at all points to seal. Paraffin should be only ⅛ inch thick. Prick any air bubbles that appear.

After jelly is cold and paraffin hardened, cover glass to protect from dust, since paraffin does not give an airtight seal.

Sealing canning jars with caps: Fill jars with hot mixture, leaving ⅛-inch space at top. Then seal one jar as manufacturer directs and invert on wire rack or towel; repeat with remaining jars. (Hot mixture destroys any microorganisms which may have settled on lid.) Then turn all jars upright to cool. Remove screw bands after jars are cold.

To Store Jams and Jellies

Fruit spreads in glasses or jars sealed with paraffin or caps may be stored in a dark, cool, dry place for up to one year if unopened. After opening, cover tightly and store in cupboard, or for best quality and longer storage life, in refrigerator.

Keep freezer jams in freezer up to 1 year. After opening, refrigerate and use within 3 weeks.

BLENDER PEACH BUTTER

about 6 8-ounce jars and caps
6 pounds peaches
2 cups sugar (about 1 pound)
½ cup orange juice
¼ teaspoon cinnamon
¼ teaspoon ground cloves

Prepare jars and caps for processing (page 692). Peel, remove seeds and quarter peaches. In covered blender container at high speed, blend peaches, one-third at a time, until smooth.

In 7-quart saucepot or Dutch oven over medium heat, heat peaches with remaining ingredients to boiling; boil 20 minutes or until thick, stirring frequently. Remove from heat; ladle mixture into jars, leaving ⅛-inch space at top. Adjust caps.

Process in boiling-water bath 10 minutes. Makes about six 8-ounce jars.

APPLE BUTTER

about 10 8-ounce jars and caps
6 pounds apples
4 cups sweet apple cider or juice
3 cups sugar (about 1½ pounds)
1½ teaspoons cinnamon
½ teaspoon ground cloves

1. Prepare jars and caps for processing (page 692). Cut apples into quarters (do not peel).
2. In heavy 7-quart saucepot over high heat, heat apples and cider to boiling. Reduce heat to medium, cover saucepot and simmer 15 to 20 minutes until apples are very tender.
3. Into very large bowl, press apple mixture through food mill or coarse sieve. Return apple pulp (about 3 quarts) to saucepot; add sugar, cinnamon and cloves; over high heat, heat to boiling. Reduce heat to medium; boil mixture, stirring occasionally, about 1 hour and 15 minutes or until mixture is thickened, dark and mounds slightly when dropped from a spoon. Remove from

heat; ladle mixture into jars, leaving ¼-inch space at top.
4. Process in boiling-water bath 10 minutes. Makes about ten 8-ounce jars.

BAR-LE-DUC

5 to 7 8-ounce jelly glasses and lids
paraffin
3 quarts fresh currants
7 cups sugar (about 3 pounds)

Prepare glasses and lids and melt paraffin (page 697). Rinse and stem currants; drain well. In heavy 7-quart Dutch oven or saucepot, with potato masher or back of spoon, thoroughly crush ⅓ of currants (about 3 cups). Add remaining currants and sugar and stir to mix well.

Over high heat, heat mixture to boiling, stirring frequently. Reduce heat to medium and boil gently 20 to 25 minutes, stirring occasionally, until mixture is slightly thickened.

Ladle mixture into glasses and seal with paraffin. When cold, cover glasses with lids. Makes about seven 8-ounce glasses.

SEEDLESS BAR-LE-DUC: If you like, with back of spoon, press cooked mixture through medium strainer into large bowl. Return strained mixture to Dutch oven and reheat to boiling; fill glasses as above. Makes about five 8-ounce glasses.

ROSE-WINE JELLY

about 4 8-ounce jelly glasses and lids
paraffin
2 cups rosé
3 cups sugar (about 1½ pounds)
½ 6-ounce bottle fruit pectin

Prepare glasses and lids and melt paraffin (page 697).

In double boiler over rapidly boiling water, stir rosé with sugar until sugar is dissolved, about 2 minutes. Remove double boiler from heat; immediately stir in fruit pectin. With metal spoon, skim off any foam.

Ladle mixture into glasses and seal with paraffin. When cold, cover glasses with lids. Makes about four 8-ounce glasses.

RED-WINE JELLY: Prepare as above but use *Burgundy*, Chianti or ruby port for rosé.

WHITE-WINE JELLY: Prepare as above but substitute *sauterne,* medium sherry or tawny port for rosé.

BLUEBERRY JAM

about 9 8-ounce jelly glasses and lids
paraffin
about 3 pints blueberries
7 cups sugar (about 3 pounds)
2 tablespoons lemon juice
1 6-ounce bottle fruit pectin

Prepare glasses and lids and melt paraffin (page 697). With potato masher, thoroughly crush blueberries to make 4 cups.

In 7-quart saucepot or Dutch oven, mix well blueberries, sugar and lemon juice. Over high heat, heat mixture, stirring constantly, until mixture comes to a rapid boil; boil rapidly 1 minute, stirring constantly. Remove from heat; stir in fruit pectin. With metal spoon, stir and skim mixture for 5 minutes to cool it slightly to prevent blueberries from floating.

Ladle mixture into glasses and seal with paraffin. When cold, cover glasses with lids. Makes about nine 8-ounce glasses.

PINEAPPLE JAM

about 5 8-ounce jelly glasses and lids
paraffin
1 20-ounce can crushed pineapple
3¼ cups sugar (about 1½ pounds)
3 tablespoons lemon juice
½ 6-ounce bottle fruit pectin

Prepare glasses and lids and melt paraffin (page 697).

In 4-quart saucepan, mix well pineapple and its liquid, sugar and lemon juice. Over high heat, heat mixture, stirring constantly, until mixture comes to a rapid boil; boil rapidly 1 minute, stirring constantly. Remove from heat; stir in fruit pectin. With metal spoon, stir and skim mixture for 5 minutes to cool it slightly to prevent fruit from floating.

Ladle mixture into glasses and seal with paraffin. When cold, cover glasses with lids. Makes about five 8-ounce glasses.

CONCORD GRAPE JELLY AND BUTTER

about 6 pounds Concord grapes
cheesecloth
about 18 8-ounce jelly glasses and lids
paraffin
14½ cups sugar (about 6¼ pounds)
1 6-ounce bottle fruit pectin

Stem grapes and place in 7-quart saucepot. With potato masher, crush grapes thoroughly; stir in ½ cup water; over high heat, heat to boiling. Reduce heat to medium-low; cover saucepot and simmer 10 minutes.

Meanwhile, line colander or very large strainer with about 4 layers damp cheesecloth. Over large bowl, pour grapes into colander; bring corners of cheesecloth together and twist to squeeze out juice. Press grape pulp through medium sieve to remove seeds. Use juice to make jelly, pulp to make butter.

JELLY: Prepare 8 glasses and lids and melt paraffin (page 697). In same saucepot, mix well *4 cups grape juice* and *7 cups sugar.* (If not quite enough grape juice, add water to make 4 cups; if any extra, add to cold juice beverages.)

Over high heat, heat mixture, stirring constantly, until mixture comes to a rapid boil; immediately stir in *½ bottle fruit pectin.* Stirring constantly, heat until mixture again boils rapidly and continue boiling 1 minute. Remove mixture from heat; with metal spoon, skim off foam.

Ladle mixture into glasses and seal with paraffin. When cold, cover glasses with lids. Makes about eight 8-ounce glasses.

BUTTER: Prepare 10 glasses and lids and melt paraffin.

In 7-quart saucepot, mix well *grape pulp* (about 5 cups) and remaining *7½ cups sugar.* Over high heat, heat mixture, stirring constantly, until mixture comes to a rapid boil; boil rapidly 1 minute, stirring constantly. Remove from heat; stir in remaining *½ bottle fruit pectin.* With metal spoon, skim off foam.

Ladle mixture into glasses and seal with paraffin. When cold, cover glasses with lids. Makes about ten 8-ounce glasses.

FREEZER STRAWBERRY JAM

about 6 8-ounce freezerproof containers and lids
1 quart fully ripened strawberries
4 cups sugar (about 1¾ pounds)
2 tablespoons orange juice
1 1¾-ounce package fruit pectin

1. Prepare containers and lids (page 697).
2. In large bowl, with potato masher or slotted spoon, thoroughly crush berries, 1 layer at a time. Stir in sugar and orange juice until thoroughly mixed; set aside.
3. In small saucepan over medium heat, heat fruit pectin with ¾ cup water until boiling; boil 1 minute, stirring constantly. Stir pectin mixture into fruit; continue stirring 3 minutes to blend well (a few sugar crystals will remain).
4. Ladle mixture into containers to ½ inch from top; cover with lids. Let stand at room temperature for 24 hours or until set. Freeze; for use within 3 weeks, store in refrigerator. Makes about six 8-ounce jars.

FREEZER RASPBERRY JAM

about 4 8-ounce freezerproof containers and lids
4 cups fully ripened red raspberries
4 cups sugar (about 1¾ pounds)
½ 6-ounce bottle fruit pectin
2 tablespoons lemon juice

1. Prepare containers and lids (page 697).
2. With potato masher or slotted spoon, thoroughly crush raspberries, 1 layer at a time. If you like, press half of the crushed berries through a strainer to remove some of the seeds. Into large bowl, measure 2 cups fruit. Stir in sugar until most of sugar is dissolved; let stand 10 minutes.
3. In small bowl, stir fruit pectin with lemon juice until thickened; stir mixture into fruit mixture; continue stirring 3 minutes to blend well (a few sugar crystals will remain).
4. Ladle mixture into containers to ½ inch from top; cover with lids. Let stand at room temperature for 24 hours or until set. Freeze; for use within 3 weeks, store in refrigerator. Makes about four 8-ounce containers.

BLENDER ORANGE MARMALADE

about 6 8-ounce jelly glasses and lids
paraffin
3 medium oranges
2 medium lemons
5 cups sugar (about 2¼ pounds)
½ 6-ounce bottle fruit pectin

1. Prepare glasses and lids and melt paraffin(page 697).
2. With vegetable peeler, cut peel from fruit; set aside fruit. In covered blender container at high speed, blend peel and 1½ cups water until peel is chopped into small pieces; pour mixture into 7-quart saucepot. Over high heat, heat mixture to boiling. Reduce heat to low; cover and simmer 20 minutes, stirring occasionally.
3. Meanwhile, remove white membrane and seeds from fruit; blender-chop orange and lemon pulp, half at a time. Add pulp to peel mixture and heat to boiling. Reduce heat to low; cover and simmer 10 minutes. Measure 3 cups (add water if necessary to make 3 cups) and return to saucepot; stir in sugar. Over high heat, heat mixture to boiling; boil rapidly 1 minute, stirring constantly. Remove from heat; stir in fruit pectin. With metal spoon, stir and skim mixture for 7 minutes.
4. Ladle mixture into glasses and seal with paraffin. When cold, cover glasses with lids; store. Makes about six 8-ounce glasses.

LEMON-LIME: Use 5 *medium lemons* and 4 *large limes;* omit oranges. Prepare as above. Makes six 8-ounce glasses.

ALL-SEASON APPLE JELLY

about 5 8-ounce jelly glasses and lids
paraffin
4 cups bottled or canned apple juice
1 1¾-ounce package fruit pectin
5 cups sugar (about 2¼ pounds)
red food color

Prepare glasses and lids and melt paraffin (page 697).

In 7-quart saucepot or Dutch oven, mix well apple juice and fruit pectin. Over high heat, heat, stirring constantly, until mixture comes to a rapid boil; immediately stir in sugar. Stirring constantly, heat until mixture again boils rapidly; continue boiling 1 minute, stirring constantly. Remove from heat; stir in few drops red food color to tint a pretty color; with metal spoon, skim off foam.

Ladle mixture into glasses and seal with paraffin. When cold, cover glasses with lids. Makes about five 8-ounce glasses.

GRAPE: Prepare as above but substitute 2 *cups unsweetened bottled grape juice* and *1 cup water* for apple juice; use only *3½ cups sugar* and omit food color. Makes about five 8-ounce glasses.

STRAWBERRY JAM

about 8 8-ounce jelly glasses and lids
paraffin
about 2 quarts fully ripened strawberries
7 cups sugar (about 3 pounds)
¼ cup lemon juice
½ 6-ounce bottle fruit pectin

Prepare glasses and lids and melt paraffin (page 697). Hull strawberries. With potato masher, crush strawberries well, a layer at a time, to make 3¾ cups.

In 7-quart saucepot or Dutch oven, mix well strawberries, sugar and lemon juice. Over high heat, heat mixture to boiling, stirring constantly; boil rapidly 1 minute, stirring constantly. Remove from heat; stir in fruit pectin. With metal spoon, stir and skim mixture for 5 minutes to cool it slightly to prevent strawberries from floating.

Ladle mixture into glasses and seal with paraffin. When cold, cover glasses with lids. Makes about eight 8-ounce glasses.

SWEET-CHERRY JAM: Prepare as above, but for strawberries, substitute about 3 *pounds Bing or other sweet cherries.* Remove stems and seeds from cherries; with sharp knife, finely chop enough cherries to make 3½ cups fruit. Use *one 6-ounce bottle fruit pectin.* Makes about nine 8-ounce glasses.

SOUR-CHERRY JAM: Prepare as above, but for strawberries, substitute about *4 cups chopped sour cherries;* omit lemon juice. Use *one 6-ounce bottle fruit pectin.* Makes about nine 8-ounce glasses.

BLENDER SPICY-APPLE JAM

about 11 8-ounce jelly glasses and lids
paraffin
3 pounds apples
7½ cups sugar (about 3¼ pounds)
¼ cup lemon juice
1 teaspoon cinnamon
½ teaspoon allspice
½ 6-ounce bottle fruit pectin

Prepare glasses and lids and melt paraffin (page 697). Peel apples; cut each into eighths and remove core. In covered blender container at high speed, blend ½ cup water and about one-fourth of apples 15 seconds or until very finely chopped; remove to large bowl. Repeat with rest of apples and additional water.

In 8-quart saucepot, mix well 5 cups apple mixture, sugar, lemon juice, cinnamon and allspice. Over high heat, heat, stirring constantly, until mixture comes to a rapid boil; boil rapidly 1 minute, stirring constantly. Remove from heat; stir in fruit pectin. With metal spoon, skim off foam.

Ladle mixture into glasses and seal with paraffin (page 698). When cold, cover glasses with lids. Makes about eleven 8-ounce glasses.

FREEZER THREE-FRUIT JAM

about 6 8-ounce freezerproof containers and lids
1 pint fully ripened strawberries
2 medium oranges
1 8¼-ounce can crushed pineapple (1 cup)
5 cups sugar (about 2¼ pounds)
1 1¾-ounce package fruit pectin

Prepare containers and lids (page 697). In large bowl, with potato masher or slotted spoon, thoroughly crush strawberries. Grate ½ teaspoon peel from 1 orange. Remove remaining peel and white membrane from oranges; crush orange pulp thoroughly and add with grated peel to strawberries. Add pineapple with its liquid; stir in sugar until most of sugar is dissolved; set aside.

In small saucepan over medium heat, heat fruit pectin with ¾ cup water until boiling; boil 1 minute, stirring constantly. Stir pectin mixture into fruit; continue stirring 3 minutes to blend well (a few sugar crystals will remain).

Ladle mixture into containers to ½ inch from top; cover with lids. Let stand at room temperature for 24 hours or until set. Freeze; for use in 3 weeks, store in refrigerator. Makes about six 8-ounce containers.

FREEZER PLUM CONSERVE

about 6 8-ounce freezerproof containers and lids
about 2 pounds fully ripened plums
5½ cups sugar (about 2½ pounds)
⅓ cup finely chopped California walnuts
1 teaspoon grated orange peel
¼ cup orange juice
1 1¾-ounce package fruit pectin

Prepare containers and lids (page 697). Remove seeds and finely chop unpeeled plums to make 2¾ cups fruit; place in large bowl; stir in sugar, walnuts, orange peel and juice until thoroughly mixed; set aside.

In small saucepan over medium heat, heat fruit pectin with ¾ cup water to boiling; boil 1 minute, stirring constantly. Stir pectin mixture into fruit mixture; continue stirring 3 minutes to blend well (a few sugar crystals will remain).

Ladle mixture into containers to ½ inch from top; cover with lids. Let stand at room temperature for 24 hours or until set. Freeze; for use within 3 weeks, store in refrigerator. Makes about six 8-ounce containers.

CARROT MARMALADE

about 6 8-ounce jelly glasses and lids
paraffin
4 medium lemons
2 medium oranges
1 pound carrots, shredded
7 cups sugar (about 3 pounds)
½ 6-ounce bottle fruit pectin

Prepare glasses and lids and melt paraffin (page 697). Into 4-cup measure, squeeze juice from lemons. Grate orange peel; remove white membrane and dice pulp of oranges; add orange peel and pulp to lemon juice with enough carrots to make 4 cups.

In 5-quart saucepot or Dutch oven over high heat, heat carrot mixture and sugar to a rapid boil; boil rapidly 2 minutes, stirring constantly. Remove from heat; stir in fruit pectin. With metal spoon, stir and skim mixture for 5 minutes to cool it slightly to prevent carrots from floating.

Ladle mixture into glasses and seal with paraffin. When cold, cover glasses with lids. Makes about six 8-ounce glasses.

CUCUMBER MARMALADE

about 8 8-ounce jelly glasses and lids
paraffin
4 large cucumbers (about 3 pounds)
7 cups sugar (about 3 pounds)
½ cup lemon juice
¼ cup shredded lemon peel
4 drops green food color
1 6-ounce bottle fruit pectin

Prepare glasses and lids and melt paraffin (page 697). Peel cucumbers; cut lengthwise in half; remove seeds. Coarsely shred cucumbers to make 4 cups.

In 7-quart saucepot, mix well cucumbers, sugar, lemon juice and peel and food color. Over high heat, heat mixture to boiling; boil rapidly 1 minute, stirring constantly. Remove from heat; stir in fruit pectin. With metal spoon, stir and skim mixture for 5 minutes to cool slightly to prevent cucumbers from floating.

Ladle mixture into glasses and seal with paraffin. When cold, cover glasses with lids. Makes about eight 8-ounce glasses.

TOMATO CONSERVE

8 pounds ripe tomatoes
1 medium orange
1 medium lemon
¾ cup sugar
1 tablespoon salt
½ teaspoon ground cloves
2 short cinnamon sticks
about 8 8-ounce jelly glasses and lids
paraffin

On cutting board, with sharp knife, chop tomatoes. Thinly slice orange and lemon. In 8-quart saucepot,* mix well tomatoes, orange, lemon, sugar, salt, cloves, cinnamon sticks and ¼ cup water. Over medium heat, heat mixture to boiling, stirring often; cook, stirring occasionally, about 1 hour or until mixture is thickened and reduced to about one-third its original volume. (Be careful mixture does not burn.) Remove cinnamon sticks.

Meanwhile, prepare glasses and lids and melt paraffin (page 697). Ladle mixture into glasses and seal with paraffin. When cold, cover glasses with lids. Makes about eight 8-ounce glasses.

* If an aluminum saucepot is used, conserve will be darker in color but will have the same good flavor.

FREEZING

Freezing is the quickest and easiest way to preserve fresh or fresh-cooked flavor, texture, appearance and nutritive value in many foods. For best results, definite procedures must be followed, starting with the selection of the food and ending with the proper technique for heating it for serving.

For freezing, it is essential that all foods should be of top quality, since freezing only preserves quality; it does not improve it. Foods in less than peak condition deteriorate more noticeably when frozen.

Fruits and vegetables should be at the stage when they would be used fresh.

Meats should be without excessive fat. Poultry, fish, eggs and dairy products should be fresh.

The ingredients of prepared dishes should also be of top quality. Some ingredients do not freeze well and may affect the finished dish when frozen; see To Freeze and Use Prepared Food (page 713).

Seasonings may change in strength during freezing; they should be used sparingly, added at serving time if necessary.

Materials for Freezing

For long-term (more than a month) freezer storage, foods should be packaged in wraps and containers specially made for freezer use. Wrapping materials must be moisture-vapor-proof—saran film, freezer-weight plastic (polyethylene) film, heavy-duty foil, specially coated or laminated papers—are all suitable for long storage. Use masking or freezer tape to secure packages.

Containers include glass canning or freezing jars, plastic boxes with tight lids and freezer cartons of all kinds; also specially designed plastic bags which can go from freezer to boiling water for heating.

For casseroles to be reheated in oven, use ovenproof containers that can double as heating and/or serving dishes. Seal covers with masking or freezer tape (remove tape before heating). Glass ovenware can go directly from freezer to oven *only if the oven has been preheated.*

For short-term storage, ordinary wraps and bags and almost any container, even fine china, can go into the freezer. The exceptions are thin crystal; thin, brittle plastic; and wood.

For labeling packages there are special gummed labels and colored tape, crayons and pens; or write on tape used to seal packages with felt-tipped or ball-point pen.

FOODS NOT TO FREEZE

Crisp vegetables to be served raw; fresh tomatoes, raw potatoes; unblanched vegetables except onions, green peppers
Eggs in the shell; hard-cooked eggs
These dairy products: buttermilk, cream cheese, creamed cottage cheese
Unbaked yeast dough (except Freezer Breads, see Index), cake batter
These meats: seasoned uncooked meat; luncheon meats; dry, semi-dry and smoked sausage
Poultry stuffed at home, cooked or uncooked
These salads and dressings: potato salad and other mixtures with mayonnaise; mayonnaise and oil-based dressings
These desserts: pies with meringue; cakes or pies with custard or pudding filling

Steps in Freezing

Packing food: Have food and liquid cold when placing in containers. Wipe clean edges to be sealed so a tight closure can be made.

With meat, poultry and fish, leave as little air space as possible in package.

Leaving head space: With fruits and vegetables, allow room for expansion; during freezing, water expands about one-tenth of its volume. For containers with wide top openings, leave a head space of about ½ inch for pints, 1 inch for quarts when foods are packed in liquids, or are packed solidly, such as mashed pumpkin, applesauce, spinach and other greens. Fruits and vegetables packed without added sugar or liquid should be packed to ½ inch from top of all containers; loosely packed vegetables such as peas may be packed right to top.

Freeze all liquids in straight-sided, wide-mouthed glass, plastic or metal containers, leaving 1½ inches head space. Liquids frozen in amounts of a quart or more can expand enough to break a glass container.

Keep packages as thin and flat as possible, so food will freeze and thaw quickly.

Wrapping food: *"Drugstore-wrap" protects food and is easy to handle.* Tear off enough freezer wrap to go around food, such as meat, 1½ times.

Place food in center of wrap; bring ends of wrap together above food and fold over about 1 inch; crease along fold. Then fold down in same-size folds as many times as needed until wrap is tight against food.

Press wrap down at both ends to press out air. Fold ends to points; then fold each

end in about 1 inch to seal points; fold ends under, tight against package. Seal package with masking or freezer tape.

To seal food in bags with metal ties, place food in bag. Label by writing on masking or freezer tape; place on outside of bag. Press out air; twist bag top, leaving head space if recipe directs. Turn top back and fasten metal tie around doubled-over top. If using sticky-back label, place on bag.

To seal food in boil-in bags, follow manufacturer's directions.

Labeling packages: Label packages so foods can be located and identified quickly. Each label should include name of food, date of packing and type of pack if food is packed in more than one form. Add other helpful information if you like, such as number of servings, maximum storage date, any special treatment needed for thawing or serving.

Loading the freezer: Package only as much food as can be frozen in 24 hours. Too much unfrozen food put in at one time will slow rate of freezing, and spoilage or loss of quality can result. Check manufacturer's instructions for your freezer to see how much unfrozen food you can safely freeze at one time.

Fill or wrap a few packages at a time and put them in freezer before packing more, or refrigerate them until all are ready. Place them in coldest part of freezer, in contact with freezer surfaces, and space at least 1 inch apart so air can circulate freely and speed freezing. Freeze food at 0°F. or below.

To freeze a maximum load and reduce it to storage temperature, set temperature control of freezer to coldest position and leave it there 24 hours, then return it to storage position. For half the maximum load or less, 8 to 12 hours at coldest temperature setting is sufficient.

After freezing, packages can be moved close together for storage.

As packages are placed in freezer, it's a good idea to keep a running record of kinds of food, number of packages and date of freezing, also maximum storage date. Keep this list near freezer and check off items as you use them.

To Store Frozen Food

Store frozen food at 0°F. or lower; keep temperature of freezer constant.

Use food within maximum storage time recommended; see Freezer Storage, page 724. If frozen food is held longer than recommended, it will probably be safe to use, but flavor, color and/or texture may not be at their best.

If You Don't Have a Home Freezer

Food can be frozen and stored for short periods even if you don't have a separate home freezer with a constant temperature of 0°F. Keep food in the freezer compartment of a refrigerator or in the separate-door freezer of a refrigerator-freezer. In the first type, temperatures range well above 0°F. and the food should be used within a month. In the second type, limited space makes it more convenient to store a variety of often-needed items rather than large amounts of a few foods.

For short-term freezing, lightweight plastic bags or wraps or household-weight foil will give sufficient protection against drying out. Many foods such as film-wrapped meats can be frozen just as they come packaged from the store. Foods also can be frozen in plastic oven bags or wraps, ready for cooking.

Because these foods are likely to be used for last-minute cooking, package them so they will thaw quickly. Chops and chicken parts, for example, will thaw faster if wrapped separately. Straight-sided containers permit removal of food when only partially thawed; jars with necks do not.

These rules for long-term storage also apply to short-term freezing:

• Never freeze food that is past its prime; freezing doesn't destroy bacteria.

• Raw vegetables (except onions and green peppers) first must be heated in boiling water, cooled quickly and then frozen in airtight containers. If the freezer temperature is above 0°F., use them within a month.

• Label all packages.

To Thaw and Use

Some foods may be cooked right from freezer; some are best served partially thawed; some must be fully thawed before cooking or serving. Many should be thawed in the sealed package, to conserve moisture and nutrients and minimize darkening. For best results, be sure to follow recommended thawing and reheating procedures for each food.

Thaw only the amount of food that will be used at one time. Once thawed, it should be cooked or used promptly.

Any food, frozen or thawed, that is reheated in oven should be reheated at original cooking temperature. Insert a meat thermometer in center of food when food is soft enough; at about 180°F., food is hot enough to serve.

Do not use prepared dishes that have been completely thawed, warmed to room temperature and left for over two hours.

Refreezing: Food frozen raw, then cooked, may be refrozen. Frozen meats and poultry, for example, may be thawed, cooked, cooled promptly and frozen again; and casseroles made with cooked frozen vegetables may be frozen.

Baked goods such as bread, plain cake and cookies can be frozen, thawed and refrozen without loss of quality.

Partially thawed food which contains ice crystals, or thawed food that is still cold (about 40°F.) and has been held no longer than 1 or 2 days at refrigerator temperature after thawing, can be refrozen safely, though flavor and texture may deteriorate with the second freezing. As a general rule, if food is safe to eat, it is safe to refreeze. However, refrozen food should be used as soon as possible, to prevent further loss of quality.

To Freeze and Use Fruit

Preparing fruit: There are three ways to pack it for freezing: in sugar syrup, in sugar, or without added sweetening. The directions that follow for specific fruits include all methods that produce good results with that particular fruit.

Wash fruit well; prepare as recipe directs for specific kind. For best results, prepare only enough for a few containers at one time, especially if fruit is a type that darkens rapidly.

Choose pack that best fits way you intend to use the fruit. The syrup pack is preferred for fruit to be served uncooked; sugar-packed or dry-packed fruit is preferred for cooking.

To pack fruit in syrup, fill container with fruit and pour in syrup to cover, leaving head space for expansion. Press fruit down under syrup and hold in place with a small piece of crumpled waxed paper, foil or saran-film; close and seal container.

To pack fruit in sugar, cut fruit into shallow pan or bowl. Sprinkle fruit with amount of sugar specified in recipe. With large spoon or pancake turner, mix fruit and sugar gently until juice is drawn out of fruit and sugar is dissolved. Then fill container as above.

To pack fruit unsweetened, place prepared fruit in container; omit syrup or sugar. If specified in Fruit Preparation Directions (page 707), cover with water, or water containing ascorbic acid; or cover crushed or sliced fruit with its own unsweetened juice. Press fruit down into liquid as above; close and seal container.

Add an anti-darkening agent, if necessary. Fruit that darkens when cut should be treated to prevent darkening; this is indicated in directions for specific fruit where needed. Use ascorbic-acid mixture for fruit in syrup or sugar as label directs. Or use ascorbic acid, available as powder, crystals or tablets.

For syrup-packed fruit, for each 4 cups syrup, dissolve ½ teaspoon ascorbic-acid powder or crystals, or crushed tablets to make 1500 milligrams, in a little cold water; add to cold syrup.

For sugar-packed fruit, sprinkle ascorbic-acid powder, crystals or tablets dissolved in small amount of water over fruit just before adding sugar. For fruit packed unsweetened, sprinkle dissolved ascorbic acid over fruit and mix thoroughly just before packing. If fruit is packed in water, dissolve ascorbic acid in the water before covering fruit.

Thawing and serving: Thaw fruit in its sealed container, in refrigerator, at room temperature or in a pan of cold water. To serve fruit uncooked, serve as soon as thawed, preferably while a few ice crystals still remain. A 1-pound package of syrup-packed fruit will take 6 to 8 hours to thaw in refrigerator, 2 to 4 hours at room temperature and ½ to 1 hour in a pan of cold water. Sugar-packed fruit will thaw slightly faster; unsweetened fruit will take longer.

To serve fruit cooked, thaw just until pieces can be separated; then cook as for fresh fruit, adding water if needed to prevent sticking. If preparation directions call for sugar, allow for any sugar that was added when fruit was packed. If thawed fruit seems too juicy, serve only part of juice or add extra thickening.

SUGAR SYRUP FOR FREEZING

EARLY IN DAY OR DAY AHEAD:
Into large bowl, measure *4 cups cold or hot water* and *sugar* (below) for desired syrup. Stir until sugar is dissolved; refrigerate until well chilled. If adding anti-darkening agent, add it just before using syrup and stir it in gently so you don't stir in air. About ½ to ⅔ cup syrup is needed for each pint package.

MEDIUM: Use 2 *cups sugar*. Makes 5 cups.

MEDIUM-HEAVY: Use 3 *cups sugar*. Makes 5½ cups.

HEAVY: Use 4 *cups sugar*. Makes 6 cups.

FRUIT PREPARATION DIRECTIONS

APPLES: Wash, peel and core firm, crisp apples. To help prevent darkening while preparing, in large bowl, stir 1 tablespoon salt into 8 cups water until dissolved. Slice apples into mixture; remove and drain on paper towels within just a few minutes.

Pack in syrup (for serving uncooked), using medium-heavy sugar syrup; add anti-darkening agent. Or, pack in sugar (for pie, cooked dishes), adding ½ to 1 cup sugar to each 4 cups fruit. Or, pack unsweetened. Leave head space. Seal, label and freeze.

APPLESAUCE: Prepare as for canning, page 693. Refrigerate until cold. Stir in ¼ to ¾ cup sugar for each 4 cups applesauce, or to taste; or leave unsweetened. Do not add spices. Pack mixture into containers; leave head space. Seal, label and freeze.

APRICOTS: Peel apricots, or freeze unpeeled. If frozen unpeeled, to keep skins from becoming tough during freezing, heat in boiling water ½ minute, then cool in iced water; drain. Cut apricots in half and remove seeds; slice if desired.

Pack in syrup (for serving uncooked), using medium-heavy syrup; add anti-darkening agent. Or, pack in sugar (for pie, cooked dishes): Sprinkle apricots with anti-darkening agent; add ½ cup sugar to each 4 cups fruit. Leave head space. Seal, label and freeze.

BERRIES (blackberries, boysenberries, dewberries, loganberries, raspberries, youngberries): Rinse and drain berries well. Pack in syrup, using medium-heavy or heavy sugar syrup depending on sweetness of fruit. Or, pack in sugar, adding ¾ cup sugar to each 4 cups fruit. Or, pack unsweetened, adding no liquid. Leave head space. Seal, label and freeze.

BLUEBERRIES: Pack unsweetened, adding no liquid; leave head space.

CHERRIES: Remove stems and seeds (or leave sweet cherries unpitted as pits give fruit almond-like flavor).

Pack tart or sour cherries in sugar (for pie, cooked dishes), adding ¾ cup sugar to each 4 cups cherries. Pack sweet cherries in syrup (for serving uncooked); use medium-heavy sugar syrup and add anti-darkening agent. Leave head space. Seal, label and freeze.

CRANBERRIES: Sort berries and remove stems. Pack unsweetened, adding no liquid; or, pack in heavy sugar syrup. Leave head space. Seal, label and freeze.

FRUIT COCKTAIL: Use any combination of fruit that can be frozen, preparing individual fruits so pieces are fairly uniform in size: melon balls or cubes, sweet cherries, sliced or cut-up peaches and apricots, pineapple chunks or other fruits as desired.

Pack in syrup, using medium or medium-heavy sugar syrup, depending on fruit used. Leave head space. Seal, label and freeze.

GOOSEBERRIES: Remove stems and blossom ends. Pack unsweetened; or pack in heavy sugar syrup. Leave head space. Seal, label and freeze.

GRAPEFRUIT: Peel and cut into sections, removing all membrane and seeds; reserve any juice for syrup. Pack in syrup, using medium-heavy sugar syrup made with reserved juice combined with water as needed; leave head space. Seal, label and freeze.

GRAPES: Remove stems. Leave seedless grapes whole; cut grapes with seeds in half and remove seeds. Pack in syrup, using medium-heavy sugar syrup; leave head space. Seal, label and freeze.

MANGOES: Cut in half and remove seed; peel. Cut into slices. Pack unsweetened, covering fruit with water; or pack in syrup, using medium-heavy sugar syrup; leave head space. Seal, label and freeze.

MELONS (cantaloupe, casaba, crenshaw, honey ball, honeydew, Persian melon, watermelon): Cut melon in half; remove seeds; scoop into balls or remove peel and cut into slices or chunks. Pack in syrup, using medium sugar syrup; leave head space. Seal, label and freeze.

NECTARINES: Peel if desired; cut in half and remove seeds. If you like, cut into quarters or slices.

Pack in syrup, using medium-heavy sugar syrup; add anti-darkening agent and cut nectarines directly into syrup. Leave head space. Seal, label and freeze.

ORANGES: Use same directions as for Grapefruit (at left); if desired, cut oranges into slices instead of sections.

PEACHES: Peel (for better-quality frozen peaches, peel without dipping into boiling water). Cut peaches in half; remove seeds; if desired, cut into slices.

Pack in syrup, using medium-heavy sugar syrup; add anti-darkening agent and cut peaches directly into syrup. Or, pack in sugar: Sprinkle peaches with anti-darkening agent and add ⅔ cup sugar to each 4 cups fruit. Leave head space. Seal, label and freeze.

PEARS: Use firm but not hard pears; peel; cut into halves or quarters and remove cores. Pack in syrup, using medium sugar syrup; add anti-darkening agent; leave head space. Seal, label and freeze.

PERSIMMONS, NATIVE: Press persimmons through food mill or coarse sieve to remove seeds. Pack without sugar. Leave head space. Seal, label and freeze.

PINEAPPLE: Prepare pineapple (see Pineapple, page 369); cut into slices, sticks, chunks or cubes. Pack in syrup, using medium sugar syrup. Or, pack unsweetened, adding no liquid. Leave head space. Seal, label and freeze.

PLUMS: Leave whole or cut in halves and remove seeds; if desired, cut into quarters. Pack cut fruit in syrup, using medium-heavy or heavy sugar syrup; add anti-darkening agent. Leave head space. Seal, label and freeze.

Pack whole fruit unsweetened, adding no liquid. Use for jam; or, to serve uncooked, dip frozen fruit into cold water a few seconds and remove skins. Cover with medium-heavy sugar syrup and let thaw.

PRUNES, ITALIAN: Use same directions as for Plums (above).

RHUBARB: Trim stalks; cut into 1-inch or 2-inch pieces or in lengths to fit containers. Pack in syrup, using medium-heavy sugar syrup. Or, pack unsweetened, adding no liquid. Leave head space. Seal, label and freeze.

STRAWBERRIES: Cut out stem caps. Large berries are better if sliced or crushed. Berries frozen packed in sugar or syrup have better eating quality than berries packed without sweetening.

Pack in syrup, using heavy sugar syrup. Or, pack in sugar, adding ¾ cup sugar for every 4 cups berries. Or, pack unsweetened, adding no liquid; however, for better color, dissolve 1 teaspoon ascorbic acid crystals in 4 cups water; pour over strawberries before sealing. Leave head space. Seal, label and freeze.

To Freeze and Use Vegetables

Preparing vegetables: Vegetables should be at peak eating quality, fresh and tender. Lima beans, peas and other vegetables protected by pods may not need to be washed. Wash other vegetables thoroughly and drain, then sort according to size unless they are to be cut up. Prepare as directed in Vegetable Preparation Directions (page 710) for specific kind.

Except for green peppers and chopped onions, raw vegetables must be heated (blanched) before freezing to slow or stop enzyme action, soften vegetables for easier packing.

Heat in boiling water; time will vary with vegetable and size of pieces. Heat just long enough to inactivate enzymes, but not long enough to cook vegetable completely. After heating, cool vegetable at once to stop the cooking.

To heat in boiling water: Heat a small amount of vegetable at a time in a large amount of boiling water, so water boils again quickly after vegetable is added.

In an 8-quart saucepot or kettle, over high heat, heat at least 4 quarts water to a rapid boil. Meanwhile, prepare a large bowl of iced water, using about 1 pound ice. Place 1 pound of prepared vegetable in wire basket, strainer or cheesecloth bag and completely immerse in boiling water. Cover saucepot and start counting time immediately.

When specified time is up, immediately lift vegetable out and plunge into iced water until vegetable is cool. Drain thoroughly. Water for heating can be reused. Water for cooling must be cold each time. Vegetable can now be packed and frozen; a smaller vegetable or pieces can be tray-frozen before packing if desired, so units won't stick together when packed.

(To tray-freeze, spread blanched, cooled, drained vegetable or pieces in a single layer on large shallow pan so units don't touch; freeze at 0°F., about 1 to 2 hours until frozen; pack in containers leaving no head space; seal, label and freeze.)

To pack vegetables: Pack without liquid, leaving head space as directed for specific kind.

Cooking frozen vegetables: Frozen vegetables should be cooked just until tender. Since they were partially cooked prior to freezing, cooking time will be short. Most can be cooked from frozen state. They may be cooked in a small amount of water or panned (see next page).

To cook in a small amount of water: For a 1-pint package frozen vegetable (except lima beans or corn-on-the-cob), use ½ cup lightly salted water. (Use 1 cup water for lima beans; water to cover for corn-on-the-cob.) Partially thaw leafy vegetables so they can be separated for even cooking; also partially thaw corn-on-the-cob so cob will be hot when kernels are done.

In 2-quart saucepan over high heat, heat water and frozen vegetable to boiling; if necessary, separate frozen pieces with fork. Cover; reduce heat to medium and start counting time. Use timetable on next page as a guide. Simmer until vegetable is just tender. Season as desired and serve.

FROZEN VEGETABLE COOKING TIMES

Frozen Vegetable	*Minutes after Water Boils*
Asparagus	
cut up	3 to 4
spears	6 to 10
Beans, green or wax	
1-inch pieces	12 to 18
French-style	5 to 10
Beans, lima	
baby	6 to 10
large	15 to 20
Beet greens, partially thawed	6 to 12
Beets, whole	16 to 20
Broccoli	5 to 8
Brussels sprouts	4 to 9
Carrots	4 to 8
Cauliflower	4 to 8
Collards partially thawed	8 to 12
Corn	
cream-style	heat
on-the-cob, partially thawed	3 to 4
whole-kernel	3 to 5
Kale, partially thawed	8 to 12
Mixed vegetables	time needed for longest-cooking vegetable
Mustard greens, partially thawed	8 to 12
Okra	10 to 20
Peas	4 to 8
Spinach, partially thawed	4 to 6
Squash	
hard-shelled	heat
soft-skinned	6 to 8
Sweet potatoes	heat
Swiss chard, partially thawed	8 to 10

To pan, partially thaw 1 pint frozen vegetable so pieces can be separated. Place about 1 tablespoon butter, margarine or salad oil in heavy skillet with cover. If desired, add 1 or 2 tablespoons water or broth. Add vegetable; cover skillet. Over low to medium heat, cook, stirring occasionally, until vegetable is just tender.

VEGETABLE PREPARATION DIRECTIONS

ASPARAGUS: Remove scales. Leave in lengths (spears) to fit package or cut into 2-inch pieces; or lay pieces flat on cutting board and cut at an angle into thin or thick pieces. Heat in boiling water 2 minutes for small stalks, 3 minutes for medium stalks, 4 minutes for large stalks. Cool at once; drain and pack into containers, leaving no head space. If spears, alternate tips and stem ends. If container is widest at top, pack spears with tips down. Seal, label and freeze.

BEANS, GREEN AND WAX: Snap off ends; cut beans into 1- or 2-inch pieces. For "French-style" green beans, slice lengthwise into strips. Heat in boiling water 3 minutes. Cool at once; drain and tray-freeze if desired. Pack into containers, leaving ½ inch head space. Seal, label and freeze.

BEANS, LIMA: Shell; or leave beans in pods to be shelled after heating and cooling. Heat in boiling water 2 minutes for small beans or pods, 3 minutes for medium beans or pods, 4 minutes for large beans or pods. Cool at once; drain. Shell, if necessary. Tray-freeze, if desired. Pack into containers, leaving ½ inch head space. Seal, label and freeze.

BEETS: Select beets not larger than 3 inches in diameter. Cut off tops and roots. Heat in boiling water until tender, about 30 minutes for small beets, about 45 minutes for medium beets. Cool at once; drain. Peel; cut into slices or cubes. Pack into containers, leaving ½ inch head space. Seal, label and freeze.

BROCCOLI: Remove large leaves; trim ends of stalks if tough or woody; peel stalks. If necessary to remove insects, soak 30 minutes in mixture of 4 teaspoons salt to 4 quarts cold water; drain well. Cut stalks lengthwise into pieces so flowerets are not more than 1½ inches across. Heat in boiling water 3 minutes. Cool at once; drain. Pack into containers, leaving no head space. Seal, label and freeze.

BRUSSELS SPROUTS: Trim coarse outer leaves. If necessary to remove insects, soak for 30 minutes in mixture of 4 teaspoons salt to 4 quarts cold water; drain well. Sort into small, medium, large sizes. Heat in boiling water 3 minutes for small heads, 4 minutes for medium heads, 5 minutes for large heads. Cool at once; drain. Pack into containers, leaving no head space. Seal, label and freeze.

CARROTS: Scrape or peel. Leave small carrots whole; cut larger carrots into ¼-inch cubes, thin slices or lengthwise strips. Heat in boiling water 5 minutes for small whole carrots, 2 minutes for cubes, slices or strips. Cool at once; drain. Tray-freeze, if desired. Pack into containers, leaving ½ inch head space. Seal, label and freeze.

CAULIFLOWER: Remove leaves and core; separate into flowerets about 1 inch across. If necessary to remove insects, soak for 30 minutes in mixture of 4 teaspoons salt to 4 quarts cold water; drain well. Heat cauliflower in boiling water 3 minutes. Cool at once; drain. Pack into containers, leaving no head space. Seal, label and freeze.

CORN, CUT: Remove husks and silk. Heat ears in boiling water 4 minutes. Cool at once; drain. For whole-kernel corn, cut kernels from cob about ⅔ depth of kernels. Tray-freeze, if desired.

For cream-style corn, cut tip ends from kernels; with back of knife, scrape out pulp.

Pack corn into containers, leaving ½ inch head space. Seal, label and freeze.

CORN-ON-THE-COB: Remove husks and silk. Sort according to size. Heat in boiling water 3 minutes for small ears, 5 minutes for medium ears and 6 minutes for large. Cool at once; drain. Pack into containers or wrap in moisture-vapor-resistant material. Seal, label and freeze.

GREENS (beet or turnip tops, collards, kale, mustard greens, spinach, Swiss chard): Trim any tough ribs or stems. Cut leaves or Swiss chard into pieces as desired. Heat in boiling water 3 minutes for collards, 2 minutes for other greens. Cool at once; drain. Pack into containers, leaving ½ inch head space. Seal, label and freeze.

OKRA: Remove stem end without cutting into pod. Heat in boiling water 3 minutes for small pods, 4 minutes for large pods. Cool at once; drain. Leave whole, or slice crosswise. Pack into containers, leaving ½ inch head space. Seal, label and freeze.

ONIONS (except green onions): Peel and chop onions. Tray-freeze, if desired. Pack (for cooked use) into containers, leaving no head space. Seal, label and freeze.

PEAS: Shell peas. Heat in boiling water 1 minute. Cool at once; drain. Tray-freeze, if desired. Pack into containers, leaving ½ inch head space. Seal, label and freeze.

PEPPERS, GREEN: Remove seeds and membrane. If desired, chop; or cut into halves, rings or strips.

To use in uncooked foods, or chopped, freeze without heating. To use in cooked foods, and for easier packing, heat peppers in boiling water 2 minutes for rings and strips, 3 minutes for halves. Cool at once; drain. Tray-freeze chopped peppers, if desired. Pack all styles of peppers in containers, leaving no head space if peppers were not heated, ½ inch head space if heated. Seal, label and freeze.

PUMPKIN, MASHED: Cook and mash pumpkin as for canning, page 696. Place pan of mashed pumpkin in cold water; stir pumpkin occasionally until cooled. Pack into containers, leaving ½ inch head space. Seal, label and freeze.

SPINACH: See Greens, opposite.

SQUASH, HARD-SHELLED: Prepare as for Pumpkin, Mashed, above.

SQUASH, SOFT-SKINNED: Cut unpeeled squash into ½-inch slices. Heat in boiling water 3 minutes. Cool at once; drain. Pack into containers, leaving ½ inch head space. Seal, label and freeze.

SWEET POTATOES: Cook or bake sweet potatoes as in To Cook, page 345. Let stand at room temperature until cool, then peel. Leave whole, cut in halves or slices, or mash with potato masher.

To keep from darkening, in medium bowl, stir ½ cup lemon juice into 4 cups water; dip whole, halved or sliced sweet potatoes into mixture; drain. Mix 2 tablespoons orange or lemon juice into each 4 cups mashed sweet potatoes.

Pack into containers, leaving ½ inch head space. Seal, label and freeze.

To Freeze and Use Meat

Don't season meat before freezing. Remove as many bones as possible, since bones take up valuable freezer space and don't enhance the flavor of cooked meat. Prepare and package meat in quantities to be cooked at one time. If it is in store wrappings, unwrap (except for short-term freezing, page 705); remove tray or backing board and re-wrap meat with suitable freezer wrap; label and store.

Salt speeds development of rancidity in fat of frozen meat; so plan to use frozen salted meats, such as cured ham, within a short time.

Thaw meat, wrapped, in refrigerator. In general, allow about 5 to 6 hours per pound. When thawed, cook immediately or keep refrigerated; use within a day or two.

Steaks and chops: To freeze, keep individual steaks and chops separated for easier handling and faster thawing. Put two thicknesses of freezer wrap or waxed paper between individual steaks and chops, keeping meat flat; freezer-wrap, label and freeze. For storage time, see Freezer Storage, page 724.

To thaw and cook: Unwrap and thaw completely in refrigerator, then cook as for fresh meat. This must be done if steaks are to be coated with egg and crumbs, batter, or flour or crumbs, or stuffed. Steaks and chops may be cooked from frozen state if extra cooking time is allowed.

Roasts: To freeze, trim off excess fat and pad sharp bone edges with fat or freezer wrap to prevent bone from puncturing wrappings. Freezer-wrap, label and freeze.

To thaw and cook: For even cooking and browning, thaw large cuts completely, unwrapped, in refrigerator; cook as for fresh meat. If necessary, a roast may be cooked from frozen or partially frozen state, but cooking time will be one-third to one-half again as long, and outside will be crusty by the time meat is done on the inside.

For best results, use a meat thermometer, but if meat is frozen or partially frozen, insert it when meat is about half done.

Ground meat: To freeze, freeze in bulk or as patties. Separate patties for freezing as for Steaks and Chops, above; freezer-wrap, label and freeze.

To thaw and cook: Thaw, wrapped, in refrigerator. Cook as for fresh meat. Patties may be broiled, baked or pan-broiled from frozen state, allowing extra time.

To Freeze and Use Poultry

Never freeze home-prepared stuffed poultry, either raw or cooked. Freeze raw poultry unstuffed; if you want stuffing, make it and stuff thawed bird just before cooking. Always remove stuffing from cooked bird within 1½ hours after roasting; cool, freezer-wrap and freeze separately.

To freeze poultry, rinse and drain bird thoroughly before packaging. Remove giblets and freeze separately since they do not keep as long as the bird. Freeze giblets and bird as below. For storage times, see Freezer Storage, page 724.

To thaw, thaw poultry, wrapped, in refrigerator, or immerse package in cold water until thawed. Chicken to be stewed need not be thawed.

To cook, as soon as possible after thawing, cook as for fresh poultry. Keep refrigerated until time to cook.

See also To Freeze Poultry and To Thaw Poultry, pages 171–172.

Whole bird: Remove giblets; tie legs and wings close to body. Freezer-wrap bird using drugstore-wrap; or place in large freezer bag, pressing out air; seal, label and freeze.

Halved bird: Place two pieces of freezer wrap between halves of bird for easy separating, then freezer-wrap entire bird; label and freeze. Or, freezer-wrap and freeze halves separately.

Cut-up bird: Press pieces together in compact pile in center of strip of freezer wrap (for easy separation, wrap pieces individually first); freezer-wrap, using drugstore-wrap, label and freeze. Or, pack in freezer bag, pressing out air, or container.

To save freezer space, freeze only meaty pieces (breast, legs, wings). Cook bony pieces (neck, back, wing tips) to make broth; remove meat from bony pieces and freeze in broth for later use in casseroles, soups, similar dishes.

Giblets: Rinse and drain giblets; freezer-wrap, label and freeze.

To Freeze and Use Fish

Rinse dressed fish thoroughly and drain. Small fish may be frozen whole; large fish, whole, or cut into fillets or steaks.

To freeze, drugstore-wrap whole fish in freezer wrap; or package in freezer bag, pressing out air.

Small whole fish may be frozen in water in waxed cartons or freezer containers. Line cartons with plastic bag; place fish in bag and cover fish with cold water, leaving head space (page 704). Seal, label and freeze.

Fillets and steaks are best if dipped in a brine before wrapping. To make brine, dissolve ⅔ cup salt in 4 quarts water. Dip fish steaks and fillets in mixture for ½ minute; drain. Freezer-wrap pieces individually; package several wrapped pieces in larger piece of freezer wrap, seal, label and freeze. For storage time, see Freezer Storage, page 724.

To use, thaw fish, wrapped, in refrigerator; or immerse package in cold water; thaw just enough to handle or separate pieces; cook promptly as for fresh fish.

To Freeze and Use Shellfish

For storage times, see Freezer Storage, page 724.

To use, leave shellfish in container and thaw in refrigerator or in cold water just until it can be separated or handled. Serve or cook promptly.

Shrimp: Shrimp is best frozen uncooked since cooked shrimp may toughen during storage. Remove heads if necessary; shell and devein shrimp; or devein, leaving shell on. Pack shrimp in freezer bags, pressing out air, or in containers. Seal, label and freeze.

Crab and Lobster: Cook seafood completely; cool completely and remove from shells. Pack dry meat in freezer bags, pressing out air, or in containers. Seal, label and freeze.

Clams, Oysters and Scallops: Scallops are ready to freeze when purchased. Pack into containers. Prepare brine: In 3 cups cold water, dissolve 1 tablespoon salt. Pour over scallops to cover. Seal, label and freeze.

Wash and shuck clams and oysters; pack into containers. Prepare brine as for scallops, or cover seafood with its own liquor from shucking. Seal, label and freeze.

To Freeze and Use Game

See Game and Wild Birds, page 247.

To Freeze Dairy Products

See Freezer Storage, page 725.

To Freeze and Use Prepared Food

When you cook food to freeze, cook it until just tender; it will cook further when reheated for serving. Meat should be tender but still firm; vegetables and macaroni products should be slightly underdone.

Keep in mind that some seasonings change during storage; pepper, onion, cloves, synthetic vanilla become stronger; salt loses flavor (but don't oversalt). Season food well but not heavily, and plan to add more during reheating if necessary.

If one ingredient in a dish doesn't freeze well, it may be possible to freeze the food without it and add it when reheating the dish for serving.

Avoid hard-cooked egg whites, potatoes or mayonnaise in mixtures. These foods change texture in storage and can affect the reheated food adversely. Sauces thickened with flour may separate after thawing; stir foods with these mixtures in them during reheating or use canned condensed soup, diluted with a little milk, instead of cream sauce; it won't separate.

Before freezing, chill cooked food in iced water or in refrigerator. Package food in meal-size amounts. If food is to be frozen in a covered dish for longer than a week, and cover doesn't fit tightly, seal cover to dish with freezer tape; or freezer-wrap covered dish and seal package with tape.

To save dishes, when freezing casserole mixtures, first line casserole with foil, extending it slightly above rim to serve as handle for removing food later; then fill with mixture. Freeze, uncovered; remove frozen block of food, freezer-wrap and store. To use, unwrap food and peel off foil; place food in casserole and reheat.

Specific information for freezing prepared foods will be found as follows:

Breads: Quick, page 415; Yeast, page 439
Cakes, page 528
Cookies, page 554
Desserts, page 478
Ice Creams and Sherbets, page 572
Pies, page 502
Rice: See Tips on Using Rice, page 298
Sandwiches, page 463

Information on freezing some other foods is as follows:

Baked apples: Prepare and bake as on page 354; cool. Pack in containers. Seal, label and freeze.

To use within 4 months, thaw in container in refrigerator or at room temperature.

Baked beans: Prepare as usual, but undercook slightly; cool. Pack in containers; cover with sauce. Seal, label and freeze.

To reheat within 2 to 4 weeks: Heat mixture in double boiler or saucepan over low heat, or electric skillet at low temperature setting, or baking dish in oven. Stir mixture occasionally to speed thawing and, if over direct heat, prevent scorching.

Braised chops: Freeze and reheat as for Baked Beans (above).

Chili con carne: Freeze and reheat as for Baked Beans (above).

Chop suey, Chow mein: Freeze and reheat as for Baked Beans (above).

Cranberry-Orange Relish: Spoon Cranberry-Orange Relish or any variations on page 384 into containers, leaving head space (page 704). Seal, label and freeze.

To use within 8 to 12 months: Thaw in container in refrigerator.

Goulash: Freeze and reheat as for Baked Beans (above).

Lasagna: Complete casserole but don't bake; cool. Place cover on dish and seal with freezer tape; or freezer-wrap dish; or place dish in freezer bag, pressing out air. Seal, label and freeze.

To use within 1 month: Preheat oven to 350°F.; remove tape or wrapping; bake frozen mixture, covered, about 1½ hours or until done.

Macaroni and cheese: Freeze and bake as for Lasagna (above).

Meat balls in gravy or sauce: Freeze and reheat as for Baked Beans (above).

Meat loaf: Freeze baked or unbaked. Freezer-wrap uncooked or cooled, baked loaf (in pan, if desired). Seal, label and freeze.

To use within 1 to 2 months: Preheat oven to 350°F. Unwrap frozen uncooked loaf; bake about 2 hours or until done.

Unwrap frozen baked loaf; bake about 1 hour or until heated through.

To serve baked loaf cold, thaw, wrapped, in refrigerator.

Potatoes, stuffed and baked: Make Twice-Baked Potatoes, page 339, but don't bake after filling. Cool; freezer-wrap individually in foil; freeze, then pack in freezer bags. Seal, label and freeze.

To use within 2 to 4 weeks: Preheat oven to 400°F. Unwrap frozen potatoes; place in baking dish. Bake 40 minutes or until heated through.

Roast meats: Bake or pot-roast beef, fresh pork, lamb, veal as usual; cool. Leave meat in as large pieces as possible; trim excess fat. Freezer-wrap meat. Or slice; pack slices in freezer container and cover with gravy, leaving head space. Seal, label and freeze.

To use within 2 to 3 months: Preheat oven to 325°F.; unwrap frozen large pieces and bake about 1 hour or until heated through. Bake slices in gravy 30 to 45 minutes until hot and bubbly.

To serve large pieces cold, thaw, wrapped, in refrigerator.

Soups: To save space, freeze ingredients for soup as they accumulate; combine with liquid to prepare soup before using; omit milk, potatoes. If soup is leftover, cool mixture; package in meal-size amounts in containers. Seal, label and freeze.

To reheat within 1 to 3 months: Place frozen soup in saucepan and heat over low heat. Add liquid, if needed; if potatoes were omitted, cook first in liquid before adding to soup. Or, thaw soup in refrigerator and reheat.

Spanish rice: Freeze and bake as for Lasagna (above).

Stew: Freeze and reheat as for Baked Beans (above).

Stuffed peppers: Fill halved or whole raw, unheated green peppers with stuffing. Freezer-wrap individually, or place in containers. Seal, label and freeze.

To use within 3 months: Preheat oven to 350°F. Unwrap frozen peppers; place in covered baking dish. Bake until stuffing is heated through or cooked.

Swiss steak: Freeze and reheat as for Baked Beans (above).

Special Freezer Recipes

Many of the recipes throughout this book are suitable for freezing. Here are some planned especially to make use of your freezer. Most have suggestions for serving as soon as they are made, if you prefer.

FREEZER TOMATO SAUCE

3 tablespoons salad oil
4 medium onions, chopped
3 small garlic cloves
4 29-ounce cans tomatoes
4 6-ounce cans tomato paste
1 pound mushrooms, sliced
1 cup chopped parsley
3 tablespoons sugar
3 tablespoons salt
4 teaspoons oregano leaves
2 bay leaves

UP TO 3 MONTHS AHEAD:
In large saucepot over medium-high heat, in hot salad oil, cook onions and garlic until onions are tender, about 10 minutes; discard garlic. Add remaining ingredients; heat to boiling. Reduce heat to low; cover and simmer 2 hours. Discard bay leaves.

If you like, reserve some of sauce to use same day; refrigerate until ready to use.

Ladle sauce into 1-pint freezer containers, leaving at least 1 inch head space. Cover and refrigerate until chilled. Label and freeze. Makes about 8 pints sauce.

FREEZER FRESH TOMATO SAUCE: Prepare sauce as above but substitute *1 peck fresh tomatoes* (about 13 pounds), peeled and cut in large chunks, for canned tomatoes. Makes about 10 pints sauce.

SAUCY BEEF PATTIES

2 pounds ground chuck
2 teaspoons salt
1 pint Freezer Tomato Sauce,* thawed (above)
8 hamburger buns, split

ABOUT 30 MINUTES BEFORE SERVING:
In large bowl, mix ground chuck with salt; shape into 8 patties. In 12-inch skillet over medium-high heat, brown patties well on both sides. Pour tomato sauce over patties; heat to boiling. Reduce heat to medium; simmer 15 minutes or until bubbly hot.

Place patties in buns, open-face style, and spoon on sauce. Makes 8 servings.

* Or, use *one 15-ounce jar marinara sauce.*

SPAGHETTI-BEEF SKILLET

1 16-ounce package spaghetti
1 pound ground lean beef
3 pints Freezer Tomato Sauce,* thawed (above)
1 8-ounce package American cheese, cut up
1½ cups halved, pitted ripe olives

ABOUT 1 HOUR BEFORE SERVING:
Cook spaghetti as label directs; drain. Meanwhile, in 12-inch skillet over medium heat, cook ground beef until browned. Stir in tomato sauce, cheese and olives and cook, stirring often, until cheese melts. Stir in spaghetti; heat. Makes 8 servings.

* Or, use *three 15-ounce jars marinara sauce.*

SHORT-CUT LASAGNA

9 lasagna noodles
1 pound ground beef
2 pints Freezer Tomato Sauce,* thawed (page 715)
1 16-ounce container ricotta cheese (2 cups)
1 pound mozzarella cheese, thinly sliced

ABOUT 1¼ HOURS BEFORE SERVING:
Cook lasagna noodles as label directs; drain; return to pan with a little cold water to prevent sticking. When ready to use, drain noodles well on paper towels.

Meanwhile, preheat oven to 350°F. In 10-inch skillet over medium-high heat, cook ground beef until well browned; pour off drippings. Add tomato sauce and heat to boiling.

In 13″ by 9″ baking pan, spread 1 cup meat mixture; lay 3 noodles lengthwise in pan; spread with 1 cup meat mixture, then half of ricotta cheese; arrange one-third of mozzarella slices evenly on top. Repeat layers. Top cheese with remaining 3 noodles, rest of meat mixture and mozzarella. Bake 30 minutes or until bubbling. Let stand 10 minutes for easier serving. Makes 6 generous servings.

* Or, use *two 15-ounce jars marinara sauce.*

VEGETABLES IN FONDUE SAUCE

3 9-ounce packages frozen French-style or cut green beans (5½ cups)
¼ cup butter or margarine
½ pound mushrooms, sliced
1 large onion, thinly sliced
1 10½-ounce can condensed cream-of-chicken soup
1 8-ounce package process Swiss cheese, shredded (2 cups)
¼ cup dry white wine
3 tablespoons diced, drained pimento

UP TO 1 MONTH AHEAD:
In 5-quart Dutch oven, prepare beans as label directs but cook just until tender-crisp; drain thoroughly. Set beans aside. Meanwhile, line 12″ by 8″ baking dish or shallow 2-quart casserole with foil.

In same Dutch oven over medium heat, in hot butter or margarine, cook mushrooms and onion until tender, about 5 minutes, stirring frequently. Add undiluted soup and cheese; cook, stirring constantly, until cheese is melted and smooth. Remove Dutch oven from heat; stir in beans and remaining ingredients; pour into casserole. Chill, then freeze. When frozen, remove bean mixture from casserole. Freezer-wrap, label and freeze.

ABOUT 1¾ HOURS BEFORE SERVING:
Preheat oven to 350°F. Peel foil from frozen vegetable mixture; place mixture in original baking dish; cover and bake 1½ hours or until hot and bubbly, stirring mixture after baking 1 hour. Makes 12 servings.

TO MAKE AND SERVE: Preheat oven to 350°F. Prepare as above but cover and bake casserole 45 minutes or until hot and bubbly.

CHICKEN BREASTS EMMENTAL

¼ cup all-purpose flour
1 teaspoon paprika
6 whole medium chicken breasts, halved
¼ cup butter or margarine
2½ teaspoons salt
¼ cup medium sherry
2 teaspoons cornstarch
1½ cups half-and-half
1 teaspoon grated lemon peel
1 tablespoon lemon juice
1 cup shredded Swiss cheese for topping
2 tablespoons chopped parsley for garnish

UP TO 3 MONTHS AHEAD:
On waxed paper, combine flour with paprika; use to coat chicken. In 12-inch skillet over medium heat, in hot butter or margarine, cook chicken, a few pieces at a time, until browned on all sides. Return chicken to skillet; sprinkle with salt; add ¼ cup water. Reduce heat to low; cover and simmer 20 minutes or until chicken breasts are almost tender. Arrange chicken breasts in freezer- and ovenproof 13″ by 9″ baking dish.

In cup, stir sherry into cornstarch until smooth; stir into drippings in skillet until blended. Over medium-low heat, stir in half-and-half, lemon peel and juice and cook, stirring constantly, until sauce is thickened; pour over chicken. Refrigerate until cold. Freezer-wrap, label and freeze.

TO THAW AND HEAT:
To thaw, let dish stand, wrapped, overnight in refrigerator until almost thawed but still cold.

To reheat, bake chicken, covered, in oven preheated to 350°F. 35 minutes or until sauce is bubbling and hot. Uncover and sprinkle chicken with cheese; bake about 3 minutes longer or until cheese is melted. Garnish with parsley. To serve, spoon sauce over chicken. Makes 12 servings.

TO MAKE AND SERVE: About 1 hour ahead, prepare as above but cook chicken breasts 30 minutes or until fork-tender; remove to broil-and-serve platter; set aside. Meanwhile, preheat broiler, if manufacturer directs. Prepare sauce as directed and pour over chicken. Sprinkle with cheese; broil until cheese is melted, about 2 minutes.

CURRIED BAKED CAULIFLOWER

1 large head cauliflower
½ teaspoon salt
1 10½-ounce can condensed cream-of-chicken soup
1 4-ounce package shredded Cheddar cheese (1 cup)
⅓ cup mayonnaise
1 teaspoon curry powder
¼ cup dried bread crumbs
2 tablespoons butter or margarine, melted

UP TO 1 MONTH AHEAD:
Break cauliflower into flowerets. In covered 2-quart saucepan over medium-low heat, in 1 inch boiling water, cook cauliflower with salt 10 minutes; drain well.

Meanwhile, in 2-quart freezer- and ovenproof casserole, stir together undiluted soup, cheese, mayonnaise and curry powder. Add cauliflower; mix well. Toss bread crumbs in melted butter; sprinkle on top. Freezer-wrap, label and freeze.

TO THAW AND HEAT:
To thaw, let dish stand, wrapped, in refrigerator overnight. To reheat, about 50 minutes before serving, preheat oven to 350°F. Bake casserole 40 minutes or until hot and bubbly. Makes 8 to 10 servings.

TO MAKE AND SERVE: About 1 hour before serving, preheat oven to 350°F. and prepare as above but bake 30 minutes.

FROZEN CHOCOLATE ROLL

5 eggs, separated, at room temperature
confectioners' sugar
3 tablespoons cocoa
dash salt
Mocha Cream (below)

UP TO 1 MONTH AHEAD:
1. Preheat oven to 400°F. Grease 15½" by 10½" jelly-roll pan; line with waxed paper; grease and flour paper.
2. In large bowl, with mixer at high speed, beat egg whites until soft peaks form; beating at high speed, gradually sprinkle in ½ cup confectioners' sugar; beat until sugar is completely dissolved; set aside.
3. In small bowl, with same beaters and with mixer at high speed, beat egg yolks until thick and lemon-colored; at low speed, beat in ½ cup confectioners' sugar, cocoa and salt. With wire whisk or rubber spatula, gently fold yolk mixture into beaten whites until blended. Spread batter evenly in pan and bake 15 minutes or until top springs back when lightly touched with finger. Sprinkle clean cloth towel with confectioners' sugar.
4. When cake is done, immediately loosen edges from sides of pan; invert cake onto towel. Gently peel paper from cake. Roll cake and towel from a narrow end, jelly-roll fashion. Cool on wire rack.
5. When cake is cool, unroll. Trim crusts from cake. Spread Mocha Cream over cake almost to edges. Starting at a short end, roll up cake without towel. Place, seam side down, on chilled platter. Freezer-wrap, label and freeze.

TO SERVE:
Unwrap cake and let stand 15 minutes for easier slicing; sprinkle with confectioners' sugar. Makes 10 servings.

MOCHA CREAM: In medium bowl with mixer at medium speed, beat *⅓ cup packed light brown sugar, 2 tablespoons instant coffee powder* and *2 cups heavy or whipping cream* just until soft peaks form.

CHICKEN SCAMPI

2 2-pound broiler-fryers, cut up
½ cup all-purpose flour
¼ cup salad oil
4 teaspoons salt
¼ teaspoon pepper
1 garlic clove
⅛ teaspoon poultry seasoning
⅛ teaspoon seafood seasoning
pinch rosemary, crushed
1 pound frozen shelled, deveined shrimp

UP TO 3 MONTHS AHEAD:
On waxed paper, coat chicken with flour. In 12-inch skillet over medium heat, in hot salad oil, cook chicken, a few pieces at a time, until browned. Spoon off fat; return chicken pieces to skillet.

Sprinkle chicken with salt and pepper; add 1¼ cups water, garlic, poultry seasoning, seafood seasoning and rosemary; heat to boiling. Reduce heat to low; cover and cook 30 minutes or until chicken is fork-tender, turning occasionally. Discard garlic. Transfer chicken to 13″ by 9″ freezer- and ovenproof pan. Freezer-wrap, label and freeze.

ABOUT 2 HOURS BEFORE SERVING:
Preheat oven to 350°F. Add frozen shrimp to frozen chicken. Cover pan and bake 1½ hours or until chicken is piping hot. Makes 8 servings.

TO MAKE AND SERVE: About 1 hour and 15 minutes ahead, thaw shrimp. In cook-and-serve skillet, prepare chicken as above but add thawed shrimp to skillet during last 10 minutes of cooking time.

FROZEN STRAWBERRY CREAM

4 cups sour cream
1⅓ cups sugar
1 tablespoon lemon juice
2 pints strawberries

UP TO 1 MONTH AHEAD:
In 13″ by 9″ baking pan, stir sour cream, sugar and lemon juice until mixed.

In covered blender container, with blender at medium speed, blend strawberries, about one-third at a time until pureed; stir into sour-cream mixture, mixing well. Cover pan with plastic wrap or foil and freeze until almost firm, about 2 hours.

Spoon mixture into chilled, large bowl; with mixer at medium speed, beat until mixture is smooth. Return mixture to pan. Cover, label and freeze until mixture is firm. Makes about 4 pints or 12 servings.

FROZEN CANTALOUPE CREAM: Prepare as above but add *1 teaspoon salt* and omit lemon juice; substitute *1 very ripe large cantaloupe,* peeled and seeded, for strawberries (about 4 cups pureed cantaloupe).

FROZEN CHOCO-NUT TORTONI

2 egg whites, at room temperature
sugar
2 cups heavy or whipping cream
2 teaspoons vanilla or rum extract
1 6-ounce package semisweet-chocolate pieces (1 cup)
2 teaspoons shortening
½ cup finely chopped toasted almonds

UP TO 1 MONTH AHEAD:
1. In small bowl with mixer at high speed, beat egg whites until soft peaks form; beating at high speed, gradually sprinkle in ¼ cup sugar, beating until sugar is completely dissolved.
2. In large bowl, with same beaters and with mixer at medium speed, beat cream with ¼ cup sugar and vanilla until soft peaks form. With rubber spatula, gently fold in beaten whites. Pour into 9″ by 9″ baking pan; freeze until frozen about ½ inch from pan edges.
3. Meanwhile, in double boiler over hot, not boiling, water, melt chocolate pieces with shortening; cool. Place a paper cup in each of 12 muffin-pan cups.
4. In large bowl, with mixer at medium speed, beat partially frozen mixture until smooth but still frozen; fold in chocolate mixture and almonds. Spoon mixture into paper cups; freeze until firm. Remove cups from muffin pan; freezer-wrap or place in freezer bag, pressing out air. Seal, label and freeze.

TO SERVE:
Let cups stand, unwrapped, at room temperature 15 minutes to soften for easier eating. Makes 12 servings.

Storage

Careful shopping does much to assure that the foods you buy are at the peak of their goodness and wholesomeness. Once you bring them home, keeping them wholesome is up to you. Storing them properly and using them in time means that, when served, they'll be safe to eat and at the peak of their flavor, texture and nutritional value.

Three types of bacteria cause most cases of food poisoning: *Salmonella, Staphylococcus* and *Streptococcus.* While present at all times, they do not normally cause trouble until certain conditions cause them to multiply rapidly (in a matter of hours) to dangerous levels. The contributing factors to bacterial growth are temperature (between 50° and 125°F.) and time.

To prevent bacterial growth, and consequent danger of food poisoning, you should: Work with well-scrubbed hands, utensils, dishes and work surfaces; cook or serve food as soon as possible after removing it from storage; and refrigerate food immediately after the meal is over. Always observe these rules, since it's often not possible to tell by taste or smell whether food has become contaminated.

Foods that need special care: Some foods need special attention in preparing and in storing. Bacteria grow readily in meat, poultry, fish and seafood, creamed mixtures, mayonnaise, puddings and stuffings.

Keep fresh meat, fish and poultry refrigerated.

Don't stuff poultry the night before roasting; the cold stuffing may not heat up to a safe temperature when you cook the bird. Never refrigerate cooked poultry or meat with the stuffing inside. Remove the stuffing and refrigerate it, any broth or gravy and the meat or poultry, each in a separate container.

Refrigerate custard, cream and meringue-topped pies and desserts with custard fillings (cream puffs, cream pies) after they have cooled slightly; keep them refrigerated. If you carry these foods on picnics, keep them in a cooler; do the same with salads and sandwiches made with salad dressings containing eggs or milk products and only a little vinegar or other acid.

If you've bought cracked eggs, use them only when they will be thoroughly cooked (baked or hard-cooked); *Salmonella,* which may be present on shells, can contaminate cracked eggs.

Refreezing frozen foods: It's safe to refreeze virtually all partially thawed foods if they still have ice crystals on them and are still firm in the center. However, many foods (ice cream and uncooked baked goods, for example) will not maintain top quality.

Meat, fish and poultry purposely thawed in the refrigerator and kept no more than one day may be refrozen. However, don't refreeze pies, stews and other combination dishes that have been thawed.

Foods thawed accidentally in the freezer over a period of days (as in the case of a power failure) should not be refrozen unless they still have ice crystals. If food is completely thawed (on purpose or by accident), warmed to room temperature and left for more than two hours, throw it out. The exceptions are fruit and juice concentrates; these ferment when spoiled. If the flavor is "off," discard the fruit or fruit juice.

Cupboard Storage

Temperature: Store food in coldest cabinets—not over range or close to refrigerator's exhaust. For large amounts of potatoes, onions and other similar vegetables, and for long storage of canned foods, use coolest spots such as the basement or cellar.

Time: Though most staples and canned foods will keep indefinitely, buy no more than you expect to use in the storage times recommended below. While foods will be safe beyond these recommended times, flavor will fade and texture wilt. Date foods, then check cabinets every six months and use up the oldest items, putting the newer foods at the back.

Buying: Buy the freshest-looking packages; messy or shopworn labels often indicate older stock. Don't buy cans with swollen ends—the food has gone bad. Dented cans are all right provided they haven't been punctured.

Home-canned foods: Use first-quality foods and the best techniques. See pages 692–693. Keep foods tightly closed or covered in a cool, dry place away from direct light.

GENERAL

Baking powder—18 months
Baking soda—18 months
Bouillon cubes, envelopes—1 year
Catchup, opened—1 month
    For longer storage, keep refrigerated.
Chocolate, cooking—1 year
Coconut
  unopened—1 year
  opened—see Refrigerator Storage
Coffee, canned
  unopened—1 year
  opened—see Refrigerator Storage
Coffee, instant
  unopened—6 months
  opened—2 weeks
Coffee lighteners, powdered form
  opened—6 months
Flour—1 year
    After opening, transfer to airtight container.
Gelatin
  flavored—18 months
  unflavored—18 months
Herbs and spices
  herbs—6 months
  ground spices—6 months
  whole spices—1 year
    Keep in glass or metal containers; if they are in paper packages, transfer to airtight containers. Red spices are most perishable; keep in refrigerator.
Honey—1 year
Jams—1 year
Macaroni and macaroni products—1 year
    After opening, transfer to airtight container.
Nonfat dry milk—6 months
    After opening, transfer to airtight container.
Noodles—6 months
    After opening, transfer to airtight container.
Nuts, shelled
  unopened—1 month
  opened—see Refrigerator Storage
Olive oil—1 month
    For longer storage, refrigerate. Olive oil will solidify but softens again quickly at warm room temperature.
Onions—1 to 2 weeks
    Keep dry, in the dark at coolest room temperature.

Parmesan cheese, grated
opened—1 month
unopened—4 months
Parmesan cheese, shredded—see Refrigerator Storage
Pasteurized process cheese, cheese food and cheese spread
opened—2 to 4 weeks
unopened—2 months
Check label directions. Some require refrigeration. See Refrigerator Storage for more information.
Peanut butter—6 months
Potatoes, sweet and white—1 to 2 weeks
Keep dry, in the dark, at coolest room temperature.
Rice
brown—6 months
white—2 years
wild—6 months
Rutabagas—1 to 2 weeks
Keep dry, in the dark, at coolest room temperature.
Salad dressings
opened—See Refrigerator Storage
unopened—3 months
Salad oil—1 to 3 months
For longer storage, refrigerate.
Shortening, solid—8 months
Soft drinks—3 months
Spaghetti, macaroni, etc. (except noodles) —1 year
After opening, transfer to airtight container.
Squash, hard-shelled—several months, use as desired
Sugar
brown—4 months
confectioners'—4 months
granulated—2 years
After opening, transfer to airtight container.
Syrup—1 year
Tea
bags—6 months
instant—1 year
loose—6 months
After opening, transfer tea bags and loose tea to airtight containers.
Worcestershire, hot pepper sauces—2 years
Yeast, active dry—see expiration date on label

CANNED AND DRIED FOODS

Fish—1 year
Fruits
canned—1 year
dried—6 months
After opening, transfer to airtight container.
Gravies
canned—1 year
mixes—6 months
Meat—1 year
Milk
evaporated—1 year
sweetened condensed—1 year
Olives, unopened—1 year
Pickles, unopened—1 year
Poultry—1 year
Sauces
canned—1 year
mixes—6 months
Soups
canned—1 year
mixes—6 months
Vegetables
canned—1 year
mixes—6 months
After opening, transfer to airtight container.

PACKAGED PREPARED FOODS AND MIXES

Bread—5 to 7 days
Bread crumbs—6 months
Cakes, prepared—1 to 2 days
Refrigerate if cake has butter-cream, whipped-cream, cream-cheese, sour-cream or custard frosting or filling.
mixes—1 year
Casserole mixes—18 months
Cereals, ready-to-eat and cooked types—2 to 3 months
Crackers—3 months
After opening, transfer to airtight container.
Frostings, canned and packaged mixes
unopened—8 months
Hot-roll mix—18 months
Instant breakfast or metered-calorie products—6 months
Pancake or baking mix—6 months
After opening, transfer to airtight container.

Piecrust mix—8 months
Pies and pastries, prepared—2 to 3 days
Refrigerate if pie has whipped-cream, custard or chiffon filling.
Potato mixes—18 months
After opening, transfer to airtight container.
Pudding mixes—1 year
Rice mixes—6 months
Toaster pop-ups—3 months
Whipped-topping mix—1 year

Refrigerator Storage

Temperature: From 34°F. to 40°F. is best. Above 40°F., foods spoil rapidly. Check temperature with a refrigerator thermometer or an outdoor thermometer.

Time: Use foods quickly; don't depend on maximum storage time.

Wraps: Use foil, plastic wrap or bags, airtight containers. When meat, poultry or fish is bought in a plastic-wrapped package, loosen ends of package to dry surface moisture. Bacteria grow faster on moist surfaces.

General care: Clean refrigerator regularly to cut down food odors. Remove spoiled foods immediately so that decay won't be passed on to other foods.

MEAT, FISH AND POULTRY

Store in coldest part of refrigerator or in meat keeper. If it comes prepackaged for self-service, leave in original wrapper. If it is not prepackaged, wrap loosely, since partial drying of surface increases keeping quality. (Exception: Ground meats and variety meats should always be tightly wrapped.)

Meats, fresh
Chops—2 days
Ground meats—1 to 2 days
Roasts—2 days
Steaks—2 days
Stew meat—1 to 2 days
Variety meats (liver, heart, etc.)—1 to 2 days

Fish and Shellfish
Cleaned fish, steaks and fillets—1 day
Clams and lobster tails in the shell—2 days
Shucked clams, oysters, shrimp, scallops—1 day

Poultry
ready-to-eat chicken, turkey, goose or duck, whole or cut-up—2 days

Meats, Smoked and Cured
The times below are for opened packages. Keep them tightly wrapped and store in coldest part of refrigerator or meat keeper. Unopened vacuum packs keep about 2 weeks. Unopened canned hams keep 6 months.
Bacon—5 to 7 days
Corned beef—5 to 7 days
Dried beef—10 to 12 days
Frankfurters—4 to 5 days
Hams, whole and halves—1 week
Luncheon meat, sliced—2 to 3 days
Sausage
dry and semi-dry, in whole pieces—2 to 3 weeks
fresh—2 to 3 days
smoked, uncooked—2 to 3 days

FRUITS AND VEGETABLES

Sort fruits and vegetables, discarding any that are bruised or decayed. Do not wash before storing—moisture encourages spoilage. Store fruits and vegetables in original package in vegetable section of refrigerator. Keep fruit juices tightly covered.

Fruits
Apples, citrus fruits, cranberries, grapes—1 to 2 weeks
Apricots, bananas, blueberries, cherries, melons—2 to 3 days
Avocados, nectarines, peaches, pears, plums, rhubarb—3 to 5 days
Blackberries, figs, pineapples, raspberries, strawberries—1 to 2 days
Citrus juices (bottled, reconstituted frozen, canned and opened)—6 days

Vegetables
Artichokes, Chinese cabbage, cardoon, cauliflower, celeriac, celery, cucumbers,

leeks, Chinese okra, green peppers, radishes, salsify, soft-skinned squashes, water chestnuts—3 to 5 days
Asparagus, bean sprouts, green and wax beans, beet tops, broccoli, Brussels sprouts, corn, eggplant, French endive, greens, kale, kohlrabi, lettuce, lima beans, mushrooms, okra, green onions, peas, spinach, tomatoes, watercress—1 to 2 days
Beets, green and red cabbage, carrots, ginger root, parsnips, turnips—1 to 2 weeks
Onions, potatoes, rutabagas, sweet potatoes, hard-shelled squash—see Cupboard Storage

DAIRY PRODUCTS

Butter or margarine—1 to 2 weeks
Keep tightly wrapped or covered.
Buttermilk, sour cream, yogurt—1 to 2 weeks
Store unopened sour-cream and yogurt containers upside down to prevent surface drying. Store opened containers tightly covered.
Cheese (Cheddar, Edam, Swiss, etc.)
unopened—3 to 6 months
opened, slices—2 weeks
opened, whole pieces—3 to 4 weeks
cottage, ricotta—5 days
cream, Neufchâtel—2 weeks
pasteurized process cheese, cheese food, cheese spread
unopened—2 months
opened—2 to 4 weeks
Check label directions for storage. Some should not be refrigerated.
Parmesan cheese, shredded; Romano
unopened—4 months
opened—1 month
See Cupboard Storage for *grated* Parmesan cheese.
Cream, all kinds—3 days
Keep tightly closed or covered. Don't return unused cream to original container; refrigerate separately to use first.
Coffee lighteners, liquid—3 weeks
Dips, sour-cream, etc.,
commercial—2 weeks
homemade—2 days
Milk
Keep tightly closed or covered. Don't return unused milk to original container; refrigerate separately to use first.
evaporated, sweetened condensed
opened—3 to 5 days
homogenized, skimmed, reliquefied nonfat dry—3 to 5 days
whipped cream in aerosol can—2 months
whipped topping in aerosol can—3 months
whipped topping prepared from a mix—3 days
whipped topping, frozen and thawed—2 weeks
Eggs
in shell—4 weeks
Keep large end of egg up to center yolk.
whites or yolks—1 week
Store in small, tightly closed container.

PACKAGED PREPARED FOODS

Keep foods tightly covered, closed or wrapped after opening. Don't feed baby from jar; saliva may liquefy food.

Baby food, opened—2 to 3 days
Coconut, opened—1 month
Coffee, ground
opened—1 week
Fish, canned, opened—1 to 2 days
Gravies
canned and opened—2 days
homemade—1 to 2 days
Meat, canned and opened—1 to 2 days
Mustard (prepared)—3 to 4 weeks
Pickles, olives, opened—1 month
Nuts—2 weeks
Poultry, canned and opened—1 to 2 days
Refrigerated biscuits, rolls, pastries—see expiration date on package
Refrigerated cookie doughs—see expiration date on package
Salad dressings, opened—3 months
Soups and broths
canned and opened—2 days
homemade—1 to 2 days
Tomato sauce, opened—5 days
Wines
table, opened—2 to 3 days
cooking, opened—2 to 3 months

HOME-COOKED FOODS

Refrigerate all cooked foods immediately. Keep tightly covered.

Meat, Fish and Poultry
- Meat and poultry
  - large cuts—3 to 4 days
  - small cuts, slices—1 to 2 days
  - stuffed poultry—1 to 2 days
    Remove stuffing from bird; refrigerate bird and stuffing separately.
- Fish and shellfish—1 to 2 days
- Meat, fish or poultry casseroles, stews, soups—1 to 3 days
  Leave meat in largest possible pieces to store. Add more milk or other liquid to casseroles when reheating, if necessary.

Desserts
- Cakes
  - whipped-cream frosting—1 day
  - butter-cream frosting—2 to 3 days
- custard, pudding—1 to 2 days
- gelatin molds—1 to 3 days
- pies, cream and custard—1 to 2 days

Fruits and Vegetables—2 to 3 days

Freezer Storage

Temperature: 0°F. or below is best; maximum temperature should be 5°F. Check temperature with freezer thermometer or outdoor thermometer, or use this rule of thumb: If freezer can't keep ice cream solid, temperature is higher than recommended. If this is the case, plan to use food within a week or so.

Time: Date foods with an "expiration date" according to maximum storage time recommended below. Longer storage is not dangerous, but flavors and textures begin to deteriorate.

Wraps: Use foil, plastic bags and wraps, freezer wrap or freezer containers. See page 704.

Commercially frozen foods: Don't buy them if they're battered, a sign that they may have been partially thawed. If foods have been partially thawed, then refrozen, use them within a few days.

Home-frozen foods: Use good-quality foods and proper techniques (pages 704–705). Freeze foods quickly in coldest part of freezer (on coils, floor), then store in another area of freezer.

MEAT, FISH AND POULTRY

Purchased frozen: Keep frozen in original package. *Home frozen:* Meat, fish or poultry which is prepackaged for self-service may be frozen in the original wrapper for 1 to 2 weeks. For longer freezer-storage, overwrap the original wrapper with foil, plastic wrap or freezer wrap, making package as airtight as possible. If not prepackaged, wrap tightly in foil, plastic wrap or freezer-wrap. If freezing individual hamburger patties, chops, steaks, separate with 2 thicknesses of freezer wrap before wrapping for easier thawing.

Meat
- Corned beef—2 weeks
- Frankfurters—1 month
- Ground beef, veal, lamb—3 to 4 months
- Ground pork—1 to 3 months
- Ham
  - whole—2 months
  - sliced—1 month
- Luncheon meats, such as bologna—do not freeze.
- Roasts and steaks
  - beef—6 to 12 months
  - lamb—6 to 9 months
  - veal—6 to 9 months
  - pork—3 to 6 months
- Sausage
  - dry, semi-dry—Do not freeze.
  - fresh pork—2 months
  - smoked—Do not freeze.

Fish and Shellfish
- Breaded fish
  - purchased frozen—3 months
  - home frozen—Do not freeze.
- Fillets and steaks from "lean" fish such as cod, flounder, sole, haddock—6 months
- Fillets and steaks from "fatty" fish such as bluefish, mackerel, perch and salmon —3 months

Shellfish
clams, crab, lobster tails, oysters, scallops—3 months
shrimp
breaded—3 months
unbreaded—1 year

Poultry
Chicken, turkey, whole or cut up—6 months
Chicken livers, other giblets—2 months
Duck—6 months
Goose—6 months

FRUITS AND VEGETABLES

Fruits
Berries, cherries, grapes, peaches, pears, pineapple—1 year
Citrus fruit—6 months
Citrus fruit juices
purchased frozen (concentrates)—1 year
home frozen—6 months

Vegetables
purchased frozen—8 months
home frozen—10 months

The following vegetables do not freeze well: celery, cabbage, green peppers, onions, potatoes, salad greens, tomatoes.

DAIRY PRODUCTS

Butter or margarine—9 months
Buttermilk, sour cream—Do not freeze.
Cheese
Cut and wrap cheese in small pieces (1 inch thick or less) for freezer storage. When frozen, cheese may show mottled color and become crumbly after thawing. Use in grated or crumbled form in salads and in cooking. Thaw cheese, wrapped, in refrigerator.
Brick, Camembert, Cheddar, Edam, Gouda, mozzarella, Muenster, Port du Salut, provolone, Swiss, pasteurized process cheese—3 months
Cottage cheese
dry curd—1 to 2 weeks
creamed—Do not freeze.
Cream cheese, Neufchâtel—Do not freeze.

Cream, all kinds—2 months
Heavy cream may not whip after thawing. Use in cooking. Thaw in refrigerator.
Ice cream, ice milk, sherbet—1 month
Cover cut surface with plastic wrap or foil to prevent surface drying.
Whipped-cream dollops—1 month
Yogurt—6 weeks

EGGS

In the shell—Do not freeze.
Whites—1 year
Store in tightly covered container, leaving some headspace, in amounts called for in favorite recipes.
Yolks—1 year
For sweet dishes: mix each cup yolks with 1 tablespoon sugar or corn syrup; for other dishes: 1 teaspoon salt.
Whites and yolks—1 year
For sweet dishes: mix each cup whole eggs with 1½ teaspoons sugar or corn syrup; for other dishes: ½ teaspoon salt.

HOME-FROZEN PREPARED FOODS

Main Dishes, Cooked
Do not freeze casseroles with homemade white-sauce base. To freeze other cooked foods, cool quickly in refrigerator (not at room temperature); then cover tightly and freeze. Leave some headspace in containers to allow for expansion, especially for casseroles and stews that contain liquid. Freeze foods in freezer-proof-and-oven-proof casseroles and baking dishes, or transfer to freezer containers.

Casseroles, stews with meat (except ham), fish and poultry—2 to 3 months
with ham—1 month
Cheese dishes—1 month
Eggs, hard-cooked—Do not freeze.
Fried foods, homemade—Do not freeze.
Gravies, thickened—Do not freeze.
Fish—Do not freeze.
Meat—2 to 3 months
Poultry—3 months

Baked Products

Cool baked products completely before freezing; then wrap tightly in foil, plastic wrap or freezer-wrap to freeze.

Breads and rolls
baked–3 months
dough (only special freezer recipes)–1 month

Cakes
with creamy or fluffy frosting–2 to 3 months
with custard or fruit filling–Do not freeze.
frosted and/or filled with whipped cream–1 month
unfrosted–3 months

Cookies, baked or dough–3 months

Fruitcake–1 year

Pies
custard–Do not freeze.
fruit (baked or unbaked)–8 months

Others

Nuts–3 months

Thaw, then allow to dry out at room temperature.

Sandwich fillings:
sliced pasteurized process or natural cheese, cream cheese, cooked and/or canned meat, fish and poultry, peanut butter, cold cuts such as ham–1 to 2 weeks

Wrap sandwiches individually in plastic wrap or bags or in foil. Thaw in wrapper. Because mayonnaise does not freeze well, use a little milk, yogurt, fruit juice or applesauce as binder for salad fillings. Do not freeze hard-cooked eggs, tomato, lettuce, onion, celery, cucumber, jam, jelly, mayonnaise and mayonnaise-based fillings such as ham and chicken salad.

PURCHASED FROZEN PREPARED FOODS

Main Dishes
Combination dinners–6 months
Meat, fish and poultry pies, casseroles, other main dishes–3 months

Baked Products
Bread and rolls
baked–3 months
dough–Follow label directions.
Cheesecake–3 months
Cakes
chocolate, yellow, pound–4 months
Pies
fruit, cream or custard–8 months

Meal planning

Properly planned meals supply the nutrition needed for good health and at the same time offer inviting variety in the flavor, color, shape and texture of food. They are geared to the family's varying nutritional needs, their likes and dislikes, the food budget and the time you yourself have to prepare them.

Planning Family Meals

Every member of the family, from baby to grandparent, has different food needs. It is possible, however, by using the Basic Four Food Groups, below, to plan meals that will provide both balanced nutrition and pleasurable eating for everyone.

This guide classifies foods in four major categories and indicates the number of servings from each that should be eaten each day to maintain good health. From these groups choose the main part of each day's eating. To make sure that your meals provide all the necessary nutrients, include at least the number of servings shown in each category. The basic outline adds up to 1200 to 1400 calories. Most family members will need more than this minimum; so serve larger quantities, or add other foods from the chart, plus supplemental foods such as butter or margarine and sugar to make meals more inviting and satisfying. Try to have one of the protein-rich foods or milk at every meal.

Plan the day's three meals at one time. That way you'll include the right number of servings from all groups (add more if you like), and you'll have greater variety with less repetition.

THE BASIC FOUR FOOD GROUPS

Meat and protein-rich foods—2 servings: These foods provide protein, iron, niacin and the other B vitamins. Choose from meats, fish, shellfish, poultry, eggs or cheese; occasionally, dry or canned beans (not green or wax beans), dry peas and lentils, or nuts or peanut butter, may be substituted for the meats.

One serving equals:

3 ounces lean, cooked meat, fish or poultry (without bone)
3 eggs
3 slices cheese (1 ounce each)
1 to 1½ cups cooked dry beans
⅓ cup peanut butter

Fruits and vegetables—4 servings: Fruits and vegetables supply vitamins A and C plus the other vitamins, minerals and roughage. Be certain to include one serving of citrus fruit or tomatoes and one serving of dark-green or leafy vegetables every day.

One serving equals:
½ cup canned or cooked fruit
1 fresh peach, pear, etc.
1 cup fresh berries or cherries
½ cup cooked vegetables
1 cup uncooked leafy vegetables

Breads, cereals and pasta—4 servings: Whole-grain, enriched and restored cereals and breads (check the labels to recognize) are important sources of the B vitamins; they also contribute supplemental amounts of protein and iron.

One serving equals:
1 slice bread
1 small biscuit, muffin or roll
½ cup potatoes, pasta or rice
¾ to 1 cup flaked or puffed ready-to-eat cereals
½ cup cooked cereals

Milk and milk products—3 to 4 servings for children, 4 or more servings for teen-agers, 2 servings for adults: Milk contributes significant amounts of calcium, protein and riboflavin as well as vitamins A and D and the B vitamins. Milk may be whole or skimmed, or reconstituted nonfat dry milk, buttermilk, diluted evaporated milk. Everyone should have some milk every day; the remaining requirement may be provided by other milk products.

One serving equals:
8-ounce glass of whole or skim milk
1 slice cheese (1-ounce slice)
½ cup cottage cheese
1 cup plain yogurt

Supplemental foods: These round out meals and help make them more satisfying, attractive and interesting. Many of these foods are used as ingredients in recipes; others are added to dishes at the table. They include butter or margarine; cream and sugar for beverages; coffee and tea; catchup and chili sauce; honey, molasses and syrups; salad dressings; candy; gravy and similar foods. Try to include some vegetable oil as part of the fats you use in cooking.

Planning for Different Age Groups

The Basic Four Food Groups guide applies to all family members, since children need the same types of foods as adults. Servings will vary in size, however; a teen-ager, for example, will eat considerably more than either a child or an adult. Or, you may want to serve different foods within one or more of the groups to different family members. A range in ages within the family can complicate meal planning. Here are suggestions to help solve this problem.

Children one to five years old: Until a child is a year old, the pediatrician will recommend the diet that best meets his individual needs. After that, the choice of foods is usually up to you. If his appetite seems to diminish, remember that his rate of growth is slowing, and that he needs and wants less to eat in proportion to his size than he did as an infant. When he isn't hungry, don't insist that he "clean his plate"; he may develop food habits that will be bad later on.

Serve small portions and make foods easy to eat. Cut chunky foods into pieces that will go into his small mouth easily; serve liquids in small paper cups or plastic glasses; cut bread and toast slices into quarters. Have seconds available.

Introduce a new food gradually and in small portions. If the child rejects it, wait a few weeks and try again.

For snacks, choose from the Basic Four Food Groups. Serve sweets as dessert only.

After the child has several teeth, start giving him foods that require chewing. If you continue to serve him only pureed food, he may be slow to accept solid food later on.

Serve meals attractively and start early to develop table manners. The young child's silverware should be small enough for him to handle, yet "grown-up" in style to enable him to make the transition to adult ware easily.

In addition to milk for drinking, use milk in other foods the child eats—cream soup, puddings, custards, cocoa. If getting him to drink milk is a real problem, add nonfat dry milk powder to mashed potatoes or cooked cereal. Reliquify double-strength nonfat dry milk and use it to make puddings, custards, soups.

Serve each day:
Meat, fish, poultry, cottage cheese: 1 to 4 level tablespoons
Eggs: 1
Cooked vegetables (mostly green or yellow): 1 to 2 servings, 2 to 4 tablespoons each serving
Potatoes (white or sweet): 2 to 4 tablespoons
Raw vegetables: 1 small serving, such as 2 or 3 short carrot sticks
Fruit (include one ¼- to ½-cup serving of citrus fruit or tomato juice daily): 2 servings
Enriched or whole-grain bread: 1½ to 3 slices
Milk: 3 to 4 cups
Butter or margarine as spread for bread or seasoning for vegetables

Children six to twelve years old: These are the years in which the child forms the eating habits that will last throughout his life. To increase his likes and interest in foods, serve him as wide a variety as possible at home, and also let him eat some meals away from home, at restaurants and in the homes of friends.

By the time he is six he will need as many calories each day as an adult woman. He will still eat smaller meals, but make up the difference with between-meal snacks. Choose these from the Basic Four Food Groups.

Teen-agers: The athletic teen-age boy needs twice as much food as his mother and half again as much as his father! The teen-age girl needs less, but still a few hundred calories a day more than the adult requirements. While the teen-ager's meals are the same as for the rest of the family, he usually makes up the difference in snacks. Here are tips to help you make sure these snacks are nutritious as well as satisfying:

Don't keep potato chips, snack crackers, soft drinks, candy or other "empty calorie" foods around the house and they won't be missed.

Do keep whole-grain or enriched crackers and cookies on hand.

Add extra cheese to homemade or frozen pizza.

Keep a bowl of fresh fruits and nuts on hand; it makes good eating as well as an attractive centerpiece.

"Food sticks," originally developed for the space program, taste like candy but are rich in protein and other nutrients.

Have foods such as carrots, cauliflower, cucumbers, celery and tomatoes washed and ready to eat in the refrigerator.

Try buttermilk, chocolate milk, cocoa made with milk, canned milk shakes, cheese fondue, cottage cheese and Swiss, Edam or other types of hard cheese as a different way of serving milk.

Add an extra tablespoon or two of nonfat dry milk powder, in addition to the regular milk used, when making cocoa.

Make this delicious Milk-rich Milk Shake in the blender: In covered blender container, at low speed, blend until smooth *½ pint ice cream, 1 cup cold milk, 1⅓ cups nonfat dry milk powder* and *1 teaspoon to 1 tablespoon flavoring* such as chocolate syrup, instant coffee powder, maple syrup or fruit jam. Makes 2 servings.

For the teen-ager in too much of a hurry to eat breakfast every day, see page 732.

Young adults: In choosing foods from the Basic Four Food Groups, remember that eating too much even of nutritious foods leads to overweight, a major factor in heart disease, arthritis, diabetes, high blood pressure and other debilitating diseases. Plan menus with an eye to their calorie content (see Calorie Values of Food, page 684). Encourage good eating habits by serving the right foods, in the right amounts to maintain proper weight.

Mature adults: The older person needs fewer calories; happily, his appetite also decreases. Nutrition requirements, however, remain the same. In using the Basic Four Food Groups, cut down on calories by using lean meats, fish and poultry and buttermilk or skim milk; serve fewer rich desserts and use less butter or margarine.

How to Plan a Menu

1. Select the main dish first; it should provide one serving from the Meat and Protein-rich Foods Group. The main dish is the most important and probably the

most expensive dish of the meal, and will influence your choice of the dishes to accompany it.

2. Next, decide on the vegetables. Most menus include one starchy vegetable—that is, one from the Breads, Cereals and Pasta Food Group—and at least one non-starchy vegetable. Choose the latter from the Fruits and Vegetables Group.

Plan vegetables that are varied in color. The plate will look more appetizing, and nutrition will be better balanced. For example, serve a green or yellow vegetable with white potatoes or rice; or serve one yellow and one green vegetable, such as acorn squash and spinach, rather than two green ones such as peas and broccoli.

Also, try to vary vegetable shapes to add interest to the plate. Asparagus spears contrast pleasantly with carrot slices, Brussels sprouts with mashed potatoes.

3. Select dessert to balance the main dish: If the main dish is a hearty one, such as beef stew, serve a light dessert such as sherbet or fruit and cookies. If the main dish is light, a salad or soup, top off the meal with a hearty sweet such as mince pie or chocolate cake. If necessary, choose a dessert that provides added protein in the form of eggs, milk or cheese. It is also a good way to provide milk for anyone who doesn't like to drink milk as is; serve custards, puddings, sweet beverages made with milk.

4. Choose a salad that will add any needed fruits or vegetables (or add supplemental ones from the Fruits and Vegetables Group). To add texture to an otherwise "soft" menu, select a crunchy vegetable salad. Serve a juicy fruit salad or molded salad when the entrée is "dry"—broiled or fried and served without sauce or gravy.

5. Bread is not an essential part of many menus; however, it can supply a delightful contrast to other dishes and add glamor when other foods are plain. If the meal is a cold one, serve a hot bread; if the main dish is soft-textured, serve a bread that is crisp and crunchy. If the menu includes only non-starchy vegetables, add a bread to supply one serving from the Breads, Cereals and Pasta Food Group.

6. Little touches (pickles, olives, jelly, butter balls, garnishes) help make a meal memorable. For ideas, see Relishes and Garnishes, page 377.

7. Use beverages to round out a menu; include milk if that has been omitted from the day's meals.

8. The last step is to go over the entire menu to be sure that flavors are harmonious, colors are varied and attractive, and textures and shapes offer agreeable variety.

Making Menus Different

Meals can be light or hearty. A light meal might consist of main dish, salad or relishes, bread and beverage. Add two or three vegetables and a dessert and you have a hearty repast.

• Plan ahead and you won't have to shop for food every day. Make a shopping list so you won't be tempted to buy on impulse; however, keep the list flexible or list alternates so you can take advantage of bargains or make substitutions if a food is temporarily unavailable.

• Contrasts make menus interesting. Try to pair crisp foods with soft ones. Serve both hot and cold dishes. Balance light with hearty foods. Include both bland and robust flavors (however, as a rule, only one highly seasoned dish is needed).

• Take a tip from restaurant menus and make up a similar listing of the family's favorite dinner foods. Include several appetizers, two or three soups, several main dishes, a few different salads and a variety of different desserts. Then plan a meal as if you were choosing in a restaurant, or let family members make the selection. Do the same with favorite breakfast and luncheon foods.

• When the family dines out, note the dishes they choose and try to duplicate the resulting menus at home.

• Keep a menu book and make notes on the family's reaction to each meal.

• Even though, thanks to today's transportation and processing techniques, many foods can now be enjoyed all year long, they are at their most plentiful, highest quality and lowest price when they are in season. Include seasonal fresh foods in your planning, to keep costs down, flavors and textures at their best.

• The so-called "meal-in-a-dish" skillet combinations, stews and casseroles make cooking as well as meal planning easy. Also, if you're cooking the main dish in the oven, and there is room, plan vegetables or a dessert that can bake along with the main dish.
• Vary dishes that must be prepared close to serving time with dishes that can be prepared well ahead. This is of particular importance when planning menus for parties. Leaving until last only the little details, such as unmolding gelatin mixtures, garnishing casseroles, heating breads, makes for pleasanter entertaining. Guests are more relaxed when the hostess isn't harried.
• Serve at least one new dish each week. Keep looking for new ideas. Check magazine and newspaper food pages; browse through cookbooks; send for booklets.
• Collect recipes for new dishes or for dishes you've had elsewhere and would like to add to your culinary repertoire. (And don't just file the recipes in a drawer—use them!)
• Change patterns. Don't serve meat-and-potato dinners every day. Try main-dish salads, skillet meals, hearty soups. Add a special hot bread and dessert and the change will be relished.
• Don't serve two or more dishes with the same major ingredients. If a cream soup is the first course, for example, don't have a creamed vegetable or a pudding dessert. (Less important ingredients, such as nuts or garnishes, may be repeated if necessary.) And don't duplicate hearty seasonings. Onion could be a part of more than one dish, but dill or cinnamon might be too much of a good thing if used in two dishes.
• Occasionally, serve fruit in place of a vegetable—pan-fried bananas, for example; or Curried Four-Fruit Bake (page 383).
• Every now and then let a beverage be the dessert. Diners often end a restaurant meal with "just coffee," and you can do the same at home. You'll save work, time, money and, in most cases, calories.
• Play up holidays; it will add to the fun of family dining. Serve cherry pie on Washington's Birthday; Irish Soda Bread (page 426) on St. Patrick's Day, etc.
• Splurge occasionally on a special roast or steak or an elegant dessert. Your family will be more willing to help you economize when they know they'll have something special from time to time. You can balance the budget with low-cost but delicious egg, cheese, pasta, or bean entrées (except green and wax beans) at other meals the same week.
• Serve biscuits, popovers, muffins or some of the Special Breads (pages 458–462). A hot bread brightens up even the simplest meal.
• Other ideas that make meals less humdrum will be found in Relishes and Garnishes, pages 377–388; Dessert Soups, pages 57–58; Hot Supper Specials (sandwiches), pages 468–471; Main-Dish Salads, pages 404–409.
• Often a piece of delicious candy, plus a beverage, makes a satisfying dessert. (Serving candy this way removes the temptation to eat too much of it.) Or, serve a sweet beverage, such as Icy Lemon Coffee (page 604) or cocoa.

Making Meals Thrifty

Plan meals when you're hungry, and shop for groceries when you're not! That way your menus will be better balanced both nutritionally and in flavor, and you'll be less likely to purchase unplanned "impulse items," which can upset the budget as well as the menu. Plan meals by the week, so you can shop for all at one time and save frequent trips to the store. When you save menu planning until you're in the supermarket, meals are likely to cost more.

When you shop, keep these pointers in mind:
• Less tender cuts of meat are usually cheaper than the more tender cuts, yet provide the same high-quality protein. They can be made tender in a number of ways: Cook slowly with moisture—braise, stew, simmer or pot roast; grind, cube, score or pound; marinate in or cook with acid ingredients such as tomatoes or vinegar; or prepare with meat tenderizer, following label directions.
• Variety meats—liver, kidney, heart, brains—are less expensive than many other cuts of meat and are fine sources of high-quality protein, plus vitamins and minerals.

Beef, pork and lamb liver are all cheaper than calves' liver.

• Plan to use every bit of the meat, fish or poultry you buy. Bones can cook in and add flavor to soups, stews and, in the case of fish, Court Bouillon. Broth makes good gravy, soup, stew, sauces; use it, too, to cook rice, macaroni and vegetables. Drippings left from roasting or frying can be used for panfrying, for seasoning vegetables and in sauces and gravies. Leftover bits can be added to casseroles, soups, sandwiches and salads.

• Stretch meat, fish and poultry by using in dishes with pasta, or adding to sauce to be served over rice, bread or mashed potatoes. Or add bread or cereals to them to make balls, patties or loaves. (Be sure also to add extra eggs, milk or cheese to insure ample protein.)

• While both chicken and turkey have a large proportion of bone to meat, quite often they are still bargains when compared to other meats. Buy the larger, meatier birds; they usually have more meat in proportion to bone. They can be cut into halves, quarters or pieces, and part can be frozen for later use; or leftovers can be frozen after cooking and used in meals weeks or months later. Whole chickens usually cost less per pound than pieces, and can easily be cut up at home.

• Other meats are also less costly if bought in larger sizes. Half a ham, or a leg of lamb, is usually less per pound than a small piece or a slice. Have the meatman cut the larger piece as you like it, or do it yourself at home.

• Serve main dishes made with dry beans, kidney beans, lentils; cottage cheese; eggs; cheese such as American or Swiss; peanut butter. Dry beans (see page 315) of many kinds are available and are a good source of protein at very low cost.

• When buying cheese, you'll find it's less expensive if: it comes in a wedge rather than sliced, cubed, shredded or grated; it is mild, not sharp or aged (if natural cheese); it is domestic, not imported. Pasteurized process cheese often costs less than natural cheese and is a more nutritious buy than cheese spread, which contains more moisture. If you like cottage cheese flavored with chives or pineapple, etc., you'll save if you add the extra ingredients yourself.

• Nonfat dry and evaporated milks cost less than fluid whole milk, and when reliquified or diluted according to label directions, can be substituted in cooking and baking. Milk in a half-gallon carton costs less than two 1-quart containers.

For drinking, try mixing equal parts of whole milk and reliquified nonfat dry milk powder. No one is likely to taste the difference, and you'll save pennies and reduce calories!

How to Make Breakfast Exciting

Start each day right by eating a nutritious breakfast. It's a fact that breakfast-eaters think better, react faster and work better than breakfast-skippers; they're also less likely to overeat at lunchtime.

If time is too short for a sit-down meal, drink one of the nutritious liquid "instant" breakfasts that can be downed even when you're on the run. There are frozen breakfast items that are ready to eat as soon as they pop out of the toaster; there are "instant" hot cereals as well as the ready-to-use cold kind.

If monotony is what's keeping you or other family members away from the breakfast table, check the ideas that follow, then create your own variations by putting together familiar foods in new combinations. The typical good breakfast consists of fruit (preferably one rich in vitamin C, such as a citrus fruit) or tomato juice, enriched or whole-grain bread or cereal and a protein-rich food such as eggs, meat or milk. Here are suggestions for making this routine pattern invitingly different:

Mixed cut-up fruit topped with cottage cheese; cinnamon toast

Scrambled egg topped with catchup in hard roll; a whole tangerine

Juice; a wedge or two of pizza topped with extra cheese

Creamed dried beef on toast or waffles; cantaloupe

Vegetable cocktail juice; macaroni and cheese

Melon balls in orange juice; puffy omelet; whole-wheat muffins

Canadian bacon; strawberry shortcake

Toasted English muffin topped with tomato

slice, poached egg, pasteurized process cheese sauce on top, heated
French toast slices topped with orange slices and plain yogurt
Scrambled eggs on pan-fried, thinly sliced pastrami or liverwurst; enriched rye-bread toast; grapefruit juice
Corned-beef hash, pan-fried pineapple slices, bran muffins
Welsh Rabbit (page 288) on toasted French bread; tomato juice
Fish sticks with chili sauce; hash-brown potatoes; orange juice

Luncheon Menus

Cream-of-Celery Soup
Bean-and-Bacon Bake (page 259)
Buttered Zucchini Spears
Thin Corn Crackers (page 424)
Dried Prunes and Apricots, Nuts in Shell
Hot Tea

❦

Cold-Cuts Platter (page 164)
Garnished with Crisp Vegetable Relishes
Mustard, Catchup,
Spicy Watermelon Pickles (page 388)
Macaroni Salad (page 397)
in Hollowed-Out Tomatoes
Buttered Slices of Pumpernickel-Rye Bread (page 445)
Warm Mince Pie (page 514) Topped with balls of Neufchâtel Cheese
Lemonade (page 608)

❦

Chilled Tomato Juice
with Lime Wedges
Dried Beef and Vegetables (page 265)
on Whole-Wheat Toast
Extra Toast
Fruit Mallow Salad (page 400)
Tea and Milk

❦

Classic Oyster Stew (page 52)
Finger Sandwiches: Canadian-style Bacon on Rye Bread
Tomato Aspic (page 398)
Pear Pie (page 510) with Cubes of Sharp Cheddar Cheese
Coffee

❦

Chilled Cocktail Vegetable Juice
Garnished with Twist of Lemon Peel
Baked Cheese Fondue (page 287)
Stir-Fried Broccoli (page 320)
Baked Apples (page 354)
Coffee and Milk

❦

Salad Plate: Stuffed Pear Salad (page 401),
Ham-and-Chicken Salad (page 404),
Indienne Rice Salad (page 404),
Pickled Beets (page 385), Gherkins
Basket of Warm Gingerbread Squares and Hot Muffins (page 42), with Softened Butter or Margarine
Chocolate-Orange Sodas (page 607)

❦

Hot Chicken Salad (page 259)
Harvard Beets (page 319)
Buttered Slices of Pumpkin Loaves (page 425)
Watermelon
Hot or Iced Tea

Supper Menus

Melon Balls with Fresh Mint Garnish
Broiled Ham Steak (page 122), Garnished with Sautéed Fresh Peaches (page 383)
Corn on the Cob with Butter or Margarine and Chives
Buttered Kohlrabi
Party-Rye-Bread Slices, Toasted in Broiler
Frozen Cheese Cream (page 575)
with Berries
Iced Coffee (page 604)

❦

Broiled Fish Steaks
with Cheese Sauce (page 217)
Shredded Carrots (page 324)
Brussels Sprouts with Buttered Crumbs
Coleslaw (page 396) on Tomato Slices
Bread Sticks
Lemon Snow Pudding (page 497)
with
Canned Apricots Garnished with Salted Peanuts
Hot Tea *Milk*

Barbecued Turkey Rolls (page 177)
Crunchy Noodles (toss cooked noodles with Buttered Crumbs, page 351)
Spinach with Grapefruit (page 330)
Perfection Salad (page 399)
Cheese Bread (page 446)
Vanilla Pudding Layered with Raspberry Jam, Topped with Slivered Almonds
Coffee

Swiss Steak with Tomato (page 87) on Noodles
Broccoli Spears
Sprinkled with Shredded Lemon Peel
Peach Halves on Lettuce with Creamy Ginger-Cheese Dressing (page 412)
Bran Muffins (page 422) with Whipped Butter or Margarine
Nesselrode Pie (page 519)
Coffee *Chocolate Milk*

Clam Juice Stinger (page 609)
Flank Steak Pinwheels (page 78)
Buttered Whole Carrots
Creamed Spinach (page 330)
Greek Salad (page 394)
Strawberry Tapioca (page 481) with Vanilla Wafers
Coffee and Milk

Carrot and Celery Sticks, Olives, Marinated Mushrooms (page 386)
Baked Stuffed Pork Chops (page 112)
Mashed Butternut Squash (page 345)
Brussels Sprouts with Water Chestnuts (page 321)
Brown-and-Serve Loaves (page 441)
Angel-Food Cake (page 537) Topped with Sliced Fresh or Canned Peaches
Hot Tea *Milk*

Shish Kebab (page 150)
on Raisin-Curry Rice (page 299)
Ratatouille (page 350)
Toasted, Buttered Thick French-Bread Slices
Orange Sherbet Topped with Preserved Kumquats and Their Syrup
Spiced Coffee (page 604)
Salted Almonds

Celery Sticks, Radishes
Crunchy Drumsticks (page 192)
Sweet Potatoes Topped with Pineapple Preserves
Buttered Cut Green Beans
Strawberry-Ice-Cream Cones
Root Beer

Chicken Pot Pie (page 194)
Crusty Rolls
Tossed Greens with Cubes of Jellied Cranberry Sauce, Thick Fruit Dressing (page 412)
Peach Melba (page 579)
Hot Chocolate

Beef Stew with Dumplings (page 88)
Grapefruit Chunks and Avocado Slices on Lettuce with Creamy Blue-Cheese Dressing (page 412)
Chocolate Ice Cream with Butter-Caramel Sauce (page 582), Salted Pecans
Coffee and Milk

Spring Vegetable Soup (page 57)
Choucroute Garni (page 128)
Cheese Bread Sticks (page 448)
Brie with Apples and Pears
Coffee and Beer

Broiled Steak (page 73)
Duchess Potatoes (page 341)
Buttered Peas
Tossed Green Salad with Mixed Herb-French Dressing (page 411)
Hot Parker House Rolls (page 439)
Deluxe Cheese Pie (page 292)
Coffee

Entertaining

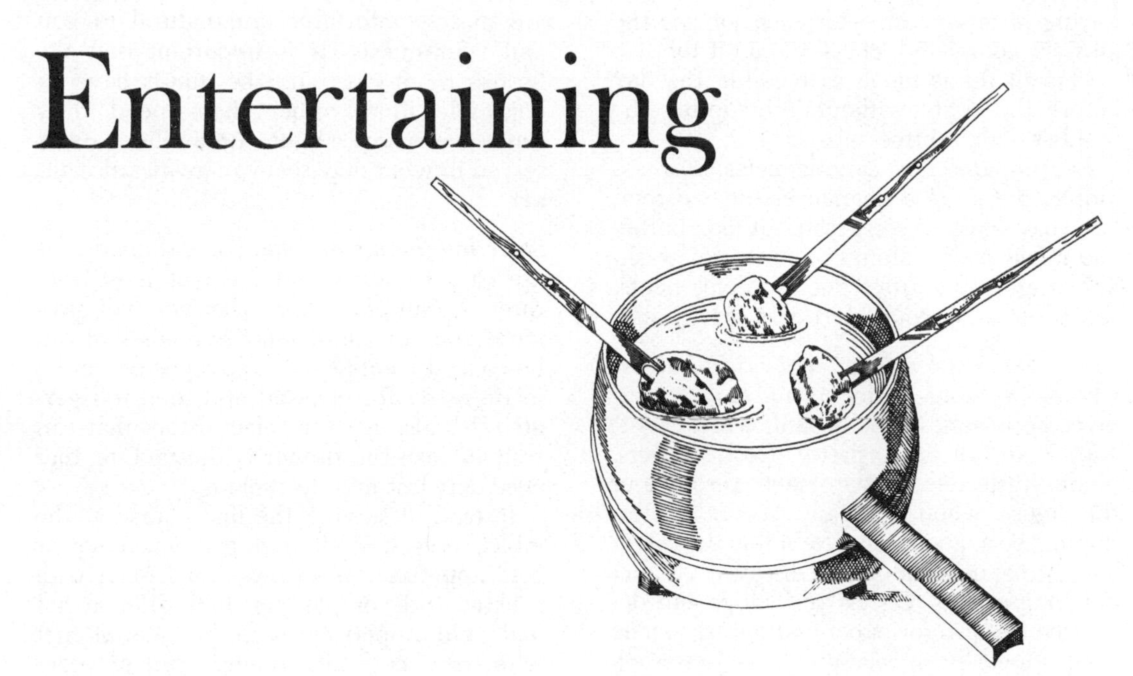

Successful entertaining is a combination of many factors—cordial hosts, appreciative guests, good food, pleasant surroundings and, sometimes, entertainment or party games.

While spur-of-the-moment entertaining can be fun, it's easier on the hostess to plan the details of a party well in advance. She will thus have time to work out special touches for the occasion—flowers or decorations, tablesettings and favors.

How to Plan

Invite the guests: Decide on the guests you want to invite and make out a guest list. For an informal meal or gathering, invite guests a week or two in advance; for a more formal dinner, bridal shower, tea or cocktail party, invite them two or three weeks ahead. If you want them to respond to a written or printed invitation, add "R.S.V.P." in the corner of the invitation and include your phone number or address.

Plan the menu: The menu should be in keeping with the occasion: For Father's Day, plan to have your husband's favorite foods; for a child's birthday, easy-to-eat foods; for dinner parties, more festive foods. Most guests welcome traditional foods for holidays: turkey for Thanksgiving, cherry pie on George Washington's birthday, fruitcake for Christmas, champagne punch for an anniversary.

Consider any special diets or allergies that your guests may have, and make allowances for their requirements. If possible, base the menu plan on the foods they can enjoy —unless their diet is too restricted. If so, plan separate foods for them.

For menus for all occasions, see each party in this chapter, as well as the menus in Meal Planning, pages 732–734.

Check equipment and dinnerware: Be sure you have enough preparation space, oven or range-top cooking space and freezer or refrigerator space for the menu you have planned. Make certain you have on hand, can borrow from friends, or rent from a supply house, necessary equipment for cooking and serving as well as all the china, silver, glassware and table linens needed for every course. If needed, borrow or rent card tables and chairs.

Make a detailed work order: Include housecleaning chores, shopping, table setting and centerpiece arrangement as well as food preparation on your list of things to do, allowing necessary time for each job. As the jobs are completed, check them off the list.

Plan to do as much as possible the day before the party without interrupting the family's daily routine.

Be prepared for contingencies. For example, if there's a change in the weather, you may have to serve the outdoor barbecue menu in the dining room; put a washable rug at the front door for wet boots; substitute a hot soup for a cold first course.

Plan the centerpiece and decorations: Choose a table arrangement and centerpiece according to the occasion. Most hostesses like to have pretty fresh flowers, plants, little decorative objects throughout the house when company comes. Entertaining is a good time to shine the silver and bring out seldom used vases, candleholders, tea sets. Check card shops and department stores for paper and papier mâché decorations for special-day functions such as Halloween, Mother's Day, Christmas and children's birthdays.

Make a shopping list: Go through the recipes for the menu and write out the grocery order; add whatever items are needed for the centerpiece and any decorations. Buy staples and decorations well ahead, perishables a day or two ahead.

Leave time for yourself: With careful planing, an hour or so can be left to get yourself ready, even relax for a few moments before the guests come. The best parties are the ones where the hostess has a good time too, so you should look and feel your best before the party starts.

The Party Dinner

The most formal of all meals, party dinners are usually given for very special occasions —anniversaries, the visits of most-loved friends, in honor of one's parents, when the boss comes to dinner. They require the most careful planning, since the presentation and serving of the food follow definite patterns. (Other special occasions follow some of these same patterns, too.)

However, when planning a party dinner, select the food and manner of serving that are most comfortable and natural to you and your guests. It is important that the hostess be at ease and the guests have an enjoyable time, rather than spend their time worrying about unfamiliar foods served in what may seem an awkward manner.

Selecting the menu: Plan party dinners that are easy to serve and have at most only three or four courses. So that you will have more time for guests, choose foods that can be cooked completely in advance or can be made ready for cooking and then refrigerated. It's also wise to select dishes that can wait in case the dinner is delayed, or that need only last-minute cooking.

Instead of serving the first course at the table, serve it in the living room. A hot or cold appetizer on an individual plate with cocktail fork, or platters of traditional hot and cold appetizers, can be offered first with wine, cocktails, punch, fruit or vegetable juices.

Serve salads before, with, or after the main course, depending on your preference or the menu. For example, fresh relishes such as carrots and celery usually give a crunchy accent to a main dish, while asparagus with vinagrette sauce would be appetizing between the first and main courses, and may even double as the first course if you like. In the continental manner, salads, usually tossed greens with a light oil and vinegar dressing, are served alone after the main course.

The main course of a party dinner should include a main dish and one or two vegetables. If the host likes to carve at the table, select a large cut of meat, whole poultry or whole fish and plan attractive as well as flavorful accompaniments for it. (See How to Plan a Menu, pages 729–730.)

Dessert should be something truly elegant, both in flavor and appearance. Many festive specialties can be prepared and frozen ahead (see page 478). Plain coffee is customary, but, for added interest, you might substitute a variation from the coffee recipes on pages 603–605, or one of the tea recipes on page 606.

Setting the table: Leaving a table uncovered shows off the beauty of its finish. However, since the finish may be marred, it's best to protect the table with an attractive tablecloth or place mats.

A damask, linen or linen-like cloth should have a felt or cotton "silence" cloth under it for added protection, and the tablecloth should hang 15 to 18 inches from the tabletop. Mats should be symmetrically spaced and placed with their edges even with the edge of the table. Use matching or coordinated napkins.

The key rule to follow when setting the table is to place china, silver, glassware and all serving dishes attractively in the order of their logical and convenient use.

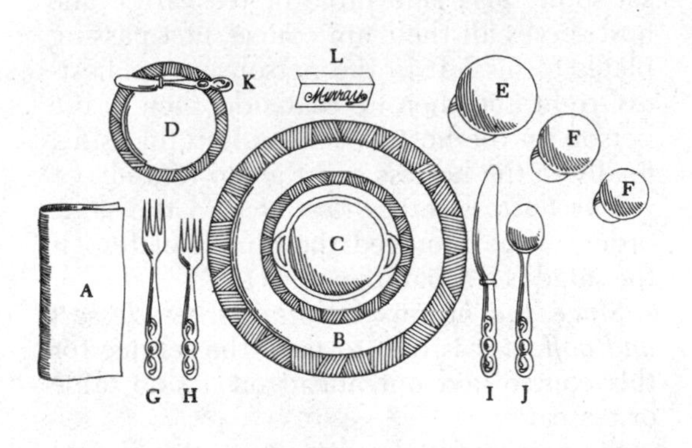

FORMAL FIRST COURSE

A. Napkin; B. Dinner or service plate; C. First-course soup bowl and liner plate; D. Bread-and-butter plate; E. Water goblet; F. Wine glass or glasses; G. Dinner fork; H. Salad fork; I. Dinner knife; J. Soup spoon (or cocktail fork); K. Butter knife; L. Place card

Place a dinner plate in the center of each place setting about 1 inch in from edge of table; arrange silverware evenly on each side so that none is hidden under the plate. (For silverware and glassware placement, see illustration.) First-course and dessert-course bowls, sherbet or parfait dishes should always have a "liner" plate under them (for used silverware). The first-course bowl and its "liner" plate are placed on top of the dinner plate (unless the host is serving, when they are placed in the center of the place setting).

Fold napkins into oblongs and place to the left of the fork, with the long edges, not the fold, facing the plate. If no first course is served at the table, napkins may be placed on the dinner plates.

Place several sets of salt and pepper shakers on the table for guests' convenience, if you like.

If the host is to serve, after the first course place the stack of dinner plates in front of him. (Have the plates ready on a side table.)

If the salad is served before the main course, place the salad plate in the center of the place setting and place a salad fork to the left of the dinner fork. If the salad is served after the main course, place the salad fork to the right of the dinner fork.

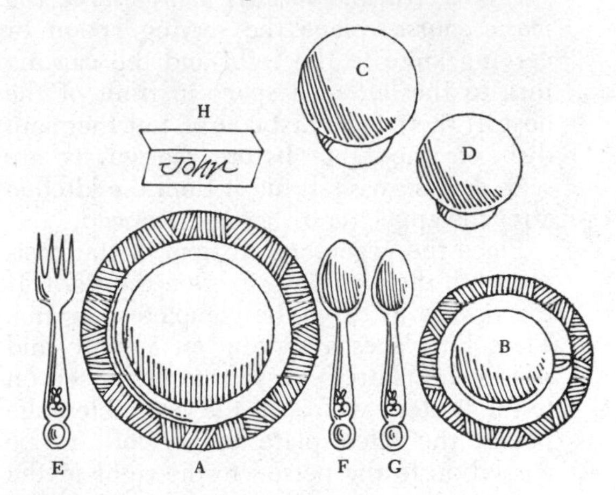

FORMAL DESSERT COURSE

A. Dessert plate (and bowl, if needed); B. Cup and saucer; C. Water goblet; D. Wine glass; E. Dessert fork; F. Dessert spoon; G. Teaspoon; H. Place card

Dessert and coffee silverware may be included in place settings before serving or may be brought in with the dessert and the coffee when they are served.

If using place cards, set them in place above the dinner plate. Place front edges of chair seats even with edges of table and squarely in front of the place settings.

Just before calling guests to the meal, put butter on the bread-and-butter plates and fill glasses three-fourths full of iced water. Light candles and give the table a final check. If there is a first course, set individual servings in place.

Seating the guests: The host should be first into the dining room, with the hostess ushering in the last guests. The host, whose place is at one end of the table, seats the female guest of honor at his right and the next "ranking" woman at his left. The hostess sits opposite the host. The male guest of honor is at her right, and the second "ranking" male guest at her left. Remaining places are usually filled by alternating men and women, seating husbands and wives apart from each other, when possible.

Arranging and serving the food: The serving dishes (platters, casseroles, etc.) and their silverware should be placed according to the manner in which the meal is to be served. See below.

If the host and hostess jointly serve the main course, place the serving spoon or carving knife to the right and the carving fork to the left of a space in front of the host. If there is no first course, put the main dish on the table before the guests are seated; otherwise, bring it from the kitchen after the appetizer dishes are removed.

Place the vegetables in front of the hostess, with their serving silver on the right. If the host is to carve, he completes carving. Then he places a serving on a plate and passes the plate to his left, to be passed on to the hostess, who adds the vegetables; she passes the filled plate to her left, to be passed on to the person to the right of the host. After serving all guests on her left, she serves the guest directly to her right and then everyone else to the right, including the host. Her own plate is last.

For convenience, a small table or cart may be placed at the hostess' end of the table for serving vegetables and other courses.

Breads, sauces, relishes and condiments may be passed around the table, usually starting with the person to the right of the host and passing right, everyone helping himself.

If wine is part of the menu, it should be opened in the kitchen in advance and placed on the table. After serving the main course, the host pours. Starting at his right and proceeding around the table, he pours wine into each glass (without lifting it from its place) filling it about one-half full.

After all are served, the hostess should take a bite of food first to signal that it is time to begin eating; however, she may ask the guests to begin before everyone is served, especially when there is a large party.

After the main course is finished, the hostess should first remove the salt and pepper shakers, bread and all other accompaniments. Starting with the guest to the right of the host, she removes the plates and silver all around the table (she does not stack several plates together but picks up one in each hand), taking the host's and hers last.

If the host alone serves the main course, place the main dish and vegetables in front of him. (If there isn't room on the table, set some on a side table or tea cart.) The host serves all the main course, first passing plates to his left to the person on the hostess' right and then up that side, then to the person on the hostess' left and up that side, finally to the hostess and then to himself.

The hostess serves the salad in the same order as she removed the dinner plates (if the salad is a separate course).

Since the hostess usually serves dessert and coffee, it is best to have the service for this course laid out ahead on a side table or tea cart.

Silverware for the dessert service should be placed after the main-course plates are removed. A dessert fork is used for cake and firmer desserts, while a fork and spoon are used for ice cream and cake; a spoon alone is used for all soft desserts.

The dessert plates are usually stacked at the hostess' place, with the dessert in front of them, for easy serving. Or, some desserts may be readied in the kitchen and served to guests like a separate salad course.

A spoon for coffee or tea should also be placed with the dessert silverware. The hostess pours the coffee at her place, passing it as she passed the dinner plates. Cream and sugar are passed by the guests so they can serve themselves. Or, cups may be filled in the kitchen and served, with spoons on saucers, to each person before dessert.

If a cheese and fruit course follows, serve it at the table just as dessert is served.

If the last course is to be served in the

living room, dessert and coffee, or perhaps only coffee, is arranged on a tray, tea cart, coffee or side table; the hostess serves from there. If cordials are served, the host pours them.

If a maid is serving the meal, be sure she knows beforehand how the food is to be served; practice with her if necessary. The maid should serve the hostess first, then the person to her right and so on around the table. If there are only four people at the table, she should serve the guest on the host's right third, then return to serve the host last. If the host is carving and serving the dinner, the maid stands at his left to receive the plate and takes it to the hostess. She then serves the person to the hostess' right and up the table to the host; then the person to the hostess' left and up to the host, who is served last.

The maid should stand at the left of a guest to place, remove and offer dishes; however, when placing or removing beverages and dessert silver, she should stand at the right to avoid reaching in front of the guest. To exchange plates, she should remove the old one with her left hand, place the new one with her right. When offering food, she should hold the platter or serving dish flat on the palm of her left hand (protected with service napkin if dish is hot), steadying it with her right hand. She should always offer the side of the platter or serving dish to the guest with handles of the serving pieces pointed toward him and low enough for easy serving.

When the guests are seated, the maid brings the first course to set on each service plate. Afterwards, she removes the service plate with the first-course plate on it and replaces it with a warm dinner plate.

It is important that she move quietly and unobtrusively around the table, offering more food, bread, butter and relishes, without disturbing the guests.

Water glasses should be refilled without being lifted from the table; a napkin held in her left hand should be used to catch any drops.

She should handle glasses only by the stem or bottom and avoid letting her thumb extend over the rims of plates while serving. Serving dishes of food, after being passed, are returned to the kitchen and rearranged with additional food for offering second helpings.

After everyone has finished one course, the hostess usually signals for the next by ringing a hostess bell or giving another prearranged signal.

Until the dessert course, an empty plate is always removed and replaced at the same time with a plate for the next course, filled or unfilled. For example, the maid removes the empty plate from the main course with her left hand, replaces it with an individual salad (or she replaces it with an empty salad plate and when all salad plates are in place, passes the salad bowl).

Before serving dessert, she removes all salt and pepper shakers, then salad plates (if salad was not served as separate course), bread-and-butter plates and dinner plates. With a clean cloth, she brushes any crumbs into a small plate.

At each place, she sets the dessert plate, with a dessert fork on the left, dessert spoon on the right. Guests are passed dessert and help themselves. Or, dessert plates may be filled in the kitchen and brought to the table after the dessert silver has been laid.

The maid pours coffee at a side table or in the kitchen and serves filled cup on saucer to each guest; then she offers each guest a tray with cream and sugar.

Jellied Madrilène Supreme (page 46)
Thin Corn Crackers (page 424)
Burgundy or Cabernet Sauvignon
Rolled Rib Roast (page 71)
with Creamy Horseradish Sauce (page 167)
and Mushroom Sauce (page 168)
Zucchini with Walnuts (page 344)
Twice-Baked Potatoes (page 339)
Orange-Spinach Salad (page 393)
Relishes: Sweet Gherkins, Stuffed Olives,
Nectarine Chutney (page 387)
Marinated Mushrooms (page 386)
Party Rolls (page 448)
Butter Molds or Curls (page 416)
Strawberry Deluxe Cheesecake (page 291)
Champagne
Demitasse (page 603)

Eggs à la Russe (page 37)
Red Snapper with Oyster Stuffing (page 216)
Peas with Lettuce (page 337)
Curried Celery (page 325)
Herbed Tomato Salad
Buttery Rye Fingers (page 459)
Crêpes Suzette (page 490)
Caffè Cappuccino (page 604)

Potted Cheese (page 34)
with Crackers,
Celery and Carrot Sticks, Cucumber Slices
Roast Turkey with
Moist Bread Stuffing or Chestnut Stuffing (page 204)
and Raspberry Gravy (page 177)
Mashed Sweet Potatoes
Lemon-Buttered Broccoli Spears
Cranberry Sauce in Orange Cups
Brown-and-Serve Rolls
Butter Balls (page 415)
Holiday Baked Pudding (page 498)
with Sunshine Foamy Sauce (page 499)
Coffee

Tomato-Ice Appetizer (page 577)
Cheese Pastry Fingers (page 421)
Lobster Thermidor
with Pilaf (page 235)
Buttered Frenched Green Beans
Skillet Cherry Tomatoes (page 347)
Seeded Savory Long Loaf (use poppy seed) (page 460)
Snow Pudding (page 497)
Caffè Espresso (page 604)

Oysters Rockefeller (page 43)
Standing Rib Roast Supreme (page 72)
Franconia Potatoes (page 340)
Peas with Macadamia Nuts
Romaine with Red Onion,
Oil and Wine-Vinegar Dressing
Relish Dish: Stuffed Olives,
Bread-and-Butter Pickles (page 388)
Crescent Rolls, Butter Balls (page 415)
Bombe Glacé with Fruit (page 580)
Coffee or Tea *Cordials*

Orange and Grapefruit Sections
Topped with Small Scoop of Lime Sherbet
Swedish-Style Pot Roast (page 81)
Spiced Carrots (page 323)
Green Beans and Celery (page 351)
Thick Lettuce Slices
with French Dressing
Rice Cream (page 486)
Coffee *Tea*

Shrimp-and-Mushroom Soup (page 48)
Parmesan Biscuits (page 420)
Roast Duckling Montmorency (page 200)
Golden Rice (page 300)
Peas Amandine (page 337)
Salad of Belgian Endives with
Tarragon-Vinegar Dressing (page 409)
Hot Rolls
Eggnog Charlotte Russe (page 496)
Coffee *Assorted Chocolates*

Chilled Tomato Juice
Appetizer Cheese Board: Sharp Cheddar, Feta, Swiss, Royal Camembert Mousse (page 38)
with Mixed Crisp Crackers
and Party Rye Bread
Beef Wellington (page 72)
Asparagus Spears with Hollandaise Sauce (page 282)
Buttered New Potatoes
Lettuce Wedges
with Tarragon-Vinegar Dressing (page 409)
Party Rolls (page 448)
Cherry-Sherry Jubilee (page 496)
Spritz (page 566)
Demitasse (page 603) *Mints*
Candied Citrus Peel (page 591)

Zucchini Wedges, Cauliflowerets,
Belgian-Endive Leaves,
with Prepared Onion Dip
Shrimp Casserole Harpin (page 242)
Buttered Small Whole Carrots
Broiled Canned Peach Halves
Artichoke Buffet Salad (page 392)
Italian Bread Sticks (page 443)
Grasshopper Pie (page 523)
Coffee

Informal and Family Dinners

Most entertaining, including all family meals, is much less formal than the dinner party. But many of the same guidelines for planning and serving apply.

Selecting the menu: Often a first course is offered, but usually informal meals include only salad, main course and dessert. Appetizers, such as crackers and cheese or spreads and dips, make easy, serve-in-the-living-room first courses. While cocktails, fruit juice or other cold drinks and appetizers are popular, for a change heat bouillon or cocktail vegetable juice and serve with crackers or raw vegetables. Or, present the first course with the main course: Place a small glass of tomato, clam or grapefruit juice to the right of the water glass on the table.

For company, it is best to select foods that can be readied ahead with only last-minute attention. Foods that can be cooked and served in the same dish—casseroles, heat-and-serve platters and skillets—are work-saving selections. A big tossed salad served from its bowl instead of on individual plates, or even a platter filled with individually arranged salads, is easy, too. Almost any dessert is suitable.

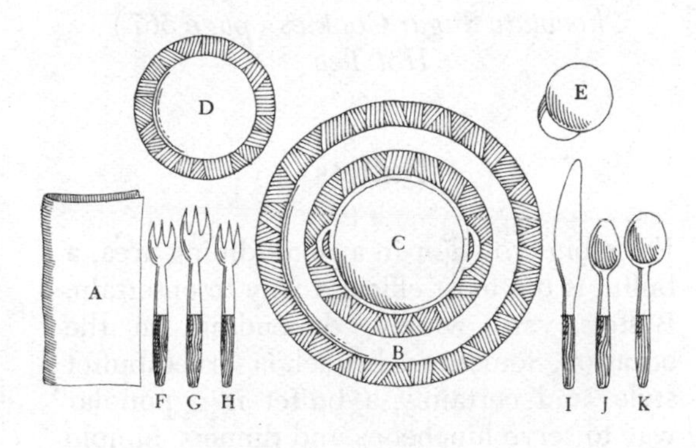

INFORMAL DINNER

A. Napkin; B. Dinner or service plate; C. First course bowl and liner plate; D. Salad plate; E. Water goblet; F. Salad fork; G. Dinner fork; H. Dessert fork; I. Dinner knife; J. Teaspoon; K. Soup spoon

Setting the table: Use a linen or linen-like tablecloth or mats and coordinated napkins. For casual and family meals, the napkins and mats may be paper. Set the table as illustrated here. If not serving a first course, place the napkin on the dinner plate, if you like. Let the salad plate act as the bread and butter plate, too, allowing room for bread next to the salad.

For family meals, put the dessert spoon or fork on the table at the beginning and simply set down the dessert plate when the dinner plate is removed. Or, serve dessert and coffee later as illustrated on page 737 for the formal dessert course.

Pour water, iced tea or iced coffee or fruit drink before guests come to the table.

Arranging and serving the food: The serving dishes (platters, casseroles, etc.) should be placed according to the manner in which the meal is to be served. See below.

Since the first course will be in place when everyone is seated, when the course is finished, the hostess, perhaps with the help of family or friends, removes the dishes.

For family-style meals, the main dish is set in front of the host; other dishes are set where table space permits. The host offers the main dish to the person on his right, who helps herself and passes it on around the table. Meanwhile, the hostess and others pick up serving dishes in front of them and pass them to the persons on their right, passing the food until everyone has been served. The host pours the wine, filling each glass about half full without lifting it from the table.

Offers for second or third helpings should be made by the host or hostess and the dishes passed around the table. Additional beverages should be poured also. When the main course is finished, the hostess removes the salt and pepper shakers, serving dishes, then the used plates and silver at each place setting.

Dessert plates should be placed at each setting and the dessert passed by the host to the right so that each person can help himself. However, sometimes the hostess prefers to serve dessert and coffee as in formal dessert service, above.

For meals served from the kitchen, the main course should be placed on warm dinner plates and brought to the table by the hostess and perhaps another member of the family or a friend. Bread, relishes and other accompaniments are passed at the table. For seconds, small dishes of food may be passed, or the hostess may take the guests' plates back to the kitchen for refills. Desserts also may be served from the kitchen.

A hostess may also combine several serving techniques, adapting them to suit her particular needs. There are no hard and fast rules about serving; the important point is to present meals as graciously as possible to both family and friends.

❦

Greek Salad (page 394)
Shrimp-Stuffed Roll-Ups (page 226)
Brussels Sprouts
with Water Chestnuts (page 321)
Mashed Potatoes (page 341)
Muffins (page 421)
Orange-Sherbet Cups (page 582)
Chewy Caramel Brownies (page 560)
Coffee

❦

Chilled Cranberry-Juice Cocktail
Baked Stuffed Pork Chops (page 112)
Orange Rice (page 301)
Cheddared Onions (page 335)
Coleslaw with Sliced Radishes
Cream-Lemon Ginger Squares (page 540)
Coffee or Tea

❦

Classic Oyster Stew (page 52)
Marinated Vegetable Salad (page 395)
in Lettuce Cups
Sesame-Seed Crackers, Rye Wafers,
Garlic Bread Sticks
Apricot-Brandy Cake (page 538)
Coffee

❦

Mugs of Apple-and-Onion Soup (page 48)
Saltines
Roast Leg of Lamb (page 145)
Cucumber Marmalade (page 703)
in Canned Pear Halves
Baked Potatoes
Topped with Pimento-Cheese Spread
Buttered Spinach
Mocha Parfaits (page 578)
Coffee

❦

Curry Soup (page 46)
Sesame Seed Crackers
Browned Beef Stew with Dumplings
(page 88)
Lettuce Wedges
with Green Goddess Dressing
Crescent Rolls
Warm Cherry Pie (page 510)
with Longhorn Cheese
Hot Tea

❦

Cranberry-Ice Relish (page 577)
Veal Stew Deluxe (page 142)
on Hot Cooked Rice
Tossed with Toasted Almonds (page 379)
Baked Parsleyed Tomatoes (page 347)
Sliced Chinese Cabbage (Nappa)
with French Dressing
French Bread
Cream Puffs (page 486)
with Hot Butterscotch Sauce (page 500)
Demitasse (page 603)

❦

Artichoke Hearts
Marinated in Italian Salad Dressing
Ham Slice in Cumberland
Sauce (page 122)
Whole Green Beans with Mushroom Caps
Shredded Carrots (page 324)
Colossal Golden Bread (page 444)
Strawberry-Orange Frost (page 575)
Chocolate Sugar Cookies (page 567)
Hot Tea

Buffets

For a big crowd or in a small dining area, a buffet is the most efficient way to entertain. Buffets vary widely, depending on the occasion. Sometimes brunch is served buffet style, and certainly a buffet is a popular way to serve luncheons and dinners. Simple refreshments such as dessert and coffee are easily presented this way too. You may want to serve from a sideboard, the dining table, a living-room table, or for a casual meal, from the kitchen counter.

Selecting the menu: Be sure to plan foods that do not "fade" quickly, since they will be standing on the buffet table for some time. Casserole and chafing-dish combinations are the best selections. When guests will be eating from plates on their laps, it is important to plan foods that can be cut with only a fork or need no cutting at all.

Pre-buttered rolls and breads, simple molded salads, and, when possible, two vegetables mixed in one bowl, all make for faster serving.

The first course may be served in the living room, as may dessert and coffee. For example, serve fresh vegetables and a sour-cream dip with cocktails first, and omit a salad on the buffet table if space is limited.

Serve iced tea, wine, water and other beverages with the main course.

Consider coffee and such finger foods as cookies and walnuts for a simple dessert.

If the crowd is a big one, plan on making two or more batches of most items on the menu and replenishing foods as needed.

Arranging the seating: If you use the sideboard or another table for the food, you can seat guests at the dining table.

However, if the dining table is also the buffet table, arrange tablecloths or mats on card tables, snack tables or coffee tables in the living room, family room or hall, and supply suitable chairs. Be sure there is a spot for each guest to put his plate and coffee cup or glass.

If you don't have enough table space, provide trays for guests to place on their laps. Young people usually don't mind sitting on the floor if there is no space at a table. Even though buffet entertaining is informal, every guest should feel comfortable.

Setting the table: If there is room for everyone at the dining table, you may want to set the table for the first and main courses and serve the first course there.

Select tablecloths or mats to suit the occasion.

It's essential that food for a buffet be arranged in logical order for help-yourself ease. The arrangement varies according to the placement of the table (see illustration for the table in the center of the room), but basically a stack of warm plates should be first, then the main-course dishes (meats, vegetables, any gravies or sauces) with the serving silver to the right of each dish. Next should be the salad, bread and relishes. (The dessert should be brought to the table after the main course has been cleared.)

Silverware and napkins go at the end, unless you set place settings at the dining or other tables. Sometimes it is convenient to wrap the silver attractively in the napkin.

The beverage may be poured and served on the serving table, on a side table or at each place setting.

If the buffet table is next to a wall, arrange the food along one side so the traffic can flow from main dish to bread.

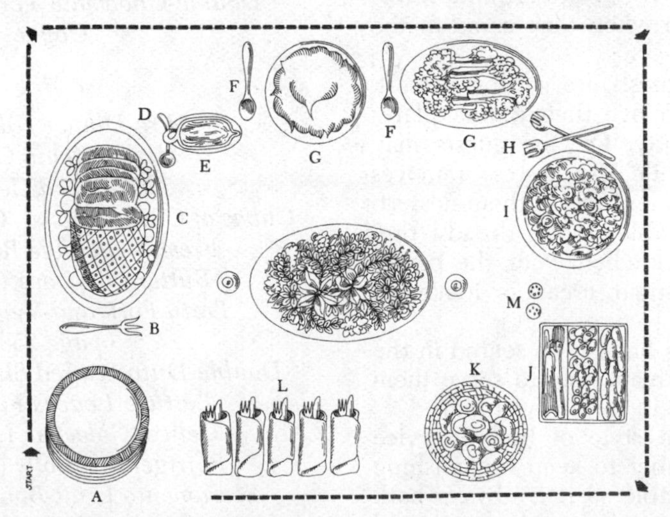

BUFFET

A. Dinner plates; B. Serving fork; C. Main dish; D. Gravy ladle; E. Gravy boat on liner plate; F. Serving spoon; G. Vegetable dish; H. Salad fork and spoon; I. Salad bowl; J. Relish tray; K. Basket of rolls; L. Napkins with knives and forks; M. Salt and pepper shakers.

If the crowd is large and you have space, plan duplicate foods, so that two lines of people can serve themselves at the same time. Steer one line down one side of the table, the other down the other side, arranging the food in logical order for both sides.

Set up the dessert and coffee service on a tea cart, small table, or even the top of a bookcase in the living room or hall, if the dining area is too crowded. Or, have it all ready on trays in the kitchen to bring out later.

Arranging and serving the food: Be sure there is enough space between serving dishes so that guests can set plates down while serving themselves. Or, perhaps the host and hostess, or a friend, may serve the main dish or salad to help move the line along. Ask people to come back for seconds.

While the guests are finishing their main course, remove those foods to the kitchen and set out dessert and coffee on the sideboard, dining table or previously prepared place. Arrange a stack of dessert dishes at the head of the table, then add the dessert (or choice of desserts) with the serving silver placed on the right. Set out dessert forks and/or spoons. At the other end of the table, arrange the coffee or tea service, cups, saucers and teaspoons.

If you like, ask guests to put their dinner plates and silver on a tray on a side table to be carried to the kitchen later, then let them help themselves to dessert and beverage or serve them when they come to the table.

Or, while the guests are getting dessert, the hostess can remove their dinner plates and silver to a tray. Or, the guests may remain seated while the hostess removes their dinner plates and serves them dessert, either from the table or an already prepared tray in the kitchen. Pour the beverage and pass the sugar, cream or lemon on a small tray.

Or, if the guests have been seated in the dining room, you may elect to serve them coffee and dessert in the living room.

No matter what style of buffet service you select, remember to keep replenishing the food on the table so it is always both attractive and as warm or cold as it should be.

When the meal is over, it is important to clear away all food and dishes, perhaps leaving the coffee out should guests want more later. Cover and refrigerate any perishable foods even though you won't do the dishes until later.

❦

Grapefruit-and-Apple Mist (page 609)
Cheddar-Cheese Thins (page 36)
Wine-Marinated Pork Roast (page 107)
Brussels Sprouts and Baby Carrots (page 349)
Candied Sweet Potatoes (page 345)
Salad of Mixed Greens
with
Deluxe Garlic French Dressing (page 411)
Seeded Savory Long Loaf (page 460)
Lemon Refrigerator Cake (page 493)
Coffee or Tea

❦

Do-Ahead Shrimp Kabobs (page 243)
Meatballs in Potato-Dill Sauce (page 100)
Roast Leg of Lamb (page 145)
Celery-Topped Ham with Dressing (page 119)
Mashed Butternut Squash (page 345)
Lemon-Buttered Peas
Radish Roses, Celery Fans
Cinnamon-Apple Salad (page 400)
One of Easy Bread sticks (page 459)
Double-Chocolate Torte (page 544)
Coffee

❦

Pre-Dinner Nibblers:
Mixed Melon Chunks
Thin-Sliced Cervelat
Cubes of Cheese: Swiss, Cheddar, Gjetost
Fresh Vegetable Relish Tray
Buttery Popcorn (page 34)
Party Pork-and-Vegetable Pie (page 258)
Double-Duty Stuffed Shells (page 306)
Lettuce Leaves Filled with
Deluxe Coleslaw (page 396)
Refrigerator Rolls (page 449)
Sacramento Fruit Bowl (page 373)
Assorted Butter Cookies
Coffee or Tea

Cold Cooked Shrimp
with
Chili-Horseradish Sauce (page 246)
Chicken à la King (page 362)
Braised Celery (page 325)
Speedy Pickled Peaches (page 384)
Spiced Prunes (page 384)
Toasted, Garlic-Buttered French Bread Slices
Chocolate-Stuffed Figs (page 593)
Orangy Fruit Compote (page 376)
Chocolate Cake (page 531)
with Fluffy Boiled Frosting (page 549)
Coffee

Mixed Platter of Fresh Fruits:
Lemon-Dipped Apple, Pear or Avocado Wedges,
Grapes, Tangerine Sections
Peach-Glazed Canadian Bacon (page 130)
Roast Boneless Turkey Roast
Special Succotash (page 349)
Frenched Green Beans with Polonaise Sauce (page 351)
Fresh Spinach
with Caesar-Salad Dressing
Filled Butter-Flake Rolls (page 461)
Mince Pie (page 514)
Coffee

Cream-Cheese-Stuffed Celery Fingers
Garnished with Red Caviar
Appetizer Kabobs (page 39)
Pan-Fried Vienna Sausages
Mustard-Sour-Cream (page 75)
Rock Cornish Hens with Currant Sauce (page 198)
Baked Sweet Potatoes (page 345)
Buttered Brussels Sprouts
Mixed Greens à la Russe (page 393)
Bran Muffins (page 422)
Quick Rum Cake de Maison (page 546)
Coffee

Brunch

Halfway between breakfast and lunch comes brunch. Although it is often served buffet style, many hostesses prefer that it be a regular sit-down affair, much like an informal luncheon.

Selecting the menu: Heartier than a breakfast, brunch menus often include eggs, bacon, pancakes or waffles, juice and coffee. Some can be quite elaborate, but hostesses should keep in mind that the meal should not be too rich, since it is the first one of the day for most of the guests. See menus below.

Setting the table: For a sit-down brunch, set the table as for a luncheon, preferably putting the first course of fruit or juice in place. Or, serve Bloody Marys (page 597), champagne punch or fruit juice in the living room. Coffee is usually served with the main course at the table.

Serving the food: Serve as for a Luncheon, page 746; or buffet style, page 742.

Mixed Berries on Melon Wedges
Buttermilk Waffles (page 432)
Butter Balls (page 415)
Scrambled Eggs (page 270)
Brown-and-Serve Sausages
Biscuits (page 416)
Bar-le-Duc (page 699)
Coffee

Sangria (page 612)
Pick-Up Fruits in Season:
Melon Balls, Papaya Chunks,
Orange Quarters, Banana Chunks,
Cherries, Strawberries
Drop Biscuits (page 416)
Topped with Dried Beef and Vegetables (page 265)
or Creamed Thin-Sliced Turkey
Buttered Broccoli
Lemon Bubble Ring (page 456)
Caffè Cappuccino (page 604)

Strawberries Manhattan (page 482)
Easy Cheese Soufflé (page 274)
or Classic Herbed Cheese Soufflé (page 275)
Bacon Curls
Honey-Peanut Butter-Flake Rolls (page 461)
Orange Marmalade
Whole-Wheat Toast
Coffee

❦

Banana Chunks and Grapes in Orange Juice
Baked Cinnamon French Toast (page 458)
Pan-Fried Canadian Bacon
Mocha Float (page 607)

❦

Fresh Pineapple Wedges Sprinkled with Pomegranate Seeds
Scrambled Eggs with Watercress Garnish
Pan-Fried Thick Liverwurst Slices
Pan-Fried Chopped-Ham Slices
Toasted Oatmeal Bread (page 446)
Freezer Plum Conserve (page 702)
Quick Kolacky (page 420)
Coffee Hot Chocolate

❦

Grapefruit Halves Sprinkled with Dry Marsala
Toasted Frozen Waffles Topped with Warm Maple Syrup and Pineapple Chunks
Pan-Fried Smoked Pork Chops (page 126)
Buttered Halved Corn Muffins
Spicy Gingerbread (page 535)
Hot Mocha Float (page 608)

Luncheons

Entertaining guests at luncheon may mean something simple like a soup-and-sandwich meal with two close friends, or an elaborate buffet meal before a concert or football game. For many hostesses, however, a luncheon is an occasion a little less formal than a dinner party but still very special. It often is a gracious way to entertain a visiting older relative or someone who has to travel too great a distance to come in the evening. It traditionally precedes afternoon card parties too (as does a dessert-and-coffee affair, opposite page).

Selecting the menu: While the first course is optional, many luncheons have a simple formula: Cold salad, hot bread, rich dessert; or hot casserole or omelet, bread and light dessert; or hot main dish, crisp salad and light or rich dessert. The first course is usually a light soup or fruit. See menus, opposite page.

Setting the table: Lace, organdy or delicately embroidered cloths or mats are suitable for a formal luncheon, while colorful cloths and napkins, often paper, are fine for more casual affairs. Candles are not appropriate for luncheons. Set the table as illustrated here. If not serving a first course, put the napkin on the luncheon plate, if you like. If serving an accompaniment salad and a bread, use the salad plate to hold both. Or, if there is room on the luncheon plate and the bread is pre-spread, place the bread there. If there is no salad but there is bread, use bread-and-butter plates.

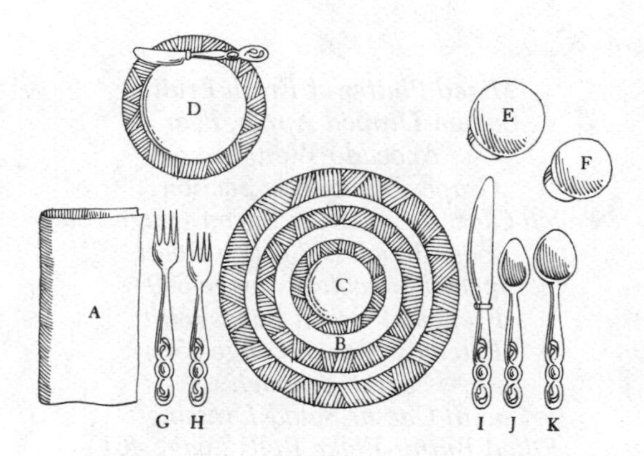

LUNCHEON

A. Napkin; B. Luncheon plate; C. First course bowl and liner plate; D. Bread-and-butter plate; E. Water goblet; F. Wine glass; G. Luncheon fork; H. Dessert fork; I. Luncheon knife; J. Teaspoon; K. Soup spoon; L. Bread-and-butter knife

Luncheon plates, available in some china patterns, are slightly smaller than dinner plates. It is correct, however, to use dinner plates for luncheons; or, if the main course is a salad or casserole that fits it, a salad plate can be used for the luncheon plate.

Set the dessert fork or spoon and dessert on the table as in Formal Dessert Course, page 737.

Seating the guests: The guest of honor—man or woman—should sit at the hostess' right if she is entertaining alone; if host and hostess are entertaining, seat the guests as for The Party Dinner (page 738).

Arranging and serving the dishes: If there is no first course, the salad may be set in place when the guests come to the table. Usually luncheon plates are brought to the table filled with food, and the bread and relishes are passed. Second helpings are always offered.

Clear the table and bring dessert as in The Party Dinner, page 739.

❦

Crème Mongole with Sherry (page 47)
Tiny Cheese Crackers
Broiled Lamb Chops
Mushroom-Capped Grilled Tomatoes (page 347)
Glazed Brown-and-Serve Rolls (page 461)
Toaster Corn Sticks
Twenty-Four-Hour Salad (page 402)
Coffee Tea

❦

Tomato Aspic Ring (page 398),
Filled with Shrimp Salad (page 406)
Toasted English Muffins (page 462)
Zabaglione (page 498)
Coffee

❦

Veal Forestier (page 140)
Broccoli Spears
Popovers (page 423)
Tossed Salad with Sliced Hearts of Palm
with Italian Salad Dressing
Orange Meringue Soufflés (page 493)
Hot Tea

❦

Beef and Bitters (page 608)
Raclette (page 288)
Rye Melba Toast
Wedges of Fresh Pineapple
with
Thick Fruit Dressing (page 412)
Sugar Bush Walnut Cake (page 537)
Coffee

❦

Vichyssoise (page 49)
Chicken en Cocotte (page 195)
Tomato Slices
Sprinkled with Lemon-Seasoned Pepper
Cinnamon Buns (page 452)
Whole-Wheat Toast Fingers
Raspberry Sherbet
Almond Lace Rolls (page 557)
Coffee or Tea

❦

Hot Bouillon with Watercress Garnish
Rye Crackers
Crab Salad in Pineapple Shells (page 406)
Herbed Corn Sticks (page 424)
Mini Nessel-Rolls (page 540)
Hot or Cold Spiced-Tea Punch (page 612)

❦

Spiced Grape-Juice Cocktail (page 609)
Mixed Salad Plate:
Tomato-Olive Aspic (page 398),
Chilled Asparagus Spears,
Crab-Stuffed Cucumbers (page 405),
Extra Mayonnaise
Boston Brown Bread (page 428)
Refrigerated Danish Rolls
Lady Napoleon (page 486)
Coffee or Tea

❦

Broiled Grapefruit (page 361)
Chicken with Endives (page 190)
Fresh Spinach and Boston Lettuce Salad
with White-Wine Vinegar and Oil Dressing
Spice Cupcakes (page 530)
with Whipped-Cream Frosting (page 551)
Coffee

❦

Vegetable Juice Cocktail
with Cucumber-Stick Stirrer
Assorted Cold Cuts
Cheddar-Macaroni Salad Mold (page 405)
Quick French Bread (page 420)
Butter Pats
Fresh Fruit
with Lemon-Sherry Dressing (page 375)
Hot or Iced Tea

Coffee and Dessert

After the theater, before an evening of bridge, or just as a pleasant way of entertaining, it is sometimes convenient to ask friends for coffee and dessert. A fancy party dessert and coffee or perhaps a coffee variation (see menus) is usually all that is served. This informal repast may be served much like the dessert course of a buffet (see page 742).

Frozen Cheese Cream (page 575)
Bittersweet Chocolate Cake (page 529)
Café Brûlot (page 604)

Cookie Plate:
Rosettes (page 430)
Cherry Bites (page 558)
Chewy Caramel Brownies (page 560)
Chocolate Sugar Cookies (page 567)
Southern Ambrosia (page 365)
Coffee

Chocolate Mousse (page 492)
Walnut Clusters (page 555)
Cinnamon Stars (page 568)
Crystallized Ginger-Tea (page 606)
Coffee

Fruit Cream Tarts (page 524)
Café Royale (page 603) or Coffee

Nesselrode Pie (page 519)
Peppermint-Chocolate Cake (page 543)
Coffee

The Formal Tea

Another formal way of entertaining is the tea party.

Selecting the menu: Both tea and coffee or a punch are served at "teas" along with party cakes, sandwiches, nuts and small candies. At some teas, especially if men are invited, dessert sherry is offered from a decanter on a sideboard or separate table. In warm weather, a punch or iced tea may replace coffee; hot tea is always served.

Finger foods that are not sticky or moist are easiest to serve and eat. Choose from cookies of all kinds, miniature cakes, tarts and cream puffs.

Although a hostess does not usually need to have enough chairs for all the guests, she should provide a few little tables and chairs if she plans to serve a cake or dessert (servings should be small) that requires a dessert plate and fork.

Setting the table: Lace, organdy or a delicately embroidered cloth should be placed directly on the table. Set the centerpiece in the center if the table is in the middle of

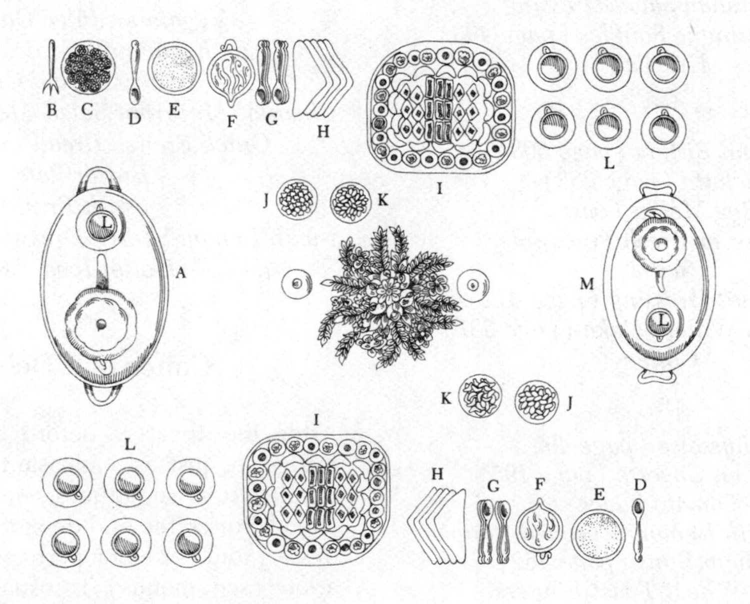

FORMAL TEA

A. Tea service (teapot and tray); B. Lemon forks; C. Plate of lemon slices; D. Sugar spoon; E. Sugar bowl; F. Creamer; G. Teaspoons; H. Napkins; I. Tray of cookies, tea sandwiches; J. Bowl of mints; K. Bowl of nuts; L. Cups and saucers; M. Coffee service (coffee pot and tray)

the room, or at the center back if the table is against the wall. Tea napkins, of paper if linen is not available, should be near the spoons. See the illustration. The tea service is placed at one end of the table, the coffee service at the other.

Serving: Usually the hostess asks two or three friends to alternate in the pouring of the tea and coffee, helping out herself if she is free for a few moments. Each guest is asked which beverage she prefers, and is directed toward the beverage of her choice.

When pouring tea, set the teacup in its saucer and fill about three-fourths full. See Hot Tea for a Crowd (page 662). Guests add lemon, milk or sugar as they prefer, take a spoon and napkin and help themselves to the party foods.

A sideboard or small table should be cleared for guests to place their used cups and saucers afterwards.

One or More of Tea Sandwiches
(page 472)
Rounds of Melba Toast
Topped with Cream Cheese, Cucumber Slice
Biscuit Halves Topped with Chicken Salad
Sandwiches of Boston Brown Bread
and Canadian Bacon, Cut into Quarters
Chocolate Date-Nut Loaf (page 427)
Thin Sandwiches of
Peanut-Butter Bread (page 426)
Filled with
Fluffy Beige Frosting (page 550)
Fruitcake Miniatures (page 591)
Shortbread (page 561)
Ladyfingers
Sherried Walnuts (page 593)
Marzipan Fruits (page 592)
Candied Violets
Hot Tea
with Candied Orange Peel for Sweetening
Lime Punch Bowl (page 610)

An Afternoon Tea

An afternoon gathering of just a few friends is a pleasant occasion for a small tea party.

Selecting the menu: Choose finger foods (little squares of gingerbread or cake, fruitcake cubes, nut bread spread with cream cheese or jam, toasted English muffins spread with jam and quartered, candied fruit, cinnamon toast, cucumber sandwiches, Decorative Frosted Fruits, page 376), or a cake to eat with a fork. And, of course, hot tea.

Arranging the tea tray and food: Select a large pretty tray and on it, place a pot of hot tea concentrate, a pot of hot water, a small bowl of lump sugar, a small pitcher of milk, a plate of lemon or orange slices with a lemon fork, and teacups, saucers and teaspoons. (If you like, omit saucers and use dessert plates.)

Place the tea tray, tea napkins and food on a handy table with a chair so you can sit and pour, yet get up easily to greet guests. If there's not enough room for the food on the table with the tea, place it nearby.

When serving: Set the teacup in the saucer (or on the dessert plate) and fill the cup about three-fourths full. See Hot Tea for a Crowd (page 662). Add lemon, milk or sugar as the guest prefers. Place the teaspoon on the back of the saucer parallel to the handle of the cup. Pass a napkin and the cup to the guest. Each guest selects a tidbit to eat. The hostess should offer more tea and may pass the food later, if she likes.

Cocktail Party

Cocktail parties are another way to entertain large groups.

Selecting the food and drink: Most hosts and hostesses, unless they know all their guests' liquor preferences, usually have an assortment of liquors, mixers and garnishes for popular drinks on hand. The time of day has a lot to do with the kind of food that should be served at a cocktail party. If the party is in the afternoon, usually a wide assortment of hot and cold snacks is suitable. If in the late afternoon, before guests go on to dinner somewhere else, a few hot and a few cold selections are satisfactory.

However, if the party is in the late afternoon and extends into the dinner hour, more hearty food is needed. See menus below.

Setting the table: If a punch is served, the food should be on a table with the punch. Other drinks should be served from a bar (or table set up as a bar) in another part of the room, or even in the kitchen. The table for the food may be covered with a festive cloth or not, depending on the occasion. Food should be arranged so guests can help themselves. Plenty of cocktail napkins, usually paper, should be stacked at both ends of the table. Small plates and cocktail or dessert forks should be near foods that are not to be eaten with the fingers. Let guests help themselves to punch, or the hostess can serve them.

Serving food and drinks: Usually the host presides at the bar, mixing drinks to each guest's order. However, for large parties, a close friend might help out, or a bartender might be hired. It is usually not a good idea to let guests mix their own drinks, since they may pour drinks wastefully, or too often.

Sometimes the bartender mixes several favorite cocktails and passes them on a tray among the guests. And sometimes the hostess circulates among the guests with a tray of special appetizers, perhaps hot from the oven.

Both the host and hostess should see that their guests have enough to eat and drink. They should also remove used glasses and plates unobtrusively and empty ashtrays from time to time.

❦

Salted Nuts
Mixed Green and Ripe Olives
Chinese Fried Walnuts (page 34)
Garlic-Broiled Shrimp (page 243)
King-Size Steak Bites (page 41)
Tiny Ham-Stuffed Tomatoes (page 37)
Stuffed Celery with Red Caviar Garnish
Guacamole (page 33) with
Crisp Corn Chips or Potato Chips
Blue-Cheese Ball (page 33)
Cocktails *Sherry*
Coffee

❦

Six-in-One Cocktail Hash (page 35)
Curried Ripe Olives (page 38)
Welsh Rabbit (page 288)
with Chunks of Crusty Bread
Cranberry-Orange Cocktail (page 609)
Cocktails *Coffee*

❦

Rye Toasties (page 659)
Sesame Mini-Drumsticks (page 193)
Egg-and-Bacon Appetizers (page 38)
Chilled Cocktail Crab Claws
with Louis Dressing (page 410)
Peppery Dip with Vegetables (page 32)
Macadamia Nuts
Pretzel Sticks
Grape Wine Spritzer (page 612)
Cocktails

❦

Appetizer Kabobs (page 39)
Salami Roll-Ups (page 39)
Cottage Cheese Dip (page 31)
with Crisp Vegetable Relishes
Cold Cooked Shrimp with
Curried Mayonnaise (page 246)
Swedish Meatballs (page 42)
Tiny Quiche Tarts (page 41)
Fresh Mushroom Salad (page 393)
Cherry Tomatoes
Garlic Sticks (page 419)
Corn-Flavor Foldovers (page 424)
Fruitcake Cubes
Grapes
Cocktails *Cold Duck* *Coffee*

❦

Plantain Chips (page 369)
Buttery Popcorn (page 34)
Deviled-Ham-Cheese Spread (page 33)
on Cucumber Slices
Cheese-and-Anchovy Spread (page 33)
on Thin Wheat Crackers
Pickled Shrimp in Crystalline Ice Bowl
(page 36)
Seafood-Stuffed Mushrooms (page 42)
Whole Smithfield Ham (page 118)
Herbed Potato Salad (page 397)
One of Some Fruit and Cheese
Combinations (page 753)
Apple-Lemon Punch (page 609)
Cocktails *Coffee*

Open House

An "open house" is an informal way of entertaining a large group. While invitations are usually extended by mail or telephone, in a small community an announcement may appear in the local paper. "Open house" is especially popular for weddings or anniversary celebrations but is just as fashionable for a housewarming or repaying social debts at Christmas.

Selecting the menu: Since an open house may extend over a period of four or five hours, the food should be both plentiful and hearty. No doubt some of the family and close friends will be on hand to help host; as the party progresses, they, as well as the guests who come later in the afternoon, will need something substantial to eat.

A buffet table filled with both hot and cold pick-up foods and a big punch bowl are necessary for this type of affair. Have extra quantities of the foods ready in the kitchen to replenish dishes so that everything looks and tastes fresh.

Cocktails and mixed drinks are frequently served from a bar; sometimes two punches are offered instead, one with and one without liquor. See menus, below.

Setting the table: The table and bar are set up the same as for the cocktail party. Rent extra glassware or punch bowls and cups, if needed; also consider using paper cups and plates. Arrange the food as for a Formal Tea, page 748, substituting punch bowls for the coffee and tea services.

Serving the food and drinks: At an open house, guests are expected to help themselves to food and drink, but the hostess should provide a handy tray or table for empty punch cups and plates and make sure used glassware and ashtrays are removed regularly. It is a good idea to recruit a couple of friends ahead of time, or even hire a maid, to replenish the foods, supply fresh glassware and dishes and remove used ones. A bartender is also helpful at a big party.

The host or hostess should be near the door at all times to welcome guests and direct them to the living room and dining room.

Pickled Shrimp (page 36)
Spicy Glazed Wieners (page 42)
Caviar-Egg Rounds (page 37)
Cucumber Slices,
Each Topped with Smoky Cheese Slice
and Halved Pitted Ripe Olives
Swiss-Cheese-Pepper Squares (page 38)
Company Bloody Mary (page 597)
Sparkling Garnet Punch (page 611)
Coffee *Tea*

Variety of Appetizer Kabobs (page 39)
Hot Biscuits
Filled with Pan-Fried Sausage Patties
Tiny Cream Puffs Filled with
Chicken Salad
Hot Mushroom Turnovers (page 44)
Bowl of Cherry Tomatoes,
Green-Pepper Squares,
Radishes, Celery Curls
Party Pumpernickel Bread Sandwiches
Filled with Spur-of-the-Moment Spreads
(page 33)
Salted Peanuts
Roasted Chestnuts (see Chestnuts,
page 20)
Glögg (page 610)
Lime Punch Bowl (page 610)
Tray of Tea Cakelets (page 662)

Wedding and Anniversary Receptions

Because wedding and anniversary receptions are often formal, written invitations are almost always issued for them. While the menu may be as extensive as the food served for an open house (at left), the refreshments may be the same as those for Afternoon Tea (page 749), with the addition of a decorated wedding or special-occasion cake and a fruit or champagne punch. Other pick-up foods from nuts and mints to party sandwiches, appetizers may be served.

Often, two punches are offered, one with liquor and one without, especially when children are present. Or, instead of an alcoholic punch, champagne or mixed drinks may be served.

Wedding Cake (page 664)
Jordan Almonds *Salted Cashew Nuts*
Assorted Chocolates
Cold Spiced-Tea Punch (page 612)
Golden Champagne Punch (page 665)

Potted Cheese (page 34)
with Pretzel-Stick Dippers
Sandwiches of Boston Brown Bread
(page 428) Filled with
Cream Cheese with Curry Added
Platter of Rolled Slices
of Rare Roast Beef Tenderloin,
Strips of Smoked Turkey and Watercress
Buttered Parker House Rolls (page 439)
Mushroom Caps Filled with
Roquefort Cheese
Tiny Patty Shells Filled with
Lobster Thermidor (page 235; omit Pilaf)
Little Fruit Kabobs:
Fresh Pineapple Chunks, Strawberries
Wedding Cake (page 664)
Melba Cream Dessert (page 576)
Mint Patties (page 663)
Miniature Chocolates
Salted Mixed Nuts
Champagne-Punch Fruit Bowl
(page 665)
Golden Anniversary Punch (page 665)
(substitute Ice Float, page 595, for
ice cubes)

Bridal and Baby Showers

Bridal showers may be given at brunch, luncheon, tea, dinner or in the evening; baby showers are more apt to be afternoon or evening functions. While a hostess often plans a few party games for a shower, the focus is on the guest of honor and the "shower" of appropriate gifts.

Attractive decorations or flowers for the table may carry out the theme of the party.

Selecting the menu: Because most showers are given in the afternoon or evening, a pretty, suitably decorated cake and tea, coffee or punch are sufficient refreshment. Party sandwiches also may be offered.

Setting the table and serving: Follow the suggestions for The Formal Tea, page 748. After the gifts have been unwrapped, serve the beverage and let guests help themselves to cake or dessert. Ask a friend to help with the serving.

Bridal-Shower Cake (page 664)
Sparkling Cinnamon Punch (page 666)
with Garnished Ice Cubes (page 595)
Mint Patties (page 663)
Divinity Drops (page 587)
Truffles (page 589)

Open-Face Sandwiches:
Buttered Halves of Small Rolls Topped
with Thin Slices of Turkey and Ham;
Cream Cheese and Quince Jelly;
Thin Slices of Smoked Salmon
Radish Roses
Kabobs of Pitted Ripe and Stuffed Olives
Lady Baltimore Cake (page 534)
Decorated with Candied Fruit
Frosted Mocha Punch (page 612)

Wine-and-Cheese Party

Either casual or more formal wine-and-cheese parties may be given as separate afternoon or evening functions or included as part of a meal. Wine and cheese may be served as a first course for a brunch, luncheon or party dinner, or after dinner or in the evening instead of dessert and coffee.

Selecting the foods: Choose wines from one of the basic classes: appetizer, white table, red table, sweet dessert or sparkling wine. (See Wine, pages 613–620.) Serve appetizer wines and flavored wines as the first course before a meal; the white and red table wines are pleasantly refreshing in the afternoon or late evening; sweet dessert wines should be served after a meal or in the evening. Champagne and the sparkling wines are suitable at any time.

Serve three or more cheeses, selecting a variety of flavors from mild to sharp, and textures from creamy to firm. Pick cheeses of different shapes, cutting some in bite-size chunks, some in slices, and leaving others in balls, wedges or bars.

Crisp, unsalted crackers and slices or chunks of crusty French or Italian bread enhance cheese flavors and add pleasing texture contrast. Set them out in an attractive basket. Also, if you like, set out a bowl of fresh fruit—grapes, apples and pears—for guests to eat with the cheese.

How much cheese and wine to buy: Allow one-third to one-half bottle of appetizer, table or sparkling wine per person. Dessert wines are heavier and sweeter; allow one-fourth to one-third bottle per person.

Allow a total of at least a quarter pound of cheese per person (remember leftovers keep well). Hard cheeses are smaller in proportion to weight than soft cheeses, so buy slightly more of a hard cheese for the sake of appearance.

Arranging and serving: Let the cheese come to room temperature for best flavor. Place it on a large board or platter and supply two or three knives for slicing or spreading. Stick toothpicks into cheese chunks.

Arrange the cheese board, basket of crackers, fruit bowl and cocktail napkins on a coffee table or side table. Nearby, arrange a tray of wines and wine glasses.

The host pours the wine, asking guests to try each kind if several are offered. Guests help themselves to cheese, breads and fruit.

When tasting an unfamiliar wine, pour a little into a clear wine glass and hold the glass to the light to see the color. Gently swirl the wine to release its bouquet, and sniff to enjoy the aroma. Then take a small sip of wine, rolling it around on the tongue to taste the full flavor, then swallow.

If tasting several wines, eat a little cheese along with some French bread or unsalted crackers after each wine to clear the palate.

CHEESE-BOARD COMBINATIONS

Wedges of Appenzeller; Gouda, scored into wedges but left whole; a bar of Neufchâtel; strips or sticks of Monterey (Jack)

Small wheel of Camembert; wedge of Stilton; slices of Colby; small cubes of Gjetost; a bar of cream cheese

Wedge of Fontina; wedge of Gorgonzola; slices of Provolone; whole Edam

Wedge of Brie; chunk of Swiss; mixed small cubes of very mild and very sharp Cheddar

Individual wedges of Gruyère; half wheel of Bel Paese; slices of Mysost; small wedges of Roquefort

Slices of baby Longhorn; chunk of Tilsiter; bar of Limburger; cubes of Neufchâtel

Fruit-and-Cheese-Tasting Party

This is an easy, informal and conversation-making way to entertain friends for dessert. Set out a variety of fruits and cheeses and let everyone sample and compare.

Selecting the fruit and cheese: See Wine-and-Cheese Party, opposite page, for tips on selecting and serving cheeses and how much cheese to buy. Select fresh fruits in season; add interest by choosing some of the more unusual varieties such as kiwi fruit, papayas, mangoes, lychees, pomegranates. To prepare, see Fruits, pages 353–373. Dried fruits also team nicely with cheese and fresh fruits.

Arranging and serving: Arrange cheeses simply on a wooden cheese board or scratch-resistant tray or platter. Arrange fruit in a basket or bowl or on a platter. Set out napkins, small knives and plates.

Let guests help themselves to cheese and fruit or, for faster self-service, cut cheeses and fruits into bite-size cubes, slices or wedges and arrange on platters or trays. Set out a basket of unsalted crackers, plain bread sticks or bland-flavored wafers, and have plenty of coffee or other beverages on hand.

SOME FRUIT AND CHEESE COMBINATIONS

Sharp Cheddar, provolone, cream cheese; grapes, strawberries, pears

Port du Salut, Gruyère, Stilton; bananas, apples, fresh figs, kiwi fruit

Brie, Neufchâtel, Tilsiter; pineapple chunks, dates, tangerines

Liederkranz, Gouda, Mysost; grapes, cantaloupes, raisins

Fontina, Stilton, Edam; cherries, dried figs, papayas

Fondue Party

A fondue party is more than a buffet. Although the food is set out ahead of time, the cooking is done in front of or by the guests. For that reason, when fondue is the main dish, it's best to limit the guest list to a very small group—unless you have more than one fondue pot.

The fondue pot is placed in the center of the table with dishes of accompaniments around it. A plate, fondue fork and napkin are given to each guest. When the fondue is cheese, guests help themselves to bread chunks from a basket, then spear the bread with a fork and dip into the hot cheese mixture. White wine and tossed green salad are favorite accompaniments. Since this is not a hearty menu, a rich dessert is appropriate.

For a beef fondue, the fondue pot is filled with salad oil at cooking temperature. Guests help themselves to chunks of raw tender beef and two or three sauces, then spear a chunk of meat on a fondue fork, cook it until of desired doneness in the hot oil and dip in one of the sauces before eating it with a luncheon or dinner fork. Crisp French bread, tossed salad and red wine are preferred accompaniments.

For an appetizer or dessert fondue, set the fondue pot on the buffet table and let people help themselves. Cheese fondue makes a hearty appetizer and chocolate fondue is a dessert favorite.

Centerpieces

Because the table setting is the showcase for the meal, the centerpiece is important in setting the mood. Its colors can be bright and bold, and the arrangement striking. However, the centerpiece should not overpower the rest of the table. It should not be so high that guests cannot see over it when they are seated.

Candles, too, should either be higher than the eye or lower; flickering candles at eye level are most distracting. Candles are party-dinner favorites but give a festive air to less formal meals, too. If they are the only source of light, enough should be used so guests can see comfortably. Candles are not appropriate for breakfast, brunches or luncheons.

Fresh flowers in a pretty arrangement are always in good taste. Many everyday foods and household items make attractive and unusual centerpieces, too.

Fall Harvest: Layer a wide row of colored leaves down the center of the table; arrange apples, grapes, nuts in shell, small pumpkins or squash down the center.

Grapes and Wheat: Top sheaths of dried wheat with bunches of purple grapes and nuts in shell.

Figurines: Set figurines on either side of a bowl of delicate greenery and sweet peas.

Pansies: Arrange pansies in two or three small bowls and place in a row.

Garnet Roses: Arrange roses in champagne glasses or other goblets and set between and above place settings.

Brunch Violets: Place bunches of violets in pretty china teacups or in eggcups and scatter around the table.

Red and Green: Place red and green peppers or green peppers and red apples in wire lettuce basket.

Wintertime: Heap onions, small zucchini, green peppers and tomatoes in a wooden bowl.

Leafy: Use red cabbage or Swiss chard with eggplant, purple and white onions.

Ivy in a Shell: Arrange ivy in a large sea shell and set candles on each side among the leaves.

Big and Little: Arrange a large floral piece for the center of a long table, then use some of the same flowers for two or four small arrangements to be placed at intervals down each side. Or, use figurines instead of small arrangements.

Potted Plants: Scrub clay pots filled with blooming plants or green leaves and arrange in a cluster on a mat.

Hawaiian: Place a pineapple with a pretty crown on a grass mat and surround with fresh flowers or fruits and leaves.

Index

A

E

H

I

J

K

M

N

S

T

U

V

W

Y

Z